Microsoft®

Microsoft® Windows Server™ 2003 Inside Out

William R. Stanek

PUBLISHED BY
Microsoft Press
A Division of Microsoft Corporation
One Microsoft Way
Redmond, Washington 98052-6399

Library of Congress Cataloging-in-Publication Data
Stanek, William R.
Microsoft Windows Server 2003 Inside Out / William R. Stanek.
p. cm.
Includes index.
ISBN 0-7356-2048-2
1. Microsoft Windows server. 2. Operating systems (Computers). 3. Microsoft .NET. I. Title.

QA76.76.O63S734515 2004
005.4'47682--dc22 2004049932

Printed and bound in the United States of America.

5 6 7 8 9 QWT 9 8 7 6

Distributed in Canada by H.B. Fenn and Company Ltd.

A CIP catalogue record for this book is available from the British Library.

Microsoft Press books are available through booksellers and distributors worldwide. For further information about international editions, contact your local Microsoft Corporation office or contact Microsoft Press International directly at fax (425) 936-7329. Visit our Web site at www.microsoft.com/learning/. Send comments to *nsideout@microsoft.com.*

Acquisitions Editor: Martin DelRe
Project Editor: Kristine Haugseth
Technical Editor: Mitch Tulloch
Indexer: Jack Lewis

Body Part No. X10-58411

Contents At A Glance

Table of Contents

Chapter 19
Storage Management 587

Chapter 20
Managing Windows Server 2003 File Systems 643

Chapter 21
File Sharing and Security 691

Chapter 23
Using Removable Media 749

Part 6
Managing Windows Server 2003 Networking and Print Services

Chapter 24
Managing TCP/IP Networking 773

Chapter 25
Managing DHCP 807

Chapter 29
Installing and Maintaining Print Services 945

Part 7
Managing Active Directory and Security

Part 8
Windows Server 2003 Disaster Planning and Recovery

Acknowledgments

No single project has ever been as challenging or as fun for me as writing *Microsoft Windows Server 2003 Inside Out*. Why? When I set out to write this book, I had no idea it would take me more than 1,500 pages to detail every quirk, every insider secret, and every sticky detail that I've learned about Windows Server 2003 since I started working with it in late 1999—back when Windows Server 2003 was known as Windows Whistler. Yet there it is all the same, and it is my sincere hope that the book you hold in your hands is the best of its class when it comes to managing a Windows Server 2003 implementation and handling everyday administration. I also hope the result of all the hard work is that *Microsoft Windows Server 2003 Inside Out* is something unique. It takes into account all the experiences I've had while consulting, conducting training courses, and writing books about Windows Server 2003. As this is my 21st Windows-related book and I've helped millions of people learn Windows over my 20+-year career, I hope that counts for an awful lot. But no man is an island and this book couldn't have been written without help from some very special people.

Without the support of my wife and children, this book would not have been possible. As I literally was writing every day since I signed on to this project—holidays included—my wife had to manage everything else and the little ones had a lot more responsibilities around the house. Thank you for your support and your extraordinary ability to put up with the clackety-clackety of my keyboard.

As I've stated in *Microsoft Windows Server 2003 Administrator's Pocket Consultant* and in *Microsoft Windows Command-Line Administrator's Pocket Consultant*, the team at Microsoft Press is top-notch. Kristine Haugseth was instrumental throughout the writing process. She helped me stay on track and coordinated the materials after I submitted chapters. Martin DelRe was the acquisitions editor for the project. He believed in the book and my unique approach and was really great to work with. Completing and publishing the book wouldn't have been possible without their help! Susan McClung headed up the editorial process for nSight, Inc. As the project manager for this and many other books I've written, she wears many hats and always helps out in many ways. Thank you! I'd also like to add that Kristine, Martin, and Susan were very understanding—writing a book of this length is very fun but also very exhausting.

Unfortunately for the writer (but fortunately for readers), writing is only one part of the publishing process. Next came editing and author review. I must say, Microsoft Press has the most thorough editorial and technical review process I've seen anywhere—and I've written a lot of books for many different publishers. Mitch Tulloch was the technical editor for the book. I believe this was the first time we worked together and it turned out to be a wonderful experience. He was very thorough and helped out every step of the way to ensure things worked as expected.

As ever I would also like to thank Michael Bolinger, Anne Hamilton, and Juliana Aldous Atkinson. They've helped out at many points of my writing career and been there when I needed them the most. Thank you also for shepherding my many projects through the publishing process!

Thanks also to Studio B literary agency and my agents, David Rogelberg and Neil Salkind. David and Neil are great to work with. Finally, I want to thank David Stanley. David, I hope we get to work together in the future!

Hopefully, I haven't forgotten anyone but if I have, it was an oversight. *Honest.* ;-)

We'd Like to Hear from You!

Our goal at Microsoft Press is to create books that help you find the information you need to get the most out of your software.

The INSIDE OUT series was created with you in mind. As part of our ongoing effort to ensure that we're creating the books that meet your learning needs, we'd like to hear from you. Let us know what you think. Tell us what you like about this book and what we can do to make it better. When you write, please include the title and author of this books in your e-mail, as well as your name and contact information. We look forward to hearing from you!

How to Reach Us

E-mail: nsideout@microsoft.com
Mail: Inside Out Series Editor
Microsoft Press
One Microsoft Way
Redmond, WA 98052

Note: Unfortunately, we can't provide support for any software problems you might experience. Please go to http://support.microsoft.com *for help with any software issues.*

About the CD

The companion CD that ships with this book contains many tools and resources to help you get the most out of your *Inside Out* book.

What's on the CD

Your *Inside Out* CD includes the following:

- **eBook** In this section you'll find the electronic version of *Microsoft Windows Server 2003 Inside Out.*
- **Resource Kit Tools** This section contains resource kit tools for Windows Server 2003.
- **Miscellaneous Tools** This section contains several tools used to manage Windows Server 2003, including Application Compatibility Analyzer, Microsoft Baseline Security Analyzer, and Windows System Resource Manager.
- **IIS Tools** A variety of tools and other resources for migrating and enhancing Microsoft Internet Information Services (IIS) 6 form this section.
- **FRS Tools** The tools in this section are used to manage File Replication Service. They include continuous monitoring tools and snapshot troubleshooting tools.
- **MOM Tools** This section contains a variety of tools relating to Microsoft Operations Manager.
- **MSA v2.0 Doc Set** The documentation in this section comprises enterprise-class architectural blueprints and implementation guidance associated with Microsoft Systems Architecture version 2.
- **Windows Server Documentation** This section contains technical documents and white papers about implementing and administering Windows Server 2003.

The companion CD provides detailed information about the files on the CD and links to Microsoft and third-party sites on the Internet.

Note The links to third-party sites are not under the control of Microsoft Corporation, and Microsoft is therefore not responsible for their content, nor should their inclusion on this CD be construed as an endorsement of the product or the site.

Software provided on this CD is only in the English language and may be incompatible with non-English-language operating systems and software.

Using the CD

To use this companion CD, insert it into your CD-ROM drive. Accept the license agreement that is presented to access the Start menu. If AutoRun is not enabled on your system, run StartCD.exe in the root of the CD or refer to the Readme.txt file. The menu provides you with links to all the resources available on the CD and also to the Microsoft Learning Support Web site.

> **Caution** The electronic version of the book and some of the other documentation included on this CD is provided in Portable Document Format (PDF). To view these files, you will need Adobe Acrobat or Acrobat Reader. For more information about these products or to download the Acrobat Reader, visit the Adobe Web site at *http://www.adobe.com*.

Support Information

Every effort has been made to ensure the accuracy of the book and the contents of this companion CD. For feedback on the book content or this companion CD, please contact us by using any of the addresses listed in the "We'd Like to Hear from You" section.

Microsoft Press provides corrections for books through the World Wide Web at *http://www.microsoft.com/learning/support/*. To connect directly to the Microsoft Press Knowledge Base and enter a query regarding a question or issue that you may have, go to *http://www.microsoft.com/learning/support/search.asp*.

For support information regarding Windows Server 2003, you can connect to Microsoft Technical Support on the Web at *http://support.microsoft.com/*.

Conventions and Features Used in this Book

This book uses special text and design conventions to make it easier for you to find the information you need.

Text Conventions

Convention	Meaning
Abbreviated menu commands	For your convenience, this book uses abbreviated menu commands. For example, "Click Tools, Track Changes, Highlight Changes" means that you should click the Tools menu, point to Track Changes, and click the Highlight Changes command.
Boldface type	**Boldface** type is used to indicate text that you enter or type.
Initial Capital Letters	The first letters of the names of menus, dialog boxes, dialog box elements, and commands are capitalized. Example: the Save As dialog box.
Italicized type	*Italicized* type is used to indicate new terms.
Plus sign (+) in text	Keyboard shortcuts are indicated by a plus sign (+) separating two key names. For example, Ctrl+Alt+Delete means that you press the Ctrl, Alt, and Delete keys at the same time.

Design Conventions

This icon identifies a new or significantly updated feature in this version of the software.

Inside Out

This statement illustrates an example of an "Inside Out" problem statement

These are the book's signature tips. In these tips, you'll get the straight scoop on what's going on with the software—inside information about why a feature works the way it does. You'll also find handy workarounds to deal with software problems.

Tip Tips provide helpful hints, timesaving tricks, or alternative procedures related to the task being discussed.

Troubleshooting

This statement illustrates an example of a "Troubleshooting" problem statement

Look for these sidebars to find solutions to common problems you might encounter. Troubleshooting sidebars appear next to related information in the chapters. You can also use the Troubleshooting Topics index at the back of the book to look up problems by topic.

Cross-references point you to other locations in the book that offer additional information about the topic being discussed.

This icon indicates information or text found on the companion CD.

Caution Cautions identify potential problems that you should look out for when you're completing a task or problems that you must address before you can complete a task.

Note Notes offer additional information related to the task being discussed.

Sidebars

The sidebars sprinkled throughout these chapters provide ancillary information on the topic being discussed. Go to sidebars to learn more about the technology or a feature.

Part 1

Windows Server 2003 Overview and Planning

Chapter 1

Introducing Windows Server 2003

Neo from the *Matrix* trilogy might not be impressed, but I certainly am. Microsoft Windows Server 2003 is the most powerful, versatile, and fully featured version of Windows Server ever, and if you've been using Windows server operating systems since Microsoft Windows NT 4, I think you'll be impressed as well. Why? For starters, in Windows Server 2003, Microsoft finally delivers a server operating system that is something more than the sum of its parts. Windows Server 2003 isn't just a server operating system or a network operating system. It is a best-of-class Internet services operating system that builds on the foundation provided by Windows NT and Microsoft Windows 2000, and it includes the foundation technologies necessary to provide networking, application, and online services that can be used over the Internet or in intranet environments.

Although many people have heard that Windows Server 2003 is little more than a service pack for Windows 2000, they've heard wrong. From top to bottom, Windows Server 2003 is dramatically different from Windows NT *and* from Windows 2000. Windows Server 2003 is in fact a major rewrite of Windows 2000 that includes significant changes to the operating system kernel; significant enhancements to core services such as the Active Directory directory service, the Domain Name System (DNS), and Remote Access; and it also offers new services.

The way you approach Windows Server 2003 will depend on your background and your implementation plans. If you are moving from Windows NT to Windows Server 2003 or switching from UNIX, you'll find that Windows Server 2003 is a significant change that requires a whole new way of thinking about the network, its services, and the interoperations between clients and servers. The learning curve will be steep, but you will find clear upgrade and migration paths to Windows Server 2003. You will also find that Windows Server 2003 has an extensive command-line interface that makes it easier to manage servers, workstations, and, indeed, the entire network using both graphical and command-line administration tools.

If you are moving from Windows 2000 to Windows Server 2003, you'll find the changes are no less significant but easier to understand. You are already familiar with administration tools such as Active Directory Users and Computers and the core technologies and administration techniques. Your learning curve might still be steep, but in only some areas, not all of them.

You can adopt Windows Server 2003 incrementally as well. For example, you might add Windows Server 2003 Routing and Remote Access Services to a Windows NT 4 or Windows 2000 environment, which can allow the organization to take advantage of the latest services and capabilities without having to implement a full upgrade or migration of existing servers. In most, but not all, cases, incremental adoption has little or no impact on the network, while allowing the organization to test new technologies and incrementally roll out features to users as part of a standard continuance or upgrade process.

Regardless of your deployment plans and whether you are reading this book to prepare for implementation of Windows Server 2003 or to manage existing implementations, my mission in this book is to help you take full advantage of all the new features in Windows Server 2003. You will find the detailed inside information you need to get up to speed quickly with Windows Server 2003 changes and technologies, to make the right setup and configuration choices the first time, and to work around the rough edges, annoyances, and faults of this complex operating system. If the default settings are less than optimal, I'll show you how to fix them so things work the way you want them to work. If something doesn't function like it should, I'll let you know and I'll also show you the fastest, surest way to work around the issue. You'll find plenty of hacks and secrets, too.

To pack as much information as possible into the 1,000-plus pages of this book, I am assuming that you have basic networking skills and some experience managing Windows-based networks but that you don't need me to explain the basic structure and architecture of an operating system. So, I'm not going to waste your time answering such questions as, "What's the point of networks?" "Why use Windows Server 2003?" or "What's the difference between the GUI and the command line?" Instead, I'm going to start with a discussion of what is new in Windows Server 2003 so that you can learn about changes that will most affect you, and then I'm going to follow this discussion with a comprehensive, informative look at Windows Server 2003 planning, installation, upgrades, and migrations.

What's New in Windows Server 2003

Windows Server 2003 brings together the best of Windows 2000 and Windows XP, building on the network services and directory features of Windows 2000 and expanding the support services and automated help systems of Windows XP. This means Windows Server 2003 is more manageable, reliable, and scalable than previous versions of the Windows operating system. It also means the operating system has improved usability, especially when it comes to remote management and administration from the command line. Add in enhancements to performance, availability, and security; a rewrite of the operating system kernel; and additional features, such as basic e-mail services and the Microsoft Data Engine (MSDE), and you have many reasons to adopt Windows Server 2003—or at the very least deploy it in engineering or development labs so that you can be ready for full implementation when the bosses say, "We gotta have it now."

A primary purpose of Windows Server 2003 is to ensure the operating system can be optimized for use in any networking scenario. An edition of the server operating system is available to meet your organization's needs whether you want to deploy a basic server for hosting applications, a network server for hosting domain services, a robust enterprise server for hosting essential applications, or a highly available datacenter server for hosting critical business solutions.

Microsoft produced multiple editions of the operating system with varying features to match the needs of any organization. In addition to offering 32-bit, 64-bit, and embedded versions of the operating system, Microsoft introduced the Web Edition as a low-cost server operating system for providing basic Web application hosting services, Standard Edition as the domain services operating system, Enterprise Edition as the robust solution for essential applications and large organizations, and Datacenter Edition as the solution for critical business operations. Thus, the four main product editions are these:

- **Windows Server 2003, Standard Edition** Available in 32-bit version only and can be used for upgrades, migrations, and new installations. This is the next evolution of Windows 2000 Server.
- **Windows Server 2003, Enterprise Edition** Available in 32-bit and 64-bit versions and can be used for upgrades, migrations, and new installations. This is the next evolution of Windows 2000 Advanced Server.
- **Windows Server 2003, Datacenter Edition** Available in 32-bit and 64-bit versions and can be used only as part of a vendor-specific original equipment manufacturer (OEM) solution. This is the next evolution of Windows 2000 Datacenter Server.
- **Windows Server 2003, Web Edition** Available in 32-bit version only and can be used for new installations. This edition has no equivalent in previous Windows editions.

The various features of each edition are discussed in the sections that follow. Afterward, I discuss the new features of Windows Server 2003, including the following:

- .NET technologies support
- Windows XP integration
- Standards support
- Interface and tool improvements
- Active Directory improvements
- Group Policy improvement
- Management and administration extras
- Security advances

For more information about the minimum and recommended system requirements for each server edition, see Chapter 3, "Preparing for the Installation and Getting Started."

Windows Server 2003, Standard Edition

Windows Server 2003, Standard Edition, is the workhorse version of the operating system. It comes with a bunch of new features that are exclusive to Windows Server 2003, as you'd expect, and it also includes a few unexpected surprises, including the aforementioned e-mail and database services, as well as Network Load Balancing. As you probably know, Network Load Balancing is included in Windows 2000 Server, but only with the Advanced Server edition—now you can get this feature without shelling out any extra cash. In fact, Network Load Balancing is now included with all four editions of the operating system, even the low-cost Web Edition.

Standard Edition is optimized to provide domain services, such as DNS, Dynamic Host Configuration Protocol (DHCP), Transmission Control Protocol/Internet Protocol (TCP/IP) networking, print, and fax, in a small to moderately sized network environment. This edition supports two- and four-way symmetric multiprocessing (SMP) and up to 4 gigabytes (GB) of memory on 32-bit systems and 32 GB on 64-bit systems.

Windows Server 2003, Enterprise Edition

Windows Server 2003, Enterprise Edition, is the robust medium- to large-enterprise solution specifically designed for multidepartmental use. It supports eight-node clusters and very large memory (VLM) configurations of up to 32 GB on 32-bit systems and 64 GB on 64-bit systems. It also allows you to boot servers from a storage area network (SAN), supports hot-add memory (you don't need to take down the system to install memory), and lets you run up to eight processors. In addition, it includes Services for Macintosh and support for Non-Uniform Memory Access (NUMA). (Don't you just hate all the acronyms you have to keep track of now?)

Inside Out

Use hot-add memory for hot swapping memory on compliant systems

With hot-add memory, you just pop the cover, insert the new random access memory (RAM), and wait a few seconds for the system to recognize the change. Then, presto! The additional RAM is made available to the operating system, its services, and applications, and just as important, no reboot is required. Watch out, though; not all server hardware supports this feature. Both the server hardware and the operating system must support this feature to use it. On the hardware, the server must be built for hot swapping of memory—this includes physical enhancements as well as machine-level coding so that hot swapping is possible. When you hot add memory, take the necessary precautions, handle the memory properly, and insert the memory carefully without touching other system components. If not, you could fry the memory or a board on the server.

Windows Server 2003, Datacenter Edition

If Windows Server 2003, Standard Edition, is plain vanilla ice cream served with a spoon, Datacenter Edition is more like an ice cream sundae made with five different flavors, nuts, and whipped cream and served with a cherry on top and spoons for everyone at your table. This edition is designed to host business-critical systems and solutions using a minimum of 8 processors and a maximum of 32 and includes all the features of the Enterprise Edition. Plus, it supports clustering for up to eight nodes and it increases VLM support, allowing for configurations of up to 64 GB on 32-bit systems and 512 GB on Itanium (IA-64) systems.

But the enhancements don't stop there. Datacenter Edition also includes Windows System Resource Manager, which allows you to specify the amount of system resources, including processors and memory, that is available to each application and to prioritize the resources. This permits tuning applications for optimal responsiveness. For example, you can specify that Microsoft Exchange Server can use up to 50 percent of the available central processing units (CPUs) and up to 75 percent of the available memory, while Microsoft SQL Server, also running on the server, can use only up to 33 percent of the available CPUs and up to 50 percent of the available memory. By further specifying that Exchange has priority over SQL Server, you can ensure that Exchange will always be optimally responsive.

Inside Out

Obtain Datacenter Edition from hardware vendors

You cannot purchase Windows Server 2003, Datacenter Edition, off the shelf. This edition of Windows Server 2003 is available only as part of a proprietary hardware system. To use the Datacenter Edition, you must choose a hardware vendor and a system from that vendor that not only meets the minimum requirements of eight CPUs and 512 gigabytes (MB) of RAM, but one that also has been through the rigorous hardware testing and certification process required by Microsoft.

Windows Server 2003, Web Edition

Windows Server 2003, Web Edition, is the fourth and newest option. It supports up to 2 GB of RAM and two CPUs and is designed, as the name implies, to provide Web services, primarily for hosting Web sites and Web-based applications on the Internet and intranets. As with all the other editions of Windows Server 2003, it supports Internet Information Services (IIS) 6, ASP.NET, and the Windows .NET Framework. These technologies work together to make the sharing of application services in Web environments possible.

However, Web Edition, doesn't include many of the other common features of Windows Server 2003. The biggest feature missing is Active Directory, which means that servers running the Web Edition cannot be domain controllers. Other servers in the datacenter can provide this functionality, however; and so servers running the Web Edition can be part of an

Active Directory domain. In addition, although Network Load Balancing support is included in Web Edition, the only other features it has in common with the other editions of Windows Server 2003 are the following:

- Distributed file system (DFS)
- Encrypting File System (EFS)
- Remote Desktop for Administration

Because of this, Web Edition cannot provide Internet connection sharing, network bridging, or faxing services, and although it includes the Remote Desktop, it doesn't include Terminal Services. This means you can access a server running Web Edition using Remote Desktop, but cannot run applications on it remotely using Terminal Services.

Caution An important security note for Web Edition is that Internet Connection Firewall is not included. Because of this, there is no built-in firewall protection. Microsoft assumes the datacenter will have its own firewall that restricts access to servers as appropriate.

Note Web Edition is available only to Microsoft customers with Enterprise and Select licensing agreements and to service providers that have a service provider licensing agreement (SPLA). You can also get Web Edition preinstalled on a system from Microsoft OEMs and System Builder partners.

64-Bit Computing

With Windows Server 2003, 64-bit computing achieves its full potential. Not only do computers running 64-bit versions of Windows perform better and run faster than their 32-bit counterparts, they are also more scalable, as they can process more data per clock cycle, address more memory, and perform numeric calculations faster. Windows Server 2003 supports two different 64-bit architectures:

- The first architecture is based on the Explicitly Parallel Instruction Computing (EPIC) processor architecture, which is implemented in Intel Itanium (IA-64) processors. This architecture offers native 64-bit processing, allowing 64-bit applications to achieve optimal performance.

- The second architecture is based on 64-bit extensions to the x86 instructions set, which is implemented in AMD Opteron (AMD64) processors and Intel Xeon processors with 64-bit extension technology. This architecture offers native 32-bit processing and 64-bit extension processing.

Inside Out

Running 32-bit applications on 64-bit hardware

In most cases, 64-bit hardware is compatible with 32-bit applications; however, 32-bit applications will perform better on 32-bit hardware. Windows Server 2003 64-bit editions support both 64-bit and 32-bit applications using the Windows on Windows 64 (WOW64) x86 emulation layer. The WOW64 subsystem isolates 32-bit applications from 64-bit applications. This prevents file system and Registry problems. The operating system provides interoperability across the 32-bit/64-bit boundary for Component Object Model (COM) and basic operations, such as cut, copy, and paste from the clipboard. However, 32-bit processes cannot load 64-bit dynamic-link libraries (DLLs), and 64-bit processes cannot load 32-bit DLLs.

64-bit computing is designed for performing operations that are memory-intensive and that require extensive numeric calculations. With 64-bit processing, applications can load large data sets entirely into physical memory (that is, RAM), which reduces the need to page to disk and increases performance substantially. The EPIC instruction set enables Itanium-based processors to perform up to 20 operations simultaneously.

x86-based and Itanium-based computers differ in many fundamental ways. x86-based computers use BIOS and the Master Boot Record (MBR) disk type. Itanium-based computers use Extensible Firmware Interface (EFI) and the GUID Partition Table (GPT) disk type. This means there are differences in the way you manage x86-based and Itanium-based computers, particularly when it comes to setup and disk configuration. For details on setting up x86-based and Itanium-based computers, see the section entitled "Getting A Quick Start" on page 72. Techniques for using MBR and GPT disks are covered in detail in Chapter 19, "Storage Management."

Note In this text, I will refer to 32-bit versions of Windows and 64-bit versions of Windows to indicate something that applies to Windows Server 2003 32-bit and Windows Server 2003 64-bit versions in general. If a feature is specific to chip architecture, I will specify the chip architecture, such as x86 (IA-32) or Itanium (IA-64). Keep in mind that the Windows Server 2003 64-bit extended systems versions run on x86 chip architectures.

.NET Technologies

All editions of Windows Server 2003 include IIS 6 and ASP.NET and support the Windows .NET Framework. IIS, as you probably already know, is a bundle of essential Web services that allow servers to act as Web servers, File Transfer Protocol (FTP) servers, Simple Mail Transfer Protocol (SMTP) hosts, and Network News Transfer Protocol (NNTP) hosts. ASP.NET is a server-side scripting environment for developing Web applications. The Windows .NET Framework is an application development environment that defines framework classes and application processes to simplify the development and deployment of Internet applications—and this is where things get really interesting.

.NET Framework Technologies

By using the .NET Framework, isolated applications can be transformed into online services that can be worked with over the Internet or in intranet environments, allowing users to access the services regardless of where the users are located. Windows Server 2003 exists within this framework, and the capabilities of the framework form the underpinnings of the operating system. Anything you can do with the Windows operating system on the corporate network, you can do over the Internet as well.

The concepts underlying the Windows .NET Framework are industry-standard technologies, including the following:

- **Extensible Markup Language** (XML) A language that can be used to describe other languages and to give form and structure to abstract data concepts. You give data concepts form by describing their components and the relationship between the components. For example, the concept of a customer could be represented by using name, address, phone number, account number, and purchase history components.

> **For more information about XML and related technologies, I recommend reading *XML Pocket Consultant* (Microsoft Press, 2002).**

- **Simple Object Access Protocol** (SOAP) A technology that facilitates message exchange in distributed environments, allowing XML-formatted information to be exchanged over the Internet or an intranet. The messages exchanged can include general requests and responses to requests.
- **Universal Description, Discovery, and Integration** (UDDI) A standard that makes it possible to locate and discover information about XML-based Web services. By using UDDI, an application can locate an available service and then discover information about it.
- **Web Service Description Language** (WSDL) A language that can be used to describe XML-based Web services. By using WSDL, function names, required parameters, and returned results from an XML-based Web service can be published so that they can be discovered through UDDI.

For organizations looking to develop Web-based applications, these technologies make it possible to create online services that communicate with each other, learn about new Web services that might become available, and then use a discovery process to structure messages properly so communication exchange is possible.

.NET Framework Layers

The Windows .NET Framework has three main layers:

- **Common language runtime engine—The bottom layer** Handles low-level services, such as verification of type safety, memory management for managed objects, and exception handling. You can think of it as a virtual machine that resides at the bottom of the framework and handles essential functions.

- **Common class library—The middle layer** Provides the common classes for the runtime engine. It includes system classes for building components, user interface creation, and input/output (I/O); enabling classes that use SOAP, UDDI, and WSDL for communications exchange; and support classes for code compilation and generation.
- **ASP.NET—The top layer** Provides the server-side scripting environment that can be used to develop Web applications. It includes server controls for working with Web forms, event-handling components, application state and session state management facilities, caching features, and Hypertext Transfer Protocol (HTTP) handlers to synchronously and asynchronously process Web service requests that are formatted using XML and SOAP.

As you can see, these layers build on one another to form a comprehensive framework. The importance of the framework is that it provides a way for applications to communicate regardless of the programming language in which they are written. Thus, .NET-enabled applications can communicate with legacy applications written in COBOL and those running on mainframes just as easily as they can communicate with applications written in Java or ASP.NET.

Windows XP and Windows Server 2003

In Windows XP, Microsoft brings the Windows family of operating systems for business and home users together and puts the operating systems on similar paths.

Windows XP Editions

Like Windows Server 2003, Windows XP has several editions:

- **Windows XP, Home Edition** The operating system designed for home users as a replacement for Microsoft Windows 3.*x*, Windows 95, Windows 98, or Windows Millennium Edition (Windows Me)
- **Windows XP, Professional Edition** The operating system designed for business users and as a replacement for Windows NT Workstation or Windows 2000 Professional

Windows XP and Active Directory

Windows XP Professional is the only edition intended for use in Active Directory domains. It includes extensions to Group Policy that require updating the Group Policy Objects (GPOs) in a domain using servers running Windows 2000. In a domain upgraded to domain controllers running Windows Server 2003, however, you are not required to update the GPOs for Windows XP Professional.

For more information about Group Policy and Windows 2000 compatibility, see "Updating GPOs for Windows XP Professional" on pages 90 and 91 of *Microsoft Windows 2000 Administrator's Pocket Consultant,* 2nd Edition (Microsoft Press, 2003).

You should be aware of some other integration issues. If you were one of the people that upgraded to Windows XP Professional when it first became available, I probably don't need to tell you there were problems using the server administration tools on the Windows XP desktop. Although the issues were fixed when a new version of the administration tools shipped, it still brings back bad memories for many, including yours truly. The good news is that Windows Server 2003 ships with a set of administration tools that can be installed on a Windows XP desktop with Service Pack 1 or later and that are used to manage both Windows 2000 and Windows Server 2003.

Installing Windows Server 2003 Administration Tools on Windows XP

You can install the Windows Server 2003 Administration Tools by following these steps:

1. Log on to the workstation using an account with administrator privileges.
2. Confirm that the computer has Service Pack 1 or later installed. The fastest way to do this is to double-click System in Control Panel, then check the System entry on the General tab.
3. Insert the Windows Server 2003 CD-ROM into the CD-ROM drive.
4. When the Autorun screen appears, click Perform Additional Tasks, and then click Browse This CD. This starts Windows Explorer.
5. Double-click I386, and then double-click Adminipak.msi. The complete set of Windows Server 2003 management tools is installed on your computer.

Increased Support for Standards

In an effort to be more standardized and less proprietary, Microsoft has introduced additional support for industry-standard technologies with each new version of the Windows operating system. Windows Server 2003 is no exception. Some of the key standards built into Windows Server 2003 include Internet Protocol version 6 (IPv6), Internet Engineering Task Force (IETF) security standards, and XML Web services.

IPv6 Support

IPv6 is the future Internet standard for TCP/IP networking, and it allows multicasting of IP addresses. Why is this important? Because the standard Internet numbering scheme used with the current Internet Protocol version 4 (IPv4) is running out of address space, and future Internet communications will need an expanded address space, which IPv6 provides. IPv6 supports IPv4 addressing, allowing organizations to use dual IP addressing or configurations that use both IPv4 and IPv6 addressing. IPv6 also supports dynamic addressing and Internet Protocol Security (IPSec).

For more information about TCP/IP networking, see Chapter 24, "Managing TCP/IP Networking."

IETF Security Standards Support

The IETF maintains a set of standards governing communications, protocols, and security. Although versions of the Windows operating system previously supported both proprietary security protocols and Internet security protocols, this is the first time Microsoft has fully supported the IETF security standards. Windows Server 2003 gains the added security benefits from trusted industry standards for security.

XML Web Services Support

Microsoft's .NET initiative is built around XML and such enabling technologies as SOAP, UDDI, and WSDL. Windows Server 2003 supports the related standards for these technologies and also supports XML Web services standards for creating and hosting dynamic Web services.

Interface and Tool Improvements

One of the first things you'll notice when you work in Windows Server 2003 is that the interface is more Windows XP–like. That is, the interface has been changed so that the two operating systems have a more consistent look and feel.

Simple and Classic Start Menus

As in Windows XP, in Windows Server 2003 you can choose to use either a newer Start menu (the default) or the older Classic Start menu of Windows 2000. The newer Start menu gives you direct access to commonly used programs and allows you to execute common tasks directly. In the default configuration, it also contains menus for Control Panel and Administrative Tools, making it easy to access the tools you want to use. As much as I hate to say it, now that I've been working with the newer Start menu for a while, I actually like it. Once you start working with this default Start menu, you'll probably get used to it and—gasp!—you might even like it.

> **Tip** **Switch to the Classic Start menu**
> Not everyone wants to be (or should be, for that matter) a convert to the kinder, gentler ways of the newer Start menu. Hey, that's why they give you the option of using a different Start menu. If you prefer the classic look, you can easily change the Start menu appearance by right-clicking the task bar and then selecting Properties. In the Taskbar And Start Menu Properties dialog box, select Classic Start Menu in the Start Menu tab, and then click OK.

At the end of the day it makes little difference which Start menu you use—it really comes down to personal preference. However, you should be aware of some important navigation differences between the two. As previously mentioned, with the newer Start menu, you have direct access to commonly used tools and tasks. These tools and tasks include the following:

- Control Panel
- Administrative Tools
- Printers And Faxes
- Recently used programs
- Any program you've pinned to the Start menu

> **Tip** **Pin programs to the simple Start menu**
> Tired of navigating through multiple menus to get to a program you want to use? I was, too, which is why I started using the Pin To Start Menu feature a lot. Here's how it works: Navigate the menu system until you get to the program you want. Right-click the program, and then click Pin To Start Menu to create a program shortcut on the Start menu. This technique works only with the newer Start menu. You can't pin shortcuts to the Classic Start menu.

On the newer Start menu, you access other programs by using the All Programs option. On the Classic Start menu, you use the Settings option to access Control Panel and Printers And Faxes, and you use the Programs option to access other programs.

Improvements for Active Directory Tools

In addition to user interface (UI) changes, Windows Server 2003 includes many interface improvements for the key Active Directory administration tools: Active Directory Domains and Trusts, Active Directory Sites and Services, and Active Directory Users and Computers. The improvements are as follows:

- **Drag and drop** You can now select objects with the mouse and drag and drop them in a new location. This is a big change from Windows 2000 in which you had to right-click an object, select Move, and then use a shortcut dialog box to specify the destination.
- **Cut and paste** You can right-click an object, select Cut, navigate to the new location for the object, right-click, and then select Paste. This is, of course, similar to drag and drop, but some people prefer to cut and paste. Sometimes one technique is easier than the other for whichever task you are trying to accomplish.
- **Multiple object selection** You can select multiple objects in a series or individually so that all the selected objects can be managed as a group. To select multiple objects individually, hold down the Ctrl key, and then click each object you want to select. To select multiple objects in a series, hold down the Shift key, select the first object, and then click the last object.
- **Edit multiple objects** You can select multiple objects for editing and then perform tasks or set their common properties all at once. To do this, select the objects you want

to work with, right-click and then select the operation, such as Add To Group, Disable Account, or Properties.

For more information about planning, managing, and implementing Active Directory, see Part 7, "Managing Active Directory and Security." Using Active Directory tools is covered in this part of the book, as well as other chapters throughout the book as appropriate.

Other Tool Improvements

Other administration tools got face-lifts, too, including the Configure Your Server Wizard. As in Windows 2000, the Configure Your Server Wizard continues to be the primary tool for configuring server roles, such as whether a server is used for file services, DNS, DHCP, or all three. In Windows Server 2003, the wizard provides quick access to Add Or Remove Programs and the Configure Your Server Logs option. It also gets a role maintenance complement called Manage Your Server.

You can access Manage Your Server from the Administrative Tools menu. Click Start, point to Programs or All Programs, click Administrative Tools, and then select Manage Your Server. Manage Your Server provides quick access to the management tools and common configuration tasks for each configured role a server has.

For more information about server roles, see Chapter 2, "Planning for Windows Server 2003." To find discussions of configuring server roles, look in the section entitled "Planning for Server Usage" on page 59, as well as in Chapter 10, "Configuring Windows Server 2003." DHCP, Windows Internet Naming System (WINS), and DNS services, and the related management of these server roles, are covered in Chapters 25 through 28.

Active Directory Improvements

Active Directory was introduced in Windows 2000, and for its second major implementation, it is a pretty decent directory service. In Windows Server 2003, you will find a number of welcome improvements. Before discussing them, however, I should mention that Active Directory is improved but not perfected. It still has its quirks and shortcomings, and it is still fairly inflexible, which will frustrate some users, to be certain. For example, there is no easy way to rearrange the structure of existing forests, merge one forest with another to form a single forest, or split domains off a forest to form a new forest. These are all tasks that most large enterprises—probably even your organization, regardless of its size—will want to perform at some point in time. So, what's changed in Active Directory? Well, a lot actually, as you'll see in the sections that follow.

Note If you are new to Active Directory and Windows Server 2003, it's okay if you are not familiar with all the terms and technologies discussed in the following introductory sections. Detailed discussions of these terms and technologies are discussed in Part 7, "Managing Active Directory and Security."

Domains Can Be Renamed

You can now rename domains, which wasn't possible in Windows 2000. For example, if your company name changes from Adventure Works to Wide World Importers, you could change your domain name from *adventure-works.com* to *wideworldimporters.com*, and the domain-renaming process changes the organization's NetBIOS name as well.

As you might imagine, changing an organization's domain name has far-reaching consequences. It affects not only DNS and Active Directory, but all other network services, as well as domain trusts. It also affects every domain controller, server, and member computer in the domain. For these reasons, many prerequisites exist, as follows:

- All the domain controllers in the forest must be running Windows Server 2003.
- The forest must be operating in Windows Server 2003 functional mode.
- You must complete fairly extensive research and implementation readiness plans prior to changing the domain name.

When you are ready to continue, you use the Microsoft-provided tool, Rendom, to change the domain name. The tool automates the change process in DNS and Active Directory. When it is finished, you must use another tool, Netdom, to rename domain controllers, and finally, you must fix the GPOs using Gpfixup. One or more reboots of domain controllers and member computers are required to complete the renaming process.

For more information about renaming domains, see the section entitled "Changing Domain Design," on page 1157.

Active Directory Can Replicate Selectively

In Windows 2000, administrators can create primary DNS zones that are integrated with Active Directory (not surprisingly, these are called Active Directory–integrated primary zones). The major benefits of integrated zones are that all DNS information is stored in Active Directory and DNS information is automatically replicated with other Active Directory information to domain controllers throughout the domain. These benefits can also be detriments, however, in cases involving large numbers of domain controllers in which only a few of them are DNS servers. DNS information is replicated to each and every domain controller (as part of normal Active Directory replication), yet only a few of the domain controllers require the information. This causes a waste of network bandwidth and system resources.

Fortunately, the Active Directory implementation in Windows Server 2003 incorporates a real solution to this problem—a solution that can be applied to other types of data that you want to store in Active Directory as well—called an application partition. Essentially, an application partition allows you to create subsets of Active Directory data that can be replicated selectively throughout the domain. With Active Directory–integrated zones, application partitions are used to ensure that DNS information is replicated only to domain controllers that are also configured as DNS servers.

The really good news is that this feature doesn't require any preparation. Any domain controller running Windows Server 2003 uses this feature automatically. For other types of data that you want to store in Active Directory, you create the application partition and specify the domain controllers to which the data should be replicated.

Note To get this benefit, you must upgrade all the domain controllers running DNS in all the domains of your forest to Windows Server 2003.

NEW FEATURE!

Active Directory–Integrated DNS Zones Can Forward Conditionally

Now you might be wondering how to fix the "split-brain" syndrome that can occur when you have multiple internal domains integrated with DNS. Am I correct? If I'm not, you probably haven't encountered this problem yet, but you might in the future.

Split-brain syndrome occurs when you have separate DNS servers set up to handle inside and outside domain name addressing. The DNS server that users inside your network see handles your internal networking needs. The DNS server that users outside your network see handles address information for the company's external Web or FTP sites and mail. This configuration works fine unless you have multiple internal domains. Because each Active Directory installation requires DNS, and if you integrate DNS zones with Active Directory, you must separate DNS servers for each domain, which causes problems.

In a normal DNS configuration, when your DNS server can't resolve a request, such as when you are trying to access a Web site on the public Internet, it simply forwards the request to your company's public DNS servers for resolution. This allows domain A to obtain internal DNS information and public DNS information. It doesn't, however, allow domain A to obtain internal DNS information on domain B, which is also part of your organization. Because of this, a request sent through the DNS server for domain A about domain B is forwarded to the public DNS server for resolution, and this public DNS server has no way to resolve the request. As far as the public DNS server is concerned, the private domain doesn't exist. See what I mean about split-brain syndrome?

By using conditional forwarding, you can tell your DNS servers that when they receive a request for such and such domain, they should not forward it to the public DNS servers for resolution. Instead, they should forward the request directly to *X* server—where *X* is the DNS server for the domain being looked up. This DNS server will then be able to answer the request, and the DNS lookup will be resolved.

Note To get this benefit, you must upgrade all the domain controllers running DNS in all the domains of your forest to Windows Server 2003.

Active Directory Schema Objects Can Be Deleted

In Windows 2000 Active Directory, you could extend the schema and make changes to the directory. However, as ironic as it sounds, you could not delete objects you created in the schema. In Windows Server 2003, however, now you can deactivate schema objects in Active Directory. Because deactivated objects are considered defunct and are unavailable, this allows you to correct any changes that shouldn't have been made and make new changes without fear of being able to undo them.

Active Directory and Global Catalog Are Optimized

For many organizations, the issue of whether to install domain controllers at remote branch offices often arises. Should you install a domain controller at each site? Should you then also install the essential services the branch office requires, such as DNS, DHCP, and WINS? These are not easy decisions to make.

One of the key factors you always must consider is the type of connection between a branch office and the central office. Although some offices have persistent T1, digital subscriber line (DSL), or cable modem connections between them, others have only Integrated Services Digital Network (ISDN) or dial-up connections. Either way, usually only one connection between sites exists, and that connection can sometimes be iffy. For example, one branch site I encountered had a DSL connection that went from good to bad to worse, depending on the day (and sometimes on the time of day). Another site had a misconfigured T1 that was even worse—if you can imagine that.

With unreliable connections, organizations might be tempted to load up the branch office with everything it is going to need. You know, give it a domain controller, and install the works—DNS, DHCP, WINS, and so forth—to ensure users in the branch office can log on and remain productive if the link goes down. But even with reliable links, putting a domain controller and all those services at the branch office location could saturate the network so that there is little network bandwidth for anything else. And imagine what would happen with a poor connection.

When you decide to install a domain controller at a branch location, you might be in for some surprises before you even complete the installation. When you install a domain controller in Windows 2000, you use a tool called Dcpromo to promote an existing member server of the domain to the role of domain controller. To complete the promotion process, Dcpromo must obtain a full copy of Active Directory, which must be transferred over the network connection. When that completes, Active Directory and the configured services at the branch office must communicate and synchronize with Active Directory and the services at the main office.

With Active Directory running in Windows 2000, typically you also must install a global catalog on the domain controller to ensure users can access the global catalog during logon (which is mandatory) and can view global Active Directory data, such as distribution lists and their membership. However, if you did that, any changes you made to Active Directory could trigger a full synchronization of the global catalog (which happens any time you add attributes to a partial attribute set, such as when you add a user to a distribution list). Just imagine how that would work over an unreliable connection—or maybe you don't need to imagine it because you've already experienced it?

In Windows Server 2003, many of the issues branch offices face go away because of improvements in Active Directory and global catalog optimization. This means Windows Server 2003 really can come to the rescue.

By using Windows Server 2003, you can back up Active Directory to a file that can be burned to a CD-ROM. You can then mail copies of the CD-ROM to branch offices, and they can start the upgrade of a member server to a domain controller by installing from media using the backup, rather than forcing a complete initial replication over the interoffice link. Afterward, all the domain controller must do is synchronize with the changes that were made since the backup occurred, which usually aren't many; hence, very little replication should occur.

Windows Server 2003 also takes care of many issues related to the global catalog. First, you might not even need to use a global catalog at a branch office because Windows Server 2003 introduces universal group membership caching, which allows the branch office domain controller to cache the universal group membership information so that it is available to users. This feature effectively solves the problem of users not being able to log on when the interoffice link is down because no local global catalog exists (otherwise, access to the global catalog is required for logon).

By using caching, the information is replicated only when it is initially requested and not each time a change is made to the directory. This means less replication traffic is transmitted over the network. In addition, Active Directory has been optimized so that when you add attributes to a partial attribute set, only the changes are replicated. This means that instead of requiring a full synchronization after a change is made, Active Directory can now replicate only the change. Active Directory in Windows Server 2003 has also been optimized to enhance the ways in which transmission of replicated data occurs.

> **Note** Good news! These features do not require you to upgrade every domain controller in all the domains of your forest. You can, in fact, take advantage of these features at a branch office simply by installing a domain controller that runs Windows Server 2003 at the branch office. However, to take advantage of other features of Active Directory, as discussed previously, you are better off upgrading all domain controllers in your forest.

Active Directory Can Compress and Route Selectively

In Windows 2000, Microsoft attempted to decrease the impact of data replication on the network by compressing data so that it uses less bandwidth for transmission and using a least-cost method of routing data from a domain controller in one office to a domain controller in another office. Unfortunately, both implementations had unintended side effects. The processes of compressing and uncompressing data require processing time and resources. The routing algorithm chosen wasn't necessarily the best one, and as a result Active Directory bogged down when replicating data to more than a few hundred sites.

The fixes in Windows Server 2003 are relatively straightforward. You can now specify whether Active Directory should use compression. You do this by disabling compression and allowing Active Directory to replicate data natively. Although this means data is raw and uncompressed and will use additional network bandwidth, it also means the domain controllers won't waste processing power compressing and uncompressing Active Directory data. If you have plenty of bandwidth but CPU power is at a premium, you might consider this option.

To resolve the routing algorithm issue, Microsoft started using industry-standard algorithms that were highly optimized rather than the routing algorithms developed in-house. The result is that Active Directory can now handle replication to thousands of sites rather than hundreds.

Note To get these benefits, however, you must upgrade all the domain controllers in all the domains of your forest to Windows Server 2003.

Forest-to-Forest Trusts

I've already mentioned Active Directory forests, and I've also mentioned that in Windows 2000 forests were fairly inflexible. This might have got you wondering whether Windows Server 2003 improves the way forests work at all. The good news is that it does. You might also have wondered what the point of a forest is. In brief, you combine Active Directory domains into a forest to gain the advantages of transitive trusts and universal group caching. For automatic transitive trusts in Active Directory, all the domains in a forest automatically trust each other. For universal group caching, the designated global catalog servers in each domain cache directory data not just about that domain but about all domains in the forest. This makes it easier for users to access resources throughout the forest and to manage permissions on an enterprise-wide basis.

A problem enters the picture, however, when you want to share resources between forests. In Windows 2000, no easy way to share resource between forests exists. Sure, if the organization acquires several forests after a merger or similar consolidation, you could migrate all the accounts for users, groups, computers, and other objects from all forests to one forest, and then you'd have only one forest. But migration is a lot of work and it might not accomplish everything you hope it would.

Fortunately, Windows Server 2003 extends the concept of trusts to the forest level. In Windows Server 2003–based forests, you can use a cross-forest trust to establish a trust relationship between forests. Once you do this, all the domains in the first forest trust all the domains in the second forest, and vice versa. Problem solved, right? Well, mostly, because the forests still separate the global catalog servers, so that the first forest has a separate global catalog from the second forest and applications that are dependent on the global catalog, such as Microsoft Exchange Server 2003, won't recognize your organization as a single forest with one directory but as two separate forests with two directories.

Note To use forest trusts, you must upgrade all the domain controllers in all the domains of *both* forests to Windows Server 2003.

Active Directory Migration Made Easier

Windows 2000 shipped with version 1 of the Active Directory Migration Tool (ADMT). The tool has since been revised and enhanced, and now version 2 is available as a download for Windows Server 2003 (*http://www.microsoft.com/windowsserver2003/downloads/tools/*). This latest version of the migration tool allows you to migrate user accounts, computer accounts, access control lists, and trusts from Windows NT 4 or Windows 2000 domains to Windows Server 2003 domains. Unlike previous versions of the tool, which migrated user accounts but not passwords, the new version migrates passwords as well.

You can also migrate objects between Active Directory forests. This allows you to set up an entirely new forest and migrate objects to the new forest. For example, if your company merges with another company or the company name changes, you could create a new forest to accommodate the changes. Or, if a branch office sets up its network in a separate forest, you could migrate it to the main forest of your organization. In the case of a merger, you could migrate the objects in company A's forest to company B's forest.

Group Policy Improvements

Some of the changes that have occurred in Group Policy include the new Group Policy Management Console, the new Software Restriction Policies feature in Group Policies, and new policies for user profiles.

Group Policy Management Console

Navigating Group Policy can be a nightmare. Heck, just trying to figure out where things are can be a challenge, not to mention trying to figure out why so and so's computer doesn't have a policy applied when everyone else's does. Often you have to work with several different tools to try to figure things out. All in all, it can be a very frustrating experience.

Enter Group Policy Management Console (GPMC), Microsoft's solution for making Group Policy management easier. GPMC does for Group Policy what the Computer Management console did for system, storage, and service management; namely, it gives you a central interface for working with Group Policy. The really good news is that GPMC can be used to manage Windows Server 2003–based as well as Windows 2000–based Group Policy implementations. This means you can use it even if you haven't fully upgraded to Windows Server 2003.

For more information about Group Policy management and the GPMC, see Chapter 38, "Managing Group Policy." You can download GPMC from the Windows Server 2003 Feature Packs page on the Microsoft Web site (*http://www.microsoft.com/windowsserver2003/downloads/featurepacks/*). GPMC is also included with Windows Server 2003 Service Pack 1.

Software Restriction Policies in Group Policy

I don't know how many administrators and help desk staff I've heard ask, "How do I keep people from running certain programs?" The problem they're describing stems from the fact that sometimes users install things they shouldn't, such as music-sharing software and other tools that should never be used in business environments—not only because of what the tools allow people to do but because of what the tools do to the computers on which they are installed.

In Windows 2000, there aren't a lot of choices. But it's a different story with Windows XP and Windows Server 2003. You can now use software restriction policies to control which programs users can install. For example, you can specify that desktop users can install only Microsoft Office applications and the Palm Desktop. Then, if users attempt to install other applications, they will not be able to do so.

Policy Changes for User Profiles

User profiles can be configured as local, mandatory, or roaming, each of which has its pluses and minuses, as you'll learn in Chapter 37, "Managing Users, Groups, and Computers." Unfortunately, there are some quirks about profiles that make them less than fun things to deal with. For example, if you are using EFS, you pretty much have to use a roaming profile (unless you copy your encryption certificate to every machine you use seriously). But roaming profiles can grow quite large (which slows you down), and they can break (which can ruin your day). So, sometimes when you are using a roaming profile, such as when you are on a slow connection, you'll want to be able to say, "Hey, don't use my roaming profile!"

In Windows Server 2003, you can configure Group Policy to handle this and other similar profile tasks for you. For starters, you can specify that only local user profiles should be used on a particular computer, which ensures roaming profiles are loaded only when you want them to be. You can also specify through policy that the system must prompt you before downloading a roaming profile when a slow link is detected (and you can configure policy that specifies exactly what a slow link is; i.e., whether it is a 56 kilobits per second [Kbps], 128 Kbps, or 512 Kbps connection). To make changes to Group Policy, you use the Group Policy Object Editor, which is discussed in Chapter 38.

Management and Administration Extras

Anyone who has managed Windows 2000 knows it is a big step forward from previous Windows operating systems when it comes to ease of management and flexibility in administration. Many of the features in Windows 2000 simply are easier to use than they were in Windows NT. Still, Windows 2000 is lacking in some key management and administration areas, with ease of remote administration being a big hit. Windows Server 2003 includes greatly improved remote administration solutions, as well as many other new features and enhancements.

Remote Administration Gets a Face-Lift

Coming from a UNIX and mainframe background, I've always missed the ease with which you could manage those systems remotely. Windows operating systems didn't contain a real "in-the-box " solution; mostly, we simply had to muddle through with third-party solutions such as Symantec's pcAnywhere. Although there's nothing wrong with pcAnywhere, it just didn't seem right that there wasn't a built-in operating system solution. Microsoft changed that with Windows 2000 by including Telnet and Terminal Services in the Server Edition of the operating system. These features allow administrators to make remote connections and to remotely control systems, but they are hardly best of class and aren't very easy to configure or manage.

What was missing was a friendly interface and ways to manage both remote control sessions and remote computers easily once you were connected. Windows XP Professional delivered the solution: Remote Desktop Connection, which is essentially a better user interface for Terminal Services that makes it easier to work with remote systems and manage your remote sessions.

Remote Desktop Connection not only brings a friendlier interface but a smarter one as well. It uses the Remote Desktop Protocol (RDP) to manage sessions and connections. Microsoft enhanced RDP so that it works well over slow connections, even over dial-up connections, which makes it seem as if you're sitting at the keyboard of the remote computer no matter where you are or what type of connection you are using. Remote Desktop Connection also gives your remote control session automatic access to your local hard disk drives and printers, which you did not have in Terminal Services in Windows 2000. Remote Desktop Connections also supports multiple screen sizes, colors, and sound. You can, in fact, set the screen size you want to use for the remote session.

Windows Server 2003 offers the remote administration features of Windows XP and extends the feature set to include remote control administration by way of Remote Desktop Web Connection. Once installed and configured, you can remotely manage systems using a Web browser. Although the feature set is limited, you can perform most management functions using the Web interface.

> **Note** It's pretty important that you know how to use remote administration in Windows Server 2003—and that's why the technology is covered in several areas of this book. You'll find the detailed examination in Chapter 30, "Using Remote Desktop for Administration."

Enhanced File Management by Using DFS

In many organizations, files are distributed across multiple servers, and each department and site usually maintains its own file shares. Users access files locally and typically also have access to files at other sites. Often, files are duplicated between sites to ensure that they are accessible to users no matter where the user is located. This creates the situation in which lots of file shares exist and many systems act as file servers.

Windows 2000 delivered DFS to help manage many distributed file shares. Windows Server 2003 builds on the features previously available and extends them to help administrators consolidate file shares to fewer servers and create file directory trees on an enterprise-wide basis. This means you can create a single enterprise-wide directory tree that spans file shares from multiple servers.

Best of all, the directory tree separates the physical files from the logical structure of the directory so you can move the data, add or remove servers, consolidate shares, and perform other physical data management functions without having to make changes to the way users see the logical DFS directory. You can also provide redundancy and fault tolerance of the physical data using DFS replicas. A *DFS replica* is essentially a copy of the physical data that serves as a file backup and can be made available to users if the primary DFS data is unavailable for some reason.

Improved Storage and File System Options

Windows 2000 introduced NTFS 5, a major revision of the NT file system (NTFS). NTFS 5 delivers support for Active Directory structures, disk quotas, and data encryption. It also increases the maximum volume size and the maximum file size that could be used with the Windows operating system. In NTFS 5, dynamic disks have a maximum size of 2 terabytes (TB) and file sizes are limited only by the volume size. By combining multiple dynamic disks into a spanned volume, you can create dynamic volumes as large as 64 TB.

Windows Server 2003 delivers a significant addition to NTFS with a feature called Volume Shadow Copy. Volume Shadow Copy can create replicas of file shares called snapshots, and as the name implies, it does this in the background without administrator intervention. Basically, you decide which file shares should have shadow copies, and then you specify the times during the day when snapshots should be taken. After a snapshot is taken, files can be read from the shadow copy to recover them to the specific point in time when the snapshot was created.

To get a better understanding of how Shadow Copy works, consider the following example: You configure the Windows operating system to create shadow copies of a data application share at 7:00 A.M. and 3 P.M. every day. If a user in Accounting accidentally deletes an important spreadsheet at 3:05 P.M., she can, without your assistance, recover the spreadsheet by obtaining it from the 3 P.M. snapshot taken that day. If she finds that the snapshot has changes that shouldn't have been made, she can recover to the 7:00 A.M. snapshot or even recover back to a snapshot taken a different day. She does this by accessing the shadow copy and selecting an archived file for retrieval.

Because Volume Shadow Copy creates point-in-time copies of files, it can also be used to back up open files. Not only has this always been an administrative challenge, it has been many an administrator's nightmare. With some backup systems, open files couldn't be backed up at all. They simply were skipped. With other backup systems, open files could be backed up, but the backup process was slowed significantly or files were backed up out of sequence.

Here's how backup of open files works by using shadow copies: Volume Shadow Copy creates a snapshot of the volume you want to back up and saves the snapshot to another volume. The backup software then uses the shadow copy to create a backup of the volume without concern for open files. In addition, because files are not in use, the backup software need not go through the normal process of unlocking each file, backing it up, and then locking it again for user access—it simply backs up the files.

Although other changes to NTFS aren't as far-reaching as Volume Shadow Copy, they are significant. For instance, in Windows 2000, NTFS clusters could not exceed 4 kilobytes (KB) in size if you wanted to be able to defragment the volume using Disk Defragmenter. However, unlike Windows 2000, Disk Defragmenter can now be used to defragment volumes of any cluster size (up to the allowed 64 KB). Encryption of files on NTFS volumes has also been improved. You can now cache encrypted files for offline use. You can also configure encrypted files so that more than one user can view them.

For more information about NTFS and its many features, see Chapter 20, "Managing Windows Server 2003 File Systems." You'll also find related discussions on auditing and sharing NTFS resources in Chapter 21, "File Sharing and Security."

Changes for Terminal Services

With Terminal Services, clients using a Web browser, a Windows terminal, or the Remote Desktop can access a centralized terminal server to gain access to network resources. Windows Server 2003 Terminal Services users gain the benefits from the improved Remote Desktop Protocol discussed previously as well as some additional features specific to client terminal services. Clients can now access local hard disk drives and printers and can get audio redirected from the central terminal server. Previously, these features were available only by using a separately purchased add-on.

Local access to hard disk drives allows users to browse local drives as well as remote drives, to drag and drop files between local and remote drives, and to copy, cut, and paste files between local and remote drives. Redirecting audio from a central terminal server to the speaker of a remote client is useful in several situations, such as when applications running on the central terminal server have text-to-speech capabilities, integrated voice mail, or other audio output capabilities.

In addition, client users now have the ability to specify the time zone to use. Previously, the only time zone used was the one on the central terminal server. In Windows Server 2003, clients can choose the default time zone on the server or their local time zone, which is useful when organizations have centralized servers and employees at many different locations.

Last, client users can specify the connection type to use as slow-speed modem, medium-speed broadband, high-speed local area network (LAN), or custom. This wasn't possible previously, and the advantage is that the terminal server optimizes the user environment based on the connection type. With a slow-speed modem connection, complex backgrounds, themes, and animations are disabled, as are other features that might slow down the display.

By specifying a medium-speed broadband connection, users get more features, but the features are balanced to ensure the connection is optimized for getting work done. For a high-speed LAN connection, all the display features and other options are enabled so the connection works just like it would if the user was sitting at a desktop in the office.

Printer Queue Redundancy

Printing is something most people—even some administrators—take for granted. Heck, when you click Print, a document is supposed to print on a printer somewhere. Well, that doesn't happen all the time. Sometimes print servers or printer queues fail. To resolve this problem for environments in which printing is a high priority, Windows Server 2003 introduces print clusters that provide redundancy for printer queues. Printer queue redundancy allows you to configure printer queues on multiple servers and configure failover from one queue to another in the event of a failure.

For more information about configuring print servers and printer queues, see Chapter 29, "Installing and Maintaining Print Services."

Remote Installation Services

Remote Installation Services (RIS) have been enhanced for Windows Server 2003. By using these services, you can create images of server configurations for use in new installations and for server recovery.

For new installations, you can use an RIS image rather than starting from scratch with the Windows Server 2003 CD-ROM. The image can include service packs, updates, security patches, services, and applications. Thus, instead of installing the operating system and then installing and configuring service packs, updates, security patches, and essential services and applications, you simply apply the image and the server is ready for use. Because RIS can store many images, you could create separate images for each server role, such as domain controllers, file servers, and application servers.

The way you use RIS for server recovery is similar to the way you use it for creating images for new servers. After you install and configure all the necessary services and applications, you create an RIS image of the server. This image stores the state of the server before system failure. Then, if the system fails, you can use RIS to recover the server to the last saved image.

For more information about RIS, see Chapter 6, "Using Remote Installation Services." There's also a supplemental discussion on using RIS to recover servers in Chapter 41, "Backup and Recovery."

Headless Servers and Out-of-Band Management

When I work with Cisco routers, I love the way that you can connect a portable computer through a serial cable to the back of the router and then use your portable computer to perform low-level management tasks. Once the router is configured, you let it run and do its work. You need not have a monitor, mouse, or keyboard connected to it because you can log in remotely from any terminal or over the Internet to make configuration changes.

In a way, you can think of routers as running in headless operations mode. They don't need input and output devices to function. In Windows Server 2003, you can run servers in headless operations mode as well. Here, you configure the server so that it doesn't expect to have a monitor, mouse, or keyboard connected to it, and then you manage the server using remote connections. This feature saves you from having to run cables to the server from a display switch or actually connecting a monitor, keyboard, or mouse.

Traditionally, one of the drawbacks of headless server operations is that if the server stops or otherwise becomes nonresponsive, there isn't a way to access the server to see what was happening. Routers solve this problem by having serial connection ports that allow direct connections, such as from your portable computer directly to the router, to perform low-level management tasks. One remote management hack to use with routers is to connect a serial cable between the router and another piece of hardware, such as a firewall, so that you could manage the router even if it is otherwise nonresponsive by using a connection from the other hardware component.

A similar out-of-band management feature, called Emergency Management Services, is now available in Windows Server 2003. By using Emergency Management Services, you can connect to a serial port on the back of the server to perform low-level management tasks from the command line. You can even recover from a blue screen, something that you could do previously only by logging on to the console. Here, you could do an image dump of the server's memory and then reboot the server. You could also reboot the server to safe mode so that you could modify system parameters before rebooting the system in normal operations mode. There are many connection options as well. You can connect through a serial port using your portable computer. You can connect through a modem or make a direct serial connection through another device, even another server—both of which work well for remote connections.

Security Advances

Windows Server 2003 has several far-reaching advances in the area of security and a few extras that make life easier as well.

Windows Server 2003 Feature Lock Down

A production goal based on the Trustworthy Computing Initiative started by Bill Gates in 2001 was for Windows Server 2003 to be the most secure version of the Windows operating system to date. It was a far-reaching goal designed to curb the perception that Windows operating systems are inherently insecure. The simple truth of the matter is that the Windows operating system is very, perhaps even extremely, secure. You can change options that lock down the server and restrict access with fine precision. The problem, however, is that the Windows operating system didn't ship in locked-down mode; it shipped with many of the major security features unlocked, making the system very open for access.

Windows Server 2003 resolves many security issues simply by locking down the security "out of the box," and that's a good thing, trust me. You'll notice right away new permissions for the volume roots and changes in how IIS is used and installed. For volume roots, permissions are changed so that the special identity Everyone has only Read and Execute permissions, while members of the Users group have Read, Execute, and limited Change permissions. (They can create only folders, not files, at the volume root level. Once they create subfolders, they can create files within the subfolders.)

IIS services are installed only if you elect to install them; and when you do install them, the default installation allows only static HTML files to be served. All other functions and types of content must be specifically enabled. You can change the settings, of course, but the default configuration does help ensure servers are inherently more secure out of the box.

IPSec and Wireless Security

IPSec provides end-to-end encryption of all data packets transferred between computers at the transport layer (level 3 of the Open System Interconnections, or OSI, model). It is considered to be one of the best ways to secure data packets and provides an enhanced layer of security against attacks, whether systems are on the public Internet or a private network. IPSec was included in Windows 2000 and has been extended in Windows Server 2003 with a new IP Security Monitor MMC snap-in, new command-line functionality in Netsh for configuring IPSec, expanded options for IPSec policies, and IPSec extensions to Group Policy for troubleshooting IPSec policies. Windows Server 2003 also supports dynamic key determination using the Institute of Electrical and Electronics Engineers (IEEE) 802.1x authentication standard for secured wireless LANs, which is an improvement over Wireless Equivalency Protocol (WEP). Both technologies can help ensure wireless communications are secure.

Windows Server 2003 also supports secure IP communications over Network Address Translation (NAT), or more specifically, IPSec NAT traversal. Yes, it's raining acronyms again, but it's all for the greater good, trust me. Standard NAT traversal, a technology first included in Windows XP and now also available in Windows Server 2003, allows computers on one private network to communicate with computers on another private network through a router when previously this wasn't possible because private IP addresses are nonroutable.

NAT comes into the picture in relation to the public Internet. NAT translates the private IP addresses used on your network to public IP addresses that can be used to make requests and communicate with computers in the public domain. NAT doesn't allow you to communicate between private networks, however, which is why NAT traversal is needed. NAT traversal allows the routers and/or firewalls between two private networks to make requests and communicate with each other by dynamically remapping port numbers. The gotcha is that standard NAT traversal isn't secure, which is why Windows Server 2003 includes IPSec NAT Traversal. With IPSec NAT Traversal, computers using NAT on separate private networks can communicate with each other using secure, encrypted communications.

Microsoft .NET Passport Support

Windows XP introduced Microsoft .NET Passport, a technology for authenticating logons and enabling secure communications with .NET Passport–enabled sites. Web software, such as MSN Instant Messenger, is .NET Passport–enabled, as are Web sites, particularly e-commerce sites. This allows easy logon authentication and secure communications once logon is complete. Now that Microsoft .NET Passport support is included in Windows Server 2003, a .NET Passport–enabled client can log on to a Windows Server 2003 network using its secure credentials. Thus, the same .NET Passport that allows users to access Web software and e-commerce sites can be used to create a secure connection to an organization's network.

Reliability and Maintenance Enhancements

System reliability and maintenance go hand in hand. For systems to be reliable and easily maintained, faster, better, and easier ways to verify system integrity; apply patches, hot fixes, and updates; and undo changes are necessary. Windows Server 2003 introduces many features that can help you in these areas.

For more information about reliability and maintenance enhancements, see Chapter 10, "Configuring Windows Server 2003," and Chapter 11, "Windows Server 2003 MMC Administration." Refer to these chapters for detailed implementation and management discussions.

Automatic System Recovery

Automatic System Recovery (ASR) is a system recovery utility included in Windows Server 2003. By using this utility, you can rebuild a failed server without having to reinstall the operating system. ASR works like this: When you run the Backup utility and select ASR, it creates a snapshot of the server and its configuration, which includes the operating system, its components, and their configurations, as well as dynamic volume settings for partitioning and fault tolerance. If the server fails, you can restore it to the same machine or another machine with the exact same system configuration as the original machine.

Because of the way the snapshot is applied, you need not reinstall the operating system or reconfigure components prior to running the utility. You simply boot the server to the Windows Server 2003 installation CD-ROM and choose to do a system recovery.

Automatic Updates

Service Pack 3 for Windows 2000 introduced the concept of Automatic Updates. Automatic Updates helps you keep the operating system up-to-date with the latest patches, hot fixes, and service packs by periodically checking to see whether compatible updates for the system are available and then downloading those updates for installation. Microsoft includes this feature in Windows Server 2003 as well, which provides an easy way to ensure servers are up-to-date with system patches and the latest security updates.

As in Windows XP, the Windows Server 2003 Automatic Updates utility gives you complete control over how the update process works. You can configure the service to do the following:

- Notify you when updates are available and then allow you to download and install them
- Download the updates automatically and then notify you before installing them
- Automatically download and install updates on a specific schedule

Automatic Updates also has a rollback feature that allows you to remove updates and restore a server to the state it was in before an update was applied.

Improved Verification and System Protection

System verification and protection utilities have been evolving since Windows 2000. Windows 2000 includes System File Protection and Driver Verifier utilities. System File Protection protects system files to ensure they are not accidentally overwritten. Driver Verifier allows you to check new device drivers and other system-level programs to ensure compatibility. If you have a problem with a kernel-level program, Driver Verifier helps you find it.

Windows XP adds System Restore, Application Verifier, and Driver Rollback. System Restore allows you to make point-in-time checkpoints of the operating system configuration and use these checkpoints to recover the Windows operating system to a previous point in time. Application Verifier allows you to check applications to ensure compatibility. If you run a program using Application Verifier and it fails, Application Verifier tells you what caused it to fail, and, even better, it has the capability to add information to the program to allow it to run normally. Driver Rollback is a simpler, friendlier version of Driver Verifier. Driver Rollback allows you to remove device drivers that have been applied by rolling the system back to use a previous version of a driver. In fact, all previous versions of drivers are saved so they can be used for rollback as necessary. Also, if you are unsure of a driver and want to test it, you can install it, let a server run with it for a while, and if it doesn't work out, you can use the Driver Rollback feature to restore the previous driver.

Except for System Restore, all of these features are included in Windows Server 2003. Windows Server 2003 continues to support System File Protection. It adopts the simpler, easier-to-use version of Driver Verifier—Driver Rollback. It includes Application Verifier. And it uses Volume Shadow Copy in place of System Restore.

Chapter 2

Planning for Windows Server 2003

Deploying Microsoft Windows Server 2003 is a substantial undertaking, even on a small network. Just the task of planning a Windows Server 2003 deployment can be a daunting process, especially in a large enterprise. The larger the business, however, the more important it is that the planning process be thorough and fully account for the proposed project's goals, as well as lay out exactly how those goals will be accomplished.

Accommodating the goals of all the business units in a company can be difficult, and it is best accomplished with a well-planned series of steps that includes checkpoints and plenty of opportunity for management participation. The organization as a whole will benefit from your thorough preparation and so will the information technology (IT) department. Careful planning can also help you avoid common obstacles by helping you identify potential pitfalls and then determine how best to avoid them, or at least be ready for any unavoidable complications.

Overview of Planning

A clear road map can help with any complex project, and deploying Windows Server 2003 in the enterprise is certainly a complex project. A number of firms have developed models to describe IT processes such as planning and systems management—often used by their consulting group—each of which offers its own structured method of approaching a complex project. This detailed description of the people who should be involved, the tasks they will perform, and the order in which they should perform the tasks can be useful when approaching a large-scale project.

These models all share a largely common path for walking through the planning process—they divide it into different phases and describe it using different phrases. The *Microsoft Solutions Framework Process Model*, described in the next section, provides an illustration of one approach.

The Microsoft Solutions Framework Process Model

Microsoft has defined its own formalized processes for implementing IT solutions and network management. Two models are used: the *Microsoft Solutions Framework (MSF)* defines deployment project methods, while operations administration is the focus of the *Microsoft Operations Framework (MOF)*. The MSF process model defines the following phases:

- **Envisioning** During the first phase, project goals are defined and clarified. Using this information, you create a vision/scope document stating the overall vision, goals, and scope of the project. The final step in this phase is approval of this document.
- **Planning** Once the goals and scope have been agreed upon, you have to translate that information into the specific features, services, and configuration options that are required to achieve the goals. A master project plan, which describes how the implementation will proceed and sets the schedule, is approved at the end of this phase.
- **Developing** During this phase, the Windows Server 2003 infrastructure, any required custom code (applications or scripting), and documentation are developed.
- **Stabilizing** When the new environment has been created in the lab, it is thoroughly tested prior to deployment. This is your chance to ensure that the platform is stable and ready to go before you begin the pilot deployment.
- **Deploying** Finally, you deploy Windows Server 2003 into the production environment. IT staff first perform a small pilot project; once that is successfully completed, Windows Server 2003 is rolled out across the rest of the environment.

These stages are seen as occurring more or less linearly, but not exclusively so, in that stages are commonly revisited at multiple points along the way.

For more information about the MSF, visit *http://www.microsoft.com/msf/*.

Tip Keep in mind that every company has its own internal politics, which can introduce quirks into many projects and processes, even those in the IT department.

Your Plan: The Big Picture

The Microsoft model is an interesting one, but it is useful to get a bit more specific. This is especially true when working with people from other departments, who might not be familiar with IT processes. For our purposes, the deployment process can be broken down into a roughly sequential set of tasks:

- **Identify the team** For all but the smallest rollouts of a new operating system, a team of people will be involved in both the planning and deployment processes. The actual size and composition of this team will be different in each situation. Collecting the right mixture of skills and expertise will help ensure the success of your project.

- **Assess your goals** Any business undertaking the move to Windows Server 2003 has many reasons for doing so, only some of which are obvious to the IT department. It is important to carefully identify the goals of the *entire* company before determining the scope of the project to ensure that all critical goals are met.
- **Analyze the existing environment** Examine the current network environment, even if you think that you know *exactly* how everything works—you will often find you are only partially correct. Gather hardware and software inventories, network maps, and lists of which servers are providing which services. Also, identify critical business processes, and examine the administrative and security approaches that are currently in place. Windows Server 2003 offers a number of security and management improvements, and it is useful to know which ones are particularly important in your environment.
- **Define the project scope** Project scope is often one of the more difficult areas to pin down, and one that deserves particular attention in the planning process. Defining scope requires prioritizing the goals of the various groups within the organization and then realistically assessing what can be accomplished within an acceptable budget and time frame. It's not often that the wish list of features and capabilities from the entire company can be fulfilled in the initial, or even later, deployment.
- **Design the new network environment** Once you have pinned down the project scope, you must develop a detailed design for the new operating system deployment and the affected portions of the network. During this time, you should create documentation describing the end state of the network, as well as the process of getting there. This design document serves as a road map for the people building the testing environment and, with refinements during the testing process, for the IT department later on.
- **Test the design** Thorough testing in the lab is an often overlooked, but critically important, phase of deploying a new network operating system. By building a test lab and putting a prototype environment through its paces, you can identify and solve many problems in a controlled environment, rather than in the field.
- **Install Windows Server 2003** After you have validated your design in the lab and management has approved the deployment, you can begin to install Windows Server 2003 in your production environment. The installation process has two phases:
    - *Pilot phase*—During the pilot phase, you will deploy and test a small group of servers running Windows Server 2003 (and perhaps clients running Microsoft Windows XP) in a production environment. You should pick a pilot group that is comfortable working with new technology, and for whom minor interruptions will not pose significant problems. In other words, this is not a good thing to do to the president of the company or the finance department just before taxes are due.
    - *Rollout*—Once you have determined that the pilot phase was a success, you can begin the rollout to the rest of the company. Make sure you schedule adequate downtime, and allow for ongoing minor interruptions and increased support demands as users encounter changed functionality.

As mentioned, these steps are generally sequential, but not exclusively so. You are likely to find that as you work through one phase of planning, you must return to activities that are technically part of an earlier phase. This is actually a good thing, because it means you are refining your plan dynamically as you discover new factors and contingencies.

Inside Out

Getting off to a quick start

People need not be assigned to all these tasks at the beginning of the planning process. If you have people who can take on the needs analysis and research on the current and new network environment (these are roughly the program management, product management, and development assignments from the MSF model), you can get the project under way while recruiting the rest of the project team.

Identifying Your Organizational Teams

A project like this requires a lot of time and effort as well as a broad range of knowledge, expertise, and experience. Unless you are managing a very small network, this project is likely to require more than one person to plan and implement. Team members are assigned to various roles, each of which is concerned with a different aspect of the project.

Each of these roles may be filled by one or more persons, devoting all or part of their workday—and beyond in some cases—to the project. No direct correlation exists between a team role and a single individual who performs it. In a large organization, a team of individuals might fulfill each of these roles, while in a small organization one person can fill more than one role.

Microsoft Solutions Framework Team Model

As with IT processes, a number of vendors and consultants have put together team models, which you can leverage in designing your own team. One such model is the *Microsoft Solutions Framework Team Model*, which uses six teams to plan and deploy an IT project.

- **Program management team** Program management's primary responsibility is ensuring that project goals are met within the constraints set forth at the beginning of the project. Program management handles the functional design, budget, schedule, and reporting.
- **Product management team** This team is responsible for identifying the business and user needs of the project and ensuring that the final plan meets those needs.
- **Development team** The development team is responsible for defining the physical design and feature set of the project and estimates the budget and time needed for project completion.

- **Testing team** The testing team is critical in ensuring that the final deployment is successful. It designs and builds the test environment, develops a testing plan, and then performs the tests and resolves any issues it discovers before the pilot deployment occurs.
- **Release management team** The release management team designs the test deployment and then performs that deployment as a means of verifying the reliability of the deployment before widespread adoption.
- **User experience team** This team manages the transition of users to the new environment. This includes developing and delivering user training, as well as analysis of user feedback during testing and the pilot deployment.

Working together, these teams cover the various aspects of a significant project, such as rolling out Windows Server 2003.

Your Project Team

The Microsoft model is just that: a model. It serves as an example, yet you will not necessarily implement it, or any other model, exactly as designed by someone else. Although all IT projects share some things in common, and therefore need someone to handle that area of the project, that's where the commonality stops.

Each company is in a different business and has IT needs related to its specific business activities. This might mean additional team members are needed to manage those aspects of the project. For example, if external clients and/or the public also access some of your IT systems as users, you have a set of user acceptance and testing requirements different than many other businesses.

The project team needs business managers who understand, and who can represent, the needs of the various business units. This requires knowledge of both the business operations and a clear picture of the daily tasks performed by line staff.

Representatives of the IT department bring their technical expertise to the table, not only to detail the inner workings of the network, but also to help business managers realistically assess how technology can help their departments and sort out the impractical goals from the realistic ones.

Make sure that all critical aspects of business operations are covered—include representatives from all departments that have critical IT needs, and the team must take the needs of the entire company into account. This means that people on the project team must collect information from line-of-business managers and the people actually doing the work. (Surprisingly enough, the latter escapes many a project team.)

Once you have a team together, management must ensure that team members have adequate time and resources to fulfill the tasks required of them for the project. This can mean shifting all or part of their usual workload to others for the project duration, or providing resources such as Internet access, project-related software, and so on. Any project is easier, and more likely to be successful, with this critical real-time support from management.

Inside Out

Hiring talent

Sometimes you don't have people available in-house with all the needed skills and must look to consultants or contracted workers. Examine which tasks should be outsourced and exactly what you must receive from the relationship. Pay particular attention to highly specialized or complex areas—the Active Directory directory service architecture, for example—and those with a high rate of change.

One-time tasks, such as creating user training programs and documentation, are also good candidates for outsourcing. For areas in which there will be an ongoing need for the lacking expertise, such as security, it might be a better idea to send a staff member to get additional training instead.

Assessing Project Goals

Carefully identifying the goals behind moving to Windows Server 2003 is an important part of the planning process. Without a clear list of objectives, you are unlikely to achieve them. Even with a clear set of goals in mind, it is unlikely you will accomplish them all. Most large business projects involve some compromise, and the process of deploying Windows Server 2003 is unlikely to be an exception.

Although deploying a new operating system is ultimately an IT task, most of the reasons behind the deployment won't be coming from the IT department. Computers are, after all, tools used by business to increase productivity, enhance communications, facilitate business tasks, and so on; the IT department is concerned with making sure that the computer environment needed by the business is implemented.

Inside Out

Creating documentation, almost painlessly

During the planning process, and as you begin to use the new network environment, you'll be creating numerous documents describing the current state of the network, the planned changes, IT standards, administrative procedures, and the like. It's a good idea to take advantage of all of this up-to-date information to create policies and procedures documents, which will help ensure that the network stays in compliance with your new standards and administration is accomplished as intended.

The same set of documents can also serve as a basis for user guides, as well as administrator and user training, and can be made available through the corporate intranet. If the people working on the project, especially those performing testing, take notes about any error conditions they encounter and the resolutions to them, you'll also have a good start on frequently asked questions (FAQs) and other technical support data.

The Business Perspective

Many discussions of the business reasons for new software deployments echo common themes: enhance productivity, eliminate downtime, reduce costs, and the like. Translating these often somewhat vague (and occasionally lofty) aspirations into concrete goals sometimes takes a bit of effort. It is well worth taking the time, however, to refine the big picture into specific objectives before moving on. An IT department should serve the needs of the business, not the other way around; if you don't understand those needs clearly, you'll have a hard time fulfilling them.

Be sure to ask for the input of people close to where the work is being done—department managers from each business area should be asked about what they need from IT, what works now and what doesn't. These people care about the day-to-day operations of their computing environment; that is, do the changes help their staff do their work? Ask about work patterns, both static and burst—the Finance department's workflow is not the same in July as it is in April. Make sure to include all departments, as well as any significant subsets—human resources (HR), finance, sales, business units, executive management, and so on.

You should also identify risks that lie at the business level, such as resistance to change, lack of commitment (frequently expressed as inadequate resources: budget, staff, time, and so on), or even the occasional bit of overt opposition. At the same time, look for positives to exploit—enthusiastic staff can help energize others, and a manager in your corner can smooth many bumps along the way. By getting people involved, you can gain allies who are vested in the success of the project.

Inside Out

Talk to the people who will use the technology

Not to put too fine a point on it, but make sure that the team members who will be handling aspects of the user experience actually talk with users. The only way to adequately assess what the people doing the work need in critical areas such as usability, training, and support is to get in the trenches and see what they are doing. If possible, have meetings at the user's workstation, because it can provide additional insight into daily operations. If passwords are visible on sticky notes stuck to monitors—a far too common practice—you know you have security issues.

Identifying IT Goals

IT goals are often fairly obvious: improve network reliability, provide better security, deliver enhanced administration, and maybe even implement a particular new feature. They are also easier to identify than those of other departments—after all, they are directly related to technology.

When you define your goals, make sure that you are specific. It is easy to say you will improve security, but how will you know when you have done so? What's improved, and how much?

In many cases, IT goals map to implementation of features or procedures; for example, to improve security you will implement Internet Protocol Security (IPSec) and encrypt all traffic to remote networks.

Don't overpromise either—eliminating downtime is a laudable goal, but not one you are likely to achieve on your network, and certainly not one on which you want your next review based.

Get to Know Each Other

Business units often seem to have little idea of the IT department's capabilities and operations—or worse, they have an idea, but it is an *extremely* unrealistic one. This can lead to expectations ranging from improbable to absurd, which is bad for everyone involved.

A major project like this brings together people from all over the company, some from departments that seldom cross paths. This is a great opportunity for members of the various areas of the company to become familiar with IT operations, and vice versa. A clearer understanding of both the big picture of the business and the workings of other departments will help smooth the interactions of IT and the rest of the company.

Examining IT–Business Interaction

A number of aspects of your business should be considered when evaluating your overall IT requirements and the business environment in which you operate. Consider things such as the following:

- **Business organization** How large is the business? Are there offices in more than one location? Does the business operate across international, legal, or other boundaries? What sorts of departmental or functional boundaries exist?
- **Stability** Does the business undergo a lot of change? Are there frequent reorganizations, acquisitions, changes, and the like in business partnerships? What is the expected growth rate of the organization? Conversely, are substantial downsizings planned in the future?
- **External relationships** Do you need to provide access to vendors, partners, and so on? Are there external networks that people operating on your network must access?
- **Impact of Windows Server 2003 deployment** How will this deployment affect the various departments in your company? Are there any areas of the company that are particularly intolerant of disruption? Are there upcoming events that must be taken into consideration in scheduling?
- **Adaptability** Is management easily adaptable to change? If not, make sure you get every aspect of your plan right the first time. Having an idea of how staff might respond to new technologies and processes can help you plan for education and support.

Predicting Network Change

Part of planning is projecting into the future and predicting how future business needs will influence the activities of the IT department. Managing complicated systems is easier when done from a proactive stance, rather than a reactive one. Predicting network change is an art, not a science, but it will behoove you to hone your skills at it.

This is primarily a business assessment, based on things such as expected growth, changes in business focus, or possible downsizing and outsourcing—each of which provides its own challenges to the IT department. Being able to predict what will happen in the business and what those changes will mean to the IT department allows you to build in room for expansion in your network design.

When attempting to predict what will happen, look at the history of the company: are mergers, acquisitions, spin-offs, and so on common? If so, this indicates a considerable need for flexibility from the IT department, as well as the need to keep in close contact with people on the business side to avoid being blindsided by a change in the future.

As people meet to discuss the deployment, talk about what is coming up for the business units. Cultivate contacts in other parts of the company, and talk with those people regularly about what's going on in their departments, such as upcoming projects, as well as what's happening with other companies in the same business sector. Reading the company's news releases and articles in outside sources can also provide valuable hints of what's to come. By keeping your ear to the ground, doing a little research, and thinking through the potential impact of what you learn, you can be much better prepared for whatever is coming up next.

The Impact of Growth on Management

Many networks start out with a single administrator (or a small team), which only makes sense, since many networks are small when first implemented. As those networks grow, it is not uncommon for a few administrative tasks to be delegated to others in the company who, although it is not their job, know how to assist the highly limited IT staff. This can lead to a haphazard approach to management, where who is doing what isn't always clear, and the methods for basics (such as data backups) vary from one department to the next, leading to potential problems as time goes by and staff moves on. If this sounds familiar to you, this is a good time to remedy the situation.

Analyzing the Existing Network

Before you can determine the path to your new network environment, you must determine where you are right now in terms of your existing network infrastructure. This requires determining a baseline for network and system hardware, software installation and configuration, operations, management, and security. Don't rely on what you think is the case; actually verify what is in place.

Project Worksheets Consolidate Information

A large network environment, with a lot of architectural and configuration information to be collected, can require juggling enormous amounts of data. If this is the case, you might find it useful to utilize project worksheets of some sort. If your company has not created customized worksheets, you can use those created by Microsoft to aid in the upgrade process. These are available in the *Microsoft Windows Server 2003 Deployment Kit.*

Evaluating the Network Infrastructure

You should get an idea of what the current network looks like before moving to a new operating system. You will require configuration information while designing the modifications to the network and deploying the servers. In addition, some aspects of Windows Server 2003, such as the sites used in Active Directory replication, are based upon your physical network configuration. (A *site* is a segment of the network with good connectivity, consisting of one or more Internet Protocol [IP] subnets.)

For reasons such as this, you'll want to assess a number of aspects related to your physical network environment. Consider such characteristics as the following:

- **Network topology** Document the systems and devices on your network, including link speeds, wide area network (WAN) connections, sites using dial-up connections, and so on. Include devices such as routers, switches, servers, and clients, noting all forms of addressing, such as both NetBIOS names and IP addresses for Windows systems.
- **Network addressing** Are you currently employing Transmission Control Protocol/Internet Protocol (TCP/IP)? Is the address space private or public? Which TCP/IP subnets are in use at each location?
- **Remote locations** How many physical locations does the organization have? Are they all using broadband connections, or are there remote offices that connect sporadically by dial-up? What is the speed of those links?
- **Traffic patterns** Monitoring network traffic can provide insights into current performance, as well as help you to identify potential bottlenecks and other problems before they occur. Examine utilization statistics, paying attention to both regularly occurring patterns and anomalous spikes or lulls, which might indicate a problem.
- **Special cases** Are there any portions of the network that have out-of-the-ordinary configuration needs, such as test labs that are isolated from the rest of the network?

Inside Out

Mapping the territory

Create a network map illustrating the location of all your current resources—this is easier by using tools such as Microsoft Visio. Collect as much detailed information as possible about those resources, starting with basics, such as what is installed on each server, the services it's providing, and so on. Additional information, such as critical workflow processes and traffic patterns between servers, can also be very useful when it comes time to consolidate servers or deploy new ones. The easier it is to cross-reference all of this information, the better.

Assessing Systems

As part of planning, you should inventory the existing network servers, identifying each system's operating system version, IP address, Domain Name System (DNS) names, as well as the services provided by that system. Collect such information by performing the following tasks:

- **Inventory hardware** Conduct a hardware inventory of the servers on your network, noting central processing unit (CPU), random access memory (RAM), disk space, and so on. Pay particular attention to older machines that might present compatibility issues if upgraded.
- **Identify network operating systems** Determine the current operating system on each computer, including the entire version number (even if it runs to many digits), as well as service packs, hot fixes, and other postrelease additions.
- **Assess your current Microsoft Windows domains** Do you have Windows domains on the network? Microsoft Windows NT 4 or Active Directory? If multiple, detail the trust relationships. List the name of each domain, what it contains (users, resources, or both), and which servers are acting as domain controllers.
- **Identify localization factors** If your organization crosses international and/or language boundaries, identify the localized versions in use and the locations in which they are used. This is critical when upgrading to Windows Server 2003, because attempting an upgrade using a different localized version of Windows Server 2003 might fail.
- **Assess software licenses** Evaluate licenses for servers and client access. This will help you select the most appropriate licensing program.
- **Identify file storage** Review the contents and configuration of existing file servers, identifying partitions and volumes on each system. Identify existing distributed file system (DFS) servers and the contents of DFS shares. Don't forget shares used to store user data.

Inside Out

Where is the data?

Locating file shares that are maintained at a departmental, team, or even individual level can take a little bit of investigation, but it can well be worth it to allow you to centralize the management of data that is important to individual groups, while providing valuable services, such as ensuring that regular data backups are performed.

You can gather hardware and software inventories of computers that run the Windows operating system by using tools such as Microsoft Systems Management Server or HP OpenView. Review the types of clients that must be supported, so that you can configure servers appropriately. This is also a good time to determine any client systems that must be upgraded (or replaced) to use Windows Server 2003 functionality.

Tip You can also gather this information with command-line scripts. To find more information on scripting, I recommend *Microsoft Windows Command-Line Administrator's Pocket Consultant* by William R. Stanek (Microsoft Press, 2004).

Identify Network Services and Applications

Look at your current network services, noting which services are running on which servers, and the dependencies of these services. Do this for all domain controllers and member servers that you'll be upgrading. You'll use this information later to plan for server placement and service hosting on the upgraded network configuration. Some examples of services to document are as follows:

- **DNS services** You must assess your current DNS configuration, especially if you're moving from Windows NT 4 to Windows Server 2003 and implementing Active Directory, which depends upon a bit of proprietary configuration. If you're currently using a non-Microsoft DNS server, you'll want to carefully plan DNS support because Active Directory relies on Windows Server 2003 DNS.
- **WINS services** You should assess the use of NetBIOS by legacy applications and computers running earlier versions of the Windows operating system to determine what type of NetBIOS support (such as Windows Internet Naming Service [WINS]) will be needed in the new network configuration.
- **Print services** List printers and the print server assigned to each one. Consider who is assigned to the various administrative tasks and whether the printer will be published in Active Directory. Also determine whether all of the print servers will be upgraded in place or whether some will be consolidated.

- **Network applications** Inventory your applications, creating a list of the applications that are currently on the network, including version number (as well as postrelease patches and such), which server hosts it, and how important each application is to your business. Use this information to determine whether upgrades or modifications are needed. Also watch for software that is never used and thus need not be purchased or supported—every unneeded application you can remove represents savings of both time and money.

This list is only the beginning. Your network will undoubtedly have many more services that you must take into account.

> **Caution** Make sure that you determine any dependencies in your network configuration. Discovering after the fact that a critical process relied upon the server that you just decommissioned is not going to make your job any easier. You can find out which Microsoft and third-party applications are certified to be compatible with Windows Server 2003 at *http://www.microsoft.com/windowsserver2003/evaluation/suppapps/default.mspx*.

Identifying Security Infrastructure

When you document your network infrastructure, you will need to review many aspects of your network security. In addition to security concerns that are specific to your network environment, the following factors should be addressed:

- Consider exactly who has access to what and why. Identify network resources, security groups, and assignment of access permissions.
- Determine which security protocols and services are in place. Are adequate virus protection, firewall protection, e-mail filtering, and so on in place? Is Kerberos or NTLM authentication being used? Have you implemented a public key infrastructure (PKI) on your network?
- Examine auditing methods and identify the range of tracked access and objects.
- Determine which staff members have access to the Internet and which sorts of access they have. Look at the business case for access that crosses the corporate firewall—does everyone that has Internet access actually need it, or has it been provided across the board because it was easier to provide blanket access than to provide access selectively? Such access might be simpler to implement, but when you look at Internet access from the security perspective, it presents many potential problems.
- Consider inbound access as well; for example, can employees access their information from home? If so, examine the security that is in place for this access.

> **Note** Security is one area in which well-established methods matter—pay particular attention to all established policies and procedures, what has been officially documented, and what isn't documented as well.

Depending upon your existing network security mechanisms, the underlying security methods can change upon deployment of Windows Server 2003. The Windows NT 4 security model (using NTLM authentication), for instance, is initially supported upon upgrade to Windows Server 2003, but is no longer supported when the forest and domain functional levels are raised to Windows Server 2003 level.

Inside Out

Thinking about Internet access

From an IT perspective, the fewer employees that have Internet access, the better. When employees have access to the Internet, their activities can open the business to potential liability. You must balance the needs of employees who require Internet access to do their jobs with the potential risks to the company of an employee doing something irresponsible or, worse, illegal.

Employee Internet access also means more work for both IT staff and management, requiring that policies be defined and enforced, requiring auditing and constant vigilance against the various problems that are introduced. When you add in lost productivity caused by Web surfing, chat, online shopping, and so on, it becomes clear that allowing Internet access is more complicated than just reconfiguring a firewall.

Reviewing Network Administration

Examining the administrative methods currently in use on your network provides you with a lot of information about what you are doing right, as well as identifying those areas that could use some improvement. Using this information, you can tweak network procedures where needed to optimize the administration of the new environment.

How Did You Get Here?

Some networks are entirely designed—actually considered, discussed, planned, and so forth—while other networks grow. At one extreme is a formally designed and carefully implemented administration scheme, complete with supporting documentation set, training, and ongoing compliance monitoring. At the other end of the spectrum is the network for which administrative methods just sort of happen organically; someone did it that way once, it worked, that person kept doing it that way and maybe even taught others to do it that way—not surprisingly, this occurs most often on small networks. In the middle, and perhaps more typically, is a looser amalgamation of policies and procedures, some of which were formally implemented, while others were created ad hoc.

Depending on the path that led to your current administrative methods, you might have more or less in the way of documentation, or actual idea, of the detailed workings of day-to-day administration. Even if you have fully documented policies and procedures, you should still assess how management tasks are actually performed—you might be surprised at what you learn.

Network Administrative Model

Each company has its own sort of approach to network administration—some are very centralized, with even the smallest changes being made by the IT department, while others are partially managed by the business units, which control aspects such as user management. Administrative models fit into these categories:

- **Centralized** Administration of the entire network is handled by one group, perhaps in one location, although not necessarily. This provides a high degree of control at the cost of requiring IT staff for every change to the network, no matter how small.
- **Decentralized** This administrative model delegates more of the control of day-to-day operations to local administrators of some sort, often departmental. Certain aspects of network management might still be managed by a central IT department, in that a network with decentralized administration often has well-defined procedures controlling exactly *how* each administrative task is performed.
- **Hybrid** On many networks, a blend of these two methods is used: A centralized IT department performs many tasks (generally, the more difficult, delicate operations, and those with the broadest impact on the network), while delegating simpler tasks (such as user management) to departmental or group administrators.

Disaster Recovery

The costs of downtime caused by service interruption or data loss can be substantial, especially in large enterprise networks. As part of your overall planning, determine whether a comprehensive IT disaster recovery plan is in place. If one is in place, this is the time to determine its scope and effectiveness, as well as to verify that it is being followed. If one isn't in place, this is the time to create and implement one.

Document the various data sets being archived, schedules, backup validation routine, staff assignments, and so on. Make sure there are provisions for offsite data storage to protect your data in the case of a catastrophic event, such as a fire, earthquake, or flood.

Examine the following:

- **Systems and servers** Are all critical servers backed up regularly? Are secondary and/or backup servers available in case of system failure?
- **Enterprise data** Are regular backups made of core enterprise data stores such as databases, Active Directory, and the like?
- **User information** Where is user data stored? Is it routinely archived? Does the backup routine get *all* of the information that is important to individuals or is some of it stored on their personal machines and thus not archived?

> **Caution** Whatever your current disaster recovery plan, make sure that it is being followed *before* you start making major changes to your network. Although moving to Windows Server 2003 should not present any major problems on the network, it's always better to have your backups and not need them than the other way around.

Network Management Tools

This is an excellent time to assess your current suite of network management tools. Pay particular attention to those that are unnecessary, incompatible, redundant, inefficient, or otherwise not terribly useful. You might find that some of the functionality of those tools is present natively in Windows Server 2003. Assess the following aspects of your management tools:

- Identify the tools currently in use, which tasks they perform, who uses them, and so on. Make note of administrative tasks that could be eased with additional tools.
- Decide whether the tools you identified are actually used. A lot of software ends up sitting on a shelf (or on your hard disk drive) and never being used. Identifying which tools are truly needed and eliminating those that aren't can save you money and simplify the learning curve for network administrators.
- Disk management and backup tools deserve special attention because of file system changes in Windows Server 2003. These tools are likely to require upgrading to function correctly under Windows Server 2003.

Inside Out

Think about compatibility issues early

Dealing with compatibility issues can take a lot of time, so examine them early in the process. The time needed to determine whether your current hardware and software will work and what changes must be made to allow them to work with Windows Server 2003 can be lengthy. When you add to that the time necessary to requisition, obtain, install, and configure new software—especially if you must write custom code—you can see why you don't want to leave this until the end of the project.

Defining Objectives and Scope

A key aspect of planning any large-scale IT deployment of an operating system is determining the overall objectives for the deployment and the scope of users, computers, networks, and organization divisions that are affected. The fundamental question of scope is: What can you realistically expect to accomplish in the given time within existing project constraints, such as staffing and budget?

Some of the objectives that you identified in the early stages of the project are likely to change as constraints become more apparent and new needs and requirements emerge. To start with, you must identify who will be affected—which organizational subdivisions, which personnel, and who will be doing what? These are questions that map to the business goals that must be accomplished.

You also must identify the systems that will be affected—which WANs, local area networks (LANs), subnets, servers, and client systems? In addition, you must determine the software that will be changed—which server software, client software, and applications?

Inside Out

Planning for scope creep

Projects grow, it's inevitable, and although the scope of some projects creeps, others gallop. Here are a few tips to help you keep it to a manageable level:

- When an addition to the project is proposed, never say yes right away. Think through the consequences thoroughly, examining the impact on the rest of the project, and the project team, before agreeing to any proposed changes.
- Insist on management buyoff on changes to the plan. In at least some cases, you won't get approval, automatically deferring the requested changes.
- Argue for trade-offs in the project when possible, so that adding one objective means removing another, rather than just adding tasks to your to-do list.
- Try to defer any noncritical proposed changes to a future project.

Specifying Organizational Objectives

Many goals of the various business units and IT are only loosely related, while others are universal—everyone wants security, for example. Take advantage of the places where goals converge to engage others in the project. If people can see that their needs are met, they are more likely to be supportive of others' goals and the project in general.

You have business objectives at this point; now they must be prioritized. You should make lists of various critical aspects of projects, as well as dependencies within the project plan, as part of the process of winnowing the big picture out into a set of realistic objectives. Determine what you can reasonably accomplish within the constraints of the current project. Also, decide what is outside the practical scope of this Windows Server 2003 deployment but is still important to implement at some later date.

The objectives that are directly related to the IT department will probably be clearer, and more numerous, after completing the analysis of the current network. These objectives should be organized to conform with existing change management procedures within your enterprise network.

When setting goals, be careful not to promise too much. Although it's tempting and sometimes easier in the short run to try to do everything, you can't. It's unlikely that you will implement every single item on every person's wish list during the first stage of this project, if at all. Knowing what you can't do is as important as knowing what you can.

Inside Out

Gauging deployment success

It is difficult to gauge the success of a project without clearly defined goals. Make sure that you define specific, measurable goals that you can use to determine when each portion of the project is complete. Everyone on the project team, particularly management, should agree on these milestones *before* the rollout gets under way.

Some goals should map to user functionality (i.e., the XYZ department is able to do ABC), while others will correspond to administrative tasks. Be granular in your goals: "Security policies will be followed" is difficult to quantify; however, "Virus definition files are updated daily" or "Operating system patches will be installed within 48 hours of release" is easy.

Setting the Schedule

You should create a project schedule, laying out the time line, tasks, and staff assignments. Including projected completion dates for milestones helps you keep on top of significant portions of the project and ensure that dependencies are managed.

It is critical that you are realistic when considering time lines; not just a little bit realistic, *really realistic*. This is, after all, your time you are allocating. Estimate too short a time and you are likely to spend evenings and weekends at the office with some of your closest coworkers.

A number of tasks will be repeated many times during the rollout of Windows Server 2003, which should make estimating the time needed for some things fairly simple: a 1-hour process repeated 25 times takes 25 hours. If, for example, you are building 25 new servers in-house, determine the actual time needed to build one and do the math.

Once you have a rough idea of the time required, do the following:

- Assign staff members to the various tasks to make sure you have adequate staff to complete the project.
- Add some time to your estimates—IT projects always seem to take more time than you thought they would. This is the only buffer you are likely to get, so make sure you build in some "extra" time from the start.
- As much as possible, verify how long individual tasks take; you might be surprised at how much time you spend doing a seemingly simple task, and if your initial estimate is significantly off, you could end up running significantly short on time.
- Develop a schedule that clearly shows who is doing what and when.
- Get drop-dead dates, which should be later than the initial target date.
- Post the schedule in a place where the team, and perhaps other staff, can view it. Keep this schedule updated with milestones reached, changes to deliverable dates, and so on.

Tip You might want to use a project management tool, such as Microsoft Project, to develop the schedule. This sort of tool is especially useful when managing a project with a number of staff members working on a set of interdependent tasks.

Shaping the Budget

Determining the budget is a process constrained by many factors, including, but not limited to, IT-related costs for hardware and licensing. In addition to fixed IT costs, you also must consider the project scope and the non-IT costs that can come from the requirements of other departments within the organization. Thus, to come up with the budget, you will need information and assistance from all departments within the organization and with consideration for all aspects of the project.

Many projects end up costing more than is initially budgeted. Sometimes this is predictable and preventable with proper research and a bit of attention to ongoing expenses. As with time lines, pad your estimates a little bit to allow for the unexpected. Even so, it helps if you can find out how much of a buffer you have for any cost overruns.

In planning the budget, also keep in mind fiscal periods. If your project is crossing budget periods, is next year's budget for the project allocated and approved?

Tip **Budget for project changes**

Keep in mind there are likely to be changes as the project is under way. Each change will probably have a cost associated with it, and you might have to fight for additional budget or go back to the department or individuals that want the change and ask them to allocate moneys from their budget to cover the requested change.

Allowing for Contingencies

No matter how carefully you plan any project, it is unlikely that everything will go exactly as planned. Accordingly, you should plan for contingencies that might present themselves; by having a number of possible responses to unforeseen events ready, you can better manage the vagaries of the project.

Start with perhaps the most common issue encountered during projects: problems in getting the assigned people to do the work. This all too common problem can derail any project, or at least cause the project manager a great deal of stress. After all, the ultimate success of any project relies upon people doing their assigned tasks. Many of these people are already stretched pretty thin, however, and you might encounter times when they aren't quite getting everything done. Your plan should include what to do in this circumstance—is the person's manager brought in, or is a backup person automatically assigned to complete the job?

Another possibility to plan for is a change in the feature set being implemented. Should such shifts occur, you must decide how to adjust to compensate for the reallocated time and money required. To make this easier, identify and prioritize the following:

- Objectives that could slip off this project and onto a later one should the need arise
- Objectives that you want to slip *into* the project if the opportunity presents itself

Items on both of these lists should be relatively small and independent of other processes and services. Avoid incurring additional expenses; you are more likely to encounter extra time than extra funding during your deployment.

In general, ask yourself what could happen to cause significant problems along the way. Then, more important, consider what you would do in response. By thinking through potential problems ahead of time, and planning what you might do in response, you can be prepared for many of the inevitable bumps along the way.

Inside Out

Padding project estimates

Many consultants pad their project estimates, primarily as a means of ensuring that the inevitable project scope creep isn't problematic later on. After all, it's preferable to have a client who is happy that the project came in early and under budget rather than one who is unhappy at the cost and time overruns. You might want to use this approach by adding in a little extra time and not allocating quite all of the available money. If you come in early and under budget, so much the better—but you probably won't.

Finalizing Project Scope

You have goals, know the time line, have a budget pinned down—now it's time to get serious. Starting with the highest-priority aspects of the project, estimate time and budget needed to complete each portion. Work your way through the planned scope, assessing the time and costs associated with each portion of the project. This will help ensure that you have enough time and budget to successfully complete the project as designed.

As you finalize the project plan, each team member should review the final project scope, noting any concerns or questions he or she has about the proposal. Encourage the team to look for weak spots, unmet dependencies, and other places where the plan might break down. Although it is tempting to ignore potential problems that are noted this late in the game, you do so at your own peril. Avoiding known risks is much easier than recovering from unforeseen ones.

Inside Out

Get management approval for your plan

Executive business and IT management should approve the deployment plan, especially if they are not on the planning team. This executive sign-off on the plan should occur at a number of points along the way. After the project team agrees upon initial goals is a good time to get approval, as are critical junctures, such as once the plan has been validated in the lab and again after a successful pilot. In any case, make sure you have management sign-off before you perform *any* installations in a production environment.

Defining the New Network Environment

Once you have determined the overall scope of your Windows deployment project and the associated network changes, you must develop the technical specifications for the project, detailing server configuration, changes to the network infrastructure, and so on. As much as possible, describe the process of transitioning to the new configuration. Care should be taken while developing this document because it will serve as the road map for the actual transition, much of which is likely to be done by staff members who were not in the planning meetings.

Defining Domain and Security Architecture

In defining the new (updated) network environment, you must review the current and projected infrastructure for your network. Analyze the domains in use on your network, and evaluate the implications for security operations and network performance.

Assess Domain Architecture and Changes

If you are implementing Active Directory for the first time, designing the domain architecture is probably going to take a substantial amount of work. Businesses already using Microsoft Windows 2000 to manage their network, on the other hand, will probably not have to change much, if they change anything at all. The amount of planning involved varies widely, depending on the current state of your network:

- **No Windows domains** If you are starting from scratch, you have a bit of work ahead of you. You should plan DNS and Active Directory carefully, taking plenty of time to consider the implications of your design before implementing it.
- **Windows NT 4 domains** This move will still entail quite a bit of change, yet it does provide the opportunity to rethink the current domain configuration before you start configuring Active Directory. Decide whether Active Directory will use existing DNS namespaces or new ones.

- **Windows 2000 domains** No changes are required, although you are free to make changes if you wish. Any changes to the domain structure will likely be made to optimize operations or support additional functionality.

Also, consider whether you are going to be changing the number of domains you currently have. Will you be getting rid of any domains through consolidation?

Impact on Network

You also must assess the impact of the projected changes on your current network operations. Consider issues such as the following:

- Will network traffic change in ways that require modifications to the network infrastructure? Assess additional loads on each network segment as well as across WAN links.
- Do you need to make changes to network naming or addressing schemes? Are new DNS namespaces needed, and, if so, have the DNS names been registered?

Identify Security Requirements

This is a good time to seriously review the security measures implemented on your network. Scrutinize the security devices, services, and protocols, as well as administrative procedures to ensure that they are adequate, appropriate, well documented, and adhered to rigorously.

Security in Windows Server 2003 is not the same as in earlier versions of Windows server operating systems—the security settings for the default (new) installation of Windows Server 2003 are much tighter than in previous versions. This might mean that services that were functioning perfectly prior to an upgrade don't work the same way afterward. Some services that were previously started by default (for example, Internet Information Services [IIS]) are now disabled when first installed.

Assign staff members to be responsible for each aspect of your security plan and have them document completion of tasks. Among the tasks that should be assigned are the following:

- **Applying regular updates of virus software** Antivirus software is only as good as its virus definition files, so make sure yours are current. This means checking the vendor site every single day, even on weekends if possible. Many antivirus packages can perform automatic updates, yet you should verify that the updates are occurring.
- **Reviewing security alerts** Someone should read the various sites that post security alerts on a regular basis and/or receive their newsletters and alerts. The sites should include Microsoft (*http://www.microsoft.com/security/*), vendors of your other software (*http://www.symantec.com/*), network device vendors (*http://www.cisco.com/*), and at least one nonvendor site (such as *http://www.SANS.org/*).
- **Checking for system software updates** IT staff should consider implementing the Software Update Service (SUS) to help keep up-to-date on security patches, service packs, and other critical updates for both servers and clients. SUS enables administrators to automatically scan and download updates and patches to a

centralized server and then configure Group Policy to automatically distribute the updates and patches to computers throughout the network.

- **Checking for hardware firmware updates** It is important that the various devices on the network, especially security-related ones such as firewalls, have up-to-date firmware.

Tip **Keep current with security updates**
It can be hard to keep up with the constantly changing set of patches and updates when you have a number of software packages in use. SUS can help you keep current with security updates as well. You'll find the SUS feature pack, as well as a detailed deployment guide, on the CD-ROM that accompanies this book.

Changing the Administrative Approach

While you are rolling out Windows Server 2003 is an excellent time to fine-tune your administration methods and deal with any issues introduced by the growth and change. Well-designed administrative methods with clearly documented procedures can make a huge difference in both the initial rollout and ongoing operations.

Management Tools

Active Directory provides the framework for flexible, secure network management, allowing you to implement the administration method that works best in your environment. There are mechanisms that support both centralized and distributed administration; group policies offer centralized control, while selected administrative capabilities can be securely delegated at a highly granular level. The combination of these methods allows administration to be handled in the method that works best for each individual business in its unique circumstances.

Tip Make sure that all administrative tasks and processes are clearly defined and that each task has a person assigned to it.

Some administrative changes will be required because of the way Windows Server 2003 works. You might find that existing administration tools no longer work or are no longer needed. So, be sure to question the following:

- Whether your existing tools work under the new operating system. A number of older tools are incompatible with Windows Server 2003—management utilities must be Active Directory–aware, work with NTFS 3.1, and so on.
- Whether current tools will be needed once you move to Windows Server 2003. If a utility such as PKZIP, for example, is in use now, it might not be required for operations under Windows Server 2003, which has incorporated the functionality of ZIP into the operating system. Eliminating unneeded tools could well be one goal of the Windows Server 2003 deployment project, and it will have a definite payoff for the IT department as well in terms of simplified management, lower costs, and so forth.

Select and Implement Standards

You will also want to select and implement standards. If your IT department has not implemented standards for naming and administration procedures, this is a good time to do so. You'll be gathering information about your current configuration, which will show you the places where standardization is in place, as well as places where it would be useful.

Make sure that any standards you adopt allow for likely future growth and changes in the business. Using an individual's first name and last initial is a very simple scheme for creating usernames and works well in a very small business. Small businesses, however, don't necessarily stay small forever—even Microsoft initially used this naming scheme, although it has been modified greatly over the years.

You can also benefit from standardization of system hardware and software configuration. Supporting 100 servers (or clients) is much easier if they share a common set of hardware, are similarly configured, and have largely the same software installed. This is, of course, possible only to a limited degree and dependent upon the services and applications that are required from each system. Still, it's worth considering.

When standardizing server hardware, keep in mind that the minimum functional hardware differs for various types of servers; that is, application servers have very different requirements than file servers. Also consider the impact of the decisions the IT department makes on other parts of the company and individual employees. There are some obvious things to watch for, such as unnecessarily exposing anyone's personal data—although surprising numbers of businesses and agencies still do.

Tip Standardization is especially important for networks that are still running Windows NT 4, because many of those environments use an eclectic, and sometimes downright *odd*, collection of computer and device names.

Inside Out

Personal information is private!

The amount of personal information that businesses have about individuals is something that should give us all pause. What's even more alarming is the casual disregard with which much of this information is treated.

Consider the use of social security numbers in the United States; they show up as student ID numbers (and are posted on professors' doors) and health insurance policy numbers (and are printed on dozens of things from insurance cards to driver's licenses), to name two of the more common and egregious misuses. If that weren't enough, portions of your social security number are used as the default "secret PIN" for some accounts at financial institutions. The same social security number that you give to several people each time anyone in your family seeks medical care. How *secret*.

This might start to change, however. For example, social security numbers are part of what is protected under the Health Information Portability and Privacy Act (HIPPA), which carries severe penalties for inadvertent or negligent exposure of the data. HIPPA has specific data management requirements that are of concern to any IT department working with patient information. Even without the threat of federal penalties, all IT departments, not just those in the medical industry, would be well served by an inspection of which sorts of personal information they are managing and how they are protecting it.

Change Management

Formalized change management processes are very useful, especially for large organizations and those with distributed administrative models. By creating structured change control processes and implementing appropriate auditing, you can control the ongoing management of critical IT processes. This makes it easier to manage the network and reduces the opportunity for error.

Although this is particularly important when dealing with big-picture issues such as domain creation or Group Policy implementation, some organizations define change control mechanisms for every possible change, no matter how small. You'll have to determine for which IT processes you must define change management processes, finding a balance between managing changes effectively or over-regulating network management.

Even if you're not planning on implementing a formal change control process, make sure that the information about the initial configuration is collected in one spot. By doing this, and collecting brief notes about any changes that are made, you will at least have data about the configuration and the changes that have been made to it. This will also help later on, if you decide to put more stringent change control mechanisms in place, by providing at least rudimentary documentation of the current network state.

Thinking about Active Directory

Active Directory is an extremely complicated, and critical, portion of Windows Server 2003, and you should plan for it with appropriate care. This book goes into detail on doing this in Part 7, "Managing Active Directory and Security"; you should read this information if you are going to be designing a new Active Directory tree.

The following section discusses, in abbreviated form, some high-level aspects of Active Directory that you must consider. It is meant to offer perspective on how Active Directory fits in the overall planning picture, not to explain how to plan for a new Active Directory installation.

Designing the Active Directory Namespace

The Active Directory tree is based on a DNS domain structure, which must be implemented prior to, or as part of, installing the first Active Directory server in the forest. Each domain in the Active Directory tree is both a DNS and Windows domain, with the associated security and administrative functionality. DNS is thoroughly integrated with Active Directory, providing location services (also called name resolution services) for domains, servers, sites, and services, as well as constraining the structure of the Active Directory tree. It is wise to keep Active Directory in mind as you are designing the DNS namespace and vice versa, because they are immutably linked.

Note Active Directory trees exist within a *forest*, which is a collection of one or more domain trees. The first domain installed in an Active Directory forest functions as the *forest root*.

The interdependence of Active Directory and DNS brings some special factors into play. For example, if your organization has outward-facing DNS servers, you must decide whether you will be using your external DNS name or another DNS domain for Active Directory. Many organizations choose not to use their external DNS name for Active Directory, unless they want to expose the directory to the Internet for a business reason, such as an Internet service provider (ISP) that uses Active Directory logon servers.

Within a domain, another sort of hierarchy exists in the form of container objects called *organizational units* (OU), which are used to organize and manage users, network resources, and security. An OU can contain related users, groups, or computers, as well as other OUs.

Tip Designing the Active Directory namespace requires the participation of multiple levels of business and IT management, so be sure to provide adequate time for a comprehensive review and sign-off on domain architecture.

Managing Domain Trusts

Domain trusts allow automatic authentication and access to resources across domains. Active Directory automatically configures trust relationships such that each domain in an Active Directory forest trusts every other domain within that forest—a vast improvement over Windows NT in which trusts require administrative planning and manual implementation.

Active Directory domains are linked by a series of such transitive trust relationships between all domains in a domain tree, and between all domain trees in the forest. By using Windows Server 2003, you can also configure transitive trust relationships between forests.

Tip **Understand explicit trust relationships**
Explicit trusts between domains can speed up authentication requests. An explicit trust relationship allows authentication queries to go directly to the domain in question rather than having to search the domain tree and/or forest to locate the domain in which to authenticate a user.

Identifying Domain and Forest Functional Level

Active Directory now has four domain functional levels and three forest functional levels, each constraining the types of domain controllers (Windows NT, Windows 2000, Windows Server 2003) that can be in use and the available feature set.

The domain functional levels are as follows:

- **Windows 2000 mixed** Windows NT, Windows 2000, and Windows Server 2003 domain controllers are supported. Use of Universal groups is limited to distribution (not security) purposes, and group nesting is supported only for distribution groups and domain local groups. This is the default mode for new installations.
- **Windows 2000 native** If you have only Windows 2000 and Windows Server 2003 domain controllers, select this mode, which offers additional features. It provides full Universal group functionality, group-nesting operations for security and distribution groups, and the ability to convert security groups to distribution groups. In addition, security principals can be migrated from one domain to another by the security identifier (SID) history.
- **Windows Server 2003 interim** If you will have only Windows NT and Windows Server 2003 domain controllers, select the Windows Server 2003 interim mode.
- **Windows Server 2003** This mode supports only Windows Server 2003 domain controllers and enables all Active Directory domain-level features. In addition to the group features specified for the other domain functional levels, this mode supports the renaming of Active Directory domains, logon timestamp updates, and passwords for InetOrgPerson users. InetOrgPersons are a special type of user, discussed in Chapter 37, "Managing Users, Groups, and Computers."

The forest functional levels are as follows:

- **Windows 2000** Supports Windows 2000 mixed or native functional levels
- **Windows Server 2003 interim** Supports Windows NT 4 domain controllers with Windows Server 2003 domain controllers
- **Windows Server 2003** Supports only domains at Windows Server 2003 functional level, which enables all Active Directory features, including the following:
  - *Replication enhancements*—Each changed value of a multivalued attribute is now replicated separately—eliminating the possibility for data conflict and reducing replication traffic. Additional changes include enhanced global catalog replication and application partitions (which segregate data, and thus the replication of that data).
  - *Schema*—Schema objects can be deactivated, and dynamic auxiliary classes are supported.
  - *Management*—Forest trusts allow multiple forests to easily share resources. Active Directory domains can be renamed, and thus the Active Directory tree can be reorganized.
  - *User management*—Last logon time is now tracked, and enhancements to InetOrgPerson password handling are enabled.

Note In forests with Windows 2000 functional level, the replication enhancements discussed for the Windows Server 2003 functional level are supported but only between two domain controllers running Windows Server 2003.

Selecting your domain and forest functional levels is generally a straightforward choice. Ultimately, the decision regarding the domain and forest functional level at which to operate mostly comes down to choosing the one that supports the domain controllers you have in place now and expect to have in the future. In most circumstances, you will want to operate at the highest possible level because it enables more functionality. Also, keep in mind that all changes to functional level are one-way and cannot be reversed.

Table 2-1 shows a summary of the types of domain controllers supported by each mode. This is in addition to Windows Server 2003, of course, which works in all modes.

Table 2-1. Domain and Forest Functional Levels

Forest Functional	Forest Functional	Supported Domain Controllers	
		Windows 2000	Windows NT
Windows 2000	Windows 2000 mixed	Yes	Yes
Windows 2000	Windows 2000 native	Yes	No
Windows Server 2003 interim	Windows Server 2003 interim	No	Yes
Windows Server 2003	Windows Server 2003	No	No

Defining Active Directory Server Roles

In addition to serving as domain controllers, a number of domain controllers fulfill special roles within Active Directory. Some of these roles provide a service to the entire forest, while others are specific to a domain or site. The Active Directory setup routine assigns and configures these roles, although you can change them later.

The Active Directory server roles are as follows:

- **Operations masters** A number of Active Directory operations must be carefully controlled to maintain the integrity of the directory structure and data. A specific domain controller serves as the *operations master* for each of these functions. That server is the only one that can perform certain operations related to that area. For example, you can make schema changes only on the domain controller serving as the schema master; if that server is unavailable, no changes can be made to the schema. There are two categories of operations masters:
  - **Forest-level operations masters** The schema master manages the schema and enforces schema consistency throughout the directory.

    The domain naming master controls domain creation and deletion, guaranteeing that each domain is unique within the forest.

  - **Domain-level operations masters** The RID master manages the pool of *relative identifiers* (RIDs). (A RID is a numeric string used to construct SIDs for security principals.)

    The infrastructure master handles user-to-group mappings, changes in group membership, and replication of those changes to other domain controllers.

    The PDC emulator emulates a Windows NT 4 primary domain controller (PDC) for down-level clients and domain controllers and serves as the Windows NT 4–style domain master browser.

- **Global catalogs** A global catalog server provides a quick index of Active Directory objects, which is used by a variety of network clients and processes to locate directory objects. Global catalog servers can be heavily used, yet must be highly available to clients, especially for user logon because the global catalog provides membership information for universal groups. Accordingly, each site in the network should have at least one global catalog server, or you should have a Windows Server 2003 domain controller with universal group caching enabled.
- **Bridgehead servers** Bridgehead servers manage intersite replication over low-bandwidth WAN links. Each site replicating with other sites usually has at least one bridgehead server, although a single site can have more than one if required for performance reasons.

Note Active Directory replication depends on the concept of sites, defined as a collected set of subnets with good interconnectivity. Replication differs depending on whether it is within a site or between sites; intrasite replication occurs automatically every 15 seconds, while intersite replication is scheduled and usually quite a bit slower.

Planning for Server Usage

When planning for server usage, consider the workload of each server: which services it is providing, the expected user load, and so on. In small network environments, it is common for a single server to act as a domain controller and to provide DNS and Dynamic Host Configuration Protocol (DHCP) services and possibly even additional services. In larger network environments, one or more stand-alone servers might provide each of these services rather than aggregating them on a single system.

Server Roles

Windows Server 2003 employs a number of *server roles*, each of which corresponds to one or more services. You can manage many Windows Server 2003 services by these roles, although not all services are included in a role.

Your plan should detail which roles (and additional services) are needed and the number and placement of servers, as well as define the configuration for each service. When planning server usage, be sure to keep expected client load in mind and account for remote sites that might require additional servers to support local operations.

The Windows Server 2003 server roles are as follows:

- **Domain controller** Active Directory domain controllers are perhaps the most important type of network server on a Windows network. Domain controllers are also one of most intensively used servers on a Windows network, so it is important to realistically assess operational requirements and server performance for each one. Remember to take into account any secondary Active Directory–related roles the server will be performing (such as global catalog, operations masters, and so on).
  - How many domain controllers are required, and which ones will fulfill which roles?
  - Which domains must be present at which sites?
  - Where should global catalogs be placed?
- **DNS server** DNS is an integral part of Windows Server 2003, with many important features (such as Active Directory) relying on it. Accordingly, DNS servers are now a required element of your suite of network services. Plan for enough DNS servers to service client requests, with adequate redundancy for fault tolerance and performance and distributed throughout your network to be available to all clients. Factor in remote sites with slow links to the main corporate network and those that might be only intermittently connected by dial-up.
  - Define both internal and external namespaces.
  - Plan name resolution path (forwarders and so on).
  - Determine the storage of DNS information (zone files, Active Directory–integrated, application partitions).

Note Microsoft DNS is the recommended method of providing domain name services on a network with Active Directory deployed, although some other DNS servers provide the required functionality. In practice, however, the intertwining of Active Directory and DNS, along with the complexity of the DNS records used by Active Directory, has meant that Microsoft DNS is the one most often used with Active Directory.

Note DNS information can be stored in traditional zone files, Active Directory–integrated zones, or in application partitions, which are new to Windows Server 2003. An application partition contains a subset of directory information used by a single application. In the case of DNS, this partition is replicated only to domain controllers that are also providing DNS services, minimizing network traffic for DNS replication. There is one application partition for the forest (ForestDnsZones) and another for each domain (DomainDnsZones).

- **DHCP server** DHCP simplifies management of the IP address pool used by both server and client systems. A number of operational factors regarding use of DHCP should be considered:
  - Determine whether DNS servers are going to act as DHCP servers also, and, if so, will all of them or only a subset?
  - Define server configuration factors such as DHCP scopes and assignment of scopes to servers, as well as client settings such as DHCP lease length.

- **WINS server** First, determine whether you still need WINS on your network. If you have a mixed environment with Windows NT and Windows Server 2003 systems, WINS might be required to translate NetBIOS names to IP addresses. If so, consider the following:
  - Which clients need to access the WINS servers?
  - What WINS replication configuration is required?
- **Remote access/VPN server** Routing and Remote Access Services for Windows provides integrated routing of packets between network segments and protocols, as well as another important function: facilitating access by remote users. Consider the following:
  - Do you need to provide routing between networks?
  - Do you want to replace existing routers?
  - Do you have external users that need access to the internal network?
- **Application server** A Windows Server 2003 application server runs IIS to support Web services and application development technologies such as ASP.NET and COM+. The application server role supports the Microsoft .NET Framework and related Web Services Description Language (WSDL), Simple Object Access Protocol (SOAP), and Universal Description, Discovery, and Integration (UDDI) services.
- **Mail server** The mail server offers basic e-mail functionality, providing Post Office Protocol 3 (POP3) and Simple Mail Transfer Protocol (SMTP) services, enabling simple sending and receiving of e-mail, and temporary storage of e-mail on the server. Active Directory manages access to e-mail accounts, providing authentication for POP3 account access.
- **File server** The role of the file server is to provide network shares used for file storage, supporting searching, indexing, shadow copying, and disk space quotas. In addition, the file server role supports DFS operations, enabling a unified logical namespace for file shares stored on distributed servers.
- **Print server** The print server fulfills the needed role of managing printer operations on the network. Windows Server 2003 enables publishing printers in Active Directory, connecting to network printers using a Uniform Resource Locator (URL), and enhanced printer control through Group Policy.
- **Streaming media server** The streaming media server role supports the Windows Media Services operations in streaming video or audio content across intranet or Internet connections to network clients.
- **Terminal server** The terminal server role supports thin client access, allowing for a single server to host network access for many users. A client with a Web browser or a Windows terminal or a Remote Desktop client can access the terminal server to gain access to network resources.

Automatic WINS Replication Partners

Automatic partner configuration allows WINS servers to detect other WINS servers and automatically configure replication—a significant improvement over manual configuration of WINS replication. Because this automated process allows replication between any two WINS servers on the network, a security mechanism has also been introduced. A list of servers with which a replication partnership can be established, as well as those that will not be allowed to replicate with a given server, can be created for each WINS server, providing more control over WINS replication.

Inside Out

Servers with multiple roles

It is common for a single server to fill more than one role, especially on smaller networks. When selecting which roles to put on a single server, try to select ones with different needs. For instance, putting one processor-intensive role (for example, an application server) and a role (such as a file server) that does a lot of network input/output (I/O) on a single system makes more sense than putting two roles that stress the same subsystem on the same machine.

Determining Which Windows Edition to Use

As discussed in Chapter 1, "Introducing Windows Server 2003," there are several versions of Windows Server 2003 and each is intended for a particular sort of usage. Which version you select for each server depends upon both the required functionality and, in the case of upgrades, the operating system that is in place.

Using Windows Server 2003, Standard Edition

This is the general-purpose version of Windows Server 2003, designed for a variety of purposes. The 32-bit version supports up to four processors and 4 gigabytes (GB) of RAM. The 64-bit version supports up to four processors and 32 GB of RAM. It functions well as a domain controller; Web, application, file, or print server; or for providing other network services (such as DNS or remote access services). Some advanced features are not supported, including the Terminal Server Session Directory feature and clustering (although Network Load Balancing *is* included).

Because it is general purpose, and less expensive than most of the specialized versions, Standard Edition is the choice for many small and medium-sized businesses. Servers running Windows NT Server 4 or Windows 2000 Server can be upgraded to Windows Server 2003, Standard Edition.

Using Windows Server 2003, Enterprise Edition

The Enterprise Edition of Windows Server 2003 provides all the same services as the Standard Edition, with a few additions, as well as improved performance, scalability, and reliability. Enterprise Edition is available in both 32-bit and 64-bit versions. Servers running Windows NT Server 4, Windows NT Server 4 Enterprise Edition, Windows 2000 Server, and Windows 2000 Advanced Server can be upgraded to Windows Server 2003, Enterprise Edition.

Hardware support is enhanced from Standard Edition, with support for eight processors and 32 GB of RAM on 32-bit platforms (up to 64 GB of RAM on 64-bit platforms), along with additional functionality such as the capability to use hot-add memory, Non-Uniform Memory Access (NUMA), and eight-node clusters. Another significant enhancement is in application performance, which is improved by *Address Windows Extensions* (AWE), which changes how the Windows operating system allocates memory, reserving only 1 GB of memory for the operating system and allowing 3 GB for applications. Standard Edition, by comparison, splits memory equally between the operating system and applications, allocating 2 GB for each.

Using Windows Server 2003, Datacenter Edition

Windows Server 2003, Datacenter Edition, is the appropriate choice if you have mission-critical, high-volume applications or services that must be available 24/7. If you are running a largely commerce site, for example, this is the version of the Windows operating system for you. Datacenter Edition supports up to 64 GB of RAM and 32 processors with 32-bit platforms and up to 512 GB of RAM and 128 processors on 64-bit platforms; it even has a *minimum* number of processors, requiring at least 8.

In keeping with the intended role of this edition of Windows Server 2003, a few features are missing. For example, functionality designed to facilitate Internet connectivity, such as Internet Connection Sharing and Internet Connection Firewall, is not available. The Datacenter Edition is available in 32- and 64-bit versions. Only Windows 2000 Datacenter Server can be upgraded to Windows Server 2003, Datacenter Edition.

Inside Out

Datacenter isn't a do-it-yourself project

The hardware support provided by the Datacenter Edition requires that each server manufacturer create a custom *hardware abstraction layer* (HAL). Datacenter Edition, in fact, is available only directly from a hardware vendor as part of a new server purchase. Once the vendor configures the server, you are not allowed to make any changes to the hardware without the vendor's authorization, and the vendor provides all support.

Using Windows Server 2003, Web Edition

Windows Server 2003, Web Edition, provides the advancements of IIS 6, along with many standard Windows services and features at a lower cost than Standard Edition. Designed to appeal to administrators running dedicated Web servers, Web Edition is optimized for providing Internet services such as Hypertext Transfer Protocol (HTTP) services, File Transfer Protocol (FTP) services, Network News Transfer Protocol (NNTP) services, and so on. Web Edition, is only available preinstalled.

Because of its focus, this edition is missing a number of features used in a corporate environment. For example, a Web Edition server cannot be a domain controller (although it can join a domain), services for other operating systems (such as UNIX and Macintosh) are not available, and Web Edition servers cannot be part of a server cluster, although they can be part of a Web farm using Network Load Balancing. There are even some Internet-related services missing from the Web Edition, such as the Internet Authentication Service and Internet Connection Sharing. Although remote access server (RAS) functionality is generally unavailable, one virtual private network (VPN) connection per media type is allowed for administrative purposes.

For more information about the supported upgrade paths for Windows Server 2003, see Table 7-1 on page 215.

Selecting a Software Licensing Program

Product licensing is, in most ways, tertiary to your daily work—it is, after all, largely a matter of tracking paperwork. You need only select a licensing program, ensure that you purchase the appropriate number of licenses, and keep track of the proof of those purchases. Just because it's simple, however, don't take it lightly; the consequences for not tracking this particular set of paperwork can be expensive, time-consuming, and awkward to deal with.

There are two kinds of licenses associated with a Windows server product. Your planning should take into consideration how you handle both sorts of licenses.

- **Server License** This license is straightforward; each system running Windows Server 2003 requires a single Server License.
- **Client Access License** Each client or device accessing a Windows server also requires a license. Client Access Licenses (CALs) are in addition to the client operating system license and can represent a significant expense for most networks, so carefully assess your client access needs.

For more information about current Microsoft product licensing, see the following URL: *http://www.microsoft.com/licensing/*.

Retail Product Licenses

If your business is very small, and you don't purchase much software, buying retail products might be the most straightforward option for you. Indeed, it can be the only option. Even when you are at a large business that is taking advantage of one of Microsoft's volume-licensing options, you might encounter an immediate need that sends you to your local computer store for software.

Volume-Licensing Programs

Microsoft has several volume-licensing options, one (or more) of which could save you a substantial amount of money when it comes time to purchase software. You should examine these licensing programs carefully and compare your options before making a commitment.

Open License Program

The Open License program allows you to purchase software licenses for a number of Microsoft programs at a discount. These agreements last 2 years. Open License discounts are fixed and don't get larger if you purchase more software, either as an initial purchase or during the two-year term of the agreement.

The Open License program has several subprograms:

- **Open License Business** This is the easiest volume licensing to qualify for because you must buy only five Microsoft products to qualify. A fixed discount is applied to your initial purchases and all covered purchases during the two-year term.
- **Open License Volume** This program assigns points to each Microsoft product and requires the purchase of software representing a certain number of points. To qualify for the Open Volume program, you must purchase 500 points worth of software from a single category: server, application, or system. The volume purchase price applies only to the categories of software for which you have fulfilled the minimum purchase requirement.
- **Open License Value** This program is designed for organizations with at least five desktops that want to use Software Assurance. It gives you the ability to spread payments annually and gives a fixed discount to your initial purchases and all covered purchases during the three-year term.

Interestingly enough, the Open License program does not include any physical items corresponding to your software purchase. You can purchase product media and documentation separately, for a nominal fee, plus shipping, of course.

Select License

Larger companies can opt to use the Select License program, which is designed for companies with 250 or more computers and a predictable pattern of software purchases. Select License uses the same sort of points-based model as the Open Volume program, with a minimum purchase of 1,500 points of software from at least one category.

If you are willing to commit to buying more software over the 3-year license term, you can get a greater discount. There are several levels of commitment to ongoing software purchases, each with its own discount amount.

Inside Out

Choose your Select License level carefully

The discount associated with the agreement level you choose is the discount that you will receive, regardless of the amount of software you actually purchase. This means that if you commit to a Level B Select License and end up buying 60,000 points worth of software, you still get only the Level B discount. For this reason, you'll want to carefully consider the amount of software you think you will purchase and compare the various options available to you before deciding.

Enterprise Agreement License

Large business organizations can take advantage of an Enterprise Agreement License, which provides a way to standardize on a set of Microsoft products and purchase all of those products at a discount. This includes the right to upgrade to new versions of software during the agreement period, as well as home use privileges for employees.

Products covered under this agreement are those that Microsoft considers to be enterprise-class, such as Microsoft Windows XP Professional, Microsoft Office Professional, and core CALs. The agreement is for 3 years and can be extended for 1 or 3 years at the end of the initial term.

Software Assurance

Software Assurance (SA) provides rolling upgrades for covered products, as well as many other benefits for both the corporation and its employees. Businesses will appreciate the access to support during "business hours," self-paced training, and special newsgroups, while employees can purchase Microsoft software at special discounts.

This program has some potential "gotchas," such as limitations on who can call for support. It's also important to remember that you must have both the server and all of the CALs that access that server covered under SA to gain the program benefits for the server.

Inside Out

Windows Product Activation

How, or even if, *Windows Product Activation* (WPA) is implemented is determined by your licensing method. If you purchase retail products, standard product activation is required. If you have a volume license agreement of some sort, you do not have to deal with WPA. A reusable *volume license key* is provided for software licensed under the Open License program, while both Enterprise Agreement and Select License customers are provided with special product CDs with embedded product keys.

Final Considerations for Planning and Deployment

If you are doing an upgrade or migration to Windows Server 2003, you should read Chapter 7, "Preparing for Upgrades and Migration," before you finalize plans and deploy the operating system. If you are doing a new installation—perhaps, for a new business or a new location of an existing one—you have a substantial amount of additional planning to do. This extends well beyond your Windows Server 2003 systems to additional computers (clients, for a start), devices, services, applications, and so on.

The details of such a project are far beyond the scope of this book; indeed, entire books have been written on the topic. If you have to implement a network from the ground up, you might want to pick one up—the *Microsoft Windows Server 2003 Deployment Kit* is worth a serious review.

You must plan the entire network, including areas such as the following:

- Infrastructure architecture (including network topology, addressing, DNS, and so on)
- Active Directory design
- Servers and services
- Administration methods
- Network applications
- Clients
- Client applications
- Client devices (printers, scanners, and the like)

This is a considerable undertaking and requires educated, dedicated staff, as well as adequate time and other resources.

Inside Out

Good news, bad news

Having the responsibility for deploying a new Windows-based network is both a good thing and a not-so-good thing.

- The not-so-good part is straightforward: It can be a staggering amount of work.
- The good thing—and it is a *very* good thing—is that you are starting with a clean slate and you have a chance to get it (at least mostly) right the first time. Many a network administrator would envy the chance to do a clean deployment, to start fresh with no existing problems, no legacy hardware or applications to maintain, no kludges or workarounds.

If you are faced with creating a new network, take advantage of this opportunity and do lots of research before you touch the first computer. With the abundance of technical information available, you should be able to avoid most problems and quickly resolve the few you encounter.

Part 2

Windows Server 2003 Installation

Chapter 3

Preparing for the Installation and Getting Started

You are likely to find yourself installing Microsoft Windows Server 2003 in various circumstances—a new installation for a new system, an upgrade of an existing Microsoft Windows installation, or perhaps even a new installation into a multiboot environment. You might need to install just a few systems, or you might need to deploy hundreds—or even thousands—in a diverse network environment.

Windows Server 2003 supports both interactive and automated setup processes, providing flexibility in how you install and configure the operating system. You can even fully automate the installation of a basic or fully configured operating system onto a brand new computer to ease the administrative burden in large deployments.

In this chapter, we discuss the things you should know to help you prepare for the installation and get started. There are three methods of performing a new installation of Windows Server 2003: interactive, unattended (using an Unattend.txt file), and by using Remote Installation Services (RIS). By using one of these three options, you can deploy Windows Server 2003 to one system or a hundred—although the latter requires a lot more planning, as you might remember from Chapter 2, "Planning for Windows Server 2003."

Installation of a new operating system involves assessment, preparation, and choices in methods and tools used for deployments. The process of preparing to install Windows Server 2003 is examined in this chapter. We highlight requirements, implementation methods, and preinstallation tasks. In Chapter 4, "Managing Interactive Installations," the interactive setup process is explained, including functionality provided by command-line parameters on the Setup program. Methods of automating the installations are explored in Chapter 5, "Managing Unattended Installations," including the steps necessary to automate setup as well as the automated setup procedures. In Chapter 6, "Using Remote Installation Services," we discuss RIS, an enhanced feature that provides improved automation and remote setup capabilities. By using RIS and the Setup Manager, you can create answer files that control automated installations and subsequent configuration of the deployed operating system. RIS provides administrative advantages in managing multiple operating system (OS) images for remote installation and deploying them to target systems by a controlled, secure process as well.

Note Chapters 3 through 6 focus on the essentials of new installations of Windows Server 2003 to the exclusion of upgrading and migrating earlier Windows servers. Information on upgrading Windows servers and migrating user, service, and server settings is covered in Part 3, "Windows Server 2003 Upgrades and Migrations."

Getting a Quick Start

To install Windows Server 2003, you can boot from the Windows CD, run Setup from within your current Windows operating system, perform a command-line installation, or use one of the automated installation options. You can also use network installations, which allow installation from a shared distribution point on your network. You should know about a few changes and enhancements in the setup processes as well.

For security reasons, most network services are not installed by default, and, unlike earlier versions of the Windows operating system, they can't be installed during the main setup procedure. Automated setup has been improved in several useful ways: Setup Manager is much easier to use and RIS now supports deploying Windows Server 2003 remotely to computers with no operating system previously installed. Licensing has also changed since Microsoft Windows 2000 Server, and product activation might now be required after installation.

New Features and Enhancements

Several aspects of installation have been improved in Windows Server 2003. Highlights of these improvements include the following:

- **Dynamic Update** You can use the Dynamic Update feature to ensure that only the latest files are installed on your computers. Dynamic Update allows you to download updated drivers and Windows setup files and easily deploy them as part of every Windows installation. This also helps ensure that all copies of the Windows operating system are using the latest security updates.
- **Windows Product Activation** Remember that to continue to operate each retail copy of Windows Server 2003 requires activation during the first 14 days after installation. Windows Product Activation (WPA) is not implemented, however, in volume-licensing programs—some sort of volume license key is used instead. This antipiracy measure requires consideration, especially by administrators of small networks who are less likely to have volume licensing and to thus be exempt from WPA. If you must deal with WPA, you must decide if you are going to do so over an Internet connection or by calling Microsoft and registering over the phone. Clearly, activating online presents advantages of speed and ease to a busy network administrator.
- **Deployment of Windows Server 2003 by using RIS** The capability to deploy server versions of the Windows operating system was added in a Windows 2000 Server Service Pack 3 and has been enhanced in Windows Server 2003. RIS now encrypts the

local administrator password, detects client hardware abstraction layer (HAL) so only OS installations with a compatible HAL are offered, performs automatic Dynamic Host Configuration Protocol (DHCP) authorization, and can automate the entire setup process—including the Client Installation Wizard (CIW) text-mode portion. RIS also provides important support for two new features of Windows Server 2003.

- *Headless servers*—To allow companies to avoid the extra cost of additional monitors, keyboards, and mice, and to facilitate operation on rack-mounted systems, Windows Server 2003 supports headless servers. RIS is important to this feature, because it can be used for the installation of these systems.
- *Emergency Management Services*—Windows Server 2003 implements a new feature for server management, Emergency Management Services (EMS). EMS allows administrators to remotely control a server in situations that would normally require local access to the machine. EMS requires serial hardware that supports out-of-bandwidth functionality. You'll find detailed guides on what EMS is and how it works on the CD-ROM that accompanies this book.

Inside Out

Product activation can recur

Although most enterprise and midsize corporate environments will be largely unaffected by WPA because they use volume license programs, it remains an ongoing concern for small businesses and users. If you are using a retail, original equipment manufacturer (OEM), or generic open-license version and change your computer hardware frequently, you are likely to be repeatedly required to perform product activation.

Keep in mind that once the product is activated, the product ID is tied to the hardware upon which the operating system is installed. If multiple components of the computer system, such as the central processing unit (CPU), hard disk, and random access memory (RAM), are changed and Windows Server 2003 is reinstalled upon this changed server hardware, the product activation is likely to fail.

In fact, you can actually change enough hardware in an existing system to elicit WPA again. Upgrade your CPU, double your system RAM, and buy a bigger hard disk—the system will work better, but you will have to get Microsoft's assistance to continue to use your operating system by reactivating Windows within three days.

Setup Methods

In performing the installation, there are two basic approaches to setting up Windows Server 2003—interactively or as an automated process. An interactive installation is what many people regard as the regular Windows installation: the kind where you walk through the setup process and enter a lot of information during setup. It can be performed from a distribution CD (by booting from the CD or running Windows Setup from a command line) or can be run across the network. The default Windows setup process when booting from the retail Windows Server 2003 CD is interactive, prompting you for configuration information throughout the process.

There are several types of automated setup, which actually have administrator-configurable amounts of user interaction. The automated setup methods available in Windows Server 2003 are as follows:

- **Unattended** The unattended setup is the only automated setup that can do upgrades. Unattended installations can be done from a distribution folder or from the Windows Server 2003 CD.
- **RIS** RIS enables the automated (or interactive) installation of operating systems to computers with no operating system previously installed. RIS requires the target computers to be Preboot Execution Environment–enabled systems.
- **Sysprep** The System Preparation Wizard supports the deployment of an operating system partition onto target computers. It does this by preparing a source computer to be imaged and then requires third-party disk-imaging software to make the actual image.

Which approach you use depends upon a number of factors: your network environment, the number of computers that must be installed, the resources available to you, the specific deployment goals, and so on.

Setup Programs

Windows Server 2003 comes with two different versions of its Setup program, with one Setup program (Winnt) designed to run on 16-bit operating systems, and the other (Winnt32) on 32-bit operating systems. Which you use depends on the environment in which you are running Setup and whether you are installing from a MS-DOS command line or from inside the Windows operating system.

- **Winnt** Winnt.exe is designed to support booting from a MS-DOS-based floppy disk with networking or CD-ROM support to enable the installation of Windows Server 2003. Winnt.exe can be run from any Microsoft 16-bit operating system platform, including MS-DOS as well as legacy Windows operating systems. Note that this 16-bit MS-DOS-based Winnt installation does not support upgrading operating systems existing on the computer, but rather provides a clean installation.
- **Winnt32** You can run Winnt32.exe from within the Windows operating system to upgrade the existing operating system or to install Windows Server 2003 to a different partition. Winnt32.exe can be run from within the following versions of the operating system: Microsoft Windows 95, Windows 98, Windows Millennium Edition (Windows Me), Windows NT (with Service Pack 5 or later), Windows 2000, Windows XP, or another Windows Server 2003 installation. In general, use Winnt32 whenever possible—it is faster and offers functionality not found in Winnt.

Tip Although you can run Winnt32 from within Windows client operating systems such as Windows NT Workstation, you cannot upgrade the client systems—a clean installation is the only option.

- **IA-64 Setup** Unlike 32-bit Intel systems that boot from CD-ROM, the Intel Architecture 64-bit (IA-64) Itanium-based systems do not—starting Setup is accomplished through the Extensible Firmware Interface (EFI) shell. To start Windows Setup, run the \IA64\Setupldr.efi Setup boot loader on the CD, and other than the partitioning method, Setup for an IA-64 system works the same as the 32-bit version.

Winnt32 on Itanium-based systems

On Itanium-based (64-bit) systems, Winnt32.exe can be executed by using the EFI for any of the 64-bit versions of Windows Server 2003. Certain command-line options normally available to Winnt32 Setup (/**Syspart**, /**Cmdcons**, and upgrade-related options) do not work in the 64-bit versions of Windows Server 2003.

Inside Out

Use Smartdrv with Winnt

In the Standard and Enterprise Editions, if you run Winnt to start the installation and haven't loaded Smartdrv, the installation will perform slowly (and can seem to hang), taking up to 4 hours to complete the process. You should run Smartdrv without any additional command-line parameters, because using them causes additional installation problems, such as Setup hanging during the file copy phase of installation. For more information, see Microsoft Knowledge Base article 317512. (*http://support.microsoft.com/default.aspx?kbid=317512*).

Controlling Setup from the Command Line

The command-line switches on the Windows Setup programs offer you numerous options for configuring the installation process as well as the installation of special consoles. The DOS-based Winnt.exe program and the Windows-based Winnt32.exe share some of the fundamental capabilities provided by Setup (such as unattended installation), yet they sometimes use different command-line parameters to accomplish the goal (i.e., **Winnt /u** versus **Winnt32 /unattend**).

Command-line options available using both programs allow you to accomplish the following:

- Set the source path and location for temporary files
- Specify an answer file and a uniqueness database file
- Create permanent or temporary folders
- Run a command at the end of setup
- Enable accessibility options

Winnt32.exe contains quite a few more command-line parameters, adding useful additional capabilities such as **/checkupgradeonly** that test your system for compatibility with Windows Server 2003.

Winnt Command-Line Parameters

The command-line parameters used with Winnt support customization of the installation process. You can specify source and temp file locations, enable accessibility options, create folders, run commands, and specify unattended installation options.

The command-line parameters for setting up Windows Server 2003 using Winnt are as follows:

- **Winnt /a** The **/a** parameter instructs Setup to enable the accessibility options during installation.
- **Winnt /e:command** To run a command at the end of the graphical user interface (GUI) portion of the installation process, use the **/e:*command*** parameter, where *command* is the name of the command to be run.
- **Winnt /r:folder** The **/r:*folder*** option designates a permanent folder to be created upon installation.
- **Winnt /rx:folder** The **/rx:*folder*** option designates a temporary folder to be copied upon installation, which is removed upon completion of the setup process.
- **Winnt /s:sourcepath** The **/s:*sourcepath*** option sets the location of Windows Server 2003 installation files to be used during setup. The source path specified has to be a complete path to the files, either as a Universal Naming Convention (UNC) value for a network location (such as *Server**Share**Directorypath* or as a local disk location; i.e., E:\I386). If this option is omitted, the current directory is assumed to be the location of the source files.
- **Winnt /t:tempdrive** The **/t:*tempdrive*** option designates the hard disk drive location where the temporary installation files will be placed and the drive to install Windows Server 2003 upon. If this value isn't specified, the available drives will be scanned and you will be prompted to select the drive during the installation process.

> **Tip Get to the command line during installation**
> If you boot from the Windows Server 2003 distribution CD to install the operating system, you won't have access to the command-line options. You can use a boot floppy disk with CD-ROM device drivers to allow you to run Winnt from the command line. Alternately, if an existing 32-bit client OS exists on the computer, you can go to a command line and run Winnt32.

- **Winnt /u:answer_file** The /u:*answer_file* parameter instructs Setup to do an unattended installation based on the values specified in the answer file (specifying an unattended installation at the command line also *requires* the /s parameter). The answer file may contain all or part of the configuration information usually prompted for during a standard installation process.
- **Winnt /udf:id,UDB_file** The **/udf:*id,UDB_file*** parameter is used in an unattended installation. It specifies the identifier that is used by Setup to determine which contents in a Uniqueness Database File (UDF) are used to replace (override) a parameter set in the answer file. The identifier (*id*) value selects the set of values to be pulled from the UDF file during unattended installation. You will be prompted for a $Unique$.udb file if one is not named on the command line.

Winnt32 Command-Line Parameters

Winnt32 has even more command-line parameters (than Winnt) to support customization of the installation process. In addition to running commands and setting file locations, accessibility, folders, and answer files, you can check the compatibility of systems you intend to upgrade, install a Recovery Console or Emergency Management Services, and implement the new Dynamic Update feature of Windows Server 2003.

The command-line parameters for Winnt32 can be divided into several groupings, based on the process the arguments support. Winnt32 provides functionality in these areas:

- General installation
- Unattended installation
- Dynamic Update
- Recovery Console
- Emergency Management Services

The first three groups are used to control Setup, and the last two install additional services.

The general installation parameters include the following:

- **Winnt32 /checkupgradeonly** The **/checkupgradeonly** parameter tests your system for compatibility with Windows Server 2003. By default, the compatibility results are displayed and are saved to disk in the %SystemRoot% folder as Upgrade.txt. The **/checkupgradeonly** parameter can be used with **/unattend** to defer the need for user responses.

- **Winnt32 /cmd:command_line** The **/cmd:*command_line*** parameter specifies the command-line argument to be run immediately prior to Setup's final phase—the command is run after the final reboot but prior to completion of the setup process.
- **Winnt32 /copydir:{i386|ia64}\folder_name** The **/copydir:{i386|ia64}*folder_name*** parameter allows you to specify custom folders that will be created within the system root folder upon installation. This could be used, for instance, to copy a folder of device drivers specific to your hardware platform as part of the standard installation process. To do this, create a custom folder (populated with files) within the distribution folder containing the Windows Server 2003 files, and then use the **/copydir** parameter to copy these drivers to the system during the installation.
- **Winnt32 /copysource:folder_name** The **/copysource:*folder_name*** parameter works the same way as the **/copydir** parameter, except that the folders that are created during installation are deleted upon completion of the installation process.
- **Winnt32 /debug[level]:filename** The **/debug[*level*]:*filename*** parameter enables the creation of a debug log with the levels of error reporting selected by the administrator. The error level is appended directly to the end of the word *debug* followed by a colon and the name of the file to which to write the debug information. Each error level is inclusive of the lower error levels (for example, error level 2 includes error levels 0 and 1).

Error Level	Description
0	Severe errors
1	Errors
2	Warnings
3	Information
4	Detailed information

- **Winnt32 /m:folder_name** The **/m:*folder_name*** option sets an alternate location for files to be used by Setup during the installation process—during setup, the alternate location is searched first, and files in the default location are used only if the installation files are not found in the specified alternate location.
- **Winnt32 /makelocalsource** The **/makelocalsource** parameter causes the installation sources files to be copied to the local drive, thus making a hard disk drive copy of the installation source files available when the CD isn't present throughout the setup process.
- **Winnt32 /noreboot** The **/noreboot** parameter prevents the rebooting of the system upon completion of the file copy phase. This is used to allow other commands or operations to be performed once the files have been copied, but prior to further Setup phases.
- **Winnt32 /s:sourcepath** The **/s:*sourcepath*** parameter sets the location of Windows Server 2003 installation files to be used during setup. The source path specified must be a complete path to the files, either as a UNC value for a network location *Server**Share**Directorypath* or as a local disk location (E:\I386). You can specify multiple

source paths (a maximum of eight) to enable simultaneous copying of files from different servers.

Caution When specifying multiple source paths, if the server specified in the first source path is not available, the setup process will stop.

- **Winnt32 /syspart:drive_letter** To create a bootable drive with Windows Setup on the system partition, use the **/syspart:*drive_letter*** parameter. The **/syspart** parameter sets a logical drive and copies the startup files used by Setup to it, then makes it an active partition. Once created, this drive can then be put into a different system, and upon boot, the new system will automatically begin the next phase of setup. For **/syspart** to work, the **/tempdrive** parameter must also be specified.

Note The **/syspart** parameter is not supported on Itanium-based systems. Systems using Windows 95, Windows 98, Windows Me, and Windows NT 4 require Service Pack 5 or 6 to use **/syspart**.

- **Winnt32 /tempdrive:drive_letter** The **/tempdrive:*drive_letter*** parameter designates the hard disk drive location where the temporary installation files will be placed and the drive upon which to install Windows Server 2003. If this value isn't specified, the available drives will be scanned and you will be prompted to select the drive during the installation process.

The unattended installation parameters include the following:

- **Winnt32 /udf:id[,UDB_file]** The **/udf:*id*[,*UDB_file*]** parameter specifies the identifier that is used by Setup to determine which portions of a UDF are used to replace (override) a parameter set in the answer file. The identifier (*id*) value selects the set of values to be pulled from the UDF file during unattended installation. If no UDF file is named on the command line, you will be prompted for a $Unique$.udb file.
- **Winnt32 /unattend** The **/unattend** parameter, when used without an answer file, instructs Setup to do an unattended upgrade installation using the values in the existing version of the Windows operating system. This parameter works only on versions of the Windows operating system that can be upgraded to Windows Server 2003, meaning Windows NT (with Service Pack 5) or Windows 2000 Server. User intervention is not required in this unattended upgrade process.
- **Winnt32 /unattend[num]:answer_file** The **/unattend[*num*]:*answer_file*** parameter, when used with an answer file, instructs Setup to do an unattended new installation (a fresh installation as opposed to an upgrade) based on the values specified in the answer file. Specifying **/unattend:*answer_file*** at the command line also requires the /s parameter to specify the location of the source files. The *num* value sets the number of seconds that Setup pauses between copying the files and rebooting the system. The answer file can contain all or part of the configuration information for which the installation process would normally prompt the user.

The Dynamic Update–related parameters include the following:

- **Winnt32 /duprepare:pathname** The **/duprepare:*pathname*** parameter is used by administrators to prepare an installation folder for Dynamic Update files (obtained through the Windows Update Web site). Folders must be prepared (by **/duprepare**) prior to using **/dushare** to provide a shared location for updated files used in client installations.
- **Winnt32 /dudisable** The **/dudisable** parameter blocks the Dynamic Update service from operating during setup, forcing Windows Server 2003 Setup to use only the original installation files (on the distribution CD or the network shared location). Note that Dynamic Update settings specified within an answer file will not override this setting.
- **Winnt32 /dushare:pathname** Use the **/dushare:*pathname*** parameter to specify the shared folder containing the Dynamic Update files to be used during setup.

Note To use the **/dushare** parameter, the Dynamic Updates files must first be downloaded from the Windows Update Web site into the specified shared folder and then the folder must be prepared using the /Duprepare parameter.

The Recovery Console–related parameter includes the following:

- **Winnt32 /cmdcons** The **/cmdcons** parameter instructs Setup to add the Recovery Console to the options available at startup, enabling the user to start or stop services and access drives from a command line. This parameter is available only after Setup has completed and only on the x86-based hardware platform.

For more information about the Recovery Console, see the section entitled "Installing and Using the Recovery Console" on page 1359.

The Emergency Management Services–related parameters are the following:

- **Winnt32 /emsport:{com1|com2|usebiossettings|off}** The **/emsport** parameter is used to specify and enable or disable the Emergency Management Services. The default value for **/emsport** is **usebiossettings** and draws its information from the Serial Port Console Redirection (SPCR) in the basic input/output system (BIOS) (for 32-bit systems) or the console device path in the Extensible Firmware Interface (EFI) of Itanium-based (64-bit) systems. If this is specified on a system that does not support SPCR or EFI, the command will be ignored.

Note The COM1 and COM2 parameters can be used only on the 32-bit x86-based platforms and are not supported on Itanium-based systems. If EMS is disabled from the command line, it can be reenabled by the boot settings—you configure EMS boot settings by using the Bootcfg command. Type **bootcfg /ems /?** at the command line to display all EMS configuration parameters. You can enable EMS, for example, on COM1 by using the following command line:

```
bootcfg /ems on /port com1 /baud 115200
```

- **Winnt32 /emsbaudrate:baudrate** The baud rate used in Emergency Management Services is set by using the **/emsbaudrate:*baudrate*** parameter, with the slowest rate (9600 baud) as the default—accepted baud rates include 19200, 57600, and 115200. The **/emsbaudrate** option is used in conjunction with the **/emsport:com1** (or **com2**) parameter. The **/emsbaudrate** parameter settings can be used only on 32-bit x86-based platforms.

Tools for Automating Setup

Several tools can be used to manage automated installations. Tools to perform automated installations are available, as is an upgrade answer file creation tool. Some tools are automation method–specific, while others (Setup Manager) are used in all methods. The primary tools used when installing the Windows operating system are the following:

- **Setup Manager** You use Setup Manager to create answer files used in automated installation. *Answer files* are text files containing information used to customize automated Windows installations. The Setup Manager Wizard presents the set of questions posed during the setup process, enabling you to configure the desired responses to each installation question. Windows Server 2003 includes improvements to Setup Manager, using a single screen to display the installation options.
- **Sysprep** The System Preparation Wizard (Sysprep) prepares an operating system installation for duplication and replication to remote computers. Sysprep relies upon you using some kind of disk-imaging software (Norton Ghost or similar software) to create and distribute the image—Sysprep only prepares the OS image (before and after OS image creation/deployment). Sysprep removes the security identifiers (SIDs) and enables the Mini-Setup program, facilitating operating system deployment on new system hardware.
- **RISetup** The Remote Installation Setup Wizard creates an operating system image in a network-accessible distribution folder for remote installation.
- **RIPrep** The Remote Installation Preparation Wizard creates a file system image of an existing master installation of an operating system.

> **Tip** **Choose the right version of Setup Manager**
> The Windows Server 2003 Setup Manager Wizard cannot create answer files for Windows 2000 installations—you must use the Windows 2000 Setup Manager Wizard if you must create an answer file for a Windows 2000 installation.

Additional ancillary tools are available in the Windows Server 2003 Deployment Kit. The following tools help in large-scale deployments of client machines running Windows Server 2003 and Windows XP:

- **Convert.exe** Converts file allocation table (FAT) and FAT32 partitions to NTFS.
- **Cvtarea.exe** Enables control over placement of files in the partition, allowing creation of contiguous files in specified partition locations.

- **DiskPart** Flexible disk management tool with scripting support.
- **Oformat.com** Formats a partition as FAT32 optimized for upgrade to NTFS.

> **Caution** Be careful with Oformat! When you invoke Oformat, it begins formatting the drive automatically without requesting further confirmation.

- **Factory.exe** Invoked by using **sysprep -factory** and causes the image to reboot with network connectivity, but without Mini-Setup or Windows Welcome. Upon initial startup, running **sysprep -factory** processes the Winbom.ini answer file, performs application install/uninstall, provides plug and play enumeration, copies drivers, and sets user information.

These tools can assist in the automated installation of client workstations and servers. For more information on these tools, refer to the "Helpful Command-Line Tools" section of the *Microsoft Windows Corporate Deployment Tools Users Guide* (Deploy.chm), which is included in the Deploy.cab file in the \Support folder on the Windows Server 2003 CD-ROM.

Product Licensing

Licensing for Windows Server 2003 has two aspects: server licenses and client access licenses (CALs). Each installation of Windows Server 2003 on a computer requires a server license. In addition to ensuring you have the required licenses for Windows Server 2003, you must decide on the client access licensing scheme you will use before installing Windows Server 2003. Your choices are as follows:

- **Per server** One CAL is required for each concurrent connection to the server. This usually means 1 CAL for every connection to that server.
- **Per device or per user** A CAL is purchased for each user or device connecting to the server—this usually corresponds to 1 CAL for every user or computer that will access the server.

Your licensing program determines how you handle both the product key and product activation. Table 3-1 describes how each type of licensing affects installation.

Table 3-1. Overview of Windows Server 2003 Product Keys and Activation

Product License	Product Key	Product Activation
Retail Product License	Unique product key needed	WPA
Open License program	Reusable product key	No WPA
Select License	On volume license CD	No WPA
Enterprise Agreement License	On volume license CD	No WPA

For more information about software licensing, see the section entitled "Product Licensing" earlier in this chapter.

Matching Product Keys to Products

The product ID used during installation of a retail version of Windows Server 2003 can be used only with the retail CD. Likewise, Open License keys are only usable with the media issued by Microsoft as part of obtaining the volume license. In enterprises using both types of software, knowing which keys go with which software makes the installation process easier.

Preparing for Windows Server 2003 Installation

Installing a server operating system requires some assessment and preparation before you actually do the work. You'll want to review the server hardware and installation details, check the latest technical notes, verify backups, and have more than a few discussions with other Information Technology (IT) staff and managers.

System Hardware Requirements

Most versions of Windows Server 2003 share baseline requirements, such as a minimum of a 133-megahertz (MHz) Pentium CPU, 128 megabytes (MB) of RAM, and 1.5 gigabytes (GB) of hard disk drive space (for three of the x86-based servers). Yet, there are differences in recommended hardware for each edition—Web, Standard, Enterprise, and Datacenter—and further differences to support the 64-bit versions on Itanium-based servers. Table 3-2 shows the hardware requirements for Windows Server 2003 on 32-bit x86 platforms, while Table 3-3 describes the requirements on the Itanium-based platform. For 64-bit extended systems, refer to Table 3-4.

Table 3-2. Hardware Requirements for x86-Based Computers (32-bit)

Version	Min. CPU Speed	Recommended CPU Speed	# of CPUs	Min.–Max. RAM	Recommended RAM	Minimum Disk Space
Web	133 MHz	550 MHz	1–2	128 MB–2 GB	256 MB	1.5 GB
Standard	133 MHz	550 MHz	1–4	128 MB–4 GB	256 MB	1.5 GB
Enterprise	133 MHz	733 MHz	1–8	128 MB–32 GB	256 MB	1.5 GB
Datacenter	400 MHz	733 MHz	8–64	512 MB–64 GB	1 GB	1.5 GB

Table 3-3. **Hardware Requirements for Itanium-Based Computers (64-bit)**

Version	Min. CPU Speed	Recommended CPU Speed	# of CPUs	Min.–Max. RAM	Recommended RAM	Minimum Disk Space
Web	NA	NA	NA	NA	NA	NA
Standard	733 MHz	733 MHz	1–4	128 MB–32 GB	256 MB	2 GB
Enterprise	733 MHz	733 MHz	1–8	128 MB–64 GB	256 MB	2 GB
Datacenter	733 MHz	733 MHz	8–64	512 MB–512 GB	1 GB	2 GB

Table 3-4. **Hardware Requirements for 64-bit Extended Systems**

Version	Min. CPU Speed	Recommended CPU Speed	# of CPUs	Min-Max RAM	Recommended RAM	Minimum Disk Space
Web	N/A	N/A	N/A	N/A	N/A	N/A
Standard	AMD Opteron 1.4 Ghz	AMD Opteron 1.4 Ghz	1-4	512 MB–32 GB	512 MB	4 GB
Enterprise	AMD Opteron 1.4 Ghz	AMD Opteron 1.4 Ghz	1-8	512 MB–64 GB	512 MB	4 GB

How a Clean Installation and an Upgrade Differ

If you have existing servers running the Windows operating system, you must decide which servers, if any, you will upgrade. The major differences between a clean installation and an upgrade are the following:

- **Upgrade** During an upgrade, user settings are retained, existing applications and application settings are kept, and basic system configuration is not required. An upgrade installation should be used when you have existing servers running the Windows operating system that support upgrade to Windows Server 2003 and you want to minimize disruption by maintaining the existing operating system and settings, user information, and application configuration.
- **Clean installation** In contrast, a clean installation does not retain any user or system settings or knowledge of any installed applications, and you must configure all aspects of the hardware and software. You should use a clean installation when the operating system cannot be upgraded, the system must boot to multiple operating systems, a standardized configuration is required, or (obviously) when no operating system is currently installed.

Tip **Install Standard Edition with more than two CPUs**

If you are performing an installation of Windows Server 2003, Standard Edition, on a system with more than two processors and there is *not* currently a copy of the Windows operating system installed, you are allowed to install, even though Standard Edition supports only two CPUs. Only two of the CPUs will function after installation.

Note that this is different from the behavior the installation does if the computer has any version of the Windows operating system installed. In this configuration, Setup will simply fail and exit.

Although the inability to upgrade to Standard Edition on a four-processor system might present limitations, the ability to do a clean install provides a workaround in case you must deploy this configuration.

Supported Upgrade Paths

Microsoft Server operating systems from Windows NT Server 4 Service Pack 5 and later can be upgraded to Windows Server 2003. In general, servers can be upgraded to a product with equal or greater capabilities, thus

- There is no supported upgrade path to Windows Server 2003, Web Edition. Windows Server 2003, Web Edition, cannot upgrade to Standard, Enterprise, or Datacenter Editions.
- Windows NT Server 4 or Windows 2000 Server can be upgraded to Standard or Enterprise Editions of Windows Server 2003.
- Windows NT Server 4, Enterprise Edition, and Windows 2000 Advanced Server, however, can be upgraded only to Windows Server 2003, Enterprise Edition.
- Only Windows 2000 Server, Datacenter Edition, can upgrade to Windows Server 2003, Datacenter Edition.

All other versions of the Windows operating system require a clean installation—no upgrade is possible.

Inside Out

Limitations on upgrading localized Windows versions

There are limitations on upgrading from one version to another, such as that servers with the Multilingual User Interface Pack can be upgraded only to an English edition of Windows Server 2003 and that localized versions cannot be upgraded to a different localized version.

Using Dynamic Update

Dynamic Update is a convenient way of ensuring that the most recently updated driver and setup files are always used during server installation. Dynamic Update connects to a distribution server containing updated files used during Windows installation. The files in dynamic updates include setup information files, dynamic libraries used during setup, file assemblies, device drivers, and system files.

The Dynamic Update files can be obtained by using two methods:

- Dynamic Update files can be obtained directly from the Windows Update site during setup, ensuring that the absolute latest setup files are used during the installation.
- Dynamic Update files can be downloaded to a server on your local network and then shared to provide clients with access to a consistent local copy of the files.

Hosting Dynamic Update files on a local network provides you with additional security and the advantage of being able to ensure that standardized setup files are applied to all systems within your network environment. You'll also want to assign permissions to the folder containing the Dynamic Update files, permissions that should commonly correspond to the permissions applied to your distribution folder for automated installations. The placement of this folder containing the Dynamic Update files should be on a server that is highly accessible to all locations on the network where installations are performed.

The Dynamic Update process does not provide new installation files, but rather supplies only updated files that replace existing files used during setup. Dynamic Update might, however, provide device drivers that are not a replacement for device drivers existing on the distribution CD (in-box device drivers) but that are new device drivers supplying additional support of devices or system hardware.

There are some basic requirements for Dynamic Update to work:

- You must use Winnt32 to install the Windows operating system.
- The target computer must be connected to the Internet (or your network if you are hosting a server with the Dynamic Update files).
- You must be upgrading the system as opposed to doing a new installation.

> **Tip** Dynamic Update is disabled by default for automated installations and must be enabled in the answer file.

Creating a Local Dynamic Update Share

To support network-based distribution of Dynamic Update files, you must download both the .cab files containing new device drivers and the Dynamic Update packages (sets of installation files). Dynamic Update package files are available from the Microsoft download center—to locate these files for your installation, select your operating system and search on "dynamic update."

You can also download new device drivers for hardware in your target computers that does not have device driver support on the Windows Server 2003 distribution CD. Use Device Manager to determine which of the devices in your standard hardware configuration for your target systems do not have device driver support by default—these devices will be highlighted with a yellow exclamation point or question mark.

> **Tip** **Try to limit use of Dynamic Update during installation**
> You should limit the use of Dynamic Update for device driver files to subsystems that are essential during the installation process, such as for the video display and hard disk subsystems. Supporting installations of new device drivers for peripheral devices such as printers should be specified in the answer file by using the OemPnPDriversPath entry in the Unattended section.

After downloading the driver and Dynamic Update .cab files to the network share you're using for distributing Dynamic Update files, you must prepare this folder and the files for use. Do so by following these steps:

1. First, extract the .cab files from the Dynamic Update package file. To do this, just run the downloaded package file. This extraction will create a folder for each supported operating system edition for which it has files. Each folder will contain four files: Duasms.cab, Winnt32.cab, Updates.cab, and Upginf.cab.

> **Tip** The Windows Server 2003 Dynamic Update package contains files for the Standard, Enterprise, and Web Editions.

2. Copy the appropriate .cab files to the folder being used for your Dynamic Update network share, then prepare the folder using the /Duprepare parameter of Winnt32. Prepare the Dynamic Update folder using the /Duprepare parameter of Winnt32, as shown in the following command line:

   ```
   Winnt32 /duprepare: path
   ```

When you use the /Duprepare parameter on the folder, Setup creates the Duasms, Winnt32, Updates, and Upginf folders—one for each of the .cab files extracted in the first step. The contents of the corresponding .cab files are then extracted into those folders, creating the Dynamic Update folder structure and populating it with files.

Controlling the Use of Dynamic Update during Setup

You can decide whether to use the Dynamic Update option each time you run Winnt32, allowing you to control the files used when installing the Windows operating system on a per-installation basis. To use Dynamic Update files in the installation process, use the

Chapter 3

following command-line option to direct Windows Setup to the network share location containing the Dynamic Update files:

```
Winnt32 /dushare:path
```

If you are using an answer file that enables Dynamic Update and you want to disable it for a specific installation, use the **/dudisable** parameter on the command line, as follows:

```
Winnt32 /dudisable
```

This overrides the setting in the answer file and disables the use of Dynamic Update during that installation.

Selecting a Distribution Method

The files used by Windows Setup must be made available for use in installation in some fashion. There are two fundamental approaches, one in which the distribution files are stored on some form of media (such as CD or DVD), and the other in which the distribution files are stored on a network share.

Using a distribution folder can reduce required administrative tasks by making all necessary Windows installation and customization files available in a single secured location on the network. This means that common changes, such as new device drivers or changes to system configuration, can be made in one location with that single change affecting all subsequent installations. This ensures a consistent configuration within the enterprise network with a minimum of administrative overhead.

There are circumstances under which you might not want to use a network distribution folder, however, such as the lack of an available server or lack of space on the file server—it takes a minimum of 650 MB to support a network distribution folder for a single OS. Likewise, if the destination computer is located at a remote site with slow or no network connectivity, using a network distribution folder for automated installation might not be practical or possible.

Creating the distribution folders varies depending upon the type of installation process you will be performing as follows:

- Distribution folders for interactive and unattended network setup are created by copying the contents of the \I386 folder manually from the Windows Server 2003 CD to a network share. Unattended installations use answer files to configure system settings and to control the process.
- The remote installation services utilities, RISetup and RIPrep, create distribution folders on a common network share on the RIS server.
- Distribution of Sysprep-based images is dependent upon the capabilities of the disk image software you use because Sysprep prepares only the computer to be imaged.

Note In the case of an unattended installation from a Windows Server 2003 CD, the product media becomes the de facto distribution folder.

Getting Ready for Automated Installations

To perform automated installations, you must establish the environment and create related answer files for each of the operating systems you want to install. In all automated installations, you must start by creating the distribution folder (or folders) containing the operating system files, answer files, and additional drivers, OEM files, or applications that will be installed.

Creating Distribution Folders

The same general question applies to distribution folders whether they are used for interactive or automated installations: do you store them on the network or on media? However, automated installations can use customized distribution folders, allowing the addition of folders containing additional drivers or applications. This facilitates a more customized, and faster, rollout of preconfigured operating environments.

The distribution folder used in automated installations stores the Windows distribution files, as well as any necessary custom files. This folder is stored on a share accessible on the local network, allowing the computers that require an operating system installed to easily access the file share.

The organization of the distribution folder differs for each automation method. In the case of an unattended installation, for example, this is a folder structure reflecting the structure of the Windows Server 2003 CD-ROM.

In cases in which you have created a distribution folder containing additional drivers or applications, and yet a server-based distribution folder is not practical, you can create your own installation media. The customized distribution folder is simply stored on a CD or DVD and the installation media provided to the remote sites.

Inside Out

No PXE support? Create startup media

Sometimes you must create the startup media, such as in the case of installing Windows Server 2003 using RIS on a computer that does not have a Preboot Execution Environment (PXE)-compliant BIOS. For systems that have supported network cards, you can create a boot floppy disk that will detect the network card, contact a DHCP server, and establish the initial network connection to a RIS server.

Using Answer Files in Automated Installations

Automated installations store configuration information in an answer file, which is read during the setup process and which holds data used to configure the system. An answer file (such as Unattend.txt) gets its name from its function—it supplies the answers to the prompts or dialogs that Windows Setup normally provides during the installation process.

An answer file is a structured text file containing discrete sections of information pertaining to the installation and initial configuration of the Windows operating system. Each section contains a number of entries that are either mandatory or optional—most are optional. An entry contains the name of a configuration setting, an equal sign, and a value supplying one of the acceptable arguments for that value (such as `TimeZone=4`).

You can either create an answer file (of one sort or another) to use in combination with a folder containing the distribution files for Windows Server 2003, or you can create an image of an existing Windows Server 2003 installation to use as your base for all computers deployed.

You create answer files using the improved Setup Manager tool (introduced in Windows 2000). Setup Manager generates answer files from information you supply using a new custom interface that lets you control the configuration settings used during an unattended installation.

Tip **Create answer files manually**
Because answer files are simple text files, you can also create them manually by using Notepad, yet this can be somewhat time-consuming. Unless you are making simple changes, or are very familiar with editing them, you might want to stick to the Setup Manager.

Preinstallation Tasks

You will want to assess the specifics of an installation and identify any tasks that must be done prior to the installation taking place. The following is a partial list—a general set of pointers to the installation-related tasks that must be performed.

- Check requirements for OS version
- Review the release notes on OS media
- Determine upgrade/new installation
- Check your system hardware compatibility

For more information about hardware compatibility, see the Microsoft Hardware Compatibility List (HCL) at *http://www.microsoft.com/HCL*. You also can check the Windows Server Catalog (*http://www.microsoft.com/windows/catalog/server*).

- Configure how the target computer boots
- Select installation type: interactive or automated

- Determine license mode
- Choose installation partition
- Select file system (usually NTFS)
- Determine network connectivity and settings
- Identify domain/workgroup membership account information
- Disconnect uninterruptible power supply (UPS)

Tip When doing a clean installation on old hardware, check to see whether an OS exists, and if so, check event or system logs for hardware errors, consider multiboot, uncompress drives, and resolve partition upgrade issues.

Tip **Plan for Dynamic Update**
Hosting Dynamic Update on a local network server—as opposed to downloading updates directly from Microsoft each time you install the operating system—can speed update and ensure consistency of driver versions across the network environment.

Migrating the User State Information

If you intend to migrate the user information, you must determine which information to migrate and establish a plan for migrating it. Then you must store this information on some form of media so that it is available to restore after the unattended installation is completed. The data that you must identify, store, and migrate include the user data, configuration settings, and application settings.

If you are migrating user information contained in Windows domain controllers (Windows NT 4, Windows 2000, etc.), you should use the Active Directory Migration Tool version 2.

You can migrate user information stored on client computer systems as well—Windows Server 2003 comes with two tools to assist in the migration of user information on client computers:

- File and Settings Transfer Wizard is a tool designed for individual Windows XP users to migrate their own information to a new system. To access this tool, click Start and point to Programs or All Programs, Accessories, System Tools, Files, and finally Settings Transfer Wizard.
- User State Migration Tool is used in enterprise deployments to migrate Windows XP client settings. This tool is on the Windows XP Professional CD-ROM in the \ValueAdd\Msft\USMT folder.

More information on these tools, as well as the process of upgrading and migrating user information from Windows NT or Windows 2000 to Windows Server 2003, is described in Chapter 9, "Migrating to Windows Server 2003."

You also must assess your installation requirements and plan the configuration of the drives and partitions on the target computers. If you must create a new partition, modify the system partition, or format the system partition before installation, you can use configuration tools such as the FDISK, FORMAT, OFORMAT, and CONVERT commands to manage partitions (prior to beginning the automated installation).

For companies that have purchased certain volume license agreements, a Windows Preinstallation Environment (WinPE) CD is available. By using this CD, you can boot the system and run the Diskpart utility to partition and format drives. The license programs providing the WinPE CD include the Select License Software Assurance, the Enterprise Agreement, and the Enterprise Subscription Agreement.

Tip On some Master Boot Record (MBR) drives, you might need to rewrite the disk signature (such as when the target computer's partition size is smaller than the size of the installation). You should use **fdisk -mbr** for this.

Chapter 4

Managing Interactive Installations

For many situations in which you're about to install Microsoft Windows Server 2003 onto a new computer system—a bare-metal or a clean installation to a computer you can sit in front of—booting from the Windows Server 2003 CD-ROM is certainly the simplest. You need only configure the server to boot from the CD-ROM by setting the boot device order in the BIOS and provide information when prompted. The exception to this is when you must specify command-line switches, which might require you to boot from a floppy disk with CD-ROM drivers (if it is a bare-metal installation) or run the command line from within an existing installation. Alternatively, if you work in an environment that maintains standing images of operating systems in use, you can do an interactive installation from a distribution folder on the network.

Windows Installation Considerations

The previous chapter covers everything you must prepare for installing Windows Server 2003 and getting started. Still, there are some additional installation considerations—just a few, I promise.

Installation on x86-Based Systems

When you are working with Windows Server 2003 on x86-based systems, you should be aware of the three special types of drive sections used by the operating system.

- **System** The system volume or partition contains the hardware-specific files needed to load the operating system.
- **Boot** The boot volume or partition contains the operating system and its support files.
- **Active** The active volume or partition is the drive section from which the computer starts. It contains the startup files, including Boot.ini, Ntdetect.com, Ntldr, and Bootsect.dos.

Note Partitions and volumes are essentially the same thing. We use two different terms at times, however, because partitions are created on basic disks and volumes are created on dynamic disks.

Note Yes, the definitions of boot partition and system partition are backward from what you'd expect. The boot partition does in fact contain the \Windows directory—that's just the way it is. Hey, you have to click Start to stop the computer, so what'd you expect?

Although these volumes or partitions can be the same, they are required nonetheless. When you install Windows Server 2003, the Setup program assesses all hard disk drive resources available. Typically, Windows Server 2003 puts boot and system on the same drive and partition and marks this partition as the active partition. The advantage of this configuration is that you don't need multiple drives for the operating system and can use an additional drive as a mirror of the operating system partitions. Contrary to some documentation, you can mirror operating system partitions—you do this by using dynamic disks as discussed in the section entitled "Using the Basic and Dynamic Store Types" on page 602.

Inside Out

Partitions should use NTFS

The active, system, and boot partitions can be formatted as file allocation table (FAT), FAT32, or NTFS. In Microsoft Windows NT, administrators often formatted these volumes as FAT on the premise that if the operating system failed, they could boot to a DOS diskette, and then from DOS, they could replace any corrupted files or reconfigure drives after installing a new drive. Unfortunately, because of its poor security, FAT reduced the overall security of the system and put the entire network at risk. On Windows Server 2003, configuring these volumes as NTFS is recommended and not only because of the added security benefits. Any time a boot fails, Windows Server 2003 enables you to boot to the Advanced Options menu. This menu gives you the option of starting the operating system in one of several safe modes that you can use to attempt to boot without certain services or system components. You can also boot to the Recovery Console, which allows you to access a command line and work with NTFS. For more information on the Recovery Mode Console, see "Chapter 40, "Disaster Planning."

Installation on 64-Bit Systems

There are a number of differences when installing to the Intel Architecture 64 (IA-64) Itanium-based hardware platform. The IA-64 Extended Firmware Interface starts up loading a firmware-based boot menu (instead of Boot.ini).

IA-64 disks have a partition structure, called a globally unique identifier (GUID) Partition Table (part of the Extensible Firmware Interface, or EFI), that differs substantially from the 32-bit platform Master Boot Record–based partitions. A GUID Partition Table (GPT)–based disk has two required partitions and one or more optional (original equipment manufacturer [OEM] or data) partitions (up to 128 total):

- EFI system partition (ESP)
- Microsoft Reserved partition (MSR)
- At least one data partition

The IA-64 boot menu presents a set of options, one of which is the EFI shell. The EFI shell provides an operating environment supporting the FAT and FAT32 file systems, as well as configuration and file management commands.

To view a list of partitions on an IA-64-based computer, use the command MAP. The following appears in the resultant display:

- blk designates partition blocks.
- fs# designates readable file systems.

Changing to a partition is like changing a logical drive—enter the partition block number followed by a colon, press Enter, and then type **DIR** to view the files.

EFI has a boot maintenance manager that allows you to configure the boot menu. By using the boot maintenance manager, you can choose to do any of the following:

- Add or remove a boot option
- Set timeout delay and the boot option to run automatically
- Define standard console devices
- Boot from a (selected) file
- Perform cold reboot

Note Any of the boot configuration settings for Windows Server 2003 can be modified by using the Bootcfg command or by using the System utility in Control Panel.

Intel's 64-bit systems do not boot from a CD-ROM; thus, Setup must be started through the EFI shell. To do this, go to the fs# alias that maps to the CD-ROM and run the \Setupldr.efi Setup boot loader.

The rest of setup for an IA-64 system is the same as the 32-bit version of setup, with the exception of the IA-64 partitioning method. Setup determines whether there is an EFI partition—if one is not present, Setup creates (and formats) the EFI and the MSR partitions and asks you to create a data partition for the operating system.

> **Caution** Because EFI does not have password protection, you must provide physical security for all IA-64 servers.

Checking System Compatibility

If possible, you should always check system compatibility with Windows Server 2003 before attempting to install the operating system. One way to check compatibility is to use **Winnt32 /Checkupgradeonly** as discussed in the section entitled "Winnt32 Command-Line Parameters," on page 77. You can start the same compatibility check from the graphical user interface (GUI) as well. Follow these steps:

1. Insert the Windows Server 2003 CD-ROM into the CD-ROM drive.
2. When the Autorun screen appears, click Check System Compatibility. (If Autorun is disabled or doesn't run, double-click the Setup.exe program on the CD-ROM.)
3. Click Check My System Automatically. The Windows operating system then analyzes the compatibility of the system and its hardware components, searching for any potential problems and displaying the results.
4. You will be prompted to get updated Setup files using Dynamic Update. Click Yes to do this or No to skip the update and continue the installation precheck.
5. Select a reported item, and then click Details to view additional information. You can also click Save As to save the report as a text file. When you are done, click Finish.

Planning Partitions

Now that you know how Windows Server 2003 uses disks on both x86-based and Itanium-based systems, consider carefully how you want to partition the hard disk drives. The boot and system files require about 1.5 gigabytes (GB) of space. To allow for flexibility, you should create a partition for the operating system with at least 4 to 10 GB minimum. This allows for the addition of service packs and other system files later. Don't forget that you should also have enough disk space for the pagefile; I recommend reserving additional disk space equivalent to twice the installed RAM for this purpose.

Although on a 32-bit system you could have a single hard disk with a single partition, it is better to have multiple partitions, even if the computer has only one drive. By using multiple partitions, you can separate operating system files from application data. Not only does this enhance security, it permits the use of services that require installation on nonsystem partitions, such as Remote Installation Services (RIS).

> **Tip** **Create additional partitions**
> If you plan to create multiple partitions, don't worry about doing it when installing the operating system. Configure the Windows operating system to use a partition of the correct size, such as 4 GB or more, and then create the other partitions that you want to use after the installation is finished.

For systems with multiple disks, this is a good time to think about whether you want to use a redundant array of independent disks (RAID) to add fault tolerance for the operating system. RAID options are discussed in the section entitled "Managing Volumes on Dynamic Disks" on page 624 and include the following:

- Disk striping (RAID 0)
- Disk mirroring or duplexing (RAID 1)
- Disk striping with parity (RAID 5)

You cannot use RAID 0 with system or boot volumes. More typically, operating system files are mirrored, while application data is striped with parity. If you plan to mirror the operating system, you will need two disks. If you plan to create a RAID-5 volume for your data, you'll need at least three disks.

RAID can be performed at the hardware level or at the operating system level. You will find that the hardware-based RAID provides the best performance and the easiest solution. Windows Server 2003 also provides software-based RAID. Software-based RAID is implemented by using dynamic disks. For a bare-metal installation, the disks on the computer should be formatted as basic disks, and then after installation, you upgrade to dynamic disks so you can implement software-based RAID. On existing installations, the computer might already have dynamic disks, such as would happen if a computer is currently using Microsoft Windows 2000 Server and you are performing a new installation of Windows Server 2003. As long as the dynamic disks are hard-linked as a result of a basic disk being upgraded to a dynamic disk, the new installation of Windows Server 2003 over the existing installation should work fine. However, the Windows Setup program has problems working with dynamic disks with soft links (that is, those disks installed initially as dynamic disks or those disks whose hard links were overwritten), and as a result, setup of a new installation fails (an upgrade would work fine, however). If you are concerned about dynamic disk issues, you might want to allow the first disk to be a basic disk.

Naming Computers

It is surprising how few organizations take the time to plan out the names they're going to use for their computers. Sure, it is fun to have servers named Lefty, Curly, Moe, Ducky, Ruddy, and Aardvark, but just what do the names say about the role and location of those servers? You guessed it—nothing, which can make it difficult for users and even other administrators to find resources they need. Not to mention the management nightmare that happens when your 6 cutely named servers grow to number 50 or 500.

Rather than using names that are cute or arbitrary, decide on a naming scheme that is meaningful to both administrators and users—and this doesn't mean naming servers after the Seven Dwarfs or Lord of the Rings characters. Okay, it might be cool—way cool—to have servers named Bilbo, Gandalf, Frodo, and Gollum. But pretty soon you'd have Galadriel, Boromir, Theoden, Eowyn, and all the rest of the cast. And at that point, you'd better be ready to field lots of questions, such as, "How do you spell Aeyowin, anyway?" or "What's Thedding and where is it again?"

To help users and ease the administration burden, you might decide to use a naming scheme that helps identify what the computer does and where it is located. For example, you could name the first server in the Engineering department Engsvr01 and the first server in the Technical Services department Techsvr01. These names identify the computers as servers and specify the departments in which they are located. You might also have servers named CorpMail01 and CorpIntranet01, which identify the corporate mail and intranet servers, respectively.

Although naming conventions can be helpful, don't go overboard. The names Engsvr01, Techsvr01, CorpMail01, and CorpIntranet01 help identify computers by role and location, but they aren't overly complex. Keeping things simple should help ensure the computer names are easy to remember and easy to work with. Stay away from overly complex names, such as SeattleSrvBldg48DC17 or SvrSeaB48F15-05, if at all possible. Overly complex names are unnecessary in most instances and probably contain information that most users don't need. For example, users won't care that a server is in building 48 or that it is on floor 15. In fact, that information might be too specific and could actually help someone who wants to break into or sabotage the corporate network. Instead of putting exact mapping information in the computer name, keep a spreadsheet that maps computer locations for administration use, and include only general information about location or department in the computer name.

Finally, keep in mind that computer names must be unique in the domain and must be 64 characters or less in length. The first 15 characters of the computer name are used as the pre–Windows 2000 computer name for NetBIOS communications and must be unique in the domain as well. Further, for DNS compatibility, the name should consist of only alphanumeric characters (A–Z, a–z, and 0–9) and the hyphen.

Network and Domain Membership Options

During installation, you must decide on several important network and domain membership options, such as the following:

- Which protocols the server will use
- Whether the server will be a member of the domain
- What networking components will be installed

Protocols

As with Microsoft Windows 2000, the only protocol that Windows Server 2003 installs by default is Transmission Control Protocol/Internet Protocol (TCP/IP). You have the option of installing additional networking components during installation, which includes Internetwork Packet Exchange (IPX) and AppleTalk. However, NetBEUI is not provided as a protocol option. It has been removed from all editions of Windows Server 2003.

To install TCP/IP, you must decide whether you want to use static Internet Protocol (IP) addressing or dynamic IP addressing. For static IP addresses, you need the following information:

- IP address
- Subnet mask
- Default gateway
- Preferred DNS server

For dynamic IP addressing, the IP information is assigned automatically by an available Dynamic Host Configuration Protocol (DHCP) server. If no DHCP server is available, the server will use Automatic Private IP Addressing (APIPA) and assign itself an IP address. Autoconfigured addressing is typically nonroutable, so you must correct this issue after installation.

Domain Membership

Just about every server you install will be a member of a domain rather than a member of a workgroup (except if your company has a datacenter or you work exclusively in an isolated development lab). You can join a computer to a domain during installation. If you want to do that, you must have a computer account created in the domain (or create one during installation using an account with Administrator or Account Operator rights). A computer account is similar to a user account in that it resides in the accounts database held in the Active Directory directory service and is maintained by domain controllers.

If a server is a member of a domain, users with domain memberships or permissions can access the server and its resources based on, of course, their individual rights and permissions without having to have a separate logon. This means that users can log on once to the domain and work with resources for which they have permissions to access, and they won't be prompted to log on separately for each server they work with. In contrast, however, if a server is a member of a workgroup, users must log on each time they want to work with a server and its resources.

Networking Components

During installation, you have the opportunity to install networking components. The common networking components for servers are selected automatically. They include the following:

- **Client for Microsoft Networks** Allows the computer to access resources on Windows-based networks
- **File and Printer Sharing for Microsoft Networks** Allows other Windows-based computers to access resources on the computer (required for remote logon)
- **Internet Protocol (TCP/IP)** Allows the computer to communicate over the network by using TCP/IP

You can install additional clients, services, and protocols during installation, including Network Load Balancing, Microsoft TCP/IP v6, and Client Service for Netware. However, try to keep additional component installation to a minimum. Install the components that you know must be installed. Don't install components you think you might need. Any additional components can be installed after the operating system installation. Remember, not only will the additional components use disk space, they might also run as services. Services use system processing time and memory, and in some cases, they also could lower the security of the system by providing an additional way for someone to break into it.

Performing an Interactive Installation

Installation of Windows Server 2003 is completed in the following phases.

- **File-copy mode** In the initial phase, all of the distribution files for Windows Server 2003 are copied to the hard disk of the target computer.
- **Text mode** During this phase of Setup, the computer hardware is analyzed, hard disk and partitions are configured, drivers are located, folders are created, and the base operating system is installed.
- **GUI mode** In the final phase of Windows Setup, a GUI interface is presented that allows you to customize the configuration—this includes hardware settings, network parameters, licensing, and regional options, as well as joining the computer to a domain or workgroup and setting the administrator password.

After installation, the Mini-Setup program runs upon first boot of the newly installed operating system to detect new device hardware, set up the operating system configuration, and prompt for required user-specific data. The Mini-Setup program is also used in conjunction with Sysprep and RIPrep operating system images to complete final configuration tasks.

The initial Windows Setup display lists the installation options. At the beginning of Windows Setup, you are prompted to press F6 if you need to install third-party drivers for the boot device. Next you can press F2 if you want to run the Automated System Recovery (ASR) component. ASR is a new Windows Server 2003 system recovery tool that automates the process of restoring the entire system after a disaster.

The initial installation files are copied and a Welcome To Setup screen is displayed, which gives you the option of repairing an existing installation using the Recovery Console, continuing installation, or quitting. If you press Enter to continue, the Windows licensing agreement is then displayed, which gives you options to either press F8 to agree with the licensing terms or press Esc to exit the installation program.

Installation Sequence

Windows Setup then conducts the installation in the following sequence:

1. **Disk partitioning during Setup** Setup searches for existing installations of the Windows operating system—in the case of a bare-metal installation, it finds none and moves on to selecting the partition on which to install. Available drives and partitions are displayed, allowing you to configure partitions and select the partition on which Windows Server 2003 should be installed.

   At this point, the location and version numbers of any existing versions of the Windows operating system are displayed. If Windows Server 2003 is already installed, its location is displayed and you are given the option to repair it.

   You can allocate the entire drive as a single partition or subdivide it into multiple smaller ones by using these methods:

   - *Single partition*—To install upon the unpartitioned space using all of it as one partition, simply press Enter; a single partition is created, and then the installation process begins.
   - *Multiple partitions*—To subdivide the unpartitioned space into multiple partitions, press C to create a partition. This allows you to specify the size of the partition (in megabytes) that you want created in this unpartitioned space. Once the size is entered, the screen shows the partition you just created, along with the existing partitions and unpartitioned space. Highlight the partition on which you want to install Windows Server 2003, and press Enter to select that partition.

> **Tip** **Select the partition to use**
> Any existing partitions are displayed. You can then select which partition to install on and press Enter to begin installation, or you can press the L key to delete a partition and create a new partition. If you delete the active partition, Setup asks you to confirm: It will then display the partition information again, requiring you to press L to actually delete the partition. You are then returned to the screen displaying the existing drives and available partition space.

2. **Selecting the file system** You next specify the file system to use—either NTFS or FAT. In most cases you want to use the NTFS file system for Windows Server 2003 installations. The FAT file system does not support the use of permissions, and thus cannot provide adequate support for Windows Server 2003 operations. In fact, a number of services require installation on an NTFS partition. Choose the option to format the partition using NTFS, and press Enter to begin formatting. Setup will display the partition and drive information, as well as a progress bar that indicates the percentage of the drive that has been formatted.

Tip **Avoid quick formatting**
Although you have the option to do a Quick format, usually you want to select a standard format. The only times you might choose the Quick formatting option is when you have very recently formatted the drive and are certain that the drive can be formatted without errors. For bare-metal installations, this usually is not the case; thus, try to avoid using the Quick format option.

3. **Hardware detection and installation of files** After the drive formatting, Setup then performs the basic installation, beginning by collecting information about the server hardware and assessing the device drivers that will be required to support the server platform. Setup then continues, preparing the files and configuration for the installation, and copying files and finalizing the installation.

Tip Unlike Windows NT 4 and Windows 2000, which used \Winnt as the default installation directory, Windows Server 2003 uses \Windows as the default.

For more information on Dynamic Update, see "Using Dynamic Update" on page 86.

Tip **Estimate installation time**
Throughout the process, Setup advises you approximately how long it will take to complete this process. The actual amount of time required to complete this process varies immensely depending upon the specifics of your hardware, including the speed of the CD-ROM drive, the speed of your processor, and the speed of your hard disk subsystem.

4. **Regional and network configuration** The Regional And Language Options dialog box is displayed, which allows you to change the location configuration, including the display of date and time, numbers, and currency. Once these settings are selected, you are prompted to enter your name and the name of your company.
5. **Product key** Next, the product key used to uniquely identify your copy of Windows Server 2003 is required (unless volume license media is used). This is an alphanumeric string, which is typically attached to the back of your CD-ROM case (or provided with an Open License agreement).

Note Companies purchasing the Select Licensing and Enterprise Agreement license programs are provided with distribution CDs that have the product key embedded, and thus they are not required to enter the product key here, nor is product activation necessary after installation.

6 **Licensing mode** Once the product key is entered correctly, Setup prompts you to select the licensing mode. You have to select one of two licensing modes, either per server or alternatively per device or per user. If per-server licensing is selected, you must set the number of client access licenses (CALs) for the server. Verify that your selections here match your Information Technology (IT) licensing allocation plans to keep CAL usage in compliance.

7 **Computer name and administrator password** Once you have established your licensing mode, you are prompted to provide the computer name and administrator password for the server. (Windows also suggests a default computer name generated from your company name and a random string.) Consider carefully the computer name and password to use.

Computer names can be up to 64 characters in length, the first 15 characters of which are used for the pre–Windows 2000 computer name. Further, for DNS compatibility, the name should consist of only alphanumeric characters (A–Z, a–z, and 0–9) and the hyphen. The best computer names follow some sort of naming scheme and help users determine where a computer is and what its role is.

Passwords should be a minimum of eight characters, for security purposes. The best passwords are as strong as possible while being fairly easy to type and memorable enough so that you won't forget them.

Tip **Use a strong password for the Administrator account**

A strong password uses a combination of uppercase letters, lowercase letters, numbers, and special characters. If your administrator password does not meet the Windows server criteria for strong passwords, a dialog box explaining the criteria for the administrator password appears and you are given the opportunity to change the password or continue with it as is. The use of a strong password for the Administrator account is a security step well worth taking. Weak passwords remain one of the more significant ways that security of a Windows network is compromised, yet they are one of the easiest to correct.

8 **Date and Time** The Date And Time Properties dialog box is displayed next, enabling you to configure your server for your time zone. As innocuous as setting the date and time seems, don't overlook its importance. In a domain setting, the time is checked during logon and a discrepancy of more than a few minutes between the domain controller and the server can cause logon failure. Of particular note is the fact that domain controllers (and Active Directory) do all their internal work in universal time, and although they don't care about the time zone, an incorrect time zone setting can lead to denial of logon. Consider the case of a domain whose domain controllers are configured for Central Time and a new server that is configured for Pacific Time (the default). Here, if the domain controllers are set to 2 P.M. Central Time and the server is set to 2 P.M. Pacific Time, there's actually 2 hours difference between their time settings because 2 P.M. Pacific Time is 4 P.M. Central Time.

9 **Installing network components** At this point, Windows Setup moves on to installing basic network components. If Windows Setup doesn't recognize your network card, or doesn't have drivers for it, it will skip the network installation portion of the setup process. In this case, you must set up and configure the network adapter and protocols manually. To do this, after installation go to Device Manager, select the network adapter's properties, in the Driver tab select Update Driver, and then specify the location of the driver for the network card. Afterward, you must install TCP/IP networking.

Note Many of the network services you might require on your network are not installed by default in the basic installation process. In fact, many services can't be installed using Setup at all. Although each network service can be installed individually (by using the Add or Remove Programs utility in Control Panel), many services are now installed by assigning the server one or more roles, such as Domain Name System (DNS) Server or DHCP Server. For each role, one or more services are installed, the server (and perhaps the network and Active Directory) are configured, and corresponding administration tools are installed.

10 **Joining a workgroup or domain** You are next able to choose whether the server should be in a workgroup or a domain. If the server should be a member of a workgroup or you are setting up a new domain, choose the No option. If the server should join an existing domain, choose the Yes option and provide the login information for an Administrator or Account Operator account when prompted. If you are using an account from a trusted domain of the domain you are joining, you must enter the full domain and account name in *Domain\Username* format, such as Adatum\WRStanek. For domains, you are next given the opportunity to create a computer account or, by electing not to, to use one you've already created for the computer (based on the computer name).

11 **Setup completes** Setup then copies the remaining files needed for installation from the CD-ROM and completes the initial installation process. Once this installation process is completed, Setup restarts the server. You can then log on and use the Manage Your Server Wizard to finish setting up the server as discussed in the "Configuring Server Roles" section later in this chapter. If Setup doesn't complete normally, try the troubleshooting options discussed next.

Activation Sequence

After you install Windows Server 2003, you should configure TCP/IP networking as discussed in Chapter 24, "Managing TCP/IP Networking." If the type of licensing you are using requires product activation after installation, you should activate Windows within 60 days of installation. You have several activation options.

Activate Windows over the Internet

Before you activate Windows over the Internet, you should change the Enhanced Security Configuration settings in Internet Explorer so that members of the Administrators group can use Internet content. This is currently required for product activation over the Internet, but the situation may change with the release of Windows Server 2003 Service Pack 2. To do this, perform the following steps:

1. In Control Panel, double-click Add Or Remove Programs.
2. In the Add Or Remove Programs dialog box, click Add/Remove Windows Components.
3. In the Windows Components Wizard, select Internet Explorer Enhanced Security Configuration and then click Details.
4. In the Internet Explorer Enhanced Security Configuration dialog box, clear the For Administrators Groups option and click OK. Optionally, you can also clear For All Other User Groups before clicking OK.
5. In the Windows Components Wizard, click Next. After the wizard updates the configuration, click Finish.

You can now activate Windows over the Internet without being restricted by the security configuration. To do this, perform the following steps:

1. Click Start, point to Programs or All Programs as appropriate, and then click Activate Windows.
2. In the Windows Product Activation Wizard, select Yes, Let's Activate Windows Over The Internet Now and then click Next.
3. Follow the prompts to complete activation and optionally register Windows Server 2003.

Activate Windows by Telephone

Activation over the telephone doesn't require changing the Internet Explorer Security Configuration. You can go straight to product activation by performing the following steps:

1. Click Start, point to Programs or All Programs as appropriate, and then click Activate Windows.
2. In the Windows Product Activation Wizard, select Yes, I Want To Telephone A Customer Service Representative To Activate Windows and then click Next.
3. Select a geographic or country location to obtain a telephone number for your area. You will also get an installation ID, which is a very long string of numbers that you will need to give to the customer service representative or enter into the automated

customer service phone system. After you call the phone number and give the installation ID, you will get an activation code, which is another long string of numbers that you have to enter on the Activate Windows page before you can continue with the activation.

4 Click Next and follow the prompts to complete activation and optionally register Windows Server 2003.

Troubleshooting Installation

Most of the time, installation completes normally and the Windows operating system starts without any problems. Some of the time, however, installation won't complete or, after installation, the server won't start up, and you must troubleshoot to figure out what's happening. The good news is that installation problems are usually the result of something simple. The bad news is that simple problems are sometimes the hardest to find.

For more information about troubleshooting and recovery, see Chapter 41, "Backup and Recovery." Beyond that, you'll also find troubleshooters in the Help And Support console and in the Microsoft Knowledge Base, which is available online at *http://support.microsoft.com/*. Both are good resources for troubleshooting.

Start with the Potential Points of Failure

Setup can fail for a variety of reasons, but more often than not it's because of incompatible hardware components or failure of the system to meet the minimum requirements for Windows Server 2003 installation. With this in mind, start troubleshooting by looking at the potential points of failure and how these failure points can be resolved.

Setup Refuses to Install or Start

If a hardware component is incompatible with Windows Server 2003, this could cause failure of the installation or failure to start up after installation. Make sure that Windows Server 2003 is detecting the system hardware and that the hardware is in the Windows Server Catalog or on the Hardware Compatibility List (HCL). As discussed previously, you can perform a compatibility check prior to installing Windows Server 2003.

Once you've started installation, however, it's too late. At this point, you have several choices. You can reboot to a working operating system and then restart the installation using Winnt or Winnt32 and the **/debug** Setup option. This puts Setup in debug mode and helps identify what is going wrong. If Setup determines you have hardware conflicts, you can try to configure the hardware and server BIOS to eliminate the conflicts. Troubleshooting BIOS involves booting the server to the firmware and then completing the following steps:

- **Examine the boot order of disk devices** You might want to configure the system so that it boots first from CD-ROM. Watch out, though; after installation, don't keep booting to CD-ROM thinking you are booting to the operating system—hey, we all get tired and sometimes we just have to stop and think for a moment. If the installation problem is that you keep going back to the installation screen after installing the operating system, you are probably inadvertently booting from CD-ROM—and you're probably way too tired by now to realize it.

- **Check Plug and Play device configuration and interrupt reservations** If a system has older components or components that aren't Plug and Play compatible, you might have a device conflict for a hard-coded interrupt. For example, a non–Plug and Play sound card could be hard-coded to use interrupt 13, which is already in use by a Plug and Play device. To work around this, you must configure interrupt 13 under your Plug and Play BIOS settings to be reserved for a non–Plug and Play device. This ensures that Plug and Play does not attempt to use that interrupt and resolves the issue in most cases.

> **Tip** The only sure way to avoid problems with non–Plug and Play devices is to avoid using them altogether.

Rather than spending time—which could run into several hours—trying to troubleshoot a hardware conflict, you might consider removing the hardware component if it's nonessential—and you might be surprised at what I consider nonessential at this stage. By nonessential, I mean most anything that isn't needed to start up and give you a display for logon. You probably don't need a network card, a sound card, a multimedia controller card, a video coder/decoder (codec), or a removable media drive. If these items are incompatible, you might resolve the problem simply by removing them. You can always try to install the components again after installation is complete.

Setup Reports a Media or CD-ROM Error

When you install directly from the Windows Server 2003 CD-ROM or perform a network install from a distribution share, you might encounter a media error that causes Setup to fail. With an actual CD-ROM, you might need to clean the CD-ROM so that it can be read or use a different CD. If the CD-ROM drive is the problem, you must replace the drive or install from a distribution share as discussed in Chapter 3, "Preparing for the Installation and Getting Started." If you are working with a distribution share, the share might not have all the necessary files, or you might encounter problems connecting to the share. Try using an actual CD-ROM.

Setup Reports Insufficient System Resources

Windows Server 2003 requires a minimum of 128 megabytes (MB) of random access memory (RAM) and about 1.5 GB of disk space. If the system doesn't have enough memory, Setup won't start. If Setup starts and detects that there isn't enough space, it might not continue or you might need to create a new partition or delete an existing partition to get enough free space to install the operating system.

Setup Cannot Connect to a Domain Controller

Sometimes installation fails because you've configured the server to join a domain and Setup is unable to access the domain. Problems accessing domains might result from a network card not working properly or because you removed a network card that was incompatible.

- If a network card isn't working, you should see an orange or red traffic indication light (rather than a green one) or no connection indication light on the card. Check the network cable connection between the server and the router.
- If you had to remove an incompatible network card, configure the server to join a workgroup temporarily. Then, after you complete installation, you can install a new network card and get TCP/IP services working, which should allow you to join the domain.

Setup can also fail to connect to a domain controller if you've improperly configured DNS or provided the wrong account information.

- If DNS is configured incorrectly, the server won't be able to connect to the domain. Check the IP address, network mask, gateway, and preferred DNS server settings. If you are using DHCP to dynamically assign the IP settings, you still might need to enter the DNS server settings.
- If you provided the wrong account information, logon to the domain will fail. You must use an account with Administrator or Account Operator permissions. If the account used has these permissions, ensure that you've entered the user name and password correctly. Remember, if you are using an account from a trusted domain of the domain you are joining, you must enter the full domain and account name in *Domain\Username* format, such as Adatum\WRStanek.

Continue Past Lockups and Freezes

If you can get past the potential points of failure, you still might find that the installation locks up or freezes. In this case, you might get a Stop error; then again, you might not.

Most Stop errors have cryptic error codes rather than clear messages telling you what's wrong. If you get a Stop error, write down the error number or code, then refer to the Microsoft Knowledge Base (available online at *http://support.microsoft.com/*) for help troubleshooting the problem. To break out of the stop, you most likely will have to press Ctrl+Alt+Del (sometimes several times) to get the server to restart. If this doesn't break out of the stop, press the Reset button on the server. Alternatively, turn off the system power, wait a few seconds, and then turn it back on.

The Windows operating system should start up and go directly back to Setup. In some cases, you will see a boot menu. If so, choose the Windows Setup option to allow the Setup program to attempt to continue the installation. Setup could freeze again. If it does, stay with it, and repeat this process—sometimes it takes several tries to get completely through the installation process.

Troubleshooting

Setup freezes at a specific point

Occasionally, Setup will continually freeze at a specific point in the installation. For example, one time I was installing a server and Setup froze every time it got to the network installation. The workaround was to change the network configuration options—I had to clear the Internet Protocol (TCP/IP) networking component installation. You might find that changing or simplifying the installation process works for you as well.

RAM and central processing units (CPUs) can also be the source of problems. Issues to watch out for include the following:

- **Incompatible RAM** Not all RAM is compatible, and you can't mix and match RAM of different speeds and types. Ensure that all RAM modules are the same type and speed. Further, RAM modules from different manufacturers could in some cases perform differently (read incompatibly), and in such a case, try changing the RAM so that all modules have the same manufacturer.
- **Malfunctioning RAM** Static discharges can ruin RAM faster than anything else. If you didn't ground yourself and use a static discharge wire before working with the RAM modules, you could have inadvertently fried the RAM so that the modules don't work at all or are malfunctioning. RAM could have also arrived in this condition from the manufacturer or distributor. There are several troubleshooting techniques for determining this. You could update BIOS to add a wait state to the RAM so that if the RAM is partially faulty the system will still boot (but you still must replace the RAM eventually). You can also try removing some RAM modules or changing their order.
- **Incompatible processors** Not all processors are created equal, and I'm not just talking about their speed in megahertz (which you generally want to be the same for all processors on a server). Some processors might have a cache or configuration that is incompatible with the server hardware or other processors. Check the processor speed and type to ensure that it is compatible with the server. In some cases, you might need to change hardware jumpers, depending on the speed and type of your processors.
- **Misconfigured processors** Adding additional processors to a server isn't a simple matter of inserting them. Often, you must change jumpers on the hardware, remove several terminators (one for a power subcomponent and one for the processor—save

them because, trust me, you might find that you need them), and then insert the new components. Check the hardware jumpers (even if you think there aren't any), and ensure the processors and the power subcomponents you've added are seated properly. If you can't get the installation to continue or the server to start up, you might need to remove the components you've added. Watch out, though; you probably don't want to continue the installation until the processor issue is resolved—single-processor systems have different threading and default configuration than multiprocessor systems, meaning this situation might not be a simple matter of adding the processor after installation and making it all work properly.

- **System processor cache problems** Sometimes there can be an issue with the system processor cache and compatibility with Windows Server 2003. Consult the server documentation to read the correct configuration settings available and how the cache can be disabled. If you suspect a problem with this, boot to BIOS and temporarily disable the system processor cache, following the server documentation. Once the installation is complete, you should be able to enable the cache to avoid a performance hit. Be sure to check both the hardware vendor support site and the Microsoft Knowledge Base to see whether any known issues with your server's processor cache exist.

Troubleshooting

RAM and CPUs are incompatible

You might be surprised at how common it is for incompatible RAM or CPUs to present problems, especially when installing enterprise-class servers. We had a problem once when we ordered all the components from a single hardware vendor that had verified the compatibility of every element down to the last detail only to find that the wrong processors and RAM were shipped for the systems ordered. The result was that every time we added the additional processors and RAM modules, the server wouldn't start up. The only recourse was to continue installation with the minimum processor and RAM configurations shipped or wait until replacements arrived. Electing to wait for replacements added time to the project but ultimately proved to be the right decision. You can bet that we were glad that we padded the project schedule to allow for the unexpected—because the unexpected usually happens.

Most of the time the installation or setup problem is caused by a compatibility issue with the Windows operating system, and that problem can be fixed by making changes to BIOS settings. Sometimes, however, the problem is the BIOS, and you'll find that you must upgrade the BIOS to resolve the problem. One problem in particular has to do with Advanced Configuration and Power Interface (ACPI)–compatible BIOS dated January 1, 2000, or earlier, which might not function properly in ACPI mode under Windows Server 2003. The result is that the Windows operating system freezes during setup and cannot get past it.

One way to fix this problem (and other BIOS problems) is to upgrade the BIOS. Check with the hardware vendor to see whether a BIOS upgrade is available. If so, install it as the hardware vendor directs. If a new BIOS version isn't available, you might be able to disable the incompatible option during setup. During setup, press F5 or other designated key at the beginning of the text-mode phase (just after it prompts you to press F6 to install third-party Small Computer System Interface [SCSI] drivers). If this doesn't work, the option you changed wasn't the source of the problem and you should reenable it before continuing.

Note Reenabling the option might be necessary because some hardware-specific BIOS settings cannot be changed after the installation. Thus, the only way to enable the option would be to reinstall the operating system.

You can also manually enable or disable advanced BIOS options. You do this by editing Txtsetup.sif in a distribution folder. This file is read after the text-mode phase of the installation and before the Windows operating system restarts to the Setup program. With ACPI, from the command line on another computer, you type **attrib –r –s –h c:\txtsetup.sif** and then type **edit c:\txtsetup.sif** so that you can edit the .sif file. In the .sif file, search for **ACPIEnable=**, change the associated line to read **ACPIEnable=0** to disable ACPI support (**ACPIEnable=1** enables ACPI support), and then save the changes. After you save the changes, restart into the Setup program.

Tip **Skip editing the Txtsetup.sif file**
You can press F7 during the portion of Setup that displays the message to press F6 for adding SCSI drivers. This configures Setup so that it won't try ACPI machine types. It also means you aren't required to edit the Txtsetup.sif file.

Finally, hard disk drive settings could also cause lockups or freezes, particularly if you are using Integrated Device Electronics (IDE) drives. When using IDE drives and controllers, you want to ensure that the system recognizes both the drives and the controllers and that both are enabled and configured properly in BIOS. You might have to check jumper settings on the drives and the cables that connect the drives. As discussed previously, check for conflicts between the drives, controllers, and other system components. You might need to temporarily remove unnecessary components, such as the sound card, to see whether this resolves a conflict. If a CD-ROM or DVD drive is on the same channel as the disk drives, try moving it to the secondary channel and configuring it as a master device. You can also try lowering the data transfer rate for the IDE drives.

Configuring Server Roles

The next step in the installation process is to install the networking services that are needed for the server. To install the networking services, you can use either of a couple of different approaches—use wizards or manually add services.

In Windows Server 2003, Microsoft has added a set of wizards that allow you to configure the server to support different roles, such as an Application Server with Internet Information Server (IIS) or a Domain Controller with Active Directory. The wizards automatically walk you through the installation of the network services needed to support the roles you select.

After the newly installed system reboots, log on as Administrator using the password assigned during installation. The Manage Your Server Wizard is displayed with two options available:

- Adding Roles To Your Server
- Managing Your Server Roles

Because only the initial installation has so far been performed, no roles have been added, and the only option available is Add Or Remove A Role. This option launches the Configure Your Server Wizard, which allows you to add and remove server roles and the corresponding services. As discussed in the section entitled "Planning for Server Usage" on page 59, it is common for a server to fill multiple roles, especially on smaller networks. The Windows Server 2003 server roles are as follows:

- Application Server
- DHCP Server
- DNS Server
- Domain Controller
- File Server
- Mail Server
- Print Server
- Remote Access/VPN Server
- Streaming Media Server
- Terminal Server
- WINS Server

> **Note** If you want to make a server a domain controller, you do this by installing Active Directory. The Active Directory Installation Wizard, Dcpromo, is discussed in the section entitled "Installing Active Directory" on page 1202.

When selecting multiple roles for a single server, try to select roles with different resource needs. For instance, putting a processor-intensive role, such as Application Server, and a role that does a lot of network input/output (I/O), such as File Server, together on a single system makes more sense than putting two roles that both require a lot of processor time or that both require a lot of network I/O.

Note Keep in mind that if your network connectivity isn't working, you cannot install any server roles. You should be able to correct this problem by installing and configuring the appropriate network components and TCP/IP networking.

Installing Additional Components Manually

The use of the server configuration wizards eases the support of server roles, yet some administrators prefer to install and configure each network service independently. Network services can also be installed in the traditional method, as part of the optional components installation process, performed from the distribution CD, or from within the Windows operating system by using the Add Or Remove Programs utility on Control Panel.

Inside Out

Recover your servers quickly

Initially installing and configuring servers takes a bit of time and effort, and thus the ability to bring them back online quickly in the event of failure can save substantial work and service downtime. Windows Server 2003 supports Automated System Recovery (ASR), an enhancement to the old Emergency Repair process, which simply scanned the registry and system files and replaced any registry entry or file that had changed since the creation of the Emergency Repair disk. ASR stores a copy of the system partition on a backup medium and writes the disk signatures, location of the backup files, and PnP device information to a floppy disk. The ASR process, like Emergency Repair, requires the earlier creation of an ASR floppy disk—the Windows Backup utility enables you to create an ASR backup, which also builds the ASR floppy disk. To activate the ASR routine, press F2 at the beginning of the setup process, and insert the ASR disk when prompted. This directs the ASR process to install the operating system (OS) and restore the system partition from the ASR backup medium. For more information on ASR, see the section entitled "Backing Up and Restoring the Registry," on page 434.

You can install and configure network services (and other optional components) by using the Add Or Remove Programs utility on Control Panel and selecting the Windows System Components option to identify and select the services and components you want to install for the server. Services include the following:

- Accessories And Utilities
- Application Server
- Internet Information Services
- Management and Monitoring Tools
- Networking Services
- Windows Media Services

Postinstallation

After you've configured server roles and installed additional components, you might be ready to call it a day. Don't do this yet because you should first perform a few final postinstallation procedures:

- **Check devices** Use Device Manager as discussed in the section entitled "Obtaining Hardware Device Information," on page 388, to look for undetected or malfunctioning hardware components. If you find problems, you might need to download and install updated drivers for the computer—you can download from another system and then transfer the files to the new server using a floppy disk or by burning the files to a CD-ROM. If you removed any system hardware prior to installation, you might want to add it back in and then check again for conflicts and issues that must be corrected. You aren't finished with Device Manager until every piece of hardware is working properly.
- **Check the TCP/IP configuration** Use the Local Area Network Connection Properties dialog box to check the TCP/IP configuration. Ensure the configuration is correct and that any additional settings are applied as necessary for the network. Test TCP/IP networking from the command line using PING or TRACERT and in the Windows operating system by trying to browse the network. See Chapter 24 for details.
- **Check event logs** Use Event Viewer to check the Windows event logs. Any startup warnings or errors will be written to the logs. See Chapter 15, "Performance Monitoring and Tuning," for details.
- **Check disk partitioning** Use the Computer Management console to check and finalize the disk partitions. Often, you must create the server's application partition or configure software RAID. See Chapter 19, "Storage Management," for details.

- **Optimize system configuration** Follow the techniques discussed in Chapter 10, "Configuring Windows Server 2003," and Chapter 12, "Managing Windows Server 2003," for tuning the operating system. For example, you might need to change the display settings, virtual memory pagefile usage, or the Server service configuration. You might also need to add local group and user accounts to the server per standard IT procedures.
- **Reboot for good measure** Once you've configured the server and optimized its settings, perform a final reboot to ensure that (1) the server starts, (2) all the server services start, and (3) no other errors occur. You should reboot even if the changes you made don't require it—better to find out about problems now rather than at 3 A.M. on a Saturday night.
- **Prepare backup and recovery** You're almost done, but not quite. Don't forget about creating an automated recovery disk for the server. You might also want to perform a full backup. For details on backing up servers and creating recovery disks, see Chapter 41.

Once these procedures are completed, you should have a server that is ready (or nearly ready) for its role in a production environment. For certain, quite a bit of extra work is involved beyond installing the operating system, but these postinstallation procedures are not only important, they're essential to ensuring the server performs as well as can be expected. As a final note, don't make the server available to users until any and all additional needed components, services, and applications are installed on it. The installation of these additional components, services, and applications could require one or more reboots or might require several time periods in which users are blocked from accessing the server or are requested not to connect to it. Remember, from the users' perspective, it's usually better to not have a resource than to be given one and then have it taken away (even temporarily). Finalize the server, then deploy it, and you'll have happier users.

Chapter 5

Managing Unattended Installations

When you have 20, 50, or 100 servers to install, you don't want to waste your time babysitting the installation for each and every server. Besides being very boring (you'll be answering the same questions over and over and over), it is a waste of your time—time you'll never get back—and this is where unattended installations come to the rescue.

An unattended installation is simply a way to automate the setup and installation process. When determining the level of user interaction you want to require during automated installation, you have several choices. Each of these choices uses an answer file to control the level of interaction. These choices are as follows:

- **User Controlled** The answer file defines the default answers to use during installation. The user can confirm the defaults or make changes as the installation progresses.
- **Fully Automated** The answer file contains all the answers needed to install computers of a specific type. Users aren't prompted during the installation process, allowing you to rapidly deploy computers. However, if settings don't work, the installation might fail.
- **Hidden Pages** The answer file specifies most of the answers needed to install computers of a specific type. Setup prompts the user to provide any information not defined in the answer file, and the user sees only these parts of the installation process. Use this option to ensure computers are configured in a specific way while at the same time allowing users to customize some parts of the process.
- **Read Only** As with hidden pages, the answer file specifies most of the answers needed to install computers of a specific type. If a dialog box in Setup has partial information, the user can complete only the unanswered portion. The rest of the values are set in read-only mode and can't be changed during the installation.
- **GUI Attended** The answer file is used to automate the text-based portion of the installation. It doesn't, however, provide answers for the graphical user interface (GUI) portion of the installation, allowing the user to configure the related settings as necessary. Use this option to help streamline and speed up the installation process while allowing users to maintain control over most of the installation.

Note Although the preceding refers specifically to Microsoft Windows Server 2003 installations, these methods can also be used for Microsoft Windows XP.

Unattended installations are most helpful on large networks where new computers are deployed frequently or must be rebuilt frequently, such as in a development lab. Besides helping you save countless hours of time, automating installation can also help the organization standardize and remove potential pitfalls from the installation process. Hey, I think we've all clicked the wrong answer once or twice during an install and didn't realize it until much later—you know, when it's after 9 P.M., you've been at work for 16 hours already and now are desperately trying to figure out what the heck is going on because server installs aren't supposed to be so troublesome, and the spouse and kids are wondering if you'll ever come home.

Another benefit of unattended installation is that it reduces the level of expertise required of the person running the installation. Once automated installation setup and configuration is in place, nonexperts can install servers by following a few simple instructions, and you can be sure the results will be the same every time. This can help in those environments in which you don't have enough experienced administrators—or the experienced administrators are typically too busy handling other tasks to manage server installations.

Automating Setup

Selecting an unattended installation method for Windows Server 2003 requires some thought and preparation regarding the target environment and the installation functionality that you need it to provide. There are three approaches to automated setup in Windows Server 2003, each providing its own particular benefits.

Determining the Method of Automation

Although it is technically possible to install all of the computers interactively from a CD-ROM, for most firms (except perhaps for the very smallest) this sort of installation is not very practical. For most companies, automating the installation process is a necessary approach and is implemented using one of three methods:

- **Creating an Unattend.txt file** When you create an Unattend.txt file, you create a file that contains answers to all the questions that Setup asks. You can then run the Unattend.txt script using Winnt or Winnt32 from the command line. You can also create an actual Windows script that provides the necessary command line so that the only thing administrators must do is enter the name of the Windows script at the command line. A boot floppy disk can be used to help simplify installation.

- **Using the Remote Installation Service** By using Remote Installation Service (RIS), you can store prebuilt Microsoft Windows 2000, Windows XP, and Windows Server 2003 installation files and scripts on a central server, called the RIS server. Then you perform a network boot of the computer you want to install, and access the installation files and scripts. If the computer isn't capable of a network boot, you can use a general-purpose floppy disk generated by RIS to perform a network boot.

> **Note** By using RIS for Windows Server 2003, you can perform RIS installations on both client machines (Windows 2000, Windows XP) and servers (Windows 2000 Server, Windows Server 2003). This is a change from Windows 2000 RIS with which you could install only client machines (Windows 2000 Professional) using RIS.

- **Using Sysprep image-based installation** By using Sysprep, you create prototype computers that are fully configured and then create images of these computers so that you can quickly deploy many computers at once. You can think of an image as a clone of the prototype computer's hard disk drive in that it contains all the essential files to make a new computer look exactly like the old one.

> **Note** Sysprep isn't new to Windows Server 2003. It was also available with Windows 2000.

So, there you have it: three different methods for automating installation. To determine the one that's right for your organization, you must answer a number of questions about your networking and software environments. The specifics of the networking environment where this automated installation is to occur can introduce some constraints and limitations on how you can perform automated installations. This might change your approach to an aspect of the automated setup process or might make it impossible for you to use a method entirely.

For example, on networks with high-speed connections, the use of a distribution folder (i.e., a share on the local network) facilitates automated installations for distributed target systems. On networks that have slow connections without a local server to house the distribution share, you might need to perform automated installations using CD media.

Unattended and Sysprep installations can be performed by using product files or images on CD media, while RIS requires network connectivity for the boot. RIS requires Preboot Execution Environment (PXE)–compliant hardware or a network adapter supported by the remote installation boot floppy disk.

There are other, less clear-cut considerations that are specific to your business environment: physical access to computers, available staff, even office politics. Once you have assessed your installation needs, you can select the most appropriate approach to automation. In this chapter, we discuss installing the Windows operating system by using the unattended method; that is, using answer files (such as Unattend.txt) at the command line. In Chapter 6, "Using Remote Installation Services," you'll find a detailed discussion specific to using RIS and Sysprep.

Establishing the Distribution Folders

Most forms of unattended installation use a distribution folder; that is, a network location of the Windows Server 2003 operating system containing the source files or images. You can have Setup Manager build this folder for you automatically when you create Unattend.txt files. The default structure of a distribution folder for unattended installations corresponds to the folder structure on the Windows Server 2003 CD media. The structure of the distribution folders used by an unattended installation is shown in Figure 5-1.

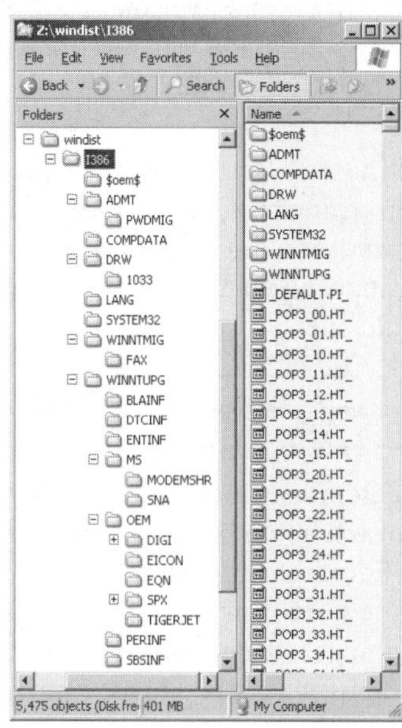

Figure 5-1. The structure of the default distribution folder.

In addition to containing a copy of the Windows Server 2003 source files, the distribution folders might also contain additional folders and files, including drivers (such as mass storage device drivers, hardware abstraction layers [HALs], as well as Plug and Play device drivers), configuration files, and applications. These files and folders are copied to the designated partition on the target computer during installation. The distribution folder could also have a Sysprep subfolder containing required Sysprep program and configuration files (used for image-based installations).

For more information about the structure of the RISetup and RIPrep distribution folders, see the section entitled "Using RIS Images" on page 181. The structure of the distribution folders used by RIS (both RISetup and RIPrep) differs substantially from that used in unattended (Unattend.txt) installations.

The consistency provided by using the distribution folder can also be helpful in subsequently creating the master installations with RIS or image-based installations. Because driver updates, service packs, security patches, and so on are constantly released, you must update your master installation periodically. If you use RISetup to create your master installation, you must update the RISetup Remote Installation folder for that operating system only periodically and regenerate the master installation (by running RIPrep to create the updated image).

How these distribution folders are established varies depending upon the form of automated installation that you are using, as follows:

- Distribution folders for unattended setup can be created automatically by Setup Manager when you create Unattend.txt files or manually by copying the contents of the I386 folder on the Windows Server 2003 CD to a network share.
- When using RIS to automate installations, the RIS Setup Wizard (RISetup) walks you through creating the Remote Installation folder.
- Sysprep-based images are posted to and downloaded from a network share by the third-party disk-imaging software employed.

Inside Out

Contents of the boot floppy disk

Boot disks can be used for most types of automated installations. The contents of the boot floppy disks are different for each type of automated install, however. The function and contents of the floppy disk used for each type of automated installation is shown in the following table:

Type of Installation	Boot Disk	CD Driver	Net Driver	Answer File
Unattended—network	Yes	No	Yes	No (on net)
Unattended—product CD	Yes	Yes	No	Yes
RIS	Only for PXE emulation	No	Yes	No (on net)

Types of Answer Files

There are several different types of answer files, each of which is used by a different type of automated installation process.

- **Unattend.txt** The Unattend.txt file allows for complete automation of the installation process, using either the distribution CD or distribution folder as the source for the distribution files. You select a new clean installation or an upgrade on the operating system currently on the computer using an Unattend.txt file.

Tip Automated installation methods using the retail CD do not allow you to choose an upgrade option, nor can you use a uniqueness file to provide modifications to the standard answer file.

- **RIS .sif files** The Setup Installation file (.sif) is a variation of the Unattend.txt file used in conjunction with RIS to automate a new, remote Windows installation usually for a new installation. The file name is assigned during creation by Setup Manager and usually is set as Winnt.sif.
- **Sysprep.inf** The Sysprep.inf file is used to automate the Mini-Setup portion of the installation; that is, the portion of setup after the initial reboot when the user normally would be prompted for configuration information. Sysprep.inf is dependent upon Sysprep.exe and Setupcl.exe being present in the %SystemDrive%\Sysprep folder on the destination computer.

Note Sysprep supports only a subset of the sections and entries that can be used in an Unattend.txt file. For detailed information on the sections and entries that can be used in a Sysprep.inf file, see the Sysprep.inf section of the "Microsoft Windows Corporate Deployment Tools User's Guide" help file in the Windows Server 2003 Deployment Kit. You'll also find a sample Sysprep.inf file later in this chapter.

You can automate some installation and configuration tasks before Mini-Setup runs using Factory mode. Factory mode is a special feature of Sysprep that uses an answer file to automate installation and configuration tasks before you prepare a computer for final delivery. Typically, Factory mode is used by computer manufacturers to customize computers after copying disk images onto those computers, but before Mini-Setup starts.

Factory mode enables disk configuration support so that you can create partitions and format disks and network connectivity so that you can connect to shared folders containing Windows Installer (.msi) packages, device drivers, and data files that should be downloaded and installed. You can also use Factory mode in the enterprise for these same purposes. Answer files used with Factory mode include the following:

- **Winbom.ini** The Winbom.ini file is a manually created answer file used to control Sysprep running in Factory mode. For a complete list of the sections and entries that can be used in a Winbom.ini file, see the Winbom.ini section of the "Microsoft Windows Corporate Deployment Tools User's Guide" help file.
- **Winpeoem.sif** The Winpeoem.sif answer file is used to configure the mass storage drivers loaded in a customized Windows preinstallation environment.
- **.ins and .isp files** The Internet settings (.ins) answer file is used to control dial-up or broadband access to the Internet. A related type of answer file is the Internet service provider (.isp) file that is used to connect to dial-up ISP services.
- **Oeminfo.ini** The Oeminfo.ini file contains the data identifying the enterprise and its product support services that is displayed in the System Properties dialog box.
- **Oobeinfo.ini** The Oobeinfo.ini file supports the customization of the Windows Welcome dialog box.

The primary answer file for Factory mode is Winbom.ini. This file includes the bill of materials (customizations) you want to make to the disk image. You tell Sysprep to use Factory mode by running **sysprep –factory** on the master computer and then creating a disk image of the master computer. When you copy the image onto the destination computer and start it, the computer starts in Factory mode and searches for the Winbom.ini file. The computer then uses this answer file to configure itself. In the [Factory] section of the Winbom.ini are Reseal and ResealMode entries, which are used to complete the customization and run Sysprep with the –Reseal parameter, which finalizes the customization and prepares the computer for final delivery. Note that Factory.exe must be in the Sysprep\I386\OEM folder with Sysprep.exe and Setupcl.exe.

Using Setup Manager for Answer Files

The Setup Manager tool provides a convenient, graphical interface for configuring settings within an answer file for specific installations, and it can write the answer file to the disk in a number of different formats (Unattend.txt, Winnt.sif, and Sysprep.inf).

By using Setup Manager, you can configure a range of installation and configuration settings, which are divided into general network and advanced settings. You can set the user and organization names, time zone, display settings, and product key. You can also configure the networking components, computer name, domain, and administrator password information, as well as the regional settings, languages, installation folder, printers, and telephony settings. Once all needed settings are configured, Setup Manager writes the information to the appropriate answer file for your mode of installation.

The Setup Manager Wizard (Setupmgr.exe) is not installed by default, but rather has to be extracted from the Deploy.cab file in the Support\Tools directory on the distribution CD. Simply access the Support\Tools directory on the CD-ROM, double-click Deploy.cab, then double-click Setupmgr.exe to begin the extraction process. While you are there, you might as well extract the rest of the files, including Deploy.chm (the Microsoft Windows Corporate Deployment Tools User's Guide) and Ref.chm (the detailed conventions and syntax reference for the Deployment Tools User's Guide).

Note Running the Support.msi file to install the Support Tools from this directory does not extract the contents of Deploy.cab.

Creating the Answer File

You start Setup Manager Wizard by running Setupmgr.exe. You are first asked whether you want to create a new answer file or to modify an existing one, as shown in the following screen:

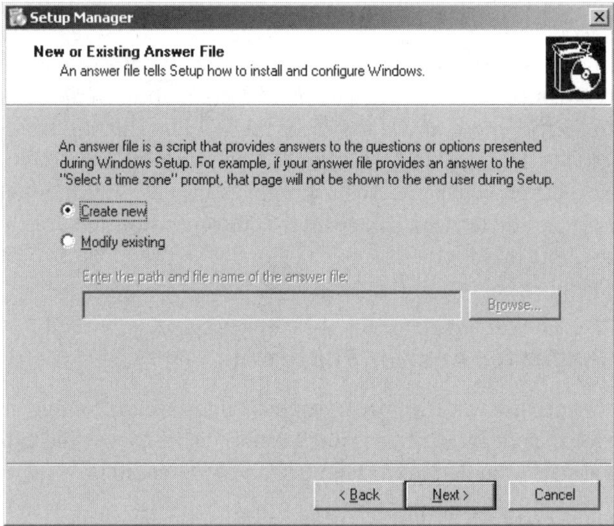

If you are creating a new answer file, you are prompted for the type of automated installation you want the answer file to support—unattended, RIS, or Sysprep-based, as shown in the screen on the following page.

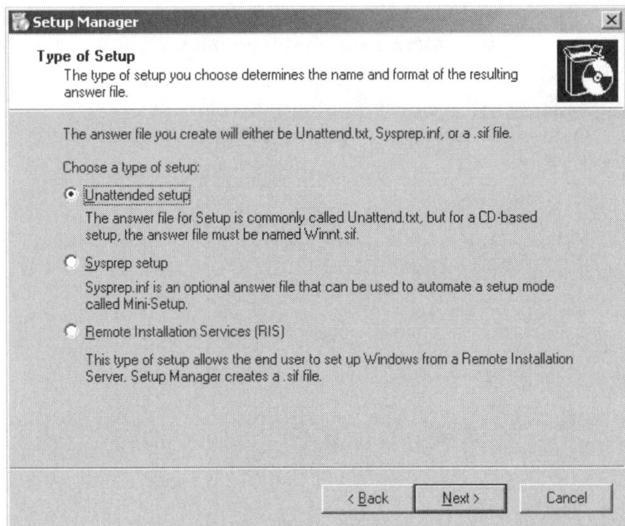

Each of these options results in an answer file with a slightly different format and name. For example, when creating an answer file for a network installation, the file name is Unattend.txt, whereas the RIS type of setup creates a file name ending with the file extension .sif, and Sysprep uses the file name Sysprep.inf.

Tip The answer file for an unattended installation using CD media is called Winnt.sif. A Setup Manager–created Unattend.txt file is renamed to Winnt.sif and placed on a floppy disk, which is used during installation.

After selecting the type of setup for which you want to create the answer file, you will be asked the version of the Windows operating system that will be installed by using this answer file. The options include the following:

- Windows XP, Home Edition
- Windows XP Professional
- Windows Server 2003, Standard Edition
- Windows Server 2003, Enterprise Edition
- Windows Server 2003, Web Edition

Note The Datacenter Edition of Windows Server 2003 is not supported for unattended installation files by the Setup Manager Wizard. Datacenter Edition supports an unattended installation, but you must use media and manually create the Unattend.txt file.

If you are performing either an unattended setup or an RIS-based setup, you'll next be prompted to specify the level of user interaction, as shown here:

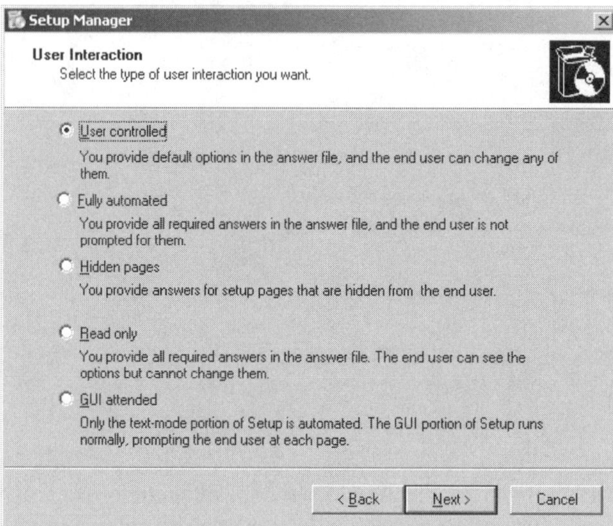

The level of user interaction can be set to the following options:

- **User Controlled** Answers are provided, but the user can modify them.
- **Fully Automated** All required answers are provided, and the user is not prompted to respond.
- **Hidden Pages** All required answers are provided, and the user does not see the dialog boxes.
- **Read-Only** All required answers are provided and are visible to the user, but are not modifiable.
- **GUI Attended** The GUI portion of the installation is interactive; only the text portion is automated.

Tip Because of the nature of image-based installations, Sysprep does not support user interaction during setup.

The distribution share (the location on the network containing the Windows source files) can then be specified, or you can designate that the files are to be pulled from the distribution CD, as shown in the screen on the following page.

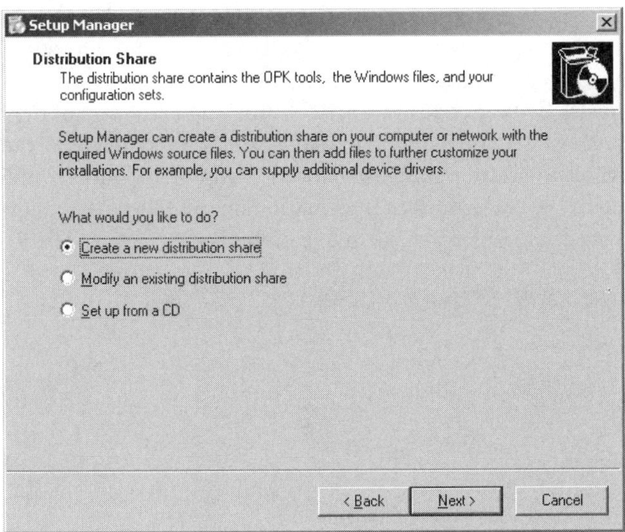

The Setup Manager Wizard also allows you to create or modify a distribution share. If you create a distribution share, you are prompted for the location of the Windows source files (specifying the CD or other location with the source files).

Once the distribution share is created or you select one to modify and you accept the terms of the End-User License Agreement, you are presented with the Setup Manager configuration dialog box.

You then must specify the distribution share location and share name for this answer file, as shown in the following screen:

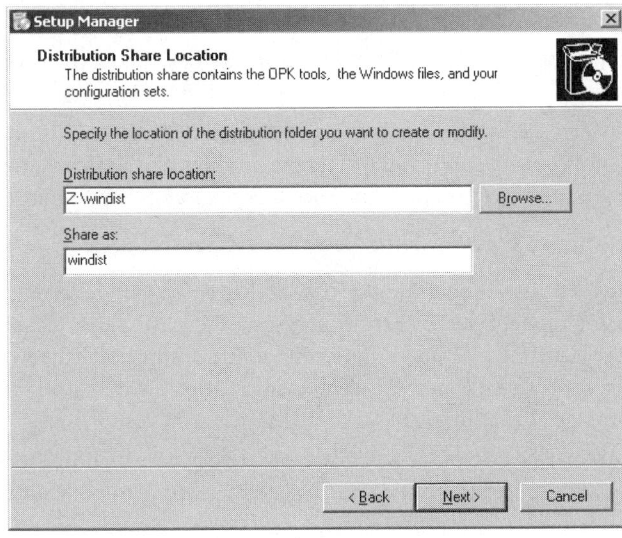

The Setup Manager interface centralizes answer file configuration. Setup Manager displays all of the configuration settings in a single window with a tree of configuration options and corresponding settings. Setup Manager divides the configuration content into three areas: General Settings, Network Settings, and Advanced Settings. The first two of these sections contain mandatory settings, yet you will undoubtedly want to investigate the range of optional settings available to preconfigure installations. Setup Manager, shown in the following screen, presents all of the configuration information on a single screen, allowing you to set all the values you need for the answer file in one place.

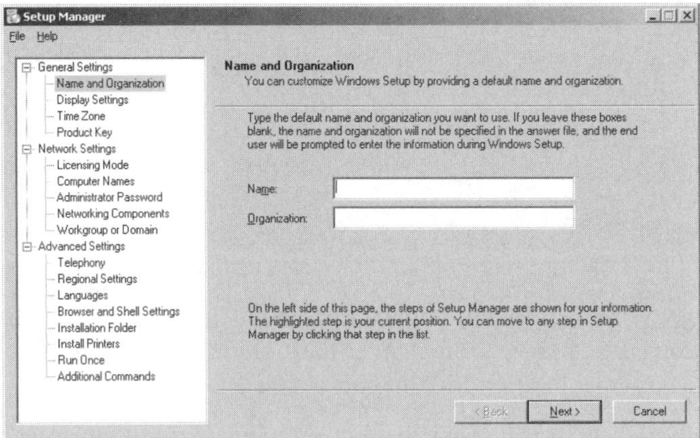

The following are the options available in the General Settings section:

- **Name And Organization** The name and organization entries are specified first, and the default user name is mandatory.
- **Display Settings** The display settings enable you to specify the color depth, screen resolution, and refresh frequency.
- **Time Zone** The time zone setting lets you specify the designated time zone for all installations using this answer file.
- **Product Key** If you are using a retail or Open License CD, this key is required—installation will not continue until you specify the product key. However, media under the Select and Enterprise Agreement volume license agreements bypass this requirement.

The following are the options available in the Network Settings section:

- **Licensing Mode** For server operating systems, the licensing mode setting lets you set the server licensing mode. Select either per server or alternatively per device or per user. If per-server licensing is selected, you must set the number of client access licenses (CALs) for the server. Verify that your selections here match your Information Technology (IT) licensing allocation plans to keep CAL usage in compliance.
- **Computer Names** The computer name is a mandatory entry. Computer names can be entered manually, imported from a text file, or generated automatically based upon the organization name.

- **Administrator Password** The administrator password that will be used for all computers installed using this answer file can be specified. You can (and should) choose to encrypt the administrator password in the answer file. You can also opt to log on as the administrator automatically when the computer boots; this is useful for engineers and administrators performing server configuration immediately following installation of the OS.
- **Networking Components** This section allows you to specify the networking components that you want included in the installation using this answer file. You can either accept the Typical Settings (which installs Transmission Control Protocol/Internet Protocol [TCP/IP] using Dynamic Host Configuration Protocol [DHCP] and the Client for Microsoft Networks) or specify Custom Settings, which enables the selection of additional clients, services, and protocols (notably, support for NetWare clients and services, as well as protocols such as NetBIOS Extended User Interface [NetBEUI], Internetwork Packet Exchange/Sequenced Packet Exchange [IPX/SPX], and AppleTalk).
- **Workgroup Or Domain** You can specify whether the computer should be joined to a workgroup or domain. You can instruct Setup to create computer accounts within a specific domain or use a precreated computer account. Both techniques require using the credentials of a user account that has sufficient permissions to add computers to domains. The password is entered in cleartext, and there is no way to encrypt it. Because of the password issue, you might instead want to allow the user to log on after installation and then join the domain manually. You could also have the installation create a computer account but not provide the user account and password, which would ensure the user is prompted for this information the first time the computer logs on to the domain after Windows Setup completes. Another workaround is to script the computer account creation as discussed in Microsoft Knowledge Base article 315273.

The following are the options available in the Advanced Settings section:

- **Telephony** The telephony settings are used to specify the country, access number, and type of line for the dial-up networking connection.
- **Regional Settings** You can opt to use the default regional settings or specify another localization option in the answer file.
- **Languages** Enables the selection of the language and character set used to display Web pages and other content.
- **Browser And Shell Settings** These settings let you specify the customization method for Microsoft Internet Explorer, using either the default settings or an autoconfiguration script or by setting the proxy and home page settings individually.
- **Installation Folder** Here, you can designate into which folder the Windows operating system will be installed, using either the default name (Windows), a generated name, or a name specified by you.

> **Note** The installation folder Name box in Setup Manager is limited to an MS-DOS 8.3 pathname (thus, Windows2003 as a folder name is not an option). This limit relates to Setup supporting Winnt and its lack of support for long file names (LFNs).

- **Install Printers** This lets you specify the printers to be installed automatically at the initial user logon.
- **Run Once** You can specify a command line to be run upon initial user logon. Postinstall commands that require user logon to run or operate correctly should be set here.
- **Additional Commands** These commands will be executed once the unattended setup has been completed but prior to user logon.

Note You cannot run commands that require a user logon with the Additional Commands option—these should be specified as a Run Once option.

Once all of the answer file options have been set, you are prompted to save the file (with the default name). You can view or modify this file in a text editor such as Notepad. We recommend using the default name only if you plan to create a limited number of answer files. If you have many answer files, you can do the following:

- Place specific types of answer files in separate folders depending on the type of system being installed and the configuration settings used.
- Name each answer file so that it helps identify the type of system being installed and the configuration settings used.

With some types of answer files, namely, unattended installations, Setup Manager also creates the Unattend.bat script needed to launch the installation. This makes it easier to start the unattended installation by typing the name of the script file rather than a complex command line.

The Unattend.bat script specifies the location of the answer file and the source files that Setup should use. It also provides a convenient way to use a complicated command line to start installation. The following text shows the batch file created by Setup Manager to start the automated installation using Unattend.txt file:

```
@rem SetupMgrTag
@echo off

rem
rem This is a SAMPLE batch script generated by Setup Manager.
rem If this script is moved from the location where it was generated,
rem it may have to be modified.
rem

set AnswerFile=.\unattend.txt
set SetupFiles=\\CORPSVR01\windist\I386

\\CORPSVR01\windist\I386\winnt32 /s:%SetupFiles% /unattend:%AnswerFile%
/copysource:lang
```

Here, the script specifies that a distribution share was set up on CorpSvr01 and that Winnt32 is to use the setup files from this share. Further, the script specifies the name of the unattended installation answer file as Unattend.txt. This file is stored in the root directory of the distribution share.

Inside Out

Manually configuring answer files

Answer files are stored as text files on the disk, and, in theory at least, you can manually create and edit them using a simple text editor such as Notepad. Given the number of different sections, however, and the range of settings within each of these sections, manually constructing an answer file could be rather laborious, not to mention subject to typographical errors. The graphical tool that Microsoft has provided (Setup Manager) is far more effective and has been improved for Windows Server 2003.

Examining Answer Files

The answer file that Setup Manager generates is different depending on the type of answer file you are creating and your answers. The answer file generated for an unattended installation (Unattend.txt) looks something like this:

```
;SetupMgrTag
[Data]
    AutoPartition=1
    MsDosInitiated="0"
    UnattendedInstall="Yes"

[Unattended]
    UnattendMode=FullUnattended
    OemSkipEula=Yes
    OemPreinstall=Yes
    TargetPath=\WINDOWS

[GuiUnattended]
    AdminPassword=f4d4b1c5a7daa210aad3b435b51404ee158daba31f78e32c5bee79add9d
    EncryptedAdminPassword=Yes
    AutoLogon=Yes
    AutoLogonCount=1
    OEMSkipRegional=1
    TimeZone=4
    OemSkipWelcome=1

[UserData]
    ProductKey=DEXHD-SSKED-IK22I-DK2DI-I5KSK
    FullName="City Power and Light User"
    OrgName="City Power and Light"
    ComputerName=*
```

```
[LicenseFilePrintData]
    AutoMode=PerSeat

[TapiLocation]
    CountryCode=1
    Dialing=Tone
    AreaCode=206

[RegionalSettings]
    LanguageGroup=1
    Language=00000409

[SetupMgr]
    DistFolder=C:\windist
    DistShare=windist

[GuiRunOnce]
    Command0="rundll32 printui.dll,PrintUIEntry /in /n
\\cprintserver03\mainprint02"

[Identification]
    JoinDomain=CPANDL
    DomainAdmin=wrstanek
    DomainAdminPassword=dudR5Ang!

[Networking]
    InstallDefaultComponents=Yes
```

As you can see, an answer file is basically an initialization (ini) file, which has been around since the earliest days of the Windows operating system. The file is written as standard American Standard Code for Information Interchange (ASCII) text and can be viewed in any standard text editor, including Notepad. It is divided into sections with headings that are enclosed in brackets. Each heading section is followed by individual configuration parameters formatted as *ParameterName=Value*. The main sections are as follows:

- **Data** Sets the essential installation parameters. AutoPartition with a value of 1 tells Setup to install the Windows operating system on the first available partition that has adequate space and that doesn't already contain an installed version of the operating system. If you enter a value of zero (0), Setup will stop and prompt for a partition to use. MSDOSInitiated determines whether the installation is running directly from the Windows CD-ROM. It should be 0 if you're doing an install from CD-ROM and 1 if you're doing an RIS install. UnattendedInstall should be set to Yes if you preinstall the Windows operating system by using the CD boot method.
- **Unattended** Specifies how much user interaction there is. UnattendMode sets the overall interaction level. Here, the installation is fully automated (FullUnattended). Installations can also be user-controlled and GUI-attended (meaning only the text mode of Setup is automated and the GUI portion runs normally). OemSkipEula specifies whether the user sees the End-User License Agreement (EULA) and must accept it.

If set to Yes, the EULA is skipped. Otherwise, the user must accept the EULA when prompted to continue. OemPreinstall controls whether Setup installs its files from distribution folders. If set to Yes, Setup copies the folders and files contained in the I386 or IA64 OEM folder during installation. The TargetPath is the folder in which you want to install the Windows operating system.

- **GuiUnattended** Controls the GUI phase of the installation. As you can see, the administrator password for the computer can be entered and encrypted. You can also preset regional and time zone information and specify that the Welcome screens be skipped. If OEMSkipRegional is set to 0, Setup stops at the Welcome screen and prompts the user before continuing. Watch out for the AutoLogon section; if it is set to Yes, the user can log on after installation as the administrator and this could pose a security threat. If it is set to No, the computer doesn't automatically log on after installation. The AutoLogonCount controls the number of times the user can log on as the administrator. Here, the user can do this only once. This means that after installation users could make configuration changes and then reboot the computer. The user couldn't log on, however, after the reboot to confirm the changes—unless AutoLogonCount were set to 2.
- **UserData** Sets the user name, computer name, and organization name, as well as the product key to use. If ComputerName is set to * (asterisk), Setup generates a random name based on the organization name. When creating an Unattend.txt file, you can also specify a list of up to 15 computer names to use sequentially during unattended installations (or you can import a list from a file). You cannot do this with Sysprep or RIS. By using Sysprep, you can enter a computer name to use or generate one. By using RIS, the computer name is taken from the *%MachineName%* environment variable stored in the RIS image.
- **LicenseFilePrintData** Sets the licensing mode to use for the computer as PerSeat or PerServer. If licensing is PerServer, there is also an AutoUsers parameter that specifies the number of client licenses purchased for the computer.
- **TapiLocation** Controls telephony options for the installation. It includes the country code for dialing, the access code for the computer's location, and the type of dialing to use for the telephony device in the computer (either tone or pulse). You can also set a long-distance access code, such as 9, which is the number to dial to access an outside line.
- **RegionalSettings** Specifies the regional settings to use during setup, including the language and the language group.
- **SetupMgr** Controls the distribution share used. DistShare sets the name of the network share for which Setup should look, and DistFolder sets the name of the local folder.
- **GuiRunOnce** Contains any configuration commands that you want to run during the installation. Typically, as shown in the example, this is used to configure any network printers that might be available for use. You could also add commands to install roles or services, such as a domain controller. If this was the first command to run,

you'd enter the line **Command0="dcpromo /answerfile:*AnswerFile*"**, where *AnswerFile* is the answer file that has the necessary configuration information for the domain controller. Or you could simply enter the line **Command0="dcpromo"** so that the program runs on first logon after installation.

- **Identification** Sets the workgroup or domain information for the computer. JoinWorkgroup sets the name of the workgroup to join when installing the computer. JoinDomain sets the name of the domain to join when installing the computer. DomainAdmin and DomainAdminPassword set the account information needed to join the computer to the domain. You'll note in the example, the password is in cleartext, which is a security issue to watch out for, especially because there is no way to encrypt this password.
- **Networking** Determines whether the default networking components are installed. If the default isn't used, custom settings for protocols, services, and components could be defined in separate sections.

Now compare this to the following answer file for a Sysprep install:

```
;SetupMgrTag
[Unattended]
    OemSkipEula=Yes
    InstallFilesPath=C:\sysprep\i386

[GuiUnattended]
    AdminPassword=f4d4b1c5a7daa210aad3b435b51404ee158daba31f78e32c5bee79add9D
    EncryptedAdminPassword=Yes
    AutoLogon=Yes
    AutoLogonCount=1
    OEMSkipRegional=1
    TimeZone=4
    OemSkipWelcome=1

[UserData]
    ProductKey=DKDKE-RWKWK-R5642-RSESV-EDDED
    FullName="City Power and Light User"
    OrgName="City Power and Light"
    ComputerName=*

[TapiLocation]
    CountryCode=1
    Dialing=Tone
    AreaCode=206

[RegionalSettings]
    LanguageGroup=1
    Language=00000409

[SetupMgr]
    DistFolder=C:\sysprep\i386
    DistShare=windist
```

```
[GuiRunOnce]
    Command0="rundll32 printui.dll,PrintUIEntry /in /n
\\corpprsvr03\corpmainprt"

[Identification]
    JoinDomain=CPANDL
    DomainAdmin=administrator
    DomainAdminPassword=d5$h71828RS

[Networking]
    InstallDefaultComponents=Yes
```

As you can see if you do a comparison, the Sysprep.inf file is very similar to the Unattend.txt file. In many ways it is streamlined, because it doesn't need to ask you basic configuration information—this is obtained from the image. A very important note is that Sysprep expects there to be a %SystemDrive%\Sysprep folder on the system to be duplicated. Setup Manager can create the %SystemDrive%\Sysprep folder with all the necessary files, which includes Sysprep.exe, Setupcl.exe, and Factory.exe. The Sysprep.inf file must also be in the %SystemDrive%\Sysprep folder on the system to be duplicated.

The final type of file you might use is the .sif file used with RIS. An RIS file looks like this:

```
;SetupMgrTag
[Data]
    AutoPartition=1
    MsDosInitiated="1"
    UnattendedInstall="Yes"
    floppyless="1"
    OriSrc="\\%SERVERNAME%\RemInst\%INSTALLPATH%"
    OriTyp="4"
    LocalSourceOnCD=1

[SetupData]
    OsLoadOptions="/noguiboot /fastdetect"

SetupSourceDevice="\Device\LanmanRedirector\%SERVERNAME%\RemInst\%INSTALLPATH%"

[Unattended]
    UnattendMode=FullUnattended
    OemSkipEula=Yes
    OemPreinstall=No
    TargetPath=\WINDOWS
    FileSystem=LeaveAlone
    NtUpgrade=No
    OverwriteOemFilesOnUpgrade=No

[GuiUnattended]
    AdminPassword=f4d4b1c5a7daa210aad3b435b51404ee158daba31f78e32c5bee79add9d9
    EncryptedAdminPassword=Yes
    AutoLogon=Yes
    AutoLogonCount=1
    OEMSkipRegional=1
    TimeZone=%TIMEZONE%
    OemSkipWelcome=1
```

```
[UserData]
    ProductKey=DFDFD-FSAFW-EFREF-AFASF-AFAAA
    FullName="City Power and Light User"
    OrgName="City Power and Light"
    ComputerName=%MACHINENAME%

[LicenseFilePrintData]
    AutoMode=PerServer
    AutoUsers=5

[SetupMgr]
    DistFolder=C:\windist
    DistShare=windist

[Identification]
    JoinDomain=%MACHINEDOMAIN%
    DoOldStyleDomainJoin=Yes

[Networking]
    InstallDefaultComponents=Yes
    ProcessPageSections=Yes

[RemoteInstall]
    Repartition=Yes
    UseWholeDrive=Yes

 [OSChooser]
    Description="Windows Server 2003 - Standard Installation"
    Help="This will install Windows Server 2003 in a standard configuration."
    LaunchFile="%INSTALLPATH%\%MACHINETYPE%\templates\startrom.com"
    ImageType=Flat
```

Although this .sif file is similar to the other types of answer files, it has many important differences. Consider these differences when comparing the files, and also note that some of these parameters could be used with other types of automatic installations:

- **Data** In installations for which you need not insert a boot floppy disk in the target machine to begin, you can set the value to 0 if you are going to use an RIS boot floppy disk primarily because the computer you are installing is non-PXE-compatible and 1 if the computer you are installing is PXE-compliant and can be network booted. OriSrc and OriTyp set the remote installation source file location and type, respectively. LocalSourceOnCD specifies whether the install is from media stored on CD-ROM that is in the computer's CD-ROM drive. If set to 1, Setup looks for the installation files on the local CD-ROM. Otherwise, Setup will look for the RIS network share.
- **Unattended** FileSystem specifies whether to convert the primary partition to NTFS or to leave it alone. NtUpgrade controls whether Setup upgrades a previous version of the Windows operating system to the version you are installing. OverwriteOemFilesOnUpgrade specifies whether to overwrite original equipment manufacturer (OEM)–supplied files that exist on the computer with Windows operating system files that have the same name during an upgrade.

- **RemoteInstall** Controls how remote installation works with disks and partitions. If Repartition is set to Yes, Setup deletes all partitions in the first hard disk of the computer being installed and reformats it with NTFS. Otherwise, Setup will use the first available existing partition (a partition must exist or remote installation will fail). If UseWholeDisk is set to Yes (or is not set, which is the default), Setup extends the partition it creates to the end of the hard disk, meaning it will repartition the first hard disk drive as a single partition. When set to No, Setup doesn't extend the partition to the end of the hard disk.
- **OSChooser** Sets remote installation information for the operating system image, including a description and help topic. LaunchFile specifies the file to execute when the user selects an operating system image from within the client interface. ImageType sets the type of image, which can be either flat, meaning it's a CD-ROM-based image, or Sysprep, meaning it's a Sysprep image created using the RIPrep Wizard.

Managing Unattended Installations

An unattended installation performs the same setup procedures as interactive installation, but doesn't necessarily prompt for information. That is, it starts with a flat directory of uninstalled Windows files and goes through the installation and configuration process using the information provided to select and configure Windows components and only prompts if you've omitted information or have configured Setup to do so. Here, where possible, the information is provided automatically by an answer file, not one data point at a time by someone sitting at a keyboard.

This is in contrast to the other traditional method of performing an automated installation, Sysprep, which uses an image of an installed operating system as its starting point for client installations.

When performing unattended installations, you must make a few basic decisions, such as how the installation files will be accessed, what sort of client interaction is desirable, and so on. Once that is done, the actual process of performing an unattended installation is simple—just invoke one of the Setup programs (Winnt or Winnt32) with a few parameters and go grab an espresso.

Customizing the Distribution Folder

The distribution folder used for unattended installations has a predefined structure for both the base operating system files and the optional folders and files that might be needed to customize the installation. The distribution folder is a single hierarchy starting with the I386 (or IA64) folder and including both mandatory and optional subfolders.

The subfolder structure used in the distribution folder is described in Table 5-1. Based on that structure, there are various ways you can customize these distribution folders.

Table 5-1. **Customizing Distribution Folders for Automated Installations**

Folder	Purpose
\I386	The root distribution folder is normally created at the root of the logical drive on the server hosting the distribution folder. This folder is created by copying the entire I386 subdirectory from the Windows Server 2003 CD.
\I386\OEM	This folder contains additional folders, tools, and files, which must use MS-DOS 8.3 names. The optional Cmdlines.txt file, which contains a set of commands to be executed at the end of GUI-mode setup, can also be in the OEM folder. For an OEM folder to exist anywhere other than under I386, the OemFilesPath entry in the answer file must specify the alternate path.
Optional Folders	
\I386\OEM\Textmode	This folder is used for supplying updated HALs and device drivers for mass storage devices. The files stored in this folder must be specified in the [OEMBootFiles] section of the answer file.
\I386\$OEM$\$$	This folder equates to the %SystemRoot%, specifying the root installation directory for Windows Server 2003. Files and subfolders of I386\$OEM$\$$ are copied to the corresponding locations in the installation directory on the target computer. The structure of these subfolders must correspond to the standard folder structure for Windows Server 2003.
\I386\$OEM$\$$\Help	The OEM help files contained in this folder are copied to the %SystemRoot%\Help folder during installation.
\I386\$OEM$\$$\System32	Any OEM files located in this folder are copied to the %SystemRoot%\System32 folder during installation.
\I386\$OEM$\$1	This folder points to the %SystemDrive%—the logical drive that Windows Server 2003 is installed in.

Table 5-1. **Customizing Distribution Folders for Automated Installations**

Folder	Purpose
\I386\$OEM$\$1\Pnpdrvers	Plug and Play device drivers that must be installed are stored in this folder.
\I386\$OEM$\$1\Sysprep	This optional folder is used to store Sysprep executable and configuration files used in image-based installations.
\I386\OEM*Drive_letter*	The contents and structure of this folder are copied to the corresponding logical drive on the target system during the Text mode part of the installation.

Preinstalling Service Packs

The distribution folder can include preinstalled service packs so that you can install the operating system with an updated service pack rather than having to install the operating system and then apply service packs.

Typically, a service pack is provided as a single download—a large executable file that you run to extract and then install the updates to the operating system files. To update the distribution folder, you must first download the service pack and then complete the following procedure to apply it to the distribution folder:

1. Create a directory on the server's hard disk, and then copy the entire contents of the I386 folder from the product CD to it. For the purposes of this example, let's call it C:\I386—and it *is* best that you call this folder I386.
2. Don't start the executable directly by running its associated .exe without options. Instead, extract the service pack to the hard disk drive by using the command ***ServicePackName*** **–x**, such as **wk3sp1_en_x86.exe –x**.
3. When prompted for the extraction folder, type the path to a temporary folder for the service pack. For the purposes of this example, let's call it C:\W2003SP.
4. Once the service pack extraction is finished, look in the temporary folder for the I386\Update folder. For example, if the temporary folder is C:\W2003SP, the folder you are looking for is C:\W2003SP\I386\Update. This folder has a program called Update.exe that you must run.
5. Run Update.exe with the –S parameter. Specify the folder in which the I386 directory is located as the value for the –S parameter. For example, if the location is C:\I386, run Update.exe using the command line **update –s:c:\I386**. Note you are specifying the complete path to the I386 folder. This technique is referred to as slipstreaming the service pack.
6. Now use C:\I386 as your distribution folder for deploying the Windows operating system with the integrated service pack.

Inside Out

Service pack update "gotchas"

You shouldn't update your existing Windows installation share. First, you want to ensure the update is completed successfully before using it, and you might have several service packs that you must apply sequentially before the update is complete. Second, if there are users currently performing installations, you could corrupt their installations or otherwise cause their installations to fail.

When you use slipstreaming to install several service packs at once, you must rename any existing Svcpack.log file before installing the next service pack update. This file is created automatically with each service pack installation and is located on the %SystemDrive% root folder.

As a final note, you can't apply service packs to Windows 2000 RIS CD-ROM-based images. There is, of course, a workaround, which is discussed in Microsoft Knowledge Base article 258868.

Preinstalling Hot Fixes and Security Updates

Hot fixes and security updates to the operating system are made available in between service packs. Although these changes do eventually make their way into service packs, you'll often find that critical fixes must be deployed either to resolve problems you're experiencing or to close security gaps. You can find hot fixes and security updates in two places: the Microsoft security Web site and Microsoft Windows Update site. The Microsoft Web site contains links to these two sites, and they are currently located at *http://www.microsoft.com/security/* and *http://windowsupdate.microsoft.com*, respectively, which addresses are entirely subject to change—Murphy's Law, right?

Most hot fixes and security updates follow a specific naming syntax. For example, the hot fix q348932_W2K3_SP1_ENU.exe tells you this fix is in relation to Microsoft Knowledge Base article 348932 and that it is a post Service Pack 1 fix for the English-language version of Windows Server 2003.

If you've installed hot fixes and security updates before, you know that basically all you must do is run them as a program. Unfortunately, you usually are prompted to reboot the computer after installing each, so you often have to work around this by forcing the Windows operating system to install quietly (without warnings and prompts) and not to reboot with the –Q and –Z options (which are available in most hot fixes and updates).

Note Windows Server 2003 supports hot-fix chaining, whereby you can install multiple hot fixes with a single restart. This means you do not need to run QChain.exe and you do not need to reboot after installing each hot fix. This feature is in fact supported with Windows 2000 Service Pack 3 or later, Windows XP, and Windows Server 2003. As an alternative to –Q and –Z, you could use the –Q and –M options to install multiple hot fixes quietly at the same time.

Although you can integrate hot fixes and security updates into the distribution folder in much the same way as previously discussed for service packs, it is not recommended. Instead, you should have Setup automatically install any necessary hot fixes and security updates during the installation of the operating system. Here's how you do this:

1. Download the hot fixes and security updates you want to use, and then copy them to the OEM directory.
2. Once all the hot fixes and security updates are in the OEM directory, create a file called Cmdlines.txt, and save it to the OEM directory. This file contains a list of commands you want to use during the installation, which in this case are the hot fixes and security updates.
3. The first line of the Cmdlines.txt file must be [Commands] on a line by itself. Then you list each of the hot fixes and security updates you want to run each on a line by itself, making sure to enclose each line in double quotation marks. The result is a file with contents similar to the following:

```
[Commands]
"q3486932_w2k3_sp1_enu -q -z"
"q124576_w2k3_sp1_enu -q -z"
```

Caution Install only hot fixes and security updates that are released after the service pack you are deploying. For example, if you've integrated Service Pack 1 into the distribution folder, you must install only hot fixes and security updates that are labeled as sp1, meaning they are post Service Pack 1. If you install hot fixes or security updates that are included in a service pack integrated with the distribution folder, you might cause the installation to fail.

4. Make sure the script generated by Setup Manager has OemPreinstall=Yes in the [Unattended] section. This tells Setup that you are preinstalling using a distribution share and will be specifying commands that should be run.

Tip **Unlock advanced installation features and options**
OemPreinstall=Yes unlocks a bunch of advanced installation features and options. Not only can you run hot fixes and security updates, you can run other commands, install device drivers, specify directories and files to copy to the new computer, and specify custom HAL settings.

Including Updated Drivers

Just as you can include hot fixes and security updates in the installation, you can also include updated drivers for Plug and Play devices. You might wonder why you would do this. Even though Windows Server 2003 includes thousands of drivers, computer hardware changes over time and the drivers included with the Windows operating system might not be the ones you need.

You can include updated drivers in automated installations by completing the following steps:

1. Create a subdirectory of the OEM directory called $1 (the full path is I386\$OEM$\$1). Then create another subdirectory for the drivers. The subdirectory name must be no more than eight characters. This subdirectory will be copied to the target computer and will remain on the target computer after Setup completes.
2. Inside the Drivers subdirectory, create individual subdirectories for each of the various types of device drivers you are going to install, such as this:
   - \$OEM$\$1\Drivers\Video for new video drivers
   - \$OEM$\$1\Drivers\Sound for new Sound drivers
   - \$OEM$\$1\Drivers\Network for new network adapter drivers
3. Copy the drivers and their .inf files into the appropriate subfolders.
4. Update the answer files to add references to the driver folder and its subfolders using the OemPnPDriversPath parameter. Separate each subfolder reference with a semicolon, but do not include OEM\$1 in the path; for instance:
   - OemPnPDriversPath="Drivers\Video; Drivers\Sound; Drivers\Network"

   Or if you used only one directory called Drivers, you could use this:
   - OemPnPDriversPath="Drivers"
5. If OemPreinstall is set to No, change this so that it is set to Yes.
6. If you are installing new drivers for RIS-based operating system images, restart the Boot Information Negotiation Layer service (BINLSVC) on the RIS server after copying the files into the distribution folder. After you log on locally or remotely to the RIS server, you can do this from a command prompt by typing

   Net stop "binlsvc"

   Net start "binlsvc"

Note You should install only signed device drivers. If you don't, Setup won't actually install the devices with Sysprep and RIS installations until an administrator logs on to the computer. You can tell Setup to bypass this policy by adding DriverSigning=Ignore to the [Unattended] section of the answer file. Keep in mind that unsigned device drivers could cause serious problems on the system.

Performing Other Preinstallation Tasks

Earlier we mentioned setting OemPreinstall=Yes and creating a Cmdlines.txt file, which must be created and saved in the OEM directory. Well, allowing you to install updates and hot fixes is not the only use for this file. You can, in fact, use the Cmdlines.txt file to handle any command that you want Setup to run. Generally, you'll want these commands to run before any hot fixes and security updates are applied. This is just a precaution in case you are running a program or installing something that might affect the drivers and system files.

Remember this example from earlier in the chapter:

```
[Commands]
"q3486932_w2k3_sp1_enu -q -z"
"q124576_w2k3_sp1_enu -q -z"
```

Here, we are running two hot fixes. Now let's add a command to run a Microsoft Software Installation (MSI) package, like this:

```
[Commands]
"msiexec /i \\corpserver01\apps\Application.msi"
"q3486932_w2k3_sp1_enu -q -z"
"q124576_w2k3_sp1_enu -q -z"
```

You can also create directories and copy over files during the installation. For example, if every computer has a C:\Data and a C:\Scripts directory, you could have Setup create these during installation. To create directories and copy over files during installation, follow these steps:

1. In the OEM directory, create a directory with a one-letter name that corresponds to the drive letter of the same name on the target computer. For example, if you want to work with the C and D drives, you would create subdirectories OEM\C and OEM\D.
2. Create the necessary directories under these directories and copy any necessary files into these directories. For example, you could create OEM\C\Data and OEM\C\Scripts directories and then copy data and scripts into the appropriate directories.

If you want to copy files into %SystemRoot% folders, place the files in the OEM\$$ directory. These files are then copied over during installation. One type of file that you might want to place in the OEM\$$ is a branding file that provides information on the computer model and manufacturer. You can also add support information, which can be any standard information that your organization wants to provide to users in the General tab of the System Properties dialog box.

The branding file is saved as Oeminfo.ini, and it contains two required sections: General and Support Information (and two optional sections: ICW and OEMSpecific). It is used like this:

```
[General]
Manufacturer=
Model=
SupportURL=

[Support Information]
Line1=
Line2=
...
LineN=
Such as:
[General]
Manufacturer= City Power and Light
Model= CP&L Primary Desktop
SupportURL= http://Intranet
```

Chapter 5

```
[Support Information]
Line1=For IT support call:
Line2=(206) 555-1212
Line3=For early morning or after hours support call:
Line4=(212) 555-6789
```

Tip **Add a logo to your computers**

While you are branding your organization's computers, you might want to use a company logo in the General tab of the System Properties dialog box. Do this by creating a bitmap image approximately 180 × 180 pixels, name it Oemlogo.bmp, and place it in the OEM\$$ directory.

Renaming Files and Folders When Using Winnt

Because Winnt doesn't support the use of LFNs, the distribution folder is restricted to short (MS-DOS 8.3) folder and file names if you use the 16-bit Setup program. Yet, applications sometimes require program files to be correctly named with LFNs to work. Thus, in certain installations, you'll need the ability to rename specific files or folders contained in the distribution folder once they are copied to the target computer.

The $$Rename.txt file can be used to rename the MS-DOS 8.3 file names after installation. Every file and folder using a short name that is to be renamed after installation must be specified in the $$Rename.txt file. To rename the files and folders, put a copy of the $$Rename.txt file in the folder containing the actual files and folders, and Setup will find the file and perform the renaming automatically at the end of the installation process.

The $$Rename.txt file is structured as a series of entries describing the path and both the short and long names of the file or folder to be renamed. Each folder with entries to be renamed has its own section, named with the path (starting at the root of the hard disk) in brackets "[*path*]" followed by the individual files to be renamed.

- The path is treated as a section name and is entered on its own line in square brackets. It points to the folder that has the files or subfolders to be renamed.
- File/folder names follow. Each pair is specified on a line in the format "*short name* = *long name.*" The short name is specified without quotation marks. If the long name has spaces in it, the long name must have quotation marks around it.

An example of a brief $$Rename.txt file is shown here:

```
[\]
InsGuide.doc = "Installation Guide.doc"
StaffHB.doc = "Employee Handbook.doc"
Frelled.chm = "IT–Escalation team.chm"
```

Using Dynamic Update in Unattended Installations

To support Dynamic Update in unattended installations, the answer file must be explicitly configured to allow the Dynamic Update operations (which are disabled by default). This is controlled by two entries in the answer file:

- A DUDisable entry in the [Unattended] section of the answer file is set to disable Dynamic Update by default. Modifying the entry to read DUDisable="No" instructs Setup to allow dynamic updates during installation. Using /Dudisable in Unattend.bat supersedes this setting in the answer file.
- In addition to enabling Dynamic Update, you must tell Setup the location of the network share containing the Dynamic Update files. This is accomplished by entering the path to the network share in the DUShare entry in the [Unattended] section of the answer file, as shown here:

  ```
  DUShare = path to network share containing files
  ```

> **Caution** You probably don't want to use Dynamic Update if you've already applied all the necessary service packs, updates, and hot fixes to the operating system.

Distribution Folder on CD

An advantage to creating a distribution folder is that you can customize it and modify it as new security patches and service packs are added and as supported hardware or applications change. In some cases, however, using CD media for unattended installations is necessary. This could occur because of a lack of adequate network connectivity, for instance, or extreme network congestion.

However, using CD media for installation requires that CDs and DVDs containing a copy of your distribution folder be re-created any time you update or change the contents or structure of your distribution folder. Every time you apply a service pack, hot fix, or even a security patch to the operating system or any included custom files—and consider how often you do that—new CD media must be made.

Thus, the amount of work involved in the creation and distribution of the CDs containing the (updated) distribution folder must be assessed, and the process of managing the implementation of these CDs in the enterprise network environment must be defined.

> **Tip** **Plan to secure CD media**
> Consider the security of distribution folder CDs carefully. Because you cannot use file system permissions to secure the contents of the CDs or DVDs containing your distribution folder, and especially because such media might well contain a Windows product key, you must plan for the physical security of each of the CDs.

Using CD Media for Automated Installations

In some cases, you might want to install Windows Server 2003 directly from the CD media provided by Microsoft. Perhaps you don't have a network distribution share that the target machine can access, or perhaps the machine has no network connectivity at all.

Several contingencies are involved in using the CD media for unattended installation, such as the following:

- The target computer must be able to boot from the CD-ROM drive, and the option to boot from the CD-ROM drive must be selected in the BIOS.
- The target computer must have a floppy disk drive.
- A correctly configured answer file must be on the floppy disk in the drive (the answer file must contain a [Data] section with the entries correctly referencing an unattended installation using the Windows Server 2003 CD.

Note For installations from CD-ROM/DVD media that are initiated by booting from a floppy disk, the floppy disk drive must contain the correct CD-ROM/DVD device drivers for the CD-ROM/DVD hardware installed in the target computer.

Before starting an automated installation process using the Windows Server 2003 CD, you must create the Winnt.sif file (an Unattend.txt file renamed as Winnt.sif) to provide answers to the Windows Setup process. The Winnt.sif file must be on a floppy disk, which must be in the floppy disk drive when Windows Setup begins. When the Windows operating system boots from CD, it checks the floppy disk drive for a Winnt.sif file and, if one is found, uses it to perform an unattended installation.

Advantages to using the Windows Server 2003 CD for unattended installation include the capabilities to install without network connectivity, repartition the hard disk, force a BIOS startup, and bypass the Mini-Setup program. Some of these actions are controlled by the use of entries in the Unattend.txt file, such as the following:

- **Partition the hard disk** You can instruct Setup to delete all existing partitions and create a new (NTFS-formatted) partition by using the Repartition=Yes entry in the [Unattended] section.
- **BIOS startup** To instruct the target computer to use the BIOS (instead of the device miniport driver) for startup, use the UseBIOSToBoot=1 entry in the [Data] section.
- **Mini-Setup bypass** To avoid running the Mini-Setup program when the system boots the first time after an unattended installation, use the UnattendSwitch=Yes entry in the [Unattended] section.

Inside Out

Limitations of the Windows Server 2003 CD

If you choose to use the Windows Server 2003 CD for unattended installations, you should be aware of some significant limitations. These restrictions include the following:

- Not allowing upgrades from any Windows platform
- No support for Dynamic Update functionality
- No support for uniqueness database files
- No capability for deploying applications as part of the Windows installation

Answer File Settings Used in Product CD–Based Unattended Installations

When using the Windows Server 2003 CD for unattended installations, you should be aware of certain key answer file settings.

There are four settings in the [Data] section that directly pertain to an automated installation from CD:

- **AutoPartition** Set to 1 to disable the /Tempdrive command-line parameter.
- **MsDosInitiated** Set to 0 to specify an unattended installation from a Windows Server 2003 CD.
- **UnattendedInstall** Must be set to Yes for an unattended installation from a Windows Server 2003 CD.
- **UseBIOSToBoot** Usually left at the default setting of 0; this must be set to 1 to use the BIOS for system startup.

The [Unattended] section contains two settings that relate to a CD-based automated installation:

- **Repartition** Set to No by default; if set to Yes, this will instruct Setup to delete all existing partitions (on the first hard disk) and to create a new NTFS partition.
- **UnattendSwitch** This parameter is used only by Winnt.exe and is set to No by default. If it is set to Yes, it instructs Setup to skip running the Mini-Setup program upon first reboot after the unattended installation completes.

Using an Answer File

Once you have an Unattend.txt file, you can use it to install Windows Server 2003 by running Winnt.exe or Winnt32.exe at the command line with the appropriate parameters, such as

```
Winnt /u:Unattend.txt /s:\\FileServer\DistributionShare\i386
```

Or

```
Winnt32 /unattend:Unattend.txt /s:\\FileServer\DistributionShare\i386
```

> **Tip** If installing from product media, name the Unattend.txt file Winnt.sif, put it on a floppy disk, and put that disk in the computer. When you boot from the CD, the answer file will be automatically recognized and used during setup.

In addition to the /Unattend command-line option that causes Setup to use the Unattend.txt file to automate installation, many other command-line parameters can be used to affect the installation. This includes whether to use Dynamic Update during installation (and many other options). For further information on these command-line options, see the sections entitled "Winnt Command-Line Parameters" on page 76, and "Winnt32 Command-Line Parameters" on page 77.

Starting the Unattended Installation

You can start an unattended installation in a number of different ways, depending on the installation programs and methods you are using, as follows:

- **Batch file** If you used Setup Manager to create your Unattend.txt file and you will be using the Windows Setup program to perform the installation, you can use the Unattend.bat file, also created by Setup Manager, to start the installation process.
- **Manually** You can also manually enter the same command sequence from the command line, with any additional parameters that might be necessary for the specific installation you're performing (for instance, a different location for the temporary files).

Extending the Unattend.txt File

The unattended installation text file in Windows Server 2003 builds on the Windows 2000 version while maintaining the familiar .inf format. Several new sections, as well as many new settings, provide finer control over the installation and configuration of Windows Server 2003 server and Windows XP operating systems.

The new sections added to the Unattend.txt file since Windows 2000 include the following:

- **[Homenet]** This section contains settings for home networking, including network adapters and Internet Connection Sharing and firewalls.
- **[PCHealth]** This section contains settings for remote assistance and detailed error-reporting management.
- **[SetupParams]** Used to run additional commands after Setup is completed (by the UserExecute entry).
- **[Shell]** Sets themes to set the style of the user interface.
- **[SystemRestore]** Sets calendar and session frequencies of backup and purging.
- **[Uninstall]** Controls uninstall options for Windows XP installations.

The number of new entries are too numerous to list here—for a complete listing of new entries, refer to the "Changes in Answer Files" section of the "Microsoft Windows Corporate Deployment Tools User's Guide."

An Unattend.txt file can contain literally hundreds and hundreds of entries, not very many of which are required. The following example of an extended Unattend.txt file demonstrates how you can add sections to the file. Although a fully configured installation with lots of customization is much longer, you probably get the idea that there's a lot you can do to optimize the configuration.

```
;SetupMgrTag
[Data]
    AutoPartition=1
    MsDosInitiated="0"
    UnattendedInstall="Yes"

[Unattended]
    UnattendMode=FullUnattended
    OemSkipEula=Yes
    OemPreinstall=Yes
    TargetPath=\Windows

[GuiUnattended]
    AdminPassword=e52cac67419a9a224a3b108f3fa6cb6d8846f7eaee8fb117ad06bdd830b
    EncryptedAdminPassword=Yes
    OEMSkipRegional=1
    TimeZone=4
    OemSkipWelcome=1

[UserData]
    ProductKey=DFDFD-FSAFW-EFREF-AFASF-AFAAA
    FullName="wrstanek"
    OrgName="City Power and Light"
    ComputerName0=corpserver01
    ComputerName1=corpserver02
    ComputerName2=corpserver03
    ComputerName3=corpserver04
    ComputerName4=corpserver05

[Display]
    BitsPerPel=32
    XResolution=1024
    YResolution=768

[LicenseFilePrintData]
    AutoMode=PerSeat

[RegionalSettings]
    LanguageGroup=1

[SetupMgr]
    DistFolder=Z:\windist
    DistShare=windist
```

```
[FavoritesEx]
    Title1="Google Home Page.url"
    URL1="http://www.google.com"
    Title2="MSN Home Page.url"
    URL2="http://www.msn.com"

[Branding]
    BrandIEUsingUnattended=Yes

[URL]
    Home_Page= http://www.cpandl.com
    Help_Page= http://www.cpandl.com/help
    Search_Page= http://search.cpandl.com

[Proxy]
    Proxy_Enable=0
    Use_Same_Proxy=1

[GuiRunOnce]
    Command0=DeleteUnnecessaryFiles.bat

[Identification]
    JoinDomain=DOMAIN
    DomainAdmin=ADomainAdmin
    DomainAdminPassword=PasswordExposed

[Networking]
    InstallDefaultComponents=No

[NetAdapters]
    Adapter1=params.Adapter1

[params.Adapter1]
    INFID=*

[NetClients]
    MS_MSClient=params.MS_MSClient

[NetServices]
    MS_SERVER=params.MS_SERVER

[NetProtocols]
    MS_TCPIP=params.MS_TCPIP
    MS_NetMon=params.MS_NetMon

[params.MS_TCPIP]
    DNS=Yes
    UseDomainNameDevolution=No
    EnableLMHosts=Yes
    AdapterSections=params.MS_TCPIP.Adapter1

[params.MS_TCPIP.Adapter1]
    SpecificTo=Adapter1
    DHCP=Yes
    WINS=No
    NetBIOSOptions=0
```

Of all these fancy extras, there are actually only a few that we haven't talked about yet. Primarily, these are the installation options you use to preconfigure networking and Internet Explorer. With networking, the sections include [Networking], [NetAdapters], [NetClients], [NetServices], and [NetProtocols], as well as individual parameter sections for the TCP/IP adapters used. In most situations, you set these parameters using Setup Manager. Occasionally, you want to tweak the parameters in the answer file, but because they are so advanced, it is often easier to create a new answer file and then copy in from the old file the additional sections that you custom created.

An exception to this is with the Internet Explorer preconfiguration options. It is really easy to preconfigure Internet Explorer in an answer file:

- The [Branding] section tells Setup that you are customizing Internet Explorer, and it must be set as this:

```
[Branding]
    BrandIEUsingUnattended=Yes
```

- The [FavoritesEx] section is used to set favorites shortcuts. Each shortcut is entered as a title/URL pair, such as these:

```
    Title1="Google Home Page.url"
    URL1="http://www.google.com"
    Title2="MSN Home Page.url"
    URL2="http://www.msn.com"
```

- The [URL] section sets the default Uniform Resource Locators (URLs) used by Internet Explorer for the home, help, and search pages, such as this:

```
[URL]
    Home_Page=http://www.cpandl.com
    Help_Page=http://www.cpandl.com/help
    Search_Page=http://search.cpandl.com
```

- The [Proxy] section configures Internet Explorer's proxy settings, such as the following:

```
[Proxy]
    Proxy_Enable=0
    Use_Same_Proxy=1
```

Chapter 6

Using Remote Installation Services

Remote Installation Services (RIS) enables you to automate the installation of new computer systems using a centralized service accessible to network clients. RIS, which was introduced with Microsoft Windows 2000 Server, has been enhanced in Microsoft Windows Server 2003. Performance and security have been improved, and completely automated remote installation processes are now possible. Enhancements to RIS in Windows Server 2003 include the following:

- Detection of client hardware abstraction layer (HAL) and subsequent HAL filtering guarantee that only images with a compatible HAL are deployed.
- The local administrator password can be encrypted, although the domain administrator password still cannot be.
- Dynamic Host Configuration Protocol (DHCP) is configured automatically during RIS setup.
- The entire setup process, including the Client Installation Wizard (CIW) Text-mode portion, can be automated, allowing for completely hands-off setup of remote systems.

RIS also supports two new features of Windows Server 2003: Out-of-Band Management and Emergency Management Services.

Introduction to RIS

RIS allows you to install the Windows operating system onto a remote bare-metal machine. Because RIS installation requires systems that can boot from the network and establish network communications with the RIS server, the client machine should have hardware that supports the Preboot Execution Environment (PXE). For computers that don't have PXE support in their system firmware, Windows Server 2003 has a remote installation boot floppy (RIBF) disk that supports a small number of network adapters.

Services and Protocols Used by RIS

RIS comprises three services running on the RIS server: the Remote Installation service, the Trivial File Transfer Protocol Daemon (TFTPD) service, and the Single Instance Store service.

In addition, RIS relies on several other services and protocols. All RIS operations are based on the Transmission Control Protocol/Internet Protocol (TCP/IP) protocol suite and related services, such as the Domain Name System (DNS) and DHCP, and require the Active Directory directory service for authentication and account management.

Following are the services required on the RIS server:

- **Remote Installation service (BINLSVC)** This service manages client requests for RIS, checks computer account configuration and the deployment method, and verifies logon credentials. Startup and shutdown of the Remote Installation service is controlled in the Services console. Configuration is performed by using RIS wizards and settings on the RIS server's computer object in Active Directory, while security is controlled by using Group Policy and NTFS file system permissions.

> **Note** The Remote Installation service was called the Boot Information Negotiation Layer (BINL) in earlier versions of the Windows operating system.

- **TFTPD** The Trivial File Transfer Protocol, or TFTP (and the TFTPD service), copies the Client Installation Wizard and other software required to start the installation of an operating system image from the RIS server to the target computer.
- **Single Instance Store service** The Single Instance Store (SIS) service works with RIS to minimize the space used to store multiple operating system images on a single RIS image partition. SIS maintains a single copy of all of the duplicate files used in all of the images on a single partition. SIS monitors the partition used for RIS images and, when duplicate files are detected, replaces the actual file with an NTFS reparse point referencing the location of a copy of that file. To accomplish this, SIS uses a special-purpose NTFS file system filter and a software agent called a groveler, which does the file management.

> **Caution** This form of optimizing storage requires that your backup software be SIS-aware, such as the Windows Server 2003 Backup application. Without SIS-aware backup software, restoration could experience errors or fail entirely.

The following are the required network services:

- **DHCP** DHCP provides the target computers with an Internet Protocol (IP) address and referral to a RIS server. The PXE specifications extended DHCP to add functionality, allowing PXE systems to locate remote installation servers.

- **DNS** DNS locates systems used in the various RIS operations, such as domain controllers and DHCP servers.
- **Active Directory** Active Directory performs user authentication to the domain and manages computer accounts; thus, Active Directory must be installed and accessible on the network for RIS to operate.

Limitations of RIS

Although RIS is a welcome new feature and will help with operating system installation in many network environments, there are some limitations to RIS that you should keep in mind, such as the following:

- RIS supports only clean installations—you cannot upgrade an existing operating system.
- Many Windows components and network services, such as DNS and Active Directory, can't be installed during setup.
- RIS distribution files used to deploy an operating system must be nonencrypted—this means a RIS distribution folder cannot be encrypted by using Encrypting File System (EFS). Likewise, encrypted files cannot be added to RIS folders and deployed by RIS.
- User-level security settings (file system security, for example) cannot be set by using RIS; rather, you must run a script after installation is complete.
- RIS requires the image folder to be on a separate partition from the boot and system partitions.
- Multihomed RIS servers require special consideration. The RIS server must also provide DHCP services to the client. The active DHCP scope must include all subnets used by the client computer, and that DHCP server must assign all IP addresses for that client computer. Adapters can be assigned IP addresses in one or more subnets.
- Not only can RIS generate massive amounts of network traffic, it can also use up many processing cycles while doing so. Don't place RIS on application servers, such as those running Microsoft Exchange or Microsoft SQL Server.
- Don't install RIS on a computer in a wireless network. Wireless clients can't support PXE, so RIS can't boot them.

> **Note** When deploying RIS into an environment where third-party remote installation servers are already in place, you should configure RIS to ignore boot requests from unknown clients. This ensures RIS won't interfere with preexisting remote installation servers that use the same remote boot protocols.

Operating Systems Installable by Using RIS

Only select Microsoft Windows operating systems can be installed using RIS—many earlier versions of clients or server operating systems are not supported. This is not likely to be much of a problem, however, because it seems unlikely that many businesses are working on large automated deployments of Microsoft Windows 95 or Microsoft Windows 98.

Windows Server 2003 RIS supports the remote installation of the following versions of the Windows operating system:

- Windows Server 2003, Standard Edition
- Windows Server 2003, Enterprise Edition
- Windows Server 2003, Enterprise Edition, 64-bit version (only by using RISetup, not RIPrep)
- Windows Server 2003, Web Edition
- Microsoft Windows 2000 Professional, Server, and Advanced Server
- Microsoft Windows XP Professional

Note When talking about RIS, the term *client computer* refers to the target computer—the system that the Windows operating system is being installing on—even when the operating system you are installing is a Windows server version. Although RIS enables the remote installation of most versions of Windows Server 2003, it is worthy to note that RIS does not support the installation of Windows Server 2003, Datacenter Edition.

Note RIS is not included with the Windows Server 2003, Web Edition. Web Edition is designed to support Internet services, not the sort of corporate environment in which you would expect to use RIS. Not surprisingly, Web Edition does not include RIS and therefore cannot be used as a RIS server. There are additional network services, such as Active Directory, that are required to support RIS operations that are not included in Web Edition, as well. Thus, to deploy RIS in your organization, you must use Windows Server 2003, Standard Edition or Enterprise Edition.

Designing the RIS Environment

Before you head off to install RIS, you should consider what the RIS server environment will look like when you are finished and what changes you must make to your existing network environment to support it. Start by considering where in the Active Directory infrastructure you plan to place the RIS server or servers. The logical structure of Active Directory is different from its physical structure. Logical structures include forests, domains, and organizational units (OUs). Physical structures include sites and subnets. Where you place your RIS server depends on how many clients the server must support; the forest, domain, and OU structures in place; and the connectivity for subnets within sites.

Typically, you want the RIS servers to be within the same site as the clients, but if connectivity between subnets is an issue, you'll want the RIS servers to be located on the same subnet as the clients. If you can't locate the RIS server in the same location or site as the RIS clients, you must ensure there is good connectivity between the subnets of the common domain. During installation, RIS clients must be able to connect to the RIS server. They find the server by sending a DHCP broadcast, which a DHCP server can respond to and use to inform the client where the RIS server is located. The RIS client's computer account must also have access to Active Directory within the domain in which the client's computer account was precreated or will be created during the installation process.

Inside Out

High-speed connectivity is essential for successful RIS deployments

The typical RIS image is between 700 megabytes (MB) and 1.5 gigabytes (GB) in size, and you need a high-speed network connection to every RIS client if you plan to transfer that amount of data over the network in a timely fashion. Have at least 100 megabytes per second (Mbps) connectivity. You might have seen charts that tell you when you transfer a RIS image of size *X* over a link of *Y* speed that it's going to take *Z* minutes (or hours). Throw them away. In the real world, it doesn't matter whether you have Gigabit Ethernet, Fast Ethernet, or T-1 connectivity; what matters is what else is going on at the same time you are trying to transfer the massive RIS image. If you kick off 50 RIS image installations along with all the other typical traffic, you will bring Fast Ethernet to its knees. If you kick off 2 RIS image installations over a T-1, you will bring the T-1 to its knees. It's all relative to the current traffic, and in either example, the network would probably slow to a crawl unless you have some bandwidth-throttling measures in place.

A single RIS server can handle between 70 and 75 simultaneous client installations. Any more than that and the server will bog down and stop handling requests. Contrary to some documentation, RIS can be configured on a server running other roles, including servers acting as domain controllers and running DHCP. In fact, in a very small environment, it is typical to have DHCP and RIS configured on the same server because this reduces the number of network packets that RIS clients send to DHCP and RIS servers and allows the simultaneous answering of requests. Combining these roles, however, does dramatically increase the load on the server, which can affect the server's response time. A more typical environment has a dedicated RIS server (or multiple RIS servers). With multiple RIS servers, you have the option of using a RIS referral server to help load balance the requests from clients.

Inside Out

RIS generates massive traffic loads

One thing to keep in mind is that client installations generate large amounts of network traffic because between 700 MB (Windows XP) and 1.5 GB (Windows Server 2003) of data is passed over the network with each installation; DHCP typically has far less traffic. In most organizations, a RIS server is an enterprise-class server that is also used for software installations. In contrast, the typical DHCP server might, in fact, be a desktop-class system running Windows Server 2003. Obviously, if the latter case is true in your environment, you shouldn't combine RIS and DHCP on the same server—no matter the size of your network.

Building a RIS Server: What's Involved

Now that you know how RIS works, its limitations, and design considerations, you are ready to deploy RIS. The procedures you must perform to get RIS up and working are as follows:

1. Install the RIS server and make it a member of the Active Directory domain in which the RIS clients are located. Be sure the server either has multiple hard disk drives or that you partition the drive so that the boot and system partitions can be separate from the RIS installation drive as it must be.
2. Add RIS to the server and then reboot it. Afterward, run the Remote Installation Services Setup Wizard (RISetup) to prepare the server to receive RIS images and put an initial image on the RIS partition or drive. When you do this, the RIS server is ready for use and you can add additional images to it by using RIPrep.

The finer details of step 2 are covered in the next section of this chapter.

Installing RIS

The RIS services, like most network services, are not installed by default when you set up Windows Server 2003. Before installing RIS, you should verify that the computer on which you are installing RIS meets the baseline system requirements for RIS operations for both hardware and software, as well as partition configuration and available free space.

RIS Server Requirements

At minimum, the RIS server must meet the following requirements:

- The computer must be running Windows Server 2003, Standard, Enterprise, or Datacenter Edition.
- The server cannot be multihomed; it must have a single supported 10- or 100-MB network interface card (NIC) with TCP/IP installed.

- The computer must be a member of an Active Directory domain.
- At minimum, a 4-GB drive should be available for RIS images.
- The location of files used by RIS must be on a local fixed drive and cannot be a network share or a distributed file system (DFS) share (although DFS can be running as an additional service on the RIS server without any problem).
- The partition upon which you install RIS must be formatted as NTFS.

Inside Out

Limitations on partitions used for RIS

The partition used for RIS has a number of limitations placed on it: It cannot be the boot or system drive, and files must be unencrypted. You should, whenever possible, give RIS its own partition, freshly formatted with NTFS, upon which to store images.

In addition, when configuring a new RIS image, access to a Windows distribution CD-ROM of each operating system the RIS server will be installing (or a network location with those files) is required.

Troubleshooting

Multihomed RIS fails to respond to clients

Multihomed RIS servers commonly fail to respond to PXE clients during the initial client boot process. The RIS server can have only one NIC installed; so, if a server has more than one NIC, you should disable or remove the additional NICs or consider using a different server.

In addition to the requirements of the RIS server, certain services must be available on the local network. These services are as follows:

- DHCP
- DNS
- Active Directory

Performing the Install

RIS is not included as a server role that you configure using the Manage Your Server Wizard. This means that to install RIS, you use Add Or Remove Programs in Control Panel.

Tip To install RIS, you must be a member of the Enterprise Admins group in Active Directory.

Preparing and Installing RIS

Use the following steps to prepare and install RIS:

1. In Control Panel, open Add Or Remove Programs.
2. Click Add/Remove Windows Components, which starts the Windows Components Wizard.
3. In the Windows Components Wizard, select the Remote Installation Services option, click Next to install RIS, and then click Finish.
4. Click Yes when prompted to reboot the system. Once the system has rebooted, you must run RISetup.exe to finish the initial configuration of RIS.

Tip **Configure the RIS server as an authorized DHCP server**
Although the RIS server must be configured as an authorized DHCP server, it doesn't have to be done manually as a separate process. DHCP configuration now happens automatically as part of the postinstallation configuration process completed by RISetup.

Configuring the RIS Server

There are several tools used to set up and configure RIS as well as the operating systems that the RIS server will deploy. These tools include the following:

- **RISetup.exe** The primary RIS setup program, RISetup, is used to perform the initial configuration of the RIS server and designate the location of the distribution folder that will contain the operating system images. RISetup also lets you specify the source location of the uninstalled product files, associate answer files with images, and provide a name and description for each of the available operating system installations.
- **RIPrep.exe** The RIPrep utility is used to create file system–based images (differing from both RISetup and Sysprep images). These images typically deploy faster than those created by using RISetup, because RIPrep images reflect an installed copy of the operating system. RIPrep prepares a master computer for imaging using a Sysprep-like process and then, rather than requiring an additional program to perform the imaging process (as Sysprep does), stores the image for deployment to client computers.
- **RBFG.exe** The Remote Boot Floppy Generator (RBFG) utility creates the remote installation boot disk that is used for client computers that do not have a PXE boot read-only memory (ROM).

Once you have installed RIS on the server, you must run the RIS Setup Wizard to configure RIS. Because you have not set up any images, nor have you had a chance to review settings, including security, RIS is not started until after this wizard has been run for the first time.

Initial RIS Configuration

To configure the Remote Installation service, follow these steps:

1. Start the RIS Installation Services Setup Wizard on the RIS server by clicking Remote Installation Services Setup on the Administrative Tools menu or by typing **risetup** at a command prompt.
2. Specify the folder to use for RIS. Here, you select the disk location to contain RIS installation images and related files, as shown in the following screen. The folder must be on a local fixed drive that is formatted with NTFS version 5 or later (meaning an NTFS folder formatted previously under Windows 2000 or later) and that is not the same drive as the server's operating system.

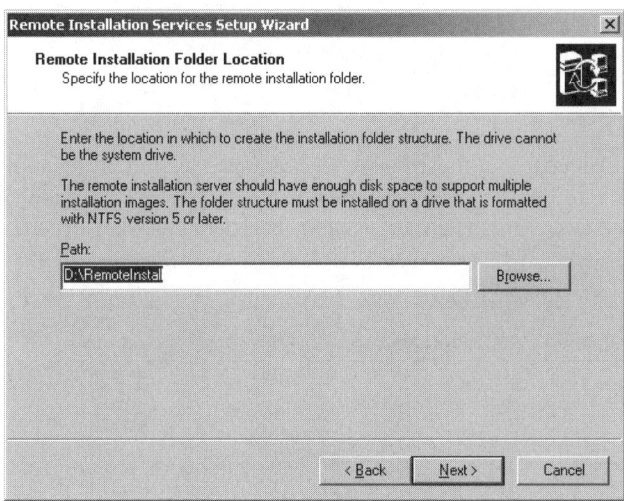

> **Tip Allocate adequate free space for RIS images**
> The RIS image folder should have substantial free disk space (4 GB minimum), because installation images average over 700 MB, and most RIS installations will house multiple installations of more than one operating system as well as image variants for the same operating systems. Depending on the range of operating system (OS) images to be supported in your environment, and the frequency of adding new OS images, you might want to put RIS on its own partition with many gigabytes of free disk space. In our installation, a separate 60-GB drive is used as the RIS image folder.

3. Set initial RIS functionality. You can define whether RIS responds to clients at all and control the initial status of the RIS service after this setup wizard is completed (as shown in the screen on the following page). When the server is configured to respond to clients, security can be tightened by instructing RIS not to respond to unknown clients.

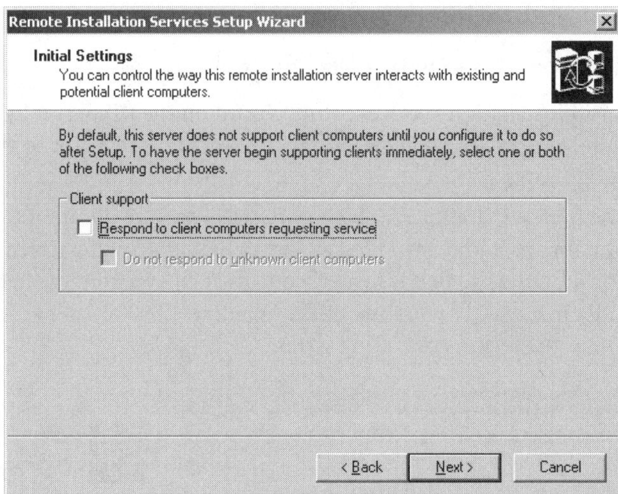

4 Specify the location of the initial source files by selecting the location of the operating system files to use as the source, which is typically the distribution CD (as shown in the following screen). The source could also be a network distribution share containing the distribution source files. In either case, these OS files are the first OS image to be made available by RIS.

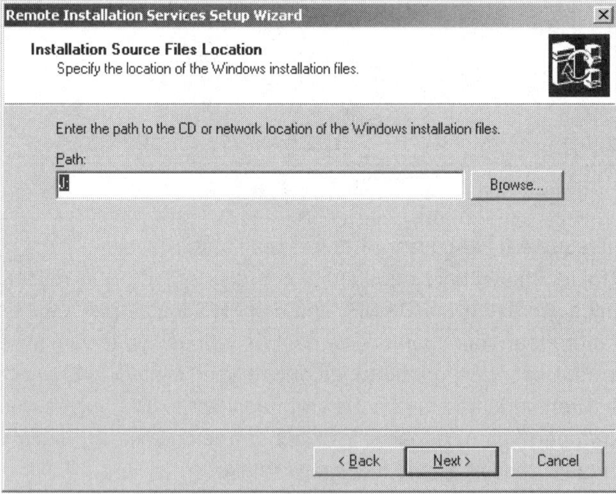

5 Create a name for the RIS installation image folder, as shown in the screen on the following page. The RIS installation image is placed in a folder named WINDOWS by default (contained under the RemoteInstall folder created by RIS in Step 1).

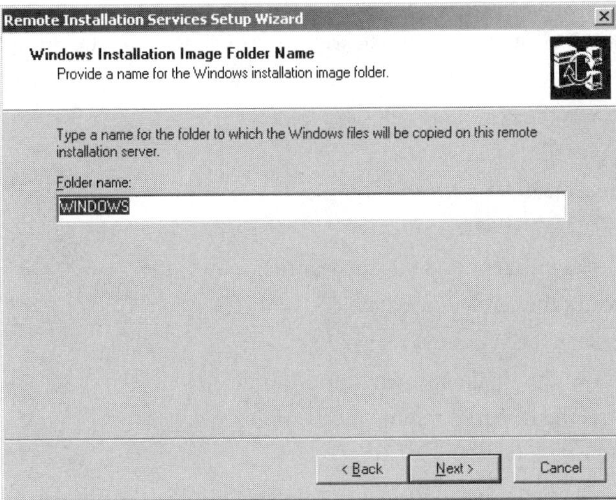

6 Define the Friendly Description and Help Text, as shown in the following screen. You can customize the Friendly Description of the RIS installation image and set the Help Text to help distinguish between the OS images available through RIS.

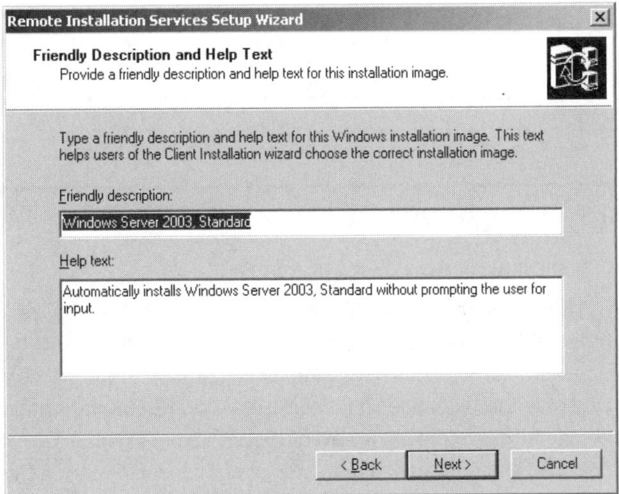

Note The Friendly Description and Help Text for a RIS image are drawn by default from the .inf files with the product's distribution files and can usually be left as is. In cases in which you will be presenting different configurations of the same operating system as options through the RIS server, however, text that is somewhat more descriptive is recommended. You should *briefly* explain the differences between the various configurations and the computers to which they are applicable.

7 The Review Settings dialog box displays the configured information prior to finishing the image creation. Once you click Finish, the Remote Installation Services Setup Wizard routine completes the following installation tasks:

- Creates the remote installation folder
- Copies files needed by RIS
- Copies Windows installation files
- Updates CIW screen files
- Creates unattended setup answer files
- Creates the services used by RIS
- Updates the Windows registry
- Creates the single instance store volume
- Starts the required remote installation services
- Authorizes DHCP

During the configuration of RIS and creation of the initial distribution folder, the root of the RIS distribution folder is shared automatically at *ServerName*\Reminst, where *ServerName* is the name of the RIS server. Three essential services were also installed and configured:

- Remote Installation service
- Single Instance Store
- Trivial FTP Daemon

These services must be running for RIS to work properly. You can check these services using the Services tool on the Administrative Tools menu. In Event Viewer, also accessible from the Administrative Tools menu, you'll find events for these services in the System log.

Inside Out

The RIS server must be authorized as a DHCP server

RISetup should automatically authorize the RIS server in Active Directory as a DHCP server, regardless of whether the server is actually running DHCP. This is necessary because it is how DHCP servers are able to locate RIS servers. You see, DHCP simply forwards the RIS request (which it can't handle) to the RIS server. If for some reason DHCP authorization fails, it can be confirmed by looking in the system log for event ID 1046 from DhcpServer that states the DHCP/BINLSVC service has determined that it is not authorized to start. If this happens, you must authorize the server manually using an account that is a member of the Enterprise Admins group. Log on to a DHCP server, and start its DHCP administration tool or use the DHCP administration tool in Administrative Tools. In the DHCP console, click Action on the menu, then choose Manage Authorized Servers. In the Manage Authorized Servers dialog box, click Authorize, and then type the IP address of the RIS server. Afterward, you must either stop and then restart the Remote Installation service in the Services node in the Computer Management console or reboot the server. A reboot is typically a good idea. Note also that the Group Policy settings control whether and how the related RIS services are started (for details, see the section entitled "Controlling Access to RIS Servers" later in this chapter).

Inside Out

Automating RIS installations

You can associate the operating system image with an answer file (Remboot.sif) to streamline the unattended installation of the operating system to the target computer. You create the answer files used by RIS in Setup Manager as discussed in Chapter 5, "Managing Unattended Installations."

Customizing RIS

You can also configure the RIS server by double-clicking its computer account in Active Directory Users and Computers and then selecting the Remote Install tab, as shown below.

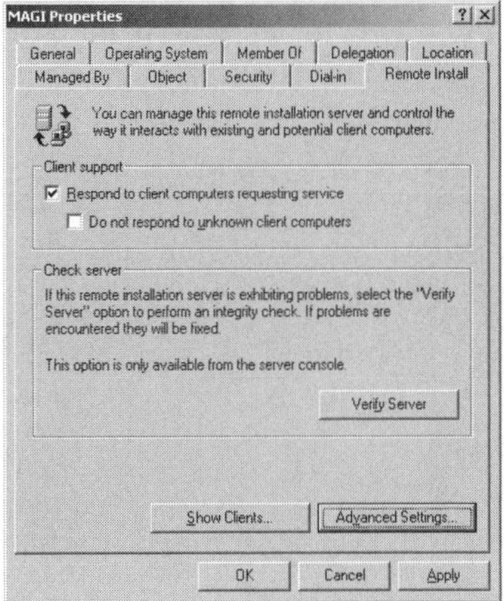

The following options are displayed:

- **Respond To Client Computers Requesting Services** This instructs the RIS services to respond to client requests, effectively making the RIS server available to RIS clients on the network.
- **Do Not Respond To Unknown Client Computers** If you select this option, the RIS server will disregard requests from unknown computers (that is, computers without an account in Active Directory). Access to the RIS servers can be restricted using this option—only prestaged computers (computers with accounts previously established in Active Directory) can access the RIS server and the OS images it hosts.

In addition to the settings in Active Directory that control how the server handles client requests, you can verify the RIS server configuration, gain administrative access to RIS clients using this server, and control management of RIS-installed computers.

To verify that the RIS server is correctly configured, click Verify Server in the Remote Install tab. RIS will analyze the configuration, repair any problems if possible, and report on the status of the server.

Clicking Show Clients loads the Find Remote Installation Clients dialog box, which lets you find and display known remote installation clients within the selected scope (the entire directory or a single domain).

Tip **Prestage client computers**
When you prestage a computer, you can specify which RIS servers can provide installation services to it or allow it to be serviced by any available RIS server. This is configured in the Remote Install tab of the client computer's properties in Active Directory. For more information on prestaging computers, see the section entitled "Prestaging Clients in Active Directory" later in this chapter.

How client computer names are generated and where they are placed in Active Directory are controlled by settings available through the Advanced button (as shown in the following screen).

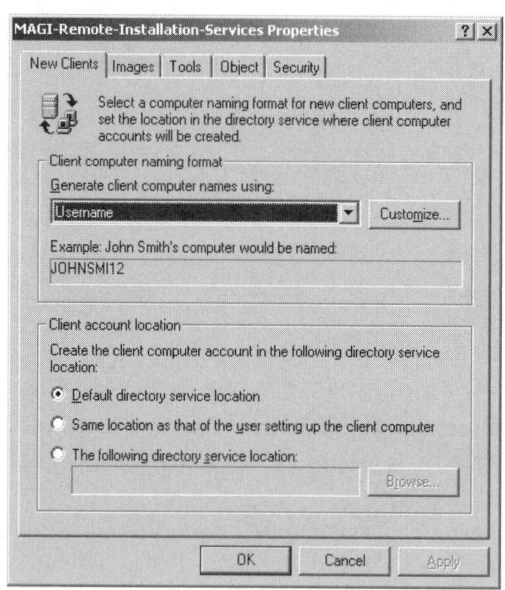

You can configure the naming format used for generating client computer names in the New Clients tab. Several naming formats are offered, including the following:

- First initial, last name
- Last initial, first name
- First name, last initial
- Last initial, first name
- User name
- The string "NP" with the Media Access Control (MAC) address appended
- Custom

You can also specify the client account location—the place in the directory where the client computer accounts are established. You can store the new computer account in the default Active Directory location in the Computers container or the same location as the user creating the account, or you can select a specific location in the directory.

Tip Computer accounts can have same name as user accounts
For the purposes of applying Group Policy, computer accounts are commonly placed in Information Technology (IT)–designated OUs. Note also that computer accounts can be the same name as user accounts, which is why the naming options using parts of the user's actual name or logon are allowed. To prevent conflicts between like-named user and computer accounts, Active Directory adds a hidden dollar sign to the computer account name. This means the computer account WRSTANEK is actually WRSTANEK$. Yes, this is a fix to resolve a naming problem found in Microsoft Windows NT. In Windows NT, you couldn't have user and computer accounts with the same name.

To configure manually how the computer account names are created, select a naming option to use as the template, and then click Customize to open the Computer Account Generation dialog box, as shown in the screen on the following page. The initial custom name format is based on the naming option you used as a template. You can then modify the format and select from several variables to create a wide variety of name templates. A box at the bottom of the dialog box previews the naming formats for you. If you make a mistake in the formatting, it shows an error.

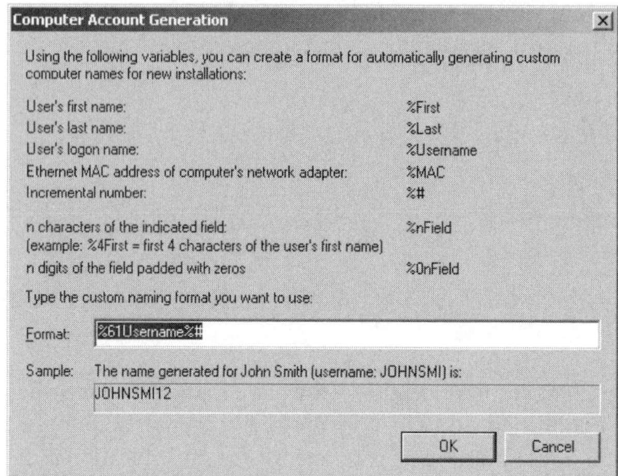

The variables that can be used in computer names include the following:

- **%First** First name of user
- **%Last** Last name of user
- **%Username** Logon name of user
- **%Mac** MAC address of the client's NIC
- **%#** Used to specify an incrementing number
- **%*n*<*field*>** Used to designate *n* characters of <*field*>
- **%0*n*<*field*>** Used to pad *n* characters with zeros

For example, to have computer names generated from the first 10 characters of the user logon name plus the first 5 characters of the MAC address of the NIC plus an incrementing number, use this syntax:

```
%10Username%5MAC%#
```

You needn't get that fancy, though. Maybe you just want to use a standard root name and increment? Well, you can do that, too. Consider the following example:

```
cpandl%#
```

Here, all computers names begin with cpandl (which is the abbreviated company name for City Power & Light) and end with a number that is automatically incremented by RIS.

> **Tip** It is important to note that name settings are ignored for prestaged clients. Prestaged clients were assigned names when their accounts were created in Active Directory.

You can view and manage the RIS installation images in the Images tab (as shown in the following screen). Information concerning each installation image is displayed—the image name, operating system it contains, platform it supports, and the language to which it is localized are all listed. You can add and remove images in this dialog box, while additional information and options are available by clicking Properties.

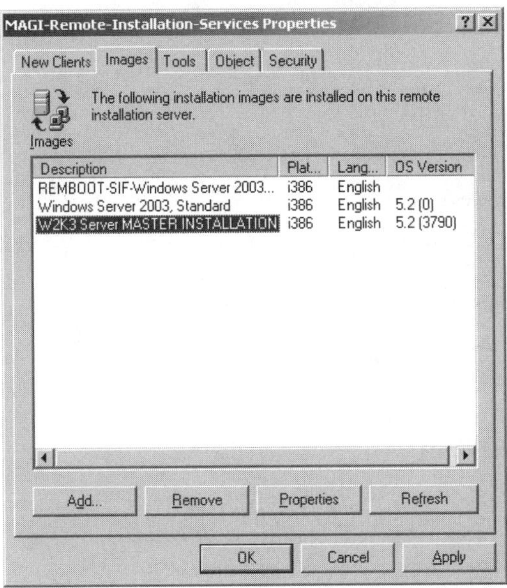

> **Note** The Add button lets you either associate an answer file with an image or create a new image.

You can modify the name and description of the image presented by the CIW (as shown in the screen on the following page). This wizard also contains additional details about the image, including version, language, date last modified, type of image, and RIS image storage folder. Security for the image is accessed by clicking Permissions. This lets you limit access to each OS image based on security group membership.

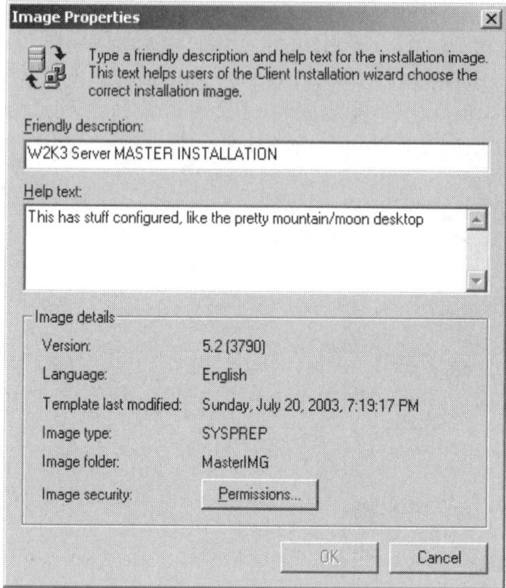

Controlling Access to RIS Servers

Access to RIS servers can be controlled by Group Policy, which allows you to manage network traffic and the workload of each RIS server. To access these settings, open a Group Policy Object, expand Computer Configuration, Windows Settings, Security Settings, Systems Services, and select Remote Installation Policy. By using this policy, you can configure the startup method for the RIS server and configure security permissions for users and groups.

Access to RIS servers can also be controlled by setting up prestaged computer accounts. During account creation, by selecting This Is A Managed Computer and specifying a globally unique identifier (GUID)/universally unique identifier (UUID), you have the option to specify which RIS server to use or to allow any available RIS server to be used. The GUID/UUID can be found in the system BIOS or it can be posted on the computer case.

Applying Security Permissions to RIS

You can set security permissions on RIS services and images to control access to remote OS installation. By setting security permissions on the image, you can specify the users and groups that are allowed to install from this OS image. You control the remote installation of the OS images by applying permissions to the default answer file for that image. For a RIPrep image, this file is Riprep.sif. For RISetup, this file is Ristndrd.sif. Right-click the file, and select Properties. In the Properties dialog box, shown in the screen on the following page, select the Security tab, and configure group and user names and the appropriate permissions.

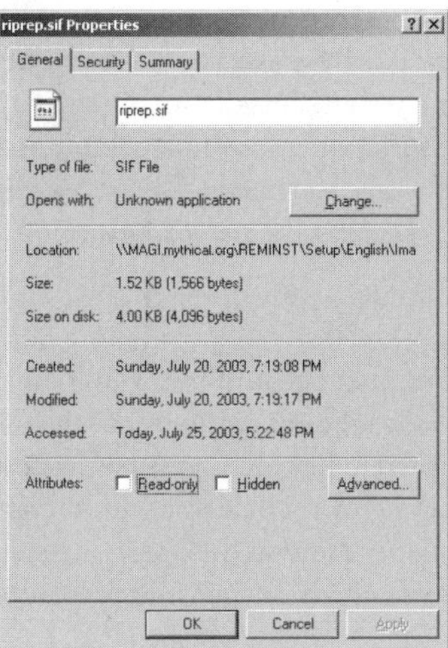

Authorizing Users to Create New Computer Accounts

When RIS installs an operating system on a computer, a computer account is created in Active Directory. Therefore, engineers and administrators who will be performing RIS installations must be able to add computers to the domain. If the individuals performing RIS installations don't already belong to a security group that can add computers to the domain, they must be granted the right to do so before they can use RIS.

To do this, set permissions in Active Directory that allow the designated security group to add computers to the domain by following these steps:

1. Log on to the domain with an account that has Administrator privileges, and then run Active Directory Users and Computers by clicking Start, pointing to Programs or All Programs, clicking Administrative Tools, and then selecting Active Directory Users And Computers.
2. Right-click the appropriate domain node, and select Delegate Control to start the Delegation Of Control Wizard.
3. Select the specific Users or Groups to delegate. Click Add, and then select a user or security group that will be responsible for using RIS. Repeat this step to add other users or groups.
4. On the Tasks To Delegate page, select Join A Computer To The Domain as the task to delegate.
5. Click Finish to complete the delegation of control.

Through delegation, you allow users to create computer accounts, but you don't miss out on the opportunity to allow users to help themselves. If Sally messes up her computer by installing things she shouldn't have installed, hand her a remote installation boot floppy disk, tell her to insert the disk, boot the machine and press F12 when prompted, and then follow the prompts, making sure to choose the appropriate image she needs. This way, Sally can help herself, and you can focus on other tasks, such as keeping the network running.

As long as Sally has been authorized to join a computer to the domain, she'll be able to complete the installation process. If she hasn't, though, she'll see an error telling her that she doesn't have permission to create or modify a computer account in the domain. Now you might be wondering why you need to authorize Sally to join a computer to the domain when any ordinary user can create a computer account. Well, if there is an existing computer account, RIS must delete the computer account and create a new one with the same name or change the password for the computer account, depending on the operating system. These procedures cannot be performed by ordinary users, which is why you must authorize the user to join a computer to the domain.

Users with the privilege to join a computer to the domain can create computer accounts and modify the computer accounts they've created. They won't, however, be allowed to modify the computer accounts other users have created. If you want to allow users to modify computer accounts created by other users, you must create a special RIS installers group, grant it this permission, and then add users who should have this permission to the group.

Creating a RIS Installers Group

To create a special group for RIS installers, follow these steps:

1. Log on to the domain with an account that has Administrator privileges, and then run Active Directory Users and Computers by clicking Start, pointing to Programs or All Programs, clicking Administrative Tools, and then selecting Active Directory Users And Computers.
2. Right-click the existing folder or organizational group into which you want to place the special group for RIS installers. Typically, this is the Users container, so right-click the Users folder, click New, and then select Group. This opens the New Object—Group dialog box.
3. Type a name for the group, such as RISInstallers (as shown in Figure 6-1), and then click OK. By default, the group is created as a Global Security Group—which you'll learn all about in Chapter 37, "Managing Users, Groups, and Computers."

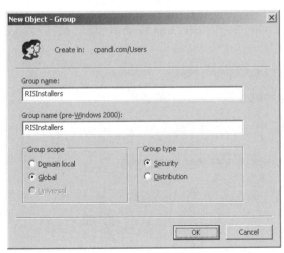

Figure 6-1. Creating the RISInstallers group.

4 In Active Directory Users and Computers, select View, and click Advanced to enable the console to show advanced properties, such as the Security tab.

5 Grant permission to add computers to the domain to the group you just created using the Delegation Of Control Wizard, as discussed in the previous procedure.

6 By default, computer accounts are created in the Computers container. You must change the permissions on this folder to allow RIS installers to delete and change computer accounts. Right-click the Computers folder, and then choose Properties. On the Computers Properties page, click the Security tab, as shown in the following screen:

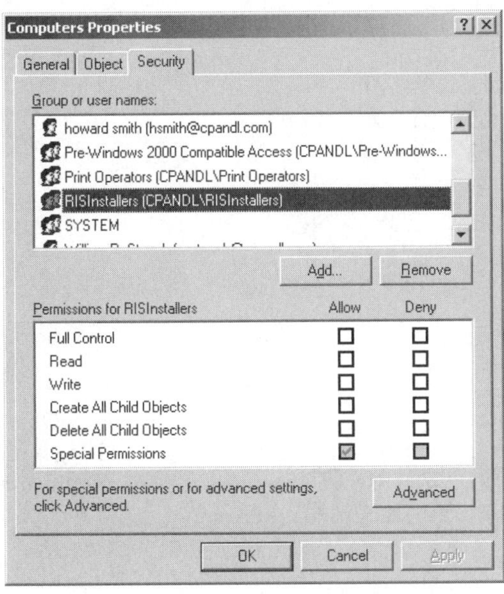

7 Find the RISInstallers group in the Group Or User Names list box, click it, and then click Advanced to display the Advanced Security Settings For Computers dialog box, as shown in the following screen:

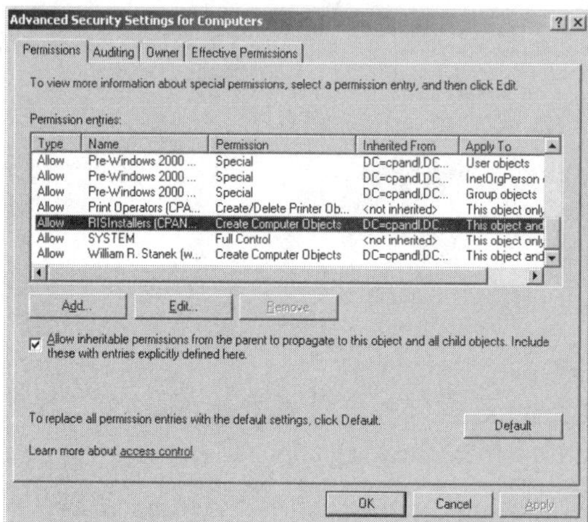

8 Scroll down the list of labeled Permissions, as shown in the following screen. You should see that the Create Computer Objects permission is set to Allow. Select this entry, and then click Edit to display the Permission Entry For Computers dialog box, as shown in the following screen:

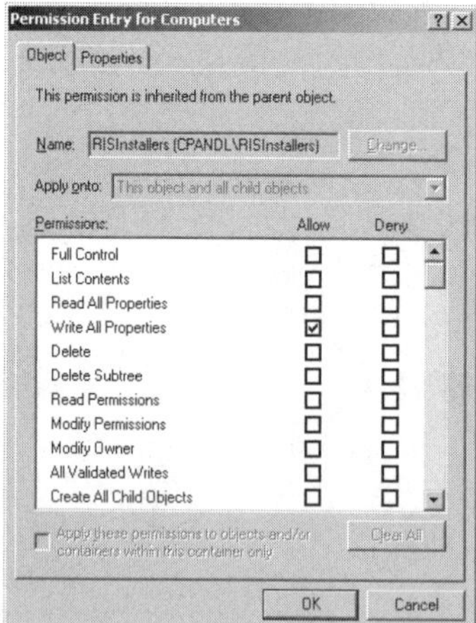

9 Select Allow for Write All Properties and for Delete Computer Objects. Click OK to return to the Advanced Security Settings For Computers dialog box. Click OK twice more to close the dialog boxes. Now all you need to do is add the users who should have these permissions to the RISInstallers group.

Adding Members to the RISInstallers Group

To add members to the special RISInstallers group, follow these steps:

1. In Active Directory Users and Computers, access the folder that contains the RISInstallers group.
2. Right-click the group entry, and then click Properties.
3. In the Members tab, click Add.
4. Find an account to add, and then click OK. Repeat this step to add other accounts.
5. Click OK to close the group Properties page.

That's it! Yes, it was a lot of work, but now you can let users help themselves.

Configuring RIS Clients

RIS clients rely on PXE to load boot code from the network and establish communications with a RIS server. A PXE-compliant computer has a PXE-enabled BIOS and a NIC that supports remote booting. PXE allows computers to boot using code from a network location, and then to remotely install an operating system—without user input, if desired. It does this using standard protocols and services, such as TCP/IP, DHCP, and Trivial File Transfer Protocol (TFTP).

> **Tip** In Windows Server 2003, RIS operates with NICs that support the PC 2001 specification.

PXE includes extensions to DHCP that allow PXE systems to locate remote installation servers. When a PXE client machine boots from the network adapter, it first locates a DHCP server and then, using information supplied by the DHCP server, contacts a RIS server. The RIS server loads and automatically runs an operating system installation process, which can be a Windows installation (automated or interactive) or an image deployment (created using RIPrep).

Not all computers support PXE in their system firmware, and Windows Server 2003 includes an alternative for those systems. If you have machines without PXE support, you can create a RIBF disk, which emulates the PXE boot process. See the section entitled "Creating a RIBF Disk" later in this chapter for details.

In addition, even if your computer is PXE-compliant, you might need to change the BIOS settings to tell the computer to boot using PXE. How you do this depends on the computer. Most of the time, when you start the computer, you'll see an option to access the BIOS setup, then from within BIOS setup you'll typically have an option that lets you change the boot order and select boot options.

On an IBM ThinkPad, for instance, restart the computer and press F1 to access the BIOS setup. Then access the Power On options on the Startup menu. Included there is a wide array of boot options, including Network Boot, Removable Devices, Hard Drive, and ATAPI CD-ROM Drive. The obvious choice seems to be Network Boot, but a Network Boot is typically for thin clients and not a standard system. The actual choice needed is under Hard Drive and is an option for Bootable Add-In Cards, which must be moved up so that the bootable card is checked for before the hard disk drive.

Tip If you're counting on using RIS for widespread deployment, verify that the systems either have firmware support for the PXE environment or are equipped with a network adapter supported by the RIBF.

Customizing Installation Options

The options presented to the person performing the RIS installation are controlled by using Group Policy settings. These settings affect whether automatic setup is supported, a failed setup can be restarted, and custom setup is available.

Tip Although using these Group Policy settings is optional, they can have significant effects on the operations of RIS-based installations. Because of this, you will usually want to take the time to customize them for your environment.

Configuring RIS Settings in Group Policy

To configure the RIS settings in a Group Policy Object (GPO), follow these steps:

1. In the Group Policy Editor, expand User Configuration, Windows Settings, Remote Installation Services.
2. Right-click Choice Options, and then select Properties (or double-click Choice Options).

Table 6-1 shows the options available for configuration.

Table 6-1. RIS Settings in Group Policy

Setup Option	Default Setting	Description
Automatic Setup	Not configured	Bypasses all CIW setup options other than selection of OS image. Active Directory searches for a target computer UUID matching a UUID in a (prestaged) Active Directory computer account and uses the Active Directory computer name. During installation, if no matching UUID is found, one is constructed from the location in Active Directory and the selected automatic-naming format.
Custom Setup	Disabled	Enables selection of Active Directory location and computer account name.
Restart Setup	Disabled	Restarts Setup upon installation failure—starts CIW before image copy phase, then users are presented with a Restart Setup option on their CIW boot display.
Tools	Disabled	Provides access to tools for troubleshooting and maintenance (diagnostics, system flash BIOS update). These tools are installed in the RemoteInstall share.

You can configure each of these settings as Enabled, Disabled, or Not Configured. You can also select both Automatic and Custom setup to support a more diverse installation environment.

Inside Out

Using specialized GPOs to customize RIS

You can configure RIS settings in the default domain policy GPO. Yet, where more flexibility is required, you can also create a specialized GPO that is limited to one or more OUs. When you use OU GPOs to customize the RIS environment, you can allow a setting from the default domain policy to apply by setting the individual option to Not Configured in the OU GPO.

Creating a RIBF Disk

Administrators can take advantage of RIS even when dealing with computers that do not have PXE hardware by using the RIBF. This disk provides PXE emulation for computers that do not support PXE but that *do* have one of a limited set of NICs. Figure 6-2 displays the Remote Boot Disk Generator interface.

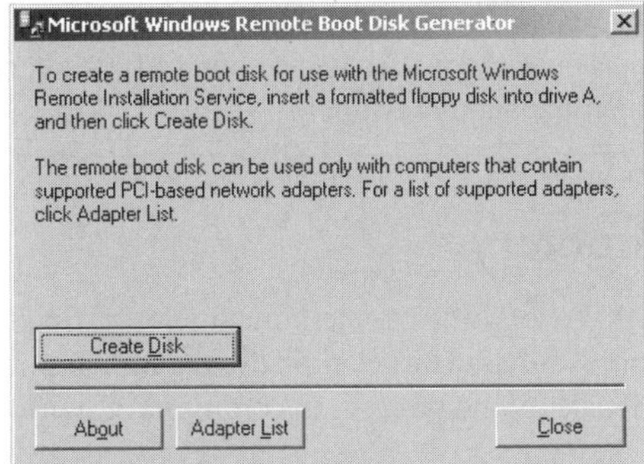

Figure 6-2. Creating the remote boot disk for non-PXE computers.

To create a remote installation boot disk, run RBFG.exe, which is located in RemoteInstall\Admin\I386 (or another RemoteInstall path specified when running the RIS Setup Wizard), and then click Create Disk. When prompted, insert a formatted floppy disk, and that's it. Now you can make copies of the disk and hand them out to RIS installers.

The remote installation boot disk provides support for a limited set of network cards on the target machine. Table 6-2 lists the network cards supported by the remote installation boot disk at the time this book was written. Support can change as additional service packs and updates become available—Murphy's Law again. Click Adapter List in the Remote Boot Disk Generator to get a current list of supported adapters.

Table 6-2. Network Adapters Supported by the RIS Boot Disk

Vendor	Network Adapter
3Com	3Com 3C900B-Combo, 3Com 3C900B-FL, 3Com 3C900B-TPC, 3Com 3C900BTPO, 3Com 3C9000-Combo, 3Com 3C9000TPO, 3Com 3C905B-Combo, 3Com 3C905B-FX, 3Com 3C905B-TX, 3Com 3C905C-TX, 3Com 3C905-T4, 3Com 3C905-TX, 3Com MiniPCI
Accton	Accton MPX5030
Allied	Telesyn 2500TX
AMD	AMD PCNet Adapters
Compaq	Compaq NetFlex 100, Compaq NetFlex 110, Compaq NetFlex 3
DEC	DEC DE450, DEC DE500
HP	HP DeskDirect 10/100TX
Intel	Intel Pro 10+, Intel Pro 100+, Intel Pro 100B
Realtek	Realtek RTL8029, Realtek RTL8139
SMC	SMC 1211TX, SMC 8432, SMC 9332, SMC 9432, SMC ENI1209D-TX5

Note The RIBF supports only a small number of network adapters, and support for additional adapters cannot be added by individual users such as you and I. Microsoft can (and probably will) change this over time, as mentioned previously.

Prestaging Clients in Active Directory

Creating computer accounts in Active Directory prior to their use in remote installations (prestaging) can enhance the security of your RIS-based installation. Prestaging computer accounts allows you to control exactly which RIS clients and servers can communicate with each other.

Prestaging involves creating a computer account for the computer before deployment using the GUID/UUID assigned to the computer. A computer's GUID/UUID is supplied by the manufacturer and must be entered in the format {*dddddddd-dddd-dddd-dddd-dddddddddddd*}, where *d* is a hexadecimal digit, such as {AEFED345-BC13-22CD-ABCD-11BB11342112}.

To obtain the GUID/UUID, you need physical access to the computer. Look for a label on the side of or within the computer case. You might need to access the computer's BIOS to find the GUID/UUID. A helpful tool for obtaining the GUID/UUID from BIOS is the BIOS Information script, which is available through the Remote Installation Scripts link on the Web Resources page. The current Uniform Resource Locator (URL) of the Web Resource page as of this writing is *http://www.microsoft.com/windows/reskits/webresources*. If you have the Windows Server 2003 Deployment Kit, use the Get RIS Client BIOS Information script (ACIRIS_14.vbs) on the CD-ROM.

Inside Out

How are GUIDs/UUIDs used with computers that aren't prestaged?

If you elect not to prestage computers, you don't have to worry about GUIDs/UUIDs. During installation, the UUID is automatically obtained or generated as necessary. For PXE-enabled systems, the UUID is obtained from the PXE-enabled NIC and is stored in Active Directory with the computer account during installation. The UUID for a non-PXE client is generated by prefixing 20 zeros to the MAC address of the installed NIC and requires a RIS remote book disk (and a compatible network adapter) to use RIS. When using the remote boot floppy disk, turn on the computer (with the boot floppy disk in the drive). The remote installation process either waits for you to press F12 (default) or automatically starts Setup (if configured).

Prestaging computer accounts increases RIS installation security by letting you control which computers can authenticate during the remote installation process. You limit which clients an RIS server responds to by selecting the Do Not Respond To Unknown Clients option during RIS setup or in the Remote Install tab of the RIS server's computer account Properties page in Active Directory.

To prestage an account in Active Directory, go to the OU where you want the computer account to reside, and create a new computer account. You are prompted for the computer name and to specify which security groups are authorized to add this computer to the domain (as shown in the following screen). Set the computer name and select the security group(s) responsible for the remote installation.

New Object - Computer
Create in: mythical.org/Computers
Computer name:
SRC000040
Computer name (pre-Windows 2000):
SRC000040
The following user or group can join this computer to a domain.
User or group:
Default: Domain Admins
Change...
Assign this computer account as a pre-Windows 2000 computer
Assign this computer account as a backup domain controller
< Back
Next >
Cancel

Next, you designate the computer account as a managed computer and specify the GUID/UUID for the computer (as shown in the following screen). This enables it to interact with RIS, functioning as the preestablished computer account in Active Directory required to complete the RIS installation.

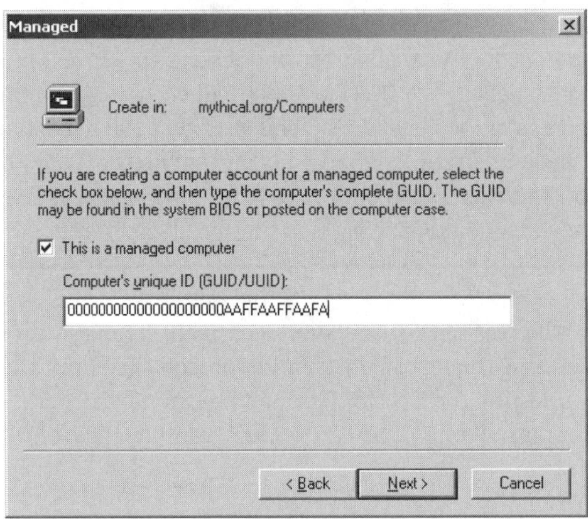

The GUID/UUID assigned to each computer account must be unique. If a duplicate is detected when you are creating computer accounts during prestaging, you are prompted to change the ID, query for duplicates, or accept it as is.

The RIS server that will be used for this computer's installation is specified next—you can choose either to allow any RIS server to be used or to configure a specific RIS server to be used. In the following screen, the Mythical.org RIS server has been selected for this prestaged computer account.

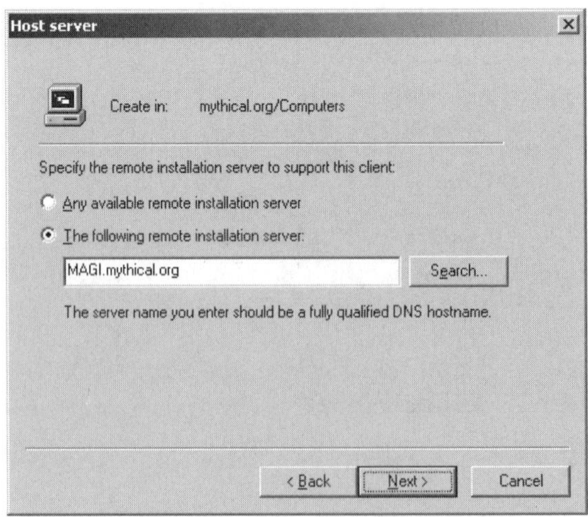

Once you complete the computer account creation, you can view the RIS client properties established for the account in the Remote Install tab, where the GUID/UUID and the designated RIS server are displayed and configurable (as shown in the following screen).

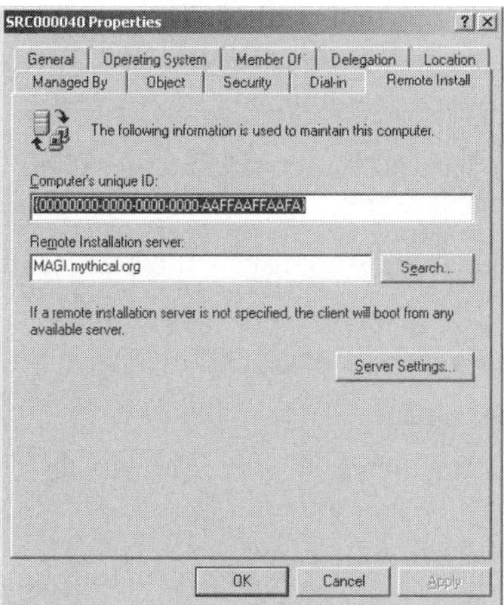

Preparing RIS-Based Installations

The process of preparing for remote installation using RIS has several aspects:

- Preparing the OS image, a process that differs depending on whether you are using RISetup or RIPrep images
- Creating and associating the answer file with an image
- Customizing CIW (if needed)

Using RIS Images

There are two different forms of operating system images supported by RIS for remote installation:

- Distribution files (as copied off the Windows Server 2003 CD or other distribution folder), which are formed into an OS image using RISetup
- A file system image made by using RIPrep, which is based on an installed operating system established as a master (template) installation

Each image created, whether by RISetup or RIPrep, has a corresponding Templates subfolder on the RIS server, and this folder contains a standard answer file called Ristndrd.sif. The Templates folder also houses additional answer files that are associated with the image.

Restricting Access to RIS Images

RIS images are stored on an NTFS partition, and the Everyone group has Full access by default (in Windows Server 2003, the Everyone group means all Authenticated Users). You might want to restrict access to some (or all) of these images, after all, many users might need to install Windows XP, yet fewer will need to install Windows Server 2003. You can control access using security settings available by following these steps:

1. Double-click the RIS server's computer account in Active Directory Users And Computers.
2. In the Remote Install tab, click Advanced Settings to display the Remote Installation Services Properties page.
3. In the Images tab, select the image you want to manage, and then click Properties.
4. Click Permissions on the Image Properties page.
5. Finally, in the actual Properties page for the image, click the Security tab to view and manage current security settings.

Alternately, you can limit the scope of users that can access RIS images (thus limiting the installation options that appear in the CIW installation display) by removing the Everyone group from a specific Templates folder and then providing access to only those security groups that must install that specific RIS image.

Either way, you ensure that users see only images for which they have access and restrict them from trying to install images they shouldn't be using. For example, if Developers should see only Developer images and not IT images, you could handle this by changing the NTFS permission on the appropriate images. Once you set restrictive permissions, RIS shows users only images for which they have access.

Note Although image-based installations can be used for server installations as discussed here, the most common use of RIPrep-based operating system images is for the deployment of network client systems.

OS Images Created by Using RISetup

Using RISetup creates an operating system image by pulling the files from the original Windows Server 2003 CD or from a customized distribution folder containing these files, such as one that has the service pack integrated.

You can further customize the installation by adding files (applications, drivers, etc.) to the distribution share and adding necessary configuration information to the answer file. Just as with an unattended installation performed by Windows Setup (Winnt or Winnt32), associating an answer file with an image enables automation and control of the installation process. This means everything discussed in the previous chapter applies to RIS, with some limitations, of course.

Configuring a RISetup OS Image

To configure a RISetup OS image, follow these steps:

1. To start the Remote Installation Services Setup Wizard, run Remote Installation Services Setup on the Administrative Tools menu or type **risetup** at a command prompt on the RIS server.
2. You are prompted to select one of the following options:
   - *Add A New OS Image To This Remote Installation Server*—This option enables the addition of multiple operating systems (or OS configurations) to be made available as installation options from the RIS server.
   - *Check This Remote Installation Server For Errors*—This option allows you to verify the operations of the RIS server, although it does not verify the integrity of the operating system images you might have previously stored.
3. Select the first option, click Next, and then specify the location of the installation source files (distribution CD or network location) on the Installation Source Files Location page.
4. Click Next, and then specify the name of the folder to which the Windows files will be copied on the RIS server. This is the name for the image in the Windows Installation Image Folder Name dialog box, which by default is WINDOWS. If you are going to have multiple images on a server, you could use names that help you identify the type of image, such as WINSVR-STD, WINSVVR-ENT, and WINXP-PRO.
5. Click Next. The Friendly Description And Help Text page lets you customize the description and help information displayed on the client computer during the installation process.
6. Click Next. If there's an existing OS image (in addition to the default image created when you set up the RIS server), you are asked what you want to do with the existing client installation screens. In most cases, you simply want to leave them alone (and you do this by selecting the Use The Old Client Installation Screens option).

> **Note** The client installation screens are saved as .osc files, and they control what users see when they first connect to the RIS server. These files use the OSC Markup Language (OSCML) and are very similar to standard Hypertext Markup Language (HTML) files. In fact, if you know anything about HTML, you could easily customize these files so that they better suit your needs. Each .osc file is a screen that the users see when connecting to the RIS server, including the Welcome, Logon, Main Menu, Operating System Choice, Client Installation, and Warning screens.

7. Click Next, and then click Finish. The wizard then copies the files and update the RIS server accordingly.

Installed (File-System-Based) Image by RIPrep

The other means of creating an operating system image for RIS is by using the Remote Installation Preparation Wizard to create an image of a preconfigured computer. This image is then stored on the RIS server and is used to install on the remote computers.

The file system image created by RIPrep is essentially the image of an installed and configured system with certain computer-specific information (such as security identifiers, or SIDs) removed. The deleted information is replaced with data specific to the target computer during deployment of the operating system image.

The process of creating a RIPrep image is similar to that of installing any new Windows computer—you install and configure the operating system, applications, and so on. In the case of an installation for RIPrep, the computer you configure is designated as the *master computer* because it is the master configuration for subsequent deployments. After the master computer is customized to meet the requirements for the computers the image will be installed upon, an image of that installation is created.

RIPrep uses answer files in a similar way to the other automated installation methods: the information in the answer files is used to control Setup and configure the computer. The RIPrep image process creates an answer file named Riprep.sif in the Image folder by default.

System Settings Stored in RIPrep Images

A RIPrep image stores the current configuration of a system and includes some desktop and application settings, as shown in Table 6-3.

Table 6-3. Settings Stored in a RIPrep Image

Category	Specific Settings
Local policy	Group Policy Administrative Template
Control Panel	Accessibility, performance, power, sound scheme, startup, and recovery
Internet Explorer	Connection, home page, privacy, security
Optional	Services for Netware, Network Monitoring, Remote Storage
Services	Logon accounts, recovery, startup
Desktop	Folder options, fonts, shortcuts, display configuration
Office	Application configuration (Microsoft Office Word, Microsoft Office Excel) for editing, saving, spelling, and viewing settings

Creating RIPrep OS images from (Select or Enterprise) volume license media is recommended, because it obviates issues with license keys and Windows product activation.

Inside Out

Retail CD not recommended for RIPrep

When a RIPrep image is created from a master installation using a non–volume license medium (such as the retail Windows Server 2003 CD), the Windows product activation (WPA) timer is reset with each RIPrep image. This causes each subsequent installation to require the target computers to complete the product activation process. Installing more than three RIPrep images created from a master installation using non–volume license media will result in the WPA grace period not being reset for subsequent RIPrep images. These WPA contingencies are specific to RIPrep and do not affect RISetup-based operating system images.

Requirements for Creating a RIPrep Image

Before you create a RIPrep-based OS image, you should know about a few constraints. First, there must be a RISetup image for the same operating system (including language and version), for example, that the master computer being used for the RIPrep image is running. The operating system version numbers of the RISetup image and the master installation that RIPrep is imaging must have the same first two numbers (i.e., 5.1).

Because Mini-Setup implements Plug and Play detection upon loading, the target computers need not have identical hardware (they simply must share the same HAL as the master installation computer).

The Plug and Play hardware detection in Mini-Setup (on the target computer) checks the HKEY_LOCAL_MACHINE\SOFTWARE\Microsoft\Windows\CurrentVersion\DevicePath registry key for the default location of device drivers. The default path for devices is the %Windir%\System32\Drivers folder.

The RIPrep.sif answer file can specify alternate locations for device drivers (as well as .inf files, catalogs, and so on) needed to support the device hardware in the target computers. You can do this by adding a device search path in the [Unattended] section using the OemPnPDriversPath parameter. The environment variable %SystemDrive% is automatically attached to the beginning of the folder path specified in the OemPnPDriversPath parameter; thus, the location of the folder containing the drivers must be on the system root partition.

Tip RIPrep creates images only from the system partition on the computer with the master installation. As a result, any special files, drivers, and applications must be located on the system partition to be integrated in the image RIS deploys.

HAL Compatibility and RIPrep Images

The HAL that the master computer uses must be compatible with the HAL that each target computer uses. A common HAL version, for example, is the Advanced Configuration and Power Interface (ACPI) HAL—if your target computers use the ACPI HAL, the master computer that you are creating the image from must also use the ACPI HAL.

Inside Out

Matching HAL versions in RIS images

You can perform an image-based RIS installation with an image created from a master computer if the HALs used by the target and master computers correspond in the following ways:

- Target and master system HALs are identical.
- Target and master systems use the Advanced Programmable Interrupt Controller (APIC) HAL (assuming both systems use either a single-processor or multiprocessor APIC HAL).
- Target and master systems use a non-ACPI HAL (assuming both systems use either a single-processor or multiprocessor non-ACPI HAL).

Note Windows Server 2003 RIS filters the images based on HAL compatibility before presenting them to the user, so there is no possibility of installing the wrong type of HAL.

There are several approaches to discovering the version of the HAL a computer is using. Some network management tools (such as Microsoft Systems Management Server) allow you to run a software inventory, which can tell you which HAL versions various computers are using. Alternately, for systems running a Windows server operating system, you can determine the HAL that is in use by viewing the properties of the Hal.dll file in the %SystemRoot%\System32 folder. In the Version tab, view the original file name—for example, in the case of an ACPI HAL, the file name is a Halacpi.dll.

Creating the Master Installation

You start the process of creating a file system image by installing the operating system on to the computer that will contain the master configuration for this image. Because you are creating an image to be used on multiple (many) target computers, begin by selecting computer system hardware that is representative of the hardware that the target systems will have. As noted previously, the HAL of the master computer must match the HAL of the target computer systems.

Install the operating system onto the master installation computer, and configure the services, applications, and desktop environment to reflect the baseline operating environment that you want the target computers to have. You should thoroughly test this OS configuration, as well as all applications, for proper functionality prior to creating the image for RIS. Again, make sure all the services and applications that will be part of the image are on the system drive.

Inside Out

User profile in master installations

The user profile used in installation and configuration of applications can affect availability or functionality of applications that store settings on a per-user basis. For instance, applications that require Administrator rights to run or configure might not allow the users of the future installations to access needed functionality. Assess the applications used in your master installation for configuration and user profile issues.

Note Remote computers booting to RIS are presented with RIPrep images the same way as images created by using RISetup are—each is simply presented by its friendly description as an installation option.

Using RIPrep to Create an OS Image

When you have configured the operating system on the master computer to meet your requirements, you use the Remote Installation Preparation Wizard (RIPrep.exe) to create the file system image of the master installation. The wizard converts the standing installation on the master computer to a file system image that is stored on the RIS server, making it accessible to remote installation client systems.

RIPrep modifies the SIDs and access control lists (ACLs) to ensure that each RIS installation using that image is unique. During RIPrep image preparation, the SIDs and ACLs are removed prior to image creation. Each computer that image is installed to will run Mini-Setup upon first boot to reassign SIDs, set ACLs, and so on.

Note Because the file system images created by RIPrep contain applications and tools, they are larger than the operating system images created by using RISetup, yet they install more quickly because they lack SIDs and ACLs initially.

The RIPrep.exe file is located in the %SystemRoot%\System32\Reminst folder (and is also copied to *ServerName*\Reminst\Admin\I386). There are two command-line parameters that can be used with RIPrep.exe:

- RIPREP /quiet disables the display of confirmation dialog boxes.
- RIPREP /pnp forces detection of Plug and Play devices during installation.

Caution Running RIPrep changes the SIDs and ACLs of an installation, so don't run RIPrep on a system unless you intend to use it as a distribution image.

Troubleshooting

Recovering from inadvertently running RIPrep or Sysprep

If one of the programs designed to prepare a computer to serve as a master computer for image-style installations is accidentally run, you must take several steps to repair the system. The details of how to recover from this are explained in Microsoft Knowledge Base article 814588. This article explains how to restore SIDs, modify the registry, and run the Recovery Console to return the computer to a functional state.

To create an image from a master installation, run RIPrep at the following location: *ServerName*\Reminst\Admin\I386.

The following are the steps of the RIPrep image creation process:

1. The Welcome page describes what RIPrep will do (converting the master installation to a file system image) and reminds you that the hardware of the target computer need not be identical to the hardware used in the image (but must share the HAL dynamic-link library).
2. You are then prompted for the server name hosting the RIS services (the existing RIS server name is provided by default).
3. The wizard then prompts you for the folder name of where the image will be stored on the RIS server (if it doesn't already exist, it will be created).

Note The RIPrep imaging process creates a folder structure on the distribution share that contains the OS of the master installation.

4. You are then prompted to provide the friendly description and help text (no default values are supplied).
5. The list of services that must be stopped before creating the installation image is displayed. Click Next, and the RIPrep Wizard will stop all of the services in the list.

Tip **Shut down services**
If all required services or programs are not stopped, the Programs Or Services Are Running dialog box is displayed, listing the processes that are still operational and directing you to use the Computer Management console (in the Services and Applications\Services nodes) to shut down the remaining services.

6. The values selected for the remote installation server, folder name, friendly description, and help text are displayed, giving you a chance to review the settings before clicking Next to confirm the selections.

7 The Completing The Remote Installation Preparation Wizard page is displayed. Once you continue, the RIPrep Wizard creates the installation image and copies it to the RIS server, then shuts down the master installation computer. During this process, the wizard performs the following steps:

- Verifies the Windows version
- Analyzes partitions
- Copies partition information
- Copies files to the server
- Copies and updates registry information
- Shuts down the computer

Upon reboot, the master installation computer runs the Mini-Setup program (like the future target computers that receive this installation image). This reassigns security-related information that was stripped off by RIPrep and enables normal operations. You will be prompted to do the following:

- Accept the license agreement
- Reenter the product key (only for a retail or Open License CD)
- Choose the keyboard and localization
- Enter the user name and organization
- Select a time zone—be sure to choose the correct one
- Determine whether typical or custom network settings should be used
- Join a workgroup or a domain

Mini-Setup goes a bit faster than normal Setup because it doesn't need to check Plug and Play hardware components, but it still takes a bit of time. As Figure 6-3 shows, the master image is stored in a separate directory from the other images you've created—and if you gave the image a clear name, such as MasterIMG, it is very easy to distinguish from any other images.

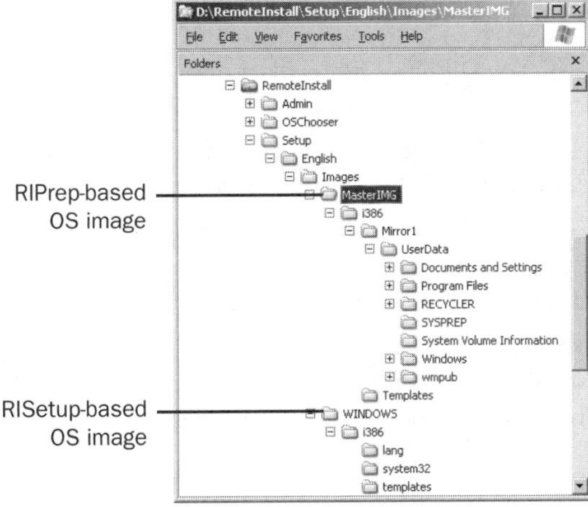

Figure 6-3. The distribution folder structure for a RIPrep image.

Inside Out

Use RISetup to create a master installation template

Using a RIS installation is recommended for creating the master installation. Because you have to create the master installation image once, and you want to be able to easily update it (say, upon the release of a service pack or critical security patch), if you create an automated RISetup installation, you can update it and regenerate the master installation quickly.

Adding "Flat" or "CD-ROM" Images to RIS

RIPrep is very useful in that it can create complete system images, but as with unattended installations, you can also use flat or CD-ROM images that include integrated service packs. All you must do is place an I386 or Intel Architecture 64 (IA-64) folder for whichever operating system you want to install on the RIS server, and then RIS clients can use that flat image. As discussed in Chapter 5, you can integrate service packs into this distribution folder and configure optional answer files to apply hot fixes, security updates, drivers, and programs to run (as you can with any RIS image).

First, you might be wondering why you would want to do this. Well, primarily because it allows you to centralize. You can store all your installation files and scripts on one server, and if you already have images with integrated service packs and scripts, why not put them on the RIS server to make the entire process easier to manage? Are you wondering how this would work? Here's what you do:

1. First, copy the I386 folder from the operating system CD-ROM to the RIS server. For example, in Windows XP Professional, you might copy the I386 folder from the CD-ROM to the C:\WINXPPRO folder on the RIS server.
2. Next, extract the service pack into a temporary folder on the RIS server, such as C:\WinXPSP1.
3. Run the update tool in the service pack's I386\Update folder. Following the example, you would change to the C:\WinXPSP1\I386\Update directory, and then type **update –s:C:\WINXPPRO\I386.**
4. Then you must tell the RIS server about the image you want to use. Start Active Directory Users and Computers by clicking Start, pointing to Programs or All Programs, clicking Administrative Tools, and selecting Active Directory Users And Computers.
5. Double-click the folder that contains the computer account. Typically, this is the Computers OU. Then double-click the Computer account name to display the properties page for the computer.
6. In the Remote Install tab (see the screen on the following page), click Advanced Settings to display the Remote Installation Services Properties page.

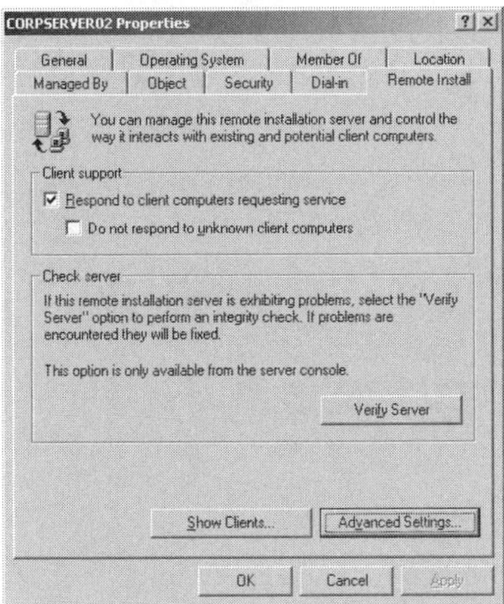

7 The Images tab contains a list of current images that are on the RIS server (see the following screen). Click Add so that you can tell RIS about the image you want to use.

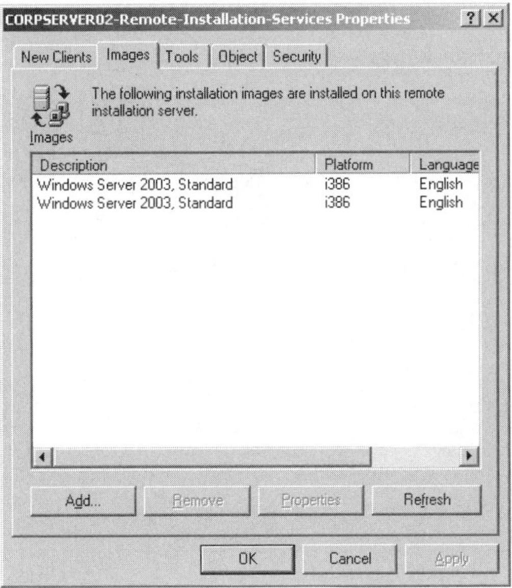

8 You can now choose to associate a new answer file with an existing image or add a new installation image. Choose Add A New Installation Image (as shown in the screen on the following page), and click Next. This starts the Remote Installation Services Setup Wizard.

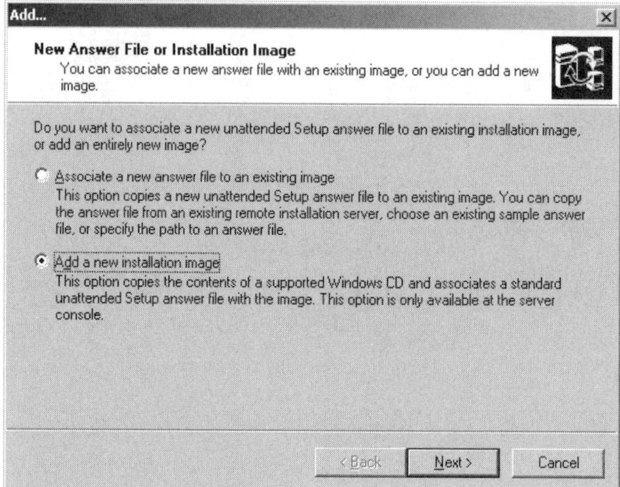

9 Specify where the image is located (as shown in the following screen). In the example, this would be C:\WINXPPRO folder.

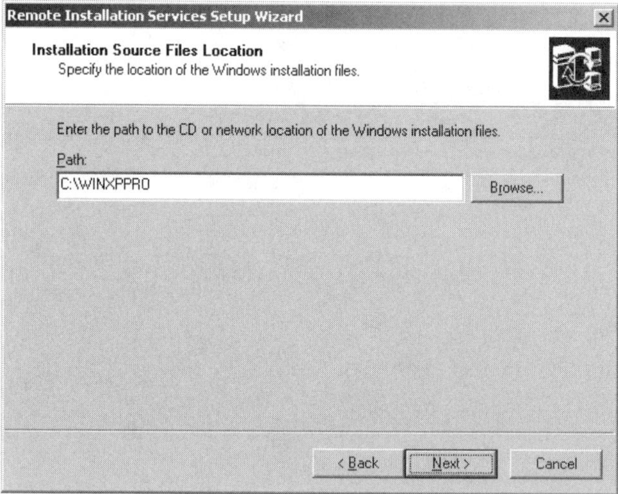

10 Click Next, and then enter the name of the folder to which the files will be copied within RIS (as shown in the screen on the following page). In the example, I called it WINXPSP1, which means that the I386 files will be stored on the remote installation folder using this name, and the path to the actual image would be RemoteInstall\Setup\English\Images\WINXPSP1.

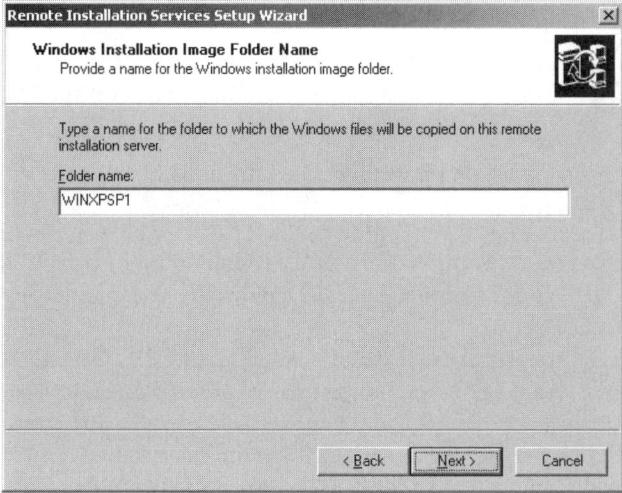

11 Click Next, and then enter the friendly name and help text for this image. Click Next again, and you'll be asked what you want to do with the previous client installation screens. The client installation screens are the .osc files that control what the user sees when first connecting to the RIS server. In most cases, you can leave these files as they are, so select Use The Old Client Installation Screens (as in the screen shown here).

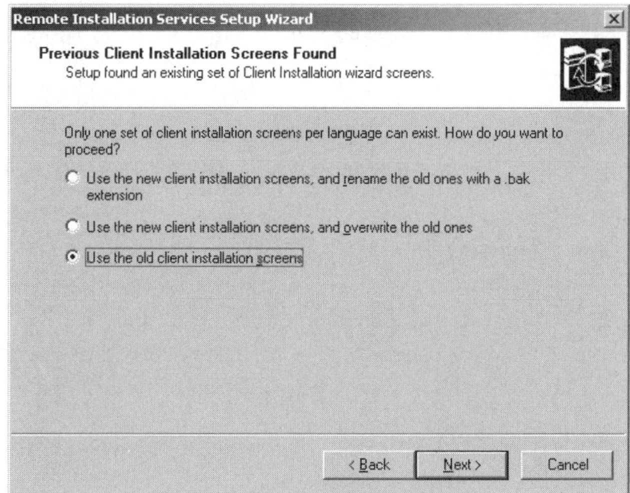

12 Click Next, and then click Finish to complete the image creation process. You'll then see the image on the list of available images, and clients will be able to use it.

RIS Answer Files

RIS answer files are highly similar to Unattend.txt files, with just a few additional or changed entries. During the RIS image creation processes, default answer files are created for each OS image:

- RISetup creates a default answer file called Ristndrd.sif.
- RIPrep creates its own answer file named Riprep.sif by default.

The easiest way to create an optional answer file (Remboot.sif by default) for RIS is by using the Setup Manager Wizard (Setupmgr.exe in Deploy.cab located in the Support\Tools folder on your product CD).

For more information about using Setup Manager to create answer files, see Chapter 5.

The internal structure of the *.sif files is much like the Unattend.txt answer files, using many of the same sections and entries to configure remote installation, but with different default entries and values. By default, a RIS answer file for either RISetup or RIPrep installations contains the [SetupData], [RemoteInstall], [OSChooser], and [SetupMgr] additional sections, and the [Data] section has additional entries such as OriSrc=\\%SERVERNAME%\RemInst\%INSTALLPATH%.

The Ristndrd.sif File

The following text shows the content of a Ristndrd.sif file created by RISetup.

```
[Data]
floppyless = "1"
msdosinitiated = "1"
OriSrc = "\\%SERVERNAME%\RemInst\%INSTALLPATH%\%MACHINETYPE%"
OriTyp = "4"
LocalSourceOnCD = 1
DisableAdminAccountOnDomainJoin = 1

[SetupData]
OsLoadOptions = "/noguiboot /fastdetect"
SetupSourceDevice = "\Device\LanmanRedirector\%SERVERNAME%\RemInst\%INSTALLPATH%"

[Unattended]
OemPreinstall = no
FileSystem = LeaveAlone
ExtendOEMPartition = 0
TargetPath = \WINDOWS
OemSkipEula = yes
InstallFilesPath = "\\%SERVERNAME%\RemInst\%INSTALLPATH%\%MACHINETYPE%"
LegacyNIC = 1
```

```
[UserData]
FullName = "%USERFIRSTNAME% %USERLASTNAME%"
OrgName = "%ORGNAME%"
ComputerName = %MACHINENAME%

[GuiUnattended]
OemSkipWelcome = 1
OemSkipRegional = 1
TimeZone = %TIMEZONE%
AdminPassword = "*"

[LicenseFilePrintData]
AutoMode = PerSeat

[Display]
BitsPerPel = 16
XResolution = 800
YResolution = 600
VRefresh = 60

[Networking]

[NetServices]
MS_Server=params.MS_PSched

[Identification]
JoinDomain = %MACHINEDOMAIN%
DoOldStyleDomainJoin = Yes

[RemoteInstall]
Repartition = Yes
UseWholeDisk = Yes

[OSChooser]
Description ="Windows Server 2003, Standard"
Help ="Automatically installs Windows Server 2003, Standard without prompting the
user for input."
LaunchFile = "%INSTALLPATH%\%MACHINETYPE%\templates\startrom.com"
ImageType =Flat
Version="5.2 (0)"
```

The RIPrep.sif file

The RIPrep installation information is written to a Riprep.sif file in the Templates subfolder. The following text is a sample Riprep.sif file:

```
[Data]
floppyless = "1"
msdosinitiated = "1"
OriSrc = "\\%SERVERNAME%\RemInst\%INSTALLPATH%\%MACHINETYPE%"
OriTyp = "4"
LocalSourceOnCD = 1
DisableAdminAccountOnDomainJoin = 1
```

```
[SetupData]
OsLoadOptions = "/noguiboot /fastdetect"
SetupSourceDevice ="\Device\LanmanRedirector\%SERVERNAME%\RemInst\%INSTALLPATH%"
SysPrepDevice="\Device\LanmanRedirector\%SERVERNAME%\RemInst\%SYSPREPPATH%"
SysPrepDriversDevice="\Device\LanmanRedirector\%SERVERNAME%\RemInst\
%SYSPREPDRIVERS%"

[Unattended]
OemPreinstall = no
FileSystem = LeaveAlone
ExtendOEMPartition = 0
TargetPath = \WINDOWS
OemSkipEula = yes
InstallFilesPath = "\\%SERVERNAME%\RemInst\%INSTALLPATH%\%MACHINETYPE%"
LegacyNIC = 1

[UserData]
FullName = "%USERFIRSTNAME% %USERLASTNAME%"
OrgName = "%ORGNAME%"
ComputerName ="%MACHINENAME%"

[GuiUnattended]
OemSkipWelcome = 1
OemSkipRegional = 1
TimeZone = %TIMEZONE%
AdminPassword = "*"

[LicenseFilePrintData]
AutoMode = PerSeat

[Display]
BitsPerPel = 16
XResolution = 800
YResolution = 600
VRefresh = 60

[Networking]

[NetServices]
MS_Server=params.MS_PSched

[Identification]
JoinDomain = %MACHINEDOMAIN%
DoOldStyleDomainJoin = Yes

[RemoteInstall]
Repartition = Yes
UseWholeDisk = Yes
```

```
[OSChooser]
Description ="W2K3 Server MASTER INSTALLATION"
Help ="This is configured for our base server deployment"
LaunchFile ="%INSTALLPATH%\%MACHINETYPE%\templates\startrom.com"
ImageType =SYSPREP
Version="5.2 (3790)"
SysPrepSystemRoot="Mirror1\UserData\W2K3"
HalName=hal.dll
ProductType=1
```

The Remboot.sif File

The following text displays the sections and entries used in the Remboot.sif file that are different or additional to those also used in common with the Unattend.txt file.

```
[Data]
    MsDosInitiated="1"
    floppyless="1"
    OriSrc="\\%SERVERNAME%\RemInst\%INSTALLPATH%"
    OriTyp="4"
    LocalSourceOnCD=1

[SetupData]
    OsLoadOptions="/noguiboot /fastdetect"

SetupSourceDevice="\Device\LanmanRedirector\%SERVERNAME%\RemInst\%INSTALLPATH%"

[Unattended]
    OemPreinstall=No
    FileSystem=LeaveAlone
    NtUpgrade=No
    OverwriteOemFilesOnUpgrade=No


[Identification]
    JoinDomain=%MACHINEDOMAIN%
    DoOldStyleDomainJoin=Yes

[Networking]
    ProcessPageSections=Yes


[RemoteInstall]
    Repartition=Yes

[OSChooser]
    Description="Windows Professional - Standard Installation"
    Help="This will install Windows Professional in a standard configuration."
    LaunchFile="%INSTALLPATH%\%MACHINETYPE%\templates\startrom.com"
    ImageType=Flat
```

Caution For security reasons, you should always encrypt the administrator passwords that you use in answer files. If you don't, they are stored in the file as plaintext, which is a security risk that many administrators don't want to take.

Associating an Answer File with a RIS Image

To automate a RIS installation, you must associate an answer file with the specific operating system image.

To associate a remote boot .sif file with a RIS installation image, follow these steps:

1. Locate the server running RIS in Active Directory Users and Computers.
2. Double-click the computer account entry, then click Advanced Settings in the Remote Install tab.
3. In the Images tab of the Advanced Settings dialog box, click Add.
4. Select Associate A New Answer File To An Existing Image, then click Next.
5. Specify the source of the new answer file (Windows Image Sample Files, Another Remote Installation Server, or An Alternate Location), and then click Next.
6. Select Installation Image To Associate The Answer File With, then click Next.
7. Select the answer file to use, and click Next. If the file name already exists, you have the option to set a new name for the answer file.
8. Provide any changes to the Friendly Description And Help Text option, click Next, and then click Finish.

The answer file you selected is then copied to the Templates directory of the designated installation image and will be used for any subsequent remote installations using that image.

Configuring the CIW

The Client Installation Wizard (CIW) is the first user interface (UI) displayed on the target computer during RIS-based installation. The CIW, also called OSChooser, is a text-based tool that guides the user through the initial steps of the installation process. Administrators can configure the CIW to provide a customized list of available operating systems.

When a client connects to the RIS server, the service sends a startup boot file to the target computer (by default, Startrom.com stored in the RemoteInstall\OsChooser\I386 folder). This startup boot file prompts you to press the F12 key. The RIS server then downloads the CIW by TFTP to the target computer. There is another startup boot file (called Startrom.n12, which can be renamed to Startrom.com if you want to use it) that does not require the F12 key to be pressed, allowing a fully automated installation.

The default CIW page displays are HTML-based *.osc files, which are put on the RIS server when you run RISetup.exe the first time. Example files are also included to show you how to modify the CIW information, displays, user logon, and setup options.

Following are tips for designing CIW pages:

- One of the pages must contain the <meta server action=dnreset> HTML tag.
- At a minimum, the CIW must contain the Welcome, Logon, and Summary pages.
- Because the user has no input with a fully automated installation, the CIW used with one should contain a minimum of setup-related data. This usually means fewer pages are needed for that CIW.

Using RIS for Automated Installations

For remote installations using RIS to work, conditions on the network (RIS server, DNS, DHCP, TFTP) and the remote target computer must support RIS-based installations. In addition to the supporting network services discussed previously, there are some server requirements. To perform an automated installation, there must be an accessible and correctly configured RIS server and one or more established OS images. Also, users performing installations must have rights to create computer accounts in the domain.

Likewise, there are requirements for the client systems. The target machine must meet certain hardware requirements to support the remote operation capabilities used by RIS. Client computers must support remote booting using PXE version 1 ROM or have one of the network cards supported by Microsoft PXE emulation software (a NIC that is supported by the RIBF). If the client has PXE-based ROM BIOS, the NIC must be set as the primary boot device. When using the RIS boot floppy disk, the floppy disk should be set as the first boot device.

Installing Windows Using RIS

A Windows OS installation by RIS simplifies deployment of remote systems. The RIS installation process is straightforward, as reflected in the following steps:

1. The process of remote installation begins when the target computer is booted from a floppy disk (or PXE-enabled ROM BIOS). The target system boots using either PXE boot ROM or RIS boot disk, detects the NIC, loads the NIC drivers, and then displays the MAC address of the network adapter.
2. The system then contacts a DHCP server (using DHCP broadcast) and gets an IP address and a referral to a RIS server. If the DHCP server and the RIS server are not the same machine, the client contacts the RIS server. If they are the same computer, the next step is done automatically.
3. The RIS server contacts Active Directory to determine whether the client is a known (prestaged) client and obtains the target computer's UUID. Otherwise, the UUID is obtained from the PXE-enabled NIC or is autogenerated based on the MAC address of the NIC.

4 The target computer then loads TFTP to copy the CIW to the client computer. If the default Startrom.com is used, CIW will prompt a user to press F12 to start the network service supporting remote installation, as follows:

```
Screen display:
Microsoft Windows Remote Installation Boot Floppy
<copyright notice>
<Network card information>
Node: <#>
DHCP...
TFTP.......................
Press F12 for network service boot
```

Caution If you have configured the RIS server to provide a fully automated installation by renaming the copy of Startrom.n12 in the RemoteInstall\OsChooser\I386 folder to Startrom.com, the prompt to press F12 is bypassed. Be sure to make a backup of the original Startrom.com before replacing it. When you are performing RIS installations, you must be very quick on the draw. The prompt to press F12 for a network service boot has a very, very short timeout of about three seconds. If you do not press the F12 key quickly enough after startup, the following error is displayed:

Exiting remote installation boot floppy. Please remove the floppy disk and reboot the workstation.

This error message seems to imply that if you remove the floppy and reboot that this will accomplish something useful—as opposed to merely failing to boot because the system has no OS on it, which is what is likely to happen.

At this point, you have to reboot the computer—if you want to continue performing the remote installation, leave in the floppy disk, and press the F12 key . . . *quickly*. Although you can work around it, it is far more convenient to rename Startrom.n12 (in the RemoteInstall\OsChooser\I386 folder) as Startrom.com and have RIS remote boot bypass F12.

5 Pressing the F12 key (if you do it quickly enough) invokes the Client Installation Wizard Welcome page and tells you the logon credentials required to use the wizard, namely, a domain name and a user name and password combination that is valid for the domain and has the permission to add computers to the domain. To continue with the installation, press Enter, and the Logon page is displayed.

6 The Logon page requires you to supply the user name, password, and domain for a valid user account with the rights to perform the remote installation. The computer name of the RIS server that the target computer is connected to is also displayed. When you press Enter, the main menu of the CIW is displayed.

7 If you have enabled user-configurable options, such as custom installation, a list of available options (Automatic Setup, Custom Setup) is displayed. Select the desired installation option, and press Enter.

8 A list of available operating system installation options is displayed next. This list can include images created by using either RIPrep, RISetup, or both. Custom answer files (such as Remboot.sif) might be associated with these images to control the installation and configuration of the installed operating system. Select the operating system you want to install, and press Enter.

9 The Warning page displays this caution: "All data on the hard drive will be deleted!" This is your reminder that the partitions on the (first) hard disk will be deleted and the drive with be formatted with NTFS. Press Esc to cancel or Enter to continue.

10 The CIW displays the Installation Information page, showing the settings for the computer account and GUID. The defaults for these settings are as follows:

- Computer account name is usually generated based on the settings on the RIS server, commonly using some derivation of the user name with an incrementing number.
- GUID is the node ID either obtained from the BIOS or generated by prefixing a string of 20 zeros ("0") to the front of the network card's MAC address. If the computer account is prestaged, the existing UUID from the computer account in Active Directory is used.
- The computer name is the name of the server providing the remote installation services and supporting this computer.

If you want to change any of this information, you can do so, then press Enter to begin the Windows Setup portion of the remote installation.

11 The CIW ends, and the Windows Setup program launches, displaying standard setup messages, and then automatically formatting the hard disk as a single partition. Windows Setup then copies files to the hard disk drive on the target computer and then reboots the target computer. At this point, the process diverges depending upon whether you are installing an operating system image from RISetup or RIPrep:

- If installing from a RISetup image, Windows Setup switches to GUI-mode setup at the Installing Windows portion. Setup continues, using the information specified by the .sif answer files and prompting you for configuration data that was left unspecified.
- If installing from a RIPrep image, the Mini-Setup is performed, and the computer is rebooted again, this time into a fully functional Windows Server 2003 installation with the configuration settings reflecting the master installation on which the RIPrep OS image is based.

Troubleshooting

This is supposed to be an automated installation, but I'm being asked questions

If information specified in the .sif file is incorrect and Setup encounters an error, Setup will prompt you to provide correct data. After correcting the error condition, Setup will continue using the .sif file.

Troubleshooting

I get a message saying, "No reply from a server"

If no RIS server is available on the network, you will get the error message "No reply from a server" after DHCP is displayed on the screen. Verify that the RIS server is operating correctly and that it has been configured to respond to this client; pay particular attention to DHCP issues with multihomed servers. Once DHCP and RIS configuration issues are resolved, reboot the target computer and retry the RIS installation.

If the RIS server is overburdened, it might not reply, as well. Each RIS server can handle only a limited number of simultaneous client installations. The optimal number is between 70 and 75, depending on the current activity. In a large enterprise where you might deploy hundreds of computers at the same time, you can have multiple RIS servers. You could then load balance requests to these servers using a RIS referral server, or you could simply configure all RIS servers to respond to all RIS clients (which undoes the added security you gain from prestaging computers).

Also, remember that if you've selected the Do Not Respond To Unknown Clients option, you will be able to install only computers that have been prestaged, as discussed in the section entitled "Prestaging Clients in Active Directory" earlier in this chapter.

More RIS Customization Tips

So far, we've covered just about everything you must know to deploy and manage RIS. You've learned how to install and configure RIS servers, how to create images and then optimize them with service packs, how to associate answer files with RIS images, and how to install clients using RIS. Before you head off and start using RIS, here are a few more tips and tricks that you should know about.

Using OEM for Hot Fixes, Security Updates, Drivers, and More

Everything you learned in Chapter 5 about using OEM folders works with RIS. After you associate a properly configured answer file with an image, you can put hot fixes and security updates along with a Cmdlines.txt file in the OEM directory. You can include drivers in driver folders and perform other preinstallation tasks as well. The catch is that RIS doesn't look for an I386\$OEM$ or IA64\$OEM$ folder. RIS looks for a OEM folder at the same level as the I386/IA64 folder. This means you must create the folder at RemoteInstall\Setup\English\Images*ImageName*\$OEM$, where *ImageName* is the name of the image folder.

After you update the folder structure of the RIS server, you should stop and then start the Remote Installation (BINLSVC) service on the RIS server after copying any necessary files into the distribution folder. To do this, log on locally or remotely to the RIS server; you can do this from a command prompt by typing

```
net stop "remote installation"
net start "remote installation"
```

Customizing the Client Installation Pages

When installation is initialized on a client, the pages shown are set by the client wizard. Each page is created as an .osc file that controls what the user sees during each stage of the installation process. There are Welcome, Logon, Main Menu, Operating System Choice, Client Installation, and Warning pages.

The .osc files are created using OSCML—a markup language very similar to plain old HTML. In fact, if you know anything about HTML, you could easily customize these files so that they better suit your needs. If you want to try this, remember that you can have only one set of client installation pages per language variant per RIS server. For the English language, the files are stored in the RemoteInstall\OsChooser\English folder, and you can make edits to these files using any standard text editor, such as Notepad.

The files you'll want to consider modifying include the following:

- **Welcome.osc** The Welcome page that is shown when the client wizard starts
- **Login.osc** The login page used to log in to the Active Directory domain
- **Oschoice.osc** The Operating System Choice page that lets you choose an OS image
- **Warning.osc** A message that warns the user that the hard disk on the computer running the client is about to be erased
- **Install.osc** The installation information page that shows the computer name, GUID, and RIS server that will be used

During the client installation, the primary pages are navigated as follows: You start on the Welcome page, continue to Login, then Oschoice, then Warning, and finally Install. You might see a few other pages, but the preceding ones are the important ones that you must examine and work with to customize the client installation.

Using Unsigned NIC Drivers

Sometimes you must use unsigned NIC drivers for a computer. If you put these drivers in a OEM\$1\Drivers\Network folder and set OemPnPDriversPath to include this path in the Ristndrd.sif script, everything should be hunky-dory, right? Well, not really. If the drivers that you want to use are unsigned, the client wizard will get to the network loading stage and then report that the network server doesn't support booting *XYZ* operating system and cannot continue. To work around this problem, you must update the [Unattended] section of the Ristndrd.sif file to include the following:

```
DriverSigningPolicy = Ignore
```

Remember, putting the driver in this folder copies it to the I386/IA64 folder on the target computer. You might need to experiment a bit to determine which .inf and .sys files the driver should use.

As discussed previously, after you update the folder structure of the RIS server, you should stop and then start the Remote Installation (BINLSVC) service on the RIS server after copying any necessary files into the distribution folder. To do this, log on locally or remotely to the RIS server; you can do this from a command prompt by typing the following:

```
net stop "remote installation"
net start "remote installation"
```

Working with Sysprep

Although Sysprep has been mentioned several times in this and the previous chapters, specific instructions on its use have not yet been provided. Primarily, this is because you really should understand all the built-in options available to you before you work with Sysprep. By using Sysprep, you can create prototype computers that are fully configured and then create images of these computers so that you can quickly deploy many computers at once. But Sysprep is special because it creates only an image; it doesn't handle the remote operating system installation. Thus, the use of Sysprep assumes that you have disk-imaging software, such as Norton Ghost from Symantec or Drive Image from PowerQuest, that can handle the remote OS installation.

Understanding Sysprep

Essentially, you use Sysprep to make a "usable" clone of the prototype computer's hard disk drive. If you've worked with other cloning tools, you can probably guess why there are quotes around usable. Basically, it is because not all cloning tools are created equal. Some cloning tools create exact copies of the prototype computer, which includes the computer's SIDs. Unfortunately, these identifiers are supposed to be unique, and copying the drives with these intact means the network sees them as two identical drives.

The creators of imaging software, such as Norton Ghost and Drive Image, worked around this by scrambling the SIDs. The problem is that Microsoft won't support computers with scrambled SIDs.

A "usable" clone has the unique SIDs removed, not just scrambled. The way you remove the SIDs is to use Sysprep to prepare the system by scrubbing or stripping them.

The primary advantage of using Sysprep-created disk images is speed. Sysprep is typically the fastest way to deploy a new computer, but it does have limitations. Before you set out to use Sysprep, keep these limitations in mind:

- Sysprep-prepared images always overwrite the existing partition, which means no operating system upgrade is possible.
- Sysprep-prepared images must share a common HAL, meaning you cannot mix ACPI systems with non-ACPI systems or uniprocessor systems with multiprocessor systems.

- Sysprep doesn't support image-based deployment of Active Directory–dependent applications. Because of this, you can't image a domain controller, for example, using Sysprep. You could, however, script the domain controller promotion (Dcpromo) process into the disk image using the answer files.
- Sysprep doesn't support imaging of servers that run certificate services or that are part of a cluster.
- Sysprep doesn't support NTFS file/folder permissions set in the master installation and doesn't work with files that are encrypted by EFS.

Other than these limitations, Sysprep can be used to prepare for imaging just about any computer running Windows 2000 or later. Sysprep requires two programs to work, Sysprep.exe and Setupcl.exe, and an answer file. Although Sysprep does not support user interaction during setup, Sysprep can be customized by an answer file, either Sysprep.inf or Winbom.ini. Sysprep.inf is used to automate the Mini-Setup portion of the installation; that is, the portion of setup after the initial reboot when normally the user would be prompted for configuration information. Winbom.ini file is a manually created answer file used to control Sysprep running in Factory mode. When used, these files along with Sysprep.exe and Setupcl.exe must be present in the %SystemDrive% folder on the destination computer.

Using Sysprep to Clone a Computer

The steps for using Sysprep are as follows:

1. Sysprep.exe and Setupcl.exe are not installed by default, but rather have to be extracted from the Deploy.cab file in the Support\Tools directory on the distribution CD. To do this, access the Support\Tools directory on the CD-ROM, and double-click Deploy.cab. Double-click Sysprep.exe, and then extract it when prompted. Next, double-click Setupcl.exe, and, again, extract it when prompted.
2. Log on as the administrator, then install and configure the Windows operating system on the prototype computer. Install and configure any applications you want to deploy to all systems using this image. The applications must be on the same drive as the Windows operating system.

Tip **Plan Sysprep-created images, partitions, and configurations carefully**

Because Sysprep-created images cannot be installed on a disk partition smaller than the one on which the image was created, plan the primary partition size carefully. Any computers that use this image will be partitioned to the same size as the prototype computer's partition. You can use the ExtendOemPartition parameter in the [Unattended] section of the Sysprep.inf answer file to extend the partition to fill the hard disk.

Remember, you can configure the prototype computer exactly as you want it. You can set simple Start menu and Classic Control Panel. You can ensure that folder options are set to display details and use single-click to open an item. And the list goes on and on.

3. On the prototype computer, copy Sysprep.exe and Setupcl.exe to a directory named Sysprep on whichever drive the operating system is on, such as C:\Sysprep.
4. To ensure the environment settings are available to all users of the computer, you must copy the Administrator profile to the Default Users profile. This way, anyone who logs on to the cloned computer uses those settings.
5. Reboot the prototype one last time, and ensure everything is working and configured correctly. You will not be able to reboot the system once you run Sysprep.
6. Run Sysprep to remove the SIDs from the system. When Sysprep finishes, it shuts down the system.
7. Don't boot the computer from the hard disk drive. Boot from a floppy disk (probably one that has DOS or was created by the disk-imaging software), and then run the disk-imaging software. If you let the computer boot to the disk drive, it realizes it doesn't have SIDs, and it will generate them—just as any new clone computers do. At that point, you'll have to run Sysprep again, because you ran it in the first place to remove the SIDs.

> **Caution** After you finish the disk imaging and have confirmed it, you can reboot the prototype computer. When you do, it will run through Mini-Setup before it can be used again.

8. Use a floppy disk to boot the new computer, that is, the computer on which you want to place the newly created disk image, and then connect to the network share containing the drive image.
9. Restart the new computer to initiate Mini-Setup. As the new computer boots, it recognizes that it doesn't have any SIDs. It then generates new ones, a process that requires the computer to rejoin the domain, obtain a product key (if applicable), and so on.

> **Note** Mini-Setup detects any additional Plug and Play devices and hides any devices that are different or missing. You can override this by using the –Pnp option, as discussed later, which tells Setup to perform a full Plug and Play device detection. You can also provide an answer file to modify the computer's configuration without having to re-create the disk image.

Several of the steps in this procedure are fairly complex.The following sections examine them more closely.

Copying the Administrator Profile

Okay, you logged on as the administrator and optimized the configuration, which is a good thing. Now you want the configuration settings to be available to other users, and to do this, you must copy the Administrator profile. The problem is you can't copy the Administrator profile while logged on as the administrator. Resolve this problem by creating a new local user on the computer and then logging on as this user so that you can copy the profile.

To create a new user account on the prototype computer, follow these steps:

1. In Control Panel, double-click Computer Management, and then double-click the Local Users And Groups node.
2. Right-click Users, and select New User.
3. In the New User dialog box, type a name for the new user account (as shown in the following screen).

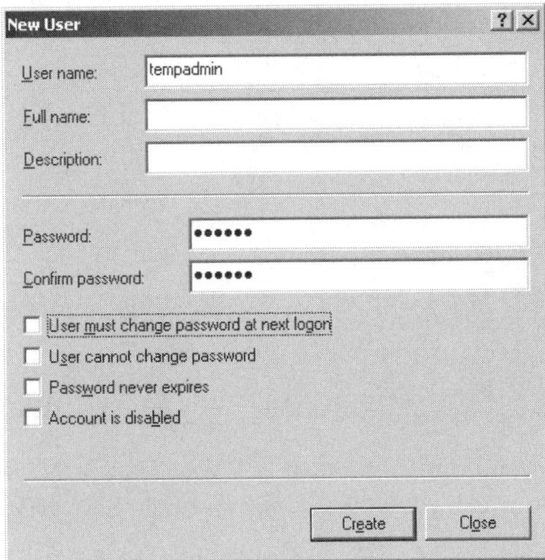

4. Enter and then confirm a password.
5. Clear the User Must Change Password At Next Logon option.
6. Click Create, and then click Close. The new user account is created.
7. In Computer Management, double-click the new user account to display the new user's Properties page.
8. In the Member Of tab of the user's Properties page, click Add.
9. Type **Administrators**, and then click OK twice.

To log on as the new user and copy the profile, follow these steps:

1. Log off as the administrator, then log on as the new user. Make sure you log on to the local computer and not the domain.
2. If the Default User profile is hidden, you must tell the Windows operating system to show hidden files. Also, you can't copy the profile files directly—you must use the System tool.
3. In Control Panel, double-click Folder Options or select Tools, and click Folder Options in Microsoft Windows Explorer.
4. Click Show Hidden Files And Folders, and then click OK.
5. In Control Panel, double-click System. Select the Advanced tab.

6 In the User Profiles panel of the Advanced tab, click Settings. This displays the User Profiles dialog box (as shown in the following screen).

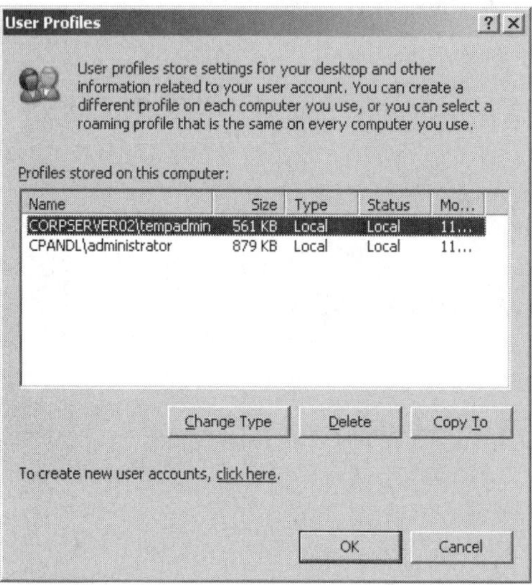

7 Select the *MachineName*\Administrator profile, where *MachineName* is the name of the local computer with which you are working. It should have a Type of Local.

8 Click Copy To, which displays the Copy To dialog box (as shown in the following screen).

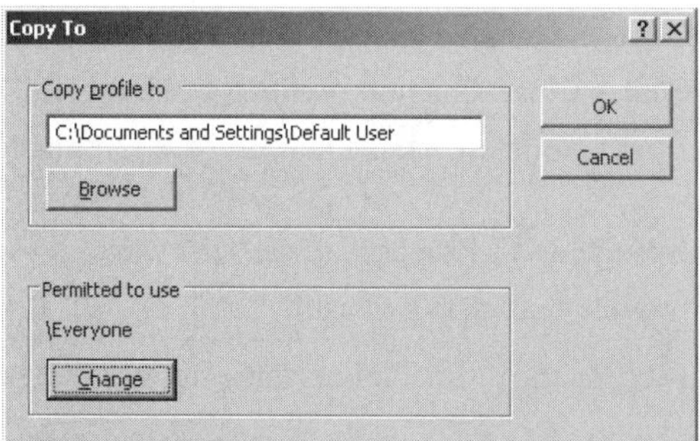

9 Under Permitted To Use, click Change. You'll see a list of all available groups on the computer, including the special group Everyone. Type **Everyone**, and click OK. Note that if Locations is set to the domain, you must change the location to the local computer. Click Locations, and then select the local computer as the search location.

10 Copy the profile to the Documents and Settings\Default User folder. To do this, either type in the full path, including the drive letter for this folder, or use the Browse button to navigate to this folder. Then click OK, and the profile is copied.

Running Sysprep

Sysprep is run from a command line and accepts quite a few parameter options. Usually when you run the command, you type the following:

```
sysprep -quiet -reseal
```

The options used here specify that confirmation dialog boxes should be shown (–Quiet) and that the SIDs that were stripped should be reset after running Factory.exe (–Reseal). In some cases, you might want to consider adding –Pnp and –Mini, such as this:

```
sysprep -quiet -reseal -pnp -mini
```

These additional options tell the cloned computer to detect its Plug and Play devices on the first boot and to run Mini-Setup. Use the options together to ensure you get what you want to happen—which is that you can copy a computer with one set of hardware and get its clone to work on a computer with very different hardware.

Part 3

Windows Server 2003 Upgrades and Migrations

Chapter 7

Preparing for Upgrades and Migration

Moving your existing network servers to Microsoft Windows Server 2003 is a significant step and requires due consideration of a somewhat complicated question—to upgrade or to migrate? A first step in this process is perhaps determining whether each server *can* be upgraded (i.e., does it meet the minimum requirements?). Once you determine that it does meet the minimum requirements, you must consider whether you want to upgrade or migrate it.

To distinguish between the use of the terms *upgrading* and *migrating* as used in this chapter:

- Upgrading involves installing Windows Server 2003 over the top of an existing Microsoft Windows server installation, maintaining all configuration settings. When you upgrade a server to Windows Server 2003, you maintain all of the existing information in place. Most applications and services operate just as they did before the upgrade, although a few, Microsoft Internet Information Services (IIS) among them, are somewhat different.
- Migrating involves creating a new installation of Windows Server 2003 and transferring the domain and user settings from another Windows server operating system (Microsoft Windows NT 4, Microsoft Windows 2000, or Windows Server 2003). During a migration, a new installation of Windows Server 2003 is done, most often on a new machine. Once the operating system is installed, information is moved from the existing server to the new one using migration tools. You can use tools from Microsoft or a number of third-party vendors such as Aelita and NetPro.

The amount of effort involved in the move to Windows Server 2003 largely depends on whether you are currently using Windows NT or Windows 2000. For example, consider one of the most significant features in Windows Server 2003, the Active Directory directory service.

- **Windows NT 4** The change in network management that the move from Windows NT domains to Active Directory entails presents a set of architectural and operational questions for both Information Technology (IT) and business management. Implementing Active Directory requires defining and creating a Domain Name System (DNS) namespace and an Active Directory forest and domain structure. Security, user rights, network administration, Group Policy, and so on are handled by Active Directory, so a large number of disparate aspects of the network and business must be taken into account in the design process—not a trivial task.
- **Microsoft Windows 2000 Server** Moving from Windows 2000 Server to Windows Server 2003, on the other hand, requires far less planning and administrative effort, because the DNS design and Active Directory namespace are already done. Although there are some new features and management changes, the changes to Active Directory between Windows 2000 and Windows Server 2003 are nominal, especially when compared to the switch from Windows NT domains to Active Directory.

The same is true to a great extent throughout the operating system—the change between Windows NT 4 and Windows Server 2003 is substantial, while the difference when moving from Windows 2000 to Windows Server 2003 is much less so.

Whether you can upgrade an existing server to Windows Server 2003 depends on hardware compatibility, available disk space, and adequate hardware resources (central processing unit [CPU], random access memory [RAM]). Upgrading to Windows Server 2003 is also dependent upon the existing version of the Windows operating system—Setup upgrades only Windows NT 4 Server (with Service Pack 5 or later) and Windows 2000 Server to Windows Server 2003.

Tip **Get tools for migrating to Windows Server 2003**

In those cases in which you want to start with a clean installation of Windows Server 2003 and migrate your users, computers, groups, and security settings to a new Active Directory forest and domain, you must determine which domains and security principals will be migrated and then select the migration tools to use. Although there are several migration tools available from independent vendors, Microsoft does supply migration capability in its Active Directory Migration Tool (ADMT). For more information on migration, see Chapter 9, “Migrating to Windows Server 2003.”

Deciding Between Upgrading and Migrating

When deciding whether to upgrade or perform a migration, you must examine several aspects of your current environment, starting with the most fundamental: Is the existing hardware adequate? It's not just a case of meeting minimum system requirements; rather, you must consider whether system performance meets your real-world needs. If it's slow now, it's not going to get any better. When considering existing systems, make sure that you factor in all the services and applications that will be running on the server.

Another thing to consider is the history of each existing server. Has it been in place for a number of years, with the inevitable wear and tear that that entails? Is a lot of additional software installed? Have a number of patches and service packs been applied? If so, you might want to start with a clean installation, even if you are using existing hardware to do so. On the other hand, if you have a server with a complex configuration and it is stable, you might want to take advantage of all the work that has gone into it and perform an upgrade.

You should consider whether sufficient hard disk drive space is available. At least 2 gigabytes (GB) of disk space—and preferably more—is required for an upgrade of Windows Server 2003. This can be an issue on systems that have small partitions, such as those using file allocation table (FAT) partitions, which might not be large enough to support an upgrade at all, rather than the NTFS file system.

Tip **Don't upgrade servers you should replace**
Hardware has dropped in price considerably over the past few years, making new servers and components more affordable than ever. This makes it easier to ensure that servers have the capabilities they need to provide the services you require. You might also find used servers that meet your needs at online auction sites, such as eBay. Bid wisely and with reputable sellers and you could get some great deals.

The current operating system is another factor to keep in mind. Is the system running some version of Windows Server? Is an upgrade to the version of Windows Server 2003 you want installed on that system supported? Table 7-1 shows the supported upgrade paths from earlier versions of the Windows operating system.

Table 7-1. Supported Upgrade Paths

Current Windows Version	Upgrades to These Editions
Windows 2000 Server	Standard, Enterprise
Windows 2000 Advanced Server	Enterprise
Windows 2000 Datacenter Server	Datacenter
Windows NT Server 4	Standard, Enterprise
Windows NT Server 4, Terminal Server Edition	Standard, Enterprise
Windows NT Server 4, Enterprise Edition	Enterprise

Note Windows Server 2003 can upgrade only Windows Server products. This means that you can't upgrade directly from Windows NT Workstation or Windows 2000 Professional, although you can upgrade the system to the server version of the current operating system and then upgrade that version if desired.

Inside Out

Sometimes a clean start is best

When you are counting on being able to gain peak performance and reliability from a server, there is a lot to be said for installing a brand new, clean copy of Windows Server 2003. Although upgrading a server is easier in the short run, that server still carries the baggage of the previous installation, which all too often means mysterious configuration settings, outdated device drivers, and fragmented drives, as well as unknown (often unused) software taking up disk space.

This is more of a problem in some situations than others. For example, there is a higher tolerance for failure with a print server that handles a couple of departmental printers than with a domain controller. In situations in which you must comprehensively control and manage the configuration of a server, you should balance the short-term convenience of an upgrade with the long-term implications of doing so. You might find that a clean installation is wiser in the long run.

Verifying Hardware and Software Compatibility

It is a good idea to check compatibility issues thoroughly for each server running the Windows operating system that you plan to upgrade. Running the provided system compatibility check and doing some research before installing Windows Server 2003 can save you many headaches later on.

Windows Server 2003 Setup can perform a hardware and software compatibility analysis on a server and provide a report with detected issues and suggested resolutions. The report includes information about hardware and software compatibility, services that will be disabled during the upgrading process, and whether the forest and domain have been prepared for upgrading Active Directory.

The analysis can be started in two ways:

- Select the Check System Compatibility option on the Setup menu that loads when the product CD is inserted.
- Run **WINNT32 /checkupgradeonly** from the command line. (Winnt32 is in the I386 folder on your product CD.)

Additional Research

In addition to the compatibility testing, you might want to do some additional research on compatibility. Some places you might check include the following:

- The Hardware Compatibility List (HCL), which provides a list of systems and components that have been tested with Windows Server 2003, is available at *http://www.microsoft.com/whdc/hcl/search.mspx.*
- The Windows Server Catalog provides software compatibility information and is located at *http://www.microsoft.com/Windows/catalog/server.*
- Software and hardware vendors generally have information about how their products operate with the various Windows operating systems—and, if they don't, you might reconsider purchasing their products. A bit of research on critical applications and common hardware can pay off if you can avoid a serious problem or even a flurry of small ones.
- Online discussion groups often yield valuable information about real-life experiences with Windows Server 2003 and various types of hardware and software. One good source for Usenet groups is Google Groups at *http://groups.google.com.* Check vendor sites for private newsgroups, which are often frequented by system administrators and, if you're lucky, tech support staff from the vendor.

Preparing for an Upgrade from Windows 2000 to Windows Server 2003

Moving servers from Windows 2000 to Windows Server 2003 is a relatively straightforward process. You will almost certainly continue to use the existing DNS and Active Directory configuration, network services, administrative methods, and so on. Obviously, this reduces considerably the amount of work involved in a network upgrade.

Upgrading Windows 2000 Forests and Domains

Moving Active Directory from Windows Server 2000 to Windows Server 2003 is a relatively simple task. However, you must take a few steps prior to installation, starting with verifying a backup of the directory, followed by running a directory preparation program (Adprep) a number of times, including once for the forest and again for each domain. The information updated in each of these steps must be replicated to every domain controller (in the forest or domain, respectively), taking a little time, but not much effort.

For more information about Adprep, see Chapter 8, "Upgrading to Windows Server 2003."

Tip **Renaming Active Directory domains isn't easy**
Windows Server 2003 introduces the capability to rename domains, which facilitates reorganizing your Active Directory tree after an upgrade. Even with the domain rename capability, however, this is not a trivial process, and you will want to approach renaming operations *cautiously*. This capability is available only once all domain controllers in the forest are running Windows Server 2003 and the forest is operating in Windows Server 2003 forest functional level.

Upgrading Domain Controllers

Review the servers currently acting as domain controllers, noting domain, Internet Protocol (IP) address, and geographic location. Branch offices require special attention because of replication issues. Identify domain controllers that will act as global catalog and bridgehead servers. You also must determine the order in which you will upgrade domain controllers. The recommended order for upgrading domain controllers from Windows 2000 to Windows Server 2003 is

1. Use the Active Directory Installation Wizard (Dcpromo) to install Active Directory on a Windows Server 2003–based member server in the forest root domain. This creates the first Windows Server 2003 domain controller in the forest.
2. Upgrade the operating system on the Windows 2000–based domain controller holding the domain naming master role. If you choose not to upgrade the domain controller, transfer the Domain Naming Master role to a domain controller running Windows Server 2003.
3. Upgrade the operating system on the Windows 2000–based domain controller holding the PDC Emulator role in each domain, or transfer the roles to Windows Server 2003–based domain controllers.
4. Upgrade all remaining Windows 2000–based domain controllers to Windows Server 2003.

You also must evaluate the disk partition and available free disk space for upgrading the Active Directory database (Ntds.dit) and extensible storage engine (Esent) log files—free space should be a minimum of 10 percent of the existing size of the Active Directory database and 20 percent of the existing size of the log files (a minimum of 300 megabytes [MB]).

Tip **Installing service packs might be required before you upgrade**
Before upgrading a Windows 2000 forest and domains by using the Active Directory Preparation Wizard, *all* Windows 2000 domain controllers within the forest must have Service Pack 1 with QFE 265089 or (perhaps more easily) Service Pack 2 or later. This is necessary to avoid domain data corruption. For more information, see Microsoft Knowledge Base article 331161.

Applications on Upgraded Servers

Some of your applications will handle the upgrade to Windows Server 2003 without problem, yet not all of them will. Determining which is which beforehand makes the upgrade process much less traumatic. Some widely used applications, such as Microsoft Exchange 2000 Server, simply won't run on Windows Server 2003—something you wouldn't want to find out in the middle of an upgrade.

Prior to upgrading your servers that run Windows 2000, review the Relnotes.htm in the Docs folder of the Windows Server 2003 product CD for information concerning your applications. You might also want to check the software vendor's Web site for relevant information and obtain the Application Compatibility Toolkit from the Microsoft Web site at *http://msdn.microsoft.com/compatibility*.

Exchange 2000 Server and Windows Server 2003

You should be aware of a number of critical issues if you are running Exchange 2000 Server and are planning to install Windows Server 2003 domain controllers. Although you can work around all of the issues, you must plan for Windows Server 2003 with Exchange 2000 Server in mind.

Some of the problems and their solutions are simple: Exchange 2000 Server won't run on Windows Server 2003. The solution is easy: Keep enough servers running Windows 2000 to host Exchange 2000 Server, or upgrade to Microsoft Exchange Server 2003.

Others are less straightforward: There are schema incompatibilities between Exchange 2000 Server and Windows Server 2003, which can result in corrupted directory information. Because of issues such as this, a number of hot fixes must be applied, schema differences must be accounted for, and so on.

Prior to installing Windows Server 2003 into a network using Exchange Server 2000, be sure to research the issues and workarounds using the Microsoft Knowledge Base articles on the subject—article number 314649 is a good place to start.

Selecting Upgrade or Migration Path

For many different deployments, upgrading versus migrating is indicated by the deployment goals and contingencies of the existing server and network operating system (NOS) infrastructure.

The decision whether to migrate or upgrade depends upon a number of factors. Start by answering the fundamental questions for each server:

- Is it possible? Do the system hardware and software support an upgrade, and, if so, to which edition of Windows Server 2003?
- Can the existing hardware support the necessary service and operations load?
- Is it desirable? Are there services or applications that are beneficial to maintain in place, or would you be better off with a new, clean installation and migrating the data?

When installing Windows Server 2003 domain controllers, you also must determine whether to upgrade or to migrate security principals from the existing domain controllers.

Upgrading vs. Migrating

Where it is possible, performing an upgrade has substantial advantages over performing a migration in that it maintains existing server and application configuration settings. Migration, on the other hand, requires that you move security principals from an existing domain controller using Microsoft or third-party migration tools.

An upgrade is an in-place installation of Windows Server 2003 on a server running Windows NT or Windows 2000. An upgrade provides operational advantages to a business that must maintain the services that the server is currently providing (without reconfiguration) while updating the operating system software.

An upgrade has certain advantages over migration, as follows:

- It is done in place, leaving existing servers intact and operational.
- Existing configuration data are incorporated.
- Current device and driver settings are leveraged.
- Configured security settings are maintained.

The following configuration data is maintained during the upgrade process:

- User accounts and settings
- Group settings
- User rights
- Permissions
- Application configuration information

Yet there are limits to the utility of upgrading servers from previous operating systems. Repeated upgrading of servers—from Windows NT 4 to Windows 2000 to Windows Server 2003—can result in the server providing less than optimal performance. Where server performance is important, a new installation will deliver better overall service performance, providing an advantage to migrating instead of upgrading.

One downside to upgrading an existing server is the possibility of installation or configuration problems that render the system unusable. This potential downside can be addressed by creating a full backup of the current server (and any data it contains), preferably an image-based backup that can be readily applied if restoration is necessary.

Review System Requirements and Compatibility

Although it is important to note the minimum requirements for Windows Server 2003 as described in Chapter 2, "Planning for Windows Server 2003," rarely do the minimum requirements allow a server to meet the operational demands placed upon it in an enterprise network environment. Consider for a moment that the performance of your servers running Windows Server 2003 will be more important than most of the other systems on your network. These servers are where a significant percentage of your network workload will reside; thus, enhancing the server hardware for Windows Server 2003 installations is a good idea.

Particularly if you are planning to upgrade a server that runs Windows NT 4, evaluate the hardware and not only from the perspective of meeting the minimum requirements, but also evaluate how effective/optimal it is for running Windows Server 2003 (and any services it is configured to provide).

To help assess server compatibility, do the following:

- Review Windows Server Catalog at *http://www.microsoft.com/Windows/catalog/server*.
- Review the HCL at *http://www.microsoft.com/whdc/hcl/search.mspx*.
- Review the \Docs\Relnotes.htm on the product CD.
- Check application compatibility at *http://msdn.microsoft.com/compatibility*.

Check Drive Partitioning

Prior to upgrading servers, review the partitioning and free disk space on drives that you intend to upgrade. The partition on which you will install Windows Server 2003 should be an NTFS partition. If upgrading, the partition must have at least 2 GB of space, though a minimum of 4 GB is recommended.

An important caveat on upgrading Windows NT 4 systems is the lack of support for drives configured with Windows NT 4 volume, mirror, or striped sets.

To handle Windows NT 4 fault-tolerant configurations, do the following:

- If you are using Windows NT 4 disk mirroring, back up all data on the mirrored volume and break the mirror set.
- If you are using a Windows NT 4 volume set, stripe set, or stripe set with parity (redundant array of independent disks [RAID] 0 or 5), back up all data on the set, remove RAID, and re-create it after the upgrade.

An important limitation for upgrading servers that run Windows 2000 is that Windows Server 2003 cannot be installed on a dynamic disk partition in a certain situation—if Windows 2000 was installed on a disk without any partitions and configured directly as a dynamic disk volume, Setup will fail. You must first revert the dynamic disk partition to basic or remove the partition during setup and create a new basic partition. Dynamic disk partitions can be reestablished (by using Disk Administrator) once Windows Server 2003 is installed.

Choosing Domain and Forest Functional Levels

In evaluating the upgrade or migration path, determine the forest and domain functional levels needed for your network environment (functional levels determine the types of domain controllers and features supported). Table 7-2 shows the types of domain controllers supported by each functional level.

Table 7-2. Domain Controllers and Functional Levels

Types of Domain Controllers on Network	Domain Functional Level	Forest Level
Windows NT 4, Windows 2000, Windows Server 2003	Windows 2000 Mixed	Windows 2000
Windows 2000, Windows Server 2003	Windows 2000 Native	Windows 2000
Windows NT 4, Windows Server 2003	Windows Server 2003 Interim	Windows Server 2003 Interim
Only Windows Server 2003	Windows Server 2003	Windows Server 2003

Advantages to Windows Server 2003 forest functional level include replication enhancements (Active Directory, global catalog, group membership), deactivating schema objects, dynamic auxiliary classes, forest-level trusts, domain renaming, linked value replication, InetOrgPerson password handling, and tracking the last logon time.

Inside Out

Setting the functional levels

Upgrading the first domain controller from Windows 2000 to Windows Server 2003 assigns the forest functional level to Windows 2000 and the domain functional level to Windows 2000 Mixed. For an upgrade from Windows NT 4 to Windows Server 2003, the domain and forest are set to Windows Server 2003 Interim function level.

To raise the forest functional level, you must be logged on using an account that is a member of the Domain Admins group in the forest root domain or a member of the Enterprise Admins group in Active Directory. Start Active Directory Domains and Trusts, and right-click the root node, then select the Raise Forest Functional Level option. In the Raise Forest Functional Level dialog box, select an available forest functional level, and click Raise. The operation cannot be reversed. All domains in the forest must be at Windows Server 2003 domain functional level to be able to change to the Windows Server 2003 forest functional level. If you are unable to raise the forest function level, click Save As in the Raise Forest Functional dialog box to save a log file detailing the domain controllers in the forest that still need to be upgraded from Windows NT or Windows 2000.

You can raise domain functional levels in much the same way. Again, you must be logged on using an account that is a member of the Domain Admins group in the forest root domain or a member of the Enterprise Admins group in Active Directory. Start Active Directory Domains and Trusts, right-click the domain, then select the Raise Domain Functional Level option. In the Raise Domain Functional Level dialog box, select an available domain functional level, and click Raise. The operation cannot be reversed. Make sure you understand the implications of raising functional levels before you do this. See "Choosing Domain and Forest Functional Levels," earlier in this chapter, for details.

Identify DNS Namespace and Storage

DNS is central to network operations in Windows Server 2003. Active Directory domains use DNS for locating domain controllers, global catalog servers, Kerberos Key Distribution Centers (KDCs), and for using Lightweight Directory Access Protocol Uniform Resource Locators (LDAP URLs). Upgrading a Windows NT network requires a defined DNS namespace, as well as organized DNS services and replication (as described in Chapter 2). Identify the DNS domain information that will be required during the upgrade, as follows:

- When upgrading Windows NT 4 domain controllers, you must implement the domain controller within the context of your IT namespace, planning for DNS and Active Directory.
- When upgrading Windows 2000 domain controllers, in most situations you will leverage the existing DNS namespace.

Consider whether the (upgraded or migrated) server(s) will be supporting DNS. If the server will be a DNS server, how you choose to store the DNS zone records has implications for replication of the DNS information. You can store DNS zone records in traditional zone files, in Windows 2000 Active Directory–integrated zones, or in the new forest and domain application partitions.

Following are the results of storing DNS data in various locations:

- DNS zone files leave replication to DNS and require administrative configuration.
- Windows 2000 Active Directory–integrated zones cause DNS data to be replicated to all domain controllers in the domain.
- The forest application partition (ForestDnsZones) causes the DNS data to be replicated to all DNS servers in the forest.
- The domain application partition (DomainDnsZones) causes the DNS data to be replicated to all DNS servers in the domain.

Identify Server Roles

You must identify the network services and server roles that an upgraded server or domain controller will need to perform. Network services commonly employed include DNS, Dynamic Host Configuration Protocol (DHCP), Windows Internet Naming Service (WINS), Routing and Remote Access Service (RRAS), Terminal Services, and Internet Authentication Service (IAS). Depending upon expected load, servers can host one or more network services.

Carefully assess servers that are domain controllers—review your ability to upgrade the server hardware and which secondary roles (such as global catalog server) the server will perform. Consider server performance and operational requirements for domain controllers on your network.

Although large networks commonly have dedicated DNS servers, on small networks a server might provide multiple network services (such as DNS and DHCP) in addition to domain controller roles such as Active Directory access, Kerberos, and global catalog operations. Evaluate which operations master roles the domain controller will support; forest-wide roles (Schema Master and Domain Naming Master) and/or domain-wide roles (RID Master, Infrastructure Master, and PDC Emulator).

> **Tip** The PDC Emulator supplies the Windows Time Services to synchronize all other domain controllers in the domain—servers that are assigned this role should receive particularly close scrutiny to ensure system reliability.

For upgrades from Windows 2000, you can continue to use the assigned operations master roles, yet operations master roles must be determined for each domain controller when upgrading a Windows NT 4 domain controller. For more information on operations master roles, see the section entitled "Establishing Operations Masters" on page 248.

Preparing for an Upgrade from Windows NT 4 to Windows Server 2003

Upgrading from a Windows NT 4 networking environment requires a substantial amount of assessment and planning. The move from a network environment employing Windows NT domains to a network based upon Active Directory is a major change, and one with far-reaching implications. In addition to the technical aspects of shifting from a NetBIOS-based network to one centered on DNS and LDAP, there are administrative issues for IT management, and the business side of the company is sure to have opinions concerning information management.

Although Active Directory might be the most significant change from Windows NT to Windows Server 2003, it is by no means the only one. Many additional services (particularly Internet-related ones) have been added—when Windows NT shipped, after all, the Internet was but a small blip on Microsoft Corporation radar.

Namespace in Windows NT vs. Active Directory

Each Windows NT 4 domain is a single flat namespace with no internal or external hierarchy, while Active Directory domains exist within a DNS tree where each domain can map to a domain within the Active Directory tree. A single Windows NT domain can contain users and a few types of resources (such as file servers), and on many small networks, they do. There are significant limits on the number of objects per Windows NT domain—the theoretical limit is 40,000, yet few servers running Windows NT perform well when approaching that limit. Accordingly, many Windows NT 4 networks employ multiple domains linked by trust relationships that are manually configured (sometimes laboriously so) to allow user authentication and access to resources.

Active Directory transcends these Windows NT limitations: a single Active Directory domain can hold millions of users, servers, computers, and many additional kinds of objects—representing a major shift in network management. By providing effectively limitless domains and automatic trusts, Active Directory offers domain structures based on IT functionality, not product limitations.

Moving from Windows NT Domains to Active Directory

You have to move your existing domain structure from one to the other—from multiple independent domains linked by explicit trust relationships to a single tree with a domain hierarchy, wherein all domains automatically trust each other.

This is a big change, and it is a good idea to take a step back from your existing domain design when considering what your Active Directory domain tree will look like. Domain design is different in Windows Server 2003; remember, the most common reason for adding an additional Windows NT domain—hitting the maximum number of objects—is no longer an issue. There are benefits to having fewer domains, such as faster searches, fewer domain controllers, simplified management, and a network that is easier to use. Unfortunately, there are also likely to be roadblocks to eliminating domains—politics and inertia, to start with.

For more information about the Active Directory planning process, see Part 7, "Managing Active Directory and Security."

You must design the DNS namespace(s) for Active Directory (the domains and domain trees), as well as any additional DNS domains you want to support. Determine which Windows NT domains will be maintained, whether additional domains will be added, and where in the DNS domain tree(s) each of your existing domains will go. When you upgrade each domain's primary domain controller, you must know where in the DNS namespace that specific domain is assigned.

Caution Support for Windows NT 4 domain controllers is provided in the initial Active Directory configuration, but it is dropped once you switch the domain to Windows Server 2003 functional level. Make sure that you are *really* finished using Windows NT before making the switch. You can't go back once you make the change.

Restructuring Domains

If you're upgrading domains from Windows NT 4 to Windows Server 2003 on a one-to-one basis, you will initially have multiple (perhaps many) domains. If so, you can collapse multiple domains into a single one to simplify your Active Directory implementation. You can perform the domain restructure operations at two times:

- **Restructuring domains after upgrading** In most circumstances, you will want to upgrade the domain controller and then migrate the user, group, and computer accounts settings to domains in your actual Active Directory forest. This method frees you from the Windows NT 4 limitations and allows you to take advantage of the ADMT as a means of restructuring your domains.
- **Restructuring domains before upgrading** If you have only a few domains to merge, you can restructure your Windows NT 4 domains prior to upgrading to Windows Server 2003. You must keep in mind, however, that all the standard Windows NT 4 limitations apply. This means that if the Security Accounts Manager (SAM) database will get too large or replication traffic will be an issue, you should wait to restructure domains until after you have upgraded the server.

Remember that the domain controllers from a domain that is subsumed go offline, so make sure there are no additional services or applications running on them before making the change.

Note **Windows NT 4 groups are converted for Active Directory**
When upgrading Windows NT 4 to Windows Server 2003, local groups are upgraded to domain local groups, and global groups are upgraded to Active Directory global groups. Down-level clients continue to see the upgraded groups as their Windows NT 4 equivalents and will regard universal groups—which don't exist in Windows NT—as global groups.

Upgrading Windows NT 4 Servers

When you're upgrading servers that run Windows NT 4, you are likely to encounter incompatible or inadequate hardware, so you should give the system hardware and installed software a thorough review. After all, the baseline requirements for Windows NT 4 server hardware are quite a bit lower than for Windows Server 2003, which requires a minimum of a Pentium 133-megahertz (MHz) processor, 128 MB of RAM, and more than 2 GB of disk space.

Another thing to remember is that Windows Server 2003 might not support some of the adapters and devices used in Windows NT 4 systems. As a result, you should expect to upgrade at least some components of the Windows NT 4 server hardware (upgrading the network adapter, for example, or adding a hard disk) to facilitate reasonable performance under Windows Server 2003.

For more information about the compatibility of specific adapters and devices, see the Windows Server Catalog at *http://www.microsoft.com/Windows/catalog/server* and the Hardware Compatibility List at *http://www.microsoft.com/whdc/hcl/search.mspx*.

Inside Out

Minimum requirements do not yield optimal results

Technically, Windows Server 2003 will run on a 133-MHz Pentium with 128 MB of RAM. Performance would be far from optimal, however, and it is questionable whether such a server would actually make it into a production environment—or how long it would last if it did.

Consider the size of your network and the expected load on the server, and decide whether each upgraded server will perform adequately in your environment. If not, replace it if possible. Hardware is relatively inexpensive, especially when compared with the long-term costs and inconvenience brought about by using an outdated, inadequate, or unstable system.

The following are additional factors to review:

- **Disk partitions** Assess the disk partitions on the servers you want to upgrade. Certain constraints apply to upgrades; you cannot upgrade servers on a FAT partition, for instance, or those using Windows NT 4 fault-tolerant configurations.
- **Windows services** Consider whether you want to phase out some legacy services, such as WINS. Don't be too hasty, though; by leaving the service installed and running for a while after the upgrade, you can ensure that network operations will continue uninterrupted during the transition away from the old service.
- **Windows applications** Look at your existing applications and assess their functionality and compatibility. Check compatibility issues carefully because there are likely to be issues with each application. Don't rely on just what the vendor has to say—do a bit of additional sleuthing, check out newsgroups (both at the vendor's site and public ones), ask colleagues what they have encountered, and so on.

Tip **No more POSIX or OS/2 support**

If you currently have applications that are operating in either the POSIX or OS/2 subsystem in a Windows NT 4 environment, you must replace these applications, because those subsystems are no longer supported. Alternatively, you could leave a server, or a few servers, in place to support the older applications. In either case, this is a decision to make early in the process, so the changeover is completed in plenty of time, and the impact on the network can be managed.

Chapter 8

Upgrading to Windows Server 2003

Whether you can upgrade an existing server to Microsoft Windows Server 2003 depends on hardware compatibility, available disk space, and adequate hardware resources (such as the CPU and RAM). Upgrading to Windows Server 2003 is also dependent upon the existing Windows version on the target system—Setup will only upgrade Microsoft Windows NT 4 Server (with Service Pack 5 or later) and Microsoft Windows 2000 Server to Windows Server 2003.

To upgrade to Windows Server 2003, you must take into account different considerations depending upon whether you are currently running a Windows NT 4 network environment or a Windows 2000–based network with the Active Directory directory service already implemented. Yet there are also issues common to each of these scenarios, such as whether the server hardware is adequate. For many companies running Windows NT 4 servers, it is questionable whether the server hardware can adequately support Windows Server 2003 operational requirements.

General Considerations for Upgrades

Before you begin the upgrade process, you must consider several areas of information, including the most basic, such as whether your existing hardware and software support upgrading to Windows Server 2003. If upgrades are not supported, starting off with a new installation on new server hardware and migrating the user and group information to the new server might be your only option.

You can upgrade a system to Windows Server 2003 only if you're currently running Windows NT 4 Server with Service Pack 5 or later or a Windows 2000 Server platform. Further, servers running Windows NT 4 Enterprise Edition or Windows 2000 Advanced Server must be upgraded to Windows Server 2003, Enterprise Edition. Additionally, Windows 2000 Server using the Remote Storage service must be upgraded to the Enterprise Edition of Windows Server 2003.

Upgrade Issues

A range of network services and applications require consideration and preparation prior to upgrading the hosting servers.

- **Itanium (IA-64) versions of Windows Server 2003** The Itanium (IA-64) versions do not support 16-bit applications (with the exception of Microsoft Windows Acme setup), nor do they support 32-bit device drivers. Likewise, 32-bit drive management utilities and 32-bit antivirus programs do not operate on 64-bit versions of Windows Server 2003, and the 32-bit Web components cannot be loaded in the 64-bit version of Microsoft Internet Explorer.
- **UDDI and SQLXML** You can't run Universal Description, Discovery, and Integration (UDDI) and Microsoft SQL Server 2000 Web Release (SQLXML) on the same machine because of their differing requirements for Microsoft Internet Information Services (IIS) support. SQLXML requires the Isolation mode used by IIS 5, while UDDI uses the new worker process Isolation mode of IIS 6.
- **Cluster service** Upgrading Windows 2000 Cluster service to Windows Server 2003 Cluster service requires that you restart the Cluster service. To restart this service, you must log on using an account that is a member of both the local Administrators group as well as the Domain Admins group. When you upgrade from Windows NT Cluster service, the security descriptor does not contain the system security identifier, or SID (see Microsoft Knowledge Base article 812876).
- **Windows 2000 SP3 required for Windows Server 2003 admin tools** Windows Server 2003 administrative tools can be used only to manage Active Directory on a server running Windows 2000 Server if it has Service Pack 3 (SP3) or is using unsigned Lightweight Directory Access Protocol (LDAP) traffic.

Inside Out

IIS is not installed by default

Although there are many changes in IIS between Windows 2000 and Windows Server 2003, the key change of interest here is that it is no longer installed by default—if IIS isn't already installed on the server that you are upgrading to Windows Server 2003, it won't be installed during the setup process. Even if IIS is installed, it will not be started automatically when the server starts up, even if it was configured to do so before the upgrade. Security is tighter by default on new installations of IIS in Windows Server 2003, yet if you upgrade an existing IIS Web server, the Windows Server 2003 default security constraints will not be applied to this installation. For further information on IIS 6, see *IIS 6 Administrator's Pocket Consultant*, by William R. Stanek (Microsoft Press, 2003). You can either set the service to start automatically after installation or preconfigure the system to support IIS. To enable IIS to retain its operational status after the upgrade, you must prepare the server by performing the following steps:

- Secure the IIS server by using the IIS Lockdown Tool, which is available at *http://www.microsoft.com/windows2000/downloads/recommended/iislockdown/default.asp.*

- Make a *dword* entry (the name is arbitrary) with a value of 1 in the following registry node:

  HKEY_LOCAL_MACHINE\SYSTEM\CurrentControlSet\Services\W3SVC\RetainW3SVCStatus
- If performing an unattended installation, set **DisableWebServiceOnUpgrade=false** (in the [Internet Server] section of the Unattend.txt file).

The following are also some baseline changes in security configuration:

- **Default is more restrictive** The default security settings for new installations of Windows Server 2003 are more restrictive than Windows 2000 Server (or Windows NT 4). Windows Server 2003 Setup will, however, retain existing security settings during an upgrade (i.e., the existing security configuration will not be enhanced by upgrading).
- **Internet Explorer is more restrictive** Internet Explorer is set up with an enhanced security configuration, which by default disables scripting, ActiveX controls, file downloading, and the browser virtual machine. Also, Internet zone security settings are set the same as Restricted zone, and by default all sites are assigned to the Internet zone. Pass-through authentication of user credentials is blocked outside of the Local Intranet zone. These Internet Explorer settings can be configured by using the Advanced tab of the Internet Options icon on Control Panel.
- **Downloading software updates** Because of the security enhancements set in Internet Explorer, you might be unable to download software updates from the Internet until you add those sites to the Trusted zones.

Verify an Upgrade Recovery Plan

Because upgrade processes can and do err, verify that you have an effective recovery plan in place prior to commencing with an upgrade. Likewise, a migration can include removing information from the source domain; thus, prior to either an upgrade or migration, you should make sure that you have verified backups.

You can create an image of the system partition prior to upgrading so that you can restore its original state quickly if needed. Verify the method of backup (network share, CD, DVD) and restoration (network connectivity, imaging software, drivers, etc.) before beginning an upgrade or migration. Create the Emergency Repair Disk in case the upgrade does not complete successfully.

If you are upgrading an existing Windows 2000 domain or forest, the Active Directory schema information must be updated before you can begin. Run the Active Directory Preparation Wizard (Adprep.exe) with the /Forestprep parameter to upgrade the forest data and with the /Domainprep parameter to upgrade the domain information. Normally, this process is successful, but it can fail, and, worst case, it can render the domain controller inoperative. To ensure that you can recover from such disasters, you should do a full backup of two domain controllers from each domain in the forest before running the ADPREP /FORESTPREP command and verify the backup media.

If you are upgrading a Windows NT 4 domain or domain controller, no previous forest and domain schema exists; thus, Windows NT 4 domains are changed to Windows Server 2003 domains as part of the upgrade process. Nevertheless, you will want to verify you have backups of the domain controller, as well as keep a current functional backup domain controller (BDC) offline and available to restore network functionality in case of abject upgrade failure.

Upgrading from Windows 2000

The easiest upgrade process for moving to Windows Server 2003 is upgrading from Windows 2000 Server, because it doesn't require planning the Domain Name System (DNS) and Active Directory namespace, nor does it normally involve restructuring domains or migration of security principals.

You must perform a couple of steps to prepare the Active Directory forest and domains for the new schema and changes and additions supplied by Windows Server 2003. Each Active Directory forest that you maintain must be updated first, prior to upgrading any of its domains. Likewise, each domain within a forest must be prepared prior to upgrading any of the domain controllers in the domain.

The Windows Setup program (Winnt32.exe) has a new /Checkupgradeonly parameter that enables it to assess the state of a server prior to installation. The Active Directory Preparation Wizard (Adprep.exe), which is used to prepare a Windows 2000 forest and domain for upgrade to Windows Server 2003, is included on the product CD.

Before you begin the upgrade process, all existing data (including all Active Directory information) should be backed up to reliable media and kept available for restoration in case of failure during the upgrade process. Further, the media should be tested to verify that you can restore from it.

Prior to rolling out Windows Server 2003 in your production environment, the upgrade process should be evaluated on a private network constructed for the purposes of testing. Use a domain controller for the domain in which you'll be starting the upgrade (a domain that is not the forest root).

> **Tip** Microsoft recommends that you install Windows Server 2003 as a member server within the forest root domain and let it run for a week or more prior to upgrading the forest and domains.

Assess every domain controller in your forest and make sure that it has the required service packs and hot fixes installed prior to beginning the upgrade. For the basic installation and upgrade of Windows Server 2003, all Windows 2000 domain controllers need Service Pack 1 with several Quick Fix Engineering (QFE) fixes, or you can simply install Service Pack 2, which incorporates those fixes. If you must run Windows Server 2003 tools on the Windows 2000 domain controllers, however, Service Pack 3 or later must be installed on those devices.

Thus, to simplify upgrade operations, unless you have a specific issue that precludes upgrading to Service Pack 3, it is recommended that you apply it (or a later service pack) to all domain controllers that run Windows 2000 in the forest.

For more information about applying service packs to Windows 2000 domain controllers, refer to Knowledge Base articles 331161 and 325465 at the Microsoft support site.

Troubleshooting

Domain controller fails to join a Windows 2000 domain or forest

You might be unable to promote a Windows Server 2003 system to be a domain controller in an existing Windows 2000 domain or to join a new domain to an existing Windows 2000 forest. This is because Windows Server 2003 has a different schema (Version 30) than Windows 2000 (Version 13). To enable a Windows Server 2003 domain controller to join a Windows 2000 domain, you must first use the Active Directory Preparation Wizard (Adprep.exe) to update the Windows 2000 forest and domain. For more detailed information on this, see the Microsoft Knowledge Base article 278875.

General Upgrade Preparation Tools

Upgrading member servers and domain controllers requires a bit of preparation and testing, both prior to installing the new operating system as well as after. A set of tools useful for testing the Active Directory and networking environments is located on the Windows Server 2003 product CD in the Support\Tools folder.

The tools include the following functionalities:

- **DNS configuration** Dnscmd.exe allows you to view the configuration of DNS zones and resource records, which is useful in analyzing the DNS configuration of DNS servers and domain controllers.
- **Replication management** To assess Active Directory replication, use the Repadmin utility to determine inbound and outbound replication partners. You can also use this tool to monitor replication status and replication consistency. Prior to upgrading a Windows 2000 domain, you must verify successful replication between at least two domain controllers in the domain (to ensure that you have rollback domain controllers in case the upgrade fails).
- **Network diagnostics** To analyze connectivity issues and verify network operations, use the Netdiag utility, which allows you to run tests on the network clients and their connectivity to the rest of the network.
- **Domain controller diagnostics** The Dcdiag utility lets you test connectivity to Active Directory and test whether the domain controller is providing the functionality required.

- **Domain trust diagnostics** To assess the trust relationships within an Active Directory forest, you can use Nltest.exe to verify the trust status and supply a list of domain controllers. This tool can also be used to shut down domain controllers.
- **Directory view and modification** To view or edit Active Directory contents, you can use the Adsiedit.msc tool, which lets you modify, delete, or add objects and attributes.

> **Tip** Adsiedit.msc can be used to identify objects created in Active Directory during /Forestprep and /Domainprep operations and to verify the successful completion of these operations.

- **Flexible Single Master Operation (FSMO) role determination** You can use the Netdom.exe tool to determine which servers are performing each of the operations master roles and what their configuration is by using the following syntax:

  ```
  netdom query /domain:DomainName /userd:UserName /passwordd:* fsmo
  ```

> **Note** The /Passwordd option is set to asterisk (*) so that Netdom prompts you to enter a password. You can also enter the password after the option so that you aren't prompted.

Windows Server 2003 provides a method to assess whether a server can be upgraded. The WINNT32 /CHECKUPGRADEONLY command instructs Setup to determine whether noncompatible software or hardware is present in the server. The /Checkupgradeonly option starts by requesting updated setup files from the Windows Update Web site (*http://windowsupdate.microsoft.com*) and then runs the upgrade check, displaying the results (and saving them in the Upgrade.txt file in the %SystemRoot% folder).

Before installing the Windows Server 2003 operating system, all Windows 2000–based domain controllers in the forest must be running Windows 2000 Service Pack 1 with QFE 265089 or Windows 2000 Service Pack 2 or later. You can use the REPADMIN /SHOWATTR command to inventory the operating system and service pack revision level for all domain controllers in a particular domain. Follow these steps:

1. Start a command prompt on a computer that has the Windows Server 2003 Support Tools installed.
2. Type the following command:

   ```
   repadmin /showattr HostName ncobj:domain: "/filter:
   (&(objectcategory=computer)(primaryGroupID=516))" /subtree /
   atts:operatingSystem,operatingSystemVersion,operatingSystemServicePack
   ```

   where *HostName* is the host name of a domain controller in the domain you want to examine, such as:

   ```
   repadmin /showattr corpsvr02 ncobj:domain: "/filter:
   (&(objectcategory=computer)(primaryGroupID=516))" /subtree /
   atts:operatingSystem,operatingSystemVersion,operatingSystemServicePack
   ```

3. The output of the command shows the distinguished name of each domain controller in the specified host's domain, followed by the operating system, operating system version, and operating system service pack, such as:

```
DN: CN=CORPSVR02,OU=Domain Controllers,DC=cpandl,DC=com
    1> operatingSystem: Windows 2000 Server
    1> operatingSystemVersion: 5.0 (2195)
    1> operatingSystemServicePack: Service Pack 1
DN: CN=CORPSVR01,OU=Domain Controllers,DC=cpandl,DC=com
    1> operatingSystem: Windows 2000 Server
    1> operatingSystemVersion: 5.0 (2195)
    1> operatingSystemServicePack: Service Pack 3
```

   Here, the first domain controller listed is running Windows 2000 Server with Service Pack 1. The second domain controller listed is running Windows 2000 Server with Service Pack 3. Keep in mind that the REPADMIN /SHOWATTR command doesn't show any hot fixes that might be installed.

4. Note domain controllers that need to have the appropriate service pack applied before upgrading, then repeat Steps 2 to 4 for each domain in the forest.

Active Directory Preparation Tool

Prior to upgrading a Windows 2000 domain controller, you must prepare the forest and domains for the Windows Server 2003 schema modifications. The Active Directory Preparation tool (Adprep.exe) is provided to update this Active Directory forest and domain structural information. You must first prepare the forest, followed by each of the domains.

Each of these processes must be run on a specific domain controller to work:

- The /Forestprep process must be performed on the Schema Master.
- The /Domainprep process must be performed on the Infrastructure Master for each domain.

Using an account that is a member of the Enterprise Admin and Schema Admins groups for the forest root domain, you can prepare the forest by running the following command:

```
adprep /forestprep
```

> **Caution** Be sure to take your Schema Master offline to perform this operation. If the schema update fails, then you can log on to another domain controller in the forest root domain and seize the Schema Master role.

Once the forest is prepared, you next prepare each of your domains by using the following command using an account that is a member of Domain Admins and Enterprise Admins groups:

```
adprep /domainprep
```

The domain preparation must be performed on each Active Directory domain prior to attempting to upgrade a domain controller. Also, prior to adding the first Windows Server 2003 system as a new domain controller in an existing (Windows 2000) domain, forest and domain preparation must be successfully completed.

The Active Directory Preparation Wizard creates a detailed log of the changes made during the preparation process, which is written to %SystemRoot%\System32\Debug\Adprep\Logs\ *DateTime*\Adprep.log, where *DateTime* is a folder name composed of the year, month, date, and time of day in seconds when Adprep was run. This file shows each step of the process and the result code of the attempt to perform each operation.

Adprep also has a couple of optional parameters to control its operations during the preparation process. Following are the Adprep parameters:

- The /Nofilecopy parameter prevents Adprep from copying any files from the source CD (or distribution folder) to the domain controller.
- The /Nospwarning parameter prevents Adprep from displaying a service pack warning when installing on domain controllers that do not have Service Pack 2 installed.

During the forest preparation process, Adprep copies the .ldf files containing the schema change from the installation folder (the CD or distribution folder) to the %SystemRoot%\ System32 folder on the domain controller. These schema change files are 17 consecutively numbered .ldf files named Sch14.ldf through Sch30.ldf.

Note The number following the *sch* indicates the version of the schema—the Windows 2000 schema is Version 13. Because Windows Server 2003 uses Version 30 schema, the schema update files begin at 14 and go to 30.

Adprep also copies the Dcpromo.csv and 409.csv files from the installation folder to the %SystemRoot%\System32\Debug\Adprep\Data folder on the domain controller.

Updating the Active Directory Forest and Domains

Before you start the upgrade process, review your Information Technology (IT) planning information that identifies the Active Directory domain controllers and the upgrade path, including which domain controllers will host which global catalog, operations masters, and bridgehead server roles and the order in which the servers should be upgraded. Because DNS is an integral part of Active Directory, you should also review your DNS namespace and planning information at this point.

When you're ready to update the Windows 2000 Active Directory forest and domains, you begin by backing up the Schema Master (domain controller) for the forest and the Infrastructure Master for each domain that will be upgraded.

Using the Active Directory Preparation tool is a required next step prior to upgrading a Windows 2000 domain controller—Windows Setup will fail if it detects that the forest and/or the domain has not been updated for Windows Server 2003.

The Active Directory Preparation tool completes the following tasks:

- Implements schema updates, integrating the Windows Server 2003 schema with existing schema.
- Improves security on directory objects, enhances security descriptor defaults, and ends reliance on the Everyone group for access to services.
- Creates new containers and directory objects. (You can view these objects to verify that the schema was updated correctly.)

Before you upgrade an Active Directory forest, verify that you have end-to-end replication of the domain information to all domain controllers in each domain and throughout the forest. At least one inbound and outbound replication partner for each directory partition must exist—the schema and configuration partitions are replicated throughout the forest, while the domain directory partition is replicated to all domain controllers in the domain. For the purposes of disaster recovery, it is critical that backups of the Schema Master and a domain controller in each domain be made prior to beginning the upgrade process.

Prior to starting the upgrade, verify that the system volume (Sysvol) information (specifically the default domain policy and the Default Domain Controller Policy) is correctly replicated to all domain controllers in the domain.

- A tool called the FRS Health Check (Health_chk.cmd)—part of the Support Tools installed from the Support\Tools folder on the Windows Server 2003 distribution CD—can be used to determine the status of the system volume replication (and many other factors).
- Alternatively, you can use Gpotool.exe (in the Windows Server 2003 Resource Kit) with the /Verbose parameter to assess whether policies are being consistently applied within the domain.

Troubleshooting

Issues with upgrading domains hosting Microsoft Exchange 2000 Server

There are problems with upgrading domains that have integrated Exchange 2000 Server—essentially, Exchange 2000 Server defines three attributes differently than Windows Server 2003 does, and upgrading domains that have been modified by Exchange 2000 Server can result in mangled attributes. For details on this problem and how to work around it, see Microsoft Knowledge Base article 314649.

Caution To avoid domain corruption, before you upgrade an Active Directory forest, all domain controllers within the forest require installation of either Service Pack 1 with QFE 265089 or Service Pack 2—see Microsoft Knowledge Base article 331161.

When running ADPREP /FORESTPREP, you will be prompted to verify that all domain controllers have the necessary service pack and QFE updates prior to ADPREP /FORESTPREP performing its operations. You can use REPADMIN /SHOWATTR to verify that service packs have been applied. Once you are certain that the correct service pack has been applied, you can press C to continue with the ADPREP /FORESTPREP process.

Preparing the Forest

There are a couple of different perspectives on how to upgrade a forest, and, interestingly enough, both of them are recommended by Microsoft.

Early Microsoft documentation (including the help files that ship with the software) encourage you to take the Schema Master offline—disconnect it from your enterprise network—prior to performing the forest and domain preparation operations on it. Later documentation in the form of Knowledge Base article 821076, "Windows Server 2003 Help Files Contain Incorrect Information About How to Update a Windows 2000 Domain" (located at *http://support.microsoft.com/default.aspx?scid=kb;en-us;821076*), states that this information is incorrect.

Although this article does not provide any further insight into why Microsoft changed its opinion about taking the Schema Master offline prior to updating the Active Directory schema information, it encourages a moment of reflection on the issue. What if the forest and domain preparation has problems—what if you encounter errors, such as corrupted directory objects or attributes? Would it replicate corrupt directory information to other domain controllers? Does it make more sense for you to take the risk of problems and the consequences of those problems in your production environment (your actual enterprise network) or to test it offline first?

By isolating the Schema Master during the upgrade, you can verify that the upgrade was completed successfully before you integrate it back into your production environment. That way, if the upgrade fails and the Schema Master is rendered unusable, you can restore from backup and retry the upgrade preparation. Once you've verified that the upgrade is successful, you can connect the Schema Master to the network so that it can replicate the changes to all domains. Then, after you've verified that the schema changes have been replicated, you can run the ADPREP /DOMAINPREP command.

To start the forest update process, you can take the Schema Master off your local network and set it up on an isolated network (or you can leave it online in your production environment as suggested by Microsoft Knowledge Base article 821076). Log on using an account that is a member of the Enterprise Admins group and the Schema Admins group. Then use the Active Directory Preparation tool (Adprep.exe) from the command line, with the /Forestprep parameter. The Adprep.exe program is located in the I386 directory of the Windows Server 2003 product CD.

From the command line, run ADPREP /FORESTPREP. A detailed step-by-step log file (Adprep.log) is created by Adprep during the forest update operations and is written to the %SystemRoot%\System32\Debug\Adprep\Logs*DateTime* folder. If you encounter errors during the forest update process, review the log file for information to assist in troubleshooting the problems.

As part of the forest preparation process, a couple of new containers (ForestUpdates and Windows2003Update) are created in Active Directory (under the Configuration container). These containers can be viewed using the Adsiedit tool:

```
CN=ForestUpdates
CN=Operations
CN=Windows2003Update
```

The presence of these containers provides verification that the ADPREP /FORESTPREP command successfully completed the update.

When Adprep has successfully completed the operation, it displays the following line at the end of the screen messages: Adprep Successfully Updated The Forest-Wide Information.

Once you are certain that the upgrade of the forest information has been completed successfully, you must let it propagate throughout the forest. The domains in Active Directory cannot be upgraded until the forest upgrade has completely replicated to all domain controllers in the forest.

To provide the forest updates to the remaining domain controllers in the forest, the Schema Master must be connected back to your actual production network. Once reconnected, you must allow time for the information from the updated Schema Master to be replicated to all of the domain controllers in the forest (including domain controllers that communicate across slow links).

Preparing the Domain(s)

The domain preparation process must be completed for each of the domains in your Active Directory forest.

The domain-updating process using Adprep is performed on the Infrastructure Master. Like the Schema Master in the forest preparation process, the domain Infrastructure Master should be backed up, taken offline, and put on the private network, and then the updating process should be performed.

To perform the domain updating, you must log on to the Infrastructure Master domain controller with an account that is a member of both the Domain Admins and Enterprise Admins groups.

Using Adsiedit, verify that the forest update completed successfully prior to preparing the domains by checking under the Configuration container for the existence of the Forest-Updates container and for the Windows2003Update container under ForestUpdates.

Before beginning the domain upgrade process, make sure that all the inbound replication traffic has completed successfully. Use the following command line to verify the replication status:

```
repadmin /showreps
```

Once the forest update and completion of the domain replication processes have been verified, use ADPREP with the /Domainprep parameter to initiate the domain update process, as follows:

```
adprep /domainprep
```


Unlike the /Forestprep operation, the /Domainprep operation does not display process information or copy files. It does, however, write log files (also named Adprep.log) into a new date- and time-stamped subfolder (%SystemRoot%\System32\Debug\Adprep\Logs*DateTime*).

When ADPREP has completed the /Domainprep operation, it displays the following line: Adprep Successfully Updated The Domain-Wide Information.

As part of the domain update, new containers (DomainUpdates, Operations, and Windows2003Update) are created in Active Directory (under the System container). These containers can be viewed by using the Active Directory Users and Computers tool (in the Advanced view):

```
DomainUpdates
Operations
Windows2003Update
```

By finding these containers, you can verify that the /Domainprep operation successfully completed.

Once the domain update is finished, you must reattach the Infrastructure Master to your network and give it time to replicate changes to all domain controllers in the domain prior to upgrading the first domain controller to Windows Server 2003.

Troubleshooting

Legacy clients can't talk to new domain controller

Security settings on the new Windows Server 2003 domain controller are set to require Server Message Block (SMB) signing (of network communications) by clients.

A Macintosh client system shows an "-Error -3: I/O" error when attempting to connect to a Windows Server 2003 domain controller using SMB signing (the default). A domain controller without client support for SMB signing produces an error, indicating either the password is incorrect or logon server access is denied.

Upgrading to Windows Server 2003

If the client is Windows NT 4 with Service Pack 2 or earlier (which also does not support SMB signing), the system indicates that the logon failed and asks you to reenter user credentials. Installing Service Pack 6a is recommended for all Windows NT 4 clients prior to connecting them to a Windows Server 2003 domain controller.

The Default Domain Controller Policy setting for SMB signing is enabled by default on Windows Server 2003, but can be disabled in the Group Policy Editor in the Microsoft Network Server node. Select Computer Configuration, select Windows Settings, Security Settings, Local Policies, Security Options, and finally Microsoft Network Server. In this node, select the Digitally Sign Communications (Always) setting, and then disable it.

Because disabling this setting reduces overall security of the network, this should be done only temporarily (until all clients are updated with the directory client on the Windows 2000 Server product CD or the newer update—see Knowledge Base article 323466).

Upgrading the Windows 2000 Domain Controllers

The next step in the upgrade process is to use the Active Directory Installation Wizard (Dcpromo) to install Active Directory on a Windows Server 2003–based member server in the forest root domain. This creates the first Windows Server 2003 domain controller in the forest. So, if you haven't yet installed a Windows Server 2003 system in the forest root domain, you should do this now and then configure the system to be a domain controller. Afterward, you should continue the upgrade process by upgrading the operating system on the Windows 2000–based domain controller holding the Domain Naming Master role. If you choose not to upgrade the domain controller, transfer the Domain Naming Master role to a domain controller running Windows Server 2003. Afterward, upgrade the operating system on the Windows 2000–based domain controller holding the PDC Emulator role in each domain, or transfer the roles to Windows Server 2003–based domain controllers. You then upgrade all remaining Windows 2000–based domain controllers to Windows Server 2003.

When upgrading domain controllers, you also must evaluate the disk partition and available free disk space for upgrading the Active Directory database (Ntds.dit) and (Esent) log files—additional free space should include at least 10 percent of the existing size of the Active Directory database and 20 percent of the existing size of the log files (a minimum of 300 megabytes [MB]).

Prior to upgrading the domain controllers operating in your enterprise network, make, or verify that you have, functional (tested) backups of at least two domain controllers for each domain (preferably those domain controllers performing key operations master roles). Verify that you have multiple functional (tested) backups of the forest root domain controllers also.

You can perform the upgrade of the domain controller either interactively (using the product CD or distribution folder) or by an automated installation that uses an Unattend.txt file specified as a command-line argument to the WINNT32 command. For further information on either of these methods, see Chapter 4, "Managing Interactive Installations."

Tip To use Windows Server 2003 administration tools with Windows 2000 domain controllers, you must install Service Pack 3 (or later) on your Windows 2000 domain controllers.

To perform an interactive upgrade process, complete the following steps:

1. Insert the CD, and select Install.
2. Setup checks compatibility, shows the compatibility screen, and then writes the Upgrade.txt file to %SystemRoot%.
3. Setup copies installation files and then reboots.
4. Setup presents the option to perform an upgrade or a new installation; you should select to perform an upgrade.
5. Setup copies files, configures settings, finalizes installation, and then reboots.

Upgrading Windows 2000 Domains

Other than the schema changes made using the Active Directory Preparation tool, Windows 2000 domains remain logically and operationally the same after upgrading to Windows Server 2003.

Similarly, domain functional levels stay the same after upgrade:

- If you are currently operating in Windows 2000 Mixed mode, upgrading leaves the domain functional level at Windows 2000 Mixed.
- If you are currently operating in Windows 2000 Native mode, upgrading leaves the domain functional level at Windows 2000 Native.

Depending upon the range of Windows server operating systems you are supporting on your network, you might want to raise the domain and forest functional levels after upgrade. For example, if after upgrade you are using Windows 2003 domain controllers, and you don't need to support domain controllers running earlier versions of Windows, you can gain extra functionality by changing the Windows Server 2003 domain and forest levels.

Selecting Active Directory Functional Levels

When you have upgraded all of the domain controllers in your environment to Windows Server 2003 Active Directory, you can then raise the forest and domain functional levels to Windows Server 2003, which enables an entire set of new features.

You can change the domain and forest functional levels using the Active Directory Domains and Trusts administrative tool.

- To modify the functional level of a forest, right-click the Active Directory Domains And Trusts node, and select Raise Forest Functional Level.
- To modify the functional level of a domain, right-click the domain name, and select Raise Domain Functional Level.

Changing Operations Masters

You must be prepared to seize (that is, forcibly take) the operational master roles held by the domain controller being upgraded in the event that the upgrade is unsuccessful.

- To seize the Infrastructure Master, RID Master (which pertains to relative identifiers, or RIDs), and PDC Emulator roles, in Active Directory Users and Computers, right-click the domain, select Operations Master, then click the needed RID, PDC, or Infrastructure tab. Select Change to transfer the operations (RID, PDC, or Infrastructure) master role to the target server.
- To seize the Domain Naming Master role, in Active Directory Domains and Trusts, right-click the Active Directory Domains And Trusts node, and select Operations Master. Select Change to switch the Domain Naming Master role to another server.
- To seize the Schema Master role, in the Active Directory Schema tool, right-click the Active Directory Schema node, and select Operations Master. Select Change to transfer the Schema Master role.
- To seize the Global Catalog role, in Active Directory Sites and Services, navigate to \Sites*Default-First-Site-Name*\Servers*ServerName*\NTDS Settings, right-click the NTDS Settings node, select Properties, and then click the Global Catalog option.

You can also seize roles from the command line:

1. Ensure that the current domain controller with the role you want to seize is permanently offline. If the server can be brought back online, don't perform this procedure unless you intend to completely reinstall this server.
2. Log on to the console of the server you want to assign as the new operations master. You can log on to the console locally or by using Remote Desktop.
3. Click Start, click Run, type **cmd** in the Open box, and then click OK.
4. At the command prompt, type **ntdsutil**. This starts the Directory Services Management tool.
5. At the Ntdsutil prompt, type **roles**. This puts the utility in Operations Master Maintenance mode.
6. At the Fsmo Maintenance prompt, type **connections**, and then, at the Server Connections prompt, type **connect to server** followed by the fully qualified domain name of the current Schema Master for the role, such as:

   ```
   connect to server engdc01.technology.adatum.com
   ```

7. Once a successful connection is established, type **quit** to exit the Server Connections prompt, and then, at the Fsmo Maintenance prompt, type **seize** and then the identifier for the role to seize. The identifiers are as follows:
   - *pdc*—For the PDC Emulator role
   - *rid master*—For the RID Master role
   - *infrastructure master*—For the Infrastructure Master role

- *schema master*—For the Schema Master role
- *domain naming master*—For the Domain Naming Master role

8 Type **quit** at the Fsmo Maintenance prompt, and type **quit** at the Ntdsutil prompt.

Upgrading Windows 2000 Users and Groups

During an upgrade of a server (or domain controller) running Windows 2000, the local (and domain) user information, including profiles, rights, permissions, and group memberships, is retained.

With minor changes (in universal groups), Windows 2000 groups are directly upgraded to the same groups in Windows Server 2003. One of the main changes (from Windows 2000) in the handling of universal groups is that the universal group information is cached on local domain controllers and no longer must contact a global catalog to authenticate a member.

Windows 2000 Member Server Upgrades

Upgrading Windows 2000 member servers to Windows Server 2003 is comparatively more straightforward than upgrading domain controllers. You still must assess the server hardware and verify its compatibility with Windows Server 2003, and you must determine whether it meets the baseline hardware requirements for the CPU (at least 128 megahertz [MHz]), 256 MB of RAM, and 2 GB or more of hard disk space.

At this point, you should review your IT planning information regarding servers that provide key network services, specifying servers to upgrade and identifying network operating system (NOS) version, services provided, and order of implementation. You must check the network services that are running on the member server and review for any specific considerations or configuration issues that must be taken into account prior to, or immediately following, the upgrade process. Your planning information should define the servers to upgrade, identify installed and updated NOS versions, and specify the roles and services the servers will provide postupgrade.

Upgrading DNS Services

Upgrading Windows 2000 DNS to Windows Server 2003 is mostly a transparent upgrade with some enhancements to DNS—namely, the capability to create application directory partitions to store DNS records that are used to replicate DNS information on a domain-wide and forest-wide basis.

In Windows 2000 Active Directory–integrated zones, all domain controllers in the domain receive the DNS replications. To remain compatible with Windows 2000 domain controllers hosting integrated zones, when you choose a replication option, opt to replicate the DNS records to all domain controllers in the domain. Once you've upgraded fully to Windows Server 2003, you change the replication so that only domain controllers that are also DNS servers get DNS information.

How to Create DNS Partitions Manually

The new DNS application directory partitions are created automatically by the Active Directory Installation Wizard (Dcpromo) when it configures DNS for Active Directory. Yet, if the automatic DNS configuration is bypassed (by you opting for manual configuration), the default DNS application partitions (ForestDnsZones and DomainDnsZones) are not created.

To create the default DNS application partitions, you can use the DNS admin tool or the DNS command-line tool. Type the following: **dnscmd *ServerName* /Createbuiltindirectory-partitions /Forest** (or **/Domain** or **/Alldomains**).

Upgrading from Windows NT 4

When upgrading servers that run Windows NT 4, review the system hardware, network services, and application software on the server. You must verify that the hardware will run Windows Server 2003, determine which Windows Server 2003 product is needed, and identify the required network services. You also must check for configuration issues, such as whether the Windows NT 4 server is using a fault-tolerant drive configuration.

Determine Server Hardware Compatibility

When preparing to upgrade servers running Windows NT 4, you might find server hardware that is incompatible and/or that would provide marginal performance for running Windows Server 2003. This is because the requirements to operate Windows NT 4 (486/33, 16 MB of RAM, 124 MB of disk space) are substantially lower than the hardware requirements to run Windows Server 2003. Windows Server 2003 hardware requirements demand a minimum of a Pentium 133-MHz processor (Datacenter Edition, however, requires at least a 400-MHz processor), 128 MB of RAM, and 1.5 GB of hard disk space (2 GB for an upgrade). Because adapters in servers that run Windows NT 4 are less likely to be supported than equivalent hardware in servers that run Windows 2000, you should closely evaluate compatibility issues by checking the Windows Server Catalog at *http://www.microsoft.com/Windows/catalog/server* and Microsoft's Hardware Compatibility List (HCL) at *http://www.microsoft.com/whdc/hcl/search.mspx*.

You can and should check the compatibility of server hardware prior to upgrading to Windows Server 2003. You can check hardware compatibility by using either of the following methods:

- Type **winnt32 /Checkupgradeonly** at the command line (in the I386 folder on the Windows Server 2003 distribution CD).
- Select the System Compatibility option on the Setup menu.

Regardless of whether you use the preceding compatibility checks, Setup will perform the compatibility analysis at the beginning of the upgrade and will report the results on-screen and store them in the %SystemRoot% folder (in the Upgrade.txt file).

If the server hardware includes a Small Computer System Interface (SCSI) hard disk drive subsystem, Windows Server 2003 might not provide drivers to support it, and you might need to use a driver from the vendor of the SCSI subsystem. To use a vendor-supplied driver during Setup, you must have it on a floppy disk. Press F6 at the beginning of the setup process (a "Press F6" message is displayed on screen) to tell Setup to use this alternative SCSI driver.

Tip **Determine driver compatibility**
When it is not clear whether your SCSI or other mass storage device driver will be compatible with Windows Server 2003, you can determine this by beginning the installation process. Setup will detect whether it recognizes the mass storage device hardware and has a device driver for it; if it does not, it will stop and display an error regarding the disk or controller.

Upgrading Different Versions of Windows NT 4

For each server running Windows NT 4 that you are upgrading, evaluate the existing operating system and determine to which version of Windows Server 2003 you can upgrade.

To select a version, assess the following:

- If upgrading from Windows NT 4 Server, you can upgrade to either Windows Server 2003, Standard Edition, or Enterprise Edition.
- If upgrading from Windows NT 4 Server Enterprise Edition, you must upgrade to Enterprise Edition.
- If upgrading an earlier version, such as Windows NT 3.51, you must upgrade to Windows NT 4 and then upgrade to Windows Server 2003.

All four versions of Windows Server 2003 (Standard, Enterprise, Datacenter, and Web) run on the Intel 32-bit platform, yet only the Enterprise and Datacenter versions run on the Intel Architecture 64 (IA-64) platform.

Tip Only a limited subset of Terminal Services functionality is supplied in Standard Edition—for full Terminal Services functionality, the Enterprise Edition of Windows Server 2003 is required.

Inside Out

Datacenter Edition is not an upgrade option

Windows Server 2003, Datacenter Edition, is not available as a stand-alone operating system, and it is not available as an upgrade product. The Datacenter Edition is original equipment manufacturer (OEM)–provided only, installed and configured on vendor-supplied hardware (from vendors such as Hewlett-Packard, Dell, and many others).

Managing Disk Partitions

Managing disk partitions in Windows NT differs from managing them in Windows Server 2003, and NTFS partitions are converted during installation (with backward compatibility supported for file allocation table [FAT] and FAT32 partitions).

Even though only 1.5 GB of disk space is required for a new installation, a little more than 2 GB of disk space is required to upgrade (thus, you cannot upgrade Windows NT server installations on FAT partitions, because doing so exceeds the partition boundaries for the FAT partition).

Windows NT 4 fault-tolerance configurations—mirroring (redundant array of independent disks [RAID] 1) and disk striping with parity (RAID 5)—are not supported by Windows Server 2003. Prior to upgrading Windows NT 4 servers that use these methods, verify you have a backup of the data contained on the fault-tolerant volumes, and then disable the fault-tolerant configuration.

Windows NT disk partitions are now referred to as basic disk (meaning, not dynamic) partitions. Beginning in Microsoft Windows 2000 (and including Microsoft Windows XP and Windows Server 2003), the use of dynamic disk partitions became available. Dynamic disk partitions cannot be modified during upgrade.

Upgrading Domain Controllers

When you're ready to begin upgrading your Windows NT 4 domain controllers, after verifying that you can and want to upgrade the server hardware, begin the process by backing up your domain controllers and taking at least one updated BDC offline for the duration of the upgrade process. Keep this offline BDC as a rollback server in case of serious upgrade errors resulting in an inoperative primary domain controller (PDC). Depending upon the criticality of your existing domain infrastructure, you might want to have multiple backups set aside for rapid recovery of your existing network functionality. For the same reason that you make and keep redundant backup tapes, when upgrading domains it makes sense to keep redundant BDCs (at least long enough to verify a successful upgrade).

- **Upgrade the PDC** To upgrade the Windows NT 4 domain controllers on your network, begin by upgrading the PDC and allow time to assess whether it has been upgraded correctly.
- **Upgrading BDCs** After the PDC is upgraded, next upgrade all of the BDCs.

Inside Out

Unlike Windows NT 4, domain controllers now require DNS

Windows NT 4 was based on NetBIOS network operations, yet this is no longer the case for Windows networking. Beginning in Windows 2000 and continuing in Windows Server 2003, Windows network operations are based on using DNS as the core location service for everything—from domain controllers and global catalogs, to Kerberos servers and other network services. To locate network services, Windows 2000 and Windows Server 2003 use service resource records, enabling identification of the Internet Protocol (IP) address and ports used to support Transmission Control Protocol/Internet Protocol (TCP/IP) network services. If your Windows NT domain already has DNS deployed, you must delegate the DNS zone for the new Windows Server 2003 domain before upgrading the PDC.

Establishing Operations Masters

Once all Windows NT 4 domain controllers have been upgraded to Windows Server 2003, assess and define the operations master roles for each of the domain controllers. Windows Server 2003 domain controllers can perform in a variety of operational roles. In fact, every Active Directory forest and domain must supply domain controllers performing the operations master roles.

The required forest roles are as follows:

- **Schema Master** A forest-wide role that manages updates to the schema within Active Directory
- **Domain Naming Master** A forest-wide role that manages the addition or removal of Active Directory domains

The required domain roles are as follows:

- **RID Master** A domain-wide role that manages the allocation of RIDs, which are combined with the domain security identifier (SID) to uniquely identify objects in the directory.
- **Infrastructure Master** A domain-wide role that is responsible for managing references from local directory objects to objects in other domains.

Tip Normally, an Infrastructure Master should not also be assigned as a global catalog, because this prevents the Infrastructure Master from functioning correctly.

- **PDC Emulator** A domain-wide role that provides backward compatibility to clients running earlier versions of Windows (supporting both NTLM and Kerberos authentication) and also provides time synchronization.

- **Global catalog** Although not one of the roles identified as an operations master, the global catalog is a required role performed by at least one domain controller in every forest (and commonly implemented with at least one global catalog per site). A global catalog contains a reference to, and a partial attribute set for, every object in the Active Directory forest.

In addition to the operations master roles and global catalog there is a server role involved in managing intersite replication for Active Directory. Servers supporting intersite replication are referred to as bridgehead servers.

Converting Windows NT 4 Groups to Windows Server 2003 Groups

The Windows NT 4 security groups are upgraded to related groups in Windows Server 2003 as follows:

- Windows NT 4 local groups become domain local groups.
- Windows NT 4 global groups become global groups.

Note Clients running earlier versions of the Windows operating system continue to work with the upgraded groups, yet they see universal groups as global groups.

Troubleshooting

Domain local groups are not correctly displayed in Windows NT 4

Windows Server 2003 domain local groups cannot be correctly referenced by Windows NT 4 administrative tools used on member servers running earlier versions of the Windows operating system. You can use administrative tools in the Windows Server 2003 Administration Tools pack (Adminpak.msi file in the I386 folder on the product CD or %SystemRoot%\System32 folder after installation) to display the local groups and manage them on servers running earlier versions of the Windows operating system.

Performing the Upgrade from Windows NT 4

Upgrading a Windows NT 4 domain begins by creating or verifying adequate backups and establishing a private network.

- **Back up the PDC** Prior to beginning the actual upgrade process of the Windows NT 4 PDC, verify that you have tested backups and (at least one) operational BDC for the domain taken offline.
- **Create an isolated network** You might want to take the upgrade off of your enterprise network (or do the upgrade during off-peak hours), so as to prevent user, application, and service access to the domain controller during the upgrade process.

Upgrade the PDC

When you are ready to begin the upgrade process, start Windows Setup from a Windows NT 4 command line, and run Windows Server 2003 Setup (Winnt32) either from the product CD or from a network distribution folder.

During the upgrade, Setup will run the Active Directory Installation Wizard, which performs the following tasks:

- Prompts you to create a new forest or join an existing forest and to create a new domain tree or join an existing one
- Establishes the directory datastore, Kerberos, which establishes parent–child trust
- Copies schema, configuration, and domain directory partitions from the parent domain
- Copies security principals stored in the Security Account Manager (SAM) into the directory and converts groups as discussed previously by establishing corresponding accounts in Active Directory. User and global group accounts are put into the Active Directory Users container, computer accounts are put into the Computers container, and Windows NT 4 local groups are put in the Builtin container. These container objects (Users, Computers, and Builtin) are not organizational units (OUs) and are not subject to administrative changes (moving, deleting, renaming).

Post-PDC Upgrade

When the upgrade of the PDC has been completed, you can commence with upgrading the BDCs until all domain controllers are running Windows Server 2003.

> **Tip** A Windows NT 4 PDC that has been upgraded to Windows Server 2003 is able to continue to replicate security principal changes to Windows NT 4 BDCs.

Once all domain controllers are upgraded (and replication has completed), proceed with upgrading member servers.

> **Tip** **Upgrading Windows NT applications**
> Prior to upgrading existing Windows NT applications, look at the Relnotes.htm file in the Docs folder of the Windows Server 2003 product CD. You can also test the compatibility of applications with Windows Server 2003 by using the Application Compatibility Toolkit (available at the Microsoft Web site at *http://msdn.microsoft.com/compatibility*). You can also use the Program Compatibility Wizard to test and enable compatibility settings that might allow applications to operate correctly. Some applications, such as disk management tools, developed for earlier versions of the Windows Server operating system will not work correctly even in compatible modes and could pose risks to the integrity of the installation.

Chapter 9

Migrating to Windows Server 2003

Migration involves moving account information from an existing domain to a new domain. You use migration instead of an upgrade process for a number of reasons, not the least of which is when the server must provide optimal performance (for instance, in environments where high server availability is essential). Likewise, when a new installation is preferred for hardware or software reasons, migration is the logical approach to providing the needed user and group information. Although it depends upon the migration scenario, once a migration has been successfully completed, the source domain often can be removed and its server hardware reallocated.

Selecting the Migration Tools

All the user, group, service, computer, domain, trust, and security information can be migrated by using an application called the Active Directory Migration Tool (ADMT). There are also several migration tools from independent vendors such as Aelita, NetIQ, and Quest (Fastlane) that provide similar functionality.

Whether you are migrating from Microsoft Windows NT, Microsoft Windows 2000, or from one Microsoft Windows Server 2003 forest to another, ADMT enables you to move account information from the source domain (from where the information is being migrated) to the destination domain (to where the information is being moved). The tasks involved in migration are centered around the transfer of information concerning security principals and security settings.

ADMT

ADMT consists of a set of wizards designed to help you migrate users, groups, computers, service accounts, trusts, and security settings on objects. ADMT also provides support for migrating accounts from the directory of Microsoft Exchange Server 5.5. The primary operations of this tool are available on the Action menu and include the following:

- User Account Migration Wizard
- Group Account Migration Wizard
- Computer Migration Wizard
- Service Account Migration Wizard
- Trust Migration Wizard
- Security Translation Wizard
- Exchange Directory Migration Wizard

Other Microsoft Migration Tools

In addition to ADMT, Microsoft provides several other tools that can assist in certain migration scenarios. These tools include User State Migration Tool (USMT), File Settings and Transfer Wizard, migration scripts, and the Movetree utility.

USMT

You can automate the migration of user settings and data by using USMT, an administrative wizard designed to assist in the deployment of Microsoft Windows XP clients in an enterprise network environment, specifically in the migration of user settings. This administrative tool was initially shipped with Windows XP in a folder off the root of the product CD called ValueAdd\Msft\Usmt.

USMT comprises a set of tools, which perform the user state acquisition and the loading operations, and a set of information files (.inf files), which determine what information gets migrated.

USMT operations (and related executable files) include the following:

- Acquire user state information (Scanstate.exe)
- Load the user state information to a new computer (Loadstate.exe)

USMT information migrated (and related .inf files) includes the following:

- Operating system settings (Migsys.inf)
- User settings (Miguser.inf)
- Application settings (Migapp.inf)

Also, the Sysfiles.inf file is used to tell USMT about files (such as operating system files) that should not be migrated, irrespective of any other USMT configuration settings.

For more information about customizing these .inf files, refer to the USMT .inf Commands.doc that is contained in the Windows Server 2003 Deployment Kit.

Migrated information includes the following:

- **File types migrated** .ch3, .csv, .dif, .doc, .doc, .dqy, .iqy, .mcw, .oqy, .pot, .ppa, .pps, .ppt, .pre, .rqy, .rtf, .scd, .sh3, .slk, .txt, .wk?, .wpd, .wps, .wq1, .wri, .xl?
- **User folders migrated** Cookies, Desktop, Favorites, My Documents, My Pictures
- **User settings migrated** Certificates, fonts, keyboard, localization, mapped network drivers, mouse, network printers, screen saver, sounds, taskbar, Microsoft Outlook/ Outlook Express configuration and mail files, dial-up configuration, Microsoft Office System configuration, and Microsoft Internet Explorer configuration.

Tip The certificates used by the Encrypting File System (EFS) are not migrated by USMT or the File and Settings Transfer Wizard. Files that are encrypted on the source computer are decrypted when written to the destination computer.

File and Settings Transfer Wizard

The File and Settings Transfer Wizard is a user-based migration tool that allows users to transfer their configuration settings and data from one computer to another. Although not designed for corporate deployments or mass migrations, it can allow users to transfer their settings, files, and folders from one computer to another without requiring administrative assistance. This tool is installed on clients running Windows XP in the System Tools menu. Click Programs or All Programs, Accessories, System Tools, File Settings And Transfer Wizard.

Migration Scripts

A set of scripts (starting with Clonepr.vbs) is provided in the Windows Support Tools for migrating security principals. Although these scripts do copy security principals to the new domain, leaving the source domain intact, they do not migrate user passwords and are used only for interforest migration of security principals (including migrating from Windows NT 4 to Windows Server 2003 or Windows 2000).

The Clonepr.vbs script completes the following tasks:

- Uses Clonegg.vbs to copy global groups, Clonelg.vbs to copy local groups, and Cloneggu.vbs to copy all global groups and users
- Adds the security identifiers (SIDs) from the source domain to the SID history for the new account in the destination domain by using Sidhist.vbs

The Movetree Utility

The Movetree utility is used in intraforest migration of security principals. Movetree is a command-line program and is part of the Support Tools provided with Windows Server 2003 (located in the Support\Tools folder on the product CD).

Movetree is used to do the following:

- Move security principals to a new domain and delete them from the source domain
- Migrate user passwords

Normally, you should use ADMT to migrate users, computers, and groups; use Movetree to move directory objects that are not migrated by ADMT (such as members of default groups such as Administrators or Domain Admins).

Third-Party Migration Tools

Independent vendors produce migration tools that provide much of the same functionality as the Microsoft tools. Each product is different, however, and the features and benefits of each must be evaluated in the context of your migration environment and process. Following are two third-party tools:

- **Quest Fastlane Migrator** *http://www.quest.com/migrator/*
- **Aelita Enterprise Directory Manager** *http://www.aelita.com*

General Considerations for Migrations

Consider your source and destination (target) domains involved in the migration. The target domain must be an Active Directory domain running in Native mode (either Windows 2000 or Windows Server 2003). When evaluating your migration scenario, you must determine which types of migration you can do.

There are two types of migrations:

- **Interforest migrations** Migrating from a Windows NT domain or a different Active Directory forest.
- **Intraforest migrations** Migrating from an Active Directory domain within the current forest. Intraforest migration can also be used to consolidate multiple Active Directory domains into a single domain, easing management of users and groups under a single set of policies.

You must establish trust relationships between the destination domain and all domains trusted by the source domain (use the Trust Migration Wizard to assess and implement domain trusts for migration).

To be migrated, the source objects must be security principals—users, security groups (including Windows NT 4 local groups, domain local groups, and global groups), or computer accounts.

Any account (or other source object) that has a SID that already exists in the destination domain or forest cannot be migrated. For example, irrespective of the domain of origin, built-in accounts such as Administrators and Power Users cannot be migrated because they use identical SIDs.

When migrating user accounts, user names are limited to 20 characters in length—anything beyond 20 characters is ignored.

> **Tip** Null values in source domains do not overwrite values in the destination domain.

Commonly, when you migrate from Windows NT Server 4, the network environment is structured into Windows NT account domains and Windows NT resource domains. During the migration process, the user and group information is copied from the account domains, and the service account and local group information is copied from the resource domains. All this information is integrated into the destination domain. When migrating from Windows NT, always migrate the account domains first and then the resource domains—this will establish the user and group accounts prior to migrating resource permissions referencing those accounts.

Determining the Approach to Migration

You can use a variety of approaches when migrating the systems on your network. These approaches can be categorized as manual, scripted, automated, and user-driven.

Manual Migration The manual migration approach uses USMT and includes the following steps:

1. Acquire the user state information (by using Scanstate.exe).
2. Deploy the new operating system.
3. Load the new operating system with the user state information (by using Loadstate.exe).

> **Tip** Manual migration is Information Technology (IT) labor-intensive, doesn't scale, and has increased error potential.

Scripted Migration Scripted migration requires that you write migration scripts to acquire and load user state information; yet, once written, the migration process involves the following steps:

1. Use scripts to acquire user state information.
2. Use the scripts for unattended installation of the new operating system.
3. Use the scripts to load user state information into the new operating system (requires you to log on as Administrator).

> **Tip** Although it still requires significant IT labor, scripting the migration can reduce error potential and speed migration.

Automated Migration By creating customized scripts (using variables such as %UserName%) to collect and restore user state information, and using Remote Installation Services (RIS) with tailored answer files to automate the new operating system (OS) installation, you can completely automate the migration process. This can minimize the amount of IT labor required, yet demands a bit more planning and design.

User-Driven Migration Although not the method most likely to be used in most corporate networks, having users perform the migration process by using the File and Settings Transfer Wizard can minimize IT labor and can allow the users greater discretion in the movement of their information from one computer to another.

Preparing for Migration

To prepare to migrate your servers or domains to Windows Server 2003, you must identify the specific users, groups, services, computers, domains, and trust relationships that are within the scope of the migration.

Identify the source domain that contains the information (users, groups, etc.) from which you want to migrate, and identify the destination (target) domain to which this information will be migrated.

To document the migration, enable auditing on both the source and destination domains by using either of the two following methods:

- In Windows 2000 and Windows Server 2003, start Active Directory Users and Computers. Right-click the domain you want to work with, and select Properties. In the Group Policy tab of the Properties dialog box, select the domain policy, and then click Edit. This displays the Group Policy Object Editor. In the Group Policy Object Editor, expand Computer Configuration, Windows Settings, Security Settings, Local Policies, and then select Audit Policies. In the right pane, double-click Audit Account Management, and then select Define These Policy Settings. Under Audit These Attempts, select Success and Failure, and then click OK.
- In Windows NT, load User Manager for Domains, go to Policies, click the Audit menu option, enable Audit These Events, and select both Success and Failure for User And Group Management.

Prior to actually performing a migration, it is useful to perform a test run to determine its effects (by viewing the logs and reports generated). To test first, select the Test The Migration Settings And Migrate Later option in each of the ADMT wizards. By doing this, you can identify errors that occur in the migration of security principals or domain information and can correct the underlying configuration factors that caused any errors before performing the actual migration. By repeating this process of doing a test run and correcting errors, you can eliminate errors in the migration.

Migrating Security Principals

One of the most critical aspects of a migration is how to move security principals (such as users, groups, and computers) from one domain to another. This can get somewhat complicated in that part of the SID for each security principal is a domain SID, which of course must be changed when moved to the new domain.

When you consider that the SIDs are used to regulate user access to resources on the network, migration must accomplish moving the users' information to the new domain while retaining their existing access to resources.

In Windows networks, user access to network resources is managed by the use of access control lists (ACLs) that specify SIDs of users and groups allowed to access the resource. For each resource (such as network shares, folders, files, printers), SIDs are applied, delineating not only which users and groups can access the resource but also the type of access that they will have, such as Read-Only permissions, Read/Write permissions, and so on.

An access token, which contains not only the user's SIDs, but also the SIDs of every group to which the user belongs, is assigned to a user at the point of logon to the network. In the process of accessing a resource, the user's SIDs are compared to the SIDs assigned to the network resource. If the ACL on the network resource indicates that the user should have the type of access requested (such as Read access), the access is granted.

By default, when you migrate a security principal from a source domain to the destination domain, the destination domain's SID becomes part of the user's SIDs; thus, although the user name remains the same, the underlying SID is different, reflecting the new domain to which the user is assigned.

Yet, in performing a migration, part of the objective is to maintain the users' existing access to network resources. To accomplish this, a history of the SIDs associated with a security principal is created (the SID history), which maintains the SIDs from the previous domain that were associated with the security principal. During network logon, in addition to the new SIDs associated with the new domain, the historic SIDs associated with the previous domain are also appended to the access token created for that user.

Inside Out

Use of SID history

Because the ACLs on network resources reference SIDs to control access, once the source accounts are no longer available because the domain is being decommissioned, the applied (source domain) SIDs in the ACLs will no longer be resolvable. Access to resources continues to work, however, because Windows Server 2003 accesses the SID history and provides name resolution. You can progressively assign the security principals defined in your new domain to these resources and clean up the SID history.

Performing the Migration: An Overview

Performing a domain migration from Windows NT or another Windows 2000 or Windows Server 2003 forest requires an existing destination domain (to which you are migrating) as well as an established trust relationship between source and destination domains.

To migrate a Windows NT account domain to Windows Server 2003, you must perform the following procedures, each of which is discussed as appropriate later in this chapter:

1. Establish the destination domain (which must be running in Windows 2000 Native mode or Windows Server 2003 mode).
2. Use Active Directory Domains and Trusts to create a trust relationship between the source and destination domains. Be sure to migrate the trusts (by using the Trust Migration Wizard in ADMT) prior to migrating user and service accounts and local groups.
3. Use the Group Migration Wizard to migrate the global groups to the destination domain. Migrating global groups with users can be a less-bandwidth-intensive means of migrating users because it avoids the enumeration of users, which can take considerable time if there are many.

Tip Migrating distribution groups to a domain that has a security group by the same name results in the migrated distribution group becoming a security group.

4. Employ the User Migration Wizard to migrate users to the destination domain (existing users in the domain are not affected by this migration process). By default, migrated users are required to change their password upon first logon, and the accounts are locked until passwords are reset. This can present problems if the User Cannot Change Password option is set in the destination domain, because users won't be able to change their password and thus will be locked out of their accounts.

Tip If migrating a resource domain, use the Service Account Migration Wizard to discover service accounts.

To migrate a resource domain, you must perform these procedures, each of which is discussed as appropriate later in the chapter:

1. Establish the destination domain.
2. Create trusts between source and destination domains by using Active Directory Domains and Trusts.
3. Use the Service Account Migration Wizard to discover service accounts.
4. Use the Computer Migration Wizard to migrate computer accounts (both servers and workstations). A software agent will reboot the computer; thus, the default startup option must be set to boot to the correct operating system. (You must log on to the source domain as Administrator to use this wizard.)

5. Use the Security Translation Wizard to migrate user profiles (which you select on the Translate Objects page).
6. Use the Group Migration Wizard to migrate shared local groups (on the Group Options page, select only the Migrate Group SIDs To Target Domain and the Do Not Rename Accounts options).
7. Use the User Migration Wizard to move service accounts to the destination domain.
8. Migrate service account rights by using the Security Translation Wizard, selecting the source domain computers containing the account rights. On the Translate Objects page, click the User Rights and Local Groups options, and on the User Account page, enter the (destination domain) account with Administrator permissions.
9. Upgrade, then migrate the domain controllers.

Migrating Group Accounts

Prior to migrating local and global groups you should use the Group Mapping and Merging Wizard to map source groups to corresponding groups in the destination domain. The Group Mapping and Merging Wizard also enables the merging of group members from multiple groups in the source domain to a group in the destination domain. You can use the Test The Migration Settings And Migrate Later option, which enables you to verify that the group mapping and/or merging will occur successfully once implemented.

The information used by the Group Mapping and Merging Wizard to specify group mapping between the source and destination domains is ignored if the group is migrated to the destination domain. If the group was originally mapped from a group in the source domain to a group in the destination domain, this mapping will be redirected to the group in the destination domain.

Tip The Default Domain Policy rights assigned to groups in a Windows 2000 source domain are ignored by the migration process.

Migrating Local Groups

During the migration process, ADMT handles local groups differently than global groups. When a source domain is using shared local groups to provide access permissions to resources, the Group Account Migration Wizard should be used to migrate the shared local groups to the destination domain.

When migrating local groups to a new domain, if the group members are being migrated as part of the process, the members are automatically added to the new local group in the destination domain. In cases in which the member belongs to a domain that is trusted by the destination and source domains, it is identified by its source domain SID, and when the member already belongs to the destination domain, it is added using its destination domain SID. In cases in which the name of the group member is not in the destination domain, nor in any domain that it trusts, the user name will not be added to the migrated local group as a member.

Tip You must move any domain local groups in Windows 2000 that are referenced by security descriptors in the source domain controller prior to migrating the server to the destination domain.

Migrating Global Groups

Migrating groups prior to migrating users from one domain to another is a good idea. Global groups are restricted to having members that exist within the (current) domain. As a result, if you migrate users from a source domain to a destination domain and groups have not yet been migrated, the migrated users cannot be part of a group that is in the source domain. They can be part of a group only in the destination domain; thus, they cannot be part of their original group. Once the groups are migrated, group membership will be restored, yet it leaves a window of opportunity for users to attempt to log on prior to the group membership being reconstructed.

Migrating the global groups from the source domain to the destination domain prior to migrating the users creates the corresponding groups in the destination domain and provides for continuity of group membership throughout the migration process. As in the migration of users, when the groups are migrated to the destination domain, they receive the SID from the new domain, and the SID from the source domain is appended to the SID history for the group.

Tip **Windows 2000 global groups migrate as universal**
Migrating global groups from a Windows 2000 Native-mode domain results in those groups being established in the destination domain as universal groups (this is done to support members from the Windows 2000 domain that have yet to be migrated).

Using the Group Account Migration Wizard

To migrate the global group accounts (and optionally the users they contain), run the Group Account Migration Wizard on the Action menu in ADMT.

The migration process for group accounts follows these steps:

1. **Choose whether to migrate or test** The Group Account Migration Wizard starts by letting you choose whether you simply want to test the effects of migrating to groups (as ADMT is currently configured). As shown in the screen on the following page, both the Test The Migration Settings And Migrate Later option and the Migrate Now option are available—if you have not yet run a migration test on migrating the global groups, you should do this prior to selecting the Migrate Now option.

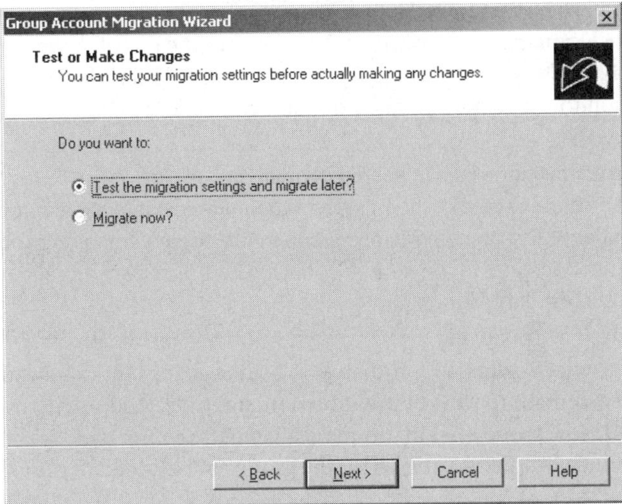

2 **Specify source and target domains** You are next prompted to specify the source of the migration information (the source domain) and the domain to which you want the information to be transferred (the target domain). The set of recognized domains is available to be selected from the drop-down list, or you can enter the name of the domain to be used in the migration (as shown in the following screen).

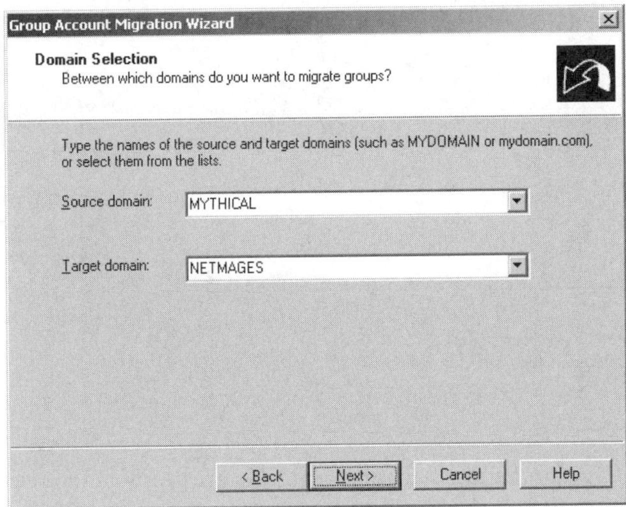

Network connectivity between source and destination domains is essential to the migration process. If you enter the name of a domain that ADMT cannot locate, it displays the error message, "The network path was not found - (Error code 53), domain =" with the domain name appended to the end of the error message.

When migrating Windows 2000 or Windows Server 2003 groups, verify that you can PING the Domain Name System (DNS) name of the remote domain controller. When migrating Windows NT 4 groups, you can use the NET USE command line to verify connection to the remote primary domain controller (PDC).

Tip **Ensure user account exists in source domain**

The user account that is running the migration tool must exist in the source domain and must be a member of the Domain Admins group in the source domain. If you do not have a corresponding user account in the source domain with the correct group membership, you will receive an access denied error.

3 **Choose groups to migrate** You must select the groups that you want to migrate from the source domain to your destination domain. Click Add, click Advanced, and then click Find Now to see a list of groups available to be migrated. Select the groups to migrate, and click OK two times for the groups to be added to the Groups Selected list.

Don't include built-in groups, such as Domain Admins or Domain Users, because they can't be migrated. For example, if you select Domain Users as shown in the following screen, it causes a migration error. To remove the group from the list, select it and then click Remove.

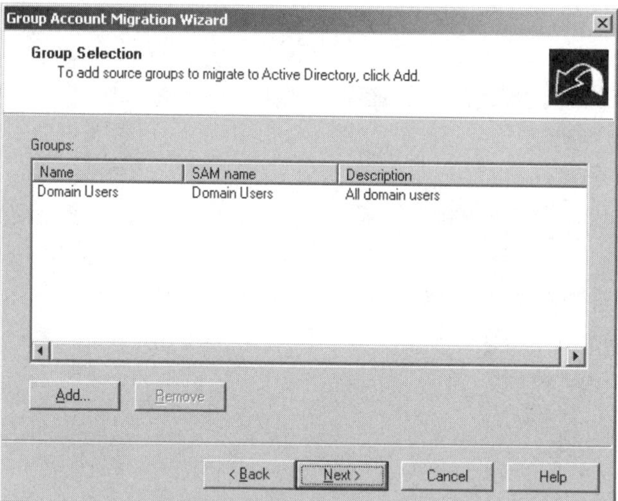

4 **Choose target organizational unit** Next you are prompted to select the organizational unit (OU) to which you want to migrate the groups (as shown in the screen on the following page). This is a significant decision, because the policies that are applied to this OU are immediately applied to the groups you are migrating.

Although selecting the target OU is an easy thing to do in the dialog box, the decisions behind the selection of the OU to which you migrate these groups require substantial consideration.

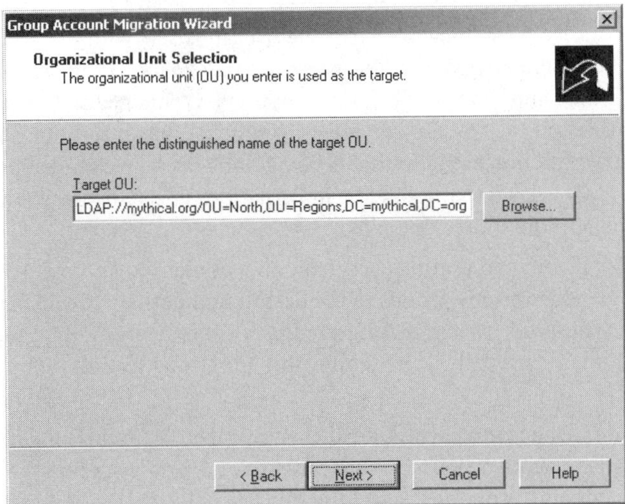

5 **Specify group information to migrate** The Group Options dialog box (as shown in the following screen) allows you to control a variety of factors about which information is migrated.

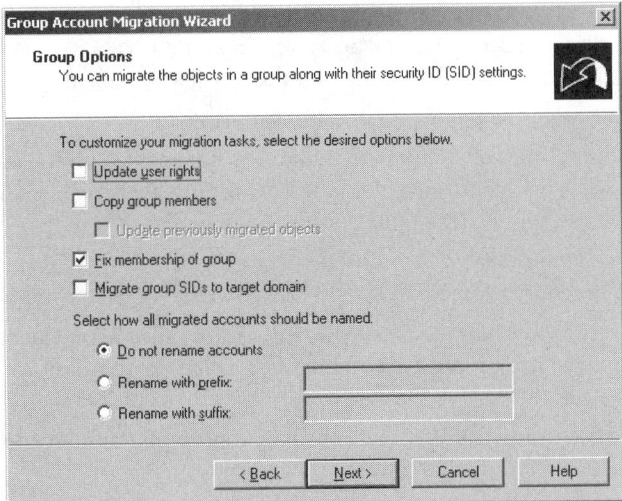

Select the Update User Rights option essentially to migrate the assigned user rights in the source domain over to the destination domain (this is the default option for Windows NT 4, but is not selected by default when migrating from Windows 2000).

You can also instruct the wizard to copy over the members of the group (by selecting the Copy Group Members option) at the same time it copies over the group to the destination domain. This option is not selected by default. If not selected, it results in a group created in the destination domain.

If you choose to have the wizard migrate over the users with the group, you also have the option to compare groups in the source and destination domains that have previously been migrated and to update information that has changed since the last migration. To do this, select the Update Previously Migrated Objects option. This is particularly useful in a migration scenario that is being done over an extended period of time because it allows you to migrate the information repeatedly until you're ready to decommission the source domains.

In general, if you're migrating users from one domain to another, you normally want them to be added to any groups in the destination domain to which they belonged in the source domain. To add all migrated users to corresponding groups in the destination domain, select the Fix Membership Of Group option (which is selected by default).

To provide user accounts with the SID history (which provides the users the capability to continue to access resources whose ACLs are dependent upon the SIDs from the previous domain), you must select the Migrate Group SIDs To Target Domain option (which is the default for Windows NT 4 but is not selected by default when migrating from Windows 2000).

In addition, you have the option to determine how the migrated accounts are named. By default, the Do Not Rename Accounts option is selected, and yet if needed, you can specify either a prefix or a suffix to be added to the account names. If a conflict between a migrated account and an existing account occurs, the settings in the Naming Conflicts dialog box determine how the account is named.

To migrate SIDs, the following conditions must exist:

- *Auditing must be enabled*—If auditing is not enabled on the source domain PDC, you are informed of this and are prompted to enable it if you want to be able to migrate SIDs to the destination domain.
- *A <domain>$$$ group must exist*—The logical group *<domain>*$$$ must exist on the source domain PDC; if it doesn't exist, you are prompted to create it.
- *A registry key must be added*—A registry key called TcpipClientSupport must be implemented on the source domain PDC; if it doesn't exist, you are prompted to create it.

Once you have the wizard set these changes, it prompts you to reboot the source domain PDC to ensure that the changes are implemented.

6 **Provide administrative credentials for migrating SID histories** When migrating from a Windows NT 4 source domain, you are prompted to supply the credentials required to migrate the group accounts (the user account must be a member of the Domain Admins group).

See the following screen:

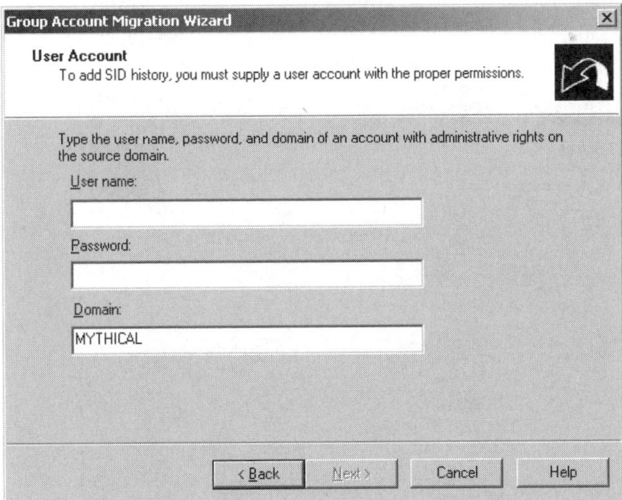

7 **Specify object properties to migrate** When you are migrating from a Windows 2000 or Windows Server 2003 domain, you can select the properties of the object to include or exclude during the migration (as shown in the following screen). All of the available properties are included by default for each of the objects (group, user, and, in the case of Windows Server 2003, InetOrgPerson).

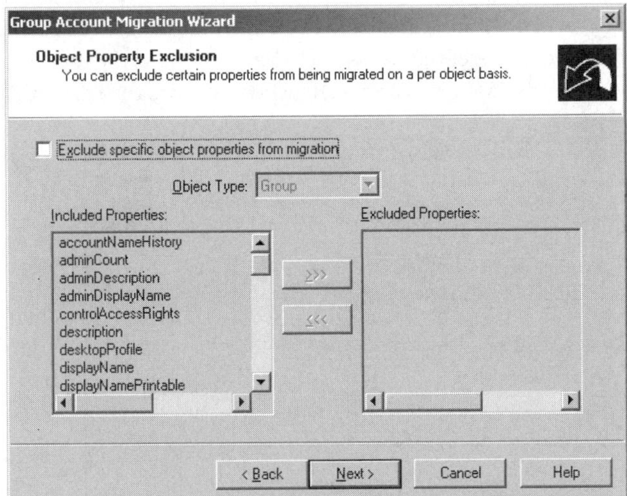

8 **Specify how naming conflicts are handled** You can configure how the wizard handles naming conflicts during the migration (see the following screen). You can select the Ignore Conflicting Accounts And Don't Migrate option to move accounts that do

not conflict with an existing account, or you can opt to replace or rename the migrated accounts. If you select the Replace Conflicting Accounts option, you can remove the existing user rights, remove the user accounts from the group, and move the existing accounts to another OU.

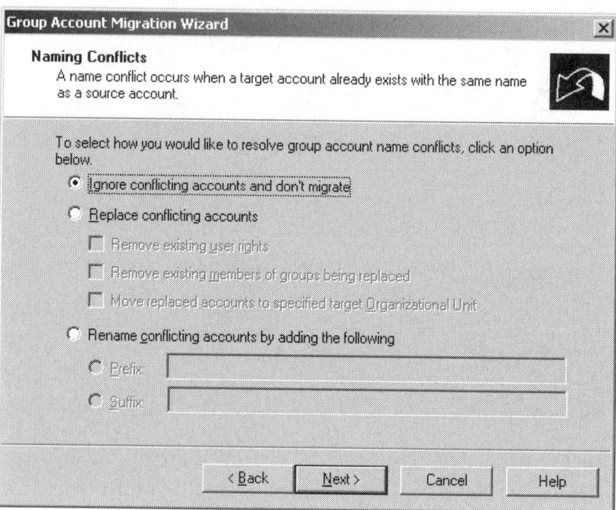

9 **Set password migration options** The password complexity level specified in the destination domain might exceed the actual password complexity of the user passwords stored in the source domain (especially for Windows NT 4 domains). In the Group Member Password Options dialog box (see the following screen), you can require complex passwords, reset the password to be the same as the user name, or migrate the existing passwords. You can also specify where to store the password file.

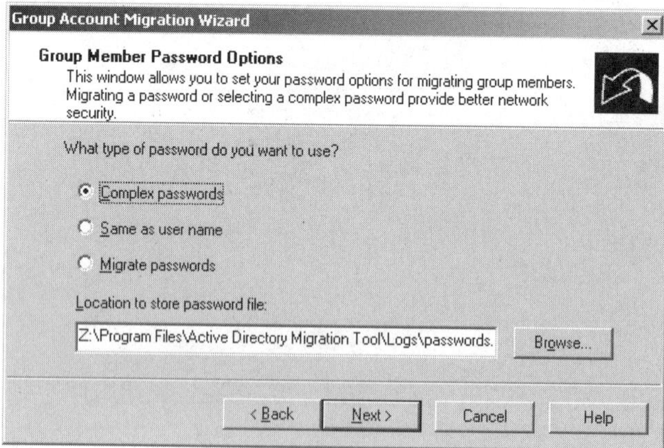

Tip Although requiring complex passwords improves network security, to prevent users from having to enter a new password upon migration, you can choose to have the wizard migrate the passwords just as they exist.

10 **Select account transition options** Next you must decide how to handle source and destination (target) versions of group accounts in the Group Member Transition Options dialog box (as shown in the following screen).

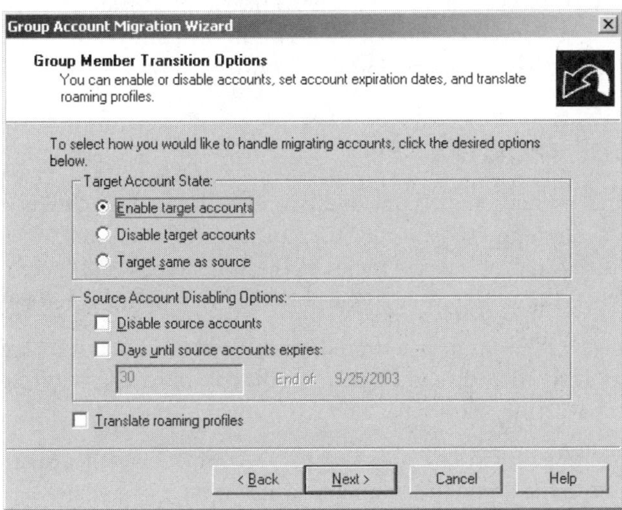

In the Target Account State section, you can enable or disable target accounts or set the target accounts to mirror the state of the account in the source domain (by default, target accounts are enabled). In the Source Account Disabling Options section, you can choose to disable the source accounts immediately or specify a predefined period of time (in days) to wait before disabling the source accounts. You can also choose to translate roaming profiles of the users in the source domain and migrate the profiles.

After you have selected the group migration options, they are summarized in the Task Description window of the final dialog box before the group migration is performed. Read these items to verify that they reflect what you want to do. For example, the Changes Will Not Be Written line indicates that this migration is running in Test mode and will not actually perform the requested changes.

When you click Finish, a progress dialog box is displayed that allows you to set the refresh rate for displaying the migration progress.

Once the migration has completed, the Progress dialog box displays the summary totals and the View Log button is enabled, allowing you to review the migration log for any errors. When you click View Log, the migration log is displayed in Notepad.

The migration log begins by listing the process configuration information as follows:

```
2004-08-27 00:02:23 Active Directory Migration Tool, Starting...
2004-08-27 00:02:23 Starting Account Replicator.
2004-08-27 00:02:23 Account MigrationWriteChanges:No NETMAGES CPANDI
CopyUsers:Yes CopyGlobalGroups:Yes CopyLocalGroups:Yes CopyComputers:No
StrongPwd:All
```

The migration log continues by listing each group and user processed and reports the results and specifies any errors or warnings. You can use the Notepad search functionality to identify the actions taken for a specific group or user. This information is stored as Migration.log in the Program Files\Active Directory Migration Tool\Logs folder.

Migrating User Accounts

Clearly, migrating user accounts is one of the core elements of domain migration, and the process takes several steps. First, the new user object must be created within the destination domain. Only then can properties of the user objects be transferred (because you cannot reference a property on an object prior to the object existing in the directory).

Before migrating user accounts, you should consider whether you must migrate passwords for the accounts. If you do, you should perform the password migration steps first, and then perform the user account migration.

An important contingency in a migration of user accounts is whether to migrate the SIDs for the user accounts to the destination domain (which creates or updates the SID history). Without the migration of the SIDs, user accounts are unable to access the network resources to which they previously had access. You must run the Security Translation Wizard to reinstate user access to network resources.

Running the User Account Migration Wizard

To migrate user accounts, run the User Account Migration Wizard on the Action menu in ADMT. This wizard uses many of the same dialog boxes as the Group Account Migration Wizard; thus, only dialog boxes unique to the User Account Migration Wizard are shown in this section. Refer to the section entitled "Migrating Group Accounts" earlier in this chapter to see the remaining dialog boxes.

Follow these steps to migrate user accounts:

1. **Choose to test only or migrate** When the User Account Migration Wizard starts, you must specify whether you want to test the effects of migrating users or actually migrate them by selecting either the Test The Migration Settings And Migrate Later option or the Migrate Now option. Prior to running the actual migration, you should run a migration test on the user accounts.

2 **Select the domains** The Domain Selection dialog box next prompts you to select or enter the names (DNS or NetBIOS) of the source and destination domains (if the destination domain is the forest root, you must provide the DNS name).

3 **Select the users** The Select Users dialog box prompts you to select the users that you want to migrate. To add users, click Add, click Advanced, click Find Now, and then select the users to migrate (you can hold down the Ctrl key while clicking to select multiples or hold down the Shift key while clicking to select a range).

4 **Choose the OU** You are next prompted to select the OU to which the users should be migrated.

5 **Select password options** You next set the password options, choosing whether to require complex passwords, reset the password as the user name, or migrate passwords (as shown in the following screen). You can prevent users from having to provide a new password after migration by having the wizard migrate the passwords. If you select the Migrate Passwords option, you must specify the name of the source domain controller in the Password Migration Source DC box. Once the source is selected, the wizard expects to find a domain controller configured as a Password Export Server.

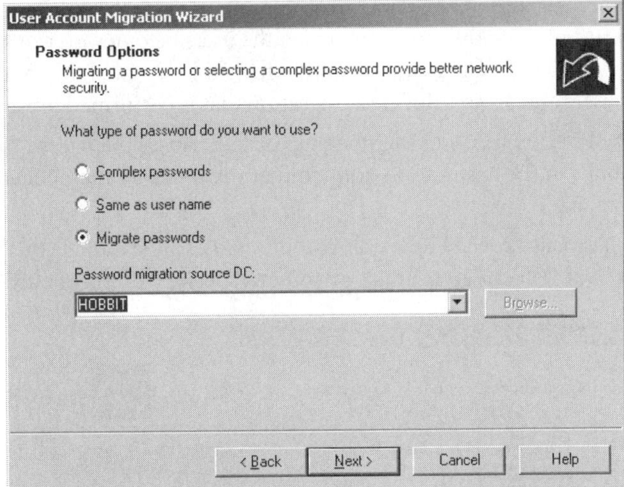

The setup for password migration has several requirements (refer to the section entitled "Migrating Passwords" later in this chapter for details on how to configure this):

- The Everyone account must be a member of the Pre–Windows 2000 Compatible Access group.
- The source domain controller must have the 128-bit high encryption pack installed and also must have the encryption key from the destination domain controller.

6 **Set the account transition options** These options tell the wizard how to move the user accounts between domains. You can enable or disable target accounts or allow target accounts to inherit account status in the source domain. You can also disable the source user accounts postmigration or wait a set number of days before disabling the accounts. The wizard will also migrate SIDs for source domain user accounts if you select the Migrate User SIDs To Target Domain option.

7 **Access authorization** When the source domain is a Windows NT 4 domain, credentials are required to authorize the migration (a user account that belongs to the Domain Admins group is required).

8 **Select user options** The User Options dialog box (as shown in the following screen) enables you to control how user accounts are handled as follows:

- The Translate Roaming Profiles option (selected by default) migrates the roaming profiles to the destination domain.
- The Update User Rights option (selected by default) migrates user rights from the source domain to the destination domain.
- The Migrate Associated User Groups option lets you migrate groups from the source domain of which the user accounts are members. When you opt to let the wizard migrate the groups to which the users belong, you can select the Update Previously Migrated Objects option to enable repeated migration of the same set of users and groups during a migration that is performed progressively over time.
- The Fix Users' Group Membership option causes the wizard to add users to all groups in the destination domain that the users are members of in the source domain.
- You can also specify how user account names are handled (this action defaults to Do Not Rename Accounts), or you can specify a prefix or suffix to be used.

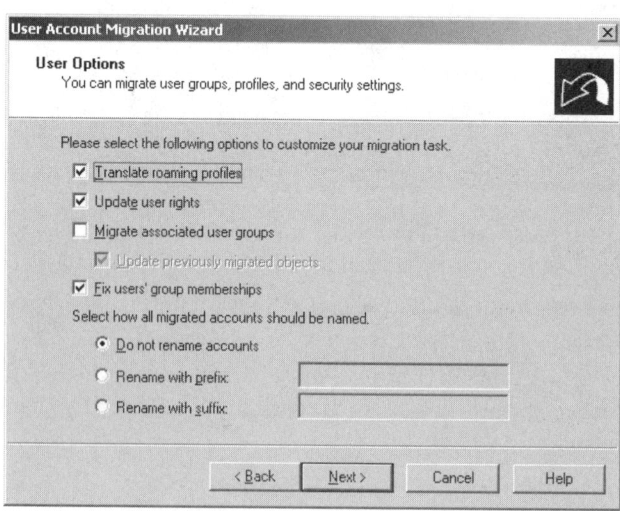

9 **Exclude object properties** When migrating a Windows 2000 or Windows Server 2003 domain, you can include or exclude the properties of the user objects during the migration. By default, all properties for user objects (user and InetOrgPerson in Windows Server 2003) are included.

10 **Manage naming conflicts** Configuring how the naming conflicts are managed lets you specify how user accounts are migrated. You can select the Ignore Conflicting Accounts And Don't Migrate option, or you can opt to replace or rename migrated user accounts. If you select the Replace Conflicting Accounts option, you have three choices:

- You can select the Remove Existing User Rights option, which instructs the wizard to remove any rights assigned to the user account in the destination domain that the user didn't have in the source domain.
- You can select the Remove Existing Members Of Groups Being Replaced option to make the destination group membership match the source group membership.
- You can select the Move Replaced Accounts To The Specified Target Organizational Unit option, which instructs the wizard to overwrite the user account information in the destination domain with the information from the source domain.

By selecting the Rename Conflicting Accounts By Adding The Following option, you can rename the user accounts by adding a prefix or suffix to the source domain user account name.

Next, the user migration information is summarized. Verify that the migration is configured the way you intend before you click Finish to begin the migration. If you are running in Test mode, verify that the line Changes Will Not Be Written is present. This line indicates that this migration is running in Test mode and will not actually perform the requested changes.

When the migration is complete, summary totals are shown and you can review the migration log list of every user and group account migrated, including a description of the action taken or related warning/error message. This log is located in the Program Files\Active Directory Migration Tool\Logs folder and is named Migration.log (previous Migration.log files are renamed as Migration 0001.log, Migration 0002.log, etc.). Especially if you have migration errors, you should review the migration log file and the audit information by using Event Viewer to assess the overall success of the user account migration.

Migrating Passwords

ADMT supports the migration of user passwords; however, it requires a bit of setup on the source and destination domain controllers.

Evaluate the password policy on the destination domain and determine whether the passwords in the user and service accounts that you're going to migrate meet the minimum password requirements for the new domain. If migrated user accounts don't meet the minimum requirements, users will be required to change their passwords at the next logon.

To prepare the destination domain for password migration, complete the following steps:

1. Modify the Default Domain Policy to enable the Everyone permissions for anonymous users. To access the policy, start Active Directory Users and Computers. Right-click the domain you want to work with, and select Properties. In the Group Policy tab of the Properties dialog box, select the domain policy, and click Edit. This displays the Group Policy Object Editor. In the Group Policy Object Editor, select Computer Configuration, Windows Settings, Security Settings, Local Policies, Security Options, and then double-click Network Access: Let Everyone Permissions Apply To Anonymous Users. In the policy dialog box, select Define This Policy Setting, choose Enabled, and then click OK.
2. On the target domain controller, locate the Pre–Windows 2000 Compatible Access group in the Builtin container, add Everyone to it, and reboot the domain controller.

> **Tip** If the destination (target) domain is a Windows NT 4 domain, the Password Export Server must have 128-bit high encryption pack support installed (which is included by default in Windows 2000 Server and Windows Server 2003 products).

3. Create the ADMT encryption key disk by changing to the drive and folder where ADMT is installed and running ADMT with the Key parameter from the command-line. Use the following syntax:

   ```
   ADMT key <sourceDomain> <drive> <password>
   ```

   where

   - *<sourceDomain>* is the NetBIOS name of the source domain from which the migration information will be collected
   - *<drive>* is the drive letter to which to write the password file
   - *<password>* is the password for the file (if you use * [asterisk], the system will prompt for the password)

Once you have performed the preceding steps to prepare the target domain, you next must prepare the source domain for password migration as follows:

1. Use the Password Migration tool (Pwdmig.exe in the I386\ADMT\Pwdmig directory on the Windows Server 2003 distribution CD), and insert the floppy disk with the encryption key created on the target domain when prompted.
2. Then set up a BDC as a Password Export Server that will be used during the migration process (the BDC must also have the 128-bit high encryption pack and be running Service Pack 5 or later). To do this, modify the registry on the BDC at HKLM\SYSTEM\CurrentControlSet\Control\Lsa, set the AllowPasswordExport value to 1, and then reboot the BDC.

Once this preparation has been done, you can specify the Password Export Server during user account migration to have the user passwords migrated at the same time.

Migrating the Computers

Not all computers can be migrated to a new domain—specifically, you cannot migrate domain controllers to a new domain. To move Windows NT domain controllers to a new Windows Server 2003 domain, the domain controllers must be upgraded to Windows Server 2003 and must join the new domain during the upgrade process. Windows 2000 domain controllers can be demoted from their domain controller mode to the status of member servers, and then you can use the Dcpromo utility to promote them to the status of domain controller and to join the new domain during that process.

Moving workstations and member servers to the destination domain automatically moves most of their information with them. The local Security Account Manager (SAM) databases (containing local user and group accounts) on member servers and client workstations are moved with the computer account during the migration process. Yet computer descriptions are not migrated from Windows NT workstations and member servers because that information isn't part of the SAM database. Whereas, with migrated Windows 2000 servers and workstations, computer descriptions are migrated with the computer accounts.

Running the Computer Migration Wizard

To migrate computer accounts, run the Computer Migration Wizard on the Action menu in ADMT. The security information (SIDs in the ACLs and secure ACLs) on accounts and objects in the same domain as the computer are migrated as part of the computer migration. Yet accounts (or objects) not part of the same domain as the computer will not have security information migrated.

The Computer Migration Wizard shares many dialog boxes in common with the Group Account Migration Wizard; therefore, only the dialog boxes unique to the Computer Migration Wizard are shown in this section. Refer to the section entitled "Migrating Group Accounts" earlier in this chapter to see the remaining dialog boxes.

To run the Computer Migration Wizard to migrate computer accounts, complete the following steps:

1. **Choose to test or migrate** When the Computer Migration Wizard starts, choose to test the computer account migration or to migrate the actual computer accounts by selecting either the Test The Migration Settings And Migrate Later option or the Migrate Now option. Testing the computer account migration enables you to identify and correct errors before an actual migration.
2. **Pick the domains** Next you must select or supply the source and destination domain names, which can be provided either as DNS or NetBIOS names (except for the forest root, which requires the DNS name).
3. **Choose the computers** The Computer Selection dialog box next prompts you to select the computers to migrate. To include the computers in the migration list, click Add, click Advanced, click Find Now, and then select the computers from the displayed list.

Note You cannot migrate domain controllers by using this wizard. To move a Windows NT domain controller to a new Windows Server 2003 domain, the domain controllers must be upgraded to Windows Server 2003 and must be joined to the new domain during the upgrade process. Windows 2000 domain controllers can be demoted from their domain controller mode to the status of member servers, then can be promoted to the status of domain controller by using Dcpromo, and finally can be joined to the new domain during that process.

4 **Select the target OU** You must next select the OU to which the computer accounts are to be migrated.

5 **Choose objects to translate** The Translate Objects dialog box, as shown in the following screen, allows you to select the objects on the source computer for which you want to migrate the security settings. That is, it translates the ACLs on the selected objects to corresponding ACLs on the computer in the destination domain. These objects include files and folders, printers, shares, local groups, and the registry, as well as user profiles and user rights. No objects are selected by default (thus, you can opt to migrate the computer without migrating any of the related security settings).

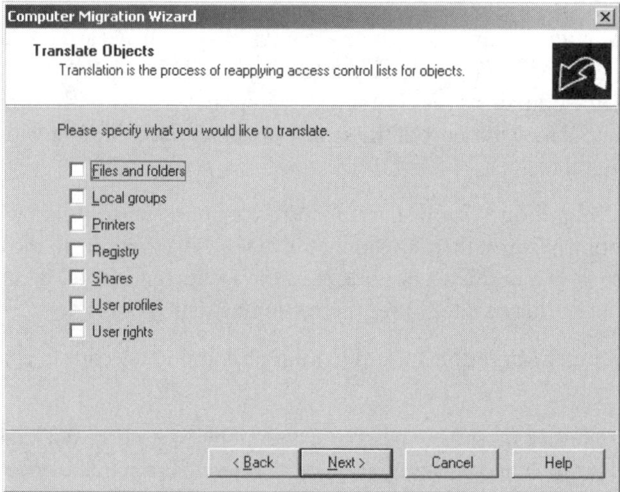

6 **Select computer options** The options in the Computer Options dialog box, as shown in the following screen, specify how the computer is handled postmigration, including how long it waits before it reboots and how it performs the renaming of the computer (if at all).

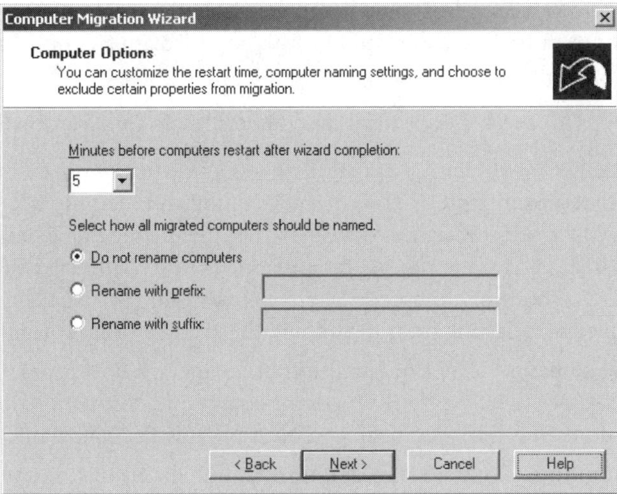

7 **Exclude object properties** When migrating a Windows 2000 or Windows Server 2003 computer, you can choose to exclude properties of computer objects during migration. By default, all computer object properties are included.

8 **Handling naming conflicts** In the event of a conflict with computer names in the destination domain, you can specify how you want the Computer Migration Wizard to deal with it. By default, the Replace Conflicting Accounts option is selected, which provides two options: You can select Remove Existing User Rights, to remove rights assigned in the destination domain that don't exist in the source domain, or Move Replaced Accounts To Specified Target Organizational Unit, which overwrites accounts in the destination domain with account data from the source domain.

   Alternatively, you can select the Rename Conflicting Accounts By Adding The Following option to rename the computer accounts by adding a prefix or suffix to the account name.

The summary of the migration information is displayed. Verify the computer migration is configured correctly before clicking Finish to complete the wizard. If you are running in Test mode, verify that the line Changes Will Not Be Written is present, which indicates that this migration is running in Test mode and will not actually perform the requested changes.

Merging Groups during Migration

To merge groups from the source domain into a group in the destination domain, run the Group Mapping and Merging Wizard on the Action menu in ADMT. The Group Mapping and Merging Wizard uses many of the same dialog boxes as the Group Account Migration

Wizard; thus, only the dialog boxes unique to the Group Mapping and Merging Wizard are displayed in this section. Refer to the section entitled "Migrating Group Accounts" earlier in the chapter to see the remaining dialog boxes.

Follow these steps to merge groups from the source domain into a group in the destination domain:

1. **Choose to test or migrate** The Group Mapping and Merging Wizard begins by allowing you to select whether you want to test the merging or actually do the merging of groups. Select the Test The Migration Settings And Migrate Later option to run the merge in Test mode or choose the Migrate Now option to actually perform the group merge operation. Testing prior to running the actual merge is recommended.
2. **Select the domains** The Domain Selection dialog box next prompts you to select or enter the names (DNS or NetBIOS) of the source and destination domains (if the destination domain is the forest root, you must provide the DNS name).
3. **Select the groups** In the Source Group Selection dialog box, you select the groups to merge from the source domain into the group in the destination domain. To do this, click Add, click Advanced, and then click Find Now, which will provide the list of groups that you can merge. Choose the groups to merge, and then click OK twice to add the groups.
4. **Choose the target group** Next, you must select the target group into which to merge the groups from the source domain, as shown in the following screen. Type in the name of the target group or click Browse to select a group.

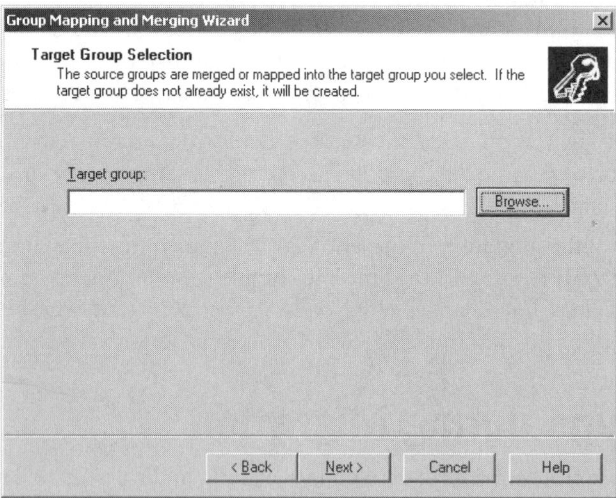

5. **Select the OU** You next must select the OU in which the target group will reside.

6 **Specify group options** The Group Options dialog box for merging the groups, as shown in the following screen, enables the copying of user rights (selected by default) and the migration of the group SIDs (by adding the SIDs from the groups in the source domain to the SID history of the target group in the destination domain) during the merge process.

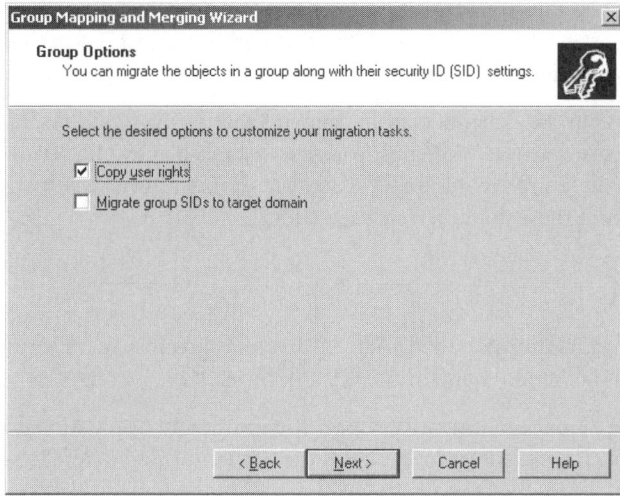

A summary of the group mapping and merging information is displayed. Verify that the information is correct before you click Finish to begin the group merge process. If you are running in Test mode, verify that the line Changes Will Not Be Written is present. This line indicates that this migration is running in Test mode and will not actually perform the requested changes. Once completed, you can click the View Log button to review each action taken during the merge process.

Migrating Domain Trusts

To enable migrated users to have the same level of access to network resources managed in multiple domains, migration of an existing domain is likely to include the migration of established domain trusts. Because Active Directory domain trusts are transitive, when migrating Windows 2000 domains, the trusts are commonly external trusts to down-level domains or trusts implemented to speed lookups between domains.

When migrating from Windows NT 4, it is common that you have both account domains and resource domains that must be migrated. Typically, the resource domains have an explicit trust relationship with the account domains, in which the resource domain trusts the account domain.

To be able to migrate the Windows NT 4 account domains and maintain the capability for users to access network resources in the established resource domains, the resource domains must also trust the new destination domain. Thus, you must establish an explicit trust relationship from each resource domain to the Windows Server 2003 destination domain prior to migrating the user accounts domain.

Likewise, when you migrate a resource domain to the new Windows Server 2003 destination domain, you must establish a trust with the existing Windows NT 4 accounts domain prior to performing the migration of the resource domains.

Groups can contain only members from domains that are trusted; thus, to migrate group accounts that exist in trusted domains, you must establish an explicit trust from the destination domain to the source Windows NT 4 accounts domain. You can use the Trust Migration Wizard to perform these domain trust migrations.

Migrating a Trust

To migrate a trust relationship to the Active Directory directory service, run the Trust Migration Wizard on the Action menu in ADMT as follows:

1. **Select the domains** You must supply the source and destination domain names. Specify from which domain to obtain the trust information and to which domain to migrate it. Enter the DNS or NetBIOS names of the domains (if the destination domain is the forest root, you must provide the DNS name).
2. **Select the trusts** The Trust Information dialog box is displayed (see the following screen), showing the trusts established in the selected domain. Once you select the trust to migrate, click Copy Trust to begin the trust migration. You are next prompted to supply credentials (user name and password) for an account with the authority to migrate the trust (Domain Admins).

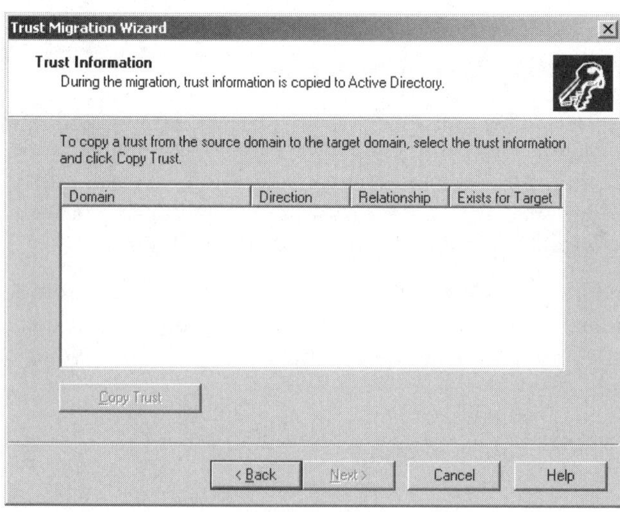

Migrating Service Accounts

Although many services operate using the local system authority, the local system authority has no rights or permissions to access network servers or services. Thus, special service accounts are used to provide credentials to network services that access other computers operating on your network. Service accounts are essentially user accounts that are designated for special purposes. They are used to run a specific network service using a unique set of user credentials assigned to the network service.

To migrate service accounts, run the Service Account Migration Wizard on the Action menu in ADMT. The Service Account Migration Wizard uses many of the same dialog boxes as the Group Account Migration Wizard; thus, only dialog boxes specific to migrating service accounts are shown in this section. Refer to the section entitled "Migrating Group Accounts" earlier in this chapter to see the remaining dialog boxes.

Follow these steps to migrate service accounts:

1. **Select the domains** You must select or supply the source and destination domain names. Enter the DNS or NetBIOS names of the domains (if the destination domain is the forest root, you must provide the DNS name).
2. **Update information** In the Update Information dialog box (as shown in the following screen), you choose either to use the service account information already collected or to reacquire the information.

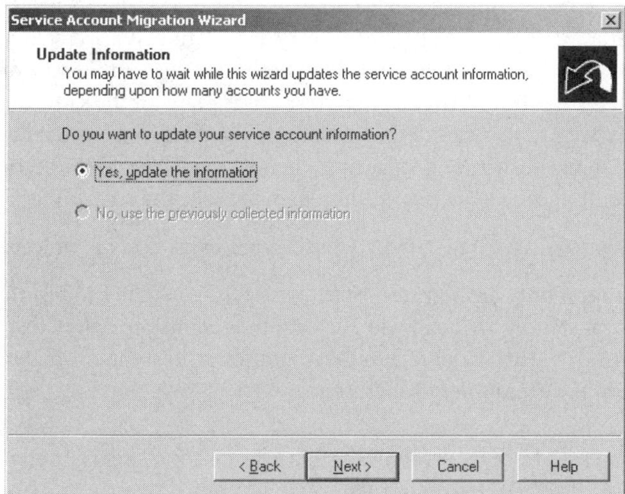

3. **Select the source of the service account data** In the Service Account Selection dialog box, you must specify the computer that contains the service accounts to migrate. To do so, click Add, click Advanced, click Find Now, and then select the computer with the service accounts.

4 **Deploy the agent** When the ADMT Agent Monitor begins, it attempts to install itself onto the specified computer (by using a remote procedure call [RPC] connection to the ADMIN$ share). The Agent Monitor displays information about the service accounts discovered in the Summary, Monitoring Settings, and Server List (default) tabs. In addition to the list of service accounts, in the Service List tab you can obtain more information about the progress of the agent (by using the Agent Detail), and you can use the View Dispatch Log option to assess each step of the process. You can also initiate or end monitoring by clicking the Start Monitoring and Stop Monitoring buttons.

5 **Discover service accounts** The Service Account Information dialog box displays the service account (by Computer, Account, Status, Service) and provides the option to select accounts to migrate (Skip/Include). If the status of an account is Update Failed, ADMT was unable to update the service. When the service is back online, select the service account, then refresh the account information by selecting the Update SCM Now option.

On the summary screen, you are congratulated on successfully defining the service account entries and are prompted to click Finish to complete the service account migration. Verify that the information is correct before doing this. Once completed, you can click View Log to review each action taken during the merge process.

Security Translation

To migrate the security settings for extra domain objects, run the Security Translation Wizard on the Action menu in ADMT. The Security Translation Wizard changes the SIDs in ACLs and SACLs on objects that do not belong to the domain or that are not migrated as part of the Computer Migration Wizard. This wizard uses many of the same dialog boxes as the Group Account Migration Wizard; therefore, only the dialog boxes that are unique to the Security Translation Wizard are displayed in this section. Refer to the section entitled "Migrating Group Accounts" earlier in this chapter to see the remaining dialog boxes.

Follow these steps to migrate the security settings for extra domain objects:

1 **Choose to test only or migrate** Start by selecting whether to test the effects of the security translation or actually to perform the migration. Select Test The Migration Settings And Migrate Later to run the migration in Test mode, or choose Migrate Now to perform the group merge operation.

> **Tip** It is a good idea to do a test run prior to performing the security translation because it will allow you to discover and resolve errors.

2 **Select translation options** In the Security Translation Options dialog box (as shown in the following screen), you can select previously migrated objects or use a SID mapping file. A SID mapping file is constructed by using comma-separated pairs of source–destination references (name or SID) specified on each line of a text file. You can use this file to migrate security for accounts that are skipped by the Group Account Migration Wizard (such as Administrators).

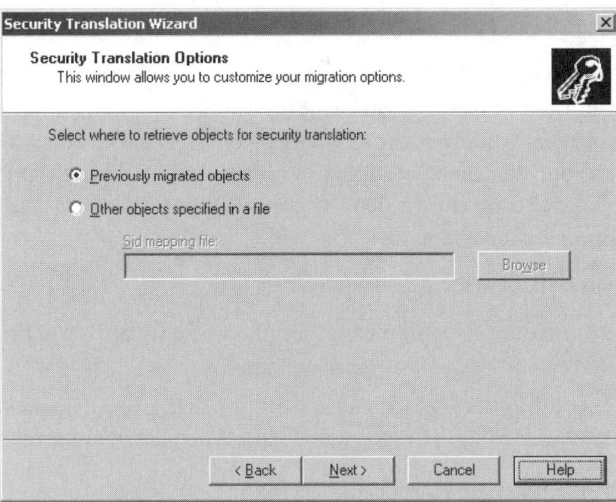

3 **Select the domains** Next you must provide the source and destination domain names. Enter the DNS or NetBIOS names of the domains (if the destination domain is the forest root, you must provide the DNS name).

4 **Select the computers** In the Computer Selection dialog box, select the computers on which to perform the security translation. Click Add, click Advanced, click Find Now, and then select the relevant computers.

5 **Select objects to translate** Locate and select the objects on the source computer for which you want to translate the security settings. The SIDs assigned to ACLs and SACLs for the selected objects are translated to corresponding security descriptors on the objects in the destination domain. Objects available for security translation include files and folders, local groups, printers, shares, registry, user profiles, and user rights, yet none are selected by default.

6 **Specify security translation options** You can decide how SIDs are translated by selecting one of the following options:

- *Replace*—Replaces SIDs referencing objects in the source domain accounts and adds the SIDs to the account in the destination domain
- *Add*—Maintains original set of SIDs references while adding SIDs to the account in the destination domain
- *Remove*—Deletes the SIDs applied to the ACLs and SACLs and removes the permissions to access source domain objects

The summary of the security translation is shown next. Check the information before you click Finish to perform the translation. If you are running in Test mode, verify that the line Changes Will Not Be Written is present, which indicates that this migration is running in Test mode and will not actually perform the requested changes. Once completed, you can click View Log to review each action taken during the merge process.

Generating Migration Reports

To review migration status information, you can produce reports on migrated user and computer accounts, account references, name conflicts, and expired accounts by using the Report Wizard. This wizard uses many of the same dialog boxes as the Group Account Migration Wizard; therefore, only the dialog boxes that are unique to the Report Wizard are displayed in this section. Refer to the section entitled "Migrating Group Accounts" earlier in this chapter to see the remaining dialog boxes.

Follow these steps to review the migration status:

1. **Select the domains** As with most other migration wizards, you first select the domains for which you want to generate reports.
2. **Select the report folder** In the Folder Selection dialog box, you must specify the folder in which you want to store the generated reports, as shown in the following screen:

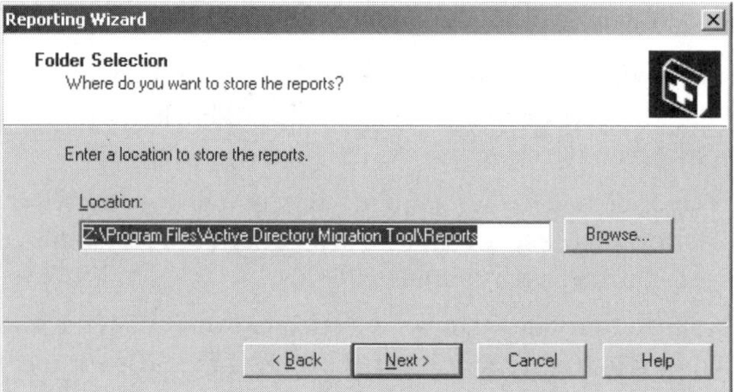

3. **Select the reports to generate** In the Report Selection dialog box, you can decide to generate reports on user and computer accounts that have been migrated, account references, and name conflicts, as well as expired accounts, as shown in the following screen:

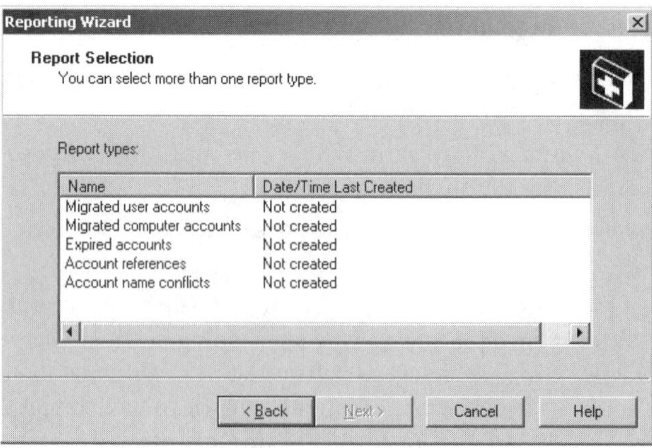

The summary information is then displayed. Click Finish to generate the selected reports.

Part 4

Managing Windows Server 2003 Systems

Chapter 10

Configuring Windows Server 2003

When you set out to work with Microsoft Windows Server 2003, one of the first things you'll notice is that the desktop and Start menu are different from previous editions of the Windows operating system. For starters, the desktop is empty—or practically so because the only item on it is the Recycle Bin—and there's a new Start menu. Beyond that, though, the interface changes from Microsoft Windows 2000 to Windows Server 2003 are minor. In fact, you'll find most of the tools that you want to work with are right where they were in Windows 2000.

However, for those coming from Microsoft Windows NT to Windows Server 2003, the interface represents a significant change, the biggest of which has to do with the use of the Microsoft Management Console (MMC). Although most system functions still are controlled through Control Panel, many administrative functions are now accessed by using the MMC. You'll find there are many prepackaged administration tools for the MMC, many of which are accessible from the Administrative Tools menu. But the true power of the MMC is in its extensible framework that lets you build your own administration tools.

This chapter is the first of two that focus on customizing the configuration of Windows Server 2003. In this chapter, you'll learn how to customize the operating system interface. In Chapter 11, "Windows Server 2003 MMC Administration," you'll learn how to use and customize the MMC using the extensible framework provided by Microsoft. As you'll see, once you optimize the environment, you'll be well on your way to mastering Windows Server 2003.

Optimizing the Menu System

Way back in Chapter 1, "Introducing Windows Server 2003," we talked about some of the interface changes in Windows Server 2003, focusing on the changes to the Start menu and discussing how you could choose to use either the simple or the Classic Start menu. Basically, you right-click the Start button, select Properties to display the Taskbar And Start Menu Properties dialog box, and then select either Start Menu (for the simple Start menu) or Classic Start Menu. That is one way to change the interface. Now let's look at other ways you can change the interface, starting with how you can control the content of the Start menu.

Modifying the Start Menu Content

Regardless of whether you choose to use the simple or Classic Start menu, you can customize the menu by adding, removing, moving, copying, sorting, and renaming menu items. The simple Start menu does have a slight advantage over the Classic Start menu in the area of customization, however. As Figure 10-1 shows, this menu has the following features:

- **Pinned items list** Appears in the upper-left corner of the menu and allows you to add items that should always appear on the menu. If you no longer want an item to appear on the list, you can remove it as well.

- **Frequently used programs list** Appears below the pinned items list and shows the most frequently used programs. The Windows operating system manages this list automatically based on your program usage, but you can control the number of items that appear here and can remove items from the list. You can't add items to this list, however.

- **All Programs button** Appears in the lower-left corner of the menu and provides access to the program menus. The items that appear here are the same as you see when you are using the Classic Start menu and click Programs, including any items that normally appear above the Programs menu. You can rearrange the items to meet your needs and preferences.

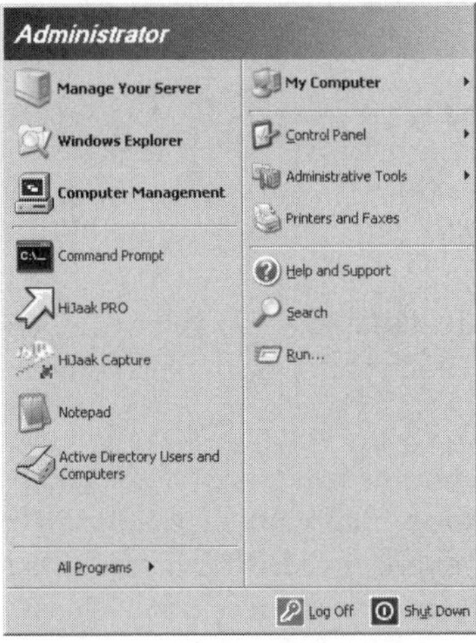

Figure 10-1. Simple Start menu has two customizable areas: the pinned items list and the most frequently used programs list.

> **Note** Items on the pinned items list and most frequently used programs list do not appear on the Classic Start menu. You can, however, add items to the top of the Start menu above the Programs folder.

Chapter 10

Adding, Copying, and Moving Menu Items

To add an item to the pinned items list, navigate the menu system until you get to the program you want to work with. When you find it, right-click it, and then click Pin To Start Menu. Now you have a program shortcut pinned to the Start menu. Alternatively, if you drag a shortcut, folder, or program icon to the Start button and release the mouse button before the menu displays, the shortcut is added to the pinned items list. Keep in mind that these techniques are for the simple Start menu—the Classic Start menu doesn't have a pinned items list.

Troubleshooting

No shortcut menus appear when I right-click

The appearance of the shortcut menu when you right-click a menu item is controlled by the drag-and-drop menu configuration option. If you don't see a shortcut menu when you right-click an item, the Enable Dragging And Dropping menu option has been disabled. To enable shortcut menus, right-click the Start button, choose Properties, and then click Customize. If you are using the simple Start menu, click the Advanced tab, and then in the Start Menu Items box, select Enable Dragging And Dropping. If you are using the Classic Start menu, click Enable Dragging And Dropping in the Advanced Start Menu Options list.

You can add a program to the top of the Classic Start menu, above the Programs folder. To do this, you drag a shortcut to the top of the menu from any location in the menu, the desktop, or a Windows Explorer window. When you do this, you'll see a shortcut menu with Copy Here, Move Here, or Cancel options. Most of the time, you'll want to create a copy of the item rather than move the shortcut. This ensures that the shortcut remains in its original location and if you later delete the item from above the Programs menu, you'll still be able to access the item in its original location.

The simple Start menu supports drag and drop, too. In fact, you can drag an item from any part of the menu to any other part of the menu, regardless of which menu you are using. This is how you add an item to any part of the menu. So, click the item you want to work with, hold down the mouse button, and navigate to where you'd like to add the item in the menu. A dark line shows where the new item will appear when you release the button.

You can use drag and drop to move items from the desktop or Windows Explorer to the menu as well. When you do this, the Windows operating system leaves the item where you got it and creates a copy on the Start menu. If the item you're dragging and dropping isn't a shortcut, that's okay as well. The operating system creates a shortcut to represent the item on the Start menu automatically. This allows you to drag a file or folder to the menu, providing a quick access shortcut to the file or folder.

Note The Windows operating system creates a shortcut only if you drag and drop a file or folder to a location within the menu. If you drag a file or folder onto the menu and then drop it into one of the document links, such as My Documents, My Music, or My Pictures, Windows Server 2003 will move the selected item to the document folder instead of creating a shortcut.

Troubleshooting

I'm unable to drag and drop items

All this talk about dragging and dropping items is fine as long as the drag and drop feature for the Start menu is enabled. If this feature is disabled, however, you won't be able to drag items to, from, or within the Start menu. To enable drag and drop, right-click Start, choose Properties, and then click Customize. If you are using the simple Start menu, click the Advanced tab, and then in the Start Menu Items box, select Enable Dragging And Dropping. If you are using the Classic Start menu, click Enable Dragging And Dropping in the Advanced Start Menu Options list.

To copy an item to a new location, press Ctrl, click the item, then hold the mouse button while dragging the item to the new location. A plus sign (+) appears next to the mouse pointer, indicating that you are copying the item not moving it. Release the mouse button and then release the Ctrl key. You can copy items from the menu to the desktop, a folder, or a toolbar using the same technique.

Note Keep in mind that when you drag an item from the left side of the simple Start menu to the All Programs menu, Windows Server 2003 always copies the item. Therefore, you don't need to hold down the Ctrl key. The same is true when you drag an item from the All Programs menu to the pinned items list.

Highlighting and Hiding Menu Items

When you work with the Start menu, you should be aware of two additional features, which you might or might not like: automatic highlighting and hiding of menu items.

For the simple Start menu, when you install new programs, by default the Windows operating system highlights the additional menus and menu items that have been created. These highlights last until you run the item (or for several days) and are designed to make it easier for you to find the new items and also ensure that you know what changes have been made to the Start menu. Some users love this feature; some users hate it. If you find the highlights distracting, you can remove them. To do this, right-click the Start button, choose Properties, and then click Customize. Click the Advanced tab, and then in the Start Menu Settings box, clear the Highlight Newly Installed Programs box, as shown in the following screen:

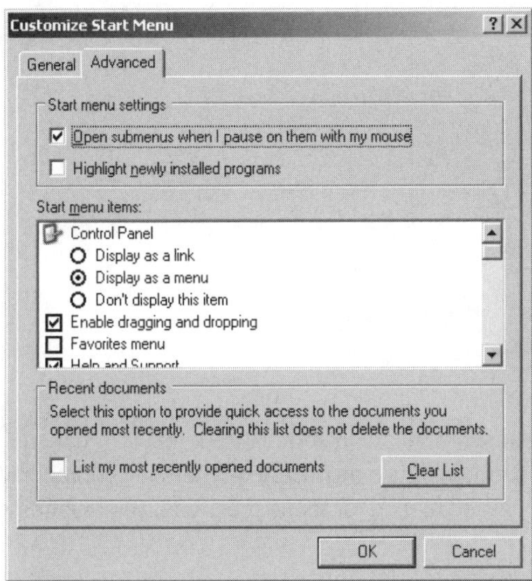

For the Classic Start menu, by default the Windows operating system displays the most frequently used items and hides the others. This feature is designed to reduce menu clutter by giving you shorter menus that make it easier for you to find the items you use the most. A double arrow at the bottom of a submenu indicates the presence of additional items that are not shown. To display these items, click the double arrow or wait a few seconds and the menu will expand automatically.

The newly displayed items are shown on a light-colored background to make them easier to see. Again, this is a feature you probably either love or hate. Don't worry, you can turn this feature off. To do this, right-click the Start button, choose Properties, and then click

Customize. In the Advanced Start Menu Options list, clear the Use Personalized Menus option, as shown in the following screen:

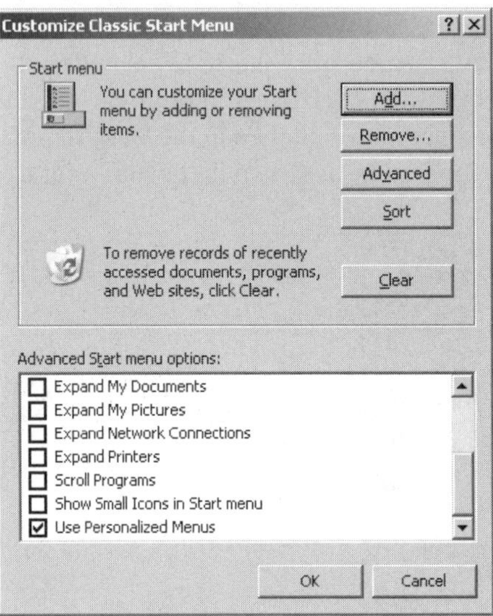

Note The Use Personalized Menus option is only for the Start menu. It doesn't affect other programs that might use this feature, such as Microsoft Internet Explorer or Microsoft Office. To enable or disable personalized menus for these programs, you must do so within each individual program.

Controlling the Frequently Used Programs List

For the default Start menu, the Windows operating system manages the frequently used programs list based on your program usage. The list includes only shortcuts to .exe files; any other executable files that you use are not shown on the list regardless of how often you use them. There are many exceptions as well. For example, if the name of the shortcut that starts the program contains any of the following strings, it is not displayed on the list:

- Documentation
- Help
- Install
- More Info
- Readme
- Read me
- Read First

- Setup
- Support
- What's New
- Remove

The list of excluded names or partial names is controlled by the AddRemoveNames value in the registry location HKEY_LOCAL_MACHINE\SOFTWARE\Microsoft\Windows\CurrentVersion\Explorer\FileAssociation. Further, the following program executables are specifically excluded from appearing on the list:

- Setup.exe
- Install.exe
- Isuninst.exe
- Unwise.exe
- Unwise32.exe
- St5unst.exe
- Rundll32.exe
- Msoobe.exe
- Lnkstub.exe

The list of excluded programs is controlled by the AddRemoveApps value in the same registry location mentioned previously. Additional programs can be registered to be excluded from the list by adding them to the KillList value in this registry location. The following programs are on the Kill list by default:

- Explorer.exe
- Dvdplay.exe
- Mplay32.exe
- Msohtmed.exe
- Quickview.exe
- Rundll.exe
- Rundll32.exe
- Taskman.exe
- Bck32api.dll

The Windows operating system uses these registry values to control the items that appear on the frequently used programs list. You can customize these values, particularly the Kill list, if you desire. You can also control whether and how the list is configured. By default, the Windows operating system shows up to six frequently used programs on the list. You can change this behavior by setting the number of programs to display using a value from 0 to 30. If you use a value of 0, no frequently used programs are displayed and you essentially disable this feature. Any other value sets the maximum number, up to and including that number, of frequently used programs that the operating system can display on the Start menu.

To specify the maximum number of programs that can appear on the frequently used programs list, right-click Start, choose Properties, and click Customize. In the General tab of the Customize Start Menu dialog box, enter the value you want to use in the Number Of Programs On Start Menu box, as shown in Figure 10-2. If you want to clear the program usage statistics, click Clear List. After you click Clear List, the Windows operating system clears out any existing program usage statistics and starts over, adding programs to the list each time you use them.

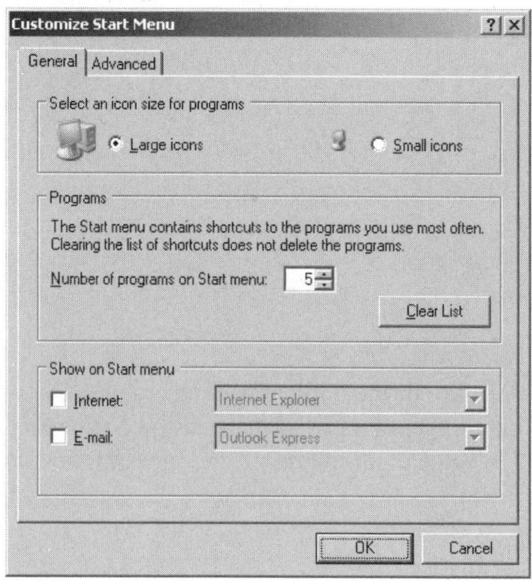

Figure 10-2. Control the maximum number of frequently used programs that is displayed by using a value from 0 to 30.

Sorting and Renaming Menu Items

As you add new programs, the Windows operating system typically adds the shortcuts for the programs to the bottom of the menu. Over time, this can result in having programs listed in a seemingly random order. To have it so programs are listed alphabetically, you can tell the operating system to re-sort a particular menu or submenu so that folders are listed in alphabetical order, followed by menu items listed in alphabetical order.

To sort the currently selected submenu, right-click an item on the menu, and choose Sort By Name from the shortcut menu. If you are using the Classic Start menu, you can sort all the submenus within the Programs menu at once. To do this, right-click Start, choose Properties, and then click Customize. In the Customize Classic Start Menu dialog box, click Sort.

> **Note** The Windows operating system maintains many menu settings separately for the Classic and simple Start menus, including drag and drop settings and sort order. This means if you change the order of a menu using the Classic Start menu, the changes don't appear if you change to using the simple Start menu.

While we're talking about sorting items, a related topic is renaming items. Unlike versions of the Windows operating system prior to Microsoft Windows XP, you can rename menu items. To do this, right-click the menu item you want to rename, and choose Rename. Edit the name of the item, and then click OK. Renaming an item can change the way the item is sorted, but Windows Server 2003 won't re-sort the menu automatically. You must do this manually using one of the techniques discussed previously.

Removing Items from the Start Menu

Windows Server 2003 gives you several options for removing items from the Start menu. If the item is on the pinned items list, you can remove it from the list by right-clicking it and choosing Unpin From Start Menu. Unfortunately, if you do this and the program is also one of your most frequently used programs, it could immediately reappear on the frequently used programs list. To ensure the program doesn't show up in either location, right-click the item, and choose Remove From This List. This is the same option you choose to remove an item from the frequently used programs list. (Unfortunately, this isn't permanent, however. If you continue to use a program, it can show up again on the frequently used programs list. So, if you really want to block a program from the frequently used programs list, exclude it as discussed in the section entitled "Controlling the Frequently Used Programs List" earlier in this chapter.)

Other types of menu items can be removed as well. To remove a regular menu item, right-click it, and choose Delete. Confirm that you want to remove the item by clicking Yes when prompted.

> **Note** Keep in mind that deleting an item from the menu doesn't uninstall the related program. It only deletes the shortcut to the program.

Customizing the Desktop and the Taskbar

By default the only items on the Windows Server 2003 desktop are the Recycle Bin and the taskbar. That's it. Everything else has been cleared away to allow you to customize the desktop anyway you want. The problem is that some of the missing items, such as My Computer, My Network Places, and Internet Explorer, were pretty useful, or at least most of us have grown so accustomed to having the items on the desktop that we expect them to be there. So, if you're like me, the first thing you'll want to do to customize the desktop is to add frequently accessed programs, files, and folders and to restore the missing items. Another thing you might want to do is to customize the taskbar so that it works the way you want it to. By default, the taskbar doesn't automatically hide or lock, and it might include items that you don't want.

Configuring Desktop Items

Windows Server 2003 allows you to drag program shortcuts, files, and folders from a Windows Explorer window onto the desktop. Simply click the item you want to move, hold down the mouse button, and drag the item to a location on the desktop. When you release the mouse button, the item is moved from its original location to the desktop. If you want to copy the item instead of moving it, press Ctrl, click the item, then hold the mouse button while dragging the item to the new location. On the desktop, release the mouse button, and then release the Ctrl key.

You can, in fact, use the copy and move techniques to add shortcuts for My Documents, My Computer, My Network Places, and Internet Explorer to the desktop. But there's another way to add these items to the desktop so that they appear as standard desktop icons instead of shortcuts. Right-click the desktop, and choose Properties. Select the Desktop tab, as shown in the following screen:

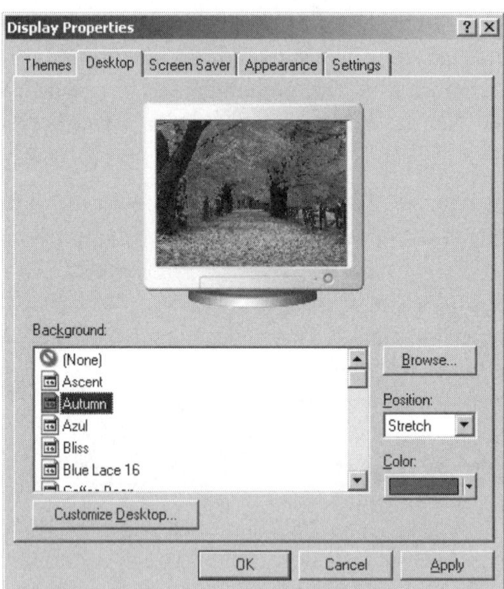

Chapter 10

While you are here, you might want to choose a new background. Simply scroll through the list of available backgrounds until you find one that you want to use. When you are ready to continue, click the Customize Desktop button in the lower-left corner of the dialog box to display the Desktop Items dialog box, as shown in the following screen:

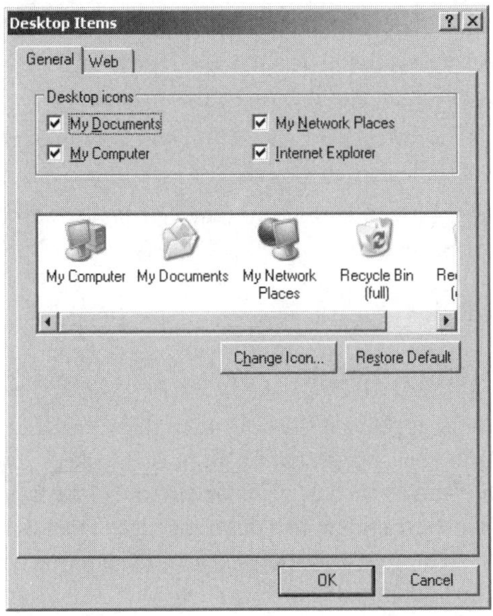

In the Desktop Items dialog box, select the items that you want to display on the desktop, for instance, My Documents, My Computer, My Network Places, and Internet Explorer. Several uses for My Computer and My Network Places aren't obvious but are great time-savers.

Use My Computer in the following ways:

- Right-click and choose Manage to start Computer Management.
- Right-click and choose Properties to display the System utility in Control Panel.
- Right-click and choose Map Network Drive or Disconnect Network Drive to manage network shares.

Use My Network Places as follows:

- Right-click and choose Search For Computers to find computers on the network.
- Right-click and choose Properties to display the Network Connections utility.
- Right-click and choose Map Network Drive or Disconnect Network Drive to manage network shares.

Configuring the Taskbar

The taskbar is one of those areas of the desktop that most people take for granted. It's sort of like people think, "Hey, there's the taskbar, what can I click?" when they should be thinking, "Hey, there's a taskbar. It tracks all the running programs for quick access and I can customize it to work the way I want it to." Beyond the Start button, the taskbar has three main areas:

- **Quick Launch** Provides quick access to the desktop and commonly used applications. Technically, it is a type of toolbar, and it is fully customizable.
- **Programs/Toolbars** Shows icons for running programs, which can be grouped according to type, as well as the toolbars that are selected for display.
- **Notification** Shows the system clock and programs that were loaded automatically at startup and that are running in the background.

You can change the behavior and properties of these taskbar areas in many ways.

Changing the Taskbar Size and Position

In the default configuration, the taskbar appears at the bottom of the screen and is sized so that one row of options is visible. As long as the taskbar position isn't locked, you can move it to any edge of the Windows desktop and resize it as necessary. To move the taskbar, simply click it and hold the mouse button while dragging it to a different edge of the desktop. When you move the mouse toward the left, right, top, or bottom edge of the desktop, you'll see a gray outline that shows you where the taskbar will appear. When you release the mouse button, the taskbar will appear in the new location.

With a left- or right-docked taskbar, you'll often have to resize the taskbar so that it is wider than usual to ensure that you can read the program names. I've found this approach useful when I am troubleshooting a system and I have lots of programs running and want to be able to switch quickly between them. In contrast, a top-docked taskbar seems to remove the clutter from the desktop, and I've found it useful when I don't want to use the Auto Hide feature.

To resize the taskbar, move the mouse pointer over the taskbar edge, and then drag it up or down, left or right, as appropriate. If you resize the taskbar so that it isn't visible (different from Auto Hide), you should still see a gray bar on the edge of the screen where the taskbar is docked. When you move the mouse pointer over the gray bar, the arrow pointer should change to the resize pointer, allowing you to resize the taskbar so that it is visible. On computers with a Windows key, you can press the Windows key and the Start menu will pop out from the edge of the screen that has the minimized taskbar, revealing the location of the taskbar as well.

Using Auto Hide and Locking

Windows Server 2003 has several features that control the visibility of the taskbar. You can enable the Auto Hide feature to hide the taskbar from view when it is not in use. You can lock the taskbar so that it cannot be resized or repositioned. You can also make the taskbar appear on top of other windows when you point to it. Once the taskbar is positioned and sized the way you want it, I recommend enabling all three of these options. In this way, the taskbar has a fixed location and is visible when it is pointed to, ensuring that it isn't accidentally hidden behind other windows.

You can enable these options as shown in the following screen by right-clicking the taskbar and then choosing Properties from the shortcut menu. Afterward, select the Lock The Taskbar, Auto-Hide The Taskbar, and Keep The Taskbar On Top Of Other Windows options as appropriate. Then click OK.

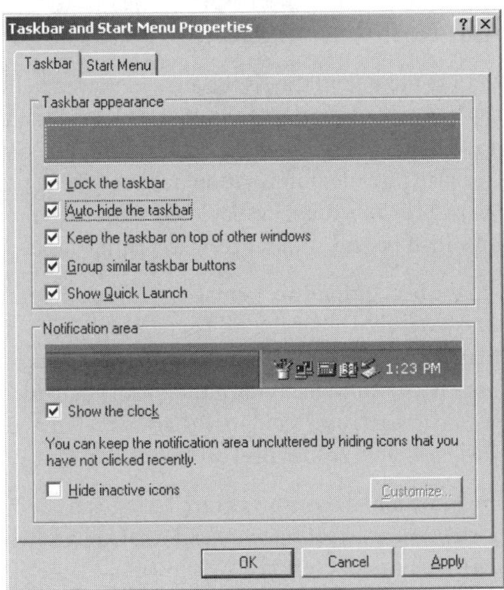

Note Locking the taskbar doesn't prevent you from changing the taskbar in the future. If you want to change the taskbar, all you must do is right-click the taskbar and then clear Lock The Taskbar. You can then make any necessary changes and, if desired, relock the taskbar to ensure the settings are protected from being accidentally changed.

Chapter 10

Grouping Similar Taskbar Items

As discussed previously, Windows Server 2003 implements many of the interface changes of Windows XP. One of these interface changes has to do with how like items are displayed on the taskbar. In versions of the Windows operating system prior to Windows XP, each item was displayed with a separate icon. Beginning with Windows XP, similar items are grouped together to reduce taskbar clutter. For example, if you open multiple MMCs and the taskbar needs additional room for other items, these consoles are grouped under a single button and are then accessible by clicking the button and selecting the individual MMC you want to use. In some ways, this is a good thing, but it can be confusing.

You can control whether similar items are grouped together by right-clicking the taskbar and then choosing Properties from the shortcut menu. Afterward, select Group Similar Taskbar Buttons to enable this option or clear Group Similar Taskbar Buttons to disable this option.

Controlling Programs in the Notification Area

The notification area, also referred to as the system tray, is the area on the far right side of the taskbar. It shows the system clock as well as icons for programs that were loaded automatically by the operating system at startup and that are running in the background. When you point to icons in the notification area, a ScreenTip provides information on the running program. You can right-click the program icon to display a menu of available options. Each program has a different menu of options, most of which provide quick access to routine tasks.

User-specified programs that run in the background are managed through the Startup folder. The Startup folder is configured at two levels. Under the All Users folder, there is a Startup folder for all users of a given system. Any program referenced in the All Users folder is run in the background regardless of which user logs on. Within the profile data for individual users, there is a Startup folder specific to each user's logon. Programs referenced in a personal Startup folder are run only when that user logs on.

You can add or remove startup programs for all users by right-clicking Start and then selecting Explore All Users from the shortcut menu. This opens Windows Explorer with the Documents And Settings\All Users\Start Menu folder selected, as shown in Figure 10-3.

In the left pane, double-click the Programs folder under Start Menu, and then click Startup. You can now add or remove startup programs for all users as follows:

- To add startup programs, create a shortcut to the program that you want to run.
- To remove a startup program, delete its shortcut from the Startup folder.

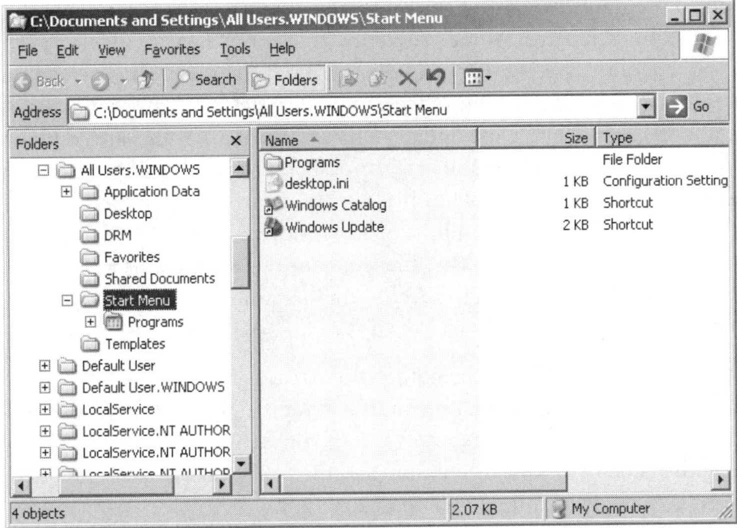

Figure 10-3. Exploring All Users gets you to the Start Menu folder for all users of the computer; then you must work your way down to the Startup folder under Programs.

You can add or remove startup programs for individual users as well, such as the administrator. To do this, log on as the user whose startup applications you want to manage. Right-click Start, and then select Explore from the shortcut menu. This opens Windows Explorer with the %UserProfile%\Start Menu folder selected. In the left pane, double-click the Programs folder under Start Menu, and then click Startup. You can now add or remove startup programs for this user as discussed previously.

Inside Out

Why log on as the user to access the Startup folder?

You might be wondering why I told you to log on as the user whose startup applications you want to control. Technically, you don't need to do this, but it is easier if you do. Why? Because when you select Explore, you'll be taken to that user's Start Menu folder—sometimes getting the right user profile folder is half the battle, especially on a system that has been upgraded or renamed or reinstalled and that contains several different profile entries for each user. If you can't log on as the user, access the Documents And Settings folder on the system drive, and work your way down through the user's profile data folders. These are listed by account name.

User-specified programs that run in the background are only one type of program that is displayed in the notification area. Some programs, such as Automatic Updates, are managed by the Windows operating system. For example, Automatic Updates runs periodically to check for updates to the operating system. When an update is detected, the user can be notified and given the opportunity to apply the update. Other types of programs are configured during installation to run in the background at startup, such as an antivirus program. You can typically enable or disable the display of notification area icons related to these programs through the setup options in the related applications. Windows Server 2003 also provides a common interface for controlling whether the icons for these programs are displayed in the notification area. This allows you to specify whether and how icons are displayed on a per-program basis.

To control the display of icons in the notification area, right-click the taskbar, and then choose Properties from the shortcut menu. If you want all icons to be displayed, clear the Hide Inactive Icons option, and then click OK. If you want to customize the appearance of icons, select the Hide Inactive Icons option, and then click Customize. This displays the Customize Notifications dialog box shown in Figure 10-4.

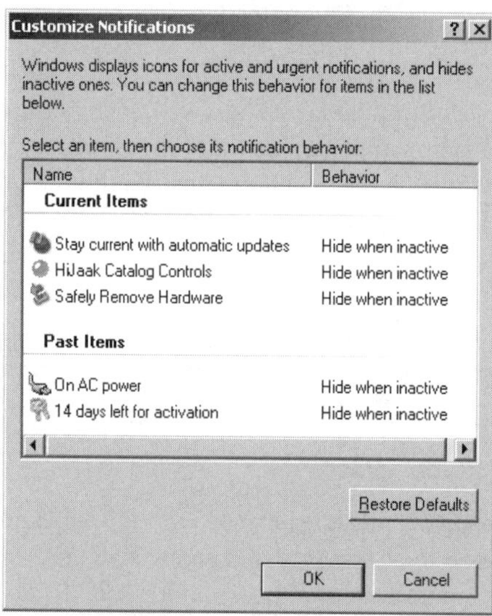

Figure 10-4. You can customize notifications for notification area items.

You can now optimize the notification behavior for current items displayed in the notification area as well as items that were displayed in the past but aren't currently active. The Name column shows the name of the program. The Behavior column shows the currently selected notification behavior, which is typically Hide When Inactive, but which can also be set to Always Hide or Always Show.

Note When the Hide Inactive Icons option is selected in the Taskbar And Start Menu Properties dialog box, you can right-click in the notification area and then select Customize Notifications to directly access the Customize Notifications dialog box.

Optimizing Toolbars

Several custom toolbars are available for the taskbar. The toolbar that most people are familiar with is the Quick Launch toolbar, which provides quick access to commonly used programs and the Windows desktop. The taskbar can display other toolbars that come with Windows Server 2003, and you can create you own toolbars as well.

Customizing the Quick Launch Toolbar

The Quick Launch toolbar includes buttons that provide quick access to the Windows desktop and the default Web browser, usually Internet Explorer. If your organization has custom applications or a preferred suite of applications, you can add buttons for these applications on the Quick Launch toolbar. If applications are no longer used, you can later remove the additional buttons.

You can add a button to the Quick Launch toolbar by clicking the item or existing shortcut that you want to place on the toolbar, holding the mouse button, and dragging the item or shortcut onto the Quick Launch toolbar. When you are in the location where you want to place the item or shortcut, release the mouse button. To remove a button from the Quick Launch toolbar, right-click the button on the toolbar, and then choose Delete from the shortcut menu. When prompted to confirm the action, click Yes.

Inside Out

Restoring the Show Desktop button

Show Desktop is the most useful button on the Quick Launch toolbar. The first time you click this button, the operating system brings the Windows desktop to the foreground in front of all open windows. The second time you click this button, the operating system restores the original view, sending the desktop to the background. If this button is accidentally deleted, you can re-create it, but the process is not like creating a regular shortcut. This is because Show Desktop is a special button that is created by using a Windows Explorer command file, and to re-create the button, you must re-create this file, called Show Desktop.scf.

As with other aspects of the menu system, the Quick Launch toolbar options have a representation in the file system. You'll find Quick Launch options in the %UserProfile%\Application Data\Microsoft\Internet Explorer\Quick Launch folder. Thus, the full file path to the Show Desktop file is %UserProfile%\Application Data\Microsoft\Internet Explorer\Quick Launch\Show Desktop.scf. To restore the button to the toolbar, you have several options. You can copy Show Desktop.scf from another user's profile, or you can re-create the file. To re-create the file, follow these steps:

1. Start Notepad, and then add the following lines of text:

   [Shell]

   Command=2

   IconFile=explorer.exe,3

   [Taskbar]

   Command=ToggleDesktop

2. Select Save from the File menu, and then save the file in the %UserProfile%\Application Data\Microsoft\Internet Explorer\Quick Launch folder. Use the file name Show Desktop.scf.

If you don't know the actual value for the %UserProfile% environment variable, open a command prompt, and type **set userprofile**. The command prompt then displays the variable value, such as D:\Documents and Settings\Administrator.CORPSVR01.

Displaying Other Custom Toolbars

In addition to the Quick Launch toolbar discussed previously, three other customizable toolbars are available for the taskbar:

- **Address** Provides an Address box into which you can type Uniform Resource Locators (URLs) and other addresses that you want to access, either on the World Wide Web, on the local network, or on the local computer. When full file paths are specified, the default application for the file is launched automatically to display the specified file, such as Internet Explorer or Microsoft Office Word. One of the things you might not realize about the Address toolbar is that it retains the same URL history as the Address bar in Internet Explorer, meaning if you previously opened a document on a network share, you could quickly access it again through the history.
- **Links** Provides access to the Links folder on the Favorites menu of Internet Explorer. To add links to files, Web pages, or other resources, drag shortcuts onto the Links toolbar. To remove links, right-click the link, and select Delete. When prompted, confirm the action by clicking Yes.
- **Desktop** Provides access to all the shortcuts on the local desktop so that you don't have to minimize windows or click Show Desktop on the Quick Launch toolbar to access them.

You can display or hide individual toolbars by right-clicking the taskbar to display the shortcut menu, pointing to Toolbars, and then selecting the toolbar you want to use. This toggles the toolbar on and off.

Tip Have toolbars use less space by turning off the title
By default, a name label is displayed for all toolbars except Quick Launch. This label wastes taskbar space, and you can turn it off. Right-click the toolbar, and then click Show Title to clear the option. The option is a toggle; if you want to see the title again, repeat the procedure.

Creating Personal Toolbars

In addition to the custom toolbars that are available, you can create personal toolbars as well. Personal toolbars are based on existing folders, and their buttons are based on the folder contents. The most common toolbars you might create are ones that point to folders on the computer or shared folders on the network. For example, if you routinely access the C:\Windist, C:\Windows\System32\LogFiles, and C:\Windows\System32\Inersvr folders, you could add to the taskbar a toolbar that provides quick access buttons to these resources. Then you could access one of the folders simply by clicking the corresponding toolbar button.

You can create personal toolbars by right-clicking the taskbar to display the shortcut menu, pointing to Toolbars, and then clicking New Toolbar. This displays the New Toolbar dialog box, as shown in the following screen:

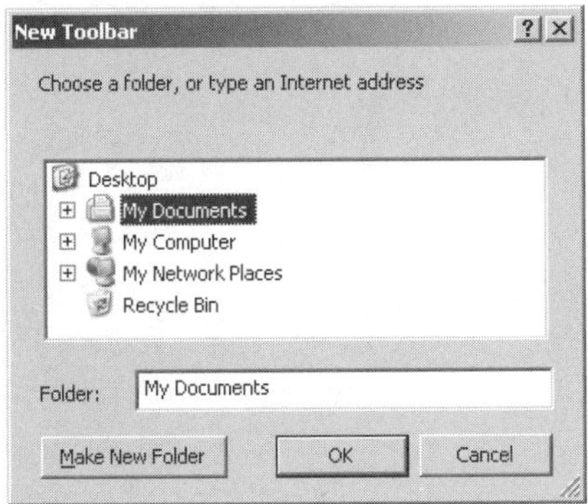

Next use the Choose A Folder list box to choose the folder you want to make into a toolbar. When you click OK, the folder is displayed as a new toolbar on the taskbar. If you add shortcuts to the folder, the shortcuts automatically appear on the toolbar as buttons that can be selected. Keep in mind that if you decide that you don't want to use the toolbar anymore and close it, you must reselect the folder before it can be viewed on the taskbar again.

Chapter 11

Windows Server 2003 MMC Administration

In this chapter, you'll learn how to work with and customize the Microsoft Management Console (MMC). You'll also find a discussion of administration tools that use the MMC. You can learn many techniques to help you better understand Microsoft Windows Server 2003, and indeed, as mentioned in the previous chapter, you must master the MMC before you can truly master Windows Server 2003.

Introducing the MMC

Compared to Microsoft Windows NT, the process of administration is much easier in Windows Server 2003. Mostly this is because of the MMC and the prepackaged administration tools that use it to help you more readily manage computers, users, and other aspects of the network environment. Not only does the MMC simplify administration, it also helps to integrate the many disparate tools that were previously available by using a single unified interface.

The advantages of having a unified interface are significant because after you learn the structure of one MMC tool, you can apply what you've learned to all the other MMC tools. Equally as significant is the capability to build your own consoles and customize existing consoles. You can in fact combine administrative components to build your own console configuration, and then store this console for future use. You would then have quick access to the tools you use the most through a single console.

If you've used the MMC in Microsoft Windows 2000, you might be wondering what's new in Windows Server 2003. For starters, the MMC in Windows Server 2003 has a new version number. It is MMC 2.0 and it offers several enhancements:

- In all of the console tools and in the MMC framework, the Console menu has been renamed as the File menu. This was done to make the console more consistent with other Microsoft tools that have a File menu.

- As discussed in Chapter 1, "Introducing Windows Server 2003," for selected snap-ins the MMC now supports multiple-item selecting and editing—another much-needed improvement. These features allow you to select multiple objects and perform the same operations on them, including editing.

- As discussed in Chapter 1, for selected snap-ins the MMC now supports drag-and-drop functionality. This brings a much-needed improvement to the administration snap-ins and allows you to perform such tasks as dragging a user, computer, or group from one organizational unit (OU) to another in Active Directory Users and Computers.

In addition, for the Active Directory Users and Computers snap-in, you can now do the following:

- Reset access permissions to the default values for objects, show the effective permission for an object, and show the parent of an inherited permission.
- Save Active Directory queries and reuse them so that you can easily perform common or complex queries.

Keep in mind that the MMC isn't a one-size-fits-all approach to administration. Some administrative functions aren't implemented for use with the MMC. Many system and operating system properties are still configured using Control Panel utilities. Many other system and administrative functions are accessed using wizards. Most administrative tools regardless of type have command-line counterparts that run as separate executables from the command line.

The really good news, however, is that you can integrate all non-MMC tools and even command-line utilities into a custom console by creating links to them. In this way, your custom console remains the central interface for administration, and you can use it to access quickly any type of tool with which you routinely work. For more information, see the section entitled "Building Custom MMCs" later in this chapter.

Using the MMC

The MMC is a framework for management applications that offers a unified interface for administration. It is not designed to replace management applications; rather, it is designed to be their central interface. As such, the MMC doesn't have any inherent management functions. It uses add-in components, called *snap-ins*, to provide the necessary administrative functionality.

MMC Snap-Ins

To take advantage of what the MMC framework has to offer, you add any of the available stand-alone snap-ins to a console. A *console* is simply a container for snap-ins that uses the MMC framework. Dozens of preconfigured snap-ins are available from Microsoft, and they provide the functionality necessary for administration. Third-party tools from independent software vendors now use MMC snap-ins as well.

> **Note** The terms *console* and *tool* are often used interchangeably. For example, in the text, I often refer to such and such as a tool when technically it is a preconfigured console containing a snap-in. For example, Active Directory Users and Computers is a tool for managing users, groups, and computers. Not all tools are consoles, however. The System tool in Control Panel is a tool for managing system properties, but it is not a console.

Although you can load multiple snap-ins into a single console, most of the preconfigured consoles have only a single snap-in. For example, most of the tools on the Administrative Tools menu consist of a preconfigured console with a single snap-in—even the Computer Management tool shown in Figure 11-1, which consists of a preconfigured console with the Computer Management snap-in added to it.

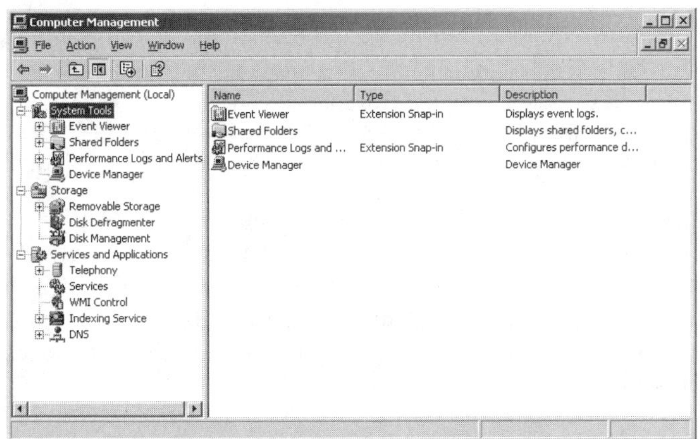

Figure 11-1. The Computer Management tool consists of a preconfigured console with the Computer Management snap-in added to it.

The many features of the Computer Management snap-in are good examples of how snap-ins can have nodes and extension components. A *node* defines a level within the console or within a snap-in. Computer Management has a root node, which is labeled Computer Management, and three top-level nodes, which are labeled System Tools, Storage, and Services and Applications. An *extension component* is a type of snap-in that is used to extend the functionality of an existing snap-in. Computer Management has many extensions. In fact, each entry under the top-level nodes is an extension—and many of these extensions can themselves have extensions.

These particular extensions are also implemented as stand-alone snap-ins, and when you use them in your own console, they add the same functionality as they do in the preconfigured administration tools. You'll find that many extensions are implemented as both extensions and stand-alone snap-ins. Many doesn't mean all: Some extensions are meant only to add functionality to an existing snap-in and they are not also implemented as stand-alone snap-ins.

Keep in mind extensions are optional and can be included or excluded from a snap-in by changing options within the console when you are authoring it. For example, if you didn't want someone to be able to use Disk Management from within Computer Management, you could edit the extension options for Computer Management on that user's computer to remove the entry for Disk Management. The user would then be unable to manage disks from within Computer Management. The user would still, however, be able to manage disks using other tools.

MMC Modes

MMC has two operating modes: author mode and user mode. In author mode, you can create and modify a console's design by adding or removing snap-ins and setting console options. In user mode, the console design is frozen, and you cannot change it. By default, the prepackaged console tools for administration open in user mode, and this is why you are unable to make changes to these console tools.

As Figure 11-2 shows, when you open a console that is in author mode, you have an extended File menu that allows you to create new consoles, open existing consoles, save the current console, add/remove snap-ins, and set console options. In contrast, when you are working with one of the preconfigured console tools or any other tool in user mode, you have a limited File menu, as shown in Figure 11-3. Here, you can access a limited set of console options or exit the console—that's it.

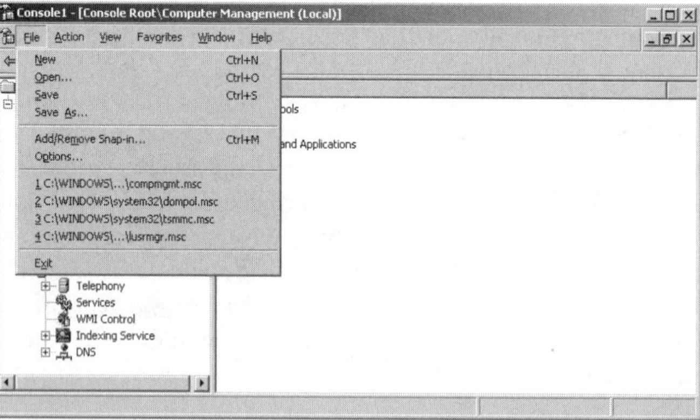

Figure 11-2. In author mode, consoles have additional options that help you design the interface.

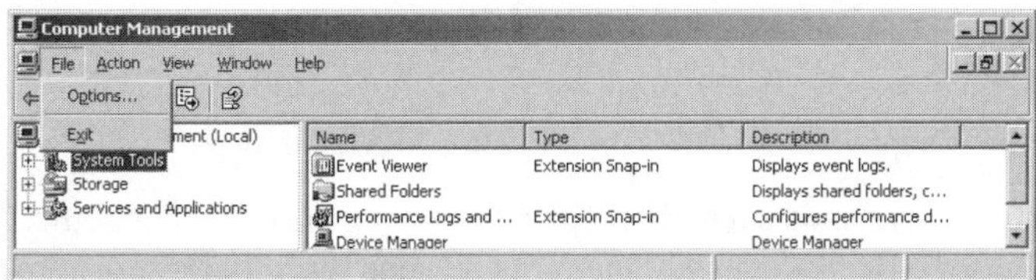

Figure 11-3. In user mode, consoles are restricted and the design cannot be changed.

In author mode, you also have a Favorites menu, which is used to add and organize favorites. The Favorites menu does not appear in the user mode.

When you are finished designing a console tool, you should change to user mode. Console tools should be run in user mode, and author mode should be used only for configuring console tools. Three user-mode levels are defined:

- **User mode—full access** Users can access all window management commands in the MMC but can't add or remove snap-ins or change console properties.
- **User mode—limited access, multiple window** Users can access only the areas of the console tree that were visible when the console was saved. Users can create new windows but cannot close existing windows.
- **User mode—limited access, single window** Users can access only the areas of the console tree that were visible when the console was saved and are prevented from opening new windows.

A console's mode is stored when you save the console and is applied when you open the console. In author mode, you can change the console mode by using the Options dialog box, which is displayed by selecting Options from the File menu. You cannot change the mode when a console is running in user mode. That doesn't mean you can't change back to author mode, however, and then make further changes as necessary.

To open any existing console tool in author mode, right-click the tool's icon, and choose Author. This works for the preconfigured administration tools as well. Simply right-click the related menu item on the Administrative Tools menu, and then choose Author. You will then have full design control over the console, but remember that if you make changes, you probably don't want to overwrite the existing .msc file for the console. So, instead of choosing Save from the File menu after you make changes, choose Save As, and save the console with a different name, location, or both.

> **Tip** Another way to enter author mode is to use the /A parameter when starting the console tool from the command line or the Run dialog box.

Inside Out

Group Policy settings can control authoring and snap-in availability

Remember that at any time, a user with appropriate permissions can enter author mode by right-clicking the console and selecting Author or by running the console tool from the command line with the /A switch. In author mode, users could change the configuration of the tool. One way to prevent this is to restrict authoring in Group Policy.

You can restrict all authoring by users at the local machine, OU, or domain level by enabling Restrict The User From Entering Author Mode in User Configuration\Administrative Templates\Windows Components\Microsoft Management Console within Group Policy.

You can set specific restricted and permitted snap-ins and extensions as well. One way to do this is first to prohibit the use of all snap-ins by enabling Restrict Users To The Explicitly Permitted List Of Snap-Ins in User Configuration\Administrative Templates\Windows Components\Microsoft Management Console within Group Policy. Then specifically enable the snap-ins and extensions that are permitted. All other snap-ins and extensions would then be prohibited.

Alternatively, you can disable Restrict Users To The Explicitly Permitted List Of Snap-Ins and then explicitly prohibit snap-ins by disabling them. All other snap-ins and extensions would then be permitted.

Be sure to read Chapter 38, "Managing Group Policy," before you try to implement Group Policy or make changes to Group Policy Objects. If you get into trouble, such as could happen if you prohibit all snap-ins but neglect to enable snap-ins needed for management, you can reset Group Policy to its default configuration by using the Dcgpofix command-line utility as discussed in the section entitled "Fixing Default Group Policy," on page 1324.

MMC Windows and Startup

As Figure 11-4 shows, the MMC window consists of two panes: console tree and details. The left pane is the console tree. It provides a hierarchical list of nodes available in the console. At the top of the tree is the console root, which could be specifically labeled Console Root, or, as with the preconfigured tools, it is simply the snap-in name. Generally, snap-ins appear as nodes below the console root. Snap-ins can also have nodes, as is the case with Computer Management. In any case, if there are nodes below the console root, you can expand them by clicking the plus sign to the left of the node label or by double-clicking the node.

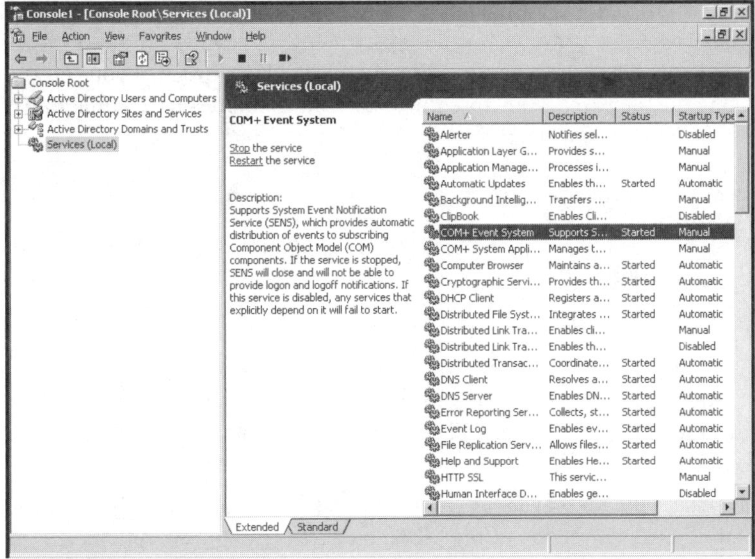

Figure 11-4. MMC windows have a console tree and a details pane.

The right pane is the details pane, and its contents change depending on the item you've selected in the console tree. When you are working with one of the lowest-level nodes in the console tree, you'll sometimes have two views to choose from: standard or extended view. The difference between the two is that the extended view typically provides quick access links to related, frequently performed tasks and a detailed description of the selected item. These are not displayed in the standard view.

One way to start a console tool is to select it on the Administrative Tools menu or double-click its icon on the desktop or in Windows Explorer. You can also start console tools from the Run dialog box and the command prompt. The executable for the MMC is Mmc.exe, and you can run it by typing **mmc** in the Run dialog box and clicking OK or by entering **mmc** at the command prompt. Either way, you'll end up with a blank (empty) console that you can use to design your custom administration tool.

To use an existing console, you can specify the console file to open when the MMC runs. This is, in fact, how the preconfigured tools and any other tools that you create are launched. For example, if you right-click Computer Management on the Administrative Tools menu, and then select Properties, you'll see that the target (the command that is run) for the menu item is as follows:

```
%SystemRoot%\System32\Compmgmt.msc /s
```

The first part of the target (%SystemRoot%\System32\Compmgmt.msc) is the file path to the associated Microsoft Saved Console (.msc) file. The second part of the target (/S) is a command parameter to use when running the MMC. It follows that you can run the MMC by specifying the file path to the .msc file to use and any necessary command parameters as well using the following syntax:

```
mmc FilePath Parameter(s)
```

where *FilePath* is the file path to the .msc file to use and *Parameter(s)* can include any of the following parameters:

- **/A** Enables author mode, which lets you make changes to preconfigured consoles as well as other consoles previously set in user mode.
- **/S** Prevents the console from displaying the splash screen that normally appears when the MMC starts in earlier versions of the Windows operating system. This parameter isn't needed when running on Windows Server 2003.
- **/32** Starts the 32-bit version of the MMC, which is needed only if you explicitly want to run the 32-bit version of the MMC on a 64-bit Windows system.
- **/64** Starts the 64-bit version of the MMC, which is available only on 64-bit Windows versions.

Inside Out

Using 32-bit and 64-bit versions of the MMC

The /32 and /64 parameters are meaningful only on 64-bit Windows versions. The 64-bit versions of the Windows operating system can run both 32-bit and 64-bit versions of the MMC. For 32-bit versions of the MMC, you use 32-bit snap-ins. For 64-bit versions of the MMC, you use 64-bit snap-ins. You can't mix and match MMC and snap-in versions, though. The 32-bit version of the MMC can be used only to work with 32-bit snap-ins. Similarly, the 64-bit version of the MMC can be used only to work with 64-bit snap-ins. In most cases, if you aren't sure which version to use, don't use the /32 or /64 parameter. This lets the Windows operating system decide which version to use based on the snap-ins contained in the .msc file you are opening.

Most console tools are found in the %SystemRoot%\System32 directory. This puts them in the default search path for executables. Because there is a file type association for .msc files, specified files of this type are opened using Mmc.exe; you can open any of the preconfigured tools stored in %SystemRoot%\System32 by specifying the file name followed by the .msc extension. For example, you can start Event Viewer by typing the following:

```
eventvwr.msc
```

This works because of the file association that specifies .msc files are executed using Mmc.exe. (You can examine file associations using the ASSOC and FTYPE commands at the command prompt.)

Some console tools aren't in the %SystemRoot%\System32 directory, or the search path for that matter. For these tools, you must type the complete file path.

MMC Tool Availability

Generally, the preconfigured MMC consoles available on a server depend on the services that are installed. As you install additional services, additional tools for administration are installed, and these tools can be both console tools and standard tools. You don't have to rely on service installation for tool availability, however. You can, in fact, install the complete administrative tool set on any computer, including servers, regardless of the services being used. The only requirement is that the computers are running Windows XP Professional Service Pack 1 or later or Windows Server 2003.

Follow these steps to install the complete administrative tool set:

1. Log on to the computer using an account with Administrator privileges.
2. Insert the Windows Server 2003 distribution CD-ROM into the CD-ROM drive.
3. When the Autorun screen appears, click Perform Additional Tasks, and then click Browse This CD. This starts Windows Explorer.
4. Double-click I386, and then double-click Adminpak.msi. The complete set of Windows Server 2003 management tools is installed on the computer.

These tools are then available from the Administrative Tools menu and can also be started quickly in the Run dialog box or at the command prompt by typing only their file name (in most cases). At times, you might find it quicker to open consoles from the command line. For example, on a server optimized for handling background services and not programs being run by users, you might find that navigating the menu is too slow. To help you in these instances, Table 11-1 provides a list of the key console tools and their .msc file names.

Table 11-1. Key Console Tools and Their .msc File Names

Tool Name	.msc File Name
Active Directory Domain and Trusts	domain.msc
Active Directory Sites and Services	dssite.msc
Active Directory Users and Computers	dsa.msc
Authorization Manager	azman.msc
Certificate Templates	certtmpl.msc
Certification Authority	certsvr.msc
Certificate Manager	certmgr.msc

Table 11-1. Key Console Tools and Their .msc File Names

Tool Name	.msc File Name
Component Services	compexp.msc
Computer Management	compmgmt.msc
Device Manager	devmgmt.msc
DHCP Manager	dhcpmgmt.msc
Disk Defragmenter	dfrg.msc
Disk Management	diskmgmt.msc
Distributed File System	dfsgui.msc
DNS Manager	dnsmgmt.msc
Domain Controller Security Policy	dcpol.msc
Domain Security Policy	dompol.msc
Event Viewer	eventvwr.msc
Group Policy Editor	gpedit.msc
Indexing Service	ciadv.msc
Internet Authentication Service	ias.msc
Internet Information Services	iis.msc
Local Security Policy	secpol.msc
Local Users and Groups	lusrmgr.msc
Performance	perfmon.msc
Remote Desktops	tsmmc.msc
Removable Storage Management	ntmsmgr.msc
Resultant Set of Policy	rsop.msc
Routing and Remote Access	rrasmgmt.msc
Services	services.msc
Shared Folders	filesvr.msc
Telephony	tapimgmt.msc
Terminal Services	tscc.msc
Windows Management Instrumentation	wmimgmt.msc

MMC and Remote Computers

Some snap-ins can be set to work with local or remote systems. If this is the case, you'll see the name of the computer with focus in parentheses after the snap-in name in the console tree. When the snap-in is working with the local computer, you'll see (Local) after the snap-in name. When the snap-in is working with a remote computer, you'll see the remote computer name in parentheses after the snap-in name, such as (CORPSERVER01).

Generally, regardless of which type of snap-in you are using, you can specify the computer to work with it in one of two ways. Within the MMC, you can right-click the snap-in node in the console tree and then select Connect To Another Computer. This displays the Select Computer dialog box, as shown in the following screen:

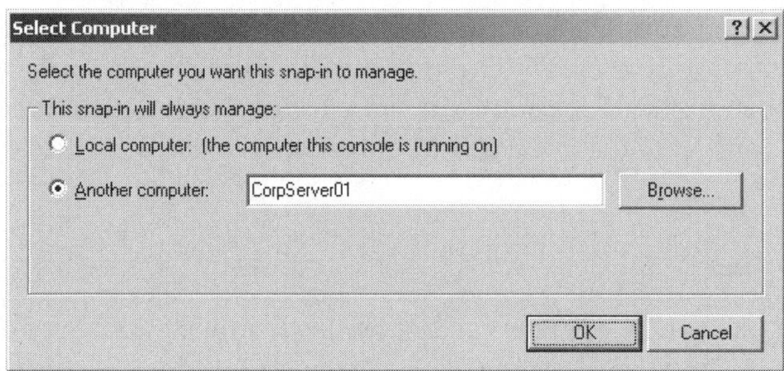

If you want the snap-in to work with the computer the console is running on, select Local Computer. Otherwise, select Another Computer, and then type the computer name or Internet Protocol (IP) address of the computer you want to use. If you don't know the computer name or IP address, click Browse to search for the computer you want to work with.

Just about any snap-in that can be set to work with local and remote systems can be started from the command line with the focus set on a specific computer. This is a hidden feature that many people don't know about or don't understand. Simply set the focus when you start a console from the command line using the following parameter:

```
/computer=RemoteComputer
```

where *RemoteComputer* is the name or IP address of the remote computer you want the snap-in to work with, such as

```
eventvwr.msc /computer=corpserver01
```

The following snap-ins use the /Computer parameter:

- Certificates Authority, certsvr.msc
- Computer Management, compmgmt.msc
- Device Manager, devmgmt.msc
- Disk Management, diskmgmt.msc
- Event Viewer, eventvwr.msc
- Indexing Service, ciadv.msc

- Internet Authentication Service, ias.msc
- Local Users and Groups, lusrmgr.msc
- Removable Storage Management, ntmsmgr.msc
- Services, services.msc
- Windows Management Instrumentation, wmimgmt.msc

Several different hidden options are available with the Active Directory–related snap-ins. For Active Directory Users and Computers, Active Directory Sites and Services, and Active Directory Domains and Trusts, you can use the /Server parameter to open the snap-in and connect to a specified domain controller. For example, if you wanted to start Active Directory Users and Computers and connect to the CORPSVR02 domain controller, you could do this by typing the following:

```
dsa.msc /server=CorpSvr02
```

For Active Directory Users and Computers and Active Directory Sites and Services, you can use the /Domain parameter to open the snap-in and connect to a domain controller in the specified domain. For example, if you wanted to start Active Directory Users and Computers and connect to the cpandl.com domain, you could do this by typing the following:

```
dsa.msc /domain=cpandl.com
```

Building Custom MMCs

If you find that the existing console tools don't meet your needs or you want to create your own administration tool with the features you choose, you can build your own custom console tools. This allows you to determine which features the console includes, which snap-ins it uses, and which additional commands are available.

The steps for creating custom console tools are as follows:

1. Create the console for the tool.
2. Add snap-ins to the console. Snap-ins you use can include Microsoft console tools as well as console tools from third-party vendors.
3. When you are finished with the design, save the console in user mode so that it is ready for use.

Each step is examined in detail in the sections that follow. Optionally, you can create one or more taskpad views containing shortcuts to menu commands, shell commands, and navigation components that you want to include in your custom tool. Techniques for creating taskpad views are discussed in the section entitled "Designing Custom Taskpads for the MMC" later in this chapter.

Step 1: Creating the Console

The first step in building a custom console tool is to create the console that you'll use as the framework. To get started, open a blank MMC in author mode. Click Start, select Run, type **mmc** in the Open box, and then click OK. This opens a blank console titled Console1 that has a default console root as shown in Figure 11-5.

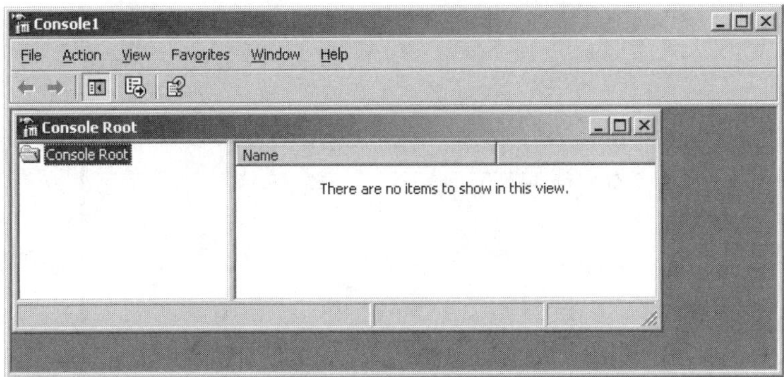

Figure 11-5. A blank console with the default console root.

If you want your custom tool to be based on an existing console, you can open its .msc file and add it to the new console. Select Open on the File menu, and then use the Open dialog box to find the .msc file you want to work with. As discussed previously, most .msc files are in the %SystemRoot%\System32 directory. Any existing console you choose will open in author mode automatically. Keep in mind that you generally don't want to overwrite the existing .msc file with the new .msc file you are creating. Because of this, when you save the custom console, be sure to choose Save As rather than Save on the File menu.

If you want to start from scratch, you'll work with the blank console you just opened. The first thing you'll want to do is rename the console root to give it and the related window a more meaningful name. For example, if you are creating a console tool to help you manage the Active Directory directory service, you could rename the console root Active Directory Management. To rename the console root and the related window, right-click the console root, and select Rename. Type the name you want to use, and then press Enter.

The next thing you'll want to do is to consider how many windows the console tool must have. Most console tools have a single window, but as shown in Figure 11-6, a console can have multiple windows, each with its own view of the console root. You add windows to the console by using the New Window option on the Window menu. After you add a window, you'll probably want the MMC to automatically tile the windows as shown in the figure. You can tile windows by selecting Tile Horizontally on the Window menu. You don't have to do this, however; anytime there are multiple windows, you can use the options on the Window menu to switch between them.

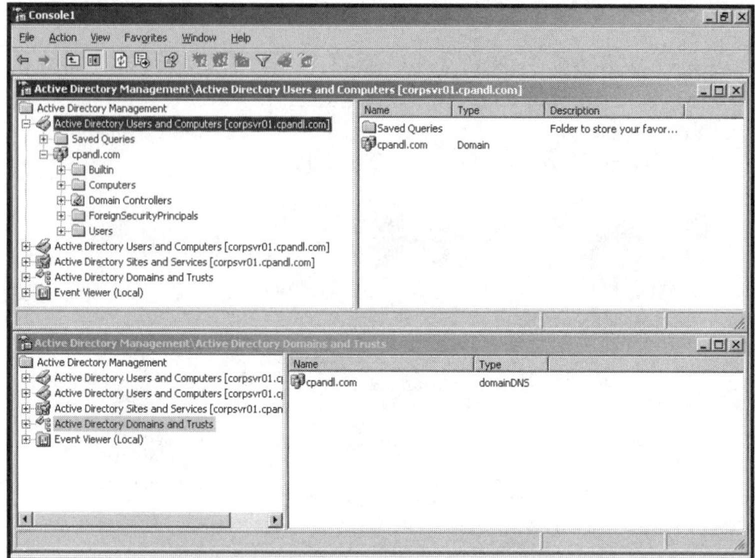

Figure 11-6. Although consoles can have multiple windows, most consoles have a single window.

Inside Out

Using multiple windows in consoles

Most console tools have a single window for a good reason: The tool creators wanted to keep the interface as simple as possible. When you introduce multiple windows, you create additional views of the console root, making the interface more complex, and often unnecessarily so. Still, there are times when a console tool with multiple windows could come in handy. For example, you might want to have multiple views of the console root where different areas of the tool are featured, and you could do this by using multiple windows.

Step 2: Adding Snap-Ins to the Console

While you are thinking about the organization of the tool and the possibility of using additional views of the console root, you should also consider the types of snap-ins that you want to add to the console. Each of the tools listed in Table 11-1 is available as a stand-alone snap-in that you can add to the console. If you've installed any third-party tools on the computer, these tools might have stand-alone snap-ins that you can use. Many other snap-ins are available from Microsoft as well.

Again, think of snap-in types or categories, not necessarily specific snap-ins that you want to use. You might want to organize the snap-ins into groups by creating folders for storing snap-ins of a specific type or category. For example, if you are creating a console tool for managing Active Directory, you might find that there are four general types of snap-ins that you want to work with: General, Policy, Security, and Support. You would then create four folders in the console with these names.

Folders are implemented as a snap-in that you add to the console root. To add folders to the console root, follow these steps:

1 Choose Add/Remove Snap-In from the File menu in the main window. As shown in Figure 11-7, you must now choose where to add the snap-in. At this point, it is possible only to add the snap-in to the console root (which is now called Active Directory Management or whichever other name you used), but after you add folders, you can add snap-ins to a folder below the console root by selecting it in the Snap-Ins Added To list.

Figure 11-7. Choose where to add the snap-in.

2 Choose Add, which displays the Add Standalone Snap-In dialog box. Note that this dialog box is set so that you can see the previous dialog box as well. This is important because when you add snap-ins they appear in the Add/Remove Snap-In list.

3 The Available Standalone Snap-Ins list shows all the snap-ins that are available. Scroll through the list until you see the Folder snap-in, as shown in Figure 11-8. Click Folder, and then choose Add. The Folder snap-in is added to the list of snap-ins in the Add/Remove Snap-In dialog box. Repeat this for each folder that you want to use. If you are following the example and want to use four folders, you would click Add three more times so that four Folder snap-ins appear in the Add/Remove Snap-In dialog box.

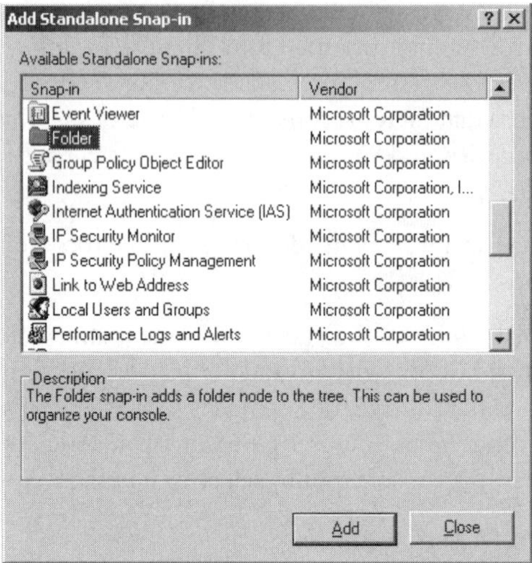

Figure 11-8. When you add a snap-in in the Add Standalone Snap-In dialog box, it appears on the Add/Remove Snap-In list.

4. Now close the Add Standalone Snap-In dialog box by clicking Close, and return to the Add/Remove Snap-In dialog box. You'll see the folders you've added. Click OK to close this dialog box and return to the console you are creating.

After you add folders, you must rename them. Right-click the first folder, and choose Rename. Type a new name, and then press Enter. If you are following the example, rename the folders: General, Policy, Security, and Support. When you are finished renaming the folders, follow a similar process to add the appropriate snap-ins to your console:

1. Choose Add/Remove Snap-In on the File menu in the main window.
2. In the Snap-Ins Added To list, choose the folder to use, and then click Add.
3. Use the Add Standalone Snap-Ins dialog box to add snap-ins to the selected folder.
4. When you are finished, click Close to return to the Add/Remove Snap-In dialog box. You'll find the snap-ins you've chosen are added to the designated folder.
5. If you want to work with a different folder, select the folder in the Snap-Ins Added To list, and repeat steps 2 to 4.
6. When you are finished adding snap-ins to folders, click OK to close the Add/Remove Snap-In dialog box and return to the console you are creating.

Some snap-ins prompt you to select a computer to manage, as shown in the following screen:

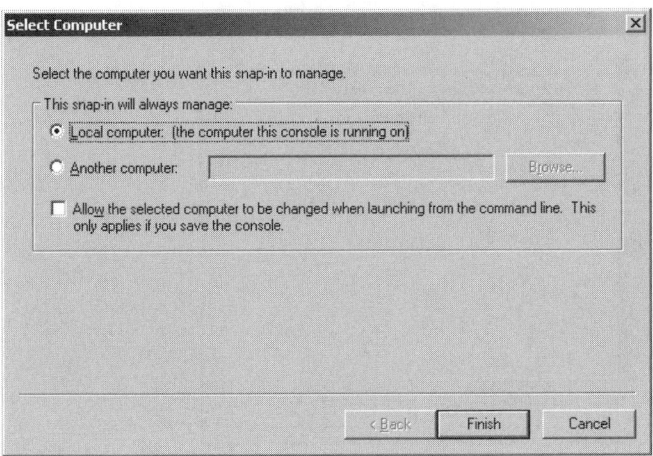

If you want the snap-in to work with whichever computer the console is running on, select Local Computer. Otherwise, select Another Computer, and then type the computer name or IP address of the computer you want to use. If you don't know the computer name or IP address, click Browse to search for the computer you want to work with.

> **Tip** **Specify which computer to manage**
> To ensure you can specify which computer to manage when running the console from the command line, you must select the Allow The Selected Computer To Be Changed option. When you use this option and save the console, you can set the computer to manage using the /Computer=*RemoteComputer* parameter.

Some snap-ins are added by using wizards with several configuration pages, so when you select these snap-ins you start the associated wizard and the wizard helps you configure how the snap-in is used. One snap-in in particular that uses a wizard is Link To Web Address. When you add this snap-in, you start the Link To Web Address Wizard, as shown in the screen on the following page, and the wizard prompts you to create an Internet shortcut. Here, you type the Uniform Resource Locator (URL) you want to use, click Next, enter a descriptive name for the URL, then click Finish. Then, when you select the related snap-in in the console tree, the designated Web page appears in the details pane.

While you are adding snap-ins, you can also examine the available extensions for snap-ins. In the Add/Remove Snap-In dialog box, click the Extensions tab, then use the Snap-Ins That Can Be Extended list to choose the snap-in that you want to work with. All available extensions are enabled by default, as shown in the following screen. So, if you want to change this behavior, you can clear the Add All Extensions option and then clear the individual options for extensions you want to exclude.

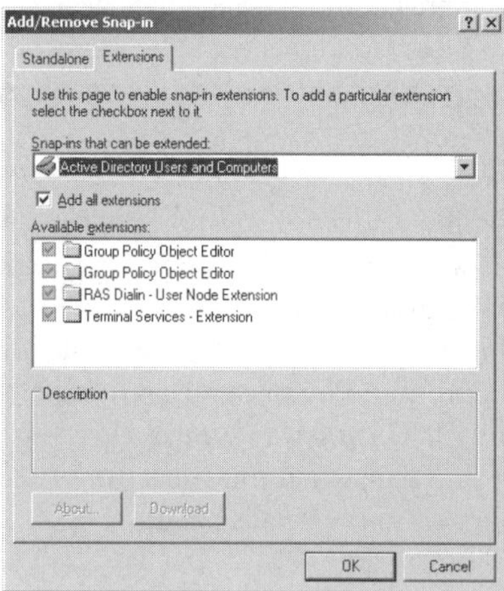

Figure 11-9 shows the example console with snap-ins organized using the previously discussed folders:

- **General** Containing Active Directory Users and Computers, Active Directory Sites and Services, and Active Directory Domains and Trusts
- **Policy** Containing Local Computer Policy, Resultant Set of Policy, and Default Domain Policy
- **Security** Containing Security Templates and Security Configuration and Analysis
- **Support** Containing links to Microsoft Knowledge Base, Microsoft Tech Support, and Windows Server Home Page

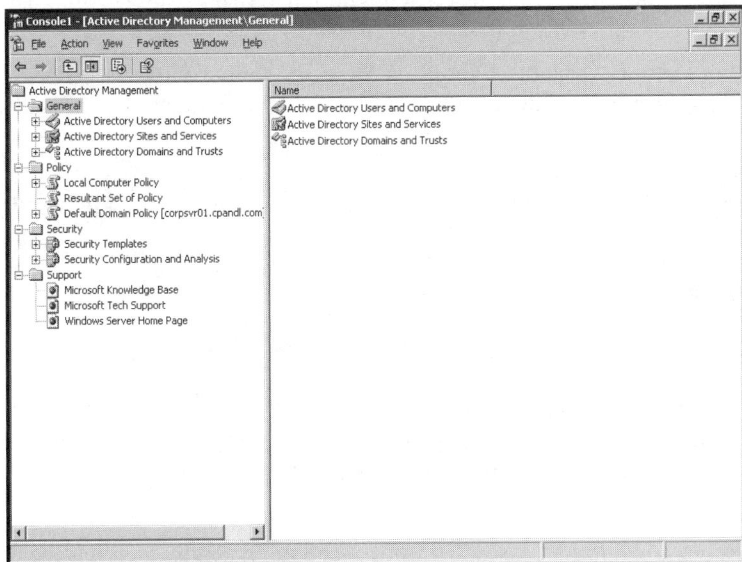

Figure 11-9. A custom console with snap-ins organized into four folders.

Step 3: Saving the Finished Console

When you are finished with the design, you are ready to save your custom console tool. Before you do this, however, there are a couple of final design issues you should consider:

- What you want the initial console view to be
- Which user mode you want to use
- Which icon you want to use
- What you want to name the console tool and where you want it to be located

Chapter 11

Setting the Initial Console View Before Saving

By default, the MMC remembers the last selected node or snap-in and saves this as the initial view for the console. In the example tool created, if you expand the General folder, select Active Directory Users and Computers, and then save the console, this selection is saved when the console is next opened.

Keep in mind that subsequent views depend on user selections. To prevent user selections from changing the view, you'll find two handy options when you select Options from the File menu:

- **Do Not Save Changes To This Console** Select this option to prevent the user from saving changes to the console. Clear this option to change the view automatically based on the user's last selection in the console before exiting.
- **Allow Users To Customize Views** Select this option to allow users to add windows focused on a selected item in the console. Clear this option to prevent users from adding customized views.

> **Note** Only the folder with the selected snap-in is expanded in the saved view. If you use folders and select a snap-in within a folder, the expanded view of the folder is saved with the snap-in selected. If you expand other folders, the console is not saved with these folders expanded.

Setting the Console Mode Before Saving

When you are finished authoring the console tool, select Options on the File menu. In the Options dialog box, as shown in the screen on the following page, you can change the console mode so that it is ready for use.

In most cases, you'll want to use User Mode—Full Access. Full access has the following characteristics:

- Users have a Window menu that allows them to open new windows, and they can also right-click a node or snap-in and choose New Window From Here to open a new window.
- Users can right-click and choose New Taskpad View to create a new taskpad view.

With user mode set to Limited Access, Multiple Window, the console has the following characteristics:

- Users have a Window menu that allows them to arrange windows, and they can also right-click a node or snap-in and choose New Window From Here to open a new window.
- Users cannot right-click and choose New Taskpad View to create a new taskpad view.

User mode set to Limited Access, Single Window has the following characteristics:

- Users do not have a Window menu and cannot right-click a node or snap-in and choose New Window From Here to open a new window.
- Users cannot right-click and choose New Taskpad View to create a new taskpad view.

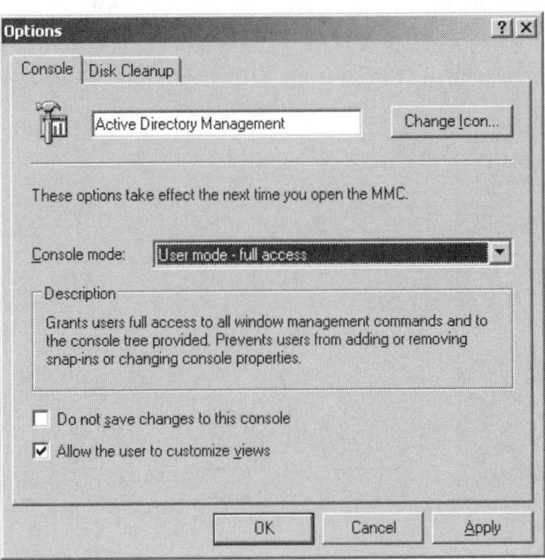

Setting the Console Icon Before Saving

While you are working in the Options dialog box, you might consider setting custom icons for your console tools. All the console tools developed by Microsoft have their own icons. You can use these icons for your console tools as well, or you could use icons from other Microsoft programs quite easily. In the Options dialog box (which is displayed when you select Options on the File menu), click Change Icon. This displays the Change Icon dialog box, as shown in the following screen:

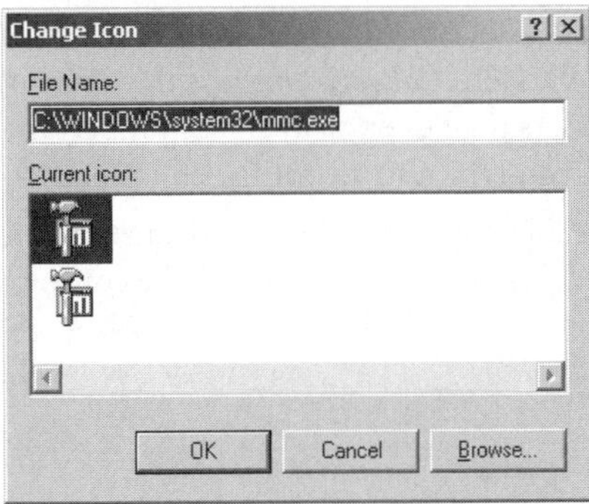

In the Change Icon dialog box, click Browse. By default, the Open dialog box should open with the directory set to %SystemRoot%\System32. In this case, type **shell32.dll** as the File Name, and click Open. You should now see the Change Icon dialog box with the Shell32.dll selected, which will allow you to choose one of several hundred icons registered for use with the operating system shell (see the following screen). Choose an icon, and then click OK. From then on, the icon will be associated with your custom console tool.

Saving the Console Tool to the Desktop, the Start Menu, or a Folder

After you set the user mode, you can save the console tool. The console tool can appear as one of the following:

- **A desktop icon** Select Save As on the File menu, and then navigate the folder structure to %SystemRoot%\Documents and Settings\%*UserName*%\Desktop. Here, %*UserName*% is the name of the user who will work with the tool or All Users if all users with an account on the computer should be able to run the tool. After you type a name for the console, click Save.
- **A menu option of the Start menu** Select Save As on the File menu, and then navigate the folder structure to %SystemRoot%\Documents and Settings\%*UserName*%\Start Menu\Programs\Administrative Tools. Here, %*UserName*% is the name of the user who will work with the tool or All Users if all users with an account on the computer should be able to run the tool. After you type a name for the console, click Save.
- **A folder icon** Select Save As on the File menu, and then navigate to the folder where you want the console tool to reside. After you type a name for the console, click Save.

> **Tip** **Change tool names using the Options dialog box**
> By default, the name shown on the console tool's title bar is set to the file name you designate when saving it. As long as you are in author mode, you can change the console tool name using the Options dialog box. Select Options on the File menu, and then type the name in the box provided at the top of the Console tab.

Designing Custom Taskpads for the MMC

When you want to simplify administration or limit the available tasks for junior administrators or Power Users, you might want to consider adding a taskpad to a console tool. By using taskpads, you can create custom views of your console tools that contain shortcuts to menu commands, shell commands, and navigation components.

Getting Started with Taskpads

Basically, taskpads let you create a page of tasks that you can perform quickly by clicking the associated shortcut links rather than using the existing menu or interface provided by snap-ins. You can create multiple taskpads in a console, each of which is accessed as a taskpad view. If you've worked with Windows XP, you've probably seen the Simple Control Panel, which is a taskpad view of the Control Panel. As with most taskpads, the Simple Control Panel has two purposes: It provides direct access to the commands or tasks so that you don't have to navigate menus, and it limits your options to a set of predefined tasks that you can perform.

You create taskpads when you are working with a console tool in author mode. Taskpads can contain the following items:

- **Menu commands** Menu commands are used to run the standard menu options of included snap-ins.
- **Shell commands** Shell commands are used to run scripts or programs or to open Web pages.
- **Navigation components** Navigation components are used to navigate to a saved view on the Favorites menu.

Taskpad commands are also called *tasks*. You run tasks simply by clicking their link. In the case of menu commands, clicking the link runs the menu command. For shell commands, clicking the link runs the associated script or program. For navigation components, clicking the link displays the designated navigation view. If you have multiple levels of taskpads, you must include navigation components to allow users to get back to the top-level taskpad. The concept is similar to having to create a home link on Web pages.

Figure 11-10 shows a taskpad created for the Active Directory Users and Computers snap-in that has been added to the custom tool created earlier in the chapter.

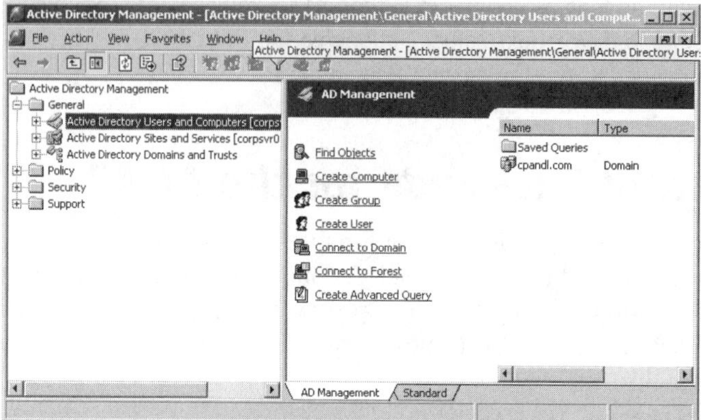

Figure 11-10. A custom console with taskpad that uses a vertical list.

As you can see, the task page view is labeled AD Management, and it provides the following commands:

- **Find Objects** Used to open the Find Users, Contacts, And Groups dialog box
- **Create Computer** Used to start the New Object—Computer Wizard
- **Create Group** Used to start the New Object—Group Wizard
- **Create User** Used to start the New Object—User Wizard
- **Connect To Domain** Used to select the domain to work with
- **Connect To Domain Forest** Used to select the domain forest to work with
- **Create Advanced Query** Used to define an Active Directory query and save it so that it can be reused

> **Note** We haven't used the taskpad to limit the options; rather, we've simply provided quick access shortcuts to commonly run tasks. In the next section, you'll learn how to limit user options.

Understanding Taskpad View Styles

Taskpads can be organized in several different ways. By default, they will have two views: an extended taskpad view and a standard view. The extended view contains the list of tasks that you've defined and can also contain the console items being managed. The standard view contains only the console items being managed. When you create the taskpad, you have the option of hiding the standard view simply by selecting the Hide Standard View option.

The extended view of the taskpad can be organized using a vertical list, a horizontal list, or no list. In a vertical list as shown previously in Figure 11-10, taskpad commands are listed to the left of the console items they are used to manage. This organization approach works well when you have a long list of tasks and you still want users to be able to work with the related snap-ins.

With a horizontal list, as shown in Figure 11-11, the console items managed by the taskpad are listed above the taskpad commands. This organization style is best when you want to display multiple columns of taskpad commands and still be able to work with the related snap-ins.

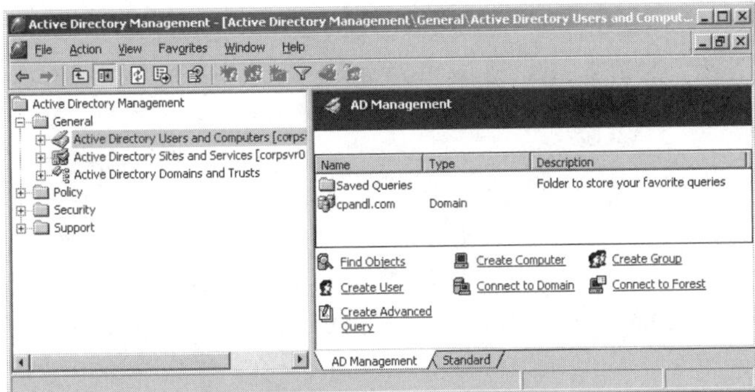

Figure 11-11. A custom console with taskpad that uses a horizontal list.

In some cases, you might not want to show the console items being managed by the taskpad on the same view as the tasks. In this case, you can specify that no list should be used. When you choose the No List option, the taskpad commands are shown by themselves in the taskpad tab (AD Management here), and users can click the Standard tab to access the related console items.

Inside Out

Limiting user options in taskpads

As discussed, you can limit the options users have in console tools by selecting both the No List and Hide Standard Tab options. Keep in mind that if the console tool doesn't include a taskpad for a snap-in, users will still be able to manage the snap-in in the usual way. For example, the taskpad shown in the figure doesn't define any tasks that manage policy or security, so the snap-ins in these folders will be fully accessible. To make it so users can't work with these snap-ins directly, you must define taskpads for those snap-ins or add tasks that use menu commands from those snap-ins to the current taskpad or another taskpad.

When you use the No List style, you can limit the options to the tasks you've defined and not allow users to access the console items being managed. To do this, you specify that the Standard tab should be hidden. From then on, when working with the console items being managed, users can perform only the tasks defined on the taskpad, such as shown in Figure 11-12.

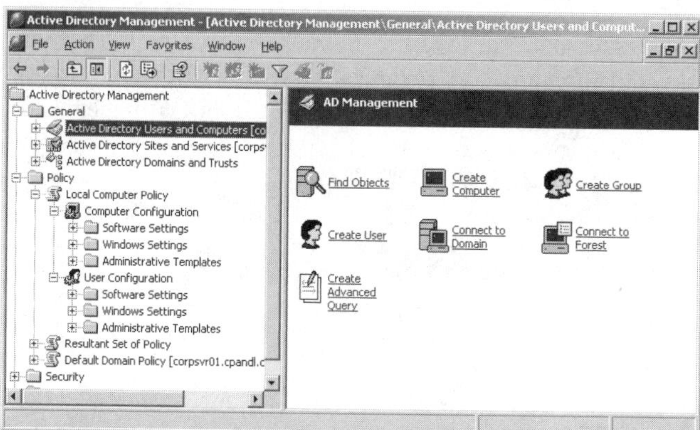

Figure 11-12. By using the No List style and hiding the Standard tab, you can limit user options.

Creating and Managing Taskpads

Any console tool that has at least one snap-in can have an associated taskpad. To create a taskpad, you must open the console in author mode, then follow these steps:

1. Right-click the console item that you want the taskpad to manage, and choose New Taskpad View to start the New Taskpad View Wizard. Keep in mind that a single taskpad can be used to manage multiple console items, and in this case, you are simply designating the object that should have initial focus when working with the taskpad.
2. In the New Taskpad View Wizard, click Next, and then configure the taskpad display by using the options shown in Figure 11-13. Select the style for the details page as Vertical List, Horizontal List, or No List, and set the task description style as Text or InfoTip. You can also choose to hide the Standard tab (which only limits the tasks that can be performed if you also select the No List style). As you make selections, the wizard provides a depiction of what the results will look like as a finished taskpad.

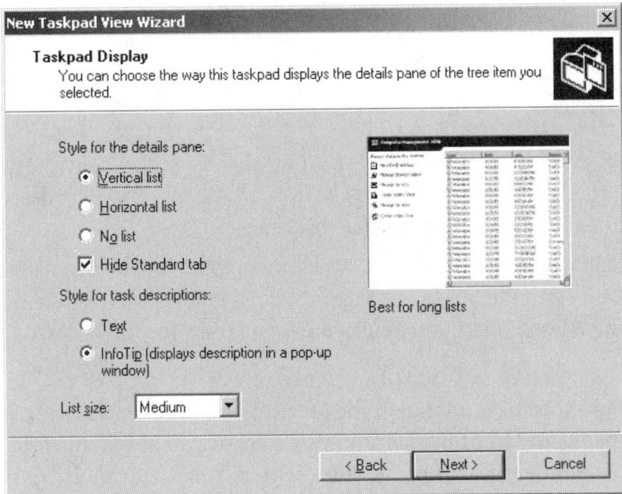

Figure 11-13. Configure the taskpad display in the New Taskpad View Wizard.

3 On the Taskpad Target page (shown in Figure 11-14), you must decide whether to apply the taskpad view to the selected tree item only (the item you right-clicked) or to any other tree item of the same type. If you choose the latter option, you also have the option to change the default display for any items used in the taskpad to the taskpad view. Typically, you'll want to do this to standardize the view, especially if you've hidden the Standard tab and don't want users to have other options.

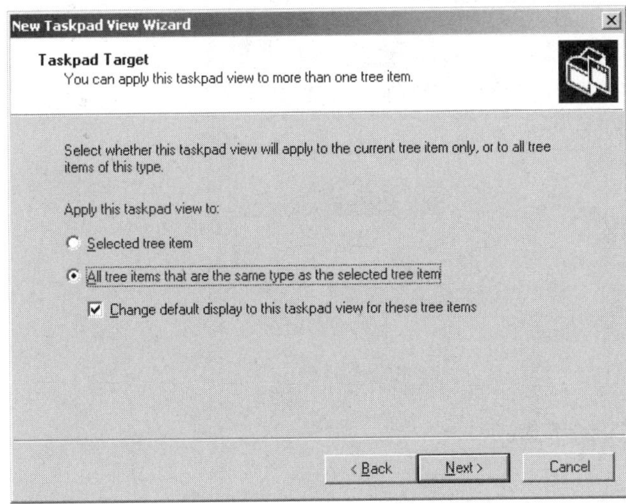

Figure 11-14. Specify a taskpad target.

Note Basically, all snap-ins are of the same type. So, if you apply the taskpad to any other tree item of the same type, the taskpad view can include any snap-in that's been added to the console.

4. Next, you set the name and description for the taskpad. The name appears at the top of the taskpad and on the tab at the bottom of the taskpad. The description appears at the top of the taskpad under the taskpad name.
5. On the final wizard page, you can click Finish to create the taskpad. The Start New Task Wizard option is selected by default, so if you click Finish without clearing this option, the wizard starts and helps you create tasks for the taskpad.

If you want to create multiple taskpads, you can repeat this procedure. For the example console, you might want to have a taskpad for each folder and so in that case would create three additional taskpads. Any additional taskpads you create can be placed at the same place in the console tree or at a different part of the console tree. You access multiple taskpads placed at the same part of the console tree by using the tabs provided in the details pane.

As long as you are in author mode, any taskpad you created can easily be edited or removed. To edit a taskpad view, right-click the item where you defined the taskpad, and then select Edit Taskpad View from the shortcut menu. This opens a Properties dialog box containing two tabs:

- **General** Use the options in the General tab shown in the following screen to control the taskpad style as well as to display or hide the Standard tab. Click Options to specify to which items the taskpad view is applied.

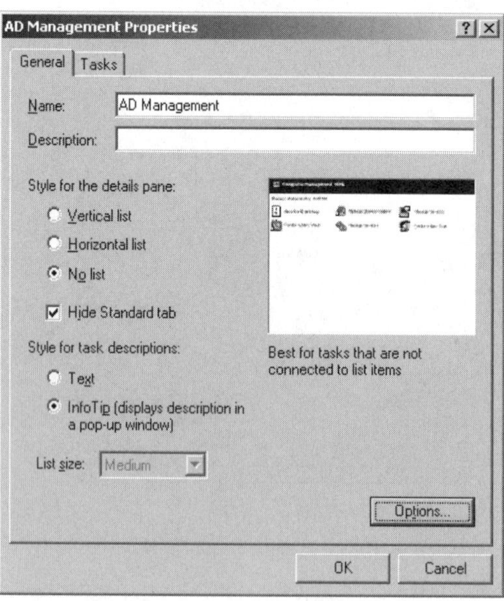

- **Tasks** Use the Tasks tab to list current tasks defined for the taskpad. Use the related options to create new tasks or manage the existing tasks.

Creating and Managing Tasks

You create tasks by using the New Task Wizard. By default, this wizard starts automatically when you finish creating a taskpad view. You can start the wizard using the taskpad Properties dialog box as well. Right-click the item where you defined the taskpad, and then select Edit Taskpad View from the shortcut menu. In the Tasks tab, click New.

Once the New Task Wizard is started, click Next, and then select the command type as follows:

- Choose Menu Command to run the standard menu options of included snap-ins.
- Choose Shell Command to run scripts or programs or to open Web pages.
- Choose Navigation to navigate to a saved view on the Favorites menu.

The subsequent screens you see depend on the type of task you are creating.

Creating Menu Command Tasks

After choosing to create a menu command, select a source for the command, as shown in Figure 11-15. You specify the source of the command as an item from the console tree or from the list in the details pane for the item selected when you started the wizard. If you choose Tree Item Task as the source, select a snap-in in the console tree, and then choose one of the available commands for that snap-in. The commands available change based on the snap-in you've selected.

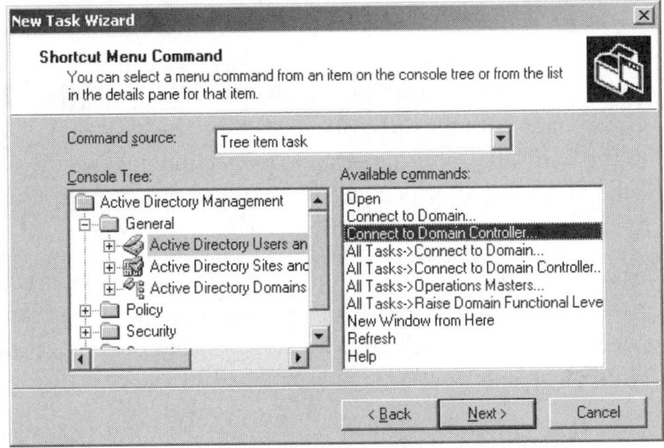

Figure 11-15. Select a command source and then choose a command from the list of available commands.

Chapter 11

Next, you set the name and description for the task, as shown in Figure 11-16. The name is used as the shortcut link designator for the task. The description is displayed as text under the shortcut link or as an InfoTip, depending on the way you configured the taskpad.

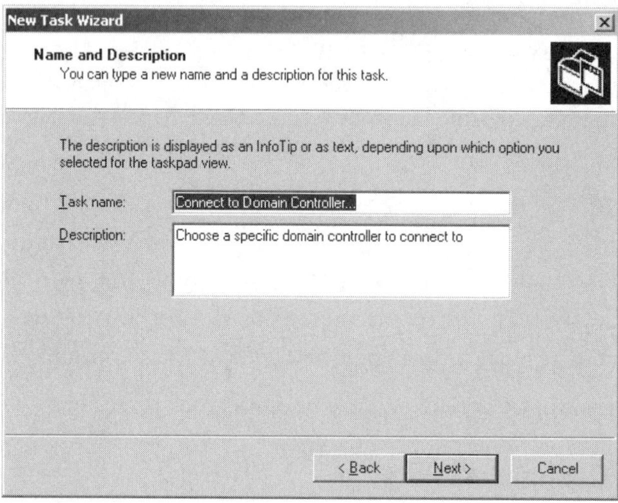

Figure 11-16. Enter a name and description for the command or simply click Next to accept the default values.

In the Task Icon dialog box, shown in Figure 11-17, you can choose an icon for the task. Select Icon Provided By MMC to choose any of the icons provided by the MMC. Click an icon to select it and to display what the icon symbolizes and its alternate meanings. In the example, the Computer icon is selected, and its alternate meanings are Client, CPU, Disconnected, and Monitor.

If you want to use a different set of icons, select Custom Icon, and then click Browse. This displays the Change Icon dialog box. Click Browse to display the Open dialog box. By default, the Open dialog box should open with the directory set to %SystemRoot%\System32. In this case, type **shell32.dll** as the File Name, and click Open. You should now see the Change Icon dialog box with the Shell32.dll selected, which will allow you to choose one of several hundred icons registered for use with the operating system shell.

When you click Next again, the wizard confirms the task creation and shows a current list of tasks on the taskpad provided you click Finish to finalize the creation of the current task. If you want to create another task, select Run This Wizard Again, and then repeat this process. Otherwise, just click Finish.

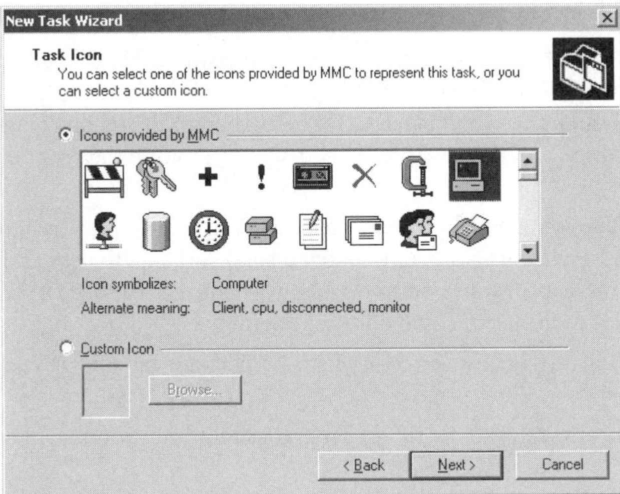

Figure 11-17. Choose an icon for the task.

Creating Shell Command Tasks

After choosing to create a shell command, specify the command line for the task, as shown in Figure 11-18.

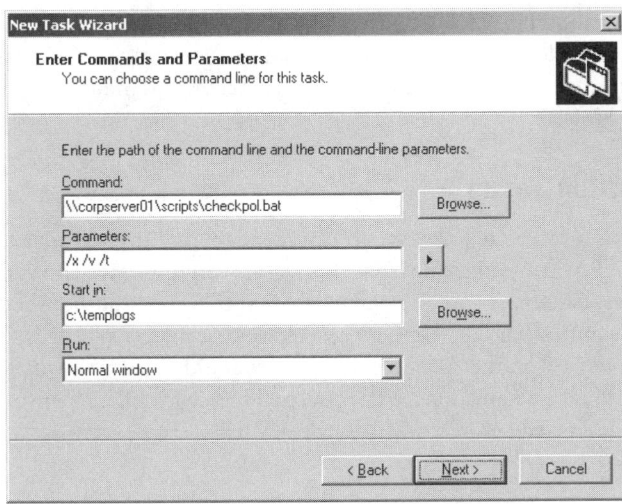

Figure 11-18. Set the command line for the script or program you want to run.

The options are as follows:

- **Command** The full file or Universal Naming Convention (UNC) path to the command to run, such as C:\Scripts\Checkpol.bat or \\Corpserver01\Scripts\Checkpol.bat. The command can be a shell or batch script or a program. If you don't know the path to use, click Browse, and then use the Open dialog box to find the program that you want to run.
- **Parameters** The command-line parameters to pass to the script or program. Click the right arrow beside the parameters field to display variables that you can use (these are related to the snap-in you selected originally when creating the taskpad). Select a variable to add it to the list of command-line parameters.
- **Start In** The startup (or base) directory for the script or program you've chosen, such as C:\Temp.
- **Run** The type of window the script or program should run within, either a normal, minimized, or maximized window.

Next, you set the name and description for the task. The name is used as the shortcut link designator for the task. The description is displayed as text under the shortcut link or as an InfoTip, depending on the way you configured the taskpad.

Next, you can choose an icon for the task. As discussed previously, you can select Icon Provided By MMC or Custom Icon. If you use custom icons, you probably want to use the Shell32.dll in the %SystemRoot%\System32 directory to provide the custom icon.

When you click Next again, the wizard confirms the task creation and shows a current list of tasks on the taskpad provided you click Finish to finalize the creation of the current task. If you want to create another task, select Run This Wizard Again, and then repeat this process. Otherwise, just click Finish.

Creating Navigation Tasks

Navigation tasks are used to create links from one taskpad to another or from a taskpad to a saved console view. Before you can create navigation tasks, you must save a console view or a view of a particular taskpad to the Favorites menu. To do this, while in author mode, navigate down the console tree until the taskpad or item to which you want to navigate is selected, and then select Add To Favorites on the Favorites menu. In the Add To Favorites dialog box, shown in Figure 11-19, type a name for the favorite, and then click OK. Then you can create a navigation task on a selected taskpad that uses that favorite.

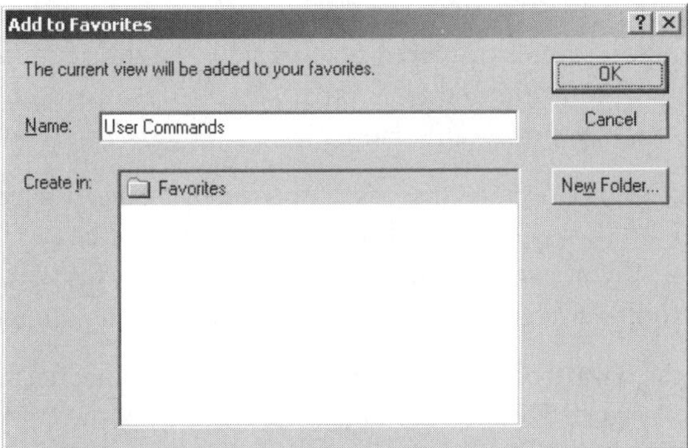

Figure 11-19. Save the current view of the console tool to the Favorites menu.

You create the navigation task using the New Task Wizard. In the New Task Wizard, choose Navigation as the task type. Next, select the favorite to which you want users to navigate when they click the related link. As shown in Figure 11-20, the only favorites available are the ones you've created as discussed previously.

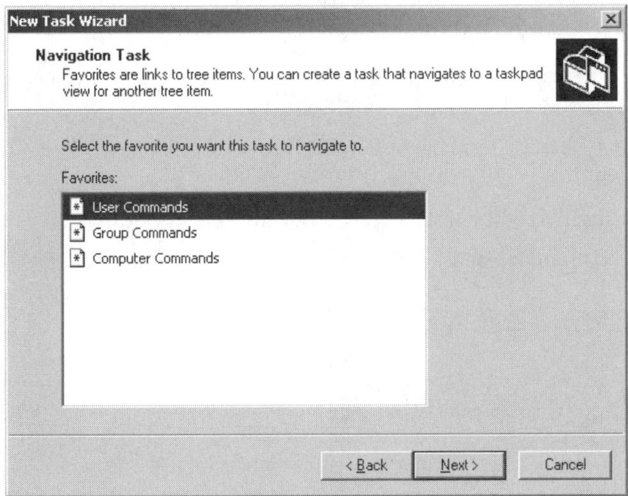

Figure 11-20. Select the previously defined favorite that you want to use.

Chapter 11

Next, you set the name and description for the task. The name is used as the shortcut link designator for the task. The description is displayed as text under the shortcut link or as an InfoTip, depending on the way you configured the taskpad. If you are creating a link to the main console tool page, you might want to call it Home.

Next, you can choose an icon for the task. As discussed previously, you can select Icon Provided By MMC or Custom Icon. If you created a link called Home, there is a Home icon provided by the MMC to use. If you use custom icons, you probably want to use the Shell32.dll in the %SystemRoot%\System32 directory to provide the custom icon.

When you click Next again, the wizard confirms the task creation and shows a current list of tasks on the taskpad provided you click Finish to finalize the creation of the current task. If you want to create another task, select Run This Wizard Again, and then repeat this process. Otherwise, just click Finish.

Arranging, Editing, and Removing Tasks

As long as you are in author mode, you can edit tasks and their properties by using the taskpad Properties dialog box. To display this dialog box, right-click the item where you defined the taskpad, and then select Edit Taskpad View from the shortcut menu. In the Tasks tab shown in Figure 11-21, you can do the following:

- **Arrange tasks** To arrange tasks in a specific order, select a task, and use Move Up or Move Down to set the task order.
- **Create new tasks** To create a new task, click New, and then use the New Task Wizard to define the task.
- **Edit existing tasks** To edit a task, select it, and then click Modify.
- **Remove tasks** To remove a task, select it, and then click Remove.

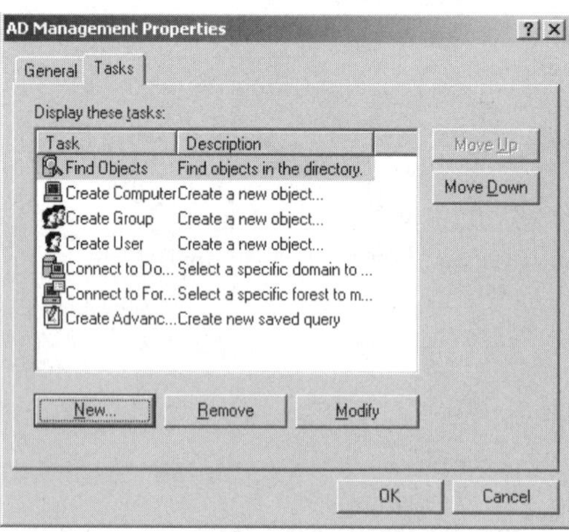

Figure 11-21. Use the Tasks tab in the taskpad Properties dialog box to arrange, create, edit, and remove tasks.

Chapter 11

Publishing and Distributing Your Custom Tools

As you've seen, the MMC provides a complete framework for creating custom tools that can be tailored to the needs of a wide range of users. For administrators, you could create custom consoles tailored for each individual specialty, such as security administration, network administration, or user administration. For junior administrators or Power Users, you could create custom consoles that include taskpads that help guide them by providing lists of common commands, and you can even restrict this list so that these individuals can perform only these commands.

Because custom consoles are saved as regular files, you can publish and distribute them as you would any other file. You could put the consoles on a network file server in a shared folder. You could e-mail the consoles directly to those who will use them. You could use Active Directory to publish the tools. You could even copy them directly to the Start menu on the appropriate computer as discussed previously.

In any case, users need appropriate access permissions to run the tasks and access the snap-ins. These permissions must be granted for a particular computer or the network. Keep in mind also that the MMC version shipped with Windows 2000 and previous versions of the Windows operating system will not run tools created using the MMC version that ships with Windows Server 2003 (MMC 2.0 version 5.2). This version runs on only Windows Server 2003 and Windows XP.

Chapter 12

Managing Windows Server 2003

Systems that run Microsoft Windows Server 2003 are the heart of any Microsoft Windows network. These are the systems that provide the essential services and applications for users and the network as a whole. As an administrator, it is your job to keep these systems running, and to do this, you must understand the administration options available and put them to the best use possible. Your front-line defense in managing systems running Windows Server 2003 is the administration and support tools discussed in this chapter.

To run most of the administration tools, you must have Administrator privileges, and if these aren't included with your current account, you must log on using an account that has these privileges. One way to do this without having to log off and log back on is to use the secondary logon so that you can run tools as an administrator.

Using the Administration Tools

Any explanation of how to manage Windows Server 2003 systems must involve the administration and support tools that are included with the operating system. These are the tools you will use every day, so you might as will learn a bit more about them. Many other tools that might come in handy are found in the Windows Server 2003 Support Tools and Resource Kit.

Understanding the Administration Tools

Most administration tools are found on the Administrative Tools menu and can be run by clicking Start, pointing to Programs or All Programs, and then selecting Administrative Tools. As Table 12-1 shows, dozens of administration tools are available for working with Windows Server 2003. The tool you use depends on what you want to do and sometimes on how much control you want over the aspect of the operating system you are seeking to manage. Several tools, including Configure Your Server, Manage Your Server, and Computer

Management, are discussed later in this section. Other tools are discussed later in this chapter or in other appropriate chapters of this book.

Table 12-1. Tools for Administration

Administrative Tool	Description
Active Directory Domains and Trusts	Used to manage trust relationships between domains.
Active Directory Sites and Services	Used to create sites and to manage the replication of Active Directory information.
Active Directory Users and Computers	Used to manage users, groups, contacts, computers, organizational units (OUs), and other objects in the Active Directory directory service.
Application Server	Used to manage the Microsoft .NET Framework, Microsoft Internet Information Services (IIS), and Component Services. This is a special console added for convenience.
Certification Authority	Used to create and manage server certificates for servers and users on the network. Certificates are used to support Public Key Infrastructure (PKI) encryption and authentication.
Cluster Administrator	Used to manage the Cluster service available with Windows Server 2003, Enterprise Edition and Datacenter Edition. Clustering allows groups of computers to work together, providing failover support and additional processing capacity.
Component Services	Used to configure and manage COM+ applications. It also lets you manage events and services.
Computer Management	Used to manage services, devices, disks, and the system hardware configuration. It is also used to access other system tools.
Configure Your Server	Used to manage server roles.
Connection Manager Administration Kit	Used to configure and customize Connection Manager.
Data Sources (ODBC)	Used to configure and manage Open Database Connectivity (ODBC) data sources and drivers.
DHCP	Used to configure and manage the Dynamic Host Configuration Protocol (DHCP) service.

Table 12-1. Tools for Administration

Administrative Tool	Description
Distributed File System	Used to create and manage distributed file systems that connect shared folders from different computers.
DNS	Used to configure and manage the Domain Name System (DNS) service, which can be integrated with Active Directory.
Domain Controller Security Policy	Used to view and modify security policy for a domain controller.
Domain Security Policy	Used to view and modify the security policy for a domain.
Event Viewer	Used to view the system event logs and manage event log configurations.
Filer Server Management	Used to manage file shares and disks. This is a special console added for convenience.
Internet Authentication Service	Used to manage authentication, authorization, and accounting (AAA) of remote Internet users.
IIS Manager	Used to configure and manage Internet services, which include Web, File Transfer Protocol (FTP), Simple Mail Transfer Protocol (SMTP), and Network News Transport Protocol (NNTP).
IP Address Management	Used to manage DHCP, Windows Internet Naming Service (WINS), and DNS. This is a special console added for convenience.
Licensing	Used to manage client access licenses for server products.
Manage Your Server	Used to manage server roles that have been configured on a system.
Microsoft .NET Framework 1.1 Configuration	Used to manage the configuration of the .NET Framework, which is used with application servers.
Microsoft .NET Framework 1.1 Configuration and Wizards	Used to install and configure the .NET Framework.
Performance	Used to monitor system performance, create performance tracking logs, and define performance alerts.
Remote Desktops	Used to configure remote connections and view remote desktop sessions.

Table 12-1. Tools for Administration

Administrative Tool	Description
Remote Storage	Used to manage the Remote Storage service, which automatically transfers data from infrequently used files to tape libraries.
Routing and Remote Access	Used to configure and manage the Routing and Remote Access service, which controls routing interfaces, dynamic Internet Protocol (IP) routing, and remote access.
Server Extensions Administrator	Used to manage server extensions, such as the Microsoft Office FrontPage Server extensions.
Services	Used to manage the startup and configuration of Windows services.
Terminal Services Configuration	Used to manage Terminal Services protocol configurations and server settings.
Terminal Services Licensing	Used to manage client access licensing for Terminal Services.
Terminal Services Manager	Used to manage and monitor Terminal Services users, sessions, and processes.
WINS	Used to manage WINS. This service resolves NetBIOS names to IP addresses and is used with computers running versions earlier than Microsoft Windows 2000.

Using Configure Your Server

As with Windows 2000, Windows Server 2003 provides the Configure Your Server Wizard to help you configure servers to handle specific roles. For example, you might want to configure a server as a domain controller, a file server, or a print server, and rather than configuring these options by hand, you can use the wizard to help you.

The Configure Your Server Wizard is in the Administrative Tools folder. Click Start, point to Programs or All Programs, click Administrative Tools, and then click Configure Your Server. When the wizard starts, click Next, and then read about the preliminary tasks (as shown in the screen on the following page) that should be performed prior to using the wizard to configure roles. Basically, you should ensure the server has a network card and is connected to the network, and also that you have the Windows Server 2003 distribution CD-ROM or can access the setup files over the network.

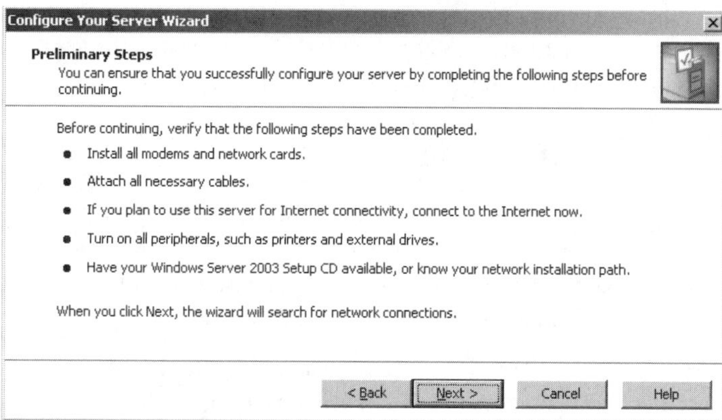

When you click Next again, Windows Server 2003 gathers information about the server's current roles, then displays a list of available server roles, and specifies whether they're configured, as shown in the following screen. You can then add or remove roles. If a role isn't configured and you want to add the role, select the role in the Server Role column, click Next, and then follow the prompts. If a role is configured and you want to remove it, select the role in the Server Role column, and then click Next. Read any warnings displayed, and then follow the prompts to remove the role.

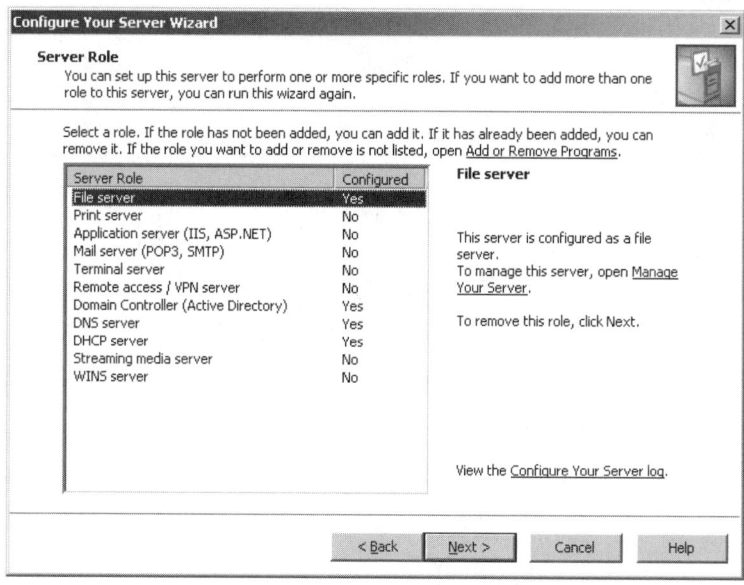

You'll find it pretty easy to configure the basic roles by following the prompts. Each role is covered in depth in other chapters of the book as well. Once a role is installed, you can manage it by using Manage Your Server, which is discussed in the next section.

Using Manage Your Server

Manage Your Server provides a central interface for managing the roles that you've configured on a server. Any role that you add by using the Configure Your Server Wizard or the standard tools is available for management, and you can also launch Configure Your Server from within this tool by clicking the Add Or Remove A Role link.

As Figure 12-1 shows, Manage Your Server lists the current roles that are configured along with quick access links for related management tools. You can use the arrow icons to the left of the role name to shrink or expand the role information provided. In the upper-right corner, you will find quick access links to Administrative Tools, Windows Update, the System Properties dialog box, Help And Support, and more under the headings Tools And Updates and See Also.

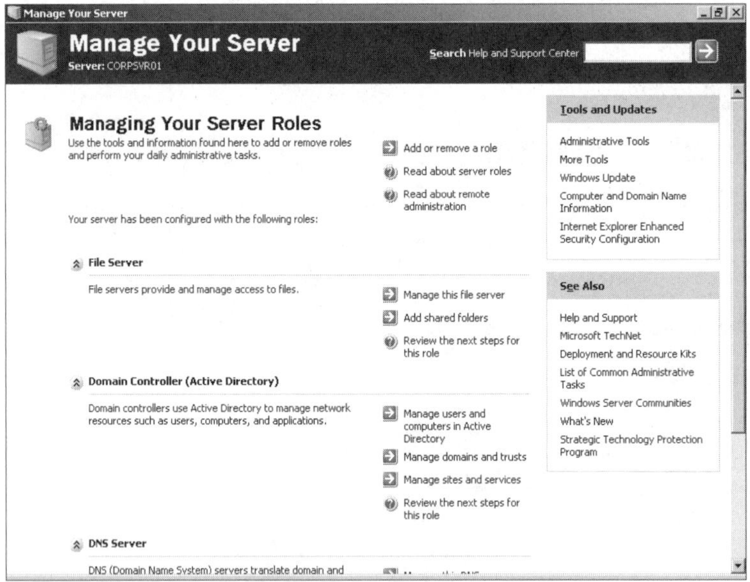

Figure 12-1. Use Manage Your Server to quickly access tools related to the roles configured on a server.

Using Computer Management

Computer Management provides tools for managing local and remote systems. The tools available through the console tree provide the core functionality and are divided into the following three categories as shown in the accompanying screen:

- System Tools
- Storage
- Services And Applications

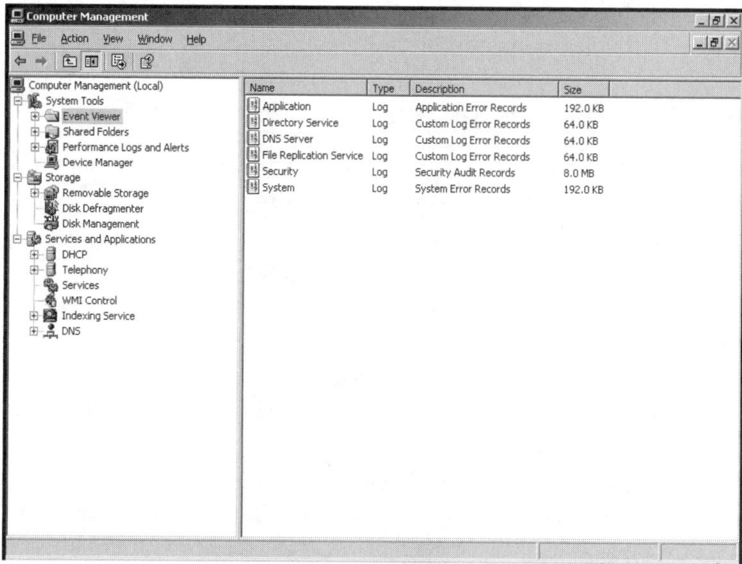

Computer Management System Tools

The Computer Management System Tools are designed to manage systems and view system information. The available system tools are these:

- **Event Viewer** Used to view the event logs on the selected computer. Event logs are covered in Chapter 15, "Performance Monitoring and Tuning."
- **Shared Folders** Used to manage the properties of shared folders as well as sessions for users working with shared folders and the files the users are working with. Managing shared folders is covered in Chapter 21, "File Sharing and Security."
- **Local Users And Groups** Used to manage local users and local user groups on the currently selected computer. Local users and local user groups aren't a part of Active Directory and are managed instead through the Local Users And Groups view. Domain

controllers don't have local users or groups, and because of this there isn't a Local Users And Groups view. Local users and groups are discussed in Chapter 37, "Managing Users, Groups, and Computers."

- **Performance Logs And Alerts** Used to monitor system performance and create logs based on performance parameters. You can also use this tool to alert users of adverse performance conditions. For more information on performance logs and alerts, see the section entitled "Performance Logging" on page 503.
- **Device Manager** Used as a central location for checking the status of any device installed on a computer and for updating the associated device drivers. You can also use it to troubleshoot device problems. Managing devices is covered in Chapter 13, "Managing and Troubleshooting Hardware."

Computer Management Storage Tools

The Computer Management Storage tools display drive information and provide access to drive management tools. The available storage tools are as follows:

- **Removable Storage** Used to manage removable media devices and tape libraries. It can also help you track work queues and operator requests related to removable media devices. Removable Storage is discussed further in Chapter 23, "Using Removable Media."
- **Disk Defragmenter** Used to correct drive fragmentation problems by locating and combining fragmented files. Defragmenting disks is discussed in the section entitled "Defragmenting Disks" on page 685.
- **Disk Management** Used to manage hard disks and the way they are partitioned. You can also use it to manage volume sets and redundant array of independent disks (RAID) arrays. Disk Management replaces the Disk Administrator utility in Microsoft Windows NT 4 and is discussed in the section entitled "Configuring Storage" on page 593.

Computer Management Services And Applications Tools

The Computer Management Services And Applications tools help you manage services and applications installed on the server. Any application or service-related task that can be performed in a separate tool can be performed through the Services And Applications node as well. For example, if the currently selected system has DHCP installed, you can manage DHCP through the server Applications And Services node. You could also use the DHCP tool in the Administrative Tools folder, and either way, you can perform the same tasks.

Computer Management Essentials

When Computer Management is selected in the console tree, you can easily connect to other computers, send console messages, and export information lists. By default, Computer Management works with the local system. To connect to a different computer, right-click the root node (labeled Computer Management) in the console tree, and then select Connect To Another Computer on the shortcut menu. In the Select Computer dialog box, which is shown in the following screen, choose Another Computer, and then type the fully qualified name of the computer you want to work with, such as **corpsvr01.microsoft.com**, where corpsvr01 is the computer name and microsoft.com is the domain name. If you don't know the computer name, click Browse to search for the computer you want to work with.

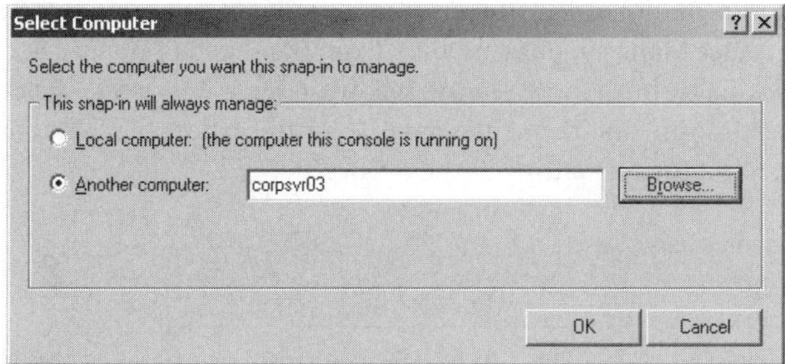

Console messages are sent to all users logged onto or connected to the system you are currently working with in Computer Management. These messages appear in a dialog box that the user must click to close and can contain whatever text you want to pass along to users working with a system. You send a console message by right-clicking the Computer Management entry in the console tree, selecting All Tasks, and then choosing Send Console Message. This displays the Send Console Message dialog box.

In the Send Console Message dialog box (shown in the following screen), type the text of the message in the Message area. In the Recipients area, you should see the name of the computer to which you're currently connected. If you want to send a message to users of this system, click Send. Otherwise, use the Add button to add recipient computers or the Remove button to delete a selected recipient. Then, when you're ready to send the message, click Send.

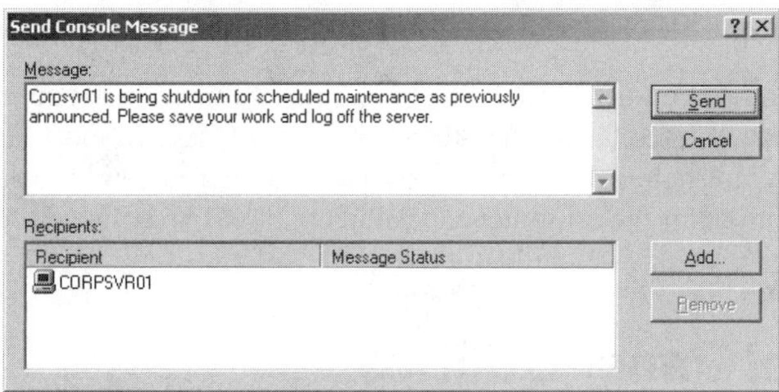

> **Note** Windows systems must be running the Messenger service to send and receive console messages. This means the service must be configured and enabled not only on the server you are using, but the user computers as well.

The Export List feature allows you to save textual information displayed in the right pane to a tab-delimited or comma-delimited text file. One of the best uses for this feature is when you want to save detailed information on all the services running on a system. To do this, right-click Services in Computer Management, and then from the shortcut menu select Export List. In the Export List dialog box (shown in the following screen), use the Save In selection list to choose the save location, and then enter a name for the export file. Next, use the Save As Type selection list to set the formatting of the export file.

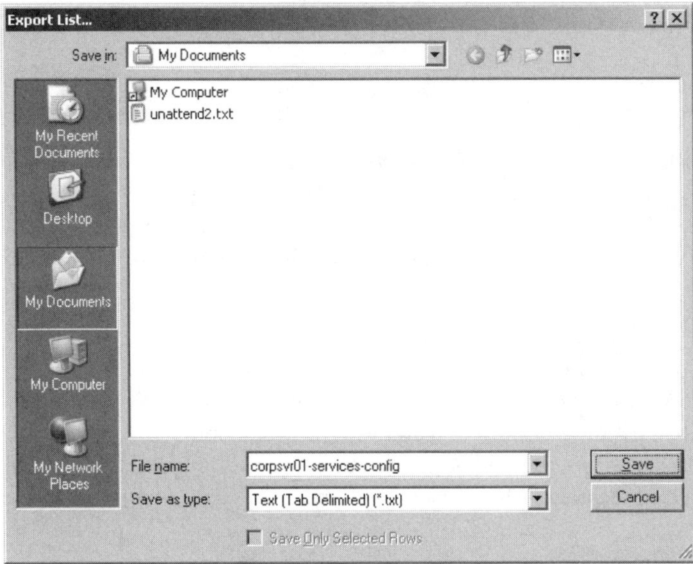

You can separate columns of information with tabs or commas and save as American Standard Code for Information Interchange (ASCII) text or Unicode text. In most cases, you'll want to use ASCII text. Finish the export process by clicking Save. You now have a detailed list of the service configuration for the computer and could use this as a baseline if you are trying to troubleshoot service-related issues in the future.

Using the Control Panel Utilities

Control Panel contains utilities for managing server hardware and operating system settings. As you might already know, some Control Panel utilities offer a fairly simple interface and are easy to work with, while others are fairly complex. Utilities that require little or no explanation are not discussed in this text; you will find a discussion of some of the more complex utilities later in this section.

Note The way you access Control Panel depends on the Start menu style. For the Classic Start menu, click Start, click Settings, and then click Control Panel. For the simple Start menu, click Start, and then click Control Panel.

Tip **Display Control Panel as a menu**
Regardless of menu style, you can configure the system to display Control Panel in a menu, which allows you to access individual utilities without having to open a separate folder. Right-click Start, select Properties, and then click Customize in the Taskbar And Start Menu Properties dialog box. Next, if you are using the Classic Start menu, select Expand Control Panel under Advanced Start Menu Options, and then click OK twice. If you are using the simple Start menu, click the Advanced tab, select Display As A Menu as a Control Panel option under Start Menu Item, and then click OK twice.

Using the Add Hardware Utility

Add Hardware is used to start the Add Hardware Wizard (shown in the following screen), which helps you add new hardware, remove hardware, and troubleshoot problems with hardware. It automatically tries to detect new Plug and Play devices that have been recently connected, and it can also be used with non–Plug and Play devices. For more information on installing hardware and managing devices, see Chapter 13.

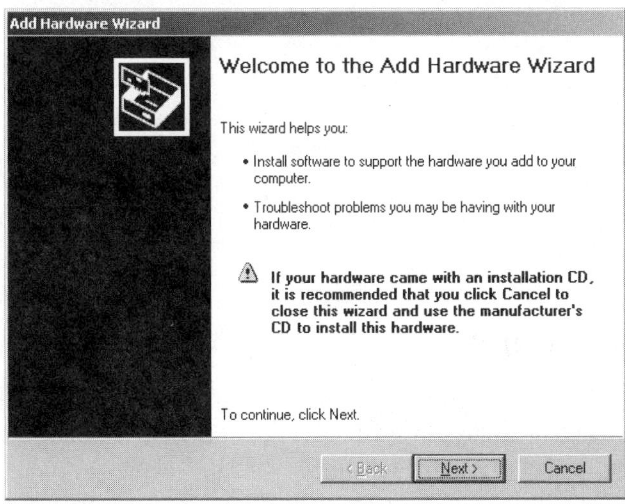

Using the Add or Remove Programs Utility

Add or Remove Programs has the following three main options, as shown in the accompanying screen:

- **Change Or Remove Programs** When you select Change Or Remove Programs, you'll see a list of the currently installed programs and the disk space those programs use. Select a program to see how often the program is used as well as when it was last used. Hot fixes installed on a computer are also listed here.
- **Add New Programs** When you select Add New Programs, you will find buttons for adding programs from CD or floppy disk as well as for adding updates downloaded from Windows Update. You'll also see a list of programs published through Active Directory and available for network installation (if any).
- **Add Or Remove Windows Components** When you select Add Or Remove Windows Components, you launch Windows Setup, which in turn starts the Windows Components Wizard. A wide variety of Windows components can be added by using this wizard, many of which are configured using server roles as well.

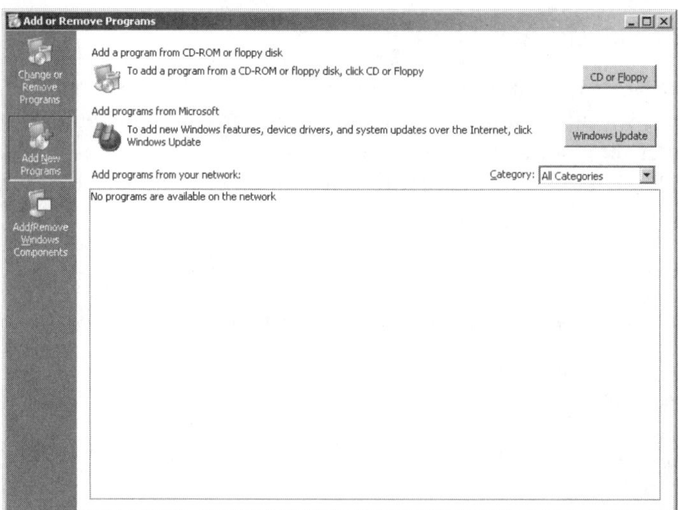

Using the Date and Time Utility

Date and Time, as shown in the screen on the following page, is used to view or set a system's date, time, and time zone. This utility can also be accessed by double-clicking the clock in the system tray. Keep in mind that some time zones within the United States and in other countries use Daylight Saving Time. If you select a time zone where this is applicable, Daylight

Saving Time is used by default and you'll see the Automatically Adjust Clock For Daylight Saving Changes option. If you do not want to use Daylight Saving Time, clear this option.

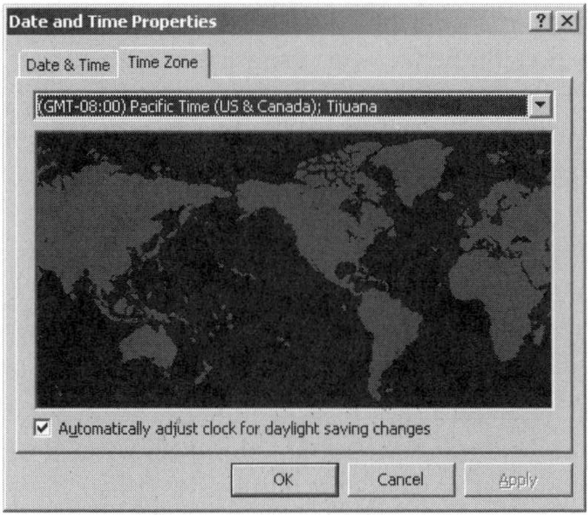

Tip Maintain accurate system time to ensure logon
Don't overlook the importance of the Date and Time settings. In a domain, the system time is checked during logon, and a discrepancy of more than a few minutes between the domain controller and the computer to which you are logging on can result in logon failure. Keep in mind that domain controllers do all their internal work in universal time and, though, they don't care about the time zone, an incorrect time zone setting can lead to denial of logon. Instead of setting the time on individual computers in the domain manually, you can use the Windows Time Service to synchronize time automatically on the network.

Using the Display Utility

Display is used to configure desktop settings, including backgrounds, screen savers, screen resolution, and appearance. You can also use this utility to specify desktop icons and to control advanced monitor settings. The tabs in this dialog box are used as follows:

- **Themes** Used to manage the theme for the computer. On most servers, you'll want to use the Windows Classic theme to reduce the amount of memory and processing time used to manage the theme.
- **Desktop** Used to set the desktop background and icons. On most servers, you'll want to use None as the background to reduce the amount of memory used when you log on. If you click Customize Desktop, you can add or remove the desktop icons for My Documents, My Computer, My Network Places, and Microsoft Internet Explorer.

- **Screen Saver** Used to specify the screen saver options. When the computer is idle for the Wait Time, the screen saver starts. Three screen savers are included: Blank, Marquee, and Windows Server 2003. With these screen savers, you should select the On Resume, Password Protect option to enhance security by requiring logon. If you select (None) as a screen saver option, the server won't use a screen saver.

> **Note** Wondering what happened to all the other screen savers? They were removed because some of them, especially the 3D screen savers, caused the processor utilization to max out, allowing the server to do little else but render the 3D art.

- **Appearance** Used to specify the window and button style, color scheme, and font size. On an LCD monitor, you might want to enable ClearType to improve text readability. Click Effects, select Use The Following Method To Smooth Edges, and then choose ClearType.

- **Settings** Used to set the screen resolution and the color quality (see the following screen). The default resolution after installation typically is 800 by 600. During the first logon after installation, Windows Server 2003 detects the available screen resolutions and will allow you to set the computer to a better resolution automatically. By clicking Advanced, you can change the dots per inch (dpi) setting from Normal Size (96 DPI) to Large Size (120 DPI), which increases the size of screen items and can make them easier to read. Other advanced settings let you examine and configure the graphics adapter, monitor settings, and graphics hardware acceleration.

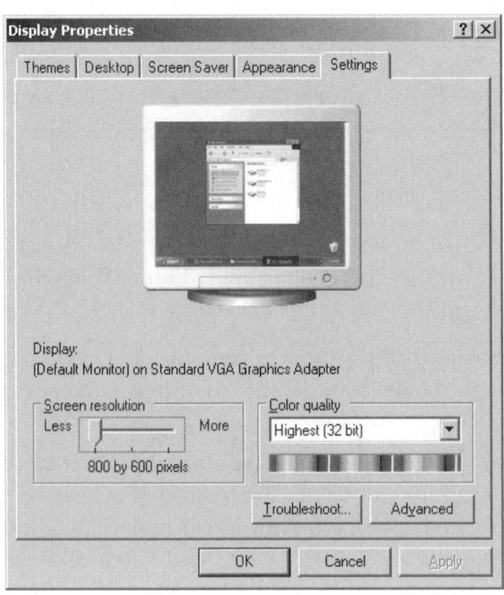

Using the Folder Options Utility

Folder Options is used to control how Windows Explorer displays files and folders and to set a wide variety of folder and file options, including the type of desktop used, the folder views used, whether offline files are used, and whether you must single-click or double-click to open items. As an administrator, you will probably want to set the following options in the View tab, as shown in the accompanying screen:

- **Show Hidden Files And Folders** Select this option to see hidden files and folders.
- **Hide Extensions For Known File Types** Clear this option to see file names as well as file extensions.
- **Hide Protected Operating System Files** Clear this option so that you can see and work with operating system files, which are otherwise hidden.

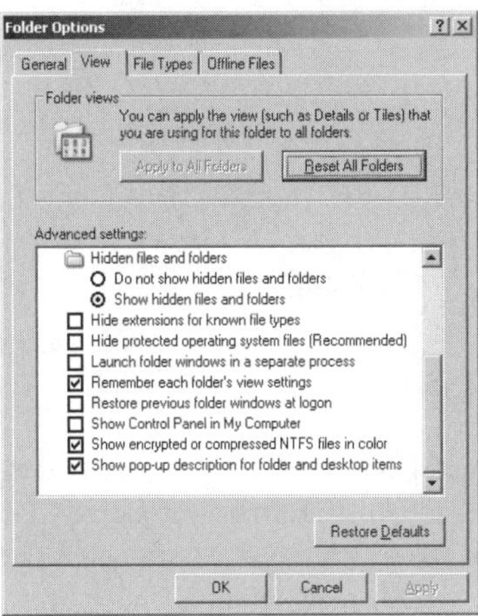

Using the Licensing Utility

Licensing is used to change the client-licensing mode of installed products, such as Windows Server 2003 or Microsoft SQL Server 2000. The licensing mode can be set to the following options, as shown in the screen on the following page:

- **Per Server** With per-server licensing, you set the number of concurrent connections allowed, and when that number is reached, additional connections are refused. A single user could have multiple client connections to a server, and each client connection a user makes counts toward the allowable maximum.
- **Per Device Or Per User** The per-device (called Per Seat in Windows 2000) mode of this option assumes you have purchased a client access license (CAL) for each computer that will access the server or application. Concurrent connections are not

tracked. If you work in a 24 × 7 environment using workers in shifts or anytime there are multiple users per computer, this option can be best.

The per-user mode assumes you have purchased a CAL for each user that will access the server or application. Concurrent connections are not tracked. If users have multiple computers, such as in an engineering or Information Technology (IT) department, this option can be best.

Note Windows Server 2003 allows you to make a one-time-only change from Per Server to Per Device Or Per User. You won't be able to change the licensing mode again without reinstalling the server.

Using the Network Connections Utility

Network Connections is used to view existing network connections and to create new ones. If you configured Transmission Control Protocol/Internet Protocol (TCP/IP) networking when you installed the operating system, the server has a default network connection called Local Area Connection. Selecting this option displays a Status dialog box that lets you determine the current networking configuration and make changes to it. For more information on configuring networking, see Chapter 24, "Managing TCP/IP Networking."

Tip **Display Network Connections as a menu**
As with Control Panel, you can configure the system to display Network Connections in a menu, which allows you to access individual utilities without having to open a separate folder. Right-click Start, select Properties, and then click Customize in the Taskbar And Start Menu Properties dialog box. Next, if you are using the Classic Start menu, select Expand Network Connections under Advanced Start Menu Options, and then click OK twice. If you are using the simple Start menu, click the Advanced tab, select Display As A Menu as a Network Connections option under Start Menu Items, and then click OK twice.

Using the Regional and Language Options Utility

Regional and Language Options is used to set country-specific standards and formats, as shown in the following screen. In different countries, the unit of measurement, currency, and date formatting can be different. To change the settings, simply select a country or region in the Standards And Formats area. By choosing a region, you choose all the appropriate settings for numbers, currency, dates, and times. Examples of the formatting standards for the selected region are displayed in the Samples section.

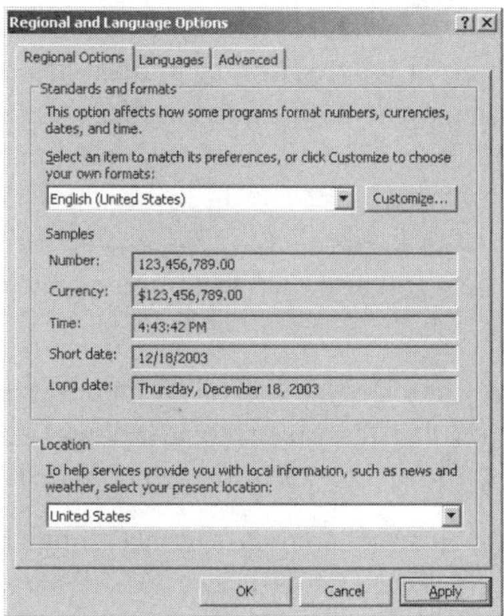

You can customize these settings by clicking Customize and then using the Customize Regional Options dialog box to modify the basic number, currency, time, and date settings for the region. Regional settings are also used to specify your present location for the purposes of presenting local information in dialog boxes and within Help And Support services windows. You set the system location by using the Location list.

Note You'll want to keep track of localized versions in use and the locations in which they are used. This is critical when upgrading to Windows Server 2003, because attempting an upgrade using a different localized version of Windows Server 2003 will fail.

Using the Scheduled Tasks Utility

Scheduled Tasks allows you to view existing scheduled tasks and add new ones. A *scheduled task* is a one-time or recurring procedure that the operating system runs to handle common administrative jobs and can be an executable program or a script. Clicking Add Scheduled

Task in the Scheduled Tasks folder starts the Scheduled Task Wizard. This wizard provides a point-and-click interface for creating tasks. Another way to create scheduled tasks is to use the Schtasks command-line utility, which is essentially the command-line counterpart to the Scheduled Task Wizard and which replaces the AT command as the preferred command-line utility for working with scheduled tasks.

Task-Scheduling Essentials

Task scheduling is managed by the Task Scheduler service. This service must be properly configured and running on all the systems on which you want to schedule tasks. When you configure tasks, you set the user account to use. This account determines the permissions and privileges the script has. Typically, however, the related user's environment settings will not be available to the script because there will be no actual user logon session. Because of this, if you use the task to run a Windows script, the script should configure whichever user settings are necessary to perform the scheduled task. In this way, you can be sure that everything the script does is under the control of the script and that domain user settings, such as drive mappings, are available as necessary.

Windows Server 2003 provides several ways to get to Scheduled Tasks. One way is, of course, through Control Panel. You can also access Scheduled Tasks by using Windows Explorer. Open Windows Explorer, click My Computer, click Control Panel, and then click Scheduled Tasks.

In a Windows domain, you can access Scheduled Tasks on a remote system through My Network Places. Open Windows Explorer, and then use the My Network Places node to navigate to the computer you want to work with. Click the computer's icon, and then click Scheduled Tasks.

For computers that are part of a workgroup, you can't access Scheduled Tasks in this way. Instead, you must establish a Remote Desktop connection to the computer you want to work with, then use Windows Explorer to access the Scheduled Tasks folder. You can also use this technique for computers in a domain.

Once you've accessed Scheduled Tasks, you can work with entries in the related folder by using any of the following techniques:

- To start the Scheduled Task Wizard, double-click Add Scheduled Task.
- To view or change a task's properties, including the account under which the task is run, double-click the task, then use the Properties dialog box to make the necessary changes. You can set advanced options in the Settings tab.
- To run a task immediately, right-click the task, and then select Run.
- To stop a running task, right-click the task, and then select End Task. This only halts the currently running task. It doesn't change the run schedule.

- To delete a task, select it, and then press Delete. Or right-click the task, and then select Delete.

Tip Consider enabling and disabling tasks instead of deleting them
Instead of deleting a task, you can disable it to stop it temporarily from running. Then, if you want to use the task again, you simply enable it rather than having to re-create it. To enable or disable a task, double-click the task in the Scheduled Tasks folder, then in the task's Properties dialog box, select or clear the Enabled option.

Creating Scheduled Tasks

You can create a scheduled task by using the Scheduled Task Wizard and following these steps:

1. Start the Scheduled Task Wizard by double-clicking Add Scheduled Task in the Scheduled Tasks folder. Click Next.
2. On the wizard page shown in Figure 12-2, click Browse to open the Select Program To Schedule dialog box. Then use the dialog box to find a command shell or Windows script you want to run.

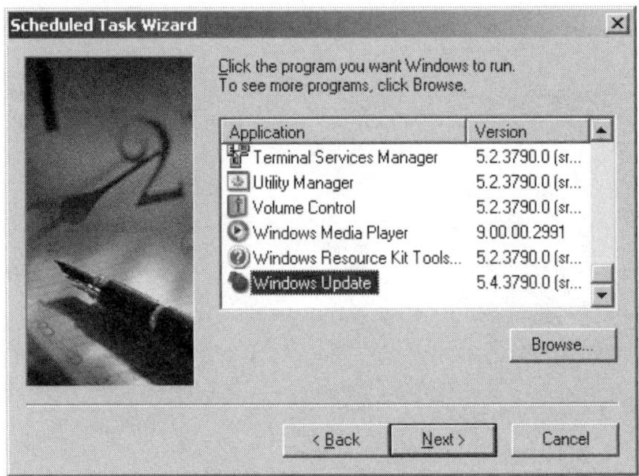

Figure 12-2. Specify the program or script to run.

3. Type a name for the task, as shown in Figure 12-3. The name should be short but descriptive so you can quickly determine what the task does. Then select a run schedule for the task. Tasks can be scheduled to run daily, weekly, monthly, or when a specific event occurs, such as when the computer starts or when the task's user logs on. You can also specify that a task should run one time only.

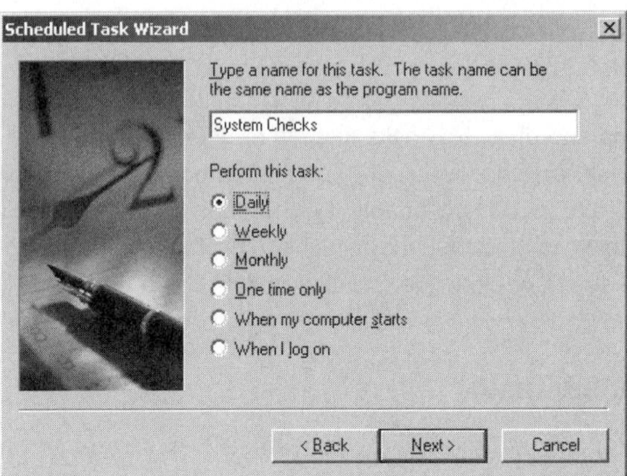

Figure 12-3. Name the task and then set the run schedule.

4 The next page you see depends on the run schedule. If you've selected a daily running task, set a start time and date as shown in Figure 12-4. Then configure the task to run one of the following ways:

- *Every Day*—Seven days a week.
- *Weekdays*—Monday through Friday only.
- *Every N Days*—Every 2, 3, . . . *N* days.

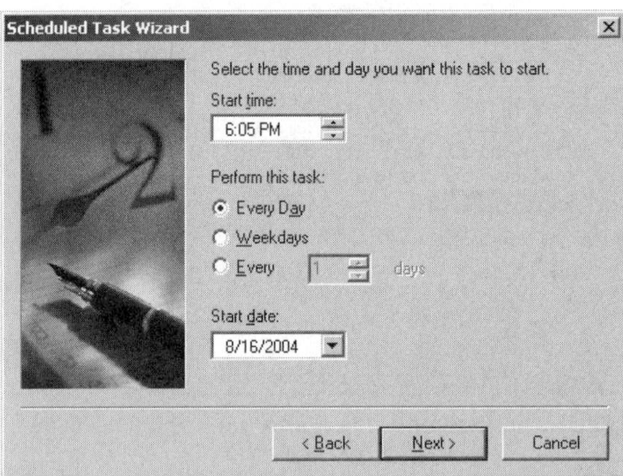

Figure 12-4. Daily tasks can be set to run Every Day, Weekdays, or Every *N* Days.

5 For a weekly running task, the date and time page appears as shown in Figure 12-5. Configure the task using these options:

- *Start Time*—Sets the start time of the task.
- *Every N Weeks*—Allows you to run the task every week, every 2 weeks, or every *N* weeks.

- *Select The Day(s) Of The Week Below*—Sets the day(s) of the week when the task runs, such as on Monday or on Monday, Wednesday, and Friday.

Figure 12-5. Weekly tasks can be set to run on specific days.

6 For a monthly running task, the date and time page appears as shown in Figure 12-6. Configure the task using these options:

- *Start Time*—Sets the start time of the task.
- *Day*—Sets the day of the month the task runs. For example, if you select 5, the task runs on the fifth day of the month.
- *The N Day*—Sets the task to run on the *N*th occurrence of a day in a month, such as the second Monday or the third Tuesday of every month.
- *Of The Month(s)*—These options let you select in which months the task runs.

Figure 12-6. Monthly tasks can be set to run on specific days.

7 For One Time Only tasks, the date and time page appears as shown in Figure 12-7. Set the start time and start date.

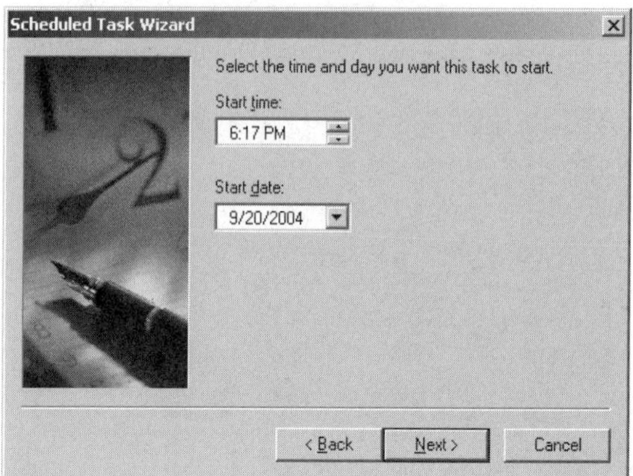

Figure 12-7. One Time Only tasks can be set to run at a specific date and time.

8 For tasks that run when the computer starts or when the task's user logs on, you don't have to set the start date and time. The task runs automatically when the startup or logon event occurs.

9 Click Next. Provide the user name and password for the account under which the task will run, as shown in Figure 12-8. This account must have the privileges and permissions necessary to run the task.

Figure 12-8. Provide the logon information for the user account under which the task will run.

> **Note** In Windows domains, be sure to enter the user name in the form: *Domain\Username*, such as CPANDL\wrstanek, where CPANDL is the domain and wrstanek is the user account.

10 Click Next. The final wizard page provides a summary of the task you're scheduling. Click Finish to complete the scheduling process.

Tip Set arguments for scripts after creating the task

For scripts, you can set command-line arguments, but only after you create the scheduled task by using the wizard. Before clicking Finish, select Open Advanced Properties For This Task When I Click Finish, or simply double-click the task in Windows Explorer after clicking Finish. Then, in the Run box, type the parameters after the task path. If the task path includes spaces, be sure to enclose the path in double quotation marks (""). Similarly, if a command-line argument includes spaces, enclose the argument in double quotation marks ("").

Troubleshooting

Correcting errors with task creation

If an error occurs when you create a task, you'll see an error prompt. The task should still be created, but you might need to edit the task's properties. In Windows Explorer, double-click the task to correct the specified error. One of the more common errors you might encounter is Access Denied. This error can occur if the user credentials provided are incorrect, such as occurs if you enter the wrong password or the user account doesn't exist in the domain.

Inside Out

Task startup problems

Task Scheduler doesn't verify the information you provide. If you don't specify the correct information, the task simply won't run or will generate errors when it does run. One way to check tasks is to view their status and last result in the Scheduled Tasks folder. Any task listed as Could Not Start should be examined. Sometimes, however, a task that is listed as Running might not in fact be running and instead can be frozen or running errant. To check for these types of tasks, use the entries in the Last Run Time column, which tell you when a task was started.

If the task has been running for more than a day, there is usually a problem. To stop the task, right-click it in the Scheduled Tasks folder, then select End Task. You could also wait for the Task Scheduler to stop the task. By default, all tasks time out after running for 72 hours. You can change the timeout in the Settings tab of the Properties dialog box for the task.

The Last Run Time tells you only the last time the scheduled task ran. It won't tell you whether there were problems running tasks prior to the last run time. This you can determine only by examining the Task Scheduler log file. You can open this log in Notepad by selecting View Log on the Advanced menu when the Scheduled Tasks folder is selected in Windows Explorer.

Using the System Utility

System allows you to configure system properties, including properties for managing the operating system configuration, startup, shutdown, hardware profiles, and user profiles. System is the most advanced Control Panel utility, and its options are organized into several tabs.

The General tab (as shown in the following screen) provides summary information about the system, including the operating system version, service pack level (if any), registered owner, Windows serial number, processor type, and system random access memory (RAM).

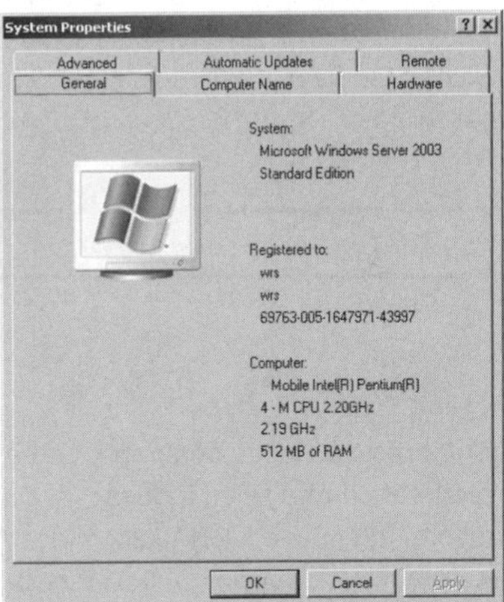

Inside Out

Determining the service pack level and hot fixes that are installed

Often, you'll want to know which service pack a server has (if any). The General tab provides one way to access this information, but a much quicker way is to type **gettype** at the command prompt. Neither technique will tell you about which hot fixes a computer has installed. To determine the hot fixes installed on a computer, use the Add or Remove Programs utility, and scroll through the list of currently installed programs under Change Or Remove Programs.

The Computer Name tab (as shown in the following screen) displays the full computer name of the system and the domain membership, if applicable. The full computer name is essentially the DNS name of the computer, which also identifies the computer's place within the Active Directory hierarchy. To change the computer name or move a computer to a new domain, use one of the following procedures:

- For member servers (not domain controllers), you can click Change to change the system name and domain associated with the computer. This displays the Computer Name Changes dialog box. If you want to change the computer's name, type a new name in the Computer Name field. If you want to change the computer's domain or workgroup membership, click Domain or Workgroup as appropriate, and then enter the new domain or workgroup name. Click OK. If you change the computer's domain, the computer will be moved to that domain and, in which case, you might be prompted to provide the appropriate credentials for joining the computer to that domain.

- For domain controllers, you can click Change to modify the name of the computer, but doing so will make the domain controller temporarily unavailable to other computers in the domain. You cannot use this feature to change the domain in which the domain controller is running. To change the domain, you must demote the domain controller using Dcpromo to make it a member server, change the computer's network ID by using the System utility, and then promote the server using Dcpromo so that it is once again a domain controller.

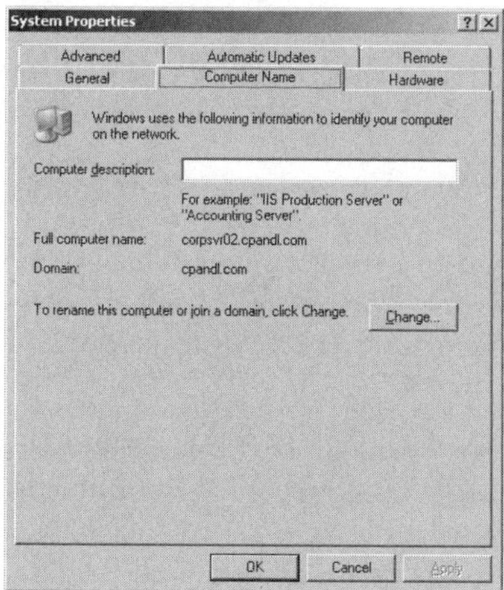

The other System utility tabs are as follows:

- **Hardware** Used to manage a server's hardware profiles and devices and to add new hardware. Hardware profiles allow a computer to have different hardware configurations for different situations, such as onsite or offsite use. You'll learn more about hardware profiles in Chapter 13.

- **Advanced** Used to control many of the key features of the Windows operating system, including application performance, user profiles, startup and recovery, environment variables, and error reporting. User profiles are discussed in Chapter 37, and application performance is discussed in Chapter 15.
- **Automatic Updates** Used to manage the Automatic Updates configuration on the server. When enabled, the Automatic Updates service compares programs, operating system components, and drivers installed on a system to a master list of items and determines whether updates should be installed.
- **Remote** Used to control Remote Assistance invitations and Remote Desktop connections. Remote Assistance invitations are primarily used with workstations and not servers. Remote Desktop is discussed in Chapter 30, "Using Remote Desktop for Administation."

Using Support Tools

If you are looking for additional tools to help you manage the network, you can install the Windows Server 2003 Support Tools. The Support Tools are a collection of graphical and command-line programs designed to help you manage the following components:

- Active Directory
- Disks, data, files, and folders
- Hardware
- Processes and services
- Performance
- Printers and fax machines
- Security

These tools are available for installation on systems running Windows Server 2003 and can be used with all versions of Windows Server 2003 and Microsoft Windows XP Professional. You install Support Tools from the Windows Server 2003 distribution CD-ROM by following these steps:

1. Insert the Windows Server 2003 distribution CD-ROM into the CD-ROM drive. When the Autorun screen appears, click Perform Additional Tasks, and then click Browse This CD to start Windows Explorer.

> **Caution** The Support Tools installation modifies the Help And Support center. You must close any instances of this console that are running before you start the installation process. Otherwise, the installation will fail.

2. In Windows Explorer, double-click Support, and then double-click Tools. Double-click Suptools.msi. This starts the Windows Support Tools Setup Wizard. Click Next.
3. Read the End-User License Agreement, and then, if you agree and want to continue, click I Agree, and then click Next. (If you do not agree, the installation will end.)
4. After you enter your user information, click Next, then select the destination directory for Support Tools. The default location is %ProgramFiles%\Support Tools. You can accept the default, type a new directory path, or click Browse to search for a location. Support Tools use about 24 megabytes (MB) of disk space.
5. To start the installation, click Install Now.

Once installation completes, you can access Support Tools through the Tools management console, as shown in Figure 12-9. To access the console, click Start, point to Programs or All Programs as appropriate, click Windows Support Tools, and then select Support Tools Help. As the figure shows, the tools are organized alphabetically by file name and by category. Clicking a tool name accesses a help page that displays the online help documentation for the tool. The tool help page also has a link for running the tool.

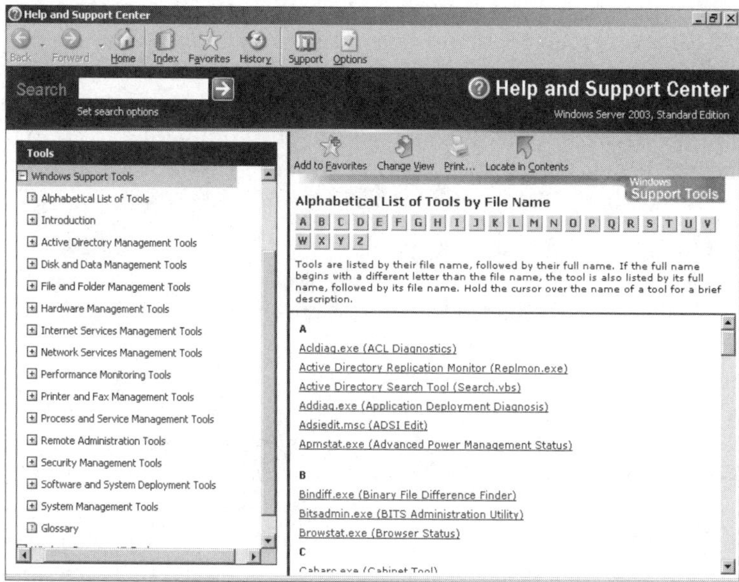

Figure 12-9. Use the Tools management console to learn about the Support Tools that are available.

Chapter 12

Inside Out

Running the Support Tools from a command prompt

Another way to run one of the support tools is to type the tool's file name at a command prompt. You will find the executables for the support tools in the installation directory, which by default is %SystemDrive%\Program Files\Support Tools. When you installed the support tools, the system path was updated to include the Support Tools installation directory. Because of this, you need not be in this directory to run the support tools and can run tools at any command prompt regardless of the current directory. As with other Windows utilities and commands, you can obtain syntax information for using most of the support tools by typing the tool's command name followed by **/?**, such as **windiff /?**.

Using Resource Kit Tools

The Windows Server 2003 Resource Kit provides an additional set of graphical and command-line programs that you can use to help you better manage the network. As with Support Tools, the Resource Kit tools are available for installation on systems running Windows Server 2003 and can be used with all versions of Windows Server 2003 as well as Windows XP Professional. To install the Resource Kit tools, you'll need the distribution CD-ROM shipped as part of the boxed Resource Kit set or Internet access so that you can obtain the free download from the Microsoft Windows Download Center. In either case, you install the Resource Kit tools as follows:

1. Start the Windows Resource Kit Setup Wizard by inserting the Windows Server 2003 Resource Kit CD-ROM into the CD-ROM drive or double-clicking the executable file you downloaded from the Microsoft Windows Download Center at *http://www.microsoft.com/downloads/*.

Caution The Resource Kit tools installation modifies the Help And Support center. You must close any instances of this console that are running before you start the installation process. Otherwise, the installation will fail.

2. Click Next. Read the End-User License Agreement, and then, if you agree and want to continue, click I Agree, and then click Next again. (If you do not agree, the installation will end.)

3 After you enter your user information, click Next, then select the destination directory for the Resource Kit tools. The default location is %ProgramFiles%\Windows Resource Kits\Tools. You can accept the default, type a new directory path, or click Browse to search for a location. The Resource Kit uses about 37 MB of disk space.

4 To start the installation, click Install Now.

Once installation completes, you access the Resource Kit tools through the Resource Kit Tools Help. Click Start, point to Programs or All Programs as appropriate, click Windows Resource Kit Tools, and then select Windows Resource Kit Tools Help. As with Support Tools, Resource Kit tools are organized alphabetically by file name and by category. Clicking a tool name accesses a help page that displays the online help documentation for the tool. The tool help page also has a link for running the tool.

> **Note** The executables for the Resource Kit tools are in the installation directory, which by default is %SystemDrive%\Program Files\Windows Resource Kits\Tools, and once again, the system path is updated to include the Resource Kit installation directory. This allows you to run the tools at any command prompt regardless of the current directory. In most cases, you can type the command name following by **/?**, such as **moveuser /?**, to display the command syntax.

Using the Secondary Logon

In UNIX, there's always been a distinction between accounts used by administrators and those used by users. You log on to UNIX systems using a user account, and if you must perform administrative tasks, you change temporarily to a secondary logon with Administrator privileges so you could perform these tasks. Switching to a secondary logon is accomplished at the command line without having to log out. Basically, you type **su –root**, enter the administrator password, and then obtain Administrator privileges as long as you use the current command line. When you are finished, you exit the secondary logon, and go back to working on everyday tasks.

Beginning with Windows 2000, Microsoft has recommended and made possible the use of a similar approach to administration, and the primary reason for this is to help maintain system and network security. Thus, instead of logging on with an account that has Administrator privileges and using it as your everyday account, it is recommended that you log on with an account that has standard user permissions and then use the secondary logon to perform administration tasks.

Inside Out

Secondary logons can help safeguard the network

Once implemented, secondary logons and the associated security precautions can help reduce the number of security incidents your organization experiences. We all know about administrators that fail to use screen savers or set their screen savers to such a long wait time that they are ineffective in protecting the system from passing users who might want to perform administration tasks. We all know how irregularly most people, including administrators, change passwords, even when password policies are enforced. But did you also know about fake logons (Trojan horses) that can be used to collect your logon information and relay it to those who want to break into your systems? Basically, if you browse the Web, a page containing the Trojan horse code could be downloaded to your computer. Once it's there, the Trojan horse could collect your logon and password and use them to wreak havoc on the computer and the network. If you are using an ordinary user account rather than an Administrator account, the intruder will have at best limited access instead of free run of the network—and it is the free run of the network offered by an Administrator account that can jeopardize the security of the entire organization.

Secondary logons are enabled by using the Secondary Logon service, which is installed and enabled by default in Windows Server 2003 (as well as in Windows 2000). When this service is running, administrators can log on to the network using an ordinary user account and then switch to the secondary logon to run programs as an administrator. Keep in mind that, by default, ordinary users cannot log on to servers, so administrators must log on locally with their Administrator accounts, which should have the Log On Locally privilege.

Note Not all tasks can be handled by using the secondary logon. Some administration tasks, such as setting system runtime parameters, require an interactive logon and do not support the secondary logon. This means that you must log on to the computer using the Administrator account to manage these tasks.

Running Programs Using the Secondary Logon

You can use one of two techniques to run programs using a different user account:

- To run administrative tools and most other programs using the secondary logon, right-click the desired program, and select Run As.
- To run Control Panel tools using the secondary logon, hold down the Shift key while right-clicking the desired tool, then select Run As.

Once the Run As utility is started, select The Following User (as shown in the following screen), and then type the user name and password for the account to use. When you click OK, Run As opens the program using the specified account credentials.

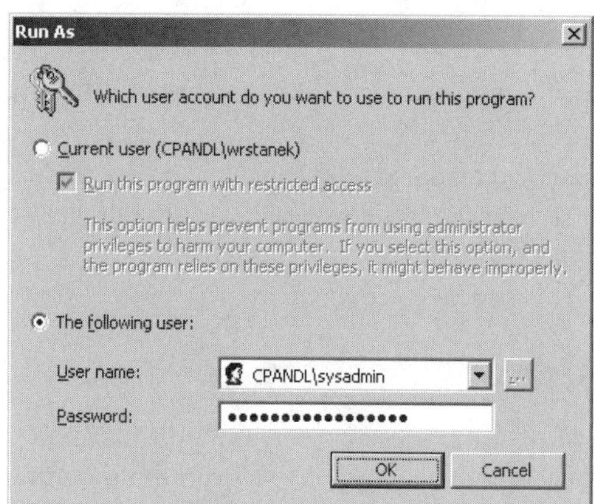

Note You can also choose to run the program with your current user account, except with restricted access. This prevents the program from using Administrator privileges.

Using the Secondary Logon at the Command Prompt

You can also use the secondary logon at the command prompt. When you do this, the basic syntax is as follows:

```
runas /user:Domain\User Program
```

where *Domain* is the optional domain name in which the user account is located, *User* is the name of the user account whose permissions you want to use, and *Program* is the program you want to run, such as

```
runas /user:CPANDL\sysadmin cmd
```

Here, you are using the RUNAS command to start the command prompt with domain Administrator privileges. If you don't specify the domain, the current domain is assumed, such as would be the case in the following example:

```
runas /user:sysadmin cmd
```

When you are working with console tools, you should start the Microsoft Management Console (MMC) using the RUNAS command. Enclose the program name and the name of the console tool to run in double quotation marks. Consider the following example:

```
runas /user:CPANDL\sysadmin "mmc %SystemRoot%\System32\compmgmt.msc"
```

Here, you are using RUNAS to start the Computer Management console as the user sysadmin.

> **Note** In all of these examples, you could also use a local logon. The syntax is `runas /user:`**`MachineName\User Program`**. This is useful if you are working with a computer in a workgroup or you want to manage only the local machine.

Running a Temporary Administrator's Desktop

The Windows desktop is launched when a user logs on, so, although you can use the secondary logon to run programs as another user, the desktop doesn't run in this context. This has subtle but far-reaching effects. For example, although you can run individual Control Panel tools as another user, the Control Panel remains in the original user context. This means when you work with Printers and Faxes and Network Connections (both of which do not support the secondary logon), you are working as the original user.

To run tasks related to Printers and Faxes, Network Connections, and other desktop features that do not support the secondary logon with different user credentials, you must create a temporary administrator's desktop. You do this by stopping the desktop shell, and then starting it again using the RUNAS command. Once you are done working with the desktop shell using this account, you stop the shell again and restart it.

To stop and restart the desktop shell, follow these steps:

1. Right-click the taskbar, and select Task Manager. Or press Ctrl+Alt+Del, and then click Task Manager.
2. Next stop the desktop shell. In the Processes tab, select Explorer.exe, and click End Process. When the warning prompt appears, click Yes. While the entire desktop exits, including the Start menu, taskbar, and system tray, any running applications and Windows Task Manager are still open.
3. In the Applications tab, click New Task, and then in the Create New Task dialog box, type **runas /user:*Domain**User* explorer.exe**, where *Domain* is the optional domain name in which the user account is located and *User* is the name of the user account whose permissions you want to use. If you don't specify the domain, the current domain is assumed. If you are logged on locally, use the command **runas /user:*MachineName**User* explorer.exe**.

4. The system then opens a command prompt. In the command prompt, enter the password for the designated user account. The desktop will restart, and the Start menu, taskbar, and system tray will return as well.
5. Don't exit the Task Manager; you'll need it again and exiting it could cause the Windows operating system to freeze. So, instead of closing Task Manager, minimize it while you use the desktop in the new context.
6. When you are ready to return to the previous desktop, use Task Manager to shut down Explorer.exe again. Afterward, click New Task in the Applications tab, and then in the Create New Task dialog box, type **explorer.exe**. This returns the desktop to normal.

Creating Run As Shortcuts for Secondary Logons

You want it to be as easy as possible to use the secondary logon. If you don't, you'll probably be tempted to use the account with Administrator privileges all the time rather than only when needed. With this in mind, one way to make it easier to work with the secondary logon is to create Run As shortcuts for commonly used tools. You can also modify the menu to use Run As shortcuts instead of running tools directly.

Creating Run As Shortcuts on the Desktop

To create Run As shortcuts on the desktop, follow these steps:

1. Right-click an open area of the desktop to display the shortcut menu.
2. On the shortcut menu, point to New, and then choose Shortcut.
3. In the Create Shortcut Wizard, shown in Figure 12-10, type the necessary RUNAS command, such as **runas /user:CPANDL\sysadmin "mmc %SystemRoot%\System32\compmgmt.msc"**, and then click Next.

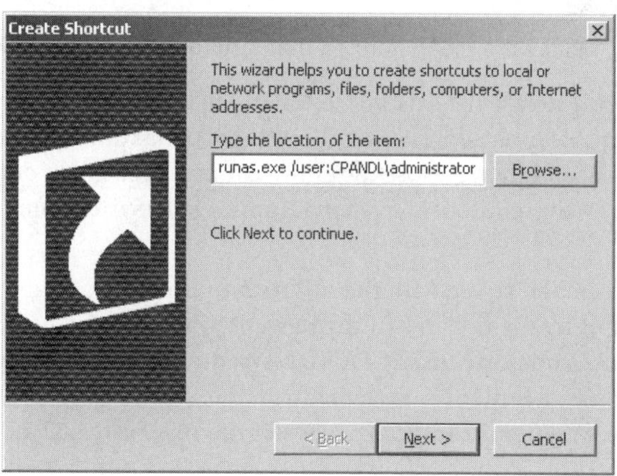

Figure 12-10. Type the RUNAS command to use, and then click Next.

4 Type a name for the shortcut, such as **Computer Management**. Click Finish.

Now whenever you use the shortcut, Run As will start automatically using the specified user account and all you need to provide is a password.

Creating Run As Menu Options

To create menu options that use RUNAS, follow these steps:

1 Navigate the Start menu until you find the menu item you want to modify, right-click it, and choose Create Shortcut. Then right-click the newly created menu item shortcut, and select Properties; it should have the same name as the original menu item with a 2 in parentheses. This displays a Properties dialog box similar to the one shown in Figure 12-11.

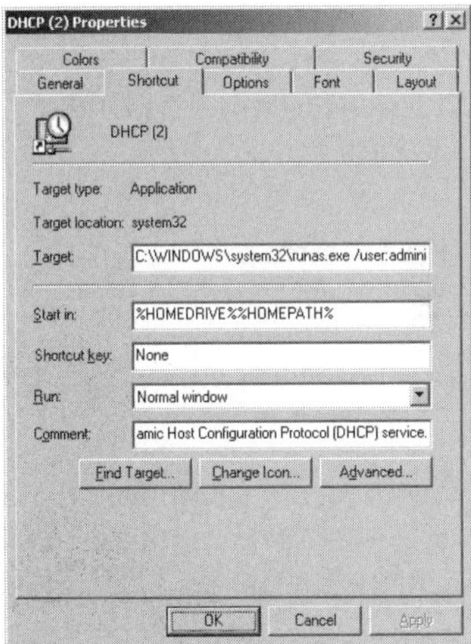

Figure 12-11. Modify the menu item so that it automatically starts Run As.

2 In the Target box, enclose the existing command in double quotations. If you are modifying a console tool, add **%SystemRoot%\System32\mmc.exe** to the beginning of the Target box, and then enclose the entire command string in double quotation marks, such as **"%SystemRoot%\System32\mmc.exe %SystemRoot%\System32\compmgmt.msc"**.

3 Precede the command string with the full path to Runas.exe, and use the User parameter to specify the user account you want to log on as, such as **%SystemRoot%\System32\runas.exe /user:CPANDL\sysadmin**. The result should be something like **%SystemRoot%\System32\runas.exe /user:CPANDL\sysadmin "%SystemRoot%\System32\mmc.exe %SystemRoot%\System32\compmgmt.msc"**.

Note Using full file paths ensures menu items are opened and displayed as quickly as possible. Neglecting or removing the file paths slows the open and display process considerably.

4. Click OK to save your changes.

Now whenever you use the menu item, Run As will start automatically using the specified user, and all you must provide is a password. Rather than having to enter a password each time, you can also add the /Savecred parameter. This parameter saves the credentials in the user profile using encryption. However, if you decide to use the /Savecred parameter, you should ensure that you don't leave yourself logged in when you step away from your computer or that your computer quickly turns on the password-protected screen saver. Otherwise, anyone could access your computer and run administration tools using your logon.

Chapter 13

Managing and Troubleshooting Hardware

Unless you've standardized on a particular hardware platform, most servers that you'll work with will have different hardware components. This means different servers will probably have different motherboards, disk controllers, graphics cards, and network adapters. Fortunately, Microsoft Windows Server 2003 is designed to work with an extensive list of hardware devices. When you install new hardware, Windows tries to detect the device automatically and then install the correct driver software so that you can use the device. If Windows has a problem with a device, you must troubleshoot the installation, which usually means finding the correct device drivers for the hardware component and installing them.

One thing to keep in mind when working with devices is that, like other software, driver software can contain bugs. These bugs can cause a variety of problems on your servers, and not only could the hardware stop working, but the server could freeze as well. Because of this, you'll want to monitor routinely for hardware problems and take corrective actions as necessary. It is also helpful to maintain a hardware inventory for servers so that you know which devices are installed and who the manufacturers are.

Working with Device Drivers

Every hardware component installed on a system has an associated device driver. Drivers are used to handle the low-level communications tasks between the operating system and hardware components. When you install a hardware component through the operating system, you tell the operating system about the device driver it uses. From then on, the device driver loads automatically and runs as part of the operating system.

Using Windows Device Drivers

Windows Server 2003 includes an extensive library of device drivers for display adapters, disk drives, drive controllers, keyboards, mice and other pointing devices, network adapters, and more. These drivers are maintained in a compressed file called Driver.cab. For i386 systems, this file is located in the %SystemRoot%\Driver Cache\I386 folder. For Intel Architecture 64 (IA-64) systems, this file is located in the %SystemRoot%\Driver Cache\IA64 folder.

All the drivers in the Driver.cab file are certified to be fully compatible with Windows Server 2003 and are digitally signed by Microsoft to assure you of their authenticity. When you install a new Plug and Play–compatible device, Windows checks this file for a compatible device driver. If one is found, the operating system automatically installs the device. Through Windows Update, Microsoft makes updates to the Driver.cab device drivers available for download and installation.

Inside Out

Installing new drivers

All device drivers provided through Windows Update have been thoroughly tested in the Windows Hardware Quality Labs (WHQL), and you should be able to count on them not to cause your system to crash or become unstable. However, just because driver updates are available doesn't mean you should install them. In a production environment, you'll rarely want to download and install new device drivers without thoroughly testing them yourself first. Better safe than sorry—always. Typically, you install new device drivers because you are experiencing problems with the old drivers. If you aren't experiencing problems, you might not want to update the drivers.

Every hardware driver has an associated Setup Information file. This file ends with the .inf extension and is a text file containing detailed information about the device being installed. The .inf file includes the names of driver files, the location where they are to be installed, version information, Registry settings, and other important configuration information. All devices with drivers included in the Driver.cab file have corresponding .inf files. These files are stored in the %SystemRoot%\Inf folder. When you install a new device driver, the driver is written to %SystemRoot%\System32\Drivers and configuration settings are stored in the Registry. The driver's .inf file is used to control the installation and write the Registry settings. If the driver doesn't already exist in the Driver.cab file (and thus does not already have an .inf file on the system), a copy of the driver's .inf file is written to the %SystemRoot%\Inf folder.

Using Signed Device Drivers

Speaking of new device drivers, Microsoft recommends that you use signed device drivers whenever possible. Signed device drivers have a digital signature that authenticates them as having passed extensive testing by the WHQL. The digital signature means that you can count on the device driver not to cause your system to crash or become unstable, and also that the device driver hasn't been tampered with by other installation programs or by a virus program.

The assurances you get with digitally signed drivers aren't applicable to unsigned device drivers. When you install an unsigned driver, there is no guarantee that it has been tested, and if the driver is poorly written, it is much more likely to cause the operating system to freeze or the server to crash than any other program you've installed. That said, there are times when you might have to use an unsigned device driver. In some situations, you might find that a particular device doesn't have a signed device driver. Here, you should check the manufacturer's Web site to see whether a signed driver is available because sometimes there is a signed driver, but it's just not distributed with the device or on the Windows Server 2003 distribution disks. If a signed driver isn't available, you might find that you have to use an unsigned driver. Keep in mind that Group Policy might prevent you from installing an unsigned driver. See the sidebar "Managing Device Driver Settings Through Group Policy" later in this chapter for details.

> **Note** If you have to install an unsigned driver, proceed cautiously and remember to monitor the system closely. If you find that the system is inexplicably freezing or crashing, the unsigned driver is probably to blame and should be rolled back or uninstalled. Remember, any type of faulty driver can cause the system to fail, even a driver for a display adapter, a network adapter, or a sound card.

Understanding and Changing Driver Installation Settings

By default, Windows Server 2003 warns you when you try to install an unsigned device driver. If you don't want to see this prompt, you can change the driver-signing options to eliminate this warning, and you can also prevent any users from trying to install unsigned drivers.

You can change driver settings by following these steps:

1. Start the System utility. In the Hardware tab, click Driver Signing.
2. In the Driver Signing Options dialog box, choose the action you want the Windows operating system to take whenever someone tries to install an unsigned device driver. The options are as follows:
   - *Ignore*—This option allows the user to install any unsigned driver without having to see and respond to a warning prompt.

- *Warn*—This option prompts the user each time either to continue with the installation of an unsigned driver or to stop the installation.
- *Block*—This options prevents the user from installing unsigned driver software. Windows Server 2003 will not install any unsigned device driver and will not display a warning prompt.

3. To apply these options to only the current user, clear the Make This Action The System Default option. Otherwise, select this option to make this the default for all users.
4. Click OK twice to apply the changes. Note that changes to driver installation made this way can be overridden by Group Policy settings at the site, domain, or organizational unit (OU) level.

Regardless of the settings you choose, Windows Server 2003 will not install drivers with known problems. If you try to install a driver with known issues that could potentially harm the server, the Windows Driver Protection facility will block the installation. A warning is displayed that states the driver is known to cause stability problems and that the Windows operating system will disable it to prevent this from happening. To complete the installation of the device, you must obtain an updated driver.

Inside Out

Managing device driver settings through Group Policy

You can manage device driver settings for computers throughout the organization by using Group Policy. When you do this, Group Policy specifies the least secure setting that is allowed. The exception is when Group Policy is set to Block. When you use this setting, unsigned device drivers can't be installed without overriding Group Policy. The Code Signing For Device Drivers policy controls device driver–signing settings on a per-user basis. This policy is located in User Configuration\Administrative Templates\System. Once you enable this policy, you can specify the action to take: Ignore, Warn, or Block. Once enabled, the system doesn't implement any setting less secure than the established setting.

If you're trying to install a device and find that you can't install an unsigned driver, you should first check the System utility settings for driver signing. If you find that the settings are set to Block and you can't change the setting, the Code Signing For Device Drivers policy has been enabled and set to Block in Group Policy. You must override Group Policy to install the unsigned device driver.

Setting Up New Hardware Devices

After you install or connect a new hardware device, you must set up the device so that it is available for use. Unlike Microsoft Windows NT, Windows Server 2003 is much better at helping you perform the related procedures, and in many cases, it will set up new devices automatically using Plug and Play.

When Plug and Play works properly, it is a wonderful thing. You simply plug in a new device, wait for the Windows operating system to detect and then configure it. The device is then ready for use. Unfortunately, although Plug and Play technology has advanced tremendously since Windows NT (and even since Microsoft Windows 2000), it doesn't always work. Sometimes, Windows will detect a new device but won't know which device driver to use. Other times, the operating system will not detect a new device at all. Usually, this happens because the device doesn't support Plug and Play.

Note You must be logged on as an administrator to install device drivers. If you're logged on using an account without Administrator privileges, you are prompted to provide a user name and password for an account that has Administrator privileges before you are allowed to install device drivers. You do not, however, need to be logged on as an administrator to install devices. As long as Windows can detect and set up the device automatically, it will do so. It is only when a new driver (meaning one that is not already on the computer) must be installed or problems occur that you must be logged on as an administrator.

Managing Plug and Play Detection and Installation

Windows Server 2003 Plug and Play is optimized to support universal serial bus (USB), FireWire (IEEE 1394), Personal Computer Memory Card International Association (PCMCIA, or PC Card), and Peripheral Component Interconnect (PCI) devices. When you connect a Plug and Play device for the first time, Windows Server 2003 reads the Plug and Play identification tag contained in the device's BIOS or firmware and then searches its master list of identification tags (which is created from the Setup Information files in the Inf folder). If the operating system finds a signed driver with a matching identification tag, it installs the driver and makes the device available for use automatically.

Unlike previous versions of Windows, which display the progress of the Plug and Play process in dialog boxes, Windows Server 2003 provides popup balloon tips in the notification area that tell you about major steps in the process only, such as device detection and finalization. For example, when installing a new disk drive, Windows Server 2003 might display Found New Hardware: Disk Drive, as shown in the screen on the following page.

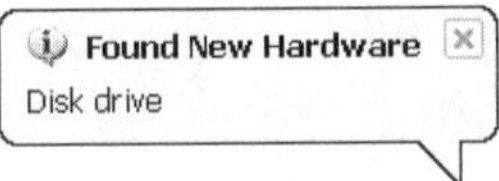

Then a balloon message is displayed to tell you that your new hardware is installed and ready to use, as shown in the following screen:

In this example, Plug and Play worked as expected. Windows Server 2003 detected the device, used the Plug and Play identification to determine which driver should be installed, and then set up the device. Because there are so many factors involved, detection and setup don't always work so smoothly, however. Sometimes the Windows operating system will warn you about something that you might need to take action to correct.

One of the more common warnings you'll see is related to Hi-Speed USB devices being connected to non-Hi-Speed USB ports, as shown in the following screen. This is important because if you are connecting an external hard disk drive or other Hi-Speed USB device, the device won't operate at the rated speed. It will in fact operate at a much slower speed.

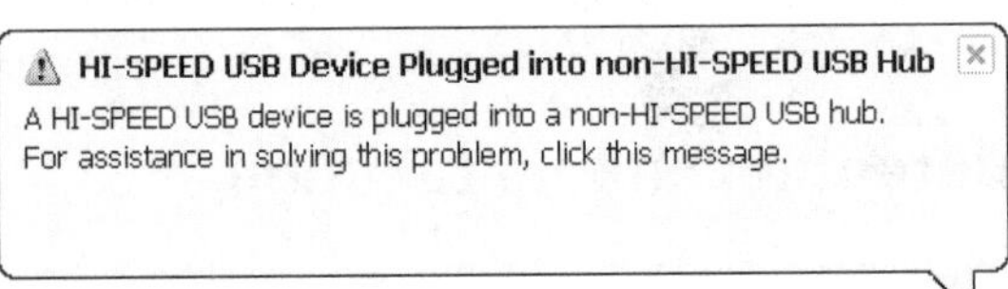

Note USB 1 is the original USB specification. USB 2 is the newer USB specification, and it is referred to as Hi-Speed USB. Although you can connect USB 2 devices to USB 1 ports, the devices operate at the USB 1 speed (which is many times slower than USB 2). If you want to achieve high-speed USB transfers, you must connect to a USB 2 port, if available. You might also want to consider upgrading the USB ports on the computer so that they are USB 2–compliant.

If Windows Server 2003 detects a Plug and Play device after you've connected it but cannot locate a suitable driver, it displays a warning that a problem occurred during installation, as shown in the following screen:

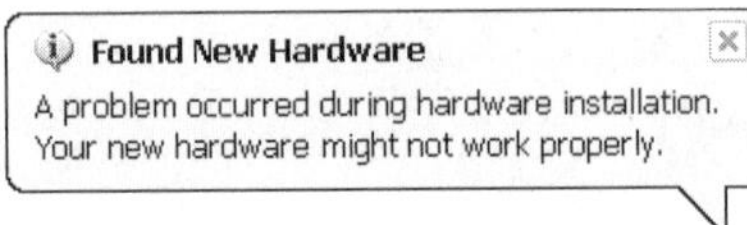

Sometimes when this happens, you must install the hardware device manually using the Add Hardware Wizard just as you do with non–Plug and Play devices. See the section entitled "Installing Non–Plug and Play Devices" later in this chapter for details.

More typically, Windows Server 2003 starts the Found New Hardware Wizard, shown in the following screen, which is designed to help you find a suitable driver for the device that was detected.

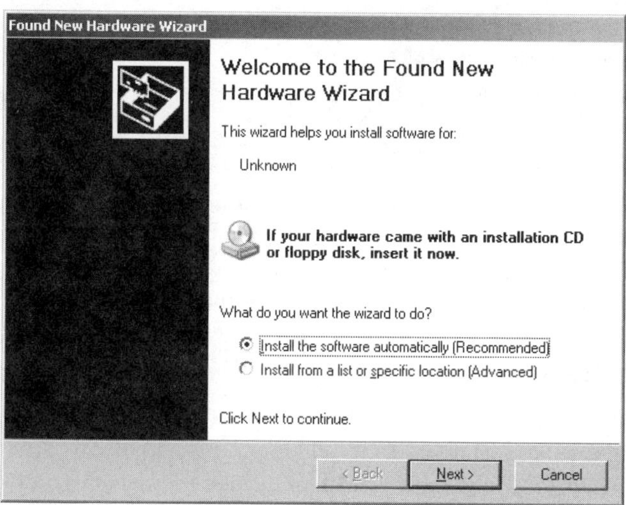

If this wizard starts, you have the following two options:

- **Install The Software Automatically** Choose this option if the device came with an installation CD or floppy disk that contains Windows Server 2003–compatible drivers.
- **Install From A List Or Specific Location** Choose this option if you've downloaded a compatible driver or want to choose a specific driver, bypassing Windows default selection.

Installing the Software Automatically

If Windows Server 2003 detects the Plug and Play device and the Found New Hardware Wizard starts automatically, you can choose the Install The Software Automatically option, which is the recommended and default option. Click Next to access the search and installation options page. By default, Windows Server 2003 searches all removable drives and looks for appropriate Setup Information files. If the wizard finds a specific driver that is compatible, it installs it. If the wizard finds multiple drivers that might be compatible, it displays a list of matching drivers and allows you to choose the driver to use.

In some cases, the wizard is unable to find a suitable device driver. If this happens, the wizard prompts, asking if it is okay to connect to the Internet, as shown in the screen on the following page.

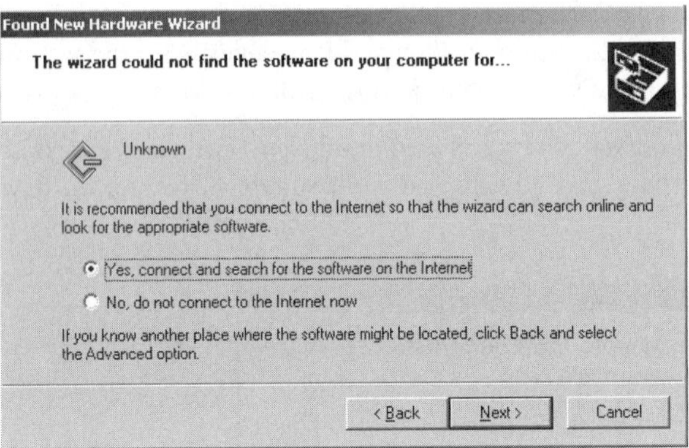

Click Yes to allow the wizard to use Windows Update to connect to the Internet and search for the device driver at the Windows Update site. If the computer doesn't have an Internet connection or you know another location where the software might be located, click Back, and then choose the Install From A List Or Specific Location option.

Installing a Downloaded Driver

If Windows Server 2003 detects the Plug and Play device and the Found New Hardware Wizard starts automatically, you can choose the Install From A List Or Specific Location option so that you can install a driver you've downloaded for the device. Select this option, and then click Next to display the search and installation options page. By default, the Search For The Best Driver In These Locations and Search Removable Media options are selected (as shown in the following screen), and Windows Server 2003 will search all removable drives if you click Next. Because you've downloaded a driver, you should select the Include This Location In The Search option instead and then enter the full file path to the folder that contains the driver you downloaded. You can click Browse to find the location as well.

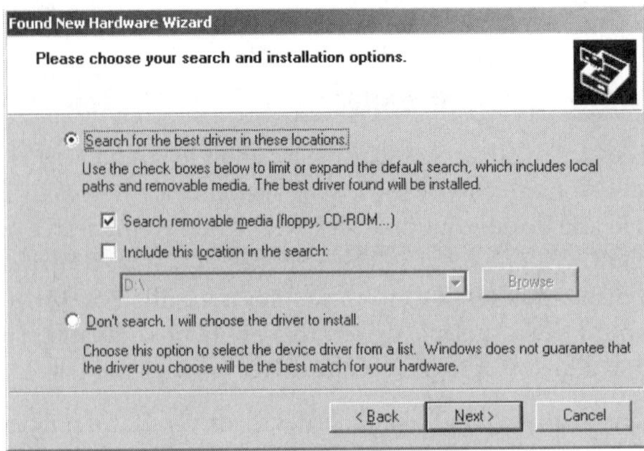

When you are ready to continue, click Next so the Windows operating system can search the specified locations for the driver. If the wizard finds a specific driver that is compatible, it installs it. If the wizard finds multiple drivers that might be compatible, it displays a list of matching drivers and allows you to choose the driver to use. As before, if no driver is found, the wizard will try to use Windows Update and find the driver on the Windows Update site.

Choosing a Specific Driver or Bypassing the Default Driver

Bypassing the default driver makes it possible to install an unsigned driver from a manufacturer rather than a signed driver included with Windows Server 2003. If you want to do this, choose the Install From A List Or Specific Location option when the Found New Hardware Wizard starts, and then click Next to display the search and installation options page. On this page, select Don't Search, I Will Choose The Driver To Install. After a short delay, the wizard shows a list of compatible drivers by model type, as shown in the following screen. If applicable, clear the Show Compatible Hardware option to display all of the drivers that are available by device type. Choose a device, and then click Next to complete the installation.

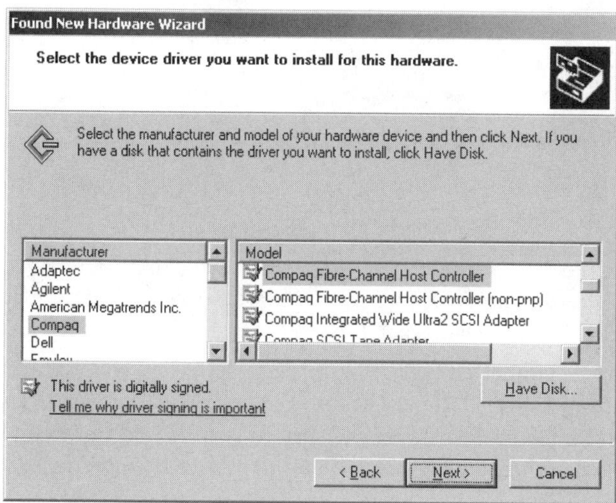

Installing Non–Plug and Play Devices

Although Windows Server 2003 doesn't detect or set up non–Plug and Play devices automatically, it does maintain a driver cache for these devices. This driver cache has hundreds of drivers, any one of which you might be able to use. You might also be able to use a Windows

2000 driver if a Windows Server 2003 device driver isn't available. In either case, you install the device using the Add Hardware Wizard. Follow these steps:

1. If the device has a CD or a downloadable Setup program, run it to copy the driver files to your hard disk.
2. Connect the device to the computer. For internal devices, such as an Industry Standard Architecture (ISA) card, you must shut down the computer, add the device, and then restart the computer.
3. Access Control Panel, and then double-click Add Hardware to start the Add Hardware Wizard.
4. Click Next to skip the Welcome page and begin searching for the device. If the wizard finds the device, you can select it to install the correct device driver and complete the setup. In most cases, however, the wizard won't find the device and will instead ask you whether the hardware is connected, as shown in the following screen:

   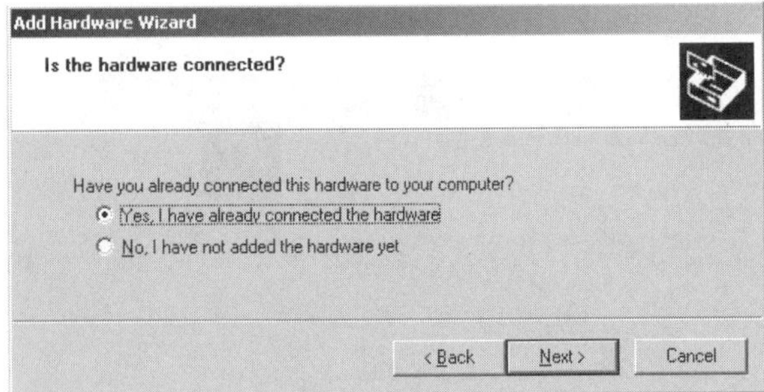

   - If you've already connected the new hardware, select Yes, I Have Already Connected The Hardware, and click Next to continue. Go on to Step 5.
   - If you haven't connected the hardware, click No, I Have Not Added The Hardware Yet, and then click Next. The only option you have now is to click Finish. You must connect the hardware and then restart the Add Hardware Wizard. Skip the remaining steps.
5. The next wizard page shows a list of all installed hardware, as shown in the screen on the following page. The device you are trying to install shouldn't already be on the list (if it is, it is already installed and you must troubleshoot the installation). To add the new hardware device, scroll to the bottom of the list and select Add A New Hardware Device. Click Next to continue.

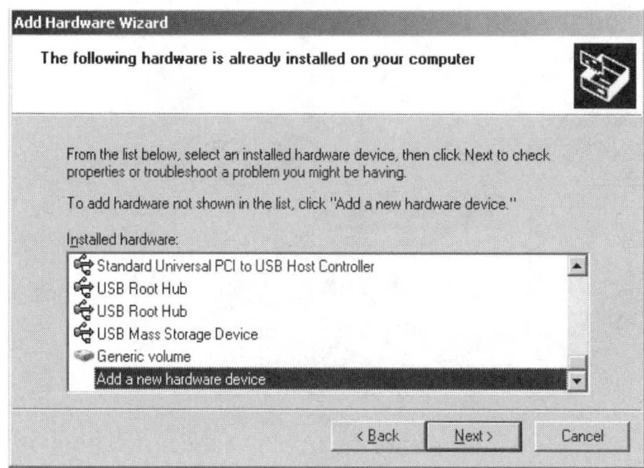

Tip **Troubleshoot device installation**
If the device you're trying to install is already listed, check the icon to determine what needs to be done to troubleshoot the installation. If the icon has a yellow warning mark with an exclamation point, the device has a configuration problem. If the icon has a red warning mark with an *x*, the device has been disabled or is improperly installed.

6 Determine whether the wizard should search for new hardware or whether you want to select the hardware from a list, as follows:

- If you choose Search For And Install, the wizard searches for and tries to detect any devices on its list of non–Plug and Play devices. The process takes a few minutes to go through all the device types and options. When the search is completed, any new devices found are displayed, and you can select a device to complete the installation. If the wizard doesn't find the device, you'll be prompted to click Next and search manually; if this happens, proceed by following the next bullet item.
- If you choose Install The Hardware That I Manually Select, or if no new devices are found in the automatic search, you'll have to select the hardware type yourself. Select the type of hardware, such as Small Computer Systems Interface (SCSI) and redundant arrays of independent disks (RAID) controllers, and then click Next. Afterward, scroll through the list of manufacturers to find the device's manufacturer, and then choose the appropriate device in the Model pane, as shown in the screen on the following page. Follow the remaining prompts to complete the wizard.

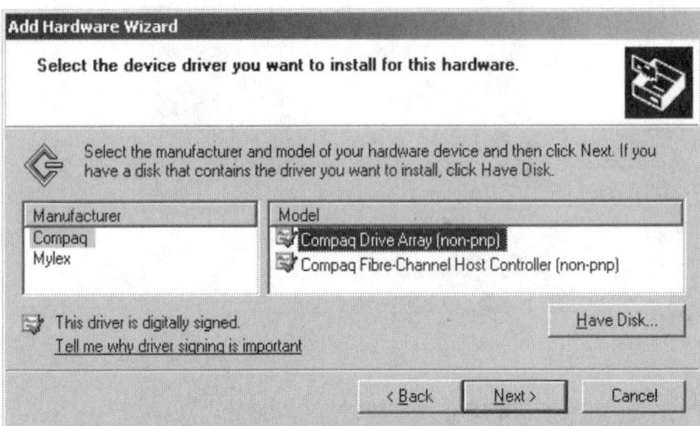

7 On the final page, the wizard shows the results of the installation. If you have problems, use the troubleshooting links.

Obtaining Hardware Device Information

When you are working with hardware devices, often you'll want to obtain information about the currently installed devices and their configuration. You can view and work with installed hardware devices using Device Manager (Devmgmt.msc). This console tool is included with Computer Management.

Viewing Device and Driver Details

In the Computer Management console, click the plus sign (+) next to the System Tools node, and then select Device Manager. You should now see a complete list of devices installed on the system. By default, this list is organized by device type, as shown in Figure 13-1, and you can click the plus sign (+) next to a device type to see a list of the specific instances of that device type.

The device list shows warning symbols if there are problems with a device. A yellow warning symbol with an exclamation point indicates a problem with a device. A red warning symbol with an *x* indicates a device that's improperly installed or that has been disabled by the user or administrator for some reason. In Figure 13-1, there is a problem with a PCI modem and a RAID controller.

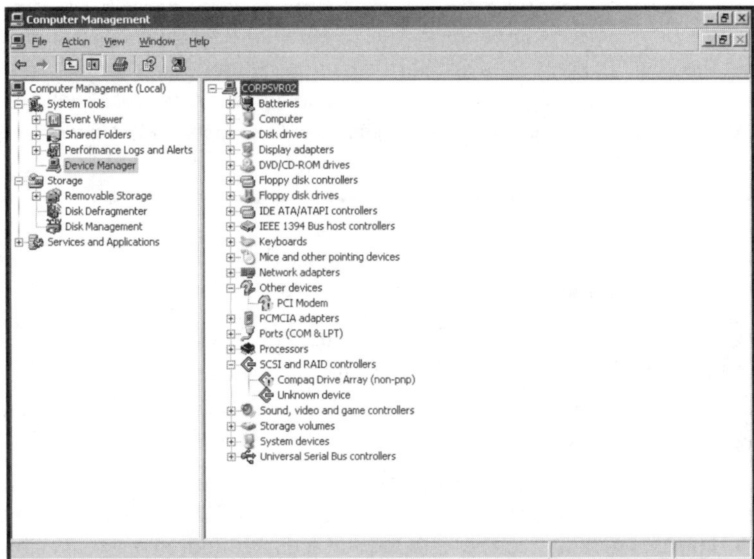

Figure 13-1. Use Device Manager to view information about installed hardware devices.

Inside Out

View and save device settings for local and remote computers

As discussed in the previous chapter, you can use Computer Management to view and work with settings on remote computers. Right-click the Computer Management entry in the console tree, and then select Connect To Another Computer on the shortcut menu. In the Select Computer dialog box, choose Another Computer, and then type the fully qualified name of the computer you want to work with, such as **entdc01.microsoft.com**, where entdc01 is the computer name and microsoft.com is the domain name. If you don't know the computer name, click Browse to search for the computer you want to work with.

If you want detailed driver lists for multiple computers, you can do this using the Driverquery command-line utility. Use the /V parameter to get verbose output and the /SI parameter to display properties of signed drivers, such as **driverquery /v /si**. If you want to write the information to a file, use the output redirection symbol (>) followed by the name of the file, such as **driverquery /v /si > system-devices.txt**.

> To list devices on remote computers, use the /S parameter followed by a computer name or Internet Protocol (IP) address to specify a remote computer to query. You can also specify the Run As permissions by using /U followed by the user name and /P followed by the user's password. Here's an example: **driverquery /v /s corpserver01 /u wrstanek /p 49iners**.

You can use the options on the View menu to change the defaults for which types of devices are displayed and how the devices are listed, as follows:

- Devices By Type is the default view, and it displays devices by the type of device installed, such as Disk Drive or Printer.
- Devices By Connection displays devices by connection type, such as System Board or Logical Disk Manager.
- Resources By Type displays the status of allocated resources by type of device using the resource. Resource types are direct memory access (DMA) channels, input/output (I/O) ports, interrupt requests (IRQs), and memory addresses.
- Resources By Connection displays the status of all allocated resources by connection type rather than device type.
- Show Hidden Devices displays non–Plug and Play devices as well as devices that have been physically removed from the computer but that haven't had their drivers uninstalled.

To view detailed information about a device, double-click its entry in Device Manager. This opens the device Properties dialog box, as shown in Figure 13-2. Most devices have two tabs, either General and Properties or General and Driver.

The most important information in the General tab is the device status. If the device is working properly, this is specifically stated. Otherwise, the error status of the device is shown, and you can click Troubleshoot to start the device troubleshooter. If the device is disabled, you have an option to enable the device instead (as shown in Figure 13-3).

The Device Usage list controls a device's status as enabled or disabled. You can temporarily disable a device by selecting Do Not Use This Device (Disable). If you later want to enable the device, you can click the Enable Device button or select the Use This Device (Enable) option on the Device Usage list.

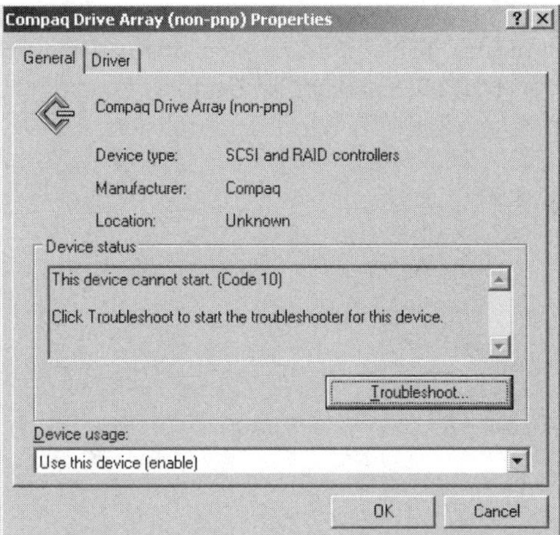

Figure 13-2. Use the device Properties dialog box to obtain essential information about a device, including whether it is functioning properly.

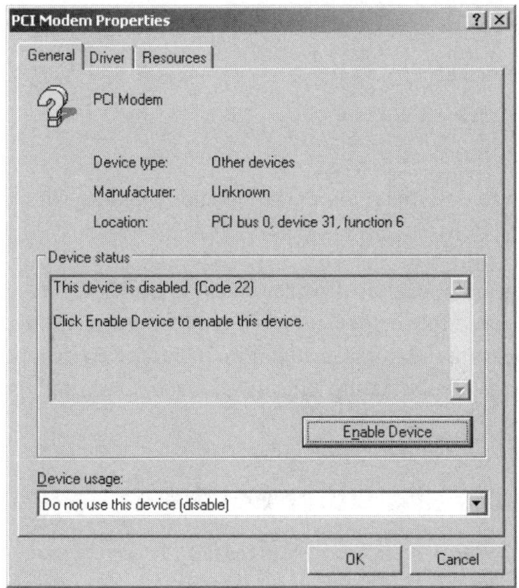

Figure 13-3. Disabled devices are listed with an error status because they aren't functioning; you can enable them by clicking Enable Device.

The Driver tab, shown in Figure 13-4, provides basic information about the driver provider, creation date, version, and digital signature. You should be wary of any drivers that list the provider as Unknown as well as drivers that are listed as Not Digitally Signed. Drivers signed by Microsoft are listed as being signed by Microsoft Windows Publisher.

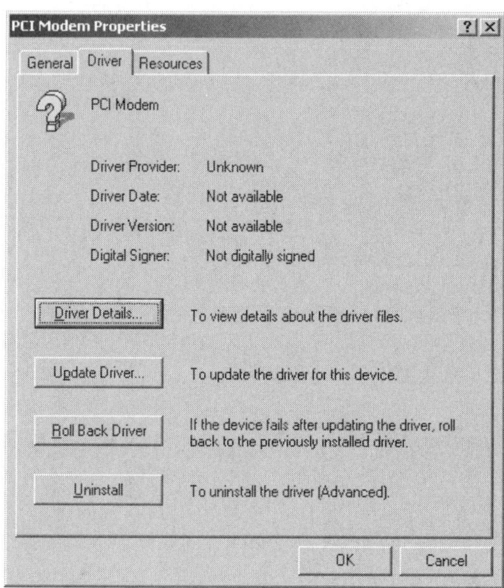

Figure 13-4. Use the Driver tab to determine the driver provider, creation date, version, and digital signature.

You can view additional information about the driver by clicking Driver Details. If no driver files are required or have been loaded for the device, you'll see a message stating this. Otherwise, you'll see the names and locations of all associated files, including an icon that indicates the signing status of each individual file. Selecting a file in this list displays details for that file in the lower section of the dialog box.

Viewing Advanced, Resources, and Other Settings

Devices often have other tabs, such as Advanced, Resources, and Power Management. Most network adapters have an Advanced tab. As shown in Figure 13-5, these options can control transmission options. You should change these options only if you are trying to resolve specific performance or connectivity issues as directed by the device manufacturer or a Microsoft Knowledge Base article. The setting that causes the most problems is Link Speed &

Duplex. Most of the time, you'll want this set to Auto Detect. Sometimes, however, to correct a specific problem, you must use a preset speed and duplex setting, such as 100Mbps/Half Duplex or 10Mbps/Full Duplex. You should do this, however, only when this setting is recommended based on your network configuration or the issue you are trying to troubleshoot.

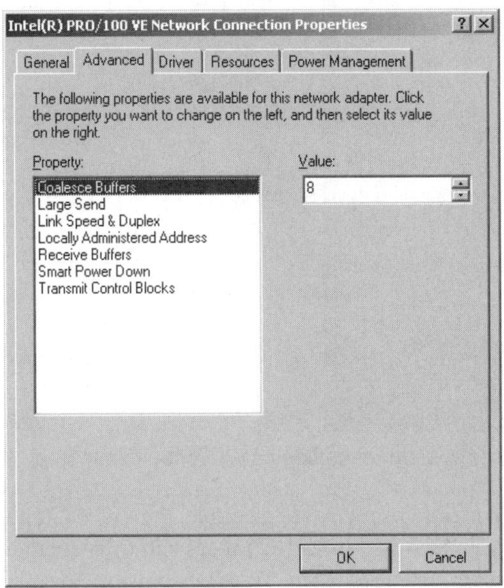

Figure 13-5. You'll find that most network adapters have an Advanced tab for setting transmission options.

Any device that uses system resources will have a Resources tab like the one shown in Figure 13-6.

The Resources tab options show the device resources that are currently assigned and their settings. There are four types of device resources:

- **DMA** The DMA channel used by the device. Values are shown as integers, such as 02.
- **Memory Range** The range of memory addresses used by the device. Values are shown in hexadecimal format, such as E8206000–E8206FFF.
- **I/O Range** The range of I/O ports used by the device. Values are shown in hexadecimal format, such as 5400–543F.
- **IRQ Line** IRQ line used by the device. Values are shown as integers, such as 10.

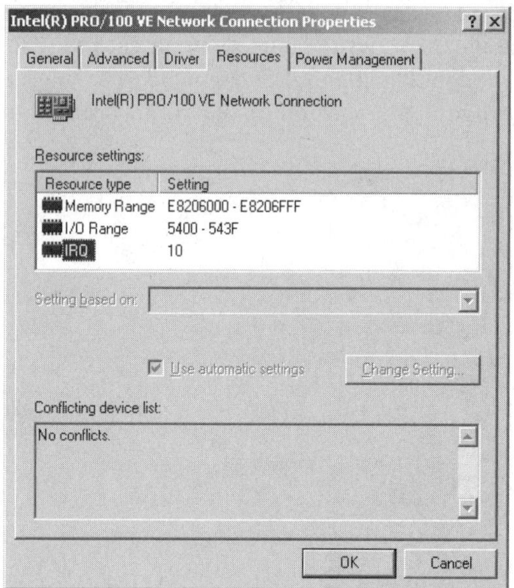

Figure 13-6. Any device that uses system resources has a Resources tab.

Devices can use multiple I/O and memory ranges. For example, the Video Graphics Adapter (VGA) adapter on one of our computers used three I/O ranges and three memory ranges. Additionally, multiple PCI devices can share the same IRQs when using Advanced Configuration and Power Interface (ACPI) BIOS. This is because ACPI BIOS allows IRQ sharing. To learn more about resource sharing and configuration options, see the section entitled "Resolving Resource Conflicts" later in this chapter.

Managing Installed Drivers

Windows Server 2003 provides three key options for managing device drivers:

- **Update Driver** As new drivers become available, you might want to update the device driver by replacing the old driver with the new driver. Primarily, you do this when you are having a hardware problem that you suspect is caused by the device driver. You may also want to update a device driver to improve performance, gain features, and so forth.
- **Roll Back Driver** If you find that a driver you've updated isn't working as expected, you can attempt to uninstall the old driver and roll back your system configuration to the previously installed driver. You can roll back only if you've updated a driver. If you haven't, clicking the rollback option displays a prompt that allows you to run a troubleshooter.

- **Uninstall** If a device does not work properly, you can uninstall it. Uninstalling a device completely removes its driver files and related Registry settings.

Updating a Device Driver

Device drivers are essential to the proper operation of Windows Server 2003. A faulty device driver can cause many problems on your systems—everything from unexpected restarts to application hangs to blue screens. To make it easier to detect and diagnose problems, you should maintain an inventory of all installed device drivers on systems you manage. Previously, we talked about using the DRIVERQUERY command to obtain a list of drivers for computers throughout the network. Ideally, the driver information should be stored on a centralized network share rather than on individual computers or could be printed out and placed in a binder where it is easily accessible. You should then periodically check manufacturer Web sites for known problems with related device drivers and for updated drivers. Windows Update can also help you because driver updates are made available through this service and can be installed automatically.

Although you can be fairly certain drivers obtained through Windows Update are newer than installed versions, this isn't the case for drivers you download yourself, and you should always double-check the driver version information before installation. As discussed previously, the current driver version is displayed in the driver's Properties dialog box, as shown in the following screen. Double-click the device in Device Manager to display the driver's Properties dialog box, then select the Driver tab. Be sure to check the driver date as well as the driver version.

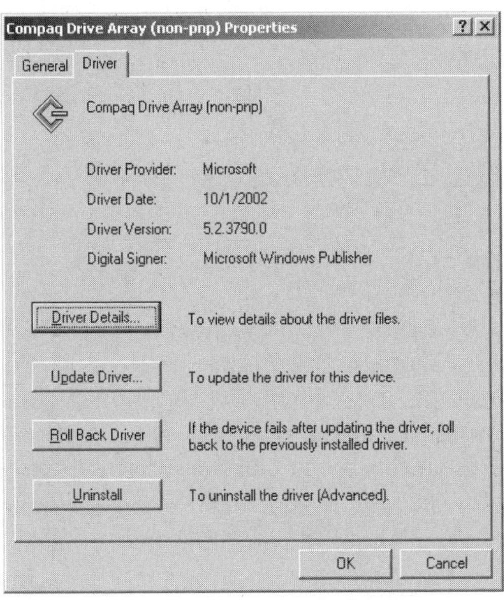

Next, check the driver version information for the driver you downloaded. To do this, unzip the downloaded driver files to a folder. In the folder, you should find .dll or .sys files. Right-click one of these files, and choose Properties. Then in the Properties dialog box, choose the Version tab to find the version information.

To continue with the installation of downloaded drivers, check to see whether the driver download includes a Setup program. If it does, run this program so that the proper files are copied to your system. Once you do this, you can use the Hardware Update Wizard to install the driver. This wizard is started by accessing the driver's Properties dialog box through Device Manager and then clicking the Update Driver button in the Driver tab. As you'll see, the Hardware Update Wizard is essentially the same as the Add Hardware Wizard (see the following screen). Because of this, you follow the same procedures as discussed in the section entitled "Setting Up New Hardware Devices" earlier in this chapter. Keep in mind that in some cases you must reboot the system to activate the updated device driver.

Rolling Back a Driver

Occasionally, you'll find that an updated driver doesn't work as expected. It could cause problems, such as device failure or system instability. In most cases, this should occur only when you've installed unsigned device drivers as a last resort or beta versions of new drivers that might have improved performance or some other benefit that outweighs their potential to crash the system. However, it can sometimes occur with signed device drivers—even those published through Windows Update.

If you suspect that an updated driver is causing the system or device problems you are experiencing, you can attempt to recover the system to the previously installed device driver. Double-click the device in Device Manager to display the driver's Properties dialog box. Then in the Driver tab, click Rollback Driver.

> **Note** You can roll back only if you've updated the driver. If you haven't, a backup driver file won't be available. Instead of being able to roll back the driver, you'll see a prompt telling you that no driver files have been backed up for this device. If you're having problems with the device, start the troubleshooter by clicking Yes.

Uninstalling and Reinstalling a Device Driver

Windows device drivers for Plug and Play devices are loaded and unloaded dynamically. You can remove the driver for a device only when the device is plugged in. This means the proper way to remove a device from a system is first to uninstall its related device driver and then to remove the device from the system.

One reason for uninstalling a device is to remove a device that is no longer used or needed. Start by uninstalling the related device driver. Double-click the device in Device Manager to display the driver's Properties dialog box. Then in the Driver tab, click Uninstall. When prompted, click OK to confirm that you want to remove the driver. Windows Server 2003 will then remove the related files and Registry settings.

At this point, you can shut down the system and remove the related hardware component if you want to. However, you might first want to check to see how the computer operates without the device in case some unforeseen problem or error occurs. So, rather than removing the device, you'll want to disable it. Disabling the device prevents Windows from reinstalling the device automatically the next time you restart the system. You disable a device by right-clicking it in Device Manager and then selecting Disable.

Sometimes when you are troubleshooting and trying to get a device to work properly, you might want to uninstall to unplug the device temporarily. Here, you could disable the device and then monitor the system to see whether problems previously experienced reoccur, or you could reinstall the device to see whether normal operations are restored. Uninstalling and then reinstalling the device forces Windows to go back to the device's original device and Registry settings, which can sometimes recover the device.

After you've uninstalled a device driver, one way to get Windows Server 2003 to reinstall the device is to reboot the computer. You can also try to rescan for devices using Device Manager by choosing Scan For Hardware Changes on the Action menu. Either way, the operating system should detect the uninstalled device as new hardware and then automatically reinstall the necessary device driver. If this doesn't happen, you must reinstall the device manually using the Add Hardware Wizard as discussed earlier in this chapter.

Managing Devices through Hardware Profiles

Developers, engineers, and information technology (IT) testers often need a way to implement or test different device configurations. You can, of course, do this by enabling and disabling devices, but this can be tedious and time-consuming. A more practical way to implement multiple device configurations is to use hardware profiles.

By using hardware profiles, you can create different device configurations and load them quickly by selecting the appropriate profile to use during startup of the operating system. Hardware profiles are most commonly used with mobile workstations and servers. On a portable computer with a Plug and Play–compatible docking station, you'll have two profiles that are created and loaded automatically as needed: a docked profile for when the computer is connected to the network, and an undocked profile for when the computer is disconnected from the docking station.

You could create hardware profiles for different device configurations as well. For example, you could have a standard profile that includes the standard devices for internal RAID controllers and drive arrays and a test profile that includes external fiber-channel devices. You could then test out the fiber-channel storage devices using the second profile and easily switch back to the standard device set when you are finished testing.

You create and manage hardware profiles by using the System utility. In the System utility, select the Hardware tab, and then click Hardware Profiles. This opens the dialog box shown in Figure 13-7.

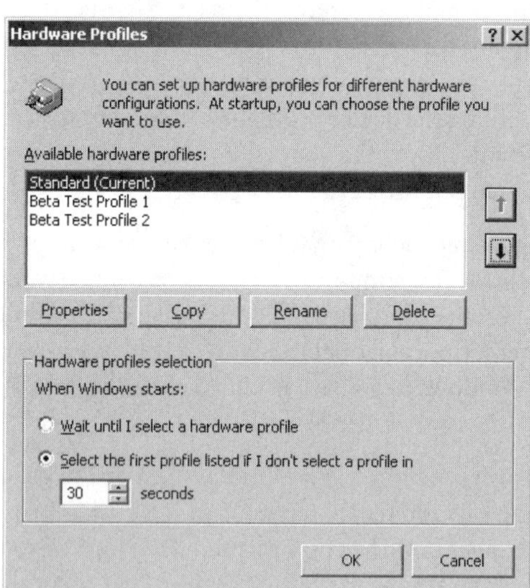

Figure 13-7. Hardware profiles are useful for testing various device configurations.

Windows Server 2003 allows you to configure the way hardware profiles are used in several ways. The active profile (that is, the one currently being used) is listed as (Current). The default profile highlighted at startup is determined by the profile's position in the Available Hardware Profiles list. To set a profile as the default, select it, and click the up arrow until the profile is at the top of the list. You can also determine how long the system displays the hardware profile menu at startup. If you don't want the hardware profile menu to be displayed, set a wait of 0 seconds.

To create new hardware profiles, you use a copy of an existing profile and then enable or disable devices as necessary. Follow these steps to create and use a new profile:

1. In Control Panel, double-click System to start the System utility.
2. Select the Hardware tab, and then click Hardware Profile.
3. In the Available Hardware Profiles list, select the profile you want to use as a template for the new profile, and then click Copy.
4. In the Copy Profile dialog box, enter a name for the profile, and then click OK.
5. Select the new profile, and then click Properties. For nonmobile servers, ensure the This Is A Portable Computer option isn't selected, as shown in Figure 13-8. For all computers, select Always Include This Profile As An Option When Windows Starts. Click OK.

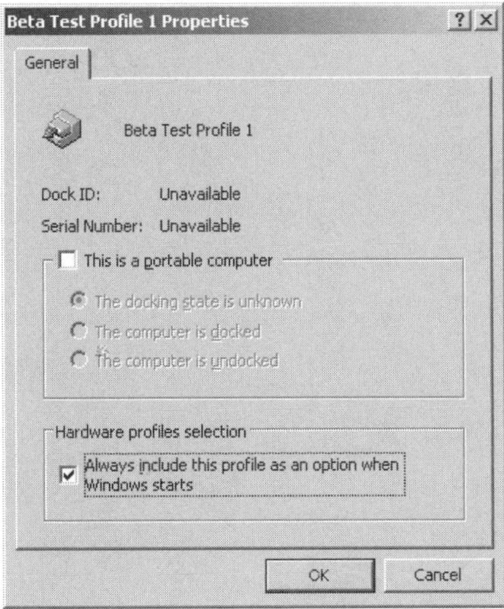

Figure 13-8. Nonmobile servers don't have docked or undocked states, so clear This Is A Portable Computer if it is selected.

6. Repeat Steps 3 through 5 to create other profiles. Then set the hardware profile selection options. In most cases, you'll want the Windows operating system to select a profile automatically after a 3- to 5-second delay. That way if you don't select a profile, the computer starts quickly using the default profile.
7. Restart the computer, and then choose the profile you want to work with. Start Device Manager, and then access the Properties dialog boxes for each of the devices you want to enable or disable in turn. In the General tab, use the Device Usage settings as follows:
   - *Use This Device (Enable)*—Choose this option for any device that you want to make available for the current profile.
   - *Do Not Use This Device In The Current Hardware Profile (Disable)*—Choose this option for any device that should be disabled in the current profile.
   - *Do Not Use This Device In Any Hardware Profiles (Disable)*—Choose this option for any device that should be disabled regardless of which profile is used.
8. To configure devices for additional profiles, repeat Step 7.

Troubleshooting Hardware Devices and Drivers

Whenever a device is installed incorrectly or has another problem, Device Manager displays a warning icon indicating the device has a problem. If you double-click the device, an error code is displayed, as shown in the following screen:

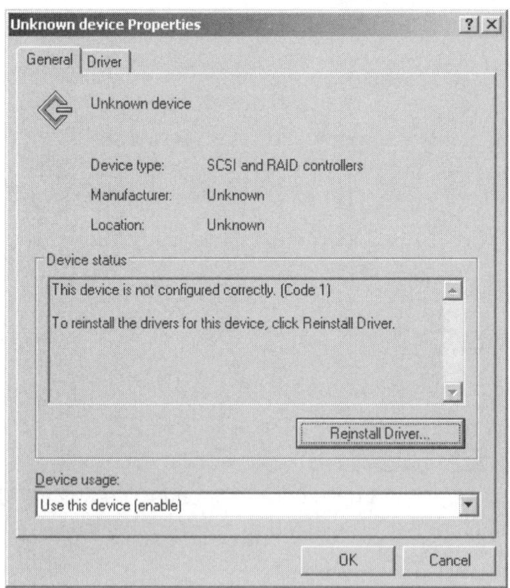

Resolving Common Device Errors

Each error code shown for a device includes a description as well as a suggested action you should take to try to resolve them. Table 13-1 summarizes the common error codes you'll see and describes the suggested actions you should take to resolve them. Most of the actions assume you have the device's Properties dialog box open to the General tab.

Table 13-1. Common Device Error Codes and Descriptions

Error Code	Error Message	Solution
Code 1	This device is not configured correctly.	Obtain a compatible driver for the device, click Reinstall Driver to start the Hardware Update Wizard. Follow the wizard as discussed in the section "Updating a Device Driver" earlier in this chapter.
Code 3	The driver for this device might be corrupted, or your system may be running low on memory or other resources.	Run the Update Driver Wizard by clicking Update Driver in the Driver tab. You might see an "Out of Memory" message at startup because of this.
Code 10	This device cannot start.	Run the Update Driver Wizard by clicking Update Driver in the Driver tab. Don't try to find a driver automatically. Instead, manually install as discussed in the section entitled "Installing Non–Plug and Play Devices" earlier in this chapter.
Code 12	This device cannot find enough free resources that it can use.	Resources assigned to this device conflict with another device, or the BIOS is incorrectly configured. Check the BIOS for resource conflicts as discussed in the section entitled "Resolving Resource Conflicts" later in this chapter.
Code 14	This device cannot work properly until you restart your computer.	Typically, the driver is installed correctly, but will not be started until you restart the computer.
Code 16	Windows cannot identify all the resources this device uses.	Check to see whether a signed driver is available for the device. If it is and you've already installed it, you must manage the resources for the device as discussed in the section entitled "Managing Installed Drivers" earlier in this chapter.

Table 13-1. Common Device Error Codes and Descriptions

Error Code	Error Message	Solution
Code 17	This device is asking for an unknown resource type.	Reinstall or update the driver using a valid, signed driver.
Code 18	Reinstall the drivers for this device.	After an upgrade, you might need to log on as an administrator to complete the device installation. If that's not the case, click Update Driver in the Driver tab to reinstall the driver.
Code 19	The Registry might be corrupted.	Remove and reinstall the device. This should clear out the incorrect or conflicting Registry settings.
Code 21	Windows is removing this device.	The system will remove the device. The Registry might be corrupted. If the device continues to display this message, restart the computer.
Code 22	This device is disabled.	This device has been disabled using Device Manager. To enable it, select Use This Device (Enable) under Device Usage.
Code 24	This device is not present, is not working properly, or does not have all its drivers installed.	Typically results from a bad device or bad hardware. Can also occur with legacy ISA devices; upgrade the driver.
Code 28	The drivers for this device are not installed.	Obtain a compatible driver for the device; click Reinstall Driver to start the Hardware Update Wizard. Follow the wizard as discussed in the section entitled "Updating a Device Driver" earlier in this chapter.
Code 29	This device is disabled because the firmware of the device did not give it the required resources.	Check the device documentation on how to assign resources. You might need to enable the device in the system BIOS or upgrade the BIOS.

Table 13-1. Common Device Error Codes and Descriptions

Error Code	Error Message	Solution
Code 31	This device is not working properly because Windows cannot load the drivers required for this device.	The device driver might be incompatible with Windows Server 2003. Obtain a compatible driver for the device; click Reinstall Driver to start the Hardware Update Wizard. Follow the wizard as discussed in the section entitled "Updating a Device Driver" earlier in this chapter.
Code 32	A driver for this device was not required and has been disabled.	A dependent service for this device has been set to Disabled. Check the event logs to determine which services should be enabled and started.
Code 33	Windows cannot determine which resources are required for this device.	Typically results from a bad device or bad hardware. Can also occur with legacy ISA devices; upgrade the driver and/or refer to the device documentation on how to set resources.
Code 34	Windows cannot determine the settings for this device.	The legacy device must be manually configured. Verify the device jumpers or BIOS settings, then configure the device resources as discussed in the section entitled "Resolving Resource Conflicts."
Code 35	Your computer's system firmware does not include enough information to properly configure and use this device.	This error occurs on multiprocessor systems. Update the BIOS; check for a BIOS option to use Microsoft Personalization System (MPS) 1.1 or MPS 1.4. Usually, you want MPS 1.4.
Code 36	This device is requesting a PCI interrupt but is configured for an ISA interrupt (or vice versa).	ISA interrupts are nonsharable. If a device is in a PCI slot but the slot is configured in BIOS as "reserved for ISA," the error might display. Change the BIOS settings.

If the suggested action doesn't resolve the problem, you might be able to use the Hardware Troubleshooter to resolve the problem. Double-click the device in Device Manager, then click Troubleshoot in the General tab. Keep in mind that if the device drivers aren't installed properly, you won't have a Troubleshoot option. Instead, you'll have a Reinstall Driver button. Clicking Reinstall Driver starts the Hardware Update Wizard discussed in the section entitled "Updating a Device Driver" earlier in this chapter.

Resolving Resource Conflicts

Anyone who remembers IRQ conflicts will be thankful that current computers support ACPI BIOS. With ACPI BIOS, resources are allocated automatically by the operating system at startup, and multiple devices can share the same IRQ settings. These changes mean IRQ conflicts are largely a thing of the past. However, ACPI depends on Plug and Play, and devices that are not fully compatible can sometimes cause problems, particularly ISA devices.

Troubleshooting

Check the device slot configuration

Some conflicts occur because PCI interrupts are sharable, while ISA interrupts are nonsharable. Typically, this is a BIOS problem. If a device is in a PCI slot but the slot is configured in BIOS as "reserved for ISA," a conflict can occur. You must change the BIOS settings rather than the resource configuration to resolve the problem.

If you suspect a device conflict is causing a problem with the current device, check the Conflicting Device list in the lower portion of the Resources tab. It will either list No Conflicts or the specific source of a known conflict. In Device Manager, you can quickly check resource allocations by choosing Resources By Type or Resources By Connection on the View menu.

In Figure 13-9, both ISA and PCI devices are using IRQ settings. You'll note each ISA device has a separate IRQ setting, while multiple PCI devices share the same IRQ settings. This is very typical. Note also that the PCI Modem device has a question mark as an icon. This is because the device isn't configured properly, not because there's a conflict. In this example, there are no conflicts.

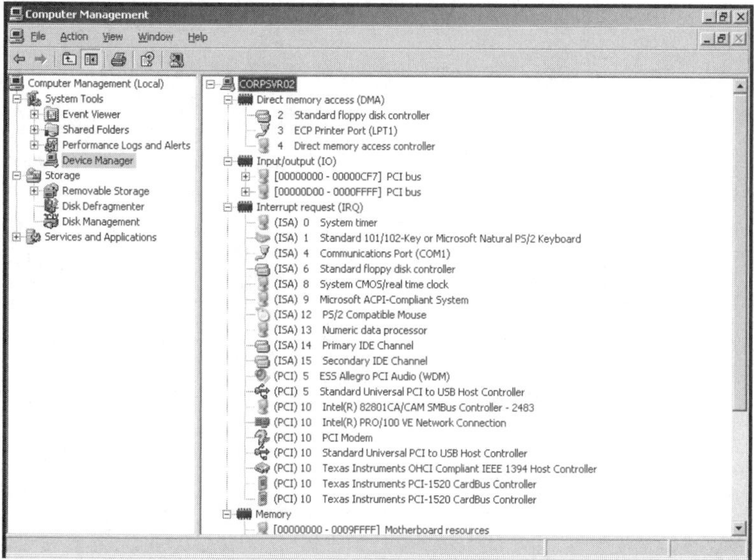

Figure 13-9. View resources by type or resources by connection to check resource settings in Device Manager.

Another way to check for conflicts is to use the System Information utility (Msinfo32.exe). Start the System Information utility by clicking Programs or All Programs, Accessories, System Tools, and then System Information. In System Information, expand Hardware Resources, and then select Conflicts/Sharing.

As shown in Figure 13-10, a list of all resources that are in use is displayed. Again, keep in mind that devices can share IRQ settings thanks to ACPI, so what you are looking for are two unrelated devices sharing the same memory addresses or I/O ports, which would cause a conflict. Keep in mind related devices *can* share memory addresses and I/O ports. In the example, the Standard VGA Graphics Adapter and the Intel 82845 Processor to AGP Controller share the same memory addresses and I/O ports. That's okay because they are related. The PCI Bus is using a memory address space with these devices as well, which is as it should be because Standard VGA Graphics Adapter and the Intel 82845 Processor to AGP Controller are both PCI devices.

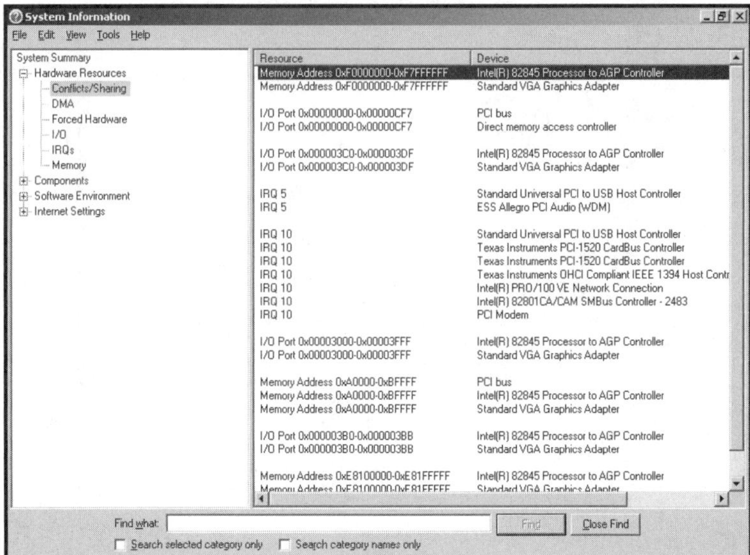

Figure 13-10. Use System Information to check for resource conflicts.

You can try to resolve resource conflicts in several different ways. Some devices use jumpers to manage resource settings, and in this case, the operating system cannot control the resource settings. To make changes, you must shut down the computer, remove the device, change the jumper settings, and then replace the device. In some cases, the jumpers are managed through software rather than an actual jumper switch. Here, you would use the device setup or configuration utility to change the resource settings.

For PCI devices, you can try swapping the cards between PCI slots. This will help if the IRQ or other resource settings are assigned on a per-slot basis, as is the case with some motherboards. You might be able to check the motherboard documentation to see which IRQ interrupts are assigned to which slots. In any case, you'll need to experiment to see which card configuration works.

For PCI devices, a conflict could also be caused by the device driver and the way it works with the ACPI BIOS. You should check to see whether an updated device driver and a BIOS update are available. Installing one or both should resolve the conflict.

As a last resort, you can change the resource settings manually for some devices in Device Manager. In the Resources tab, shown in Figure 13-11, select the resource type that you want to work with. If you can make a change, you should be able to clear the Use Automatic Settings option and then see whether any of the alternate configurations in the Setting Based On box resolve the conflict. Keep in mind that you are now manually managing the resource settings. To allow the Windows operating system once again to manage the settings automatically, you must select Use Automatic Settings.

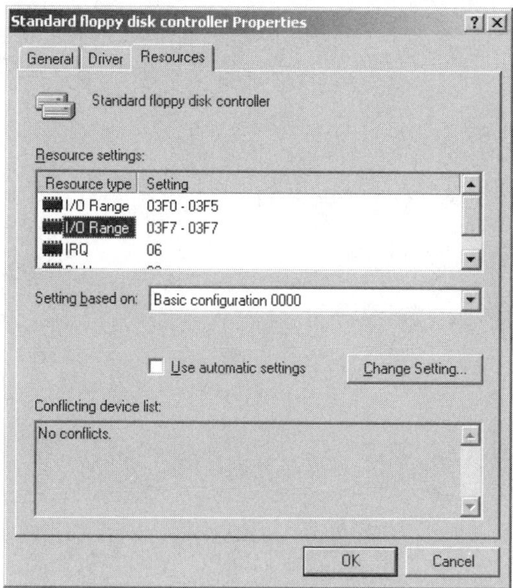

Figure 13-11. For legacy devices, you can use a different configuration to see whether this resolves a conflict.

Chapter 14

Managing the Registry

Everyone who accesses a computer, whether in a workgroup or on a domain, at one time or another has worked with the Microsoft Windows Registry whether the person realizes it or not. Whenever you log on, your user preferences are read from the Registry. Whenever you make changes to the system configuration, install applications or hardware, or make other changes to the working environment, the changes are stored in the Registry. Whenever you uninstall hardware, applications, or system components, these changes are recorded in the Registry as well.

The Registry is the central repository for configuration information in Microsoft Windows Server 2003. Applications, system components, device drivers, and the operating system kernel all use the Registry to store settings and to obtain information about user preferences, system hardware configuration, and system defaults. The Registry also stores information about security settings, user rights, local accounts, and much more. Unlike Microsoft Windows NT, in domains, it no longer stores information about domain accounts or network objects because the related settings are managed by the Active Directory directory service as discussed in Part 7, "Managing Active Directory and Security."

With so much information being read from and written to the Registry, it is not only important for administrators to understand its structures and uses, it is essential. You should know the types of data the Registry works with, what type of data is stored where, and how to make changes if necessary. This is important because often when you must fine-tune system configuration or correct errors to stabilize systems, you'll be instructed to access the Registry and make such and such a change. Generally, the instructions assume you know what you're doing. Unfortunately, if you attempt such a change and really don't know what you're doing, you could make it so the system won't boot at all. So, with this in mind, let's look at how the Registry works and how you can work with it.

Introducing the Registry

The Registry is written as a binary database with the information organized in a hierarchy. This hierarchy has a structure much like that used by a file system and is an inverted tree with the root at the top of the tree. Any time the operating system must obtain system default values or information about your preferences, it obtains this information from the Registry. Any time you install programs or make changes in Control Panel, these changes usually are written to the Registry.

Note I say "usually" because in Windows domains some configuration information is written to Active Directory. For example, beginning with Microsoft Windows 2000, information about user accounts and network objects is stored in Active Directory. In addition, when you promote a member server to a domain controller, key Registry settings that apply to the server, such as the default configuration values, are transferred to Active Directory and thereafter managed through Active Directory. If you were later to demote the domain controller, the original Registry settings would not be restored either. Instead, the default settings are restored as they would appear on a newly installed server.

The Registry's importance is that it stores most of a system's state. If you make preference and settings changes to a system, these changes are stored in the Registry. If a system dies and cannot be recovered, you don't have to install a new system and then configure it to look like the old one. You could instead install Windows Server 2003 and then restore a backup of the failed system's Registry. This would restore all the preferences and settings of the failed system on the new system.

Although it's great that the Registry can store settings that you've made, you might be wondering what else the Registry is good for. Well, in addition to storing settings that you've made, the Registry stores settings that the system makes as well. For example, whenever a system boots, it uses Ntdetect.com to take an inventory of its hardware, and then stores this information in the Registry. The operating system kernel in turn uses this information, read from the Registry at startup, to determine which device drivers to load and in which order. The kernel also stores information needed by those drivers in the Registry, including the driver initialization parameters, which allows the device drivers to configure themselves to work with the system's hardware.

Many other system components make use of the Registry as well. When you install Windows Server 2003, the setup choices you make are used to build the initial Registry database. Setup modifies the Registry whenever you add or remove hardware from a system. Similarly, application setup programs modify the Registry to store the application installation settings and to determine whether components of the application are already installed.

Then, when you run applications, the applications store any changes you make to the default settings in the Registry.

Beyond this, many administration tools are little more than friendly user interfaces for managing the Registry, especially when it comes to Control Panel. So, rather than having you work directly with a particular area of the Registry, Microsoft provides a tool that you can use to make the necessary changes safely and securely. Use these tools—that's what they are for.

Caution The importance of using the proper tools to make Registry changes cannot be overstated. If there's a tool that lets you manage an area of the Registry, you should use it. Don't fool around with the Registry just because you can. Making improper changes to the Registry can cause a system to become unstable, and in some cases, it could even make it so the system won't boot.

As you can see, nearly everything you do with the operating system affects the Registry in one way or another. That's why it's so important to understand what the Registry is used for, how you can work with it, how you can secure it, and how you can maintain it.

Understanding the Registry Structure

The Registry is first a database. Like any other database, the Registry is designed for information storage and retrieval. Any Registry value entry can be identified by specifying the path to its location. For example, the path HKEY_LOCAL_MACHINE\SOFTWARE\Microsoft\Windows NT\CurrentVersion\Winlogon\AllowMultipleTSSessions specifies a Registry value that can be used to enable or disable the use of offline files with Terminal Services.

Figure 14-1 shows this value in the Registry. Because of its hierarchical structure, the Registry appears to be organized much like a file system. In fact, its structure is often compared to that of a file system. However, this is a bit misleading because there is no actual folder/file representation on a system's hard disk to match the structure used by the Registry. The Registry's actual physical structure is separate from the way Registry information is represented. Locations in the Registry are represented by a logical structure that has little correlation to how value entries are stored.

Unlike Windows 2000 and Windows NT, Windows Server 2003 supports larger Registry sizes than were previously possible and no longer keeps the entire Registry in paged pool memory. Instead, 256-kilobyte (KB) views of the Registry are mapped into system cache as needed. This is an important change from the original architecture of the Registry, which effectively limited the Registry to about 80 percent of the total size of paged pool. The new Registry implementation is limited only by available space in the paging file.

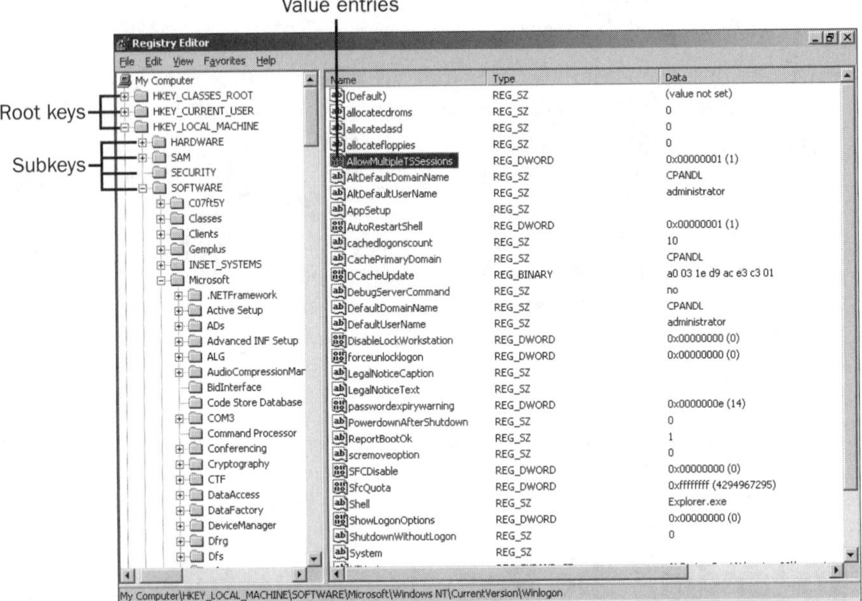

Figure 14-1. Accessing a value according to its path in the Registry.

At startup, 256-KB mapped views of the Registry are loaded into system cache so that Windows Server 2003 can quickly retrieve configuration information. Some of the Registry's information is created dynamically based on the system hardware configuration at startup and doesn't exist until it is created. For the most part, however, the Registry is stored in persistent form on disk and read from a set of files called hives. *Hives* are binary files that represent a grouping of keys and values. You'll find the hive files in the %SystemRoot%\System32\Config directory. Within this directory, you'll also find .sav and .log files, which serve as backup files for the Registry.

Inside Out

Windows Server 2003 manages the Registry size and memory use

Windows NT and Windows 2000 store the entire Registry in paged, pooled memory. For 32-bit systems, this limits the Registry to approximately 160 megabytes (MB) because of the layout of the virtual address space in the operating system kernel. Unfortunately, in this configuration as the Registry grows in size it uses a considerable amount of paged, pooled memory and can leave too little memory for other kernel-mode components.

Windows Server 2003 resolves this problem by changing the way the Registry is stored in memory. Under the new implementation, 256-KB mapped views of the Registry are loaded into the system cache as necessary by the Cache Manager. The rest of the Registry is stored in the paging file on disk. Because the Registry is written to system cache, it can exist in system random access memory (RAM) and be paged to and from disk as needed. In previous versions of the Windows operating system, the operating system allowed you to control the maximum amount of memory and disk space that could be used by the Registry. With the improved memory management features of Windows Server 2003, the operating system has now taken over control of managing how much memory the Registry uses. Most member servers running Windows Server 2003 use between 20 and 25 MB of memory for the Registry. Domain controllers or servers that have many configuration components, services, and applications use considerably more. For example, one of my key domain controllers uses between 25 and 30 MB of memory for the Registry. Quite a change from the old architecture, when the in-memory requirements of the Registry could be up to 160 MB.

To read the Registry you need a special editor. The editor provided in Windows Server 2003 is Registry Editor. By using Registry Editor, you can navigate the Registry's logical structure from the top of the database to the bottom. From the top down, the levels of the database are defined as root keys, subkeys, and value entries.

Inside Out

Regedit replaces Regedt32 in Windows Server 2003

Unlike previous versions of the Windows operating system that included two versions of Registry Editor, Windows Server 2003 ships with a single version. This version, Regedit.exe, integrates all of the features of the previous Registry editors. From the original Regedit.exe it gets its core features. From Regedt32.exe, which is no longer available, it gets its security and favorites features. By using the security features, you can view and manage permissions for Registry values. By using the favorites feature, you can create and use favorites to quickly access stored locations within the Registry.

Regedt32 *really* is gone—although I, like many administrators, still refer to it. It is, after all, the editor administrators used because it gave us the ability to manage Registry security and it is the one that was recommended for administrators over Regedit. Because old habits die hard, Windows Server 2003 still has a stub file for Regedt32. However, if you run Regedt32, the operating system will in fact start Regedit.

At the top of the Registry hierarchy are the root keys. Each root key contains several subkeys, which contain other subkeys and value entries. The names of value entries must be unique within the associated subkey, and the value entries correspond to specific configuration parameters. The settings of those configuration parameters are the values stored in the value entry. Each value has an associated data type that controls the type of data it can store. For example, some value entries are used to store only binary data, while others are used to store only strings of characters, and the value's data type controls this.

We can now break down the Registry path HKEY_LOCAL_MACHINE\SOFTWARE\Microsoft\Windows NT\CurrentVersion\Winlogon\AllowMultipleTSSessions so that it is more meaningful. Here, *HKEY_LOCAL_MACHINE* is the root key. Each entry below the root key until we get to *AllowMultipleTSSessions* represents a subkey level within the Registry hierarchy. Finally, *AllowMultipleTSSessions* is the actual value entry.

The Registry is very complex and it is often made more confusing because documentation on the subject uses a variety of different terms beyond those already discussed. When reading about the Registry in various sources, you might see references to the following:

- **Subtrees** A *subtree* is a name for the tree of keys and values stemming from a root key down the Registry hierarchy. In documentation, you often see root keys referred to as subtrees. What the documentation means when it refers to a subtree is the branch of keys and values contained within a specified root key.
- **Keys** Technically, root keys are the top of the Registry hierarchy, and everything below a root key is either a subkey or a value entry. In practice, subkeys are often referred to as keys. It's just easier to refer to such and such a key—sort of like when we refer to "such and such a folder" rather than saying "subfolder."
- **Values** A *value* is the lowest level of the Registry hierarchy. For ease of reference, value entries are often simply referred to as values. Technically, however, a value entry comprises three parts: a name, a data type, and a value. The name identifies the configuration setting. The data type identifies the format for the data. The value is the actual data within the entry.

Now that you know the basics of the Registry's structure, let's dig deeper, taking a closer look at the root keys, major subkeys, and data types.

Registry Root Keys

The Registry is organized into a hierarchy of keys, subkeys, and value entries. The root keys are at the top of the hierarchy and form the primary branches, or subtrees, of Registry information. There are two physical root keys, HKEY_LOCAL_MACHINE and HKEY_USER. These physical root keys are associated with actual files stored on the disk and are divided into additional logical groupings of Registry information. As shown in Table 14-1, the logical groupings are simply subsets of information gathered from HKEY_LOCAL_MACHINE and HKEY_USER.

Table 14-1. Registry Subtrees

Subtree	Description
Physical Subtree	
HKEY_LOCAL_MACHINE (HKLM)	Stores all the settings that pertain to the hardware currently installed on the machine.
HKEY_USERS (HKU)	Stores user profile data for each user who has previously logged on to the computer locally as well as a default user profile.
Logical Subtree	
HKEY_CLASSES_ROOT (HKCR)	Stores all file associations and object linking and embedding (OLE) class identifiers. This subtree is built from HKEY_LOCAL_MACHINE\SOFTWARE\Classes and HKEY_CURRENT_USER\SOFTWARE\Classes.
HKEY_CURRENT_CONFIG (HKCC)	Stores information about the hardware configuration with which you started the system. This subtree is built from HKEY_LOCAL_MACHINE\SYSTEM\CurrentControlSet\Hardware Profiles\Current, which in turn is a pointer to a numbered subkey that has the current hardware profile.
HKEY_CURRENT_USER (HKCU)	Stores information about the user currently logged on. This key has a pointer to HKEY_USER*UserSID*, where *UserSID* is the security identifier for the current user as well as for the default profile discussed previously.

Inside Out

The Registry on 64-bit Windows systems

The Registry on 64-bit Windows systems is divided into 32-bit and 64-bit keys. Many keys are created in both 32-bit and 64-bit versions, and although the keys belong to different branches of the Registry, they have the same name. On these systems, Registry Editor (Regedit.exe) is designed to work with both 32-bit and 64-bit keys. The 32-bit keys, however, are represented with the WOW64 Registry redirector and appear under the HKEY_LOCAL_MACHINE\SOFTWARE\WOW6432Node key. If you want to work directly with the 32-bit keys, you can do so by using the 32-bit Registry editor located in the file path %SystemRoot%\Syswow64\Regedit.

To support both 32-bit and 64-bit interoperability through the Component Object Model (COM) and the use of 32-bit programs, the WOW64 redirector mirrors COM-related Registry keys and values between the 64-bit and 32-bit Registry views. In some cases, the keys and values are modified during the reflection process to adjust pathnames and other values that might be version-dependent. This, in turn, means that the 32-bit and 64-bit values might differ.

HKEY_LOCAL_MACHINE

HKEY_LOCAL_MACHINE, abbreviated as HKLM, contains all the settings that pertain to the hardware currently installed on a system. It includes settings for memory, device drivers, installed hardware, and startup. Applications are supposed to store settings in HKLM only if the related data pertains to everyone who uses the computer.

As Figure 14-2 shows, HKLM contains the following major subkeys:

- HARDWARE
- SAM
- SECURITY
- SOFTWARE
- SYSTEM

These subkeys are discussed in the sections that follow.

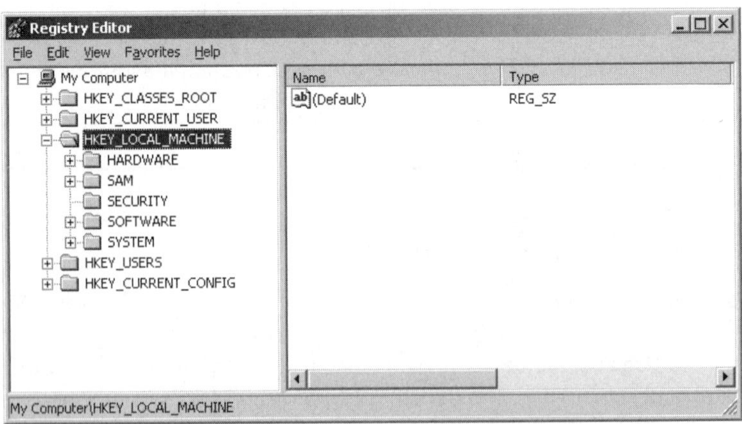

Figure 14-2. Accessing HKEY_LOCAL_MACHINE in the Registry.

HKLM\HARDWARE

HKLM\HARDWARE stores information about the hardware configuration for the computer. This key is re-created by Ntdetect.com each time you start Windows Server 2003, and it exists only in memory, not on disk. To build this key, Ntdetect.com enumerates every device it can find by scanning the system buses and by searching for specific classes of devices, such as serial ports, keyboards, and pointer devices.

Under HKLM\HARDWARE, you'll find four standard subkeys that are dynamically created at startup and contain the information gathered by Ntdetect.com. These subkeys are as follows:

- **ACPI** Contains information about the Advanced Configuration Power Interface (ACPI), which is a part of system BIOS that supports Plug and Play and advanced power management. This subkey doesn't exist on non-ACPI-compliant computers.
- **DESCRIPTION** Contains hardware descriptions including those for the system's central processor, floating-point processor, and multifunction adapters. For portable computers, one of the multifunction devices lists information about the docking state. For any computer with multipurpose chip sets, one of the multifunction devices lists information about the controllers for disks, keyboards, parallel ports, serial ports, and pointer devices. There's also a catchall category for other controllers, such as when a computer has a PC Card controller.
- **DEVICEMAP** Contains information that maps devices to device drivers. You'll find device mappings for keyboards, pointer devices, parallel ports, Small Computer System Interface (SCSI) ports, serial ports, and video devices. Of particular note is that within the VIDEO subkey is a value entry for the Video Graphics Adapter (VGA)–compatible video device installed on the computer. This device is used when the computer must start in VGA display mode.
- **RESOURCEMAP** Contains mappings for the hardware abstraction layer (HAL), for the Plug and Play manager, and for available system resources. Of particular note is the Plug and Play manager. It uses this subkey to record information about devices it knows how to handle.

Additional nonstandard subkeys can exist under HKLM\HARDWARE. The subkeys are specific to the hardware used by the computer.

HKLM\SAM

HKLM\SAM stores the Security Accounts Manager (SAM) database. When you create local users and groups on member servers and workstations, the accounts are stored in HKLM\SAM as they were in Windows NT. This key is also used to store information about built-in user and group accounts, as well as group membership and aliases for accounts.

By default, the information stored in HKLM\SAM is inaccessible through Registry Editor. This is a security feature designed to help protect the security and integrity of the system.

Inside Out

Browsing HKLM\SAM and HKLM\SECURITY

As an administrator, you, like me, probably hate getting locked out of an area of the operating system, especially when you might be curious to know just what information is stored within these secret keys. If you want to browse the information in these subkeys, you can do this by running Regedit in the LocalSystem security context. As the LocalSystem, you have full access to these subkeys. However, you should only browse these subkeys. You should never try to make changes because this could cause serious damage to the computer.

With that said, the easiest way to browse the Registry in the LocalSystem context is to start Regedit in interactive mode by using the scheduler service. Type the following:

```
at HH:MM /interactive regedit
```

where *HH:MM* is a time slightly ahead of the current time. The at scheduler uses a 24-hour clock, so if it is currently 8:29 A.M., you could use a time of 08:30, or if it is 8:29 P.M., you could use a time of 20:30. Either way, you give the system just enough time to schedule and then run the task.

HKLM\SECURITY

HKLM\SECURITY stores security information for the local machine. It contains information about cached logon credentials, policy settings, service-related security settings, and default security values. It also has a copy of the HKLM\SAM. As with the HKLM\SAM subkey, this subkey is inaccessible through Registry Editor. This is a security feature designed to help protect the security and integrity of the system.

HKLM\SOFTWARE

HKLM\SOFTWARE stores machine-wide settings for every application and system component installed on the system. This includes setup information, executable paths, default configuration settings, and registration information. Because this subkey resides under HKLM, the information here is applied globally. This is different from the HKCU\ SOFTWARE configuration settings, which are applied on a per-user basis.

As Figure 14-3 shows, you'll find many important subkeys within HKLM\SOFTWARE, including the following:

- **Classes** Contains all file associations and OLE class identifiers. This is also the key from which HKEY_CLASSES_ROOT is built.
- **Clients** Stores information about protocols and shells used by every client application installed on the system. This includes the calendar, contacts, mail, media, and news clients.
- **Microsoft** Contains information about every Microsoft application and component installed on the system. This includes their complete configuration settings, defaults, registration information, and much more. You'll find most of the graphical user interface (GUI) preferences in HKLM\SOFTWARE\Microsoft\Windows\CurrentVersion. You'll find the configuration settings for most system components, language packs, hot fixes, and more under HKLM\SOFTWARE\Microsoft\Windows NT\CurrentVersion.
- **ODBC** Contains information about the Open Database Connectivity (ODBC) configuration on the system. It includes information about all ODBC drives and ODBC file Data Source Names (DSNs).
- **Policies** Contains information about local policies for applications and components installed on the system.

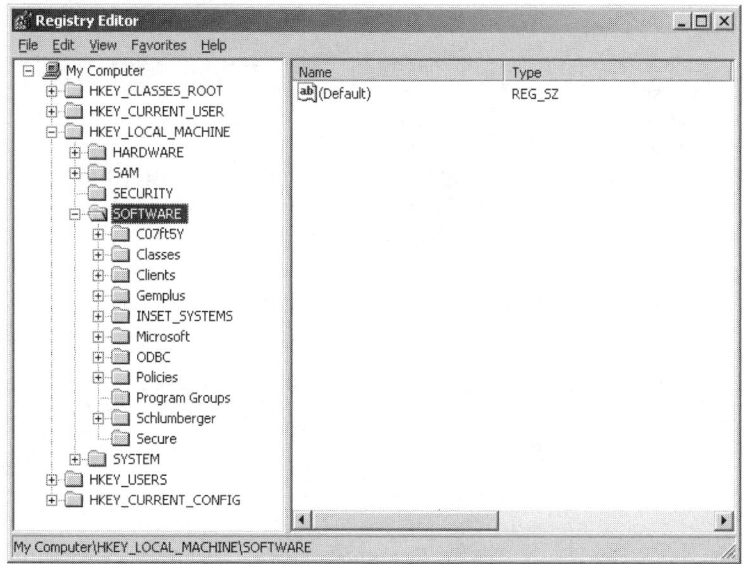

Figure 14-3. Accessing HKEY_LOCAL_MACHINE\SOFTWARE in the Registry.

HKLM\SYSTEM

HKLM\SYSTEM stores information about device drivers, services, startup parameters, and other machine-wide settings. You'll find several important subkeys within HKLM\SYSTEM. One of the most important is HKLM\SYSTEM\CurrentControlSet, as shown in Figure 14-4.

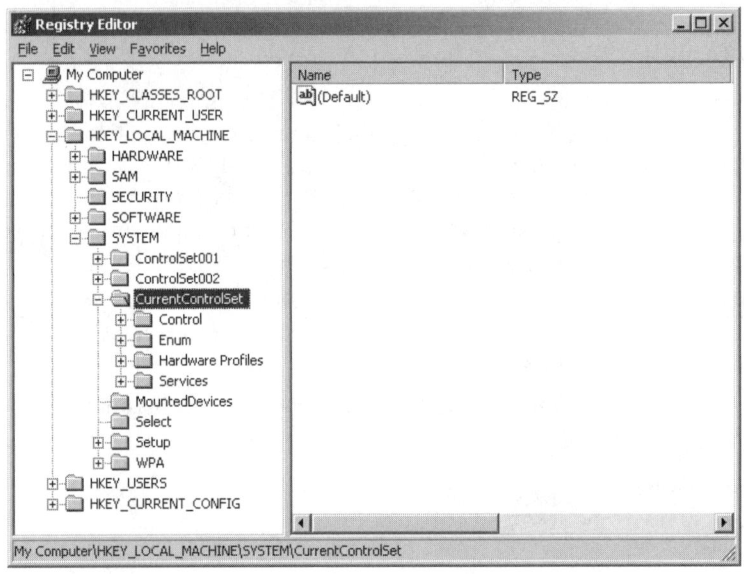

Figure 14-4. Accessing HKEY_LOCAL_MACHINE\SYSTEM\CurrentControlSet in the Registry.

CurrentControlSet contains information about the set of controls and services used for the last successful boot of the system. This subkey always contains information on the set of controls actually in use and represents the most recent successful boot. The control set is written as the final part of the boot process so that the Registry is updated as appropriate to reflect which set of controls and services was last used for a successful boot. This is, in fact, how you can boot a system to the last known good configuration after it crashes or experiences a Stop error.

HKLM\SYSTEM also contains previously created control sets. These are saved under the subkeys named ControlSet001, ControlSet002, and so forth. Within the control sets, you'll find four important subkeys:

- **Control** Contains control information about key operating system settings, tools, and subcomponents, including the HAL, keyboard layouts, system devices, interfaces, and device classes. Under BackupRestore, you'll find the saved settings for Backup, which include lists of Automated System Recovery (ASR) keys, files, and Registry settings not to restore. Under the SafeBoot subkey, you'll find the control sets used for minimal and network-only boots of the system.

- **Enum** Contains the complete enumeration of devices found on the system when Ntdetect.com scans the system buses and searches for specific classes of devices. This represents the complete list of devices present at boot time.
- **Hardware Profiles** Contains a subkey for each hardware profile available on the system. The first hardware profile, 0000, is an empty profile. The other numbered profiles, beginning with 0001, represent profiles that are available for use on the system. The profile named Current always points to the profile selected at boot time.
- **Services** Contains a subkey for each service installed on the system. These subkeys store the necessary configuration information for their related services, which can include startup parameters as well as security and performance settings.

Another interesting subkey is HKLM\SYSTEM\MountedDevices. This key is created by the Logical Volume Manager service and is used to store the list of mounted and available disk devices. Disk devices are listed according to logical volume configuration and drive letter designator.

HKEY_USERS

HKEY_USERS, abbreviated as HKU, contains user profile data for every user who has previously logged on to the computer locally, as well as a default user profile. Each user's profile is owned by that user unless you change permissions or move profiles. Profile settings include the user's desktop configuration, environment variables, folder options, menu options, printers, and network connections.

User profiles are saved in subkeys of HKEY_USERS according to their security identifiers (SIDs). There is also a SecurityID_Classes subkey that represents file associations that are specific to a particular user. For example, if a user sets Adobe Photoshop as the default program for .jpeg and .jpg files and this is different from the system default, there are entries within this subkey that show this association.

When you use Group Policy as discussed in Part 7, the policy settings are applied to the individual user profiles stored in this key. The default profile specifies how the machine behaves when no one is logged on and is also used as the base profile for new users who log on to the computer. For example, if you wanted to ensure that the computer used a password-protected screen saver when no one was logged on, you would modify the default profile accordingly. The subkey for the default user profile is easy to pick out because it is named HKEY_USERS\.DEFAULT.

> **Note** The profile information stored in HKU is loaded from the profile data stored on disk. The default location for profiles is %SystemDrive%\Documents and Settings*UserName*, where *UserName* is the user's pre–Windows 2000 logon name.

HKEY_CLASSES_ROOT

HKEY_CLASSES_ROOT, abbreviated as HKCR, stores all file associations that tell the computer which document file types are associated with which applications, as well as which action to take for various tasks, such as open, edit, close, or play, based on a specified document type. For example, if you double-click a .doc file, the document typically is opened for editing in Microsoft Office Word. This file association is added to HKCR when you install Microsoft Office. If Microsoft Office isn't installed, a .doc file is opened instead in WordPad because of a default file association created when the operating system is installed.

HKCR is built from HKEY_LOCAL_MACHINE\SOFTWARE\Classes and HKEY_CURRENT_USER\SOFTWARE\Classes. The former provides computer-specific class registration, and the latter, user-specific class registration. Because the user-specific class registrations have precedence, this allows for different class registrations for each user of the machine. This is different from previous versions of the Windows operating system for which the same class registration information was provided for all users of a particular machine.

HKEY_CURRENT_CONFIG

HKEY_CURRENT_CONFIG, abbreviated as HKCC, contains information about the hardware configuration with which you started the system, which is also referred to as the machine's boot configuration. This key contains information about the current device assignments, device drivers, and system services that were present at boot time.

HKCC is built from HKEY_LOCAL_MACHINE \SYSTEM\CurrentControlSet\Hardware Profiles\Current, which in turn is a pointer to a numbered subkey that contains the current hardware profile. If a system has multiple hardware profiles, the key points to a different hardware profile, depending on the boot state or the hardware profile selection made at startup. For example, portable computers typically have docked and undocked hardware profiles. If a portable computer were started using the docked profile, it would use one hardware configuration, and if it were started using the undocked profile, it would use another hardware configuration.

HKEY_CURRENT_USER

HKEY_CURRENT_USER, abbreviated as HKCU, contains information about the user currently logged on. This key has a pointer to HKEY_USER*UserSID*, where *UserSID* is the security identifier for the current user as well as for the default profile discussed previously. Microsoft requires that applications store user-specific preferences under this key. For example, Microsoft Office settings for individual users are stored under this key. Additionally, as discussed previously, HKEY_CURRENT_USER\SOFTWARE\Classes stores the user-specific settings for file associations.

> **Tip Restrict changes to global settings by using the Classes subkey**
> If you don't want users to be able to set their own file associations, you could change the permissions on HKLM\SOFTWARE\Classes so users can't alter the global settings you want them to have. For more information about Registry permissions, see the section entitled "Securing the Registry" later in this chapter.

Registry Data: How It Is Stored and Used

Now that you know more about the Registry's structure, let's take a look at the actual data within the Registry. Understanding how Registry data is stored and used is just as important as understanding the Registry structure.

Where Registry Data Comes From

As mentioned previously, some Registry data is created dynamically at boot time and some is stored on disk so it can be used each time you boot a computer. The dynamically created data is volatile, meaning that when you shut down the system, it is gone. For example, as part of the boot process Ntdetect.com scans for system devices and uses the results to build the HKEY_LOCAL_MACHINE\HARDWARE subkey. The information stored in this key exists only in memory and isn't stored anywhere on disk.

On the other hand, Registry data stored on disk is persistent. When you shut down a system, this Registry data remains on disk and is available the next time you boot the system. Some of this stored information is very important, especially when it comes to recovering from boot failure. For example, by using the information stored in HKEY_LOCAL_MACHINE\SYSTEM\CurrentControlSet, you can boot using the Last Known Good configuration. If the Registry data was corrupted, however, this information might not be available and the only way to recover the system would be to try repairing the installation or reinstalling the operating system.

To help safeguard the system and ensure that one section of bad data doesn't cause the whole Registry to fail to load, Windows Server 2003 has several built-in redundancies and fail safes. For starters, the Registry isn't written to a single file. Instead, it is written to a set of files called hives. There are six main types of hives, each representing a group of keys and values. Most of the hives are written to disk in the %SystemRoot%\System32\Config directory. Within this directory, you'll find these hive files:

- .DEFAULT, which corresponds to the HKEY_USERS\.DEFAULT subkey
- SAM, which corresponds to the HKEY_LOCAL_MACHINE\SAM subkey
- SECURITY, which corresponds to the HKEY_LOCAL_MACHINE\SECURITY subkey
- SOFTWARE, which corresponds to the HKEY_LOCAL_MACHINE\SOFTWARE subkey
- SYSTEM, which corresponds to the HKEY_LOCAL_MACHINE\SYSTEM subkey

The remaining hive files are stored in individual user profile directories with the default name of Ntuser.dat. These files are in fact hive files that are loaded into the Registry and used to set the pointer for the HKEY_CURRENT_USER root key. When no user is logged on to a system, the user profile for the default user is loaded into the Registry. When an actual user logs on, this user's profile is loaded into the Registry.

Note The root keys not mentioned are HKEY_CURRENT_CONFIG and HKEY_CLASSES_ROOT. The on-disk data for HKEY_CURRENT_CONFIG comes from the subkey from which it is built: HKEY_LOCAL_MACHINE \SYSTEM\CurrentControlSet\Hardware Profiles\Current. Similarly, the on-disk data for HKEY_CLASSES_ROOT comes from HKEY_LOCAL_MACHINE \SOFTWARE\Classes and HKEY_CURRENT_USER\SOFTWARE\Classes.

Every hive file has an associated .log file—even Ntuser.dat, whose log file is Ntuser.dat.log. Windows Server 2003 uses the log files to help protect the Registry during updates. When a hive file is to be changed, the change is first written to the associated log file. It is then written to disk. The system then uses the change log to write the changes to the actual hive file. If the system were to crash while a change is being written to a hive file, the change log could later be used by the system to roll back the change, resetting the hive to its previous configuration.

Inside Out

How Windows Server 2003 starts over with a clean Registry

Examine %SystemRoot%\System32\Config closely and you'll see several files with the .sav extension. These files represent the postinstallation state of the Registry. If you ever wonder how Windows Server 2003 can reset the Registry to that of a clean install after you demote a domain controller, this is the answer. By loading these files into the Registry and then writing them to disk as the original hive files, the server is returned to its postinstallation state with a clean Registry.

Types of Registry Data Available

When you work your way down to the lowest level of the Registry, you see the actual value entries. Each value entry has a name, a data type, and a value associated with it. Although value entries have a theoretical size limit of 1024 KB, most value entries are less than 1 KB in size. In fact, many value entries contain only a few bits of data. The type of information stored in these bits depends on the data type of the value entry.

The data types defined include the following:

- **REG_BINARY** Raw binary data without any formatting or parsing. You can view binary data in several forms, including standard binary and hexadecimal. In some cases, if you view the binary data, you will see the hexadecimal values as well as the text characters these values define.
- **REG_DWORD** A binary data type in which 4-byte integer values are stored. REG_DWORD is often used to track values that can be incremented, status codes, or Boolean flags. With Boolean flags, a value of 0 means the flag is off (false) and a value of 1 means the flag is on (true).
- **REG_SZ** A fixed-length string of Unicode characters. REG_SZ is used to store values that are meant to be read by users and can include names, descriptions, and so on, as well as stored file system paths.
- **REG_EXPAND_SZ** A variable-length string that can include environment variables that are to be expanded when the data is read by the operating system, its components, or services, as well as installed applications. Environment variables are enclosed in percentage signs (%) to set them off from other values in the string. For example, %SystemDrive% refers to the SystemDrive environment variable. A REG_EXPAND_SZ value that defines a path to use could include this environment variable, such as %SystemDrive%\Program Files\Common Files.
- **REG_MULTI_SZ** A multiple-parameter string that can be used to store multiple string values in a single entry. Each value is separated by a standard delimiter so that the individual values can be picked out as necessary.
- **REG_FULL_RESOURCE_DESCRIPTOR** A value with an encoded resource descriptor, such as a list of resources used by a device driver or a hardware component. REG_FULL_RESOURCE_DESCRIPTOR values are associated with hardware components, such as a system's central processors, floating-point processors, or multifunction adapters.

The most common data types you'll see in the Registry are REG_SZ and REG_DWORD. The vast majority of value entries has this data type. The most important thing to know about these data types is that one is used with strings of characters and the other is used with binary data that is normally represented in hexadecimal format. And don't worry, if you have to create a value entry—typically because you are directed to by a Microsoft Knowledge Base article in an attempt to resolve an issue—you'll usually be told which data type to use. Again, more often than not, this data type is either REG_SZ or REG_DWORD.

Managing the Registry

Windows Server 2003 provides several tools for working with the Registry. The main tool, of course, is Registry Editor, which is started by typing **regedit** or **regedt32** at the command line or in the Run dialog box. Another tool for working with the Registry is the REG command.

Both tools can be used to view and manage the Registry. Keep in mind that although both tools are considered editors, any changes you make are applied immediately. Thus, any change you make is applied automatically to the Registry without you having to save the change.

Caution As an administrator, you have permission to make changes to most areas of the Registry. This allows you to make additions, changes, and deletions as necessary. However, before you do this, you should always make a backup of the system state along with the Registry first, as discussed in the section "Choosing a Backup Method for the Registry" later in this chapter. This will help ensure that you can recover the Registry in case something goes wrong when you are making your modifications.

Searching the Registry

One of the common tasks you'll want to perform in Registry Editor is to search for a particular key. You can search for keys, values, and data entries using the FIND command on the Edit menu (see the following screen).

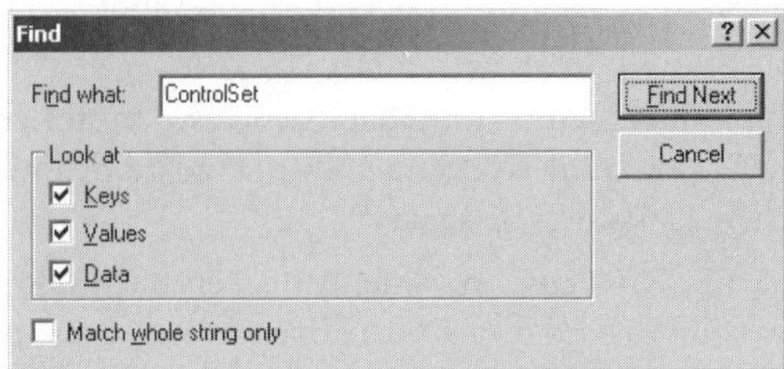

Don't let the simplicity of the Find interface fool you—there is a bit more to searching the Registry than you might think. So, if you want to find what you're looking for, do the following:

- The Find function in the Registry searches from the current node forward to the last value in the final root key branch. So, if you want to search the complete Registry, you must select the My Computer node in the left pane before you select Find on the Edit menu or press Ctrl+F.
- Type the text you want to find in the Find What box. You can search only for standard American Standard Code for Information Interchange (ASCII) text. So, if you're searching for data entries, Registry Editor will search only string values (REG_SZ, REG_EXPAND_SZ, and REG_MULTI_SZ) for the specified text.
- Use the Look At options to control where Registry Editor looks for the text you want to find. You can search on key names, value names, and text within data entries. If you want to match only whole strings instead of searching for text within longer strings, select Match Whole Strings Only.

After you make your selections, click Find Next to begin the search. If Registry Editor finds a match before reaching the end of the Registry, it selects and displays the matching item. If the match isn't what you're looking for, press F3 to search again from the current position in the Registry.

Modifying the Registry

When you want to work with keys and values in the Registry, you typically are working with subkeys of a particular key. This allows you to add a subkey and define its values and to remove subkeys and their values. You cannot, however, add or remove root keys or insert keys at the root node of the Registry. Default security settings within some subkeys might also prohibit you from working with their keys and values. For example, by default you cannot create, modify, or remove keys or values within HKLM\SAM and HKLM\SECURITY.

Modifying Values

The most common change you'll make to the Registry is to modify an existing value. For example, a Knowledge Base article might recommend that you change a value from 0 to 1 to enable a certain feature in Windows Server 2003 or from 1 to 0 to disable it. To change a value, locate the value in Registry Editor, and then in the right pane double-click the value name. This opens an Edit dialog box, the style of which depends on the type of data you are modifying.

The most common values you'll modify are REG_SZ, REG_MULTI_SZ, and REG_DWORD. Figure 14-5 shows the Edit String dialog box, which is displayed when you modify REG_SZ values. In the dialog box, you would typically replace the existing value with the value you need to enter.

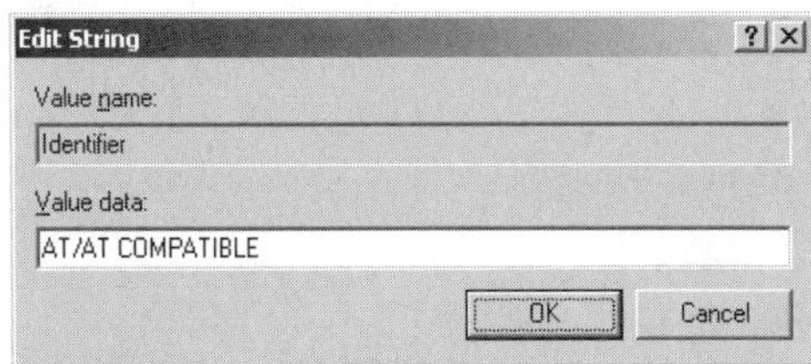

Figure 14-5. Using the Edit String dialog box.

Figure 14-6 shows the Edit Multi-String dialog box, which is displayed when you modify REG_MULTI_SZ values. In this example, there are four separate string values. In the dialog box, each value is separated by a new line to make the values easier to work with. If directed to change a value, you would typically need to replace an existing value, making sure you don't accidentally modify the entry before or after the entry you are working with. If directed to add a value, you would begin typing on a new line following the last value.

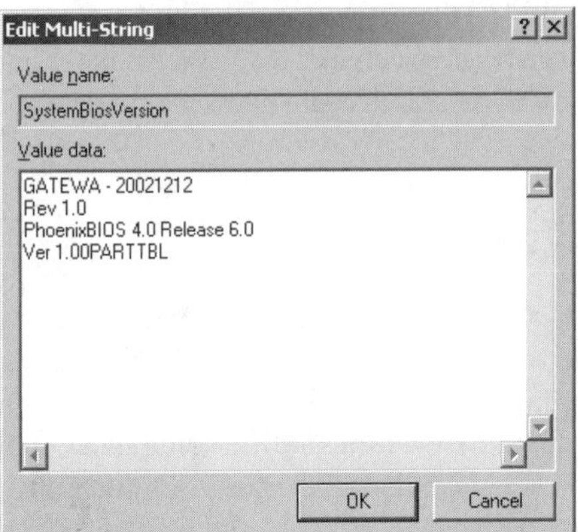

Figure 14-6. Using the Edit Multi-String dialog box.

Figure 14-7 shows the Edit DWORD Value dialog box, which is displayed when you modify REG_DWORD values. In this example, the value is displayed in hexadecimal format. Typically, you won't need to worry about the data format. You will simply enter a new value as you've been directed. For example, if the Count value entry represented a flag, the data entry of 1 would indicate the flag is on (or true). To turn off the flag (switch it to false), you would replace the 1 with a 0.

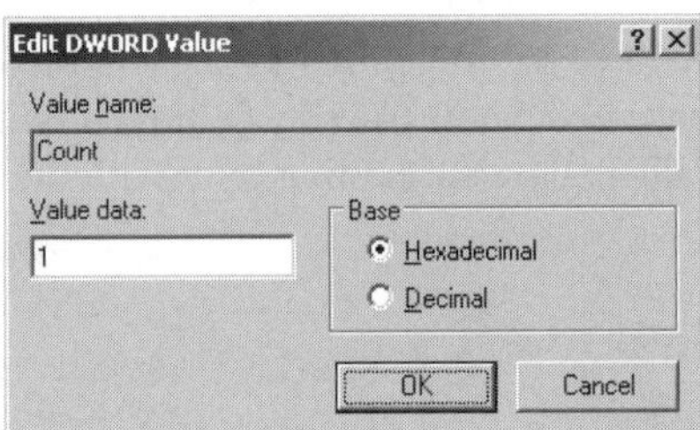

Figure 14-7. Using the Edit DWORD Value dialog box.

> **Tip** **Copy and paste using the Clipboard to get values right**
> The Windows Clipboard is available when you are working with Registry Editor. This means you can use copy, cut, and paste just as you do with other Windows programs. If there is a value in a Knowledge Base article that's difficult to type, you might want to copy it to the Clipboard and then paste it into the Value Data box of the Edit dialog box.

Adding Keys and Values

As noted previously, you can add or remove keys in most areas of the Registry. The exceptions pertain to the root node, the root keys, and areas of the Registry where permissions prohibit modifications.

You add new keys as subkeys of a selected key. Access the key with which you want to work, and then add the subkey by right-clicking the key and selecting New, Key. Registry Editor creates a new key and selects its name so that you can set it as appropriate. The default name is New Key #1.

The new key has a default value entry associated with it automatically. The data type for this default value is REG_SZ. Just about every key in the Registry has a similarly named and typed value entry, so don't delete this value entry. Either set its value by double-clicking it to display the Edit String dialog box, or create additional value entries under the selected key.

To create additional value entries under a key, right-click the key, then select one of these values:

- **String Value** Used to enter a fixed-length string of Unicode characters; type REG_SZ
- **Binary Value** Used to enter raw binary data without any formatting or parsing; type REG_BINARY
- **DWORD Value** Used to enter binary data type in which 4-byte integer values are stored; type REG_DWORD
- **Multi-String Value** Used to enter a multiple-parameter string; type REG_MULTI_SZ
- **Expandable String Value** Used to enter a variable-length string that can include environment variables that are to be expanded when the data is read; type REG_EXPAND_SZ

Creating a new value adds it to the selected key and gives it a default name of New Value #1, New Value #2, and so on. The name of the value is selected for editing so that you can change it immediately. After you change the value name, double-click the value name to edit the value data.

Removing Keys and Values

Removing keys and values from the Registry is easy but should never be done without careful forethought to the possible consequences. That said, you delete a key or value by selecting it, and then pressing the Delete key. Registry Editor will ask you to confirm the deletion. Once you do this, the key or value is permanently removed from the Registry.

Modifying the Registry of a Remote Machine

You can modify the Registry of remote computers without having to log on locally. To do this, select Connect Network Registry on the File menu in Registry Editor, then use the Select Computer dialog box to specify the computer with which you want to work. In most cases, all you must do is type the name of the remote computer and then click OK. If prompted, you might need to enter the user name and password of a user account that is authorized to access the remote computer.

Once you connect, you get a new icon for the remote computer under your My Computer icon. Double-click this icon to access the physical root keys on the remote computer (HKEY_LOCAL_MACHINE and HKEY_USERS). The logical root keys aren't available because they are either dynamically created or simply pointers to subsets of information from HKEY_LOCAL_MACHINE and HKEY_USERS. You can then edit the computer's Registry as necessary. When you are done, you can select Disconnect Network Registry on the File menu and then choose the computer from which you want to disconnect. Registry Editor will then close the Registry on the remote computer and break the connection.

When working with remote computers, you can also load or unload hives as discussed in the section "Loading and Unloading Hives" later in this chapter. If you're wondering why you would do this, the primary reason is to work with a specific hive, such as the hive that points to Jo Brown's user profile because she inadvertently changed the display mode to an invalid setting and can no longer access the computer locally. With her user profile data loaded, you could then edit the Registry to correct the problem and then save the changes so that she can once again log on to the system.

Importing and Exporting Registry Data

Sometimes you might find that it is necessary or useful to copy all or part of the Registry to a file. For example, if you've installed a service or component that requires extensive configuration, you might want to use it on another computer without having to go through the whole configuration process again. So, instead, you would install the service or component baseline on the new computer, then export the application's Registry settings from the previous computer, copy them over to the other computer, and then import the Registry settings so that the service or component is properly configured. Of course, this technique works only if the complete configuration of the service or component is stored in the Registry, but you can probably see how useful being able to import and export Registry data can be.

By using Registry Editor, it is fairly easy to import and export Registry data. This includes the entire Registry, branches of data stemming from a particular root key, and individual subkeys and the values they contain. When you export data, you create a .reg file that contains the designated Registry data. This Registry file is a script that can then be loaded back into the Registry of this or any other computer by importing it.

> **Note** Because the Registry script is written as standard text, you could view it and, if necessary, modify it in any standard text editor as well. Be aware, however, that double-clicking the .reg file launches Registry Editor, which prompts you as to whether you want to import the data into the Registry. If you are concerned about this, save the data to a file with the .hiv extension because double-clicking files with this extension won't start Registry Editor. Files with the .hiv extension must be manually imported (or you could simply change the file extension to .reg when it is time to use the data).

To export Registry data, right-click the branch or key you want to export, and then select Export. You can also right-click the root node for the computer you are working with, such as My Computer for a local computer, to export the entire Registry. Either way, you'll see the Export Registry File dialog box as shown in Figure 14-8. Use the Save In selection list to choose a save location for the .reg file, and then type a file name. The Export Range panel shows you the select branch within the Registry that will be exported. You can change this as necessary or select All to export the entire Registry. Then click Save to create the .reg file.

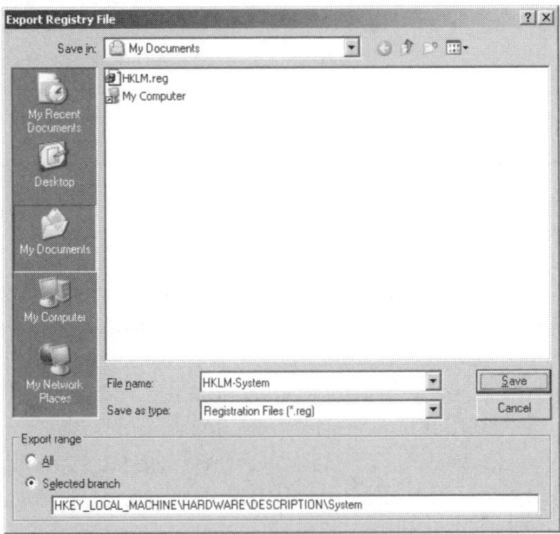

Figure 14-8. Exporting Registry data to a .reg file so that it can be saved and, if necessary, imported on this or another computer.

> **Tip Want to export the entire Registry quickly?**
> You can export the entire Registry at the command line by typing **regedit /e *SaveFile***, where *SaveFile* is the complete file path to the location where you want to save the copy of the Registry. For example, if you wanted to save a copy of the Registry to C:\Corpsvr06-regdata.reg, you would type **regedit /e C:\corpsvr06-regdata.reg**.

Importing Registry data adds the contents of the Registry script file to the Registry of the computer you are working with, either creating new keys and values if they didn't previously exist or overwriting keys and values if they did previously exist. You can import Registry data in one of two ways. You can double-click the .reg file, which starts Registry Editor and prompts you as to whether you want to import the data. Or you can select Import on the File menu, then use the Import Registry File dialog box to select and open the Registry data file you want to import.

Inside Out

Using export and import processes to distribute Registry changes

The export and import processes provide a convenient way to distribute Registry changes to users. You could, for example, export a subkey with an important configuration change and then mail the associated .reg file to users so they could import it simply by double-clicking it. Alternately, you could copy the .reg file to a network share where users could access and load it. Either way, you have a quick and easy way to distribute Registry changes. Officially, however, distributing Registry changes in this manner is frowned upon because of the potential security problems associated with doing so. The preferred technique is to distribute Registry changes through Group Policy as discussed in Part 7.

Loading and Unloading Hive Files

Just as you sometimes must import or export Registry data, you'll sometimes need to work with individual hive files. The most common reason for doing this, as discussed previously, is when you must modify a user's profile to correct an issue that prevents the user from accessing or using a system. Here, you would load the user's Ntuser.dat file into Registry Editor and then make the necessary changes. Another reason for doing this would be to change a particular part of the Registry on a remote system. For example, if you needed to repair an area of the Registry, you could load the related hive file into the Registry of another machine and then repair the problem on the remote machine.

Loading and unloading hives affects only HKEY_LOCAL_MACHINE and HKEY_USERS, and you can perform these actions only when one of these root keys is selected. Rather than replacing the selected root key, the hive you are loading then becomes a subkey of that root key. HKEY_LOCAL_MACHINE and HKEY_USERS are of course used to build all the logical root keys used on a system, so you could in fact work with any area of the Registry.

After you select either HKEY_LOCAL_MACHINE or HKEY_USERS in Registry Editor, you can load a hive for the current machine or another machine by selecting Load Hive on the File menu. Registry Editor then prompts you for the location and name of the previously saved hive file. Select the file, and then click Open. Afterward, enter a name for the key under which the hive will reside while it is loaded into the current system's Registry, and then click OK.

Note You can't work with hive files that are already being used by the operating system or another process. You could, however, make a copy of the hive and then work with it. At the command line, type **reg save** followed by the abbreviated name of the root key to save and the file name to use for the hive file. For example, you could type **reg save hkcu c:\curr-hkcu.hiv** to save HKEY_LOCAL_MACHINE to a file called Curr-hkcu.hiv on drive C. Although you can save the logical root keys (HKCC, HKCR, HKCU) in this manner, you can save only subkeys of HKLM and HKU using this technique.

When you are finished working with a hive, you should unload it to clear it out of memory. Unloading the hive doesn't save the changes you've made—as with any modifications to the Registry, your changes are applied automatically without the need to save them. To unload a hive, select it, and choose Unload Hive on the File menu. When prompted to confirm, click Yes.

Working with the Registry from the Command Line

If you want to work with the Registry from the command line, you can do so using the REG command. REG is run using the permissions of the current user and can be used to access the Registry on both local and remote systems. As with Registry Editor, you can work only with HKEY_LOCAL_MACHINE and HKEY_USERS on remote computers. These keys are, of course, used to build all the logical root keys used on a system, so you can in fact work with any area of the Registry on a remote computer.

REG has different subcommands for performing various Registry tasks. These commands include the following:

- REG ADD Adds a new subkey or value entry to the Registry
- REG COMPARE Compares Registry subkeys or value entries
- REG COPY Copies a Registry entry to a specified key path on a local or remote system
- REG DELETE Deletes a subkey or value entries from the Registry
- REG EXPORT Exports Registry data and writes it to a file

Note These files have the same format as files you export from Registry Editor. Typically, however, they are saved with the .hiv extension because double-clicking files with this extension won't start Registry Editor.

- REG IMPORT Imports Registry data and either creates new keys and value entries or overwrites existing keys and value entries
- REG LOAD Loads a Registry hive file
- REG QUERY Lists the value entries under a key and the names of subkeys (if any)

- **REG RESTORE** Writes saved subkeys and entries back to the Registry
- **REG SAVE** Saves a copy of specified subkeys and value entries to a file
- **REG UNLOAD** Unloads a Registry hive file

You can learn the syntax for using each of these commands by typing **reg** followed by the name of the subcommand you want to learn about and then **/?**. For example, if you wanted to learn more about REG ADD, you would type **reg add /?** at the command line.

Backing Up and Restoring the Registry

By now it should be pretty clear how important the Registry is and that it should be protected. I'll go so far as to say that part of every backup and recovery plan should include the Registry. Backing up and restoring the Registry isn't done from within Registry Editor, however. It is handled through the Windows Backup utility or through your preferred third-party backup software. Either way, you have an effective means to minimize downtime and ensure that the system can be recovered if the Registry becomes corrupted.

Choosing a Backup Method for the Registry

You can make a backup of the entire Registry very easily at the command line. Simply type **regedit /e *SaveFile***, where *SaveFile* is the complete file path to the save location for the Registry data. Following this, you could save a copy of the Registry to C:\Backups\Regdata.reg by typing **regedit /e c:\backups\regdata.reg**. You would then have a complete backup of the Registry.

You can also easily make backups of individual root keys. To do this, you use REG SAVE. Type **reg save** followed by the abbreviated name of the root key you want to save and the file name to use. For example, you could type **reg save hkcu c:\backups\hkcu.hiv** to save HKEY_CURRENT_USER to a file in the C:\Backups directory. Again, although you can save the logical root keys (HKCC, HKCR, HKCU) in this manner, you can save only subkeys of HKLM and HKU using this technique.

Okay, so now you have your fast and easy backups of Registry data. What you do not have, however, is a sure way to recover a system in the event the Registry becomes corrupted and the system cannot be booted. Partly this is because you have no way to boot the system to get at the Registry data.

In Windows NT, you created an Emergency Repair Disk (ERD) to help you recover the Registry and get a system to a bootable state. The ERD contained system data as well as Registry data that could be used to recover and boot a system. Some of this data was stored on a floppy disk and some of it was written to the %SystemRoot%\Repair directory.

In Windows Server 2003, Microsoft replaces the ERD with Automated System Recovery (ASR). ASR data includes essential system files, partition boot sector information, the startup environment, and Registry data. When you complete installation of a Windows Server 2003 system, basic recovery information is saved in %SystemRoot%\Repair. This basic data include a copy of the local SAM database and other essential system files but don't include a full backup of the Registry. At first opportunity, you should create a complete ASR backup. Whenever you apply a service pack or change device drivers, you should perform an ASR backup as well.

You can create ASR backups using the Backup utility provided with the operating system. When you do this, the recovery data is stored in two locations. The primary data is stored on the backup medium you choose, such as a tape backup device or hard disk drive. Additional information needed to boot the system and access the primary data is stored on a floppy disk.

By using the Windows Backup utility, you can also back up the entire system state. Although the system state data includes a copy of the system's Registry, this type of backup isn't used in the same way as an ASR backup. Normally, you back up the system state when you perform a normal (full) backup of the rest of the data on the system.

For systems that aren't domain controllers, the system state data includes essential boot files, key system files, and the COM+ class registration database as well as the Registry data. For domain controllers, the Active Directory database and System Volume (Sysvol) files are included as well. Thus, if you are performing a full recovery of a server rather than a repair, you use the complete system backup as well as system state data to recover the server completely. Performing full system backups is discussed in Chapter 41, "Backup and Recovery."

Creating Registry Backups

You create Registry backups by using the Backup utility. You can start Backup by typing **ntbackup** at the command line or in the Run dialog box or by clicking Start, pointing to Programs or All Programs, and selecting Accessories, System Tools, Backup. By default, Backup starts in wizard mode. To change this behavior, clear Always Start In Wizard Mode, and then click Advanced Mode. This takes you to the main Backup interface, as shown in the following screen:

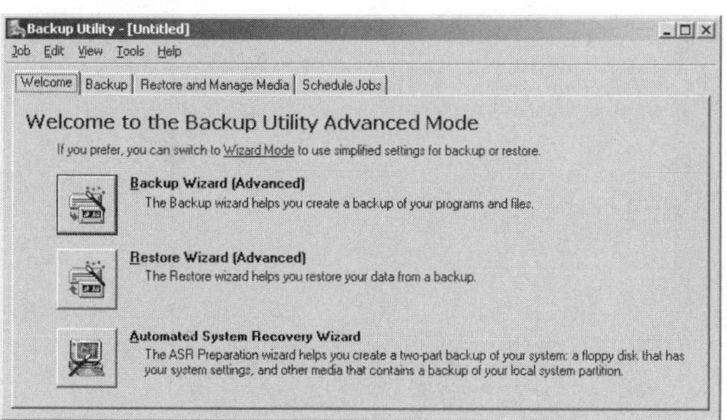

If you want to back up the Registry data along with the system state, select the Backup tab, then select the System State option, as shown in the following screen. You can then configure the rest of the backup as you would any other backup. This includes selecting the other data you want to back up, specifying the backup medium to use, and clicking Start Backup to begin the backup process—all of which is discussed in detail in Chapter 41. When you back up the system state, a backup copy of the Registry is also created in the %SystemRoot%\Repair directory.

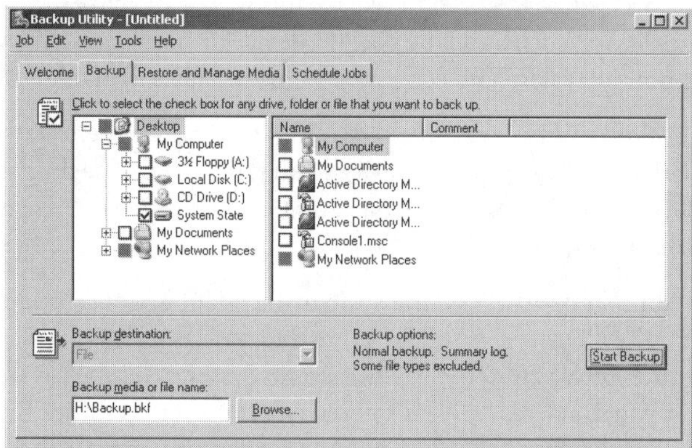

To make a backup for ASR, follow these steps:

1 Start the Backup utility in Advanced Mode, then click the Automated System Recovery Wizard button in the Welcome tab. This starts the Automated System Recovery Preparation Wizard, as shown in the following screen:

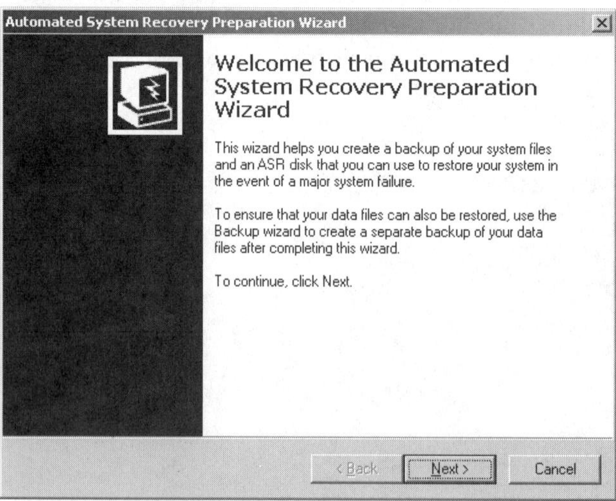

2. Click Next. Select a medium type for the primary ASR data, such as File, and then type the path to the backup medium or file to use.
3. Click Next, and then click Finish.
4. After the wizard creates the backup of the system files, you will be prompted to insert a floppy disk. The floppy disk and the primary backup data can then later be used to restore the system.

Recovering a System Using the ASR Backup

Microsoft recommends using ASR to recover a system only as a last resort. If you've tried other techniques to recover the system and haven't succeeded, use ASR. The ASR restoration process requires the backup medium with the primary ASR data, the ASR floppy disk, and the Windows Server 2003 distribution CD-ROM. You start the ASR recovery by booting the system off the installation CD-ROM. During the text portion of the setup, press F2. ASR then guides you through the recovery process, the exact details of which depend on the system you are recovering.

Note ASR performs a backup or restore only of essential system information. It doesn't back up or restore other data or the disk drives on the system. To back up or restore a system and all its data fully, you must follow the backup and restore procedures discussed in Chapter 41.

Tip **Recover domain controllers using a two-step process**
Domain controllers deserve special consideration during backup and recovery because they store a copy of Active Directory. Not only is additional information backed up when you save the system state, but the recovery of Active Directory requires a change in technique. For domain controllers, you must perform a two-step recovery process. First, you restore the Registry, which contains the local SAM so you can log on, and then you restore the Active Directory store.

Maintaining the Registry

The Registry is a database, and like any other database it works best when it is optimized. Optimize the Registry by reducing the amount of clutter and information it contains. This means uninstalling unnecessary system components, services, and applications. One way to uninstall components, services, and applications is to use the Add or Remove Programs utility in Control Panel. This utility allows you to remove Windows components and their related services safely as well as applications installed using the Windows Installer.

Most applications include uninstall utilities that attempt to remove the application, its data, and its Registry settings safely and effectively as well. Sometimes, however, applications either do not include an uninstall utility or for one reason or another do not fully remove their Registry settings, and this is where Registry maintenance utilities come in handy.

In the Windows Support Tools, you'll find two useful utilities for helping you maintain the Registry:

- Windows Installer CleanUp utility (Msicuu.exe)
- Windows Installer Zapper (Msizap.exe)

Both tools are designed to work with programs installed using the Windows Installer and must be run using an account with Administrator permissions. In addition to being able to clear out Registry settings for programs you've installed then uninstalled, you can also use these utilities to recover the Registry to the state it was in prior to a failed or inadvertently terminated application installation. This works as long as the application used the Windows Installer.

Using the Windows Installer CleanUp Utility

Windows Installer CleanUp Utility removes Registry settings for applications that were installed using the Windows Installer. It is most useful for cleaning up Registry remnants of applications that were partially uninstalled or whose uninstall failed. It is also useful for cleaning up applications that can't be uninstalled or reinstalled because of partial or damaged settings in the Registry. It isn't, however, intended to be used as an uninstaller because it won't clean up the applications files or shortcuts and will make it necessary to reinstall the application to use it again.

Note Keep in mind that the profile of the current user is part of the Registry. Because of this, Windows Installer CleanUp Utility will remove user-specific installation data from this profile. It won't, however, remove this information from other profiles.

If you've already installed the Support Tools, you can run this utility by typing **msicuu** at the command line. When the Windows Installer Clean Up Utility dialog box is displayed, as shown in the screen on the following page, select the program or programs to clean up, and then click Remove. The Windows Installer CleanUp Utility keeps a log file to record the applications that users delete in this manner. The log is stored in the %SystemDrive%\Documents and Settings\UserName\Local Settings\Temp directory and is named Msicuu.log.

Note The Windows Installer CleanUp Utility is a GUI for the Windows Installer Zapper discussed in the next section. When you use this utility, it runs the Windows Installer CleanUp Utility with the /T parameter to delete an application's Registry entries. It has an added benefit because it creates a log file, which is not used with Windows Installer Zapper.

Caution Windows Installer CleanUp Utility is meant to be used as a last resort only. Don't use this program if you can uninstall programs by other means.

Using the Windows Installer Zapper

The Windows Installer Zapper (Msizap.exe) is a command-line utility for removing Registry settings for applications that were installed using the Windows Installer. Like the Windows Installer CleanUp Utility, it can be used to clean up Registry settings for applications that were partially uninstalled or for which the uninstall failed, as well as applications that can't be uninstalled or reinstalled because of partial or damaged settings in the Registry. Additionally, it can be used to remove Registry settings related to failed installations or failed rollbacks of installations. It can also be used to correct failures related to multiple instances of a setup program running simultaneously and in cases when a setup program won't run.

The complete syntax for the Windows Installer Zapper is as follows:

```
msizap [*] [!] [A] [P] [S] [W] [T] [G] [AppToZap]
```

where

- **AppToZap** Specifies an application's product code or the file path to the application Windows Installer (.msi) program
- * Deletes all Windows Installer configuration information on the computer, including information stored in the Registry and on disk. Must be used with the ALLPRODUCTS flag

- ! Turns off warning prompts asking you to confirm your actions
- A Gives administrators Full Control permissions on the applicable Windows Installer data so that it can be deleted even if the administrator doesn't have specific access to the data
- P Deletes Registry information related to active installations
- S Deletes Registry information saved for rollback to the previous state
- T Used when you are specifying a specific application to clean up
- W Examines all user profiles for data that should be deleted
- G Removes orphaned Windows Installer files that have been cached for all users

Caution Windows Installer Zapper is meant as a last resort only. Don't use this program if you can uninstall programs by other means.

Removing Registry Settings for Active Installations That Have Failed

Application installations can fail during installation or after installation. When applications are being installed, an InProgress key is created in the Registry under the HKLM\SOFTWARE\Microsoft\Windows\CurrentVersion\Installer subkey. In cases when installation fails, the system might not be able to edit or remove this key, which could cause the application's setup program to fail the next time you try to run it. Running Windows Installer Zapper with the P parameter clears out the InProgress key, which should allow you to run the application's setup program.

After installation, applications rely on their Registry settings to configure themselves properly. If these settings become damaged or the installation becomes damaged, the application won't run. Some programs have a repair utility that can be accessed simply by rerunning the installation. During the repair process, the Windows Installer might attempt to write changes to the Registry to repair the installation or roll it back to get back to the original state. If this process fails for any reason, the Registry can contain unwanted settings for the application. Running Windows Installer Zapper with the S parameter clears out the rollback data for the active installation. Rollback data is stored in the HKLM\SOFTWARE\Microsoft\Windows\CurrentVersion\Installer\Rollback key.

Any running installation also has rollback data, so you typically use the P and S parameters together. This means you would type **msizap ps** at the command line.

Removing Partial or Damaged Settings for Individual Applications

When an application can't be successfully uninstalled you can attempt to clean up its settings from the Registry using the Windows Installer Zapper. To do this, you need to know the product code for the application or the full path to the Windows Installer file used to install the application. The installer file ends with the .msi extension and usually is found in one of the application's installation directories.

You then type **msizap t** followed by the product code or .msi file path. For example, if the installer file path is C:\Apps\KDC\KDC.msi, you would type **msizap t c:\apps\kdc\kdc.msi** at the command line to clear out the application's settings. Because the current user's profile is a part of the Registry, user-specific settings for the application will be removed from this profile. If you want to clear out these settings for all user profiles on the system, add the W parameter, such as **msizap wt c:\apps\kdc\kdc.msi**.

> **Note** If you use Run As, you can delete installer data and settings for a specific user rather than the current user or all users.

Securing the Registry

The Registry is a critical area of the operating system. It has some limited built-in security to reduce the risk of settings being inadvertently changed or deleted. Additionally, some areas of the Registry are available only to certain users. For example, HKLM\SAM and HKLM\SECURITY are available only to the LocalSystem user. This security in some cases might not be enough, however, to prevent unauthorized access to the Registry. Because of this, you might want to set tighter access controls than the default permissions, and you can do this from within the Registry. You can also control remote access to the Registry and configure access auditing.

Preventing Access to the Registry Utilities

One of the best ways to protect the Registry from unauthorized access is to make it so users can't access the Registry in the first place. For a server, this means tightly controlling physical security and allowing only administrators the right to log on locally. For other systems or when it isn't practical to prevent users from logging on locally to a server, you can configure the permissions on Regedit.exe and Reg.exe so that they are more secure. You could also remove Registry Editor and the REG command from a system, but this can introduce other problems and make managing the system more difficult, especially if you also prevent remote access to the Registry.

To modify permissions on Registry Editor, access the %SystemRoot% folder, right-click Regedit.exe, and then select Properties. In the Properties dialog box, select the Security tab, as shown in Figure 14-9. Add and remove users and groups as necessary, then set permissions as appropriate. Permissions work the same as with other types of files. You select an object and then allow or deny specific permissions. See Chapter 21, "File Sharing and Security," for details.

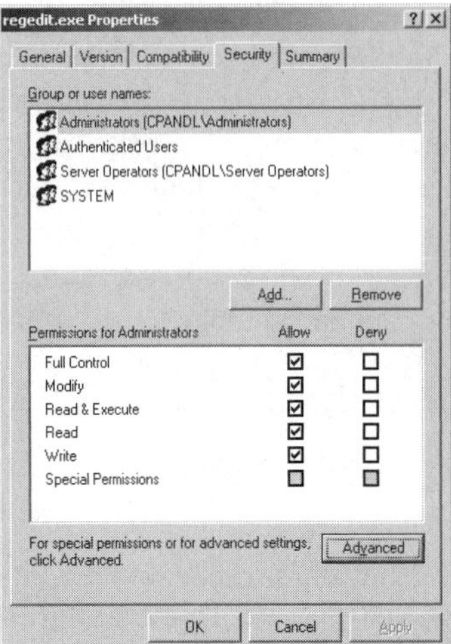

Figure 14-9. Tighten controls on Registry Editor to limit access to it.

To modify permissions on the REG command, access the %SystemRoot%\System32 folder, right-click Reg.exe, and then select Properties. In the Properties dialog box, select the Security tab. As Figure 14-10 shows, this command by default can be used by administrators, BATCH (scripts), INTERACTIVE (from the command line), SERVICE (LocalService user), and SYSTEM (LocalSystem user). Add and remove users and groups as necessary, then set permissions as appropriate.

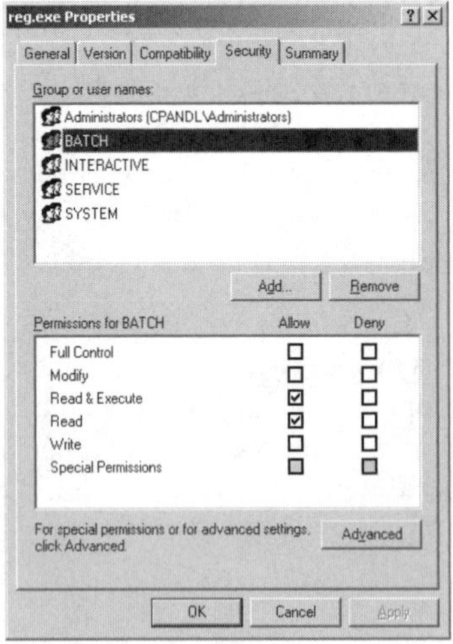

Figure 14-10. Reg.exe is designed to be used by administrators and to be run from the command line; its permissions reflect this.

> **Note** I'm not forgetting about Regedt32. It's only a link to Regedit.exe, so you don't really need to set its access permissions. The permission on Regedit.exe will apply regardless.

Applying Permissions to Registry Keys

Keys within the Registry have access permissions as well. Rather than editing these permissions directly, I recommend you use an appropriate security template as discussed in Chapter 38, "Managing Group Policy." Using the right security template locks down access to the Registry for you, and you won't have to worry about making inadvertent changes that will prevent systems from booting or applications from running.

That said, you might in some limited situations want to or have to change permissions on individual keys in the Registry. To do this, start Registry Editor and then navigate to the key you want to work with. When you find the key, right-click it, and select Permissions, or select the key, then choose Permissions on the Edit menu. This displays a Permissions For dialog box similar to the one shown in Figure 14-11. Permissions work the same as for files. You can add and remove users and groups as necessary. You can select an object and then allow or deny specific permissions.

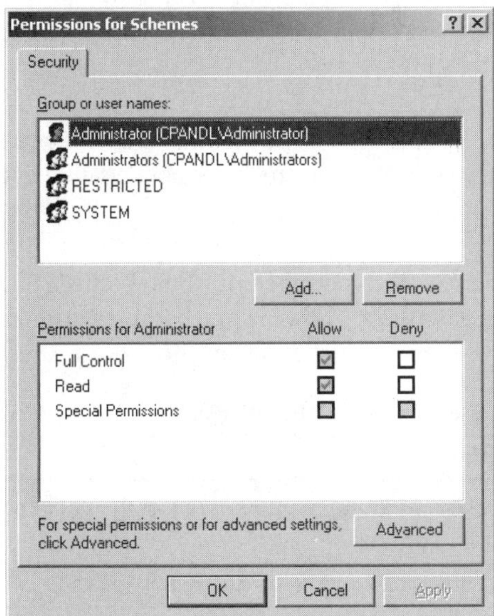

Figure 14-11. Use the Permissions For dialog box to set permissions on specific Registry keys.

Many permissions are inherited from higher-level keys and are unavailable. To edit these permissions, you must access the Advanced Security Settings dialog box by clicking the Advanced button. As Figure 14-12 shows, the Advanced Security Settings dialog box has four tabs:

- **Permissions** The Inherited From column in the Permissions tab shows from where the permissions are inherited. Usually, this is the root key for the key branch you are working with, such as CURRENT_USER. You can use the Add and Edit buttons in the Permissions tab to set access permissions for individual users and groups. Table 14-2 shows the individual permissions you can assign.

> **Caution** Before you click OK to apply changes, consider whether you should clear the Allow Inheritable Permissions From The Parent To Propagate option. If you don't do this, you'll change permissions on the selected key and all its subkeys.

- **Auditing** Allows you to configure auditing for the selected key. The actions you can audit are the same as the permissions listed in Table 14-2. See the section entitled "Registry Root Keys" earlier in this chapter.
- **Owner** Shows the current owner of the selected key and allows you to reassign ownership. By default, only the selected key is affected, but if you want the change to apply to all subkeys of the currently selected key, choose Replace Owner On Subcontainers And Objects.

> **Caution** Be sure you understand the implications of taking ownership of Registry keys. Changing ownership could inadvertently prevent the operating system or other users from running applications, services, or application components.

- **Effective Permissions** Lets you see which permissions would be given to a particular user or group based on the current settings. This is helpful because permission changes you make in the Permissions tab aren't applied until you click OK or Apply.

Table 14-2. Registry Permissions and Their Meanings

Permission	Meaning
Full Control	Allows user or group to perform any of the actions related to any other permission
Query Value	Allows querying the Registry for a subkey value
Set Value	Allows creating new values or modifying existing values below the specified key
Create Subkey	Allows creating a new subkey below the specified key

Table 14-2. Registry Permissions and Their Meanings

Permission	Meaning
Enumerate Subkey	Allows getting a list of all subkeys of a particular key
Notify	Allows registering a callback function that is triggered when the select value changes
Create Link	Allows creating a link to a specified key
Delete	Allows deleting a key or value
Write DAC	Allows writing access controls on the specified key
Write Owner	Allows taking ownership of the specified key
Read Control	Allows reading the discretionary access control list (DACL) for the specified key

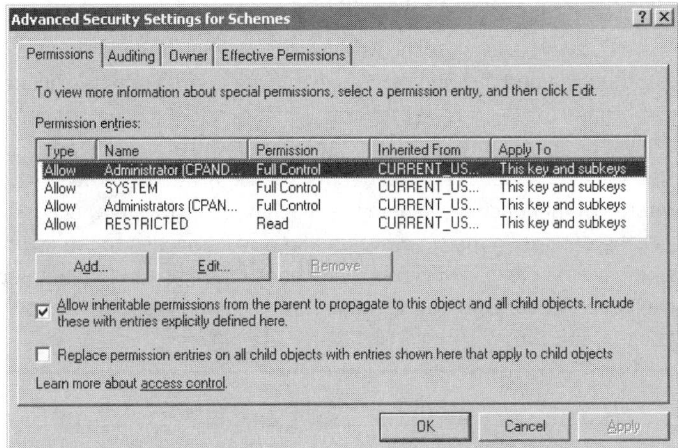

Figure 14-12. Use the Advanced Security Settings dialog box to change the way permissions are inherited or set and to view auditing settings, ownership, and effective permissions.

Controlling Remote Registry Access

Hackers and unauthorized users can attempt to access a system's Registry remotely just like you do. If you want to be sure they are kept out of the Registry, you can prevent remote Registry access. Remote access to a system's Registry is controlled by the Registry key HKLM\SYSTEM\CurrentControlSet\Control\SecurePipeServers\Winreg. If you want to limit remote access to the Registry, you can start by changing the permissions on this key.

If this key exists, then the following occurs:

1. Windows Server 2003 uses the permissions on the key to determine who can access the Registry remotely, and by default any authenticated user can do so. In fact, authenticated users have Query Value, Enumerate Subkeys, Notify, and Read Control permissions on this key.
2. Windows Server 2003 then uses the permissions on the keys to determine access to individual keys.

If this key doesn't exist, Windows Server 2003 allows all users to access the Registry remotely and uses the permissions on the keys only to determine which keys can be accessed.

Inside Out

Services might need remote access to the Registry

Some services require remote access to the Registry to function correctly. This includes the Directory Replicator service and the Spooler service. If you restrict remote access to the Registry, you must bypass the access restrictions. Either add the account name of the service to the access list on the Winreg key or list the keys to which services need access in the Machine or Users value under the AllowedPaths key. Both values are REG_MULTI_SZ strings. Paths entered in the Machine value allow machine (LocalSystem) access to the locations listed. Paths entered in the Users value allow users access to the locations listed. As long as there are no explicit access restrictions on these keys, remote access is granted. After you make changes, you must restart the computer so that Registry access can be reconfigured on startup.

Note Windows Server 2003 has an actual service called Remote Registry service. This service does in fact control remote access to the Registry. You want to disable this service only if you are trying to protect isolated systems from unauthorized access, such as when the system is in a perimeter network and is accessible from the Internet. If you disable Remote Registry service before starting the Routing and Remote Access service, you cannot view or change the Routing and Remote Access configuration. Routing and Remote Access reads and writes configuration information to the Registry, and any action that requires access to configuration information could cause Routing and Remote Access to stop functioning. To resolve this, stop the Routing and Remote Access service, start the Remote Registry service, and then restart the Routing and Remote Access service.

Auditing Registry Access

Access to the Registry can be audited as can access to files and other areas of the operating system. Auditing allows you to track which users access the Registry and what they're doing. All the permissions listed previously in Table 14-1 can be audited. However, you usually limit what you audit to only the essentials to reduce the amount of data that is written to the security logs and to reduce the resource burden on the affected server.

Before you can enable auditing of the Registry, you must enable the auditing function on the system you are working with. You can do this either through the server's local policy or through the appropriate Group Policy Object. The policy that controls auditing is Computer Configuration\Windows Settings\Security Settings\Local Policies\Auditing. For more information on auditing and Group Policy, see Chapter 21 and Chapter 38, respectively.

Once auditing is enabled for a system, you can configure how you want auditing to work for the Registry. This means configuring auditing for each key you want to track. Thanks to inheritance, this doesn't mean you have to go through every key in the Registry and enable auditing for it. Instead, you can select a root key or any subkey to designate the start of the branch for which you want to track access and then ensure the auditing settings are inherited for all subkeys below it (this is the default setting).

Say, for example, you wanted to audit access to HKLM\SAM and its subkeys. To do this, you would follow these steps:

1. After you locate the key in Registry Editor, right-click it, and select Permissions, or select the key, then choose Permissions on the Edit menu. This displays the Permissions For SAM dialog box.
2. In the Permissions For SAM dialog box, click the Advanced button.
3. In the Advanced Security Settings dialog box, select the Auditing tab.
4. Click Add to select a user or group whose access you want to track.
5. After you select the user or group, click OK. The Auditing Entry For SAM dialog box is displayed, as shown in Figure 14-13.

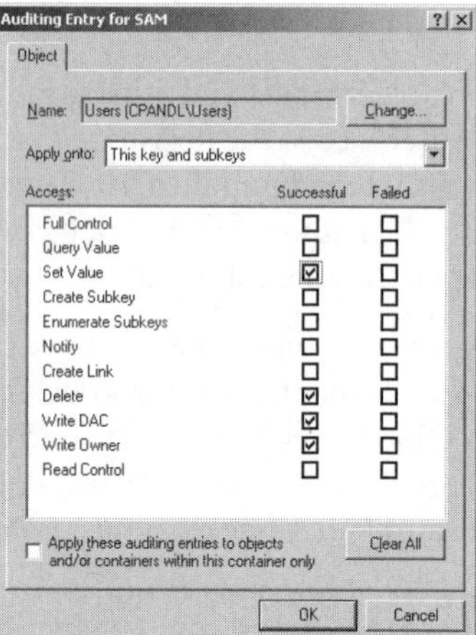

Figure 14-13. Use the Auditing Entry For dialog box to specify the permissions you want to track.

6. For each permission, select the type of auditing you want to track. If you want to track successful use of the permission, select the adjacent Successful option. If you want to track failed use of the permission, select the adjacent Failed option. Click OK to close the dialog box.
7. Repeat Step 6 to audit other users or groups.
8. If you want auditing to apply to subkeys, ensure the Allow Inheritable Permissions From The Parent To Propagate option is selected.
9. Click OK twice.

Chapter 15

Performance Monitoring and Tuning

Performance monitoring and tuning is the process of tracking system performance to establish baselines and to identify and resolve problems. When you install a server, you should create a performance baseline to see how the server is performing given its current resources and typical usage. If a server isn't performing as expected, is unresponsive, or is generating errors, you'll want to try to investigate. Many tools are designed to help you monitor server performance and troubleshoot performance issues. This chapter discusses the key tools for fine-tuning the system configuration, tracking system health, and troubleshooting the event logs. In the next chapter, you'll learn more about comprehensive monitoring techniques you can use for establishing performance baselines and pinpointing performance bottlenecks.

Tuning Performance, Memory Usage, and Data Throughput

Out of the box, Microsoft Windows Server 2003 is optimized for general network environments. The operating system might not, however, be optimized for the way a particular system is being used in your organization. You can often improve Windows operating system and application performance considerably simply by fine-tuning the way a system uses resources. While you are fine-tuning resource usage, you should also take a look at the server's data throughput configuration. Optimizing data throughput options can help ensure the server is configured appropriately to support user requests, file handles, and client connections.

Tuning Windows Operating System Performance

One of the reasons the Windows operating system no longer ships with 3D screen savers is that when these screen savers turn on, they use a considerable amount of processing power to render the 3D art. In some cases, the screen saver alone put the processor at 99 percent utilization, and you can probably imagine how well servers performed when the processor was maxed out. Similarly, you don't want the Windows operating system to tie up too much processing power displaying visual effects when administrators or other users are logged on to a server. So, if you're wondering why all the fancy visuals are turned off in the standard configuration of Windows Server 2003, this is why—the processing power is better used supporting the server's roles and applications than displaying fancy visuals to users that log on.

In most cases, you want to keep the visual effects to the bare minimum as per the default configuration after installation. This ensures that users who log on either locally or remotely won't severely impact the performance of the system just by logging on and displaying menus and dialog boxes. You can check or change the visual effects options by using the Performance Options dialog box. Click the Advanced tab in the System utility, and then click the Settings button in the Performance panel to display the Visual Effects tab in the Performance Options dialog box, as shown in the following screen:

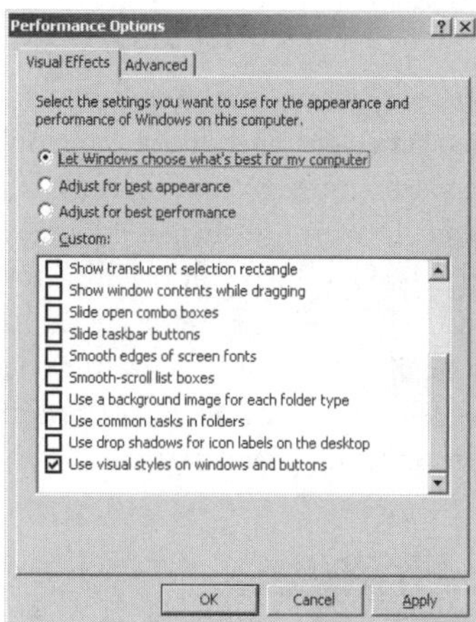

Tuning Processor Scheduling and Memory Usage

The way the Windows operating system performs for applications and installed services is determined by the processor-scheduling and memory usage configuration. Processor-scheduling options control how much processor resources are allocated to applications running on a server, which in turn determines the responsiveness of applications. You can optimize processor scheduling for the following application types:

- **Programs** When processor scheduling is optimized for programs, the active (foreground) application running on the system gets the best response time and the greatest share of available resources. Generally, you'll want to use this option only on development servers.

- **Background services** When processor scheduling is optimized for background services, all applications receive equal amounts of processor resources, and the active application doesn't get the best response time. Generally, you'll want to use this option for production servers.

Memory caching controls how much physical memory is reserved for the system cache, which in turn determines the way the system cache is used. You can optimize memory caching for the following application types:

- **Programs** When memory caching is optimized for programs, the operating system reserves less memory for the system cache and relies on applications to have their own cache. Generally, you'll want to use this option only on development servers, with the exception that you could use this setting on production servers that run services like IIS that can use their own separate cache.
- **System cache** When memory caching is optimized for the system cache, the operating system reserves more memory for the system cache. Generally, you'll want to use this option for production servers, particularly if installed applications don't maintain their own cache and instead rely on the system cache for their caching needs.

How Much Do the System Cache Settings Really Affect Performance?

The system cache settings affect servers much more than you might think. Consider the following example. A Microsoft Internet Information Services (IIS) server running Windows Server 2003 had 512 megabytes (MB) of random access memory (RAM). The IIS server was very busy and serviced a large Web site with many pages.

With memory caching optimized for system cache, the server reserved approximately 140 MB of RAM for the system cache. IIS reserves 50 percent of the available RAM for its file cache, which in this case was about 186 MB of RAM (half the 372 MB that remained). By using this setting, the server performed well but not as good as was expected.

With memory caching optimized for programs, the server reserved approximately 72 MB of RAM for the system cache, which freed up an additional 68 MB of RAM for applications. This allowed IIS to reserve 220 MB of RAM (50 percent of the available 440 MB of RAM) for its file cache. The server performed considerably better because it had more RAM available for file cache and had to access the disk less often. The downside of this approach however is that the smaller system cache can negatively affect the performance of other services running on the server, so a more practical solution would be to choose the system cache option and add more RAM.

You can check or change processor-scheduling and memory usage configuration by using the Advanced tab of the Performance Options dialog box. Click the Advanced tab in the System utility, and then click the Settings button in the Performance panel to display the Performance Options dialog box. Then select the Advanced tab, as shown in the following screen, in the Performance Options dialog box.

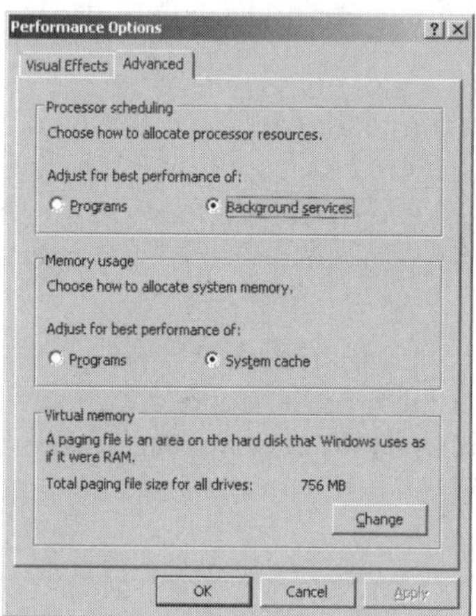

Tuning Data Throughput

Behind the scenes when you optimize the way a server uses system cache, the server makes several assumptions about how it should be configured to handle user requests, file handles, and client connections, collectively referred to as *data throughput* options. If the server is configured to adjust for best performance of the system cache, the system increases the amount of memory reserved for the system cache and it maximizes data throughput for file sharing. Here, the server dedicates as many resources as possible to handling user requests, file handles, and client connections. This improves responsiveness and can also improve performance for user, file, and client actions and should be used with Active Directory, file, print, and Network And Communications servers.

If the server is configured to adjust for best performance of programs, the system reduces the amount of memory reserved for the system cache and it maximizes data throughput for network applications. Here, the server optimizes itself for distributed applications that manage their own memory cache, such as IIS and Microsoft SQL Server. This reduces the size of the system cache because fewer resources are allocated for user requests, file handles, and client connections and should be used with application, Web, and streaming media servers.

In most cases, these data throughput configurations work well. However, if servers have mixed usage, such as a server that provides Active Directory services and application services, you might need to change the data throughput options. Usually this means configuring the server to balance the needs of the mixed-usage environment. When the server attempts to balance data throughput, it allocates some additional resources for handling requests, file handles, and client connections, but not as much as when it is configured to maximize data throughput for file sharing.

You might also find that you want the server to reserve as little memory as possible for data throughput. In this minimal-memory configuration, you free up memory for other purposes, but the server is set to serve a small number of users.

Data throughput is optimized by using File and Printer Sharing for Microsoft Networks. You access this networking component by using the system's Local Area Connections Properties dialog box. Servers with multiple network adapters have multiple network connections, and you should optimize each of the related local area network connections as appropriate.

To get started, access Network Connections in Control Panel. Right-click Local Area Connection, and then select Properties. This displays the Properties dialog box. In this dialog box, double-click File And Printer Sharing For Microsoft Networks to display the File And Printer Sharing For Microsoft Networks dialog box, as shown in the following screen. In the Server Optimization tab, select the appropriate optimization setting, and then click OK. You must reboot the server for these changes to take effect.

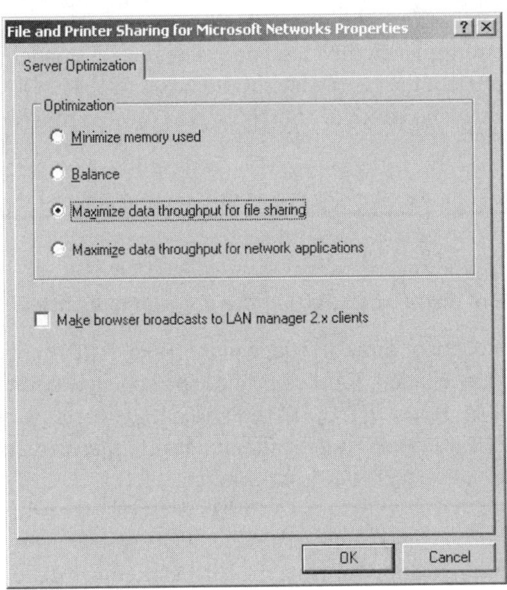

Tuning Virtual Memory

Windows Server 2003 uses virtual memory to allow a system to page parts of memory to disk. This makes it possible for a system to create a paging file on disk and use more memory space than is physically available. All servers have an initial paging file. It is created automatically on the drive containing the operating system during installation and setup.

In some cases, you can improve a server's performance by optimizing the way the paging file is used. You can configure the size of the paging file so that it is optimal given the server's RAM and usage. Although Windows Server 2003 can expand paging files incrementally as needed, you'll want to size the paging file so that it is as large as it needs to be for average usage conditions. This helps reduce fragmentation of data within the paging file and also keeps the server from having to expand the paging file continually.

You can also fix the paging file size so that the server needn't spend any resources expanding the paging file. If you do this, I recommend setting the total paging file size so that it's twice the physical RAM size on the system (the default paging file size is 1.5 times RAM). For instance, on a server with 512 MB of RAM, you could configure the paging file to use 1024 MB. This is a general rule of thumb, however, and not an absolute. On servers with 2 gigabytes (GB) or more of RAM, it's best to follow the hardware manufacturer's guidelines for setting the paging file size.

If a server has multiple hard disk drives, you might consider creating a paging file for each physical hard disk drive on the system. Multiple paging files can incrementally improve the performance of virtual memory on SMP machines with eight or more processors and a large amount of RAM. When you use multiple paging files, you create several smaller paging files rather than one big one. For example, if the paging file should be set to 1024 MB of RAM and the system has two disk drives, you could configure both drives to use a paging file 512 MB in size.

Inside Out

Consider the RAID configuration of disks when setting the paging file location

You should always consider the redundant array of independent disks (RAID) configuration of disks when setting the paging file location. RAID configurations can slow down read/write performance for the paging file. By using RAID 1, you typically get better write performance than RAID 5. By using RAID 5, you typically get better read performance than RAID 1. So, there's a trade-off to be made with either RAID configuration.

You can manage the paging file configuration by using the Virtual Memory dialog box. Click the Advanced tab in the System utility, and then click the Settings button in the Performance panel to display the Performance Options dialog box. Then select the Advanced tab in the

Performance Options dialog box, and click Change in the Virtual Memory panel, as shown in the following screen.

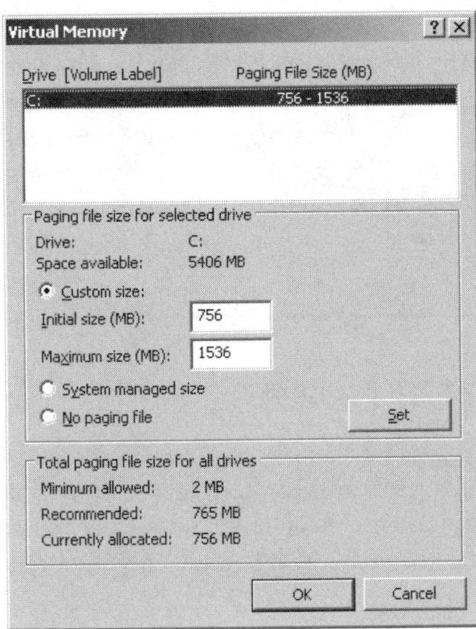

The upper section of the Virtual Memory dialog box shows the current paging file location and size. The initial paging file size is shown followed by a dash, and then the maximum size is shown. If the paging file has a size that can be incremented, the initial and maximum sizes will be different, such as 768–1536 MB. If the paging file has a fixed size (recommended), the initial and maximum sizes will be the same, such as 1024–1024 MB.

Selecting a disk drive in the top portion of the Virtual Memory dialog box allows you to configure whether and how the paging file is used. Usually, you want to select Custom Size and then set the Initial Size and Maximum Size options. Then click Set to apply the changes before you configure another disk drive. When you are finished configuring paging file usage, click OK. You then will be prompted to restart the server for the changes to take effect. Click OK. When you close the System utility, you will be prompted to restart the system for the changes to take effect. Click Yes to restart the computer now, or click No if you plan to restart the server later.

> **Caution** Don't set the total paging file size to 0 MB. As you set the paging file for individual drives, pay particular attention to the Total Paging File Size For All Drives information. You don't want to configure a server so that the Currently Allocated value is 0 MB. This means no paging file is configured, and it will drastically reduce the server's performance.

Troubleshooting

Be careful when setting or moving the paging file

Some documentation recommends that you move the paging file from the system drive to a different drive to improve performance. Don't do this without understanding the implications of doing so. The paging file is also used for debugging purposes when a Stop error occurs. On the system volume, the initial size of the paging file must be as large as the current physical RAM. If it isn't, Windows Server 2003 won't be able to write Stop information to the system drive when fatal errors occur. Because of this, my recommendation is to leave the paging file on the system drive.

Tracking a System's General Health

The fastest, easiest way to track a system's general health is to use Task Manager or Process Resource Monitor. Unlike some of the other performance tools that require some preparation before you can use them, you can start and use these tools without any preparation. This makes them very useful when you want to see what's going on with a system right now.

Task Manager and Process Resource Monitor Essentials

By using Task Manager, you can track running applications and processes and determine resource usage. This can help you understand how a server is performing and whether there are any problems, such as applications that aren't running or processes that are hogging system resources. Task Manager is available on both workstations and servers by pressing Ctrl+Alt+End.

To work with Task Manager, the key issue you must understand is the distinction between an application, an image name, and a process. Basically, the executable name of an application, such as Taskmgr.exe, is known to the operating system as its *image name,* and any time that you start an application the operating system starts one or more processes to support it. As Figure 15-1 shows, Task Manager has five tabs:

- **Applications** Shows programs run in a user context on the system and displays whether they're running or not responding. Also allows you to interact with applications and halt their execution
- **Processes** Lists the image name of the processes running on the system, including those run by the operating system and users. Includes usage statistics for system resources allocated to each process and allows you to interact with and stop processes
- **Performance** Displays current processor and memory usage. Includes graphs as well as detailed statistics

- **Networking** Displays current network usage for each of the system's connections to the network
- **Users** Details the users currently logged on to the system. Includes local users as well as users connected through Remote Desktop sessions and allows you to disconnect, log off, and send console messages to these users

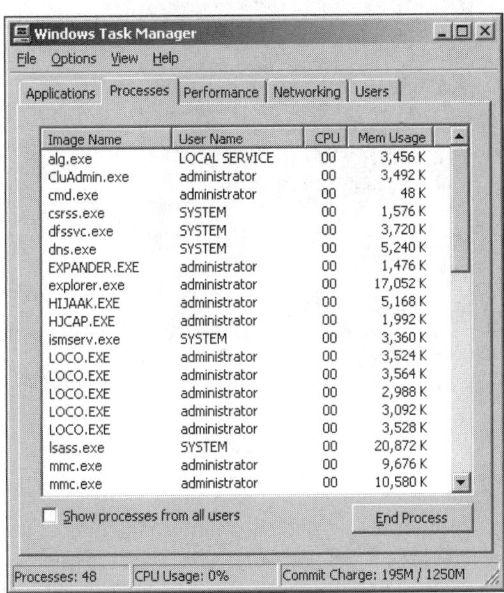

Figure 15-1. Use the Task Manager to track running applications and processes and to determine resource usage.

> **Caution** Task Manager uses system resources while it's running. Because of this, you should run it only while you are tracking performance.

No single command-line tool performs all the same functions as Task Manager. The closest tool in functionality is Process Resource Manager (Pmon.exe). Pmon is included in the Support Tools and performs the following tasks:

- Displays current processor and memory usage
- Lists the image name of the processes running on the system
- Shows current per-process resource usage statistics and activity

As Figure 15-2 shows, Pmon is much more detailed than the default Task Manager view, especially when it comes to current per-process resource usage and activity. To run Pmon, access a command prompt, and then type **pmon**.

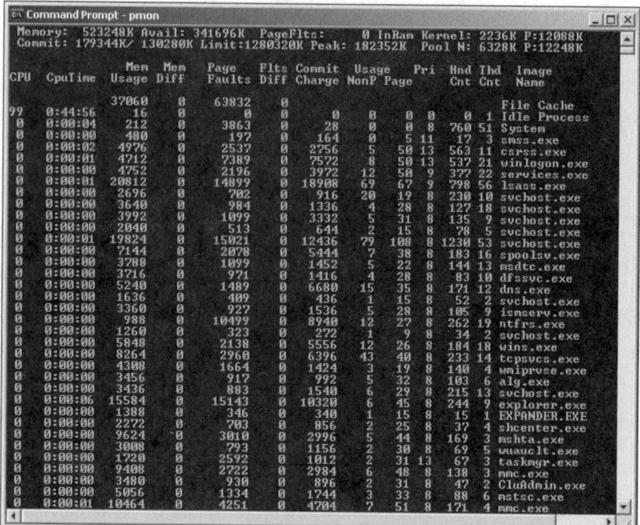

Figure 15-2. Use the Process Resource Manager to track running applications and processes and to determine resource usage.

> **Tip** **Use Pmon to reduce resource usage**
> Because Pmon is a text-based rather than graphical utility, it will, in most cases, use fewer system resources than Task Manager. On systems for which you are very concerned about resource usage and the possibility of bogging down a system by tracking performance information, you might initially want to start tracking performance by using Pmon.

Unlike most commands that run and then exit, Pmon runs continuously until you press the Q key to quit. While it is running, Pmon gathers resource and process statistics every 5 seconds and redisplays them automatically. If you press any key other than Q, Pmon updates the statistics, allowing for more frequent refreshes if desired. Like Task Manager, Pmon can be run only locally, so if you wanted to work with a remote system, you must start a Remote Desktop Connection.

The sections that follow discuss how to use these tools to gather information about systems and resolve problems. The focus of the discussion is on Task Manager, which should be your primary tool for tracking a system's general health.

Getting Processor and Memory Usage for Troubleshooting

The Performance tab in Task Manager, shown in Figure 15-3, should be the first tab you check if you suspect a performance issue with a system. It shows current processor and memory usage and also graphs some historical usage statistics based on data collected since you started Task Manager.

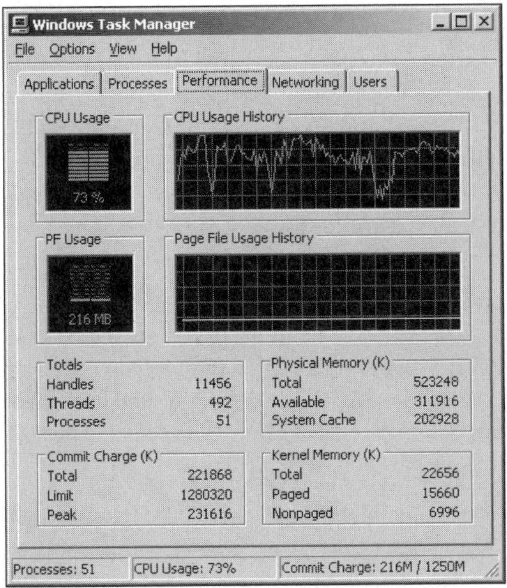

Figure 15-3. The Performance tab provides a summary of current processor and memory usage as well as some historical usage statistics based on data collected since you started Task Manager.

Some of the performance data is fairly self-explanatory. The CPU Usage and CPU Usage History graphs show the percentage of processor resources being used. The PF Usage and Page File Usage History graphs show the size of the paging file being used by the system. The paging file is an area of memory written to disk, also referred to as virtual memory. The tough data to interpret here is the information below the graphs.

Totals shows summary statistics for input/output (I/O), threads, and processes. Handles shows the number of I/O file handles in use. Because each handle requires system memory to maintain, this is important to note. Threads shows the number of threads in use. Threads allows concurrent execution of process requests. Processes shows the number of processes in use.

Commit Charge shows how much memory is committed to processes currently and is not available for other processes. Total lists all physical and virtual memory currently in use. Limit lists the total physical and virtual memory available. Peak lists the maximum memory used by the system since it was started.

Physical Memory shows the total RAM on the system. Total shows the amount of physical RAM. Available shows the RAM not currently being used and available for use. System Cache shows the amount of memory used for system caching.

Kernel Memory shows the memory used by the operating system kernel. Total lists all memory being used by the operating system kernel, including physical memory (RAM) and virtual memory. Nonpaged reflects memory used by the operating system kernel that can't be written to disk. Paged reflects memory that can be paged to virtual memory if necessary.

In Figure 15-3 on the previous page, you see an example of a system with moderate to fairly high central processing unit (CPU) usage but with very little ongoing paging file activity. A system with CPU usage consistently at these levels would warrant some additional monitoring to determine whether resources should be added to the system. Basically, you'd want to determine whether these were average usage conditions or whether you were seeing peak usage.

If these are average usage conditions, increasing the processor speed or adding processors could improve performance and allow for better handling of peak usage situations. If these statistics represent peak usage conditions, the system probably wouldn't need additional resources. Sometimes the CPU usage can be high if the system has too little memory as well. A quick check of the memory usage of the server, including its current and peak usage, shows, however, that this isn't the case for this particular system.

Figure 15-4 shows performance data for a different system. This system has high CPU usage and in many cases, CPU usage is at 100 percent. If CPU usage were consistent at 100 percent, I might suspect a runaway process and look for a process that is causing the problem. Here, however, there are times when CPU usage isn't maxed out, and you'd definitely want to take a closer look at what's going on starting with memory usage. One thing to note right away is that the system has very little available RAM—around 45 MB—and the paging file (as shown in the Commit Charge section) is quite large—around 550 MB.

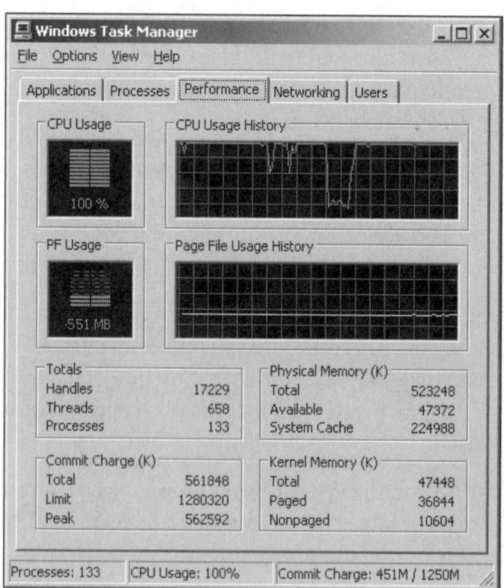

Figure 15-4. Heavy activity on the system is causing CPU usage to soar and in many cases to max out.

Such a small amount of available RAM would be a concern, and if this level of usage were consistent, you might consider changing the way applications use RAM, adding RAM, or both. Such a large amount of virtual memory being used (relative to available physical RAM) is also an area of possible concern that might make you consider adding physical RAM. Although increasing the amount of RAM could offer some relief to the CPU, it might not be enough, so you could consider increasing the processor speed or adding processors. You might also consider offloading some of the system's load. For example, you could move one of its roles or applications to a different server.

Getting Information on Running Applications

The Applications Tab in Task Manager, shown in Figure 15-5, lists applications being run by users on the computer along with status details that show whether the applications are running or not responding. If an application has an open file, such as a Microsoft Word document, the name of the file is shown as well.

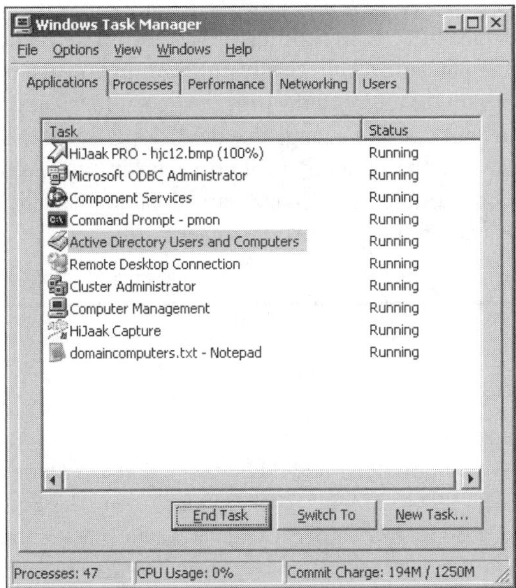

Figure 15-5. Task Manager tracks applications users are running in the Applications tab.

To work with an application, select it by clicking it in the Task list. You can then right-click the application name to select the Switch To, Bring To Front, Minimize, or Maximize options. Don't overlook the usefulness of the Go To Process option when you right-click: Use this when you're trying to find the primary process for a particular application because selecting this option highlights the related process in the Processes tab.

If you see an application with a status of Not Responding, that's an indicator that an application might be frozen, and you might want to select it and then click End Task. Keep in mind that the Not Responding message can also be an indicator that an application is busy and should be left alone until it finishes. Generally, don't use End Task to stop an application that is running without errors. Instead, select the Switch To option to switch to the application and then exit as you normally would.

Monitoring and Troubleshooting Processes

You can view information about processes running on a system by using the Processes tab of Task Manager or by running Pmon. The Task Manager display differs greatly from the output provided by Pmon. By default, the Processes tab shows only processes run by the operating system, local services, network services, and the interactive user. The interactive user is the user account logged on to the local console. To see processes run by remote users, such as those users connecting by using a Remote Desktop Connection, you must select the Show Processes From All Users option.

The default view of the Processes tab shows each running process by image name and user name. The CPU column shows the percentage of processor utilization for each process. The Mem Usage column shows the amount of memory the process is currently using. By default, processes are sorted by user name, but you can change this by clicking any of the available column headers to sort the information based on that column. Clicking again on the same column reverses the sort order. For example, click Image Name to alphabetically sort the image names. Click Image Name again to reverse sort the image names.

Troubleshooting

Isolate 32-bit or 64-bit processes

By default, 32-bit Windows systems show both 16-bit and 32-bit tasks that are running on the system, and 64-bit systems show both 32-bit and 64-bit tasks that are running on the system. To show only 32-bit tasks on 32-bit systems, click Options, then click Show 16-Bit Tasks. To show only 64-bit tasks on 64-bit systems, click Options, then click Show 32-Bit Tasks. This should clear the option for the related item on the Option menu.

As you may recall from Figure 15-2, Pmon shows much more detailed information for each process. This information is useful for troubleshooting. If you click View and choose Select Columns, you'll see a dialog box that allows you to add columns to the Processes tab. To get the additional information shown by Pmon, the following columns should be selected:

- Image Name
- CPU Usage

- CPU Time
- Memory Usage Delta
- Page Faults
- Page Faults Delta
- Virtual Memory Size
- Paged Pool
- Nonpaged Pool
- Base Priority
- Handle Count
- Thread Count

You will then have a process display like the one shown in Figure 15-6.

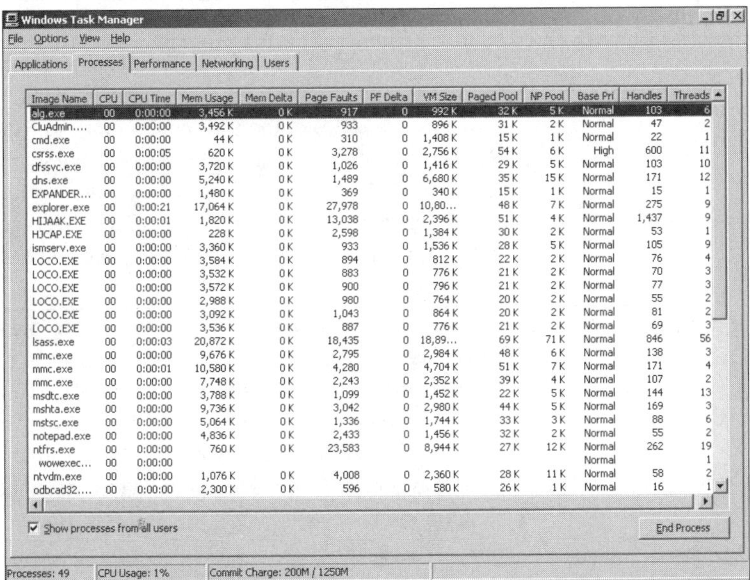

Image Name	CPU	CPU Time	Mem Usage	Mem Delta	Page Faults	PF Delta	VM Size	Paged Pool	NP Pool	Base Pri	Handles	Threads
alg.exe	00	0:00:00	3,456 K	0 K	917	0	992 K	32 K	5 K	Normal	103	6
CluAdmin....	00	0:00:00	3,492 K	0 K	933	0	896 K	31 K	2 K	Normal	47	2
cmd.exe	00	0:00:00	44 K	0 K	310	0	1,408 K	15 K	1 K	Normal	22	1
csrss.exe	00	0:00:05	620 K	0 K	3,278	0	2,756 K	54 K	6 K	High	600	11
dfssvc.exe	00	0:00:00	3,720 K	0 K	1,026	0	1,416 K	29 K	5 K	Normal	103	10
dns.exe	00	0:00:00	5,240 K	0 K	1,489	0	6,680 K	35 K	15 K	Normal	171	12
EXPANDER...	00	0:00:00	1,480 K	0 K	369	0	340 K	15 K	1 K	Normal	15	1
explorer.exe	00	0:00:21	17,064 K	0 K	27,978	0	10,80...	48 K	7 K	Normal	275	9
HIJAAK.EXE	00	0:00:01	1,820 K	0 K	13,038	0	2,396 K	51 K	4 K	Normal	1,437	9
HJCAP.EXE	00	0:00:00	228 K	0 K	2,598	0	1,384 K	30 K	2 K	Normal	53	1
ismserv.exe	00	0:00:00	3,360 K	0 K	933	0	1,536 K	28 K	5 K	Normal	105	9
LOCO.EXE	00	0:00:00	3,584 K	0 K	894	0	812 K	22 K	2 K	Normal	76	4
LOCO.EXE	00	0:00:00	3,532 K	0 K	883	0	776 K	21 K	2 K	Normal	70	3
LOCO.EXE	00	0:00:00	3,572 K	0 K	900	0	796 K	21 K	2 K	Normal	77	3
LOCO.EXE	00	0:00:00	2,988 K	0 K	980	0	764 K	20 K	2 K	Normal	55	2
LOCO.EXE	00	0:00:00	3,092 K	0 K	1,043	0	864 K	20 K	2 K	Normal	81	2
LOCO.EXE	00	0:00:00	3,536 K	0 K	887	0	776 K	21 K	2 K	Normal	69	3
lsass.exe	00	0:00:03	20,872 K	0 K	18,435	0	18,89...	69 K	71 K	Normal	846	56
mmc.exe	00	0:00:00	9,676 K	0 K	2,795	0	2,984 K	48 K	6 K	Normal	138	3
mmc.exe	00	0:00:01	10,580 K	0 K	4,280	0	4,704 K	51 K	7 K	Normal	171	4
mmc.exe	00	0:00:00	7,748 K	0 K	2,243	0	2,352 K	39 K	4 K	Normal	107	2
msdtc.exe	00	0:00:00	3,788 K	0 K	1,099	0	1,452 K	22 K	5 K	Normal	144	13
mshta.exe	00	0:00:00	9,736 K	0 K	3,042	0	2,980 K	44 K	5 K	Normal	169	3
mstsc.exe	00	0:00:00	5,064 K	0 K	1,336	0	1,744 K	33 K	3 K	Normal	88	6
notepad.exe	00	0:00:00	4,836 K	0 K	2,433	0	1,456 K	32 K	2 K	Normal	55	2
ntfrs.exe	00	0:00:00	760 K	0 K	23,583	0	8,944 K	27 K	12 K	Normal	262	19
wowexec...	00	0:00:00								Normal		1
ntvdm.exe	00	0:00:00	1,076 K	0 K	4,008	0	2,360 K	28 K	11 K	Normal	58	2
odbcad32....	00	0:00:00	2,300 K	0 K	596	0	580 K	26 K	1 K	Normal	16	1

Figure 15-6. The Processes tab provides detailed information on running processes according to image name and user name.

> **Tip** For multiprocessor systems, you can configure the CPU history to show one graph per CPU or one graph for all CPUs. To change this behavior, click View, point to CPU History, and then choose a viewing style.

Okay, so now that you've added all these extra columns of information, you are probably wondering what it all means and why you want to track it. As stated previously, you primarily use this information for troubleshooting. It helps you pinpoint which processes are hogging system resources and the type of resources the resource hogs are using. Once you know what's going on with processes, you can modify the system or its applications accordingly to resolve a performance problem.

Table 15-1 summarizes the information provided by the process statistics. The value in parentheses following the Task Manager column name is the name of the corresponding column in Pmon. If by monitoring processes you notice what looks like a problem, you will probably want to start more detailed monitoring of the system. One tool to consider is System Monitor, which is discussed in Chapter 16, "Comprehensive Performance Analysis and Logging." You can also stop processes that you suspect aren't running properly. To do this, right-click the process, and choose End Process to stop the process or End Process Tree to stop the process as well as any other processes it started.

Table 15-1. Process Statistics and How They Can Be Used

Column Name	Description
CPU (CPU)	Shows the percentage of CPU utilization for the process. The System Idle Process shows what percentage of CPU power is idle. A 99 in the CPU column for the System Idle Process means 99 percent of the system resources currently aren't being used. If the system has low idle time (meaning high CPU usage) during peak or average usage, you might consider upgrading to faster processors or adding processors.
CPU Time (CpuTime)	Shows the total amount of CPU time used by the process since it was started. Click the column header to quickly see the processes that are using the most CPU time. If a process is using a lot of CPU time, the related application might have a configuration problem. This could also indicate a runaway or nonresponsive process that is unnecessarily tying up the CPU.
Mem Usage (Mem Usage)	Shows the amount of memory the process is currently using. If memory usage for a process slowly grows over time and doesn't go back to the baseline value, this can be an indicator of a memory leak.
Mem Delta (Mem Diff)	Shows the change in memory usage for the process recorded since the last update. A constantly changing memory delta can be an indicator that a process is in use, but it could also indicate a problem. Generally, the memory delta might show increasing memory usage when a process is being used and then show a negative delta (indicated by parentheses in Task Manager) as activity slows.

Table 15-1. Process Statistics and How They Can Be Used

Column Name	Description
Page Faults (Page Faults)	Shows page faults caused by the process. Page faults occur when a process requests a page in memory and the system can't find it at the requested location. If the requested page is elsewhere in memory, the fault is called a *soft page fault*. If the requested page must be retrieved from disk, the fault is called a *hard page fault*. Most processors can handle large numbers of soft faults. Hard faults, on the other hand, can cause significant delays. If there are a lot of hard faults, you might need to increase the amount of memory or reduce the system cache size.
PF Delta (Flts Diff)	Shows the change in the number of page faults for the process recorded since the last update. As with memory usage, you might see an increase in page faults when a process is active and then a decrease as activity slows.
VM Size (Commit Charge)	Shows the amount of virtual memory allocated to and reserved for a process. Virtual memory is memory on disk and is slower to access than pooled memory. By configuring an application to use more physical RAM, you might be able to increase performance. To do this, however, the system must have available RAM. If it doesn't, other processes running on the system might slow down.
Paged Pool (Usage Page)	Shows paged pool memory usage. The paged pool is an area of RAM for objects that can be written to disk when they aren't used. As process activity increases, so does the amount of pool memory the process uses. Most processes have more paged pool than nonpaged pool requirements.
NP Pool (Usage NonP)	Shows nonpaged pool memory usage. The nonpaged pool is an area of RAM for objects that can't be written to disk. You should note processes that require a high amount of nonpaged pool memory. If there isn't enough free memory on the server, these processes might be the reason for a high level of page faults.
Base Pri (Pri)	Shows the priority of the process. Priority determines how much of the system resources are allocated to a process. The standard priorities are Low (4), Below Normal (6), Normal (8), Above Normal (10), High (13), and Real-Time (24). Most processes have a Normal priority by default, and the highest priority is given to real-time processes.

Table 15-1. Process Statistics and How They Can Be Used

Column Name	Description
Handles (Hnd Cnt)	Shows the number of file handles maintained by the process. The number of handles used is an indicator of how dependent the process is on the file system. Some processes have thousands of open file handles. Each file handle requires system memory to maintain.
Threads (Thd Cnt)	Shows the number of threads that the process is using. Most server applications are multithreaded, which allows concurrent execution of process requests. Some applications can dynamically control the number of concurrently executing threads to improve application performance. Too many threads, however, can actually reduce performance, because the operating system has to switch thread contexts too frequently.

Getting Network Usage Information

As Figure 15-7 shows, the Networking tab in Task Manager displays current network usage for each of the system's connections to the network.

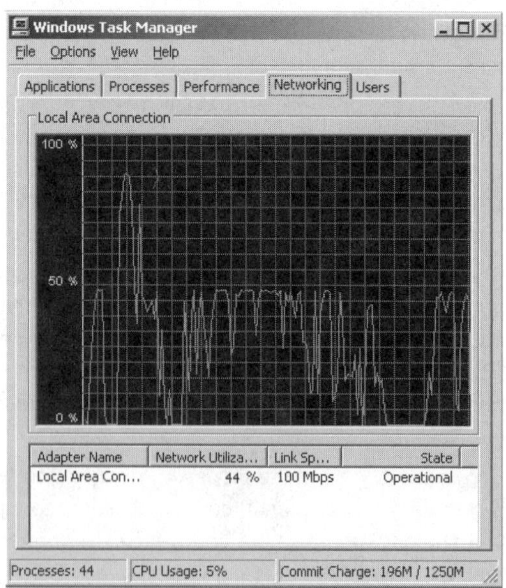

Figure 15-7. Use the Networking tab to track network activity.

You can use the information provided to determine the following quickly:

- The number of network adapters installed on the computer
- The percentage of utilization of each network adapter
- The link speed of each network adapter
- The state of each network adapter

The network activity graph shows traffic going to and from the computer as well as how much of the network capacity is in use. If a system has one network adapter, the graph details network traffic on this adapter over time. If a system has multiple network adapters, the graph displays a composite index of all network connections, which represents all network traffic.

Troubleshooting

Get separate views of bytes received and sent for troubleshooting

For troubleshooting, it is sometimes useful to have separate views of traffic going to the computer (Bytes Received) and traffic going from the computer (Bytes Sent). To do this, click View, choose Network History, and then select Bytes Sent. Then click View, choose Network History, and then select Bytes Received. Afterward, Bytes Sent are shown in red, Bytes Received in yellow, and Bytes Total in green.

You can also get more detailed information for each adapter. This information is useful for troubleshooting. If you click View and choose Select Columns, you'll see a dialog box that will let you add columns for summary statistics to the Networking tab. Table 15-2 summarizes the key network statistics available.

Table 15-2. Network Statistics and How They Can Be Used

Column Name	Description
Bytes Sent Throughput	Shows percentage of current connection bandwidth used by traffic sent from the system.
Bytes Received Throughput	Shows percentage of current connection bandwidth used by traffic received by the system.
Bytes Throughput	Shows percentage of current connection bandwidth used for all traffic on the network adapter. If this shows 50 percent or more utilization consistently, you'll want to monitor the system more closely and consider adding network adapters.

Table 15-2. Network Statistics and How They Can Be Used

Column Name	Description
Bytes Sent	Shows cumulative total bytes sent on the connection since bootup.
Bytes Received	Shows cumulative total bytes received on the connection since bootup.
Bytes Total	Shows cumulative total bytes on the connection since bootup.
Unicasts	Shows cumulative number of unicast packets received or sent since bootup.
Unicasts Sent	Shows total packets sent by unicast since bootup.
Unicasts Received	Shows total packets received by unicast since bootup.
Nonunicasts	Shows total number of broadcast packets sent or received since bootup. Too much broadcast traffic on the network can be an indicator of networking problems. If you see a lot of nonunicast traffic, monitor the amount received during the refresh interval.
Nonunicasts Sent	Shows total broadcast packets sent since bootup.
Nonunicasts Received	Shows total broadcast packets received since bootup.

Getting Information on User and Remote User Sessions

Members of the Administrators group and any users to which you specifically grant remote access can connect to systems using Terminal Services or a Remote Desktop Connection. Both techniques allow users to access systems remotely and use the systems as if they were sitting at the keyboard. In the standard configuration, however, remote access is disabled. You can enable the remote access feature by using the System utility in Control Panel. Start the System utility, then click the Remote tab. In the Remote Desktop panel, select Allow Users To Connect Remotely To This Computer, and then click OK.

With Remote Desktop, Windows Server 2003 allows one console session and two remote administration sessions. Most remote sessions are created as console sessions. The reason for this is that the console session provides full functionality for administration. If you log on locally to the console and someone is logged on remotely to the console, you will be prompted to end his or her user session so that you can log on. If you click Yes, the user's session is disconnected, halting all user-started applications without saving application data. If you click No, you will not be allowed to log on. See Chapter 30, "Using Remote Desktop for Administration," for details on how you can use Remote Desktop to configure remote sessions for administration rather than console sessions.

If you configure a server by using Terminal Services, multiple users can log on to a system up to a maximum allowed by licensing. To keep track of sessions once you've configured Terminal Services, you can use the Users tab of Task Manager. As shown in Figure 15-8, the Users tab lists user connections according to the following factors:

- **User** The pre–Windows 2000 logon name of the user account, such as Wrstanek or Administrator. If you want to see the logon domain as well as the logon name, select Show Full Account Name on the Options menu.
- **ID** The session ID. All user connections have a unique session ID. The session ID for any user logged on locally is 0.
- **Status** The status of the connection (Active or Disconnected).
- **Client Name** The name of the computer from which the user is connecting. This field is blank for console sessions.
- **Session** The type of session. Console is used for users logged on locally. Otherwise, indicates the connection type and protocol, such as RDP-TCP for a connection using the Remote Desktop Protocol (RDP) with Transmission Control Protocol (TCP) as the transport protocol.

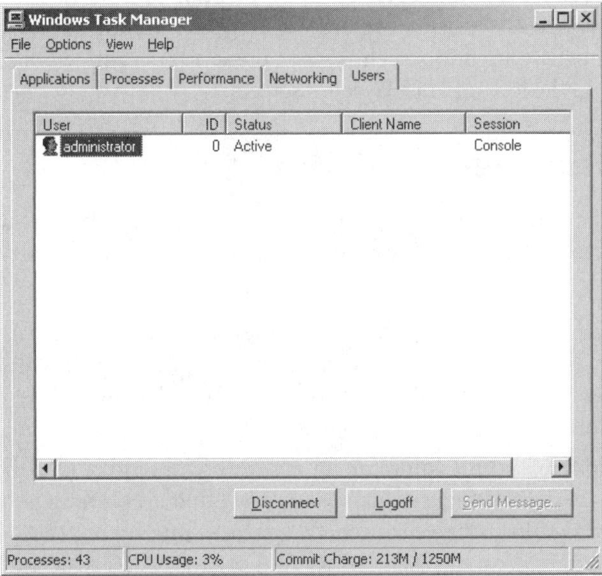

Figure 15-8. Use the Users tab to track and manage remote user sessions.

The Users tab can help you determine who is logged on and whether that user's status is either Active or Inactive. Right-click an active session and you can choose Send Message to send a console message to the user. This message is displayed on the screen of that user's session.

If you must end a user session, you can do this in one of two ways. Right-clicking the session and choosing Log Off logs the user off using the normal logoff process. This allows application data and system state information to be saved as during a normal logoff. Right-clicking the session and choosing Disconnect forcibly ends a user's session without saving application data or system state information.

You can also connect to an inactive session. Right-click the inactive session, and then choose Connect. When prompted, provide the user's password.

Finally, by default the hot keys used to end a remote control session are Ctrl+* (Ctrl+Shift+8). If you want a session to use different hot keys, right-click the session you want to work with, and then select Remote Control. You can then set the hot keys to end the remote control session.

Tracking Events and Troubleshooting by Using Event Viewer

The Windows operating system defines an event as any significant occurrence in the operating system or an application that should be recorded for tracking purposes. Informational events can be tracked as well as events that record warnings, errors, and auditing. Critical errors that deserve immediate attention, such as when the server has run out of disk space or memory, are recorded in the logs and displayed on screen.

Understanding the Event Logs

The Windows service that controls event logging is the Event Log service. When this service is started, events are recorded in one of the available event logs. On member servers, you'll find three event logs:

- **Application** Contains events logged by applications. You'll find events in this log for Exchange Server, SQL Server, IIS, and other installed applications. It is also used to record events from printers and, if you've configured alert logging, alerts. The default location is %SystemRoot%\System32\Config\AppEvent.evt.
- **Security log** Contains events you've set for auditing with local or global group policies. Depending on the auditing configuration, you'll find events for logon, logoff, privilege use, and shutdown, as well as general system events, such as the loading of the authentication package by the Local Security Authority (LSA). The default location is %SystemRoot%\System32\Config\SecEvent.evt.

> **Note** Only administrators are granted access to the Security log by default. If other users need to access the Security log, you must specifically grant them the Manage Auditing and the Security Log user rights. You can learn more about assigning user rights in Chapter 37, "Managing Users, Groups, and Computers."

- **System Log** Contains events logged by Windows Server 2003 and its components. You should routinely check this log for warnings and errors, especially those related to the failure of a service to start at bootup or the improper configuration of a service. The default location is %SystemRoot%\System32\Config\SysEvent.evt.

On domain controllers, you'll find the Application, Security, and System logs as well as these additional event logs:

- **Directory Service** Contains events logged by the Active Directory directory service. The primary events relate to the Active Directory database and global catalogs. You'll find details on database consistency checks, online defragmentation, and updates. The default location is %SystemRoot%\System32\Config\NTDS.evt.
- **DNS Server** Contains Domain Name System (DNS) queries, responses, and other DNS activities. You might also find details on activities that relate to DNS integration with Active Directory. The default location is %SystemRoot%\System32\Config\DNSEvent.evt.
- **File Replication Service** Contains events logged by the File Replication Service, a service used to replicate Active Directory changes to other domain controllers. You'll find details on any important events that took place while a domain controller attempted to update other domain controllers. The default location is %SystemRoot%\System32\Config\NtFrs.evt.

By default, the logs are sized as appropriate for the type of system you are working with and its configuration. In a standard configuration of Windows Server 2003, most logs have a maximum size of 16 MB. This includes the DNS Server, System, and Application logs. Because they are less critical, the Directory Service and File Replication Service logs on domain controllers have a maximum size of 512 kilobytes (KB). Because the Security log is so important, it is usually configured with a maximum size of 128 MB. Primarily, this is to allow the server to record a complete security audit trail for situations in which the server is under attack and a large number of security events are generated.

Windows Server 2003 logs are configured to overwrite old events as needed by default. So, when the log reaches its maximum size, the operating system overwrites old events with new events. This is different from Microsoft Windows NT. In Windows NT, the event logs were configured to overwrite only events that were older than 7 days. If desired, you can configure Windows Server 2003 logs in the same way. However, the problem with doing it that way is, when the maximum size is reached, events less than 7 days old can't be overwritten and the system will generate an error message telling you that such and such an event log is full each time it tries to write an event—and you can quickly get to where there are dozens of these errors on-screen.

> **Note** The log configuration can be controlled through Group Policy as well. This means changes to Group Policy could in turn change the maximum log size and which action to take when the maximum log size is reached. For more information about Group Policy, see Chapter 38, "Managing Group Policy."

Accessing the Event Logs and Viewing Events

You can view the event logs using Event Viewer, as shown in Figure 15-9. Event Viewer is a Microsoft Management Console (MMC) snap-in that can be started from the Administrative Tools menu or by typing **eventvwr** at the command line. The main view shows event logs by name and also displays the current size of each log. When you select the log you want to view in the left pane, the events recorded in the log are displayed in the right pane.

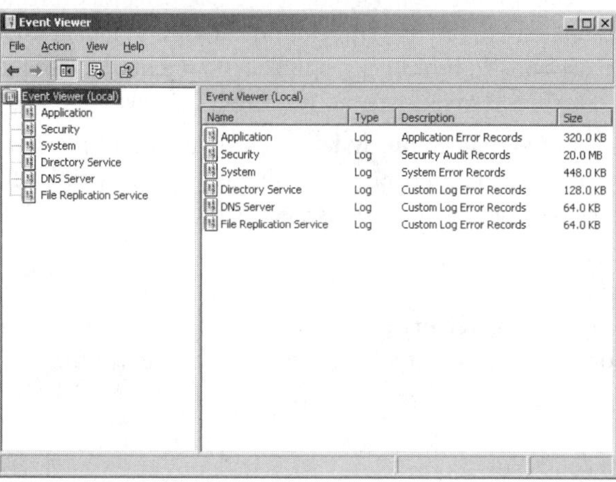

Figure 15-9. The main view in Event Viewer lists the available logs and shows their current size.

As Figure 15-10 shows, individual event entries provide an overview of the event that took place. Each event is recorded according to the date and time the event took place as well as the event type. For all the logs except Security, the event types are classified as Information, Warning, or Error. For the Security log, the event types are classified as Success Audit or Failure Audit. These event types have the following meanings:

- **Information** Generally relates to a successful action, such as the success of a service starting up. If you've configured Alert logging, the alerts are also recorded with this event type to show they've been triggered.
- **Warning** Describes events that aren't critical but could be useful in preventing future system problems. Most warnings should be examined to determine whether a preventative measure should be taken.
- **Error** Indicates a fatal error or significant problem occurred, such as the failure of a service to start. All errors should be examined to determine what corrective measure should be taken to prevent the error from reoccurring.
- **Success Audit** Describes an audited security event that completed as requested, such as when a user logs on or logs off successfully.

- **Failure Audit** Describes an audited security event that didn't complete as requested, such as when a user tries to log on and fails. Failed audit events can be useful in tracking down security issues.

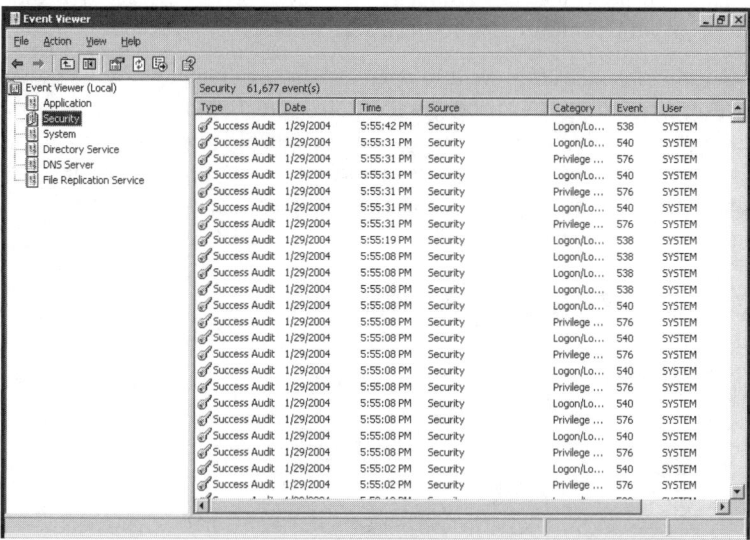

Figure 15-10. Events are logged according to the date and time they occurred as well as by type.

> **Note** Any attempt by users, services, or applications to perform a task for which they don't have appropriate permissions can be recorded as a failure audit. If someone is trying to break into a system, you might see a large number of failure audit events. If a service or application doesn't have the permissions it needs to perform certain tasks, you might also see a large number of failure audit events.

Other pertinent information recorded with an event includes the event source, category, event ID, user name, and computer name. The Source column lists the application, service, or component that logged the event. The Category column details the category of the event and is sometimes used to further describe the event. The Event column provides an identifier for the specific event that occurred. You can sometimes look up events in the Microsoft Knowledge Base to get more detailed information.

The User column shows the name of the user that was logged on when the event occurred. If a server process triggered the event, the user name usually is that of the special identity that caused the event. This includes the special identities Anonymous Logon, Local Service, Network Service, and System. Although events can have no user associated with them, they can also be associated with a specific user who was logged on at the time the event occurred.

The Computer column shows the name of the computer that caused the event to occur. Because you are working with a log from a particular computer, this is usually the account name of that computer. However, this is not always the case. Some events can be triggered because of other computers on the network. Some events triggered by the local machine are stored with the computer name as MACHINENAME.

You can double-click any event to open its Properties dialog box. As shown in Figure 15-11, the Properties dialog box provides additional information about the event including a text description and, for some events, any binary data or error code generated by the event. Most of the event descriptions aren't easy to understand, so if you need a little help deciphering the event, click Copy To Clipboard. You can then paste the event description into an e-mail message to another administrator.

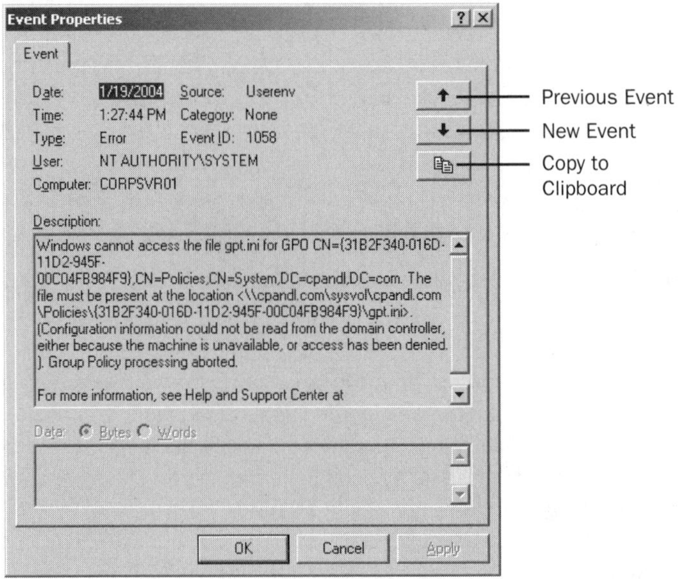

Figure 15-11. Event details include a description of the event and in some cases binary data generated by the event.

> **Tip** Within every event description is a Help And Support Center link that you can click. This link provides access to the Microsoft Web site where you can query for any additional information that might be available on the event. As of the time of this writing, the response is often that there's no additional information available. Hopefully this will improve over time.

Viewing Event Logs on Remote Systems

You can use Event Viewer to view events on other computers on your network. Start Event Viewer, right-click Event Viewer (Local) in the left pane, and then choose Connect To Another Computer. In the Select Computer dialog box, type the domain name or Internet Protocol (IP) address of the computer whose event log you want to view, and then click OK. Or you can click Browse to search for the computer you want to use. Keep in mind that you must be logged on as an administrator or be a member of the Administrators group to view events on a remote computer.

You can view events on systems running Windows Server 2003, Windows XP, Windows 2000, and Windows NT. If you are connecting to a computer over a low-speed connection and you see timeouts when you try to work with the logs, you can configure Event Viewer to use longer wait and transfer times by specifying that you are using a low-speed connection. You do this on a per–log file basis. Right-click the log you want to work with, and choose Properties to display the log's Properties dialog box. In the lower-left corner of the dialog box, select Using A Low-Speed Connection, and then click OK.

Sorting, Finding, and Filtering Events

Event Viewer provides several ways for you to organize and search for events in the logs. You can sort events based on date or other stored information. You can search a particular event log for specific events and view events one at a time. You can also filter events so that only the specific events you want to see are shown.

Sorting the Event Logs

By default, logs are sorted so that the newest events are listed first. If you'd rather see the oldest events first, you can do this by clicking View and then selecting Oldest First. This change must be made for each log in which you want to see the oldest events first.

You can also sort events based on information in a particular column. For example, if you wanted to sort the events based on the user name, you would click the User column header. Sort any event log in this way and all the event logs will be sorted in the same way.

Searching the Event Logs

By using the Find feature, you can search for events within a selected log and view matching events one at a time. Say, for instance, a Microsoft Knowledge Base article says to look for an event with such and such an event source and you want to search for it quickly. You can use the Find feature to do this.

To search the selected event log, click View, and then click Find. This displays the Find In dialog box, as shown in the screen on the following page. Choose the find options you want to use as described in Table 15-3, and then click Find Next. The first event that matches the search criteria is highlighted in the log. You can double-click the event to get more detailed information or click Find Next to find the next match.

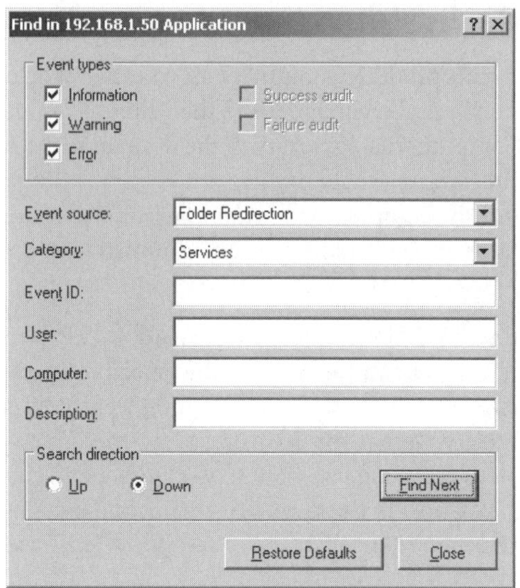

Table 15-3. Find and Filter Options for Event Logging

Option	Description
Event Types	Allows you to include or exclude events by type. The most important event types are warnings, which indicate that something might pose a future problem and might need to be examined, and errors, which indicate a fatal error or significant problem occurred.
Event Source	Includes events only from a specified source, such as an application, service, or component that logged the event.
Category	Includes events only within a given category. The categories available change based on the event source you choose.
Event ID	Includes events only with the event ID you specify. Only one event ID can be entered.
User	Includes events associated with a particular user account that was logged on when the event was triggered. Server processes can log events with the special identities Anonymous Logon, Local Service, Network Service, and System. Not all events have a user associated with them.
Computer	Includes all events associated with a particular computer. Usually this is the name of the computer whose logs you are working with.

Table 15-3. Find and Filter Options for Event Logging

Option	Description
Search Direction	With Find, use these options to specify whether you want to search forward from the current position in the log (Down) or backward from the current position in the log (Up).
From/To	With filters, all events from the first to the last are displayed by default. To specify the date with which to start, select Events On in the From selection list, then set the start date. To specify the date with which to end, select Events On in the To selection list, then set the end date.

Filtering the Event Logs

The Find option works well if you want to perform quick searches, such as for a single event of a specific type. If you want to perform an extended search, however, such as when you want to review all events of a particular type, there's a better way to do it and that's to filter the event log so that only the specific events you want to see are shown.

To filter the selected event log, click View, and then click Filter. This displays the log's Properties dialog box with the Filter tab selected, as shown in the following screen. Choose the filter options you want to use, as described in Table 15-3, and then click OK. Once you've applied the filter, only events with the options you specify are displayed in the selected event log.

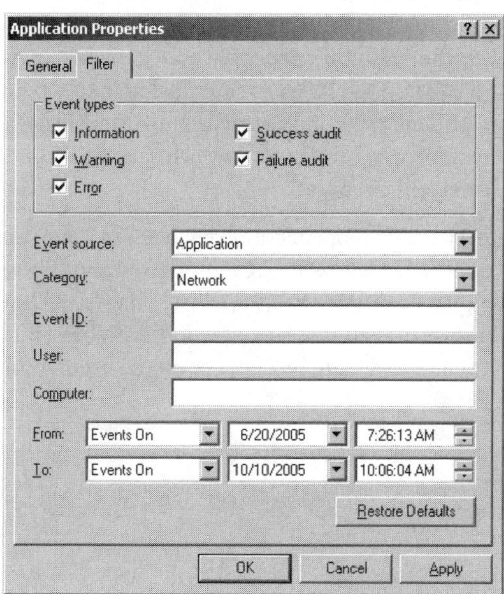

Tip **Set filter options**
You can set as many filter options as you want to narrow the results. Keep in mind, however, that each filter option you apply sets a search criterion that must be matched for an event to be displayed. The options are cumulative so that an event must match all filter options.

If you later want to restore the log to its original view, click View, and then click Filter to display the log's Properties dialog box with the Filter tab selected. Then click Restore Defaults.

Caution Don't click Restore Defaults in the General tab in the log's Properties dialog box. This button has a different purpose—it restores the log size options to their defaults.

Archiving Event Logs

In most cases, you'll want to have several months' worth of log data available in case you must go back through the logs and troubleshoot. One way to do this, of course, is to set the log size so that it is large enough to accommodate this. However, this usually isn't practical because individual logs can grow quite large. So, as part of your routine, you might want to archive the log files on critical systems periodically, such as for domain controllers or application servers.

To create a log archive, right-click the log in the left pane of Event Viewer, and then select Save Log File As. In the Save As dialog box, select a directory and a log file name. In the Save As Type dialog box, Event Log (*.evt) is the default file type. This saves the file in event log format for access in Event Viewer. You can also select .txt to save the log in tab-delimited text format, such as for accessing it in a text editor or importing it into a spreadsheet, or .csv to save the log in comma-delimited text format, such as for importing it into a spreadsheet or database. After you select a log format, choose Save.

Logs saved in Event Log format (.evt) can be reopened in Event Viewer at any time. To do this, right-click the Event Viewer node in the left pane of Event Viewer, and choose Open Log File. Use the Open dialog box to select a directory and a log file. Then use Log Type to specify the type of log, such as Application. Next type a display name to use. When you click Open, the saved event log is loaded into Event Viewer and will appear on the list of available logs in the left pane, as shown in Figure 15-12.

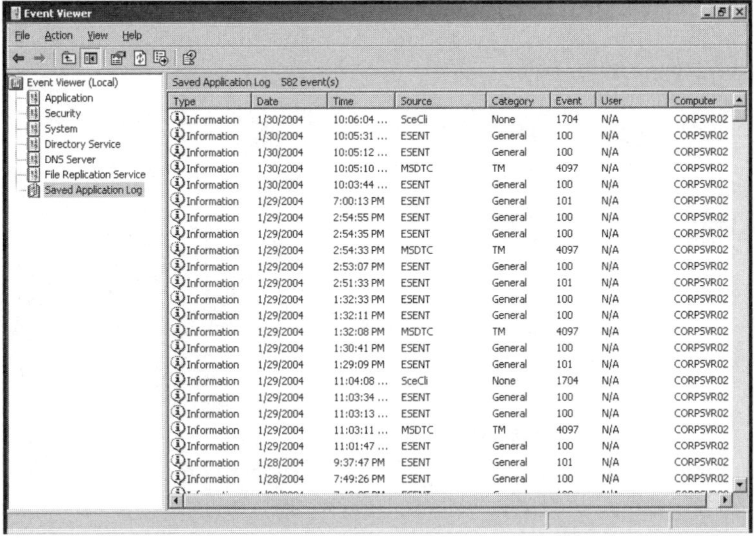

Figure 15-12. Archived logs can be reopened in Event Viewer.

Tracking Events on Multiple Computers

When you are working with a specific system or trying to track down issues, Event Viewer is an excellent tool to use and should be your tool of choice. As you've seen, Event Viewer can also be used to access logs on remote systems. It isn't particularly useful, however, when you must work with many systems as might be the case if you routinely check the event logs on all critical systems in the organization. For checking the event logs on many systems, you need a power tool, and two such power tools are available:

- **Eventquery** A command-line tool for examining the event logs on local and remote systems
- **EventComb** A Windows Server 2003 Resource Kit tool for searching the event logs on multiple systems

Quick Look: Using Eventquery

By using Eventquery within a batch script, you can quickly and easily automate the process of checking event logs on multiple systems using a variety of filters. You could then write this information to a central log file or a Web page, either of which could be easily viewed in a Web browser, giving you a one-stop location for checking the event logs.

The most common search you'll perform in the event logs using Eventquery is a search in a specific log for warning or error events. You can search for warning events on a local computer by typing the following:

```
eventquery /l "LogName" /fi "type eq warning"
```

where *LogName* is the name of the event log you want to search. You can search for error events on a local computer by typing this:

```
eventquery /l "LogName" /fi "type eq error"
```

For example, if you want to search the Application log on the local system for error events, you'd type:

```
eventquery /l "Application" /fi "type eq error"
```

To search for events on remote systems, add the /S parameter followed by the name or IP address of the remote system. Consider the following example:

```
eventquery /s corpsrv02 /l "Application" /fi "type eq error"
```

Here, you search the Application log on CORPSERVER02 for error events.

By default, Eventquery returns the 50 most recent events that match the particular filter you've defined. For the previous example that would mean you'd get a list of up to 50 errors, sorted in time order, such as the following:

```
------------------------------------------------------------------------------
Listing the events in 'application' log of host 'CORPSVR02'
------------------------------------------------------------------------------
Type        Event  Date                   Time               Source            ComputerName
----------- ------ ---------------------- ----------------- ----------------- --------------
Error       11706  1/28/2004    2:55:03 PM    MsiInstaller      CORPSVR02
Error       8019   1/25/2004    1:26:07 PM    NTBackup          CORPSVR02
Error       8001   1/25/2004    1:26:05 PM    NTBackup          CORPSVR02
Error       1053   1/18/2004    1:16:39 PM    Userenv           CORPSVR02
Error       1053   1/18/2004    1:11:37 PM    Userenv           CORPSVR02
Error       1053   1/18/2004    1:06:35 PM    Userenv           CORPSVR02
Error       1030   1/18/2004    1:01:34 PM    Userenv           CORPSVR02
Error       1058   1/18/2004    1:01:34 PM    Userenv           CORPSVR02
Error       1030   1/18/2004    12:56:34 PM   Userenv           CORPSVR02
Error       1058   1/18/2004    12:56:34 PM   Userenv           CORPSVR02
Error       1058   1/18/2004    12:51:34 PM   Userenv           CORPSVR02
Error       1030   1/18/2004    12:46:34 PM   Userenv           CORPSVR02
Error       1058   1/18/2004    12:46:34 PM   Userenv           CORPSVR02
Error       1030   1/18/2004    12:41:34 PM   Userenv           CORPSVR02
Error       1058   1/18/2004    12:41:34 PM   Userenv           CORPSVR02
Error       1053   1/18/2004    12:34:42 PM   Userenv           CORPSVR02
Error       1000   1/17/2004    2:26:17 PM    Application Error CORPSVR02
Error       1000   1/17/2004    2:26:04 PM    Application Error CORPSVR02
Error       1000   1/17/2004    2:25:07 PM    Application Error CORPSVR02
```

To control the maximum number of events returned, you use the /R parameter. Follow /R with the number of events to return. For example, to return the 100 most recent events that match the filter, you'd type **/r 100**. To learn more about Eventquery and its possible uses, type **eventquery /?** at the command line.

> **Note** Other useful command-line tools for working with the event logs include Eventcreate and Eventtriggers. Eventcreate can be used to create custom events in the event logs. Eventtriggers can be used to monitor event logs for specific events, and then it acts on those events by running tasks or commands.

Quick Look: Using EventComb

EventComb, shown in Figure 15-13, is a Windows Server 2003 Resource Kit tool used for searching the event logs on multiple systems. If you've installed the Resource Kit as discussed in Chapter 1, "Introducing Windows Server 2003," you can start EventComb by typing **eventcombmt** at the command line.

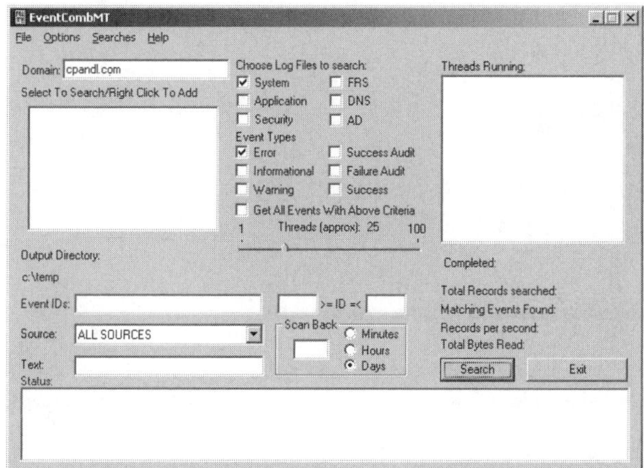

Figure 15-13. EventComb let's you search multiple systems in a domain for events by event ID, source, and search text.

By using EventComb, you can search multiple systems in a specified domain for events that match a set of search criteria you specify. Before you can start a search, you must first specify the domain to work with and the computers to search in that domain. By default, the current domain is entered in the Domain field. If you want to work with computers in another domain, type the fully qualified domain name in the Domain field, such as Tech.cpandl.com. Next, right-click the text area labeled Select To Search/Right-Click To Add. This displays a shortcut menu that allows you to select computers to search. The options include the following:

- **Get DCs In Domain** Polls the network to obtain a list of all domain controllers in the domain
- **Add Single Server** Allows you to add servers by name or IP address

- **Add All GCs In This Domain** Polls the network to obtain a list of all global catalog servers in the domain
- **Get All Servers** Polls the network to obtain a list of all servers in the domain
- **Get Servers From File** Gets a list of servers to use from a text file

Any computers you choose are added to the search list, as shown in Figure 15-14. Adding computers to the list doesn't select them for searches, however. Use Shift+Click or Ctrl+Click to select the computers in the list that you want to search. Then specify the log files to search and the type of events to look for. Logs you can search include System, Application, Security, FRS (the File Replication Service log), DNS (the DNS Server log), and AD (the Active Directory Service log). Event types you can search for include Error, Warning, Informational, Success Audit, and Failure Audit.

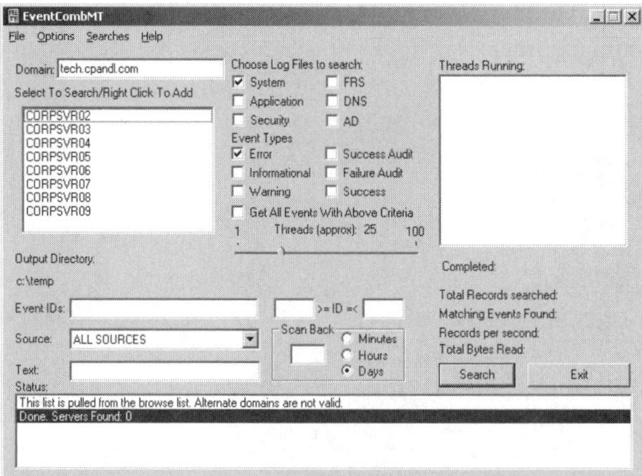

Figure 15-14. To specify computers to search, right-click the text area labeled Select To Search/Right-Click To Add.

> **Tip** Set the output directory
> By default, EventComb uses C:\Temp as the output directory for files it creates. To change the output directory, select Options, Set Output Directory, and then choose a new output directory by using the Browse For Folder dialog box.

After you specify the logs to search and the type of events to look for, you specify which events should be returned in the result set. To get all events with the specified event types, select Get All Events With Above Criteria, and then click Search. To add filters so that only matching events are returned, you can use the following options:

- **Event IDs** Includes only events with the event ID you specify. You can also enter a range. For example, if you wanted to include event IDs 0 to 1000, you'd enter **1000** in the first Event ID box and **0** in the >= ID box. If you wanted to include event IDs 5000 to 9999, you'd enter **5000** in the first Event ID box and **9999** in the <= ID box.

- **Source** Includes only events from a specified source, such as an application, service, or component that logged the event.
- **Text** Includes only events that contain the specified filter text.

> **Tip** **Specify how far to search back**
> If desired, you can limit the search so that only recent events are examined. To do this, use the Scan Back panel to specify how for back in minutes, hours, or days to search.

Finally, when you are ready to comb the logs, click Search, and EventComb will go to work examining the logs on the designated systems. Results are written to an output directory, which by default is C:\Temp. EventComb creates a status log (EventCombMT.txt) in the output directory. This log records EventComb's actions as it searches the logs on the specified systems. If any errors occur during log retrieval, this is where you'll find them.

In the output directory, you'll also find comma-delimited text files for each log on each server that had events matching your search criteria. So, if you search many logs on many systems, you could end up with dozens or hundreds of separate files. Each log contains only events that match your filter criteria and is named using the format *ComputerName-LogType_*LOG.txt, such as CORPSVR02-System_LOG.txt for the system log from CORPSVR02. Figure 15-15 shows an example log.

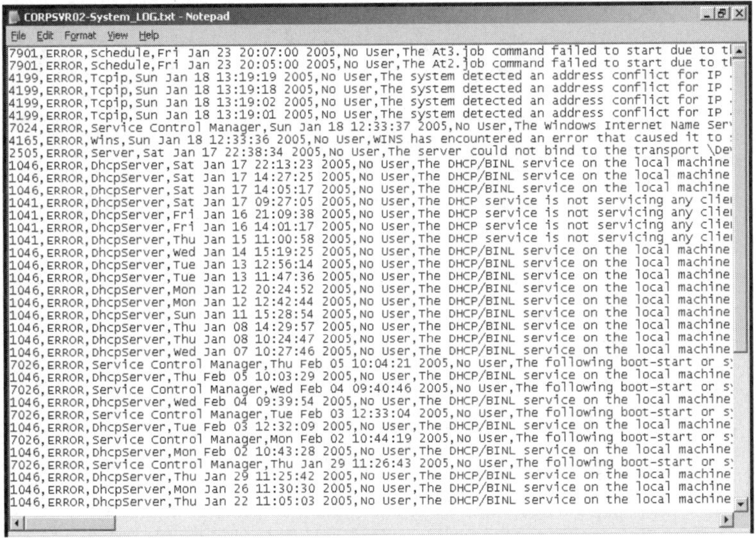

Figure 15-15. Events that match your search criteria are written to a computer- and log-specific text file.

Chapter 15

Chapter 16

Comprehensive Performance Analysis and Logging

Microsoft Windows Server 2003 provides many tools to help you track performance. In the previous chapter, we looked at tuning performance through configuration settings; using Task Manager to track running processes, users, and network utilization; and using the event logs to track important occurrences recorded by the operating system. Although these tools are excellent and do their jobs well, you might need to dig deeper to establish comprehensive performance baselines, diagnose complex system problems, and optimize system performance.

The key comprehensive monitoring and optimization tools available include the following:

- **System Monitor** System Monitor can be used to track and display performance information in real time. It gathers information on any performance parameters you've configured for monitoring and presents it using a graphical display.
- **Performance Logs And Alerts** Performance logs can be considered to be the logging counterpart to System Monitor. By using performance logs, you can record performance information in real time and store it in a log so that it can be analyzed later. Performance alerts can be used to notify users when certain events occur or when certain performance thresholds are reached. For example, you could configure a performance alert that lets you know when the C drive is running low on free space or the central processing unit (CPU) is operating at 95 percent or more of capacity.

Before discussing each of these tools in turn, let's look at how you can establish performance baselines.

Establishing Performance Baselines

One of the key reasons for tracking performance information is to establish a baseline for a computer that allows you to compare past performance with current performance. There are several types of baselines you can use, including the following:

- **Postinstallation baselines** A postinstallation baseline is a performance level that is meant to represent the way a computer performs after installing all the system components, services, and applications that will be used on the system.
- **Typical usage baselines** A typical usage baseline is a performance level that is meant to represent average usage conditions and serve as a starting point against which you can measure future performance.
- **Test baselines** A test baseline is a performance level that you use during testing of a system. In the test lab, you might want to simulate peak usage loads and test how the system performs under these conditions.

Although it is important to obtain postinstallation and typical usage baseline values, the more important of the two is the typical usage baseline. This is the baseline you get when you simulate user loads or when users actually start working with a server. Ideally, it represents typical or average loads. Once you have a typical usage baseline, you can gather information in the future to try to determine how resource usage has changed and how the computer is performing comparatively.

To be able to establish a baseline, you must collect a representative set of performance statistics. By that I mean collect the data that you actually need to determine resource usage and performance in future scenarios. If possible, you should also collect several data samples at the same time each day over a period of several days. This will give you a more meaningful data sample.

You must work to keep the baseline in sync with how the server is used. As you install new components, services, and applications, you must establish new baselines. This ensures that future comparisons with the baseline are accurate and that they use the most current system configuration to determine how resource usage has changed and how the computer is performing comparatively.

Comprehensive System Monitoring

System Monitor is a tool designed to track and display performance information in real time. It gathers information on any performance parameters you've configured for monitoring and presents it using a graphical display.

Using System Monitor

System Monitor is a snap-in that's added to the Performance Monitor utility. You can start Performance Monitor by clicking Start, selecting Programs or All Programs, Administrative Tools, and then Performance, or you can type **perfmon** at the command line.

When you start Performance Monitor, the System Monitor node is selected by default, as shown in Figure 16-1, and the right pane graphs any performance items you've configured for monitoring. Each performance item you want to monitor is defined by the following three components:

- **Performance objects** Represent any system component that has a set of measurable properties. A performance object can be a physical part of the operating system, such as the memory, the processor, or the paging file; a logical component, such as a logical disk or print queue; or a software element, such as a process or a thread.
- **Object instances** Represent single occurrences of performance objects. If a particular object has multiple instances, such as when a computer has multiple processors, you can use an object instance to track a specific occurrence of that object. You could also elect to track all instances of an object, such as whether you want to monitor all processors on a system.
- **Performance counters** Represent measurable properties of performance objects. For example, with a processor, you can measure the percentage of processor utilization using the %Processor Time counter.

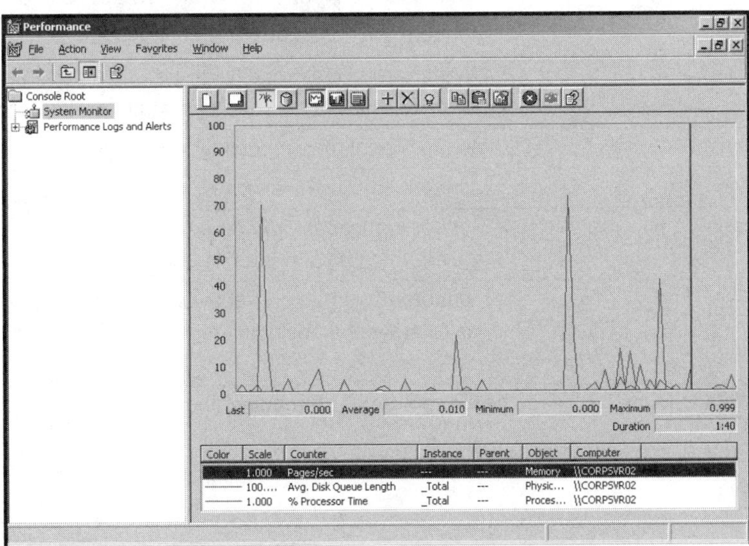

Figure 16-1. System Monitor graphs the performance data you are tracking.

In a standard installation of Windows Server 2003, many performance objects are available for monitoring. As you add services, applications, and components, additional performance objects can become available. For example, when you install the Domain Name System (DNS), the DNS object becomes available for monitoring on that computer.

The most common performance objects you'll want to monitor are summarized in Table 16-1. Like all performance objects, each performance object listed here has a set of counters that can be tracked.

Table 16-1. Commonly Tracked Performance Objects

Performance Object	Description
Browser	Monitors the Browser service for a domain or workgroup
Cache	Monitors disk cache usage
LogicalDisk	Monitors the logical volumes on a computer
Memory	Monitors memory performance for system cache (including pooled paged and pooled nonpaged memory), physical memory, and virtual memory
Network Interface	Monitors the network adapters configured on the computer
NTDS	Monitors the Active Directory directory service
Objects	Monitors the number of events, mutexes, processes, sections, semaphores, and threads on the computer
Paging File	Monitors page file current and peak usage
PhysicalDisk	Monitors hard disk read/write activity as well as data transfers, hard faults, and soft faults
Print Queue	Monitors print jobs, spooling, and print queue activity
Process	Monitors all processes running on a computer
Processor	Monitors processor idle time, idle states, usage, deferred procedure calls, and interrupts
Server	Monitors current server activity and important server usage statistics, including logon errors, access errors, and sessions
Server Work Queues	Monitors server threading and client requests

Table 16-1. Commonly Tracked Performance Objects

Performance Object	Description
System	Monitors system-level counters, including processes, threads, context switching of threads, file system control operations, system calls, and system uptime
Thread	Monitors all running threads and allows you to examine usage statistics for individual threads by process ID

Selecting Performance Objects and Counters to Monitor

The most commonly tracked performance objects are Memory, PhysicalDisk, and Processor. This is why when you first start Performance Monitor, System Monitor is configured to graph basic counters for these objects. Many other performance counters are available for tracking. To track additional counters, you use the Add Counters dialog box, as shown in Figure 16-2. After you access System Monitor, you display this dialog box by pressing Ctrl+I or right-clicking the graph in the details pane and selecting Add Counters.

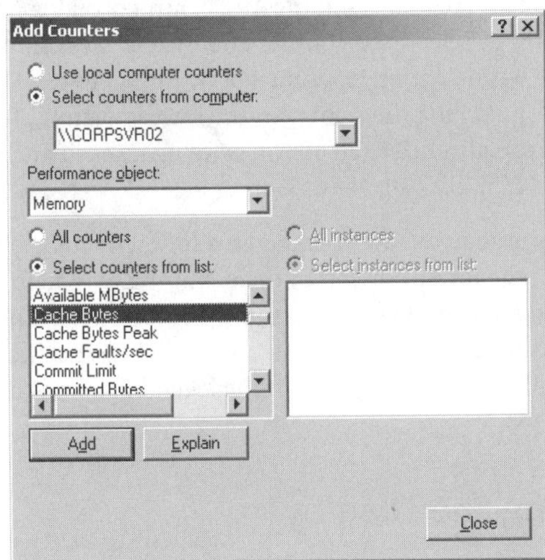

Figure 16-2. Select the objects and the counters that you want to track.

Adding counters to track is easy. Select the type of object you want to work with, such as Memory, and then choose the counters for that object that you want to track. To add all counters for the object, click All Counters, and then click Add. To choose the individual counters to add, click Select Counters From List, and then select the counters to add. Use

Ctrl+Click or Shift+Click to select multiple counters, and then click Add. Or select one counter at a time and then click Add. Any counters you've added will be displayed in System Monitor. You can then repeat this process, as necessary, to add counters for other performance objects. Click Close when you're finished adding counters.

Inside Out

Selecting counters when objects have multiple instances

If you select an object that has multiple instances, you'll be able to select counters for a specific instance or all instances of that object. Choose All Instances to monitor the counter for all instances of the object. Choose Select Instances From List to monitor the counter for specific instances of the object. You can use Ctrl+Click or Shift+Click to select multiple instances. Then click Add to track the counter for the specified instances.

As you've seen, it's easy to add counters to track. What isn't so easy is determining which counters you should track. While you are working with the Add Counters dialog box, you can get a detailed explanation of a counter by selecting a counter and then clicking Explain. If you add too many counters or track the wrong counters, don't worry. In the System Monitor view, you can delete counters later by clicking their entry in the lower portion of the details pane and then clicking Delete. You can also delete all counters being tracked and start over with a clean graph by pressing Ctrl+E or clicking New Counter Set.

System Monitor displays each counter that you are tracking in a different color and line thickness. You can use the legend in the lower portion of the details pane to help you determine which counter is being graphed where. If you are unsure, double-click a line in the graph to select the corresponding counter in the legend list. To highlight a specific counter so that it is easy to pick out in the graph, select the counter in the legend list, and then press Ctrl+H.

Choosing Views and Controlling the Display

System Monitor can present counter statistics in several different ways. By default, it graphs the statistics. A graph is useful when you are tracking a limited number of counters because you can view historical data for each counter that you are working with. By default, System Monitor samples the counters once every second and updates the graph. This means at any given time there can be up to 100 seconds worth of data on the graph. If you increase the sample interval, you can get more information into the chart. For example, if you set the sample interval to once every 10 seconds, you can get up to 1,000 seconds (or about 17 minutes) worth of data on the graph.

You can set the sample interval by using the General tab of the System Monitor Properties dialog box, as shown in Figure 16-3. To display this dialog box, press Ctrl+Q or click Properties. Then set the sample interval using the Sample Automatically Every *x* Seconds option.

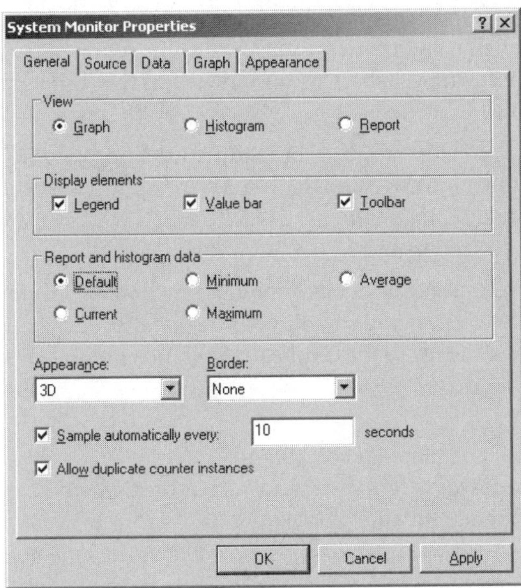

Figure 16-3. Configure the display properties.

The options on the Display Elements panel control the availability of the Legend, Value Bar, and Toolbar. The Legend is displayed at the bottom of the details pane, and it shows the color and line style that are used for each counter. The Value Bar is displayed between the graph and the legend. It shows values related to the counter you've selected in the graph or in the legend. The Toolbar is displayed above the graph and provides the basic toolbar functions for working with System Monitor. You might find that it is much easier to use the shortcut keys than to click the Toolbar buttons. The Toolbar buttons and their shortcut keys are as follows:

- **New Counter Set** Ctrl+E; deletes all counters being tracked so you can use a different counter set.
- **Clear Display** Ctrl+D; clears the display so that you can start with a clean display.
- **View Current Activity** Ctrl+T; switches the view so that current activity being logged is displayed.
- **View Log Data** Ctrl+L; switches the view so that data from a performance log can be replayed.
- **View Histogram** Ctrl+B; switches the view to represent the performance information using a bar graph.
- **View Report** Ctrl+R; switches the view to display the report list format.

- **View Graph** Ctrl+G; switches the view to display the graph format.
- **Add** Ctrl+I; displays the Add Counter dialog box, which lets you add counters to track.
- **Delete** Delete key; removes the counter so that it is no longer tracked.
- **Highlight** Ctrl+H; highlights the counter using a white line so that it is more easy to see. Highlighting works best with graphs. If you want to turn the Highlight function off, press Ctrl+H again.
- **Copy Properties** Ctrl+C; creates a copy of the counter list along with the individual configuration of each counter and puts it on the Windows Clipboard. The information is formatted as an Extensible Markup Language (XML) file. If you open a text editor, you could paste in this information and save it for later use.
- **Paste Counter List** Ctrl+V; pastes a copied counter list into System Monitor so that it is used as the current counter set. If you saved a counter list to a file, you simply open the file, copy the contents of the file to the Clipboard, and then press Ctrl+V in System Monitor to use that counter list.

Tip **Save the counter list or use it on different computers**

You can use the copy and paste features to track the same set of counters quickly and easily at a later date or to use the set on other computers. Press Ctrl+C to copy the counter list and save it to a file. Then you or someone else could access the counter list when you want to use the same setup again. You could also paste the counter list into an e-mail message so that it could be sent to someone who wants to use the same counter list.

- **Properties** Ctrl+Q; displays the System Monitor Properties dialog box.
- **Freeze Display** Ctrl+F; freezes the display so that System Monitor no longer updates the performance information. Press Ctrl+F a second time to resume sampling.
- **Update Data** Ctrl+U; updates the display by one sampling interval. When you freeze the display, System Monitor still gathers performance information; it just doesn't update the display using the new information. If you want to update the display while it is frozen, use this option.
- **Help** F1; displays the System Monitor Help information.

The histogram and report views deserve a bit of additional discussion. In the histogram view, System Monitor represents the performance information by using a bar graph with the last sampling value for each counter displayed on an individual bar within the graph. The sizes of the bars within the graph are adjusted automatically based on the number of performance counters being tracked and can be adjusted to accommodate hundreds of counters. That is, in fact, the biggest advantage of the histogram—it allows you to track a lot of counters more easily. In the screen on the following page, approximately 100 counters are being tracked, and it is easy to pick out which counter is which.

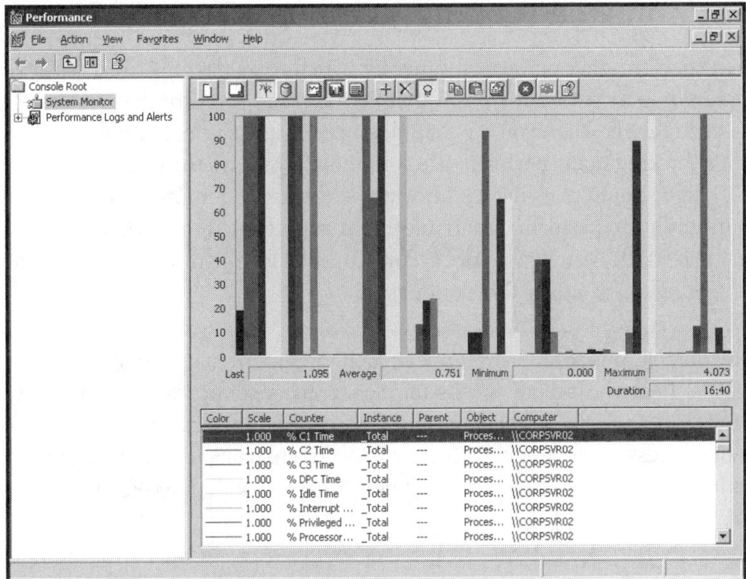

In the report view, as shown in the following screen, System Monitor represents the performance information by using a report list format. In this view, objects and their counters are listed in alphabetical order. The performance information is displayed numerically rather than graphed. If you are trying to determine specific performance values for many different counters, this is the best view to use because the actual values are always shown.

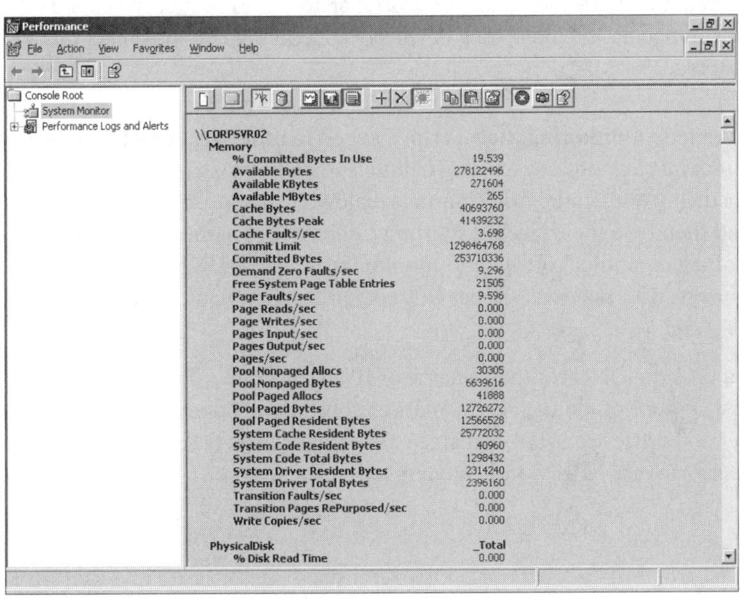

Monitoring Performance Remotely

Monitoring performance on the computer for which you are trying to establish a baseline can skew the results. The reason for this is that Performance Monitor uses resources when it is running, particularly when you are graphing performance information, taking frequent samples, or tracking many performance counters. To remove the resource burden (or at least most of it), you should consider monitoring performance remotely. Here, you use one computer to monitor the performance of another computer. Although this does generate some extra network traffic, you'll get more accurate results for the monitored computer because you're not using its resources for monitoring.

Note By default, only administrators can monitor performance remotely. Like remote access to the Registry, remote access for monitoring is controlled by the Registry key HKLM\ SYSTEM\CurrentControlSet\Control\SecurePipeServers\Winreg. If you want to limit remote access to the Registry, you can start by changing the permissions on this key. For more information, see the section entitled "Controlling Remote Registry Access" on page 445.

Tip **Configure remote monitoring**

You can use any computer running Microsoft Windows 2000 or later to perform remote monitoring, and that computer can monitor any computer running Windows 2000 or later. The only exceptions are for Microsoft Windows Millennium Edition (Windows Me) and Windows XP Home Edition. The computer you are using for monitoring can even monitor multiple computers. Don't, however, use a Remote Desktop Connection to connect to the computer you want to monitor and then start monitoring. Even though you are viewing from a different computer, the monitoring is still being performed on the computer to which you are connected.

To begin remote monitoring, start Performance Monitor, press Ctrl+E to start with a new counter set and clear out any existing counters, then press Ctrl+A to display the Add Counters dialog box. In the Add Counters dialog box, choose Select Counters From Computer, and then type the Universal Naming Code (UNC) name or Internet Protocol (IP) address of the computer you want to monitor remotely. A UNC computer name or IP address begins with two back slashes (\\). So, for instance, you could type **\\CorpServer03** or **\\192.168.1.56**.

After you type the UNC computer name or IP address, press Tab or click the Performance Object list. When you do this, Performance Monitor will attempt to connect to the remote computer and retrieve a list of available performance objects to monitor. You can then choose performance objects and counters to track just as you would for a local computer.

Troubleshooting

Try the IP address if you can't connect

Performance Monitor should be able to find any computer in any trusted domain of your organization's forest. Sometimes, however, it isn't able to do this and returns an error. If this happens, ensure you entered the correct computer name. If you did and you still get an error, try entering the UNC path with the computer's IP address. Using an IP address saves Performance Monitor from having to perform a DNS lookup to resolve the computer's name to its IP address.

Tip **Compare performance of multiple systems**
The Legend area shows the associated UNC computer name or IP address for each performance counter you are tracking. If you want to see how performance compares on different computers, use your monitoring computer to track the same performance counters on these computers. You can then make direct comparisons of how these computers perform relative to each other.

Resolving Performance Bottlenecks

Generally, a bottleneck is any condition that keeps a computer from performing at its best. Bottlenecks can also apply to situations in which one resource is preventing another resource from performing optimally. For example, if a system doesn't have enough physical memory, it doesn't matter whether it has a fast processor or a slow processor. The system will still perform poorly because it doesn't have enough physical memory available and must rely heavily on the paging file, reading and writing to disk frequently.

Memory is usually the main bottleneck on both workstations and servers. It is the resource you should examine first to try to determine why a system isn't performing as expected. But memory isn't the only bottleneck. The processor, disk subsystem, and the networking components are also sources of potential performance bottlenecks.

Resolving Memory Bottlenecks

Windows applications use a lot of memory. If you install a server with the minimum amount of memory required, it isn't going to perform at its optimal level. The server cannot perform at its optimal level when you install the recommended amount of memory either. The reason for this is that a server's memory requirements depend on many factors, including the services, components, and applications that are installed on the server as well as the server's configuration.

Computers use both physical and virtual memory. Physical memory is represented by the amount of random access memory (RAM) installed. Virtual memory is memory written to a paging file on disk. Reading from and writing to the paging file involves the disk subsystem, and it is much slower than accessing physical memory. Because of this, you don't want a system to have to use the paging file too frequently.

Before you set out to monitor memory usage, you should check to ensure the computer has the recommended amount of memory for the operating system and the applications it is running. You should also check the system cache configuration. If the system cache is too large, the system might page to disk more often than it needs to, which in turn can impact the system's performance. The size of the system cache depends on the Memory Caching setting, as discussed in the section entitled "Tuning Processor Scheduling and Memory Usage" on page 450, and on the Data Throughput setting, as discussed in the section entitled "Tuning Data Throughput" on page 452.

Once you've optimized the system, you can determine how the system is using memory and check for problems. Look closely at the amount of memory available and the amount of virtual memory being used. If the server has very little available memory, you might need to add memory to the system. In general, you want the available memory to be no less than 5 percent of the total physical memory on the server. If the server has a high ratio of virtual memory being used to total physical memory on the system, you might need to add physical memory as well.

Look at the way the system is using the paged pool and nonpaged pool memory. The *paged pool* is an area of system memory for objects that can be written to disk when they aren't used. The *nonpaged pool* is an area of system memory for objects that can't be written to disk. If the size of the paged pool is large relative to the total amount of physical memory on the system, you might need to add memory to the system. If the size of the nonpaged pool is large relative to the total amount of virtual memory allocated to the server, you might want to increase the virtual memory size.

Look at the way the system is using the paging file. A page fault occurs when a process requests a page in memory and the system can't find it at the requested location. If the requested page is elsewhere in memory, the fault is called a *soft page fault*. If the requested page must be retrieved from the paging file on disk, the fault is called a *hard page fault*. Most processors can handle large numbers of soft faults. Hard faults, however, can cause significant delays. If there are a high number of hard page faults, you might need to increase the amount of memory or reduce the size of the system cache.

Counters you can use to check for memory bottlenecks include the following:

- **Memory\Available Bytes** Records the number of bytes of physical memory available to processes running on the server. When there is less than 5 percent of memory free, the system is low on memory and performance can suffer. The server might page excessively to disk to try to keep up with resource demands. Memory is critically short if there is less than 4 megabytes (MB) of memory free, and in this case, the system might page excessively to disk and try to borrow memory from running processes to keep up with resource demands. If the system is very low on memory, it could also point to a possible memory leak.

- **Memory\Committed Bytes** Records the number of bytes of committed virtual memory. This represents memory that has been paged to disk and is in use. If a server is using too much virtual memory relative to the total physical memory on the system, you might need to add physical memory.
- **Memory\Commit Limit** Shows the total physical and virtual memory available. As the number of committed bytes grows, the paging file is allowed to grow up to its maximum size, which can be determined by subtracting the total physical memory on the system from the commit limit. If you set the initial paging file size too small, the system will repeatedly extend the paging file and this requires system resources. It is better to set the initial page size as appropriate for typical usage or simply use a fixed paging file size. For a fixed paging file, set the size to at least two times the size of RAM.
- **Memory\Page Faults/Sec** Records the average number of page faults per second. It includes both hard and soft page faults. Soft faults result in memory lookups. Hard faults require access to disk.
- **Memory\Pages/Sec** Records the number of memory pages that are read from disk or written to disk to resolve hard page faults. It is the sum of Memory\Pages Input/Sec and Memory\Pages Output/Sec.
- **Memory\Pages Input/Sec** Records the rate at which pages are read from disk to resolve hard page faults. Hard page faults occur when a requested page isn't in memory and the computer has to go to disk to get it. Too many hard faults can cause significant delays and hurt performance.
- **Memory\Pages Output/Sec** Records the rate at which pages are written to disk to free up space in physical memory. If the server has to free up memory too often, this is an indicator that there isn't enough physical memory (RAM) on the system.
- **Memory\Pool Paged Bytes** Represents the size in bytes of the paged pool. The paged pool is an area of system memory for objects that can be written to disk when they aren't used. If the size of the paged pool is large relative to the total amount of physical memory on the system, you might need to add memory to the system. If this value slowly increases in size over time, a kernel mode process might have a memory leak.
- **Memory\Pool Nonpaged Bytes** Represents the size in bytes of the nonpaged pool. The nonpaged pool is an area of system memory for objects that can't be written to disk. If the size of the nonpaged pool is large relative to the total amount of virtual memory allocated to the server, you might want to increase the virtual memory size. If this value slowly increases in size over time, a kernel mode process might have a memory leak.

- **Paging File\%Usage** Records the percentage of the paging file currently in use. If this value approaches 100 percent for all instances, you should consider either increasing the virtual memory size or adding physical memory to the system. This will ensure the server has additional memory if it needs it, such as when the server load grows.
- **Paging File\%Usage** Records the peak size of the paging file as a percentage of the total paging file size available. A high value can mean that the paging file isn't large enough to handle increased load conditions.
- **Physical Disk\%Disk Time** Records the percentage of time that the selected disk spent servicing read and write requests. Keep track of this value for the physical disks that have paging files. If you see this value increasing over several monitoring periods, you should more closely monitor paging file usage and you might consider adding physical memory to the system.
- **Physical Disk\Avg Disk Queue Length** Records the average number of read and write requests that were waiting for the selected disk during the sample interval. Keep track of this value for the physical disks that have paging files. If you see this value increasing over time and the Memory\Page Reads/Sec is also increasing, the system is having to perform a lot of paging file reads.
- **Physical Disk\Avg Disk Sec/Transfer** Records the length in seconds of the average disk transfer. Track this value for the physical disks that have paging files in conjunction with Memory\Pages/Sec. Memory\Pages/Sec tracks the number of reads and writes for the paging file. If you multiply the Physical Disk\Avg Disk Sec/Transfer by the Memory\Pages/Sec value, you have an excellent indicator of how much of the disk access time is being used by paging. Use the result to help you decide whether to move the paging files to faster disks or add physical memory to the system.

Resolving Processor Bottlenecks

After you've eliminated memory as a potential bottleneck, you should examine the system's processor usage to determine whether there are any potential bottlenecks. Processor bottlenecks can occur if a process's threads need more processing time than is available. This in turn causes the processor queue to grow because threads have to wait to get processing time. As a result, the system response suffers and the system appears sluggish or nonresponsive.

Excess interrupts are another common reason for processor bottlenecks. Each time drivers or disk subsystem components, such as hard disk drives or network components, generate an interrupt, the processor has to stop what it is doing to handle the request because requests from hardware take priority. However, poorly designed drivers and components can generate false interrupts, which tie up the processor for no reason. System boards or components that are failing can generate false interrupts as well.

Tip Watch out for bad device drivers and system components
Generally, you'll see more interrupt problems with beta or nonsigned drivers than with signed drivers. A poorly designed driver could by itself generate several thousand interrupts per second, and a processor can get overloaded quickly under those conditions.

Troubleshooting

Rule out processor affinity as an issue on multiprocessor systems

On multiprocessor systems, you might need to rule out processor affinity as a cause of a processor bottleneck. By using processor affinity, you can set a program or process to use a specific processor to improve its performance. Assigning processor affinity can, however, block access to the processor for other programs and processes.

If a system's processors are the performance bottleneck, adding memory, drives, or network connections won't overcome the problem. Instead, you might need to upgrade the processors to faster clock speeds or add processors to increase the server's upper capacity. You could also move processor-intensive applications, such as Microsoft Exchange Server, to another server.

Counters you can use to check for processor bottlenecks include the following:

- **System\Processor Queue Length** Records the number of threads waiting to be executed. These threads are queued in an area shared by all processors on the system. If this counter has a sustained value of 10 or more threads, you might need to upgrade the processors to faster clock speeds or add processors to increase the server's upper capacity.
- **Processor\%Processor Time** Records the percentage of time the selected processor is executing a nonidle thread. You should track this counter separately for all processor instances on the server. If the %Processor Time values for all instances are high (above 75 percent) while the network interface and disk input/output (I/O) throughput rates are relatively low, you might need to upgrade the processors to faster clock speeds or add processors to increase the server's upper capacity.
- **Processor\%User Time** Records the percentage of time the selected processor is executing a nonidle thread in User mode. *User mode* is a processing mode for applications and user-level subsystems. A high value for all process instances might indicate that you need to upgrade the processors to faster clock speeds or add processors to increase the server's upper capacity.
- **Processor\%Privileged Time** Records the percentage of time the selected processor is executing a nonidle thread in Privileged mode. *Privileged mode* is a processing mode for operating system components and services, allowing direct access to hardware and

memory. A high value for all processor instances might indicate that you need to upgrade the processors to faster clock speeds or add processors to increase the server's upper capacity.

- **Processor\Interrupts/Sec** Records the average rate, in incidents per second, that the processor received and serviced hardware interrupts. Compare this value to your baselines. If this value changes substantially (I mean by thousands of interrupts) without a corresponding increase in activity, the system might have a hardware problem. To resolve this problem, you must identify the device or component that is causing the problem. Start with devices that have drivers you've updated recently.

Resolving Disk I/O Bottlenecks

With the high-speed disks available today, a system's hard disks are rarely the primary reason for a bottleneck. It is more likely that a system is having to do a lot of disk reads and writes because there isn't enough physical memory available and the system has to page to disk. Because reading from and writing to disk is much slower than reading and writing memory, excessive paging can degrade the server's overall performance. To reduce the amount of disk activity, you want the system to manage memory as efficiently as possible and page to disk only when necessary.

That said, you can do several things with a system's hard disks to improve performance. If the system has faster drives than the ones used for the paging file, you might consider moving the paging file to those disks. If the system has one or more drives that are doing most of the work and other drives that are mostly idle, you might be able to improve performance by balancing the load across the drives more efficiently.

To help you better gauge disk I/O activity, use the following counters:

- **PhysicalDisk\%Disk Time** Records the percentage of time the physical disk is busy. Track this value for all hard disk drives on the system in conjunction with Processor\%Processor Time and Network Interface Connection\Bytes Total/Sec. If the %Disk Time value is high and the processor and network connection values aren't high, the system's hard disk drives might be creating a bottleneck. You might be able to improve performance by balancing the load across the drives more efficiently or by adding drives and configuring the system so that they are used.

> **Note** Redundant array of independent disks (RAID) devices can cause the PhysicalDisk\%Disk Time value to exceed 100 percent. For this reason, don't rely on PhysicalDisk\%Disk Time for RAID devices. Instead, use PhysicalDisk\Current Disk Queue Length.

- **PhysicalDisk\Current Disk Queue Length** Records the number of system requests that are waiting for disk access. A high value indicates that the disk waits are impacting system performance. In general, you want there to be very few waiting requests.

> **Note** Physical disk queue lengths are relative to the number of physical disks on the system and proportional to the length of the queue minus the number of drives. For example, if a system has two drives and there are 6 waiting requests, that can be considered a proportionally large number of queued requests; but if a system has eight drives and there are 10 waiting requests, that is considered a proportionally small number of queued requests.

- **PhysicalDisk\Avg. Disk Write Queue Length** Records the number of write requests that are waiting to be processed.
- **PhysicalDisk\Avg. Disk Read Queue Length** Records the number of read requests that are waiting to be processed.
- **PhysicalDisk\Disk Writes/Sec** Records the number of disk writes per second. It is an indicator of how much disk I/O activity there is. By tracking the number of writes per second and the size of the write queue, you can determine how write operations are impacting disk performance. If lots of write operations are queuing and you are using RAID 5, it could be an indicator that you would get better performance by using RAID 1. Remember that by using RAID 5 you typically get better read performance than RAID 1. So, there's a trade-off to be made by using either RAID configuration.
- **PhysicalDisk\Disk Reads/Sec** Records the number of disk reads per second. It is an indicator of how much disk I/O activity there is. By tracking the number of reads per second and the size of the read queue, you can determine how read operations are impacting disk performance. If lots of read operations are queuing and you are using RAID 1, it could be an indicator that you would get better performance by using RAID 5. Remember that by using RAID 1 you typically get better write performance than RAID 5. So, as mentioned, there's a trade-off to be made by using either RAID configuration.

Resolving Network Bottlenecks

The network that connects your computers is critically important. Its responsiveness, or lack thereof, weighs heavily on the way users perceive the responsiveness of their computers and any computers to which they connect. It doesn't matter how fast their computers are or how fast your servers are. If there's a big delay (and big network delays are measured in tens of milliseconds) between when a request is made and the time it's received, users might think systems are slow or nonresponsive.

Unfortunately, in most cases, the delay (latency) users experience is beyond your control. It's a function of the type of connection the user has and the route the request takes to your server. The total capacity of your server to handle requests and the amount of bandwidth available to your servers are factors you can control, however. Network capacity is a function of the network cards and interfaces configured on the servers. Network bandwidth availability is a function of your organization's network infrastructure and how much traffic is on it when a request is made.

Counters you can use to check network activity and look for bottlenecks include the following:

- **Network Interface\Bytes Total/Sec** Records the rate at which bytes are sent and received over a network adapter. Track this value separately for each network adapter configured on the system. If the Bytes Total/Sec for a particular adapter is substantially slower than what you'd expect given the speed of the network and the speed of the network card, you might want to check the network card configuration. Check to see whether the link speed is set for half duplex or full duplex. In most cases, you'll want to use full duplex.
- **Network Interface\Current Bandwidth** Estimates the current bandwidth for the selected network adapter in bits per second. Track this value separately for each network adapter configured on the system. Most servers use 10/100 network cards or Gigabit Ethernet cards, which can be configured in many ways. Someone might have configured a card for 10 megabits per second (Mbps). If that is the case, the current bandwidth might be off by a factor of 10.
- **Network Interface\Bytes Received/Sec** Records the rate at which bytes are received over a network adapter. Track this value separately for each network adapter configured on the system.
- **Network Interface\Bytes Sent/Sec** Records the rate at which bytes are sent over a network adapter. Track this value separately for each network adapter configured on the system.

Troubleshooting

Compare network activity to disk time and processor time

Compare these values in conjunction with PhysicalDisk\%Disk Time and Processor\%Processor Time. If the disk time and processor time values are low but the network values are very high, a capacity problem might exist. Solve the problem by optimizing the network card settings or by adding an additional network card.

Performance Logging

By using performance logs you can record performance information for replay in Performance Monitor at a later date. You can also export logging data to spreadsheets or databases for analysis and report generation. Performance logging is configured as a Windows service called Performance Logs and Alerts. Because this service runs under the special identity Network Service by default, a user needn't be logged on to the computer you are monitoring to collect performance information.

> **Note** The Performance Logs and Alerts service is configured to start manually and is stopped by default. You shouldn't start it yourself. It is started by the Performance Logs and Alerts snap-in as necessary.

Creating Performance Logs

You create performance logs by using Performance Monitor. In Performance Monitor, expand the Performance Logs And Alerts node, and then select the type of performance log you want to create. Two types of performance logs are available: counter logs and trace logs.

Counter logs record performance data at a specific interval by using the performance objects and counters discussed previously. You can save data in several formats, including comma-delimited and tab-delimited text and binary. When using a text file, you can export the data to a spreadsheet or database for further analysis. When using the binary format, logged data can be replayed in real time in System Monitor.

Trace logs monitor continuously for specific types of events from Windows system providers and subcomponents and record performance data whenever those events occur. Trace logs can also obtain information from nonsystem providers such as Active Directory, Netlogon, and the Security Accounts Manager (SAM). To interpret the trace log output, you need a parsing tool that can read the raw data and convert it into a usable format. One tool available in Windows Server 2003 is Tracerpt. Tracerpt is a command-line utility that processes trace logs and allows you to generate trace analysis reports and comma-delimited text files for the events generated.

For both trace and counter logs, parameters that you track in log files are recorded separately from parameters that you chart in Performance Monitor. You can configure performance logging to start manually or automatically. Logging can be manually started in Performance Monitor. Automatic monitoring can be scheduled to start at a specific date and time.

Using Counter Logs

After you select the Counter Logs node in the left pane of Performance Monitor, you should see a list of current logs (if any) in the right pane. A green log symbol next to the log name, as shown in the following screen, indicates logging is active. A red log symbol indicates logging is stopped.

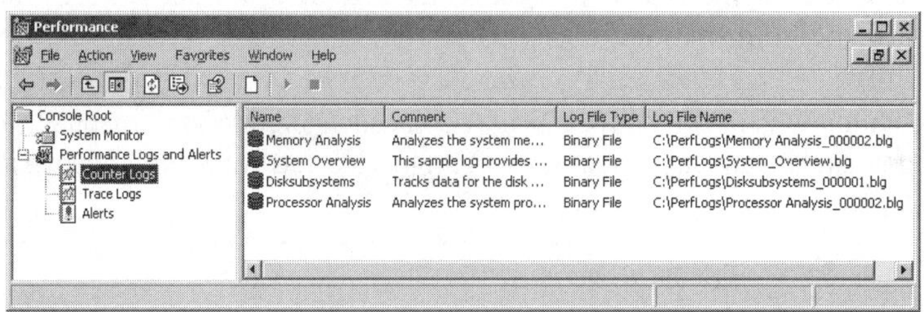

You can manage an existing counter log by right-clicking its entry in the right pane, and then selecting one of the available shortcut options. Choose Delete to delete the log. Choose Properties to display the log's Properties dialog box. Choose Start to activate logging. Choose Stop to halt logging. Choose Save Settings As to save the log configuration as a Web page that can be viewed in a browser, such as Microsoft Internet Explorer, or imported into a new counter log using New Log Settings From.

Tip **View performance data from the Web**

The Web page created by using the Save Settings As option has an embedded System Monitor that you can use to view the performance data you've configured. If you save the settings to a folder published under Microsoft Internet Information Services (IIS), you are able to view performance data remotely. All you must do is type the appropriate Uniform Resource Locator (URL) in the Web browser's Address box.

You can create a new counter log by right-clicking in the right pane and selecting New Log Settings from the shortcut menu. A New Log Settings dialog box is displayed asking you to name the new log settings. Type a descriptive name here before continuing, and then click OK. A Properties dialog box similar to the one in Figure 16-4 is displayed.

You have two options for tracking performance data. To add all counters for specific performance objects, click Add Objects, and then use the Add Object dialog box to select the objects you want to add. All counters for these objects will be logged. To add specific counters for objects, click Add Counters, and then use the Select Counters dialog box to select the counters you want to add.

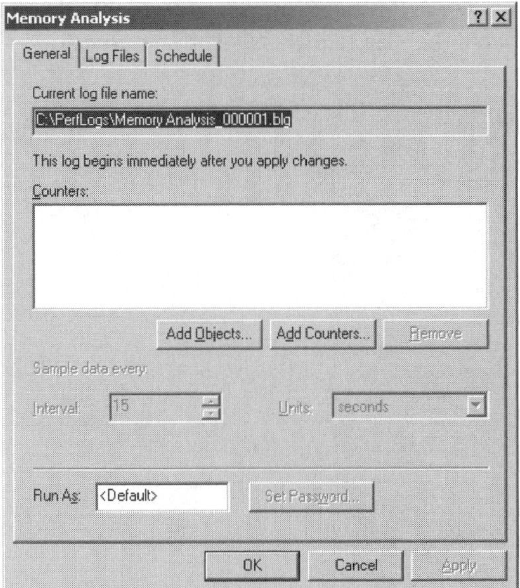

Figure 16-4. After you name the counter log, you can specify the performance objects and counters you want to track.

In the Properties dialog box, any counters you've selected are added to the Counters list in the General tab. By default, each counter is sampled once every 15 seconds. For most monitoring, this is too rapid because you'll want to collect data over a period of several hours and the data set grows too large with so much sampling going on. Lots of sampling also requires lots of processing power. So, to reduce overhead and get a more useful sample, set a longer sampling interval, such as once every 5 minutes or once every 15 minutes.

Inside Out

Use an account with appropriate access permissions when necessary

By default, the Performance Logs and Alerts service runs as the special identity Network Service. If this special identity doesn't have sufficient permissions to collect the performance data, such as when you are remotely monitoring, you might want to specify an administrator account to use. In the Run As box, type the name of the account under which the counter log will run, and then click Set Password. After you type the password for the account and then confirm the password, click OK to close the Set Password dialog box. To run the log under the default account later, type **<Default>**.

Next, select the Log Files tab, as shown in Figure 16-5. By default, counter logs are saved as sequentially numbered binary files in the %SystemDrive%\PerfLogs directory.

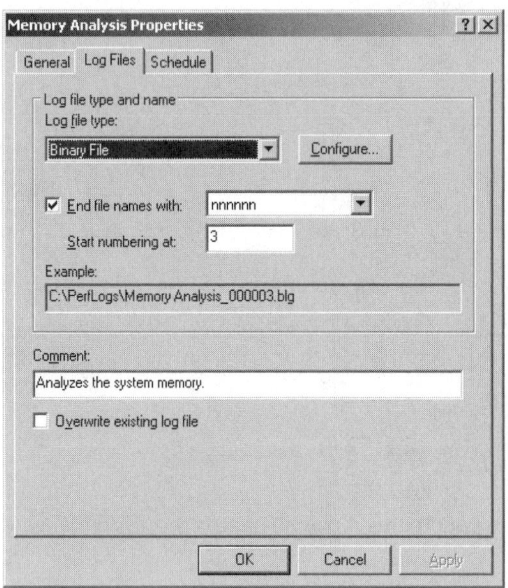

Figure 16-5. After you specify counters to track, configure the logging options.

If desired, you can change the logging options. Use Log File Type to set the log type as one of the following formats:

- Text File (Comma Delimited) creates a log file with comma-separated entries.
- Text File (Tab Delimited) creates a log file with tab-separated entries.
- Binary File creates a binary file that Performance Monitor can read.
- Binary Circular File creates a binary file that overwrites old data with new data when the file reaches a specified size limit.
- SQL Database writes the performance data to a Microsoft SQL database.

> **Tip** If you plan to use Performance Monitor to analyze or view the log, use one of the binary file formats.

If you want the counter logs to use a particular naming style, Use End File Names With to set an automatic suffix for each new file created when you run the counter log. Logs can have a numeric suffix or a suffix in a specific date format. With a numeric suffix, use Start Numbering At to set the first serial number for a log that uses an automatic numeric suffix.

After you set the log file type, click Configure to configure the log file location. If you selected SQL Database as the file type, use the Configure SQL Logs dialog box to select a previously configured system Data Source Name (DSN). The DSN is used to establish a connection to a structured query language (SQL)–compliant database. If you selected another file type, you'll be able to set the log file name and folder location. By choosing either selection, you have the option of limiting the log file size to a specific value, such as 1 MB, as shown in the following screen:

When you've set all of the log file options, click the Schedule tab, shown in Figure 16-6, and then specify when logging should start and stop. You can configure the logging to start manually or automatically at a specific date. Select the appropriate option, and then specify a start date if necessary.

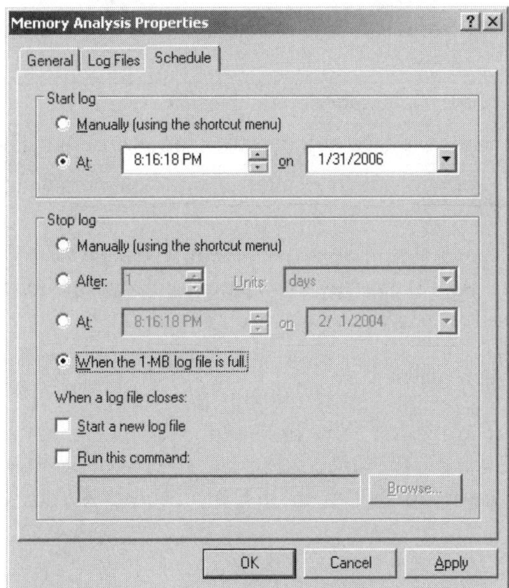

Figure 16-6. Specify when logging should start and stop.

Chapter 16

Once logging is started, it will continue until you manually shut it off. You can configure the log file to stop manually after a specified period of time, such as seven days, at a specific date and time, or when the log file is full (if you've set a specific file size limit). When a log file closes, you can start a new log file or run a command automatically as well.

Click OK when you've finished setting the logging schedule and the new log will be added to the Counter Logs list. The log's icon will be red until logging starts.

Monitoring Performance from the Command Line

Windows Server 2003 includes a command-line utility called Typeperf for writing performance data to the command line. You can use it to monitor the performance of both local and remote computers. The available parameters for Typeperf are summarized in Table 16-2.

Table 16-2. Parameters for Typeperf

Parameter	Description
–cf <*filename*>	Specifies a file containing a list of performance counters to monitor.
–config <*filename*>	Specifies the settings file containing command options.
–f <CSV|TSV|BIN|SQL>	Sets the output file format. The default is .csv for comma separated values.
–o <*filename*>	Sets the path of an output file or SQL database.
–q [*object*]	Lists installed counters for the specified object.
–qx [*object*]	Lists installed counters with instances.
–s <*ComputerName*>	Sets the server to monitor if no server is specified in the counter path.
–sc <*samples*>	Sets the number of samples to collect.
–si <[[*hh*:]*mm*:]ss>	Sets the time between samples. The default is 1 second.
–y	Answers Yes to all questions without prompting.

Looks complicated, I know, but Typeperf is fairly easy to use once you get started. In fact, all you really need to provide to get basic monitoring information is the pathname to the performance counter you want to track. The performance counter path has the following syntax:

```
\\ComputerName\ObjectName\ObjectCounter
```

Here, the path starts with the UNC computer name or IP address of the local or remote computer you are working with and includes the object name and the object counter to use. If you wanted to track System\Processor Queue Length on CORPSVR02, you'd type:

```
typeperf "\\corpsvr02\System\Processor Queue Length"
```

Note You might have noticed that I enclosed the counter path in double quotation marks. Although this is good form for all counter paths, it is required in this example because the counter path includes spaces.

You can also easily track all counters for an object by using an asterisk (*) as the counter name, such as in the following:

```
typeperf "\\corpsvr02\Memory\*"
```

Here, you track all counters for the Memory object.

A slight problem is introduced for objects that have multiple instances. For these objects, such as the Processor object, you must specify the object instance you want to work with. The syntax for this is as follows:

```
\\ComputerName\ObjectName(ObjectInstance)\ObjectCounter
```

Here, you follow the object name with the object instance in parentheses. To work with all instances of an object that has multiple instances, you use _Total as the instance name. To work with a specific instance of an object, use its instance identifier. For example, if you want to examine the Processor\%Processor Time counter, you must use either this to work with all processor instances:

```
typeperf "\\corpsvr02\Processor(_Total)\%Processor Time"
```

or this to work with a specific processor instance:

```
typeperf "\\corpsvr02\Processor(0)\%Processor Time"
```

In this case, that is the first processor on the system.

By default, Typeperf writes its output to the command line in a comma-delimited list. You can redirect the output to a file using the –O parameter and set the output format using the –F parameter. The output format indicators are CSV for a comma-delimited text file, TSV for a tab-delimited text file, BIN for a binary file, and SQL for a SQL binary file. Consider the following example:

```
typeperf "\\corpsvr02\Memory\*" -o perf.bin -f bin
```

Here, you track all counters for the Memory object and write the output to a binary file called Perf.bin in the current directory.

If you need help determining the available counters, type **typeperf –q** followed by the object name whose counters you want to view, such as in the following:

```
typeperf -q Memory
```

If an object has multiple instances, you can list the installed counters with instances by using the –QX parameter, such as in the following:

```
typeperf -qx PhysicalDisk
```

You can use this counter information as input to Typeperf as well. Add the –O parameter and write the output to a text file, such as in the following:

```
typeperf -qx PhysicalDisk -o perf.txt
```

Then edit the text file so that only the counters you want to track are included. You can then use the file to determine which performance counters are tracked by specifying the –CF parameter followed by the file path to this counter file. Consider the following example:

```
typeperf -cf perf.txt -o c:\perflogs\perf.bin -f bin
```

Here, Typeperf reads the list of counters to track from Perf.txt and then writes the performance data in binary format to a file in the C:\PerfLogs directory.

The one problem with Typeperf is that it will sample data once every second until you tell it to stop by pressing Ctrl+C. This is fine when you are working at the command line and monitoring the output. It doesn't work so well, however, if you have other things to do—and most administrators do. To control the sampling interval and set how long to sample, you can use the –SI and –SC parameters, respectively. For example, if you wanted Typeperf to sample every 60 seconds and stop logging after 120 samples, you could type this:

```
typeperf -cf perf.txt -o C:\perf\logs\perf.bin -f bin -si 60 -sc 120
```


Using Trace Logs

You use trace logs to monitor continuously for specific types of events generated by system providers and subcomponents of the operating system, then you can record performance data whenever those events occur. For Windows system providers, you can track the following general events:

- **Process creations/deletions** Records performance data related to the creation and deletion of processes.
- **Threads creations/deletions** Records performance data related to the creation and deletion of threads.
- **Disk I/O** Records disk I/O operations. You should select this data if you plan to monitor file details.
- **Network TCP/IP** Records Transmission Control Protocol/Internet Protocol (TCP/IP) send and receive requests.

- **Page faults** Records page faults.
- **File details** Records file I/O operations.

Trace logs can also obtain information from nonsystem providers, including these:

- Active Directory: Core
- Active Directory: Kerberos
- Active Directory: Netlogon
- Active Directory: SAM
- DNS Trace
- Local Security Authority (LSA)
- NTLM Security Protocol
- Processor Trace Information
- Spooler Trace Control

After you select the Trace Logs node in the left pane of Performance Monitor, you should see a list of current logs (if any) in the right pane. A green log symbol next to the log name, as shown in the following screen, indicates logging is active. A red log symbol indicates logging is stopped.

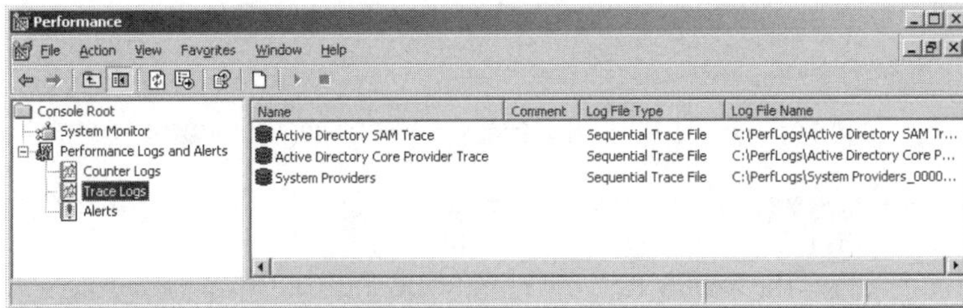

You can manage an existing trace log by right-clicking its entry in the right pane, and then selecting one of the available shortcut options. Choose Delete to delete the log. Choose Properties to display the log's Properties dialog box. Choose Start to activate logging. Choose Stop to halt logging. Choose Save Settings As to save the log configuration as a Web page that can be viewed in a browser, such as Internet Explorer, or imported into a new counter log using the New Log Settings From option.

> **Tip** **View performance data from the Web**
> The Web page created by using Save Settings As has an embedded System Monitor that you can use to view the performance data you've configured. If you save the settings to a folder published under IIS, you are able to view performance data remotely. All you must do is type the appropriate URL in the Web browser's Address box.

You can create a new trace log by right-clicking in the right pane and selecting New Log Settings from the shortcut menu. A New Log Settings dialog box is displayed asking you to name the new log settings. Type a descriptive name here before continuing, and then click OK. A Properties dialog box similar to the one in Figure 16-7 is displayed.

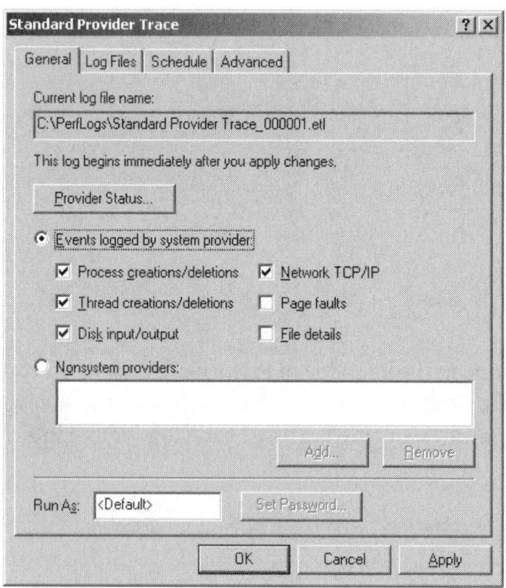

Figure 16-7. After you name the trace log, you can specify the provider to track.

To trace operating system events, select the Events Logged By System Provider option, then select system events to trace. Collecting page faults and file details events puts a heavy load on the server and causes the log file to grow rapidly. Because of this, you should collect page faults and file details only for a limited amount of time.

To trace events from nonsystem providers, select the Nonsystem Providers option, and then click Add. This displays the Add Nonsystem Providers dialog box, which you use to select the provider to trace.

In the Run As box, type the name of the account under which the counter log will run, and then click Set Password. After you type the password for the account and then confirm the password, click OK to close the Set Password dialog box. To run the log under the default account, Network Services, type <**Default**>.

Next, select the Log Files tab, as shown in Figure 16-8. For trace logs, you have two log types: Sequential Trace File, which writes events to the trace log sequentially up to the maximum file size (if any), and Circular Trace File, which overwrites old data with new data when the file reaches a specified size limit. By default, counter logs are saved as sequentially numbered binary files in the %SystemDrive%\PerfLogs directory.

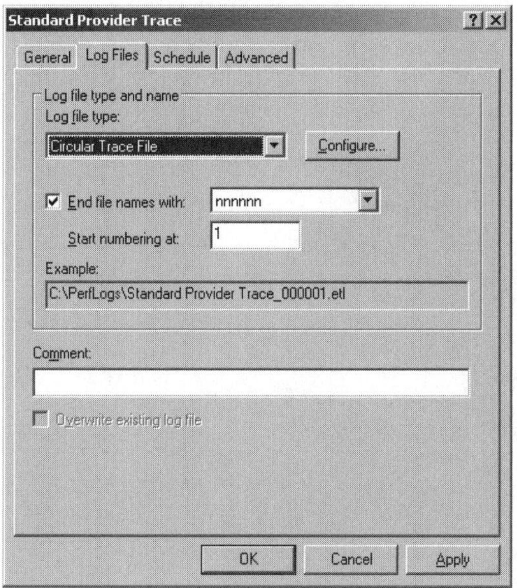

Figure 16-8. After you specify providers to use, configure the logging options.

If you want the trace logs to use a particular naming style, use the End File Names With option to set an automatic suffix for each new file created when you run the trace log. Logs can have a numeric suffix or a suffix in a specific date format. For a numeric suffix, use the Start Numbering At option to set the first serial number for a log that uses an automatic numeric suffix.

After you set the log file type, click Configure to configure the log file location. You are able to set the log file name and folder location. You also have the option of limiting the log file size to a specific value, such as 1 MB, as shown in the following screen:

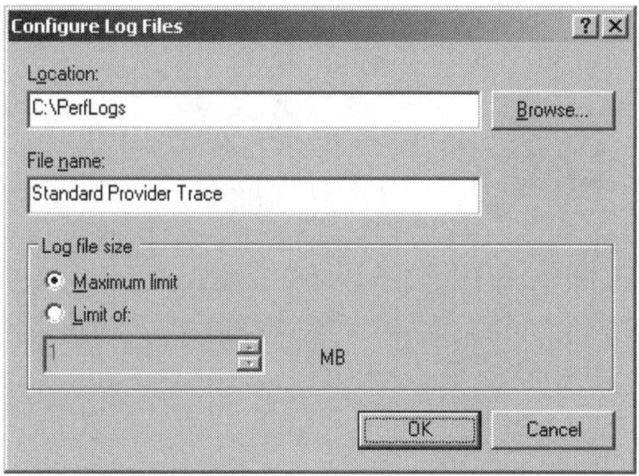

When you've set all of the log file options, click the Schedule tab, shown in Figure 16-9, and then specify when logging should start and stop. You can configure the logging to start manually or automatically at a specific date. Select the appropriate option, and then specify a start date if necessary.

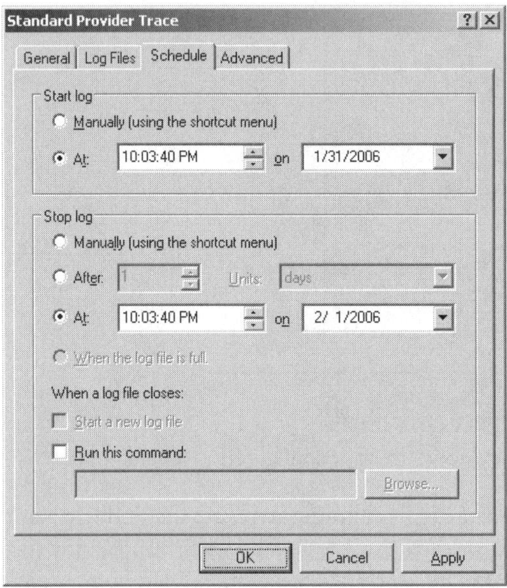

Figure 16-9. Specify when logging should start and stop.

Once logging is started, it will continue until you manually shut it off. You can configure the log file to stop manually after a specified period of time, such as seven days, at a specific date and time, or when the log file is full (if you've set a specific file size limit). When a log file closes, you can start a new log file or run a command automatically.

Click OK when you've finished setting the logging schedule and the new log will be added to the Trace Logs list. The log's icon will be red until logging starts.

Analyzing Performance Logs

Once you set up performance logging, you can use the logs to record performance data. When you are ready at a later date to view and work with the data, you must access and view the logs to try to interpret the data using the techniques previously discussed. The method of viewing the log data depends on the log type and its format.

Analyzing Counter Logs

After you create a counter log, you can replay data collected in binary format to analyze the results much like you do with live performance information you're collecting in System Monitor. In Performance Monitor, select the System Monitor entry in the left pane, and then press Ctrl+Q to display the System Monitor Properties dialog box. Alternately, you can right-click the System Monitor details pane and select Properties from the shortcut menu.

Next, as shown in Figure 16-10, click the Source tab. In the Data Source panel, select Log Files, and then click Add to open the Select Log File dialog box. You can now select the log file you want to analyze. By default performance logs are stored in C:\PerfLogs.

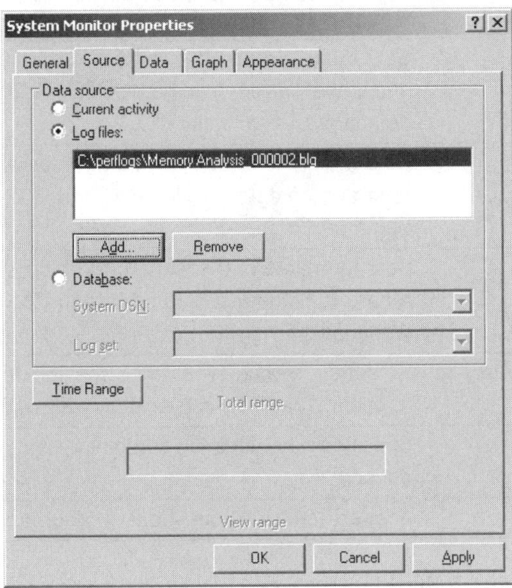

Figure 16-10. Select the saved counter log.

Click Time Range so you can specify the time window that you want to analyze by dragging the Total Range bar to specify the appropriate starting and ending times. Drag the left edge to the right to move up the start time. Drag the right edge to the left to move down the end time.

Afterward, select the Data tab so that you can choose the performance counters to view. Click the Add button. This displays the Add Counter dialog box, which you can use to select the counters that you want to analyze. Only counters that you logged are available. If you don't see a counter that you want to work with, you must modify the log properties, restart the logging process, and then check the logs another time.

When you are finished configuring counters to view, click Close, and then click OK. In System Monitor, use the View Graph, View Histogram, and View Report options on the toolbar to display performance information based on the counters selected.

Analyzing Trace Logs

You can examine trace log data by using the Tracerpt command-line utility. Tracerpt processes trace logs and allows you to generate trace analysis reports and comma-delimited text files for the events generated. The parameters for Tracerpt are summarized in Table 16-3.

Table 16-3. Parameters for Tracerpt

Parameter	Description
–o [*filename*]	Sets the text output file to which the parsed data should be written in comma-delimited format. The default is Dumpfile.csv.
–summary [*filename*]	Sets the name of the text file to which a summary report of the data should be written. The default is Summary.txt.
–report [*filename*]	Sets the name of the text file to which a detailed report of the data should be written. The default is Workload.txt.
–rt <*session_name* [*session_name* ...]>	Sets the real-time event trace session data source to use instead of a converted log file.
–config <*filename*>	Specifies a settings file containing command options.
–y	Answers Yes to all questions without prompting.

The most basic way to use Tracerpt is to specify the name of the trace log to use. By default trace logs are written to C:\PerfLogs, so if a log in this directory was named SysP_000002.etl, you could analyze it by typing the following:

```
tracerpt C:\Perflogs\SysP_000002.etl
```

Here, three files are created in the current directory: The parsed output is written to Dumpfile.csv, a summary report is written to Summary.txt, and a detailed report is written to Workload.txt.

You could also specify the exact files to use for output as shown in the following example:

```
tracerpt C:\Perflogs\ SysP_000002.etl -o c:\sysp.csv -summary c:\sysp-summary.txt
-report sysp-report-.txt
```

Creating Performance Alerts

You can use performance alerts to notify you and others when certain events occur or when certain performance thresholds are reached. You can also use performance alerts to generate events that are logged in the Application event log and to start applications and performance logs.

After you select the Alerts node in the left pane of Performance Monitor, you should see a list of current alerts (if any) in the right pane. A green log symbol next to an alert, as shown in the following screen, indicates it is active. A red log symbol indicates the alert is inactive and won't be triggered even if the performance alert condition is reached.

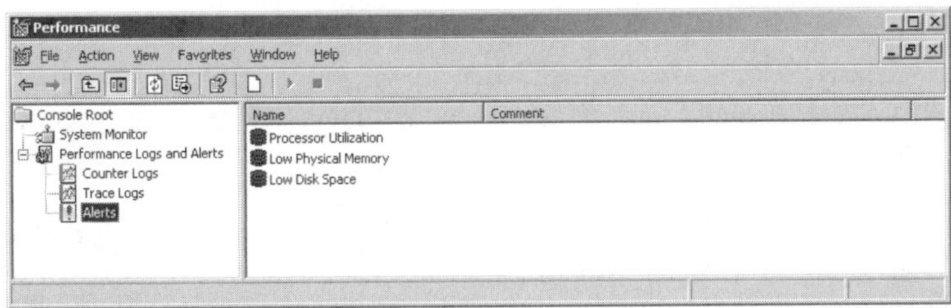

You can manage an existing alert by right-clicking its entry in the right pane and then selecting one of the available shortcut options. Choose Delete to delete the alert. Choose Properties to display the alert's Properties dialog box. Choose Start to activate the alert. Choose Stop to stop the alert. Choose Save Settings As to save the alert configuration as a Web page that can be viewed in a browser, such as Internet Explorer, or imported into a new alert by using the New Alert Settings From option.

You can create a new alert by right-clicking in the right pane and selecting New Alert Settings from the shortcut menu. A New Alert Settings dialog box is displayed asking you to name the new alert. Type a descriptive name here before continuing, and then click OK. A Properties dialog box similar to the one in Figure 16-11 is displayed.

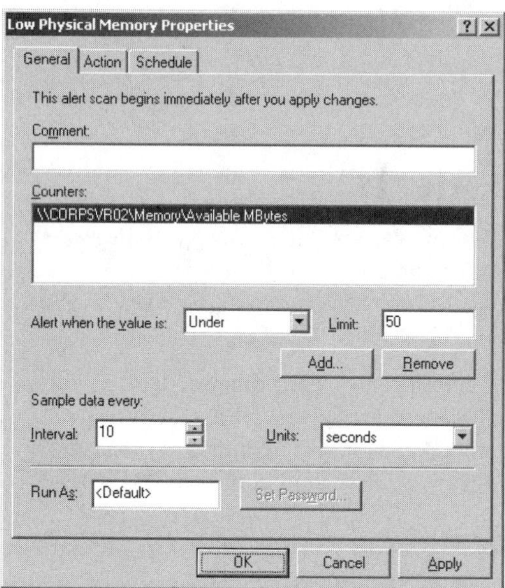

Figure 16-11. Create a new alert by adding counters and setting the alert conditions for those counters.

Click Add to display the Add Counters dialog box, then add the counters for which you want to define alert conditions. When you are finished, click Close to return to the Properties dialog box of the alert. In the Counters panel, select the first counter, and then use the Alert When Value Is box to specify when an alert for this counter is triggered. Alerts can be triggered when the counter is over or under a specific value. Select Over or Under, and then set the trigger value. The unit of measurement is whatever makes sense for the currently selected counter(s). For example, to alert if the available megabytes of memory is less than 50, you would select Under and then type **50**. Repeat this process to configure other counters you've selected.

In the Sample Data Every box, type in a sample interval, and select a time unit in seconds, minutes, hours, or days. The sample interval specifies how frequently the alert condition is checked for. By default, each counter will be sampled once every 5 seconds. Because you don't want to overburden the system by checking alert conditions, you should set a sampling interval that makes the most sense given the counters you are tracking and the load on the system.

In the Run As box, type the name of the account under which the counter log will run, and then click Set Password. After you type the password for the account and then confirm the password, click OK to close the Set Password dialog box. To run alert logging under the default account, Network Service, type **<Default>**.

Next, select the Action tab, as shown in Figure 16-12. You can now specify any of the following actions to happen when an alert is triggered:

- The Log An Entry In The Application Event Log option creates entries in the Application log for alerts.
- The Send A Network Message To option sends a network message to the computer specified.
- The Start Performance Data Log option sets a counter log to start when an alert occurs.
- The Run This Program option sets the complete file path of a program or batch file script to run when the alert occurs.

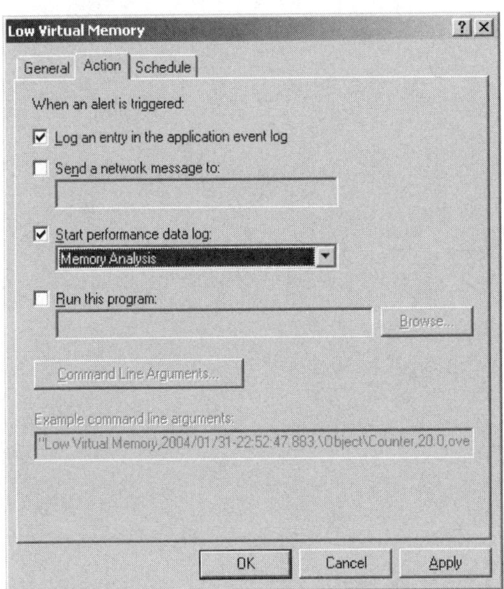

Figure 16-12. Set the actions to take if the alert is triggered.

When you've set the actions to use, click the Schedule tab, and then specify when alerting should start and stop. You can configure the alerting to start manually or automatically at a specific date. Select the appropriate option, and then specify a start date if necessary.

Once alerting is started, it will continue until you manually shut it off. Unlike performance logs, for which you usually want a specific stop date, you will usually want performance alerts to keep running. That way, you can be sure you will be alerted if a performance condition is met. Click OK when you are finished setting the alerting schedule and the new alert will be added to the Alerts list. The alert's icon will be red until alerting starts.

Part 5

Managing Windows Server 2003 Storage and File Systems

Chapter 17

Planning for High Availability

The enterprise depends on highly available, scalable, and manageable systems. High availability refers to the ability of the system to withstand hardware, application, or service outages while maintaining system availability. High scalability refers to the ability of the system to expand processor and memory capacity, as business needs demand. High manageability refers to the ability of the system to be managed locally and remotely and the ease with which components, services, and applications can be administered.

Planning for high availability is critical to the success of using Microsoft Windows Server 2003, Enterprise Edition, and Microsoft Windows Server 2003, Datacenter Edition, and you need a solid understanding of the recommendations and operating principles for deploying and maintaining high-availability servers before you deploy servers running these editions. You should also understand the types of hardware, software, and support facilities needed for enterprise computing. These concepts are all covered in this chapter.

Planning for Software Needs

Software should be chosen for its ability to support the high-availability needs of the business system. Not all software is compatible with clustering or load balancing. Not all software must be compatible, either. Instead of making an arbitrary decision, you should let the uptime needs of the application determine the level of availability required.

An availability goal of 99 percent uptime is usual for most noncritical business systems. If an application must have 99 percent uptime, the application might not need to support clustering or load balancing. To achieve 99 percent uptime means that the application can have about 88 hours of downtime in an entire year, or 100 minutes of downtime a week.

To have 99.9 percent uptime is the availability goal for highly available business systems. If an application must have 99.9 percent uptime, the application must support clustering or load balancing. To achieve 99.9 percent uptime means that the application has less than 9 hours of downtime in an entire year, or, put another way, less than 10 minutes of downtime a week.

Inside Out

Clustering support alone isn't enough

Applications that support clustering are said to be cluster-aware. Microsoft SQL Server and Microsoft Exchange Server are examples of applications that are cluster-aware. Although both applications can be configured to provide high availability in the enterprise, they don't achieve high availability through cluster support alone. High-availability applications must support online backups and be tested for compatibility with Windows Server 2003. Support for online backups ensures that you don't have to take the application offline to back up critical data. Compatibility testing ensures that the software has been thoroughly evaluated for operation with Windows Server 2003.

To evaluate the real-world environment prior to deployment, you should perform integration testing on applications that will be used together. The purpose of integration testing is to ensure that disparate applications interact as expected and to uncover problem areas if they don't. During integration testing, testers should look at system performance and overall system utilization, as well as compatibility. Testing should be repeated prior to releasing system or application changes to a production environment.

You should standardize the software components needed to provide system services. The goal of standardization is to set guidelines for software components and technologies that will be used in the enterprise. Standardization accomplishes the following:

- Reduces the total cost of maintaining and updating software
- Reduces the amount of integration and compatibility testing needed for upgrades
- Improves recovery time because problems are easier to troubleshoot
- Reduces the amount of training needed for administration support

Software standardization isn't meant to limit the organization to a single specification. Over the life of the datacenter, new application versions, software components, and technologies will be introduced, and the organization can implement new standards and specifications as necessary. The key to success lies in ensuring there is a standard process for deploying software updates and new technologies. The standard process must include the following:

- Software compatibility and integration testing
- Software support training for personnel
- Predeployment planning
- Step-by-step software deployment checklists
- Postdeployment monitoring and maintenance

The following checklist summarizes the recommendations for designing and planning software for high availability:

- Choose software that meets the availability needs of the solution or service.
- Choose software that supports online backups.
- Test software for compatibility with other applications.
- Test software integration with other applications.
- Repeat testing prior to releasing updates.
- Create and enforce software standards.
- Define a standard process for deploying software updates.

Planning for Hardware Needs

Sound hardware strategy helps increase system availability while reducing total cost of ownership and improving recovery times. Windows Server 2003 is designed and tested for use with high-performance hardware, applications, and services. To ensure that hardware components are compatible, choose only components that are listed in the Windows Server Catalog (*http://www.microsoft.com/windows/catalog/server/*) or that are on the Hardware Compatibility List (HCL) (*http://www.microsoft.com/hcl/*).

Note All components on the HCL undergo rigorous testing in the Microsoft Windows Hardware Quality Labs (WHQL). The initial testing is 14 days with a 7-day retest for firmware revision, service pack updates, and other minor revisions. Once certified through testing, hardware vendors must maintain the configuration through updates and resubmit for testing and certification. The program requirements and the tight coordination with vendors greatly improve the reliability and availability of Windows Server 2003.

You should standardize on a hardware platform and this platform should have standardized components. Standardization accomplishes the following:

- Reduces the amount of training needed for support
- Reduces the amount of testing needed for upgrades
- Requires fewer spare parts because subcomponents are the same
- Improves recovery time because problems are easier to troubleshoot

Standardization isn't meant to restrict the datacenter to a single type of server. In an *n*-tier environment, standardization typically means choosing a standard server configuration for the front-end servers, a standard server configuration for middle-tier business logic, and a standard server configuration for back-end data services. The reason for this is that Web servers, application servers, and database servers all have different resource needs. For example, although a Web server might need to run on a dual-processor system with limited hardware RAID control and 1 gigabyte (GB) of random access memory (RAM), a database server might need to run on an eight-way system with dual-channel RAID control and 64 GB of RAM.

Standardization isn't meant to limit the organization to a single hardware specification either. Over the life of the datacenter, new equipment will be introduced and old equipment likely will become unavailable. To keep up with the pace of change, new standards and specifications should be implemented when necessary. These standards and specifications, as with the previous standards and specifications, should be published and made available to you.

Redundancy and fault tolerance must be built into the hardware design at all levels to improve availability. You can improve hardware redundancy by using the following components:

- **Clusters** Clusters provide failover support for critical applications and services.
- **Standby systems** Standby systems provide backup systems in case of total failure of a primary system.
- **Spare parts** Spare parts ensure replacement parts are available in case of failure.
- **Fault-tolerant components** Fault-tolerant components improve the internal redundancy of the system.

Storage devices, network components, cooling fans, and power supplies all can be configured for fault tolerance. For storage devices, you should be sure to use multiple disk controllers, hot-swappable drives, and redundant drive arrays. For network components, you should look well beyond the network adapter and also consider whether fault tolerance is needed for routers, switches, firewalls, load balancers, and other network equipment.

A standard process for deploying hardware must be defined and distributed to all support personnel. The standard process must include the following:

- Hardware compatibility and integration testing
- Hardware support training for personnel
- Predeployment planning
- Step-by-step hardware deployment checklists
- Postdeployment monitoring and maintenance

The following checklist summarizes the recommendations for designing and planning hardware for high availability:

- Choose hardware that is listed on the HCL.
- Create and enforce hardware standards.
- Use redundant hardware whenever possible.
- Use fault-tolerant hardware whenever possible.

- Provide a secure physical environment for hardware.
- Define a standard process for deploying hardware.

If possible, add these recommendations to the preceding checklist:

- Use fully redundant internal networks from servers to border routers.
- Use direct peering to major tier-1 telecommunications carriers.
- Use redundant external connections for data and telephony.
- Use direct connection with high-speed lines.

Planning for Support Structures and Facilities

The physical structures and facilities supporting your server room are critically important. Without adequate support structures and facilities, you will have problems. The primary considerations for support structures and facilities have to do with the physical environment of the servers. These considerations also extend to the physical security of the server environment.

Just as hardware and software have availability requirements so should support structures and facilities. Factors that affect the physical environment are as follows:

- Temperature and humidity
- Dust and other contaminants
- Physical wiring
- Power supplies
- Natural disasters
- Physical security

Temperature and humidity should be carefully controlled at all times. Processors, memory, hard drives, and other pieces of physical equipment operate most efficiently when they are kept cool; between 65 and 70 degrees Fahrenheit is the ideal temperature in most situations. Equipment that overheats can malfunction or cease to operate altogether otherwise. Servers should have multiple redundant internal fans to ensure these and other internal hardware devices are kept cool.

> **Tip** You should pay particular attention to fast-running processors and hard drives. Typically, fast processors and hard drives can become overheated and need additional cooling fans—even if the surrounding environment is cool.

Humidity should be kept low to prevent condensation, but the environment shouldn't be dry. A dry climate can contribute to static electricity problems. Antistatic devices and static guards should be used in most environments.

Dust and other contaminants can cause hardware components to overheat or short out. Servers should be protected from these contaminants whenever possible. You should ensure an air filtration system is in place in the server room or hosting facility that is used. The regular preventive maintenance cycle on the servers should include checking servers and their cabinets for dust and other contaminants. If dust is found, the servers and cabinets should be carefully cleaned.

Few things affect the physical environment more than wiring and cabling. All electrical wires and network cables should be tested and certified by qualified technicians. Electrical wiring should be configured to ensure that servers and other equipment have adequate power available for peak usage times. Ideally, multiple dedicated circuits are used to provide power.

Improperly installed network cables are the cause of most communications problems. Network cables should be tested to ensure their operation meets manufacturer specifications. Redundant cables should be installed to ensure availability of the network. All wiring and cabling should be labeled and well maintained. Whenever possible, use cable management systems and tie wraps to prevent physical damage to wiring.

Ensuring servers and their components have power is also important. Servers should have hot-swappable, redundant power supplies. Being hot swappable ensures that the power supply can be replaced without having to turn off the server. Redundancy ensures that one power supply can malfunction and the other will still deliver power to the server. You should be aware that having multiple power supplies doesn't mean that a server or hardware component has redundancy. Some hardware components require multiple power supplies to operate. In this case, an additional (third or fourth) power supply is needed to provide redundancy.

The redundant power supplies should be plugged into separate power strips, and these power strips should be plugged into separate local uninterruptible power supply (UPS) units if other backup power sources aren't available. Some facilities have enterprise UPS units that provide power for an entire room or facility. If this is the case, redundant UPS systems should be installed. To protect against long-term outages, gas- or diesel-powered generators should be installed. Most hosting and colocation facilities have generators. But having a generator isn't enough; the generator must be rated to support the peak power needs of all installed equipment. If the generator cannot support the installed equipment, brownouts (temporary outages) will occur.

> **Tip** **Protect equipment against earthquakes**
> To protect against earthquakes, server racks should have seismic protection. Seismic protection should be extended to other components and to wiring. All cables should be securely attached at both ends and, whenever possible, should be latched to something other than the server, such as a server rack.

> **Caution** A fire-suppression system should be installed to protect against fire. Dual gas-based systems are preferred, because the systems do not harm hardware when they go off. Water-based sprinkler systems, on the other hand, can destroy hardware.

In addition, access controls should be used to restrict physical access to the server room or facility. Use locks, key cards, access codes, or biometric scanners to ensure only designated individuals can gain entry to the secure area. If possible, use surveillance cameras and maintain recorded tapes for at least a week. When the servers are deployed in a hosting or colocation facility, ensure locked cages are used and that fencing extends from the floor to the ceiling.

The following checklist summarizes the recommendations for designing and planning structures and facilities:

- Maintain temperature at 65 to 70 degrees Fahrenheit.
- Maintain low humidity (but not dry).
- Install redundant internal cooling fans.
- Use an air filtration system.
- Check for dust and other contaminants periodically.
- Install hot-swappable, redundant power supplies.
- Test and certify wiring and cabling.
- Use wire management to protect cables from damage.
- Label hardware and cables.
- Install backup power sources, such as UPS and generators.
- Install seismic protection and bracing.
- Install dual gas-based fire-suppression systems.
- Restrict physical access by using locks, key cards, access codes, and so forth.
- Use surveillance cameras and maintain recorded tapes (if possible).
- Use locked cages, cabinets, and racks at offsite facilities.
- Use floor-to-ceiling fencing with cages at offsite facilities.

Planning for Day-to-Day Operations

Day-to-day operations and support procedures must be in place before deploying mission-critical systems. The most critical procedures for day-to-day operations involve the following activities:

- Monitoring and analysis
- Resources, training, and documentation

- Change control
- Problem escalation procedures
- Backup and recovery procedures
- Postmortem after recovery
- Auditing and intrusion detection

Monitoring is critical to the success of business system deployments. You must have the necessary equipment to monitor the status of the business system. Monitoring allows you to be proactive in system support rather than reactive. Monitoring should extend to the hardware, software, and network components but shouldn't interfere with normal systems operations—that is, the monitoring tools chosen should require limited system and network resources to operate.

Note Keep in mind that too much data is just as bad as not collecting any data. The monitoring tools should gather only the data required for meaningful analysis.

Without careful analysis, the data collected from monitoring is useless. Procedures should be put in place to ensure personnel know how to analyze the data they collect. The network infrastructure is a support area that is often overlooked. Be sure you allocate the appropriate resources for network monitoring.

Inside Out

Use monitoring to ensure availability

A well-run and well-maintained network should have 99.99 percent availability. There should be less than 1 percent packet loss and packet turnaround of 80 milliseconds or less. To achieve this level of availability and performance the network must be monitored. Any time business systems extend to the Internet or to wide area networks (WANs), internal network monitoring must be supplemented with outside-in monitoring that checks the availability of the network and business systems.

Resources, training, and documentation are essential to ensuring you can manage and maintain mission-critical systems. Many organizations cripple the operations team by staffing minimally. Minimally manned teams will have marginal response times and nominal effectiveness. The organization must take the following steps:

- Staff for success to be successful.
- Conduct training before deploying new technologies.

- Keep the training up-to-date with what's deployed.
- Document essential operations procedures.

Every change to hardware, software, and the network must be planned and executed deliberately. To do this, you must have established change control procedures and well-documented execution plans. Change control procedures should be designed to ensure that everyone knows what changes have been made. Execution plans should be designed to ensure that everyone knows the exact steps that were or should be performed to make a change.

Change logs are a key part of change control. Each piece of physical hardware deployed in the operational environment should have a change log. The change log should be stored in a text document or spreadsheet that is readily accessible to support personnel. The change log should show the following information:

- Who changed the hardware
- What change was made
- When the change was made
- Why the change was made

> **Tip Establish and follow change control procedures**
> Change control procedures must take into account the need for both planned changes and emergency changes. All team members involved in a planned change should meet regularly and follow a specific implementation schedule. No one should make changes that aren't discussed with the entire implementation team.

You should have well-defined backup and recovery plans. The backup plan should specifically state the following information:

- When full, incremental, differential, and log backups are used
- How often and at what time backups are performed
- Whether the backups must be conducted online or offline
- The amount of data being backed up as well as how critical the data is
- The tools used to perform the backups
- The maximum time allowed for backup and restore
- How backup media is labeled, recorded, and rotated

Backups should be monitored daily to ensure they are running correctly and that the media is good. Any problems with backups should be corrected immediately. Multiple media sets should be used for backups, and these media sets should be rotated on a specific schedule. With a four-set rotation, there is one set for daily, weekly, monthly, and quarterly backups. By rotating one media set offsite, support staff can help ensure that the organization is protected in case of a disaster.

The recovery plan should provide detailed step-by-step procedures for recovering the system under various conditions, such as procedures for recovering from hard disk drive failure or troubleshooting problems with connectivity to the back-end database. The recovery plan should also include system design and architecture documentation that details the configuration of physical hardware, application logic components, and back-end data. Along with this information, support staff should provide a media set containing all software, drivers, and operating system files needed to recover the system.

Note One thing administrators often forget about is spare parts. Spare parts for key components, such as processors, drives, and memory, should also be maintained as part of the recovery plan.

You should practice restoring critical business systems using the recovery plan. Practice shouldn't be conducted on the production servers. Instead, the team should practice on test equipment with a configuration similar to the real production servers. Practicing once a quarter or semiannually is highly recommended.

You should have well-defined problem escalation procedures that document how to handle problems and emergency changes that might be needed. Many organizations use a three-tiered help desk structure for handling problems:

- Level 1 support staff form the front line for handling basic problems. They typically have hands-on access to the hardware, software, and network components they manage. Their main job is to clarify and prioritize a problem. If the problem has occurred before and there is a documented resolution procedure, they can resolve the problem without escalation. If the problem is new or not recognized, they must understand how, when, and to whom to escalate it.
- Level 2 support staff include more specialized personnel that can diagnose a particular type of problem and work with others to resolve a problem, such as system administrators and network engineers. They usually have remote access to the hardware, software, and network components they manage. This allows them to troubleshoot problems remotely and to send out technicians once they've pinpointed the problem.
- Level 3 support staff include highly technical personnel who are subject matter experts, team leaders, or team supervisors. The level 3 team can include support personnel from vendors as well as representatives from the user community. Together, they form the emergency response or crisis resolution team that is responsible for resolving crisis situations and planning emergency changes.

All crisis situations and emergencies should be responded to decisively and resolved methodically. A single person on the emergency response team should be responsible for coordinating all changes and executing the recovery plan. This same person should be responsible for writing an after-action report that details the emergency response and resolution process used. The after-action report should analyze how the emergency was resolved and what the root cause of the problem was.

In addition, you should establish procedures for auditing system usage and detecting intrusion. In Windows Server 2003, auditing policies are used to track the successful or failed execution of the following activities:

- **Account logon events** Tracks events related to user logon and logoff
- **Account management** Tracks those tasks involved with handling user accounts, such as creating or deleting accounts and resetting passwords
- **Directory service access** Tracks access to the Active Directory directory service
- **Object access** Tracks system resource usage for files, directories, and objects
- **Policy change** Tracks changes to user rights, auditing, and trust relationships
- **Privilege use** Tracks the use of user rights and privileges
- **Process tracking** Tracks system processes and resource usage
- **System events** Tracks system startup, shutdown, restart, and actions that affect system security or the security log

You should have an incident response plan that includes priority escalation of suspected intrusion to senior team members and provides step-by-step details on how to handle the intrusion. The incident response team should gather information from all network systems that might be affected. The information should include event logs, application logs, database logs, and any other pertinent files and data. The incident response team should take immediate action to lock out accounts, change passwords, and physically disconnect the system if necessary. All team members participating in the response should write a postmortem that details the following information:

- What date and time they were notified and what immediate actions they took
- Who they notified and what the response was from the notified individual
- What their assessment of the issue is and the actions necessary to resolve and prevent similar incidents

The team leader should write an executive summary of the incident and forward this to senior management.

The following checklist summarizes the recommendations for operational support of high-availability systems:

- Monitor hardware, software, and network components 24/7.
- Ensure monitoring doesn't interfere with normal systems operations.
- Gather only the data required for meaningful analysis.
- Establish procedures that let personnel know what to look for in the data.

- Use outside-in monitoring any time systems are externally accessible.
- Provide adequate resources, training, and documentation.
- Establish change control procedures that include change logs.
- Establish execution plans that detail the change implementation.
- Create a solid backup plan that includes onsite and offsite tape rotation.
- Monitor backups and test backup media.
- Create a recovery plan for all critical systems.
- Test the recovery plan on a routine basis.
- Document how to handle problems and make emergency changes.
- Use a three-tier support structure to coordinate problem escalation.
- Form an emergency response or crisis resolution team.
- Write after-action reports that detail the process used.
- Establish procedures for auditing system usage and detecting intrusion.
- Create an intrusion response plan with priority escalation.
- Take immediate action to handle suspected or actual intrusion.
- Write postmortem reports detailing team reactions to the intrusion.

Planning for Deploying Highly Available Servers

You should always create a plan before deploying a business system. The plan should show everything that must be done before the system is transitioned into the production environment. Once in the production environment, the system is deemed operational and should be handled as outlined in the section entitled "Planning for Day-to-Day Operations" earlier in this chapter.

The deployment plan should include the following items:

- Checklists
- Contact lists
- Test plans
- Deployment schedules

Checklists are a key part of the deployment plan. The purpose of a checklist is to ensure that the entire deployment team understands the steps they need to perform. Checklists should list the tasks that must be performed and designate individuals to handle the tasks during each phase of the deployment—from planning to testing to installation. Prior to executing a checklist, the deployment team should meet to ensure that all items are covered and that the necessary interactions among team members are clearly understood. After deployment, the preliminary checklists should become a part of the system documentation and new checklists should be created any time the system is updated.

The deployment plan should include a contact list. The contact list should provide the name, role, telephone number, and e-mail address of all team members, vendors, and solution provider representatives. Alternative numbers for cell phones and pagers should be provided as well.

The deployment plan should include a test plan. An ideal test plan has several phases. In Phase I, the deployment team builds the business system and support structures in a test lab. Building the system means accomplishing the following tasks:

- Creating a test network on which to run the system
- Putting together the hardware and storage components
- Installing the operating system and application software
- Adjusting basic system settings to suit the test environment
- Configuring clustering or network load balancing as appropriate

The deployment team can conduct any necessary testing and troubleshooting in the isolated lab environment. The entire system should undergo burn-in testing to guard against faulty components. If a component is flawed, it usually fails in the first few days of operation. Testing doesn't stop with burn-in. Web and application servers should be stress tested. Database servers should be load tested. The results of the stress and load tests should be analyzed to ensure the system meets the performance requirements and expectations of the customer. Adjustments to the configuration should be made to improve performance and optimize for the expected load.

In Phase II, the deployment team tests the business system and support equipment in the deployment location. They conduct similar tests as before but in the real-world environment. Again, the results of these tests should be analyzed to ensure the system meets the performance requirements and expectations of the customer. Afterward, adjustments should be made to improve performance and optimize as necessary. The team can then deploy the business system.

After deployment, the team should perform limited, nonintrusive testing to ensure the system is operating normally. Once Phase III testing is completed, the team can use the operational plans for monitoring and maintenance.

The following checklist summarizes the recommendations for predeployment planning of mission-critical systems:

- Create a plan that covers the entire testing to operations cycle.
- Use checklists to ensure the deployment team understands the procedures.
- Provide a contact list for the team, vendors, and solution providers.
- Conduct burn-in testing in the lab.
- Conduct stress and load testing in the lab.
- Use the test data to optimize and adjust the configuration.
- Provide follow-on testing in the deployment location.
- Follow a specific deployment schedule.
- Use operational plans once final tests are completed.

Chapter 18

Preparing and Deploying Server Clusters

Clustering technologies allow servers to be connected into multiple-server units called *server clusters*. Each computer connected in a server cluster is referred to as a node. Nodes work together, acting as a single unit, to provide high availability for business applications and other critical resources, such as Microsoft Internet Information Services (IIS), Microsoft SQL Server, or Microsoft Exchange Server. Clustering allows administrators to manage the cluster nodes as a single system rather than as individual systems. Clustering allows users to access cluster resources as a single system as well. In most cases, the user doesn't even know the resources are clustered.

Microsoft Windows Server 2003 supports three cluster technologies:

- **Network Load Balancing** Network Load Balancing provides failover support for Internet Protocol (IP)–based applications and services that require high scalability and availability. By using Network Load Balancing, organizations can build groups of clustered computers to support load balancing of Transmission Control Protocol (TCP), User Datagram Protocol (UDP), and Generic Routing Encapsulation (GRE) traffic requests. Front-end Web servers are ideal candidates for Network Load Balancing.
- **Component Load Balancing** Component Load Balancing provides dynamic load balancing of application components that use COM+. By using Component Load Balancing, COM+ components can be load balanced over multiple nodes to enhance the availability and scalability of software applications. Middle-tier application servers are ideal candidates for Component Load Balancing.

- **Server cluster** Server cluster provides failover support for applications and services that require high availability, scalability, and reliability. By using server clustering, organizations can make applications and data available on multiple servers linked together in a cluster configuration. Back-end applications and services, such as those provided by database servers, are ideal candidates for Server cluster.

These cluster technologies are discussed in this chapter so that you can plan for and implement your organization's high-availability needs.

Introducing Server Clustering

A server cluster is a group of two or more servers functioning together to provide essential applications or services seamlessly to enterprise clients. The servers are physically connected together by a network and might share storage devices. Server clusters are designed to protect against application and service failure, which could be caused by application software or essential services becoming unavailable; system and hardware failure, which could be caused by problems with hardware components such as central processing units (CPUs), drives, memory, network adapters, and power supplies; and site failure, which could be caused by natural disaster, power outages, or connectivity outages.

You can use cluster technologies to increase overall availability while minimizing single points of failure and reducing costs by using industry-standard hardware and software. Each cluster technology has a specific purpose and is designed to meet different requirements. Network Load Balancing is designed to address bottlenecks caused by Web services. Component Load Balancing is designed to address the unique scalability and availability needs of Web-based applications. Server cluster is designed to maintain data integrity and provide failover support.

The clustering technologies can be and often are combined to architect a comprehensive service offering. The most common scenario in which all three solutions are combined is a commercial Web site where the site's Web servers use Network Load Balancing, application servers use Component Load Balancing, and back-end database servers use Server cluster.

Benefits and Limitations of Clustering

A server cluster provides high availability by making application software and data available on several servers linked together in a cluster configuration. If a server stops functioning, a failover process can automatically shift the workload of the failed server to another server in the cluster. The failover process is designed to ensure continuous availability for critical applications and data.

Although clusters can be designed to handle failure, they are not fault tolerant with regard to user data. The cluster by itself doesn't guard against loss of a user's work. Typically, the recovery of lost work is handled by the application software, meaning the application software must be designed to recover the user's work or it must be designed in such a way that the user session state can be maintained in the event of failure.

Clusters help to resolve the need for high availability, high reliability, and high scalability. *High availability* refers to the ability to provide user access to an application or a service a high percentage of scheduled times while attempting to reduce unscheduled outages. A cluster implementation is highly available if it meets the organization's scheduled uptime goals. Availability goals are achieved by reducing unplanned downtime and then working to improve total hours of operation for the related applications and services.

High reliability refers to the ability to reduce the frequency of system failure while attempting to provide fault tolerance in case of failure. A cluster implementation is highly reliable if it minimizes the number of single points of failure and reduces the risk that failure of a single component or system will result in the outage of all applications and services offered. Reliability goals are achieved by using redundant, fault-tolerant hardware components, application software, and systems.

High scalability refers to the ability to add resources and computers while attempting to improve performance. A cluster implementation is highly scalable if it can be scaled up and out. Individual systems can be scaled up by adding more resources such as CPUs, memory, and disks. The cluster implementation can be scaled out by adding more computers.

> **Tip** **Design for availability**
> A well-designed cluster implementation uses redundant systems and components so that the failure of an individual server doesn't affect the availability of the related applications and services. Although a well-designed solution can guard against application failure, system failure, and site failure, cluster technologies do have limitations.

Cluster technologies depend on compatible applications and services to operate properly. The software must respond appropriately when failure occurs. Cluster technology cannot protect against failures caused by viruses, software corruption, or human error. To protect against these types of problems, organizations need solid data protection and recovery plans.

Cluster Organization

Clusters are organized in loosely coupled groups often referred to as farms or packs. A *farm* is a group of servers that run similar services but don't typically share data. They are called a farm because they handle whatever requests are passed out to them using identical copies of data that is stored locally. Because they use identical copies of data rather than sharing data, members of a farm operate autonomously and are also referred to as *clones*.

A *pack* is a group of servers that operate together and share partitioned data. They are called a pack because they work together to manage and maintain services. Because members of a pack share access to partitioned data, they have unique operations modes and usually access the shared data on disk drives to which all members of the pack are connected.

In most cases, Web and application services are organized as farms, while back-end databases and critical support services are organized as packs. Web servers running IIS and using Network Load Balancing are an example of a farm. In a Web farm, identical data is replicated to all servers in the farm and each server can handle any request that comes to it by using local copies of data. For example, you might have a group of five Web servers using Network Load Balancing, each with its own local copy of the Web site data.

Database servers running SQL Server and Server cluster with partitioned database views are an example of a pack. Here, members of the pack share access to the data and have a unique portion of data or logic that they handle rather than handling all data requests. For example, in a two-node SQL Server cluster, one database server might handle accounts that begin with the letters A through M and another database server might handle accounts that begin with the letters N through Z.

Servers that use clustering technologies are often organized using a three-tier structure. The tiers in the architecture are composed as follows:

- Tier 1 includes the Web servers, which are also called front-end Web servers. Front-end Web servers typically use Network Load Balancing.
- Tier 2 includes the application servers, which are often referred to as the middle-tier servers. Middle-tier servers typically use Component Load Balancing.
- Tier 3 includes the database servers, file servers, and other critical support servers, which are often called back-end servers. Back-end servers typically use Server cluster.

Inside Out

Organize Component Load Balancing clusters based on usage

When you use Component Load Balancing in three-tier architecture, you typically have two clusters. One cluster handles the message routing between the front-end Web servers and the application servers and is referred to as the component routing cluster. The other cluster activates and runs the components installed on the application servers and is referred to as the application server cluster.

Although the component routing cluster could be configured on the Web tier without needing additional servers, you get the best availability benefits by using a separate cluster. Here, the routing would take place on separate servers that are clustered using Server cluster. The application servers would then be clustered using Component Load Balancing.

As you set out to architect your cluster solution, you should try to organize servers according to the way they will be used and the applications they will be running. In most cases, Web servers, application servers, and database servers are all organized in different ways.

By using proper architecture, the servers in a particular tier can be scaled out or up as necessary to meet growing performance and throughput needs. When you are looking to scale out by adding servers to the cluster, the clustering technology and the server operating system used are both important:

- All editions of Windows Server 2003 support up to 32-node Network Load Balancing clusters.
- Enterprise Edition and Datacenter Edition support up to 8-node Component Load Balancing clusters.
- Enterprise Edition and Datacenter Edition support Server cluster, allowing up to 8-node clusters.

When looking to scale up by adding CPUs and random access memory (RAM), the edition of the server operating system used is extremely important. In terms of both processor and memory capacity, Datacenter Edition is much more expandable. Standard Edition supports up to 4 processors and 4 gigabytes (GB) of RAM on 32-bit systems and 32 GB of RAM on 64-bit systems. Enterprise Edition supports up to 8 processors and 32 GB of RAM on 32-bit platforms and up to 64 GB of RAM on 64-bit platforms. Datacenter Edition supports up to 64 GB of RAM and 32 processors on 32-bit platforms and up to 512 GB of RAM and 128 processors on 64-bit platforms.

As you look at scalability requirements, keep in mind the real business needs of the organization. The goal should be to select the right edition of the Windows operating system to meet current and future needs. The number of servers needed depends on the anticipated server load as well as the size and types of requests the servers will handle. Processors and memory should be sized appropriately for the applications and services the servers will be running as well as the number of simultaneous user connections.

Cluster Operating Modes

For Network Load Balancing and Component Load Balancing, cluster nodes usually are identical copies of each other. Because of this, all members of the cluster can actively handle requests, and they can do so independently of each other. When members of a cluster share access to data, however, they have unique operating requirements, as is the case with Server cluster.

For Server cluster, nodes can be either active or passive. When a node is active, it is actively handling requests. When a node is passive, it is idle, on standby waiting for another node to fail. Multinode clusters can be configured by using different combinations of active and passive nodes.

When you are architecting multinode clusters, the decision as to whether nodes are configured as active or passive is extremely important. If an active node fails and there is a passive node available, applications and services running on the failed node can be transferred to the passive node. Because the passive node has no current workload, the server should be able to assume the workload of the other server without any problems (providing all servers have the same hardware configuration). If all servers in a cluster are active and a node fails, the applications and services running on the failed node can be transferred to another active node. Unlike a passive node, however, an active server already has a processing load and must be able to handle the additional processing load of the failed server. If the server isn't sized to handle multiple workloads, it can fail as well.

In a multinode configuration where there is one passive node for each active node, the servers could be configured so that under average workload they use about 50 percent of processor and memory resources. In the four-node configuration depicted in Figure 18-1, in which failover goes from one active node to a specific passive node, this could mean two active nodes (A1 and A2) and two passive nodes (P1 and P2) each with four processors and 4 GB of RAM. Here, node A1 fails over to node P1, and node A2 fails over to node P2 with the extra capacity used to handle peak workloads.

In a configuration in which there are more active nodes than passive nodes, the servers can be configured so that under average workload they use a proportional percentage of processor and memory resources. In the four-node configuration also depicted in Figure 18-1, in which nodes A, B, C, and D are configured as active and failover could go between nodes A and B or nodes C and D, this could mean configuring servers so that they use about 25 percent of processor and memory resources under an average workload. Here, node A could fail over to B (and vice versa) or node C could fail over to D (and vice versa). Because the servers must handle two workloads in case of a node failure, the processor and memory configuration would at least be doubled, so instead of using four processors and 4 GB of RAM, the servers would use eight processors and 8 GB of RAM.

When Server cluster has multiple active nodes, data must be shared between applications running on the clustered servers. In many cases, this is handled by using a shared-nothing database configuration. In a shared-nothing database configuration, the application is partitioned to access private database sections. This means that a particular node is configured with a specific view into the database that allows it to handle specific types of requests, such as account names that start with the letters A through F, and that it is the only node that can update the related section of the database (which eliminates the possibility of corruption from simultaneous writes by multiple nodes). Both Exchange Server 2003 and SQL Server 2000 support multiple active nodes and shared-nothing database configurations.

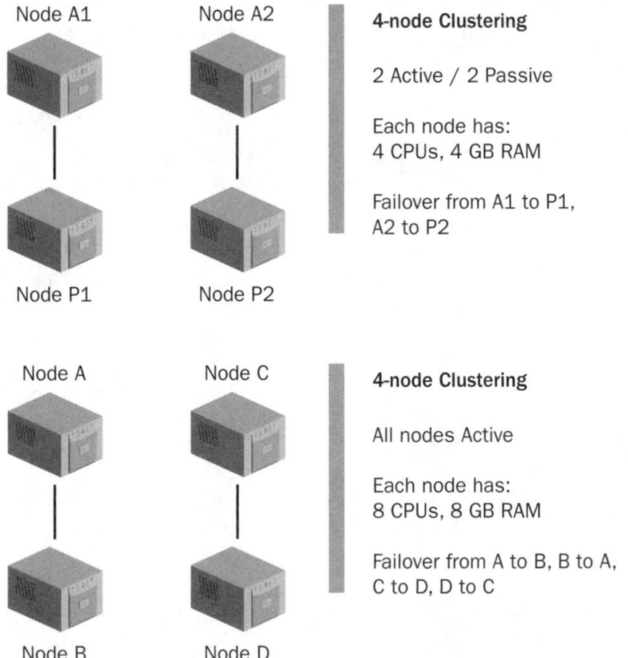

Figure 18-1. Clustering can be implemented in many ways; these are examples.

As you consider the impact of operating modes in the cluster architecture, you should look carefully at the business requirements and the expected server loads. By using Network Load Balancing and Cluster Load Balancing, all servers are active and the architecture is scaled out by adding more servers, which typically are configured identically to the existing Network Load Balancing and Cluster Load Balancing nodes. By using Server cluster, nodes can be either active or passive, and the configuration of nodes depends on the operating mode (active or passive) as well as how failover is configured. A server that is designated to handle failover must be sized to handle the workload of the failed server as well as the current workload (if any). Additionally, both average and peak workloads must be considered. Servers need additional capacity to handle peak loads.

Multisite Options for Clusters

Some large organizations build disaster recovery and increased availability into their infrastructure using multiple physical sites. Multisite architecture can be designed in many ways. In most cases, the architecture has a primary site and one or more remote sites. Figure 18-2 shows an example of a primary site and a remote site for a large commercial Web site.

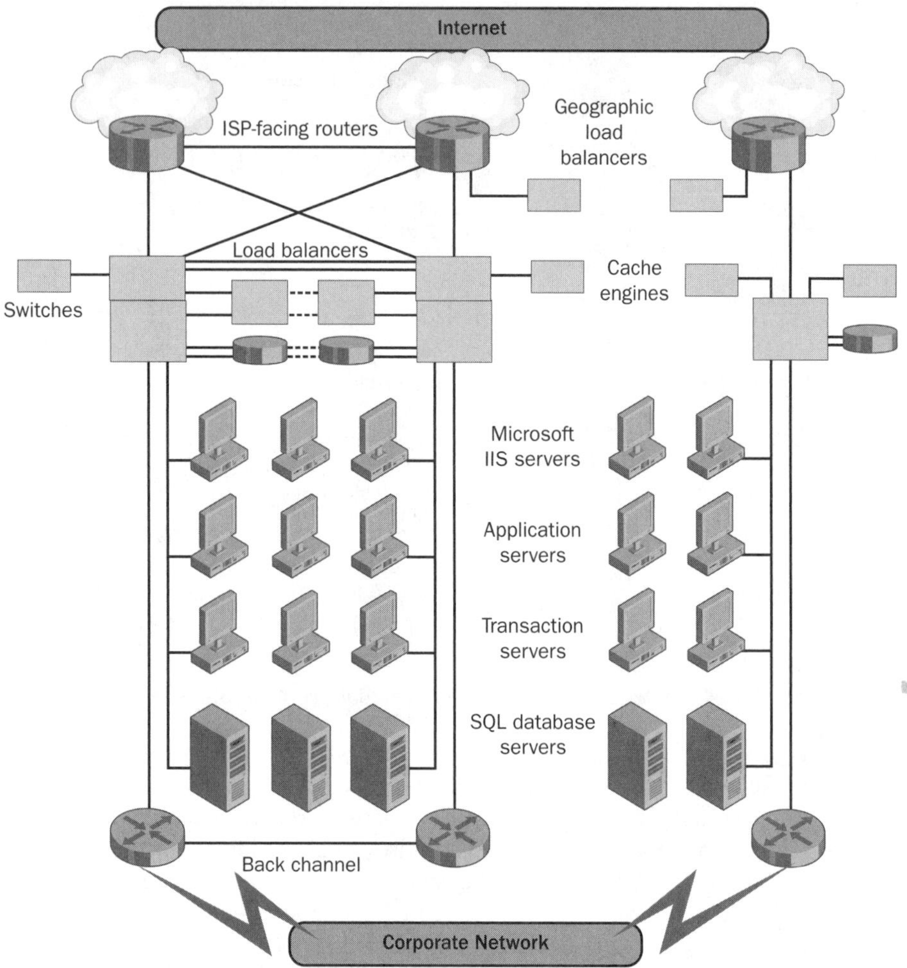

Figure 18-2. Enterprise architecture for a large commercial Web site that has multiple physical locations.

As shown in Figure 18-2, the architecture at the remote site mirrors that of the primary site. The level of integration for multiple sites and the level at which components are mirrored between sites depends on the business requirements. With a full implementation, the complete infrastructure of the primary site could be re-created at remote sites. This allows for a remote site to operate independently or to handle the full load of the primary site if necessary. Here, the design should incorporate real-time replication and synchronization for databases and applications. Real-time replication ensures a consistent state for data and application services between sites. If real-time updates are not possible, databases and applications should be replicated and synchronized as rapidly as possible.

With a partial implementation, only essential components are installed at remote sites with the goal of handling overflow in peak periods, maintaining uptime on a limited basis in case the primary site fails, or providing limited services on an ad hoc basis. One technique is to replicate static content on Web sites and read-only data from databases. This would allow remote sites to handle requests for static content and other types of data that is infrequently changed. Users could browse sites and access account information, product catalogs, and other services. If they must access dynamic content or modify information (add, change, delete), the sites' geographical load balancers could redirect the users to the primary site.

Another partial implementation technique is to implement all layers of the infrastructure but with fewer redundancies in the architecture or to implement only core components, relying on the primary site to provide the full array of features. By using either technique, the design might need to incorporate near real-time replication and synchronization for databases and applications. This ensures a consistent state for data and application services.

A full or partial design could also use geographically dispersed clusters running Server cluster. Geographically dispersed clusters use virtual local area networks (VLANs) to connect storage area networks (SANs) over long distances. A VLAN connection with latency of 500 milliseconds or less ensures that cluster consistency can be maintained. If the VLAN latency is over 500 milliseconds, the cluster consistency cannot be easily maintained. Geographically dispersed clusters are also referred to as stretched clusters.

For geographically dispersed clusters, Windows Server 2003 supports a majority node set quorum resource. Majority node clustering changes the way the cluster quorum resource is used to allow cluster servers to be geographically separated while maintaining consistency in the event of node failure. In a standard cluster configuration, the quorum resource writes information on all cluster database changes to the recovery logs, ensuring that the cluster configuration and state data can be recovered. The quorum resource resides on the shared disk drives and can be used to verify whether other nodes in the cluster are functioning.

In a majority node cluster configuration, the quorum resource is configured as a majority node set resource. This allows the quorum data, which includes cluster configuration changes and state information, to be stored on the system disk of each node in the cluster. Because the data is localized even though the cluster is geographically dispersed, the cluster can be maintained in a consistent state. As the name implies, the majority of nodes must be available for this cluster configuration to operate normally. Should the cluster state become inconsistent, you can force the quorum to get a consistent state. An algorithm also runs on the cluster nodes to help ensure the cluster state.

Using Network Load Balancing

Each server in a Network Load Balancing cluster is referred to as a *node*. Network Load Balancing nodes work together to provide availability for critical IP-based resources, which can include TCP, UDP, and GRE traffic requests.

Using Network Load Balancing Clusters

Network Load Balancing provides failover support for IP-based applications and services that require high scalability and availability. You can use Network Load Balancing to build groups of up to 32 clustered computers, starting with as few as 2 computers and incrementally scaling out as demand increases. Network Load Balancing is ideally suited to improving the availability of Web servers, media servers, terminal servers, and e-commerce sites. Load balancing these services ensures that there is no single point of failure and that there is no performance bottleneck.

Network Load Balancing uses a virtual IP address, and client requests are directed to this virtual IP address, allowing for transparent failover and failback. When a load-balanced resource fails on one server, the remaining servers in the group take over the workload of the failed server. When the failed server comes back online, the server can automatically rejoin the cluster group, and Network Load Balancing starts to distribute the load to the server automatically. Failover takes less than 10 seconds in most cases.

Network Load Balancing doesn't use shared resources or clustered storage devices. Instead, each server runs a copy of the TCP/IP application or service that is being load balanced. Local storage is used in most cases as well. As with Server cluster, users usually don't know that they're accessing a group of servers rather than a single server. The reason for this is that the Network Load Balancing cluster appears to be a single server. Clients connect to the cluster using a virtual IP address and, behind the scenes, this virtual address is mapped to a specific server based on availability.

Anyone familiar with load-balancing strategies might be inclined to think of Network Load Balancing as a form of round robin Domain Name System (DNS). In round robin DNS, incoming IP connections are passed to each participating server in a specific order. For example, an administrator defines a round robin group containing Server A, Server B, and Server C. The first incoming request is handled by Server A, the second by Server B, the third by Server C, and then the cycle is repeated in that order (A, B, C, A, B, C, . . .). Unfortunately, if one of the servers fails, there is no way to notify the group of the failure. As a result, the round robin strategy continues to send requests to the failed server. Windows Network Load Balancing doesn't have this problem.

To avoid sending requests to failed servers, Network Load Balancing sends heartbeats to participating servers. These heartbeats are similar to those used by the Cluster service. The purpose of the heartbeat is to track the condition of each participant in the group. If a server in the group fails to send heartbeat messages to other servers in the group for a specified interval, the server is assumed to have failed. The remaining servers in the group take over the workload of the failed server. While previous connections to the failed host are lost, the IP-based application or service continues to be available. In most cases, clients automatically retry the failed connections and experience only a few seconds delay in receiving a response. When the failed server becomes available again, Network Load Balancing automatically allows the server to rejoin the group and starts to distribute the load to the server.

Network Load Balancing Configuration

Although Network Load Balancing is normally used to distribute the workload for an application or service, it can also be used to direct a specific type of traffic to a particular server. For example, an administrator might want to load Hypertext Transfer Protocol (HTTP) and File Transfer Protocol (FTP) traffic to a group of servers but might want a single server to handle other types of traffic. In this latter case, Network Load Balancing allows traffic to flow to a designated server and reroutes traffic to another server only in case of failure.

Network Load Balancing runs as a network driver and requires no hardware changes to install and run. Its operations are transparent to the TCP/IP networking stack. Because Network Load Balancing is IP-based, IP networking must be installed on all load-balanced servers. At this time, Network Load Balancing supports Ethernet and Fiber Distributed Data Interface (FDDI) networks but doesn't support Asynchronous Transfer Mode (ATM). Future versions of Network Load Balancing might support these network architectures. There are four basic models for Network Load Balancing:

- **Single network adapter in unicast mode** This model is best for an environment in which ordinary network communication among cluster hosts is not required and in which there is limited dedicated traffic from outside the cluster subnet to specific cluster hosts.
- **Multiple network adapters in unicast mode** This model is best for an environment in which ordinary network communication among cluster hosts is necessary or desirable and in which there is moderate to heavy dedicated traffic from outside the cluster subnet to specific cluster hosts.
- **Single network adapter in multicast mode** This model is best for an environment in which ordinary network communication among cluster hosts is necessary or desirable but in which there is limited dedicated traffic from outside the cluster subnet to specific cluster hosts.
- **Multiple network adapters in multicast mode** This model is best for an environment in which ordinary network communication among cluster hosts is necessary and in which there is moderate to heavy dedicated traffic from outside the cluster subnet to specific cluster hosts.

Network Load Balancing uses unicast or multicast broadcasts to direct incoming traffic to all servers in the cluster. The Network Load Balancing driver on each host acts as a filter between the cluster adapter and the TCP/IP stack, allowing only traffic bound for the designated host to be received. Network Load Balancing controls only the flow of TCP, UDP, and GRE traffic on specified ports. It doesn't control the flow of TCP, UDP, and GRE traffic on nonspecified ports, and it doesn't control the flow of other incoming IP traffic. All traffic that isn't controlled is passed through without modification to the IP stack.

To provide high-performance throughput and responsiveness, Network Load Balancing normally uses two network adapters, as shown in Figure 18-3. The first network adapter, referred to as the cluster adapter, handles network traffic for the cluster, and the second adapter, referred to as the dedicated adapter, handles client-to-cluster network traffic and other traffic originating outside the cluster network.

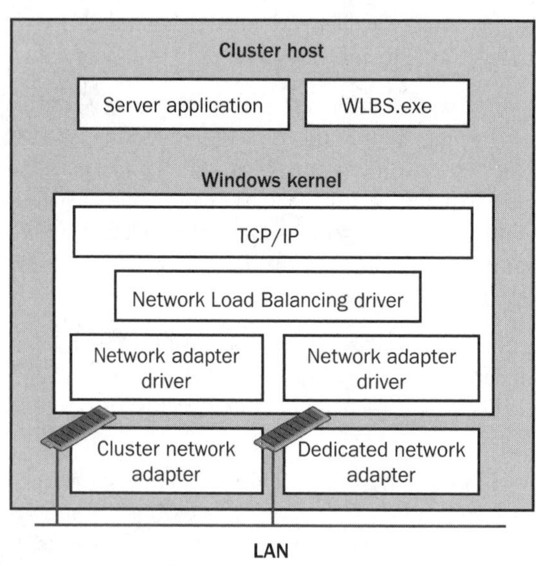

Figure 18-3. Network Load Balancing with two network adapters.

Network Load Balancing can also work with a single network adapter. When it does so, there are limitations. With a single adapter in unicast mode, node-to-node communications are impossible, meaning nodes within the cluster cannot communicate with each other. Servers can, however, communicate with servers outside the cluster subnet. By using a single adapter in multicast mode, node-to-node communications are possible as are communications with servers outside the cluster subnet. However, the configuration is not optimal for handling moderate to heavy traffic from outside the cluster subnet to specific cluster hosts. For handling node-to-node communications and moderate to heavy traffic, two adapters should be used.

Regardless of whether a single adapter or multiple adapters are used, all servers in the group operate in either unicast or multicast mode—not both. In unicast mode, the cluster's Media Access Control (MAC) address is assigned to the computer's network adapter and the network adapter's built-in MAC address is disabled. All participating servers use the cluster's MAC address, allowing incoming packets to be received by all servers in the group and passed to the Network Load Balancing driver for filtering. Filtering ensures that only packets intended for the server are received and all other packets are discarded. To avoid problems with Layer 2 switches, which expect to see unique source addresses, Network Load Balancing uniquely modifies the source MAC address for all outgoing packets. The modified address shows the server's cluster priority in one of the MAC address fields.

Because the built-in MAC address is used, the server group has some communication limitations when a single network adapter is configured. Although the cluster servers can communicate with other servers on the network and with servers outside the network, the cluster servers cannot communicate with each other. To resolve this problem, two network adapters are needed in unicast mode.

In multicast mode, the cluster's MAC address is assigned to the computer's network adapter and the network adapter's built-in MAC address is maintained so that both can be used. Because each server has a unique address, only one adapter is needed for network communications within the cluster group. Multicast offers some additional performance benefits for network communications as well. However, multicast traffic can flood all ports on upstream switches. To prevent this, a virtual LAN should be set up for the participating servers.

Inside Out

Using Network Load Balancing with routers

If Network Load Balancing clients are accessing a cluster through a router, be sure that the router is configured properly. For unicast clusters, the router should accept a dynamic Address Resolution Protocol (ARP) reply that maps the unicast IP address to its unicast MAC address. For multicast clusters, the router should accept an ARP reply that has a MAC address in the payload of the ARP structure. If the router isn't able to do this, you can also create a static ARP entry in the router to handle these requirements. Some routers will require a static ARP entry because they do not support the resolution of unicast IP addresses to multicast MAC addresses.

Network Load Balancing Client Affinity and Port Configurations

Several options can be used to optimize performance of a Network Load Balancing cluster. Each server in the cluster can be configured to handle a specific percentage of client requests, or the servers can handle client requests equally. The workload is distributed statistically and does not take into account CPU, memory, or drive usage. For IP-based traffic, the technique does work well, however. Most IP-based applications handle many clients, and each client typically has multiple requests that are short in duration.

Many Web-based applications seek to maintain the state of a user's session within the application. A session encompasses all the requests from a single visitor within a specified period of time. By maintaining the state of sessions, the application can ensure the user can complete a set of actions, such as registering for an account or purchasing equipment. Network

Load Balancing features allow administrators to configure client affinity to help maintain application sessions. Client affinity uses a combination of the source IP address and source and destination ports to direct multiple requests from a single client to the same server. Three client affinity settings can be used:

- **None** Specifies that Network Load Balancing doesn't need to direct multiple requests from the same client to the same server
- **Single** Specifies that Network Load Balancing should direct multiple requests from the same client IP address to the same server
- **Class C** Specifies that Network Load Balancing should direct multiple requests from the same Class C address range to the same server

Class C affinity is useful for clients that use multiple proxy servers to access the cluster.

Network Load Balancing clusters use filtering to ensure that only packets intended for the server are received and all other packets are discarded. Port rules specify how the network traffic on a port is filtered. Three filtering modes are available:

- **Disabled** No filtering
- **Single Host** Direct traffic to a single host
- **Multiple Hosts** Distribute traffic among the Network Load Balancing servers

Port rules are used to configure Network Load Balancing on a per-port basis. For ease of management, port rules can be assigned to a range of ports as well. This is most useful for UDP traffic when many different ports can be used.

Planning Network Load Balancing Clusters

Many applications and services can work with Network Load Balancing, provided they use TCP/IP as their network protocol and use an identifiable set of TCP or UDP ports. Key services that fit these criteria include the following:

- FTP over TCP/IP, which normally uses TCP ports 20 and 21
- HTTP over TCP/IP, which normally uses TCP port 80
- HTTPS over TCP/IP, which normally uses TCP port 443
- IMAP4 over TCP/IP, which normally uses TCP ports 143 and 993 (SSL)
- POP3 over TCP/IP, which normally uses TCP ports 110 and 995 (SSL)
- SMTP over TCP/IP, which normally uses TCP port 25

Network Load Balancing can be used with virtual private network (VPN) servers, terminal servers, and streaming media servers as well. For Network Load Balancing, most of the capacity planning focuses on the cluster size. *Cluster size* refers to the number of servers in the cluster. Cluster size should be based on the number of servers necessary to meet anticipated demand.

Stress testing should be used in the lab to simulate anticipated user loads prior to deployment. Configure the tests to simulate an environment with increasing user requests. Total requests should simulate the maximum anticipated user count. The results of the stress tests will determine whether additional servers are needed. The servers should be able to meet demands of the stress testing with 70 percent or less server load with all servers running. During failure testing, the peak load shouldn't rise above 80 percent. If either of these thresholds is reached, the cluster size might need to be increased.

Servers that use Network Load Balancing can benefit from optimization as well. Servers should be optimized for their role, the types of applications they will run, and the anticipated local storage they will use. Although you might want to build redundancy into the local hard drives on Network Load Balancing servers, this adds to the expense of the server without significant availability gains in most instances. Because of this, Network Load Balancing servers often have drives that do not use redundant array of independent disks (RAID) and do not provide fault tolerance; the idea being that if a drive causes a server failure, other servers in the Network Load Balancing cluster can quickly take over the workload of the failed server.

If it seems odd not to use RAID, keep in mind that servers using Network Load Balancing are organized so they use identical copies of data on each server. Because many different servers have the same data, maintaining the data with RAID sets isn't as important as it is with server clusters. A key point to consider when using Network Load Balancing, however, is data synchronization. The state of the data on each server must be maintained so that the clones are updated whenever changes are made. The need to synchronize data periodically is an overhead that must be considered when designing the server architecture.

Managing Network Load Balancing Clusters

Network Load Balancing Manager (Nlbmgr.exe) is a new tool for Windows Server 2003. It provides the graphical interface for managing, monitoring, and configuring Network Load Balancing clusters. Its command-line counterpart is Nlb.exe. Both tools use the NLB application programming interface (API) to manage Network Load Balancing.

Creating a New Network Load Balancing Cluster

You create Network Load Balancing clusters using the Network Load Balancing Manager (see Figure 18-4). Start Network Load Balancing Manager from the Administrative Tools menu or by typing **nlbmgr** at the command prompt.

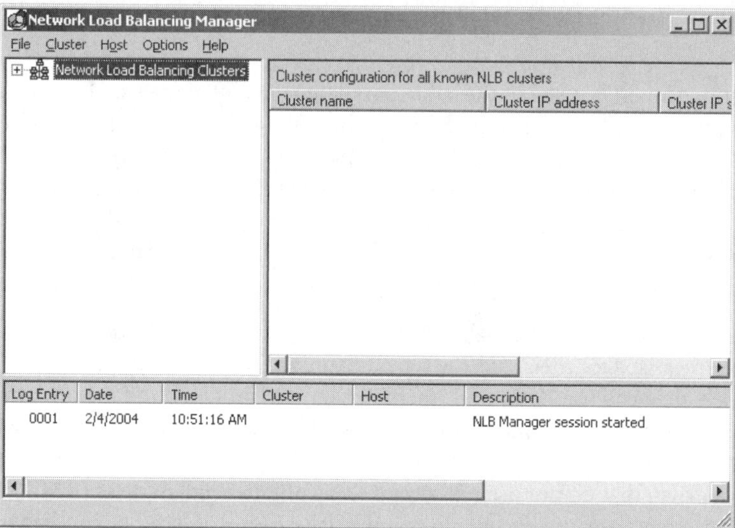

Figure 18-4. Use Network Load Balancing Manager to create and manage Network Load Balancing clusters.

Once you've started Network Load Balancing Manager, you can create the new Network Load Balancing cluster by following these steps:

1 Right-click Network Load Balancing Clusters in the left pane, and then choose New Cluster. This displays the Cluster Parameters Wizard, as shown in Figure 18-5.

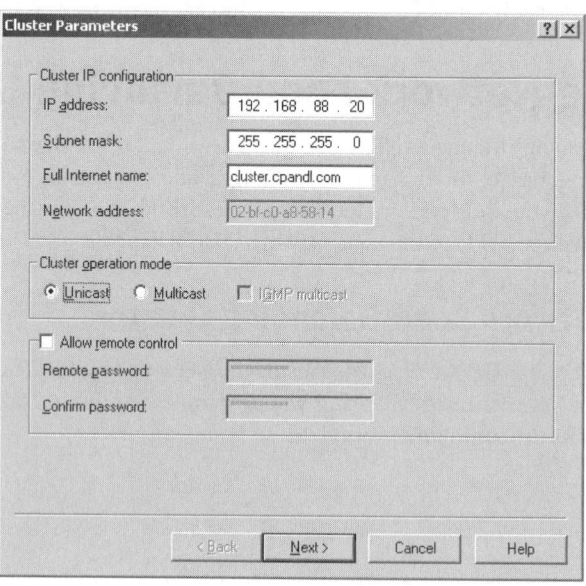

Figure 18-5. Use the Cluster Parameters Wizard to configure the new cluster.

2. In the IP Address field, type the virtual IP address for the cluster. The IP address you assign is used to address the cluster as a whole and should be the IP address that maps to the full Internet name of the cluster that you provide in the Full Internet Name field.

> **Note** For clusters operating in unicast mode, the IP address can be any Class A, B, or C IP address, but typically is a private IP address, such as 192.168.88.20. For clusters operating in multicast mode, the IP address typically is a Class D IP address (224.0.0.0 to 239.255.255.255).

> **Tip** The virtual IP address is used for addressing throughout the cluster. You must use this IP address for all hosts in the cluster, and it is fixed, so it cannot be a Dynamic Host Configuration Protocol (DHCP) address.

3. In the Subnet Mask field, type the subnet mask for the cluster or accept the default. In most cases, if you aren't using subnetting, the default subnet mask value is what you should use. Check with your organization's network administrator if you are unsure.
4. In the Full Internet Name field, type the fully qualified domain name for the cluster, such as cluster.cpandl.com. This is the domain name by which the cluster will be known.
5. Next, set the Cluster Operations Mode as either Unicast or Multicast. By selecting Multicast, you can also enable IGMP Multicast. However, the multicast IP address is then restricted to the standard Class D address range (224.0.0.0 to 239.255.255.255).

> **Tip** **Limit switch flooding**
> If the cluster hosts are directly connected to a hub and Internet Group Membership Protocol (IGMP) support is not enabled, incoming client traffic is automatically sent to all switch ports and can produce switch flooding. By enabling IGMP support for multicast clusters, you can limit switch flooding.

> **Note** Keep in mind that if you are working from a computer that has a single network adapter and that computer uses Network Load Balancing in unicast mode, you cannot use Network Load Balancing Manager on this computer to configure and manage other hosts. A computer with a single network adapter operating in unicast mode cannot communicate with other hosts in the cluster. You can, however, communicate with computers outside the cluster.

6. Optionally, you can enable Remote Control to allow the cluster to be managed remotely from another computer running the Windows operating system. Select Allow Remote Control, and then type and confirm the remote control password.

Caution Allowing remote control of a Network Load Balancing cluster presents serious security risks, and before you do this, you should consider the consequences carefully. The security risks include the possibility of data tampering, denial of service, and disclosure of cluster traffic. If you decide to enable remote control, you should use a strong password that follows the strict security rules for user passwords in Windows domains.

7. Click Next. If the cluster will have additional virtual IP addresses, click Add, enter the virtual IP address and subnet mask information, then click OK. Repeat this process for each additional virtual IP address, and then click Next.
8. Using the Port Rules page, as shown in Figure 18-6, you can specify how the network traffic on a port is filtered. When you've configured multiple IP addresses for the cluster, you might want to configure filtering on a per–IP address basis. By default all TCP and UPD traffic directed to any cluster IP address that arrives on ports 0 to 65535 is balanced across all members of the cluster based on the load weight of each cluster member.

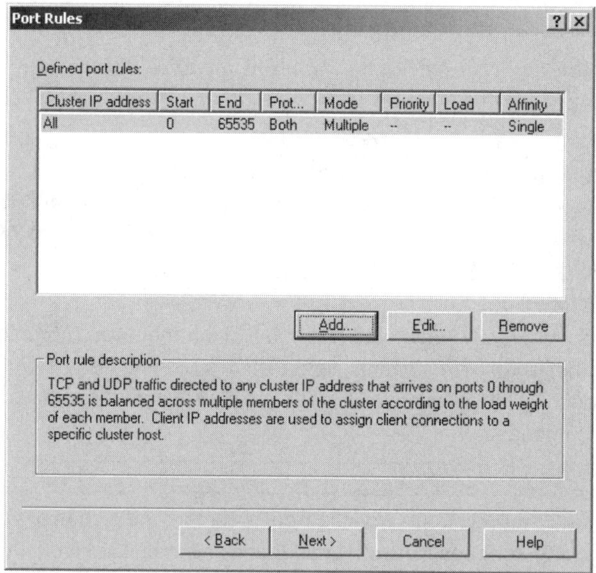

Figure 18-6. Use the Port Rules page to specify how network traffic on a port is filtered.

9. Click Next. Enter the domain name or IP address of the first host that will be a member of the cluster. Click Connect to connect to the server and display a list of available network interfaces. Select the network adapter that you want to use for Network Load Balancing, and then click Next. The IP address configured on this network adapter will be the dedicated IP address for this host and will be used for the public traffic of the cluster (as opposed to the private, node-to-node traffic).

10 On the Host Parameters page, shown in Figure 18-7, set the priority for this host in the cluster and the dedicated IP address that will be used to connect to this specific server. Afterward, set the initial state of this host when the Windows operating system is started. In most cases with deployed systems, you want the default state to be set as Started.

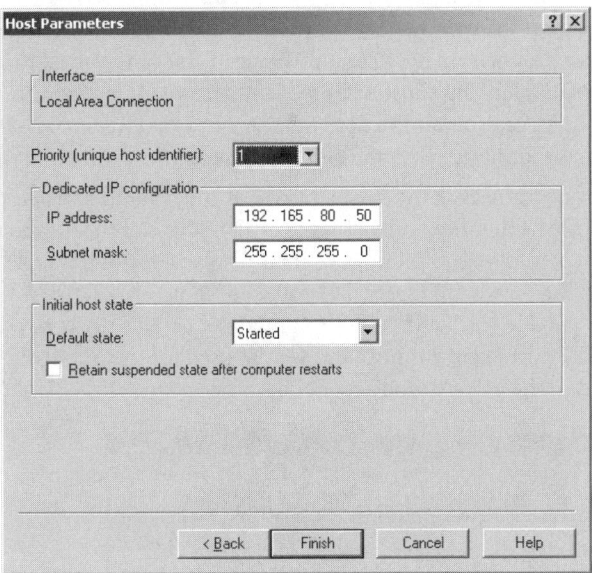

Figure 18-7. Use the Host Parameters page to specify the host priority and dedicated IP address.

> **Note** The *host priority* is a unique host identifier that indicates the order in which traffic is routed among members of the cluster, and it ranges from 1 to 32. The host with ID 1 is the first to receive traffic, the host with ID 2 is the second, and so on. The dedicated IP address for the host is used for private node-to-node traffic (as opposed to the public traffic for the cluster). Again, it must be a fixed IP address and not a DHCP address.

11 Click Finish to start the Network Load Balancing service and configure the cluster using the specific initial host. You can then add hosts into the cluster as appropriate. If you need to change the cluster parameters later, right-click the cluster in the left pane, and select Cluster Properties. You are then able to change the cluster IP configuration, operation mode, and port rules.

Adding Nodes to a Network Load Balancing Cluster

Once you've created a cluster and added an initial host, at any time you can add other nodes to the cluster, up to a maximum of 32. Additional hosts automatically inherit the cluster port rules from the initial host. As mentioned previously, if you are working from a computer that has a single network adapter and that computer uses Network Load Balancing in unicast mode, you cannot use Network Load Balancing Manager on this computer to configure and manage other hosts.

To add a node to a Network Load Balancing cluster, follow these steps:

1 Start Network Load Balancing Manager from the Administrative Tools menu or by typing **nlbmgr** at the command prompt. If the cluster you want to work with isn't shown in the Network Load Balancing Manager, you can connect to it by right-clicking Network Load Balancing Clusters in the left pane and selecting Connect To Existing. On the Connect page, enter the domain name or IP address of any host in the cluster, and then click Connect. Select the cluster name to work with, and then click Finish.

2 In the left pane right-click the cluster to which you want to add a node, and select Add Host To Cluster. Enter the domain name or IP address of the host to add to the cluster. Click Connect to connect to the server and display a list of available network interfaces. Select the network adapter that you want to use for Network Load Balancing, as shown in Figure 18-8. The IP address configured on this network adapter will be the dedicated IP address for this host and will be used for the public traffic of the cluster (as opposed to the private, node-to-node traffic).

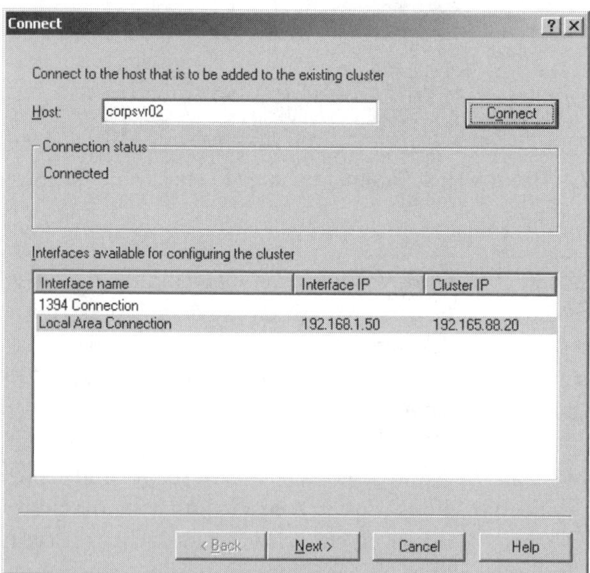

Figure 18-8. Type the domain name or IP address of the host to add.

3 Click Next to display the Host Parameters page. Set the unique priority for this host in the cluster and the dedicated IP address that will be used to connect to this specific server. Afterward, set the initial state of this host when the Windows operating system is started. In most cases with deployed systems, you want the default state to be set as Started.

4 Click Finish to add the host to the cluster. When the host is added to the cluster, the cluster status changes to Converged temporarily while Network Load Balancing updates the cluster configuration. If you must change the host parameters later, right-click the host in the left pane, and select Host Properties. You are then able to change the host priority, IP configuration, and initial state.

Removing Nodes from a Network Load Balancing Cluster

Network Load Balancing Manager provides several techniques for temporarily removing a node from a cluster, including the capability to suspend and resume load balancing on a per-node basis. If you no longer want a node to be a member of a Network Load Balancing cluster, you can remove it permanently from the cluster as well. To do this, start Network Load Balancing Manager from the Administrative Tools menu or by typing **nlbmgr** at the command prompt. Right-click the node in the left pane to remove it, and then select Delete Host. When prompted to confirm the action, click Yes.

> **Note** If the cluster you want to work with isn't shown in the Network Load Balancing Manager, you can connect to it by right-clicking Network Load Balancing Clusters in the left pane and selecting Connect To Existing. In the Connect dialog box, enter the domain name or IP address of any host in the cluster, and click Connect. Select the cluster name to work with, and then click Finish.

Configuring Event Logging for Network Load Balancing Clusters

Events related to the Network Load Balancing service (the Windows Load Balancing Service, or WLBS) are stored in the System logs and can be accessed in Event Viewer. You can also enable logging related to the use of Network Load Balancing Manager. These events show the operations being performed in Network Load Balancing Manager.

To enable Network Load Balancing Manager logging, click Log Settings on the Options menu, check Enable Logging, and specify the full file path to the file you want to use for logging. Because this file contains sensitive information regarding the cluster, it should be stored in a secure folder accessible only to administrators.

Controlling Cluster and Host Traffic

Network Load Balancing Manager allows you to control operations on the cluster as a whole as well as for individual hosts within the cluster. You control cluster operations by right-clicking the cluster in the left pane of Network Load Balancing Manager, pointing to Control Hosts, and then selecting one of the following options:

- **Stop** Stops all Network Load Balancing cluster traffic. Cluster operations are immediately stopped, and all existing connections are immediately closed.
- **Drainstop** Disables all new traffic to the cluster but allows hosts to continue servicing active connections.

- **Suspend** Stops all Network Load Balancing cluster traffic and also suspends cluster-control commands, including remote control, except for resume and query. Cluster operations are immediately stopped, and all existing connections are immediately closed.
- **Resume** Reenables the use of cluster-control commands for the cluster, including remote control. This option doesn't restart cluster operations, however.
- **Start** Starts or restarts the handling of Network Load Balancing traffic for the cluster.

You can manage the Cluster service on a specific host by right-clicking the host, pointing to Control Host, and then selecting one of the following options:

- **Stop** Stops Network Load Balancing on the host, and all existing connections to the host are immediately closed.
- **Drainstop** Disables all new traffic to the host but allows the host to continue servicing any active connections.
- **Suspend** Stops all Network Load Balancing on the host and also suspends cluster-control commands, including remote control, except for resume and query.
- **Resume** Reenables the use of cluster-control commands for the host, including remote control. This option doesn't restart cluster operations, however.
- **Start** Starts or restarts the handling of Network Load Balancing traffic for the host.

Component Load Balancing Architecture

Unlike Server cluster and Network Load Balancing, which are built into the Enterprise Edition and Datacenter Edition of Windows Server 2003, Component Load Balancing is a feature of Microsoft Application Center and is designed to provide high availability and scalability for transactional components. Component Load Balancing is scalable on up to eight servers and is ideally suited to building distributed solutions.

Using Component Load Balancing Clusters

Component Load Balancing makes use of the COM+ services supplied as part of the Windows operating system. COM+ services provide enterprise functionality for transactions, object management, security, events, and queuing. COM+ components use the Component Object Model (COM) and COM+ services to specify their configuration and attributes. Groups of COM+ components that work together to handle common functions are referred to as COM+ applications.

Figure 18-9 provides an overview of Component Load Balancing. Component Load Balancing uses several key structures:

- Component Load Balancing software, which handles the load balancing and is responsible for determining the order in which cluster members activate components.

- A router, which can be implemented through component routing lists stored on front-end Web servers or a component routing cluster configured on separate servers. The router handles message routing between the front-end Web servers and the application servers.
- Application server clusters, which activate and run COM+ components. The application server cluster is managed by Application Center.

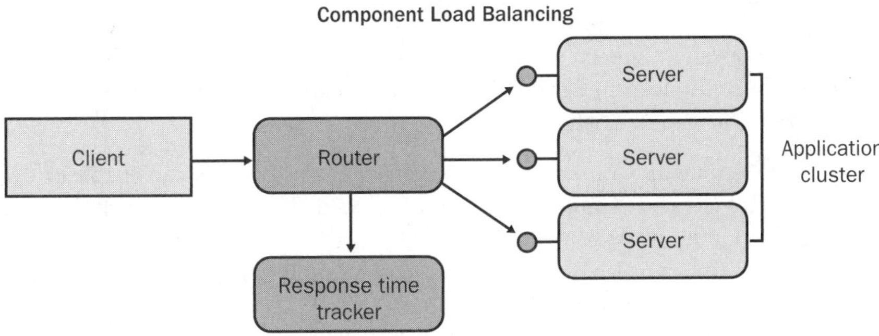

Figure 18-9. Component Load Balancing relies on software for load balancing.

The routing list made available to the router is used to track the response time of each application server from the Web servers. If the routing list is stored on individual Web servers, each server has its own routing list and uses this list to check the response times of the application servers periodically. If the routing listed is stored on a separate routing cluster, the routing cluster servers handle this task.

The goal of tracking the response time is to determine which application server has the fastest response time from a given Web server. The response times are tracked as an in-memory table and are used in round robin fashion to determine to which application server an incoming request should be passed. Because of this, the application server with the fastest response time (and theoretically the one that is least busy and most able to handle a request) is given the next request. The next request goes to the application server with the next fastest time, and so on.

Understanding Application Center

Application Center (Appcenter.exe) can run on Windows Server 2003, Standard Edition, Enterprise Edition, or Web Edition. It includes both server and client components. Typically, server components are installed on the systems responsible for the Component Load Balancing clusters—the application servers and client components are installed on the front-end Web servers. The command-line counterpart to Application Center is Ac.exe.

Application Center provides many ways of changing the state of the systems it administers and features integration with Network Load Balancing, allowing you to view and manage the Network Load Balancing configuration. Using Application Center, you can take servers online or offline, deploy new content, and add or remove members to the cluster. In most cases, you do this in Application Center. Sometimes you want to do this by using a script, and this is where the command-line tool comes in handy.

In terms of the Application Center architecture, an *application* is a collection of software resources for a Web site or COM+ application. This collection can include a COM+ application, a Web site, Registry keys, certificates, and more. When creating and managing applications, Application Center allows you to create, rename, or delete applications and to add or remove resource definitions.

When you work with Component Load Balancing clusters, you can enable or disable load balancing for cluster members. When you enable load balancing on a cluster member, the member is put online. When you disable load balancing on a cluster member, the member is taken offline. You can also determine how load balancing is implemented by setting Network Load Balancing weights for cluster members.

Planning Component Load Balancing Clusters

The architecture of Component Load Balancing clusters should be designed to meet the availability requirements of the service offering. For small to moderate-sized implementations, the front-end Web servers can host the routing list for the application server cluster. For larger implementations, dedicated routing clusters are desirable to ensure high-availability requirements can be met.

As with Network Load Balancing, servers in Component Load Balancing clusters should be optimized for their role, the types of applications they will run, and the anticipated local storage they will use. Routing servers maintain in-memory routing lists and need high-speed connections to the network. Whether configured separately or as part of the front end, this feature doesn't require a lot of storage, but a limited amount of additional RAM might be required.

Application servers, on the other hand, typically need a lot of RAM, fast CPUs, and limited redundancy in the drive array configuration. If redundant drive arrays are used, a basic configuration, such as RAID 1 or RAID 5, might be all that is needed to maintain the level of availability required.

Using Server Cluster

Server cluster is implemented using the Microsoft Cluster service and is used to provide failover support for applications and services. A server cluster can consist of up to eight nodes. Each node is attached to one or more cluster storage devices. Cluster storage devices allow different servers to share the same data and thus, by reading this data, provide failover for resources. You can use shared Small Computer System Interface (SCSI) or fibre channel devices. The preferred technique is fibre channel, and it is recommended when you have three or more nodes. For server clusters running 64-bit editions of Windows Server 2003, fibre channel is the only technique that should be used.

Server Cluster Configurations

Server clusters can be set up using many different configurations. Servers can be either active or passive, and different servers can be configured to take over the failed resources of another server. Failover can take several minutes, depending on the configuration and the application being used, but is designed to be transparent to the user.

When a node is active, it makes its resources available. Clients access these resources through dedicated virtual servers. The Cluster service uses the concept of virtual servers to specify groups of resources that fail over together. Thus, when a server fails, the group of resources configured on that server for clustering fail over to another server. The server that handles the failover should be configured for the extra capacity needed to handle the additional workload. When the failed server comes back online, the Cluster service can be configured to allow failback to the original server or to allow the current server to continue to process requests.

Windows Server 2003 supports three basic types of server clusters:

- Single-node clusters
- Single quorum device multinode clusters
- Majority node clusters

Figure 18-10 shows an example of a single-node cluster. A single-node cluster doesn't make use of failover but does provide easier administration for sharing resources and network storage. The main advantage of a single-node cluster is that the Cluster service monitors and automatically restarts applications and dependent resources that fail or freeze. A single-node cluster could work with file, print, or Web shares when the primary concern is to make it easy for users to access resources, but it isn't practical otherwise. Single-node clusters are also useful for test and development purposes, allowing you to develop cluster-aware applications and test them using limited hardware.

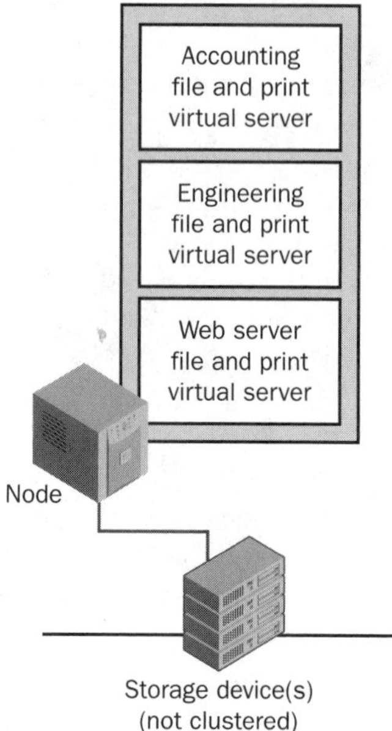

Figure 18-10. A single-node server cluster.

To get the full benefit of clustering, administrators must implement a multinode cluster. The key multinode cluster models are active/passive and active/active. In an active/passive configuration, one or more nodes are actively processing user, application, and system requests, while one or more other nodes are idle. The nodes processing requests are referred to as *active*, or *primary*, nodes. The idle nodes are referred to as *standby*, or *passive*, nodes. The passive nodes are ready to be used when a failover occurs on a primary node. By contrast, in an active/active configuration all nodes actively process user, application, and system requests and there are no standby nodes. Then when an active node fails the other primary nodes temporarily take up the slack until the failed node can be restarted.

Figure 18-11 shows a multinode cluster with a single quorum device configuration. The nodes are configured so that every node is attached to one or more cluster storage devices that all nodes share and the cluster configuration data is stored on a single cluster storage device called the quorum device.

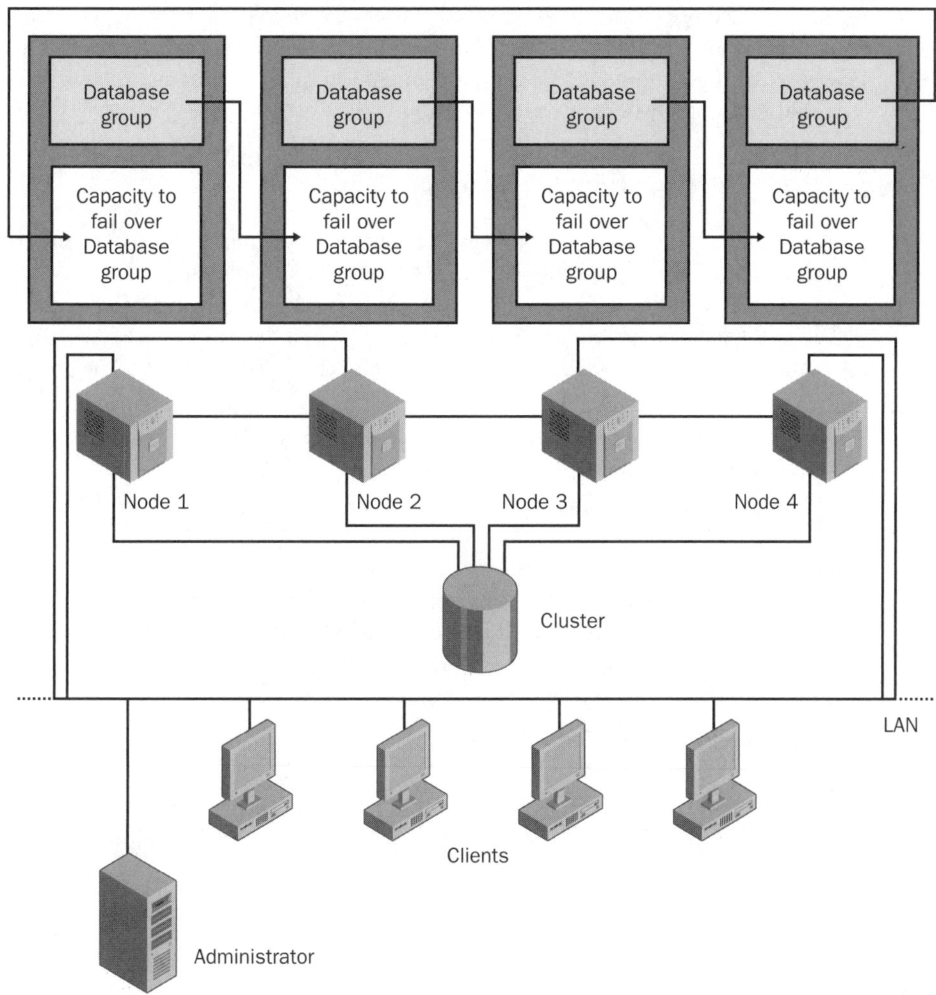

Figure 18-11. Server cluster using shared storage.

The final type of server cluster is the majority node set, which is primarily used in larger end-to-end solutions developed by original equipment manufacturers and independent hardware vendors. In a majority node cluster configuration, nodes don't have to be connected to shared storage devices. Each node can have its own storage device. The cluster configuration data is stored on multiple disks across the cluster. This allows each node to have a local quorum device.

As discussed previously, majority node clusters are often used with geographically separated servers. Primarily, this is because each node can have its own storage and its own copy of the cluster configuration data. Geographic separation isn't a requirement, however. The servers could just as easily be in the same location.

Server Cluster Resource Groups

A resource group is a unit of failover. Resources that are related or dependent on each other are associated through resource groups. All resources grouped together must be from the same node. If any of the resources in a group fails, all the resources fail over together according to the failover policy defined for the group. When the cause of a failure is resolved, the group fails back to its original location based on the failback policy of the group.

Note Only applications that need high availability should be part of a resource group. Other applications can run on a cluster server but don't need to be a part of a resource group.

Before adding an application to a resource group, you must determine whether the application can work within the cluster environment. Applications that can work within the cluster environment and support cluster events are called cluster-aware. Cluster-aware applications can register with the Server cluster to receive status and notification information. Applications and services that are cluster-aware include the following:

- Distributed File System (DFS)
- DHCP
- Exchange Server
- File shares
- IIS
- Microsoft Distributed Transaction Coordinator (MS DTC)
- Microsoft Message Queuing (MSMQ)
- Network News Transfer Protocol (NNTP)
- Print spooler
- Simple Mail Transfer Protocol (SMTP)
- SQL Server
- Windows Internet Naming Service (WINS)

Generic applications and services can also be cluster-aware. Check with the software vendor to determine compatibility with the Cluster service.

Applications that do not support cluster events are called cluster-unaware. Some cluster-unaware applications can be assigned to resource groups and can be failed over. The following provisions apply:

- IP-based protocols are used for cluster communications. The application must use an IP-based protocol for its network communications. Applications cannot use NetBIOS Extended User Interface (NetBEUI), Internetwork Packet Exchange (IPX), AppleTalk, or other protocols to communicate.
- Nodes in the cluster access application data through shared storage devices. If the application isn't able to store its data in a configurable location, the application data won't be available on failover.
- Client applications experience a temporary loss of network connectivity when failover occurs. If client applications cannot retry and recover from this, they will cease to function normally.

Applications that meet these criteria can be assigned to resource groups.

Optimizing Hardware for Server Clusters

After determining which applications and services need high availability and which don't, administrators should focus on selecting the right hardware to meet the needs of the business system. A cluster model should be chosen to adequately support resource failover and the availability needs of the system. Based on the model chosen, excess capacity should be added to ensure resources are available in the event a resource fails and failover to a server substantially increases the workload.

The configuration of the hardware should be adjusted to maximize total throughput and optimize performance for the types of applications and services that will experience the greatest demand. Different servers have different optimization needs. A Web server with static HTML pages might need fast hard disk drives and additional RAM to cache files in memory but typically doesn't need high-end CPUs. A typical database server needs high-end CPUs, fast hard disk drives, and additional RAM.

Administrators should carefully optimize performance of each server in the cluster node. A key area where optimization can have huge benefits is with paging files. Key rules for paging files are as follows:

- Paging files should have a fixed size to prevent excess paging and shouldn't be located on the shared cluster storage device.
- Whenever more than 4 GB of RAM is installed, the paging file size should be reduced. Try setting it to 2060 megabytes (MB) to ensure effective use of disk space.
- If multiple local drives are available, place the paging file on separate drives to improve performance.

With a clustered SQL Server configuration, you should consider using high-end CPUs, fast hard disk drives, and additional memory. SQL Server 2000 and standard services together use over 100 MB of memory as a baseline. User connections consume about 24 kilobytes (KB) each. Although the minimum memory for query execution is 1 MB of RAM, the average query can require 2 to 4 MB of RAM. Other SQL Server processes use memory as well.

Cluster storage devices should be optimized based on performance and availability needs. Table 18-1 provides an overview of common hardware RAID configurations for clusters. The table entries are organized listing the highest RAID level to the lowest.

Table 18-1. Hardware RAID Configurations for Clusters

RAID Level	RAID Type	RAID Description	Advantages and Disadvantages
5+1	Disk striping with parity + mirroring	Uses at least six volumes, each on a separate drive. Each volume is configured identically as a mirrored stripe set with parity error checking.	Provides very high level of fault tolerance but has a lot of overhead.
5	Disk striping with parity	Uses at least three volumes, each on a separate drive. Each volume is configured as a stripe set with parity error checking. In the case of failure, data can be recovered.	Provides fault tolerance with less overhead than mirroring. Better read performance than disk mirroring.
1	Disk mirroring	Uses two volumes on two drives. The drives are configured identically and data is written to both drives. If one drive fails, there is no data loss because the other drive contains the data. This approach does not include disk striping.	Provides redundancy with better write performance than disk striping with parity.

Table 18-1. Hardware RAID Configurations for Clusters

RAID Level	RAID Type	RAID Description	Advantages and Disadvantages
0+1	Disk striping with mirroring	Uses two or more volumes, each on a separate drive. The volumes are striped and mirrored. Data is written sequentially to drives that are identically configured.	Provides redundancy with good read and write performance.
0	Disk striping	Uses two or more volumes, each on a separate drive. Volumes are configured as a stripe set. Data is broken into blocks, called stripes, and then written sequentially to all drives in the stripe set.	Provides speed and performance without data protection.

Optimizing Networking for Server Clusters

The network configuration of the cluster can also be optimized. All nodes in a cluster must be a part of the same domain and can be configured as domain controllers or member servers. Ideally, multinode clusters have at least two nodes that act as domain controllers and provide failover for critical domain services. If this isn't the case, the availability of cluster resources might be tied to the availability of the controllers in the domain.

Typically, nodes in a cluster are configured with both private and public network addresses. Private network addresses are used for node-to-node communications, and public network addresses are used for client-to-cluster communications. However, some clusters might not need public network addresses and instead can be configured to use two private networks. Here, the first private network is for node-to-node communications and the second private network is for communicating with other servers that are a part of the service offering.

Increasingly, clustered servers and storage devices are connected over SANs. SANs use high-performance interconnections between secure servers and storage devices to deliver higher bandwidth and lower latency than comparable traditional networks. Enterprise Edition and Datacenter Edition implement a feature called Winsock Direct that allows direct communication over a SAN using SAN providers.

SAN providers have user-mode access to hardware transports. When communicating directly at the hardware level, the individual transport endpoints can be mapped directly into the address space of application processes running in user mode. This allows applications to pass messaging requests directly to the SAN hardware interface, which eliminates unnecessary system calls and data copying.

SANs typically use two transfer modes. One mode is for small transfers, which primarily consist of transfer control information. For large transfers, SANs can use a bulk mode whereby data is transferred directly between the local system and the remote system by the SAN hardware interface without CPU involvement on the local or remote system. All bulk transfers are prearranged through an exchange of transfer-control messages.

In addition to improved communication modes, SANs have other benefits. They allow you to consolidate storage needs, using several highly reliable storage devices instead of many. They also allow you to share storage with non-Windows operating systems, allowing for heterogeneous operating environments.

Running Server Clusters

Cluster Administrator (Cluadmin.exe) provides the graphical interface for managing, monitoring, and configuring server clusters. Its command-line counterpart is Cluster.exe. Both tools use the Cluster API to manage the Cluster service.

The Cluster Service and Cluster Objects

The Cluster service is responsible for all aspects of server cluster operation and also maintains the cluster database. The Cluster service uses objects to control the physical and logical units within the cluster. Many types of cluster objects are defined, including those pertaining to the following components:

- Cluster networks
- Cluster interfaces
- Nodes
- Cluster resources
- Resource types
- Groups

Cluster objects have properties that define their behavior within the cluster. The Cluster API contains the control codes and management functions needed to manage the object through the Cluster service. As shown in Figure 18-12, each node in a cluster runs an instance of the Cluster service (Clussvc.exe), the Cluster Network Driver (Clusnet.sys), and the Cluster

Disk Driver (Clusdisk.sys). The Cluster Network Driver is responsible for the following activities:

- Providing reliable, guaranteed communication between nodes
- Monitoring network paths between nodes
- Routing cluster messages
- Detecting communication failure

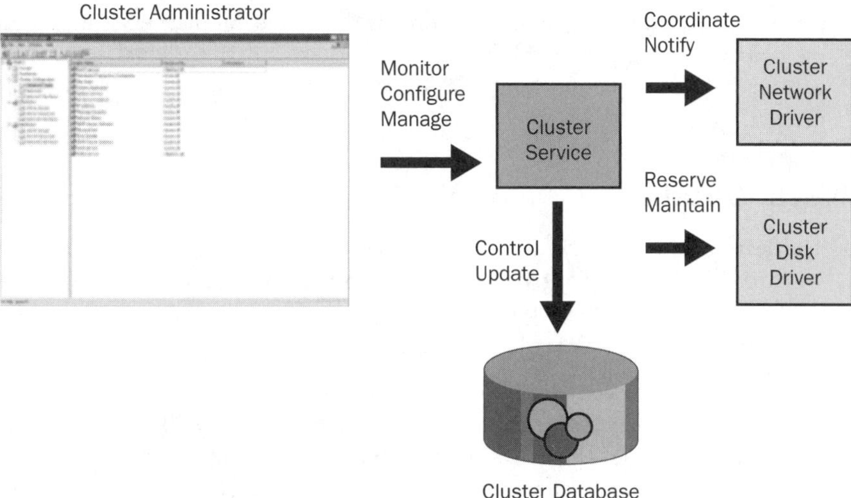

Figure 18-12. Overview of cluster administration.

Each node's Cluster Network Driver periodically exchanges messages called *heartbeats* with other active nodes. The heartbeat is a UDP packet that is sent between cluster nodes. If a node fails to respond to a heartbeat message, the Cluster Network Driver on the node that detects the failure notifies the Cluster service.

Each node's Cluster Disk Driver is responsible for maintaining exclusive ownership of shared disks. Only the node that owns the physical disk resource can access the disk. All other nodes cannot access the disk resource. The Cluster Disk Driver also is responsible for replacing reservations on disks for the local system.

The Cluster Heartbeat

The Cluster service transmits heartbeat messages on a dedicated network adapter, called the cluster adapter, to other computers in the server cluster. The number of nodes in the server cluster determines how these additional network adapters are connected. With a four-node cluster and standard Ethernet cabling, the dedicated network adapters are normally connected to a dedicated hub or switch. For redundancy, communications can be transmitted over multiple networks as well.

As the name implies, the heartbeat is used to track the condition of each node in the cluster. If the Cluster service doesn't receive a heartbeat from a server in the cluster within a specified time, the service assumes the server has failed and initiates failover. The Cluster service uses the concept of virtual servers to specify groups of resources that fail over together. Failover occurs when a clustered resource fails on one server and another server takes over management of the resource. When the failed resource is restored, the original server is able to regain control of the resource and come back online. The process of returning to service is called *failback.*

The Cluster Database

The heartbeat isn't the only traffic transmitted between clusters. The clusters also exchange synchronization and management data. Most management information is stored in the cluster database. This database contains information on the configuration of the cluster and the resources it uses.

The cluster database contains information on all physical and logical elements in the cluster, referred to as cluster objects, as well as configuration data. The Cluster service maintains the database by using global updates and periodic check pointing. Global updates are used to replicate changes across all nodes. Any changes that the Cluster service fails to replicate to all nodes are logged to a recovery log. These changes are synchronized at a subsequent checkpoint.

The Cluster Quorum Resource

Every cluster has a single resource that is responsible for maintaining the recovery logs. This resource is called the quorum resource. The quorum resource writes information on all cluster database changes to the recovery logs, ensuring that the cluster configuration and state data can be recovered. The importance of the quorum resource is evident in any failover situation. Consider the following scenario:

1. Nodes in a cluster are using the quorum resource and then node 1 fails. Nodes 2, 3, and 4 continue to operate. Node 2 takes over resources of the failed node.
2. Node 2 writes configuration changes to the recovery logs.
3. Node 2 fails before node 1 comes back online. Nodes 3 and 4 take over the resources of the failed nodes.
4. Shortly afterward, node 1 comes back online and must update its private copy of the cluster database with the changes made by node 2.

5 The Cluster service uses the quorum resource's recovery logs to synchronize changes and perform the configuration updates. Node 1 is then able to rejoin and regain control of its resources.

The only standard cluster resource that can act as a quorum resource is the Physical Disk resource. Developers can create their own quorum resource types for resources, provided those resources have the following characteristics:

- Enable a single node to gain physical control of and maintain control of the resource
- Provide physical storage that can be accessed by any node in the cluster
- Use NTFS

The Cluster Interface and Network States

The network adapter used to transfer cluster management and state data is referred to as the cluster adapter. Traffic between nodes in the cluster is transmitted over the cluster network, which is typically a private network used only by the cluster nodes. To determine failure, the Cluster service tracks the status of the cluster adapter interface and the cluster network.

The cluster adapter interface states are shown in Table 18-2. Administrators can use the CLUSTER NETINTERFACE command or Cluster Administrator to check the interface state.

Table 18-2. Cluster Adapter Interface States

Network Interface State	Description
Up	The normal operation state. The interface is active and can communicate with all other interfaces on the network (except those that are Failed or Unavailable).
Unknown	The state cannot be determined at this time.
Unavailable	The interface is disabled for cluster use or the node associated with the network interface is down.
Unreachable	The node cannot communicate through the interface. The reason is unknown.
Failed	The node associated with the interface is active but cannot communicate through its interface. The Cluster service has isolated the error to the interface as determined by failure to receive heartbeats from the node and receipt of hardware failure notifications from an adapter that supports Network Driver Interface Specification (NDIS).

The network states are shown in Table 18-3. Administrators can use the CLUSTER NETWORK command or Cluster Administrator to check network state.

Table 18-3. Cluster Network States

Network State	Description
Up	The normal operation state. The network is functioning normally.
Unknown	The state cannot be determined at this time.
Unavailable	The network is disabled for cluster use or all the nodes attached to the network are inactive.
Partitioned	The network has partially failed. Some active clusters cannot communicate with one another over the network.
Down	The network has failed. None of the active clusters can communicate with another using the network.

When a network interface enters the Failed state, the Cluster service triggers failover of all IP Address resources that use the network interface. The Cluster service does not do this when a network interface is unreachable. When the interface is unreachable, the Cluster service cannot isolate the problem in a way that is sufficient to implement a recovery policy. Additionally, if the interface is in the Unavailable state, the Cluster service assumes the node is down.

The cluster network should normally be in the Up state. When in the Up state, the cluster network is working normally and all active nodes are communicating. If the network enters the Partitioned state, it means one or more of the nodes is having communication problems or has recently failed. The Down state indicates the cluster network has failed and isn't functioning. In the Down state, clusters cannot communicate with each other over this network.

Creating Server Clusters

After you finish the cluster planning and set up the server hardware, you can create the cluster. You create the cluster using Cluster Administrator, which can be started from the Administrative Tools menu or by typing **cluadmin** at the command prompt. Before you do this, however, you should ensure that all the nodes in the system have the same default language and country or region selected. Start the Regional And Language Options utility in Control Panel, and then select the options for Standards And Formats and Location.

> **Caution** If you are using a shared storage device, only one node in the cluster should have access to the cluster disk while you are creating the cluster. Otherwise, the cluster disk can become corrupted. To prevent this, either shut down all but the primary node or use another technique such as logical unit number (LUN) masking to keep the other nodes from accessing the cluster disk.

When you start Cluster Administrator for the first time, the Open Connection To Cluster dialog box should be displayed, as shown in Figure 18-13.

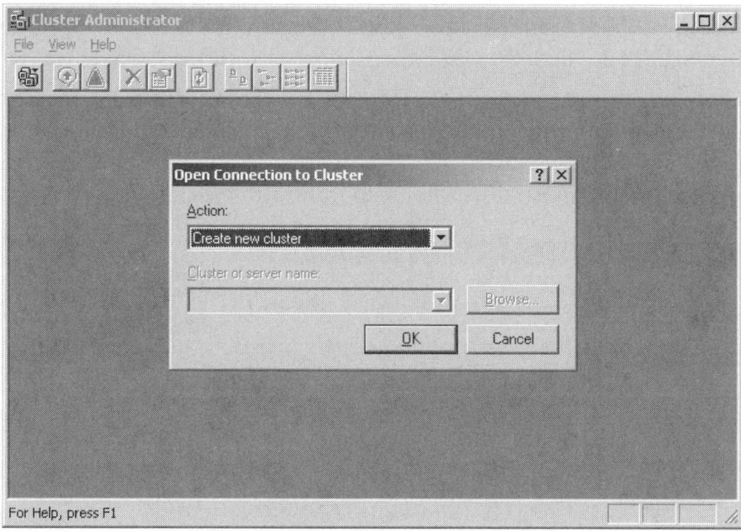

Figure 18-13. Cluster Administrator.

In this dialog box, you can select the following options:

- **Open Connection To Cluster** To connect to an existing cluster by name or IP address
- **Create New Cluster** To set up a new server cluster using the New Server Cluster Wizard
- **Add Nodes To Cluster** To add nodes to an existing cluster using the Add Cluster Node Wizard

The sections that follow detail how to create a new cluster and add nodes to it.

Troubleshooting

Check the cluster configuration logs

The New Cluster Service Wizard and the Add Nodes Wizard generate a cluster configuration log that by default is located at %SystemRoot%\System32\LogFiles\Cluster\ClCfgSrv.log. You can use any standard text editor, including Notepad, to view the contents of the log. These logs include the complete configuration of the cluster and as such should be safeguarded to protect the security of the cluster. For help troubleshooting cluster installation, see Microsoft Knowledge Base article 295648. For help troubleshooting clusters after installation, you can check the cluster diagnostic log. This log is saved at %SystemRoot%\Cluster\Cluster.log.

Creating a Server Cluster

To create a new cluster in Cluster Administrator, follow these steps:

1. Select Create New Cluster in the Open Connection To Cluster dialog box, then click OK. Or click File, New, Cluster. Either action starts the New Server Cluster Wizard.
2. As shown in Figure 18-14, use the Domain and Cluster Name options to set the fully qualified domain name for the cluster. This is the domain name by which the cluster will be known. Because users will connect to the cluster using virtual servers, this is the name that administrators will use to work with the cluster.

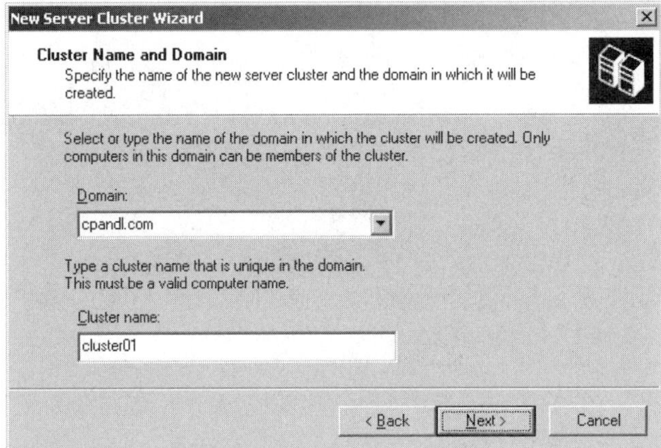

Figure 18-14. Set the fully qualified domain name of the cluster; this is the name for administrators.

3. Click Next to display the Select Computer page, as shown in Figure 18-15. Enter the name or IP address of the computer that will be the first computer in the new cluster.

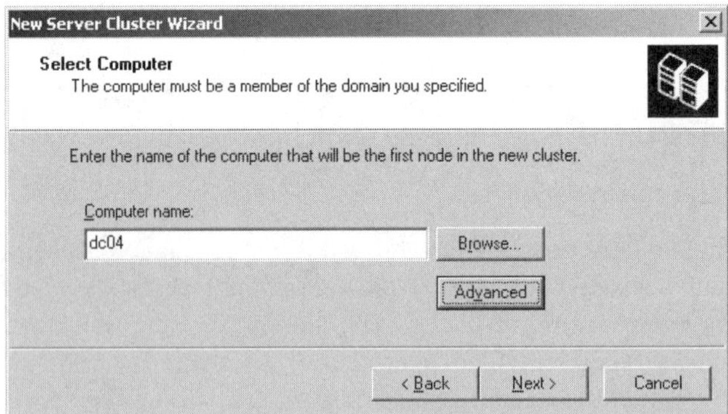

Figure 18-15. Specify the name or IP address of the first node.

Chapter 18

4 Click Next to display the Analyzing Configuration page, as shown in Figure 18-16. The wizard automatically begins analyzing the configuration and highlights any problems found, as follows:

- First, the wizard checks for any existing cluster using the fully qualified domain name you've specified.
- Second, the wizard tries to establish a connection to the computer you designated as the first node, either by computer name or IP address.
- Third, the wizard determines whether the designated computer can be a member of a cluster.
- Fourth, the wizard determines common resources on the node that can be managed by the cluster.
- Finally, the wizard checks the feasibility of the cluster.

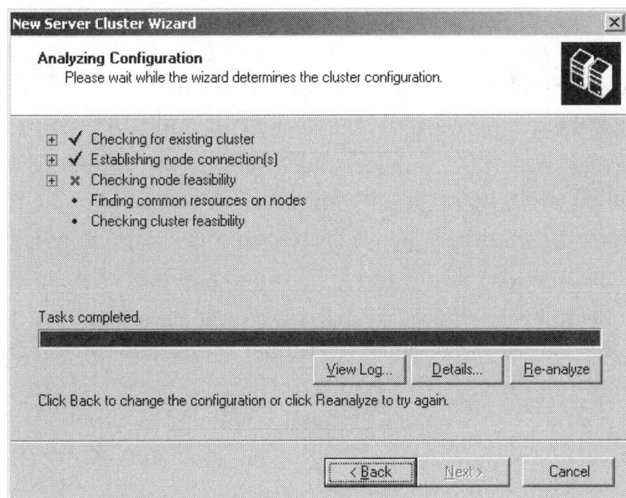

Figure 18-16. The wizard analyzes the configuration and highlights any problems found.

5 If the taskbar turns red, the wizard has encountered a fatal error in the configuration and you will not be able to continue. In this case, you can choose one of the following steps:

- Select View Log to open the configuration log for viewing in Notepad. As mentioned previously, Microsoft Knowledge Base article 295648 can help you make sense of this log.
- Select a configuration item in the analysis list, and then click Details to view detailed information regarding the analysis entry. Detailed entries include links to the Microsoft Web site where you can get more information.
- Select Reanalyze to have the wizard analyze the configuration again. This is useful if you made a change to the network or make another correction that should allow the configuration to pass the analysis test.

6 Once the configuration passes analysis, you can click Next to display the IP Address page. Enter the IP address that will be used by cluster management tools to connect to the cluster, and then click Next.

7 Use the Cluster Service Account page to specify the logon information for the account under which the Cluster service will run. The account will be granted local administrative privileges on all nodes of the cluster and can be a new account or an existing account.

8 Click Next, then use the Proposed Cluster Configuration page to review the cluster configuration. If you see something that should be corrected, you can click Back to make the necessary changes.

9 Optionally, click Quorum to display the Proposed Cluster Configuration page. This lets you select a quorum type other than the default. Choose Local Quorum, Physical Disk, or Majority Node Set as appropriate.

10 Click Next to start configuring the cluster. When the configuration is finalized, you'll see a status page very similar to the Analyzing Configuration page. This page shows the progress of each step of the configuration as follows:

- First, the wizard reanalyzes the cluster configuration.
- Second, the wizard configures the Cluster service, installing the service and configuring it to use the account you specified.
- Third, the wizard configures the resource types for the cluster.
- Finally, the wizard configures the common resources of the cluster.

11 Again, if the taskbar turns red, the wizard has encountered a fatal error in the configuration and you will not be able to continue. In this case, you can choose one of the following steps:

- Select View Log to open the configuration logs for viewing in Notepad
- Select a configuration item in the analysis list, and then click Details to view detailed information regarding the analysis entry
- Select Retry to have the wizard try to configure the cluster again after you make a correction that should allow the configuration to complete

12 Click Next, and then click Finish to complete the process. You can then define cluster resource groups, configure resources, and add nodes to the cluster.

Add a Node to a Cluster

Once you've created a cluster and added an initial node, at any time you can add other nodes to the cluster, up to a maximum of eight. Additional nodes automatically inherit the quorum and resource configuration from the initial host.

To add a node to a server cluster, start Cluster Administrator, which can be started from the Administrative Tools menu or by typing **cluadmin** at the command prompt. In the Open Connection To Cluster dialog box, select Add Nodes To Cluster, type the cluster name or IP address of the cluster you want to work with, and then click OK. This starts the Add Nodes Wizard. When the wizard starts, enter the domain name or IP address of the host to add to the cluster, and then click Next.

The wizard begins analyzing the configuration with the new node and notes any problems found. The rest of configuration works much the same as a new node configuration. If there are problems with using the node, you can use View Logs or Details to get troubleshooting information.

Managing Server Clusters and Their Resources

After you create the cluster, you can specify the resources that you want to be highly available and configure the policies that you want to follow to administer those resources. You can, for example, specify how resources fail over and fail back as well as which nodes are the primary owners of resources.

Creating Clustered Resources

Once you create a cluster, you can specify the resources that you want to be highly available. Each primary resource, such as a file share or print spooler, has a group of resources that it depends on. These resources should all be placed in the same group to allow seamless failover from one node in the cluster to another. Although you could place the resources in the main Cluster group, it is usually better to group resources together by dependencies as discussed previously.

Cluster Resource Types

The Cluster service defines specific resource types that can be configured for high availability and added to resource groups. The available resource types include the following:

- **Physical Disk** The Physical Disk resource type is used to manage disks that are on a shared cluster storage device. You can assign drive letters to disks that are on a cluster storage device or use mount points. If you assign drive letters, the disks must have the same drive letters on all cluster nodes. Physical Disk resources are created automatically for cluster disks when you use drive letters and must be manually created when you use mount points.
- **DHCP** DHCP provides dynamic IP addressing in the domain. When you can run it as a resource of the cluster, you provide for high availability. For DHCP to fail over successfully, the DHCP database must be on the shared cluster storage. Be sure to use the full directory path and end the path with a backslash (\), such as **g:\dchp\data**.

- **WINS** WINS provides resolution of NetBIOS names to IP addresses. When you can run it as a resource of the cluster, you provide for high availability. For WINS to fail over successfully, the WINS database must be on the shared cluster storage. Be sure to use the full directory path and end the path with a backslash (\), such as **g:\wins\data**.
- **File Share** For file servers, the File Share resource type provides for high availability of the shared folders. You can manage file shares in several ways. As a normal file share, only the top-level folder is visible as the share name. This is the most basic type of file share. As shared subfolders, the top-level folder and each of its immediate subfolders are shared with separate names. This allows you to create a large number of related file shares easily, such as those for user's home directories. As a stand-alone DFS root, you can share DFS roots that aren't configured to be fault tolerant. This is ideal when the DFS data changes frequently and you don't want to have to replicate changes to DFS replicas frequently.
- **Print Spooler** For print servers, the Print Spooler resource type provides for high availability of network-attached print devices. Printers connected directly to print servers cannot be included because there is no way to fail over control to a different server. If a print server fails, all jobs that are currently spooling are restarted. Jobs that are in the process of spooling are discarded and must be respooled or reprinted to the Print Spooler resource. Although multiple Print Spooler resources can be configured in a cluster, each resource group can have only one Print Spooler.
- **Internet Protocol Address** The Internet Protocol Address resource type is used to manage the IP addresses of the cluster. When an IP Address resource is included with a resource group with a Network Name resource, the resource group can be accessed by network clients as a virtual server. Virtual servers allow clients to continue to use the same name to access the cluster even after a failover has occurred. Failover happens seamlessly for clients and no change is required on the clients.
- **Network Name** The Network Name resource type is used to provide an alternate computer name. When included in a resource group with an IP Address resource, the resource group can be accessed by network clients as a virtual server.
- **Local Quorum** The Local Quorum resource type is used to manage the system disk on the local node of a single-node cluster. This resource type cannot fail over to another node because there are no other nodes available. If you create a Local Quorum resource on one node of a multinode cluster, you migrate the node so that it uses the Local Quorum as its quorum resource. That node then acts as a one-node cluster and is isolated from the other nodes, which is useful for troubleshooting in some cases.
- **Majority Node Set** The Majority Node Set resource type allows the quorum data, which includes cluster configuration changes and state information, to be stored on the system disk of each node in the cluster. It is used to ensure the data remains consistent across nodes that might be geographically dispersed. Only one Majority Node Set can exist in a server cluster.

- **Generic Application** The Generic Application resource type is used to manage cluster-unaware applications that can be failed over. Generic applications must use an IP-based protocol for their network communications and must be able to store their data in a configurable location.
- **Generic Script** The Generic Script resource type is used to manage Windows scripts as cluster resources. Only the most basic clustering functionality is provided. If the script is running, it is assumed that it is online.
- **Generic Service** The Generic Script resource type is used to manage Windows services as cluster resources. Only the most basic clustering functionality is provided. If the service is running, it is assumed that it is online.
- **Volume Shadow Copy Service Task** The Volume Shadow Copy Service Task resource type allows you to create jobs in the Scheduled Tasks folder that must be run on the node that is currently hosting a particular resource group. This allows you to define scheduled tasks that can fail over from one cluster node to another. The functionality is limited because it is primarily designed to support shadow copies of shared folders in server clusters.

Planning Resource Groups

When planning resource groups, you should list all server-based applications and services that will run in the cluster environment, regardless of whether they will need high availability. Be sure to look at applications and services running on front-end servers, application logic servers, and back-end servers. Afterward, divide the list into three sections: Support, HA, and Non-HA. The Support section should include all applications and services that run on severs that aren't part of the cluster and on which clustered resources do not depend. The HA section should include all applications and services running on the cluster servers that need high availability. This section should also include the resources these applications and services are dependent on. The Non-HA section should include all applications and services running on the cluster servers that do not need or do not support failover. Put an asterisk next to any items that need further research or discussion as a reminder that the deployment team should reexamine the items later.

Support applications and services often interact with clustered applications and services, and these interactions should be clearly understood and tracked. Failure of a support application or service shouldn't impact the core functions of the business system. If it does, the support application or service might need to be clustered or load balanced.

Applications and services in the HA section represent resources that should be placed into resource groups. Resources should be grouped together according to their dependencies. Resources cannot span groups. For example, if several applications depend on a particular resource, the applications and the resource must be placed into a single resource group.

Applications and services in the Non-HA section represent resources that might not need to be placed into resource groups. Before making the final determination, administrators should ensure that failure of a support application or service doesn't impact other applications or services. If it does, the application or service represents a dependency for another application or service—and all dependent resources must be together in a single resource group. Failure of a support application or service shouldn't impact the core functions of the business system. If it does, the application or service might need to be clustered or load balanced. In the case of dependent services that don't support clustering, you might want to provide backup planning in case these services fail or might want to attempt to make the services cluster-aware by using Windows scripts.

Each application and service that you've identified as HA, such as a file share or print spooler, has a group of resources that it depends on. These resources should all be placed in the same resource group to allow seamless failover from one node in the cluster to another. Although you could place the resources in the main Cluster group, it is usually better to group resources together by dependencies.

To get a better understanding of dependencies, you should draw a dependency tree for each resource group. This will help you understand not only which resources that an application or service is dependent upon, but also how those dependencies are interrelated. For example, a high-availability print server is dependent on a Print Spooler resource, which in turn is dependent on a Physical Disk resource and a Network Name resource. The Network Name resource is in turn dependent on the IP Address resource, and ultimately the dependency tree is similar to that shown in Figure 18-17.

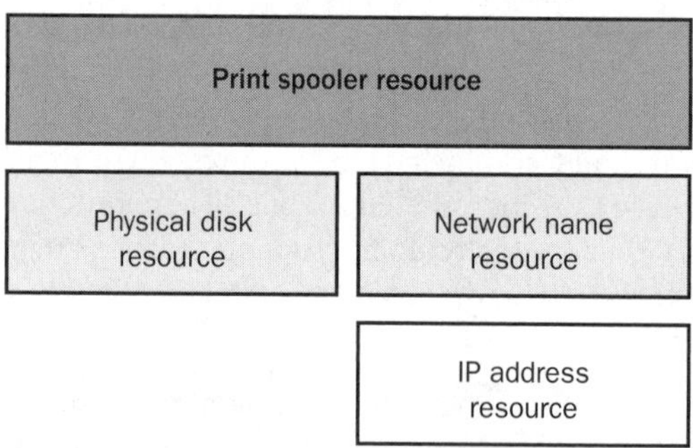

Figure 18-17. The dependency tree for a Print Spooler resource.

Controlling the Cluster Service

By using the Cluster service you can control operations on a per-node basis. To stop the Cluster service on a node, select the node in Cluster Administrator, and then click File and then Stop Cluster Service. When you stop the Cluster service, you prevent clients from accessing resources on that node. If the node's failover policies are configured to move resources to another node, all resource groups on the node are moved to another node. If no failover policies are configured, however, clients cannot access the node's resources. To start the Cluster service again, select the node in Cluster Administrator, and then click File and then Start Cluster Service.

The key reason for stopping and starting nodes is to repair a node. Here, you stop the Cluster service, make the necessary repairs, and then when you are finished you bring the node back online by starting the Cluster service. If the server must be rebooted to complete the repairs, you should follow these steps after making repairs and before rebooting:

1. Set the Cluster service to start manually before you shut down. To do this, start Services from the Administrative Tools menu. In the details pane, right-click Cluster Service, and then choose Properties. In the General tab of the Properties dialog box, set the Startup Type to Manual, and then click OK.
2. Restart the server. When it comes back online, access the node in Cluster Administrator, and then choose File and then Start Cluster Service.
3. Start services from the Administrative Tools menu. In the details pane, right-click Cluster Service, and then choose Properties. In the General tab of the Properties dialog box, set the Startup Type to Automatic, and then click OK.

Troubleshooting

Resolve problems with the quorum resource

You can start the Cluster service from the command line as well. This is useful if there are problems with the quorum resource and you want to try to repair them. In this case, stop the Cluster service by selecting File, Stop Cluster Service. Then, at the command line, type **clussvc /debug /fixquorum**. (Only one node can be started at a time using this approach.) The server will start the Cluster service but won't bring any resources online. You can then try to bring the quorum resource online manually and troubleshoot, or you could switch to another quorum resource. For Majority Node Set server cluster when one of the nodes loses communication with the nodes in another location, you can try to restore the quorum using the force quorum technique, which involves stopping the Cluster service on all remaining nodes, making a change to the HKEY_LOCAL_MACHINE\SYSTEM\CurrentControlSet\Services\ClusSvc\Parameters subkey in the Registry for the current node and then starting the Cluster service on the remaining nodes. When you access this subkey, you'll want to create a String value called ForceQuorum and set the value of this string to a comma-separated list of the names of the nodes that are to be part of the quorum set.

You also have the option of using Pause and Resume. To pause a node, select the node in Cluster Administrator, and then click File, Pause Node. When you pause a node, existing groups and resources stay online, but additional groups and resources cannot be brought online. You can later allow new groups and resources to be brought online by selecting File, Resume Node.

Controlling Failover and Failback

The resources in a group fail over and fail back together according to the failover and failback policies set on the group as a whole. Basically, the failover policy for a group sets a threshold for the maximum number of times that the group is allowed to fail over in a specified period before it is left in a failed state. If a group fails over more often than the failover policy allows, the Cluster service leaves it offline. For example, if a group failover threshold is set to 4 and its failover period to 2, the Cluster service will fail over the group at most four times within a 2-hour period.

You can set group failover policy in Cluster Administrator by clicking the Groups folder in the left pane, selecting the group you want to work with in the right pane, and then clicking File, Properties. In the Failover tab, set the Threshold and Period options as appropriate for the type of resources in the group.

For a failback policy, you specify whether and how the resource group is returned to its preferred owner. You set group failback policy in Cluster Administrator by clicking the Groups folder in the left pane, selecting the group you want to work with in the right pane, and then clicking File, Properties. In the Failback tab, select either Prevent Failback or Allow Failback. If you click Allow Failback, select Immediately to allow immediate failback, or click Failback Between and set the time interval during which it is permissible to fail back the group. Enter numbers between 0 and 23 to specify the beginning and end of the interval. These numbers correspond to the local time of the cluster group with regard to a 24-hour clock.

Creating and Managing Resource Groups

When you create a resource group in Cluster Administrator, you assign the group a name, description, and preferred owner. The group name and description are for administrative purposes only. They have no relation to the virtual server name that clients use to connect to the group. All resources within a group fail over together. If you want a group to fail back to a certain node, assign that node as the preferred owner, and set the failback policy as discussed in the previous section. If it doesn't matter to which node the resource fails back, don't assign a preferred owner.

Tip Balance the load

One of your goals in defining groups and assigning them to nodes should be to balance the load among all nodes and maximize the performance of the cluster. If a group has very little impact on performance, you might not want to assign it a preferred owner. That way, if the group fails, it can fail over to a new node but won't fail back to the previous node.

You can create a new group in Cluster Administrator by clicking File, New, Group. This starts the New Group Wizard. Enter a name and description for the group, then click Next. If you want to assign a preferred owner, select the nodes you want to be the preferred owners for the group, and then click Add. The owner listed first has priority, meaning it will be the first node attempted for failback. You can change the priority of an owner by selecting the owner and clicking Move Up or Move Down. When you are finished, click Finish.

After you create a group, you can assign resources to the group as discussed in the section entitled "Creating and Managing Resource Groups" earlier in this chapter. Once resources are assigned, you can manage the group in several ways:

- **Bring a group online** You can bring a group online so that the resources are available to clients. Double-click the Groups folder, select the group you want to bring online, and then click File, Bring Online. Resources in a group come online in the order of their dependencies.
- **Take a group offline** You can bring a group offline so that the resources are no longer available to clients. Double-click the Groups folder, select the group you want to bring offline, and then click File, Bring Offline. Resources in a group go offline in the order of their dependencies.
- **Move a group to another node** You can move a group to another node to help balance resource usage or in case you need to bring a server offline. Double-click the Groups folder, select the group you want to move, and then click File, Move Group. In clusters with three or more nodes, choose Best Possible or select the specific node to which you want to move the group. Once the group is moved, the new node owns all resources in the group and the Owner option in the details pane should reflect this.
- **Delete a group** You can delete a group that you no longer want to use. Double-click the Groups folder, and select the group you want to delete. Delete or move all resources in the group, then click File, Delete.

Creating and Managing Resources

When you create a resource in Cluster Administrator, you specify the group to which the resource will belong first and then set the resource's properties. Double-click the Groups folder, select the group to which you want the resource to belong, and then click File, New, Resource. When the New Resource Wizard starts, enter a name and description for the resource, select the appropriate resource type using the Resource Type list, and then click Next. If you want to assign possible owners, select the nodes that can host this resource. Click Next so that you can configure the dependencies for the resource.

If this is the first resource you are defining for the group, there will be no other resources to assign as dependencies. For other resources, you might have dependencies to assign. To add dependencies, click a resource, then click Add. To remove dependencies, click a resource, then click Remove. You can also assign dependencies later.

When you click Next again, the page you see depends on the type of resource you are creating, as follows:

- For Physical Disk, you'll see the Disk Parameters page that will let you choose the physical disk drive for the resource.
- For IP Address, you'll see the TCP/IP Parameters page that lets you specify the IP address, subnet mask, and network adapter to associate with the resource. You can also enable NetBIOS name resolution.
- For Network Name, you'll see the Network Name Parameters page that lets you specify the name for the virtual server.

After you configure the necessary parameters, click Finish to create the resource and assign it to the designated group. When you are done creating resources for a group, you can bring the group online by selecting it, then clicking File, Bring Online.

Once you create resources, you can manage them in several ways:

- **Bring a resource and its dependent resources online** Double-click the Resources folder, select the primary resource, and then click File, Bring Online.
- **Take a resource and its dependent resources offline** Double-click the Resources folder, select the primary resource, and then click File, Take Offline.
- **Move a resource and all its dependent resources to a new group** Double-click the Resources folder, select the primary resource, click File, Change Group, and then click the name of the group to which you want to transfer ownership. You can also select the resource you want to move, then drag and drop it in another group.
- **Initiate a resource failure to trigger a restart or failover** Double-click the Groups folder, select the group that contains the resource in the left pane, and then in the right pane select the resource on which you want to initiate failure. Click File, Initiate Failure. When a resource fails, it automatically restarts according to its restart policy (if any). If a resource fails repeatedly, the entire group to which the resource belongs can fail over, depending on the failover policy defined (if any).

Scenario: Creating a Clustered Print Service

For clustered print services, you should create a resource group to hold the printer's dependent resources. You would then complete the following steps:

1. Create a Physical Disk resource for the drive on which the print spool folder is located.
2. Create an IP Address resource, which is used in conjunction with the Network Name resource so the print service can be accessed by network clients as a virtual server.
3. Create a Network Name resource and add IP Address as a dependency.
4. Create a Print Spooler resource and add as dependencies the Physical Disk, IP Address, and Network Name resources.

Afterward, you add these resources to the resource group you previously defined. You then bring the virtual server containing the print spooler resource online by selecting it and then choosing File, Bring Online. Afterward, you prepare the printer for high availability use by completing the following:

- Installing a print port monitor on all nodes in the cluster
- Installing print drivers on the virtual server
- Installing a printer port for the printer on the virtual server
- Adding a print queue on the virtual server

Scenario: Creating a Clustered File Share

Cluster-managed file shares work in much the same way. You start by creating a folder on the cluster disk to which the Cluster service account has Full Control rights. Create a resource group to hold the file share's dependent resources, and then complete the following steps:

1. Create a Physical Disk resource for the drive on which the shared folders are located.
2. Create an IP Address resource, which is used in conjunction with the Network Name resource so the shared folders can be accessed by network clients as a virtual server.
3. Create a Network Name resource and add IP Address as a dependency.
4. Create a File Share resource and add as dependencies the Physical Disk, IP Address, and Network Name resources.

After you add these resources to the resource group you previously defined, you select the File Share resource that you created and edit its properties by clicking File, Properties. In the Parameters tab, use the Path field to set the path to the folder whose subfolders you want to share. Then click Permissions to configure the File Share permissions according to the users and groups who should have access to the file share. The File Share permissions are different from the NTFS permissions assigned locally on the computer. When you are finished assigning permissions, you can bring the File Share resource online by selecting it and then choosing File, Bring Online.

Chapter 19

Storage Management

This chapter introduces Microsoft Windows Server 2003 storage management. Data is stored throughout the enterprise on a variety of systems and storage devices, the most common of which are hard disk drives but also can include storage management devices and removable media devices. Managing and maintaining the myriad of systems and storage devices is the responsibility of administrators. If a storage device fails, runs out of space, or encounters other problems, serious negative consequences can result. Servers could crash, applications could stop working, users could lose data, all of which affect the productivity of users and the organization's bottom line. You can help prevent such problems and losses by implementing sound storage management procedures that allow you to evaluate your current and future storage needs and also help you meet current and future performance, capacity, and availability requirements. You then must configure storage appropriately for the requirements you've defined.

Essential Storage Technologies

One of the few constants in Microsoft Windows operating system administration is that data storage needs are ever increasing. It seems that only a few years ago a 120-gigabyte (GB) hard disk was huge and something primarily reserved for Windows servers rather than Windows workstations. Now Windows workstations ship with 120-GB hard disks as standard equipment, and some even ship with striped drives that allow workstations to have a single large volume that spans over several drives—and all of that must be stored somewhere other than on the workstations, which has meant that back-end storage solutions have had to scale dramatically as well. Server solutions that were once used for enterprise-wide implementations are now being used increasingly at the departmental level, and the underlying architecture for the related storage solutions has had to change dramatically to keep up.

Using Internal and External Storage Devices

To help meet the increasing demand for data storage and changing requirements, servers are being deployed with a mix of internal and external storage. In internal storage configurations, drives are connected inside the server chassis to a local disk controller and are said to be directly attached. You'll sometimes see an internal storage device referred to as direct-attached storage (DAS).

In external storage configurations, servers connect to external, separately managed collections of storage devices that are either network-attached or part of a storage area network. Although the terms *network-attached storage (NAS)* and *storage area network (SAN)* are sometimes used as if they are one and the same, the technologies differ in how servers communicate with the external drives.

NAS devices are connected through a regular Transmission Control Protocol/Internet Protocol (TCP/IP) network. All server-storage communications go across the organization's local area network (LAN), as shown in Figure 19-1. This means the available bandwidth on the network can be shared by clients, servers, and NAS devices. For best performance, the network should be running at 100 megabits per second (Mbps) or 1000 Mbps. Networks operating at slower speeds can experience a serious performance impact as clients, services, and storage devices try to communicate using the limited bandwidth.

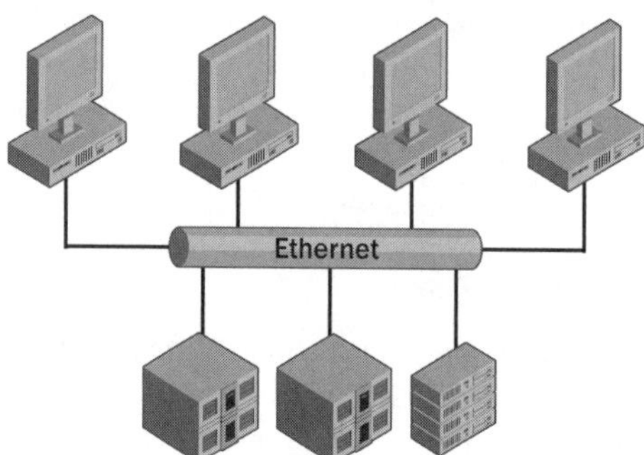

Figure 19-1. In a NAS, server-storage communications are on the LAN.

A SAN is physically separate from the LAN and is independently managed. As shown in Figure 19-2, this isolates the server-to-storage communications so that traffic doesn't impact communications between clients and servers. Several SAN technologies are implemented, including fibre channel, a more traditional SAN technology that delivers high reliability and performance, and Internet SCSI (iSCSI), a newer SAN technology that delivers good reliability and performance at a lower cost than fibre channel. As the name implies, Internet SCSI uses TCP/IP networking technologies on the SAN, allowing servers to communicate with storage devices using the IP protocol. The SAN is still isolated from the organization's LAN.

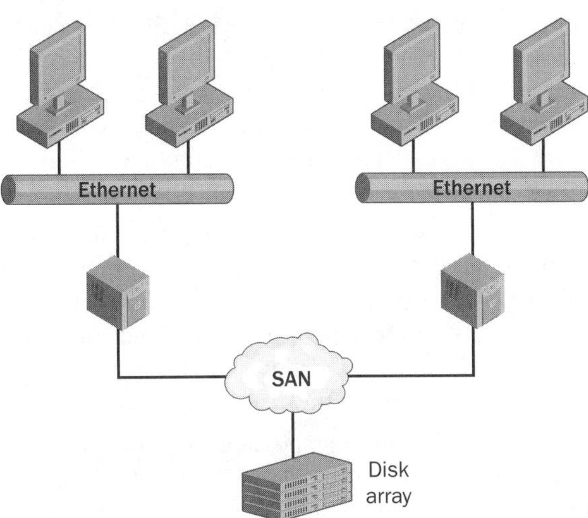

Figure 19-2. In a SAN, server-storage communications don't affect communications between clients and servers.

Improving Storage Management

Because of the increasing use of SANs, Windows Server 2003 includes many new and enhanced features for working with SANs and handling storage management in general. These improvements include the following:

- **Volume Shadow Copy service (VSS)** VSS allows administrators to create point-in-time copies of volumes and individual files called *snapshots*. This makes it possible to back up these items while files are open and applications are running and to restore them to a specific point in time. VSS also makes it possible to create point-in-time copies of documents on shared folders called shadow copies.

Note Users can recover their own files when VSS is enabled. Once you configure shadow copy, point-in-time backups of documents contained in the designated shared folders are created automatically, and users can quickly recover files that have been deleted or unintentionally altered as long as the Shadow Copy Client has been installed on their computer. For more information about VSS and the Shadow Copy Client, see Chapter 22, "Using Volume Shadow Copy."

- **Virtual Disk Service (VDS)** VDS makes it possible for storage devices from multiple vendors to interoperate. To do this, VDS provides application programming interfaces (APIs) that management tools and storage hardware can use, allowing for a unified interface for managing storage devices from multiple vendors and making it easier for administrators to manage a mixed-storage environment.

- **Volume automounting** Volume automounting makes it possible to manage better the way volumes are mounted. By using the MOUNTVOL command, administrators can turn off volume automounting. By using volume mount points, administrators can mount volumes to empty NTFS folders, giving the volumes a drive path rather than a drive letter. This means it is easier to mount and unmount volumes, particularly with SANs.

- **Multipath I/O** Multipath I/O makes it possible to configure as many as 32 separate physical paths to external storage devices that can be used simultaneously and load balanced if necessary. The purpose of having multiple paths is to have redundancy and possibly increased throughput. If you have multiple host bus adapters as well, you improve the chances of recovery from a path failure. However, if a path failure occurs, there might be a short period of time when the drives on the SAN aren't accessible.
- **Distributed File System (DFS)** DFS makes it possible to create a single directory tree that includes multiple file servers and their file shares. The DFS tree can contain more than 5000 shared folders in a domain environment (or 50,000 shared folders on a stand-alone server), located on different servers, allowing users to find files or folders distributed across the enterprise easily. DFS directory trees can also be published in the Active Directory directory service so that they are easy to search.

Tip **DFS now supports multiple roots and closest-site selection**
New for Windows Server 2003 is the capability for a single server to host multiple DFS roots and use closest-site selection. The capability to host multiple DFS roots allows you to consolidate and reduce the number of servers needed to maintain DFS. By using closest-site selection, DFS uses Active Directory site metrics to route a client to the closest available file server.

- **File Replication Services (FRS)** FRS makes it possible to synchronize data across the enterprise and is in fact the synchronization technology used by Active Directory. FRS works in conjunction with DFS to replicate data on file shares and automatically maintain synchronization of copies on multiple servers. New for Windows Server 2003 is the DFS Microsoft Management Console (MMC), which allows administrators to configure replication. FRS is now capable of compressing replication traffic as well.

Windows Server 2003 adds several command-line tools for managing local storage. These tools include the following:

- **DiskPart** Used to manage disks, partitions, and volumes. It is the command-line counterpart to the Disk Management tool and also includes features not found in the graphical user interface (GUI) tool, such as the capability to extend partitions on basic disks.

- **Dfsutil** Used to configure DFS, back up and restore DFS directory trees (namespaces), copy directory trees, and troubleshoot DFS. This tool is in the Windows Server 2003 Support Tools.
- **Fsutil** Used to get detailed drive information and perform advanced file system maintenance. You can manage sparse files, reparse points, disk quotas, and other advanced features of NTFS.
- **Health_Chk** Used to monitor or troubleshoot FRS. It works in conjunction with a number of other utilities, using them to retrieve and log the data necessary for troubleshooting. This tool is part of the Windows Server 2003 Support Tools.
- **Vssadmin** Used to view and manage the Volume Shadow Copy service and its configuration.

Booting from SANs and Using SANs with Clusters

Windows Server 2003 supports booting from a SAN, having multiple clusters attached to the same SAN, and having a mix of clusters and stand-alone servers attached to the same SAN. To boot from a SAN, the external storage devices and the host bus adapters of each server must be configured appropriately to allow booting from the SAN.

When multiple servers must boot from the same external storage device, either the SAN must be configured in a switched environment or it must be directly attached from each host to one of the storage subsystem's fibre channel ports. A switched or direct-to-port environment allows the servers to be separate from each other, which is essential for booting from a SAN.

> **Tip** **Fibre Channel–Arbitrated Loop isn't allowed**
> The use of a Fibre Channel–Arbitrated Loop (FC-AL) configuration is not supported because hubs typically don't allow the servers on the SAN to be isolated properly from each other—and the same is true when you have multiple clusters attached to the same SAN or a mix of clusters and stand-alone servers attached to the same SAN.

Each server on the SAN must have exclusive access to the logical disk from which it is booting, and no other server on the SAN should be able to detect or access that logical disk. For multiple-cluster installations, the SAN must be configured so that a set of cluster disks is accessible only by one cluster and is completely hidden from the rest of the clusters. By default, Windows Server 2003 will attach and mount every logical disk that it detects when the host bus adapter driver loads, and if multiple servers mount the same disk, the file system can be damaged.

To prevent file system damage, the SAN must be configured in such a way that only one server can access a particular logical disk at a time. You can configure disks for exclusive access using a type of logical unit number (LUN) management such as LUN masking, LUN zoning, or a preferred combination of these techniques. Keep in mind that LUN management isn't normally configured within Windows. It is instead configured at the level of the switch, storage subsystem, or host bus adapter.

Troubleshooting

Detecting SAN configuration problems

On an improperly configured SAN, multiple hosts are able to access the same logical disks. This isn't what you want to happen, but it does happen and you might be able to detect this configuration problem when you are working with the logical disks. Try using Windows Explorer from multiple hosts to access the logical disks on the SAN. If you try to access a logical disk and receive an "Access Denied," "Device Not Ready," or a similar error message, this can be an indicator that another server has access to the logical disk you are attempting to use. You might see another indicator of an improperly configured SAN when you add or configure logical disks. If you notice that multiple servers report that they've found new hardware when adding or configuring logical disks, there is a configuration problem with the SAN. If there is a configuration problem with clusters, you can see the following error events in the System logs:

- Warning event ID 11 with event source %HBADriverName%, "The driver detected a controller error on Device\ScsiPort*N*."
- Warning event ID 50 with event source Disk, "The system was attempting to transfer file data from buffers to \Device\HarddiskVolume*N*. The write operation failed, and only some of the data may have been written to the file."
- Warning event ID 51 with event source FTDISK, "An error was detected on device during a paging operation."
- Warning event ID 9 with event source %HBADriverName%, "Lost Delayed Write Data: The device, \Device\ScsiPort*N*, did not respond within the timeout period."
- Warning event ID 26 with event source Application Popup, "Windows—Delayed Write Failed: Windows was unable to save all the data for the file \Device\Harddisk Volume*N*\MFT$. The data has been lost. This error may be caused by a failure of your computer hardware or network connection. Please try to save this file elsewhere."

Meeting Performance, Capacity, and Availability Requirements

Whether you are working with internal or external disks, you should follow the same basic principles to help ensure the chosen storage solutions meet your performance, capacity, and availability requirements. Storage performance is primarily a factor of the disk's access time (how long it takes to register a request and scan the disk), seek time (how long it takes to find the requested data), and transfer rate (how long it takes to read and write data). Storage capacity relates to how much information you can store on a volume or logical disk.

Although NTFS as implemented on Microsoft Windows NT 4 (NTFS 4) had a maximum volume size and file size limit of 32 GB, NTFS 5 as introduced with Windows NT 4 Service

Pack 4 and Microsoft Windows 2000 Server extended this limit to 2 terabytes (TB). In Windows Server 2003, you have greatly extended limits. You can have a maximum NTFS volume size of 256 TB minus 64 KB using 64-KB clusters and 16 TB minus 4 KB using 4-KB clusters. Windows Server 2003 has a maximum file size on an NTFS volume of up to 16 TB minus 64 KB. Further, Windows Server 2003 supports a maximum of 4,294,967,294 files on each volume, and a single server can manage hundreds of volumes (theoretically, around 2000).

Storage availability relates to fault tolerance. As discussed in Chapter 18, "Preparing and Deploying Server Clusters," you ensure availability for essential applications and services by using cluster technologies. If a server has a problem or a particular application or service fails, you have a way to continue operations by failing over to another server. In addition to clusters, you can help ensure availability by saving redundant copies of data, keeping spare parts, and if possible making standby servers available. At the disk and data level, availability is enhanced by using redundant array of independent disks (RAID) technologies. RAID allows you to combine disks and to improve fault tolerance.

RAID can be implemented in software or in hardware. By using software RAID, the operating system maintains the disk sets at some cost to server performance. Windows Server 2003 supports RAID 0 (disk striping), RAID 1 (disk mirroring), and RAID 5 (disk striping with parity). Each of these software-implemented RAID levels requires processing power and memory resources to maintain. By using hardware RAID, you use separate hardware controllers (RAID controllers) to maintain the disk arrays. Although this requires the purchase of additional hardware, it takes the burden off the server and can improve performance. Why? In a hardware-implemented RAID system, processing power and memory aren't used to maintain the disk arrays. Instead, the hardware RAID controller handles all the necessary processing tasks. Some hardware RAID controllers have integrated disk caching as well, which can give a further boost to overall RAID performance.

The RAID levels available with a hardware implementation depend on the hardware controller and the vendor's implementation of RAID technologies. Some hardware RAID configurations include RAID 0 (disk striping), RAID 1 (disk mirroring), RAID 0+1(disk striping with mirroring), RAID 5 (disk striping with parity), and RAID 5+1 (disk striping with parity plus mirroring).

For more information about the advantages and disadvantages of various RAID levels, see Table 18-1, "Hardware RAID Configurations for Clusters," on page 566.

Configuring Storage

When you install disks, you must configure them for use by choosing a partition style and a storage type to use. After you configure drives, you prepare them to store data by partitioning them and creating file systems in the partitions. Partitions are sections of physical drives that function as if they were separate units. This allows you to configure multiple logical disk units even if a system has only one physical drive and to apportion disks appropriately to meet the needs of your organization.

Using the Disk Management Tools

When you want to manage storage, the primary tool you use is Disk Management, as shown in Figure 19-3. Disk Management is a snap-in included in Computer Management and can be added to any custom MMC you create. As long as you are a member of the Administrators group, you can use Disk Management to configure drives and software RAID.

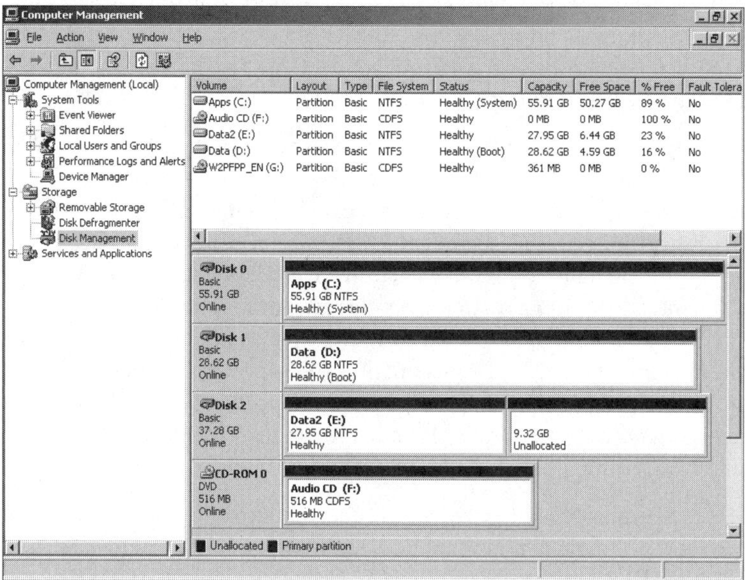

Figure 19-3. Disk Management is the primary tool for managing storage.

Disk Management makes it easy to work with any available internal and external drives on both local and remote systems. You can start Disk Management by clicking Start, pointing to Programs or All Programs as appropriate, selecting Administrative Tools, Computer Management. You're automatically connected to the local computer on which you're running Computer Management. In Computer Management, expand Storage, and then select Disk Management. You can now manage the drives on the local system.

To use Disk Management to work with a remote system, right-click the Computer Management entry in the left pane, and select Connect To Another Computer on the shortcut menu. This displays the Select Computer dialog box (shown in the following screen). Type the domain name or IP address of the system whose drives you want to view, and then click OK.

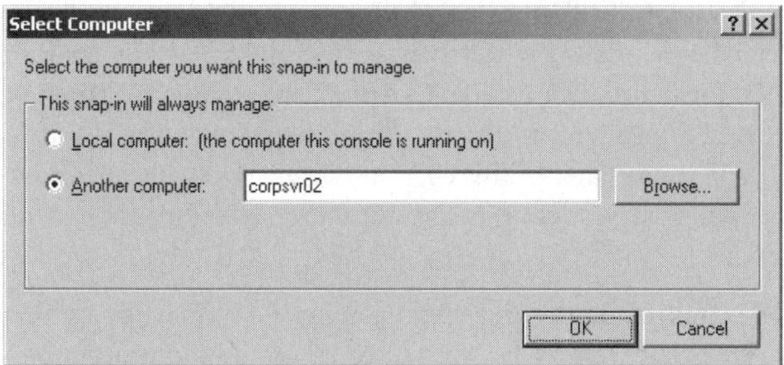

Disk Management has three views:

- **Disk List** Shows a list of physical disks on or attached to the selected system with details on type, capacity, unallocated space, and status. It is the only disk view that shows the device type, such as Small Computer System Interface (SCSI) or Integrated Device Electronics (IDE), and the partition style, such as Master Boot Record (MBR) or GUID Partition Table (GPT).
- **Graphical View** Displays summary information for disks graphically according to disk capacity and the size of disk regions. By default, disk and disk region capacity are shown on a logarithmic scale, meaning the disks and disk regions are displayed proportionally.

Tip Change the scaling options to get different disk views
You can also specify that you want all disks to be the same size regardless of capacity (which is useful if you have many disk regions on disks) or that you want to use a linear scale in which disk regions are sized relative to the largest disk (which is useful if you want to get perspective on capacity). To change the size settings for the Graphical View, click View, Settings, and then in the Settings dialog box, select the Scaling tab.

- **Volume List** Shows all volumes on the selected computer (including hard disk partitions and logical drives) with details on volume layout, type, file system, status, capacity, and free space. It also shows whether the volume has fault tolerance and the related disk usage overhead. The fault tolerance information is for software RAID only.

Volume List and Graphical View are the default views. In Figure 19-3, the Volume List view is in the upper-right corner, and the Graphical View is in the lower-right corner. To change the top view, select View, choose Top, and then select the view you want to use. To change the bottom view, select View, choose Bottom, and then select the view you want to use.

Disk Management's command-line counterpart is the DiskPart utility. You can use DiskPart to perform all Disk Management tasks with the exception of formatting partitions, logical drives, and volumes. To format partitions, logical drives, and volumes from the command line, you use the FORMAT command, as discussed in the section entitled "Formatting a Partition, Logical Drive, or Volume" later in this chapter. DiskPart can also perform some tasks that Disk Management can't, such as configuring automount settings and extending disk partitions on basic disks.

DiskPart is a text-mode command interpreter that you invoke so that you can manage disks, partitions, and volumes. As such, DiskPart has a separate command prompt and its own internal commands. You invoke the DiskPart interpreter by typing **diskpart** at the command prompt. DiskPart is designed to work with physical hard disks installed on a computer, which can be internal, external, or a mix of both. Although it will list other types of disks, such as CD/DVD drives, removable media, and universal serial bus (USB)–connected flash random access memory (RAM) devices, and allow you to perform some minimal tasks, such as assigning a drive letter, these devices are not supported.

After you invoke DiskPart, you can list available disks, partitions, and volumes by using the following list commands:

- **LIST DISK** Lists all internal and external hard disks on the computer
- **LIST VOLUME** Lists all volumes on the computer (including hard disk partitions and logical drives)
- **LIST PARTITION** Lists partitions, but only on the disk you've selected

Then you must give focus to the disk, partition, or volume you want to work with by selecting it. Giving a disk, partition, or volume focus ensures that any commands you type will act only on that disk, partition, or volume. To select a disk, type **select disk** ***N***, where *N* is the number of the disk you want to work with. To select a volume, type **select volume** ***N***, where *N* is the number of the volume you want to work with. To select a partition, first select its related disk by typing **select disk** ***N***, and then select the partition you want to work with by typing **select partition** ***N***.

If you use the list commands again after selecting a disk, partition, or volume, you'll see an asterisk (*) next to the item with focus. When you are finished working with DiskPart, type **exit** at the DiskPart prompt to return to the standard command line.

Listing 19-1 shows a sample DiskPart session. As you can see, when you first invoke DiskPart, it shows the operating system and DiskPart version you are using as well as the name of the computer you are working with. When you list available disks, the output shows you the disk number, status, size, and free space. It also shows the disk partition style and type. If there's an asterisk in the Dyn column, the disk is a dynamic disk. Otherwise, it is a basic disk. If there's an asterisk in the Gpt column, the disk uses the GPT partition style. Otherwise, it is an MBR disk. You'll find more information on partition styles in the section entitled "Using the MBR and GPT Partition Styles" later in this chapter.

Listing 19-1 Using DiskPart: An Example

```
C:\> diskpart

Microsoft DiskPart version 5.2.3790
Copyright (C) 1999-2001 Microsoft Corporation.
On computer: CORPSVR02

DISKPART> list disk

Disk ###      Status        Size       Free       Dyn     Gpt
--------      ----------    -------    ------     ---     ---
  Disk 0      Online        56 GB      0 B        *       *
  Disk 1      Online        29 GB      0 B
  Disk 2      Online        37 GB      9 GB

DISKPART> list volume

  Volume ###  Ltr  Label        Fs     Type        Size     Status     Info
  ----------  ---  ---------    -----  ---------   -------  -------    -------
  Volume 0    F                        DVD-ROM        0 B
  Volume 1    G    W2PFPP_EN    CDFS   CD-ROM      361 MB
  Volume 2    C    Apps         NTFS   Partition     56 GB  Healthy    System
  Volume 3    D    Data         NTFS   Partition     29 GB  Healthy
  Volume 4    N    Data2        NTFS   Partition     28 GB  Healthy
  Volume 5    S                        Partition     47 MB  Healthy

DISKPART> select disk 0

Disk 0 is now the selected disk.

DISKPART> list partition

  Partition ###    Type                Size       Offset
  -------------    ----------------    ------ -  -------
  Partition 1      Primary             56 GB      32 KB

DISKPART> select partition 1

Partition 1 is now the selected partition.

DISKPART> list partition

  Partition ###    Type                Size       Offset
  -------------    ----------------    --------   ------
* Partition 1      Primary             56 GB      32 KB

DISKPART> exit

Leaving DiskPart...

C:\>
```

Adding New Disks

Thanks to hot swapping and Plug and Play technologies—both supported by Windows Server 2003—the process of adding new disks has changed considerably from the days of Windows NT 4. If a computer supports hot swapping of disks, you can install new disks without having to shut down the computer. Simply insert the hard disk drives you want to use. If the computer doesn't support hot swapping, you will need to shut down the computer, insert the drives, and restart the computer.

Either way, after you insert the drives you want to use, log on and access Disk Management in the Computer Management tool. If the new drives have already been initialized, meaning they have disk signatures, they should be brought online automatically when you select Rescan Disks from the Action menu. If you are working with new drives that haven't been initialized, meaning they lack a disk signature, Windows Server 2003 will start the Initialize And Convert Disk Wizard when you select the Disk Management node in the Computer Management tool. As the name implies, this wizard initializes the disks you've added and allows you to convert them to dynamic disks.

When the Initialize And Convert Disk Wizard starts, follow these steps to configure the disks:

1. Click Next to get to the Select Disks To Initialize page. The disks you added are selected for initialization automatically, but if you don't want to initialize a particular disk, you can clear the related option.
2. Click Next to display the Select Disks To Convert page. The new disks aren't selected by default. Select the disks you want to convert to dynamic disks (if any), and then click Next.
3. The final page shows you the options you've selected and the actions that will be performed on each disk. If the options are correct, click Finish. The wizard then performs the designated actions. If you've elected to initialize a disk, the wizard writes a disk signature to the disk. If you've elected to convert a disk, the wizard converts the disk to a dynamic disk after writing the disk signature.
4. When the wizard finishes, the disk is ready for partitioning and formatting.

Inside Out

Windows Server 2003 can use disk write caching

As discussed previously, storage performance is primarily a factor of a disk's access time (how long it takes to register a request and scan the disk), seek time (how long it takes to find the requested data), and transfer rate (how long it takes to read and write data). By enabling disk write caching, you could reduce the number of times the operating system accesses the disk by caching disk writes and then performing several writes at once. In this way, disk performance is primarily influenced by seek time and transfer rate.

The drawback of disk write caching is that in the event of a power or system failure the cached writes might not be written to disk, and this can result in data loss. Windows Server 2003 disables disk write caching by default, but you can enable it on a per-disk basis. Keep in mind that some server applications require disk write caching to be enabled or disabled, and if these applications use a particular set of disks, these disks must use the required setting for disk write caching.

To configure disk write caching, start Computer Management, expand the System Tools node, and select Device Manager. In the details pane, expand Disk Drives, right-click the disk drive you want to work with, and then select Properties. In the properties dialog box, select the Policies tab. Select or clear Enable Write Caching On This Disk as appropriate, and click OK.

Using the MBR and GPT Partition Styles

The term *partition style* refers to the method that Windows Server 2003 uses to organize partitions on a disk. Two partition styles are available: MBR and GPT. The partition style you use really depends on whether the computer is an x86-based computer or an Itanium-based computer. x86-based computers can use only the MBR partition style. Itanium-based computers running 64-bit versions of Windows can use the MBR partition style as well as the GPT partition style. The GPT partition style is preferred, however, because it is optimized for 64-bit versions of Windows and is the only partition style from which you can boot Itanium-based computers. The key difference between the MBR partition style and the GPT partition style has to do with how partition data is stored.

Note For this discussion, I focus on the basic storage type and won't get into the details of the dynamic storage type. That's covered in the next section.

Working with MBR Disks

MBR uses a partition table that describes where the partitions are located on the disk. The first sector on a hard disk contains the MBR and a master boot code that's used to boot the system. The boot sector is unpartitioned and hidden from view to protect the system.

MBR disks support a maximum volume size of up to 4 TB unless they're dynamic disks and use RAID. MBR disks have two special types of partitions associated with them. The first partition type, called a primary partition, is used with drive sections that you want to access directly for file storage. You make a primary partition accessible to users by creating a file system on it and assigning it a drive letter or mount point. The second partition type, called an extended partition, is used when you want to divide a section of a disk into one or more logical units called logical drives. Here, you create the extended partition first, then create the logical drives within it. You then create a file system on each logical drive and assign a drive letter or mount point.

Each MBR drive can have up to four primary partitions or three primary partitions and one extended partition. It is the extended partition that allows you to divide a drive into more than four parts.

> **Note** These rules apply to MBR disks that use the basic storage type. There's also a storage type called dynamic. I discuss basic and dynamic storage types in the section entitled "Using the Basic and Dynamic Storage Types" later in this chapter.

Working with GPT Disks on 64-Bit Windows Editions

Instead of using BIOS, Itanium-based computers use the Extensible Firmware Interface (EFI). EFI acts as the interface between a computer's hardware and its operating system. It also defines the GPT style. GPT disks don't have a single MBR. With GPT disks, critical partition data is stored in the individual partitions, and there are redundant primary and backup partition tables. Further, checksum fields are maintained to allow for error correction and to improve partition structure integrity.

Inside Out

GPT headers and error checking

GPT disks use a primary and backup partition table. Each partition table has a header that defines the range of logical block addresses on the disk that can be used by partition entries. The GPT header also defines its location on the disk, its globally unique identifier (GUID), and a 32-bit cyclic redundancy check (CRC32) checksum that is used to verify the integrity of the GPT header. The primary GPT header is created directly after the protected boot sector on the disk. The backup GPT header is located in the last sector on the disk.

EFI verifies the integrity of the GPT headers by using the CRC32 checksum. The checksum is a calculated value used to determine whether there are errors in a GPT header. If the primary GPT header is damaged, EFI checks the backup header. If the backup header's checksum is valid, the backup GPT header is used to restore the primary GPT header. The process of restoring the GPT header works much the same way if it is determined that the backup header is damaged—only in reverse. If both the primary and backup GPT headers are damaged, the Windows operating system won't be able to access the disk.

GPT disks support partitions of up to 18 exabytes (EB) and up to 128 partitions per disk. Itanium-based computers using GPT disks have two required partitions and one or more optional original equipment manufacturer (OEM) or data partitions. The required partitions are the EFI system partition (ESP) and the Microsoft Reserved (MSR) partition.

Although the optional partitions that you see depend on the system configuration, the optional partition type you see the most is the primary partition. Primary partitions are used to store user data on GPT disks.

If you install Windows Server 2003 64-bit edition on a new system with clean disks or an existing system with a clean disk, Setup will initialize the disk as a GPT disk. Setup will offer to create the ESP and then will automatically create the MSR partition. The ESP is formatted automatically using file allocation table (FAT). The ESP is required only on the first GPT disk, however. Additional GPT disks do not require an ESP. Further, a basic GPT disk might not contain primary partitions. For example, when you install a new disk and configure it as a GPT disk, the Windows operating system automatically creates the ESP and MSR partition, but does not create primary partitions.

Although GPT offers a significant improvement over MBR, it does have limitations. First, as discussed previously, only Itanium-based computers can have local disks formatted using GPT. You cannot use GPT with removable disks, disks that are direct-attached using USB or IEEE 1394 (FireWire) interfaces, or disks attached to shared storage devices on server clusters.

Caution It is recommended that you don't use disk editing tools such as DiskProbe to make changes to GPT disks. Any change that you make using these tools renders the CRC32 checksums in the GPT headers invalid, and this can cause the disk to become inaccessible. To make changes to GPT disks, you should use only Disk Management or DiskPart. If you are working in the firmware environment, you'll find there's a version of DiskPart available as well—DiskPart.efi.

Using and Converting MBR and GPT Disks

Tasks for using MBR and GPT disks are similar but not necessarily identical. On an x86-based computer, you can use only MBR disks. On an Itanium-based computer, you can have both GPT and MBR disks, but you must have at least one GPT disk that contains the ESP and a primary partition or simple volume that contains the operating system.

Partitions and volumes on MBR and GPT disks can be formatted using FAT, FAT32, and NTFS. When you create partitions or volumes in Disk Management, you have the opportunity to format the disk and assign it a drive letter or mount point as part of the volume creation process. Although Disk Management lets you format the partitions and volumes on MBR disks using FAT, FAT32, and NTFS, you can format partitions and volumes on GPT disks using only NTFS. If you want to format GPT disks by using FAT or FAT32, you must use the FORMAT command at the command prompt.

You can change partition table styles from MBR to GPT or from GPT to MBR. Changing partition table styles is useful when you want to move disks between x86-based computers and Intel Architecture 64 (IA-64)–based computers or you receive new disks that are formatted for the wrong partition table style. You can convert partition table styles only on empty disks, however. This means the disks must either be new or newly formatted. You could, of course, empty a disk by removing its partitions or volumes.

Both Disk Management and DiskPart can be used to change the partition table style. To use Disk Management to change the partition style of an empty disk, start Computer Management from the Administrative Tools menu or by typing **compmgmt.msc** at the command line, expand the Storage node, and then select Disk Management. All available disks are displayed. Right-click the disk to convert in the Graphical View, and then click Convert To GPT Disk or Convert To MBR Disk as appropriate.

To use DiskPart to change the partition style of an empty disk, invoke DiskPart by typing **diskpart**, and then select the disk you want to convert. For example, if you want to convert disk 3, type **select disk 3**. Once the disk is selected, you can convert it from MBR to GPT by typing **convert gpt**. To convert a disk from GPT to MBR, type **convert mbr**.

Using the Basic and Dynamic Storage Types

The term *storage type* refers to the method that Windows Server 2003 uses to structure disks and their contents. Windows Server 2003 offers two storage types: basic disk and dynamic disk. Unlike partition style, which depends on whether the computer is x86-based or Itanium-based, the storage type you use doesn't depend on the processor architecture. You can use either or both storage types on any edition of Windows Server 2003.

Working with Basic and Dynamic Disks

Basic disks use the same disk structure as earlier versions of the Windows operating system. When using basic disks, you are limited to creating four primary partitions per disk, or three primary partitions and one extended partition. Within an extended partition, you can create one or more logical drives. For ease of reference, primary partitions and logical drives on basic disks are known as basic volumes. Dynamic disks were introduced in Windows 2000 as a way to improve disk support by requiring fewer restarts after disk configuration changes and improved support for combining disks and fault tolerance using RAID configurations. All volumes on dynamic disks are known as dynamic volumes.

Inside Out

Disk issues when upgrading to Windows Server 2003

When you install Windows Server 2003 on a new system with unpartitioned disks, disks are initialized as basic disks. When you upgrade to Windows Server 2003, disks with partitions are initialized as basic disks. Windows 2000 had limited support for the fault-tolerant features found in Windows NT 4. In Windows 2000, you can use basic disks to maintain existing spanning, mirroring, and striping configurations and to delete these configurations. You cannot, however, create new combined or fault-tolerant drive sets using the basic disk type.

In Windows Server 2003, fault-tolerant sets that you created in Windows NT are not supported in Windows Server 2003. Before upgrading to Windows Server 2003, it is recommended that you remove the fault-tolerant features. Start by backing up the data. If you have a mirror set, break the mirror set and then run Windows Server 2003 Setup. If you have a volume set, stripe set, or stripe set with parity, you must delete the set before you upgrade. As long as you have a working backup, you can upgrade the disks to dynamic after installation, re-create the fault-tolerant set, and then restore the data from backup.

Windows Server 2003 systems can use both basic and dynamic disks. You cannot, however, mix disk types when working with volume sets. All disks, regardless of whether they are basic or dynamic, have three special types of drive sections:

- **System** The system volume contains the hardware-specific files needed to load the operating system.
- **Boot** The boot volume contains the operating system and its support files. The system and boot volume are usually the same.
- **Active** The active volume, usually the system/boot volume, is the drive section from which the computer starts.

The system and boot volumes are set when you install the operating system. On an x86-based computer, you can mark a partition as active to ensure that it is the one from which the computer starts. You can do this only for partitions on basic disks. You can't mark an existing dynamic volume as the active volume, but you can convert a basic disk containing the active partition to a dynamic disk. Once the update is complete, the partition becomes a simple volume that's active.

You can mark a partition as active on a basic disk by using Disk Management. Right-click the primary partition you want to mark as active, and select Mark Partition As Active. Before you do this, however, make sure that the necessary startup files are on the primary partition that you want to make the active partition. Typically, these files are Boot.ini, Ntdetect.com, Ntldr, and Bootsect.dos. You might also need Ntbootdd.sys.

Troubleshooting

Dynamic disks have limitations

You can't use dynamic disks on portable computers or with removable media. You can only configure disks for portable computers and removable media as basic disks with primary partitions. For computers that are multibooted, keep in mind that only Windows 2000 or later versions of the Windows operating system can use dynamic disks.

Using and Converting Basic and Dynamic Disks

Basic disks and dynamic disks are managed in different ways. For basic disks, you use primary and extended partitions. Extended partitions can contain logical drives. Dynamic disks allow you to combine disks to create spanned volumes, to mirror disks to create mirrored volumes, and to stripe disks using RAID 0 to create striped volumes. You can also create RAID-5 volumes for high reliability on dynamic disks.

You can change storage types from basic to dynamic and from dynamic to basic. When you convert a basic disk to a dynamic disk, existing partitions are changed to volumes of the appropriate type automatically and existing data is not lost. Converting a dynamic disk to a basic disk isn't so easy and can't be done without taking some drastic measures. You must delete the volumes on the dynamic disk before you can change the disk back to a basic disk. Deleting the volumes destroys all the information they contain, and the only way to get it back is to restore the data from backup.

You should consider a number of things when you want to change the storage type from basic to dynamic. To be converted successfully, an MBR disk must have 1 megabyte (MB) of free space at the end of the disk. This space is used for the dynamic disk database, which tracks volume information. Without this free space at the end of the disk, the conversion will fail. Because both Disk Management and DiskPart reserve this space automatically, primarily only if you've used third-party disk management utilities you will need to be concerned about whether this space is available. However, if the disk was formatted using another version of the Windows operating system, this space might not be available either.

A GPT disk must have contiguous, recognized data partitions to be converted successfully. If the GPT disk contains partitions that the Windows operating system doesn't recognize, such as those created by another operating system, you won't be able to convert a basic disk to a dynamic disk. When you convert a GPT disk, the Windows operating system creates LDM Metadata and LDM Data partitions as discussed in the section entitled "LDM Metadata and LDM Data Partitions" later in this chapter.

With either type of disk, you can't convert drives that use sector sizes larger than 512 bytes. If the disk has large sector sizes, you must reformat the disk before converting. You can't convert a disk if the system or boot partition uses software RAID. You must stop using the software RAID before you convert the disk.

Both Disk Management and DiskPart can be used to change the storage type.

Using Disk Management to Convert a Basic Disk to a Dynamic Disk To use Disk Management to convert a basic disk to a dynamic disk, start Computer Management from the Administrative Tools menu or by typing **compmgmt.msc** at the command line, expand the Storage node, and then select Disk Management. In Disk Management, right-click a basic disk that you want to convert, either in Disk List View or in the left pane of Graphical View, and select Convert To Dynamic Disk.

In the Convert To Dynamic Disk dialog box (as shown in the following screen), select the disks you want to convert. If you're converting a RAID volume, be sure to select all the basic disks in the set because they must be converted together. Click OK when you're ready to continue.

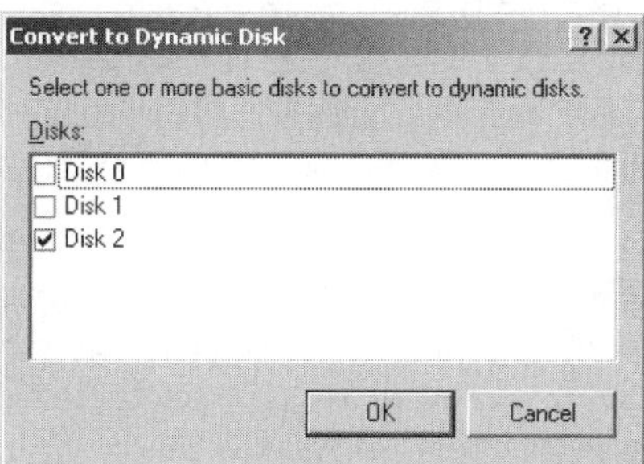

Next, the Disks To Convert dialog box shows the disks you're converting along with details of the disk contents. To see the drive letters and mount points that are associated with a disk, select the disk in the Disks list, and then click Details. If a disk cannot be converted for some reason, the Will Convert column will show No and the Disk Contents column will provide a reason, as shown in the following screen. You must correct whatever problem is noted before you can convert the disk.

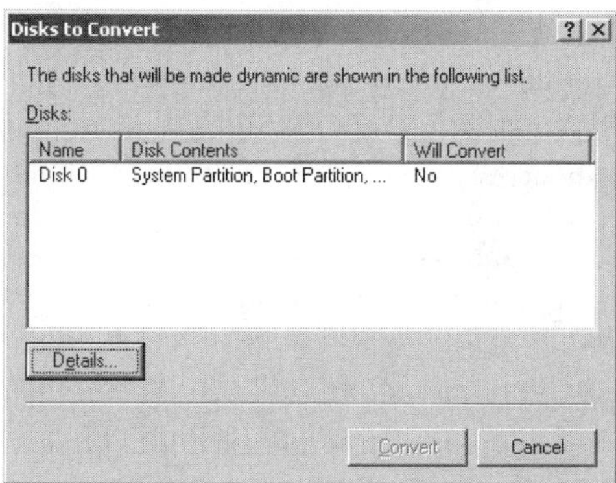

When you're ready to start the conversion, click Convert. Disk Management will then warn you that once you finish the conversion you won't be able to boot previous versions of the Windows operating system from volumes on the selected disks. Click Yes to continue. If a selected drive contains the boot partition, system partition, or a partition in use, you'll see another warning telling you that the computer will need to be rebooted.

Using DiskPart to Convert a Basic Disk to a Dynamic Disk To use DiskPart to convert a basic disk to a dynamic disk, invoke DiskPart by typing **diskpart**, and then select the disk you want to convert. For example, if you want to convert disk 2, type **select disk 2**. Once the disk is selected, you can convert it from basic to dynamic by typing **convert dynamic**.

Using Disk Management to Change a Dynamic Disk Back to a Basic Disk To use Disk Management to change a dynamic disk back to a basic disk, you must first delete all dynamic volumes on the disk. Then right-click the disk, and select Convert To Basic Disk. This changes the dynamic disk to a basic disk, and you can then create new partitions and logical drives on the disk.

Using DiskPart to Convert a Dynamic Disk to a Basic Disk To use DiskPart to convert a basic disk to a dynamic disk, invoke DiskPart by typing **diskpart**, and then select the disk you want to convert. For example, if you want to convert disk 2, type **select disk 2**. If there are any existing volumes on the disk, you must delete them. You can do this by typing **clean**. However, be sure to move any data the disk contains to another disk prior to deleting the disk volumes.

After you delete all the volumes on the disk, you can convert the disk from dynamic to basic by typing **convert basic**. This changes the dynamic disk to a basic disk, and you can then create new partitions and logical drives on the disk.

Converting FAT or FAT32 to NTFS

On both MBR and GPT disks, you can convert FAT or FAT32 partitions, logical drives, and volumes to NTFS by using the CONVERT command. This preserves the file and directory structure without the need to reformat. Before you use CONVERT, you should check to see whether the volume is being used as the active boot volume or is a system volume containing the operating system. If it is, CONVERT must have exclusive access to the volume before it can begin the conversion. Because exclusive access to boot or system volumes can be obtained only during startup, you will see a prompt asking if you want to schedule the drive to be converted the next time the system starts.

As part of preparation for conversion, you should check to see if there's enough free space to perform the conversion. You'll need a block of free space that's about 25 percent of the total space used by the volume. For example, if the volume stores 12 GB of data, you should have about 3 GB of free space. CONVERT checks for this free space before running, and if there isn't enough, it won't convert the volume.

> **Caution** Conversion is one-way only. You can convert only from FAT or FAT32 to NTFS. You can't convert from NTFS to FAT or NTFS to FAT32 without deleting the volume and re-creating it using FAT or FAT32.

You run CONVERT at the command line. Its syntax is as follows:

```
convert volume /FS:NTFS
```

where *volume* is the drive letter followed by a colon, drive path, or volume name. So, for instance, if you want to convert the E drive to NTFS, type **convert e: /fs:ntfs**. This starts CONVERT. As shown in the following example, CONVERT checks the current file system type and then prompts you to enter the volume label for the drive:

```
The type of the file system is FAT32.
Enter current volume label for drive E:
```

Provided you enter the correct volume label, CONVERT will continue as shown in the following example:

```
Volume CORPDATA created 12/16/2004 7:41 PM
Volume Serial Number is 4BE3-234A
Windows is verifying files and folders...
File and folder verification is complete.
Windows has checked the file system and found no problems.
    9,717,848 KB total disk space.
    9,717,840 KB are available.

         8,192 bytes in each allocation unit.
    1,214,731 total allocation units on disk.
    1,214,730 allocation units available on disk.

Determining disk space required for file system conversion...
Total disk space:9727357 KB
Free space on volume:717840 KB
Space required for conversion:99904 KB
Converting file system
Conversion complete
```

Here, CONVERT examines the file and folder structure and then determines how much disk space is needed for the conversion. If there is enough free space, CONVERT performs the conversion. Otherwise, it exits with an error, stating there isn't enough free space to complete the conversion.

Several additional parameters are available as well, including /V, which tells CONVERT to display detailed information during the conversion, and /X, which tells CONVERT to force the partition or volume to dismount before the conversation if necessary. You can't dismount a boot or system drive—these drives can be converted only when the system is restarted.

On converted boot and system volumes, CONVERT applies default security the same as that applied during Windows setup. On other volumes, CONVERT sets security so the Users group has access but doesn't give access to the special group Everyone. If you don't want security to be set, you can use the /Nosecurity parameter. This parameter tells CONVERT to remove all security attributes and make all files and directories on the disk accessible to the group Everyone. In addition, you can use the /Cvtarea parameter to set the name of a contiguous file in the root directory to be a placeholder for NTFS system files.

Managing MBR Disk Partitions on Basic Disks

A disk using the MBR partition style can have up to four primary partitions and up to one extended partition. This allows you to configure MBR disks in one of two ways: using one to four primary partitions or using one to three primary partitions and one extended partition. After you partition a disk, you format the partitions to assign drive letters or mount points.

Inside Out

Drive letter assignment is initiated during installation

The drive letters that are available depend on how a system is configured. The initial drive letters used by a computer are assigned during installation of the operating system. Setup does this by scanning all fixed hard disks as they are enumerated.

For MBR disks, Setup assigns a drive letter to the first primary partition starting with C. Setup then scans floppy/Zip disks and assigns drive letters starting with A. Afterward, Setup scans CD/DVD-ROM drives and assigns the next available letter starting with D. Finally, Setup scans all fixed hard disks and assigns drive letters to all remaining primary partitions.

With GPT disks, Setup assigns drive letters to all primary partitions on the GPT disk starting with C. Setup then scans floppy/Zip drives and assigns the next available drive letter starting with A. Finally, Setup scans CD/DVD-ROM drives and assigns the next available letter starting with D.

Creating a Primary or Extended Partition

In Disk Management you can create primary or extended partitions using Graphical View. The steps you use to create primary and extended partitions are as follows:

1. In Disk Management Graphical View, right-click an area marked Unallocated on a basic disk, and then choose New Partition. This starts the New Partition Wizard, as shown in Figure 19-4. To continue, click Next.

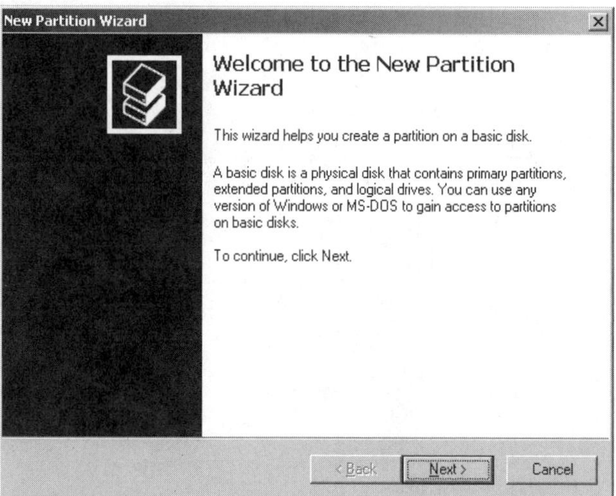

Figure 19-4. The New Partition Wizard guides you through the process of creating partitions.

2 As shown in Figure 19-5, you can select a partition type. As discussed previously, a disk can have up to four primary partitions or three primary partitions and one extended partition. Keep the following in mind:

- You can size a primary partition to fill an entire disk, or you can size it as appropriate for the system you're configuring. Because of the availability of FAT32 and NTFS, you no longer must worry about the 4-GB volume size and 2-GB file size limits that applied to 16-bit FAT systems. This allows you to size partitions as you see fit.
- You can size extended partitions to fill any available unallocated space on a disk. Because an extended partition can contain multiple logical drives, each with their own file system, consider carefully how you might want to size logical drives before creating the extended partition. Additionally, if a drive already has an extended partition or is removable, you won't be able to create an extended partition.

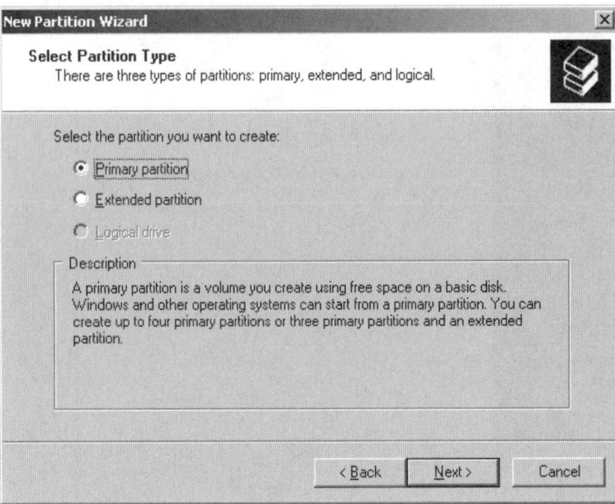

Figure 19-5. Select the type of partition as either primary or extended.

3 Click Next to display the Specify Partition Size page, as shown in Figure 19-6. Then use the Amount Of Disk Space To Use field to specify how much of the available disk space you want to use for the partition. Click Next again.

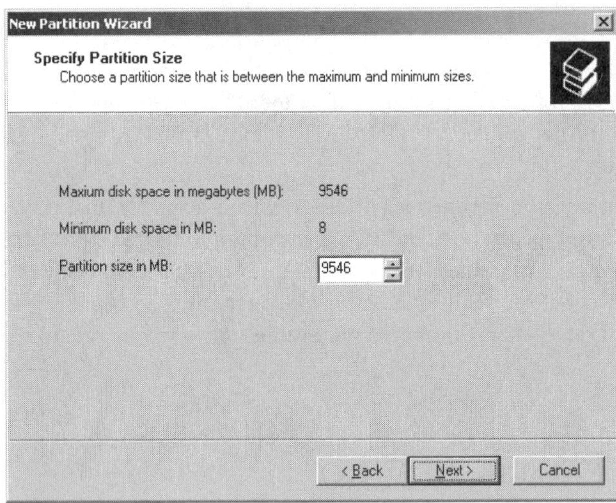

Figure 19-6. Size the partition appropriately.

4 If you are creating a primary partition, use the Assign Drive Letter Or Path page, as shown in Figure 19-7, to assign a drive letter or path. You can do one of the following:

- Assign a drive letter by choosing Assign The Following Drive Letter To and then selecting an available drive letter in the selection list provided. Generally, the drive letters E through Z are available for use (drive letters A and B are used with floppy/Zip drives, drive C is for the primary partition, and drive D is for the computer's CD/DVD-ROM drive).
- Mount a path by choosing Mount In The Following Empty NTFS Folder and then typing the path to an existing folder. You can also click Browse to search for or create a folder.
- Use Do Not Assign A Drive Letter Or Drive Path To if you want to create the partition without assigning a drive letter or path.

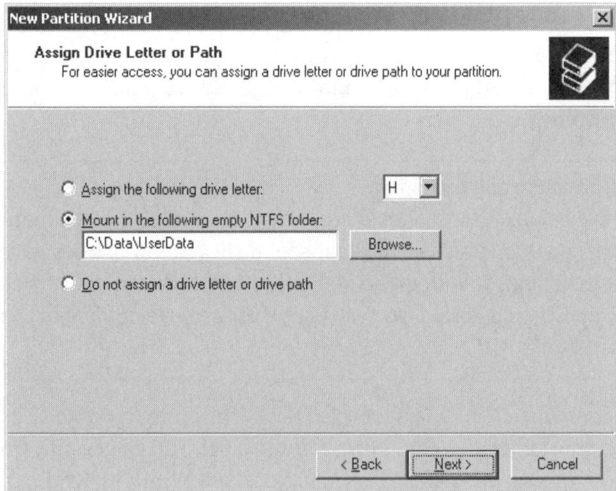

Figure 19-7. Specify how the partition should be used.

5 Using the Format Partition page, as shown in Figure 19-8, you can opt to not format the partition at this time or to select the formatting options to use. Formatting creates a file system in the new partition and permanently deletes any existing data. The formatting options are as follows:

- File System sets the file system type as FAT, FAT32, or NTFS. FAT volumes can be up to 4 GB in size and have a maximum file size limit of 2 GB. FAT32 volumes can be up to 32 GB in size (a limitation of Windows Server 2003) and have a maximum file size of 4 GB. NTFS files and volumes can be up to 2 TB in size on MBR disks and up to 18 EB on GPT disks.

Tip **Choose the partition format with care**

If you don't know which file system to use, it is best in most cases to use NTFS. Only NTFS volumes can also use advanced file access permissions, compression, encryption, disk quotas, shadow copies, remote storage, and sparse files. There are exceptions, of course. If you want to be able to boot multiple operating systems, you might want to use FAT or FAT32. When a boot partition is formatted using FAT, you are able to boot to just about any operating system. When a boot partition is FAT32, you are able to boot to any version of the Windows operating system except Windows NT 4 and Microsoft Windows 95 OSR1. Further, because FAT32 doesn't have the journaling overhead of NTFS, it is more efficient at handling large files that change frequently, and particularly files that have small incremental changes, such as log files. This means in some cases that FAT32 will read and write files faster than NTFS. However, if you use FAT32, you won't be able to use any of the advanced file system features of Windows Server 2003.

- Allocation Unit Size sets the cluster size for the file system. This is the basic unit in which disk space is allocated, and by default, it is based on the size of the volume.

Tip **Choosing an allocation unit size**

In most cases the default size is what is best but you can override this feature by setting a different value. If you use lots of small files, you might want to use a smaller cluster size, such as 512 or 1024 bytes. With these settings, small files use less disk space. While sizes of up to 256 KB are allowed, you will not be able to use compression on NTFS if you use a size larger than 4 KB.

- Volume Label sets a text label for the partition that is used as its volume name. If you must change a partition's volume label, you can do this from the command line by using the LABEL command or from Windows Explorer by right-clicking the volume, selecting Properties, and then typing a new label in the General tab.
- Perform A Quick Format specifies that you want to format the partition without checking for errors. Although you can use this option to save you a few minutes, it's better to check for errors because this allows Disk Management to mark bad sectors on the disk and lock them out.
- Enable File And Folder Compression turns on compression so that files and folders on this partition are compressed automatically. Compression is available only for NTFS. For more information about using compression, see the section entitled "Using File-Based Compression" on page 666.

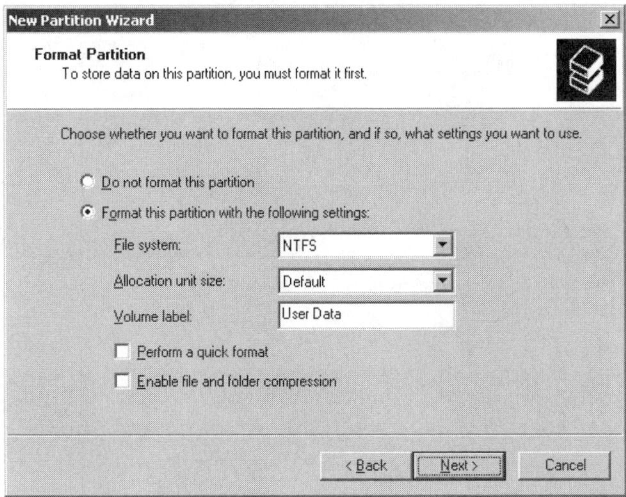

Figure 19-8. Format the partition now or opt to format the partition later.

6 Click Next. The final page shows you the options you've selected. If the options are correct, click Finish. The wizard then creates the partition and configures it.

> **Note** If you add partitions to a physical drive that contains the Windows Server 2003 operating system, you might inadvertently change the number of the boot partition. Windows Server 2003 will display a prompt warning you that the number of the boot partition will change. Click Yes to confirm this change. In most cases, Windows Server 2003 will make the appropriate changes in Boot.ini to ensure the system can be booted. To be sure, however, you should examine the Boot.ini file. It is located on the root directory of the system drive. You can determine the system drive by typing **set systemdrive** at the command prompt.

Creating a Logical Drive in an Extended Partition

In Disk Management, you can create a logical drive within an extended partition by completing the following steps:

1 In Disk Management Graphical View, right-click an area marked Free Space in the extended partition, and then choose New Partition. This starts the New Partition Wizard, as shown previously in Figure 19-4. Click Next.

2 As shown in Figure 19-9, the only option you have for partition type is Logical Drive, which is what you want to use, so click Next.

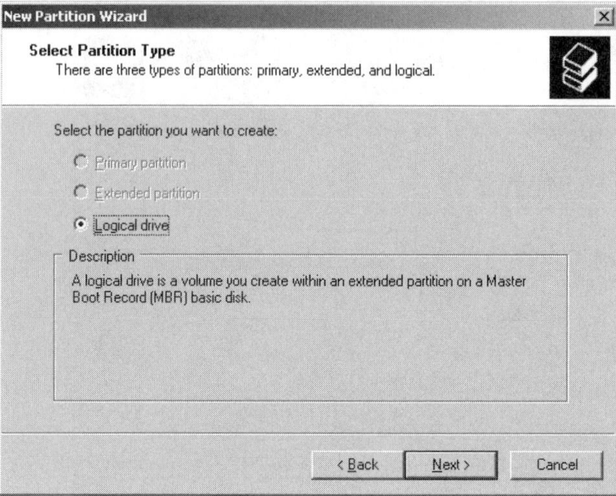

Figure 19-9. Select the partition type.

3 Use the Assign Drive Letter Or Path page to assign a drive letter or path. You can also choose Do Not Assign A Drive Letter Or Drive Path To if you want to create the partition without assigning a drive letter or path. Click Next.

4 Using the Format Partition page to set the formatting options or opt not to format the partition at this time. Click Next.

5 The final page shows you the options you've selected. If the options are correct, click Finish. The wizard then creates the logical drive and configures it. If you want to create additional logical drives on the extended partition, repeat these steps.

Formatting a Partition, Logical Drive, or Volume

Before a primary partition, logical drive, or volume can be used, it must be formatted. Formatting creates the file structures necessary to work with files and folders. If you want to clean out a partition, logical drive, or volume and remove all existing data, you can use formatting to do this as well.

Tip **You need not format if you want to convert to NTFS**

Although you can use formatting to change the type of file system, you don't have to do this to change from FAT or FAT32 to NTFS. Instead, to convert to NTFS you can use the CONVERT command, which preserves any existing data. For more information about CONVERT, see the section entitled "Converting FAT or FAT32 to NTFS" earlier in this chapter.

To format a primary partition, logical drive, or volume, follow these steps:

1. In Disk Management, right-click the primary partition, logical drive, or volume you want to format, and then choose Format. This displays the Format dialog box, as shown in Figure 19-10.

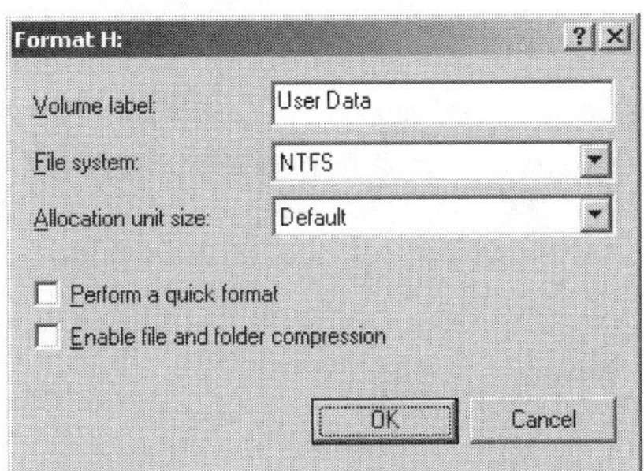

Figure 19-10. Set the formatting options, then click OK.

2. In the Volume Label box, type a descriptive label for the primary partition, logical drive, or volume. In most cases, you'll want to use a label that helps you and other administrators determine what type of data is stored in the partition or on the logical drive.
3. Select the file system type as FAT, FAT32, or NTFS. Keep in mind that only NTFS allows you to use the advanced file system features of Windows Server 2003, including advanced file access permissions, compression, encryption, disk quotas, shadow copies, remote storage, and sparse files.
4. Use the Allocation Unit Size field to specify the basic unit in which disk space should be allocated. In most cases the default size is what is best.
5. Select Perform A Quick Format if you want to format the partition without checking for errors. Although this option can save you a few minutes, Disk Management won't mark bad sectors on the disk or lock them out, and this can lead to problems with data integrity later on.
6. If you want files and folders to be compressed automatically, select Enable File And Folder Compression. Compression is available only for NTFS; you can learn more about compression in the section entitled "Using File-Based Compression" on page 666.
7. Click OK to begin formatting using the specified options.

Configuring Drive Letters

Each primary partition, logical drive, or volume on a disk can have one drive letter and one or more drive paths associated with it. You can assign, change, or remove driver letters and mount points at any time without having to restart the computer. Windows Server 2003 also allows you to change the drive letter associated with CD/DVD-ROM drives. You cannot, however, change or remove the drive letter of a system volume, boot volume, or any volume that contains a paging file. Additionally, on GPT disks, you can assign drive letters only to primary partitions. You cannot assign driver letters to other types of partitions on GPT disks.

Inside Out

Changing the drive letter of a system or boot volume

If you installed the operating system on a drive with an odd drive letter, such as F or H, it would seem that you are stuck with it, which might not be for the best if you really want the operating system to be on a different drive letter, such as C. Although Disk Management and DiskPart won't let you change the drive letter of a system volume, boot volume, or any volume that contains a paging file, there are workarounds. For volumes containing paging files, you must first move the paging file to a different volume, and then reboot the computer. You are then able to assign the volume a different drive letter—provided it isn't also a system or boot volume. To change the system or boot volume drive letter, you must edit the Registry using an account that is a member of the Administrators group. Don't do this without creating a full backup of the computer and its system state first.

Start Registry Editor by typing **regedit**, and then access the HKEY_LOCAL_MACHINE\SYSTEM\MountedDevices key. This key has value entries for each of the drive letters used on the computer. Find the value entry for the system or boot volume that you want to change. Right-click it, and choose Rename so that you can edit the name. Change the name of the value entry so that it points to the drive letter you want to use. If that drive letter is in use, you must rename two value entries. For example, if you want to rename D as C and C is already in use, you must rename C to an unused drive letter and then rename D as C. Afterward, restart the computer.

After you make a change, the new drive letter or mount point assignment is made automatically as long as the volume or partition is not in use. If the partition or volume is in use, Windows Server 2003 displays a warning. You must exit programs that are using the partition or volume and try again or allow Disk Management to force the change by clicking Yes when prompted.

To add, change, or remove a drive letter, right-click the primary partition, logical drive, or volume in Disk Management, and choose Change Drive Letter And Paths. This displays the dialog box shown in the following screen:

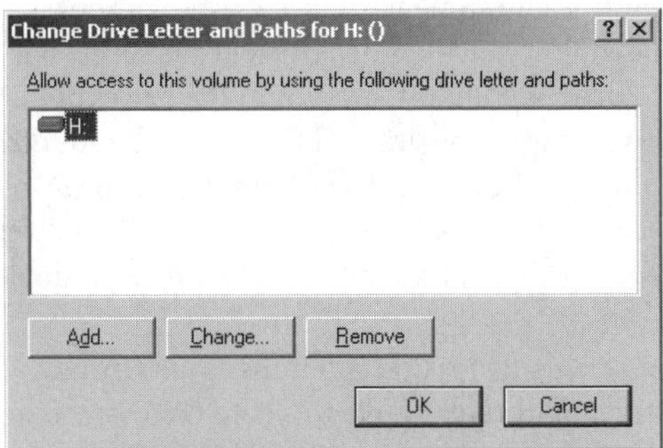

Any current drive letter and mount points associated with the selected drive are displayed. You have the following options:

- **Add a drive letter** If the primary partition, logical drive, or volume doesn't yet have a drive letter assignment, you can add one by clicking Add. In the Add Drive Letter Or Path dialog box that appears, select the drive letter to use from the drop-down list, and then click OK.
- **Change an existing drive letter** If you want to change the drive letter, click Change, select the drive letter to use from the drop-down list, and then click OK. Confirm the action when prompted by clicking Yes.
- **Remove a drive letter** If you want to remove the drive letter, click Remove, and then confirm the action when prompted by clicking Yes.

> **Note** When you change or remove a drive letter, the volume or partition will no longer be accessible using the old drive letter, and this can cause programs using the volume or can cause the partition to stop running.

Configuring Mount Points

Any volume or partition can be mounted to an empty NTFS folder as long as the folder is on a fixed disk drive rather than a removable media drive. A volume or partition mounted in such a way is called a mount point. Each volume or partition can have multiple mount points associated with it. For example, you could mount a volume to the root folder of the C drive as both C:\EngData and C:\DevData, giving the appearance that these are separate folders.

The real value of mount points, however, lies in how they allow you the capability to create the appearance of a single file system from multiple hard disk drives without having to use spanned volumes. Consider the following scenario: A department file server has four data drives—drive 1, drive 2, drive 3, and drive 4. Rather than mount the drives as D, E, F, and G, you decide it'd be easier for users to work with the drives if they were all mounted as folders of the system drive, C:\Data. You mount drive 1 to C:\Data\UserData, drive 2 to C:\Data\CorpData, drive 3 to C:\Data\Projects, and drive 4 to C:\Data\History. If you were then to share the C:\Data folder, users would be able to access all the drives using a single share.

> **Note** Wondering why I mounted the drives under C:\Data rather than C:\ as is recommended in some documentation? The primary reason I did this is to help safeguard system security. I didn't want users to have access to other directories, which includes the operating system directories, on the C drive.

To add or remove a mount point, right-click the volume or partition in Disk Management, and choose Change Mount Point And Paths. This displays the Change Mount Point And Paths dialog box (as shown in the following screen), which shows any current mount point and mount points associated with the selected drive.

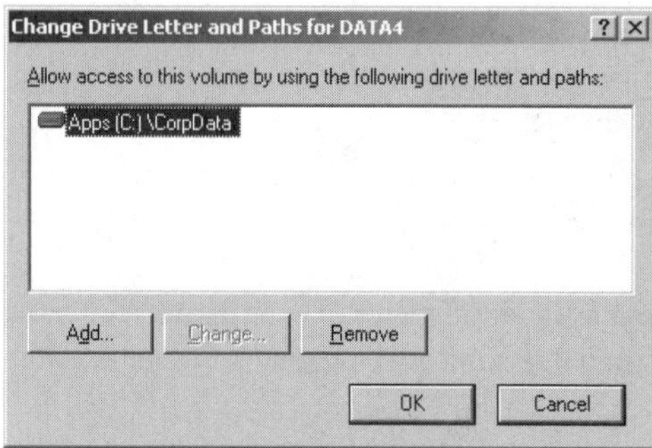

You now have the following options:

- **Add a mount point** Click Add, then in the Add Drive Letter Or Path dialog box, select Mount In The Following Empty NTFS Folder, as shown in the screen on the following page. Type the path to an existing folder or click Browse to search for or create a folder. Click OK to mount the volume or partition.

- **Remove a mount point** If you want to remove a mount point, select the mount point, and then click Remove. When prompted to confirm the action, click Yes.

> **Note** You can't change a mount point assignment after making it. You can, however, simply remove the mount point you want to change and then add a new mount point so that the volume or partition is mounted as appropriate.

Extending Partitions on Basic Disks

By using DiskPart, you can extend partitions on basic disks. This is handy if you create a partition that's too small and you want to extend it so you have more space for programs and data. Here's how this feature works: If a disk has free space and has as its last or only partition a nonboot or nonsystem partition that is formatted as NTFS, you can extend the partition to the end of the disk or to fill a designated amount of free space on the disk.

To extend an NTFS-formatted partition, invoke DiskPart by typing **diskpart** at the command prompt. List the disks on the computer by typing **list disk.** After you check the free space of each disk, select the disk by typing **select disk *N***, where *N* is the disk you want to work with. Next, list the partitions on the selected disk by typing **list partition**. Select the last partition in the list by typing **select partition *N***, where *N* is the disk you want to work with.

Now that you've selected a partition, you can extend it. To extend the partition to the end of the disk, type **extend**. To extend the partition a set amount, type **extend size=*N***, where *N* is the amount of space to add in megabytes. For example, if you want to add 1200 megabytes to the partition, type **extend size=1200.**

Listing 19-2 shows an actual DiskPart session in which a disk is extended. You can use this as an example to help you understand the process of extending basic disks. Here, disk 2 has 19 GB of free space, and its primary partition is extended so that it fills the disk.

Listing 19-2 Extending Basic Disks

```
C:\> diskpart

Microsoft DiskPart version 5.2.3790
Copyright (C) 1999-2001 Microsoft Corporation.
On computer: CORPSVR02

DISKPART> list disk

  Disk ###    Status      Size     Free     Dyn    Gpt
  --------    ----------  ------   -------  ---    ---
  Disk 0      Online      56 GB      0 B     *      *
  Disk 1      Online      29 GB      0 B
  Disk 2      Online      37 GB     19 GB

DISKPART> select disk 2

Disk 2 is now the selected disk.

DISKPART> list partition

  Partition ###  Type              Size     Offset
  -------------  ----------------  -------  -------
  Partition 1    Primary           37 GB    32 KB

DISKPART> select partition 1

Partition 1 is now the selected partition.

DISKPART> extend

DiskPart successfully extended the partition.

DISKPART> exit

Leaving DiskPart...

C:\>
```

Deleting a Partition, Logical Drive, or Volume

Deleting a partition, logical drive, or volume removes the associated file system and all associated data. When you delete a logical drive, the logical drive is removed from the associated extended partition and its space is marked as free. When you delete a partition or volume, the entire partition or volume is deleted and its space is marked as Unallocated. If you want to delete an extended partition that contains logical drives, however, you must delete the logical drives before trying to delete the extended partition.

In Disk Management, you can delete a partition, logical drive, or volume by right-clicking it and then choosing Delete Partition, Delete Logical Drive, or Delete Volume, as appropriate. When prompted to confirm the action, click Yes. Keep in mind that if you delete a partition on a physical drive that contains the Windows Server 2003 operating system, the number of the boot partition might change. If so, you should check the Boot.ini file to ensure the Windows Server 2003 entry points to the right partition.

Note In Windows NT and Windows 2000, deleting a partition on a physical drive that contains the operating system is likely to cause the boot partition number to change. In Windows Server 2003, this behavior has been fixed—but better safe than sorry, so I always check the Boot.ini file anyway.

Managing GPT Disk Partitions on Basic Disks

GPT disks can have the following types of partitions:

- ESP
- MSR partition
- Primary partition
- Logical Disk Manager (LDM) Metadata partition
- LDM Data partition
- OEM or Unknown partition

Each of these partition types is used and managed in a different way.

ESP

An Itanium-based computer must have one GPT disk that contains an ESP. This partition is similar to the system volume on an x86-based computer in that it contains the files that are required to start the operating system. Windows Server 2003 creates the ESP during setup and formats it by using FAT. The partition is sized so that it is at least 100 MB in size or 1 percent of the disk up to a maximum size of 1000 MB.

The ESP is shown in Disk Management but isn't assigned a drive letter or mount point. All Disk Management commands associated with the ESP are disabled, however, and you cannot store data on it, assign a drive letter to it, or delete it by using Disk Management or DiskPart. The ESP has several directories, including EFI\Microsoft\WINNT50, which contains Ia64ldr.efi and other files that are necessary to start the operating system, and Msutil, which contains utilities such as Diskpart.efi and Nvrboot.efi. Other directories are created as necessary by the operating system.

The only way to access these directories is to use the EFI firmware's Boot Manager or the MOUNTVOL command. If you access the ESP, don't make changes, additions, or deletions unless you've been specifically directed to by a Microsoft Knowledge Base article or other official documentation by an OEM vendor. Any changes you make could prevent the system from starting.

Inside Out

You can create an ESP if necessary—but do so only if directed to

Although the ESP is normally created for you automatically when you install Windows Server 2003, there are some limited instances when you might be directed to create an ESP after installing an additional GPT disk on a server, such as when you want to use the new disk as a boot device rather than the existing boot device. You can create the necessary ESP by using DiskPart. Select the disk you want to work with, and then type the following command: **create partition efi size=*N***, where *N* is at least 100 MB or 1 percent of the disk, up to a maximum size of 1000 MB. After you create the partition, follow the vendor- or Microsoft-directed guidelines for preparing the partition for use. Never create an ESP unless you are directed to do so, however. One instance in which you must create an ESP is when you want to establish and boot to mirrored GPT disks. Here, you must prepare the second disk of the mirror so that it can be booted, and you do this by creating the necessary ESP and MSR partition.

MSR Partitions

An Itanium-based computer must have an MSR partition on every GPT disk. The MSR partition contains additional space that might be needed by the operating system to perform disk operations. For example, when you convert a basic GPT disk to a dynamic GPT disk, the Windows operating system takes 1 MB of the MSR partition space and uses it to create the LDM Metadata partition, which is required for the conversion.

The MSR partition is not shown in Disk Management and does not receive a drive letter or mount point. The Windows operating system creates the MSR partition automatically. For the book disk, it is created along with the ESP when you install the operating system. An MSR partition is also created automatically when a disk is converted from MBR to GPT and any time you access a GPT disk that doesn't already have an MSR partition in Disk Management or DiskPart.

If a GPT disk contains an ESP as the first partition on the disk, the MSR partition is usually the second partition on the disk. If a GPT disk does not contain an ESP, then the MSR partition is typically the first partition on the disk. However, if a disk already has a primary partition at the beginning of the disk, the MSR partition is placed at the end of the disk.

The MSR partition is sized according to the size of the associated disk. For disks up to 16 GB in size, it is 32 MB in size. For all other disks, it is 128 MB in size.

Inside Out

You can create an MSR partition if necessary—but do so only if directed to

The MSR partition is normally created for you automatically when you install Windows Server 2003. It can also be created automatically when you access a secondary GPT disk that doesn't already have an MSR partition in Disk Management or DiskPart. You shouldn't attempt to create a Microsoft Reserved partition unless you are directed to by vendor- or Microsoft-specific documentation. In this case, you can use DiskPart to create the partition. Select the disk you want to work with, and then type the following command: **create partition msr size=*N***, where *N* is 32 for disks up to 16 GB in size and 128 for all other disks.

Primary Partitions

You create primary partitions on basic disks to store data. GPT disks support up to 128 partitions, which can be a mix of required and optional partitions. Every primary partition you create appears in the GUID partition entry array within the GPT header. If you convert a basic disk that contains primary partitions to a dynamic disk, the primary partitions become simple volumes, and information about them is then stored in the dynamic disk database and not in the GUID partition entry array.

To create a primary partition, complete the following steps:

1. In Disk Management Graphical View, right-click an area marked Unallocated on a basic disk, and then choose New Partition. This starts the New Partition Wizard. Click Next.
2. The only option you have for partition type is Primary, which is what you want to use, so click Next.
3. Use the Assign Drive Letter Or Path page to assign a drive letter or path. You can also choose Do Not Assign A Drive Letter Or Drive Path To if you want to create the partition without assigning a drive letter or path. Click Next.
4. Use the Format Partition page to set the formatting options. If you opt not to format the partition at this time you can format the partition later as discussed in the section entitled "Formatting a Partition, Logical Drive, or Volume" earlier in this chapter.
5. Click Next. The final page shows you the options you've selected. If the options are correct, click Finish. The wizard then creates the partition and configures it.

LDM Metadata and LDM Data Partitions

Windows Server 2003 64-bit edition creates LDM Metadata and LDM Data partitions when you convert a basic GPT disk to a dynamic GPT disk. The LDM Metadata partition is 1 MB in size and is used to store the partitioning information needed for the conversion. The LDM Data partition is the partition in which the actual dynamic volumes are created.

The LDM Data partition is used to represent sections of unallocated space on the converted disk as well as sections that had basic partitions that are now dynamic volumes. For example, if a disk had a primary boot partition that spanned the whole disk, the converted disk will have a single LDM Data partition. If a disk had a boot partition and other primary partitions, it will have two LDM Data partitions after the conversion: one for the boot volume, and one for all the rest of the partitions. Although the LDM Metadata and LDM Data partitions are not shown in Disk Management and do not receive drive letters or mount points, you are able to use this space by creating primary partitions as discussed in the previous section.

OEM or Unknown Partitions

GPT disks can have partitions that are specific to OEM implementations, and your vendor documentation should describe what they are used for. The Windows operating system displays these partitions in Disk Management as Healthy (Unknown Partition). You cannot, however, manipulate these partitions in Disk Management or DiskPart. Additionally, if an unknown partition lies between two known partitions on a GPT disk, you won't be able to convert the disk from the basic disk type to the dynamic disk type.

Managing Volumes on Dynamic Disks

Any disk using the MBR or GPT partition style can be configured as a dynamic disk. Unlike basic disks, which have basic volumes that can be created as primary partitions, extended partitions, and logical drives, dynamic disks have dynamic volumes that can be created as the following types:

- **Simple volumes** A simple volume is a volume that's on a single drive and has the same purpose as a primary partition.
- **Spanned volumes** A spanned volume is a volume that spans multiple drives.
- **Striped volumes** A striped volume is a volume that uses RAID 0 to combine multiple disks into a stripe set.
- **Mirrored volumes** A mirrored volume is a volume that uses RAID 1 to mirror a primary disk onto a secondary disk that is available for disaster recovery.
- **RAID-5 volumes** A RAID-5 volume is a volume that uses RAID 5 to create a fault-tolerant striped set on three or more disks.

Techniques for creating and managing these volume types are discussed in the sections that follow.

Creating a Simple or Spanned Volume

You create simple and spanned volumes in much the same way. The difference between the two is that a simple volume uses free space from a single disk to create a volume, while a spanned volume is used to combine the disk space on multiple disks to create the appearance of a single volume. If you later need more space, you can extend either volume type by using Disk Management. Here, you select an area of free space on any available disk and add it to the volume. When you extend a simple volume onto other disks, it becomes a spanned volume. Any volume that you want to expand should be formatted using NTFS because only NTFS volumes can be extended.

Simple and spanned volumes aren't fault tolerant. If you create a volume that spans disks and one of those disks fails, you won't be able to access the volume. Any data on the volume will be lost. You must restore the data from backup after you replace the failed drive and re-create the volume.

To create a simple or spanned volume, complete the following steps:

1. In Disk Management Graphical View, right-click an area marked Unallocated on a dynamic disk, and then choose New Volume. This starts the New Volume Wizard, as shown in Figure 19-11. Click Next.

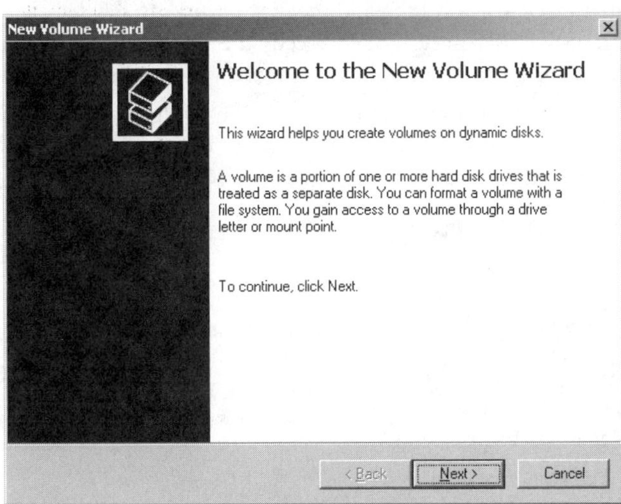

Figure 19-11. The New Volume Wizard.

2. Select Simple to create a volume on a single disk or Spanned to create a volume on multiple disks, and then click Next. You should see the Select Disks page shown in Figure 19-12. Use this page to select dynamic disks that should be part of the volume and to size the volume segments on the designated disks.

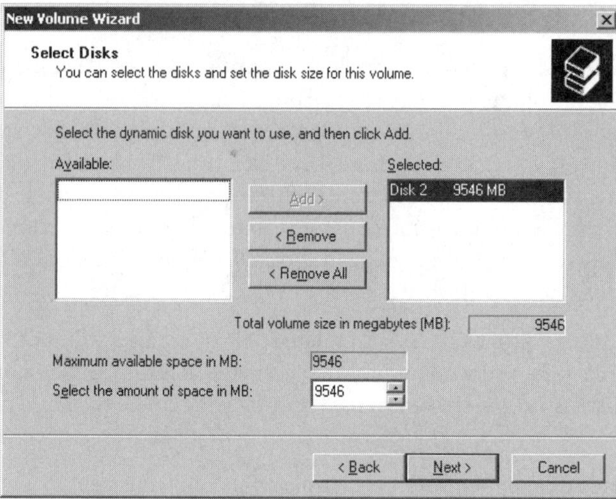

Figure 19-12. Select the disks that should be part of the volume, and then specify how much space to use on each disk.

3 Select one or more disks from the list of dynamic disks that are available and have unallocated space. Click Add to add the disk or disks to the Selected list box. Next, select each of the disks in turn, then specify the amount of space you want to use on the selected disk. Click Next when you are ready to continue.

4 Use the Assign Drive Letter Or Path page shown in Figure 19-13 to assign a drive letter or path. You can also choose Do Not Assign A Drive Letter Or Drive Path if you want to create the partition without assigning a drive letter or path. Click Next.

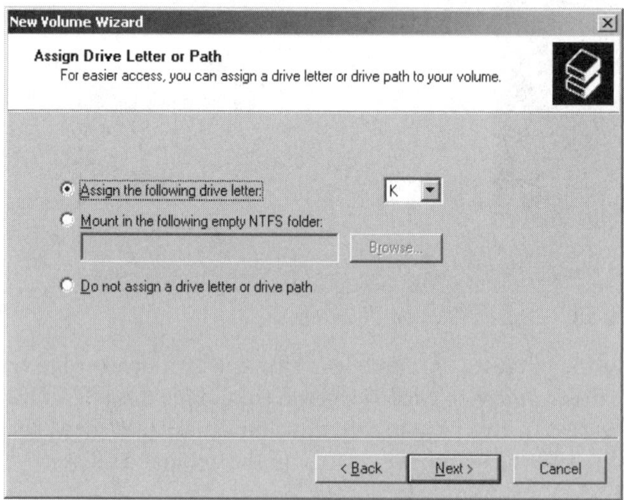

Figure 19-13. Assign the volume a drive letter or mount point.

5 Use the Format Volume page, as shown in Figure 19-14, to set the formatting options. Simple and spanned volumes can be formatted by using FAT, FAT32, or NTFS. If you think you might need to expand the volume at a later date, you might want to use NTFS because only volumes using NTFS can be expanded. If you opt not to format the partition at this time you can format the partition later as discussed in the section entitled "Formatting a Partition, Logical Drive, or Volume" earlier in this chapter.

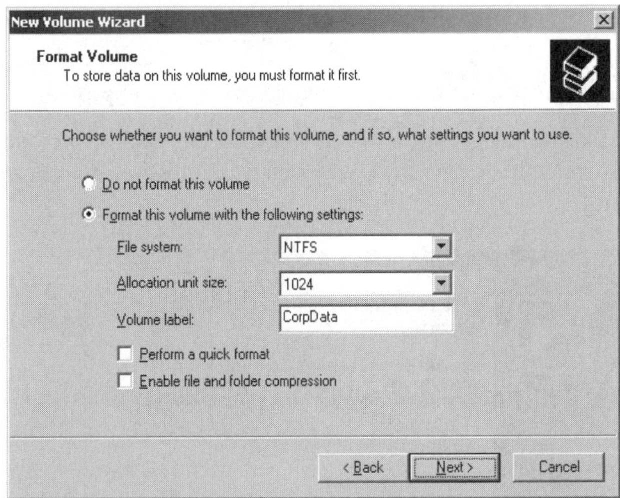

Figure 19-14. Format the volume preferably by using NTFS so that it can be expanded if necessary.

6 Click Next. The final page shows you the options you've selected. If the options are correct, click Finish. The wizard then creates the volume and configures it.

Note If you add volumes to a physical drive that contains the Windows Server 2003 operating system, you might inadvertently change the number of the boot volume. Windows Server 2003 will display a prompt warning you that the number of the boot volume will change. Click Yes to confirm this change. In most cases, Windows Server 2003 will make the appropriate changes in Boot.ini to ensure the system can be booted. To be sure, however, you should examine the Boot.ini file. It is located on the root directory of the system drive. You can determine the system drive by typing **set systemdrive** at the command prompt.

Extending a Simple or Spanned Volume

Unlike mirrors, striped, and RAID-5 volumes, which cannot be extended after they are created, both simple and spanned volumes can be extended. When you extend a simple or spanned volume, you add areas of free space either from the current disk or disks being used or from other disks to create a single volume.

Before you can extend a volume, the volume must be formatted as NTFS. You can convert FAT and FAT32 volumes to NTFS by using the CONVERT command discussed in the section entitled "Converting FAT or FAT32 to NTFS" earlier in this chapter. The volume also cannot be a boot or system volume, and there's a limitation of 32 disks for expansion, meaning a volume can span up to 32 disks, but no more. Additionally, you can't extend simple or spanned volumes that were upgraded from basic disks, either.

To extend a simple or spanned volume formatted as NTFS, complete the following steps:

1. In Disk Management Graphical View, right-click the volume you want to extend, and choose Extend Volume. This starts the Extend Volume Wizard, as shown in Figure 19-15. Click Next.

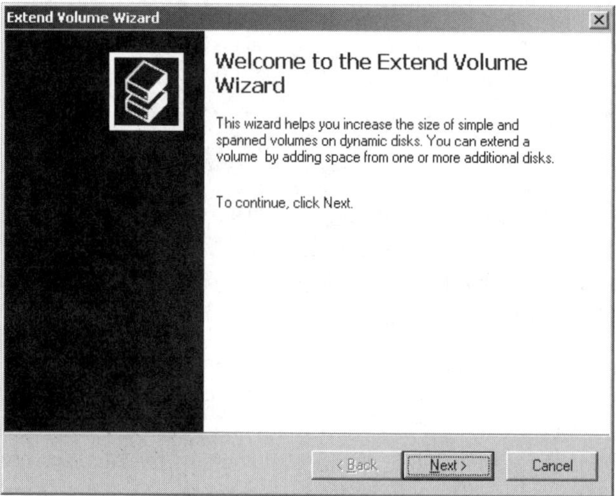

Figure 19-15. The Extend Volume Wizard.

2. Use the Select Disks page shown in Figure 19-16 to select one or more disks from the list of dynamic disks that are available and have unallocated space. Click Add to add the disk or disks to the Selected list box. Afterward, select each of the disks in turn, then specify the amount of space you want to use on the selected disk. Click Next when you are ready to continue.

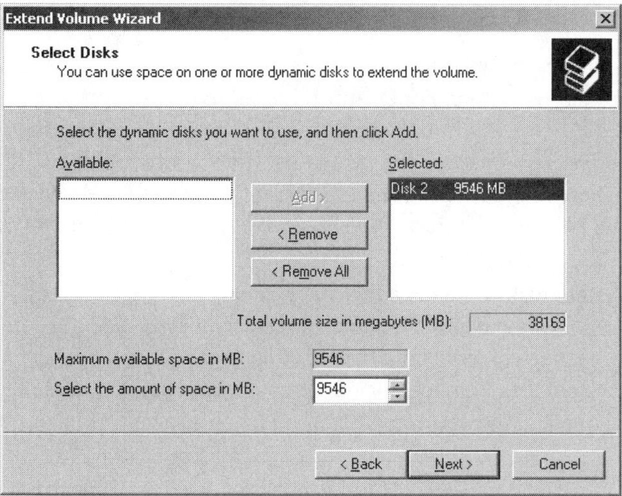

Figure 19-16. Select the disks to use to extend the volume.

3. Click Next. The final page shows you the options you've selected. If the options are correct, click Finish. The wizard then extends the volume as appropriate.

> **Caution** Extended volumes aren't fault tolerant. If you create a volume that extends across multiple disks and one of those disks fails, you won't be able to access the volume, and any data on the volume will be lost. To recover, you must restore the data from backup after you replace the failed drive and re-create the volume.

Recovering a Failed Simple or Spanned Disk

Simple disks are the easiest to troubleshoot and recover because there is only one disk involved. Spanned disks, on the other, might have multiple disks, and the failure of any one disk makes the entire volume unusable. The drive status might show it is Missing, Failed, Online (Errors), Offline, or Unreadable.

The Missing (and sometimes Offline) status usually happens if drives have been disconnected or powered off. If the drives are part of an external storage device, check the storage device to ensure it is connected properly and has power. Reconnecting the storage device or turning on the power should make it so the drives can be accessed. You then must start Disk Management and rescan the missing drive. Right-click the missing drive, and choose Rescan Disks. When Disk Management finishes, right-click the drive, and then choose Reactivate.

The Failed, Online (Errors), and Unreadable statuses indicate input/output (I/O) problems with the drive. As before, try rescanning the drive, and then try to reactivate the drive. If the drive doesn't come back to the Healthy state, you might need to replace it.

Moving Dynamic Disks

One of the advantages of dynamic disks over basic disks is that you can easily move them from one computer to another. For example, if after setting up a server, you decide that you don't really need its two additional hard disk drives, you could move them to another server where they could be better used. Before you move disks, you should access Disk Management on the server where the dynamic disks are currently installed and check their status. The status should be Healthy. If it isn't, you should fix any problems before moving the disks.

> **Tip** **Moving system disks requires additional planning**
> Before you move a system disk from one computer to another, you must ensure that the computers have identically configured hard disk subsystems. If they don't, the Plug and Play ID on the system disk from the original computer won't match what the new computer is expecting. As a result, the new computer won't be able to load the right drivers and boot will fail.

Next check to see whether any dynamic disks that you want to move are part of a spanned, extended, mirrored, striped, or RAID-5 set. If they are, you should make a note of which disks are part of which set and plan on moving all disks in a set together. If you are moving only part of a disk set, you should be aware of the consequences. For spanned, extended, or striped volumes, moving only part of the set will make the related volumes unusable on the current computer and on the computer to which you are planning to move the disks. If you plan to move only one disk of a mirrored volume, you should break the mirror before you move it. This ensures you can keep using the disks on both computers. For RAID-5 volumes, you should move all of the disks in the set if possible. If you move only part of the RAID-5 set, you might find that you can't use the set on either computer.

To move the disks, Start Computer Management and then in the left pane, select Device Manager. In the Device List, expand Disk Drives. This shows a list of all the physical disk drives on the computer. Right-click each disk that you want to move, and then select Uninstall. If you are unsure which disks to uninstall, right-click each disk and select Properties. In the Properties dialog box, select the Volumes tab, and then choose Populate. This shows you the volumes on the selected disk. In Computer Management, select Disk Management. Right-click each disk that you want to move, and then select Remove Disk.

Once you perform these procedures, you can move the dynamic disks. If the disk are hot swappable and this feature is supported on both computers, remove the disks from the original computer and then install them on the destination computer. Otherwise, turn off both computers, remove the drives from the original computer, and then install them on the destination computer. When you're finished, restart the computers. On the destination computer, access Disk Management, and then select Rescan Disks from the Action menu. When Disk Management finishes scanning the disks, right-click any disk marked Foreign, and click Import. You should now be able to access the disks and their volumes on the destination computer.

Note When you move dynamic disks, the volumes on those disks should retain the drive letters they had on the previous computer. If a drive letter is already used on the destination computer, a volume receives the next available drive letter. If a dynamic volume previously did not have a drive letter, it does not receive a drive letter when moved to another computer. Additionally, if automounting is disabled, the volumes aren't automatically mounted and you must manually mount volumes and assign drive letters.

Caution You should move GPT disks only to other Itanium-based computers. If you move GPT disks to an x86-based computer, Disk Management shows the GPT disk as containing one partition that covers the entire disk and you will be unable to access any data on the disk.

Configuring RAID 1: Disk Mirroring

For RAID 1, disk mirroring, you configure two volumes on two drives identically. Data is written to both drives. If one drive fails, there is no data loss because the other drive contains the data. After you repair or replace the failed drive, you can restore full mirroring so that the volume is once again fault tolerant.

By using disk mirroring, you gain the advantage of redundancy. Because disk mirroring doesn't write parity information, mirrored volumes can usually offer better write performance than disk striping with parity. The key drawback, however, is that disk mirroring has a 50 percent overhead, meaning it effectively cuts the amount of storage space in half. For example, to mirror a 60-GB drive, you need another 60-GB drive. That means you use 120 GB of space to store 60 GB of information.

As with disk striping, you'll often want the mirrored disks to be on separate disk controllers. This provides redundancy for the disk controllers. If one of the disk controllers fails, the disk on the other controller is still available. When you use two separate disk controllers to duplicate data, you're using a technique known as disk duplexing rather than disk mirroring—but why mince words?

You can create a mirrored set either by using two new disks or by adding a mirror to an existing volume. As with other RAID techniques, mirroring is transparent to users. Users see the mirrored set as a single volume that they can access and use like any other drive.

Creating a Mirrored Set Using Two New Disks

To create a mirrored set using two new disks, start Disk Management. In Graphical View, right-click an area marked Unallocated on a dynamic disk, and then choose New Volume. This starts the New Volume Wizard. Click Next. Select Mirrored as the volume type. Create the volume as described in the section entitled "Creating a Simple or Spanned Volume" earlier in this chapter. The key difference is that you must create two identically sized volumes and these volumes must be on separate dynamic drives. The volumes can be formatted as FAT, FAT32, or NTFS. You won't be able to continue past the Selected Disks page until you've selected the two disks that you want to work with.

When you click Finish, you'll return to the main Disk Management window, and Disk Management will create the mirrored set. During the creation of the mirror, you'll see a status of Resynching, as shown in Figure 19-17. This tells you that Disk Management is creating the mirror. When this process finishes, you'll have two identical volumes. Both volumes will show the same drive letter in Disk Management, but the separation of volumes is transparent to users. Users see the mirror set as a single volume. The volume status should be listed as Healthy. This is the normal status for volumes. If the status changes, you might need to repair or resync the mirrored set, as discussed in the section entitled "Resolving Problems with Mirrored Sets" later in this chapter.

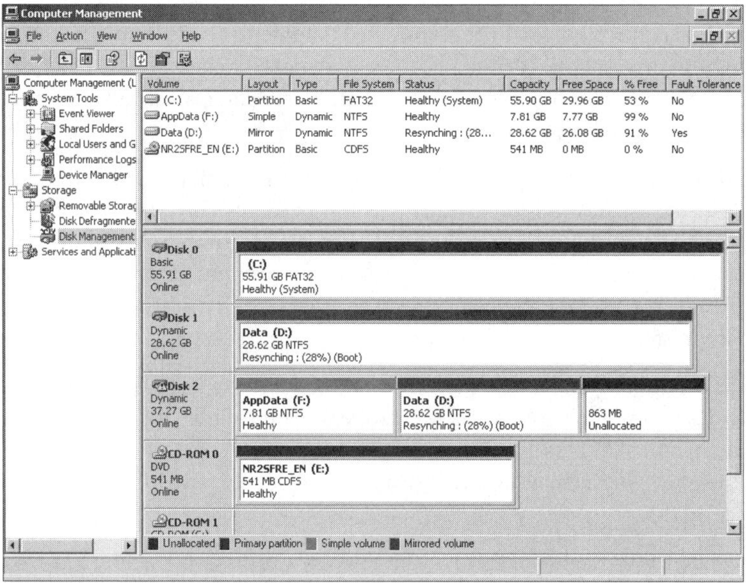

Figure 19-17. Disk Management creates the mirror and shows its progress.

Adding a Mirror to an Existing Volume

You can also use an existing volume to create a mirrored set. For this to work, the volume you want to mirror must be a simple volume and you must have an area of unallocated space on a second dynamic drive of equal or larger space than the existing volume. When you add a mirror onto this unallocated space, Disk Management creates a volume that is the same size and file system type as the simple volume you are mirroring. It then copies the data from the simple volume to the new volume using a process called resynching.

To add a mirror to an existing volume, start Disk Management. In Graphical View, right-click the simple volume you want to mirror, and then select Add Mirror. This displays the Add Mirror dialog box. Use the Disks list to select a location for the mirror, and then click Add Mirror. Windows Server 2003 begins the mirror creation process, and you'll see a status of Resynching on both volumes.

When the resynching is complete, you have two identical copies of the original volume. Although both volumes show the same drive letter in Disk Management, the separation of volumes is transparent to users. Users see the mirror set as a single volume.

Mirroring Boot and System Volumes

Disk mirroring is often used to mirror boot and system volumes. Mirroring these volumes ensures that you'll be able to boot the server in case of a single drive failure.

Mirroring Boot and System Volumes on MBR Disks

When you want to mirror boot or system volumes on MBR disks, the process is fairly straightforward. You start with two disks, which I'll call Disk 0 and Disk 1, where Disk 0 has the system files and Disk 1 is a new disk. Because Setup won't let you install Windows Server 2003 on a dynamic disk, the system disk is typically a basic disk that must be upgraded to a dynamic disk before you can mirror it—mirroring is only possible on dynamic disks.

To begin, upgrade Disk 0 to a dynamic disk and then upgrade Disk 1 as discussed in the section entitled "Using and Converting Basic and Dynamic Disks" earlier in this chapter. In Disk Management, right-click the boot or system volume that you want to mirror, and then select Add Mirror. This displays the Add Mirror dialog box. Select the disk onto which you want to add the mirror (Disk 1 in the example), and then click Add Mirror. Windows Server 2003 begins the mirror creation process, and you'll see a status of Resynching on both volumes. When the resynching is complete, the status should change to Healthy.

During the creation of the mirror, Windows Server 2003 adds an entry on the Boot menu for the second volume and labels it "Boot Mirror—Secondary Plex." If the primary mirror fails, you can use this entry to boot the computer to the second volume as discussed in the section entitled "Repairing a Mirrored System Volume to Enable Boot" later in this chapter.

Mirroring Boot and System Volumes on GPT Disks

Mirroring boot and system volumes on GPT disks isn't the same as for MBR disks. Primarily, this is because GPT disks used to boot the operating system have an ESP and an MSR partition that must be created on the disk in a certain order. Thus, to mirror boot and system volumes on GPT disks, you must create the necessary partitions on the second disk of the mirrored set and tell the operating system that these partitions can be used for booting.

To get started, you need two disks that use the GPT partition style and the basic storage type. One of the disks should already be designated as the boot volume. I'll refer to this volume as Disk 0. The other disk should be identical in size or larger than the boot volume. I'll refer to this volume as Disk 1. Disk 1 should be a clean disk, meaning it can't already have partitions on it; so, if necessary, copy any data on the disk to another disk or make a backup of the data and then delete any existing partitions. You can use DiskPart to do this by completing the following steps:

1. At the command prompt, invoke DiskPart by typing **diskpart.** List the disks available on the system by typing **list disk.**
2. Select the disk you are going to use as the secondary boot disk. Following the example, this is Disk 1, so you would type **select disk 1**.
3. List the partitions on this disk by typing **list partition.**
4. If there are any existing partitions, select and delete each partition in turn. For example, if the disk had Partition 1, you'd type **select partition 1**, and then type **delete partition override.** The Override parameter ensures that you can delete nonuser partitions.

Once you've made sure the second disk doesn't contain any partitions, list the available disks again by typing **list disk**, then select the disk you are going to use as the current boot disk. Following the example, this is Disk 0, so you would type **select disk 0**. List the partitions on this disk by typing **list partition.** The output you'll see will be similar to the following:

```
Partition ###        Type                   Size         Offset
-------------        ----------------     -------       -------
Partition 1          System                316 MB         32 KB
Partition 2          Primary              9992 MB        312 MB
Partition 3          Reserved               32 MB          9 GB
```

The output shows you which partitions are being used as the ESP and MSR partition. The ESP is listed with the partition type System. The MSR partition is listed with the partition type Reserved. Note the size of each partition. Here, System is 316 MB and Reserved is 32 MB.

You now must create the ESP and the MSR partition on the second disk by completing the following steps:

1. In DiskPart, select this disk to give it focus. Following the example, you'd type **select disk 1.**
2. Afterward, you would create the ESP first by typing **create partition efi size=*N***, where *N* is the size previously noted, such as **size=316.**
3. Create the MSR partition by typing **create partition msr size=*N***, where *N* is the size previously noted, such as **size=32.**

4. If you type **list partition**, you should see that both partitions have been created and are sized appropriately, such as follows:

```
Partition ###    Type                   Size        Offset
-------------    ----------------       -------     -------
Partition 1      System                 316 MB       32 KB
Partition 2      Reserved                32 MB      316 MB
```

Next you must prepare the ESP for use by assigning it a drive letter, formatting it, and copying over the necessary startup files from the current boot volume. To do this, follow these steps:

1. In DiskPart, select the partition by typing **select partition** 1.
2. Assign a drive letter by typing **assign letter=X**, where *X* is the drive letter, such as **letter=H.**
3. Exit DiskPart by typing **exit.**
4. Format the ESP as FAT using the drive letter you just assigned. Following the example, you'd type **format h: /fs:fat /q /y.**
5. Once formatting is complete, invoke DiskPart by typing **diskpart**, and then select the current boot volume. Following the example, you'd type **select disk 0.**
6. Type **select partition** 1 to select the ESP on the current boot volume.
7. Assign this partition a drive letter by typing **assign letter=X**, where *X* is the drive letter to assign, such as **letter=I.**
8. Exit DiskPart by typing **exit.**
9. Use the XCOPY command to copy all the files from the ESP on the current boot volume to the ESP on the second disk. Following the example, you'd type **xcopy i:*.* h: /s /h.** The /S and /H parameters ensure that hidden system files are copied.

You now must convert both drives to the dynamic storage type. Start with the second disk and then convert the current boot disk. Follow these steps:

1. Invoke DiskPart by typing **diskpart.**
2. Select the disk you are going to use as the secondary boot disk. Following the example, this is Disk 1, so you would type **select disk** 1.
3. Convert the disk by typing **convert dynamic.**
4. Select the current boot disk. Following the example, this is Disk 1, so you would type **select disk 0.**
5. Convert the disk by typing **convert dynamic.**
6. Exit DiskPart by typing **exit.**

7 You must shut down and restart the computer to complete the conversion process for the current boot disk. In some cases, this process takes several reboots to complete.

Note You don't have to delete the drive letters assigned in the previous procedure. These drive letters will not be reassigned after the restart.

When the conversion process is complete, log on to the system, and then follow these steps to mirror the boot drive:

1 Invoke DiskPart by typing **diskpart**.
2 Select the current boot disk. Following the example, this is Disk 1, so you would type **select disk 0**.
3 Add the disk to use as the second drive to this volume to create the mirrored set. Following the example, you'd type **add disk=1**.
4 DiskPart will then begin the mirror creation process by synchronizing the data on both volumes.

During the creation of the mirror, Windows Server 2003 adds an entry on the Boot menu for the second volume and labels it "Boot Mirror—Secondary Plex." If the primary mirror fails, you can use this entry to boot the computer to the second volume, as discussed in the section entitled "Repairing a Mirrored System Volume to Enable Boot" later in this chapter. However, this doesn't protect you from complete failure of the primary boot disk. Why? Because you haven't told the operating system about the ESP on the second disk.

To tell the operating system about the ESP on the second disk and safeguard the system against complete failure of the primary boot disk, you clone the ESPs on the primary and secondary boot disks, and thereby create new entries that allow the system to boot from the secondary boot disk regardless of whether the primary boot disk is available. Follow these steps:

1 List the current boot entries for the computer by typing **bootcfg** at the command prompt. The output shows you the current default boot device and the configuration of each boot entry, as follows:

```
Boot Loader Settings
--------------------
timeout: 30
default: \Device\HarddiskDmVolumes\PhysicalDmVolumes\BlockVolume1\WIN03
CurrentBootEntryId: 1

Boot Entries
------------
Boot entry ID:    1
OS Friendly Name:Windows 2003 Server, Enterprise
OsLoadOptions:    N/A
BootFilePath:     \Device\HarddiskVolume1\EFI\Microsoft\WINNT50\ia64ldr.efi
OsFilePath:       \Device\HarddiskDmVolumes\PhysicalDmVolumes\BlockVolume1\WIN03
```

```
Boot entry ID:    2
OS Friendly Name:CDROM

Boot entry ID:    3
OS Friendly Name:EFI Shell

Boot entry ID:    4
OS Friendly Name:Boot Mirror D: - secondary plex
OsLoadOptions:    N/A
BootFilePath:     \Device\HarddiskVolume1\EFI\Microsoft\WINNT50\ia64ldr.efi
OsFilePath:       \Device\HarddiskDmVolumes\PhysicalDmVolumes\BlockVolume1\WIN03
```

2. Display the boot entry details of each partition on the primary boot disk. Following the example, you'd type **bootcfg /list 0**. The partition listings look like this:

```
Partition No:      1
Partition Style:   GPT
Starting  offset:  32,256
Partition length:  211,000,512
Partition GUID:    {344b23d1-003b-125c-3522-5e2c34515322}
GUID type:         {d01b1234-d234-e235-b34a-00b12c34234a}
Partition name:    EFI system partition
```

3. Copy the GUID of the ESP to the Clipboard and paste it into a Notepad window. Here, you would copy {344b23d1-003b-125c-3522-5e2c34515322} and paste it to Notepad. This is the source GUID value needed to clone the boot entry.
4. Display the boot entry details of each partition on the secondary boot disk. Following the example, you'd type **bootcfg /list 1**. As before, copy the GUID of the ESP to the Clipboard and paste it into a Notepad window. This is the target GUID value needed to clone the boot entry.
5. Use the BOOTCFG /CLONE command to create the boot entries needed to boot to the secondary boot disk. Type **bootcfg /clone /sg *SourceGUID* /tg *TargetGUID* /d+ Secondary_Boot**, where *SourceGUID* is the GUID for the primary boot disk and *TargetGUID* is the GUID for the secondary boot disk. Paste or type in the GUIDs carefully, making sure to include the curly braces {}.

Before you press Enter, ensure the syntax is exact and that the GUIDs are correctly entered. This command creates two boot entries, one for the source and one for the target. BOOTCFG will report the status of each, and the output should report success, as follows:

```
INFO: Boot entry whose id is '1' successfully cloned.
INFO: Boot entry whose id is '4' successfully cloned.
SUCCESS: The operation completed successfully.
```

Here, BOOTCFG reports that it successfully cloned boot entries 1 and 4. These entries should be added to the Boot menu with the next available ID. In this case, that would be if you typed **bootcfg** again, you'd see the additional entries, as follows:

```
Boot entry ID:      5
OS Friendly Name:   Windows 2003 Server, Enterprise Secondary_Boot
OsLoadOptions:      N/A
BootFilePath:       \Device\HarddiskVolume2\EFI\Microsoft\WINNT50\ia64ldr.efi
OsFilePath:         \Device\HarddiskDmVolumes\PhysicalDmVolumes\BlockVolume1\WIN03

Boot entry ID:      6
OS Friendly Name:   Boot Mirror D: - secondary plex Secondary_Boot
OsLoadOptions:      N/A
BootFilePath:       \Device\HarddiskVolume2\EFI\Microsoft\WINNT50\ia64ldr.efi
OsFilePath:         \Device\HarddiskDmVolumes\PhysicalDmVolumes\BlockVolume1\WIN03
```

Note The boot file path (BootFilePath) of the cloned entry points to a different hard disk drive than the original entries. This is as expected, because these entries are for the secondary disk.

Now if you shut down the system and restart, you should be able to boot successfully to either the primary or secondary boot disk.

Configuring RAID 5: Disk Striping with Parity

RAID 5, disk striping with parity, offers fault tolerance with less overhead and better read performance than disk mirroring. To configure RAID 5, you use three or more volumes, each on a separate drive, as a striped set, similar to RAID 0. Unlike RAID 0, however, RAID 5 adds parity error checking to ensure that the failure of a single drive won't bring down the entire drive set. In the event of a single drive failure, the set continues to function with disk operations directed at the remaining disks in the set. The parity information can also be used to recover the data using a process called regeneration.

RAID 5 works like this: Each time the operating system writes to a RAID-5 volume, the data is written across all the disks in the set. Parity information for the data, used for error checking and correction, is written to disk as well, but always on a separate disk from the one used to write the data. For example, if you are using a three-volume RAID-5 set and save a file, the individual data bytes of the file are written to each of the disks in the set. Parity information is written as well, but not to the same disk as one of the individual data bytes. Thus, a disk in the set could have a chunk of the data or the corresponding parity information, but not both, and this in turn means that the loss of one disk from the set doesn't cause the entire set to fail.

Like any type of RAID, RAID 5 has its drawbacks as well. First, if multiple drives in the set fail, the entire set will fail and you won't be able to regenerate the set from the parity information. Why? If multiple drives fail, there won't be enough parity information to use to recover the set. Second, having to generate and write parity information every time data is written to disk slows down the write process (and, in the case of software RAID, processing power). To compensate for the performance hit, hardware RAID controllers have their own processors that handle the necessary processing—and this is why hardware RAID is preferred over software RAID.

Okay, so RAID 5 gives you fault tolerance at some cost to performance. It does, however, have less overhead than RAID 1. By using RAID 1, you have a 50 percent overhead, which effectively cuts the amount of storage space in half. By using RAID 5, the overhead depends on the number of disks in the RAID set. With three disks, the overhead is about one-third. If you had three 60-GB drives using RAID 5, you'd use 180 GB of space to store about 120 GB of information. If you have additional disks, the overhead is reduced incrementally, but not significantly.

To create a RAID-5 set, start Disk Management. In Graphical View, right-click an area marked Unallocated on a dynamic disk, and then choose New Volume. This starts the New Volume Wizard. Click Next. Select RAID 5 as the volume type. Create the volume as described in the section entitled "Creating a Simple or Spanned Volume" earlier in this chapter. The key difference is that you must select free space on three or more separate dynamic drives.

When you click Finish, you'll return to the main Disk Management window and Disk Management will create the RAID-5 set. During the creation of the mirror, you'll see a status of Resynching. This tells you that Disk Management is creating the RAID-5 set. When this process finishes, you'll have three or more identical volumes, all of which will show the same drive letter in Disk Management. Users, however, will see the RAID-5 set as a single volume. The volume status should be listed as Healthy. This is the normal status for volumes. If the status changes, you might need to repair or regenerate the RAID-5 set as discussed in the section entitled "Resolving Problems with RAID-5 Sets" later in this chapter.

Breaking or Removing a Mirrored Set

Windows Server 2003 provides two ways to stop mirroring. You can break a mirrored set, creating two separate but identical volumes. Or you can remove a mirror, which deletes all the data on the removed mirror.

To break a mirrored set, follow these steps:

1. In Disk Management, right-click one of the volumes in the mirrored set, and then choose Break Mirrored Volume.

2. Confirm that you want to break the mirrored set by clicking Yes. If the volume is currently in use, you'll see another warning dialog box. Confirm that it's okay to continue by clicking Yes.
3. Windows Server 2003 will then break the mirrored set, creating two independent volumes.

To remove a mirror, follow these steps:

1. In Disk Management, right-click one of the volumes in the mirrored set, and then choose Remove Mirror. This displays the Remove Mirror dialog box.
2. In the Remove Mirror dialog box, select the disk from which to remove the mirror. If the mirror contains a boot or system volume, you should remove the mirror from the secondary drive rather than the primary. For example, if Drive 0 and Drive 1 are mirrored, remove Drive 1 rather than Drive 0.
3. Confirm the action when prompted. All data on the removed mirror is deleted.

Resolving Problems with Mirrored Sets

Occasionally, data on mirrored volumes can get out of sync. Typically, this happens if one of the drives in the set goes offline or experiences temporary I/O problems and, as a result, data can be written only to the drive that's online. To reestablish mirroring, you must get both drives online and then resynchronize the mirror. The corrective action you take depends on the drive status.

The Missing or Offline status usually happens if drives have been disconnected or powered off. If the drives are part of an external storage device, check the storage device to ensure it is connected properly and has power. Reconnecting the storage device or turning on the power should make it so the drives can be accessed. You then must start Disk Management and rescan the missing drive. Right-click the missing drive, and choose Rescan Disks. When Disk Management finishes, right-click the drive, and choose Reactivate. The drive status should change to Regenerating and then to Healthy. If the volume doesn't return to the Healthy status, right-click the volume, and then click Resynchronize Mirror.

A status of Failed, Online (Errors), or Unreadable indicates I/O problems with the drive. As before, try rescanning the drive, and then try to reactivate the drive. The drive status should change to Regenerating and then to Healthy. If the volume doesn't return to the Healthy status, right-click the volume, and then click Resynchronize Mirror.

If these actions don't work, you must remove the failed mirror, replace the bad drive, and then rebuild the mirror. To do this, follow these steps:

1. Right-click the failed volume, and then select Remove Mirror.
2. You now must mirror the volume on an Unallocated area of free space on a different disk. If you don't have free space, you must create space by deleting other volumes or replacing the failed drive.

3. When you are ready to continue, right-click the remaining volume in the original mirror, and then select Add Mirror. This displays the Add Mirror dialog box.
4. Use the Disks list to select a location for the mirror, and then click Add Mirror. Windows Server 2003 begins the mirror creation process, and you'll see a status of Resynching on both volumes.

Repairing a Mirrored System Volume to Enable Boot

When you mirror a system volume, an entry that allows you to boot to the secondary mirror is added to the system's Boot.ini file. So, if a system fails to boot to the primary system volume, restart the system, and select the Boot Mirror—Secondary Plex option for the operating system you want to start. The system should start up normally. Once you successfully boot the system to the secondary drive, you can schedule the maintenance necessary to rebuild the mirror if desired.

Rebuilding Mirrored System Volumes on MBR Disks

To rebuild the mirror, you must complete the following steps:

1. Shut down the system and replace the failed drive, and then restart the system using the secondary drive.
2. In Disk Management, right-click the remaining volume in the mirrored set, and choose Break Mirrored Volume. Click Yes at the prompts to confirm the action.
3. Next, right-click the volume again, and choose Add Mirror. Use the Add Mirror dialog box to select the second disk to use for the mirror, and then click Add Mirror.
4. Check Boot.ini to ensure that the designated boot volumes are correct.

If you want the primary mirror to be on the drive you added or replaced, perform these additional steps:

1. Use Disk Management to break the mirrored set again.
2. Make sure that the primary drive in the original mirror set has the drive letter that was previously assigned to the complete mirror. If it doesn't, assign the appropriate drive letter.
3. Right-click the original system volume, select Add Mirror, and then re-create the mirror.
4. Check Boot.ini to ensure that the original system volume is used during startup.

Rebuilding Mirrored System Volumes on GPT Disks

For GTP disks, rebuilding mirrored system volumes is a bit different. To rebuild the mirror, shut down the system and replace the failed drive, and then restart the system using the secondary drive. In Disk Management, right-click the remaining volume in the mirrored set, and choose Break Mirrored Volume. Click Yes at the prompts to confirm the action. After this, you can use the secondary boot disk as your primary boot disk and follow the procedures outlined in the section entitled "Mirroring Boot and System Volumes on MBR Disks" earlier in this chapter to reenable mirroring properly using the secondary disk as the primary.

Resolving Problems with RAID-5 Sets

Most problems with RAID-5 sets have to do with the intermittent or permanent failure of a drive. If one of the drives in the set goes offline or experiences temporary I/O problems, parity data cannot be properly written to the set and, as a result, the set's status will show as Failed Redundancy and the failed volume's status changes to Missing, Offline, or Online (Errors).

You must get all drives in the RAID-5 set online. If the status of the problem volume is Missing or Offline, make sure that the drive has power and is connected properly. You then must start Disk Management and rescan the missing drive. Right-click the missing drive, and choose Rescan Disks. When Disk Management finishes, right-click the drive, and choose Reactivate. The drive status should change to Regenerating and then to Healthy. If the volume doesn't return to the Healthy status, right-click the volume, and then click Regenerate Parity.

A status of Failed, Online (Errors), or Unreadable indicates I/O problems with the drive. As before, try rescanning the drive, and then try to reactivate the drive. The drive status should change to Regenerating and then to Healthy. If the volume doesn't return to the Healthy status, right-click the volume, and then click Regenerate Parity.

If one of the drives still won't come back online, you must repair the failed region of the RAID-5 set. Right-click the failed volume, and then select Remove Volume. You now must right-click an unallocated space on a separate dynamic disk and choose Repair Volume. This space must be at least as large as the region to repair, and it can't be on a drive that's already being used by the RAID-5 set. If you don't have enough space, the Repair Volume option is unavailable and you must free space by deleting other volumes or replacing the failed drive.

Chapter 20

Managing Windows Server 2003 File Systems

The previous chapter discussed storage management, which primarily focuses on storage technologies and techniques for configuring storage. As discussed in that chapter, disks can be apportioned in many ways but ultimately must be formatted with a particular file system. The file system provides the environment for working with files and folders. Microsoft Windows Server 2003 provides two basic file system types: File Allocation Table (FAT) and NTFS file system (NTFS). These file systems are discussed in this chapter.

Understanding Disk and File System Structure

The basic unit of storage is a disk. Regardless of the partition style or disk type, Windows Server 2003 reads data from disks and writes data to disks using the disk input/output (I/O) subsystem. The I/O subsystem understands the physical and logical structures of disks, which allows it to perform read and write operations. The basic physical structure of a disk includes:

- Platters
- Cylinders
- Tracks
- Clusters
- Sectors

Each disk has one or more platters. Platters are the physical media from which data is read and to which data is written. The disk head travels in a circular path over the platter. This circular path is called a track. Tracks are magnetically encoded when you format a disk. Tracks that reside in the same location on each platter form a cylinder. For example, if a disk has four platters, Cylinder 1 consists of Track 1 from all four platters.

Tracks are divided into sectors. Sectors represent a subsection within a track and are made up of individual bytes. The number of sectors in a track depends on the disk type and the location of the track on the platter. Tracks closer to the outside of the platter can have more sectors than tracks near the center of the platter.

When you format a disk with a file system, the file system structures the disk using clusters, which are logical groupings of sectors. Both FAT and NTFS use a fixed sector size of 512 bytes but allow the cluster size to be variable. For example, the cluster size might be 4096 bytes, and if there are 512 bytes per sector, each cluster is made up of eight sectors. Table 20-1 provides a summary of the default cluster sizes for FAT, FAT32, and NTFS. You have the option of specifying the cluster size when you create a file system on a disk, or you can accept the default cluster size setting. Either way, the cluster sizes available depend on the type of file system you are using.

Tip **Three Different FAT File Systems**

There are actually three FAT file systems used by Windows platforms: FAT12, FAT16, and FAT32. The difference between them is the number of bits used for entries in their file allocation tables, namely 12, 16, or 32 bits. From a user's perspective, the main difference in these file systems is the theoretical maximum volume size, which is 16 MB for a FAT12 volume, 4 GB for FAT16, and 2 TB for FAT32. When the term *FAT* is used without an appended number, however, it always refers to FAT16.

Table 20-1. Default Cluster Sizes for FAT16, FAT32, and NTFS

Volume Size	Cluster Size		
	FAT16	**FAT32**	**NTFS**
7 MB to 16 MB	2 KB	Not supported	512 bytes
17 MB to 32 MB	512 bytes	Not supported	512 bytes
33 MB to 64 MB	1 KB	512 bytes	512 bytes
65 MB to 128 MB	2 KB	1 KB	512 bytes
129 MB to 256 MB	4 KB	2 KB	512 bytes
257 MB to 512 MB	8 KB	4 KB	512 bytes
513 MB to 1024 MB	16 KB	4 KB	1 KB
1025 MB to 2 GB	32 KB	4 KB	2 KB
2 GB to 4 GB	64 KB	4 KB	4 KB
4 GB to 8 GB	Not supported	4 KB	4 KB
8 GB to 16 GB	Not supported	8 KB	4 KB
16 GB to 32 GB	Not supported	16 KB	4 KB
32 GB to 2 TB	Not supported	Not supported	4 KB

The important thing to know about clusters is that they are the smallest unit in which disk space is allocated. Each cluster can hold one file at most. So, if you create a 1-kilobyte (KB) file and the cluster size is 4 KB, there will be 3 KB of empty space in the cluster that isn't available to other files. That's just the way it is. If a single cluster isn't big enough to hold an entire file, then the remaining file data will go into the next available cluster and the next until the file is completely stored. For FAT, for example, the first cluster used by the file has a pointer to the second cluster, and the second cluster has a pointer to the next, and so on until you get to the final cluster used by the file, which has an End Of File (EOF) marker.

While the disk I/O subsystem manages the physical structure of disks, Windows Server 2003 manages the logical disk structure at the file system level. The logical structure of a disk relates to the basic or dynamic volumes you create on a disk and the file systems with which those volumes are formatted. You can format both basic volumes and dynamic volumes using FAT or NTFS. As discussed in the next section, each file system type has a different structure, and there are advantages and disadvantages of each as well.

Using FAT

FAT is available in 16-bit and 32-bit versions, which are referred to as FAT16 and FAT32. FAT volumes use an allocation table to store information about disk space allocation.

File Allocation Table Structure

Disks formatted using FAT are organized as shown in Figure 20-1. They have a boot sector that stores information about the disk type, starting and ending sectors, the active partition, and a bootstrap program that executes at startup and boots the operating system. This is followed by a reserve area that can be one or more sectors in length.

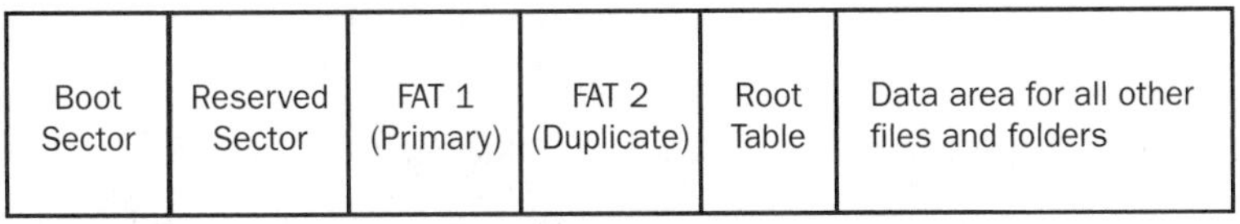

Boot Sector	Reserved Sector	FAT 1 (Primary)	FAT 2 (Duplicate)	Root Table	Data area for all other files and folders

Figure 20-1. An overview of FAT16 volume structure.

The reserve area is followed by the primary file allocation table, which provides a reference table for the clusters on the volume. Each reference in the table relates to a specific cluster and defines the cluster's status as follows:

- Available (unused)
- In use (meaning it is being used by a file)
- Bad (meaning it is marked as bad and won't be written to)
- Reserved (meaning it is reserved for the operating system)

If a cluster is in use, the cluster entry identifies the number of the next cluster in the file or that it is the last cluster of a file, in which case the end of the file has been reached.

FAT volumes also have the following features:

- Duplicate file allocation table, which provides a backup of the primary file allocation table and can be used to restore the file system if the primary file allocation table gets corrupted
- Root directory table, which defines the starting cluster of each file in the file system
- Data area, which stores the actual data for user files and folders

When an application attempts to read a file, the operating system looks up the starting cluster of the file in the root directory table and then uses the file allocation table to find and read all the clusters in the file.

FAT Features

Although FAT supports basic file and folder operations, its features are rather limited. By using FAT, you have the following capabilities:

- You can't control local access to files and folders using Microsoft Windows file and folder access permissions.
- You can't use any advanced file system features of NTFS, including compression, encryption, disk quotas, and remote storage.
- You can use Windows file sharing but have limited control over remote access to files and folders.
- You can use long file names, meaning file and folder names containing up to 255 characters.
- You can use FAT with floppy disks and removable disks.
- You can use Unicode characters in file and folders names.
- You can use upper- and lowercase letters in file and folder names.

In addition, although FAT16 supports small cluster sizes, FAT32 does not. Table 20-2 provides a summary of FAT16 and FAT32.

Table 20-2. Comparison of FAT16 and FAT32 Features

Feature	FAT16	FAT32
File allocation table size	16-bit	32-bit
Minimum volume size	See following Inside Out sidebar	33 MB
Maximum volume size	4 GB; best at 2 GB or less	2 TB; limited in Windows Server 2003 to 32 GB
Maximum file size	2 GB	4 GB

Table 20-2. Comparison of FAT16 and FAT32 Features

Feature	FAT16	FAT32
Supports small cluster size	Yes	No
Supports NTFS features	No	No
Use on floppy disks	Yes	Yes
Use on removable disks	Yes	Yes

Note While Windows Server 2003 can read to or write from FAT32 volumes as large as 2 TB, the operating system can only format FAT32 volumes up to 32 GB in size.

Inside Out

FAT on very small media

It is important to note that FAT volumes are structured differently depending on volume size. When you format a volume that is less than 32,680 sectors (16 megabytes [MB]), the format program uses 12 bits for FAT12. This means less space is reserved for each entry in the table and more space is made available for data. This technique is meant to be used with very small media, such as floppy disks.

In FAT, disk sectors are 512 bytes. By default Windows Server 2003 sets the size of clusters and the number of sectors per cluster based on the size of the volume. Disk geometry also is a factor in determining cluster size because the number of clusters on the volume must fit into the number of bits used by the file system. The actual amount of data you can store on a single FAT volume is a factor of the maximum cluster size and the maximum number of clusters you can use per volume. This can be written out as a formula:

ClusterSize × MaximumNumberOfClusters = MaximumVolumeSize

FAT16 supports a maximum of 65,526 clusters and a maximum cluster size of 64 KB. This is where the limitation of 4 gigabytes (GB) for volume size comes from. With disks less that 32 MB but more than 16 MB in size, the cluster size is 512 bytes and there is one sector per cluster. This changes as the volume size increases up to the largest cluster size of 64 KB with 128 sectors per cluster on 2-GB to 4-GB volumes.

FAT32 volumes using 512-byte sectors can be up to 2 terabytes (TB) in size and can use clusters of up to 64 KB. To control the maximum number of clusters allowed, the Windows operating system reserves the upper 4 bits, however, limiting FAT32 to a maximum 28 bits worth of clusters. With a maximum recommended cluster size of 32 KB (instead of the maximum allowable 64 KB), this means a FAT32 volume on the Windows operating system can be up to 32 GB in size. Because the smallest cluster size allowed for FAT32 volumes is 512 bytes, the smallest FAT32 volume you can create is 33 MB.

Tip **FAT32 volumes of any size can be mounted**
Windows Server 2003 does support mounting FAT32 volumes of up to the theoretical limit of 2 TB. This allows you to mount volumes larger than 32 GB that were created on other operating systems or by using third-party utilities.

Inside Out

Getting volume format and feature information

A quick way to check the file system type and available features of a volume is to type **fsutil fsinfo volumeinfo *DriveDesignator*** at the command prompt, where *DriveDesignator* is the drive letter of the volume followed by a colon, such as C:. For a FAT or FAT32 volume, you'll see output similar to the following:

```
Volume Name : LogData
Volume Serial Number : 0x70692a2e
Max Component Length : 255
File System Name : FAT32
Preserves Case of filenames
Supports Unicode in filenames
```

Using NTFS

NTFS is an extensible and recoverable file system that offers many advantages over FAT and FAT32. Because it is extensible, the file system can be extended over time with various revisions. As you'll learn shortly, the version of NTFS that ships with Windows Server 2003 is in fact a revision of the NTFS version that shipped with Microsoft Windows 2000 Server. Because it is recoverable, volumes formatted with NTFS can be reconstructed if they contain structure errors. Typically, restructuring NTFS volumes is a task performed at startup.

NTFS Structures

NTFS volumes have a very different structure and feature set than FAT volumes. The first area of the volume is the boot sector, which is located at sector 0 on the volume. The boot sector stores information about the disk layout, and a bootstrap program executes at startup and boots the operating system. A backup boot sector is placed at the end of the volume for redundancy and fault tolerance.

Instead of a file allocation table, NTFS uses a relational database to store information about files. This database is called the master file table (MFT). The MFT stores a file record of each file and folder on the volume, pertinent volume information, and details on the MFT itself. The first 16 records in the MFT store NTFS metadata as summarized in Table 20-3.

Table 20-3. NTFS Metadata

MFT Record	Record Type	File Name	Description
0	MFT	$Mft	Stores the base file record of each file and folder on the volume. As the number of files and folders grows, additional records are used as necessary.
1	MFT mirror	$MftMirr	Stores a partial duplicate of the MFT used for failure recovery. Also referred to as MFT2.
2	Log file	$LogFile	Stores a persistent history of all changes made to files on the volume, which can be used to recover files.
3	Volume	$Volume	Stores volume attributes, including the volume serial number, version, and number of sectors.
4	Attribute definitions	$AttrDef	Stores a table of attribute names, numbers, and descriptions.
5	Root file name index	$	Stores the details on the volume's root directory.
6	Cluster bitmap	$Bitmap	Stores a table that details the clusters in use.
7	Boot sector	$Boot	Stores the bootstrap program on bootable volumes. Also includes the locations of the MFT and MFT mirror.
8	Bad cluster file	$BadClus	Stores a table mapping bad clusters.
9	Security file	$Secure	Stores the unique security descriptor for all files and folders on the volume.
10	Upcase table	$Upcase	Stores a table used to convert lowercase to matching uppercase Unicode characters.
11	NTFS extension file	$Extend	Stores information on enabled file system extensions.
12–15	To be determined	To be determined	Reserved records for future use.

The MFT mirror stores a partial duplicate of the MFT that can be used to recover the MFT. If any of the records in the primary mirror become corrupted or are otherwise unreadable and there's a duplicate record in the MFT mirror, NTFS uses the data in the MFT mirror and if possible uses this data to recover the records in the primary MFT. It is also important to note that the NTFS version that ships with Windows Server 2003 (NTFS 5.1) has a slightly different metadata mapping than the version that originally shipped with Windows 2000 (NTFS 5.0). In the current version, the $LogFile and $Bitmap metadata files are located on a different position on disk than they were in Windows 2000. This gives a performance advantage of 5 to 8 percent to disks that are formatted under Windows Server 2003 and comes close to approximating the performance of FAT.

The rest of the records in the MFT store file and folder information. Each of these regular entries includes the file or folder name, security descriptor, and other attributes, including file data or pointers to file data. The MFT record size is set when a volume is formatted and can be 1024 bytes, 2048 bytes, or 4096 bytes, depending on the volume size. If a file is very small, all of its contents might be able to fit in the data field of its record in the MFT. When all of a file's attributes, including its data, can be stored in the MFT record, the attributes are called resident attributes. Figure 20-2 shows an example of a small file with resident attributes.

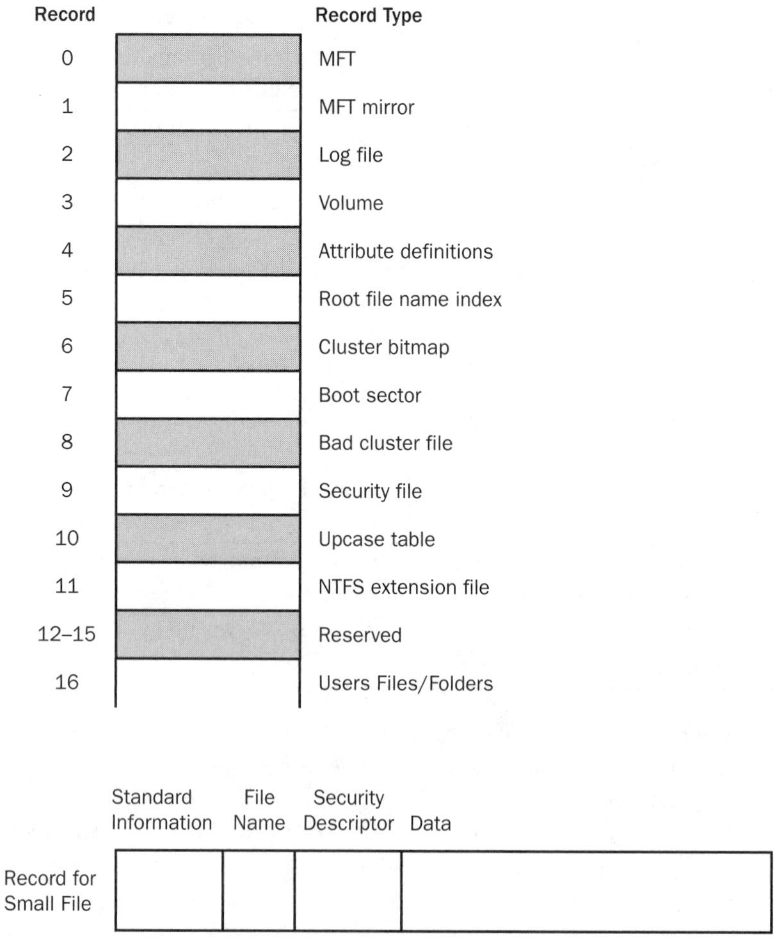

Record	Record Type
0	MFT
1	MFT mirror
2	Log file
3	Volume
4	Attribute definitions
5	Root file name index
6	Cluster bitmap
7	Boot sector
8	Bad cluster file
9	Security file
10	Upcase table
11	NTFS extension file
12–15	Reserved
16	Users Files/Folders

	Standard Information	File Name	Security Descriptor	Data
Record for Small File				

Figure 20-2. A graphical depiction of the MFT and its records.

If a file is larger than a single record, it has what are called nonresident attributes. Here, the file has a base record in the MFT that details where to find the file data. NTFS creates additional areas called runs on the disk to store the additional file data. The size of data runs is dependent on the cluster size of the volume. If the cluster size is 2 KB or less, data runs are 2 KB. If the cluster size is over 2 KB, data runs are 4 KB.

As Figure 20-3 shows, clusters belonging to the file are referenced in the MFT using virtual cluster numbers (VCNs). VCNs are numbered sequentially starting with VCN 0. The Data field in the file's MFT record maps the VCNs to a starting logical cluster number (LCN) on the disk and details the number of clusters to read for that VCN. When these mappings use up all the available space in a record, additional MFT records are created to store the additional mappings.

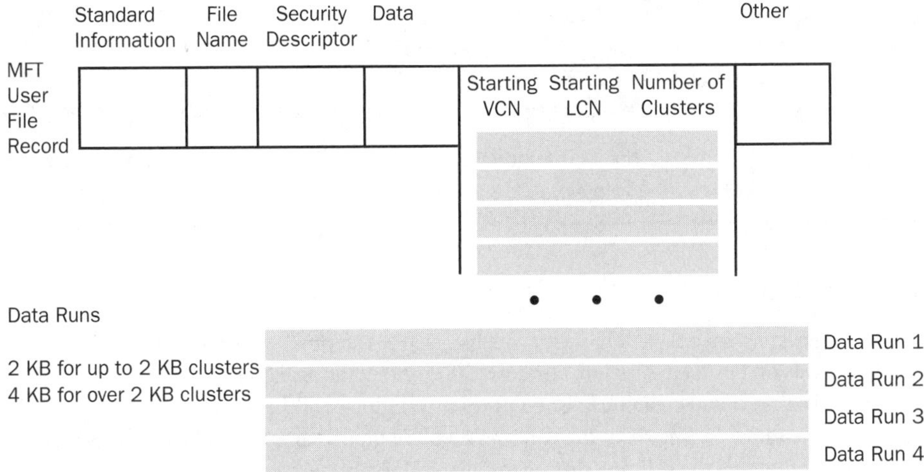

Figure 20-3. A graphical depiction of a user file record with data runs.

In addition to the MFT, NTFS reserves a contiguous range of space past the end of the MFT called the MFT zone. By default the MFT zone is approximately 12.5 percent of the total volume space. The MFT zone is used to allow the MFT to grow without becoming fragmented. Typically, the MFT zone shrinks as the MFT grows.

The MFT zone is not used to store user data unless the remainder of the volume becomes full. Fragmentation can and still does occur, however. On volumes with lots of small files, the MFT zone can get used up by the MFT, and as additional files are added, the MFT has to grow into unreserved areas of the volume. On volumes with but a few large files, the unreserved space on a volume can get used up before the MFT, and in this case, the files start using the MFT zone space.

Inside Out

The MFT zone can be optimized

By default, the MFT is optimized for environments that have a mix of large and small files. This setting works well if the average file size is 8 KB or larger. It doesn't work so well if a volume has many very small files, such as when the average size of files is less than 2 KB or between 2 KB and 7 KB. Here, you might want to configure the volume so that it has a larger MFT zone than normal to help prevent the MFT from becoming fragmented. The MFT zone size is set in eighths of the disk.

You can determine the current MFT zone setting by typing the following command at the command prompt: **fsutil behavior query mftzone**. If this command returns "mftzone is not currently set," the MFT zone is using the default setting. The default setting, 1, specifies that the MFT zone should use one-eighth (12.5 percent) of the total volume space. You can also use a setting of 2, 3, or 4 to set the MFT zone to use two-eighths (25 percent), three-eighths (37.5 percent), or four-eighths (50 percent) of the total volume space.

You can configure the MFT zone by typing the command **fsutil behavior set mftzone *Value***, where *Value* is the relative size setting to use, such as 2.

NTFS Features

Several versions of NTFS are available. NTFS 4 shipped with Microsoft Windows NT 4. NTFS 5 was first implemented in Windows 2000 and made available to Windows NT 4 through Service Pack 4. If you created NTFS volumes in Windows NT 4 and upgraded to Windows 2000 or Windows Server 2003, the volumes aren't upgraded automatically to NTFS 5. You must choose to upgrade the volumes during installation of the operating system or when you install the Active Directory directory service.

You have the following capabilities when you use NTFS 4:

- You can use advanced file and folder access permissions.
- You can use file sharing and full-control remote access to files and folders.
- You can use long file names, meaning file and folder names can contain up to 255 characters.
- You can use Unicode characters in file and folder names.
- You can use upper- and lowercase letters in file and folder names.
- You can't use NTFS with floppy disks but can use NTFS with removable disks.

By using NTFS 5, you have all the features of NTFS 4 plus additional features:

- You can use Encrypting File System (EFS).
- You can use sparse files, disk quotas, and object identifiers.

- You can use reparse points, remote storage, and shadow copies.
- You can use data streams and change journals.

> **Note** For NTFS, you typically refer to major version numbers rather than the major version and the revision number. Technically, however, Shadow Copy is a feature of NTFS 5.1 or later. NTFS 5.1 is the version of NTFS that was first included in Windows XP (and is available with Windows 2000 Server Service Pack 4 or later). With NTFS 5.1 you gain some additional enhancements, primarily the ability to use shadow copies.

Table 20-4 provides a comparison of key features of NTFS 4 and NTFS 5.

Table 20-4. Comparison of NTFS 4 and NTFS 5 Features

Feature	NTFS 4	NTFS 5
Maximum volume size	32 GB	2 TB on basic Master Boot Record (MBR) disks; 256 TB on dynamic MBR disks; 18 (exabytes) EB on GUID Partition Table (GPT) disks. See the section entitled "Configuring Storage" on page 593 for details on MBR and GPT disks.
Maximum file size	32 GB	Only limited by volume size
Supports object identifiers	No	Yes
Supports advanced file access permissions	Yes	Yes
Supports disk quotas	No	Yes
Supports remote storage	No	Yes
Supports sparse files	No	Yes
Supports file-based compression	Yes	Yes
Supports EFS	No	Yes
Supports reparse points	No	Yes
Use on floppy disks	No	No
Use on removable disks	Yes	Yes

With NTFS, disk sectors are 512 bytes. Windows Server 2003 automatically sets the size of clusters and the number of sectors per cluster based on the size of the volume. Cluster sizes range from 512 bytes to 4 KB. As with FAT, NTFS has the following characteristics:

- Disk geometry also is a factor in determining cluster size because the number of clusters on the volume must fit into the number of bits used by the file system.

- The actual amount of data you can store on a single NTFS volume is a factor of the maximum cluster size and the maximum number of clusters you can use per volume.

Thus, although volumes have a specific maximum size, the cluster size used on a volume can be a limiting factor. For example, a dynamic volume with a 4-KB cluster size can have dynamic volumes up to 16 TB, which is different from the maximum allowed dynamic volume size on NTFS.

Analyzing NTFS Structure

If you want to examine the structure of a volume formatted using NFTS, you can use the FSUTIL FSINFO command to do this. Type **fsutil fsinfo ntfsinfo *DriveDesignator*** at the command prompt, where *DriveDesignator* is the drive letter of the volume followed by a colon. For example, if you want to obtain information on the C drive, you'd type

```
fsutil fsinfo ntfsinfo c:
```

The output would be similar to the following:

```
NTFS Volume Serial Number :             0x2c64a9b264a97f68
Version :                               3.1
Number Sectors :                        0x0000000006fcf9c2
Total Clusters :                        0x0000000000df9f38
Free Clusters  :                        0x0000000000c8a5e5
Total Reserved :                        0x0000000000000030
Bytes Per Sector  :                     512
Bytes Per Cluster :                     4096
Bytes Per FileRecord Segment    :       1024
Clusters Per FileRecord Segment :       0
Mft Valid Data Length :                 0x00000000049d9000
Mft Start Lcn  :                        0x00000000000c0000
Mft2 Start Lcn :                        0x00000000006fcf9c
Mft Zone Start :                        0x00000000002801e0
Mft Zone End   :                        0x0000000000283c00
```

As Table 20-5 shows, FSUTIL FSINFO provides detailed information on NTFS volume structure, including space usage and configuration.

Table 20-5. Details from FSUTIL FSINFO

Field	Description
NTFS Volume Serial Number	The unique serial number of the selected NTFS volume.
Version	The internal NTFS version. Here, 3.1 refers to NTFS 5.1.
Number Sectors	The total number of sectors on the volume in hexadecimal.

Table 20-5. Details from FSUTIL FSINFO

Field	Description
Total Clusters	The total number of clusters on the volume in hexadecimal.
Free Clusters	The number of unused clusters on the volume in hexadecimal.
Total Reserved	The total number of clusters reserved for NTFS metadata.
Bytes Per Sector	The number of bytes per sector.
Bytes Per Cluster	The number of bytes per cluster.
Bytes Per FileRecord Segment	The size of MFT file records.
Clusters Per FileRecord Segment	The number of clusters per file record segment, which is valid only if the file record size is as large as or larger than the volume cluster size.
Mft Valid Data Length	The current size of the MFT.
Mft Start Lcn	The location of the first LCN on the disk used by the MFT.
Mft2 Start Lcn	The location of the first LCN on the disk used by the MFT mirror.
Mft Zone Start	The cluster number that marks the start of the region on the disk reserved by the MFT.
Mft Zone End	The cluster number that marks the end of the region on the disk reserved by the MFT.

Using FSUTIL, you can also obtain detailed statistics on NTFS metadata and user file usage since a system was started. To view this information, type **fsutil fsinfo statistics *DriveDesignator*** at the command prompt, where *DriveDesignator* is the drive letter of the volume followed by a colon. For example, if you want to obtain information on the C drive, you'd type

```
fsutil fsinfo statistics c:
```

The output is shown in two sections. The first section of the statistics details user file and disk activity as well as the overall usage of NTFS metadata. As shown in this example, the output shows the number of reads and writes as well as the number of bytes read or written:

```
File System Type :        NTFS
UserFileReads :           28737
UserFileReadBytes :       458655232
UserDiskReads :           28518
UserFileWrites :          22402
```

```
UserFileWriteBytes :       387661568
UserDiskWrites :           23494
MetaDataReads :            3327
MetaDataReadBytes :        18976768
MetaDataDiskReads :        4553
MetaDataWrites :           11953
MetaDataWriteBytes :       59817984
MetaDataDiskWrites :       19326
```


The second section of the statistics details usage of individual NTFS metadata files. As shown in this example, the output details the number of reads and writes as well as the number of bytes read or written for each NTFS metadata file:

```
MftReads :                 2757
MftReadBytes :             16642048
MftWrites :                9590
MftWriteBytes :            48275456
Mft2Writes :               0
Mft2WriteBytes :           0
RootIndexReads :           0
RootIndexReadBytes :       0
RootIndexWrites :          0
RootIndexWriteBytes :      0
BitmapReads :              487
BitmapReadBytes :          1994752
BitmapWrites :             2108
BitmapWriteBytes :         10493952
MftBitmapReads :           3
MftBitmapReadBytes :       12288
MftBitmapWrites :          254
MftBitmapWriteBytes :      1044480
UserIndexReads :           1198
UserIndexReadBytes :       4907008
UserIndexWrites :          7332
UserIndexWriteBytes :      32956416
LogFileReads :             6
LogFileReadBytes :         24576
LogFileWrites :            21983
LogFileWriteBytes :        157179904
```

Advanced NTFS Features

NTFS has many advanced features that administrators should know about and understand. These features include the following:

- Hard links
- Data streams
- Change journals

- Object identifiers
- Reparse points
- Remote storage
- Sparse files

Each of these features is discussed in the sections that follow.

Hard Links

Every file created on a volume has a hard link. The hard link is the directory entry for the file and it is what allows the operating system to find files within folders. On NTFS volumes, files can have multiple hard links. This allows a single file to appear in the same directory with multiple names or to appear in multiple directories with the same name or different names. As with file copies, applications can open a file using any of the hard links you've created and modify the file. If you use another hard link to open the file in another application, the application can detect the changes.

Wondering why you'd want to use hard links? Hard links are useful when you want the same file to appear in several locations. For example, you might want a document to appear in a folder of a network share that is available to all users but have an application that requires the document to be in another directory so that it can be read and processed on a daily basis. Rather than moving the file to the application directory and giving every user in the company access to this protected directory, you decide to create a hard link to the document so that it can be accessed separately by both users and the application.

Regardless of how many hard links a file has, however, the related directory entries all point to the single file that exists in one location on the volume—and this is how hard links differ from copies. With a copy of a file, the file data exists in multiple locations. With a hard link, the file appears in multiple locations but exists in only one location. Thus, if you modify a file using one of its hard links and save, and then someone opens the file using a different hard link, the changes are shown.

> **Note** Hard links have advantages and disadvantages. Hard links are not meant for environments where multiple users can modify a file simultaneously. If Sandra opens a file using one hard link and is working on the file at the same time Bob is working on the file, there can be problems if they both try to save changes. Although this is a disadvantage of hard links, the really big advantage of hard links shouldn't be overlooked: If a file has multiple hard links, the file will not be deleted from the volume until all hard links are deleted. This means that if someone were to accidentally delete a file that had multiple hard links, the file wouldn't actually be deleted. Instead, only the affected hard link would be deleted and any other hard links and the file itself would remain.

Because there is only one physical copy of a file with multiple hard links, the hard links do not have separate security descriptors. Only the source file has security descriptors. Thus, if you were to change the access permissions of a file using any of its hard links, you would actually change the security of the source file and all hard links that point to this file would have these security settings.

You can create hard links by using the FSUTIL HARDLINK command. Use the following syntax:


```
fsutil hardlink create NewFilePath CurrentFilePath
```

where *NewFilePath* is the file path for the hard link you want to create and *CurrentFilePath* is the name of the existing file to which you are linking. For example, if the file ChangeLog.doc is found in the file path C:\CorpDocs and you want to create a new hard link to this file with the file path C:\UserData\Logs\CurrentLog.doc, you would type

```
fsutil hardlink create C:\UserData\Logs\CurrentLog.doc C:\CorpDocs\ChangeLog.doc
```

Hard links can be created only on NTFS volumes, and you cannot create a hard link on one volume that refers to another volume. Following this, you couldn't create a hard link to the D drive for a file created on the C drive.

Data Streams

Every file created on a volume has a data stream associated with it. A data stream is a sequence of bytes that contains the contents of the file. The main data stream for a file is unnamed and is visible to all file systems. On NTFS volumes, files can also have named data streams associated with them. Named data streams contain additional information about a file, such as custom properties or summary details. This allows you to associate additional information with a file but still be able to manage the file as a single unit.

Once you create a named data stream and associate it with a file, any applications that know how to work with named data streams can access the streams by their name and read the additional details. Many applications support named data streams, including Microsoft Office, Adobe Acrobat, and other productivity applications. This is how you can set summary properties for a Microsoft Word document, such as Title, Subject, and Author, and save that information with the file. In fact, if you were to right-click any file on an NTFS volume and select Properties and then click the Summary tab, you can view or set this same information as shown in Figure 20-4.

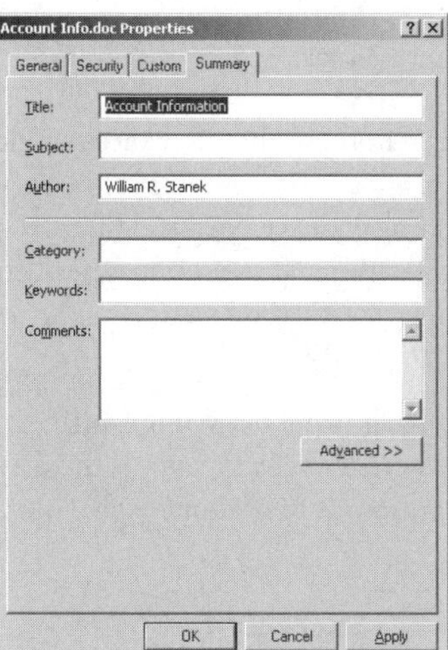

Figure 20-4. Information entered in the Summary tab is saved to a named data stream.

Generally speaking, the named data streams associated with a file are used to set the names of its property tabs and to populate the fields of those tabs. This is how some document types can have other tabs associated with them and how the Windows operating system can store a thumbnail image within an NTFS file containing an image.

The most important thing to know about streams is that they aren't supported on FAT. If you move or copy a file containing named streams to a FAT volume, you will see the warning prompt labeled "Confirm Stream Loss" telling you the file has additional information associated with it and asking you to confirm that it's okay that the file is saved without this information. If you click Yes, only the contents of the file are copied or moved to the FAT volume—and not the contents of the associated data streams. If you click No, the copy or save operation is canceled.

Change Journals

In Windows Server 2003, an NTFS volume can use an update sequence number (USN) change journal. A change journal provides a complete log of all changes made to the volume. It records additions, deletions, and modifications regardless of who made them or how the additions, deletions, and modifications occurred. As with system logs, the change log is persistent, so it isn't reset if you shut down and restart the operating system. The operating system writes records to the NTFS change log when an NTFS checkpoint occurs. The checkpoint tells the operating system to write changes that would allow NTFS to recover from failure to a particular point in time.

The change journal is enabled when you install any of the following services:

- File Replication Service
- Indexing Service

- Remote Installation Services (RIS)
- Remote Storage

Domain controllers and any other computer in the domain that uses these services rely heavily on the change journal. The change journal allows these services to be very efficient at determining when files, folders, and other NTFS objects have been modified. Rather than checking time stamps and registering for file notifications, these services perform direct lookups in the change journal to determine all the modifications made to a set of files. Not only is this faster, it uses system resources more efficiently as well.

You can gather summary statistics about the change journal by typing **fsutil usn queryjournal *DriveDesignator*** at the command prompt, where *DriveDesignator* is the drive letter of the volume followed by a colon. For example, if you want to obtain change journal statistics on the C drive, you'd type

```
fsutil usn queryjournal c:
```

The output is similar to the following:

```
Usn Journal ID    :  0x01c2ed7bd1b73670
First Usn         :  0x000000001b700000
Next Usn          :  0x00000000237ceb40
Lowest Valid Usn  :  0x0000000000000000
Max Usn           :  0x00000fffffff0000
Maximum Size      :  0x0000000008000000
Allocation Delta  :  0x0000000000100000
```

The details show the following information:

- **Usn Journal ID** The unique identifier of the change journal.
- **First Usn** The first USN in the change journal.
- **Next Usn** The next USN that can be written to the change journal.
- **Lowest Valid Usn** The lowest valid USN that can be written to the change journal.
- **Max Usn** The highest USN that can be assigned.
- **Maximum Size** The maximum size in bytes that the change journal can use. If the change journal exceeds this value, older entries are overwritten.
- **Allocation Delta** The size in bytes of memory allocation that is added to the end and removed from the beginning of the change journal when it becomes full.

Individual records written to the change journal look like this:

```
File Ref#         :   0x18e90000000018e9
ParentFile Ref#   :   0x17c00000000017c0
Usn               :   0x0000000000000000
SecurityId        :   0x00000119
Reason            :   0x00000000
Name (024)        :   ocmanage.dll
```

The most important information here is the name of the affected file and the security identifier of the object that made the change. You can get the most recent change journal entry for a file by typing **fsutil usn readdata *FilePath***, where *FilePath* is the name of the file for which you want to retrieve change information. For example, if you want to obtain the most recent change journal information on a file with the path C:\DomainComputers.txt, you'd type

```
fsutil usn readdata c:\domaincomputers.txt
```

The output is similar to the following:

```
Major Version    :   0x2
Minor Version    :   0x0
FileRef#         :   0x000800000001c306
Parent FileRef#  :   0x0005000000000005
Usn              :   0x00000000237cf7f0
Time Stamp       :   0x0000000000000000
Reason           :   0x0
Source Info      :   0x0
Security Id      :   0x45e
File Attributes  :   0x20
File Name Length :   0x26
File Name Offset :   0x3c
FileName         :   domaincomputers.txt
```

This data shows the file's reference number in the root file index and that of its parent. It also shows the current USN associated with the file and the file attributes flag. The File Name Length element shows the total length in characters of the file's long and short file names together. This particular file has a file name length of 38 (0 × 26). That's because the file name has more than eight characters followed by a dot and a three-letter extension. This means the file is represented by NTFS using long and short file names. The long file name is domaincomputers.txt. This is followed by an offset pointer that indicates where the short file name, domain~1.txt, can be looked up, which is where the total file name length of 38 characters comes from.

> **Tip** You can examine a file's short file name by typing **dir /x *FilePath*** at the command prompt, where *FilePath* is the path to the file you want to examine, such as: **dir /x c:\domaincomputers.txt**.

Object Identifiers

Another feature of NTFS is the ability to use object identifiers. Object identifiers are 16 bytes in length and are unique on a per-volume basis. Any file that has an object identifier also has the following:

- Birth volume identifier (BirthVolumeID), which is the object identifier for the volume in which the file was originally created

- Birth object identifier (BirthObjectID), which is the object identifier assigned to the file when it was created
- Domain identifier (DomainID), which is the object identifier for the domain in which the file was created

These values are also 16 bytes in length. If a file is moved within a volume or moved to a new volume, it is assigned a new object identifier, but information about the original object identifier assigned when the object was created can be retained using the birth object identifier.

Object identifiers are used by the File Replication Service (FRS) and the Distributed Link Tracking (DLT) Client service to uniquely identify files and the volumes with which they are associated. FRS uses object identifiers to locate files for replication. The DLT Client service uses object identifiers to track linked files that are moved within an NTFS volume, to another NTFS volume on the same computer, or to an NTFS volume on another computer.

Any file used by FRS or the DLT Client service has an object identifier field set containing values for the object ID, birth volume ID, birth object ID, and domain ID. The actual field set looks like this:

```
Object ID :         52eac013e3d34445334345453533ab3d
BirthVolume ID :    a23bc3243a5a3452d32424332c32343d
BirthObject ID :    52eac013e3d34445334345453533ab3d
Domain ID :         00000000000000000000000000000000
```

Here, the file has a specific object ID, birth volume ID, and birth object ID. The domain ID isn't assigned, however, because this is not currently used. You can tell that the file is used by the DLT Client service because the birth volume ID and birth object ID have been assigned and these identifiers are used only by this service. Because the birth volume ID and birth object ID remain the same even if a file is moved, the DLT Client service uses these identifiers to find files no matter where they have been moved.

In contrast, FRS uses only the object ID, so the object identifier field set for a file used by FRS looks like this:

```
Object ID :         52eac013e3d34445334345453533ab3d
BirthVolume ID :    00000000000000000000000000000000
BirthObject ID :    00000000000000000000000000000000
Domain ID :         00000000000000000000000000000000
```

If you are trying to determine whether a file is used by FRS or the DLT Client service, you could use the FSUTIL OBJECTID command to see if the file has an object identifier field set. Type **fsutil objectid query *FilePath*** at the command prompt, where *FilePath* is the path to the file or folder you want to examine. If the file has an object identifier field set, it is displayed. If a file doesn't have an object identifier field set, an error message is displayed stating "The specified file has no object ID."

Reparse Points

On NTFS volumes, a file or folder can contain a reparse point. Reparse points are file system objects with special attribute tags that are used to extend the functionality in the I/O subsystem. When a program sets a reparse point, it stores an attribute tag as well as a data segment. The attribute tag identifies the purpose of the reparse point and details how the reparse point is to be used. The data segment provides any additional data needed during reparsing.

Reparse points are used for directory junction points and volume mount points. Directory junctions enable you to create a single local namespace using local folders, local volumes, and network shares. Mount points enable you to mount a local volume to an empty NTFS folder. Both directory junction points and volume mount points use reparse points to mark NTFS folders with surrogate names.

When a file or folder containing a reparse point used for a directory junction point or a volume mount point is read, the reparse point causes the pathname to be reparsed and a surrogate name to be substituted for the original name. For example, if you were to create a mount point with the file path C:\Data that is used to mount a hard disk drive, the reparse point is triggered whenever the file system opens C:\Data and points the file system to the volume you've mounted in that folder. The actual attribute tag and data for the reparse point would look similar to the following:

```
Reparse Tag Value :  0xa0000003
Tag value: Microsoft
Tag value: Name Surrogate
Tag value: Mount Point
Substitute Name offset:    0
Substitute Name length:    98
Print Name offset:        100
Print Name Length:        0
Substitute Name:          \??\Volume{3796c3c1-5106-11d7-911c-806d6172696f}\

Reparse Data Length: 0x0000006e
Reparse Data:
0000:  00 00 62 00 64 00 00 00  5c 00 3f 00 3f 00 5c 00  ..b.d...\.?.?.\.
0010:  56 00 6f 00 6c 00 75 00  6d 00 65 00 7b 00 33 00  V.o.l.u.m.e.{.3.
0020:  37 00 39 00 36 00 63 00  33 00 63 00 31 00 2d 00  7.9.6.c.3.c.1.-.
0030:  35 00 31 00 30 00 36 00  2d 00 31 00 31 00 64 00  5.1.0.6.-.1.1.d.
0040:  37 00 2d 00 39 00 31 00  31 00 63 00 2d 00 38 00  7.-.9.1.1.c.-.8.
0050:  30 00 36 00 64 00 36 00  31 00 37 00 32 00 36 00  0.6.d.6.1.7.2.6.
0060:  39 00 36 00 66 00 7d 00  5c 00 00 00 00 00        9.6.f.}.\.....
```

The reparse attribute tag is defined by the first series of values, which identifies the reparse point as a Microsoft Name Surrogate Mount Point and specifies the surrogate name to be substituted for the original name. The reparse data follows the attribute tag values and in this case provides the fully expressed surrogate name.

> **Tip** Examine reparse points
> Using the FSUTIL REPARSEPOINT command, you can examine reparse information associated with a file or folder. Type **fsutil reparsepoint query *FilePath*** at the command prompt, where *FilePath* is the path to the file or folder you want to examine.

Reparse points are also used by file system filter drivers to mark files so they are used with that driver. When NTFS opens a file associated with a file system filter driver, it locates the driver and uses the filter to process the file as directed by the reparse information. Reparse points are used in this way to implement Remote Storage, which is discussed in the next section.

Remote Storage

Remote Storage is Microsoft's implementation of Hierarchical Storage Management (HSM). By using Remote Storage, you can define a set of rules that allow infrequently used files to be moved automatically and transparently to long-term storage on tape or other media yet still be accessible to users. How this works is that Remote Storage moves the data for a file that meets your rule set to long-term storage and replaces the file with a stub file that contains a reparse point. When a file or folder containing this reparse point is read, the reparse point causes the pathname to be reparsed, and the actual location of the file in long-term storage is substituted for the original file path. This allows NTFS to retrieve the file from long-term storage.

To users, the retrieval process is fairly transparent. They simply access a file at its regular location on a disk or shared folder and Windows handles the task of retrieving the file from long-term storage. Because retrieval from tape storage is slower than from disk, the user will see a dialog box specifying that the file is being recalled from Remote Storage and asking the user to wait.

With the cheap price of hard disk drives today, Remote Storage isn't used as frequently as it once was. Still, it is worth consideration if you have already made an investment in a storage system, such as an autoloader tape system or an optical jukebox, that uses magneto optical disks. What Remote Storage allows you to do is to extend a disk-based volume onto the storage system. Say, for instance, you have a 60-GB disk-based volume and an autoloader tape system that can automatically mount any of its 16 tapes into one of the available tape drives. If each tape has a 100-GB capacity, as with AIT-3 tapes (uncompressed), you would have about 1600 GB of tape storage.

When you extend the volume onto the available tape storage space using Remote Storage, the total space available appears to be about 1660 GB. When users write data to the volume, the data is written first to the disk area, and then as the drive spaces fill, older files are moved to tape storage. Very handy, if users don't mind the delays they might encounter when trying to access files that have been moved to tape.

Sparse Files

Often scientific or other data collected through sampling is stored in large files that are primarily empty except for sparsely populated sections that contain the actual data. For example, a broad-spectrum signal recorded digitally from space might have only several minutes of audio for each hour of actual recording. In this case, a multiple-gigabyte audio file such as the one depicted in Figure 20-5 might have only a few gigabytes of meaningful information. Because there are large sections of empty space and limited areas of meaningful data, the file is said to be sparsely populated and can also be referred to as a sparse file.

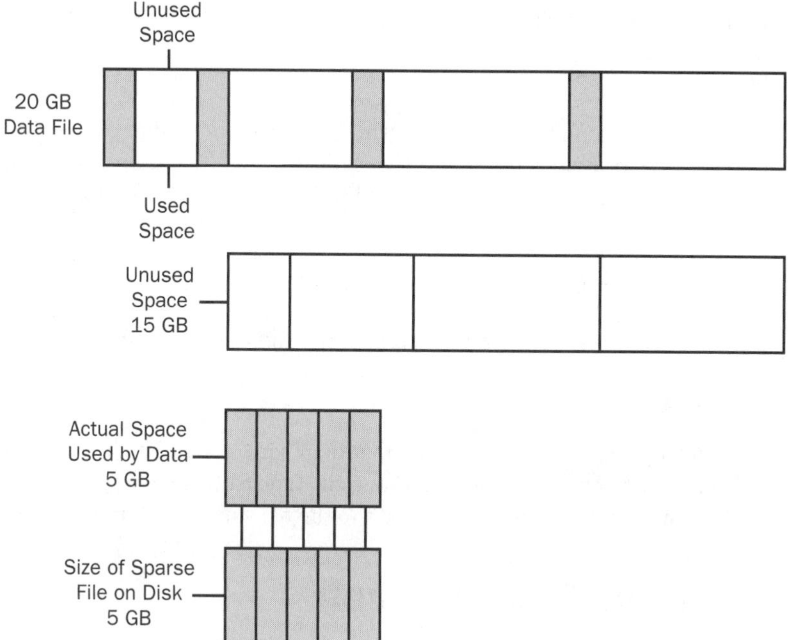

Figure 20-5. Using sparse files.

Stored normally, the file would use 20 GB of space on the volume. If you mark the file as sparse, however, NTFS allocates space only for actual data and marks empty space as nonallocated. In other words, any meaningful or nonzero data is marked as allocated and written to disk, and any data composed of zeros is marked as nonallocated and is not explicitly written to disk. In this example, this means the file uses only 5 GB of space, which is marked as allocated, and has nonallocated space of 15 GB.

For nonallocated space, NTFS records only information about how much nonallocated space there is, and when you try to read data in this space, it returns zeros. This allows NTFS to store the file in the smallest amount of disk space possible while still being able to reconstruct the file's allocated and nonallocated space.

In theory, all this works great, but it is up to the actual program working with the sparse file to determine which data is meaningful and which isn't. Programs do this by explicitly specifying the data for which space should be allocated. In Windows Server 2003, several services use sparse files. One of these is the Indexing Service, which stores its catalogs as sparse files.

Using the FSUTIL SPARSE command, you can easily determine whether a file has the sparse attribute set. Type **fsutil sparse queryflag *FilePath*** at the command prompt, where *FilePath* is the path to the file you want to examine, such as


```
fsutil sparse queryflag c:\data\catalog.wci\00010002.ci
```

If the file has the sparse attribute, this command returns

```
This file is set as sparse
```

You can examine sparse files to determine where the byte ranges that contain meaningful (nonzero) data are located by using FSUTIL SPARSE as well. Type **fsutil sparse queryrange *FilePath*** at the command prompt, where *FilePath* is the path to the file you want to examine, such as

```
fsutil sparse queryrange c:\data\catalog.wci\00010002.ci
```

The output is the byte ranges of meaningful data within the file, such as

```
sparse range [0] [28672]
```

In this particular case, the output specifies that there's meaningful data at the start of the file to byte 28672. You can mark files as sparse as well. Type **fsutil sparse setflag *FilePath*** at the command prompt, where *FilePath* is the path to the file you want to mark as sparse.

Using File-Based Compression

File-based compression allows you to reduce the number of bits and bytes in files so that they use less space on a disk. The Windows operating system supports two types of compression: NTFS compression, which is a built-in feature of NTFS, and compressed (zipped) folders, which is an additional feature of Windows available on both FAT and NTFS volumes.

NTFS Compression

Windows allows you to enable compression when you format a volume using NTFS. When a drive is compressed, all files and folders stored on the drive are automatically compressed when they are created. This compression is transparent to users, who can open and work with compressed files and folders just as they do with regular files and folders. Behind the scenes, Windows decompresses the file or folder when it is opened and compresses it again when it is closed. Although this can decrease a computer's performance, it saves space on the disk because compressed files and folders use less space.

You can turn on compression after formatting volumes as well, or if desired turn on compression only for specific files and folders. Once you compress a folder, any new files added or copied to the folder are compressed automatically and they remain compressed even if you later move them to an uncompressed folder on an NTFS volume.

Moving uncompressed files to compressed folders affects their compression attribute as well. If you move an uncompressed file from a different drive to a compressed drive or folder, the file is compressed. However, if you move an uncompressed file to a compressed folder on the same NTFS drive, the file isn't compressed. Finally, if you move a compressed file to a FAT16 or FAT32 volume, the file is uncompressed because FAT16 and FAT32 volumes do not support compression.

To compress or uncompress a drive, follow these steps:

1. Right-click the drive that you want to compress or uncompress in Windows Explorer or in the Disk Management Volume List view, and then select Properties. This displays the disk's Properties dialog box, as shown in Figure 20-6.

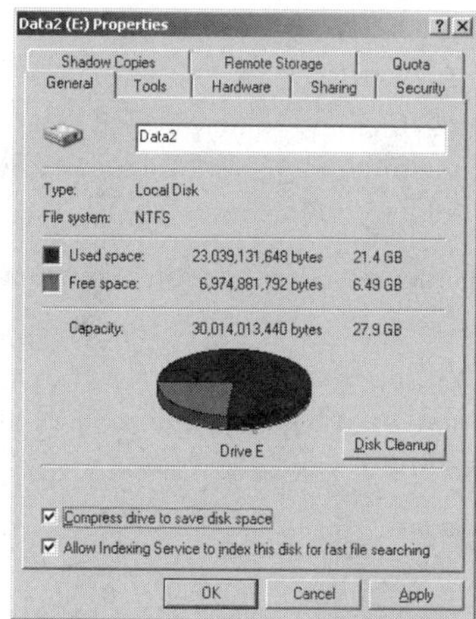

Figure 20-6. You can compress entire volumes or perform selective compression for specific files and folders.

2. Select or clear Compress Drive To Save Disk Space as appropriate. When you click OK, the Confirm Attribute Changes dialog box shown in Figure 20-7 is displayed.

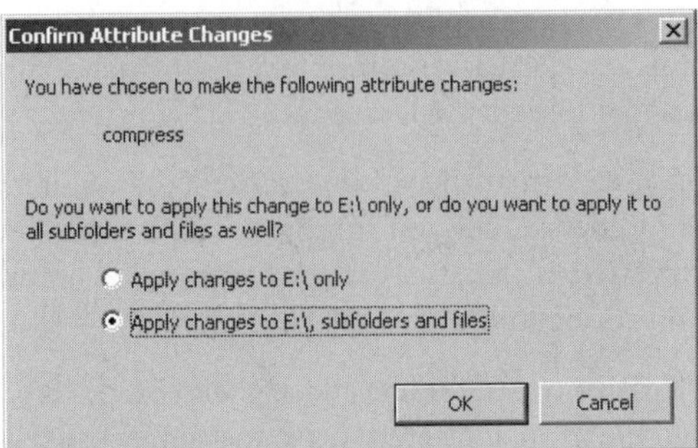

Figure 20-7. Choose a compression option.

3 If you want to apply changes only to the root folder of the disk, select Apply Changes To *X* Only. Otherwise, accept the default, which will compress the entire contents of the disk. Click OK.

> **Caution** Although Windows Server 2003 will let you compress system volumes, this is not recommended because the operating system will need to decompress and compress system files each time they are opened, which can seriously impact server performance. Additionally, you can't use compression and encryption together. You can use one feature or the other, but not both.

You can selectively compress and uncompress files and folders as well. The advantage here is that this affects only a part of a disk, such as a folder and its subfolders, rather than the entire disk. To compress or uncompress a file or folder, follow these steps:

1 In Windows Explorer, right-click the file or folder that you want to compress or uncompress, and then select Properties.

2 In the General tab of the related Properties dialog box, click Advanced. This displays the Advanced Attributes dialog box shown in Figure 20-8. Select or clear Compress Contents To Save Disk Space as appropriate. Click OK twice.

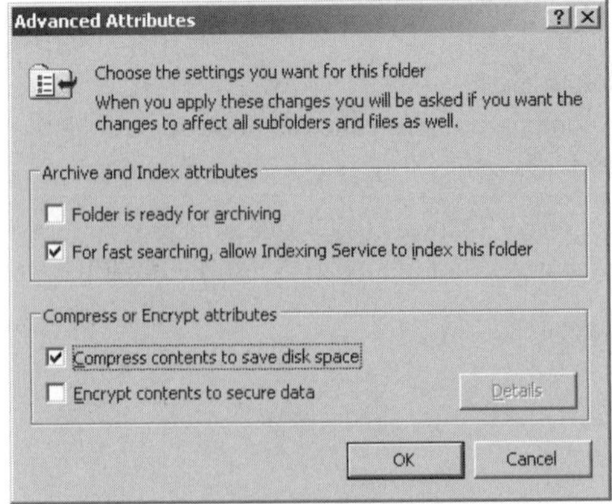

Figure 20-8. Use the Advanced Attributes dialog box to compress the file or folder.

3 If you are changing the compression attributes of a folder with subfolders, the Confirm Attribute Changes dialog box is displayed. If you want to apply the changes only to the files in the folder and not files in subfolders of the folder, select Apply Changes To *X* Only. Otherwise, accept the default, which will apply the changes to the folder, its subfolders, and files. Click OK.

Windows Server 2003 also provides command-line utilities for compressing and uncompressing your data. The compression utility is called Compact (Compact.exe). The decompression utility is called Expand (Expand.exe).

Compressed (Zipped) Folders

Compressed (zipped) folders are another option for compressing files and folders. When you compress data using this technique, you use Zip compression technology to reduce the number of bits and bytes in files and folders so that they use less space on a disk. Compressed (zipped) folders are identified with a zipper on the folder icon and are saved with the .zip file extension.

> **Note** At the time of this writing, compressed (zipped) folders were not available on 64-bit editions of Windows Server 2003. Further, if you install a Zip utility, the compressed folder icon for this utility might be used and some of the built-in compressed (zipped) folder features can change.

Compressed (zipped) folders have several advantages over NTFS compression. Because zip technology is an extension of the operating system rather than the file system, compressed (zipped) folders can be used on both FAT and NTFS volumes. Zipped folders can be password protected to safeguard their contents and can be sent by e-mail. They can also be transferred using File Transfer Protocol (FTP), Hypertext Transfer Protocol (HTTP), or other protocols. An added benefit of zipped folders is that some programs can be run directly from compressed folders without having to be decompressed. You can also open files directly from zipped folders.

You can create a zipped folder by selecting a file, folder, or a group of files and folders in Windows Explorer, right-clicking, pointing to Send To, and clicking Compressed (Zipped) Folder. The zipped folder is named automatically by using the file name of the last item selected and adding the .zip extension. If you double-click a zipped folder in Windows Explorer, you can access and work with its contents. As shown in Figure 20-9, the zipped folder's contents are listed according to file name, type, and date. The file information also shows the packed file size, the original file size, and the compression ratio. Double-clicking a program in a zipped folder runs it (as long as it doesn't require access to other files). Double-clicking a file in a zipped folder opens it for viewing or editing.

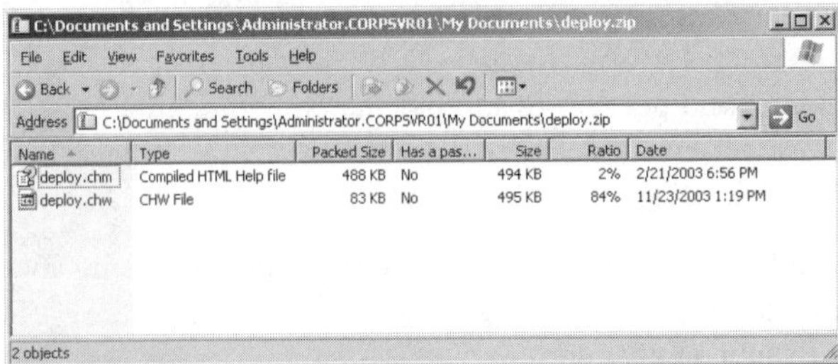

Figure 20-9. Compressed (zipped) folders can be accessed and used like other folders.

While you're working with a zipped folder, you can perform tasks similar to those you can with regular folders. You can do the following:

- Add other files, programs, or folders to the zipped folder by dragging them to it.
- Copy a file in the zipped folder and paste it into a different folder.
- Remove a file from the zipped folder using CUT so that you can paste it into a different folder.
- Delete a file or folder by selecting it and clicking Delete.

You also have the option to perform additional tasks, which are unique to zipped folders. You can click File, Extract All to start the Extraction Wizard, which can be used to extract all the files in the zipped folder and copy them to a new location. You can click File, Add A Password to add a password to the zipped folder to control access to it.

Managing Disk Quotas

Even with the large disk drives available today, you'll often find that hard disk space is at a premium, and this is where disk quotas come in handy. Disk quotas are a built-in feature of NTFS that help you manage and limit disk space usage.

How Quota Management Works

Using disk quotas, you can monitor and control the amount of disk space people who access the network can use. Without quota management it is hard to monitor the amount of space being used by individual users and even harder to control the total amount of space they can use. I refer to monitoring and controlling separately because there's a very important difference between monitoring disk space usage and controlling it—and the disk quota system allows you to perform these tasks separately or together. You can, in fact, do the following:

- Configure the disk quota system to monitor disk space usage only, allowing administrators to check disk space usage manually

- Configure the disk quota system to monitor disk space usage and generate warnings when users exceed predefined usage levels
- Configure the disk quota system to monitor disk space usage, generate warnings when users exceed predefined usage levels, and enforce the limits by denying disk space to users who exceed the quota limit

Your organization's culture will probably play a major role in the disk quota technique you use. In some organizations the culture is such that it is acceptable to monitor space usage and periodically notify users that they are over recommended limits, but it wouldn't be well received if administrators enforced controls that limited disk space usage to specific amounts. In other organizations, especially larger organizations where there might be hundreds or thousands of employees on the network, it can make sense to have some controls in place and users might be more understanding of specific controls. Controls at some point become a matter of necessity to help ensure that the administrative staff can keep up with the disk space needs of the organization.

Disk quotas are configured on a per-volume basis. When you enable disk quotas, all users who store data on a volume will be affected by the quota. You can set exceptions for individual users as well that either set new limits or remove the limits all together. As users create files and folders on a volume, an ownership flag is applied that says that this particular user owns the file or folder. Thus, if a user creates a file or folder on a volume that user is the owner of, the file or folder and the space used counts toward the user's quota limit. However, because each volume is managed separately, there is no way to set a specific limit for all volumes on a server or across the enterprise.

> **Note** For NTFS compressed files and sparse files, the space usage reported can reflect total space of files rather than the actual space the files use. This happens because the quota system reads the total space used by the file rather than its reduced file size.

Ownership of files and folders can change in several scenarios. If a user creates a copy of a file owned by someone else, the copy is owned by that user. This occurs because a file is created when the copy is made. File and folder ownership can also change when files are restored from backup. This can happen if you restore the files to a volume other than the one the files were created on and copy the files over to the original volume. Here, during the copy operation, the administrator becomes the owner of the files. A workaround for this is to restore files and folders to a different location on the same volume and then move the files and folders rather than copying them. When you move files and folders from one location to another on the same volume, the original ownership information is retained.

Administrators can be assigned as the owner of files in other ways as well, such as when they install the operating system or application software. To ensure that administrators can always install programs, restore data, and perform other administrative tasks, members of the

Administrators group don't have a quota limit as a general rule. This is true even when you enforce disk quotas for all users. In fact, for the Administrators group, the only type of quota you can set is a warning level that warns administrators when they've used more than a set amount of space on a volume. When you think about it, this makes a lot of sense—you don't want to get into a situation where administrators can't recover the system because of space limitations.

That said, you can apply quotas to individual users—even those who are members of the Administrators group. You do this by creating a separate quota entry for each user. The only account that cannot be restricted in this way is the built-in Administrator account. If you try to set a limit on the Administrator account, the limit is not applied.

Finally, it is important to note that all space used on a volume counts toward the disk quota—even space used in the Recycle Bin. Thus, if a user who is over the limit deletes files to get under the limit, the disk quota might still give warnings or if quotas are enforced, the user still might not be able to write files to the volume. To resolve this issue, the user would need to delete files and then empty the Recycle Bin.

Configuring Disk Quotas

By default, disk quotas are disabled. If you want to use disk quotas, you must enable quota management for each volume on which you want to use disk quotas. You can enable disk quotas on any NTFS volume that has a drive letter or a mount point. Before you configure disk quotas, think carefully about the limit and warning level. Set values that make the most sense given the number of users that store data on the volume and the size of the volume. For optimal performance of the volume, you won't want to get in a situation where all or nearly all of the disk space is allocated. For optimal user happiness, you want to ensure the warning and limit levels are adequate so the average user can store the necessary data to perform job duties. Quota limits and warning levels aren't one size fits all either. Engineers and graphic designers can have very different space needs than a typical user. In the best situations you'll have configured network shares so that different groups of users have access to different volumes, and these volumes should be sized to meet the typical requirements of a particular group.

In some organizations, I've seen administrators set very low quota limits and warning levels on data shares. The idea behind this was that the administrators wanted users to save most of their data on their workstations and only put files that needed to be shared on the data shares. I would discourage this for two reasons. Low quota limits and warning levels frustrate users—you don't want frustrated users; you want happy users. Second, you should be encouraging users to store more of their important files on central file servers, not less. Central file servers should be a part of regular enterprise-wide backup routines because corporate servers and backing up data safeguards it from loss. In addition, with the Volume Shadow Copy service, shadow copies of files on shared folders can be created automatically, allowing users to perform point-in-time file recovery without needing help from administrators.

To enable disk quotas on an NTFS volume, follow these steps:

1. In Computer Management, expand Storage, and then select Disk Management. In the details pane, right-click the volume on which you want to enable quotas, and then select Properties.
2. Choose the Quota tab, and then choose Enable Quota Management as shown in Figure 20-10.

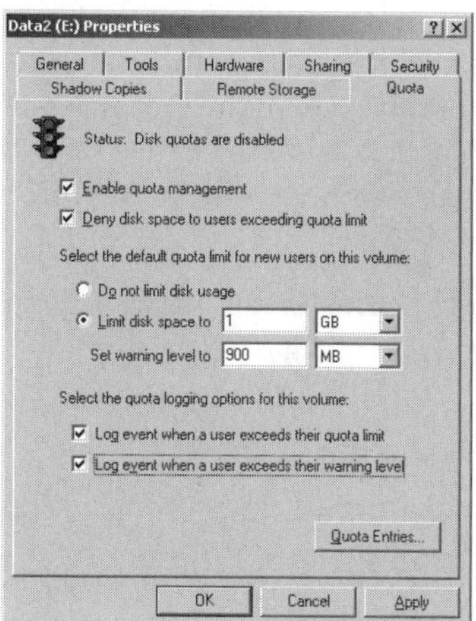

Figure 20-10. Enable quota management on the volume, and then configure the disk quota settings.

3. Define a default disk quota limit for all users by selecting Limit Disk Space To and then using the fields provided to set a limit in KB, MB, GB, TB, PB, or EB. Afterward, use the Set Warning Level To field to set the default warning limit. In most cases, you'll want the disk quota warning limit to be 90 to 95 percent of the disk quota limit. This should give good separation between when warnings occur and when the limit is reached.
4. To prevent users from going over the disk quota limit, select Deny Disk Space To Users Exceeding Quota Limit. This sets a physical limitation for users that will prevent them from writing to the volume once the limit is reached.
5. NTFS sends warnings to users when they reach a warning level or limit. To ensure that you have a record of these warnings, you can configure quota logging options. Select the Log Event options as appropriate.
6. Click OK. If the quota system isn't currently enabled, you'll see a prompt asking you to enable the quota system. Click OK to allow Windows Server 2003 to rescan the volume and update the disk usage statistics. Keep in mind that actions might be taken against users who exceed the current limit or warning levels, which can include preventing additional writing to the volume, notifying users the next time they try to access the volume that they've exceeded a warning level or have reached a limit, and logging applicable events in the Application log.

Customizing Quota Entries for Individual Users

Once you enable disk quotas, the configuration is set for and applies to all users who store data on the volume. The only exception, as noted previously, is for members of the Administrators group. The default disk quotas don't apply to these users. If you want to set a specific quota limit or warning level for an administrator, you can do this by creating a custom quota entry for that particular user account. You can also create custom quota entries for users who have special needs, requirements, or limitations.

To view and work with quota entries access Disk Management, right-click the volume on which you enabled quotas, and then select Properties. In the Properties dialog box for the disk, select the Quota tab, and then click Quota Entries. You'll then see a list of quota entries for everyone who has ever stored data on the volume, as shown in Figure 20-11. The entries show the following information:

- **Status** The status of the disk entries. Normal status is OK. If a user has reached a warning level, the status is Warning. If a user is at or above the quota limit, the status is Above Limit.
- **Name** The display name of the user account.
- **Logon Name** The logon name and domain (if applicable).
- **Amount Used** The amount of disk space used by the user.
- **Quota Limit** The quota limit set for the user.
- **Warning Level** The warning level set for the user.
- **Percent Used** The percentage of disk space used toward the limit.

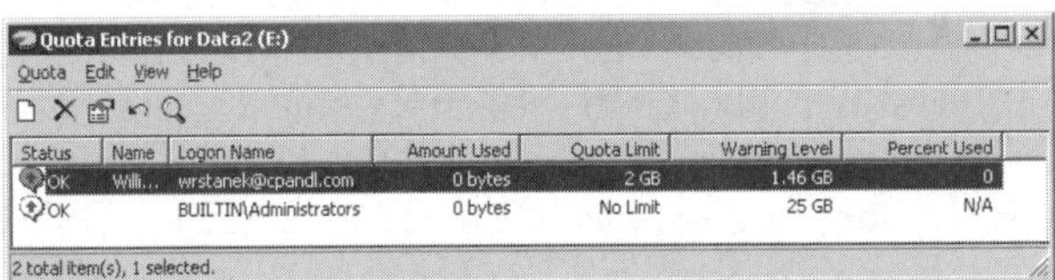

Figure 20-11. Any existing quota entries are shown.

Quota entries get on the list in one of two ways: either automatically if a user has ever stored data on the volume or by an administrator creating a custom entry for a user. You can customize any of these entries—even the ones automatically created—by double-clicking them, which displays the Quota Settings For dialog box shown in Figure 20-12, and selecting the appropriate options either to remove the disk quota limits or set new ones.

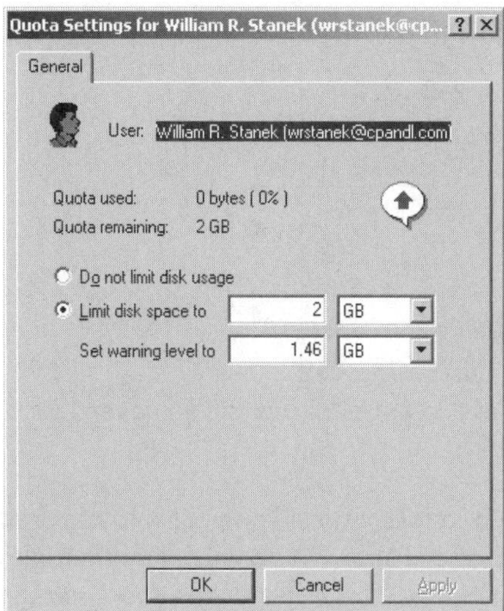

Figure 20-12. You can customize quota entries for individual users as necessary.

> **Note** You can't create quota entries for groups. The only group entry that is allowed is the one for the Administrators account, which is created automatically.

If a user doesn't have an entry in the Quota Entries For dialog box, it means that user has not yet saved files to the volume. You can still create a custom entry for the user if you want. To do this, click Quota, New Quota Entry. This displays the Select Users dialog box shown in Figure 20-13. Use this dialog box to help you find the user account you want to work with. Type the name of the user account or part of the name, and click Check Names. If multiple names match the value you entered, you'll see a list of names and will be able to choose the one you want to use. Otherwise, the name will be filled in for you, and you can click OK to display the Add New Quota Entry dialog box, which has the same options as the Quota Settings For dialog box shown in Figure 20-12.

> **Tip** **Use Locations to access user accounts from other domains**
> By default, the Select Users dialog box is set to work with users from your logon domain. If you want to add a user account from another domain, click Locations to display the Locations dialog box. Then either select the entire directory or the specific domain in which the account is located, and click OK.

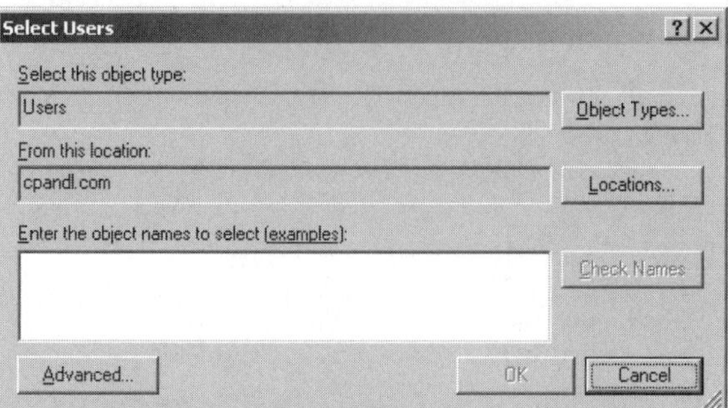

Figure 20-13. Type the name of the user account or part of the name, and click Check Names.

In the Quota Entries dialog box, there are a couple of tricks you can use to add or manage multiple quota entries at once. If you want to add identical quota entries for multiple users, you can do this by clicking Quota, New Quota Entry. This displays the Select Users dialog box. Click Advanced to display the advanced Select Users dialog box, as shown in Figure 20-14.

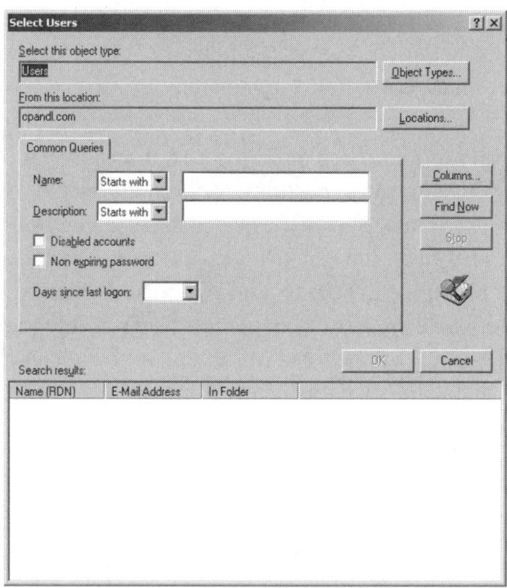

Figure 20-14. The advanced Select Users dialog box has additional options.

You can now search for users by name and description or by clicking Find Now without entering any search criteria to display a list of available users from the current location. You can select any of the users listed. Select multiple user accounts by holding down the Ctrl key and clicking each account you want to select or by holding down the Shift key, selecting the first account name, and then clicking the last account name to choose a range of accounts. Click OK twice, and then use the Add New Quota Entry dialog box to configure the quota options for all the selected users.

To manage multiple quota entries simultaneously, access the Quota Entries dialog box, then select the entries by holding down the Ctrl key and clicking each entry you want to select or by holding down the Shift key, selecting the first entry, and then clicking the last entry to choose a range of entries. Afterward, right-click one of the selected entries, and then click Properties. You'll then be able to configure quota options for all the selected entries at once.

Managing Disk Quotas After Configuration

Users are notified that they have reached a warning level or quota limit when they access the volume on which you've configured disk quotas. As an administrator, you'll want to check for quota violations periodically, and there's several ways you can do this. One way is to access Disk Management, right-click the volume that you want to check on, and then select Properties. In the Properties dialog box for the disk, select the Quota tab, and then click the Quota Entries button. You can then check the current disk usage of users and see whether there are any quota violations. You can also copy selected entries to the Clipboard by pressing Ctrl+C and then pasting them into other applications, such as Microsoft Excel, using Ctrl+V to help you create reports or lists of disk space usage.

You can check quota entries from the command line as well. Type **fsutil quota query *DriveDesignator*** at the command prompt, where *DriveDesignator* is the drive letter of the volume followed by a colon, such as D:. If disk quotas are enabled on the volume, you'll then get a summary of the disk quota settings on the volume, as follows:

```
FileSystemControlFlags    =  0x00000032
    Quotas are tracked and enforced on this volume
    Logging enable for quota limits and threshold
    The quota values are up to date

Default Quota Threshold   =  0x0000000038400000
Default Quota Limit       =  0x0000000040000000

SID Name         =   edwardh@cpandl.com
Change time      =   Sat Dec 26 23:02:44 2004
Quota Used       =   528164252
Quota Threshold  =   943718400
Quota Limit      =   1073741824

SID Name         =   williams@cpandl.com
Change time      =   Sat Dec 26 23:02:05 2004
Quota Used       =   627384965
Quota Threshold  =   943718400
Quota Limit      =   1073741824
```

In this example, disk quotas are tracked and enforced on the volume, logging is enabled for both quota limits, and the warning levels and the disk quota values are current. In addition, the default warning limit (listed as the quota threshold) is set to 900 MB (0 × 038400000 bytes) and the default quota limit is set to 1 GB (0 × 040000000 bytes).

The disk quota summary is followed by the individual disk quota entries for each user that has stored data on the volume or has a custom entry regardless of whether the user has ever written data to the volume. The entries show the following information:

- **SID Name** The logon name and domain of user accounts or the name of a built-in or well-known group that has a quota entry.
- **Change Time** The last time the quota entry was changed or updated.
- **Quota Used** The amount of space used in bytes.
- **Quota Threshold** The current warning level set for the user in bytes.
- **Quota Limit** The current quota limit set for the user in bytes.

When you configure disk quotas, you also have the option of logging two types of events in the system logs. One for when a user exceeds the quota limit and another for when a user exceeds the warning level. By default, quota violations are written to the system log once an hour, so if you checked the logs periodically, you could see events related to any users who have disk quota violations. It's much easier to check for quota violations from the command line, however. Simply type **fsutil quota violations** at the command prompt, and the FSUTIL QUOTA command will check the system and application event logs for quota violations.

> **Note** Wondering why FSUTIL QUOTA VIOLATIONS checks the system and application logs? Well, in some cases, quota violations for programs running under user accounts are logged in the application log rather than the system log. So, to ensure all quota violations are checked for, FSUTIL QUOTA VIOLATIONS checks both logs.

If there are no quota violations found, the output is similar to the following:

```
Searching in System Event Log...
Searching in Application Event Log...
No quota violations detected
```

If there are quota violations, the output shows the event information related to each violation. In the following example, a user reached the warning level (listed as the quota threshold):

```
Searching in System Event Log...
**** A user hit their quota threshold ! ****
    Event ID : 0x40040024
    EventType : Information
    Event Category : 2
    Source : Ntfs
    User: BUILTIN\Administrators
    Data: D:
Searching in Application Event Log...
```

As you can see, the output shows you the event ID, type, category, and source. It also shows the user who violated the disk quota settings and the volume on which the violation occurred.

Inside Out

You can change the notification interval for quota violations

As mentioned previously, quota violations are written to the event logs once an hour by default. You can check or change this behavior using the FSUTIL BEHAVIOR command. Keep in mind, however, that any changes you make apply to all volumes on the system that use disk quotas. To check the notification interval, type **fsutil behavior query quotanotify**. If the notification interval has been set by you or another administrator, the notification interval is shown in seconds. To set the notification interval, type **fsutil behavior set quotanotify *Interval***, where *Interval* is the notification interval you want to set expressed as the number of seconds. For example, if you want to receive less-frequent notifications, you might want to set the notification interval to 7200 seconds (2 hours), and you would do this by typing **fsutil behavior set quotanotify 7200**.

Exporting and Importing Quota Entries

If you want to use the same quotas on more than one NTFS volume, you can do this by exporting the quota entries from one volume and importing them on another volume. When you import quota entries, if there isn't a quota entry for the user already, a quota entry will be created. If a user already has a quota entry on the volume, you'll be asked if you want to overwrite it.

To export and import quota entries, access Disk Management, right-click the volume on which you want to enable quotas, and then select Properties. In the Properties dialog box for the disk, select the Quota tab, and then click the Quota Entries button. You'll then see the Quota Entries dialog box. Select Export from the Quota menu. This displays the Export Quota Settings dialog box.

Use the Save In selection list to choose the save location for the file containing the quota settings, and then set a name for the file using the File Name field. Afterward, click Save.

Next, access the Quota Entries dialog box for the drive on which you want to import settings. Select Import on the Quota menu. Then, in the Import Quota Settings dialog box, select the quota settings file that you saved previously. Click Open.

If prompted about whether you want to overwrite an existing entry, click Yes to replace an existing entry or click No to keep the existing entry. Select Do This For All Quota Entries prior to clicking Yes or No to use the same option for all existing entries.

Maintaining File System Integrity

As part of routine maintenance, you should periodically check disks for errors. The primary tool to do this is Check Disk, which is implemented in both a graphical and a command-line version.

How File System Errors Occur

File data is stored in clusters, and the Windows operating system uses a file table to determine where a file begins and on which clusters it is stored. With FAT, the file table used is called the root directory table. It defines the starting cluster of each file in the file system. This cluster has a pointer to the second cluster, and the second cluster has a pointer to the next, and so on until you get to the final cluster used by the file, which has an EOF marker. With NTFS, an MFT is used. If a file's data can't fit within a single record in this table, clusters belonging to the file are referenced using VCNs that map to starting LCNs on the disk. If a file's pointer or mapping is lost, you might not be able to access the file. Errors can also occur for pointers or mappings that relate to the file tables themselves and to the pointers or mappings for folders.

FAT tries to prevent disk integrity problems by maintaining a duplicate file allocation table that can be used to recover the primary file allocation table if it becomes corrupted. Beyond this, however, FAT doesn't do much else to ensure disk integrity. NTFS, on the other hand, has several mechanisms for preventing and correcting disk integrity problems automatically. NTFS stores a partial duplicate of the MFT, which can be used for failure recovery. NTFS also stores a persistent history of all changes made to files on the volume in a log file, and the log file can be used to recover NTFS metadata files, regular data files, and folders. What these file structure recovery mechanisms all have in common is that they are automatic and you as an administrator don't need to do anything to ensure these disk housekeeping tasks are performed. These mechanisms aren't perfect, however, and errors can occur.

The most common errors relate to the following areas:

- Internal errors in a file's structure
- Free space being marked as allocated
- Allocated space being marked as free
- Partially or improperly written security descriptors
- Unreadable disk sectors not marked as bad

Fixing File System Errors by Using Check Disk

Using Check Disk, you can check for and correct any of the common disk errors discussed previously. Check Disk works on FAT, FAT32, and NTFS volumes and primarily looks for inconsistencies in the file system and its related metadata. It locates errors by comparing the volume bitmap to the disk sectors assigned to files. For files, Check Disk looks at structural integrity, but won't check for or attempt to repair corrupted data within files that appear to be structurally intact.

Check Disk has two modes in which it can be run. It can analyze a disk, checking for errors, but not repairing them. Or it can analyze a disk and attempt to repair any errors found. New for Windows Server 2003 is that Check Disk has been optimized so that it runs faster than previous versions.

You can run the graphical version of Check Disk by using either Windows Explorer or Disk Management. Right-click the volume, and choose Properties. In the Tools tab of the Properties dialog box, click Check Now to display the Check Disk dialog box, as shown in Figure 20-15. If you want to analyze the disk but not repair errors, click Start without selecting either of the available options. If you want to check for errors and repair them, select Automatically Fix File System Errors, and click Start. You can also check for and repair bad sectors by selecting Scan For And Attempt Recovery Of Bad Sectors.

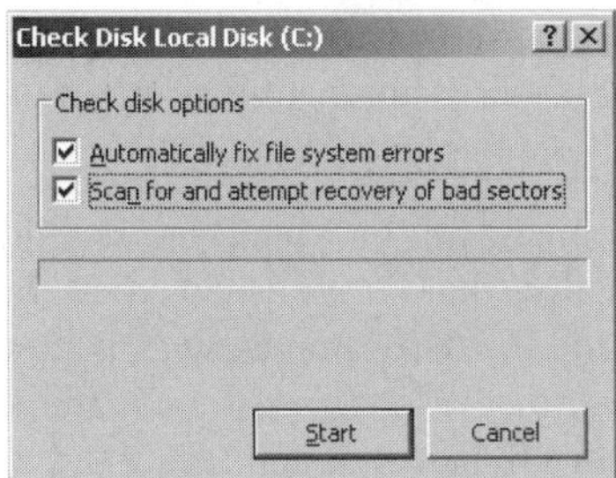

Figure 20-15. Check the disk for errors and repair them or perform analysis only.

To fix errors, Check Disk needs exclusive access to the volume. If Check Disk can't get exclusive access to files (because they have open file handles), Check Disk will prompt you, as shown in Figure 20-16. If you click Yes, Check Disk will analyze and repair the disk the next time the system is started.

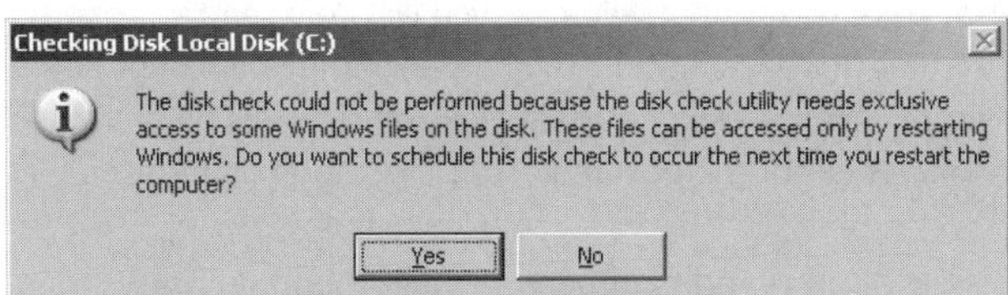

Figure 20-16. Check Disk needs exclusive access to some Windows files to fix errors.

Inside Out

Marking disks for checking on startup

Check Disk can't get exclusive access to a volume if it has open file handles. As a result, you must either use the command-line version and dismount the volume or schedule Check Disk to run the next time the system is started. When you schedule Check Disk to run, the operating system marks the disk as dirty, which means it needs to be checked and repaired. You can mark a disk as dirty using the FSUTIL DIRTY command. Type **fsutil dirty set** followed by the drive designator, such as **fsutil dirty set c:**. If you want to determine if Check Disk is set to run the next time the system is started, you can use the FSUTIL DIRTY command to do this as well. Type **fsutil dirty query** followed by the drive designator, such as **fsutil dirty query c:**.

Check Disk can also be run at the command line using ChkDsk (Chkdsk.exe). The key advantage of using the command-line version is that you get a detailed report of the analysis and repair operations as detailed in the sections of this chapter entitled "Analyzing FAT Volumes by Using ChkDsk" and "Analyzing NTFS Volumes by Using ChkDsk."

You can run ChkDsk in analysis mode at the command line by typing **chkdsk** followed by the drive designator. For example, if you want to analyze the C drive, you'd type **chkdsk c:**. To have ChkDsk analyze and repair volumes, you add the /F parameter, such as **chkdsk c: /f**. If you want to check for bad sectors and try to repair them as well, use the /R parameter (which implies /F as well, meaning ChkDsk will perform a full analysis and repair and then check and repair bad sectors).

The complete syntax for ChkDsk is as follows:

```
chkdsk [volume[[path]filename]] [/f] [/v] [/r] [/x] [/i] [/c] [/l:size]
```

Note The command-line version of Check Disk also needs exclusive access to some Windows files to fix errors. For nonsystem volumes, you will be given the opportunity to dismount the volume so that ChkDsk can run. You can also force dismount of a nonsystem volume by using the /X parameter. For system volumes, you will be prompted to schedule the analysis and repair for the next restart of the operating system.

Table 20-6 summarizes the options and parameters available and their uses.

Table 20-6. Command-Line Parameters for ChkDsk

Option/Parameter	Description
Volume	Set the volume to work with.
Filename	On FAT/FAT32, specifies files to check for fragmentation.

Table 20-6. Command-Line Parameters for ChkDsk

Option/Parameter	Description
/F	Tells ChkDsk to analyze the disk and fix any errors noted.
/C	On NTFS only, tells ChkDsk to not check for cycles within the folder structure. A cycle is a very rarely occurring type of error in which a directory contains a pointer to itself, causing an infinite loop.
/I	On NTFS only, tells ChkDsk to perform a minimum check of indexes.
/L[:*Size*]	On NTFS only, changes the transaction log file size. The default size is 4096 KB, which is sufficient most of the time.
/R	Tells ChkDsk to analyze the disk and fix any errors noted and also to check for bad sectors. Any bad sectors found are marked as bad. (/F is implied when you use this parameter.)
/V	On FAT/FAT32, lists the full path of every file on the volume. On NTFS, displays cleanup messages related to fixing file system errors or other discrepancies.
/X	Forces the volume to dismount if necessary.

Analyzing FAT Volumes by Using ChkDsk

When you run ChkDsk, you can get an analysis report. For FAT volumes, a disk analysis report looks like this:

```
The type of the file system is FAT.
Volume DATA3 created 2/19/2004 5:58 PM
Volume Serial Number is 7D11-2345
Windows is verifying files and folders...
File and folder verification is complete.
Windows has checked the file system and found no problems.

    209,489,920 bytes total disk space.
         24,576 bytes in 6 hidden files.
         12,288 bytes in 3 folders.
    200,679,936 bytes in 279 files.
      8,773,120 bytes available on disk.

          4,096 bytes in each allocation unit.
         51,145 total allocation units on disk.
          1,970 allocation units available on disk.
```

Here, ChkDsk examines each record in the file allocation table for consistency. It lists all the file and folder records in use and determines the starting cluster for each using the root directory table. It checks each file and notes any discrepancies in the output. Any clusters that were marked as in use by files or folders but that weren't actually in use are noted and during repair the clusters can be marked as available. Other discrepancies noted in the output can be fixed during repair as well.

Analyzing NTFS Volumes by Using ChkDsk

Disk analysis for NTFS volumes is performed in three stages, and ChkDsk reports its progress during each stage as shown in this sample report:

```
The type of the file system is NTFS.
Volume label is Data.

WARNING!  F parameter not specified.
Running CHKDSK in read-only mode.
CHKDSK is verifying files (stage 1 of 3)...
File verification completed.
CHKDSK is verifying indexes (stage 2 of 3)...
Index verification completed.
CHKDSK is verifying security descriptors (stage 3 of 3)...
Security descriptor verification completed.
Correcting errors in the master file table's (MFT) BITMAP attribute.
Correcting errors in the Volume Bitmap.
Windows found problems with the file system.
Run CHKDSK with the /F (fix) option to correct these.

   30009388 KB total disk space.
   25116620 KB in 44945 files.
      14456 KB in 2557 indexes.
          0 KB in bad sectors.
     114972 KB in use by the system.
      65536 KB occupied by the log file.
    4763340 KB available on disk.

    4096 bytes in each allocation unit.
       7502347 total allocation units on disk.
       1190835 allocation units available on disk.
```

During the first stage of analysis, ChkDsk verifies file structures. This means ChkDsk examines each file's record in the MFT for consistency. It lists all the file records in use and determines which clusters the file records are stored in and then compares this with the volume's cluster bitmap stored in the $Bitmap metadata file. Any discrepancies are noted in the ChkDsk output. For example, any clusters that were marked as in use by files but that weren't actually in use are noted, and during repair the clusters can be marked as available.

During the second stage of analysis, ChkDsk verifies directory structure by examining directory indexes, starting with the volume's root directory index, which is stored in the $Metadata file. ChkDsk examines index records, making sure that each index record corresponds to an actual directory on the disk and that each file that is supposed to be in a directory is in the directory. It also checks to see whether there are files that have an MFT record but that don't actually exist in any directory, and during repair these lost files can be recovered.

During the third stage of the analysis, ChkDsk verifies the consistency of security descriptors for each file and directory object on the volume using the $Secure metadata file. It does this by validating that the security descriptors work. It doesn't actually check to see if the users or groups assigned in the security descriptors exist.

Repairing Volumes and Marking Bad Sectors by Using ChkDsk

If problems are found, ChkDsk will repair them only if you've used the /F parameter. Alternately, you can use the /X or /R parameter as well, and each implies the /F parameter. If you use the /R parameter, ChkDsk will perform an additional step in the analysis and repair that involves checking each sector on the disk to make sure it can be read from and written to correctly. If it finds a bad sector, ChkDsk will mark it so data won't be written to that sector. If the sector was part of a cluster that was being used, ChkDsk will move the good data in that cluster to a new cluster. The data in the bad sector can be recovered only if there's redundant data from which to copy it. The bad sector won't be used again, so at least it won't cause problems in the future. Checking each sector on a disk is a time-intensive process—and one that you won't perform often. More typically, you'll use ChkDsk /F to check for and repair common errors.

Defragmenting Disks

As files are created, modified, and moved, fragmentation can occur both within the volume's allocation table and on the volume itself. This happens because files are written to clusters on disk as they are used. The file system uses the first clusters available when writing new data, so as you modify files, different parts of files can end up in different areas of the disk. If you delete a file, an area of the disk is made available, but it might not be big enough to store the next file that is created and as a result, part of a new file might get written to this newly freed area and part of it might get written somewhere else on the disk.

Although the file system doesn't care if the file data is on contiguous clusters or spread out across the disk, the fact that data is in different areas of the disk can slow down read/write operations. This means it will take longer than usual to open and save files. It also makes it more difficult to recover files in case of serious disk error. Windows Server 2003 provides a tool for defragmenting volumes called the Disk Defragmenter.

Fixing Fragmentation by Using Disk Defragmenter

Using Disk Defragmenter, you can check for and correct volume fragmentation problems on FAT, FAT32, and NTFS volumes. The areas checked for fragmentation include the volume, files, folders, the page file if one exists on the volume, and the MFT. Being able to check the MFT is a new feature for Windows Server 2003. Another new feature is the ability to defragment volumes with cluster sizes greater than 4 KB.

You can run the graphical version of Disk Defragmenter using either Windows Explorer or Computer Management. In Windows Explorer, right-click the volume, and choose Properties. In the Tools tab of the Properties dialog box, click Defragment Now to display the Disk Defragmenter dialog box. In Computer Management, expand Storage, and select Disk Defragmenter as shown in Figure 20-17. Select the volume you want to work with by clicking it, and then determine the level of fragmentation on the volume by clicking Analyze.

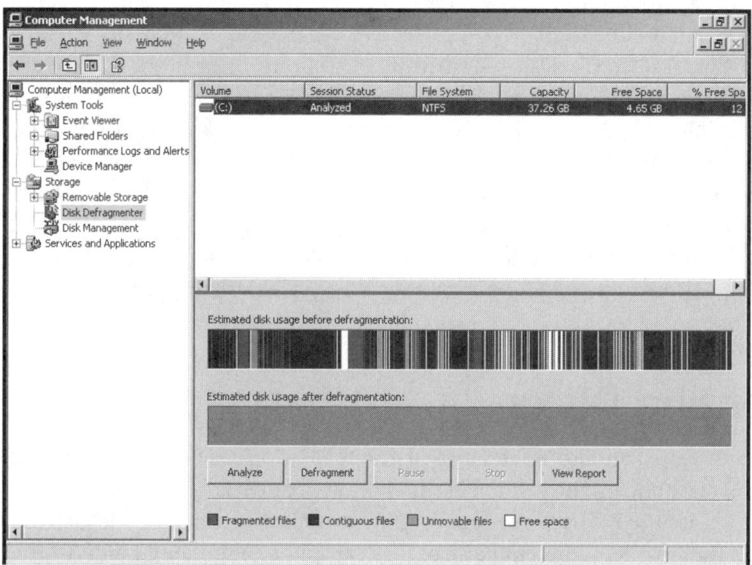

Figure 20-17. Use Disk Defragmenter to check disks for fragmentation.

If the disk is marked to be checked the next time the operating system is started, you won't be able to analyze it. Instead, you will be told that Check Disk is scheduled to run on the volume, and you must run it before you can analyze the disk. If the disk is possibly corrupt and has been marked as such, you won't be able to analyze it either. In this case, you will be told that you should run Check Disk. Otherwise, Disk Defragmenter will then analyze the disk and graphically display the current disk usage, indicating the following information:

- **Fragmented files** Files that are fragmented
- **Contiguous files** Files that are written in consecutive clusters

- **Unmovable files** Files that can't be moved, typically because they are system files, such as the page file
- **Free Space** Space that is available on the volume

When Disk Defragmenter finishes the analysis, it displays a recommendation, as shown in Figure 20-18. You will be told either that you should defragment the volume now or that the volume doesn't need to be defragmented. If you click View Report, you can view a report of the analysis, as shown in Figure 20-19. You also have the option to print or save the report. If you save the report, it is saved to a text file that can be viewed in any standard text editor.

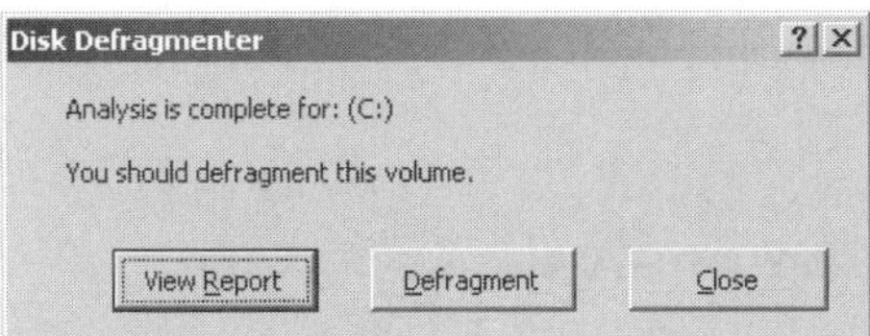

Figure 20-18. After analysis, Disk Defragmenter will recommend an action and let you view an analysis report.

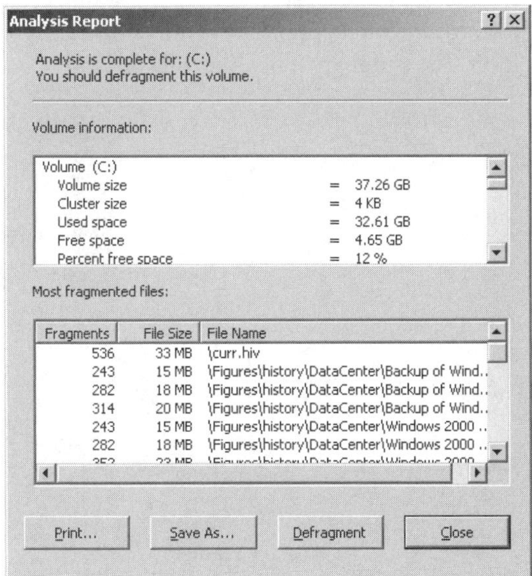

Figure 20-19. The Analysis Report dialog box allows you to view the results of running Disk Defragmenter.

After you analyze the disk, you can defragment it by clicking the Defragment button. Disk Defragmenter needs at least 15 percent free space to defragment a disk completely. Disk Defragmenter uses this space as a sorting area for file fragments. If a volume has less than 15 percent free space, Disk Defragmenter will only partially defragment it.

Disk Defragmenter can also be run at the command line using Defrag (Defrag.exe). You can run Disk Defragmenter in analysis mode at the command line by typing **defrag –a** followed by the drive designator. For example, if you want to analyze the fragmentation of the D drive, you'd type **defrag –a d:**. To analyze and then defragment a volume if defragmentation is necessary, type **defrag** followed by the drive designator, such as **defrag d:**. No parameters are necessary.

The complete syntax for Defrag is this:

```
defrag volume [-a] [-v] [-f]
```

The –V parameter is used to display detailed output and the –F parameter is used to force defragmentation even if there is low free space on the volume.

Understanding the Fragmentation Analysis

You can perform fragmentation analysis using the report generated from the graphical user interface (GUI) or the command line. Both techniques produce similar results as long as you use the –V parameter at the command line. The graphical report is in two sections: The first section provides a summary of fragmentation in all areas checked, and the second section provides information on individual file fragmentation. The command-line report shows only the summary of fragmentation. The summary looks like this:

```
Volume Apps (D:)
    Volume size                              = 55.91 GB
    Cluster size                             = 4 KB
    Used space                               = 50.18 GB
    Free space                               = 5.73 GB
    Percent free space                       = 11 %

Volume fragmentation
    Total fragmentation                      = 13 %
    File fragmentation                       = 24 %
    Free space fragmentation                 = 3 %

File fragmentation
    Total files                              = 116,409
    Average file size                        = 210 KB
    Total fragmented files                   = 11,874
    Total excess fragments                   = 68,585
    Average fragments per file               = 1.58

Pagefile fragmentation
    Pagefile size                            = 768 MB
    Total fragments                          = 1
```

```
Folder fragmentation
    Total folders                                    = 7,477
    Fragmented folders                               = 610
    Excess folder fragments                          = 3,418

Master File Table (MFT) fragmentation
    Total MFT size                                   = 123 MB
    MFT record count                                 = 124,119
    Percent MFT in use                               = 98 %
    Total MFT fragments                              = 255
```

Disk Defragmenter provides a summary of the volume's configuration and space usage. In addition, depending on the type of volume you are working with, it reports on the following areas:

- **Volume Fragmentation** Gives on overview of fragmentation on the volume. Total Fragmentation details the percentage of the total volume that is fragmented. File Fragmentation details the percentage of used space that is fragmented. Free Space Fragmentation details the percentage of unused space that is fragmented.
- **File Fragmentation** Gives an overview of file-level fragmentation showing the total number of files on the volume, the average size of those files, how many files are fragmented, and the average number of fragments per file. Ideally, you want the number of fragments per file to be as close to 1.00 as possible. In this example, the fragments per file ratio is 1.58, indicating that about 58 percent of files are fragmented into two or more clusters.
- **Pagefile Fragmentation** Gives an overview of how fragmented the page file is (if there's one on the volume). If you followed my advice of setting a fixed page file size, as discussed in the section entitled "Tuning Virtual Memory" on page 454, the page file shouldn't be fragmented, which is the case here. Otherwise, the page file can get fragmented as it grows in size and is written to new areas of the disk.
- **Folder Fragmentation** Gives an overview of folder-level fragmentation showing the total number of folders on the volume and how many folders are fragmented.
- **Master File Table (MFT) Fragmentation** For NTFS volumes only, gives an overview of fragmentation in the MFT, showing the current size of the MFT, the number of records it contains, the percentage of the MFT in use, and the total number of fragments in the MFT. In this example, the MFT has some fragmentation. But the real concern is that it is at 98 percent of its maximum size. Because of this, the MFT could become more fragmented over time—there is still 11 percent free space on the volume, and if it needs to grow it will grow into the free space.

That's it. If you click Defragment or run Defrag again without the -A parameter, the Disk Defragmenter will set about cleaning up the drive to give optimal space usage. This won't clear up all fragmentation, but it will help so that disk space is used more efficiently—and on a moderately fragmented volume like the one shown, you should see some performance improvements after defragmentation as well.

Chapter 21

File Sharing and Security

Sharing files means that you allow users to access those files from across the network. The most basic way to share files is to create a shared folder and make it accessible to users through a mapped network drive. In most cases, you don't want everyone with access to the network to be able to read, modify, or delete the shared files. So, when you share files, the access permissions on the shared folder and the local NTFS permissions are very important in helping to grant access as appropriate and to restrict access to files when necessary. File sharing and file security go hand in hand. You don't want to share files indiscriminately, and to help safeguard important data you can configure auditing. Auditing allows you to track who accessed files and what they did.

File Sharing Essentials

File sharing is one of the most fundamental features of a server, and servers running Microsoft Windows Server 2003 have many file sharing features. The basic component that makes file sharing possible is the Server service, which is responsible for sharing file and printer resources over the network.

Using and Finding Shares

You share file resources over the network by creating a shared folder that users can map to as a network drive. For example, if the D:\Data directory on a computer is used to store user data, you might want to share this drive as UserData. This would allow users to map to it using a driver letter on their machines, such as X. Once the drive is mapped, users can access it in Windows Explorer or by using other tools just like they would a local drive on their computer.

All shared folders have a share name and a folder path. The share name is the name of the shared folder. The folder path is the complete path to the folder on the server. In the previous example, the share name is UserData and the associated folder path is D:\Data. Once you share a folder, it is available to users automatically. All they have to know to map to the shared folder is the name of the server on which the folder is located and the share name.

In Windows Explorer, you map network drives by selecting Map Network Drive from the Tools menu. This displays the Map Network Drive dialog box shown in Figure 21-1. You use the Drive field to select a free drive letter to use and the Folder field to enter the path to the network share. You use the Universal Naming Convention (UNC) path to the share. For example, to access a server called CORPSVR02 and a shared folder called CorpData, you would type **\\CorpSvr02\CorpData**. If you don't know the name of the share, you could click Browse to search for available shares.

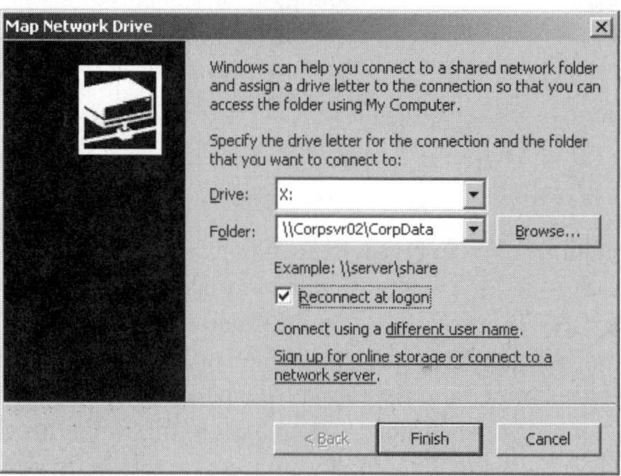

Figure 21-1. The Map Network Drive dialog box.

Users can browse My Network Places in Windows Explorer to find shares that have been made available, as shown in Figure 21-2. Here, you expand My Network Places, Entire Network, and Microsoft Windows Network to display the available domains, and then expand the domain node to display servers on the network. When you expand a server node, any publicly shared resources on that server are listed and can be connected to simply by clicking the associated folder.

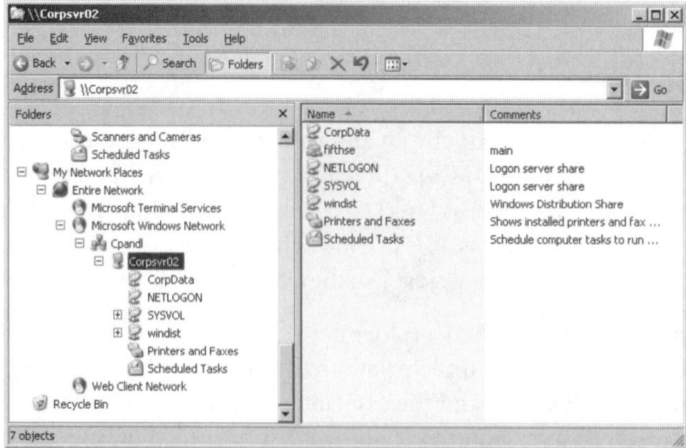

Figure 21-2. My Network Places shows shares published in Active Directory on a per-server basis.

To make it easier for users to find shared folders, you can also publish information about shares in the Active Directory directory service. When you publish shared resources, Microsoft Windows XP users can use My Network Places to find them, and administrators can use Active Directory Users and Computers. The procedures are similar regardless of which tool you are using. An example of how you can find shared folders follows:

1 In My Network Places, click Search Active Directory under Network Tasks. Or in Active Directory Users and Computers, right-click the domain name in the left pane, and click Find.

2 As shown in Figure 21-3, in the Find List, choose Shared Folders.

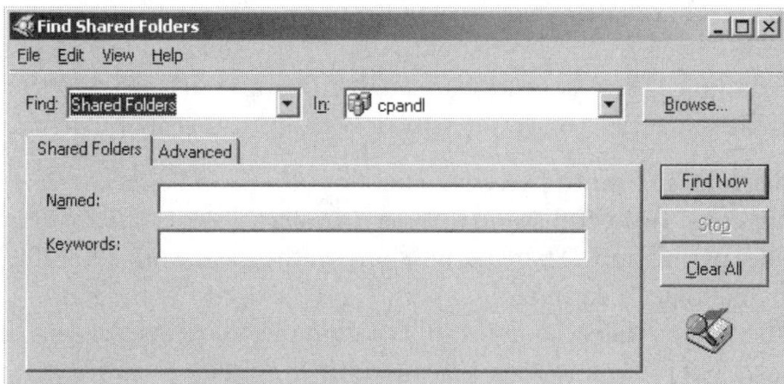

Figure 21-3. Using the Find Shared Folders dialog box to find shared resources, such as folders and printers.

3 In the Named field, type the name of the folder you want to find, and then click Find Now.

4 In the Search Results, right-click any of the shared folders to display a shortcut menu, as shown in Figure 21-4. You will then be able to open the shared folder, map a network drive to the folder, and perform other tasks.

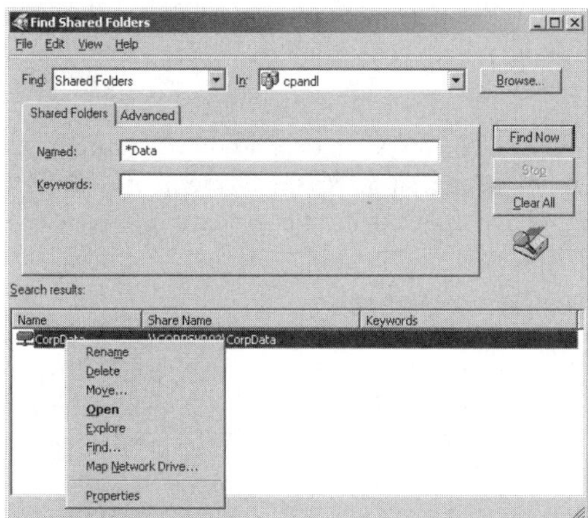

Figure 21-4. Right-click the shared folder you want to work with to display its shortcut menu.

Tip **Use wildcards to match partial names**
If you know part of the name, you can use the asterisk (*) to match partial names. For example, if you know that the folder name ends with the word "data," you could type ***Data** to search for all folders that end with the word "data."

Hiding and Controlling Share Access

Because there are times when you don't want everyone to see or know about a share, Windows Server 2003 also allows you to create hidden shares. Hidden shares are shares that are made available to users but that are not listed in the normal file share lists or published in Active Directory. You can create hidden shares by adding the dollar sign ($) to the end of the share name. For example, if you want to share E:\DataDumps but don't want it to be displayed in the normal file share lists, you could name it Backup$ rather than Backup.

Hiding a share doesn't control access to the share, however. Access to shares is controlled using permissions. Two permissions sets apply to shared folders: share permissions and local file and folder permissions. Share permissions set the maximum allowable actions available within a shared folder. File and folder permissions assigned to the share's contents further constrain the actions users can perform. For example, share permissions can allow a user to access a folder, but file and folder permissions might not allow a user to view or modify files.

By default, when you create a share, everyone with access to the network has Read access to the share's contents. This is an important security change from previous versions of Windows in which the default permission was to give everyone Full Control over a share's contents.

Special and Administrative Shares

In Windows Server 2003, you'll find that several shares are created automatically. These shares are referred to as special or default shares. Most special shares are hidden because they are created for administrative purposes. Thus, they are also referred to as administrative shares.

The special shares that are available on a system depend on its configuration. This means a domain controller might have more special shares than a member server. Or that a server that handles network faxing might have shares that other systems don't.

C$, D$, E$, and Other Drive Shares

All drives, including CD/DVD-ROM drives, have a special share to the root of the drive. These shares are known as C$, D$, E$, and so on and are created to allow administrators to connect to a drive's root folder and perform administrative tasks. For example, if you map to C$, you are connecting to C:\ and have full access to this drive.

On workstations and servers, members of the Administrators or Backup Operators groups can access drive shares. On domain controllers, members of the Server Operators group can also access drive shares.

> **Note** Windows allows you to delete drive shares. However, the next time you restart the computer or the Server service, the drive shares will be re-created.

ADMIN$

The ADMIN$ share is an administrative share for accessing the %SystemRoot% folder in which the operating system files reside. It is meant to be used for remote administration. For administrators working remotely with systems, it is a handy shortcut for directly accessing the operating system folder. Thus, rather than having to connect to C$ or D$ and then look for the operating system folder, which could be named WINDOWS, WINNT, or just about anything else, you can connect directly to the right folder every time.

On workstations and servers, members of the Administrators or Backup Operators groups can access the ADMIN$ share. On domain controllers, members of the Server Operators group can also access the ADMIN$ share.

FAXCLIENT and FXSSRVCP$

The FAXCLIENT and FXSSRVCP$ shares are used to support network faxes. Fax clients use the FAXCLIENT share when sending faxes. FXSSRVCP$ is an administrative share used to store common cover pages. By default, the special group Everyone has Read permissions on these shared folders. This means that anyone with access to the network can access these folders.

IPC$

The IPC$ share is an administrative share used to support named pipes. Named pipes are used for interprocess (or process-to-process) communications. Because named pipes can be redirected over the network to connect local and remote systems, they also enable remote administration and are what allow you to manage resources remotely.

NETLOGON

The NETLOGON share is used by domain controllers. It supports the Netlogon service and is used by this service during processing of logon requests. Once users log on, Windows accesses their user profile and, if applicable, any related logon scripts. Logon scripts contain actions that should be run automatically when users log on to help set up the work environment, perform housekeeping tasks, or complete any other task that must be routinely performed every time users log on.

Microsoft UAM Volume

The Microsoft UAM Volume supports Macintosh file and printer services. It is used by the File Server For Macintosh and Print Server For Macintosh services.

PRINT$

The PRINT$ share supports printer sharing by providing access to printer drivers. Any time you share a printer, the system puts the printer drivers in this share so that other computers can access them as needed.

SYSVOL

The SYSVOL share is used to support Active Directory. Domain controllers have this share and use it to store Active Directory data, including policies and scripts.

Accessing Shares for Administration

As Figure 21-5 shows, administrators can view information about existing shares on a computer including the special shares by using Computer Management. In Computer Management, expand System Tools and Shared Folders, and then select Shares.

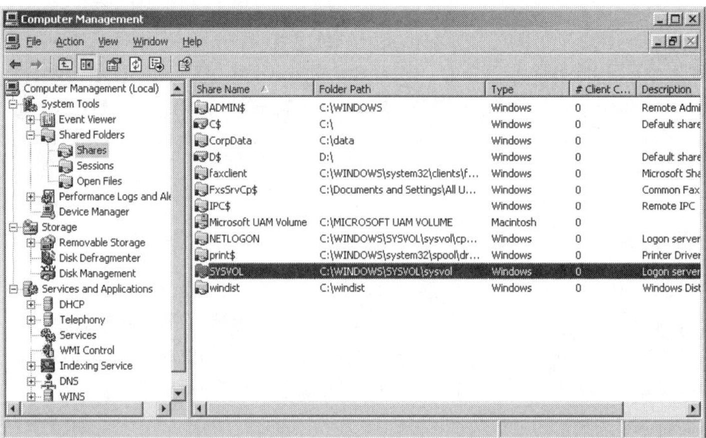

Figure 21-5. Use Computer Management to access shared folders.

If you want to work with shares on a remote computer, right-click the Computer Management node in the left pane and select Connect To Another Computer. This displays the Select Computer dialog box. Select Another Computer, and then type the computer name or Internet Protocol (IP) address of the computer you want to use. If you don't know the computer name or IP address, click Browse to search for the computer you want to work with.

Creating and Publishing Shared Folders

To create shares on a server running Windows Server 2003, you must be a member of the Administrators or Server Operators group. You can create shares using Windows Explorer, Computer Management, or NET SHARE from the command line.

- Windows Explorer works well when you want to share folders on the computer to which you are logged on.
- Using Computer Management, you can share the folders on the local computer and on any computer to which you can connect.
- Using NET SHARE, you can create shares from the command line or in scripts. Type **net share /?** at the command prompt for details on using this command.

As an administrator, Computer Management is the tool you'll use the most for creating and managing shares. After you create a share, you might want to publish it in Active Directory so it is easier to find.

Creating Shares by Using Windows Explorer

By using Windows Explorer, you can share folders on the computer to which you are logged on. In Windows Explorer, right-click the folder you want to share, and select Sharing And Security. This displays the folder's Properties dialog box with the Sharing tab selected. Select Share This Folder, as shown in Figure 20-6.

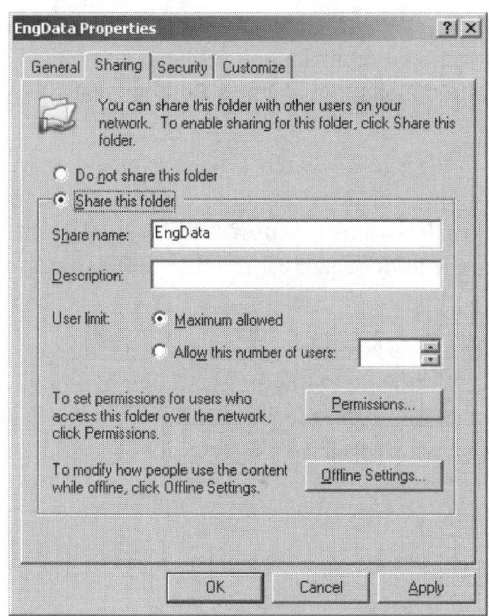

Figure 21-6. Configuring sharing using the folder's Sharing tab.

In the Share Name field, type a name for the share. This is the name of the folder to which users will connect. The key thing to keep in mind when naming shares is that the names must be unique for each system. Share names can be up to 80 characters in length and can contain spaces. If you want to provide support for MS-DOS clients, you should limit the share name to eight characters with a three-letter extension and no spaces. Optionally, type a description of the share in the Description field. The description is displayed as comments when you view shares in My Network Places and other Windows dialog boxes.

Tip **Create hidden shares to hide the share from view**

If you want to hide the share from users (which means that they won't be able to see the shared resource when they try to browse to it in Windows Explorer or at the command line), type **$** as the last character of the share name. Keep in mind that you can hide shares only from normal users. If users have Administrator privileges, they would be able to get a list of the shares.

Click Permissions to view and set the share permissions as discussed in the section entitled "Managing Share Permissions" later in this chapter. Share permissions provide the top-level access controls to the share. By default, all users have Read access to the share, but they don't have other permissions. This is an important security change for Windows Server 2003 that is designed to help ensure permissions aren't given to users unless you grant them.

Note After you set share permissions, you might want to configure the share for offline use. By default, the share is configured so that only files and programs that users specify are available for offline use. If you want to prohibit the offline use of files or programs in the share or specify that all files and programs in the share are available for offline use, click Change, and then select the appropriate options in the Offline Settings dialog box.

Finally, click OK to create the share, and it is immediately available for use. In Windows Explorer, you'll see that the folder icon now includes a hand to indicate it is a share. If you access the folder's Sharing tab again, you'll see a new button at the bottom of the tab labeled New Share. This button lets you share the folder again using a different name and a different set of access permissions.

If you create multiple shares, the Share Name box of the Sharing tab becomes a selection list that allows you to select a share to work with and configure, as shown in Figure 21-7. Once you've selected a share to work with, the options in the Sharing tab apply to that share only. You'll also have a Remove Share option, which you can use to remove the additional share.

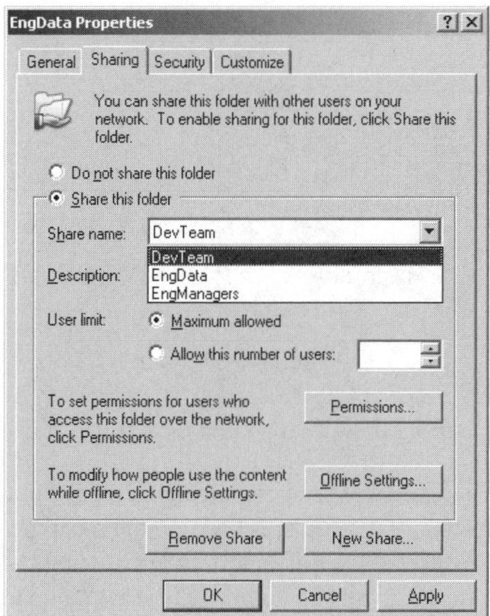

Figure 21-7. You can configure different shares with different names and permissions as well.

Creating Shares by Using Computer Management

By using Computer Management, you can share the folders of any computer to which you can connect on the network. This is handy for when you are sitting at your desk and don't want to have to log on locally to share a server's folders. After you start Computer Management, you can connect to the computer you want to work with by right-clicking Computer Management in the console tree and then selecting Connect To Another Computer. Use the Select Computer dialog box to choose the computer you want to work with. When you are finished, expand System Tools and Shared Folders, and then select Shares to display the current shares on the system you are working with.

You can then create a shared folder by right-clicking Shares and then selecting New Share. This starts the Share A Folder Wizard. Click Next to display the Folder Path page as shown in Figure 21-8. In the Folder Path field, type the full path to the folder you want to share. If you don't know the full path, click Browse, and then use the Browse For Folder dialog box to find the folder you want to share. The Browse For Folder dialog box will also let you create a new folder that you can then share. Click Next when you are ready to continue.

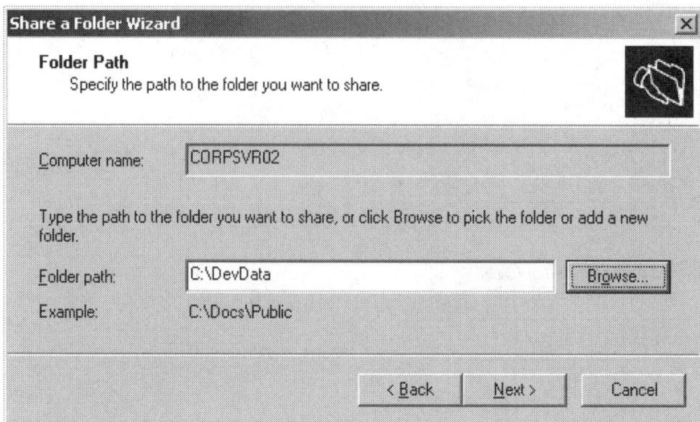

Figure 21-8. Specify the folder path or click Browse to search for a folder to use.

In the Share Name field, type a name for the share, as shown in Figure 21-9. This is the name of the folder to which users will connect, and it must be unique on the computer you are working with. Share names can be up to 80 characters in length and can contain spaces. If you want to provide support for MS-DOS clients, you should limit the share name to eight characters with a three-letter extension. If you want to hide the share from users (which means that they won't be able to see the shared resource when they try to browse to it in Windows Explorer or at the command line), type $ as the last character of the share name.

Optionally, type a description of the share in the Description field. The description is displayed as comments when you view shares in My Network Places and other Windows dialog boxes.

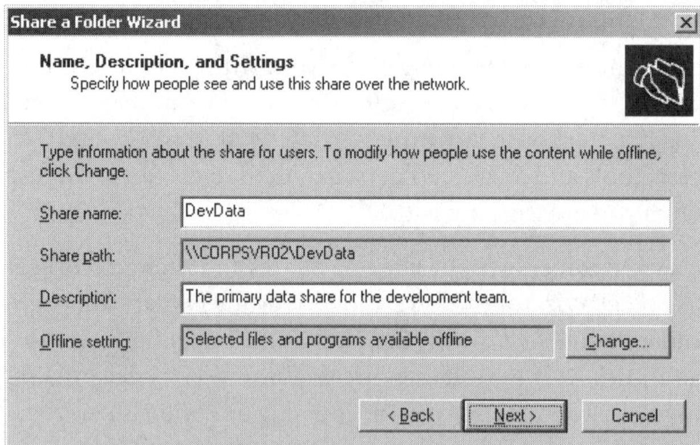

Figure 21-9. Set the share name and description.

When File Sharing For Macintosh is installed, the options on this wizard page change considerably, as shown in Figure 21-10. Here, you can do the following:

- Enable or disable the shared folder for usage by Microsoft Windows Users. The Microsoft Windows Users option is selected by default. If you clear Microsoft Windows Users, the folder will be configured for use only by Apple Macintosh Users.

- Enable or disable the shared folder for usage by Apple Macintosh Users. The Apple Macintosh Users option isn't selected by default. If you select Apple Macintosh Users, the folder will be configured for use by Apple Macintosh Users. You can then either accept the default share name (which is set the same as the Windows share name if applicable) or type a new share name.

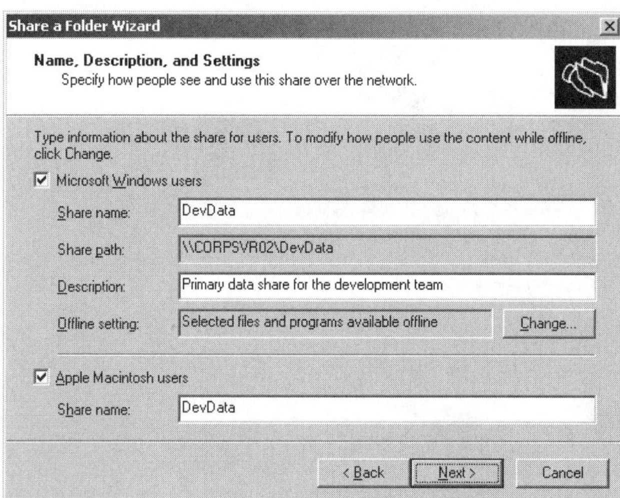

Figure 21-10. Set the share name and description.

When you are ready to continue, click Next to display the Permissions page shown in Figure 21-11. The available options are as follows:

- **All Users Have Read-Only Access** This is the default option. When you create shared folders in Windows Explorer, this permission is set automatically to give users the right to view files and read data but to restrict them from creating, modifying, or deleting files and folders.

Note Granting Read access instead of Full Control by default is an important security change for Windows Server 2003. It is designed to help ensure permissions aren't given to users unless you specifically grant them. Although it is a start on better controls, it isn't perfect because this permission is assigned to the special group Everyone, which means anyone with access to the network—even Guests—have Read access to the share.

- **Administrators Have Full Access; Other Users Have Read-Only Access** This option gives administrators full access to the share. This allows administrators to create, modify, and delete files and folders. On NTFS it also gives administrators the right to change permissions and to take ownership of files and folders. Other users can only view files and read data. They can't create, modify, or delete files and folders.

- **Administrators Have Full Access; Other Users Have Read And Write Access** This option gives administrators full access to the share and allows other users to create, modify, or delete files and folders.
- **Use Custom Share And Folder Permissions** This option allows you to configure access for specific users and groups, which is usually the best technique to use. Setting share permissions is discussed fully later in this chapter in the section entitled "Managing Share Permissions."

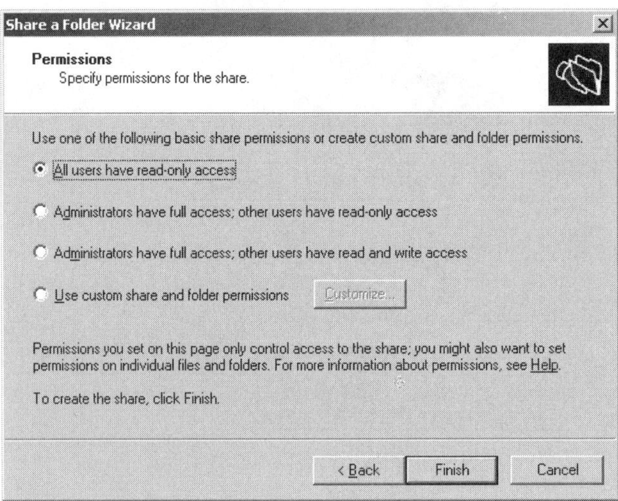

Figure 21-11. Set the share permissions.

After you set up permissions on the share, click Finish. The wizard displays a status report, which should state "Sharing Was Successful" as shown in Figure 21-12. Click Close.

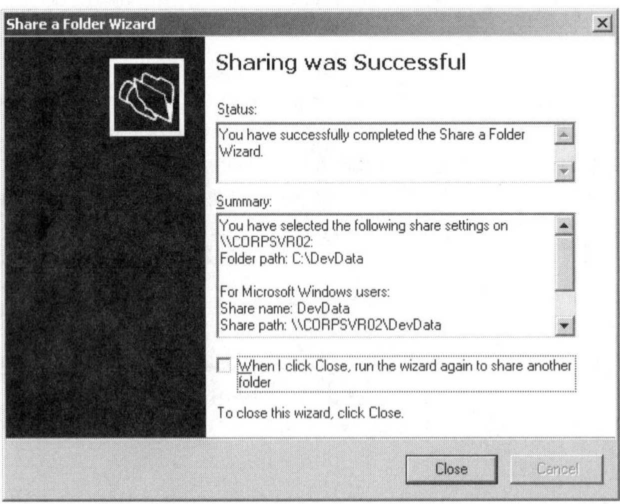

Figure 21-12. Shows a summary of the share that you created.

Publishing Shares in Active Directory

Sometimes, you'll also want to publish shares in Active Directory to make them easier to find. The quickest way to do this is to use Computer Management. After you start computer management and connect to the computer you want to work with, expand System Tools And Shared Folders, and then select Shares to display the current shares on the system you are working with.

You can then publish a shared folder by right-clicking the share in the details pane and then selecting Properties. In the share's Properties dialog box, select the Publish tab as shown in Figure 21-13. Finally, select Publish This Share In Active Directory, and then click OK.

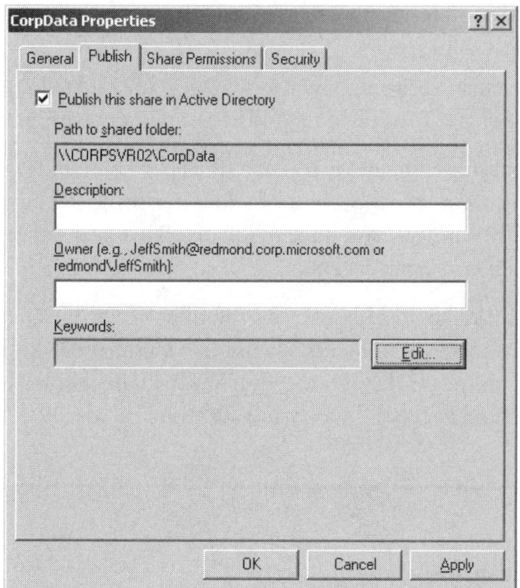

Figure 21-13. Publish the share in Active Directory.

Managing Share Permissions

As discussed previously, Windows Server 2003 has two levels of permissions for shared folders: share permissions and file and folder permissions. Share permissions are applied any time you access a file or folder over the network. These top-level permissions set the maximum allowable actions available within a shared folder. Although share permissions can get you in the door when you work remotely, the file and folder permissions can further constrain access and the allowable actions.

When accessing files locally, only the file and folder permissions are applied. However, when accessing files remotely, first the share permissions are applied and then the file and folder permissions. In the case of file allocation table (FAT) volumes, the share permissions are the only permissions, and if a user has local access to the folder, the user can perform any action.

Understanding Share Permissions

With shared folders, you use share permissions to set the maximum allowed access level. Share permissions are applied only when you access a folder remotely, and they can be used to grant access directly to users or implicitly through the groups to which users belong.

The share permissions available are as follows:

- **Full Control** By granting this permission, users have Read and Change permissions, as well as the following additional capabilities to change file and folder permissions and take ownership of files and folders.
- **Change** By granting this permission, users have Read permissions and the additional capability to create files and subfolders, modify files, change attributes on files and subfolders, and delete files and subfolders.
- **Read** By granting this permission, you allow users to view file and subfolder names, access the subfolders of the share, read file data and attributes, and run program files.

If you have Read permissions on a share, the most you can do is perform read operations. If you have Change permissions on a share, the most you can do is perform read operations and change operations. If you have Full Control, you have full access. However, in any case, file and folder permissions can further constrain access.

Permissions assigned to groups work like this: If a user is a member of a group that is granted share permissions, the user also has those permissions. If a user is a member of multiple groups, the permissions are cumulative. This means that if one group of which the user is a member has Read access and another has additional access, the user has additional access as well.

Inside Out

Changes might be needed to enhance security

When you create a shared folder, default access permissions are assigned. Watch out, though, because the default in most cases is to give Read access to the special group Everyone, which means that even Guests have access to shares—it doesn't mean they can read files, however, because this is determined by the base-level file and folder permissions. In most cases, it is more prudent to lock down access and only grant permissions to those users that truly need access to a shared folder. If you really want to grant wide access to a shared folder, you might want to use the Domain Users group to do this rather than the Everyone group. In this case, you would remove the Everyone group and add the Domain Users group. By using Domain Users, you require users to have a logon account to access the shared folder, which excludes Guests.

To override this behavior, you must specifically deny an access permission. Denying permission is the trump card—it takes precedence and overrides permissions that have been granted. When you want to single out a user or group and not let it have a permission, configure the share permissions to specifically deny that permission to the user or group. For example, if a user is a member of a group that has been granted Full Control over a share, but the user should have only Change permissions, configure the share to deny Full Control to that user.

Configuring Share Permissions

The easiest way to configure share permissions is to use Computer Management. After you start Computer Management, connect to the computer you want to work with by right-clicking Computer Management in the console tree and then selecting Connect To Another Computer. Then use the Select Computer dialog box to choose the computer you want to work with. When you are finished, expand System Tools And Shared Folders, and then select Shares to display the current shares on the system you are working with.

To view or manage the permissions of a share, right-click the share, and then select Properties. In the share Properties dialog box, select the Share Permissions tab, as shown in Figure 21-14. You can now view the users and groups that have access to the share and the type of access they have.

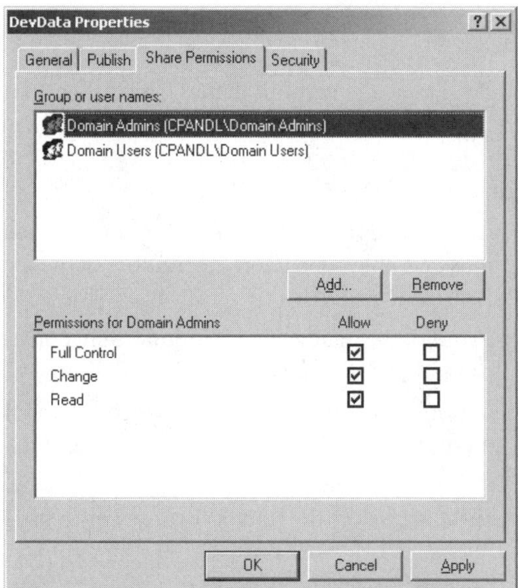

Figure 21-14. View or set share permissions.

In this example, members of the Domain Admins group have Full Control over the share and members of the Domain Users group have Change access. The group Everyone was removed to enhance security as discussed in the sidebar "Changes Might Be Needed to Enhance Security" earlier in this chapter.

You can grant or deny permission to access a share by following these steps:

1. In Computer Management, right-click the share, and then select Properties. In the share Properties dialog box, select the Share Permissions tab.
2. In the Share Permissions tab, choose Add. This opens the Select Users, Computers, Or Groups dialog box, as shown in Figure 21-15.

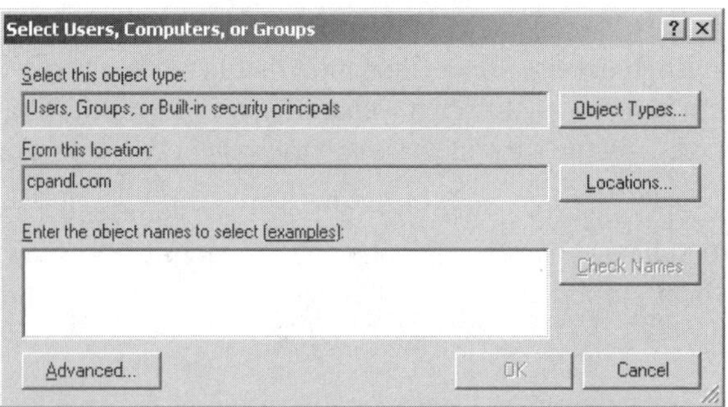

Figure 21-15. Specify the users or groups to add.

3. The Locations button allows you to access account names from other domains. Click Locations to see a list of the current domains, trusted domains, and other resources that you can access. Because of the transitive trusts in Windows Server 2003, you can usually access all the domains in the domain tree or forest.
4. Type the name of a user or group account in the selected or default domain, and then click Check Names. The options available depend on the number of matches found, as follows:
   - When a single match is found, the dialog box is automatically updated as appropriate and the entry is underlined.
   - When no matches are found, you've either entered an incorrect name part or you're working with an incorrect location. Modify the name and try again, or click Locations to select a new location.
   - If multiple matches are found, select the name(s) you want to use, and then click OK.
5. To add additional users or groups, type a semicolon (;), and then repeat this process.
6. When you click OK, the users and groups are added to the Name list for the share.
7. Configure access permissions for each user and group added by selecting an account name and then allowing or denying access permissions. If a user or group should be

granted access permissions, select the permission in the Allow column. If a user or group should be denied access permissions, select the permission in the Deny column.

8 When you're finished, click OK.

Managing File and Folder Permissions

You can think of file and folder permissions as the base-level permissions—the permissions that are applied no matter what. For NTFS volumes, you use file and folder permissions and ownership to further constrain actions within the share as well as share permissions. For FAT volumes, share permissions provide the only access controls. The reason for this is that FAT volumes have no file and folder permission capabilities.

File and folder permissions are much more complex than share permissions, and to really understand how they can be used and applied, you must understand ownership and inheritance as well as the permissions that are available.

Inside Out

Changes to basic file and folder attributes are sometimes necessary

As administrators, we often forget about the basic file and folder attributes that can be assigned. However, basic file and folder attributes can affect access, so let's look at these attributes first and then at the file and folder permissions you can apply to NTFS volumes. All files and folders have basic attributes regardless of whether you are working with FAT or NTFS. These attributes can be examined in Windows Explorer by right-clicking the file or folder icon and then selecting Properties. Folder and file attributes include Hidden and Read-Only. Hidden determines whether the file is displayed in file listings. You can override this by telling Windows Explorer to display hidden files. On NTFS, the Read-Only attribute for folders is initially shown as unavailable. Here, this means the attribute is in a mixed state regardless of the current state of files in the folder. If you override the mixed state by selecting Read-Only for a folder, all files in the folder will be read-only. If you override the mixed state and clear Read-Only for a folder, all files in the folder will be writable.

File and Folder Ownership

Before working with file and folder permissions, you should understand the concept of ownership as it applies to files and folders. In Windows Server 2003, the file or folder owner isn't necessarily the file or folder's creator. Instead, the file or folder owner is the person who has direct control over the file or folder. File or folder owners can grant access permissions and give other users permission to take ownership of a file or folder.

The way ownership is assigned initially depends on where the file or folder is being created. By default, the user who created the file or folder is listed as the current owner. Ownership can be taken or transferred in several ways. Any administrator can take ownership. Any user or group with the Take Ownership permission can take ownership. Any user who has the right to Restore Files And Directories, such as a member of the Backup Operators group, can take ownership as well. Any current owner can transfer ownership to another user as well.

Taking Ownership of a File or Folder

You can take ownership using a file or folder's Properties dialog box. Right-click the file or folder, and then select Properties. In the Security tab of the Properties dialog box, display the Access Security Settings dialog box by clicking Advanced. Next, select the Owner tab, as shown in Figure 21-16. In the Change Owner To list box, select the new owner. If you're taking ownership of a folder, you can take ownership of all subfolders and files within the folder by selecting the Replace Owner On Subcontainers And Objects option. Click OK twice when you are finished.

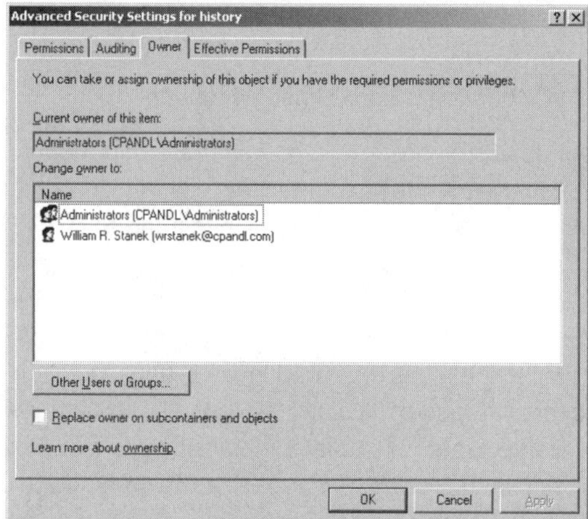

Figure 21-16. Transferring ownership is done by using the Owner tab.

Transferring Ownership

If you are an administrator or a current owner of a file or folder, you can transfer ownership to another user by using a file or folder's Properties dialog box. In Windows Explorer, right-click the file or folder, and then select Properties. In the Security tab of the Properties dialog box, display the Advanced Security Settings dialog box by clicking the Advanced button. Next, select the Owner tab, as shown in Figure 21-16.

Click Other Users Or Groups to display the Select User, Computer, Or Group dialog box. Type the name of a user or group, and click Check Names. If multiple names match the value you entered, you'll see a list of names and will be able to choose the one you want to use. Otherwise, the name will be filled in for you, and you can click OK to close the Select User, Computer, Or Group dialog box. Under Change Owner To in the Owner tab of the Advanced Security Settings dialog box, the user you added is listed and selected. When you click OK, ownership is transferred to this user.

Permission Inheritance for Files and Folders

By default, when you add a folder or file to an existing folder, the folder or file inherits the permissions of the existing folder. For example, if the Domain Users group has access to a folder and you add a file to this folder, members of the Domain Users group will be able to access the file. Inherited permissions are automatically assigned when files and folders are created.

When you assign new permissions to a folder, the permissions propagate down and are inherited by all subfolders and files in the folder and supplement or replace existing permissions. If you add permissions on a folder to allow a new group to access a folder, these permissions are applied to all subfolders and files in the folder, meaning the additional group is granted access. On the other hand, if you were to change the permissions on the folder so that, for instance, only members of the Engineering group could access the folder, these permissions would be applied to all subfolders and files in the folder, meaning only members of the Engineering group would have access to the folder, its subfolders, and its files.

Inheritance is automatic. If you do not want the permissions of subfolders and files within folders to supplement or replace existing permissions, you must override inheritance starting with the top-level folder from which the permissions are inherited. A top-level folder is referred to as a parent folder. Files and folders below the parent folder are referred to as child files and folders. This is identical to the parent/child structure of objects in Active Directory.

Changing Shaded Permissions and Stopping Inheritance

If a permission you want to change is shaded, the file or folder is inheriting the permission from a parent folder. To change the permission, you must do one of the following:

- Access the parent folder and make the desired changes. These changes will then be inherited by child folders and files.
- Select the opposite permission to override the inherited permission if possible. In most cases, Deny overrides Allow, so if you explicitly deny permission to a user or group for a child folder or file, this permission should be denied to that user or group of users.
- Stop inheriting permissions from the parent folder and then copy or remove existing permissions as appropriate.

To stop inheriting permissions from a parent folder, right-click the file or folder in Windows Explorer, and then select Properties. In the Security tab of the Properties dialog box, click Advanced to display the Advanced Security Settings dialog box shown in Figure 21-17.

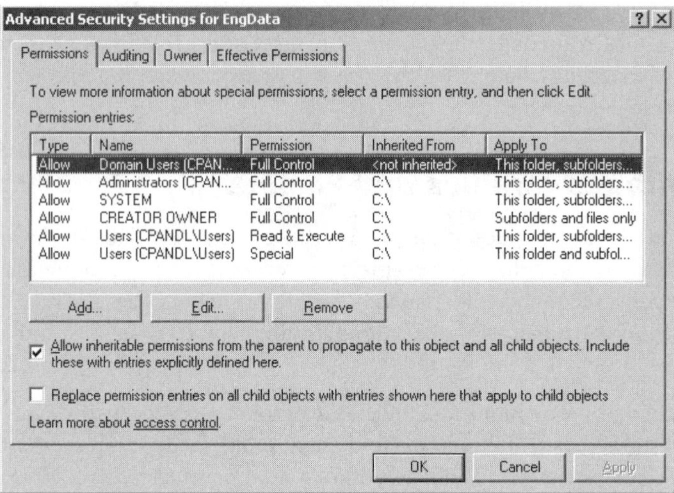

Figure 21-17. Change inheritance as necessary.

Clear Allow Inheritable Permissions From The Parent To Propagate To This Object. As shown in Figure 21-18, you now have the opportunity to copy over the permissions that were previously applied or remove the inherited permission and only apply the permissions that you explicitly set on the folder or file. Click Copy or Remove as appropriate.

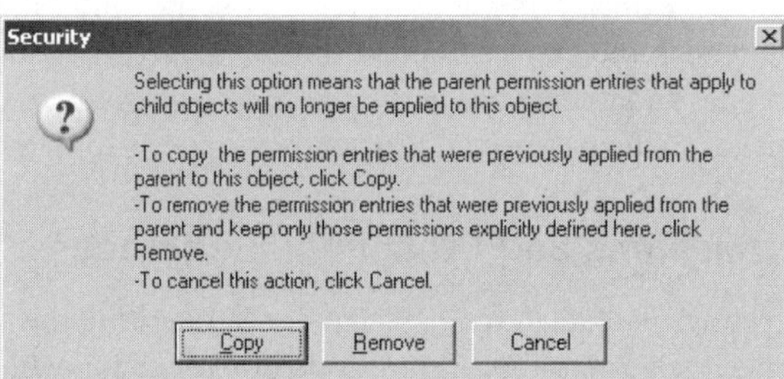

Figure 21-18. Copy over or remove the inherited permissions.

Resetting and Replacing Permissions

Another way to manage permissions is to reset the permissions of subfolders and files within a folder, replacing their permissions with the current permissions assigned to the folder you are working with. In this way, subfolders and files get all inheritable permissions from the parent folder and all other explicitly defined permissions on the individual subfolders and files are removed.

To reset permissions for subfolders and files of a folder, right-click the file or folder in Windows Explorer, and then select Properties. In the Security tab of the Properties dialog box, click Advanced to display the Advanced Security Settings dialog box shown previously in Figure 21-17.

Select Replace Permission Entries On All Child Objects With Entries Shown Here, and click OK. As shown in Figure 21-19, you will see a prompt explaining that this action will remove all explicitly defined permissions and enable propagation of inheritable permissions. Click Yes.

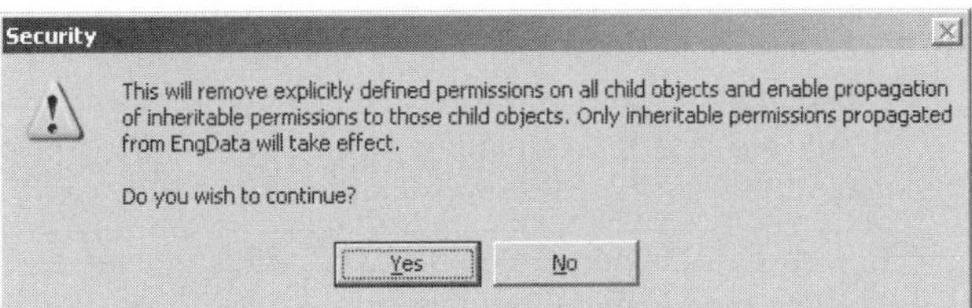

Figure 21-19. Confirm that you want to replace the existing permissions on subfolders and files.

Configuring File and Folder Permissions

On NTFS volumes, you can assign access permissions to files and folders. These permissions grant or deny access to users and groups.

Basic Permissions

In Windows Explorer you can view basic permissions by right-clicking the file or folder you want to work with, selecting Properties on the shortcut menu, and then in the Properties dialog box selecting the Security tab, as shown in Figure 21-20. The Group Or User Names list shows groups and users with assigned permissions. If you select a group or user in this list, the applicable permissions are shown in the Permissions For list. If permissions are unavailable, it means the permissions are inherited from a parent folder as discussed previously.

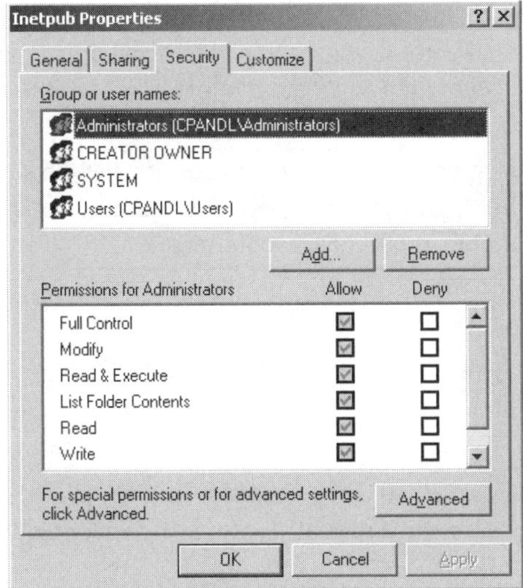

Figure 21-20. The Security tab shows the basic permissions assigned to each user or group.

The basic permissions you can assign to folders and files are shown in Table 21-1 and Table 21-2. These permissions are made up of multiple special permissions.

Table 21-1. Basic Folder Permissions

Permission	Description
Full Control	This permission permits reading, writing, changing, and deleting files and subfolders. If a user has Full Control over a folder, she can delete files in the folder regardless of the permission on the files.
Modify	This permission permits reading and writing of files and subfolders; allows deletion of the folder.
List Folder Contents	This permission permits viewing and listing files and subfolders as well as executing files; inherited by folders only.
Read & Execute	This permission permits viewing and listing files and subfolders as well as executing files; inherited by files and folders.
Write	This permission permits adding files and subfolders.
Read	This permission permits viewing and listing files and subfolders.

Table 21-2. Basic File Permissions

Permission	Description
Full Control	This permission permits reading, writing, changing, and deleting the file.
Modify	This permission permits reading and writing of the file; allows deletion of the file.
Read & Execute	This permission permits viewing and accessing the file's contents as well as executing the file.
Write	This permission permits writing to a file. Giving a user permission to write to a file but not to delete it doesn't prevent the user from deleting the file's contents.
Read	This permission permits viewing or accessing the file's contents. Read is the only permission needed to run scripts. Read access is required to access a shortcut and its target.

You can set basic permissions for files and folders by following these steps:

1. In Windows Explorer, right-click the file or folder you want to work with, and select Properties. In the Properties dialog box select the Security tab, shown previously in Figure 21-20.
2. Users or groups that already have access to the file or folder are listed in the Name list box. You can change permissions for these users and groups by selecting the user or

group you want to change and using the Permissions list box to grant or deny access permissions.

3. The Locations button allows you to access account names from other domains. Click Locations to see a list of the current domain, trusted domains, and other resources that you can access. Because of the transitive trusts in Windows Server 2003, you can usually access all the domains in the domain tree or forest.
4. Type the name of a user or group account in the selected or default domain, and then click Check Names. The options available depend on the number of matches found as follows:
   - When a single match is found, the dialog box is automatically updated as appropriate and the entry is underlined.
   - When no matches are found, you've either entered an incorrect name part or you're working with an incorrect location. Modify the name and try again, or click Locations to select a new location.
   - If multiple matches are found, select the name(s) you want to use, and then click OK.
5. To add additional users or groups, type a semicolon (;), and then repeat this process.
6. When you click OK, the users and groups are added to the Name list for the share. Configure access permissions for each user and group added by selecting an account name and then allowing or denying access permissions. If a user or group should be granted access permissions, select the permission in the Allow column. If a user or group should be denied access permissions, select the permission in the Deny column.
7. When you're finished, click OK.

Special Permissions

In Windows Explorer you can view special permissions by right-clicking the file or folder you want to work with and selecting Properties on the shortcut menu. In the Properties dialog box, select the Security tab, and then click Advanced to display the Advanced Security Settings dialog box, as shown in Figure 21-21.

The special permissions available are as follows:

- **Traverse Folder/Execute File** Traverse Folder lets you directly access a folder even if you don't have explicit access to read the data it contains. Execute File lets you run an executable file.
- **List Folder/Read Data** List Folder lets you view file and folder names. Read Data lets you view the contents of a file.
- **Read Attributes** Lets you read the basic attributes of a file or folder. These attributes include Read-Only, Hidden, System, and Archive.
- **Read Extended Attributes** Lets you view the extended attributes (named data streams) associated with a file. As discussed in Chapter 20, "Managing Windows Server

2003 File Systems," these include Summary fields, such as Title, Subject, and Author, as well as other types of data.

- **Create Files/Write Data** Create Files lets you put new files in a folder. Write Data allows you to overwrite existing data in a file (but not add new data to an existing file because this is covered by Append Data).
- **Create Folders/Append Data** Create Folders lets you create subfolders within folders. Append Data allows you to add data to the end of an existing file (but not to overwrite existing data because this is covered by Write Data).
- **Write Attributes** Lets you change the basic attributes of a file or folder. These attributes include Read-Only, Hidden, System, and Archive.
- **Write Extended Attributes** Lets you change the extended attributes (named data streams) associated with a file. As discussed in Chapter 20, these include Summary fields, such as Title, Subject, and Author, as well as other types of data.
- **Delete Subfolders and Files** Lets you delete the contents of a folder. If you have this permission, you can delete the subfolders and files in a folder even if you don't specifically have Delete permission on the subfolder or file.
- **Delete** Lets you delete a file or folder. If a folder isn't empty and you don't have Delete permission for one of its files or subfolders, you won't be able to delete it. You can do this only if you have Delete Subfolders and Files permission.
- **Read Permissions** Lets you read all basic and special permissions assigned to a file or folder.
- **Change Permissions** Lets you change basic and special permissions assigned to a file or folder.
- **Take Ownership** Lets you take ownership of a file or folder. By default administrators can always take ownership of a file or folder and can also grant this permission to others.

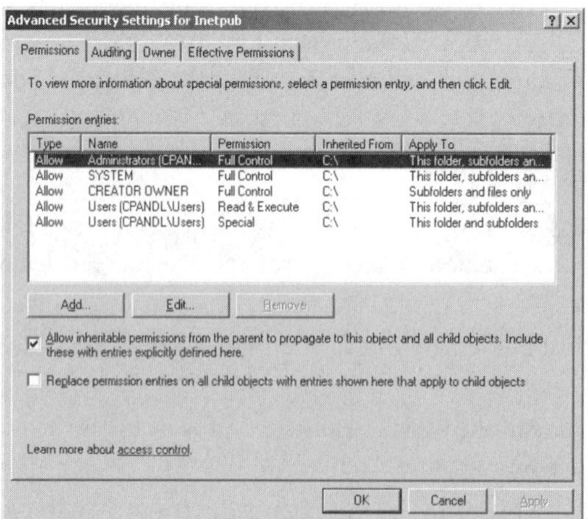

Figure 21-21. The Advanced Security Settings dialog box can be used to access the special permissions assigned to each user or group.

Tables 21-3 and 21-4 show how special permissions are combined to make the basic permissions for files and folders. Because special permissions are combined to make the basic permissions, they are also referred to as *atomic permissions*.

Table 21-3. Special Permissions for Folders

Special Permissions	Full Control	Modify	Read & Execute	List Folder Contents	Read	Write
Traverse Folder/ Execute File	X	X	X	X		
List Folder/Read Data	X	X	X	X	X	
Read Attributes	X	X	X	X	X	
Read Extended Attributes	X	X	X	X	X	
Create Files/Write Data	X	X				X
Create Folders/ Append Data	X	X				X
Write Attributes	X	X				X
Write Extended Attributes	X	X				X
Delete Subfolders And Files	X					
Delete	X	X				
Read Permissions	X	X	X	X	X	X
Change Permissions	X					
Take Ownership	X					

Table 21-4. Special Permissions for Files

Special Permissions	Full Control	Modify	Read & Execute	Read	Write
Traverse Folder/ Execute File	X	X	X	–	–
List Folder/Read Data	X	X	X	X	–
Read Attributes	X	X	X	X	–
Read Extended Attributes	X	X	X	X	–

Chapter 21

Table 21-4. Special Permissions for Files

Special Permissions	Full Control	Modify	Read & Execute	Read	Write
Create Files/Write Data	X	X	–	–	X
Create Folders/ Append Data	X	X			X
Write Attributes	X	X			X
Write Extended Attributes	X	X			X
Delete Subfolders and Files	X				
Delete	X	X			
Read Permissions	X	X	X	X	X
Change Permissions	X				
Take Ownership	X				

You can set special permissions for files and folders in Windows Explorer. Right-click the file or folder you want to work with, and then select Properties. In the Properties dialog box, select the Security tab, and then click Advanced. This displays the dialog box shown previously in Figure 21-21. You now have the following options:

- **Add** Adds a user or group. Click Add to display the Select User, Computer, Or Group dialog box. Type the name of a user or group, and click Check Names. If multiple names match the value you entered, you'll see a list of names and will be able to choose the one you want to use. Otherwise, the name will be filled in for you. When you click OK, the Permissions Entry For dialog box shown in Figure 21-22 is displayed.

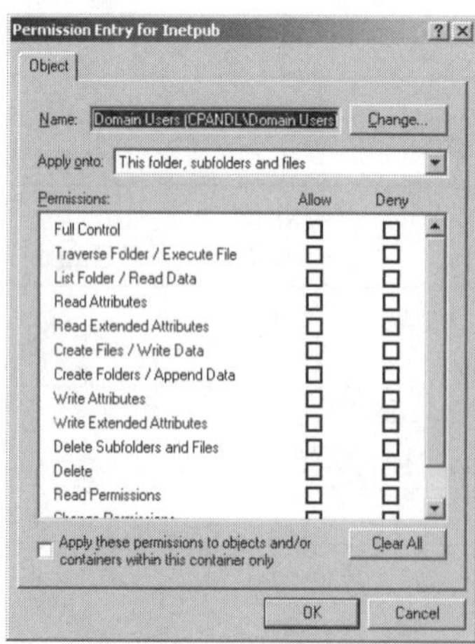

Figure 21-22. Use the Permission Entry For dialog box to set special permissions.

Chapter 21

- **Edit** Edits an existing user or group entry. Select the user or group whose permissions you want to modify, and then click Edit. The Permissions Entry For dialog box shown in Figure 21-22 is displayed.
- **Remove** Removes an existing user or group entry. Select the user or group whose permissions you want to remove, and then click Remove.

If you are adding or editing entries for users or groups, you use the Permission Entry For dialog box to grant or deny special permissions. Select Allow or Deny for each permission as appropriate. When finished, use the Apply Onto options shown in Table 21-5 to determine how and where these permissions are applied. If you want to prevent subfolders and files from inheriting these permissions, select Apply These Permissions To Objects And/Or Containers Within This Container Only. When you do this, all the related entries in Table 21-5 are No. This means the settings no longer apply onto subsequent subfolders or to files in subsequent subfolders.

Table 21-5. Special Permissions Apply Onto Options

Apply Onto	Applies to Current Folder	Applies to Subfolders in the Current Folder	Applies to File in the Current Folder	Applies to Subsequent Subfolders	Applies to Files in Subsequent Subfolders
This folder only	Yes	No	No	No	No
This folder, subfolders, and files	Yes	Yes	Yes	Yes	Yes
This folder and subfolders	Yes	Yes	No	Yes	No
This folder and files	Yes	No	Yes	No	Yes
Subfolders and files only	No	Yes	Yes	Yes	Yes
Subfolders only	No	Yes	No	Yes	No
Files only	No	No	Yes	No	Yes

> **Note** When Apply These Permissions To Objects And/Or Containers Within This Container Only is selected, all the values under Applies To Subsequent Subfolders and Applies To Files In Subsequent Subfolders are No. The settings no longer apply onto subsequent subfolders or to files in subsequent subfolders.

Determining Effective Permissions

Navigating the complex maze of permissions can be daunting even for the best administrators. Sometimes it won't be clear how a particular permission set will be applied to a particular user or group. If you ever want to know exactly how the current permissions will be applied to a particular user or group, you can use a handy tool called Effective Permissions.

Effective Permissions applies only to file and folder permissions—not share permissions—and is an option of the Advanced Security Settings dialog box. To get to it from Windows Explorer, right-click the file or folder you want to work with, and select Properties. In the Properties dialog box, select the Security tab, and then click Advanced. To see how permissions will be applied to a user or group, click the Effective Permissions tab, click Select, type the name of the user or group, and then click OK. The Effective Permissions for the selected user or group are displayed as shown in Figure 21-23.

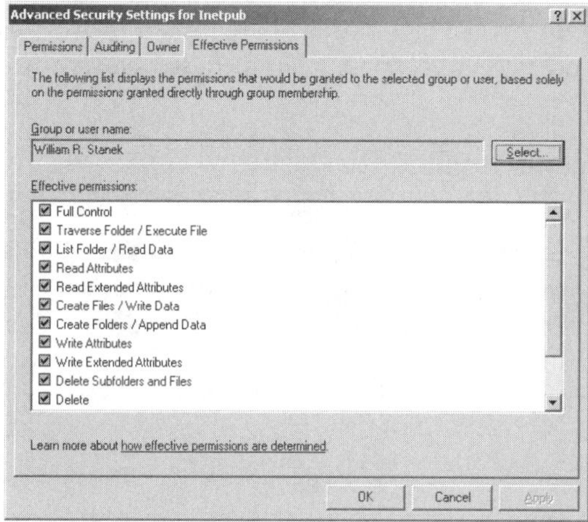

Figure 21-23. Use Effective Permissions to help you determine how permissions will be applied to a specific user or group.

Effective Permissions does have the following limitations:

- You need the proper access permissions to view the effective permissions of a user or group. That goes without saying, pretty much. But it is important to point out.
- You cannot determine permissions for global or universal security groups that are nested in domain local groups. For example, by default Users has access to most folders, and one of its members is Domain Users, which is a global security group. If you try to determine the effective permissions for Domain Users, no permissions are displayed.
- You cannot determine the effective permissions for implicit groups or special identities, such as Everyone, Interactive, Domain Controllers, Local Service, or Network Service.

Managing File Shares After Configuration

Configuring shares can be a time-consuming process especially if you are trying to troubleshoot why a particular user doesn't have access or set up a new server with the same file shares as a server you are decommissioning. Fortunately, there are two tools you can use to help you better manage file shares and the way they are implemented:

- SrvCheck
- PermCopy

Both tools are found in the Windows Server 2003 Resource Kit, and each is discussed in the sections that follow. Keep in mind that you should use an account with administrative privileges to run these tools.

Tracking and Logging File Share Permissions by Using SrvCheck

SrvCheck is a handy tool for helping you track file share and print share permissions on both local and remote systems. You can use it to display a list of shares and who has access. If you redirect the output of SrvCheck, you can save the share configuration and access information to a file, and this file can become a log that helps you track share permission changes over time.

To run SrvCheck, type **srvcheck *ComputerName***, where *ComputerName* is the domain name or IP address of the computer whose file share and print share information you want to display. For example, if you wanted to display the share information for CORPSVR02, you'd type

```
srvcheck \\CorpSvr02
```

The output of SrvCheck shows you the name of each share on the server, who has access to it, and which access permissions these users have. Here is an example:

```
\\corpsvr02\SYSVOL
                NT AUTHORITY\Authenticated Users        Full Control
                BUILTIN\Administrators    Full Control
                Everyone                  Read

\\corpsvr02\NETLOGON
                BUILTIN\Administrators    Full Control
                Everyone                  Read

\\corpsvr02\print$
                BUILTIN\Server Operators                Full Control
                BUILTIN\Print Operators                 Full Control
                BUILTIN\Administrators    Full Control
                Everyone                  Read
```

```
\\corpsvr02\fifthse
                BUILTIN\Server Operators                Full Control
                BUILTIN\Print Operators                 Full Control
                BUILTIN\Administrators    Full Control
                Everyone                  Full Control

\\corpsvr02\CorpData
                CPANDL\Domain Users       Change
                CPANDL\Domain Admins      Full Control

\\corpsvr02\FxsSrvCp$
                Everyone                  Read
                BUILTIN\Administrators    Full Control

\\corpsvr02\faxclient
                Everyone                  Read

\\corpsvr02\EngData
                CPANDL\Domain Users       Change
                CPANDL\Domain Guests      Read
                CPANDL\Domain Controllers               Read
                CPANDL\Domain Computers                 Read
                CPANDL\Domain Admins      Full Control

\\corpsvr02\DevData
                CPANDL\Domain Users       Change
                CPANDL\Domain Guests      Read
                CPANDL\Domain Controllers               Read
                CPANDL\Domain Computers                 Read
                CPANDL\Domain Admins      Full Control
```


The list of shares shown for CORPSVR02 includes the file shares SYSVOL, NETLOGON, PRINT$, CORPDATA, FXSRVCP$, ENGDATA, and DEVDATA, as well as the FIFTHSE print share. Administrative shares created and managed by Windows, including ADMIN$, IPC$, and any drive shares, are not included in the list. You'll also find that any Macintosh shares that you've configured aren't listed. Still, this tool is very handy for helping you track file share and print share permissions.

If you want to redirect the output to a file, you can do this by typing **srvcheck *ComputerName* > *FileName.txt***, where *ComputerName* is the domain name or IP address of the computer whose file share and print share information you want to display and *FileName.txt* is the name of the file to create and to which you want to write, such as

```
srvcheck \\CorpSvr02 >  C:\logs\fileshares-Dec05.txt
```

Copying File Share Permissions

Whether you are setting up a new file share with the same permissions as an existing file share or configuring a new file server with the same file shares as a server you are decommissioning, you can use PermCopy to help you out. PermCopy is a tool that you can use to copy share permissions from one file share to another. Not only will this save you time, but this will also ensure that share permissions are exact—something that is often hard to do if you have a complicated permission set or a lot of different users and groups with assigned permissions. Thus, rather than going back and forth from one folder's Share Permissions to another's, you can simply copy the permissions from one to the other.

The syntax for PermCopy is as follows:

```
permcopy \\SourceServer ShareName1 \\DestinationServer ShareName2
```

where

- *SourceServer* is the domain name or IP address of the source computer. This is the computer with the file share whose permissions you want to copy.
- *ShareName1* is the name of the source file share. This is the file share with the permissions you want to copy.
- *DestinationServer* is the domain name or IP address of the destination computer. This is the computer to which you are copying file share permissions.
- *ShareName2* is the name of the destination file share. This is the file share whose permissions you want to replace.

Consider the following example:

```
permcopy \\corpsvr01 DevData \\corpsvr17 EngData
```

Here, you copy the permissions of the DevData share on CORPSVR01 to the EngData share on CORPSVR17. It's important to note that any existing permissions for the EngData share are deleted and replaced with those of DevData.

The source and destination computer can be the same. In the following example, you copy the permissions of the History share on CORPSVR02 to the Q405 share in the same server:

```
permcopy \\corpsvr02 History \\corpsvr17 Q405
```

When you run the command, it should display the message "The command completed successfully." If you get an error, check the syntax and make sure you can connect to both the source and destination server.

Sharing Files on the Web

With Web shares, you share files over your intranet or the Internet. Web shares are accessible in Web browsers using the Hypertext Transfer Protocol (HTTP). If the system you're currently logged on to has Microsoft Internet Information Services (IIS) installed on it, you can create Web shares by using Windows Explorer. In Windows Explorer, right-click the local folder you want to share, and then, from the shortcut menu, select Properties. In the Properties dialog box, select the Web Sharing tab, which is shown in Figure 21-24.

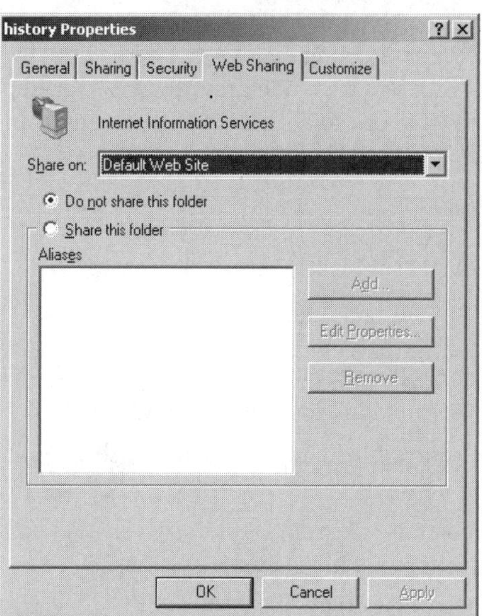

Figure 21-24. Use the Web Sharing tab to share a folder using HTTP.

In the Web Sharing tab, use the Share On drop-down list box to select the local Web site on which you want to share the folder. If this is the first share for this folder, select the Share This Folder option to display the Edit Alias dialog box shown in Figure 21-25. Otherwise, click Add to configure an additional share.

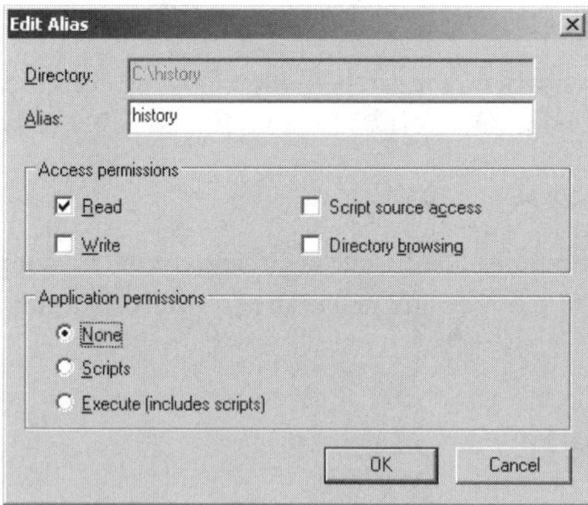

Figure 21-25. Set the share alias and access permissions.

The Edit Alias dialog box allows you to set the alias and access permissions for the folder. In the Alias box, type an alias for the folder. The alias is the name you'll use to access the folder on the Web server. This name must be unique and must not conflict with existing folders used by the Web server. For example, if you type the alias MyDir, you could access the folder as http://Localhost/MyDir/.

Next, set the access permissions for the folder. You use the available options as follows:

- **Read** Allows Web users to read files in the folder
- **Write** Allows Web users to write data in the folder
- **Script Source Access** Allows Web users to access the source code for scripts
- **Directory Browsing** Allows Web users to browse the folder and its subfolders

Tip **Directory browsing isn't required**
Directory browsing isn't required to read or access files in a directory. This permission is required only if you want to allow users to browse the contents of folders when you don't provide a default document (such as Default.htm or Index.htm). Generally, it's a poor security practice to allow directory browsing when the server is accessible to the public Internet; you don't want external users going through lists of files (in most cases). On a private network where the Web share is meant to provide quick access to a set of documents, however, you might want users to be able to browse directories; users could then browse a directory and select a file to work with.

After you set the access permissions, set application permissions for the folder. You use the available options as follows:

- **None** Disallows the execution of programs and scripts
- **Scripts** Allows scripts in the folder to be run from the Web
- **Execute (Includes Scripts)** Allows programs and scripts in the folder to be run from the Web

When you're finished setting permissions, click OK. To further restrict access to contents of a shared folder on an NTFS volume, set file and folder permissions as outlined in the section entitled "Managing File and Folder Permissions" earlier in this chapter.

Note Web shares are subject to the access controls enforced by the Web server and the server running Windows Server 2003. If you have problems accessing a share, check the Web server permissions first, and then check the Windows Server 2003 file and folder permissions.

Auditing File and Folder Access

Access permissions will only help protect data; they won't tell you who deleted important data or who was trying to access files and folders inappropriately. To track who accessed files and folders and what they did, you must configure auditing for file and folder access. Every comprehensive security strategy should include auditing.

To track file and folder access, you must

- Enable auditing

- Specify which files and folders to audit
- Monitor the security logs

Enabling Auditing for Files and Folders

You configure auditing policies by using Group Policy or local security policy. Group Policy is used when you want to set auditing policies for an entire site, domain, or organizational unit and is used as discussed in Part 7 of this book, "Managing Active Directory and Security." Local security policy settings apply to an individual workstation or server and can be overridden by Group Policy.

To enable auditing of files and folders for a specific computer, start the Local Security Policy tool by clicking Start, Programs or All Programs, Administrative Tools, and Local Security Policy. On a domain controller, select the Default Domain Controller Security Policy tool. Expand Local Policies, and then Audit Policy, as shown in Figure 21-26.

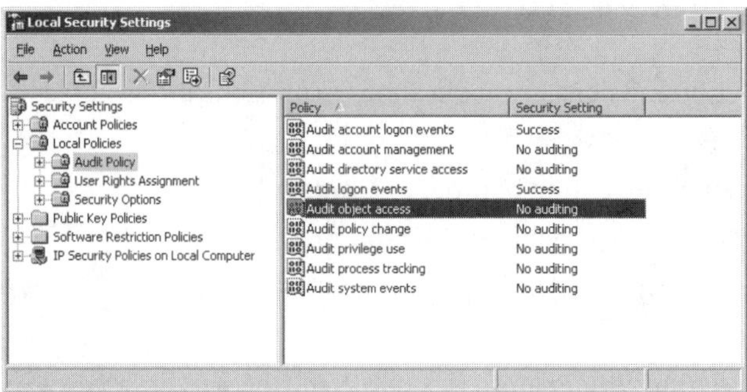

Figure 21-26. Access the local auditing policy settings.

Next, double-click Audit Object Access. This displays the Audit Object Access Properties dialog box shown in Figure 21-27. Under Audit These Attempts, select Success to log successful access attempts, Failure to log failed access attempts, or both options, and then click OK. This enables auditing but it doesn't specify which files and folders should be audited.

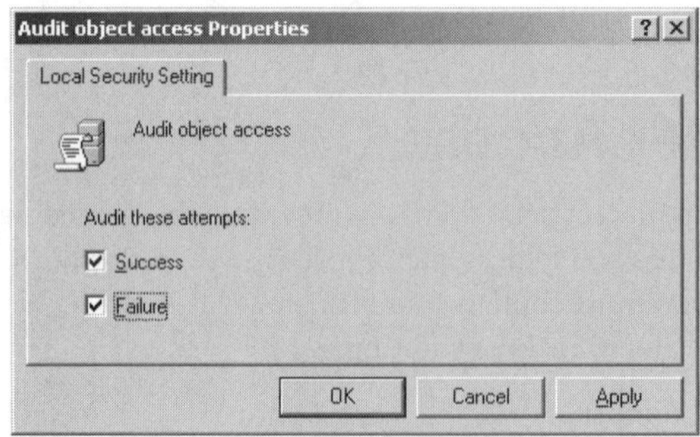

Figure 21-27. Configure auditing for object access.

Specifying Files and Folders to Audit

Once you have configured enable Audit Object Access, you can set the level of auditing for individual folders and files. This allows you to control whether and how folder and file usage is tracked. Keep in mind auditing is available only on NTFS volumes. In addition, everything discussed about inheritance applies to files and folders as well—and this is a good thing. This allows you, for example, to audit access to every file or folder on a volume simply by specifying that you want to audit the root folder of the volume.

You specify files and folders to audit using Windows Explorer. In Windows Explorer, right-click the file or folder to be audited, and then, from the shortcut menu, select Properties. In the Properties dialog box, select the Security tab, and then click Advanced. In the Access Control Settings dialog box, select the Auditing tab, as shown in Figure 21-28.

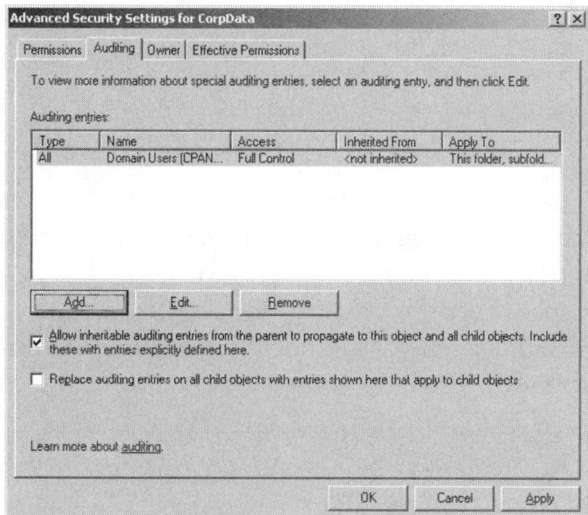

Figure 21-28. Specify to which users and groups auditing should apply.

You have the same two inheritance options discussed earlier in the chapter:

- If you want to inherit auditing settings from a parent object, ensure Allow Inheritable Permissions From The Parent To Propagate To This Object And All Child Objects is selected.
- If you want child objects of the current object to inherit the settings you are setting on the current folder, select Replace Auditing Entries On All Child Objects With Entries Shown Here.

Now use the Auditing Entries list box to select the users, groups, or computers whose actions you want to audit. To add specific accounts, click Add, and then use the Select User, Computer, Or Group dialog box to select an account name to add. If you want to audit actions for all users, use the special group Everyone. Otherwise, select the specific user groups or users, or both, that you want to audit. When you click OK, you'll see the Auditing Entry For dialog box, as shown in Figure 21-29.

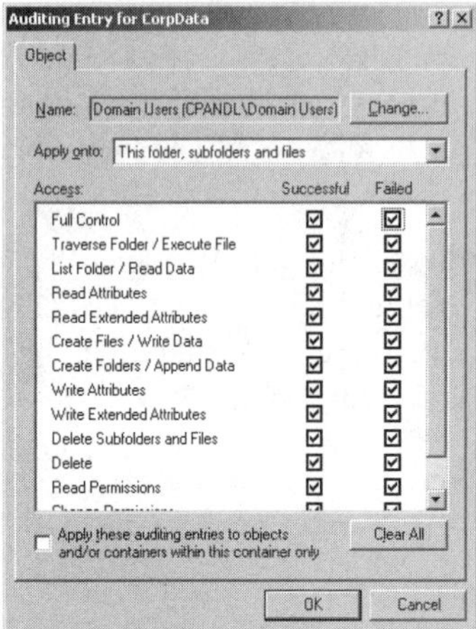

Figure 21-29. Determine the actions to audit for the designated user, group, or computer.

The Apply Onto drop-down list box allows you to specify which actions should be audited. Select the Successful or Failed options, or both, for the events you want to audit. The events you can audit are the same as the special permissions listed in Table 21-3 and 21-4, except you can't audit synchronizing of offline files and folders. Choose OK when you're finished. Repeat this process to audit other users, groups, or computers.

> **Note** Often you'll want to track only failed actions. This way, you know if someone was trying to perform an action and failed. Keep in mind a failed attempt doesn't always mean someone is trying to break into a file or folder. A user simply might have double-clicked a folder or file to which he or she didn't have access. In addition, some types of actions can cause multiple failed attempts to be logged even when the user performed the action only once. Regardless, as an administrator, you should always check multiple failed attempts because of the possibility that someone is attempting to breach your system's defenses.

Monitoring the Security Logs

Any time files and folders that you've configured for auditing are accessed, the action is written to the system's Security log, where it's stored for your review. The Security log is accessible from Event Viewer. Successful actions can cause successful events, such as successful file reads, to be recorded. Failed actions can cause failed events, such as failed file deletions, to be recorded.

Chapter 22

Using Volume Shadow Copy

Volume Shadow Copy service is a new feature of Microsoft Windows Server 2003. It offers two important features:

- **Shadow copying of files in shared folders** Allows you to configure volumes so that shadow copies of files in shared folders are created automatically at specific intervals during the day. This allows you to go back and look at earlier versions of files stored in shared folders. You can use these earlier versions to recover deleted, incorrectly modified, or overwritten files. You can also compare versions of files to see what changes were made over time. Up to 64 versions of files are maintained.
- **Shadow copying of open or locked files for backups** Allows you to use backup programs, such as Windows Backup, to back up files that are open or locked. This means you can back up when applications are using the files and no longer have to worry about backups failing because files were in use. Backup programs must implement the Volume Shadow Copy application programming interface (API).

Both features are independent of each other. You do not need to enable shadow copying of a volume to be able to back up open or locked files on a volume. This chapter primarily focuses on shadow copying of files in shared folders. Chapter 41, "Backup and Recovery," examines backups.

Shadow Copy Essentials

Shadow copying of files in shared folders is a feature administrators can use to create backup copies of files on designated volumes automatically. You can think of these backup copies as point-in-time snapshots that can be used to recover previous versions of files. Normally, when a user deletes a file from a shared folder, it is immediately deleted and doesn't go to the local Recycle Bin. This means the only way to recover it is from backup. The reason for this is that when you delete files over the network, the files are permanently deleted on the remote server and never make it to the Recycle Bin. This changes with shadow copying. If a user deletes a file from a network share, she can go back to a previous version and recover it—and she can do this without needing assistance from an administrator.

Using Shadow Copies of Shared Folders

Shadow copies of shared folders are designed to help recover files that were accidentally deleted, corrupted, or inappropriately edited. Once you configure shadow copies on a server, the server creates and maintains previous versions of all files and folders created on the volumes you've specified. It does this by creating snapshots of shared folders at predetermined intervals and storing these images in shadow copy storage in such a way that users and administrators can easily access the data to recover previous versions of files and folders.

Ideally, once you implement shadow copies throughout the organization and show users how to use the feature, users will be able to recover files and folders without needing assistance. This allows users to manage their own files, resolve problems, and fix mistakes. It also saves time and money because previous versions can be recovered quickly and easily and resources that would have been used to recover files and perform related tasks can be used elsewhere.

When planning to deploy shadow copies in your organization, look at the shared folders that are in use. When you identify the ones that would benefit from this feature, note the volumes on which those shares are located. Those are the volumes for which you will need to configure shadow copying. You might also want to consider changing the way users' personal data is stored. In Windows Server 2003, you can centrally manage user data folders through file shares, and then if you configure shadow copies on these file shares, users will have access to previous versions of all their data files and folders. The folders you can centrally manage are the following:

- Application Data
- Desktop
- Start Menu
- My Documents
- My Pictures

You configure central management of these folders through Group Policy. When you do this, you want to redirect the root path for these folders to a file share.

How Shadow Copies Works

Shadow Copies for Shared Folders is made possible through the Shadow Copy API. The shadow copy driver (Volsnap.sys) and the Volume Shadow Copy service executable (Vssvc.exe) are key components used by this API. When you enable shadow copies on a server, the server is configured to a client-accessible shadow copy service provider. The default provider is the Microsoft Software Shadow Copy Provider, and it is responsible for providing the necessary interface between clients that want to access shadow copies and clients that write shadow copies or information pertaining to shadow copies, called Volume Shadow Copy service writers.

A number of shadow copy service writers are installed by default and other writers can be installed when you install other programs, such as third-party backup software. The default writers installed depend on the system configuration and include the following:

- **System Writer** The standard shadow copies writer used by the operating system
- **File Replication Service (FRS) Writer** Shadow copies writer used by FRS so that in-use files can be backed up, primarily on domain controllers
- **Event Log Writer** Shadow copies writer used by other writers to write events in the event logs. Most shadow copy events are written to the Application log with the event source as VolSnap
- **Registry Writer** Shadow copies writer used by other writers to make Registry changes
- **DHCP Jet Writer** Shadow copies writer used to make backups of files in use by the Dynamic Host Configuration Protocol (DHCP)
- **WINS Jet Writer** Shadow copies writer used to make backups of files in use by the Windows Internet Naming Service (WINS)
- **NT Directory Service (NTDS) Writer** Shadow copies writer used to make backups of files in use by NTDS
- **Microsoft Data Engine (MSDE) Writer** Used to write shadow copy data
- **IIS Metabase Writer** Shadow copies writer used to make backups of Microsoft Internet Information Services (IIS) metabase files
- **Windows Management Instrumentation (WMI) Writer** Standard WMI writer for shadow copies
- **Remote Storage Writer** Shadow copies writer used to make backups of file in use by Remote Storage
- **Certification Authority Writer** Shadow copies writer used to make backups of files in use by Microsoft Certificate service
- **Microsoft Exchange Writer** Shadow copies writer used to make backups of files in use by Microsoft Exchange Server

Tip You can list available shadow copy providers by typing **vssadmin list providers** at the command line. To list shadow copy writers, type **vssadmin list writers**.

To create copies of previous versions of files, Shadow Copies for Shared Folders uses a differential copy procedure. With this technique, only copies of files that have changed since the last copy are marked for copying. During the copy procedure, Shadow Copies for Shared Folders creates the previous version data in one of two ways:

- If the application used to change a file stored details of the changes, Shadow Copies for Shared Folders performs a block-level copy of any changes that have been made to files since the last save. Thus, only changes are copied, not the entire file.
- If the application used to change a file rewrote the entire file to disk, Shadow Copies for Shared Folders saves the entire file as it exists at that point in time.

If you're wondering exactly how this works, I was too at first, then I started experimenting. An example of an application that can save changes or full copies is Microsoft Word. If you enable Fast Saves in Word, only changes to a file are written to disk. If you clear the Fast Saves option, Word writes a complete copy of the file when you save it.

As mentioned previously, Shadow Copies for Shared Folders runs at predefined intervals. These predefined intervals are set as the run schedule when you configure shadow copying of a volume. As with other processes that have a run schedule, a scheduled task is created that is used to trigger shadow copying at the specified times. Because of this, Shadow Copies for Shared Folders is dependent on the Schedule Task service. If this service is stopped or improperly configured, shadow copying will not work.

Implementing Shadow Copies for Shared Folders

Implementing Shadow Copies for Shared Folders isn't something you should do haphazardly. You should take the time to plan out the implementation. Key issues that you should consider include the following:

- **Copy volumes** For which volumes should shadow copying be configured?
- **Disk space** How much disk space will be needed for shadow copying, and is there enough available space on existing volumes?
- **Shadow storage** Where should the shadow copies be stored and on which volumes?
- **Run schedule** How often should shadow copies be made?

Start your planning by considering for which volumes you want to configure shadow copies. Once you configure this feature, shadow copies will be created of files in the shared folders on these volumes. To implement shadow copying of files of shared folders, you enable shadow copying of the volume in which the shared folders are located. The initial shadow copy requires at least 100 megabytes (MB) of free space to create, regardless of how much data is stored in the volume's shared folders. The disk space used by Shadow Copies of Shared Folders is referred to as shadow storage. Shadow Copies uses this space to store previous versions of files and as a work area when it is taking snapshots. Because of this, the actual amount of space used for shadow storage is different from the amount of space allocated for shadow storage.

The amount of disk space available shouldn't be overlooked. The Shadow Copy service will save up to 64 versions of each file in shared folders and, by default, will configure its maximum space usage as up to 10 percent of the volume. Once set, the maximum size is fixed unless you change it. The service won't, however, reexamine free space later to determine if this maximum value should be changed. If a volume runs out of space, shadow copying will fail and errors will be generated in the event logs.

When you plan out your shadow copies implementation, you should think carefully about where shadow storage will be located. Shadow storage can be created on the volumes for which you are creating shadow copies or on different volumes. If you have busy file servers or you must scale this feature to serve many users or an increasing number of users, it might be best to use a separate volume on a separate drive for shadow storage.

Tip **Use the command-line tools to examine shadow storage**
You can determine how much space is allocated to and used by shadow storage by using the VSSADMIN LIST SHADOWSTORAGE command. Working with this command is discussed in the section entitled "Configuring Shadow Copies at the Command Line" later in this chapter.

Inside Out

Increase shadow copy storage

The initial shadow copy storage requires at least 100 MB. On busy servers with high input/output (I/O) on the drives, it is recommended that the initial shadow copy storage space be set to at least 300 MB—and you can do this manually when you set up shadow copy. This allows Shadow Copies for Shared Folders to have more disk space for its working set and helps prevent timeouts during shadow copy write operations. A hot fix is provided that changes the initial shadow copy storage size to 300 MB and also includes improvements to the shadow copy driver (Volsnap.sys) and the Volume Shadow Copy service executable (Vssvc.exe) to improve performance of Shadow Copies for Shared Folders. The hot fix and the changes are discussed in Microsoft Knowledge Base article 826936. Several other important hot fixes for shadow copies are available as discussed in Microsoft Knowledge Base article 833167. These hot fixes are applied when you install Windows Server 2003 Service Pack 1.

Shadow copying is a resource-intensive process. By default, when you configure shadow copying on a volume, copies are made at two scheduled intervals during the day: once in the morning at 7:00 A.M. and once at midday at 12:00 P.M. The morning copy allows you to save the work from the previous day and is meant to occur before users come in to work in the morning. The midday copy allows you to save work up to that point in the day and is meant to occur when users are taking a break for lunch. In this way, a user would lose at most, a half day's work and the resource impact caused by creating shadow copies is minimized.

When you configure the shadow copy schedule for your organization, you should take these same issues into consideration. Start by determining the best times of the day to create shadow copies. Ideally, this is when the server's resources are being used the least. Then determine how much potential data loss is acceptable, given the resources, the type of data stored, and the available disk space.

> **Tip** **Plan shadow copies around backups**
> When planning the run schedule for shadow copies be sure to take into account the backup schedule for the related volumes. If you schedule shadow copies during backup, the shadow copy service writers will experience time out errors and any shadow copies that should have been created at that time will be lost. If you suspect a scheduling conflict, you can use the VSSADMIN LIST WRITERS command to check the last error status of the shadow copy writers.

You can change the default shadow copy times, add new scheduled run times, and schedule recurring tasks that create copies at specific time intervals during the day. However, it is recommended that you avoid creating shadow copies more frequently than once per hour. When configuring run schedules, keep in mind how much work is saved and how long users will have to retrieve versions of files. If you save changes 2 times a day during weekdays, the maximum of 64 shadow copies means that users have about 32 working days during which they could retrieve the oldest version of a file before it is automatically deleted.

After you configure shadow copying, you must install a client on computers throughout the organization. Two clients are available: the Previous Versions Client and the Shadow Copy Client. The installation of these clients is discussed in the section entitled "Using Shadow Copies on Clients" later in this chapter.

With either client, users can access the Previous Versions tab by right-clicking a shared file or folder, selecting Properties, and choosing Previous Versions. Users will then be able to view a version of a file, save a version of a file to a new location, or restore a previous version of a file. The clients can be distributed through Group Policy or Microsoft Systems Management Server (SMS).

Managing Shadow Copies in Computer Management

Shadow copies are configured on a per-volume basis. Each volume on a server that has shared folders must be configured separately for shadow copying.

> **Tip** **Defragment volumes before enabling shadow copies**
> Shadow copies can become corrupted on volumes that are heavily fragmented. It is recommended that you defragment volumes before enabling shadow copies.

Troubleshooting

Be careful when defragmenting

If you defragment a volume while shadow copies are enabled, the oldest shadow copies can be lost. Shadow copy loss can occur because the shadow copy provider uses a copy-on-write approach that uses a 16-kilobyte (KB) block level. If the volume's cluster size is smaller than 16 KB, the shadow copy provider cannot distinguish disk defragmentation I/O and normal write I/O operations and as a result can create an extra shadow copy. If there are already 64 copies of a file, the oldest file is then deleted, which is how the oldest shadow copy gets deleted accidentally. To prevent this, it is recommended that cluster size of volumes that use shadow copies be set to 16 KB or larger.

Configuring Shadow Copies in Computer Management

You can use Computer Management to configure shadow copying by following these steps:

1. Start Computer Management, expand Storage, and select Disk Management. Right-click a volume in the Disk Management Volume List or Graphical View, and select Properties.
2. In the Properties dialog box, select the Shadow Copies tab, as shown in Figure 22-1.

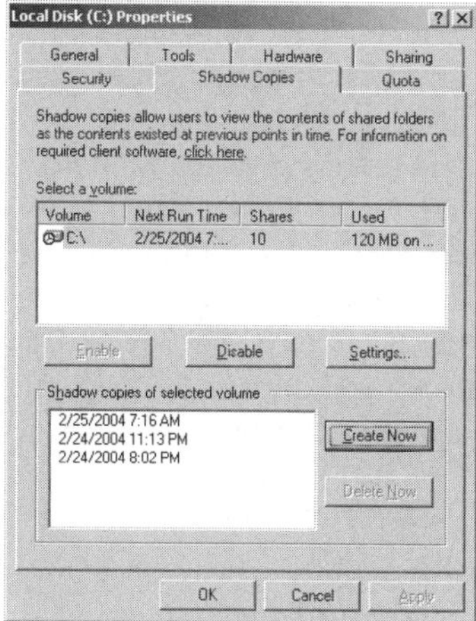

Figure 22-1. Enable shadow copies on a per-volume basis.

3 Select the volume for which you want to configure shadow copies, and then click Settings. This displays the Settings dialog box shown in Figure 22-2.

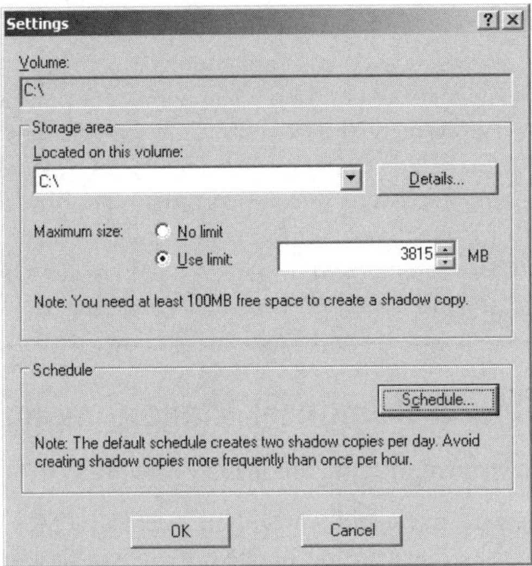

Figure 22-2. Set storage limits for shadow copies.

> **Tip** **Configure mount points separately**
> There's a limitation for volumes that have mount points. With a mount point, a volume is attached to an empty folder on an NTFS volume and made to appear as part of that volume. If you enable shadow copies on a volume with mounted drives, the mounted drives are not included and users will not be able to access previous versions of files on the mounted volume. The workaround is to share the mounted volume and enable shadow copies for this share. Users then must access the share path to the mounted volume to view previous versions. For example, if you have a folder F:\Eng\Data, and the Data folder is a mount point for G, you enable shadow copies on both drives F and G. You share F:\Eng as \\CorpSvr01\Eng, and you share F:\Eng\Data as \\CorpSvr01\Data. In this example, users can access previous versions of \\CorpSvr01\Eng and \\CorpSvr01\Data, but not \\CorpSvr01\Eng\Data.

4 Use the Located On This Volume selection list to specify where the shadow copies should be created. Shadow copies can be created on the volume you are configuring or any other volume available on the computer.

5 Click Details to see the free space and total available disk space on the selected volume, and then click OK.

Using Volume Shadow Copy

6 Use the Maximum Size options to set the maximum size that shadow copies for this volume can use.

7 Click Schedule to display the dialog box shown in Figure 22-3. Two run schedules are set automatically. Use the selection list to view these schedules. If you don't want to use a scheduled run time, select it, and then click Delete. To add a run schedule, configure the run times using the Schedule Task, Start Time, and Schedule Task Weekly options, then click New. When you are finished configuring run times, click OK twice to return to the volume's Properties dialog box.

Tip Check cluster configuration to ensure scheduling can work after failover

To ensure the VolumeShadowCopy task runs after failover on a clustered file server, the %SystemRoot% should be the same on the cluster to which the service is failed over. If it isn't in the same location and failover occurs, the VolumeShadowCopy task might not run. For example, if the %SystemRoot% on node 1 is C:\Windows and then %SystemRoot% on node 2 is C:\Winnt, the task might not run when the service fails over from node 1 to node 2. This is because the task runs in the %SystemRoot%\System32 folder and the Start In property setting for the task changes the environment variable to the actual folder location rather than using the environment variable once the task is set. See Chapter 18, "Preparing and Deploying Server Clusters," for more information about clustering.

Figure 22-3. Set the schedule for when shadow copies are made.

8. Select the volume on which you want to enable shadow copies and click Enable. When prompted, click Yes to confirm the action. Windows will then create a snapshot of the volume.
9. Configure any additional volumes for shadow copying by repeating steps 3 through 8. Click OK when you are finished.

Troubleshooting

Shadow copy relies on the Task Scheduler

The schedule you set for shadow copies is set as a scheduled task on the server. Scheduled tasks are run by the Task Scheduler service and can be viewed in the Scheduled Tasks folder as discussed in Chapter 12, "Managing Windows Server 2003." The Task Scheduler service must be running and properly configured for shadow copying to work correctly. In addition, you should not modify ShadowCopyVolume tasks using the Scheduled Tasks folder. Instead, only configure the run schedule using a volume's Properties dialog box.

Maintaining Shadow Copies After Configuration

Once you configure shadow copying, snapshots are made according to the schedule you've set. Keep the following in mind:

- Individual snapshots taken of a volume can be deleted. Start Computer Management, expand Storage, and select Disk Management. Right-click a volume in the Disk Management Volume List or Graphical View, and select Properties. In the Properties dialog box, select the Shadow Copies tab. Click the volume you want to work with. Its snapshots are listed in the Shadow Copies Of Selected Volume list. To delete a specific snapshot, select it in the list and then click Delete Now.
- If you ever want to make a snapshot manually, you can do this by clicking Create Now in the Shadow Copies tab.
- You can change the settings and run schedule at a later date as well. Access the Shadow Copies tab, select the volume you want to change, and then click Settings. Make the necessary changes, and then click OK.

Caution Changing the maximum allowed size can cause existing shadow copies to disappear. This could happen if you set the maximum allowed size smaller than the amount of space currently in use.

- To delete a shadow copy of a volume, select the shadow copy in bottom list box of the Shadow Copies tab, and then click Delete Now. When prompted to confirm the action, click Yes.

- To disable Shadow Copies for a volume, select the volume in top list box of the Shadow Copies tab, and then click Disable. When prompted to confirm the action, click Yes.

> **Caution** Disabling shadow copies deletes all previously saved snapshot images. Because of this, only disable snapshots when you are sure previously saved snapshot images are no longer needed.

> **Tip** **Disable shadow copies before removing the associated volume**
> If you want to remove a volume on which shadow copies have been enabled, you should first disable shadow copies or delete all scheduled tasks that create the shadow copies for the volume. This will ensure error events aren't written to the system logs when the Scheduled Task service can't create the snapshot images.

Configuring Shadow Copies at the Command Line

The command-line tool for configuring shadow copies is VSSAdmin. Using VSSAdmin, you can configure shadow copying of volumes on the computer you're logged on to locally or remotely through Remote Desktop. As with Computer Management, each volume on a server that has shared folders must be configured separately for shadow copying.

Enabling Shadow Copying from the Command Line

To enable shadow copying of a volume, you use the ADD SHADOWSTORAGE command. The syntax is as follows:

```
vssadmin add shadowstorage /for=ForVolumeSpec /on=OnVolumeSpec
```

Here, /for=*ForVolumeSpec* is used to specify the local volume for which you are configuring or managing shadow copies and /on=*OnVolumeSpec* is used to specify the volume on which the shadow copy data will be stored.

Consider the following example:

```
vssadmin add shadowstorage /for=c: /on=d:
```

Here, you are configuring the C volume to use shadow copies, and the shadow copy data is stored on D. Both values can be set to the same volume as well, such as

```
vssadmin add shadowstorage /for=e: /on=e:
```

Here, you are configuring the E volume to use shadow copies, and the shadow copy data is stored on that same volume.

With VSSAdmin, shadow copying is configured by default so that there is no maximum size limit for shadow storage. To set a specific limit, you can use the /MaxSize parameter. This parameter expects to be passed a numeric value with a suffix of KB, MB, GB, TB, PB, or EB to indicate whether the value is set in kilobytes, megabytes, gigabytes, terabytes, petabytes, or exabytes. This parameter must be set to 100 MB or greater. Consider the following example:

```
vssadmin add shadowstorage /for=c: /on=d: /maxsize=2GB
```

Here, you are configuring the C volume to use shadow copies, and the shadow copy data is stored on D. The maximum size allowed for the shadow storage is 2 GB.

The most common errors that occur when you are configuring shadow copies from the command line relate to improper syntax. If you enter the wrong syntax, VSSAdmin shows the error message "Error: Invalid command" and will display the command syntax. If shadow copying is already configured for a volume, the error message states "Error: The specified shadow copy storage association already exists."

Create Manual Snapshots from the Command Line

When you enable shadow copying, snapshots of shared folders are created automatically according to the default run schedule. If you ever want to make a snapshot manually, you can do this using the CREATE SHADOW command. Type **vssadmin create shadow /for=*ForVolumeSpec***, where *ForVolumeSpec* is the local volume for which you are creating the snapshot. Consider the following example:

```
vssadmin create shadow /for=e:
```

Here, you create a snapshot of shared folders on the E volume.

Tip **Set the AutoRetry interval to retry creation automatically**
Occasionally, the Shadow Copy service is busy, typically because it is creating a snapshot of this or another volume. Here, you can try again in a few minutes, or, by using the /AutoRetry parameter, you can specifically set the length of time during which CREATE SHADOW should continue to try to create the snapshot. For example, if you want to retry automatically for 15 minutes, you'd use /AutoRetry=15.

Viewing Shadow Copy Information

VSSAdmin provides several utility commands for viewing shadow copy information. The most useful are LIST SHADOWS and LIST SHADOWSTORAGE.

LIST SHADOWS lists the existing shadow copies on a volume. By default, all shadow copies on all volumes are displayed. The command accepts /for=*ForVolumeSpec* to list only the information for a particular volume and /shadow=*ShadowId* to list only the information for a particular shadow copy. However, it is much easier just to type **vssadmin list shadows** and go through the information to find what you are looking for.

The output from LIST SHADOWS shows summary information for each snapshot created according to its shadow copy identifier, such as:

```
Contents of shadow copy set ID: {ff70e4e6-4117-446a-8ffe-1708632664ff}
   Contained 1 shadow copies at creation time: 2/26/2004 2:03:55 AM
      Shadow Copy ID: {5ba0f3d3-afa8-4e4e-a00e-64a44e11bf81}
        Original Volume: (C:)\\?\Volume{3796c3c0-5106-11d7-911c-806d6172696f}\
         Shadow Copy Volume: \\?\GLOBALROOT\Device\HarddiskVolumeShadowCopy3
         Originating Machine: corpsvr02.cpandl.com
         Service Machine: corpsvr02.cpandl.com
         Provider: 'Microsoft Software Shadow Copy provider 1.0'
         Type: ClientAccessible
      Attributes: Persistent, Client-accessible, No auto release, No writers,
 Differential

Contents of shadow copy set ID: {6cb7fba8-afbb-415f-b47a-6800b332af9a}
   Contained 1 shadow copies at creation time: 2/26/2004 2:34:09 AM
      Shadow Copy ID: {3f44a086-2034-4c6b-bf3f-3489a5e98bd8}
        Original Volume: (C:)\\?\Volume{3796c3c0-5106-11d7-911c-806d6172696f}\
         Shadow Copy Volume: \\?\GLOBALROOT\Device\HarddiskVolumeShadowCopy4
         Originating Machine: corpsvr02.cpandl.com
         Service Machine: corpsvr02.cpandl.com
         Provider: 'Microsoft Software Shadow Copy provider 1.0'
         Type: ClientAccessible
         Attributes: Persistent, Client-accessible, No auto release, No writers,
 Differential

Contents of shadow copy set ID: {25f354e1-003a-4e54-8ba6-2f09bc499ef4}
   Contained 1 shadow copies at creation time: 2/26/2004 3:08:37 AM
      Shadow Copy ID: {f3899e11-613a-4a7d-95de-cb264d1dbb7b}
        Original Volume: (C:)\\?\Volume{3796c3c0-5106-11d7-911c-806d6172696f}\
         Shadow Copy Volume: \\?\GLOBALROOT\Device\HarddiskVolumeShadowCopy5
         Originating Machine: corpsvr02.cpandl.com
         Service Machine: corpsvr02.cpandl.com
         Provider: 'Microsoft Software Shadow Copy provider 1.0'
         Type: ClientAccessible
      Attributes: Persistent, Client-accessible, No auto release, No writers,
 Differential
```

Here, there is a data set for each snapshot that has been created. The most important information is the following:

- **Shadow Copy ID** The unique identifier for the snapshot image. This identifier can be copied and used to delete a particular snapshot if desired.
- **Original Volume** The volume for which shadow copies are configured.
- **Originating Machine** The name of the computer you are working with.

LIST SHADOWSTORAGE displays all shadow copy storage associations on the system. The command accepts /for=*ForVolumeSpec* and /on=*OnVolumeSpec* parameters to limit the output. But again, it is much easier just to type **vssadmin list shadowstorage** and go through the information to find what you are looking for. Here is an example of the output from this command:

```
Shadow Copy Storage association
   For volume: (C:)\\?\Volume{3796c3c0-5106-11d7-911c-806d6172696f}\
   Shadow Copy Storage volume: (C:)\\?\Volume{3796c3c0-5106-11d7-911c-806d617269
6f}\
   Used Shadow Copy Storage space: 39.516 MB
   Allocated Shadow Copy Storage space: 122.297 MB
   Maximum Shadow Copy Storage space: 3.726 GB
```

Here, the output shows you the following information:

- **For Volume** The volume for which shadow copies are configured
- **Shadow Copy Storage Volume** The volume on which shadow copy data is stored
- **Used Shadow Copy Storage Space** The actual amount of disk space used on the storage volume
- **Allocated Shadow Copy Storage Space** The amount of disk space allocated on the storage volume for shadow copies
- **Maximum Shadow Copy Storage Space** The maximum size allowed for shadow copies on the storage volume

Deleting Snapshot Images from the Command Line

If you want to delete individual snapshots on a volume, you can use the DELETE SHADOWS command to do this. You can delete the oldest snapshot on the specified volume by typing **vssadmin delete shadows /for=*ForVolumeSpec* /oldest**, where /for=*ForVolumeSpec* specifies the local volume for which the snapshot is used. For example, if you configured shadow copying on the C volume and want to delete the oldest snapshot on this volume, you'd enter the command:

```
vssadmin delete shadows /for=c: /oldest
```

When prompted to confirm that you really want to delete the snapshot, press Y. VSSAdmin should then report "Successfully deleted 1 shadow copies."

To delete a snapshot by its shadow identifier use the /Shadow=*ShadowID* parameter instead of the /For=*ForVolumeSpec* and /Oldest parameters. Here, *ShadowID* is the globally unique identifier for the snapshot image, including the brackets {}. For example, if you want to delete the snapshot image with the ID {f3899e11-613a-4a7d-95de-cb264d1dbb7b} from the C volume, you'd use the following command:

```
vssadmin delete shadows /for=c: /shadow={f3899e11-613a-4a7d-95de-cb264d1dbb7b}
```

Again, when prompted to confirm that you really want to delete the snapshot, press Y. VSSAdmin doesn't actually check to see if the snapshot exists until you confirm that you want to delete the snapshot. In this case, if the shadow copy ID is invalid or the snapshot has already been deleted, VSSAdmin reports a "not found" error, such as:

```
Error: Shadow Copy ID: {f3899e11-613a-4a7d-95de-cb264d1dbb7b} not found.
```

DELETE SHADOWS also lets you delete all snapshots on all volumes configured for shadow copy on the computer. To do this, type **delete shadows /all**. When prompted to confirm that you really want to delete all snapshots, press Y. VSSAdmin should then report, "Successfully deleted *N* shadow copies." Deleting all the shadow copies, doesn't disable shadow copy on the volumes, however. To do this, you must use the DELETE SHADOWSTORAGE command.

Disabling Shadow Copies from the Command Line

To disable shadow copy on a volume, you can use the DELETE SHADOWSTORAGE command. However, unlike the graphical user interface (GUI), you cannot disable shadow copying until all previously saved snapshot images on the affected volume are deleted. Because of this, you must first delete all the snapshots on the volume and then disable shadow copying. Type the command **vssadmin delete shadowstorage /for=*ForVolumeSpec***, where /for=*ForVolumeSpec* is used to specify the local volume for which you are disabling shadow copy. For example, if you want to disable shadow copying of the C volume, you'd use the command:

```
vssadmin delete shadowstorage /for=c:
```

As long as the shadow storage isn't in use, you will be able to delete and VSSAdmin will report, "Successfully deleted the shadow copy storage association(s)."

Using Shadow Copies on Clients

After you configure shadow copying, you must install the client on computers throughout the organization. The client installs a new tab called Previous Versions on files and folders that are shared.

Obtaining and Installing the Client

Before users can access previous versions, the client must be installed on their computer. Two clients are available:

- Previous Versions Client
- Shadow Copy Client

You can use Group Policy or SMS to distribute either client. You can also simply copy the file to a user's computer. Both clients are made available as MSI packages that require Microsoft Windows Installer 2 or later, which is available automatically on Microsoft Windows XP or later versions of the Windows operating system.

> **Note** Both clients offer the same features as of the time of this writing. If you want one client for all your systems, the Previous Versions client may be the best one to use. Otherwise, you may want to install the Shadow Copy Client on systems as this one has the most current APIs.

Installing the Previous Versions Client

The Previous Version client is stored in the %SystemRoot%\System32\Clients\Twclient\X86 folder. Its installer is named Twcli32.msi. Computers running Windows Server 2003, Windows XP, Microsoft Windows 2000 Service Pack 3 or later, and Microsoft Windows 98 can use this client.

Once the client is on the user's computer, you run it by double-clicking it. This starts the Previous Versions Client Setup Wizard. The wizard automatically installs the client, and you only need to click Next and then click Finish (see Figure 22-4).

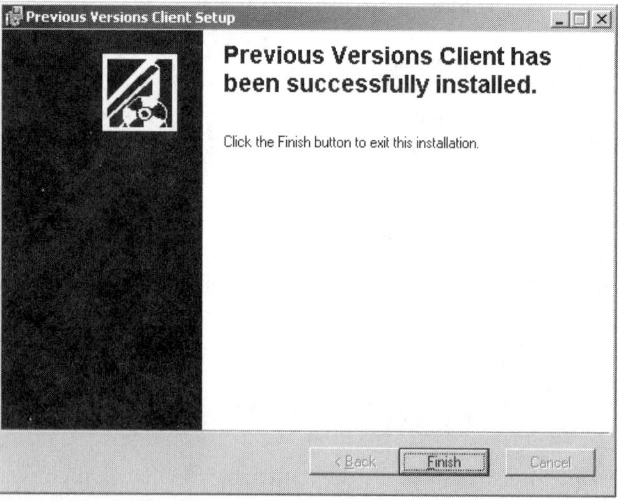

Figure 22-4. The Previous Versions Client Setup Wizard installs automatically when you double-click the Installer Package.

Installing the Shadow Copy Client

The Shadow Copy Client can be downloaded from the Microsoft Web site. Its installer is ShadowCopyClient.msi. Computers running Windows Server 2003, Windows XP, and

Windows 2000 Service Pack 3 or later can use this client. If you use this client with earlier versions of the Windows operating system, you must install the Shadow Copy Client on both the servers using shadow copies and the user computers that must access shadow copies.

Once the client is on the user's computer, you run it by double-clicking it. This starts the Shadow Copy Client Installation Wizard, as shown in Figure 22-5. When the wizard starts, click Next. If you accept the terms of the licensing agreement, select I Accept The Terms In The License Agreement, and then click Next again. The wizard will then install the client, and you only need to click Finish.

Figure 22-5. Start the Shadow Copy Client Installation Wizard.

Accessing Shadow Copies on Clients

You can access shadow copies on a client that has either the Previous Versions Client or the Shadow Copy Client installed from the following components:

- **Microsoft Windows Explorer** In Windows Explorer, right-click the network drive for which you want to access previous file versions, choose Properties, and then click the Previous Versions tab, as shown in Figure 22-6.
- **My Network Places** In My Network Places, expand Entire Network and Microsoft Windows Network to display the available domains, and then expand the domain node to display servers on the network. When you expand a server node, any publicly shared resources on that server are listed. Right-click the share for which you want to access previous file versions, choose Properties, and then click the Previous Versions tab, as shown in Figure 22-7.

> **Tip** **For local logon use My Network Places**
> If you are logged on locally to the server and want to examine previous versions, use My Network Places. This way, you can access the folder as a share and see the previous versions. Otherwise, if you access the folder directly, the option won't be available.

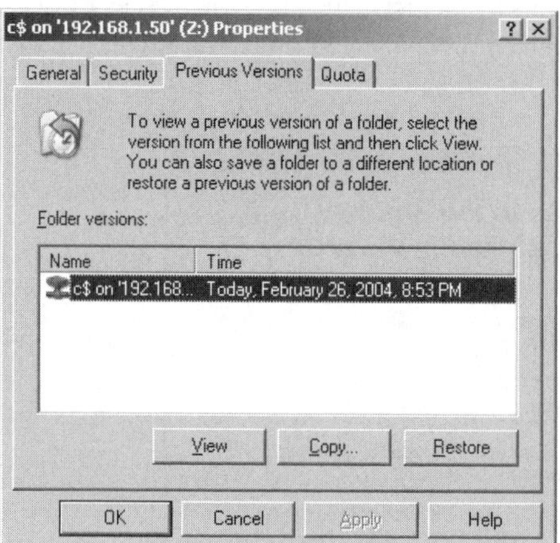

Figure 22-6. The Previous Versions tab is available for network drives that are mapped to shared folders using shadow copies.

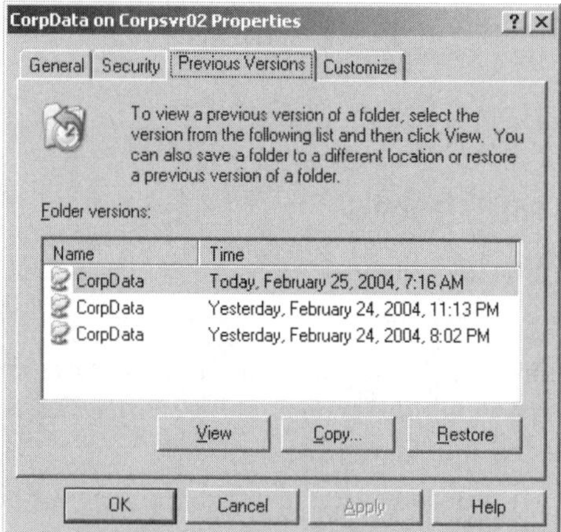

Figure 22-7. When you access shared folders directly, you see the shared folder name rather than the network drive letter and mapping information.

> **Tip Access the full path for mount points**
> If a volume is a mount point, you must access the full mount point path to see its previous versions. For example, if you have a folder F:\Eng\Data, and the Data folder is a mount point for G, you enable shadow copies on both volumes F and G. You share F:\Eng as \\CorpSvr01\Eng, and you share F:\Eng\Data as \\CorpSvr01\Data. In this example, users can access previous versions of \\CorpSvr01\Eng and \\CorpSvr01\Data, but not \\CorpSvr01\Eng\Data.

After you access the Previous Versions tab, select the folder version that you want to work with. Each folder has a date and time stamp. Then click the button corresponding to the action you want to perform:

- **View** Clicking View opens the shadow copy in Windows Explorer. You can then work with the files it contains much like a normal folder. You won't, however, be able to delete files from this folder or save files to this folder—you can of course copy files to other locations.
- **Copy** Clicking Copy displays the Copy Items dialog box, which lets you copy the snapshot image of the folder to the location you specify.
- **Restore** Clicking Restore rolls back the shared folder to its state as of the snapshot image you selected. Because this could result in losing any changes subsequent to the date and time of the snapshot image, you are prompted to confirm the action. Click Yes to proceed with the restore.

Restoring Shadow Copies from the Command Line

In the *Windows Server 2003 Resource Kit*, you'll find a command-line tool for working with shadow copies called VolRest. You can use VolRest to search for a file on a server and list the available versions and to locate previous versions of a file and restore those versions to a specific folder.

Searching for a File and Listing Available Versions

The easiest way to work with VolRest is to use the Universal Naming Convention (UNC) path of the server and shared folder you want to examine. The UNC path has the following syntax:

```
\\ServerName\SharedFolderName
```

where *ServerName* is the domain name or Internet Protocol (IP) address of the server and *SharedFolderName* is the name of the shared folder. If you know the server and folder name, you can search for files within the shared folder by adding the name or part of the name to the UNC pathname. Consider the following examples:

```
volrest \\CorpSvr02\EngData\QuarterlyReport.doc
```

Here, you are looking for previous versions of the QuarterlyReport.doc file in the EngData share on CORPSVR02.

If you know only part of the name, you could use wildcards as well, such as follows:

```
volrest \\CorpSvr02\EngData\*Report.doc
```

Here, VolRest would return any files whose names end in Report.doc. It is important to note that VolRest searches aren't case-sensitive. This means you could type **volrest \\CorpSvr02\EngData*report.doc** or even **volrest \\CorpSvr02\EngData*REPORT.DOC**.

Tip If you want to search subdirectories of the shared folder, add the /S parameter.

The output from VolRest shows each available version of the file according to the timestamp of the snapshot, such as follows:

```
10/01/2004 09:05 AM      65,203,203 \\corpsvr02\corpdata\@GMT-2004.10.01-
12.05.09\quarterlyreport.doc
10/02/2004 03:42 PM      65,224,896 \\corpsvr02\corpdata\@GMT-2004.10.02-
07.12.34\quarterlyreport.doc
10/03/2004 08:35 AM      64,123,083 \\corpsvr02\corpdata\@GMT-2004.10.03-
12.20.12\quarterlyreport.doc
10/04/2004 12:35 PM      67,965,072 \\corpsvr02\corpdata\@GMT-2004.10.05-
07.30.23\quarterlyreport.doc
```

Here several versions of the file are available. The first was last modified on 10/01/2004 at 09:05 A.M., the second was last modified on 10/02/2004 at 03:42 P.M., and so on. The large number following the last modified time stamp is the size of the file in bytes. Finally, the file path includes the date and time stamp of the snapshot. This is the time when the snapshot of a particular file version was made.

Additionally, if you mapped a network drive to a share, you can use the drive designator instead of the UNC server and file share name. For example, if you mapped \\Eng08\EngData to the X drive, you could search for versions of QuarterlyReport.doc by typing **volrest x:\quarterlyreport.doc** or **volrest x:*report.doc**.

Locating and Restoring Previous Versions from the Command Line

If you want to restore these versions of the file to another location, you can use the /R parameter to specify the folder to which the files should be restored. The syntax is as follows:

```
volrest \\ServerName\SharedFolderName\FileName /r:RestorePath
```

where *RestorePath* is the local or network path to the folder to which you want to restore the file's versions. Consider the following example:

```
volrest \\CorpSvr02\EngData\QuarterlyReport.doc /r:c:\data
```

Here, you restore previous versions of QuarterlyReport.doc to the C:\Data folder. By default, each version of the file after the first is sequentially numbered. In this example, that means the files would be named as follows:

- QuarterlyReport(Friday, October 1, 2004, 12.05.09).doc
- QuarterlyReport(Saturday, October 2, 2004, 07.12.34).doc
- QuarterlyReport(Sunday, October 3, 2004, 12.20.12).doc
- QuarterlyReport(Tuesday, October 5, 2004, 07.30.23).doc

Chapter 23

Using Removable Media

Removable media are important aspects of Microsoft Windows Server 2003 networks, especially when it comes to backups. In Windows Server 2003, you can create backups on fixed drives or removable drives. Managing backups on fixed drives is fairly straightforward. Backups are written to backup files and restored from backup files on a hard disk. By using removable drives, you have tapes or discs to manage as well as media pools and media libraries. If you use a tape drive, for example, tapes are your media. The tapes and the tape drive form a library in which backups are written to one or more tapes. Sets of tapes are managed through media pools, which reflect the usage and state of the media.

Introducing Removable Media

To help administrators better manage media, media pools, and media libraries, Windows Server 2003 uses the Removable Storage snap-in and the Removable Storage service. You use the snap-in to manage removable media and, in turn, the snap-in relies on the related service to handle necessary tasks. You can use the Removable Storage Management snap-in to perform many media management tasks, including the following:

- Mounting and dismounting media
- Creating media pools and managing media pool properties
- Inserting and ejecting media in an automated tape library
- Configuring operators that can manage removable storage
- Managing operators requests and the request queue

Removable Storage is only available on servers running Microsoft Windows 2000 or later, and only authorized users can manage Removable Storage. To manage Removable Storage, you must be an administrator, a member of Backup Operators, or an authorized user.

The sections that follow examine essential media management concepts and administrative tasks.

Understanding Media Libraries

Storage media and the storage device used to read and write to the media form a media library in much the same way as books and shelves form a traditional library. Windows Server 2003 supports both automated media libraries and nonautomated libraries:

- Automated media libraries hold multiple media sets and can have multiple drives for reading and writing media. These libraries support automated library management and can have robotic subsystems for loading and unloading media. Other features can include bar-code readers, built-in support for cleaner cartridges, doors for inserting and ejecting tapes, and more. Another name for an automated media library is a robotic library.
- Nonautomated libraries are single-drive devices without robotic subsystems. You manually insert media sets and there is no automated system for switching between multiple media sets. Another name for a nonautomated library is a stand-alone drive.

The library unit and the media used in the library form a Removable Storage system. As in a real library, Removable Storage keeps tracks of all media used in the system whether they are in the library unit or offline on a shelf. You can use this feature to create media inventories and to track down files for recovery. Whenever you bring a new library unit online, Removable Storage attempts to configure the library automatically.

> **Note** With Small Computer System Interface (SCSI)–based robotic libraries, the automated configuration might fail. If this happens, it is usually because the library unit uses multiple drives and those drives aren't on the same SCSI bus as the media changer. The drives and the media changer must be on the same SCSI bus. In addition, robotic libraries must support drive-element address reporting. Otherwise, automatic configuration fails.

Understanding Media Pools

A media pool is a collection of tapes or discs that are managed together. With Removable Storage all media belongs to a pool of a specific media type. The concept of a media pool is very dynamic. Libraries can have multiple media pools, and some media pools can span multiple libraries.

Media pools can also be used to establish a hierarchy in which top-level media pools contain lower-level media pools, and these media pools in turn contain collections of tapes or discs. For example, you could create top-level media pools called IS_Data, Marketing_Data, and HR_Data. The IS_Data pool could in turn have media pools called Exchange, SQL_Server, and ServerApps. A media pool that contains other media pools cannot contain individual tapes or discs.

Removable Storage categorizes media pools into types. The different types of media pools are these:

- **Unrecognized** Unrecognized media pools contain media that Removable Storage does not recognize as well as new media that hasn't been written to yet. To make Unrecognized media available for use, move the media to the Free media pool. If you eject the media prior to doing this, the media are automatically deleted from the Removable Storage database and no longer are tracked.
- **Free** Free media pools contain media that are not currently in use and do not contain useful data. These media are available for use by applications.
- **Import** Import media pools contain media that Removable Storage recognizes but that have not been used before in a particular Removable Storage system. For example, if you are transferring media from one office to another, the media might be listed as Import. To reuse the media at the new location, move the media to a Free media or application media pool.
- **Application** Application media pools contain media that are allocated to and controlled by an application, such as Windows Server 2003 Backup. Administrators and Backup Operators can control application media pools as well. Application media pools can be configured to draw media automatically from Free media pools as necessary. Once allocated, application media cannot be moved between media pools.

Free, Unrecognized, and Import media pools are referred to as system media pools. Unlike application media pools that you can delete, you cannot delete system media pools.

Working with the Removable Storage Snap-In

You access the various types of media through Computer Management. Start Computer Management. Expand Storage, Removable Storage, and then Media Pools. As Figure 23-1 shows, you'll see nodes labeled Free, Import, and Unrecognized. These media types are managed by Remote Storage.

Free, Import, and Unrecognized are configured as top-level media pools that contain other media pools. In most cases, they contain the media pools Removable Media and CD-ROM. If your system has robotic library units or other types of removable drives, you might see additional media pools. These media pools can be configured to store other media pools or media of a specific type. For details, see the section entitled "Changing Library Media Types" later in this chapter.

Note Media pools for removable drives that don't contain media might not be displayed. If this happens, insert media into the drive and the necessary pool is added automatically.

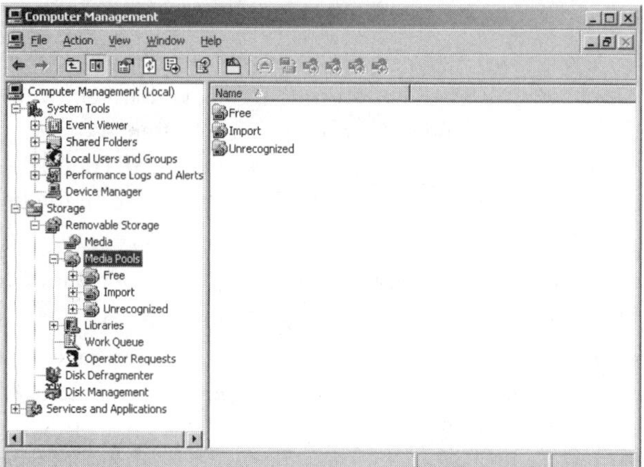

Figure 23-1. Removable Storage is used to manage media pools, libraries, and individual tapes or discs.

Following the system media types, you'll find media pools for application media. In most cases, the default application media pools are Backup and Remote Storage. You use the Backup media pool with Windows Server 2003 Backup and the Remote Storage media pool with Windows Server 2003 Remote Storage. You can create additional media pools for use by applications or configure applications to create their own media pools.

Other nodes of Removable Storage are used as follows:

- **Libraries** Shows the libraries available for use and provides menu options for managing their drives and media. Also provides tracking for offline media.
- **Work Queue** Shows the status of operations and allows you to manage entries in the work queue to resolve conflicts and cancel requests.
- **Operator Requests** Shows service requests that have been submitted by Removable Storage or by another application. These requests are messages asking a specific operator to perform a necessary task, such as inserting media, servicing a library unit, or cleaning a drive.

Understanding Media State and Identification

The media state tells you the operational status of media. You can view media state through the related library or the related media pool.

- To access media through the related library, start Computer Management, expand Storage, Removable Storage, and then select Libraries. Select the library you want to work with.

- To access media through the related media pool, start Computer Management, expand Storage, Removable Storage, and then select Media Pools. Select the media pool you want to work with.

All media has two states: a physical state that reflects movement, and a side state that reflects usage (of a particular side of the media). The physical and side states that you can see are summarized in Table 23-1.

Table 23-1. Physical and Side States for Media

State Type	State	Description
Physical	Idle	Media is currently not in use or is shelved offline.
	In-Use	Media is being used.
	Loaded	Media is mounted and data is available for read/write operations.
	Mounted	Media is mounted but data is not available for read/write operations.
	Unloaded	Media has been dismounted and is ready to be removed.
Side	Allocated	Media has been allocated for use by a specific application.
	Available	Media is available for use by an application.
	Completed	Media is available for use but cannot be used for write operations. The media is full.
	Decommissioned	Media has reached its allocation maximum and is no longer available for use.
	Imported	Media's label type is recognized, but its label ID is not.
	Incompatible	The media type is not compatible with the library and should be removed.
	Reserved	Media is two-sided. One side has already been allocated to an application, and the other is reserved for use by the application.
	Unprepared	Media is in a Free media pool but does not have a Free media label.
	Unrecognized	Media's label type and label ID are not recognized.

As you see in Table 23-1, the media label type and ID play an important role in determining the state of the media. The label type identifies the format used to record information on the media, such as the Microsoft Tape Format (MTF). The label ID is a unique identifier that is based on the library and location of the media.

- If Removable Storage recognizes the label type but not the label ID, it usually means that you've moved the media from one location to another and this is why the media has the Imported state and is placed in the Import media pool.
- If Removable Storage doesn't recognize the label type or label ID, you're trying to use a tape of unknown origin. The tape might have come from a different operating system or an unsupported application.

> **Note** With read-only or write-once optical media, such as CD-ROM or DVD-ROM, Removable Storage doesn't use media identifiers. Instead, Removable Storage uses the volume and serial number on the disc.

Together, the label type and label ID are referred to as media identifiers. Media identifiers are recorded on the media the first time you insert it into a library and are thereafter used to track the media. If the library supports bar codes, you can use bar codes to identify media as well. The advantage of using bar codes is that you don't have to mount the media to read its identifier and then dismount it. This makes searching and inventory tracking quick and efficient.

Media must be formatted properly for it to be recognized by Removable Storage. Compact discs must be formatted with the CD-ROM File System (CDFS). Other types of removable media must be formatted with the File Allocation Table (FAT), FAT32, or NTFS file system (NTFS).

Understanding Access Permissions for Removable Storage

Like other objects in Windows Server 2003, Removable Storage has specific access permissions. You can set access permissions for all of Removable Storage as well as for individual media pools, libraries, and media. Table 23-2 summarizes the available user permissions from lowest to highest. Higher-level permissions inherit the capabilities of lower-level permissions.

> **Note** Keep in mind these permissions apply to the Removable Storage system and not the files that might be stored on media. NTFS access permissions still apply to files on NTFS-formatted media.

Table 23-2. Access Permissions for Removable Storage

Permission	Meaning for Removable Storage	Meaning for Media, Media Pools, or Libraries
Use	Grants Read access to Removable Storage but not necessarily to media, media pools, or libraries.	Grants Read access to the individual media, media pool, or library. Allows user to insert and eject media and take inventory in a library.
Modify	Grants Read/Write access. User can create media pools, manage the work and requests queues.	Grants Read/Write access. User can change properties of the media, media pool, or library.
Control	Grants complete control to user. User can change permissions, delete media pools, and delete libraries.	Grants complete control. User can change permissions, delete media pools, and delete libraries.

Initially, Removable Storage is configured for management by the operating system and administrators. Backup Operators can use and control Remote Storage. Normal users are granted only limited access, which might be necessary when working with both Removable Storage and Remote Storage. If you use Removable Storage for purposes other than backup and recovery operations, you might want to grant access to other users and groups. However, only administrators and Backup Operators have the necessary permissions to back up and restore files on computers. Thus, even if you grant an operator control, that user might not be able to back up and restore files.

Managing Media Libraries and Media

You commonly perform many tasks when you work with media libraries and media. These tasks are examined in this section.

Inserting Media into a Library

You use different techniques to insert media into automated and nonautomated libraries. For nonautomated libraries, you insert media manually into the drive. Then the media is mounted and placed in a media pool (if possible). Otherwise, you must mount the media you want to work with.

To insert media into a robotic library, follow these steps:

1. Access Removable Storage in Computer Management, then double-click Libraries in the console tree.
2. Right-click the library you want to work with, then click Inject. This starts the Media Inject Wizard, as shown in Figure 23-2. Click Next.

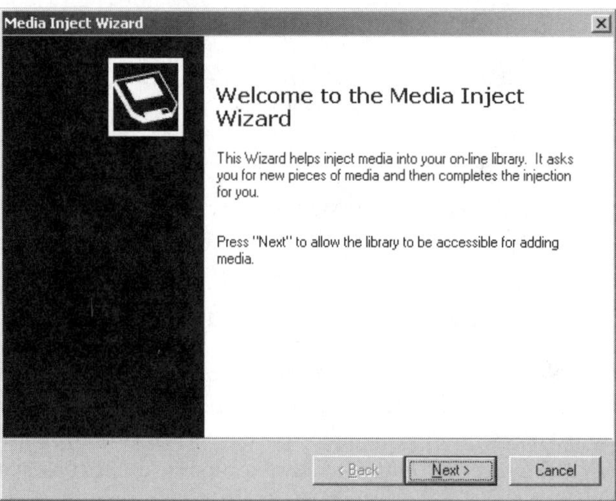

Figure 23-2. The Media Inject Wizard.

3. The wizard accesses the library and prepares it to accept new media. If the library is full, you'll see a note explaining that no slots are available and that you must eject media before you can insert media.
4. When prompted as shown in Figure 23-3, place the media into the inject/eject port. Make sure you use the correct slots. If the library doesn't have an inject/eject port, use the tape library door.

> **Note** Inserting or ejecting media through the tape library door means that media will be reinventoried. In addition, if the media isn't bar-coded, you must perform a full inventory as detailed in the section entitled "Configuring Library Inventory" later in this chapter.

5. If the inject/eject port doesn't close automatically, click Next. The media is then loaded into the library and added to the appropriate pool.
6. Specify whether you want to inject more media or complete the operation. If you want to add media, repeat step 5. Otherwise, click Next, and then click Finish.

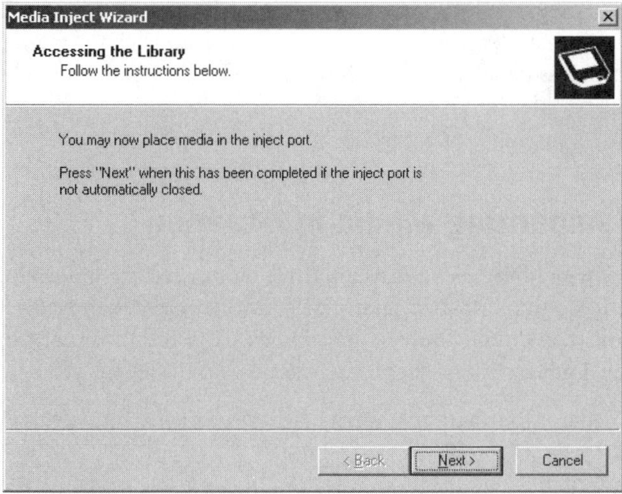

Figure 23-3. Insert media into the inject/eject port or the tape library door.

You must mount the media you want to work with.

Ejecting Media from a Library

As with inserting media into a library, you use different techniques to eject media from a library based on whether the library is nonautomated or automated. To eject media from a nonautomated library, access Removable Storage in Computer Management, then double-click Libraries in the console tree. Next right-click the library you want to work with, then click Eject.

> **Note** If the media is in use or busy, you might not be able to eject it. Check the work queue as detailed in the section entitled "Managing Work Queues, Requests, and Security" later in this chapter.

To eject media from an automated library, follow these steps:

1. Access Removable Storage in Computer Management, and then double-click Libraries.
2. Expand the library and the library's Drives folder by double-clicking them.
3. Right-click the media you want to eject, then click Eject. This starts the Media Eject Wizard. Click Next.

4. The wizard prepares the library to eject the media. If successful, you'll be able to select additional media that you want to eject. Otherwise, check the work queue and resolve any problems as detailed in the section entitled "Managing Work Queues, Requests, and Security" later in this chapter.
5. Click Next, and then click Finish to complete the operation.

Mounting and Dismounting Media in Libraries

When you work with libraries that have multiple tapes, you might need to mount and dismount media. To do this with a nonautomated library, access Removable Storage in Computer Management, and then double-click Libraries. Expand the library and the library's Drives folder by double-clicking them. You can now do one of the following:

- **Mount media** To mount media, right-click the media you want to mount, then click Mount.
- **Dismount media** To dismount media, right-click the media you want to dismount, then click Dismount.

> **Tip** Trying to dismount media in use can cause problems on the drive. Check the work queue as described in the section entitled "Managing Work Queues, Requests, and Security" later in this chapter.

To mount and dismount media in automated libraries, access Removable Storage in Computer Management, and then double-click Libraries. You can now do one of the following:

- **Mount media** To mount media, expand the library and the library's Drives folder by double-clicking them. Right-click the media you want to mount, then click Mount.
- **Dismount media** To dismount media, expand the library and the library's Drives folder by double-clicking them. Right-click the drive from which you want to dismount media, then click Dismount.

> **Tip** Trying to dismount media in use can cause problems with the library. Check the work queue as described in the section entitled "Managing Work Queues, Requests, and Security" later in this chapter.

Enabling and Disabling Media

Sometimes you'll want to disable media so that it cannot be used. You might want to do this to ensure that a bad tape isn't used or to prevent media from being used temporarily. You enable or disable media as follows:

1. Access Removable Storage in Computer Management, and then double-click Libraries.

2. Expand the library and the library's Drives folder by double-clicking them. Right-click the media you want to enable or disable, then click Properties.
3. In the General tab of the Properties dialog box, select or clear Enable Media.

Enabling and Disabling Drives

You can disable drives temporarily as well. You might want to do this if you have a bad drive in a library with multiple drives or if you need to clean a dirty drive but must first perform other operations.

When a library has a single drive, you must enable or disable the entire library. See the section entitled "Enabling and Disabling Libraries" later in this chapter. When a library has multiple drives, you enable or disable a drive as follows:

1. Access Removable Storage in Computer Management, and then double-click Libraries.
2. Expand the library and the library's Drives folder by double-clicking them. Right-click the drive you want to enable or disable, then click Properties.
3. In the General tab of the Properties dialog box, select or clear Enable Drive.

Cleaning Drives

You must periodically clean drives in both nonautomated and automated libraries. You clean drives in a nonautomated library by inserting a cleaner cartridge and then cleaning the drive manually. In Removable Storage, access the library and the Drives folder where the drive is listed. Right-click the drive, then click Mark As Clean. This makes a record of the cleaning.

You clean drives in an automated library by using a wizard. In Removable Storage, right-click the library you want to clean. Then select Cleaner Management. This starts the Cleaner Management Wizard. Click Next. The wizard prepares the library. Insert the cleaner cartridge when prompted.

Working with Library Doors and Ports

Robotic libraries can have automated doors and ports that you can use to insert and eject media. If you must open the library doors, you can do so by right-clicking the library, selecting Door Access, and then opening the door when prompted. If you must access an inject/eject port, follow the procedures in the sections entitled "Inserting Media into a Library" and "Ejecting Media from a Library" earlier in this chapter.

To specify how long the doors and port wait for media to be inserted, right-click the library you want to work with, then select Properties. In the Properties dialog box, select the Components tab. Set a new timeout for the library doors using the Time-Out field in the Doors area, then set the timeout for the port using the Time-Out field in the Ports area. Click OK.

Configuring Library Inventory

Inventories are used with automated libraries to help you track the whereabouts of online and offline media. By default, libraries are configured to update the inventory only when the status of a slot changes between occupied and unoccupied, which happens when you mount, dismount, insert, or eject media. To change the default library inventory method, follow these steps:

1. Access Removable Storage, then double-click Libraries.
2. Right-click the library you want to set an inventory method for, and then click Properties.
3. In the General tab, in Inventory Method, select one of the following methods:
   - *None*—Select this method if you do not want to inventory media.
   - *Fast*—Select this method to inventory only storage slots that have changed status between being occupied and unoccupied. This is the default inventory method.
   - *Full*—Select this method to always perform complete inventories. For bar-coded media, this means reading the bar-code information. For other media, this means mounting the media, reading the media identifier, and then dismounting the media.

> **Note** When a mount operation fails, a full inventory is always performed regardless of the default inventory method selected. You can disable this feature by clearing the Perform Full Inventory On Mount Failure option.

4. The chosen inventory method is performed each time a library door is accessed.

Starting Library Inventory

Inventories are performed on automated libraries whenever you access the library door. You can also start an inventory manually by right-clicking the library you want to inventory and selecting Inventory.

Changing Library Media Types

The media types used by libraries are displayed as media pools under the Free, Import, and Unrecognized media pools in Removable Storage. You can add and remove media types (and their associated media pools) by completing the following steps:

1. In Removable Storage, right-click the library you want to work with, then select Properties.
2. In the Properties dialog box, select the Media tab, then click Change to display the Change Media Types dialog box.
3. Available Types shows additional media types available for use. To add a new media type, select the entry you want to add in Available Types, then click Add.
4. Selected Types shows existing media types configured for use. To remove an existing media type, select the entry you want to remove in Selected Types, then click Remove.
5. Repeat steps 5 and 6 as necessary, then click OK when finished. The changes you make are reflected in the Free, Import, and Unrecognized media pools.

Enabling and Disabling Libraries

You disable libraries to make them unavailable for use. This ensures no one can use a library you need to repair, replace, or service. To enable or disable libraries, access Removable Storage in Computer Management, and then double-click Libraries. Right-click the library you want to enable or disable, then click Properties. In the General tab of the Properties dialog box, select or clear Enable Library as appropriate.

Managing Media Pools

Collections of tapes are organized into media pools. The tasks you use to manage media pools are examined in the sections that follow.

Preparing Media for Use in the Free Media Pool

If media has information that you don't need anymore, you can initialize the media and prepare it for use in the Free media pool. When you do this, you destroy the information on the media and move it to the Free media pool.

To prepare media and move it to the Free media pool, access Removable Storage in Computer Management, and then double-click Media Pools. Expand Free Media pools. Right-click the media you want to prepare, then click Prepare. Confirm the action by clicking Yes.

> **Caution** Moving media to the Free media pool destroys the data on the media. In addition, you cannot move read-only media to the Free media pool.

Moving Media to a Different Media Pool

You can move media to a different media pool to make it available for use or to allocate it to an application. Access Removable Storage in Computer Management, and then double-click Media Pools. Expand the pool you want to work with. In the details pane, drag the media you want to move to the applicable media pool in the console tree.

Creating Application Media Pools

The only type of media pool you can create is an application media pool. In Removable Storage, right-click Media Pools, then click Create Media Pool. Or right-click an existing application media pool, and then click Create Media Pool.

In the Create A New Media Pool Properties dialog box, shown in Figure 23-4, enter a name and description of the media pool. If the media pool will contain other media pools, select Contains Other Media Pools. Otherwise, click Contains Media Of Type, and select an appropriate media type from the list.

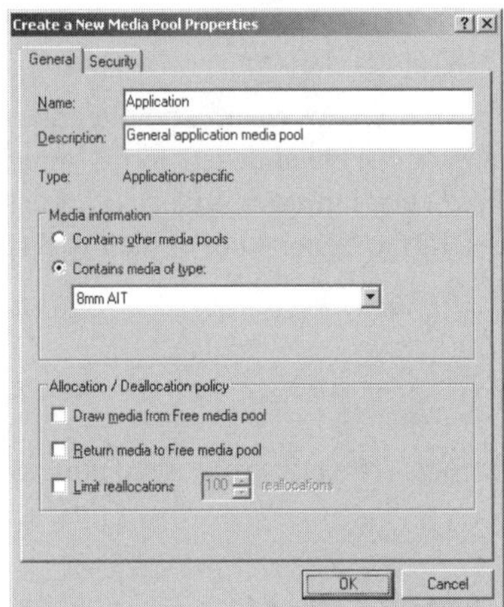

Figure 23-4. Create the media pool.

Complete the process by clicking OK. As necessary, allocate media and configure security. These tasks are described in the sections entitled "Setting Allocation and Deallocation Policies" and "Setting Access Permissions for Removable Storage," respectively, later in this chapter.

Changing the Media Type in a Media Pool

Each media pool can contain only one type of media. Normally, the media type is assigned when the media pool is created, but you can change the media type, provided no media is currently assigned to the media pool.

In Removable Storage, double-click Media Pools. Right-click the media pool you want to work with, then select Properties. In the General tab, select Contains Media Of Type, then select an appropriate media type from the list. Click OK.

Setting Allocation and Deallocation Policies

Application media pools can be configured to allocate and deallocate free media automatically. By enabling this process, you ensure that when an application needs media, the application can obtain it, and then when the media is no longer needed, it can be returned to the Free media pool.

You configure allocation and deallocation of media in Removable Storage. Double-click Media Pools. Right-click the media pool you want to work with, then select Properties. This displays the dialog box shown in Figure 23-5.

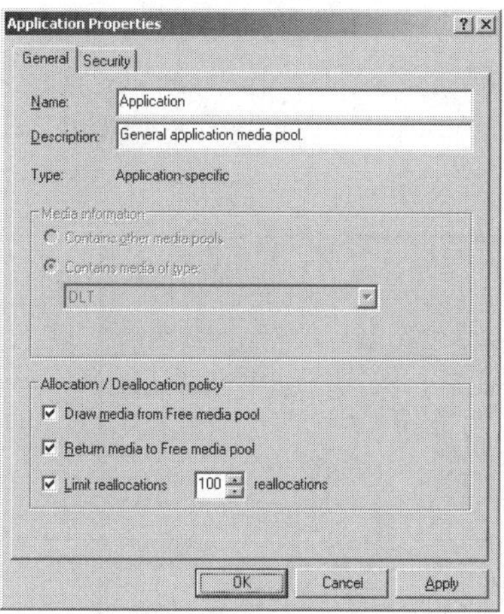

Figure 23-5. Set the allocation and deallocation policies.

The media pool must contain media of a specific type and cannot be a container for other media pools. In the General tab, use the following options under Allocation/Deallocation Policy to control media allocation:

- **Draw Media From Free Media Pool** Select this option to draw unused media automatically from the Free media pool when needed.
- **Return Media To Free Media Pool** Select this option to return media automatically to the Free media pool when no longer needed.
- **Limit Reallocations** Select this option if you want to limit the number of times tapes or discs can be reused. Then use the combo box provided to set a specific limit.

When you are finished, click OK.

Deleting Application Media Pools

In Removable Storage, you delete application media pools by right-clicking them and selecting Delete. Only do this if the media pool is no longer needed.

> **Caution** You shouldn't delete application media pools created by Windows Server 2003, such as Backup and Remote Storage. These are used by the operating system.

Managing Work Queues, Requests, and Security

Whenever you work with removable media, you must keep a close eye on the work queues, operator requests, and security.

Using the Work Queue

Work Queue is the area where Removable Storage displays the status of operations (see Figure 23-6). You access Work Queue by expanding Removable Storage and then clicking Work Queue in the console tree.

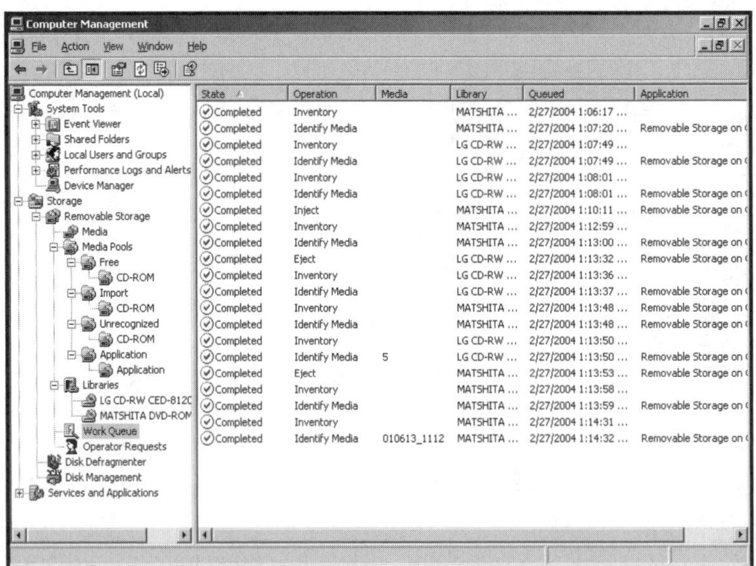

Figure 23-6. Work Queue shows the status of operations for Removable Storage.

Operations are tasks initiated by administrators, Backup Operators, and other authorized users. Each operation listed in the queue has a specific state, which indicates the status of the operation. Operation states include the following:

- **Waiting** Operation is waiting to execute.
- **In Progress** Operation is executing.
- **Completed** Operation has completed successfully.
- **Canceled** Operation was canceled by an administrator or other operator.
- **Failed** Operation failed to complete.

By default, completed, canceled, and failed requests stay in the queue for 72 hours. Waiting or in-progress operations stay in the queue until their status changes. If waiting or in-progress operations are causing problems, such as delaying priority operations, you can manage the requests in one of these ways:

- **Reorder mount operations** Changing the mount order can allow priority operations to execute before lower-priority operations. For example, if you are backing up a database, you can make your mount operation the next one in the queue, pushing it ahead of others. You change the mount order as described in the section entitled "Changing Mount Operations" later in this chapter.
- **Cancel pending operations** Canceling a pending operation can free up drives and media when operations are waiting on another operation to complete. For example, processes that are waiting to be run can often hold up other processes, and in this case, you might need to cancel the process to allow other processes to run. You cancel a waiting operation by right-clicking it and then selecting Cancel Request.
- **Deleting operations** You can delete completed, canceled, or failed operations manually or automatically. You configure when operations are deleted as described in the section entitled "Controlling When Operations Are Deleted" later in this chapter.

Troubleshooting Waiting Operations

Operations that have a status of Waiting can be an indicator that something has gone wrong. For example, an operation could be waiting because a resource it needs is not in the correct state. If the operation has been waiting for a long time, this can mean that the resource is not mounted, enabled, or otherwise working properly and that you might need to dismount, enable, or correct a problem with the resource.

To correct the problem you might need to cancel the operation, perform a corrective action, and then issue a new operation. You cancel a waiting operation by right-clicking it and then selecting Cancel Request.

Changing Mount Operations

When there are two or more mount operations waiting, you can change the order of the operations to allow priority operations to proceed ahead of other operations. To do this, right-click the waiting mount operation you want to manipulate, then select Re-Order Mounts. This displays the Change Mount Order dialog box.

The current order of the mount operation is shown. The options available allow you to do one of the following:

- Move the mount operation to the front of the queue, which ensures it is the next mount operation run
- Move the mount operation to the end of the queue, which ensures it is run after existing mount operations
- Move the mount operation to a specific location in the queue, which allows you to move the operation ahead of or behind other operations without making it the highest or lowest priority

When you are finished changing mount operations, click OK.

Controlling When Operations Are Deleted

By default, completed, canceled, and failed operations are deleted from the work queue after 72 hours. You can control when operations are deleted by using one of the following methods:

- **Deleting individual operations** You can delete operations individually by right-clicking them and then selecting Delete.
- **Deleting all operations** To delete all completed, canceled, and failed operations, right-click Work Queue, select Properties, then click Delete All Now.
- **Reconfiguring automatic deletion times** To change the automatic deletion time, follow these steps:
    1. Right-click Work Queue, then select Properties. This displays the dialog box shown in Figure 23-7.
    2. To stop automatic deletion of all operations, clear the Automatically Delete Completed Requests option, and complete the process by clicking OK.

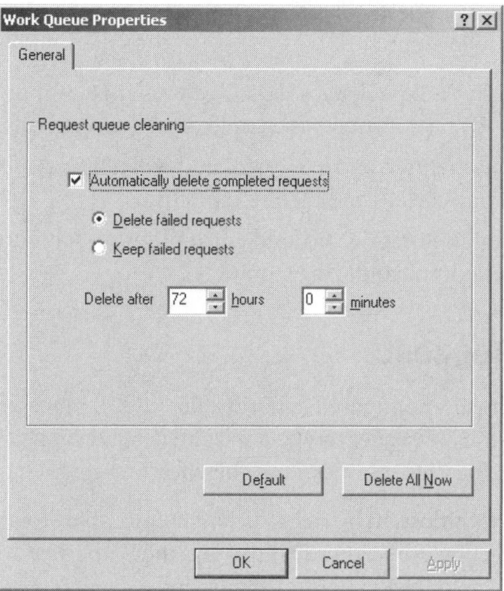

Figure 23-7. You can control when operations are deleted from the queue by using the Work Queue Properties dialog box.

3. To enable automatic deletion, select the Automatically Delete Completed Requests option. Completed requests will now be deleted automatically.
4. Select Delete Failed Requests to delete failed requests automatically as well. Or to save failed requests, select Keep Failed Requests.
5. In the Delete After settings, change the deletion interval using the Hours and Minutes boxes. The default is 72 hours.
6. Click OK.

Using the Operator Requests Queue

Operator Requests is the area where Removable Storage displays the status of requests that need the attention of administrators or Backup Operators. You access Operator Requests by expanding Removable Storage and then clicking Operator Requests in the console tree.

Each entry in the queue represents a task that you or another operator must perform. These requests are issued by Removable Storage or a compliant application for operations that are performed manually, such as inserting a cleaning cartridge, inserting offline tapes, or servicing a library. Each request has a specific state, which indicates the status of the request. You can respond to requests by either completing or refusing them. By default, completed or refused requests stay in the queue for 72 hours.

To help you track the status of requests, all requests are listed according to their current state. Request states include the following:

- **Completed** Request was completed as specified by an operator or detected by Removable Storage. To mark a request as completed, right-click it, and select Complete.
- **Refused** Request was refused by an operator and will not be performed. To mark a request as refused, right-click it, and then select Refuse.
- **Submitted** Removable Storage or a compliant application submitted the request and is waiting for an operator to handle the request.

Notifying Operators of Requests

By default, Removable Storage is configured to notify operators of requests. Notifications are sent to the local system by the Messenger service and as an icon that appears on the Windows taskbar. If you aren't receiving these notifications, these features might have been disabled.

You can reenable operator notification by right-clicking Removable Storage in Computer Management and then selecting Properties. This displays the Properties dialog box shown in Figure 23-8. Select one of the following notification options:

- To receive requests by the Messenger service, select Display Operator Request Dialogs.
- To display an icon on the Windows taskbar when requests are waiting, select Use Status Area Icon For Notifying About Mounts.

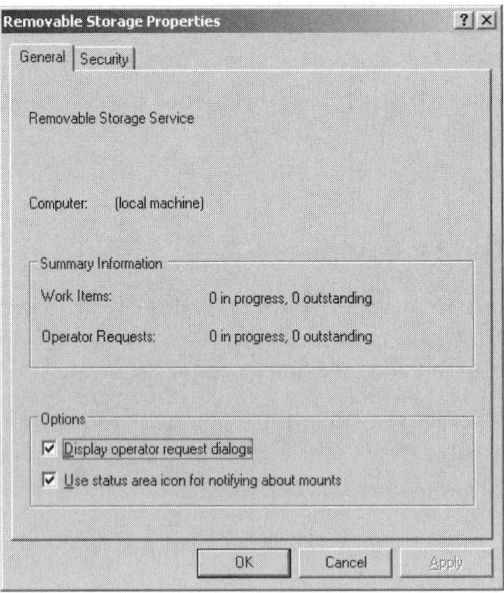

Figure 23-8. Configure operator notification.

Completing or Refusing Requests

As an administrator or authorized operator, you can mark requests as completed or refused. Simply right-click the request, then select Complete or Refuse as appropriate.

When you mark a request as completed, Removable Storage attempts to continue whatever operation was waiting on the request. For example, if Removable Storage was waiting on a cleaner cartridge and you inserted the cartridge, Removable Storage can continue with cleaning.

When you mark a request as refused, Removable Storage might cancel pending operations that were waiting on the request. These pending operations can be marked as Failed, and if you read the comments, you'll see that the operation failed because a request was canceled.

Controlling When Requests Are Deleted

By default, completed or refused requests are deleted from the request queue after 72 hours. You can control when requests are deleted in the same way that you control when operations are deleted. The only difference is that you right-click Operator Requests to display the necessary Properties dialog box. For complete details, see the section entitled "Controlling When Operations Are Deleted" earlier in this chapter.

Setting Access Permissions for Removable Storage

You can set access permissions for Removable Storage, media pools, libraries, and media. The available permissions are Use, Modify, and Control. These permissions are summarized in the section entitled "Understanding Access Permissions for Removable Storage" earlier in this chapter.

You set or view permissions as follows:

1. In Removable Storage, right-click the element you want to work with.
2. Select Properties from the shortcut menu, then click the Security tab, as shown in Figure 23-9.
3. Users or groups that already have access to the element are listed in the Name box. Change permissions by selecting a group or user, then using the Permissions list box to grant or deny access permissions.
4. To set access permissions for additional users, computers, or groups, click Add. Then use the Select Users, Computers, Or Groups option to add users, computers, or groups.

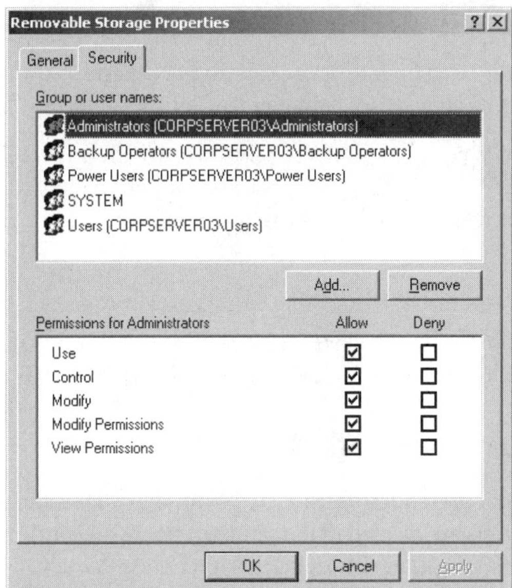

Figure 23-9. Use the Security tab to configure access permissions.

5 Select the user, computer, or group you want to configure in the Name list box, then use the fields in the Permissions area to allow or deny permissions. Repeat for other users, computers, or groups.

6 Click OK when you are finished.

Part 6

Managing Windows Server 2003 Networking and Print Services

Chapter 24

Managing TCP/IP Networking

TCP/IP is a protocol suite consisting of Transmission Control Protocol (TCP) and Internet Protocol (IP). TCP is a connection-oriented protocol designed for reliable end-to-end communications. IP is an internetworking protocol that is used to route packets of data called datagrams over a network. An IP datagram consists of an IP header and an IP payload. The IP header contains information about routing the datagram, including source and destination IP addresses. The IP payload contains the actual data being sent over the network.

TCP/IP is the backbone for Microsoft Windows networks. It is required for internetwork communications and for accessing the Internet. Before you can implement TCP/IP networking, you should understand IP addressing conventions, subnetting options, and name resolution techniques—all of which are covered in this chapter.

Understanding IP Addressing

The most important thing IP gives us is the IP address. It is the existence of IP addresses that allows information to be routed from point A to point B over a network. An IP address is a 32-bit logical address that has two components: a network address and a node address. Typically, IP addresses are divided into four 8-bit values called octets and written as four separate decimal values delimited by a period (referred to as a dot). The binary values are converted to decimal equivalents by adding the numbers represented by the bit positions that are set to 1. The general way to write this value is in the form *w.x.y.z*, where each letter represents one of the four octets.

IP addresses can be used in three ways:

- **Unicast** Unicast IP addresses are assigned to individual network interfaces that are attached to an IP network and are used in one-to-one communications.
- **Multicast** Multicast IP addresses are addresses for which one or multiple IP nodes can listen on the same or different network segments and are used in one-to-many communications.
- **Broadcast** Broadcast IP addresses are designed to be used by every IP node on a particular network segment and are used for one-to-everyone communications.

Each of these IP addressing techniques is discussed in the sections that follow.

Tip **IPv4 and IPv6**

The primary version of IP in use today on networks, including the Internet, is IP version 4 (IPv4). IPv4 has 32-bit addresses and is the version of IP discussed in this chapter. The next version of IP is IP version 6 (IPv6). IPv6 has 128-bit addresses. Windows Server 2003 fully supports IPv6, and you can install IPv6 in much the same way as you installed TCP/IP.

Unicast IP Addresses

Unicast IP addresses are the ones you'll work with the most. These are the IP addresses that are assigned to individual network interfaces. In fact, each network interface that uses TCP/IP must have a unique unicast IP address. A unicast IP address consists of two components:

- **A network ID** The network ID or address identifies a specific logical network and must be unique within its boundaries. Typically, IP routers set the boundaries for a logical network, and this boundary is the same as the physical network defined by the routers. All nodes that are on the same logical network must share the same network ID. If they don't, routing or delivery problems occur.
- **A host ID** The host ID or address identifies a specific node on a network, such as a router interface or server. As with a network ID, it must be unique within a particular network segment.

Address classes are used to create subdivisions of the IP address space. With unicast IP addresses, the classes A, B, and C can be applied. Each describes a different way of dividing a subset of the 32-bit IP address space into network addresses and host addresses.

Note Classes D and E are defined as well. Class D addresses are used for multicast, as discussed in the next section of this chapter. Class E addresses are reserved for experimental use. Class D addresses begin with a number between 224 and 239 for the first octet. Class E addresses begin with a number between 240 and 247 for the first octet. Although Windows Server 2003 supports the use of Class D addresses, it does not support Class E addresses.

Class A Networks

Class A networks are designed for when you need a large number of hosts but only a few network segments and have addresses that begin with a number between 1 and 127 for the first octet. As shown in Figure 24-1, the first octet (the first 8 bits of the address) defines the network ID, and the last three octets (the last 24 bits of the address) define the host ID. As you'll learn shortly, the Class A address 127 has a special meaning and isn't available for your use. This means that there are 126 possible Class A networks and each network can have 16,277,214 nodes. For example, a Class A network with the network address 100 contains all IP addresses from 100.0.0.0 to 100.255.255.255.

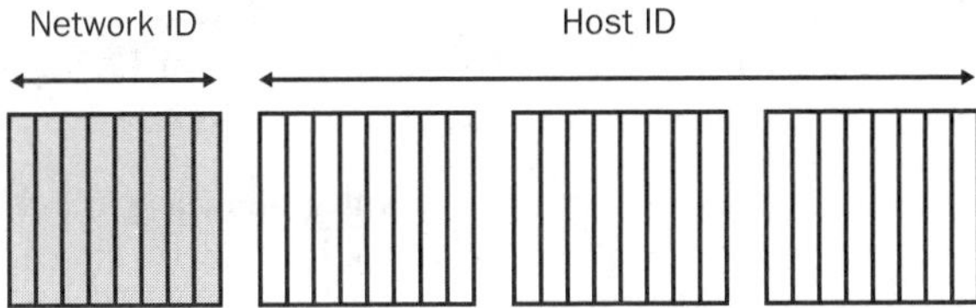

Figure 24-1. IP addressing on Class A networks.

Class B Networks

Class B networks are designed for when you need a moderate number of networks and hosts and have addresses that begin with a number between 128 and 191 for the first octet. As shown in Figure 24-2, the first two octets (the first 16 bits of the address) define the network ID, and the last two octets (the last 16 bits of the address) define the host ID. This means that there are 16,384 Class B networks and each network can have 65,534 nodes.

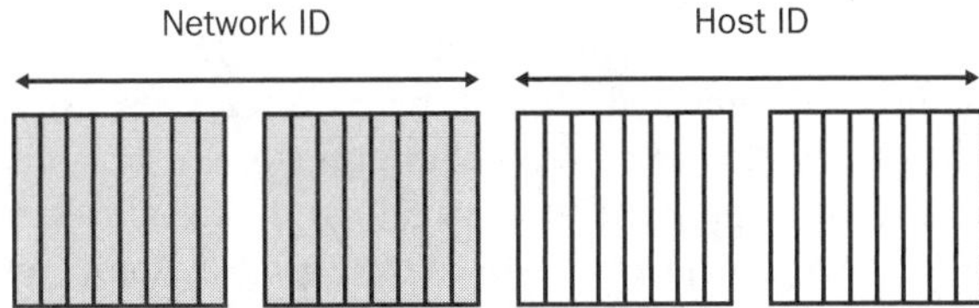

Figure 24-2. IP addressing on Class B networks.

Class C Networks

Class C networks are designed for when you need a large number of networks and relatively few hosts and have addresses that begin with a number between 192 and 223 for the first octet. As shown in Figure 24-3, the first three octets (the first 24 bits of the address) define the network ID, and the last octet (the last 8 bits of the address) defines the host ID. This means that there are 2,097,152 Class C networks and each network can have 254 nodes.

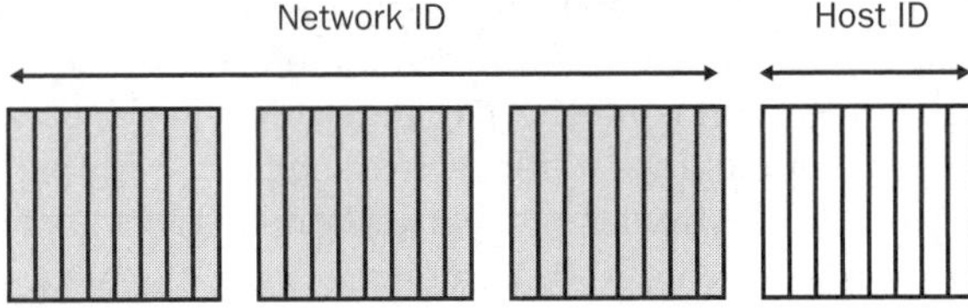

Figure 24-3. IP addressing on Class C networks.

Loopback, Public, and Private Addresses

When using any of the IP address classifications, there are certain rules that must be followed. The network ID cannot begin with 127 as the first octet. All IP addresses that begin with 127 are reserved as loopback addresses. Any packets sent to an IP address beginning with 127 are handled as if they've already been routed and reached their destination, which is the local network interface. This means any packets addressed to an IP address of 127.0.0.0 to 127.255.255.255 are addressed to and received by the local network interface.

In addition, some addresses in the ranges are defined as public and others as private. Public IP addresses are assigned by Internet service providers (ISPs). ISPs obtain allocations of IP addresses from a local Internet registry (LIR) or national Internet registry (NIR) or from their appropriate regional Internet registry (RIR). Private addresses are addresses reserved for organizations to use on internal networks. Because they are nonroutable, meaning they are not reachable on the Internet, they do not affect the public Internet and do not have to be assigned by an addressing authority.

The private IP addresses defined are as follows:

- **Class A private IP addresses** 10.0.0.0 through 10.255.255.255
- **Class B private IP addresses** 172.16.0.0 through 172.31.255.255
- **Class C private IP addresses** 192.168.0.0 through 192.168.255.255

Because hosts on an organization's private network shouldn't be directly connected to the Internet, they should be indirectly connected using Network Address Translation (NAT) or a gateway program such as a proxy. When NAT is configured on the organization's network, a device, such as a router, is responsible for translating private addresses to public addresses, allowing nodes on the internal network to communicate with the nodes on the public Internet. When proxies are configured on the organization's network, the proxy acts as the go-between. It receives requests from nodes on the internal network and sends the requests to the public Internet. When the response is returned, the proxy sends the response to the node that made the original request. In both cases, the device providing NAT or proxy services has private addresses on its internal network interface and public addresses on its Internet interface.

Multicast IP Addresses

Multicast IP addresses are used only as destination IP addresses and allow multiple nodes to listen for packets sent by a single originating node. In this way, a single packet can be delivered to and received by many hosts. Here's how it works: A sending node addresses a packet using a multicast IP address. If the packet is addressed to the sending node's network, nodes on the network that are listening for multicast traffic receive and process the packet. If the packet is addressed to another network, a router on the sending node's network forwards the packet as it would any other packet. When it is received on the destination network, any nodes on the network that are listening for multicast traffic receive and process the packet.

The nodes listening for multicast packets on a particular IP address are referred to as the host group. Members of the host group can be located anywhere—as long as the organization's routers know where members of the host group are located so that the routers can forward packets as appropriate.

One address class is reserved for multicast: Class D. Class D addresses begin with a number between 224 and 239 for the first octet.

Multicast IP addresses in the range of 224.0.0.0 through 224.0.0.255 are reserved for local subnet traffic. For example, the address 224.0.0.1 is an all-hosts multicast address and is designed for multicasting to all hosts on a subnet. The address 224.0.0.2 is an all-routers multicast address and is designed for multicasting to all routers on a subnet. Other addresses in this range are used as specified by the Internet Assigned Numbers Authority (IANA). For details, see the IANA Web site at *http://www.iana.org/assignments/multicast-addresses*.

Broadcast IP Addresses

Broadcast IP addresses are used only as destination IP addresses and allow a single node to direct packets to every node on the local network segment. When a sending node addresses a packet using a broadcast address, every node on that network segment receives and processes the packet.

To understand how broadcasts are used, you must understand the difference between classful networks and nonclassful networks. A *classful network* is a network that follows the class rules as defined, meaning a Class A, B, or C network is configured with network addresses and host addresses as described previously. A *nonclassful network* is a network that doesn't strictly follow the class rules. Nonclassful networks might have subnets that don't follow the normal rules for network and host IDs. You'll learn more about subnets in the section entitled "Using Subnets and Subnet Masks" later in this chapter.

> **Note** A nonclassful network can also be referred to as a classless network. However, classless interdomain routing (CIDR) and all it implies are specifically spelled out in Request For Comments (RFCs), such as RFC 1812. RFC 1812 provides rules that supersede those of some previous RFCs, such as RFC 950, which prohibited the use of all-zeros subnets.

All nodes listen for and process broadcasts. Because IP routers usually do not forward broadcast packets, broadcasts are generally limited by router boundaries. The broadcast address is obtained by setting all the network or host bits in the IP address to 1 as appropriate for the broadcast type. Three types of broadcasts are used:

- **Network broadcasts** Network broadcasts are used to send packets to all nodes on a classful network. For network broadcasts, the host ID bits are set to 1. For a nonclassful network, there is no network broadcast address, only a subnet broadcast address.
- **Subnet broadcasts** Subnet broadcasts are used to send packets to all nodes on nonclassful networks. For subnet broadcasts, the host ID bits are set to 1. For a classful network, there is no subnet broadcast address, only a network broadcast address.
- **Limited broadcasts** Limited broadcasts are used to send packets to all nodes when the network ID is unknown. For a limited broadcast, all network ID and host ID bits are set to 1.

Tip DHCP uses limited broadcasts
Limited broadcasts are sent by nodes that have their IP address automatically configured as is the case with Dynamic Host Configuration Protocol (DHCP). With DHCP, clients use a limited broadcast to advertise that they need to obtain an IP address. A DHCP server on the network acknowledges the request by assigning the node an IP address, which the client then uses for normal network communications.

Note Previously, a fourth type of broadcast was available called an all-subnets-directed broadcast. This broadcast type was used to send packets to all nodes on all the subnets of a nonclassful network. Because of the changes specified in RFC 1812, all-subnets-directed broadcasts have been deprecated, meaning they are no longer to be supported.

Special IP Addressing Rules

As you've seen, certain IP addresses and address ranges have special uses:

- The addresses 127.0.0.0 through 127.255.255.255 are reserved for local loopback.
- The addresses 10.0.0.0 through 10.255.255.255, 172.16.0.0 through 172.31.255.255, and 192.168.0.0 through 192.168.255.255 are designated as private and as such are nonroutable.
- On classful networks, the Class A addresses *w*.255.255.255, Class B addresses *w.x*.255.255, and Class C addresses *w.x.y*.255 are reserved for broadcasts.
- On nonclassful networks, the broadcast address is the last IP address in the range of IP addresses for the associated subnet.

Note Certain IP addresses are also reserved for other purposes as well. For example, the IP addresses 169.254.0.1 to 169.254.255.254 are used for Automatic Private IP Addressing (APIPA) as discussed in the section entitled "Configuring TCP/IP Networking" later in this chapter.

On classful networks, all the bits in the network ID cannot be set to 0 because this expression is reserved to indicate a host on a local network. Similarly, on a classful network all the bits in the host ID cannot be set to 0 because this is reserved to indicate the IP network number.

Table 24-1 lists the ranges of network numbers based on address classes. You cannot assign the network number to a network interface. The network number is common for all network interfaces attached to the same logical network. On a nonclassful network, the network number is the first IP address in the range of IP addresses for the associated subnet—as specified in RFC 1812.

Table 24-1. Network IDs for Classful Networks

Address Class	First Network Number	Last Network Number
Class A	1.0.0.0	126.0.0.0
Class B	128.0.0.0	191.255.0.0
Class C	192.0.0.0	233.255.255.0

When you apply all the rules for IP addresses, you find that many IP addresses cannot be used by hosts on a network. This means the first available host ID and last available host ID are different from the range of available IP addresses. Table 24-2 shows how these rules apply to classful networks. On a nonclassful network, the same rules apply—you lose the first and last available host ID from the range of available IP addresses.

Table 24-2. Available Host IDs on Classful Networks

Address Class	First Host ID	Last Host ID
Class A	*w*.0.0.1	*w*.255.255.254
Class B	*w*.*x*.0.1	*w*.*x*.255.254
Class C	*w*.*x*.*y*.1	*w*.*x*.*y*.254

Inside Out

Routers, gateways, and bridges connect networks

A router is needed for hosts on a network to communicate with hosts on other networks. It is standard convention for the network router to be assigned the first available host ID. On Windows systems, you identify the address for the router as the gateway IP address for the network. Although the terms "gateways" and "routers" are often used interchangeably, the two technically are different. A *router* is a device that sends packets between network segments. A *gateway* is a device that performs the necessary translation so that communication between networks with different architectures is possible, such as between Novell NetWare and Windows networks. When working with networks, you might also hear the term "bridge." A *bridge* is a device that directs traffic between two network segments using physical machine addresses (Media Access Control, or MAC, addresses). Routers, gateways, and bridges can be implemented in hardware as separate devices or in software so that a system on the network can handle the role as a network router, gateway, or bridge as necessary.

Using Subnets and Subnet Masks

Anyone that works with computers should learn about subnetting and what it means. A *subnet* is a portion of a network that operates as a separate network. Logically, it exists separately from other networks even if hosts on those other networks share the same network ID. Typically, such networks are also physically separated by a router. This ensures the subnet is isolated and doesn't affect other subnets.

Subnetting is designed to make more efficient use of the IP address space. Thus, rather than having networks with hundreds, thousands, or millions of nodes, you have a subnet that is sized appropriately for the number of nodes that you use. This is important, especially for the crowded public IP address space where it doesn't make sense to assign the complete IP address range for a network to an individual organization. Thus, instead of getting a complete network address for the public Internet, your organization is more likely to get a block of consecutive IP addresses to use.

Subnet Masks

You use a 32-bit value known as a subnet mask to configure nodes in a subnet to communicate only with other nodes on the same subnet. The mask works by blocking areas outside the subnet so that they aren't visible from within the subnet. Because it is a 32-bit value, subnet masks can be expressed as an address for which each 8-bit value (octet) is written as four separate decimal values delimited by a period (dot). As with IP addresses, the basic form is *w.x.y.z.*

The subnet mask identifies which bits of the IP address belong to the network ID and which bits belong to the host ID. Nodes can see only the portions of the IP address space that aren't masked by a bit with a value of 1. If a bit is set to 1, it corresponds to a bit in the network ID that isn't accessible from within the subnet. If a bit is set to 0, it corresponds to a bit in the host ID that is accessible from within the subnet.

Because a subnet mask must be configured for each IP address, nodes on both classful and nonclassful networks have subnet masks. On a classful network, all the bits in the network ID portion of the IP address are set to 1 and can be presented in dotted decimal as shown in Table 24-3.

Table 24-3. Standard Subnet Masks for Classful Networks

Address Class	Bits for Subnet Mask	Subnet Mask
Class A	11111111 00000000 00000000 00000000	255.0.0.0
Class B	11111111 11111111 00000000 00000000	255.255.0.0
Class C	11111111 11111111 11111111 00000000	255.255.255.0

Inside Out

Blocks of IP addresses on the public Internet

For internal networks that use private IP addresses, you'll often be able to use the standard subnet masks. This isn't true, however, when you need public IP addresses. Most of the time, you'll be assigned a small block of public IP addresses to work with. For example, you might be assigned a block of eight (six usable) addresses. In this case, you must create a subnet that uses the subnet mask to isolate your nodes as appropriate for the number of nodes you've been assigned. I say there are six usable addresses out of eight because the lowest address is reserved as the network number and the highest address is reserved as the broadcast address for the network. This is always the case, as any good Cisco Certified Network Associate (CCNA) will tell you.

Network Prefix Notation

With subnetting, an IP address alone doesn't help you understand how the address can be used. To be sure, you must know the number of bits in the network ID. As discussed, the subnet mask provides one way to determine which bits in the IP address belong to the network ID and which bits belong to the host ID. If you have a block of IP addresses, writing out each IP address and the subnet mask is rather tedious. A shorthand way to do this is to use network prefix notation, which is also referred to as the Classless Inter-Domain Routing (CIDR) notation.

In network prefix notation, the network ID is seen as the prefix of an IP address, and the host ID as the suffix. To write a block of IP addresses and specify which bits are used for the network ID, you write the network number followed by a forward slash and the number of bits in the network ID, as in

```
NetworkNumber/# of bits in the network ID
```

The slash and the number of bits in the network ID are referred to as the network prefix. Following this, you could rewrite Table 24-3 as shown in Table 24-4.

Table 24-4. Standard Network Prefixes for Classful Networks

Address Class	Bits for Subnet Mask	Network Prefix
Class A	11111111 00000000 00000000 00000000	/8
Class B	11111111 11111111 00000000 00000000	/16
Class C	11111111 11111111 11111111 00000000	/24

You now have two ways of detailing which bits are used for the network ID and which bits are used for the host ID. With the network number 192.168.1.0, you could use either of the following to specify that the first 24 bits identify the network ID:

- 192.168.1.0, 255.255.255.0
- 192.168.1.0/24

With either entry, you know that the first 24 bits identify the network ID and the last 8 bits identify the host ID. This in turn means the usable IP addresses are 192.168.1.1 through 192.168.1.254.

Subnetting

When you use subnetting, nodes no longer follow the class rules for determining which bits in the IP address are used for the network ID and which bits are used for the host ID. Instead, you set the 32 bits of the IP address as appropriate to be either network ID bits or host ID bits based on the number of subnets you need and then number nodes for each subnet. There is an inverse relationship between the number of subnets and the number of nodes per subnet that can be supported. As the number of subnets goes up by a factor of 2, the number of hosts per subnet goes down by a factor of 2.

Because Class A, B, and C networks have a different number of host ID bits to start with, borrowing bits from the host ID yields different numbers of subnets and hosts. The technique is the same, however. Each bit represented as a 1 in the subnet mask corresponds to a bit that belongs to the network ID. This means the value of each bit can be represented as shown in Figure 24-4.

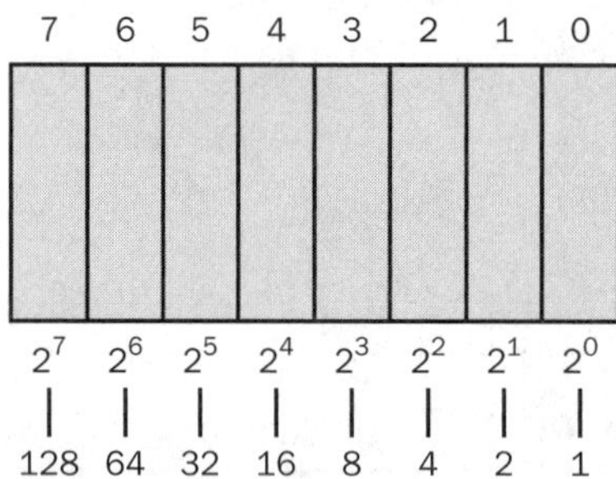

Figure 24-4. Represents the value of each bit when it is set to 1.

You start with the high-order bits and work your way to the low-order bits. When you borrow 1 bit of the host ID, you raise the number of possible subnets by a factor of 2 and reduce the number of possible hosts by a factor of 2.

Subnetting Class A Networks

The network entry mask for a standard Class A network can be defined as follows:

Address Class	Bits for Subnet Mask	Network Prefix	Decimal
Class A	11111111 00000000 00000000 00000000	/8	255.0.0.0

If you want to divide a Class A network into two separate subnets, you can borrow the high-order bit from the host ID in the second octet and add this bit to the network ID. Because the value of this bit taken from the host ID is 128, the corresponding subnet mask is 255.128.0.0. Thus, the network entry for the subnetted Class A network can be defined as follows:

Address Class	Bits for Subnet Mask	Network Prefix	Decimal
Class A	11111111 10000000 00000000 00000000	/9	255.128.0.0

Note Each time you borrow a bit from the host ID, the network prefix bits go up by 1.

If you take an additional bit from the host ID bits, you allow the Class A network to be divided into up to four subnets. The value of this bit taken from the host ID is 64. When you add this value to the value of the previous bit taken from the host ID, the sum is 192 (128 + 64) and the corresponding subnet mask is 255.192.0.0. This means the network entry for a subnetted Class A network that can be divided into up to four subnets can be defined as follows:

Address Class	Bits for Subnet Mask	Network Prefix	Decimal
Class A	11111111 11000000 00000000 00000000	/10	255.192.0.0

Table 24-5 shows how Class A networks can be subnetted and how this affects the number of possible subnets and hosts per subnet.

Table 24-5. Subnetting Class A Networks

Maximum Subnets	Bits for Subnet Mask	Network Prefix	Decimal	Maximum Nodes
1	11111111 00000000 00000000 00000000	/8	255.0.0.0	16,777,214
2	11111111 10000000 00000000 00000000	/9	255.128.0.0	8,388,606

Table 24-5. Subnetting Class A Networks

Maximum Subnets	Bits for Subnet Mask	Network Prefix	Decimal	Maximum Nodes
4	11111111 11000000 00000000 00000000	/10	255.192.0.0	4,194,302
8	11111111 11100000 00000000 00000000	/11	255.224.0.0	2,097,150
16	11111111 11110000 00000000 00000000	/12	255.240.0.0	1,048,574
32	11111111 11111000 00000000 00000000	/13	255.248.0.0	524,286
64	11111111 11111100 00000000 00000000	/14	255.252.0.0	262,142
128	11111111 11111110 00000000 00000000	/15	255.254.0.0	131,070
256	11111111 11111111 00000000 00000000	/16	255.255.0.0	65,534
512	11111111 11111111 10000000 00000000	/17	255.255.128.0	32,766
1,024	11111111 11111111 11000000 00000000	/18	255.255.192.0	16,382
2,048	11111111 11111111 11100000 00000000	/19	255.255.224.0	8,190
4,096	11111111 11111111 11110000 00000000	/20	255.255.240.0	4,094
8,192	11111111 11111111 11111000 00000000	/21	255.255.248.0	2,046
16,384	11111111 11111111 11111100 00000000	/22	255.255.252.0	1,022
32,768	11111111 11111111 11111110 00000000	/23	255.255.254.0	510
65,536	11111111 11111111 11111111 00000000	/24	255.255.255.0	254
131,072	11111111 11111111 11111111 10000000	/25	255.255.255.128	126
262,144	11111111 11111111 11111111 11000000	/26	255.255.255.192	62
524,288	11111111 11111111 11111111 11100000	/27	255.255.255.224	30

Table 24-5. Subnetting Class A Networks

Maximum Subnets	Bits for Subnet Mask	Network Prefix	Decimal	Maximum Nodes
1,048,576	11111111 11111111 11111111 11110000	/28	255.255.255.240	14
2,097,152	11111111 11111111 11111111 11111000	/29	255.255.255.248	6
4,194,304	11111111 11111111 11111111 11111100	/30	255.255.255.252	2

Subnetting Class B Networks

The network entry mask for a standard Class B network can be defined as follows:

Address Class	Bits for Subnet Mask	Network Prefix	Decimal
Class B	11111111 11111111 00000000 00000000	/16	255.255.0.0

A standard Class B network can have up to 65,534 hosts. If you want to divide a Class B network into two separate subnets, you can borrow the high-order bit from the host ID in the third octet and add this bit to the network ID. Because the value of this bit taken from the host ID is 128, the corresponding subnet mask is 255.255.128.0. Thus, the network entry for the subnetted Class B network can be defined as follows:

Address Class	Bits for Subnet Mask	Network Prefix	Decimal
Class B	11111111 11111111 10000000 00000000	/17	255.255.128.0

If you take an additional bit from the host ID bits, you allow the Class B network to be divided into up to four subnets. The value of this bit taken from the host ID is 64. When you add this value to the value of the previous bit taken from the host ID, the sum is 192 (128 + 64) and the corresponding subnet mask is 255.255.192.0. This means the network entry for a subnetted Class B network that can be divided into up to four subnets can be defined as follows:

Address Class	Bits for Subnet Mask	Network Prefix	Decimal
Class B	11111111 11111111 11000000 00000000	/18	255.255.192.0

Table 24-6 shows how Class B networks can be subnetted and how this affects the number of possible subnets and hosts per subnet.

Table 24-6. Subnetting Class B Networks

Maximum Subnets	Bits for Subnet Mask	Network Prefix	Decimal	Maximum Nodes
1	11111111 11111111 00000000 00000000	/16	255.255.0.0	65,534
2	11111111 11111111 10000000 00000000	/17	255.255.128.0	32,766
4	11111111 11111111 11000000 00000000	/18	255.255.192.0	16,382
8	11111111 11111111 11100000 00000000	/19	255.255.224.0	8,190
16	11111111 11111111 11110000 00000000	/20	255.255.240.0	4,094
32	11111111 11111111 11111000 00000000	/21	255.255.248.0	2,046
64	11111111 11111111 11111100 00000000	/22	255.255.252.0	1,022
128	11111111 11111111 11111110 00000000	/23	255.255.254.0	510
256	11111111 11111111 11111111 00000000	/24	255.255.255.0	254
512	11111111 11111111 11111111 10000000	/25	255.255.255.128	126
1,024	11111111 11111111 11111111 11000000	/26	255.255.255.192	62
2,048	11111111 11111111 11111111 11100000	/27	255.255.255.224	30
4,096	11111111 11111111 11111111 11110000	/28	255.255.255.240	14
8,192	11111111 11111111 11111111 11111000	/29	255.255.255.248	6
16,384	11111111 11111111 11111111 11111100	/30	255.255.255.252	2

Subnetting Class C Networks

The network entry mask for a standard Class C network can be defined as follows:

Address Class	Bits for Subnet Mask	Network Prefix	Decimal
Class C	11111111 11111111 11111111 00000000	/24	255.255.255.0

A standard Class C network can have up to 254 hosts. If you want to divide a Class C network into two separate subnets, you can borrow the high-order bit from the host ID in the fourth octet and add this bit to the network ID. Because the value of this bit taken from the host ID is 128, the corresponding subnet mask is 255.255.255.128. Thus, the network entry for the subnetted Class C network can be defined as follows:

Address Class	Bits for Subnet Mask	Network Prefix	Decimal
Class C	11111111 11111111 11111111 10000000	/25	255.255.255.128

If you take an additional bit from the host ID bits, you allow the Class C network to be divided into up to four subnets. The value of this bit taken from the host ID is 64. When you add this value to the value of the previous bit taken from the host ID, the sum is 192 (128 + 64) and the corresponding subnet mask is 255.255.255.192. This means the network entry for a subnetted Class C network that can be divided into up to four subnets can be defined as follows:

Address Class	Bits for Subnet Mask	Network Prefix	Decimal
Class C	11111111 11111111 11111111 11000000	/26	255.255.255.192

Table 24-7 shows how Class C networks can be subnetted and how this affects the number of possible subnets and hosts per subnet.

Table 24-7. Subnetting Class C Networks

Maximum Subnets	Bits for Subnet Mask	Network Prefix	Decimal	Maximum Nodes
1	11111111 11111111 11111111 00000000	/24	255.255.255.0	254
2	11111111 11111111 11111111 10000000	/25	255.255.255.128	126

Table 24-7. Subnetting Class C Networks

Maximum Subnets	Bits for Subnet Mask	Network Prefix	Decimal	Maximum Nodes
4	11111111 11111111 11111111 11000000	/26	255.255.255.192	62
8	11111111 11111111 11111111 11100000	/27	255.255.255.224	30
16	11111111 11111111 11111111 11110000	/28	255.255.255.240	14
32	11111111 11111111 11111111 11111000	/29	255.255.255.248	6
64	11111111 11111111 11111111 11111100	/30	255.255.255.252	2

Getting and Using IP Addresses

As discussed previously, there are two categories of IP addresses:

- **Public** Public addresses are assigned by Network Solutions (formerly this was InterNIC) and can be purchased as well from IANA. Most organizations don't need to purchase their IP addresses directly, however. Instead, they get the IP addresses they need from their Internet service provider (ISP).
- **Private** Private addresses are reserved for Class A, B, and C networks and can be used without specific assignment. Most organizations follow the private addressing scheme as determined by their information technology (IT) department, and in which case, they would request IP addresses from the IT department.

> **Note** Technically, if your organization doesn't plan to connect to the Internet, you can use any IP address. However, I still recommend using private IP addresses in this case and taking the time to plan out the IP address space carefully. If you do this and you later must connect the organization to the Internet, you won't have to change the IP address of every node on the network. Instead, you'll only need to reconfigure the network's Internet-facing nodes, such as a proxy server or NAT router, to connect your organization to the Internet.

If you are planning out your organization's network infrastructure, you must determine how you want to structure the network. In many cases, you'll want to isolate the internal systems from the public Internet and place them on their own private network. An example of this is shown in Figure 24-5.

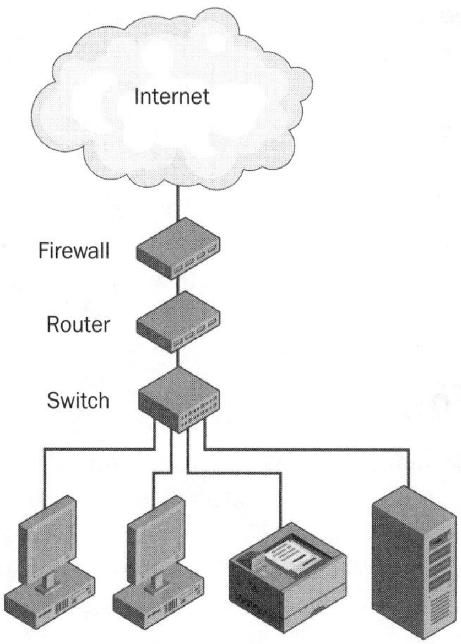

Figure 24-5. Overview diagram for connecting a private network to the Internet.

In this example, hosts on the internal network connect to a switch. The switch in turn connects to a router, which performs the necessary internal to external IP address translation using NAT. The NAT router is in turn connected to a firewall, and the firewall connects to the Internet. If the internal network ID is 192.168.1.0/24, the internal IP addresses would range from 192.168.1.1 to 192.168.1.254 and all hosts would use the network mask 255.255.255.0. After this occurs, the hosts might include the following:

- A router with IP address 192.168.1.1 on the interface facing the internal network
- A manageable switch with IP address 192.168.1.2
- Computers with IP addresses 192.168.1.20 to 192.168.149
- Servers with IP addresses 192.168.1.150 to 192.168.199
- A network printer with the IP address 192.168.1.200

Tip **Follow an IP addressing plan**

Notice how the IP addresses are assigned. I generally recommend reserving blocks of IP addresses for the various types of hosts you'll have on a network. On an internal network with the ID 192.168.1.0/24 you might designate that IP addresses 192.168.1.1 to 192.168.1.19 are reserved for network hardware, IP addresses 192.168.1.20 to 192.168.1.149 are reserved for workstations, IP addresses 192.168.1.150 to 192.168.1.199 are reserved for servers, and IP addresses above 192.168.1.200 are reserved for other types of network hardware, such as printers.

You can then determine the number of public IP addresses you need by assessing the number of public Internet-facing nodes you need. In this example, the NAT router needs a public IP address as does the external firewall. To be able to send and receive e-mail, you'll need an IP address for the organization's e-mail server. To set up a public Web site, you'll need an IP address for the organization's Web server.

That's a total of four IP addresses (six, including the network ID address and the broadcast address). In this case, your ISP might assign you a /29 subnet, giving you a total of six usable addresses. If you think you might need more than this, you could ask for a /28 subnet. However, keep in mind that you might have to pay a per–IP address leasing fee.

Understanding Name Resolution

Although IP addressing works well for computer-to-computer communications, it doesn't work so well when you and I want to access resources. Could you imagine having to remember the IP address of every computer that you work with? That would be difficult, and it would make working with computers on networks a chore. This is why computers are assigned names. Names are easier to remember than numbers—at least for most people.

When a computer has a name, you can type that name rather than its IP address to access it. This name resolution doesn't happen automatically. In the background, a computer process translates the computer name you type into an IP address that computers can understand. On Windows networks, computer names are handled and resolved using one of two naming systems:

- Domain Name System (DNS)
- Windows Internet Naming Service (WINS)

DNS is the primary name system. WINS is maintained for backward support and compatibility with pre–Microsoft Windows 2000 computers.

Domain Name System

DNS provides a distributed database that enables computer names to be resolved to their corresponding IP addresses. When working with DNS, it is important to understand what is meant by the terms "host name," "domain name," "fully qualified domain name," and "name resolution."

Host Names

A *host name* identifies an individual host in DNS. Ordinarily, you might call this a computer name. The difference, however, is that there is an actual record in the DNS database called a *host record* that corresponds to the computer name and details how the computer name is used on the network. Host names can be assigned by administrators and other members of the organization.

Domain Names

A *domain name* identifies a network in DNS. Domain names follow a specific naming scheme that is organized in a tree-like structure. Periods (dots) are used to separate the name components or levels within the domain name.

The first level of the tree is where you'll find the top-level domains. *Top-level domains* describe the kinds of networks that are within their domain. For example, the .edu top-level domain is for educational domains, the .gov top-level domain is for U.S. government domains, and .com is for commercial domains. As you can see, these top-level domains are organized by category. There are also top-level domains organized geographically, such as .ca for Canada and .uk for United Kingdom.

The second level of the tree is where you'll find parent domains. *Parent domains* are the primary domain names of organizations. For example, City Power & Light's domain name is cpandl.com. The domain name cpandl.com identifies a specific network in the .com domain. No parent domain can be used on the public Internet without being reserved and registered. Name registrars, such as Network Solutions, charge a fee for this service.

Additional levels of the tree belong to individual hosts or subsequent levels in the organization's domain structure. These subsequent levels are referred to as *child domains*. For example, City Power & Light might have Tech, Support, and Sales child domains, which are named tech.cpandl.com, support.cpandl.com, and sales.cpandl.com, respectively.

Tip **Connect the network to the Internet**
If your organization's network must be connected to the Internet, you should obtain a public domain name from a name registrar or use a similar service as provided by an ISP. Because many domain names have already been taken, you should have several previously agreed upon alternative names in mind when you go to register. After you obtain a domain name, you must configure DNS hosting for that domain. You do this by specifying the addresses of two or more DNS servers that will handle DNS services for this domain. Typically, these DNS servers belong to your ISP.

Fully Qualified Domain Name (FQDN)

All hosts on a TCP/IP network have what is called a fully qualified domain name (FQDN). The FQDN combines the host name and the domain name and serves to uniquely identify the host. For a host named CPL05 in the cpandl.com domain, the FQDN would be cpl05.cpandl.com. For a host named CORPSVR17 in the tech.cpandl.com domain, the FQDN would be corpsvr17.tech.cpandl.com.

Name Resolution

Name resolution is the process by which host names are resolved to IP addresses and vice versa. When a TCP/IP application wants to communicate with another host on a network, it needs the IP address of that host. Typically, the application knows only the name of the host it is looking for, so it has to resolve that name to an IP address.

To do this, the application first looks in its local DNS cache of names that it has previously looked up. If the name is in this cache, the IP address is found without having to look elsewhere and the application can connect to the remote host. If the name isn't in the cache, the application must ask the network's DNS server or servers to help resolve the name. These servers perform a similar lookup. If the name is in their database or cache, the IP address for the name is returned. Otherwise, the DNS server has to request this information from another DNS server.

That's the way it works—the simplified version at least. Most of the time, a TCP/IP application has the host name and needs to find the corresponding IP address. Occasionally, a TCP/IP application will have an IP address and needs the corresponding host name. To do this, the application must perform a reverse lookup, so instead of requesting an IP address, the application requests a host name using the IP address.

The application first looks in its local cache of information that has been previously looked up. If the IP address is in this cache, the name is found without having to look elsewhere and the application can perform whichever tasks are necessary. If the IP address isn't in the cache, the application must ask the network's DNS server or servers to help resolve the IP address. These servers perform a similar lookup. If the IP address is in their reverse lookup database or cache, the name for the IP address is returned. Otherwise, the DNS server has to request this information from another DNS server.

Windows Internet Naming Service (WINS)

WINS is another name resolution service provided by Windows Server 2003. Under WINS, computers have NetBIOS names. WINS provides a similar service for NetBIOS names as DNS provides for DNS host names. That is to say, WINS provides the necessary services for mapping NetBIOS names to IP addresses for hosts running NetBIOS over TCP/IP.

NetBIOS is an interface developed to allow applications to perform basic network operations, such as sending data, connecting to remote hosts, and accessing network resources. NetBIOS is used by earlier versions of Windows, including Windows 95, Windows 98, and Windows NT, to identify and locate computers on the network.

NetBIOS computer names can be up to 15 characters long. They must be unique on the network and can be looked up on a server called a WINS server. WINS supports both forward lookups (NetBIOS computer name to IP address) and reverse lookups (IP address to NetBIOS computer name).

Your organization must set up WINS only if you are using Windows 95, Windows 98, Windows NT, or applications that rely on NetBIOS over TCP/IP. If you are currently using WINS, you can eliminate the need for this service by moving workstations and servers to Windows 2000 or a later version of Windows.

Configuring TCP/IP Networking

As you've seen, computers use IP addresses to communicate over TCP/IP and are also assigned names to make it easier for people to work with networked computers. Although name resolution can be performed using DNS, WINS, or a combination of both, the preferred technique on Windows Server 2003 domains is DNS.

IP addresses can be static or dynamic. A *static* IP address is an IP address that is assigned manually and is fixed once it is assigned. A *dynamic* IP address is assigned automatically at startup by a DHCP server and can change over time. Most of the time, you assign static IP addresses to servers and configure workstations with dynamic IP addresses.

A third type of addressing, Automatic Private IP Addressing (APIPA), is also available. APIPA is used whenever a DHCP server can't be reached at startup or when the current IP address lease expires and cannot be renewed.

Note Unless an IP address is specifically reserved, DHCP servers assign IP addresses for a specific period of time, known as an *IP address lease*. If this lease expires and cannot be renewed, then the client is assigned an automatic private IP address.

Note To perform most TCP/IP configuration tasks, you must be a member of the Administrators group.

Preparing for Installation of TCP/IP Networking

Before you can configure TCP/IP networking on individual computers, you need the following information:

- **Domain name** The name of the domain in which the computer will be located. This can be a parent or a child domain as discussed previously.
- **IP address type, value, or both** The IP address information to assign to the computer.
- **Subnet mask** The subnet mask for the network to which the computer is attached.
- **Default gateway address** The address of the router that will function as the computer's gateway.

- **DNS server address** The address of the DNS server or servers that provide DNS name resolution services on the network.
- **WINS server address** The address of the WINS server or servers that provide WINS name resolution services on the network.

If you are unsure of any of this information, you should ask the IT staff. In many cases, even if you are an administrator, there is a specific person you must ask for the IP address setup that should be used. Typically, this is your organization's network administrator and it is that person's job to maintain the spreadsheet or database that shows how IP addresses are assigned within the organization.

If no one in your organization has this role yet, this role should be assigned to someone or jointly managed to ensure that IP addresses are assigned following a specific plan. The plan should detail the following information:

- The address ranges that are reserved for network equipment and hardware and which individual IP addresses in this range are currently in use
- The address ranges that are reserved for DHCP and as such cannot be assigned using a static IP address
- The address ranges that are for static IP addresses and which individual IP addresses in this range are currently in use

Installing TCP/IP Networking

TCP/IP is installed by default during the installation of the operating system if a network adapter was detected. If no network adapter was available or you elected not to install TCP/IP during installation, you can add TCP/IP by following these steps:

1. In Control Panel, access Network Connections, and then select or double-click the connection you want to work with. A connection called Local Area Connection is created automatically when you install a computer.
2. In the Status dialog box, click Properties. This displays the Properties dialog box shown in Figure 24-6. If Internet Protocol (TCP/IP) isn't shown in the list of installed components, click Install, select Protocol, and then click Add.
3. In the Select Network Protocol dialog box, click Internet Protocol (TCP/IP), and then click OK.
4. In the Local Area Connection Properties dialog box, make sure that Internet Protocol (TCP/IP) is selected, and click OK.
5. TCP/IP is now installed on the computer. Next you must configure TCP/IP to use the correct IP addressing information. The details of this process are discussed in the remaining sections of this chapter.

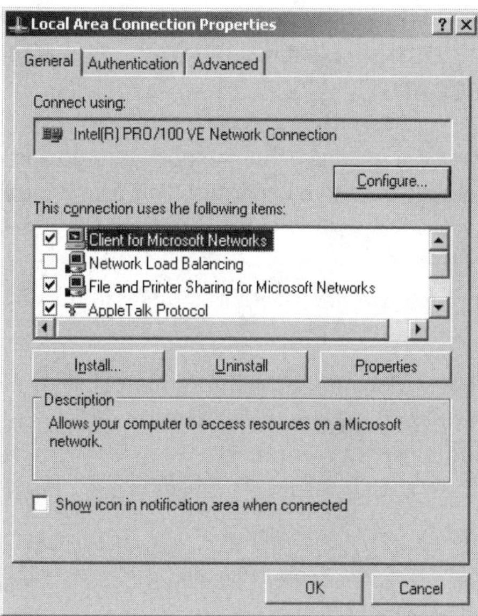

Figure 24-6. A list of currently installed networking components is displayed.

Configuring Static IP Addressing

You can manually assign an IP address to a computer by giving the computer a static IP address. A static IP address is an IP address that is fixed once it is assigned. Check with your organization's network administrator or whoever else is in charge of assigning IP addresses and get a static IP address that you can use.

Before you use any address—even one assigned to you—you should make sure it doesn't conflict with any existing IP address that has been assigned. One way to do this is to open a command prompt and type **ping** followed by the IP address, such as **ping 192.168.1.100**. If no current host on the network uses this IP address, the PING command output should be similar to the following:

```
Pinging 192.168.1.100 with 32 bytes of data:

Request timed out.
Request timed out.
Request timed out.
Request timed out.

Ping statistics for 192.168.1.100:
Packets: Sent = 4, Received = 0, Lost = 4 (100% loss)
```

You can then use the IP address. On the other hand, if you receive a reply when you ping the IP address, someone on the network is using that IP address. You should then inform the network administrator and obtain a different address.

Note Pinging an IP address will work as long as all the hosts are up and running on the network at the time you ping the address. More important is to plan the assignment of static addresses to machines on your network carefully.

You can configure IP addressing for a computer with a static IP address by following these steps:

1. In Control Panel, access Network Connections, and then select or double-click the connection you want to work with. A connection called Local Area Connection is created automatically when you install a computer.
2. In the Status dialog box, click Properties. This displays the Properties dialog box shown previously in Figure 24-6.
3. Open the Internet Protocol (TCP/IP) Properties dialog box, as shown in Figure 24-7, by double-clicking Internet Protocol (TCP/IP).

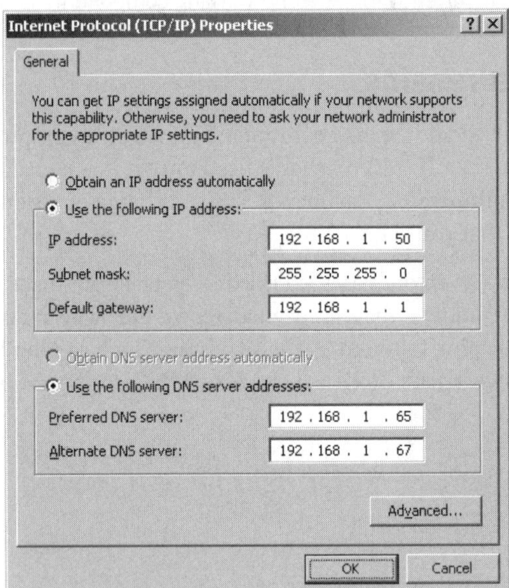

Figure 24-7. Using a static IP address.

4. Click Use The Following IP Address, and then type the IP address you want to use in the IP Address field. If you press Tab, the subnet mask is filled in for you automatically based on the IP address class. As necessary, change the subnet mask to match the subnet mask in use for the subnet in which the computer is located.

5. Type the IP address of the network's default gateway or router in the Default Gateway field. The default gateway is responsible for forwarding and routing packets for any nodes that are outside the local subnet, which could include another intranet subnet or the Internet.
6. Type the IP addresses of the preferred and alternate DNS servers in the fields provided. These IP addresses are needed for domain name resolution.
7. When you're finished, click OK. If the computer has additional network adapters, repeat this process for those adapters. Be sure to use a unique IP address for each network adapter.

Configuring Dynamic IP Addressing

Many organizations use DHCP servers to dynamically assign IP addresses. To receive an IP address, client computers use a limited broadcast to advertise that they need to obtain an IP address. DHCP servers on the network acknowledge the request by offering the client an IP address. The client acknowledges the first offer it receives, and the DHCP server in turn tells the client that it has succeeded in leasing the IP address for a specified amount of time.

The message from the DHCP server can, and typically does, include the IP addresses of the default gateway, the preferred and alternate DNS servers, and the preferred and alternate WINS servers. This means these settings wouldn't need to be manually configured on the client computer.

> **Tip** **DHCP is primarily for clients**
> Dynamic IP addresses aren't for all hosts on the network, however. Typically, you'll want to assign dynamic IP addresses to workstations and, in some instances, member servers that perform noncritical roles on the network. But if you use dynamic IP addressing for member servers, these servers should have reservations for their IP addresses. For any server that has a critical network role or provides a key service, you'll definitely want to use static IP addresses. Finally, with domain controllers and DHCP servers, you must use static IP addresses, so don't try to assign dynamic IP addresses to these servers.

You configure a computer to use dynamic IP addressing by completing the following steps:

1. In Control Panel, access Network Connections, and then select or double-click the connection you want to work with. A connection called Local Area Connection is created automatically when you install a computer.
2. In the Status dialog box, click Properties. This displays the Properties dialog box.
3. Open the Internet Protocol (TCP/IP) Properties dialog box by double-clicking Internet Protocol (TCP/IP).

4 Select Obtain An IP Address Automatically, as shown in Figure 24-8. If your DHCP servers are configured to provide the DNS server addresses, select Obtain DNS Server Address Automatically. Otherwise, select Use The Following DNS Server Addresses, and then type a preferred and alternate DNS server address in the fields provided.

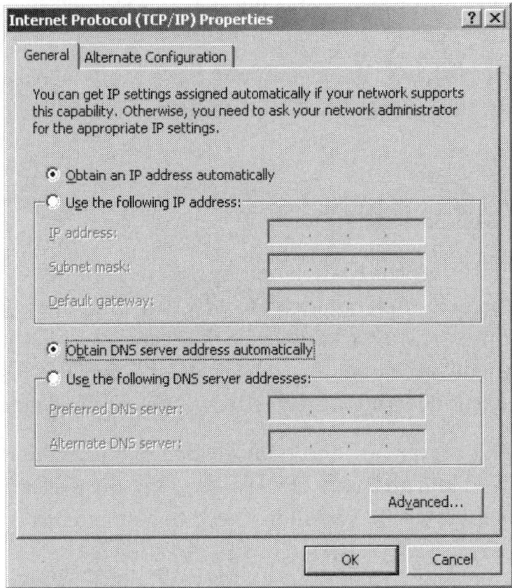

Figure 24-8. Using a dynamic IP address.

5 When you're finished, click OK. If the computer has additional network adapters, repeat this process for those adapters. Be sure to use a unique IP address for each network adapter.

Configuring Automatic Private IP Addressing

Computers using DHCP can be assigned an automatic private IP address, which is also referred to as an *alternate address*. An alternate address is used when a DHCP server can't be reached at startup or when the current IP address lease expires and cannot be renewed. By default, with Windows 2000 and later, the alternate IP address is in the range of 169.254.0.1 to 169.254.255.254 with a subnet mask of 255.255.0.0 and doesn't include default gateway, DNS, or WINS server settings. This means a computer using the alternate IP addressing is essentially isolated on its own network segment.

To ensure that a computer uses a specific IP address when no DHCP server is available, you must specify an alternate configuration manually by completing the following steps:

1. In Control Panel, access Network Connections, and then select or double-click the connection you want to work with. A connection called Local Area Connection is created automatically when you install a computer.
2. In the Status dialog box, click Properties. This displays the Properties dialog box.
3. Open the Internet Protocol (TCP/IP) Properties dialog box by double-clicking Internet Protocol (TCP/IP).
4. Select the Alternate Configuration tab, as shown in Figure 24-9. As long as you've already configured the adapter to obtain an IP address automatically, this tab is available.

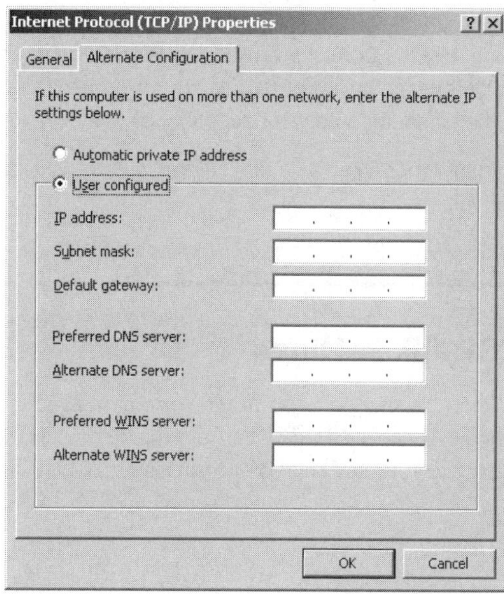

Figure 24-9. Using an alternate IP address.

5. Select User Configured, and then, in the IP Address field, type the alternate IP address you want to use when no DHCP server is available. The IP address should be a private IP address that isn't in use anywhere else at the time the settings are applied. If you press Tab, the subnet mask is filled in for you automatically based on the IP address class. As necessary, change the subnet mask to match the subnet mask for the subnet the computer should use in the alternate configuration.
6. If you want the computer to be able to communicate with other computers in the alternate configuration, type the default gateway, DNS server, and WINS server addresses as necessary, and then click OK to save the settings.

Inside Out

Disabling APIPA

Whenever DHCP is used, APIPA is enabled by default. If you don't want a computer to use APIPA, you can either assign a static TCP/IP address or disable APIPA. For example, if your network uses routers or your network is connected to the Internet without a NAT or proxy server, you might not want to use APIPA. You can disable APIPA in the Registry.

On Windows 98 or Microsoft Windows Millennium Edition, you disable APIPA by creating the IPAutoconfigurationEnabled as a DWORD value-entry under HKEY_LOCAL_MACHINE\SYSTEM\CurrentControlSet\Services\VxD\DHCP and setting the value to 0×0.

On Windows 2000 or later, you can disable APIPA by creating the IPAutoconfigurationEnabled as a DWORD value-entry under HKEY_LOCAL_MACHINE\SYSTEM\CurrentControlSet\Services\Tcpip\Parameters\Interfaces*AdapterGUID*, where *AdapterGUID* is the globally unique identifier (GUID) for the computer's network adapter. Set the value to 0×0.

If you create the IPAutoconfigurationEnabled as a DWORD value-entry, you can enable APIPA at any time by changing the value to 0×1.

For more information about disabling APIPA, see Microsoft Knowledge Base article 220874.

Configuring Advanced TCP/IP Settings

When you are using static IP addressing on a computer, you might need to configure additional TCP/IP settings using the Advanced TCP/IP Settings dialog box. As Figure 24-10 shows, this dialog box lets you customize four key areas of a computer's TCP/IP configuration:

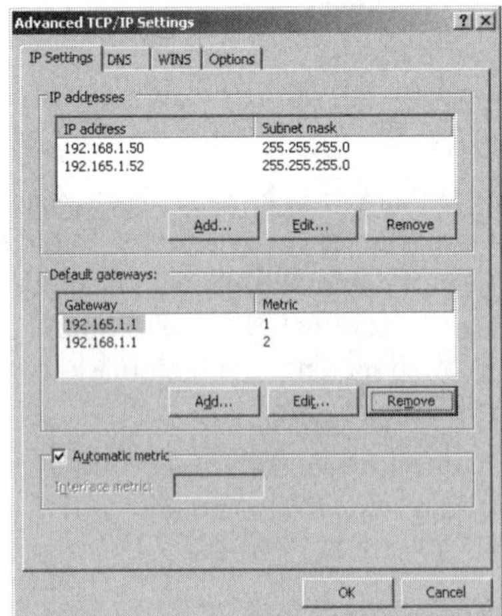

Figure 24-10. Customize the TCP/IP configuration using advanced options.

- **IP Settings** Allows you to configure additional IP addresses and gateways to use
- **DNS** Allows you to optimize the DNS configuration as well as to add and prioritize the order of DNS servers
- **WINS** Allows you to optimize the WINS configuration as well as to add and prioritize the order of WINS servers
- **Options** Allows you to configure advanced options, such as TCP/IP filtering

Configuring Advanced IP Settings

Using advanced IP settings, you can configure a single network interface on a computer to use multiple IP addresses and multiple gateways. This allows a computer to appear to be several computers and to access multiple logical subnets to route information or to provide internetworking services. In the example shown in Figure 24-10, the computer has the IP address 192.165.1.52 to communicate on the 192.165.1/24 subnet and the IP address 192.168.1.50 to communicate on the 192.168.1/24 subnet. To get to these subnets, the computer must know the gateways to use, which is why one default gateway for each subnet is configured.

You can configure advanced IP settings by completing the following steps:

1. In Control Panel, access Network Connections, and then select or double-click the connection you want to work with. A connection called Local Area Connection is created automatically when you install a computer.
2. In the Status dialog box, click Properties. This displays the Properties dialog box.
3. Open the Internet Protocol (TCP/IP) Properties dialog box by double-clicking Internet Protocol (TCP/IP).
4. Display the dialog box shown previously in Figure 24-10 by clicking Advanced.
5. To add an IP address, click Add in the IP Addresses area to display the TCP/IP Address dialog box. After you type the IP address in the IP Address field and the subnet mask in the Subnet Mask field, click Add to return to the Advanced TCP/IP Settings dialog box. Repeat this step for each IP address you want to add.
6. To add a default gateway, click Add in the Default Gateways area to display the TCP/IP Gateway Address dialog box. Type the gateway address in the Gateway field. By default, Windows Server 2003 automatically assigns a metric to the gateway, which determines in which order the gateway is used. To assign the metric manually, clear the Automatic Metric option, and then enter a metric in the field provided. Click Add, and then repeat this step for each gateway you want to add.
7. When you are finished, click OK to apply the changes.

Configuring Advanced DNS Settings

The standard DNS settings are designed to work in network environments where there is a primary and an alternate DNS server and these DNS servers are running Microsoft DNS in a standard configuration. If you want to specify additional DNS servers or your network uses custom DNS settings, you might need to configure advanced DNS settings.

You can configure advanced DNS settings by completing the following steps:

1. In Control Panel, access Network Connections, and then select or double-click the connection you want to work with. A connection called Local Area Connection is created automatically when you install a computer.
2. In the Status dialog box, click Properties. This displays the Properties dialog box.
3. Open the Internet Protocol (TCP/IP) Properties dialog box by double-clicking Internet Protocol (TCP/IP).
4. Click Advanced to display the Advanced TCP/IP Settings dialog box, and then select the DNS tab, as shown in Figure 24-11.

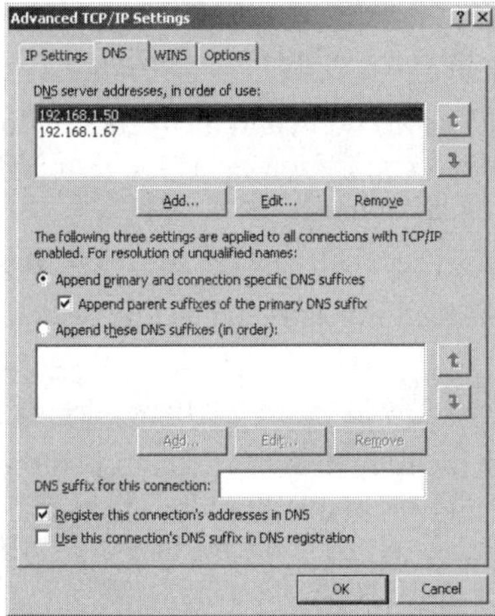

Figure 24-11. Configure advanced DNS options.

5. To add a DNS server address, click Add in the DNS Server Addresses area to display the TCP/IP DNS Server dialog box. After you type the DNS server address in the IP Address field, click Add to return to the Advanced TCP/IP Settings dialog box. Repeat this step for each DNS server address you want to add.

6 DNS servers are used for name resolution according to the priority order you specified. If the first server isn't available to respond to a host name resolution request, the next DNS server on the list is accessed, and so on. To change the position of a server in the list box, click it, and then use the Up or Down arrow button.

7 The additional DNS options are used as follows:

- *Append Primary And Connection Specific DNS Suffixes*—Ensures unqualified computer names are resolved in the primary domain (and optionally in the connection-specific domain specified under DNS Suffix For This Computer). If the computer name is CP05 and the parent domain is cpandl.com, DNS attempts to resolve the computer name to cp05.cpandl.com. If the FQDN exists, the lookup succeeds. Otherwise, it fails. The parent domain used is the one set in the Network Identification tab of the System Properties dialog box.
- *Append Parent Suffixes Of The Primary DNS Suffix*—Ensures unqualified computer names are resolved using the parent/child domain hierarchy. If a query fails in the immediate parent domain, the suffix for the parent of the parent domain is used to try to resolve the query. This process continues until the top of the organization's domain hierarchy is reached. If the computer name is CP05 and the parent domain is tech.cpandl.com, DNS attempts to resolve the computer name to cp05.tech.cpandl.com. If this fails, DNS attempts to resolve the computer name to cp05.cpandl.com.
- *Append These DNS Suffixes (In Order)*—Ensures unqualified computer names are resolved using only the suffix provided rather than resolving through the parent domain. If you use this option, the primary and connection-specific DNS suffixes are not applied. When selected, you use the Add button to add a domain suffix to the list, the Remove button to remove a domain suffix from the list, and the Edit button to edit a selected entry. When you specify multiple domain suffixes, these suffixes are used in the order specified. To change the order of the domain suffixes, select the suffix, and then use the Up or Down arrow button to change its position.
- *DNS Suffix For This Connection*—Designates a specific DNS suffix for the connection that overrides DNS names already configured for use on this connection. If you type a suffix here, DNS attempts to resolve in the parent domain and then in the DNS suffix domain. For example, if the parent domain is eng.cpandl.com and the suffix domain is tech.cpandl.com, DNS attempts to resolve the computer name CP05 to cp05.eng.cpandl.com first, and then if this fails, it tries cp05.tech.cpandl.com.

- *Register This Connection's Addresses In DNS*—Ensures all IP addresses for this connection are registered in DNS under the computer's FQDN.
- *Use This Connection's DNS Suffix In DNS Registration*—Ensures all IP addresses for this connection are registered in DNS under the parent domain (and if used, the domain specified under DNS Suffix For This Computer).

Configuring Advanced WINS Settings

The standard WINS settings are designed to work in network environments where there is a primary and an alternate WINS server and these WINS servers are running Microsoft WINS in a standard configuration. If you want to specify additional WINS servers or your network uses custom WINS settings, you might need to configure advanced WINS settings.

To configure advanced WINS settings, complete the following steps:

1. In Control Panel, access Network Connections, and then select or double-click the connection you want to work with. A connection called Local Area Connection is created automatically when you install a computer.
2. In the Status dialog box, click Properties. This displays the Properties dialog box.
3. Open the Internet Protocol (TCP/IP) Properties dialog box by double-clicking Internet Protocol (TCP/IP).
4. Click Advanced to display the Advanced TCP/IP Settings dialog box, and then select the WINS tab, as shown in Figure 24-12.

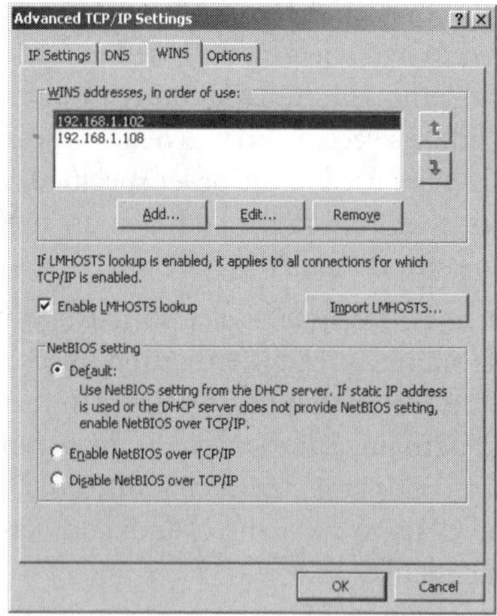

Figure 24-12. Configure advanced WINS options.

5. To add a WINS server address, click Add in the WINS Addresses area to display the TCP/IP WINS Server dialog box. After you type the WINS server address in the IP Address field, click Add to return to the Advanced TCP/IP Settings dialog box. Repeat this step for each WINS server address you want to add.
6. WINS servers are listed in priority order. If the first server isn't available to respond to a host name resolution request, the next WINS server on the list is accessed, and so on. To change the position of a server in the list, click it, and then use the Up or Down arrow button.
7. To enable LMHOSTS lookups, select the Enable LMHOSTS Lookup option. If you want the computer to use an existing LMHOSTS file defined somewhere on the network, retrieve this file by clicking the Import LMHOSTS button. In most cases, you use LMHOSTS only when other name resolution methods fail. Because LMHOSTS files are maintained locally on a computer-by-computer basis, you must configure an LMHOSTS file on each computer for which name resolution is failing.
8. NetBIOS Over TCP/IP services are required for WINS name resolution. You have three configuration options:
   - If you use DHCP and NetBIOS settings are provided by the DHCP servers, you can get the NetBIOS setting from the DHCP servers. Select Default, Use NetBIOS Setting From The DHCP Server.
   - If you use static IP addresses or the DHCP servers don't provide NetBIOS settings, select Enable NetBIOS Over TCP/IP.
   - If WINS and NetBIOS aren't used on the network, select Disable NetBIOS Over TCP/IP. This eliminates the NetBIOS broadcasts that would otherwise be sent by the computer.

Configuring Advanced TCP/IP Options

Advanced TCP/IP options are primarily used for configuring TCP/IP filtering. TCP/IP filtering provides a very basic way to control IP traffic to and from a computer and is useful when you don't want to use IP Security or the built-in Internet Connection Firewall. TCP/IP filtering is a global option and applies to all network interfaces configured on a computer.

To configure TCP/IP filtering, complete the following steps:

1. In Control Panel, access Network Connections, and then select or double-click the connection you want to work with. A connection called Local Area Connection is created automatically when you install a computer.
2. In the Status dialog box, click Properties. This displays the Properties dialog box.
3. Open the Internet Protocol (TCP/IP) Properties dialog box by double-clicking Internet Protocol (TCP/IP).

4 Click Advanced to display the Advanced TCP/IP Settings dialog box, and then select the Options tab.

5 In the Options tab, select TCP/IP Filtering, and then click Properties. This displays the TCP/IP Filtering dialog box, as shown in Figure 24-13.

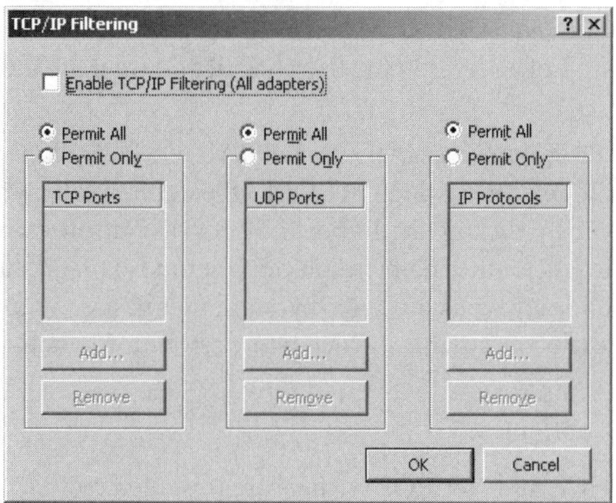

Figure 24-13. TCP/IP filtering can be configured as well.

6 If you want to configure TCP/IP filtering, select Enable TCP/IP Filtering, and then configure traffic for TCP ports, User Datagram Protocol (UDP) ports, and IP protocols to permit all or permit only those ports or protocols you've specifically listed.

Chapter 25

Managing DHCP

Most Microsoft Windows network should be configured to use Dynamic Host Configuration Protocol (DHCP). DHCP simplifies administration and makes it easier for users to get their computer on the organization's network. How does DHCP do this? DHCP is a protocol that allows client computers to start up and automatically receive an Internet Protocol (IP) address and other related Transmission Control Protocol/Internet Protocol (TCP/IP) settings such as the subnet mask, default gateway, Domain Name System (DNS) servers and Windows Internet Naming Service (WINS) servers. This chapter describes how DHCP works and how to use it.

DHCP Essentials

DHCP is a standards-based protocol that was originally defined by the Internet Engineering Task Force (IETF) and based on the Bootstrap Protocol (BOOTP). It is defined in Requests for Comments (RFCs) 3396 and 3442 and has been implemented on a variety of operating systems including UNIX and Windows. Because DHCP is a client/server protocol, there is a server component and a client component necessary to implement the protocol on a network. To make it easier to deploy DHCP in the enterprise, all server editions of Windows Server 2003 include the DHCP Server service, which can be installed to support DHCP, and all versions of the Windows operating system from Windows 98 to Windows Server 2003 automatically install the DHCP Client service as part of TCP/IP.

Because of the client/server model, a computer that gets its configuration from DHCP is referred to as a *DHCP client,* and the computer that provides the DHCP services to the client is referred to as a *DHCP server*. It's the job of the DHCP server to maintain a database about the IP addresses that are available and the related configuration information. When an IP address is given out to a client, the client is said to have a lease on the IP address. The term "lease" is used because the assignment generally is not permanent. The DHCP server sets the duration of the lease when the lease is granted and can also change it later as necessary, such as when the lease is renewed.

DHCP also provides a way to assign a lease on an address permanently. To do this, you can create a *reservation* by specifying the IP address to reserve and the Media Access Control (MAC) address of the computer that will hold the IP address. The reservation thereafter ensures the client computer with the specified MAC address always gets the designated IP address.

Note MAC addresses are tied to the network interface card (NIC) of a computer. If you remove a NIC or install an additional NIC on a computer, the MAC address of the new or additional card will be different from the MAC address of the original NIC.

Tip **Consider DHCP for non-DHCP member servers**

You'll find that configuring member servers to use DHCP and then assigning them a reservation is an easy way to ensure member servers have a fixed IP address while maintaining the flexibility provided by DHCP. Once configured for DHCP, the member servers get all of their TCP/IP options from DHCP, including their IP addresses. If you ever need to change their addressing, you can do this from within DHCP rather than on each member server—and changing IP addressing and other TCP/IP options in one location is much easier than having to do so in multiple locations. Keep in mind that some server applications or roles might require a static IP address in order to work properly.

Microsoft recommends that a single DHCP server service no more than 10,000 clients. You define a set of IP addresses that can be assigned to clients using a scope. A *scope* is a set of IP addresses and related configuration options. The IP addresses set in a scope are continuous and are associated with a specific subnet mask. To define a subset of IP addresses within a scope that should not be used, you can specify an exclusion. An *exclusion* defines a range of IP addresses that you can exclude so that it isn't assigned to client computers.

Windows Server 2003 supports integration of DHCP with dynamic DNS. When configured, this ensures the client's DNS record is updated when it receives a new IP address. To ensure client names can be resolved to IP addresses, you should configure integration of DHCP and DNS.

DHCP can also be integrated with the Routing and Remote Access Service (RRAS). When configured, dial-up networking or virtual private network (VPN) clients can log on to the network remotely and use DHCP to configure their IP address and TCP/IP options. The server managing their connection to the network is called a remote access server, and it is the responsibility of this server to obtain blocks of IP addresses from a DHCP server for use by remote clients. If a DHCP server is not available when the remote access server requests IP addresses, the remote clients are configured with automatic private IP addresses.

DHCP Security Considerations

DHCP is inherently insecure. Anyone with access to the network can perform malicious actions that could cause problems for other clients trying to obtain IP addresses. A user could take the following actions:

- Initiate a denial of service (DoS) attack by requesting all available IP addresses or by using large numbers of IP addresses, either of which could make it impossible for other users to obtain IP addresses.
- Initiate an attack on DNS by performing a large number of dynamic updates through DHCP.
- Use the information provided by DHCP to set up rogue services on the network, such as using a non-Microsoft DHCP server to provide incorrect IP address information.

To reduce the risk of attacks, you should limit physical access to the network. Don't make it easy for unauthorized users to connect to the network. If you use wireless technologies, configure the network so that it doesn't broadcast the service set identifier (SSID) and use Wired Equivalent Privacy (WEP) encryption, which prohibits wireless users from obtaining a DHCP lease until they provide an appropriate WEP key.

To reduce the risk of a rogue DHCP server, configure the Active Directory directory service on the network and use it to determine which DHCP servers are authorized to provide services. By using Active Directory, any computer running Microsoft Windows 2000 or later must be authorized to provide DHCP services. Once a server is authorized, it is available for clients to use. This, unfortunately, doesn't restrict the use of unauthorized Microsoft Windows NT or non-Microsoft servers running DHCP, but it is a start.

In addition, the DHCP Server service should not be placed on an Active Directory domain controller if this can be avoided. The reason for this is because this changes security related to service locator (SRV) records, which domain controllers are responsible for publishing. SRV records detail the location of domain controllers, Kerberos servers, and other servers, and the changes to the security of these records when you install DHCP means that the records could be altered by any client on the network.

The reason this happens is because DHCP servers must be able to update client records dynamically if a client's IP address changes. Because of this, they are made members of the DNSUpdateProxy group, and members of this group do not have any security applied to objects they create in the DNS database. If you can't avoid placing DHCP on a domain controller, it is recommended that you remove the DHCP server from the DNSUpdateProxy group. This should avoid the security problem outlined here, but will also prevent the DHCP server from dynamically updating client records in DNS when the client IP addresses change.

Planning DHCP Implementations

Planning a new DHCP implementation or revamping your existing DHCP implementation requires a good understanding of how DHCP works. You need to know the following information:

- How DHCP messages are sent and received
- How DHCP relay agents are used
- How multiple servers should be configured

DHCP Messages and Relay Agents

When a DHCP client is started, it uses network broadcasts to obtain or renew a lease from a DHCP server. These broadcasts are in the form of DHCP messages. A client obtains its initial lease as shown in Figure 25-1. Here, the client broadcasts a DHCP Discover message. All DHCP servers on the network respond to the broadcast with a DHCP Offer message, which offers the client an IP lease. The client accepts the first offer received by sending a DHCP Request message back to the server. The server accepts the request by sending the client a DHCP Acknowledgment message.

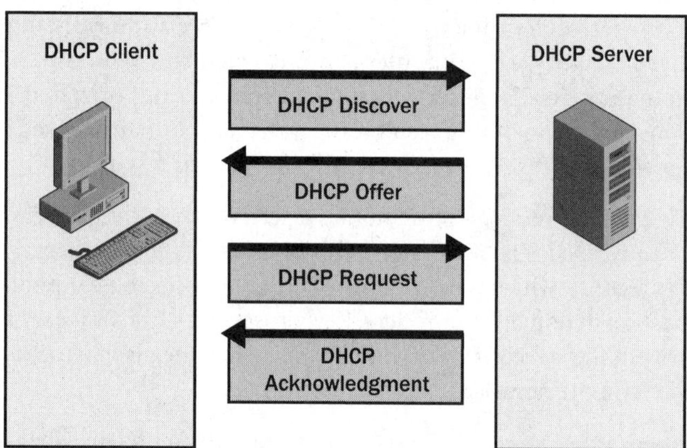

Figure 25-1. Obtaining an initial lease.

DHCP clients must renew their leases periodically, either at each restart or when 50 percent of the lease time has passed. If the renewal process fails, the client tries to renew the lease again when 87.5 percent of the lease time has passed. Renewing the lease involves the client sending the DHCP server a DHCP Request and the server accepting the request by sending a DHCP Acknowledgment. This streamlined communication process is shown in Figure 25-2.

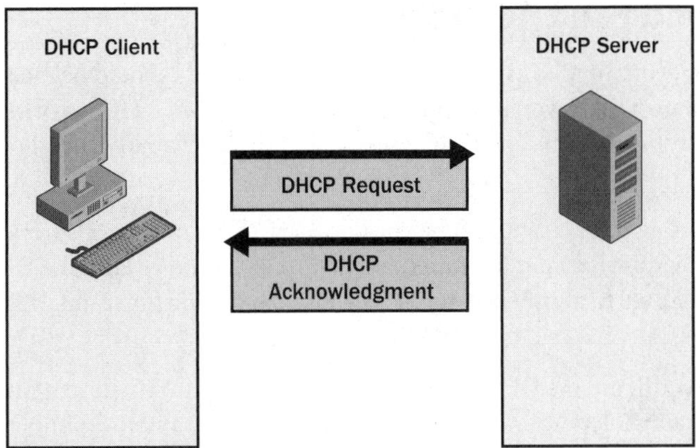

Figure 25-2. Renewing a lease.

If a DHCP client is unable to reach a DHCP server at startup or to renew its lease, it pings the the default gateway that was previously assigned. If the default gateway responds, the client assumes it is on the subnet from which the lease was originally obtained and continues to use the lease. If the default gateway doesn't respond, the client assumes it has been moved to a new subnet and that there is no DHCP server on this subnet. It then configures itself to use an automatic private address. The client will continue to check for a DHCP server when it is autoconfigured. By default, it does this by sending a DHCP Discover message every five minutes. If the client gets a DHCP Offer back from a DHCP server, it sends a DHCP Request to the server. When it gets back a DHCP Acknowledgment, it abandons its autoconfiguration and uses the address and other configuration settings sent by the DHCP server.

Typically, the messages sent by DHCP clients and servers are limited by the logical boundaries of the network. As a result, DHCP client broadcasts aren't routed and stay on only the originating network. In this configuration, you need at least one DHCP server per subnet.

To reduce the number of DHCP servers needed for your organization, you can configure a DHCP relay agent on any subnet that has no DHCP server. This relay agent is a router or a computer on the network that is configured to listen for DHCP broadcasts from clients on the local subnet and forward them as appropriate to a DHCP server on a different subnet. A router that supports BOOTP can be configured as a relay agent. You can also configure Windows Server 2003 computers on the network to act as DHCP relay agents.

Tip **Relay agents are best for LANs**
Relay agents work best in local area network (LAN) environments where subnets are all in the same geographic location. In a wide area network (WAN) environment where you are forwarding broadcasts across links, you might not want to use relay agents. If a WAN link goes down, clients won't be able to obtain or renew leases, and this could cause the clients to use Automatic Private IP Addressing (APIPA).

DHCP Availability and Fault Tolerance

As part of planning, you must consider how many DHCP servers should be made available on the network. In most cases, you'll want to configure at least two DHCP servers. If they are configured properly, having multiple DHCP servers increases reliability and allows for fault tolerance.

In a large enterprise, a server cluster can be your primary technique for ensuring DHCP availability and providing for fault tolerance. Here, if a DHCP server fails, the DHCP Server service can be failed over to another server in the cluster, allowing for seamless transition of DHCP services.

Although you can configure the DHCP Server service for failover on a cluster, much simpler and less expensive fault-tolerance implementations are available, and these implementations work with large networks as well as small and medium networks. The implementations include the following:

- 50/50 failover approach
- 80/20 failover approach
- 100/100 failover approach

50/50 Failover

By configuring the 50/50 failover approach, you use two DHCP servers to make an equal amount of IP addresses available to clients for leasing. Here, each DHCP server is configured with an identical scope range but with different exclusions within that range. The first server gets the first half of the scope's IP address range and excludes the second half. The second server gets the second half of the scope's IP address range and excludes the first half.

To see how this would be implemented, consider the following example. The organization has two DHCP servers:

- Server A's primary scope is configured to use the IP address range 192.168.10.1 to 192.168.10.254 and has an exclusion range of 192.168.10.125 to 192.168.10.254.
- Server B's primary scope is configured to use the IP address range 192.168.10.1 to 192.168.10.254 and has an exclusion range of 192.168.10.1 to 192.168.10.124.

Here, 254 IP addresses are available, which could be used to service 200 or more clients. When a client starts up on the network, both DHCP servers respond. The client accepts the first IP address offered, which could be on either Server A or Server B and which is often the server that is closest to the client. Because both servers are configured to use the same IP address range, both servers can service clients on that subnet. If one of the servers fails, a client using an IP address in the excluded range of the remaining server would be allowed to obtain a new lease. Why? The DHCP server is on the same subnet and its scope is configured for IP addresses in this range. It sees the exclusion and knows that IP addresses in this range cannot be assigned, but it can assign the client an IP address from the nonexcluded range. Thus, you achieve basic fault tolerance and availability.

Although this approach is designed to provide some redundancy and fault tolerance, it is possible that one of the servers would assign more IP addresses than the other. This could lead to a situation in which one of the servers doesn't have any available IP addresses, and if it is the other server that fails, no IP addresses would be available to clients seeking new leases and they would be configured to use APIPA.

80/20 Failover

By configuring the 80/20 failover approach, you use two DHCP servers to make a disproportionate amount of IP addresses available to clients for leasing. Here, you have a primary DHCP server that is configured with 80 percent of the available IP addresses and a backup DHCP server that is configured with 20 percent of the available IP addresses. This situation is ideal when the DHCP servers are separated from each other, such as when the primary DHCP server is on the primary subnet and the backup DHCP server is on a smaller remote subnet.

To see how this would be implemented, consider the following example. The organization has two DHCP servers, as follows:

- Server A's primary scope is configured to use the IP address range 192.168.10.1 to 192.168.10.254 and has an exclusion range of 192.168.10.203 to 192.168.10.254.
- Server B's primary scope is configured to use the IP address range 192.168.10.1 to 192.168.10.254 and has an exclusion range of 192.168.10.1 to 192.168.10.202.

Here, 254 IP addresses are again available, which could be used to service 200 or more clients—the bulk of which are located on the primary subnet. You are using the remote DHCP server on a smaller subnet as a backup. If the primary server were to go down, the backup could respond to client requests and handle their leases. When the primary came back online, it would handle the majority of client leases because it is located on the primary subnet closer to the bulk of the client computers. Again, you achieve basic fault tolerance and availability.

Although this approach is designed to provide some redundancy and fault tolerance, it is possible that the primary would be offline too long and the backup DHCP server would run out of available IP addresses. If this were to happen, no IP addresses would be available to clients seeking new leases, and they would be configured to use APIPA.

100/100 Failover

By configuring the 100/100 failover approach, you make twice as many IP addresses available as are needed. Thus, if you must provide DHCP services for 200 clients, you make at least 400 IP addresses available to those clients. As with 50/50 failover, each DHCP server is configured with an identical scope range but with different exclusions within that range. The first server gets the first half of the scope's IP address range and excludes the second half. The second server gets the second half of the scope's IP address range and excludes the first half.

To make twice as many IP addresses available as are needed, you must think carefully about the IP address class you use and would most likely want to use a Class A or Class B network. With this in mind, the organization's two DHCP servers might be configured as follows:

- Server A's primary scope is configured to use the IP address range 10.0.1.1 to 10.0.10.254 and has an exclusion range of 10.0.6.1 to 10.0.10.254. You also must block the potential broadcast addresses in the nonexcluded range, so you also exclude 10.0.1.255, 10.0.2.255, 10.0.3.255, 10.0.4.255, and 10.0.5.255.
- Server B's primary scope is configured to use the IP address range 10.0.1.1 to 10.0.10.254 and has an exclusion range of 10.0.1.1 to 10.0.5.254. You also must block the potential broadcast addresses in the nonexcluded range, so you also exclude 10.0.6.255, 10.0.7.255, 10.0.8.255, 10.0.9.255, and 10.0.10.255.

Here, over 2,500 IP addresses are again available, which is more than two times what is needed to service the network's 1,000 clients. When a client starts up on the network, both DHCP servers respond. The client accepts the first IP address offered, which could be on either Server A or Server B and which is often the server that is closest to the client. Because both servers are configured to use the same IP address range, both servers can service clients on that subnet. If one of the servers fails, a client using an IP address in the excluded range of the remaining server would be allowed to obtain a new lease.

Because more than two times as many IP addresses are available, every client on the network can obtain a lease even if one of the DHCP servers goes offline. Not only does this approach offer availability and fault tolerance, it gives you flexibility. You are able to take one of the DHCP servers offline and perform maintenance or upgrades without worrying about running out of available IP addresses.

Setting Up DHCP Servers

The approach you use to set up DHCP servers depends on many factors, including the number of clients on the network, the network configuration, and the Windows domain implementation you are using. From a physical server perspective, the DHCP Server service doesn't use a lot of system resources and can run on just about any system configured with Windows Server 2003. The DHCP Server service is in fact often installed as an additional service on an existing infrastructure server or on an older server that isn't robust enough to offer other types of services. Either approach is fine as long as you remember the security precaution discussed previously about not installing DHCP on a domain controller if possible. Personally, however, I prefer to install the DHCP Server service on hardware that I know and trust. Rather than installing it on an older system that might fail, I install it on either a workstation-class system running Windows Server 2003 or an existing infrastructure server that can handle the additional load.

Speaking of server load, a single DHCP server can handle about 10,000 clients and about 1,000 scopes. This is, of course, if the system is a dedicated DHCP server with adequate processing power and memory. Because DHCP is so important for client startup and network access, I don't trust the service to a single server, and you shouldn't either. In most cases, you'll want to have at least two DHCP servers on the network. If you have multiple subnets, you might want two DHCP servers per subnet. However, configuring routers to forward DHCP broadcasts or having DHCP relay agents reduces the need for additional servers.

Many organizations have standby DHCP servers available as well. A standby DHCP server is a server that has the DHCP Server service fully configured but has its scopes deactivated. Then, if a primary DHCP server fails and can't be recovered immediately, the scopes can be activated to service clients on the network as necessary.

After you select the server hardware, you should plan out the IP address ranges and exclusions you want to use. The section entitled "Planning DHCP Implementations" earlier in this chapter should have given you some good ideas on how to configure IP address ranges and exclusions for availability and fault tolerance. At the implementation stage, don't forget about IP addresses that might have been or will be assigned to computers using static IP addresses. You should either specifically exclude these IP address ranges or simply not include them in the scopes you configure.

The way you set up DHCP services depends on whether the network in which the DHCP server will be placed is using Active Directory domains or workgroups. With Active Directory domains, you set up DHCP services by completing the following steps:

1. Installing the DHCP Server service
2. Authorizing the DHCP server in Active Directory
3. Configuring the DHCP server with the appropriate scopes, exclusions, reservations, and options
4. Activating the DHCP server's scopes

With workgroups, you don't need to authorize the DHCP server in Active Directory. This means the steps for setting up DHCP services look like this:

1. Installing the DHCP Server service
2. Configuring the DHCP server with the appropriate scopes, exclusions, reservations, and options
3. Activating the DHCP server's scopes

The sections that follow examine the related procedures in detail.

Installing the DHCP Server Service

You can install the DHCP Server service using the Add Or Remove Programs utility or using the Configure Your Server Wizard. Follow these steps for using the Add Or Remove Programs utility to do this:

1. In Control Panel, double-click Add Or Remove Programs.
2. In the Add Or Remove Programs dialog box, click Add Windows Components to start the Windows Components Wizard.
3. On the Windows Components page, select Networking Services, and then click Details.
4. In the Networking Services dialog box, shown in the following screen, ensure the correct components are selected, but don't clear selections if a service has already been installed.

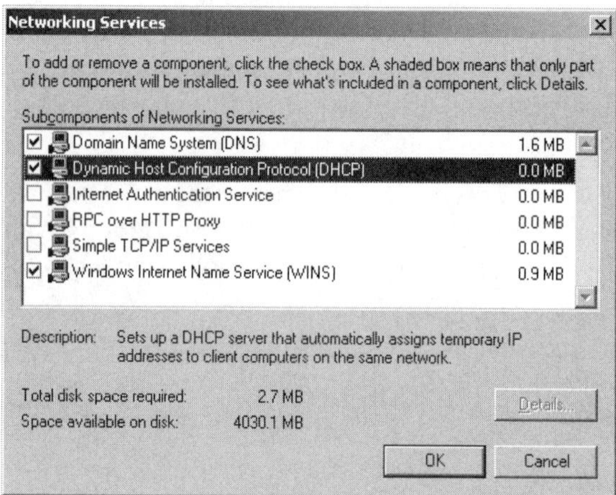

5. Click OK. Click Next to begin the installation, and then click Finish.

Follow these steps for using the Configure Your Server Wizard to do this:

1. Select Configure Your Server Wizard on the Administrative Tools menu. When the wizard starts, click Next twice.
2. The server's current roles are shown, as in the screen at the top of the following page. Select DHCP Server, and then click Next.
3. The wizard will then install DHCP and begin configuring the server. When it finishes, the wizard launches the New Scope Wizard.
4. If you want to create the initial scope for the DHCP server, click Next and follow the steps outlined in the section entitled "Creating and Configuring Scopes" later in this chapter. Otherwise, click Cancel, and create the scope later. Click Finish.

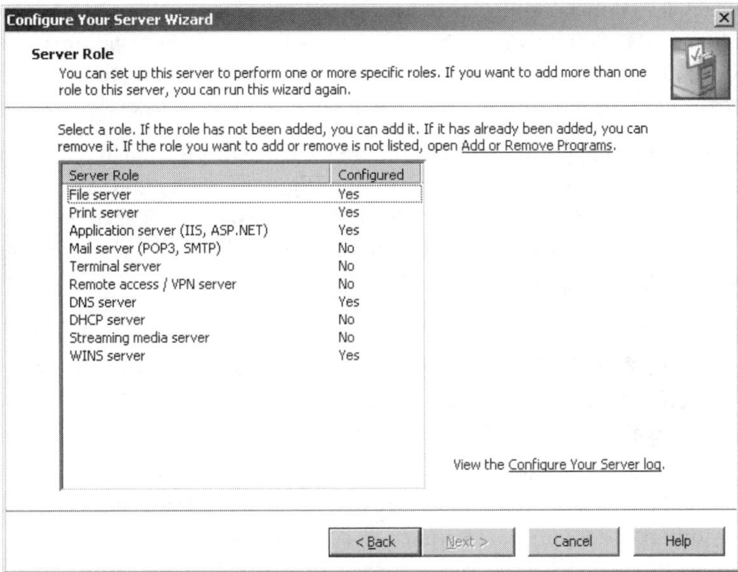

After you install the DHCP Server service, the DHCP console is available on the Administrative Tools menu. Start the console by clicking Start, Programs or All Programs as appropriate, Administrative Tools, DHCP. Then select the DHCP server you are working with to see its status. If you haven't yet created a scope, the details pane will appear, as shown in Figure 25-3. This tells you to create a scope so that the clients can get IP addresses dynamically assigned by this server.

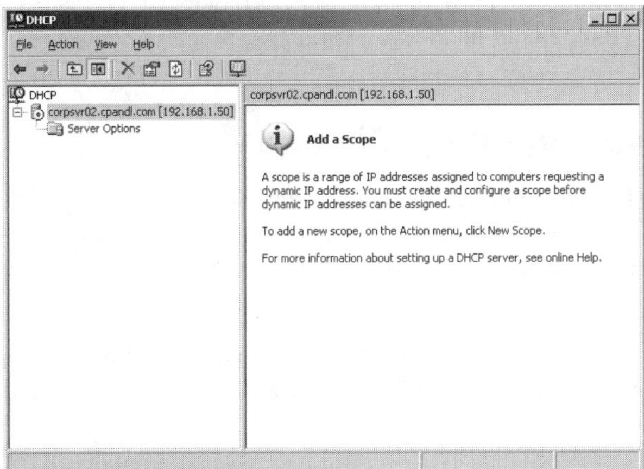

Figure 25-3. The DHCP console.

You don't have to complete the rest of the configuration at the server. If you've installed the Administrative Tools (Adminpak.msi) as discussed in the section entitled "Installing Windows

Server 2003 Administration Tools on Windows XP" on page 12, you can remotely manage and configure DHCP. Simply start the DHCP console on your workstation, right-click the DHCP node in the left pane, and select Add Server. In the Add Server dialog box, select This Server, type the name or IP address of the DHCP server, and then click OK.

The command-line counterpart to the DHCP console is the **netsh dhcp** command. From the command prompt on a computer running Windows Server 2003 you can use Netsh DHCP to perform all the tasks available in the DHCP console as well as to perform some additional tasks that can't be performed in the DHCP console. To start Netsh DHCP and access a particular DHCP server, follow these steps:

1. Start a command prompt, and then type **netsh** to start Netsh. The command prompt changes to netsh>.
2. Access the DHCP context within Netsh by typing **dhcp**. The command prompt changes to netsh dhcp>.
3. Type **server** followed by the Universal Naming Convention (UNC) name or IP address of the DHCP server, such as **\\corpsvr02** or **\\192.168.1.50**. If the DHCP server is in a different domain from your logon domain, you should type the fully qualified domain name (FQDN) of the server, such as **\\corpsvr02.cpandl.com**.
4. The command prompt changes to netsh dhcp server>. You can now work with the selected server. If you later want to work with a different server, you can do this without having to start over. Simply type **server** followed by the UNC name or IP address of that server.

> **Note** Technically, you don't need to type \\ when you specify an IP address. You must, however, type \\ when you specify a server's name or FQDN. Because of this discrepancy, you might want to use \\ all the time so that you remember that it is needed.

Authorizing DHCP Servers in Active Directory

Before you can use a DHCP server on an Active Directory domain, you must authorize the server in Active Directory. In the DHCP console, any unauthorized DHCP server to which you connect will have an icon showing a red down arrow. Authorized DHCP servers have an icon showing a green up arrow.

In the DHCP console, you can authorize a DHCP server by right-clicking the server entry in the console tree and selecting Authorize. To remove the authorization later, right-click the server entry in the console tree and select Unauthorize.

In Netsh, you can authorize a server by typing the following command:

```
netsh dhcp server ServerID initiate auth
```

where *ServerID* is the UNC name or IP address of the DHCP server on which you want to create the scope, such as \\CORPSVR03 or \\192.168.1.1. Keep in mind that if you are already at the netsh dhcp server prompt, you only need to type **initiate auth**.

> **Note** If you install DHCP on a server acting as a domain controller, the DHCP server is automatically authorized and you cannot remove the authorization. Also note that if you install DHCP in a workgroup, you don't need to authorize the server for it to work. However, if you later install Active Directory, DHCP servers will detect this automatically and will stop running until they are authorized.

Creating and Configuring Scopes

After you install the DHCP Server service, the next thing you must do is create the scopes that will provide the range of IP addresses and TCP/IP options for clients. The DHCP Server service supports three types of scopes:

- **Normal scope** A normal scope is a scope with Class A, B, or C network addresses. Normal scopes have an IP address range assignment that includes the subnet mask and can also have exclusions and reservations as well as TCP/IP options that are specific to the scope. When you create normal scopes, each scope must be in its own subnet. This means if you add a normal scope, it must be on a different subnet than any of the existing scopes configured on the server.
- **Multicast scope** A multicast scope is a scope with Class D network addresses. Multicast scopes are created in the same way as normal scopes except that they do not have an associated subnet mask, reservations, or related TCP/IP options. This means there is no specific subnet association for multicast scopes. Instead of a subnet mask, you assign the scope a Time to Live (TTL) value that specifies the maximum number of routers the messages sent to computers over multicast can go through. The default TTL is 32. Additionally, because multicast IP addresses are used for destination addresses only, they have longer lease duration than unicast IP addresses, typically, from 30 to 60 days.
- **Superscope** A superscope is a container for scopes. If you configure multiple scopes on a server and want to be able to activate or deactivate them as a unit or view the usage statistics for all the scopes at once, you can use a superscope to do this. Create the superscope and then add to it the scopes you want to manage as a group.

Before you create a normal scope, you should plan out the IP address range you want to use as well as any necessary exclusions and reservations. You also must know the IP address of the default gateway and any DNS or WINS servers that should be used.

Creating Normal Scopes Using the DHCP Console

In the DHCP console, you can create a normal scope by right-clicking the server on which you want to create the scope and choosing New Scope. If the server isn't listed, right-click DHCP in the console tree, and select Add Server so that you can specify the server you want to work with.

In the New Scope Wizard, click Next to display the Scope Name page, as shown in Figure 25-4. Type a descriptive name for the scope and a description that will be used as a comment.

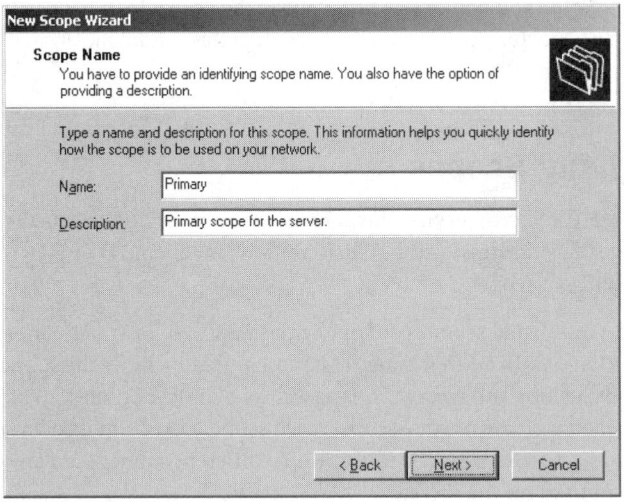

Figure 25-4. Set the scope name and description.

Click Next to display the IP Address Range page, as shown in Figure 25-5. Enter the start and end IP address to use for the scope in the Start IP Address and End IP Address boxes. Be sure to specify the first and last usable IP address only, which means you shouldn't include the *x.x.x.*0 and *x.x.x.*255 addresses. When you enter an IP address range, the bit length and subnet mask are filled in automatically for you. Change the default values if you use subnets.

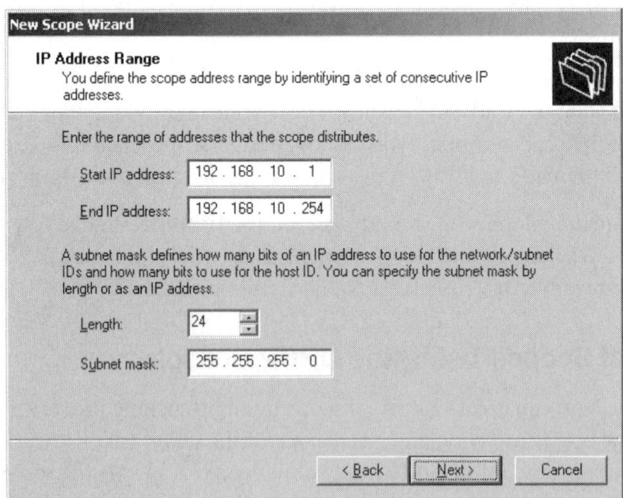

Figure 25-5. Set the IP address range and subnet information.

Click Next. If the IP address range you entered is on multiple subnets, you'll see a Create Superscope page as shown in Figure 25-6 instead of the Exclusion Range page. This page gives you the opportunity to create a superscope that contains separate scopes for each subnet. Click Yes to continue to the Lease Duration page.

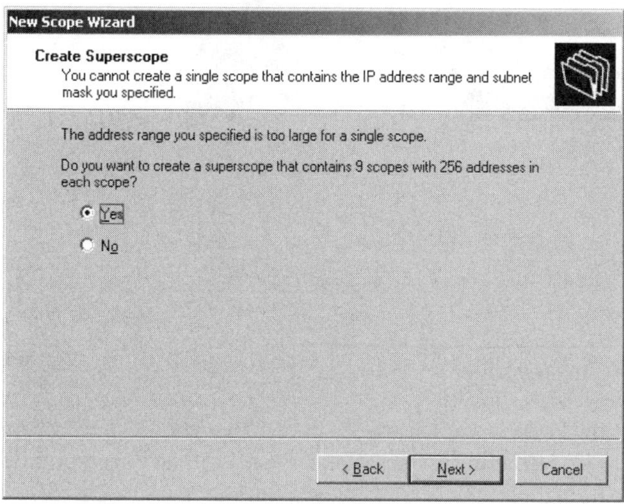

Figure 25-6. The New Scope Wizard knows when you cross subnet boundaries and will let you create a superscope with multiple scopes automatically.

Inside Out

Multiple subnets on same physical network

If you're wondering how it would work to have multiple subnets on the same network segment, it should work just fine and it generally won't matter to which subnet a client connects as long as you've set up DHCP to give clients the appropriate TCP/IP options. The physical network provides the boundaries for these subnets unless you've configured routers or DHCP relay agents to forward DHCP broadcasts. Incidentally, if you want to be sure that clients use a specific subnet, there is a way to do that using reservations. However, you wouldn't want to create reservations for a lot of clients. Instead, you might want to create a user- or vendor-defined class and allow clients to connect to any subnet to get their class-specific TCP/IP options.

If all the IP addresses you entered are on the same subnet, you'll have the opportunity to specify an exclusion range, as shown in Figure 25-7. Use the Exclusion Range boxes to define IP address ranges that are to be excluded from the scope, such as servers that have static IP addresses assigned to them. After you enter the Start IP Address and End IP Address for the exclusion range, click Add. You can then add additional exclusion ranges as necessary.

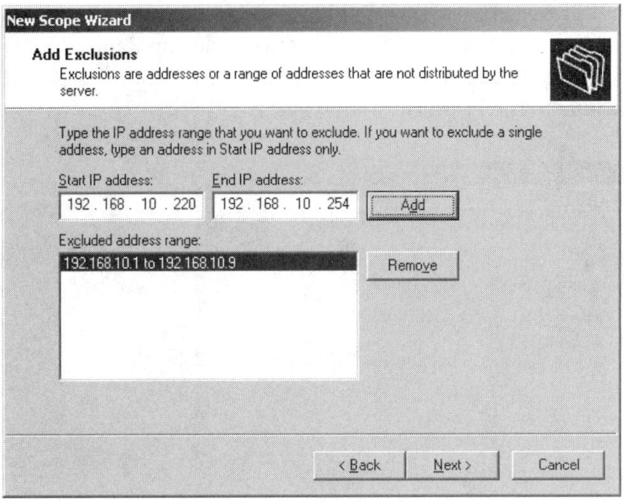

New Scope Wizard

Add Exclusions
Exclusions are addresses or a range of addresses that are not distributed by the server.

Type the IP address range that you want to exclude. If you want to exclude a single address, type an address in Start IP address only.

Start IP address: 192 . 168 . 10 . 220
End IP address: 192 . 168 . 10 . 254
Add

Excluded address range:
192.168.10.1 to 192.168.10.9
Remove

< Back | Next > | Cancel

Figure 25-7. Set exclusion ranges.

Click Next to display the Lease Duration page, as shown in Figure 25-8. Specify the duration of leases for the scope. The default lease duration is 8 days, but don't accept the default without first giving some thought to how leases will be used. A lease duration that's too long or too short can reduce the effectiveness of DHCP. If a lease is too long, you could run out of IP addresses because the DHCP server is holding IP addresses for computers that are no longer on the network, such as when there are a lot of mobile users who connect and disconnect their portable computers. If a lease is too short, this could generate a lot of unnecessary broadcast traffic on the network as clients attempt to renew leases.

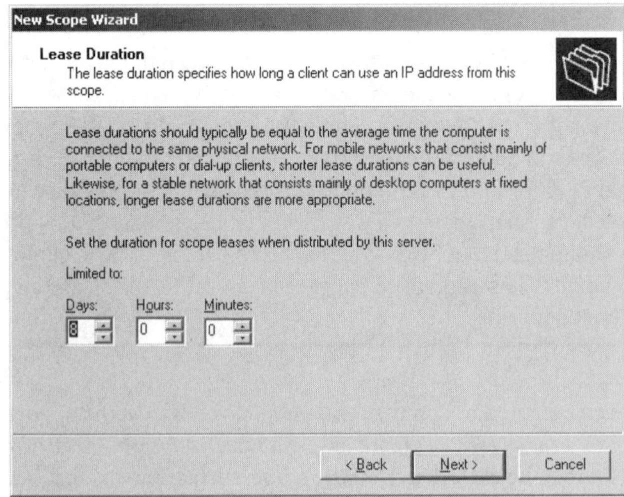

Figure 25-8. Set the lease duration.

By default, clients try to renew lease when 50 percent of the lease time has passed and then again when 87.5 percent of the lease time has passed if the first attempt fails. With this in mind, you generally want to find a balance in the lease time that serves the type of clients on the subnet. If there are only fixed desktops and servers, you could use a longer lease duration of 14 to 21 days. If there are only mobile users with portable computers, you could shorten the lease duration to 2 to 3 days. If there's a mix of fixed systems and mobile systems, a lease duration of 5 to 7 days might be more appropriate.

Click Next to display the Configure DHCP Options page. If you want to set TCP/IP options now, click Yes, and then click Next to continue to the Router (Default Gateway) page, as shown in Figure 25-9. If you don't want to set TCP/IP options now, click No, click Next, and then click Finish to create the scope and exit the wizard.

In the IP Address box enter the IP address of the primary default gateway, and then click Add. You can repeat this process to specify other default gateways. Keep in mind clients try to use gateways in the order they are listed, and you can use the Up and Down buttons to change the order of the gateways, as necessary.

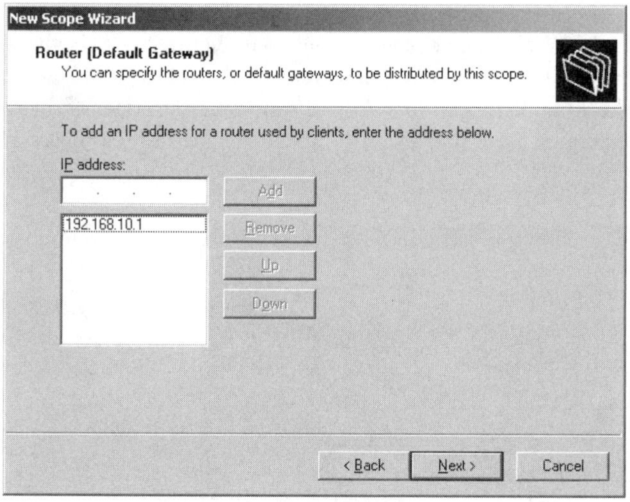

Figure 25-9. Set the default gateways.

Click Next to display the Domain Name And DNS Servers page, as shown in Figure 25-10. In the Parent Domain box, type the name of the parent domain to use for DNS resolution of computer names that aren't fully qualified. In the IP Address box, type the IP address of the primary DNS server, and then click Add. You can repeat this process to specify additional DNS servers. As with gateways, the order of the entries determines which DNS server is used first, and you can change the order as necessary using the Up and Down buttons.

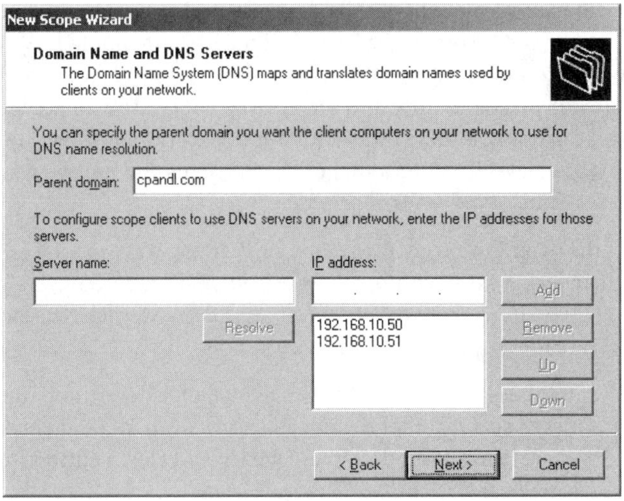

New Scope Wizard

Domain Name and DNS Servers

The Domain Name System (DNS) maps and translates domain names used by clients on your network.

You can specify the parent domain you want the client computers on your network to use for DNS name resolution.

Parent domain: cpandl.com

To configure scope clients to use DNS servers on your network, enter the IP addresses for those servers.

Server name:

IP address:

Add

Resolve

192.168.10.50
192.168.10.51

Remove

Up

Down

< Back

Next >

Cancel

Figure 25-10. Set the DNS servers to use.

Click Next to display the WINS Servers page, as shown in Figure 25-11. In the IP Address box, type the IP address of the primary WINS server, and then click Add. You can repeat this process to specify additional WINS servers. As with gateways, the order of the entries determines which WINS server is used first, and you can change the order as necessary using the Up and Down buttons.

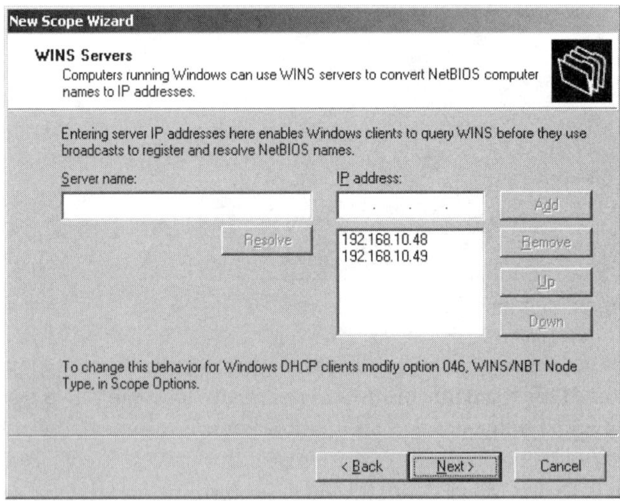

Figure 25-11. Set the WINS servers to use.

Click Next to display the Activate Scope page. If you want to activate the scope, click Yes, I Will Activate This Scope Now. Otherwise, click No, I Will Activate This Scope Later. Click Next, and then click Finish to create the scope and exit the wizard.

Creating Normal Scopes Using Netsh

Using Netsh, you can create a scope by typing the following command:

```
netsh dhcp server ServerID add scope NetworkID SubnetMask ScopeName
```

where the following is true:

- *ServerID* is the UNC name or IP address of the DHCP server on which you want to create the scope, such as \\CORPSVR03 or \\192.168.1.1.
- *NetworkID* is the network ID of the scope, such as 192.168.1.0.
- *SubnetMask* is the subnet mask of the scope, such as 255.255.255.0.
- *ScopeName* is the name of the scope, such as Primary.

After you create the scope, you must use separate commands to set the scope's IP address, exclusions, reservations, and options. You can add an IP range to the scope using the ADD IPRANGE command for the NETSH DHCP SERVER SCOPE context. Type the following:

```
netsh dhcp server ServerID scope NetworkID add iprange StartIP EndIP
```

where

- *ServerID* is the UNC name or IP address of the DHCP server on which you want to create the scope, such as \\CORPSVR03 or \\192.168.1.1.
- *NetworkID* is the network ID of the scope, such as 192.168.1.0.
- *StartIP* is the first IP address in the range, such as 192.168.1.1.
- *EndIP* is the last IP address in the range, such as 192.168.1.254.

Other commands available when you are working with the NETSH DHCP SERVER SCOPE context include the following:

- ADD EXCLUDERANGE *StartIP EndIP*—adds a range of excluded IP addresses to the scope.
- DELETE IPRANGE *StartIP EndIP*—deletes an IP address range from the scope.
- DELETE EXCLUDERANGE *StartIP EndIP*—deletes an exclusion range from the scope.
- SHOW IPRANGE—shows currently configured IP address ranges for the scope.
- SHOW EXCLUDERANGE—shows currently configured exclusion ranges for the scope.
- SHOW CLIENTS—lists clients using the scope.
- SHOW STATE—shows the state of the scope as active or inactive.

Using Exclusions

To exclude IP addresses from a scope, you can define an exclusion range. In the DHCP console, any existing exclusions for a scope can be displayed by expanding the scope and selecting Address Pool, as shown in Figure 25-12. To list exclusions at the command line, type the following:

```
netsh dhcp server ServerID scope NetworkID show excluderange
```

where *ServerID* is the UNC name or IP address of the DHCP server on which you want to create the scope, such as \\CORPSVR03 or \\192.168.1.1, and *NetworkID* is the network ID of the scope, such as 192.168.1.0.

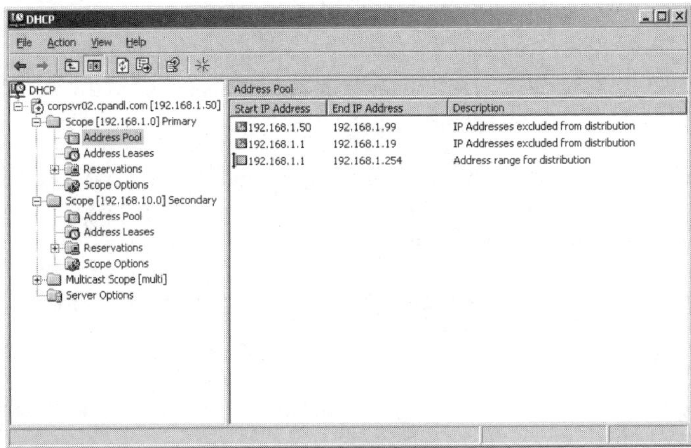

Figure 25-12. Exclusions are listed under the Address Pool node.

In the DHCP console, you can define an exclusion range by right-clicking Address Pool within the scope you want to work with and choosing New Exclusion Range. In the Add Exclusion dialog box, enter a start address and an end address for the exclusion range, as shown in Figure 25-13, and then click Add. Keep in mind the range excluded must be a subset of the scope's range and must not currently be in use by DHCP clients.

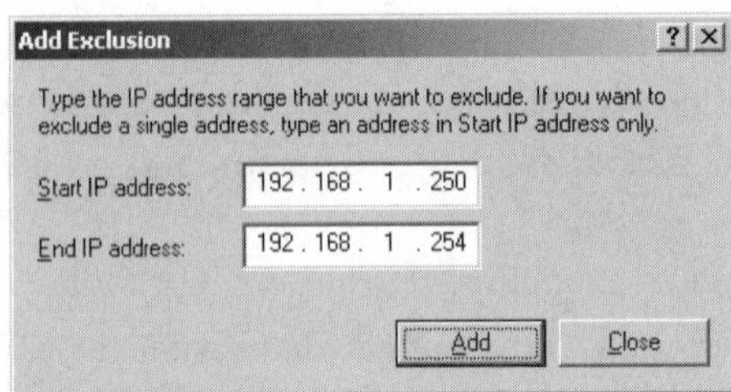

Figure 25-13. Set the exclusion range.

Using Netsh, you can add an exclusion range in much the same way. Type the following:

```
netsh dhcp server ServerID scope NetworkID add excluderange StartIP EndIP
```

where the following is true:

- *ServerID* is the UNC name or IP address of the DHCP server on which you want to create the scope, such as \\CORPSVR03 or \\192.168.1.1.
- *NetworkID* is the network ID of the scope, such as 192.168.1.0.
- *StartIP* is the first IP address in the exclusion range, such as 192.168.1.200.
- *EndIP* is the last IP address in the exclusion range, such as 192.168.1.219.

Using Reservations

Reservations provide a way to assign a permanent lease on an IP address to a client. In this way, the client has a fixed IP address, but you retain flexibility in that you could change the IP address at any time if necessary through DHCP rather than having to do so on the client. In the DHCP console, any existing reservations for a scope can be displayed by expanding the scope and selecting Reservations. As shown in Figure 25-14, existing reservations are shown according to the reservation name and IP address reserved. You can right-click a reservation and select Properties to see the associated MAC address. To list reservations by IP address and MAC address at the command line, type the following:

```
netsh dhcp server ServerID scope NetworkID show reservedip
```

where *ServerID* is the UNC name or IP address of the DHCP server on which you want to create the scope, such as \\CORPSVR03 or \\192.168.1.1, and *NetworkID* is the network ID of the scope, such as 192.168.1.0.

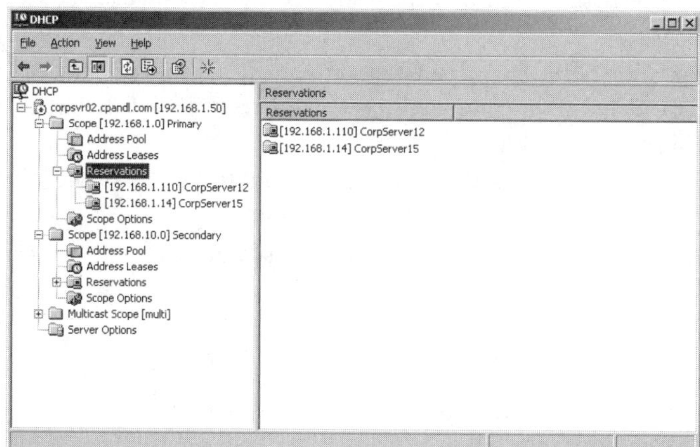

Figure 25-14. Current reservations are listed by reservation name and IP address.

To create a reservation, you need to know the MAC address of the computer that will hold the IP address. The MAC address is specific to an individual network interface configured on the client and can be viewed by typing **ipconfig /all** at the command prompt. The output will list the MAC address as the Physical Address of the network interface, as it does under Physical Address in the following example:

```
Windows IP Configuration

      Host Name. . . . . . . . . . . . . : corpsvr06
      Primary Dns Suffix . . . . . . . . :  cpandl.com
      Node Type. . . . . . . . . . . . . :  Hybrid
      IP Routing Enabled . . . . . . . . :  No
      WINS Proxy Enabled . . . . . . . . :  No
      DNS Suffix Search List . . . . . . :  cpandl.com

Ethernet adapter Local Area Connection:

      Connection-specific DNS Suffix . . :
      Description. . . . . . . . . . . . :  Intel(R) PRO/100
      Physical Address . . . . . . . . . :  23-24-AE-67-B4-E8
      Dhcp Enabled . . . . . . . . . . . :  Yes
      Autoconfiguration Enabled. . . . . :  Yes
      IP Address . . . . . . . . . . . . :  192.168.1.20
      Subnet Mask. . . . . . . . . . . . :  255.255.255.0
      Default Gateway. . . . . . . . . . :  192.168.1.1
      DHCP Server. . . . . . . . . . . . :  192.168.1.50
      Lease Obtained . . . . . . . . . . :  Thursday, August 12, 2004 12:03:40 PM
      Lease Expires. . . . . . . . . . . :  Friday, August 20, 2004 12:03:40 PM
```

In the DHCP console, you can reserve a DHCP address for a client as follows:

1. After you expand the scope you want to work with, right-click the Reservations folder, and choose New Reservation. This opens the New Reservation dialog box, as shown in Figure 25-15.
2. In the Reservation Name box, type a descriptive name for the reservation. This doesn't have to be the name of the computer to which the reservation belongs, but that does help simplify administration.
3. In the IP Address box, enter the IP address you want to reserve for the client. This IP address must be valid for the currently selected scope.
4. In the MAC Address box, type the MAC address as previously obtained using the IPCONFIG /ALL command.
5. If desired, enter an optional comment in the Description box.
6. By default, the reservation is configured to accept both DHCP and BOOTP clients. Only change the default if you want to exclude a particular type of client. DHCP clients include computers running the standard version of the DHCP client as with most Windows operating systems. BOOTP clients are clients running other operat-

ing systems and could also include devices such as printers that can use dynamic IP addressing.

7 Click Add to create the address reservation.

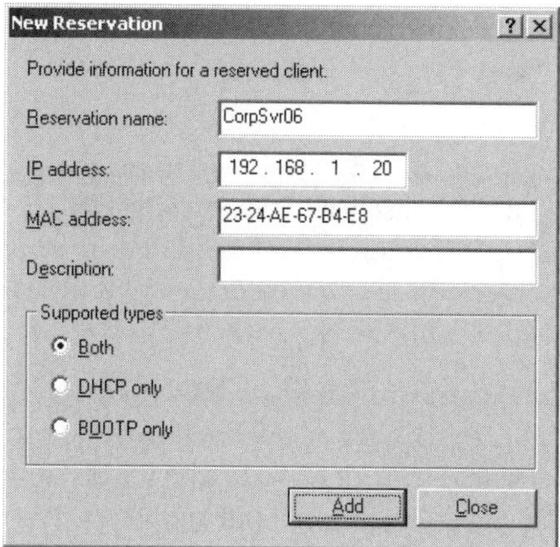

Figure 25-15. Create a reservation for an IP address using the MAC address of the client.

In Netsh, you can create a reservation by typing the following command:

```
netsh dhcp server ServerID scope NetworkID add reservedip ReservedIP MacAddress
Name Comment
```

where the following is true:

- *ServerID* is the UNC name or IP address of the DHCP server on which you want to create the scope, such as \\CORPSVR03 or \\192.168.1.1.
- *NetworkID* is the network ID of the scope, such as 192.168.1.0.
- *ReservedIP* is the IP address you are reserving, such as 192.168.1.20.
- *MacAddress* is the MAC address of the client (excluding the dashes), such as 2324AE67B4E8.
- *Name* is the descriptive name of the reservation.
- *Comment* is the optional comment describing the reservation.

When you assign reservations, keep in mind that a client with an existing lease won't automatically use the reservation. If a client has a current lease, you must force the client to release that lease and then request a new one. If a client has an existing address and you want to force it to start using DHCP, you must force the client to stop using its current IP address and request a new IP address from DHCP.

To force a client to release an existing lease or drop its current IP address, log on to the client, and type **ipconfig /release** at the command prompt. Next, if the client isn't already configured to use DHCP, you must configure the client to use DHCP as discussed in the section entitled "Configuring Dynamic IP Addressing" on page 797.

To get a client to request a new IP address from DHCP, log on to the client, and type **ipconfig /renew** at the command prompt.

Activating Scopes

Scopes are available only when they are activated. If you want to make a scope available to clients, you must right-click it in the DHCP console and then select Activate. Activating a scope won't make clients switch to that scope. If you want to force clients to switch to a different scope or to use a different DHCP server, you can terminate the client leases in the DHCP console and then deactivate the scope the clients are currently using.

To terminate a lease, you expand the scope you want to work with in the DHCP console and then select Address Leases. You will then see a list of current leases and can terminate a lease by right-clicking it and selecting Delete. The next time the client goes to renew its lease, the DHCP server will tell the client the lease is no longer valid and that a new one must be obtained.

To prevent clients from reusing the original scope, you can deactivate that scope by right-clicking it in the DHCP console and then selecting Deactivate.

You can perform these same actions using Netsh. To terminate a lease, type the following command:

```
netsh dhcp server ServerID scope NetworkID delete lease IPAddress
```

where the following is true:

- *ServerID* is the UNC name or IP address of the DHCP server on which you want to create the scope, such as \\CORPSVR03 or \\192.168.1.1.
- *NetworkID* is the network ID of the scope, such as 192.168.1.0.
- *IPAddress* is the IP address for the lease you want to remove, such as 192.168.1.8.

To activate or deactivate a scope, type the following:

```
netsh dhcp server ServerID scope NetworkID state StateVal
```

where the following is true:

- *ServerID* is the UNC name or IP address of the DHCP server on which you want to create the scope, such as \\CORPSVR03 or \\192.168.1.1.
- *NetworkID* is the network ID of the scope, such as 192.168.1.0.
- *StateVal* is set to 0 to deactivate the scope and 1 to activate it. If you are using a switched network where multiple logical networks are hosted on a single physical network, use 2 to deactivate the scope and 3 to activate the scope.

Configuring TCP/IP Options

The messages clients and servers broadcast to each other allow you to set TCP/IP options that clients can obtain by default when they obtain a lease or can request if they need additional information. It is important to note, however, that the types of information you can add to DHCP messages is limited in several ways:

- DHCP messages are transmitted using User Datagram Protocol (UDP), and the entire DHCP message must fit into the UDP datagram. On Ethernet with 1500-byte datagrams, this leaves 1236 bytes for the body of the message (which contains the TCP/IP options).
- BOOTP messages have a fixed size of 300 bytes as set by the original BOOTP standard. Any clients using BOOTP are likely to have their TCP/IP options truncated.
- Although there are many options that you can set, clients understand only certain TCP/IP options. Thus, the set of options available to you is dependent upon the client's implementation of DHCP.

With that in mind, let's look at the levels at which options can be assigned and the options that Windows clients understand.

Levels of Options and Their Uses

Each individual TCP/IP option such as a default gateway is configured separately. DHCP administrators can manage options at five levels within the DHCP server configuration:

- **Predefined options** Allow DHCP administrators to specify the way in which options are used and to create new option types for use on a server. In the DHCP console, you can view and set predefined options by right-clicking the server node in the console tree and selecting Set Predefined Options.
- **Server options** Allow DHCP administrators to configure options that are assigned to all scopes created on the DHCP server. Think of server options as global options that would be assigned to all clients. Server options can be overridden by scope, class, and client-assigned options. In the DHCP console, you can view and set server options by expanding the entry for the server you want to work with, right-clicking Server Options, and then choosing Configure Options.
- **Scope options** Allow DHCP administrators to configure options that are assigned to all clients that use a particular scope. Scope options are assigned only to normal scopes and can be overridden by class and client-assigned options. In the DHCP console, you can view and set scope options by expanding the scope you want to work with, right-clicking Scope Options, and then choosing Configure Options.

- **Class options** Allow DHCP administrators to configure options that are assigned to all clients of a particular class. Client classes can be user- or vendor-defined. Two classes included with DHCP Server are Windows 98, which is used to assign specific options to clients running Windows 98, and Windows 2000, which is used to assign specific options to clients running Windows 2000 or later. Class options can be overridden by client-assigned options. You define new user and vendor classes by right-clicking the server entry and selecting either Define User Classes or Define Vendor Classes as appropriate. Once defined, class options can be configured in the Advanced tab of the Server Options, Scope Options, and Reservation Options dialog boxes.
- **Reservation options** Allow administrators to set options for an individual client that uses a reservation. Also referred to as client-specific options. After you create a reservation for a client, you can configure reservation options by expanding the scope, expanding Reservations, right-clicking the reservation, and selecting Configure Options. Only TCP/IP options manually configured on a client can override client-assigned options.

Options Used by Windows Clients

RFC 3442 defines many TCP/IP options that you can set in DHCP messages. Although you can set all of these options on a DHCP server, the set of options available is dependent upon the client's implementation of DHCP.

Table 25-1 shows the options that can be configured by administrators and used by Windows computers running the DHCP Client service. Each option has an associated option code, which is used to identify it in a DHCP message, and a data entry, which contains the value setting of the option. These options are requested by clients to set their TCP/IP configuration.

Table 25-1. Standard TCP/IP Options That Administrators Can Configure

Option Name	Option Code	Description
Router	003	Sets a list of IP addresses for the default gateways that should be used by the client. IP addresses are listed in order of preference.
DNS Servers	006	Sets a list of IP addresses for the DNS servers that should be used by the client. IP addresses are listed in order of preference.
DNS Domain Name	015	Sets the DNS domain name that clients should use when resolving host names using DNS.
WINS/NBNS Servers	044	Sets a list of IP addresses for the WINS servers that should be used by the client. IP addresses are listed in order of preference.

Table 25-1. Standard TCP/IP Options That Administrators Can Configure

Option Name	Option Code	Description
WINS/NBT Node Type	046	Sets the method to use when resolving NetBIOS names. The acceptable values are: 0x1 for B-node (broadcast), 0x2 for P-node (peer-to-peer), 0x4 for M-node (mixed), and 0x8 for H-node (hybrid). See the section entitled "NetBIOS Node Types"on page 928.
NetBIOS Scope ID	047	Sets the NetBIOS scope for the client.

Using User- and Vendor-Specific TCP/IP Options

DHCP uses classes to determine which options are sent to clients. The user classes let you assign TCP/IP options according to the type of user the client represents on the network. The default user classes include the following:

- **Default User Class** An all-inclusive class that includes clients that don't fit into the other user classes, such as computers running Windows NT 4. Any computer running a version of the Windows operating system earlier than Windows 2000 is in this class.
- **Default BOOTP Class** Any computer running Windows 2000 or later has this user class if it is connected to the local network directly. This means Windows 2000, Microsoft Windows XP, and Windows Server 2003 computers connected with a wired network interface have this class.
- **Default Routing And Remote Access Class** Any computer that connects to the network using RRAS has this class. Any settings applied to this class are used by dial-in and VPN users, which allows you to set different TCP/IP options for these users.

Clients can be a member of multiple user classes, and you can view the user class memberships for each network interface by typing **ipconfig /showclassid** * at the command prompt. (The asterisk tells the command that you want to see all the network interfaces.) The output you'll see on a computer running Windows 2000 or later will be similar to the following:

```
Windows IP Configuration
DHCP Classes for Adapter "Local Area Connection":

     DHCP ClassID Name. . . . . . . . : Default Routing and Remote Access Class
     DHCP ClassID Description . . . . : User class for remote access clients

     DHCP ClassID Name. . . . . . . . : Default BOOTP Class
     DHCP ClassID Description . . . . : User class for BOOTP Clients
```

Here, the client is a member of the Default Routing And Remote Access Class and the Default BOOTP Class. The client doesn't, however, get its options from both classes. Rather the class from which the client gets its options depends on its connection state. If the client is connected directly to the network, it uses the Default BOOTP Class. If the client is connected by Routing and Remote Access, it uses the Default Routing And Remote Access Class.

Vendor classes work a bit differently because they define the set of options available to and used by the various user classes. The default vendor class, DHCP Standard Options, is used to set the standard TCP/IP options, and the various user classes all have access to these options so that they can be implemented in a user-specific way. Additional vendor classes beyond the default define extensions or additional options that can be implemented in a user-specific way. This means that the vendor class defines the options and makes them available, while the user class settings determine which of these additional options (if any) are used by clients.

The default vendor classes that provide additional (add-on) options are as follows:

- **Microsoft Options** Add-on options available to any client running any version of Windows
- **Microsoft Windows 98 Options** Add-on options available to any client running Windows 98 or later
- **Microsoft Windows 2000 Options** Add-on options available to any client running Windows 2000 or later

When it comes to these classes, a client applies the options from the most specific add-on vendor class. Thus, a Windows 98 client would apply the Microsoft Windows 98 Options vendor class, and a Windows 2000 or later client would apply the Microsoft Windows 2000 Options vendor class. Again, these options are in addition to the standard options provided through the DHCP Standard Options vendor class and can be implemented in a manner specific to a user class. This means you can have one set of add-on options for directly connected clients (Default BOOTP Class) and one set for remotely connected clients (Default Routing And Remote Access Class).

The add-on options that can be set for a client running Windows 2000 or later are listed in Table 25-2.

Table 25-2. Additional TCP/IP Options That Administrators Can Configure

Option Name	Option Code	Description
Microsoft Disable NetBIOS Option	001	Disables NetBIOS if selected as an option with a value of 0x1.
Microsoft Release DHCP Lease On Shutdown Option	002	Specifies that a client should release its DHCP lease on shutdown if selected as an option with a value of 0x1.
Microsoft Default Router Metric Base	003	Specifies that the default router metric base should be used if selected as an option with a value of 0x1.

Settings Options for All Clients

On the DHCP server, you can set TCP/IP options at several levels. You can set options for the following components:

- **All scopes on a server** In the DHCP console, expand the entry for the server you want to work with, right-click Server Options, and then choose Configure Options.
- **A specific scope** In the DHCP console, expand the scope you want to work with, right-click Scope Options, and then choose Configure Options.
- **A single reserved IP address** In the DHCP console, expand the scope, expand Reservations, right-click the reservation you want to work with, and select Configure Options.

Regardless of the level at which you are setting TCP/IP options, the dialog box displayed has the exact same set of choices as that shown in Figure 25-16. You can now select each standard TCP/IP options you want to use in turn, such as Router, DNS Servers, DNS Domain Name, WINS/NBNS Servers, and WINS/NBT Node Type, and configure the appropriate values. Click OK when you are finished.

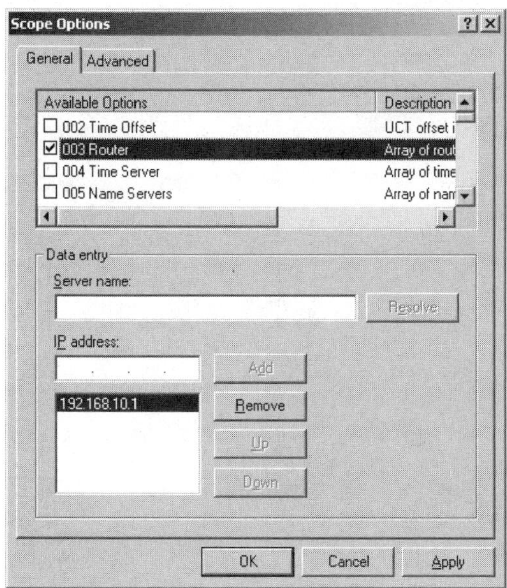

Figure 25-16. Set class-specific options using the General tab.

Settings Options for Routing and Remote Access Clients Only

On the DHCP server, you can set TCP/IP options for RRAS clients at several levels. You can set options for the following components:

- **All scopes on a server** In the DHCP console, expand the entry for the server you want to work with, right-click Server Options, and then choose Configure Options.
- **A specific scope** In the DHCP console, expand the scope you want to work with, right-click Scope Options, and then choose Configure Options.
- **A single reserved IP address** In the DHCP console, expand the scope, expand Reservations, right-click the reservation you want to work with, and select Configure Options.

Regardless of the level at which you are setting TCP/IP options, the dialog box displayed has the exact same set of choices. You can now complete the following steps:

1. Click the Advanced tab, as shown in Figure 25-17. Select DHCP Standard Options as the vendor class and Default Routing And Remote Access Class as the user class.

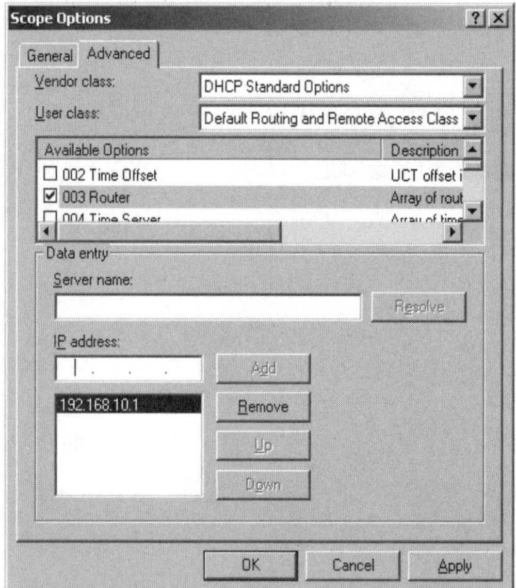

Figure 25-17. Set the DHCP Standard Options.

2. Select each standard TCP/IP option you want to use in turn, such as Router, DNS Servers, DNS Domain Name, WINS/NBNS Servers, and WINS/NBT Node Type, and configure the appropriate values.
3. For clients running Windows 2000 or later, select Microsoft Windows 2000 Options as the vendor class and Default Routing And Remote Access Class as the user class, as shown in Figure 25-18.

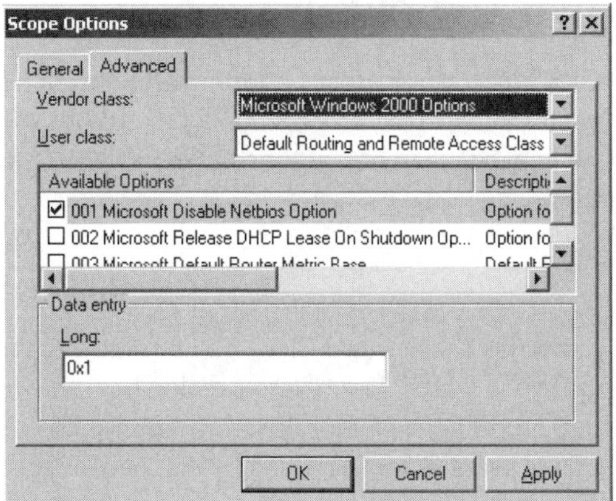

Figure 25-18. Set the add-on options for remote access clients.

4. Select each add-on TCP/IP option you want to use in turn, such as Microsoft Disable NetBIOS Option and Microsoft Release DHCP Lease On Shutdown Option, and accept the default value (0x1) to turn on the option.
5. Click OK.

Setting Add-On Options for Directly Connected Clients

You can set add-on options for directly connected clients that are different from those of remote access clients. Access the TCP/IP options dialog box at the appropriate level, and then click the Advanced tab. For Windows 2000 or later clients, select Microsoft Windows 2000 Options as the vendor class and Default BOOTP Class as the user class, as shown in Figure 25-19. Now select each add-on TCP/IP option you want to use in turn, such as Microsoft Disable NetBIOS Option and Microsoft Release DHCP Lease On Shutdown Option, and accept the default value (0x1) to turn on the option. Then click OK when you are finished.

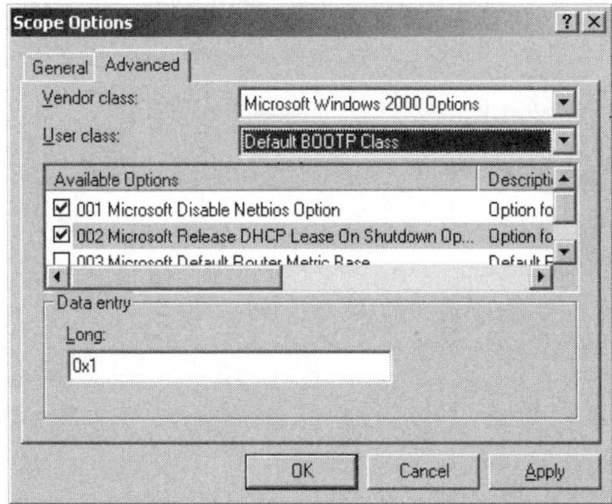

Figure 25-19. Set the add-on options for directly connected clients.

Defining Classes to Get Different Option Sets

If you want a group of DHCP clients to use a set of options different than other computers, you can use classes to do this. It is a two-part process. First, create your own user-defined class on each DHCP server to which the clients might connect. Then configure the network interfaces on the clients to use the new class.

Creating the Class

In the DHCP console, you can define the new user class by right-clicking the server entry and selecting Define User Classes. In the DHCP User Classes dialog box, shown in Figure 25-20, the existing classes are listed, including the Default Routing And Remote Access Class and then Default BOOTP Class. The Default User Class isn't listed, however, because it is the base user class.

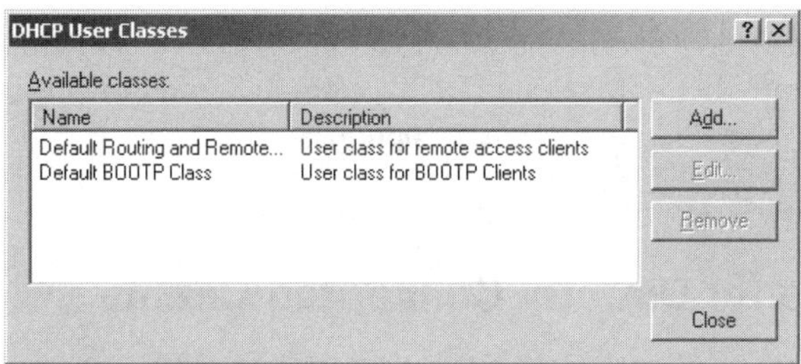

Figure 25-20. User classes in addition to the base class.

Click Add to display the New Class dialog box shown in Figure 25-21. In the Display Name box, type the name of the class you are defining. The name is arbitrary and should be short but descriptive enough so that you know what that class is used for by seeing its name. You can also type a description in the Description box. Afterward, click in the empty area below the word ASCII. In this space, type the class identifier, which is used by DHCP to identify the class. The class identifier cannot have spaces. Click OK to close the New Class dialog box, and then click Close to return to the DHCP console.

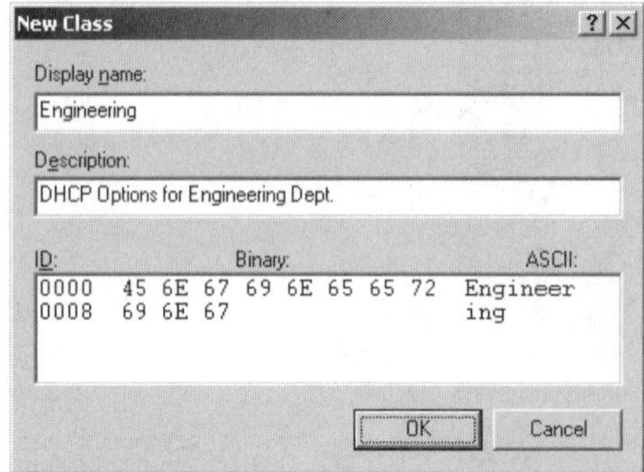

Figure 25-21. Set the class name, description, and class ID.

Next, you must configure the TCP/IP options that should be used by this class. In the DHCP console, expand the entry for the server you want to work with, right-click Server Options, and then choose Configure Options. In the Server Options dialog box, click the Advanced tab. As shown in Figure 25-22, select DHCP Standard Options as the vendor class and the class you created as the user class.

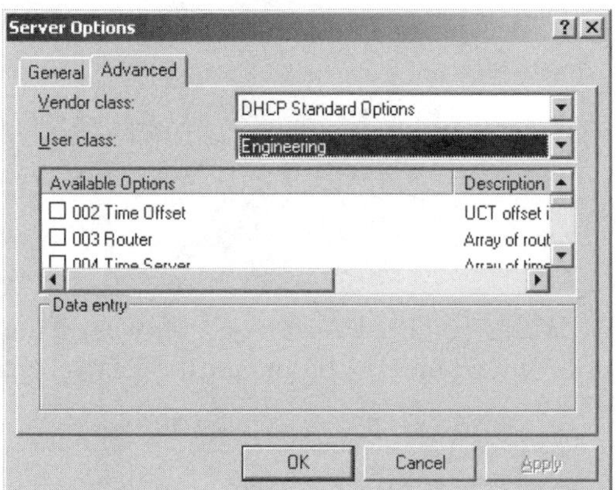

Figure 25-22. Set the TCP/IP options for the new class.

Select each standard TCP/IP option you want to use in turn, such as Router, DNS Servers, DNS Domain Name, WINS/NBNS Servers, and WINS/NBT Node Type, and configure the appropriate values. If you want to set Windows options, select Microsoft Windows 2000 Options as the vendor class. Don't change the user class. Then select each add-on TCP/IP option you want to use in turn, such as Microsoft Disable NetBIOS Option and Microsoft Release DHCP Lease On Shutdown Option, and accept the default value (0x1) to turn on the option. Click OK to complete the configuration of the new class.

Configuring Clients to Use the Class

Now you must configure the network interfaces on the clients to use the new class. Assuming "Local Area Connection" is the name of the network interface on the client, you would type the following command to do this:

```
ipconfig /setclassid "Local Area Connection" ClassID
```

where *ClassID* is the ID of the user class to use. For example, if the class ID is Engineering, you would type

```
ipconfig /setclassid "Local Area Connection" Engineering
```

In these examples, I use "Local Area Connection" as the network interface name because that is the default connection created by Windows. If a client has multiple network interfaces or a user has changed the name of the default network interface, you must use the name of the appropriate interface. You can get a list of all network interfaces on a client by typing **ipconfig /all** at the command prompt.

After you set the class ID, type **ipconfig /renew** at the command prompt. This tells the client to renew the lease and because the client has a new class ID it also forces the client to request new TCP/IP options. The output should be similar to the following:

```
Windows IP Configuration
Ethernet adapter Local Area Connection:

      Connection-specific DNS Suffix . . :
      IP Address . . . . . . . . . . . . : 192.168.1.22
      Subnet Mask. . . . . . . . . . . . : 255.255.255.0
      Default Gateway. . . . . . . . . . : 192.168.1.1
      DHCP Class ID. . . . . . . . . . . : Engineering
```

That's it. Because the class ID is persistent, you need to set it only once. So, if the client is restarted, the class ID will remain. To remove the class ID and use the defaults again, type the following command:

```
ipconfig /setclassid "Local Area Connection"
```

Troubleshooting

Class ID problems

Sometimes the network interface won't report that it has the new class ID. If this happens, try releasing the DHCP lease first by typing **ipconfig /release** and then obtain a new lease by typing **ipconfig /renew**.

Advanced DHCP Configuration and Maintenance

When you install the DHCP Server service, many advanced features are configured for you automatically, including audit logging, network bindings, integration with DNS, and DHCP database backups. All of these features can be fine-tuned to optimize performance, and many of these features, such as auditing, logging, and backups, should be periodically monitored.

Configuring DHCP Audit Logging

Auditing logging is enabled by default for the DHCP Server service and is used to track DHCP processes and requests in log files. The DHCP logs are stored in the %SystemRoot%\System32\DHCP folder by default. In this folder you'll find a different log file for each day of the week. For example, the log file for Monday is named DhcpSrvLog-Mon.log. When you start the DHCP Server service or a new day arrives, a header message is written to the log file. As shown in

Listing 25-1, the header provides a summary of DHCP events and their meanings. The header is followed by the actual events logged by the DHCP Server service. The event IDs and descriptions are entered because different versions of the DHCP Server service can have different events.

Listing 25-1 DHCP Server Log File

```
Microsoft DHCP Service Activity Log
Event ID  Meaning
00        The log was started.
01        The log was stopped.
02        The log was temporarily paused due to low disk space.
10        A new IP address was leased to a client.
11        A lease was renewed by a client.
12        A lease was released by a client.
13        An IP address was found to be in use on the network.
14        A lease request could not be satisfied because the scope's
          address pool was exhausted.
15        A lease was denied.
16        A lease was deleted.
17        A lease was expired.
24        IP address cleanup operation has began.
25        IP address cleanup statistics.
30        DNS update request to the named DNS server
31        DNS update failed
32        DNS update successful
50+       Codes above 50 are used for Rogue Server Detection information.

ID,Date,Time,Description,IP Address,Host Name,MAC Address
00,03/04/04,11:30:26,Started,,,,
55,03/04/04,11:30:27,Authorized(servicing),,cpandl.com,,
10,03/04/04,11:56:03,Assign,192.168.1.1,corpserver03.cpandl.com,2324AE67B4E8,
12,03/04/04,11:56:32,Release,192.168.1.1,corpserver03.cpandl.com,2324AE67B4E8,
10,03/04/04,12:01:45,Assign,192.168.1.20,corpserver03.cpandl.com,2324AE67B4E8,
15,03/04/04,12:03:41,NACK,192.168.0.100,,2324AE67B4E8,
11,03/04/04,12:03:42,Renew,192.168.1.20,becka.,2324AE67B4E8,
24,03/04/04,12:30:30,Database Cleanup Begin,,,,
25,03/04/04,12:30:30,0 leases expired and 0 leases deleted,,,,
25,03/04/04,12:30:30,0 leases expired and 0 leases deleted,,,,
24,03/04/04,13:30:35,Database Cleanup Begin,,,,
25,03/04/04,13:30:35,0 leases expired and 0 leases deleted,,,,
25,03/04/04,13:30:35,0 leases expired and 0 leases deleted,,,,
01,03/04/04,14:10:23,Stopped,,,,
00,03/04/04,14:10:37,Started,,,,
55,03/04/04,14:10:37,Authorized(servicing),,cpandl.com,,
01,03/04/04,20:15:50,Stopped,,,,
```

The events in the audit logs can help you troubleshoot problems with a DHCP server. As you examine Listing 25-1, the first event entry with ID 00 tells you the DHCP Server service was started. The second event entry with ID 55 tells you the DHCP Server is authorized to service the cpandl.com domain. Every hour that the service is running, it also performs cleanup operations. Database cleanup is used to check for expired leases and leases that no longer apply.

The audit logs also serve as a record of all DHCP connection requests by clients on the network. Events related to lease assignment, renewal, and release are recorded according to the IP address assigned, the client's FQDN, and the client's MAC address.

Declined leases are listed with the event ID 13 and the description of the event is DECLINE. A DHCP client can decline a lease if it detects that the IP address is already in use. The primary reason this happens is that a system somewhere on the network is using a static IP address in the DHCP range or has leased it from another DHCP server during a network glitch. When the server receives the decline, it marks the address as bad in the DHCP database. See the section "Enabling Conflict Detection on DHCP Servers" later in this chapter for details on how IP address conflicts can be avoided.

Denied leases are listed with the event ID 15 and the description of the event is NACK. DHCP can deny a lease to a client that is requesting an address that cannot be provided. This could happen if an administrator terminated the lease or if the client moved to a different subnet where the original IP address held is no longer valid. When a client receives a NACK, the client releases the denied IP address and requests a new one.

As discussed previously, audit logging is enabled by default. If you want to check or change the logging setting, you can do this in the DHCP console. Right-click the server you want to work with, and then select Properties. This displays the dialog box shown in Figure 25-23.

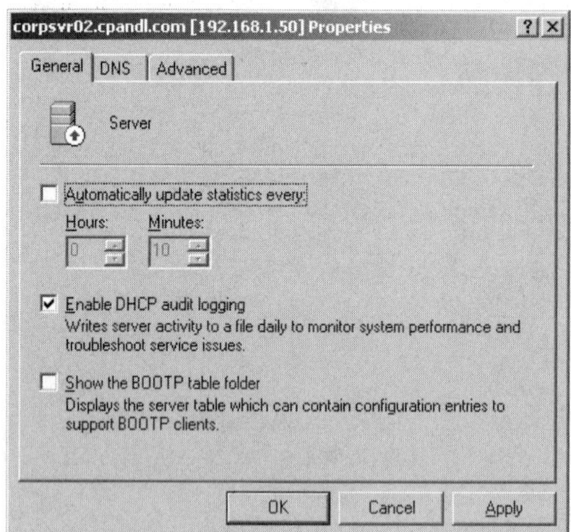

Figure 25-23. Audit logging is enabled by default.

In the General tab, select or clear Enable DHCP Audit Logging as necessary. Afterward, select the Advanced tab. The Audit Log File Path box shows the current folder location for log files. Enter a new folder location or click Browse to find a new location. Click OK. If you change the audit log location, Windows Server 2003 will need to restart the DHCP Server service. When prompted to confirm that this is OK, click Yes.

Binding the DHCP Server Service to a Network Interface

The DHCP Server service should bind automatically to the first NIC on the server. This means that the DHCP Server service should use the IP address and TCP/IP configuration of this network interface to communicate with clients. In some instances, the DHCP Server service might not bind to any available network interface or it might bind to a network interface that you don't want it to use. To resolve this problem, you must bind the DHCP Server service to a specific network interface by following these steps:

1. In the DHCP console, right-click the server you want to work with, and then select Properties.
2. In the Advanced tab of the Properties dialog box, click Bindings to display the Bindings dialog box. This dialog box displays a list of available network connections for the DHCP server.
3. If you want the DHCP Server service to use a connection to service clients, select the option for the connection. If you don't want the service to use a connection, clear the related option.
4. Click OK.

Integrating DHCP and DNS

Using the DNS Dynamic Update protocol, DHCP clients running Windows 2000 or later can automatically update their forward (A) and reverse lookup (PTR) records in DNS or request that the DHCP server does this for them. Clients running versions of the Windows operating system earlier than Windows 2000 can't dynamically update any of their records, so DHCP must do this for them. In either case, when the DHCP server is required to update DNS records, this requires integration between DHCP and DNS.

In the default configuration of DHCP, a DHCP server will update DNS records for clients only if requested but will not update records for clients running versions of the Windows operating system earlier than Windows 2000. To change this behavior, start the DHCP console, right-click the server you want to work with, and then select Properties. Select the DNS tab, as shown in Figure 25-24, then choose Dynamically Update DNS A And PTR Records For DHCP Clients That Do Not Request Updates. Don't change the other settings. These settings are configured by default, and you don't need to modify the configuration in most cases.

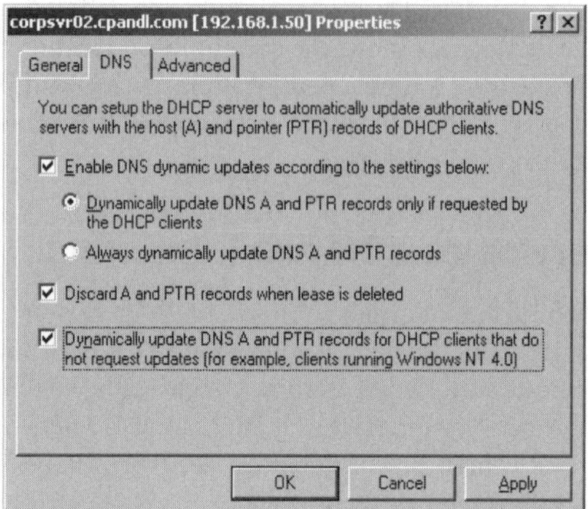

Figure 25-24. DHCP and DNS integration.

Enabling Conflict Detection on DHCP Servers

No two computers on the network can have the same unicast IP address. If a computer is assigned the same unicast IP address as another, one or both of the computers might become disconnected from the network. To prevent this from happening, DHCP has built-in conflict detection that enables clients to check the IP address they've been assigned by pinging the address on the network. If a client detects that an IP address it has been assigned is in use, it sends the DHCP server a Decline message telling the server that it is declining the lease because the IP address is in use. When this happens, the server marks the IP address as bad in the DHCP database, and then client requests a new lease. This process works fairly well but requires additional time because the client is responsible for checking the IP address, declining a lease, and requesting a new one.

To speed up the process, you can configure DHCP servers to check for conflicts before assigning an IP address to a client. When conflict detection is enabled, the process works in much the same way as before, except the server checks the IP address to see if it is in use and, if so, marks it as bad without interaction with the client. You can configure conflict detection on a DHCP server by specifying the number of conflict detection attempts that the DHCP server will make before it leases an IP address to a client. The DHCP server checks IP addresses by sending a ping request over the network.

You can configure conflict detection in the DHCP console by right-clicking the server you want to work with and then selecting Properties. In the Advanced tab, set Conflict Detection Attempts to a value other than zero. At the command line, type the following command:

```
netsh dhcp server ServerID set detectconflictretry Attempts
```

where *ServerID* is the name or IP address of the DHCP server and *Attempts* is the number of conflict detection attempts the server should use. You can confirm the setting by typing the following:

```
netsh dhcp server ServerID show detectconflictretry
```

Saving and Restoring the DHCP Configuration

After you finish configuring a DHCP server, you should save the configuration settings so that you can easily restore the server to a known state or use the same settings on another server. To do this, type the following command at the command prompt:

```
netsh dhcp server dump ServerID > SaveFile
```

where *ServerID* is the name or IP address of the DHCP server and *SaveFile* is the name of the file in which you want to store the configuration settings. Here is an example:

```
netsh dhcp server dump > dhcpconfig.dmp
```

If you examine the file Netsh creates, you'll find that it is a Netsh configuration script. To restore the configuration, run the script by typing the following command:

```
netsh exec SaveFile
```

where *SaveFile* is the name of the file in which you stored the configuration settings. Here is an example:

```
netsh exec dhcpconfig.dmp
```

> **Tip** **Copy to a new DHCP server**
> You can run the script on a different DHCP server to configure it the same as the original DHCP server whose configuration you saved. Copy the configuration script to a folder on the destination computer, and then run it. The DHCP server will be configured like the original server.

Managing and Maintaining the DHCP Database

Information about leases and reservations used by clients is stored in database files on the DHCP Server. Like any other data set, the DHCP database has properties that you can set and techniques you can use to maintain it.

Setting DHCP Database Properties

In the default configuration, these files are stored in the %SystemRoot%\System32\Dhcp folder, and automatically created backups of the files are stored in %SystemRoot%\

System32\Dhcp\Backup. The DHCP Server service performs two routine actions to maintain the database:

- Database cleanup during which the DHCP Server service checks for expired leases and leases that no longer apply
- Database backup during which the DHCP Server service backs up the database files

By default, both maintenance tasks are performed every 60 minutes, and you can confirm this as well as the current DHCP folders being used by typing the following command at the command prompt:

```
netsh dhcp server ServerID show dbproperties
```

where *ServerID* is the name or IP address of the DHCP server, such as

```
netsh dhcp server 192.168.1.50 show dbproperties
```

The output of this command shows you the current database properties for the DHCP server:

```
Server Database Properties :

      DatabaseName                = dhcp.mdb
      DatabasePath                = C:\WINDOWS\System32\dhcp
      DatabaseBackupPath          = C:\WINDOWS\System32\dhcp\backup
      DatabaseBackupInterval      = 60 mins.
      DatabaseLoggingFlag         = 1
      DatabaseRestoreFlag         = 0
      DatabaseCleanupInterval     = 60 mins.
```

Note the DatabaseLoggingFlag and DatabaseRestoreFlag properties. DatabaseLoggingFlag tracks whether audit logging is enabled. If the flag is set to 0, audit logging is disabled. If the flag is set to 1, audit logging is enabled. DatabaseRestoreFlag is a special flag that tracks whether the DHCP Server service should restore the DHCP database from backup the next time it starts. If the flag is set to 0, the main database is used. If the flag is set to 1, the DHCP Server service restores the database from backup, overwriting the existing database.

You can use the following commands to set these properties:

- Netsh dhcp server *ServerID* set databasename *NewFileName*—Sets the new file name for the database, such as Dhcp1.mdb.
- Netsh dhcp server *ServerID* set databasepath *NewPath*—Sets the new path for the database files, such as C:\Dhcp\Dbfiles.
- Netsh dhcp server *ServerID* set databasebackupinterval *NewIntervalMinutes*—Sets the database backup interval in minutes, such as 120.
- Netsh dhcp server *ServerID* set databasebackuppathname *NewPath*—Sets the new path for the database backup files, such as C:\Dhcp\Dbbackup.

- Netsh dhcp server *ServerID* set databaseloggingflag *FlagValue*—Enables or disables audit logging. Set to 0 to disable or 1 to enable.
- Netsh dhcp server *ServerID* set databaserestoreflag *FlagValue*—Forces DHCP to restore the database from backup when it is started. Set to 1 to restore.
- Netsh dhcp server *ServerID* set databasecleanupinterval *NewIntervalMinutes*—Sets the database backup interval in minutes, such as 120.

Note If you change the database name or folder locations, you must stop the DHCP server and then start it again for the changes to take effect. To do this, type **net stop "dhcp server"** to stop the server and then type **net start "dhcp server"** to start the server again.

Backing Up and Restoring the Database

The DHCP database is backed up automatically. You can manually back it up as well at any time. In the DHCP console, right-click the server you want to back up, and then choose Backup. In the Browse For Folder dialog box, select the backup folder, and then click OK.

If a server crash corrupts the database, you might need to restore and then reconcile the database. Start by restoring a good copy of the contents of the backup folder from tape or other archive source. Afterward, start the DHCP console, right-click the server you want to restore, and then choose Restore. In the Browse For Folder dialog box, select the folder that contains the backup you want to restore, and then click OK. During restoration of the database, the DHCP Server service is stopped and then started automatically.

Inside Out

Moving the DHCP database to a new server

You can use the backup and restore procedure to move the DHCP database to a new server. For example, before upgrading a DHCP server or decommissioning it, you could configure a new DHCP server and move the current DHCP database from the old server to the new server. Start by installing the DHCP Server service on the destination server and then restart the server. When the server restarts, log on, and at the command prompt type **net stop "dhcp server"** to stop the DHCP Server service. Remove the contents of the %SystemRoot%\System32\Dhcp folder on this server.

Afterward, log on to the original (source) server, and at the command prompt type **net stop "dhcp server"** to stop the DHCP Server service. In the Services node of Computer Management, disable the DHCP Server service so that it can no longer be started, then copy the entire contents of the %SystemRoot%\System32\Dhcp folder to the %SystemRoot%\System32\Dhcp folder on the destination server. Once all the necessary files are on the destination server, type **net start "dhcp server"** to start the DHCP Server service on the destination server, which completes the migration.

Repairing the DHCP Database

DHCP databases can become corrupt, especially if they've been in use for a long time. If this happens, you'll see error messages in the system event log that have DHCP Server as the event source and reference JET database errors. A typical error might look like this: "The JET database returned the following Error: 510."

You can use the Jetpack.exe utility to repair the database. First, stop the DHCP Server service by typing **net stop "dhcp server"** at the command prompt. In the command prompt, change to the DHCP database directory, which by default is %SystemRoot%\System32\Dhcp. To repair the database, type **jetpack dhcp.mdb dhcptemp.mdb**, where *dhcp.mdb* is the current name of the DHCP database and *dhcptemp.mdb* is the name of a temporary file that can be used by the Jetpack utility.

If the Jetpack utility fails to repair the database, you must restore the database from backup or force the DHCP Server service to re-create the database from backup. To do this, stop the DHCP Server service by typing **net stop "dhcp server"** at the command prompt. Set the DatabaseRestoreFlag using the following command:

```
netsh dhcp server ServerID set databaserestoreflag 1
```

where *ServerID* is the name or IP address of the DHCP server and the database restore flag is set to 1 to restore the database from backup. Afterward, start the DHCP Server service by typing **net start "dhcp server"** at the command prompt.

Setting Up DHCP Relay Agents

In an ideal configuration, you'll have multiple DHCP servers on each subnet. However, because this isn't always possible, you can configure your routers to forward DHCP broadcasts or configure a computer on the network to act as a relay agent. Any computer running Windows Server 2003 can act as a relay agent. Doing so requires that Routing and Remote Access be configured and enabled on the computer first, and then you can configure the computer as a relay agent using the Routing And Remote Access console.

Configuring and Enabling Routing and Remote Access

To start the Routing And Remote Access console, click Start, Programs or All Programs, Administrative Tools, Routing And Remote Access. If the computer you want to use as the relay agent isn't listed as an available server, right-click the Routing And Remote Access node in the left pane, and select Add Server. In the Add Server dialog box, select The Following Computer, type the name or IP address of the computer, and then click OK.

If the computer isn't already configured for Routing and Remote Access, right-click the computer node in the left pane, and then select Configure And Enable Routing And Remote Access. This starts the Routing And Remote Access Setup Wizard. Click Next. Choose Custom Configuration, as shown in Figure 25-25, and then click Next again. On the Custom Configuration page, select LAN Routing. Click Next, and then click Finish. Click Yes when prompted to start the Routing and Remote Access Service.

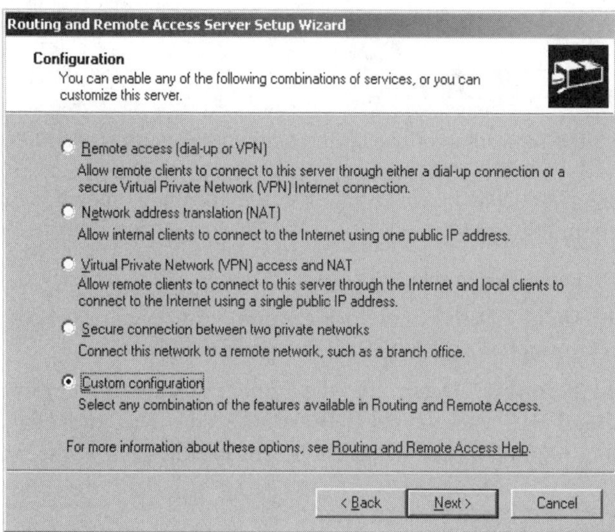

Figure 25-25. Configure and enable Routing and Remote Access.

Adding and Configuring the DHCP Relay Agent

In the Routing And Remote Access console, expand the node for the computer you just configured, and then expand IP Routing. Right-click the General node, and then choose New Routing Protocol. In the New Routing Protocol dialog box, select DHCP Relay Agent, and then click OK. This adds an entry under IP Routing labeled DHCP Relay Agent.

In the Routing And Remote Access console, right-click the DHCP Relay Agent entry, and choose New Interface. The New Interface For DHCP Relay Agent dialog box is displayed, as shown in Figure 25-26, showing the currently configured network interfaces on the computer. Select the network interface that is connected to the same network as the DHCP clients whose DHCP broadcasts need forwarding, and then click OK.

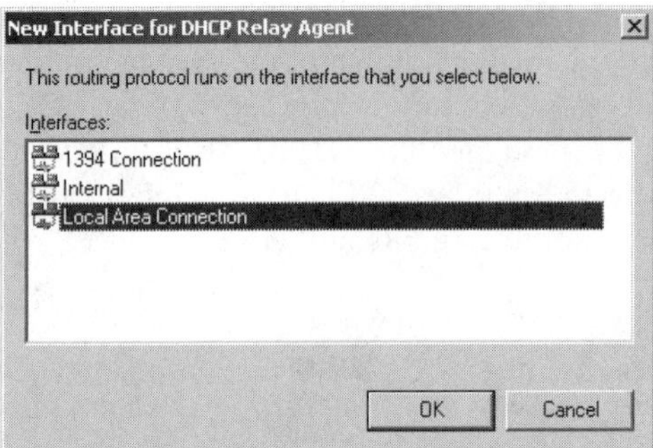

Figure 25-26. Select the network interface on the same network as the DHCP clients.

The DHCP Relay Properties dialog box is displayed automatically, as shown in Figure 25-27. You have several configurable options:

- **Relay DHCP Packets** When selected ensures DHCP packets are relayed.
- **Hop-Count Threshold** Determines the maximum number of relay agents a DHCP request can pass through. The default is 4. The maximum is 16.
- **Boot Threshold (Seconds)** Determines the number of seconds the relay agent waits before forwarding DHCP packets. The delay is designed so that local DHCP servers will be the first to respond if they are available. The default delay is 4 seconds.

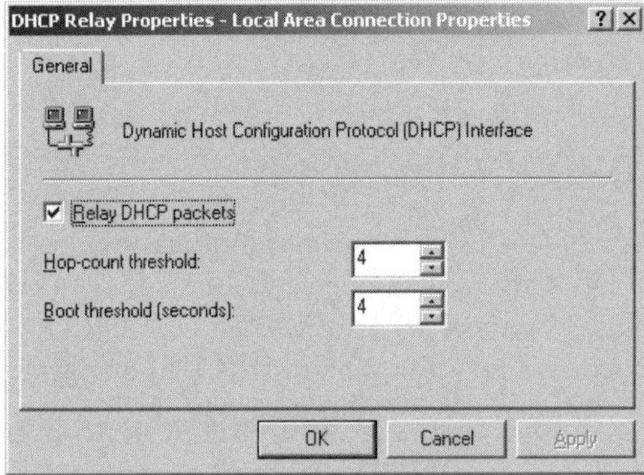

Figure 25-27. Set the relay options.

After you set the relay options, click OK. In the Routing And Remote Access console, right-click the DHCP Relay Agent entry, and choose Properties. This displays the DHCP Relay Agent Properties dialog box. Type the IP address of the DHCP server to which DHCP packets should be forwarded, and then click Add. Click OK. The computer is then configured as a DHCP relay agent.

Chapter 26

Architecting DNS Infrastructure

The Domain Name System (DNS) is an Internet Engineering Task Force (IETF) standard name service. Its basic design is described in Request for Comments (RFCs) 1034 and 1035, and it has been implemented on many operating systems including UNIX and Microsoft Windows. All versions of Windows automatically install a DNS client as part of Transmission Control Protocol/Internet Protocol (TCP/IP). To get the server component, you must install the DNS Server service. All editions of Microsoft Windows Server 2003 include the DNS Server service. Because DNS is the name resolution service for the Active Directory directory service, DNS is installed automatically if you install Active Directory on a network.

DNS Essentials

Like Dynamic Host Configuration Protocol (DHCP), DNS is a client/server protocol. This means there is a client component and a server component necessary to successfully implement DNS. Because of the client/server model, any computer seeking DNS information is referred to as a DNS client, and the computer that provides the information to the client is referred to as a DNS server. It's the job of a DNS server to store a database containing DNS information, to respond to DNS queries from clients, and to replicate DNS information to other DNS servers as necessary.

DNS provides for several types of queries, including forward lookup queries and reverse lookup queries. Forward lookup queries allow a client to resolve a host name to an Internet Protocol (IP) address. A DNS client makes a forward lookup using a name query message that asks the host address record for a specific host. The response to this query is sent as a name query response message. If there's a host address record for the specified host, the name server returns this. If the host name is an alias, the name server returns the record for the alias (CNAME) as well as the host address record to which the alias points.

Reverse lookup queries allow a client to resolve an IP address to a host name, as Figure 26-1 shows. Reverse lookups are primarily used by computers to find out who is contacting them so that they can communicate directly using an IP address rather than a host name. This can speed up communications in some cases because name queries aren't necessary. A DNS client makes a reverse lookup using a reverse name query message. The response to the query is set as a reverse name query response message. This message contains the reverse address record (PTR) for the specified host.

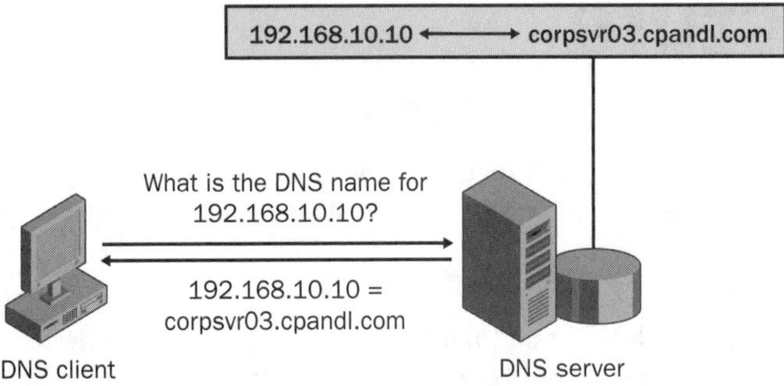

Figure 26-1. A reverse lookup query.

DNS also provides a way to cache DNS information to reduce the number of queries that are required. So, instead of having to send a query to a name server each time the host wants to resolve a particular name, the DNS client checks its local cache for the information first. DNS information in the cache is held for a set amount of time, referred to as the Time to Live (TTL) value of a record. When a record exists in cache and its TTL has not expired, it is used to answer subsequent queries. Not only does this reduce traffic on the network, it also speeds up the name resolution process. A record's TTL is set in the query response from a name server.

Planning DNS Implementations

Planning a new DNS implementation or revamping your existing DNS implementation requires good planning. You need a solid understanding of how DNS works, and the areas you should know about include the following:

- How DNS namespaces are assigned and used
- How DNS name resolution works and can be modified
- What resource records are available and how are they used
- How DNS zones and zone transfers can be used
- How internal and external servers can be used

Public and Private Namespaces

The DNS domain namespace is a hierarchical tree in which each node and leaf in the tree represents a named domain. Each level of the domain namespace tree is separated by a period (called a "dot"). As discussed in the section entitled "Understanding Name Resolution" on page 790, the first level of the tree is where you'll find the top-level domains, and these top-level domains form the base of the DNS namespace. The second level of the tree is for second-level or parent domains, and subsequent levels of the tree are for subdomains. For example, cpandl.com is the parent domain of the child domains sales.cpandl.com and tech.cpandl.com.

Note Although the actual root of the DNS namespace is represented by "." and doesn't have a name, each level in the tree has a name, which is referred to as its label. The fully qualified domain name (FQDN) of a node in the DNS namespace is the list of all the labels in the path from the node to the root of the namespace. For example, the FQDN for the host named CORPSVR02 in the cpandl.com domain is corpsvr02.cpandl.com.

To divide public and private namespaces, the top-level domains are established and maintained by select organizations. The top authority, Internet Corporation for Assigned Names and Numbers (ICANN), is responsible for defining and delegating control over the top-level domains to individual organizations. Top-level domains are organized functionally and geographically. Table 26-1 lists the functions of the generic top-level domains that are currently defined; the list can be extended to include other generic top-level domains (see *http://www.iana.org/gtld/gtld.htm* for the most current list). The geographically organized top-level domains are identified by two-level country codes. These country codes are based on the International Organization for Standardization (ISO) country name and are used primarily by organizations outside the United States.

Note The United Kingdom is the exception to the ISO naming rule. Although the ISO country code for the United Kingdom is GB (Great Britain), its two-letter designator is UK.

Table 26-1. Top-Level Domain Names for the Internet

Domain	Purpose
.aero	For aerospace firms, including airlines
.biz	For businesses, extends the .com area
.com	For commercial organizations
.coop	For business cooperatives
.edu	For educational institutions
.gov	For U.S. government agencies
.info	For information sources
.int	For organizations established by international treaties
.mil	For U.S. military departments and agencies
.museum	For museums
.name	For use by individuals
.net	For use by network providers

Table 26-1. Top-Level Domain Names for the Internet

Domain	Purpose
.org	For use by organizations, such as those that are nongovernmental or nonprofit
.pro	For professional groups such as doctors and lawyers

Once ICANN delegates control over a top-level domain, it is the responsibility of the designated organization to maintain the domain and handle registrations. After an organization registers a domain name with one of these authorities, the organization controls the domain and can create subdomains within this domain without having to make a formal request. For example, if you register the domain cpandl.com, you can create the subdomains seattle.cpandl.com, portland.cpandl.com, and sf.cpandl.com without having to ask the registration authority for permission.

Private namespaces aren't controlled by ICANN. You can create your own private namespace for use within your company. For example, you could use .local for your top-level domain. This keeps your internal network separate from the public Internet. You would then need to rely on Network Address Translation (NAT) or proxy servers to access the public Internet.

Name Resolution Using DNS

In DNS, name resolution is made possible using a distributed database. The resource records in this database detail host name and IP address information relating to domains. It is the job of DNS name servers to store the DNS database and respond to queries from clients about the information the database contains. A portion of the DNS namespace that is controlled by a DNS name server or a group of name servers is referred to as a zone.

Zones establish the boundaries within which a particular name server can resolve requests. On clients, it is the job of DNS resolvers to contact name servers and perform queries about resource records. Thus, the three main components of DNS are as follows:

- Resource records stored in a distributed database
- DNS name servers that are responsible for maintaining specific zones
- DNS resolvers running on clients

These key components are used to perform DNS operations, which can consist of query operations, query replies, and DNS update operations. A basic query and reply work as shown in Figure 26-2. Here, a DNS client wants information from a DNS name server, so it sends a DNS query. The DNS server to which the query is sent checks its local database and forwards the request to an authoritative server. The authoritative server sends back a response to the local DNS server, and that response is forwarded to the client.

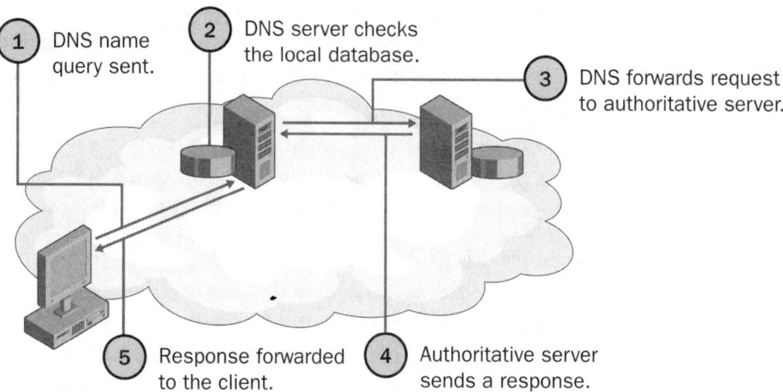

Figure 26-2. DNS query and reply.

As Figure 26-3 shows, things get a bit more complicated when a client requests the name of an external resource, such as a Web site. If you were on an internal domain and requested a resource on the public Internet, such as the IP address for the www.cpandl.com server, the DNS client on your computer queries the local name server as specified in its TCP/IP configuration. The local name server forwards the request to the root server for the external resource domain. This domain contacts the name server for the related top-level domain, which in turn contacts the name server for the cpandl.com domain. This authoritative server sends a response, which is forwarded to the client, who can then access the external resource.

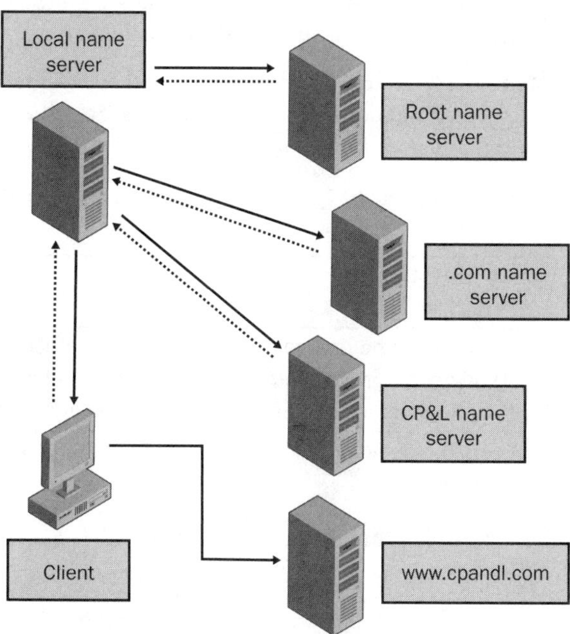

Figure 26-3. Name resolution using the DNS tree.

As you can see, in a normal DNS configuration, if your DNS name server can't resolve a request, it simply forwards the request to another name server for resolution. This allows your organization's name servers to get internal DNS information and external DNS information on the public Internet. However, what if the domain you were trying to reach was a resource in another one of your own internal domains. In this case, you wouldn't want requests to be forwarded to a public DNS name server for resolution. The public DNS server would have no idea how to resolve the request.

There are several ways to resolve this problem and one of these ways is to use conditional forwarding. By using conditional forwarding, you can tell your DNS name servers that if you see a request for domain XYZ, don't forward it to the public DNS name servers for resolution. Instead, forward the request directly to the XYZ name server—which is the authoritative name server for the domain being looked up. This name server will then be able to reply to the query and the DNS lookup will be resolved. For more information on resolving name resolution problems and conditional forwarding, see the section entitled "Secondary Zones, Stub Zones, and Conditional Forwarding" later in this chapter.

DNS Resource Records

Resource records are used to store domain information. DNS name servers contain resource records for those portions of the DNS namespace for which they are authoritative. It is the job of administrators who maintain an authoritative DNS name server to maintain the resource records and ensure that they are accurate. DNS name servers can also cache resource records for those areas for which they can answer queries sent by hosts. This means DNS name servers can cache resource records relating to any part of the domain tree.

Although many types of resource records are defined and supported by DNS servers, only a few record types are actually used on a Windows Server 2003 network. So, with that in mind, Table 26-2 provides an overview of the resource records that you'll use.

Table 26-2. Common Resource Records Used on Windows Server 2003 Networks

Record Type	Common Name	Description
A	Host address	Contains the name of a host and its Internet Protocol version 4 (IPv4) address. Any computer that has multiple network interfaces or IP addresses should have multiple address records.
AAAA	IPv6 host address	Contains the name of a host and its Internet Protocol version 6 (IPv6) address.

Table 26-2. Common Resource Records Used on Windows Server 2003 Networks

Record Type	Common Name	Description
CNAME	Canonical name	Creates an alias for a host name. This allows a host to be referred to by multiple names in DNS. The most common use is when a host provides a common service, such as World Wide Web (WWW) or File Transfer Protocol (FTP), and you want it to have a friendly name rather than a complex name. For example, you might want www.cpandl.com to be an alias for the host dc06.cpandl.com.
MX	Mail exchanger	Indicates a mail exchange server for the domain, which allows mail to be delivered to the correct mail servers in the domain. For example, if an MX record is set for the domain cpandl.com, all mail sent to *username*@cpandl.com will be directed to the server specified in the MX record.
NS	Name server	Provides a list of authoritative servers for a domain, which allows DNS lookups within various zones. Each primary and secondary name server in a domain should be declared through this record.
PTR	Pointer	Enables reverse lookups by creating a pointer that maps an IP address to a host name.
SOA	Start of authority	Indicates the authoritative name server for a particular zone. The authoritative server is the best source of DNS information for a zone. Because each zone must have an SOA record, the record is created automatically when you add a zone. The SOA record also contains information about how resource records in the zone should be used and cached. This includes refresh, retry, and expiration intervals as well as the maximum time that a record is considered valid.
SRV	Service location	Makes it possible to find a server providing a specific service. Active Directory uses SRV records to locate domain controllers, global catalog servers, Lightweight Directory Access Protocol (LDAP) servers, and Kerberos servers. SRV records are created automatically. For example, Active Directory creates an SRV record when you set a domain controller as a global catalog. LDAP servers can add an SRV to indicate they are available to handle LDAP requests in a particular zone. SRV records are created in the forest root zone as discussed in the section entitled "Using DNS with Active Directory" on page 873.

DNS Zones and Zone Transfers

DNS name servers that have complete information for a part of the DNS namespace are said to be authoritative. A portion of the namespace over which an authoritative name server has control is referred to as a zone. Zones establish the boundaries within which a particular name server can resolve requests and are the main replication units in DNS. Zones can contain resource records for one or more related DNS domains.

Windows Server 2003 supports four types of zones:

- **Standard primary** Stores a writable master copy of a zone as a text file. All changes to a zone are made in the primary zone. The information in as well as changes to a primary zone can be replicated to secondary zones.
- **Standard secondary** Stores a read-only copy of a zone as a text file. It is used to provide redundancy and load balancing for a primary zone. The information in and changes to a primary zone are replicated to a secondary zone using zone transfers.
- **Active Directory–integrated** Integrates zone information in Active Directory and uses Active Directory to replicate zone information. This is a proprietary zone type that is only possible when you deploy Active Directory on the network. Active Directory–integrated zones were first introduced in Microsoft Windows 2000 and are new for previous Microsoft Windows NT users. A new feature in Windows Server 2003 is the ability to selectively replicate DNS information.

Tip **Active Directory–integrated zones are only on domain controllers**

Designating a zone as Active Directory–integrated means that only domain controllers can be primary name servers for the zone. These domain controllers can accept dynamic updates, and Active Directory security is used automatically to restrict dynamic updates to domain members. Any DNS servers in the zone that aren't domain controllers can act only as secondary name servers. These secondary name servers cannot accept dynamic updates.

- **Stub** Stores a partial zone that can be used to identify the authoritative DNS servers for a zone. A stub zone has no information about the hosts in a zone. Instead, it has information only about the authoritative name servers in a zone so queries can be forwarded directly to those name servers. Stub zones are new to Windows Server 2003.

Each of these four DNS zone types can be created for forward or reverse lookups. A forward lookup zone is used to resolve DNS names into IP addresses and provide information about available network services. A reverse lookup zone is used to resolve IP addresses to DNS names.

Zones That Aren't Integrated with Active Directory

With standard zones that aren't integrated with Active Directory, a master copy of the zone is stored in a primary zone on a single DNS server, called a *primary DNS server*. This server's

SOA record indicates that it is the primary zone for the related domain. Secondary zones are used to improve performance and provide redundancy. A server storing a copy of a secondary zone is referred to as a *secondary DNS server*.

A primary DNS server automatically replicates a copy of the primary zone to any designated secondary servers. The transfer of zone information is handled by a zone replication process and is referred to as a zone transfer. Although the initial zone transfer after configuring a new secondary server represents a full transfer of the zone information, subsequent transfers are made incrementally as changes occur. Here's how it works: When changes are made to a primary zone, the changes are made first to the primary zone and then transferred to the secondary zone on the secondary servers. Because only changes are transferred, rather than a complete copy of the zone, the amount of traffic required to keep a secondary zone current is significantly reduced.

You can implement DNS zones in many ways. One way to do this is to mimic your organization's domain structure. Figure 26-4 shows an example of how zones and zone transfers could be configured for child domains of a parent domain. Here, you have separate zones that handle name services for the cpandl.com, tech.cpandl.com, and sales.cpandl.com domains. Zone transfers are configured so that copies of the primary zone on cpandl.com are transferred to the name servers for the tech.cpandl.com and sales.cpandl.com domains. The reason for this is that users in these zones routinely work with servers in the cpandl.com zone. This makes lookups faster and reduces the amount of DNS traffic as well.

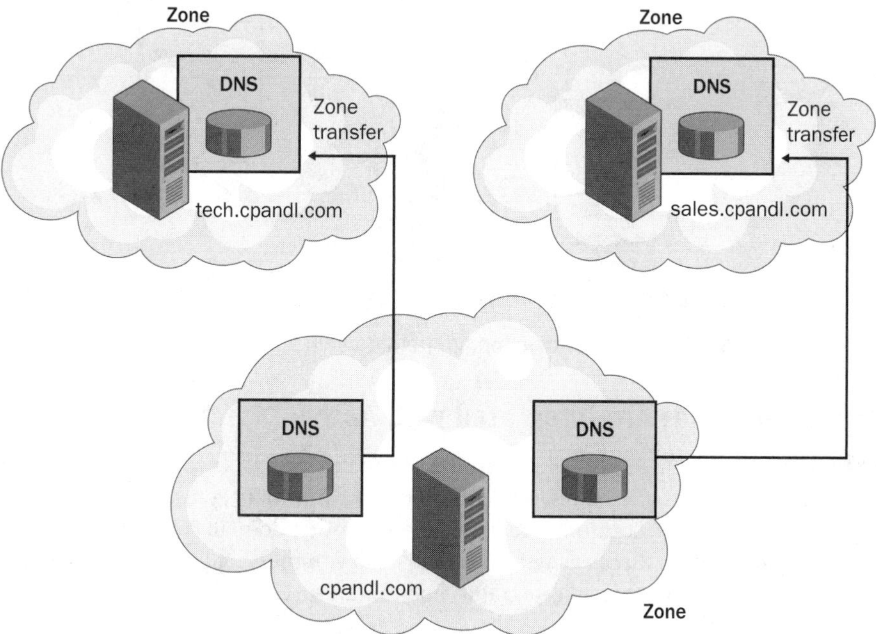

Figure 26-4. DNS zones on separate servers.

Although you can configure DNS services in this way, your organization's domain structure is separate from its zone configuration. If you create subdomains of a parent domain, they can either be part of the same zone or belong to another zone and these zones can be on separate DNS servers or the same DNS servers.

The example in Figure 26-5 shows a wide area network (WAN) configuration. The branch offices in Seattle and New York are separate from the company headquarters, and key zones are organized geographically. At company headquarters there's an additional zone running on the same DNS name server as the zone for the cpandl.com domain. This zone handles services.cpandl.com, tech.cpandl.com, and sales.cpandl.com.

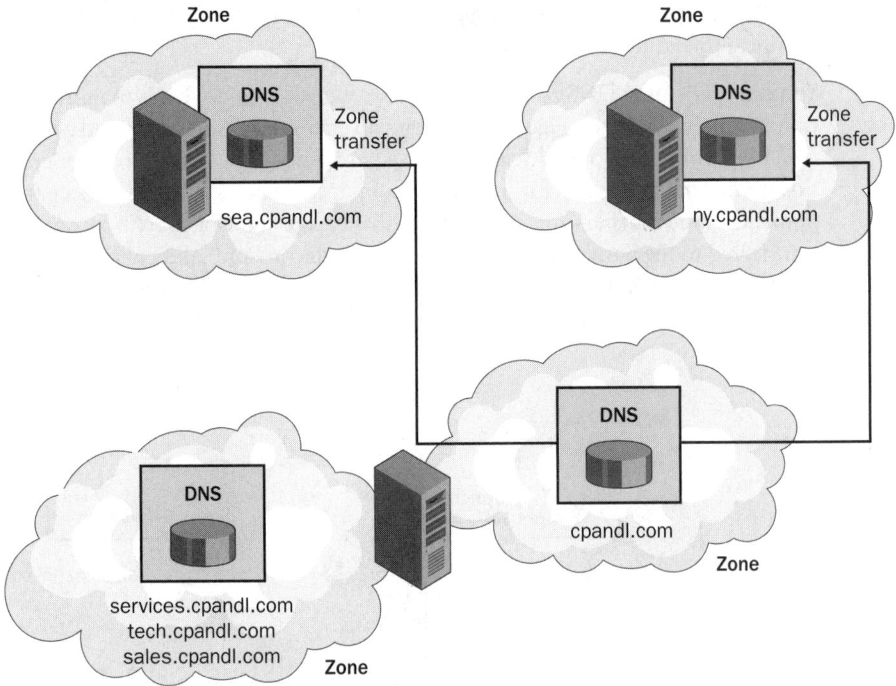

Figure 26-5. Zones can be separate from domain structure.

Zones That Are Integrated with Active Directory

Using Active Directory–integrated zones, you can store DNS zone information within Active Directory. This gives you several advantages. Any primary zone or stub zone integrated with Active Directory is automatically replicated to other domain controllers using Active Directory replication. Because Active Directory can compress replication data between sites, you can more efficiently replicate traffic, and this is especially important over slow WAN links.

Figure 26-6 shows an example of Active Directory–integrated zones and replication. Here, zone information for cpandl.com, seattle.cpandl.com, portland.cpandl.com, and sf.cpandl.com has been integrated with Active Directory. This allows any DNS changes made at branch offices or at company headquarters to be replicated throughout the organization to all the available name servers. Because the decision to integrate zones with Active Directory isn't an all-or-nothing approach, there are also standard primary and secondary zones, and standard DNS zones transfers are used to maintain these zones.

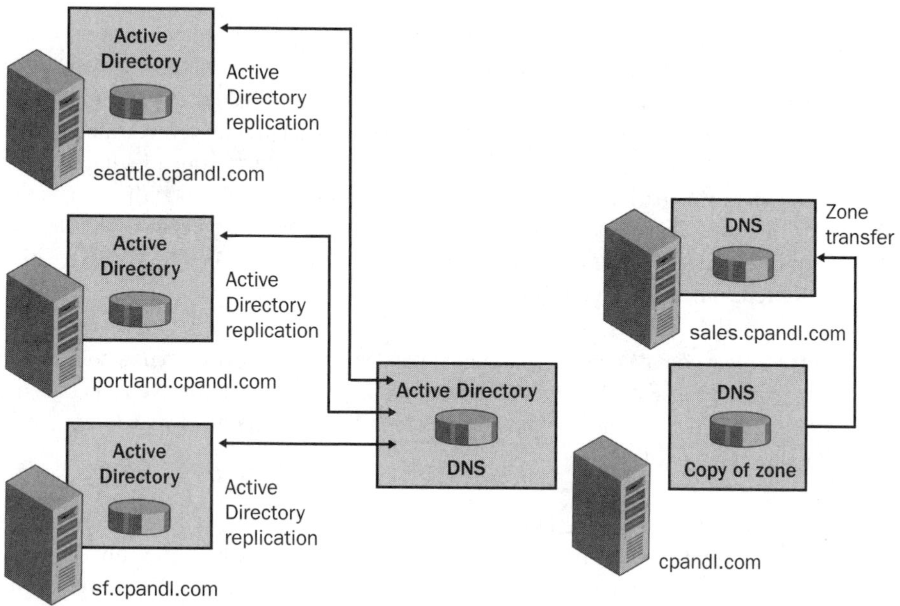

Figure 26-6. Active Directory–integrated zones.

Inside Out

Multimaster replication for DNS changes

By using Active Directory integration, copies of zone information are maintained on all domain controllers that are also configured as DNS servers. This is different from standard DNS zones. When you use standard zones, there's a single authoritative DNS server for a zone, and it maintains a master copy of the zone. All updates to the primary zone must be made on the primary server. With Active Directory–integrated zones, each domain controller configured as a DNS server in a domain is an authoritative server for that domain. This means clients can make updates to DNS records on any of these servers and the changes will be automatically replicated.

Active Directory–integrated zones have changed substantially since they were first implemented. In Windows 2000, DNS information is stored in the same context as other Active Directory information. This means updates to DNS records are automatically replicated to all domain controllers in the domain regardless of whether those domain controllers are also DNS name servers. In an organization with many domain controllers but only a few DNS name servers, this means there is a lot of unnecessary traffic on the network. Additional planning is also required to ensure all domain controllers are able to resolve the forest-side locator records stored in the _msdcs subdomain in the forest root domain.

In Windows Server 2003, default application partitions are used to ensure that DNS information is replicated only to domain controllers that are also configured as DNS servers. Here's how it works: For every domain in an Active Directory forest, a separate application partition is created and used to store all records in each Active Directory–integrated zone configured for that domain. Because the application partition context is outside that of other Active Directory information, DNS information is no longer replicated with other Active Directory information. There's also a default application partition that stores DNS information and replicates that information to all DNS servers in an Active Directory forest. This simplifies DNS replication for organizations with multiple domains.

Note Only domain controllers running Windows Server 2003 can use default application partitions to replicate DNS information in this way. Because of this, you can take advantage of this feature when the domain controllers in all the domains of your forest are running Windows Server 2003.

Another benefit of Active Directory integration is the ability to perform conditional forwarding. By using conditional forwarding, you can eliminate the split-brain syndrome when internal requests get incorrectly forwarded to external DNS servers. Finally, with dynamic updates using DHCP, clients gain the ability to use secure dynamic updates. Security dynamic updates ensure that only those clients that created a record can subsequently update the record. You'll find more on secure dynamic updates in the section entitled "Security Considerations" later in this chapter.

Secondary Zones, Stub Zones, and Conditional Forwarding

Secondary zones, stub zones, and conditional forwarding can all be used to resolve name resolution problems—chiefly the split-brain scenario in which internal DNS servers blindly forward any requests that they can't resolve to external servers. Rather than blindly forwarding requests, you can configure internal servers so that they know about certain DNS domains. This ensures name resolution works for domains that aren't known on the public Internet and can also be used to speed up name resolution for known domains, which makes users much happier than if name resolution fails or they have to wait all the time for name requests to be resolved.

By using a secondary zone, you create a complete copy of a zone on a DNS server that can be used to resolve DNS queries without having to go to the authoritative name server for that domain. Not only can this be used for subdomains of a parent domain that exists in different zones, but for different parent domains as well. For example, on the name servers for cpandl.com you could create secondary zones for a partner company, such as The Phone Company whose domain is thephone-company.com. In this way, DNS clients in the cpandl.com domain can perform fast lookups for hosts in thephone-company.com domain.

The downside is that you must replicate DNS traffic between the domains. If this replication takes place over the public Internet, the administrators at The Phone Company would need to configure firewalls on their network to allow this and make other security changes as well, which might not be acceptable. Because you are maintaining a full copy of the zone, any change generates replication traffic.

With a stub zone, you create a partial copy of a zone that has information about only the authoritative name servers in a zone. As Figure 26-7 shows, this allows a DNS server to forward queries directly to a name server for a particular domain and bypass the normal name server hierarchy. This speeds up the lookup because you don't have to go through multiple name servers to find the authoritative name server for a domain.

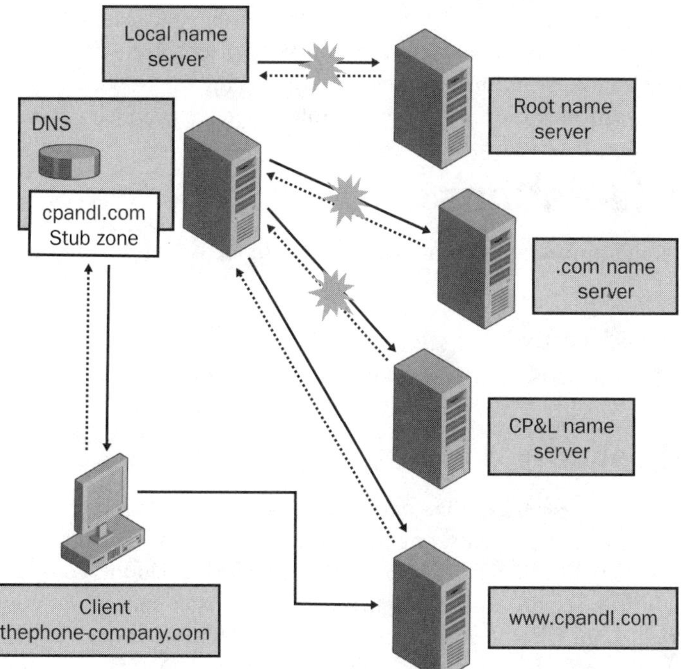

Figure 26-7. Using stub zones for lookups.

Stub zones work like this: When you set up a stub zone for a domain, only the resource records needed to identify the authoritative name servers for the related domain are transferred to the name server. These records include the SOA and NS records as well as the related A records for these servers (referred to as glue records). These records can be maintained in one of two ways. If you use Active Directory integration, the normal Active Directory replication process can be used to maintain the stub zone. If you use a standard stub zone, standard zone transfers are used to maintain the stub zone. Both techniques require access to the domain specified in the stub zone, which can be a security issue. Replication traffic isn't an issue, however, because you are maintaining a very small amount of data.

Conditional forwarding is very similar to stub zones except that you don't need to transfer any information from the domain to which you want to forward requests. Instead, you configure names servers in domain A so that they know the IP address of the authoritative name servers in domain B, allowing these name servers to be used as forwarders. There's no access requirement, so you don't need permission to do this, and there's no bandwidth requirement, so you don't need to worry about extra replication traffic.

By using conditional forwarding, there are some trade-offs to be made, however. If the authoritative name servers change, the IP addresses aren't updated automatically as they are with stub zones or secondary zones. This means you would have to reconfigure name servers manually in domain A with the new IP addresses of the authoritative name servers in domain B. When you configure conditional forwarders on a name server, the name server has to check the forwarders list each time it resolves a name. As the list grows, it requires more and more time to work through the list of potential forwarders.

Security Considerations

DNS security is an important issue, and this discussion focuses on three areas:

- DNS queries from clients
- DNS dynamic updates
- External DNS name resolution

DNS Queries and Security

A client that makes a query trusts that an authoritative DNS name server gives it the right information. In most environments, this works fine. Users or administrators specify the initial DNS name servers to which DNS queries should be forwarded in a computer's TCP/IP configuration. In some environments where security is a major concern, administrators might be worried about DNS clients getting invalid information from DNS name servers. Here, administrators might want to look at the DNS Security (DNSSEC) protocol. DNSSEC is especially useful for companies that have many branch locations, and DNS information is transferred over the public Internet using zone transfers.

Note Windows Server 2003 provides basic support for DNSSEC, which enables a DNS name server running Windows Server 2003 to act as a secondary for a DNS Berkeley Internet Name Domain (BIND) server using DNSSEC. Additionally, the standard DNS Client for Windows computers doesn't validate any DNSSEC data that is returned to it.

Tip **Configure DNSSEC support**
In Windows Server 2003, you can configure DNSSEC support for a DNS server using the DNSCMD command, which is included in the Support Tools folder on the Windows Server 2003 CD. To enable DNSSEC support, type **dnscmd *ServerName* /config /enablednssec 1**, where *ServerName* is the name or IP address of the DNS server you want to configure, such as NS2 or 192.168.18.17. To disable DNSSEC support, type **dnscmd *ServerName* /config /enablednssec 0**.

DNSSEC provides authentication of DNS information. Using DNSSEC, you can digitally sign zone files so that they can be authenticated. These digital signatures can be sent to DNS clients as resource records from DNS servers hosting signed zones. The client can then verify that the DNS information sent from the DNS server is authentic.

DNSSEC digital signatures are encrypted using private key encryption on a per-zone basis. In private key encryption, there is a public key and a private key. A zone's public key is used to validate a digital signature. Like the digital signature itself, the public key is stored in a signed zone in the form of a resource record. A zone's private key is not stored in the zone; it is private and used only by the name server to sign the related zone or parts of the zone. The records used with DNSSEC are summarized in Table 26-3.

Table 26-3. DNSSEC Resource Records

Record Type	Common Name	Description
KEY	Key	Contains the public key for a digitally signed zone.
NXT	Next	Indicates the next record in a digitally signed zone and states which records exist in a zone. It can be used to validate that a particular record doesn't exist in the zone. For example, if there's a record for corpsvr07.cpandl.com and the Next record points to corpsvr09.cpandl.com, there isn't a record for corpsvr08.cpandl.com, so that server doesn't exist in the zone.
SIG	Signature	Contains the digital signature for a zone or part of a zone.

DNS Dynamic Updates and Security

Windows Server 2003 fully supports DNS dynamic updates. Dynamic updates are used in conjunction with DHCP to allow a client to update its A record if its IP address changes and allow the DHCP server to update the PTR record for the client on the DNS server. DHCP servers can also be configured to update both the A and PTR records on the client's behalf. Dynamic DNS is also supported for IPv6 AAAA records, which allows for dynamic updating of host addresses on systems that use IPv6 and DHCP.

If dynamic updates are enabled, the DNS name server trusts the client to update its own DNS record and trusts the DHCP server to make updates on behalf of the client. There are two types of dynamic updates:

- **Secure dynamic updates** Using secure dynamic updates allows you to put security mechanisms in place to ensure only a client that created a record can update a record.
- **Nonsecure dynamic updates** By using nonsecure dynamic updates there is no way to ensure that only a client that created a record can update a record.

Secure dynamic updates are the default setting for Active Directory–integrated zones. By using secure updates, only clients capable of using secure dynamic updates can update their records. This means clients running Windows 2000 or later can update their own records, but clients running earlier versions of the Windows operating system cannot. DHCP servers can be configured to make updates on behalf of these clients. For more information on this, see the section entitled "Integrating DHCP and DNS" on page 843.

With standard zones, the default setting is to allow both secure and nonsecure dynamic updates. The reason standard zones are configured for both secure and nonsecure dynamic updates is that this allows clients running Windows 2000 or later as well as earlier versions of Windows to update records dynamically. Although it seems to imply that security is involved, it is in fact not. Here, allowing secure updates simply means that the dynamic update process won't break when a secure update is made. DNS doesn't validate updates and this means dynamic updates are accepted from any client. This creates a significant security vulnerability because updates can be accepted from untrusted sources.

Caution If you install DHCP on a domain controller, the DHCP server is made a member of the DNSUpdateProxy group. Because members of this group do not have security set on records they create, any records the DHCP server creates will have no security. This means they could be updated by any client.

Inside Out

Hidden "gotchas" with secure updates

There are hidden "gotchas" when you use secure dynamic updates that people don't often think about. When a DHCP server creates a record on a DNS server, the DHCP server becomes the owner of the record. If a DHCP server is replaced or its scopes are migrated to another computer, then the server no longer exists and no one else can update the records it created. Thus, any records that the server owns become outdated (stale) and nonupdateable (orphaned).

In addition, if you upgrade a client from a version of Windows earlier than Windows 2000 to Windows 2000 or later, the client's DNS records can become stale and orphaned as well. This happens because DHCP servers update the DNS records for pre–Windows 2000 clients but do not do so for clients using Windows 2000 or later.

The best solution for these hidden "gotchas" is to change ownership of records manually as appropriate after upgrades.

External DNS Name Resolution and Security

Typically, as part of a standard DNS configuration, you'll configure DNS servers on your internal network to forward queries that they can't resolve to DNS servers outside the organization. Normally, these servers are the name servers for the Internet service provider (ISP) that provides your organization's Internet connection. In this configuration, you know that internal servers forward to designated external servers. However, if those servers don't respond, the internal servers typically will forward requests directly to the root name servers, and this is where security problems can be introduced.

By default, DNS servers include a list of root servers that can be used for name resolution to the top-level domains. This list is maintained in what is called a *root hints file*. If this file is not updated regularly, your organization's internal name servers could point to invalid root servers, and this leaves a hole in your security that could be exploited. To prevent this, periodically update the root hints file.

On a DNS server that doesn't use Active Directory, the root hints are read from the %SystemRoot%\System32\DNS\Cache.dns file. You can obtain an update for this file from *ftp://ftp.rs.internic.net/domain/named.cache*. To determine whether an update is needed, compare the version information in your current root hints file with that of the published version. Within the root hints file, you'll find a section of comments like this:

```
;       This file holds the information on root name servers needed to
;       initialize cache of Internet domain name servers
;       (e.g. reference this file in the "cache  .  <file>"
;       configuration file of BIND domain name servers).
;
;       This file is made available by InterNIC
;       under anonymous FTP as
;          file                            /domain/named.root
;          on server                       FTP.INTERNIC.NET
;
;          last update:                    Nov 5, 2002
;          related version of root zone:   2002110501
```

Here, the version information is in the last two lines of the comments. If you changed the root hints file, you must stop and then start the DNS Server service so that the root hints file is reloaded. In the DNS console, you can do this by right-clicking the server entry, pointing to All Tasks, and selecting Restart.

On a DNS server that uses Active Directory–integrated zones, the root hints are read from Active Directory and the Registry at startup. You can view and modify the root hints in the DNS console. To do this, right-click the DNS server entry and then select Properties. In the Properties dialog box, select the Root Hints tab. You can then manage each of the individual root hint entries using Add, Edit, or Remove as necessary. To update the entire root hints using a known good DNS server, click Copy From Server, type the IP address of the DNS server, and then click OK. If you suspect the root hints file is corrupted, see Microsoft Knowledge Base article 249868 for details on reloading the file into Active Directory using the %SystemRoot%\System32\DNS\Cache.dns file.

Inside Out

Consider whether external root servers should be used

In some instances, you might not want to use a root hint file, or you might want to bypass using root servers. Here are two scenarios to consider:

- If your organization isn't connected to the Internet, your name servers don't need pointers to the public root servers. Instead, you should remove the entries in the Cache.dns file and replace them with NS and A records for the DNS server authoritative for the root domain at your site. For example, if you use a private top-level domain, such as .local, you must set up a root name server for the .local domain, and the Cache.dns file should point to these root name servers. You must then restart the DNS Server service so that the root hints file is reloaded. In the DNS console, you can do this by right-clicking the server entry, pointing to All Tasks, and selecting Restart.
- Making a connection to the root name servers exposes your internal name servers. The internal name server must connect through your organization's firewall to the root name server. While this connection is open and your name server is waiting for a response, there is a potential vulnerability that could be exploited. Here, someone could have set up a fake name server that is waiting for such connections and then could use this server to perform malicious activity on your DNS servers. To prevent this, you can configure forwarding to specific external name servers and tell your name servers not to use the root name servers. You do this by configuring the Do Not Use Recursion For This Domain option when you set up forwarding.

For more information, see the section entitled "Configuring Forwarders and Conditional Forwarding" on page 893.

Architecting a DNS Design

After you complete your initial planning, you should consider an overall design architecture. There are two primary DNS designs used:

- Split-brain design
- Separate-name design

Split-Brain Design: Same Internal and External Names

Most DNS implementations are architected to use a split-brain design. What this means is that your organization uses the same domain name internally as it does externally, and DNS is designed so that the name services for your organization's internal network are separate from that used for the organization's external network. Put another way, an organization's private network should be private and separate from its presence on the public Internet, so your internal name servers should be separate from your external name servers. You don't want a situation in which you have one set of name servers and they are used for both users within the organization and users outside the organization. That's a security no-no that could open your internal network to attack.

The concern with this design—and this is why it is called split-brain—is that if your internal network uses the same domain namespace as that of your public Internet presence, you can get in a situation in which users within the organization can't look up information related to the organization's public Internet presence and users outside the organization can't look up information for the organization's private network.

From an internal user perspective, it is a bad thing that users can't access the organization's public Internet resources. There's an easy fix, however. You simply create records on the authoritative name server for the internal network that specifies the IP address for the organization's public Internet resources. For example, to allow users on the internal cpandl.com domain to access www.cpandl.com on the public Internet, you create a host record on the internal DNS server for www in the cpandl.com domain that specifies its IP address.

From a security perspective, it is a good thing that outside users can't look up information for the organization's private network—you don't want them to be able to do this. If you have business partners at other locations that need access to the internal network, you should set up a secure link between your organizations or make other arrangements, such as using an extranet.

To implement split-brain design, you should do the following:

- **Complete your planning** Complete your planning and decide how many DNS servers you are going to use on the internal network. Decide on the host names and IP addresses these servers will use. In most cases, you'll need only two DNS servers for a domain. It is a standard convention to set the host names of DNS servers as Primary and Secondary if there are two servers and as NS01, NS02, and so on if there are more than two servers. You can use this naming convention or adopt a different one.

- **Install and configure the DNS Server service** Install the DNS Server service on each of the designated DNS servers. If you are using Active Directory, DNS is already implemented on some servers because it is required. With Active Directory–integrated zones, every DNS server in a domain that is also configured as a domain controller is a primary name server—and any DNS server not configured as a domain controller can be only a secondary in that zone. With standard primary and secondary zones, you can have only one primary server for a zone—and every other DNS server in that zone must be a secondary.
- **Create records on internal name servers for your public resources** For each of the organization's public Internet resources to which internal users need access, you must create records on the internal name servers. This allows the internal users to access and work with these resources. This includes the organization's WWW, FTP, and mail servers.
- **Configure forwarding to your ISP's name servers** The ISP that provides your connection to the Internet should provide you with the host names and IP addresses of name servers to which internal users can forward DNS queries. Configure your internal name servers so that they forward to your ISP's name servers DNS queries that they cannot resolve. As necessary, configure secondary zones, stub zones, or conditional forwarding to any domains for which you desire direct lookups.
- **Configure internal systems to use your internal DNS servers** Every workstation and server on your internal network should be configured with the IP address of your primary and secondary DNS name servers. If you have more than two name servers, set the name servers that should be used as appropriate. Normally, you'll point a system to only one or two internal name servers. Don't point internal systems to external name servers—you don't want internal systems trying to resolve requests on these name servers.
- **Configure external name servers for internal resources as necessary** Consider whether you need to create resource records on your ISP's external name servers for servers on your internal network that need to be resolvable from the Internet, such as by mobile users. If you do, provide the necessary information to your ISP to set up these resource records.

Separate-Name Design: Different Internal and External Names

Another approach to DNS design is to use separate-name design in which your internal network uses different domain names than that of your organization's public Internet presence. This creates actual physical separation of your organization's internal and external namespaces by placing them in different parent domains. For example, your organization could use cohovineyard.com for its internal network and cohowinery.com for its external network. Now you have a situation in which completely different namespaces are used to create separation.

As with split-brain design, you have different internal name servers and different external name servers. Unlike split-brain design, internal users should be able to look up information related to the organization's public Internet presence, and you won't need to create additional records to do this. Here, it is only a matter of ensuring the internal name servers forward to external name servers, which can perform the necessary lookups.

If you use different names that are in the public domain hierarchy, you should register all the internal and external domain names you use. In the previous example, you would register cohovineyard.com and cohowinery.com. This ensures someone else can't register one of the domain names you use internally, which could mess up name resolution in some instances. You wouldn't need to register a domain name, such as cohowinery.local, however, because .local is not a public top-level domain.

To implement separate-name design, you should do the following:

- **Complete your planning** Complete your planning and decide how many DNS servers you are going to use on the internal network. Decide on the host names and IP addresses these servers will use. In most case, you'll need only two DNS servers for a domain. It is a standard convention to set the host names of DNS servers as Primary and Secondary if there are two servers and as NS01, NS02, and so on if there are more than two servers. You can use this naming convention or adopt a different one.
- **Install and configure the DNS Server service** Install the DNS Server service on each of the designated DNS servers. If you are using Active Directory, DNS is already implemented on some servers because it is required. With Active Directory–integrated zones, every DNS server in a domain that is also configured as a domain controller is a primary name server—and any DNS server not configured as a domain controller can be only a secondary in that zone. With standard primary and secondary zones, you can have only one primary server for a zone—and every other DNS server in that zone must be a secondary.
- **Configure forwarding to your ISP's name servers** The ISP that provides your connection to the Internet should provide you with the host names and IP addresses of name servers to which internal users can forward DNS queries. Configure your internal name servers so that they forward DNS queries that they cannot resolve to your ISP's name servers. As necessary, configure secondary zones, stub zones, or conditional forwarding to any domains for which you desire direct lookups.
- **Configure internal systems to use your internal DNS servers** Every workstation and server on your internal network should be configured with the IP address of your primary and secondary DNS name servers. If you have more than two name servers, set the name servers that should be used as appropriate. Normally, you'll point a system to only one or two internal name servers. Don't point internal systems to external name servers—you don't want internal systems trying to resolve requests on these name servers.
- **Configure external name servers for internal resources as necessary** Consider whether you need to create resource records on your ISP's external name servers for servers on your internal network that need to be resolvable from the Internet, such as by mobile users. If you do, provide the necessary information to your ISP to set up these resource records.

Chapter 27

Implementing and Managing DNS

Name services are essential for communications for Transmission Control Protocol/Internet Protocol (TCP/IP) networking. Microsoft Windows Server 2003 uses the Domain Name System (DNS) as its primary method of name resolution. DNS enables computers to register and resolve DNS domain names. DNS defines the rules under which computers are named and how names are resolved to IP addresses. Windows Server 2003 also supports Windows Internet Naming Service (WINS), which is covered in detail in Chapter 28, "Implementing and Maintaining WINS." WINS provides a similar service for NetBIOS names as DNS provides for DNS domain names. WINS maps NetBIOS names to IP addresses for hosts running NetBIOS over TCP/IP.

Installing the DNS Server Service

The way you install the DNS Server service depends on whether you plan to use DNS with the Active Directory directory service or without Active Directory. Once you make that decision, you can install DNS as necessary using the Add Or Remove Programs utility or using the Configure Your Server Wizard.

Using DNS with Active Directory

On a domain with Active Directory, DNS is required to install the first domain controller in a domain. Active Directory doesn't necessarily require Windows DNS, however. Active Directory is designed to work with any DNS server that supports dynamic updates and

Service Location (SRV) records. This means Active Directory can work with any DNS server running Berkeley Internet Name Domain (BIND) version 8.1.2 or later. If you have DNS servers that use BIND version 8.1.2 or later, you can use those servers. If you don't already have BIND servers, you probably won't want to set these up because there are many benefits to using the Microsoft DNS Server service.

When you install the DNS Server service as part of the Active Directory installation process, you can use Active Directory–integrated zones and take advantage of the many replication and security benefits of Active Directory. Here, any server configured as a domain controller with DNS and using Active Directory–integrated zones is an Active Directory primary name server.

Here's how installation of DNS on the first domain controller in a domain works:

1. You use the Domain Controller Promotion tool (Dcpromo) to install the first domain controller. During the installation process, you are prompted to specify the Active Directory domain name, as shown in the following screen. This sets the DNS name for the domain as well.

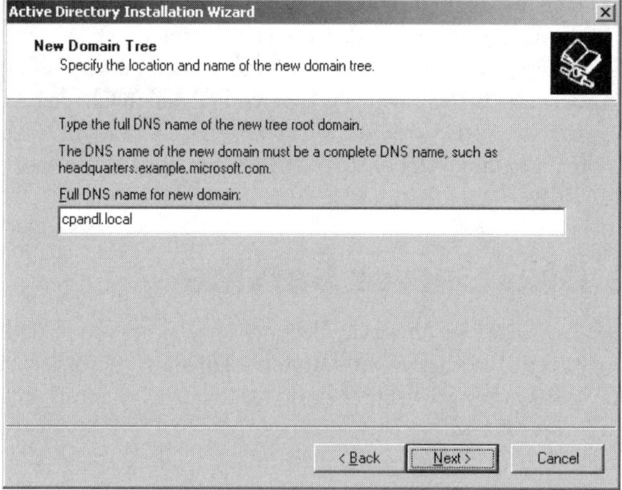

For more information about promoting domain controllers, see the section entitled "Installing Active Directory" on page 1202.

2 When the Active Directory installation process begins, the Active Directory Installation Wizard will check the currently configured DNS servers on the server. If the IP addresses aren't valid or can't be reached, you will be prompted to install DNS as shown in the following screen:

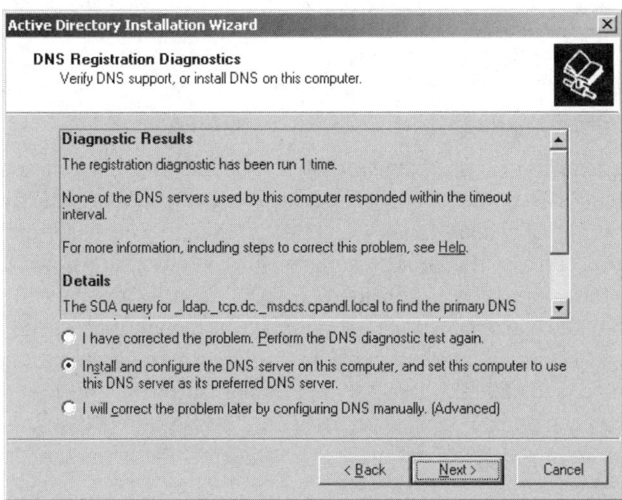

3 In most cases, you'll want to install DNS. If you install DNS, the Active Directory Installation Wizard will install and then configure DNS. As the next screen shows, this means a forward lookup zone will be created for the domain. The forward lookup zone will have a Start Of Authority (SOA), Name Server (NS), and Host address (A) record for the server you are working with. This designates it as the authoritative name server for the domain. If desired, you can also create reverse lookup zones to allow for IP-address-to-host-name lookups.

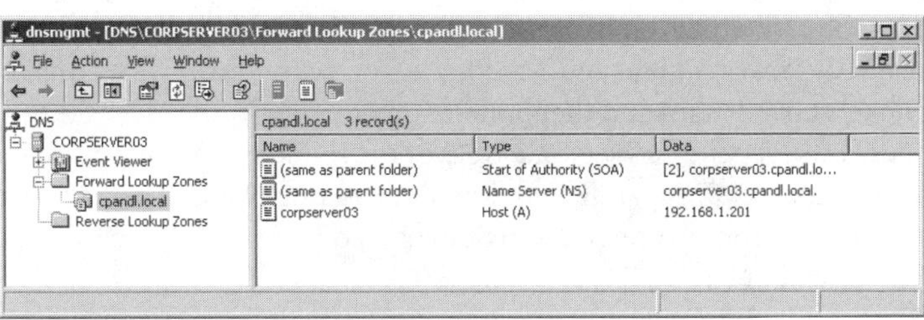

4 For the first DNS server in a forest, the Active Directory Installation Wizard creates the forest-side locator records and stores them in the _msdcs subdomain. Unlike Microsoft Windows 2000, Windows Server 2003 creates this as a separate zone, which is referred to as the *forest root zone*.

Inside Out

Forest root zones

The forest root zone is an important part of Active Directory. It is in this zone that Active Directory creates SRV resource records used when clients are looking for a particular resource such as global catalog servers, Lightweight Directory Access Protocol (LDAP) servers, and Kerberos servers. The _msdcs subdomain was moved to its own zone to improve performance with remote sites. With Windows 2000, remote sites have to replicate the entire DNS database to access forest root records, which means increased replication and bandwidth usage. As a separate zone, only the zone can be replicated to the DNS servers in remote sites as long as Active Directory application partitions are used. In Windows Server 2003, you can enable application partitions for use with DNS as discussed in the section entitled "Configuring Default Application Directory Partitions and Replication Scope" later in this chapter.

On subsequent domain controllers, you must specifically install the DNS Server service. You do this using the Add or Remove Programs utility or the Configure Your Server Wizard as detailed in the section entitled "DNS Setup" later in this chapter.

In an Active Directory domain, secondary and stub zones can also be useful, as discussed in the section entitled "DNS Zones and Zone Transfers" on page 858. In fact, in certain situations you might have to use a secondary or stub zone for name resolution to work properly. Consider the case when you have multiple trees in a forest, each in their own namespace. For instance, City Power & Light and The Phone Company are both part of one company and use the domains cpandl.com and thephone-company.com, respectively. If the namespaces for these domains are set up as separate trees of the same forest, your organization would have two namespaces. In the cpandl.com domain, you might want users to be able to access resources in thephone-company.com domain and vice versa. To do this, you would configure DNS as shown in Figure 27-1.

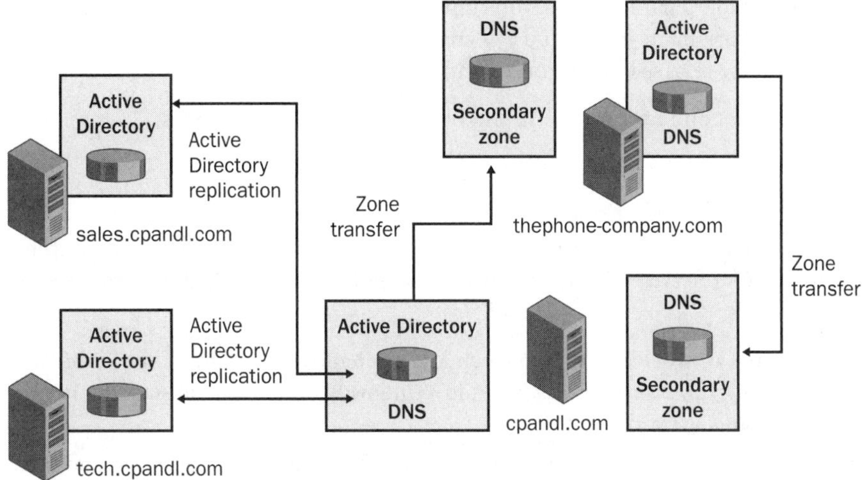

Figure 27-1. Using secondary zones with Active Directory.

The implementation steps for this example are as follows:

1. Set up a secondary or stub zone for thephone-company.com on the authoritative name server for cpandl.com.
2. Set up a secondary or stub zone for cpandl.com on the authoritative name server for thephone-company.com.
3. Configure zone transfers between cpandl.com and thephone-company.com.
4. Configure zone transfers between thephone-company.com and cpandl.com.

Using DNS Without Active Directory

On a domain without Active Directory, DNS servers act as standard primary or standard secondary name servers. You must install the DNS Server service on each primary or secondary server. You do this using the Add or Remove Programs utility or the Configure Your Server Wizard as detailed in the section entitled "DNS Setup" later in this chapter.

On primary name servers, you configure primary zones for forward lookups and as necessary for reverse lookups. The forward lookup zone will have an SOA, NS, and A record for the server you are working with. This designates it as the authoritative name server for the domain. You can also create reverse lookup zones to allow for IP-address-to-host-name lookups.

On secondary name servers, you configure secondary zones to store copies of the records on the primary name server. You can create secondary zones for the forward lookup zones as well as the reverse lookup zones configured on the primary.

Stub zones and forwarders are also options for these DNS servers.

DNS Setup

You can install the DNS Server service using the Add or Remove Programs utility or the Configure Your Server Wizard. Follow these steps for using the Add or Remove Programs utility to do this:

1. In Control Panel, double-click Add Or Remove Programs. Then in the Add Or Remove Programs dialog box, click Add Windows Components to start the Windows Components Wizard.
2. On the Windows Components page, select Networking Services, and then click Details.
3. In the Networking Services dialog box, shown in the following screen, ensure the correct components are selected, but don't clear selections if a service has already been installed.

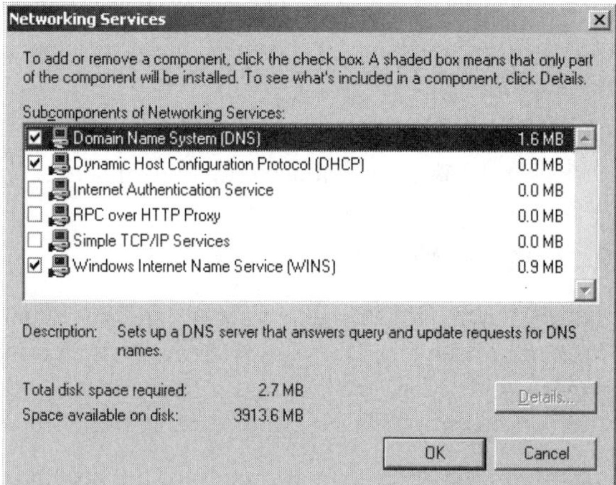

4. Click OK. Click Next to begin the installation, and then click Finish.

Follow these steps for using the Configure Your Server Wizard to do this:

1. Select Configure Your Server Wizard on the Administrative Tools menu. When the wizard starts, click Next twice.
2. The server's current roles are shown. Select DNS Server, and then click Next.

3. The wizard will then install DNS. When it finishes, the wizard launches the Configure A DNS Server Wizard, shown in the following screen.
4. If you want to create the initial DNS setup using the wizard, click Next and follow the steps outlined in the section entitled "Configuring DNS Using the Wizard" later in this chapter.
5. Otherwise, click Next when the wizard displays the Select Configuration Action page shown in the following screen. Select Configure Root Hints Only, click Next, and then click Finish. You will then need to configure zones, forwarders, and other DNS settings manually.

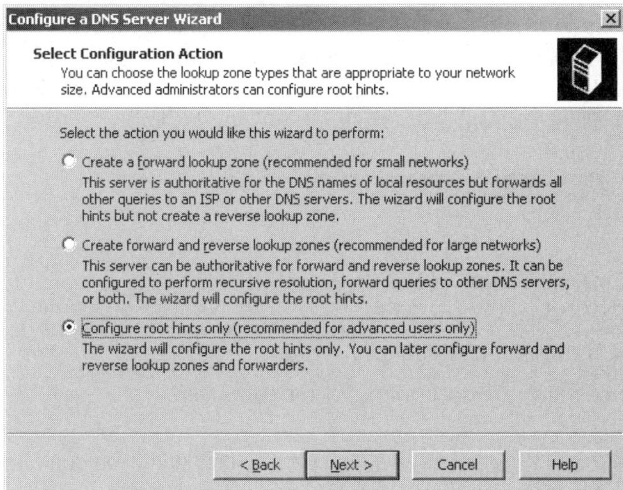

After you install the DNS Server service, the DNS console is available on the Administrative Tools menu. Start the console by clicking Start, Programs or All Programs as appropriate, Administrative Tools, DNS. Then select the DNS server you are working with to see its status. If you haven't yet created zones, the details pane will appear as shown in Figure 27-2. This is telling you to create a scope so that the clients can get IP addresses dynamically assigned by this server.

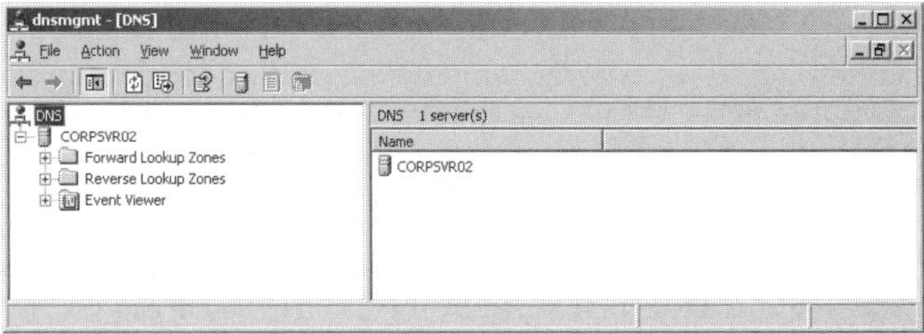

Figure 27-2. The DNS console.

You don't have to complete the rest of the configuration at the server. If you've installed the Administrative Tools (Adminpak.msi) as discussed in the section entitled "Installing Windows Server 2003 Administration Tools on Windows XP" on page 12, you can remotely manage and configure DNS. Simply start the DNS console on your workstation, right-click the DNS node in the left pane, and select Connect To DNS Server. In the Connect To DNS Server dialog box, select The Following Computer, type the name or IP address of the DNS server, and then click OK.

The command-line counterpart to the DNS console is DNSCMD. DNSCMD is included in the Windows Support Tools. From the command prompt on a computer running Windows Server 2003, you can use DNSCMD to perform most of the tasks available in the DNS console as well as to perform many troubleshooting tasks that are specific to DNSCMD. Unlike NETSH, DNSCMD doesn't offer internal command prompts. You can specify only the server you want to work with followed by the command and the command-line options to use for that command. Thus, the syntax is as follows:

```
dnscmd ServerName Command CommandOptions
```

where

- *ServerName* is the name or IP address of the DNS server you want to work with, such as CORPSVR03 or 192.168.10.15.
- *Command* is the command to use.
- *CommandOptions* are the options for the command.

Note If you are working on the server you want to configure, you don't have to type the server name or IP address.

After you set up a DNS server, you should configure the server's TCP/IP settings so that the server attempts to resolve its own DNS queries. You do this by setting the server's primary DNS server address to its own IP address. In Control Panel, access Network Connections, and then select or double-click the primary network connection. In the Status dialog box, click Properties.

In the Properties dialog box, open the Internet Protocol (TCP/IP) Properties dialog box by double-clicking Internet Protocol (TCP/IP). Select the Use The Following DNS Server Address. For Preferred DNS Server, type the computer's own IP address. Set an alternate DNS server as necessary. When you're finished, click OK.

You can also set the preferred DNS server IP address from the command line. Type the following command:

```
netsh interface ip set dns ConnectionName static ServerIPAddress
```

where *ConnectionName* is the name of the local area connection and *ServerIPAddress* is the IP address of the server.

Consider the following example:

```
netsh interface ip set dns "Local Area Connection" static 192.168.1.100
```

Here, you set the preferred DNS server address for the network connection named Local Area Connection to 192.168.1.100. The Static option says that you want to use the local setting for DNS rather than the Dynamic Host Configuration Protocol (DHCP) setting when applicable.

You can confirm the new setting by typing **ipconfig /all** at the command prompt and checking for the DNS server entry. The server should have the same setting for IP address and primary DNS server.

Configuring DNS Using the Wizard

From the DNS console, you can start the Configure A DNS Server Wizard and use it to help you set up a DNS server. This wizard is useful for helping you configure small networks that work with Internet service providers (ISPs) and large networks that use forwarding.

Inside Out

Are reverse lookups needed?

For small networks, the Configure A DNS Server Wizard creates only a forward lookup zone. For large networks, the Configure A DNS Server Wizard creates a forward lookup zone and a reverse lookup zone. This might get you to thinking whether reverse lookup zones are needed on your network. Computers use reverse lookups to find out who is contacting them. Often this is so that they can display a host name to users rather than an IP address. So, although a reverse lookup zone isn't created by the Configure A DNS Server Wizard for small networks, you might still want to create one. If so, follow the procedure discussed in the section entitled "Creating Reverse Lookup Zones" later in this chapter.

Configuring a Small Network Using the Configure A DNS Server Wizard

For a small network, you can use the wizard to set up your forward lookup zone and query forwarding to your ISP or other DNS servers. You can also choose to configure this zone as a primary or secondary zone. You use the primary zone option if your organization maintains its own zone. You use the secondary zone if your ISP maintains your zone. This gives you a read-only copy of the zone that can be used by internal clients. Because small network don't normally need reverse lookup zones, these are not created. You can, of course, create these zones later if needed.

To configure a small network using the Configure A DNS Server Wizard, follow these steps:

1. Click Next to continue in the Configure A DNS Server Wizard. If the wizard isn't already started, right-click the server entry in the DNS console, and select Configure A Server, then when the wizard starts, click Next.

> **Note** If the server you want to work with isn't shown, right-click the DNS node in the left pane, and select Connect To DNS Server. In the Connect To DNS Server dialog box, select The Following Computer, type the name or IP address of the DNS server, and then click OK.

2. Choose Create A Forward Lookup Zone (Recommended For Small Networks), as shown in Figure 27-3, and then click Next.

> **Note** If Active Directory is installed on the network, this zone will be automatically integrated with Active Directory. To avoid this, you can choose the second option, Create Forward And Reverse Lookup Zones (Recommended For Large Networks), and then proceed as discussed in the section entitled "Configuring a Large Network Using the Wizard" later in this chapter. When the wizard gets to the reverse lookup zone configuration part, you can skip this if you don't want to create a reverse lookup zone.

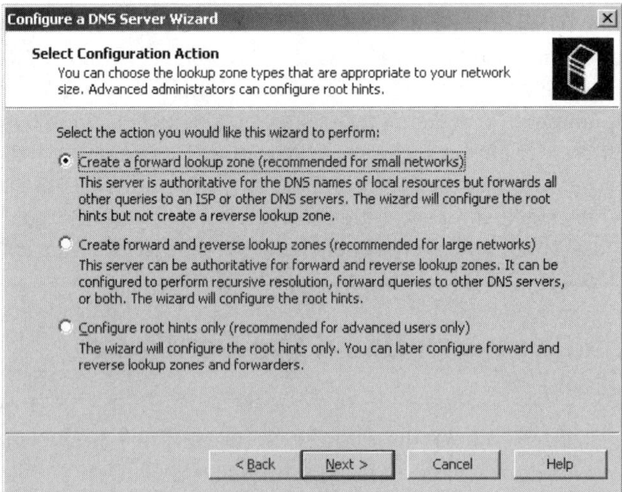

Figure 27-3. Select the first option to configure DNS for a small network.

3 As shown in Figure 27-4, you can now choose whether the DNS server or your ISP maintains the zone and then click Next. Keep the following in mind:

- If the DNS server maintains the zone, the wizard configures a primary zone that you control. This allows you to create and manage the DNS records for the organization.
- If your ISP maintains the zone, the wizard configures a secondary zone that will get its information from your ISP. This means the staff at the ISP will need to create and manage the DNS records for the organization—and you will need to pay them to do so.

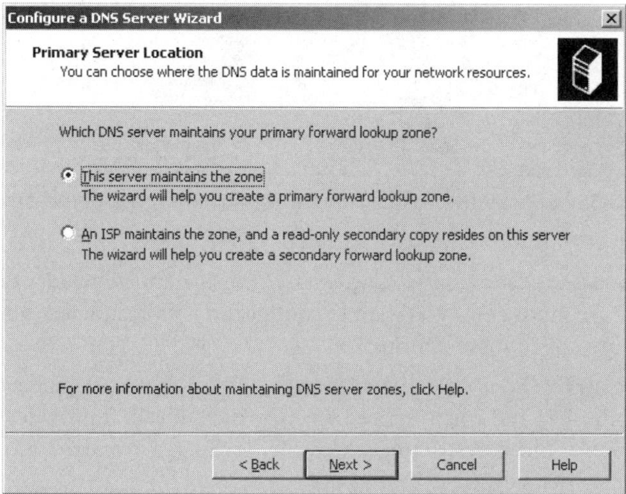

Figure 27-4. Specify whether the zone will be maintained on the server or by your ISP.

4 In the Zone Name page, type the full DNS name for the zone. The zone name should help determine how the zone fits into the DNS domain hierarchy. For example, if you're creating the primary server for the cpandl.com domain, you should type **cpandl.com** as the zone name. Click Next.

5 If your ISP maintains the zone, you see the Master DNS Servers page, as shown in Figure 27-5. Type the IP address of the primary DNS server that's maintaining the zone for you, and then click Add. Repeat this step to specify additional name servers at your ISP. Zone transfers will be configured to copy the zone information from these DNS servers.

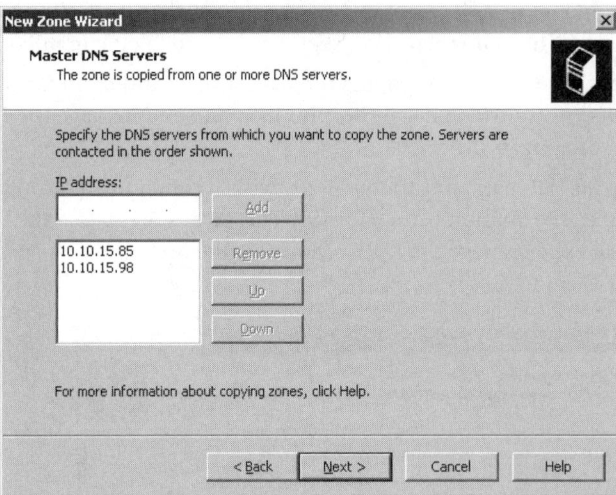

Figure 27-5. Specify the primary name server and other name servers at the ISP.

6 If you choose to maintain the zone, you see the Dynamic Update page, as shown in Figure 27-6. Choose how you want to configure dynamic updates, and then click Next. You can use one of these options:

- *Allow Only Secure Dynamic Updates*—This option is available only on domain controllers and when Active Directory is deployed. It provides for the best security possible by restricting which clients can perform dynamic updates.
- *Allow Both Nonsecure and Secure Dynamic Updates*—This option allows any client to update resource records in DNS. Although it allows both secure and nonsecure updates, it doesn't validate updates, which means dynamic updates are accepted from any client.
- *Do Not Allow Dynamic Updates*—Choosing this option disables dynamic updates in DNS. You should use this option only when the zone isn't integrated with Active Directory.

7 The Forwarders page allows you to configure forwarding of DNS queries. If you want internal DNS servers to forward queries that they can't resolve to another server, type the IP address for that server. You can optionally include the IP address for a second forwarder as well. If you don't want to use forwarders, select No, It Should Not Forward Queries.

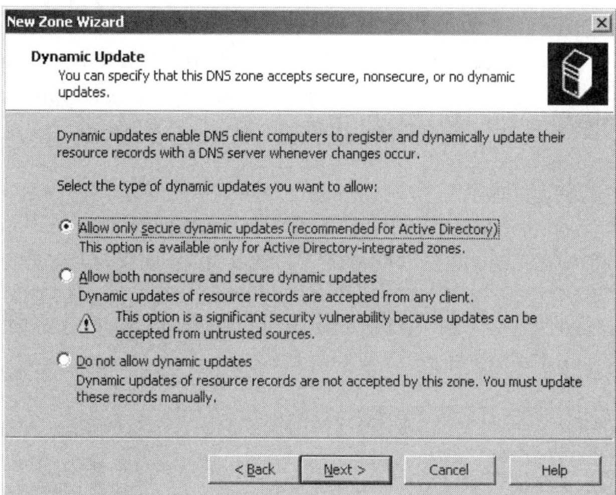

Figure 27-6. Set the dynamic updates options.

> **Note** Selecting the No, It Should Not Forward Queries option won't prevent internal name servers from forwarding queries altogether. A root hints file will still be created, which lists the root name servers on the public Internet. Thus, if you don't designate forwarders, such as the primary and secondary name servers of your ISP, the internal name servers will still forward queries. To prevent this, you must modify the root hints file as discussed in the section entitled "Security Considerations" on page 864.

8 When you click Next, the wizard will search for and retrieve the current root hints. Click Finish to complete the configuration and exit the wizard.

Configuring a Large Network Using the Configure A DNS Server Wizard

For a large network, you can use the wizard to set up your forward and reverse lookup zones and to set up forwarding with or without recursion. With recursion, queries for external resources are first forwarded to your designated servers, but if those servers are unavailable, the DNS server forwards queries to the root name servers. Without recursion, queries for external resources are only forwarded to your designated servers.

To configure a large network using the Configure A DNS Server Wizard, follow these steps:

1. Click Next to continue in the Configure A DNS Server Wizard. If the wizard isn't already started, right-click the server entry in the DNS console, and select Configure A Server. When the wizard starts, click Next.

Note If the server you want to work with isn't shown, right-click the DNS node in the left pane, and select Connect To DNS Server. In the Connect To DNS Server dialog box, select The Following Computer, type the name or IP address of the DNS server, and then click OK.

2. Choose Create Forward And Reverse Lookup Zones (Recommended For Large Networks), as shown in Figure 27-7, and then click Next.

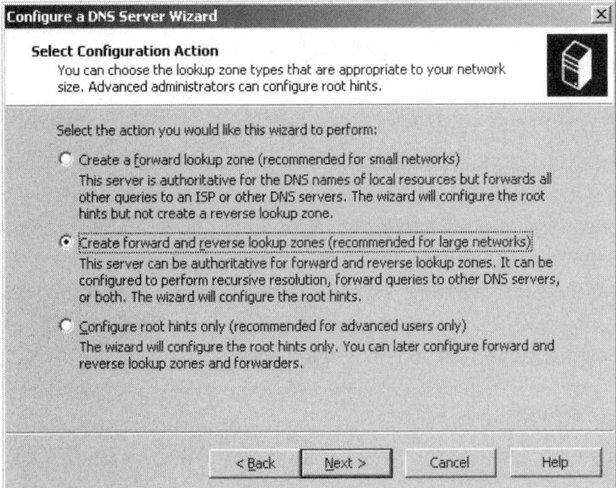

Figure 27-7. Select the second option to configure DNS for a large network.

3. To create a forward lookup zone, accept the default option on the Forward Lookup Zone page, and then click Next. Otherwise, click No, and skip to step 10.
4. As Figure 27-8 shows, you can now select the zone type. Choose one of the following options, and then click Next:
   - *Primary Zone*—Use this option to create a primary zone and designate this server to be authoritative for the zone. Ensure that Store The Zone In Active Directory is selected if you want to integrate DNS with Active Directory. Otherwise, clear this option so that a standard primary zone is created.
   - *Secondary Zone*—Use this option to create a secondary zone. This means the server will have a read-only copy of the zone and must use zone transfers to get updates.

- *Stub Zone*—Use this option to create a stub zone. This creates only the necessary glue records for the zone. Optionally, specify that this zone should be integrated with Active Directory. This means the zone will be stored in Active Directory and be updated using Active Directory replication.

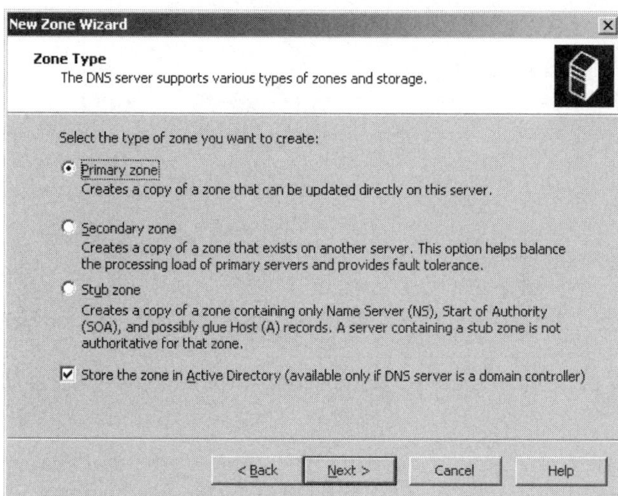

Figure 27-8. Select the zone type.

5 If you created an Active Directory–integrated zone, specify the replication scope, and then click Next. As Figure 27-9 shows, you have the following options:

- *To All DNS Servers In The Active Directory Forest*—Enables replication of the zone information to all domains in the Active Directory forest. Each DNS server in the forest will receive a copy of the zone information and get updates through replication.
- *To All DNS Servers In The Active Directory Domain*—Enables replication of the zone information in the current domain. Each DNS server in the domain will receive a copy of the zone information and get updates through replication.
- *To All Domain Controllers In The Active Directory Domain*—Replicates zone information to all domain controllers in the Active Directory domain. As with a Windows 2000 domain, all domain controllers will get a copy of the zone information and get updates through replication regardless of whether they are also running the DNS Server service.
- *To All Domain Controllers Specified In The Scope Of The Following Application Partition*—If you've configured application partitions other than the default partitions, you can limit the scope of replication to a designated application partition. Any domain controllers configured with the application partition will get a copy of the zone information and get updates through replication regardless of whether they are also running the DNS Server service.

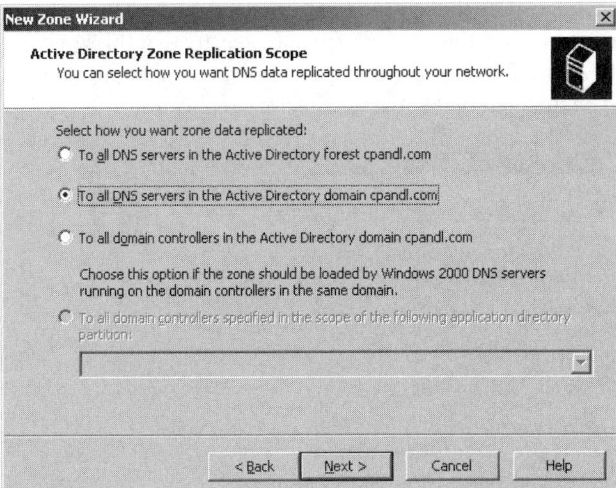

Figure 27-9. Select the replication scope if you are using Active Directory integration.

6 In the Zone Name page, type the full DNS name for the zone. The zone name should help determine how the zone fits into the DNS domain hierarchy. For example, if you're creating the primary server for the cpandl.com domain, you should type **cpandl.com** as the zone name. Click Next.

7 If you're creating a standard primary zone, you see the Zone File page. This page allows you to create a new zone file or use an existing zone file. In most cases, you'll simply accept the default name and allow the wizard to create the file for you in the %SystemRoot%\System32\Dns folder. If you are migrating from a BIND DNS server or have a preexisting zone file, you can select Use This Existing File, and then type the name of the file that you've copied to the %SystemRoot%\System32\Dns folder. Click Next when you are ready to continue.

8 If you're creating a secondary zone, you see the Master DNS Servers page. Type the IP address of the primary DNS server that's maintaining the zone, and then click Add. Repeat this step to specify additional name servers. Zone transfers will be configured to copy the zone information from these DNS servers.

9 On the Dynamic Update page, choose how you want to configure dynamic updates and then click Next. You can use one of the following options:

- *Allow Only Secure Dynamic Updates*—This option is available only on domain controllers and when Active Directory is deployed. It provides for the best security possible by restricting which clients can perform dynamic updates.

- *Allow Both Nonsecure And Secure Dynamic Updates*—This option allows any client to update resource records in DNS. Although it allows both secure and nonsecure updates, it doesn't validate updates, which means dynamic updates are accepted from any client.
- *Do Not Allow Dynamic Updates*—Choosing this option disables dynamic updates in DNS. You should use this option only when the zone isn't integrated with Active Directory.

10 To create a reverse lookup zone, accept the default option in the Reverse Lookup Zone page, and then click Next. Otherwise, click No, and skip to step 16.

11 On the Zone Type page, you can select the zone type. The options available are the same as before. Click Next after making a selection.

12 If you created an Active Directory–integrated zone, specify the replication scope, and then click Next.

13 In the Reverse Lookup Zone Name Page, type the network ID for the reverse lookup zone, as shown in Figure 27-10, and then click Next. If you have multiple subnets on the same network, such as 192.168.1, 192.168.2, and 192.168.3, you should enter only the network portion for the zone name, such as 192.168 rather than the complete network ID. The DNS Server service will then fill in the necessary subnet zones as you use IP addresses on a particular subnet.

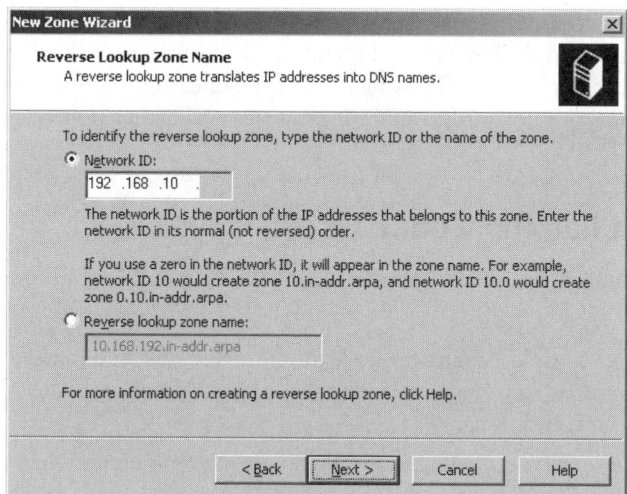

Figure 27-10. Set the network ID for the reverse lookup zone.

14 If you're creating a standard secondary zone, you see the Zone File page. This page allows you to create a new zone file or use an existing zone file.

15 On the Dynamic Update page, choose how you want to configure dynamic updates, and then click Next.

16 The Forwarders page allows you to configure forwarding of DNS queries. If you want internal DNS servers to forward queries that they can't resolve to another server, type the IP address of that server. You can optionally include the IP address for a second forwarder as well. If you don't want to use forwarders, select No, It Should Not Forward Queries.

Note Selecting the No, It Should Not Forward Queries option won't prevent internal name servers from forwarding queries altogether. A root hints file will still be created, which lists the root name servers on the public Internet. Thus, if you don't designate forwarders, such as the primary and secondary name servers of your ISP, the internal name servers will still forward queries. To prevent this, you must modify the root hints file as discussed in the section entitled "Security Considerations" on page 864.

17 When you click Next, the wizard will search for and retrieve the current root hints. Click Finish to complete the configuration and exit the wizard.

Configuring DNS Zones, Subdomains, Forwarders, and Zone Transfers

Windows Server 2003 supports primary, secondary, Active Directory–integrated, and stub zones, each of which can be created to support either forward lookups or reverse lookups. Forward lookup queries allow a client to resolve a host name to an IP address. Reverse lookups allow a client to resolve an IP address to a host name. At times you might also need to configure subdomains, forwarders, and zone transfers. All of these topics are discussed in this section.

Creating Forward Lookup Zones

To create the initial forward lookup zone or additional forward lookup zones on a server, follow these steps:

1 In the DNS console, expand the node for the server you want to work with. Right-click the Forward Lookup Zone entry, and then choose New Zone. Afterward, in the New Zone Wizard, click Next.

2 Select the zone type. Choose one of the following options, and then click Next:

- *Primary Zone*—Use this option to create a primary zone and designate this server to be authoritative for the zone. Ensure that Store The Zone In Active Directory is selected if you want to integrate DNS with Active Directory. Otherwise, clear this option so that a standard primary zone is created.

- *Secondary Zone*—Use this option to create a secondary zone. This means the server will have a read-only copy of the zone and will need to use zone transfers to get updates.
- *Stub Zone*—Use this option to create a stub zone. This creates only the necessary glue records for the zone. Optionally, specify that this zone should be integrated with Active Directory. This means the zone will be stored in Active Directory and be updated using Active Directory replication.

3 If you created an Active Directory–integrated zone, specify the replication scope, and then click Next. You have the following options:

- *To All DNS Servers In The Active Directory Forest*—Enables replication of the zone information to all domains in the Active Directory forest. Each DNS server in the forest will receive a copy of the zone information and get updates through replication.
- *To All DNS Servers In The Active Directory Domain*—Enables replication of the zone information in the current domain. Each DNS server in the domain will receive a copy of the zone information and get updates through replication.
- *To All Domain Controllers In The Active Directory Domain*—Replicates zone information to all domain controllers in the Active Directory domain. As with a Windows 2000 domain, all domain controllers will get a copy of the zone information and get updates through replication regardless of whether they are also running the DNS Server service.
- *To All Domain Controllers Specified In The Scope Of The Following Application Partition*—If you've configured application partitions, you can limit the scope of replication to a designated application partition. Any domain controllers configured with the application partition will get a copy of the zone information and get updates through replication regardless of whether they are also running the DNS Server service.

4 In the Zone Name page, type the full DNS name for the zone. The zone name should help determine how the zone fits into the DNS domain hierarchy. For example, if you're creating the primary server for the cpandl.com domain, you should type **cpandl.com** as the zone name. Click Next.

5 If you're creating a standard primary zone, you see the Zone File page. This page allows you to create a new zone file or use an existing zone file. In most cases, you'll simply accept the default name and allow the wizard to create the file for you in the %SystemRoot%\System32\Dns folder. If you are migrating from a BIND DNS server or have a preexisting zone file, you can select Use This Existing File and then type the name of the file that you've copied to the %SystemRoot%\System32\Dns folder. Click Next when you are ready to continue.

6 If you're creating a secondary zone, you see the Master DNS Servers page. Type the IP address of the primary DNS server that's maintaining the zone, and then click Add. Repeat this step to specify additional name servers. Zone transfers will be configured to copy the zone information from these DNS servers.

7 On the Dynamic Update page, choose how you want to configure dynamic updates, and then click Next. You can use one of these options:

- *Allow Only Secure Dynamic Updates*—This option is available only on domain controllers and when Active Directory is deployed. It provides for the best security possible by restricting which clients can perform dynamic updates.
- *Allow Both Nonsecure and Secure Dynamic Updates*—This option allows any client to update resource records in DNS. Although it allows both secure and nonsecure updates, it doesn't validate updates, which means dynamic updates are accepted from any client.
- *Do Not Allow Dynamic Updates*—Choosing this option disables dynamic updates in DNS. You should use this option only when the zone isn't integrated with Active Directory.

8 Click Next and then click Finish to complete the configuration and exit the wizard.

Creating Reverse Lookup Zones

To create the initial reverse lookup zone or additional reverse lookup zones on a server, follow these steps:

1 In the DNS console, expand the node for the server you want to work with. Right-click the Reverse Lookup Zone entry, and choose New Zone. Afterward, in the New Zone Wizard, click Next.

2 On the Zone Type page, you can select the zone type. The options available are the same as for forward lookup zones. Click Next after making a selection.

3 If you created an Active Directory–integrated zone, specify the replication scope, and then click Next.

4 In the Reverse Lookup Zone Name Page, type the network ID for the reverse lookup zone, and then click Next. If you have multiple subnets on the same network, such as 192.168.1, 192.168.2, and 192.168.3, you should enter only the network portion for the zone name, such as 192.168, rather than the complete network ID. The DNS Server service will then fill-in the necessary subnet zones as you use IP addresses on a particular subnet.

5 If you're creating a standard secondary zone, you see the Zone File page. This page allows you to create a new zone file or use an existing zone file.

6 On the Dynamic Update page, choose how you want to configure dynamic updates, and then click Next.

7 Click Next and then click Finish to complete the configuration and exit the wizard.

Configuring Forwarders and Conditional Forwarding

In a normal configuration, if a DNS name server can't resolve a request, it forwards the request for resolution. A server to which DNS queries are forwarded is referred to as a forwarder. You can specifically designate forwarders that should be used by your internal DNS servers. For example, if you designate your ISP's primary and secondary name servers as forwarders, queries that your internal name servers can't resolve will be forwarded to these servers. Forwarding still takes place, however, even if you don't specifically designate forwarders. The reason for this is that the root hints file specifies the root name servers for the public Internet.

Any time forwarders are not specified or available requests are forwarded to the root name servers. The root name servers then forward the request to the appropriate top-level domain name server, which forwards it to the next level domain server, and so on. This process is referred to as *recursion*, and, as you can see, this involves a number of forwarding actions.

Another forwarding option is to configure what is called a conditional forwarder. When using conditional forwarding, you can tell your DNS name servers that if they see a request for domain XYZ, they should not forward it to the public DNS name servers for resolution. Instead, the name servers should forward the request directly to the authoritative name server for the XYZ domain.

You can configure these forwarding options in the DNS console. In the DNS console, right-click the server you want to work with, and select Properties. In the Properties dialog box, select the Forwarders tab, as shown in Figure 27-11.

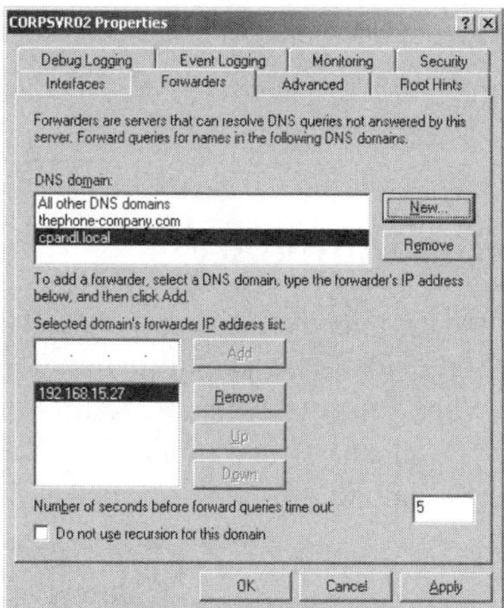

Figure 27-11. The Forwarders tab.

You can now do one of the following:

- **Configure a forwarder** To forward queries that internal servers can't resolve to another server, select All Other DNS Domains, type the IP address for this server, and click Add. You can optionally include the IP address for a second forwarder as well.
- **Configure a conditional forwarder** To forward queries conditionally for a specific domain, click New to the right of the DNS domain boxes. In the New Forwarder dialog box, type the DNS domain name for which conditional forwarding should be configured, such as thephone-company.com, and click OK. With the conditional domain selected under DNS Domain, type the IP address for the primary server in the conditional domain, and then click Add. You can optionally include the IP address for a second forwarder in the conditional domain as well.
- **Set forwarder query timeout** Use the Number Of Seconds Before Forward Queries Time Out to set a timeout for queries in seconds. By default, a DNS server will continue to attempt to contact and use a listed forwarded for 5 seconds. When the timeout expires, the server moves to the next forwarder on the list and does the same. When there are no additional forwarders, the server uses the root hints to locate a root server to which the query can be forwarded.
- **Disable recursion** To disable recursion, select Do Not Use Recursion For This Domain. If this option is selected and no forwarders are configured, a query automatically fails. If this option is selected and forwarders don't respond in the timeout interval, a query automatically fails. Clients configured with another DNS server would then try to resolve the query on this server.

> **Note** A DNS server configured to use forwarders and to not use recursion is called a *subordinate name server*. The reason for this is that the server can forward queries only to designated servers and isn't free to try to resolve the query using the root hints.

Configuring Subdomains and Delegating Authority

Your organization's domain structure is separate from its zone configuration. If you create subdomains of a parent domain, you can add these subdomains to the parent domain's zone or create separate zones for the subdomains. When you create separate zones, you must tell DNS about the other servers that have authority over a particular subdomain. You do this by telling the primary name server for the parent domain that you've delegated authority for a subdomain.

When you add subdomains of a parent domain to the same zone as the parent domain, you have a single large namespace hosted by primary servers. This gives you a single unit to manage, which is good when you want central control over DNS in the domain. The disadvantage is that as the number of subdomains in the zone grows, there's more and more to manage, and at some point, the DNS server can become overburdened, especially if dynamic updates are allowed and there are hundreds or thousands of host records.

When you create a separate zone for a subdomain, you have an additional unit of management that can be placed on the same DNS server or on a different DNS server. This means that you can delegate control over the zone to someone else, which would allow branch offices or other departments within the organization to manage their own DNS services. If the zone is on another DNS server, you shift the load associated with that zone to another server. The disadvantage is that you lose central control over DNS.

> **Note** It isn't possible to combine domains from different branches of the namespace and place them in a single zone. As a result, domains that are part of the same Active Directory forest but on different trees must be in separate zones. Thus, you would need separate zones for cohowinery.com and cohovineyards.com.

To create subdomains in separate zones on the same server as the parent domain, complete the following steps:

1. Create the necessary forward and reverse lookup zones for the subdomains as described earlier in this chapter in the sections "Creating Forward Lookup Zones" and "Creating Reverse Lookup Zones," respectively.
2. You don't need to delegate authority because these subdomains are on the primary name server for the parent domain. This server automatically has control over the zones.

To create subdomains in separate zones and on separate servers, complete the following steps:

1. Install a DNS server in each subdomain, and then create the necessary forward and reverse lookup zones for the subdomains as described earlier in this chapter in the sections "Creating Forward Lookup Zones" and "Creating Reverse Lookup Zones," respectively.
2. On the primary DNS server for the parent domain, you must delegate authority to each subdomain. In the DNS console, expand the node for the server on which the parent domain is located, and then expand the related Forward Lookup Zones folder.
3. Right-click the parent domain entry, and then select New Delegation. This starts the New Delegation Wizard. Click Next.
4. As shown in Figure 27-12, type the name of the subdomain, such as **ny**. Check the fully qualified domain name (FQDN) to ensure that it is correct, and then click Next.

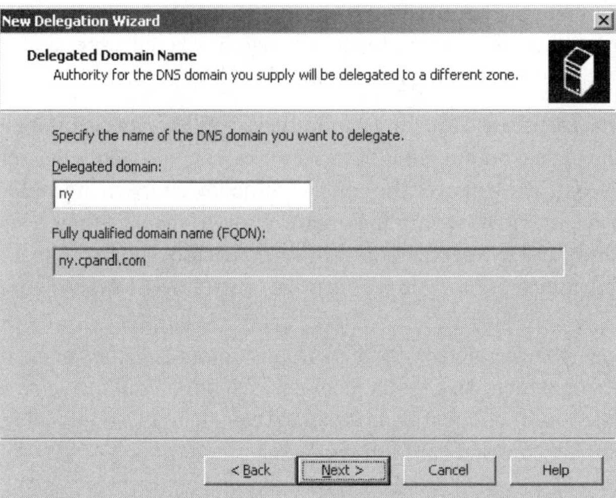

Figure 27-12. Specify the subdomain name.

5 In the Name Servers page, click Add. As shown in Figure 27-13, the New Resource Record dialog box is displayed.

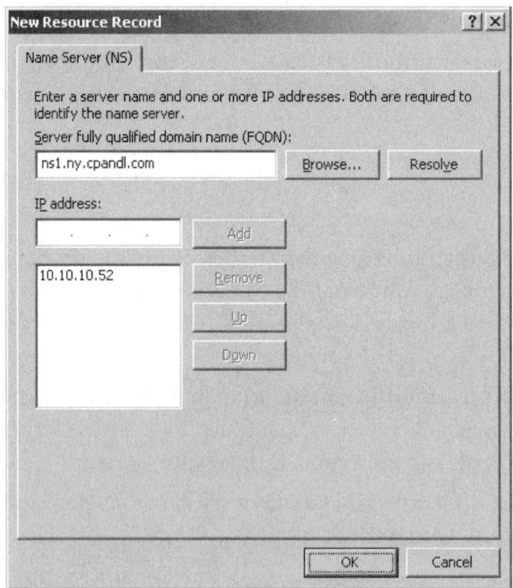

Figure 27-13. Specify the server name and IP address.

6 In the Server Fully Qualified Domain Name (FQDN) box, type the fully qualified host name of a DNS server for the subdomain, such as ns1.ny.cpandl.com, and then click Resolve. If the IP address of the name server is filled in for you, click Add, and then add other IP addresses for this name server as necessary.

> **Note** You must specify the server name and at least one IP address. The order of the entries determines which IP address is used first. You can change the order as necessary using the Up and Down buttons.

7. Click OK to close the New Resource Record dialog box. Repeat steps 5 and 6 to specify other authoritative DNS servers for the subdomain.
8. Click Next, and then click Finish.

Configuring Zone Transfers

Zone transfers are used to send a read-only copy of zone information to secondary DNS servers, which can be located in the same domain or in other domains. Windows Server 2003 supports three zone transfer methods:

- Standard zone transfers in which a secondary server requests a full copy of a zone from a primary server.
- Incremental zone transfers in which a secondary server requests only the changes that it needs to synchronize its copy of the zone information with the primary server's copy.
- Active Directory zone transfers in which changes to zones are replicated to all domain controllers in the domain (or a subset if application partitions are configured) using Active Directory replication.

Active Directory zone transfers are automatically used and configured when you use Active Directory–integrated zones. If you have secondary name servers, these name servers can't automatically request standard or incremental zone transfers. To allow this, you must first enable zone transfers on the primary name server. Zone transfers are disabled by default to enhance DNS server security. Speaking of security, although you can allow zone transfers to any DNS server, this opens the server to possible attack. It is better to designate specific name servers that are permitted to request zone transfers.

Inside Out

Incremental zone transfers

To manage incremental transfers, DNS servers track changes that have been made to a zone between each increment of a zone's serial number. Secondary servers use the zone's serial number to determine whether changes have been made to the zone. If the serial number matches what the secondary server has for the zone, no changes have been made and an incremental transfer isn't necessary. If the serial number doesn't match, the secondary server's copy of the zone isn't up-to-date and the secondary server then requests only the changes that have occurred since the last time the secondary zone was updated.

Zone transfers can be enabled for domains and subdomains in forward lookup zones and subnets in reverse lookup zones. You enable zone transfers on primary name servers. If a server is a secondary name server, it is already configured to perform zone transfers with the primary name server in the zone.

Using the DNS console, you can enable zone transfers on a primary name server and restrict the secondary name servers that can request zone transfers. In the DNS console, expand the node for the primary name server, and then expand the related Forward Lookup Zones or Reverse Lookup Zones folder as appropriate. Right-click the domain or subnet you want to configure, and then choose Properties. In the Properties dialog box, select the Zone Transfers tab, as shown in Figure 27-14.

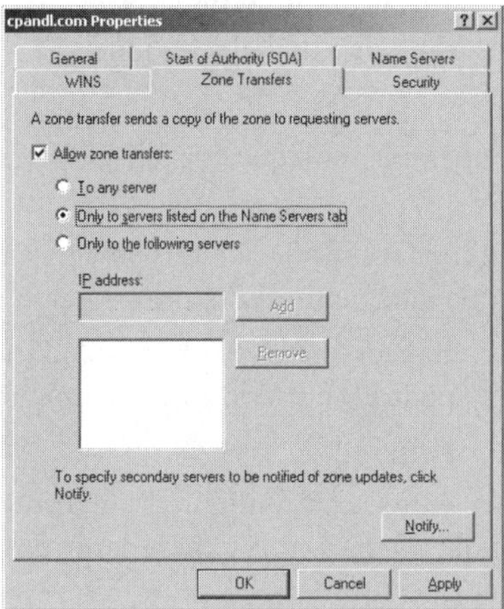

Figure 27-14. Configure zone transfers for a domain or subnet.

Select Allow Zone Transfers. You have three zone transfer options:

- **To Any Server** Select To Any Server to allow any DNS server to request zone transfers.
- **Only To Servers Listed On The Name Servers Tab** Select Only To Servers Listed On The Name Servers Tab to restrict transfers to name servers listed in the Name Servers tab, and then click the Name Servers tab. Then complete these steps:
  1. The Name Servers list shows the DNS servers currently configured to be authoritative for the zone and includes DNS servers that host secondary zones. If a secondary server isn't listed and you want to authorize the server to request zone transfers, click Add. This displays the New Resource Record dialog box.
  2. In the Server Fully Qualified Domain Name (FQDN) field, type the fully qualified host name of a secondary server for the domain, and then click Resolve. If

the IP address of the name server is filled in for you, click Add, and then add other IP addresses for this name server as necessary.

3. Click OK to close the New Resource Record dialog box. Repeat this process to specify other secondary DNS servers for the domain or subnet.

- **Only The Following Servers** Select Only The Following Servers to restrict transfers to a list of approved servers. Then complete these steps.

    1. Type the IP addresses of a secondary server that should receive zone transfers, and then click Add.
    2. Repeat this process to specify other secondary DNS servers for the domain or subnet.

When you are finished, click OK to close the Properties dialog box.

Configuring Secondary Notification

When changes are made to a zone on the primary server, secondary servers can be automatically notified of the changes. This allows the secondary servers to request zone transfers. You can configure automatic notification of secondary servers using the DNS console.

In the DNS console, expand the node for the primary name server, and then expand the related Forward Lookup Zones or Reverse Lookup Zones folder as appropriate. Right-click the domain or subnet you want to configure, and then choose Properties. In the Properties dialog box, select the Zone Transfers tab. Click Notify in the lower-right corner of the Zone Transfers tab. This displays the Notify dialog box, as shown in Figure 27-15.

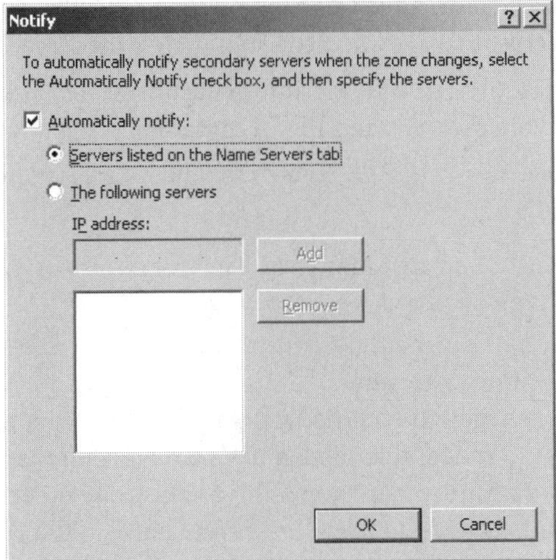

Figure 27-15. Configure secondary notification.

Select Automatically Notify. You have two notification options:

- **Servers Listed On The Name Servers Tab** Select Servers Listed On The Name Servers Tab to notify name servers listed in the Name Servers tab.
- **The Following Servers** Select The Following Servers to specify the name servers that should be notified. Then complete these steps:
  1. Type the IP addresses of a secondary server that should receive notification, and then click Add.
  2. Repeat this process to notify other secondary DNS servers for the domain or subnet.

When you are finished, click OK twice.

Adding Resource Records

When you create a zone in Windows Server 2003, several records are created automatically.

- For a forward lookup zone, these records include an SOA record, an NS record, and an A record. The SOA record contains information about how resource records in the zone should be used and cached. The NS record contains the name of the authoritative name server, which is the server on which the zone was configured. The A record is the host address record for the name server.
- For a reverse lookup zone, these records include an SOA record, an NS record, and a PTR record. The SOA record contains information about how resource records in the zone should be used and cached. The NS record contains the name of the authoritative name server, which is the server on which the zone was configured. The PTR record is the pointer record for the name server that allows reverse lookups on the server's IP address.
- When you use Active Directory, SRV records are automatically created as well for domain controllers, global catalog servers, and PDC Emulators.
- When you allow dynamic updates, A and PTR records for clients are automatically created for any computer using DHCP.

Any other records that you need must be created manually. The technique you use to create additional records depends on the type of record.

> **Tip** **Create and change records on primary servers**
> When you create records or make changes to records, you should do so on a primary server. For Active Directory–integrated zones, this means any domain controller running the DNS Server service. For standard zones, this means the primary name server only. After you make changes to standard zones, right-click the server entry in the DNS console and select Update Server Data File. This increments the serial number for zones as necessary to ensure secondary name servers know changes have been made. You do not need to do this for Active Directory–integrated zones because Active Directory replicates changes automatically.

Host Address (A) and Pointer (PTR) Records

Host Address (A) records contain the name of a host and its IPv4 address. Any computer that has multiple network interfaces or IP addresses should have multiple address records. Pointer (PTR) records enable reverse lookups by creating a pointer that maps an IP address to a host name.

You do not need to create A and PTR records for hosts that use dynamic DNS. These records are created automatically. For hosts that don't use dynamic DNS, you can create a new host entry with A and PTR records by completing the following steps:

1. In the DNS console, expand the node for the primary name server, and then expand the related Forward Lookup Zones folder. Right-click the domain to which you want to add the records, and then choose New Host (A). This displays the dialog box shown in Figure 27-16.

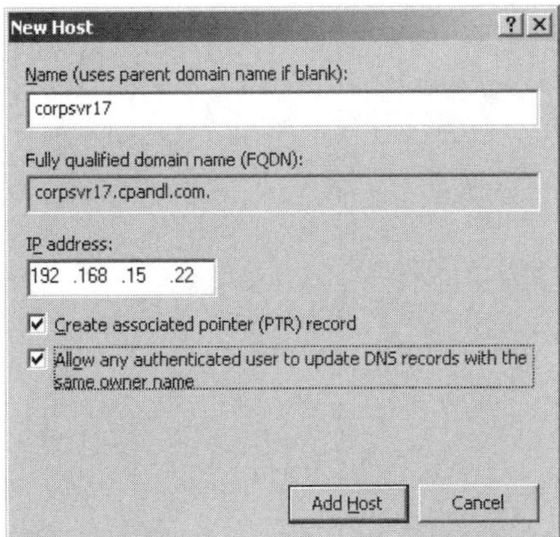

Figure 27-16. Create a host record.

2. Type the host name, such as **corpsrv17**, and then type the IP address, such as **192.168.15.22**.
3. If a reverse lookup zone has been created for the domain and you want to create a PTR record for this host, select the Create Associated Pointer (PTR) Record option.

> **Note** If you are working with an Active Directory–integrated zone, you have the option of allowing any authenticated client with the designated host name to update the record. To enable this, select Allow Any Authenticated User To Update DNS Records With The Same Owner Name. This is a nonsecure dynamic update where only the client host name is checked.

4 Click Add Host. Repeat this process as necessary to add other hosts.

5 Click Done when you're finished.

If you opt not to create a PTR record when you create an A record, you can create the PTR later as necessary. In the DNS console, expand the node for the primary name server, and then expand the related Reverse Lookup Zones folder. Right-click the subnet to which you want to add the record, and then choose New Pointer (PTR). This displays the dialog box shown in Figure 27-17. Type the Host IP Number for the designated subnet, such as **206**, and then type the FQDN for the host, such as **corpsvr05.cpandl.com**. Click OK.

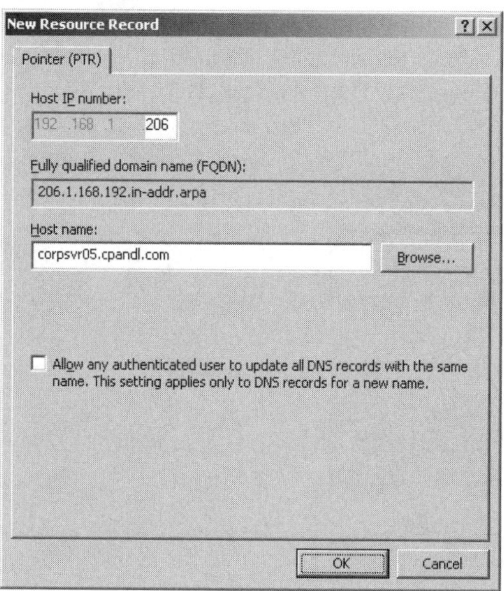

Figure 27-17. Create a PTR record.

Inside Out

Using round robin for load balancing

If a host name has multiple A records associated with it, the DNS Server service will use round robin for load balancing. With round robin, the DNS server cycles between the A records so that queries are routed proportionally to the various IP addresses that are configured. Here's how round robin works: Say that your organization's Web server gets a ton of hits—so much that the single Web server you've set up can't handle the load anymore.

To spread the workload, you configure three machines, one with the IP address 192.168.12.18, one with the IP address 192.168.12.19, and one with the IP address 192.168.12.20. On the DNS server, you configure a separate A record for each IP address, but use the same host name: www.cpandl.com. This tells the DNS server to use round robin to balance the incoming requests proportionally. As requests come in, DNS will respond in a fixed circular fashion with an IP address. For a series of requests, the first user might be directed to 192.168.12.18, the next user to 192.168.12.19, and the next user to 192.168.12.20. The next time around the order will be the same so the fourth user is directed to 192.168.12.18, the next user to 192.168.12.19, and the next user to 192.168.12.20. As you can see, with three servers, each server will get approximately one-third of the incoming requests and hopefully about one-third of the workload as well.

Round robin isn't meant to be a replacement for clustering technologies, but it is an easy and fast way to get basic load balancing. Support for round robin is enabled by default. If you have to disable round robin, type **dnscmd *ServerName* /config /roundrobin 0**. To enable round robin again later, type **dnscmd *ServerName* /config /roundrobin 1**. In both cases, *ServerName* is the name or IP address of the DNS server you want to configure.

Canonical Name (CNAME) Records

Canonical Name (CNAME) records create aliases for host names. This allows a host to be referred to by multiple names in DNS. The most common use is when a host provides a common service, such as World Wide Web (WWW) or File Transfer Protocol (FTP) service, and you want it to have a friendly name rather than a complex name. For example, you might want www.cpandl.com to be an alias for the host dc06.cpandl.com.

To create an alias for a host name in the DNS console, expand the node for the primary name server, and then expand the related Forward Lookup Zones folder. Right-click the domain to which you want to add the records, and then choose New Alias (CNAME). This displays the dialog box shown in Figure 27-18. Type the alias for the host name, such as **www**, and then type the FQDN for the host, such as **corpsvr17.cpandl.com**. Click OK.

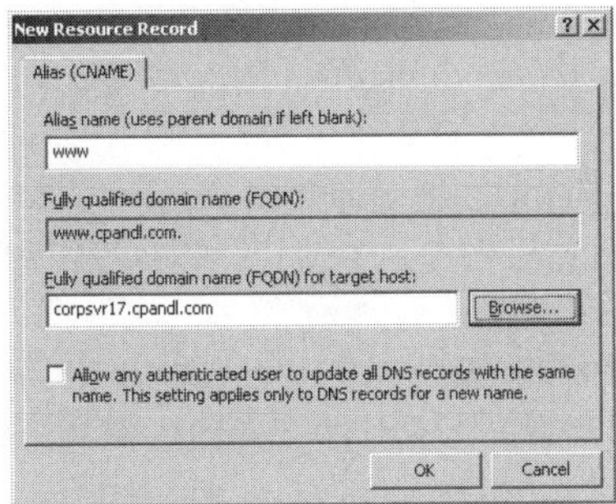

Figure 27-18. Create a new alias.

Mail Exchanger (MX) Records

Mail Exchanger (MX) records designate a mail exchange server for the domain, which allows mail to be delivered to the correct mail servers in the domain. For example, if an MX record is set for the domain cpandl.com, all mail sent to *Username*@cpandl.com will be directed to the server specified in the MX record.

You can create an MX record by completing the following steps:

1. In the DNS console, expand the node for the primary name server, and then expand the related Forward Lookup Zones folder. Right-click the domain to which you want to add the records, and then choose New Mail Exchanger (MX). This displays the dialog box shown in Figure 27-19.

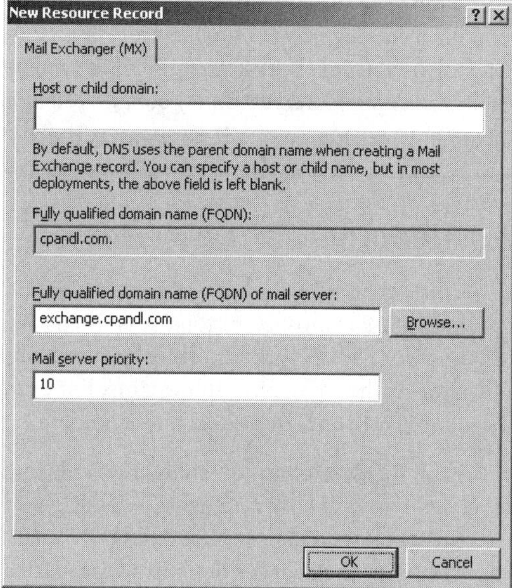

Figure 27-19. Create an MX record.

2. Consider leaving the Host Or Child Domain box blank. A blank entry specifies the mail exchanger name is the same as the parent domain name, which is typically what is desired.
3. Type the FQDN of the mail exchanger in the Fully Qualified Domain Name (FQDN) Of Mail Server box, such as **exchange.cpandl.com**. This is the name used to route mail for delivery.
4. Specify the priority of the mail server relative to other mail servers in the domain. The mail server with the lowest priority is the mail server that is tried first when mail must be routed to a mail server in the domain.
5. Click OK.

Name Server (NS) Records

Name Server (NS) records provide a list of authoritative servers for a domain, which allows DNS lookups within various zones. Each primary and secondary name server in a domain should be declared through this record. These records are created automatically when Active Directory–integrated zones are used. For standard zones, you can create an NS record by doing the following:

1. In the DNS console, expand the node for the primary name server, and then expand the related Forward Lookup Zones or Reverse Lookup Zones folder as appropriate.
2. Right-click the domain of the subnet for which you want to create name servers, and then select Properties. In the Properties dialog box select the Name Servers tab, as shown in Figure 27-20.

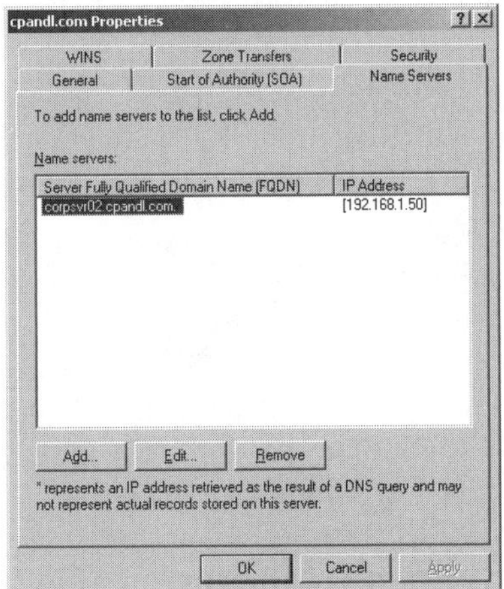

Figure 27-20. The Name Servers tab lists current name servers for the domain or subnet.

3. The Name Servers list shows the DNS servers currently configured to be authoritative for the zone and includes DNS servers that host secondary zones. If a name server isn't listed and you want to add it, click Add. This displays the New Resource Record dialog box.
4. In the Server Fully Qualified Domain Name (FQDN) field, type the fully qualified host name of a secondary server for the domain, and click Resolve. If the IP address of the name server is filled in for you, click Add, and then add other IP addresses for this name server as necessary.
5. Click OK to close the New Resource Record dialog box. Repeat this process to specify other name servers for the domain.

Start Of Authority (SOA) Records

Start Of Authority (SOA) records indicate the authoritative name server for a particular zone. The authoritative server is the best source of DNS information for a zone. Because each zone must have an SOA record, the record is created automatically when you add a zone. The SOA record also contains information about how resource records in the zone should be used and cached. This includes refresh, retry, and expiration intervals as well as the maximum time that a record is considered valid.

To view the SOA record for a zone in the DNS console, expand the node for the primary name server, and then expand the related Forward Lookup Zones or Reverse Lookup Zones folder as appropriate. Right-click the domain or subnet whose SOA record you want to view, and then select Properties. In the Properties dialog box select the Start Of Authority (SOA) tab, as shown in Figure 27-21.

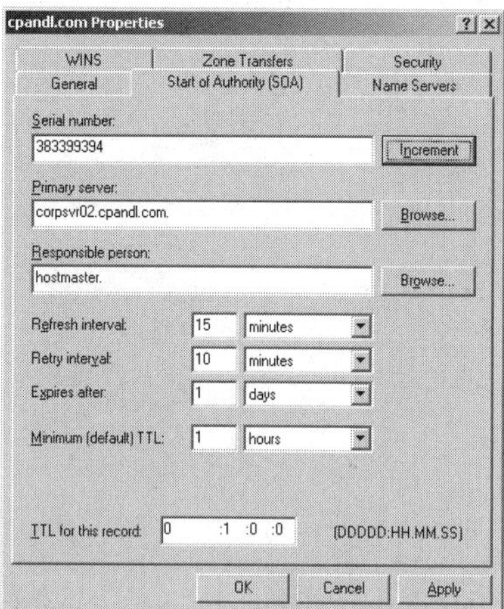

Figure 27-21. The Start Of Authority (SOA) tab for a domain or subnet.

The key field here is the Serial Number field. When you make changes manually to records in standard zones, you must update the serial number in the related zone or zones to show that changes have been made. Rather than updating the serial number manually for each individual zone, you can have the DNS server do this automatically for all zones as applicable. In the DNS console, right-click the server entry, and then choose Update Server Data File. As discussed previously, you do not need to do this with Active Directory–integrated zones as changes are replicated automatically.

Service Location (SRV) Records

Service Location (SRV) records make it possible to find a server providing a specific service. Active Directory uses SRV records to locate domain controllers, global catalog servers, LDAP servers, and Kerberos servers. SRV records are created automatically. For example, Active Directory creates an SRV record when you promote a domain controller. LDAP servers can add an SRV to indicate they are available to handle LDAP requests in a particular zone.

In the forest root zone, SOA, NS, CNAME, and SRV records are created. The SOA record contains information about the forest root zone. The NS records indicate the primary DNS servers for the forest root zone. The CNAME records are used to designate aliases that allow Active Directory to use the globally unique identifier (GUID) of a domain to find the forest root name servers for that domain. The SRV records used to locate Active Directory resources are organized by function as follows:

- **DC** Contains SRV records for domain controllers. These records are organized according to the Active Directory site in which domain controllers are located.
- **Domains** Contains SRV records for domain controllers by domain. Folders for each domain in the forest are organized by the domain's GUID.
- **GC** Contains SRV records for global catalog servers in the forest. These records are primarily organized according to the Active Directory site in which domain controllers are located.
- **PDC** Contains SRV records for PDC Emulators in the forest.

In the forward lookup zone for a domain, you'll find similar SRV records used to locate Active Directory resources. These records are organized by the following criteria:

- Active Directory site
- The Internet protocol used by the resource; either TCP or UDP
- Zone, either DomainDnsZones or ForestDnsZones

As Figure 27-22 shows, each record entry identifies a server that provides a particular service according to the following:

- **Domain** The DNS domain in which the record is stored.
- **Service** The service being made available. LDAP is for directory services on a domain controller. Kerberos indicates a Kerberos server that enables Kerberos authentication. GC indicates a global catalog server. KPasswd indicates Kerberos password service.
- **Protocol** The protocol the service uses, either TCP or User Datagram Protocol (UDP).

- **Priority** The priority or level of preference given to the server providing the service. The highest priority is 0. If multiple servers have the same priority, clients can use the weight to load balance between available servers.
- **Weight** The relative weight given to the server for load balancing when multiple servers have the same priority level.
- **Port Number** The TCP/IP port used by the server to provide the service.
- **Host Offering This Service** The FQDN of the host providing the service.

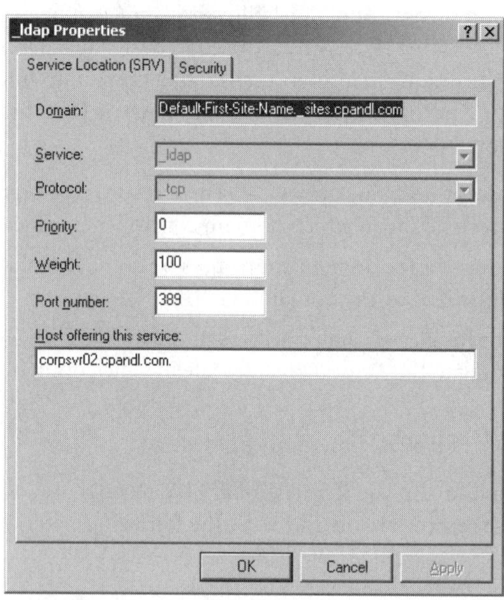

Figure 27-22. An SRV record.

Maintaining and Monitoring DNS

When using DNS, you can perform many routine tasks to maintain and monitor domain name resolution services. Key tasks you might need to perform include the following:

- Configuring default application directory partitions and replication scope
- Setting aging and scavenging
- Configuring logging and checking event logs

Configuring Default Application Directory Partitions and Replication Scope

When the domain controllers running DNS in all the domains of your forest are using Windows Server 2003, you can create default application directory partitions for DNS. This reduces DNS replication traffic because DNS changes are replicated only to domain controllers also configured as DNS servers. There are two ways to configure default application directory partitions:

- **Forest-wide** Creates a single application directory partition that stores DNS zone data and replicates that data to all DNS servers in the forest. The default partition name is ForestDnsZones.*DnsForestName*, where *DnsForestName* is the domain name of the forest.
- **Domain-wide** Creates a single application directory partition that stores DNS zone data and replicates that data to all DNS servers in a designated domain. The default partition name is DomainDnsZones.*DnsDomainName*, where *DnsDomainName* is the domain name of the domain.

> **Tip** **Check the DNS configuration fast**
> A fast way to check for the default application partitions and other DNS server configuration settings is to use DNSCMD. At a command prompt, type **dnscmd *ServerName* /info**, where *ServerName* is the name or IP address of a DNS server, such as CORPSVR03 or 192.168.10.15.

By default, the DNS Server service will try to create the default application directory partitions when you install it. You can verify this by connecting to the primary DNS server in the forest root domain and looking for subdomains of the forest root domain named DomainDnsZones and ForestDnsZones. Figure 27-23 shows an example in which these partitions have been created.

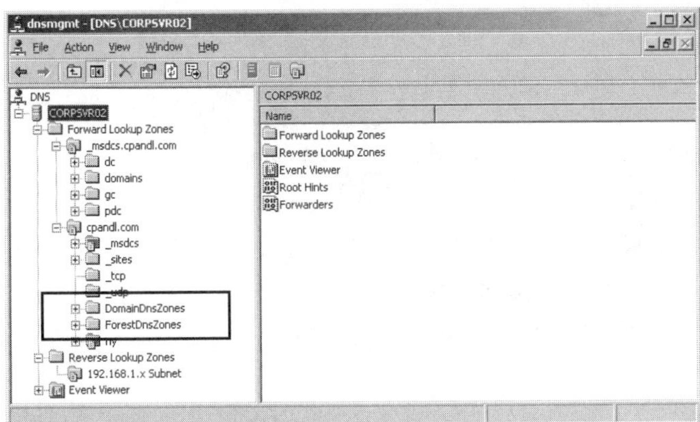

Figure 27-23. The default application partitions.

If the DNS Server service is unable to create these partitions, you will need to create the partitions manually. To do so, you must use an account that is a member of the Enterprise Admins group. If the default application partitions are currently available, the option to create them should not be available in the DNS console.

If the default application partitions have not yet been created, you can create them in the DNS console by following these steps:

1. In the DNS console, connect to the DNS server handling the zone for the parent domain of your forest root, such as cpandl.com rather than tech.cpandl.com.
2. Right-click the server entry, and select Create Default Application Directory Partitions. The DNS dialog box is displayed, as shown in Figure 27-24.

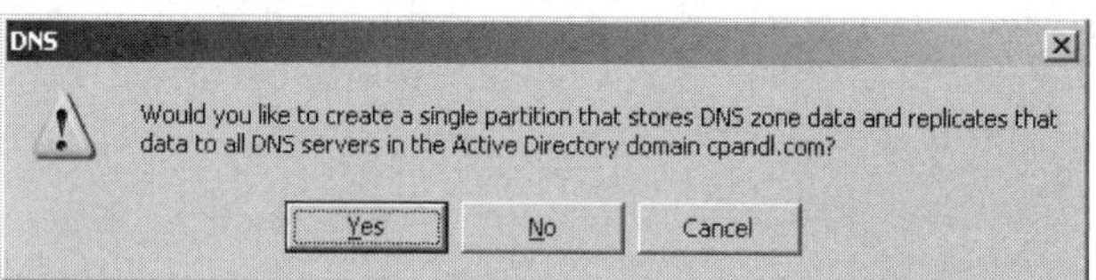

Figure 27-24. Creating the default domain partition.

3. The first prompt asks: Would You Like To Create A Single Partition That Stores DNS Zone Data And Replicates That Data To All DNS Servers In The Active Directory Domain *DomainName*? Click Yes if you want to create the DomainDnsZones.*Dns-DomainName* default partition.
4. As Figure 27-25 shows, the next prompt states: Would you like to create a single partition that stores DNS zone data and replicates that data to all DNS servers in the Active Directory forest *ForestName*. Click Yes if you want to create the ForestDnsZones.*Dns-ForestName* default partition.

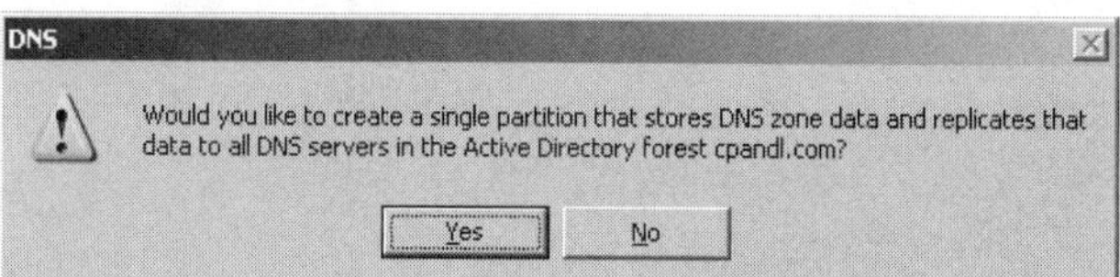

Figure 27-25. Creating the default forest partition.

When you create Active Directory–integrated zones, you have the option of setting the replication scope. Four replication scopes are available:

- All DNS Servers In The Active Directory Forest
- All DNS Servers In The Active Directory Domain

- All Domain Controllers In The Active Directory Domain
- All Domain Controllers Specified In The Scope Of The Following Application Partition

To check or change the replication scope for a zone in the DNS console, right-click the related domain or subnet entry, and select Properties. In the Properties dialog box, the current replication scope is listed to the right of the Replication entry. If you click the related Change button, you can change the replication scope using the dialog box shown in Figure 27-26.

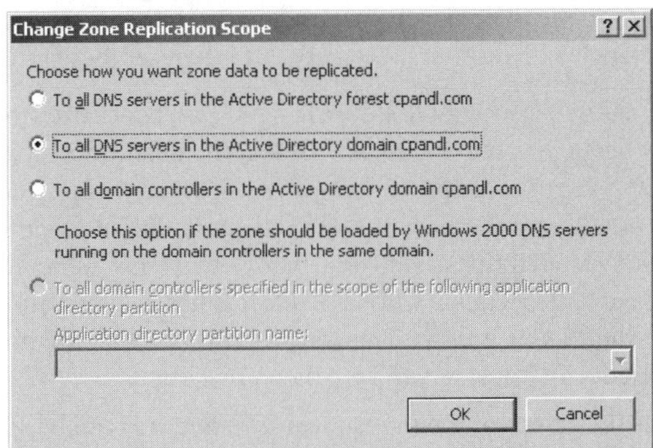

Figure 27-26. Change the replication scope as necessary.

Setting Aging and Scavenging

By default, the DNS Server service doesn't clean out old records. In some ways this is a good thing, because you don't want records you created manually to be deleted. However, for records created automatically through dynamic DNS, you might want to clear out old records periodically. Why? Consider the case of systems that register with DNS and then are removed from the network. Records for these systems will not be cleared automatically, which mean the DNS database might contain records for systems that are no longer in use.

DNS can help you clear out old records by using aging and scavenging. These rules determine how long a record created through a dynamic DNS update is valid, and if a record isn't reregistered within the allotted time, it can be cleared out. Aging and scavenging rules are set at two levels:

- **Zone** Zone aging/scavenging properties apply to an individual zone on a DNS server. To set zone-level options, right-click a zone entry, and select Properties. In the Properties dialog box, click Aging in the General tab. After you enable and configure aging/scavenging, click OK.

- **Server** Server aging/scavenging properties apply to all zones on a DNS server. To set server-level options in the DNS console, right-click a server entry, and select Set Aging/Scavenging For All Zones. After you enable and configure aging/scavenging, click OK. You'll see a prompt telling you these settings will be applied to new Active Directory–integrated zones created on the server. To apply these settings to existing zones, select Apply These Settings To The Existing Active Directory–Integrated Zones before you click OK.

In either case, the dialog box you see is similar to the one shown in Figure 27-27. To enable aging/scavenging, select Scavenge Stale Resource Records, and then set these intervals:

- **No-Refresh Interval** Sets a period of time during which a DNS client cannot reregister its DNS records. When aging/scavenging is enabled, the default interval is 7 days. This means that if a DNS client attempts to reregister its record within 7 days of creating it, the DNS server will ignore the request. Generally, this is what is wanted because each time a record is reregistered this is seen as a change that must be replicated. The no-refresh interval doesn't affect clients whose IP address has changed and who therefore need to reregister their DNS records. The reason for this is that the previous records are actually deleted and new records are then created.
- **Refresh Interval** Sets the extent of the refresh window. Records can be scavenged only when they are older than the combined extent of the no-refresh interval and the refresh interval. When aging/scavenging is enabled, the default no-refresh interval is 7 days and the default refresh interval is 7 days. This means their combined extent is 14 days, and the DNS server cannot scavenge records until they are older than 14 days.

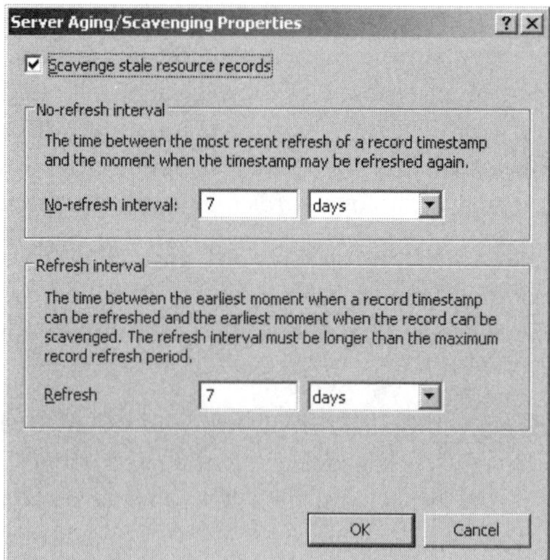

Figure 27-27. Set scavenging/aging options.

> **Tip Scavenge stale records manually**
> In addition to configuring automatic aging/scavenging, you can manually scavenge for stale (old) records. To do this in the DNS console, right-click a server entry, and select Scavenge Stale Resource Records. When prompted to confirm the action, click Yes. You can start scavenging at the command prompt by typing **dnscmd *ServerName* /startscavenging**, where *ServerName* is the name or IP address of the DNS server to work with, such as NS1 or 10.10.1.52.

Configuring Logging and Checking DNS Server Logs

By default the DNS Server service is configured to record all types of events (error, warning, and informational events) in the DNS Server log. You change this behavior in the DNS console; right-click a server entry, and then select Properties. In the Properties dialog box, select the Event Logging tab. Select the appropriate logging option so that no events, errors only, or errors and warnings are logged, and then click OK.

Using the DNS console, you can view only DNS-related events that have been logged in the system log by expanding the Event Viewer node in the left pane and selecting DNS events. As Figure 27-28 shows, you'll then see the current DNS events for the server. The primary events you will want to examine are error and warning events.

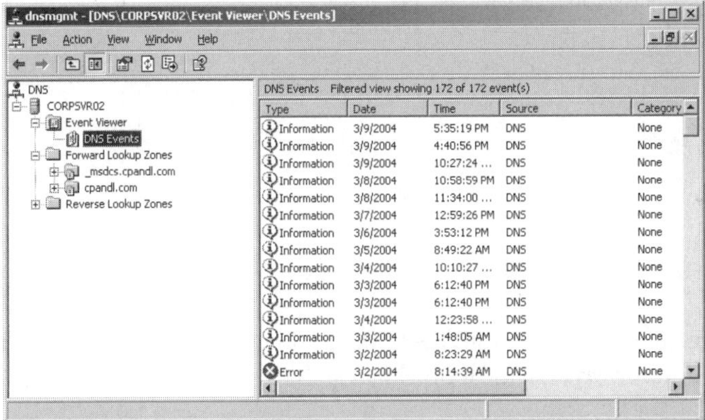

Figure 27-28. Check the event logs for warnings and errors.

Troubleshooting DNS Client Service

Frequently, when you are trying to troubleshoot DNS problems, you will want to start on the client that is experiencing the problem. If you don't find a problem on the client, then try troubleshooting the DNS Server service.

Try Reregistering the Client

If the problem has to do with a client not showing up in DNS, force the client to reregister itself in DNS by typing **ipconfig /registerdns**. This works only for dynamic updates. For clients with fixed IP addressing, you must create or update the A and PTR records.

> **Note** Although Windows NT 4 computers have an IPCONFIG command, most of the features discussed here are available only on computers running Windows 2000 or later. In addition, on Windows 95, the related command is WINIPCFG, and for Windows 98 the IPCONFIG command has a slightly different syntax.

Check the Client's TCP/IP Configuration

If the problem has to do with the client making lookups, start by checking the DNS servers configured for the client to use. You can display this information by typing **netsh interface ip show config**. The output will show you the basic TCP/IP configuration including the primary DNS server for the client. If the DNS server is configured through DHCP, the output will look similar to the following:

```
Configuration for interface "Local Area Connection"
   DHCP enabled:                         Yes
   InterfaceMetric:                      0
   DNS servers configured through DHCP:  192.168.0.1
   WINS servers configured through DHCP: 192.168.0.12
   Register with which suffix:           Primary only
If the DNS server is configured locally, the output will look similar to the following:
Configuration for interface "Local Area Connection"
   DHCP enabled:                         No
   IP Address:                           192.168.1.50
   SubnetMask:                           255.255.255.0
   Default Gateway:                      192.165.1.1
   GatewayMetric:                        1
   Statically Configured DNS Servers:    192.168.1.50
   Statically Configured WINS Servers:   192.168.1.102
   Register with which suffix:           Primary only
```

If you see a problem with the client's DNS configuration, you can change a locally assigned DNS server IP address by typing the following command:

```
netsh interface ip set dns ConnectionName static ServerIPAddress
```

where *ConnectionName* is the name of the local area connection and *ServerIPAddress* is the IP address of the server, such as

```
netsh interface ip set dns "Local Area Connection" static 192.168.0.1
```

Chapter 27

If you see a problem with a DHCP-assigned DNS server IP address, try renewing the client's IP address lease by typing **ipconfig /renew**.

Check the Client's Resolver Cache

If you don't see a problem with the client's DNS configuration, you will want to check the client's DNS resolver cache. All systems running Windows 2000 or later have a built-in DNS resolver cache that caches resource records from query responses that the DNS Client service receives. When performing lookups, the DNS client first looks in the cache. Records remain in the cache until one of the following events occurs:

- Their Time to Live (TTL) expires.
- The system or the DNS Client service is restarted.
- The cache is flushed.

You can display the records in a cache by typing **ipconfig /displaydns** at the command prompt. Records in the cache look like this:

```
Windows IP Configuration

         1.0.0.127.in-addr.arpa
         ----------------------------------------
         Record Name........... : 1.0.0.127.in-addr.arpa.
         Record Type........... : 12
         Time To Live.......... : 573686
         Data Length........... : 4
         Section............... : Answer
         PTR Record............ : localhost

         www.activetopic.com
         ----------------------------------------
         Record Name........... : www.activetopic.com
         Record Type........... : 5
         Time To Live.......... : 12599
         Data Length........... : 4
         Section............... : Answer
         CNAME Record ......... : activetopic.com
```

If you suspect a client has stale records in its cache, you can force it to flush the cache. Type **ipconfig /flushdns** at the command prompt.

Perform Lookups for Troubleshooting

Another useful command to use when troubleshooting DNS is NSLOOKUP. You can use NSLOOKUP to query the default DNS server of a client and check to see the actual records it is using. To perform a basic lookup simply follow NSLOOKUP with the FQDN of the host to look up. Consider the following example:

```
nslookup www.microsoft.com
```

The response shows the information that the default DNS server has on that host, such as

```
C:\Documents and Settings\WS>nslookup www.microsoft.com
DNS request timed out.
    timeout was 2 seconds.
Non-authoritative answer:
Name:    www2.microsoft.akadns.net
Addresses: 207.46.244.188, 207.46.156.252, 207.46.144.222, 207.46.245.92
         207.46.134.221, 207.46.245.156, 207.46.249.252, 207.46.156.220
Aliases: www.microsoft.com, www.microsoft.akadns.net
```


If you want to look up a particular type of record, follow these steps:

1. Type **nslookup** at the command prompt. The prompt changes to nslookup>.
2. Type **set query=*RecordType***, where *RecordType* is the type of record, such as **set query=mx**, **set query=soa**, or **set query=ns.**
3. Type the FQDN for the domain in which you want to search, such as **microsoft.com.**

The output shows you matching records in the specified domain, such as

```
microsoft.com  MX preference = 10, mail exchanger = mailb.microsoft.com

microsoft.com  nameserver = dns1.cp.msft.net
microsoft.com  nameserver = dns1.dc.msft.net
mailb.microsoft.com internet address = 131.107.3.122
mailb.microsoft.com internet address = 131.107.3.123
```

Troubleshooting DNS Server Service

If you suspect the DNS problem is on the server itself, you can begin troubleshooting on the server. There are, of course, many troubleshooting techniques. This section covers the key ones you'll want to use.

Check the Server's TCP/IP Configuration

When you are troubleshooting DNS on a DNS server, start with the server's TCP/IP configuration. As discussed previously, display the TCP/IP configuration by typing **netsh interface ip show config** at the command prompt. After you verify or modify the TCP/IP configuration as necessary, you can continue to troubleshoot. Like DNS clients, DNS servers have a resolver cache. The cache on servers is for query responses to lookups the server has performed either on behalf of clients or for its own name resolution purposes.

Check the Server's Cache

If the problem with DNS is that you think the server has stale records, you can check the DNS Server cache (as opposed to DNS Client cache) by using the following command:

```
dnscmd ServerName /zoneprint .
```

where *ServerName* is the name or IP address of the DNS server and "." indicates that you want to examine the server cache. This cache list includes the root name servers being used by the server.

If necessary, you can force a server to clear out its cache. In the DNS console, right-click the server entry, and select Clear Cache. You can clear the cache at the command prompt by typing the following:

```
dnscmd ServerName /clearcache
```

where *ServerName* is the name or IP address of the DNS server whose cache you want to clear.

Check Replication to Other Name Servers

Active Directory replication of changes to DNS zones is automatic. By default, Active Directory checks for changes to zones every 180 seconds. This interval is called the directory service polling interval. For advanced configuration needs, you can set the directory service polling interval using DNSCMD. Type **dnscmd *ServerName* /config /dspollinginterval *Interval***, where *ServerName* is the name or IP address of the DNS server you want to configure and *Interval* is the polling interval in seconds.

If the problem has to do with failure to replicate changes to secondary servers, start by ensuring zone transfers are enabled as discussed in the section entitled "Configuring Zone Transfers" earlier in this chapter. If zone transfers are properly configured, try updating the serial number on the zone records on the primary server. In the DNS console, right-click the server entry in the DNS console, and select Update Server Data Files. This increments the serial number for zones as necessary, which should trigger zone transfers if they are necessary.

Examine the Configuration of the DNS Server

Frequently, DNS problems have to do with a DNS server's configuration. Rather than trying to navigate multiple tabs and dialog boxes to find the configuration details, you can use DNSCMD to help you out. You can view a DNS server's configuration by typing **dnscmd *ServerName* /info** at the command prompt, where *ServerName* is the name or IP address of the DNS server you want to check, such as Primary or 10.10.1.52. The output looks like this:

```
Query result:
Server info
        server name                 = corpsvr02.cpandl.com
        version                     = 0ECE0205 (5.2 build 3790)
        DS container                = cn=MicrosoftDNS,cn=System,DC=cpandl,DC=com
        forest name                 = cpandl.com
        domain name                 = cpandl.com
        builtin domain partition    = ForestDnsZones.cpandl.com
        builtin forest partition    = DomainDnsZones.cpandl.com
        last scavenge cycle         = not since restart (0)
  Configuration:
        dwLogLevel                  = 00000000
        dwDebugLevel                = 00000000
        dwRpcProtocol               = FFFFFFFF
        dwNameCheckFlag             = 00000002
        cAddressAnswerLimit         = 0
        dwRecursionRetry            = 3
        dwRecursionTimeout          = 15
        dwDsPollingInterval         = 180
  Configuration Flags:
        fBootMethod                 = 3
        fAdminConfigured            = 1
        fAllowUpdate                = 1
        fDsAvailable                = 1
        fAutoReverseZones           = 1
        fAutoCacheUpdate            = 0
        fSlave                      = 0
        fNoRecursion                = 0
        fRoundRobin                 = 1
        fStrictFileParsing          = 0
        fBindSecondaries            = 1
        fWriteAuthorityNs           = 0
        fLocalNetPriority           = 1
```

Chapter 27

```
  Aging Configuration:
          ScavengingInterval        = 0
          DefaultAgingState         = 0
          DefaultRefreshInterval    = 168
          DefaultNoRefreshInterval  = 168
  ServerAddresses:
Addr Count = 1
          Addr[0] => 192.168.1.50
  ListenAddresses:
          NULL IP Array.
  Forwarders:
          NULL IP Array.
          forward timeout      = 5
          slave                = 0
```

Table 27-1 summarizes section by section the output from DNSCMD /Info. Using DNSCMD /Config, you can configure most of these options. The actual subcommand to use is indicated in parentheses in the first column, and examples of acceptable values are indicated in the final column. For example, if you wanted to set the fBindSecondaries configuration setting to allow maximum compression and efficiency (assuming you are using Windows 2000 or later DNS servers or BIND 4.9.4 or later), you would type **dnscmd *ServerName* /config /bindsecondaries 0**, where *ServerName* is the name or IP address of the DNS server you want to configure. This overrides the default setting to support other DNS servers.

Table 27-1. DNS Server Configuration Parameters

Section/Entry (Command)	Description	Example/Accepted Values
Server Info		
Server name	The FQDN of the DNS server.	corpsvr02.cpandl.com
Version	The operating system version and build. Version 5.2 is Windows Server 2003.	CE0205 (5.2 build 3790)
DS container	The directory services container for a DNS server that uses Active Directory–integrated zones.	cn=MicrosoftDNS, cn=System, DC=cpandl,DC=com
Forest name	The name of the Active Directory forest in which the server is located.	cpandl.com

Table 27-1. DNS Server Configuration Parameters

Section/Entry (Command)	Description	Example/Accepted Values
Domain name	The name of the Active Directory domain in which the server is located.	cpandl.com
Builtin domain partition	The default application partition for the domain.	ForestDnsZones.cpandl.com
Builtin forest partition	The default application partition for the forest.	DomainDnsZones.cpandl.com
Last scavenge cycle	The last time records were aged/scavenged.	not since restart (0)
Configuration		
dwLogLevel (/loglevel)	Indicates whether debug logging is enabled. A value other than zeros means it is enabled.	0x0; default, no logging.
dwDebugLevel	The debug logging level, not used. dwLogLevel is used instead.	00000000
dwRpcProtocol (/rpcprotocol)	The RPC protocol used.	0x0; disables remote procedure call (RPC) for DNS. 0x1; default, uses TCP/IP. 0x2; uses named pipes. 0x4; uses LPC.
dwNameCheckFlag (/namecheckflag)	The name-checking flag. By default, DNS names can be in multibyte Unicode format as indicated by the example entry.	0; Strict RFC (ANSI). 1; Non RFC (ANSI). 2; Multibyte (UTF8). 3; All Names.
cAddressAnswerLimit (/addressanswerlimit)	The maximum number of records the server can send in response to a query.	0; default with no maximum. [5–28]; sets a maximum.
dwRecursionRetry (/recursionretry)	The number of seconds the server waits before trying to contact a remote server again.	3
dwRecursionTimeout (/recursiontimeout)	The number of seconds the server waits before stopping contact attempts.	15

Chapter 27

Table 27-1. DNS Server Configuration Parameters

Section/Entry (Command)	Description	Example/Accepted Values
dwDsPollingInterval (/dspollinginterval)	How often in seconds Active Directory polls for changes in Active Directory–integrated zones.	180
Configuration Flags		
fBootMethod (/bootmethod)	The source from which the server gets its configuration information.	1; loads from BIND file. 2; loads from Registry. 3; loads from Active Directory and the Registry.
fAdminConfigured	Indicates whether the settings are administrator-configured.	1; default for yes.
fAllowUpdate	Indicates whether dynamic updates are allowed.	1; default dynamic updates are allowed. 0; dynamic updates not allowed.
fDsAvailable	Indicates whether Active Directory directory services are available.	1; Active Directory is available. 0; Active Directory isn't available.
fAutoReverseZones (/disableautoreversezone)	Indicates whether automatic creation of reverse lookup zones is enabled.	1; default enabled. 0; disabled.
fAutoCacheUpdate (/secureresponses)	Indicates how server caching works.	0; default, saves all responses to name queries to cache. 1; saves only records in same DNS subtree to cache.
fSlave (/isslave)	Determines how the DNS server responds when forwarded queries receive no response.	0; default, recursion is enabled. If the forwarder does not respond, the server attempts to resolve the query itself using recursion. 1; recursion is disabled. If the forwarder does not respond, the server terminates the search and sends a failure message to the resolver.

Table 27-1. DNS Server Configuration Parameters

Section/Entry (Command)	Description	Example/Accepted Values
fNoRecursion (/norecursion)	Indicates whether the server performs recursive name resolution.	0; default, DNS server performs if requested. 1; DNS server doesn't perform recursion.
fRoundRobin (/roundrobin)	Indicates whether server allows round robin load balancing when there are multiple A records for hosts.	1; default, automatically load balances using round robin for any hosts with multiple A records. 0; disables round robin.
fStrictFileParsing (/strictfileparsing)	Indicates server behavior when it encounters bad records.	0; default, continues to load, logs error. 1; stops loading DNS file and logs error.
fBindSecondaries (/bindsecondaries)	Indicates the zone transfer format for secondaries. By default, DNS server is configured for compatibility with other DNS server types.	1; default, for pre-BIND 4.9.4 compatibility. 0; enables compression and multiple transfers on Windows secondaries and others with BIND 4.9.4 or later.
fWriteAuthorityNs (/writeauthorityns)	Indicates whether the server writes NS records in the authority section of a response.	0; default, writes for referrals only. 1; writes for all successful authoritative responses.
fLocalNetPriority (/localnetpriority)	Determines the order in which host records are returned when there are multiple host records for the same name.	1; returns records with similar IP addresses first. 0; returns records in the order in which they are in DNS.
Aging Configuration		
ScavengingInterval (/scavenginginterval)	Indicates the number of hours between scavenging intervals.	0x0; scavenging is disabled.
DefaultAgingState (/defaultagingstate)	Indicates whether scavenging is enabled by default in new zones.	0; default, scavenging is disabled. 1; scavenging is enabled.

Chapter 27

Table 27-1. DNS Server Configuration Parameters

Section/Entry (Command)	Description	Example/Accepted Values
DefaultRefreshInterval (/defaultrefreshinterval)	Indicates the default refresh interval in hours.	168 (set in hexadecimal)
DefaultNoRefreshInterval (/defaultnorefreshinterval)	Indicates the default no-refresh interval in hours.	168 (set in hexadecimal)
ServerAddresses		
Addr Count	The number of IP addresses configured on the server and the IP address used.	1 Addr[0] => 192.168.1.50
ListenAddresses		
Addr Count	The number and value of IP addresses configured for listening for requests from clients. NULL IP Array when there are no specific IP addresses are designated for listening for requests from clients.	1 Addr[0] => 192.168.1.50
Forwarders		
Addr Count	The number and value of IP addresses of servers configured as forwarders. NULL IP Array when there are no forwarders.	1 Addr[0] => 192.168.12.8
Forward timeout (/forwardingtimeout)	Timeout for queries to forwarders in seconds.	5
Slave	Indicates whether recursion is enabled.	0; recursion is enabled 1; recursion is disabled

Another useful command for troubleshooting DNS Server is DNSCMD /Statistics. This command shows you the following information:

- DNS server time statistics, including server start time, seconds since start, stats of last cleared date and time

- Details on queries and responses, including total queries received, total responses sent. The number of UDP queries received and sent, UDP responses received and sent. The number of TCP queries received and sent, TCP responses received and sent
- Details on queries by record, including the exact number of each type of record sent
- Details on failures and where they occurred, including recursion failures, retry limits reached, and partial answers received
- Details on the total number of dynamic updates, the status for each update type. Later breakdowns on number and status of secure updates, the number of updates that were forwarded, and the types of records updated
- Details on the amount of memory used by DNS, including total amount of memory used, standard allocations, allocations from standard to the heap

Tip **Save the stats to a file**
Write the output of DNSCMD /STATISTICS to a file so that you don't overflow the history buffer in the command prompt. This also allows you to go through the stats at your leisure. Type **dnscmd *ServerName* /statistics > *FileName***, where *ServerName* is the name or IP address of the DNS server and *FileName* is the name of the file to use, such as **dnscmd corpsvr02 /statistics > dns-stats.txt**.

Examine Zones and Zone Records

DNSCMD provides several useful commands for helping you pinpoint problems with records. To get started, list the available zones by typing **dnscmd *ServerName* /enumzones**, where *ServerName* is the name or IP address of the DNS server you want to check. The output shows a list of the zones that are configured as follows:

```
Enumerated zone list:

        Zone count = 4

Zone name                 Type         Storage       Properties

.                         Cache        File
_msdcs.cpandl.com         Primary      AD-Forest     Secure
1.168.192.in-addr.arpa    Primary      AD-Legacy     Secure Rev
cpandl.com                Primary      AD-Domain     Secure Aging
```

The zone names you can work with are listed in the first column. The other values tell you the type of zone and the way it is configured as summarized in Table 27-2.

Table 27-2. Zone Entries and Their Meanings

Column/Entry	Description
Type	
Cache	A cache zone (server cache).
Primary	A primary zone.
Secondary	A secondary zone.
Stub	A stub zone.
File	
AD-Forest	Active Directory–integrated with forest-wide replication scope.
AD-Legacy	Active Directory–integrated with legacy replication scope to all domain controllers in the domain.
AD-Domain	Active Directory–integrated with domain-wide replication scope.
File	Indicates the zone data is stored in a file.
Properties	
Secure	Zone allows secure dynamic updates only and is a forward lookup zone.
Secure Rev	Zone allows secure dynamic updates only and is a reverse lookup zone.
Secure Aging	Zone allows secure dynamic updates only and is configured for scavenging/aging.
Aging	Zone is configured for scavenging/aging but isn't configured for dynamic updates.
Update	Zone is a forward lookup zone configured to allow both secure and nonsecure dynamic updates.
Update Rev	Zone is a reverse lookup zone configured to allow both secure and nonsecure dynamic updates.
Down	Secondary or stub zone hasn't received a zone transfer since startup.

After you examine the settings for zones on the server, you can print out the zone records of a suspect zone by typing **dnscmd *ServerName* /zoneprint *ZoneName*** at the command prompt, where *ServerName* is the name or IP address of the DNS server and *ZoneName* is the name of the zone as reported previously.

Consider the following example:

```
dnscmd corpsvr02 /zoneprint cpandl.com
```

Here, you want to examine the cpandl.com zone records on the CORPSVR02 server. The output from this command shows the records in this zone and their settings. Here is a partial listing:

```
;
;  Zone:    cpandl.com
;  Server:  corpsvr02.cpandl.com
;  Time:    Wed Mar 10 18:38:14 2004 UTC
;
@ [Aging:3534235] 600 A 192.168.1.50
       [Aging:3534235] 3600 NS          corpsvr02.cpandl.com.
       3600 SOA       corpsvr02.cpandl.com. hostmaster. 383 900 600 86
400 3600
                3600 MX       10 exchange.cpandl.com.
_msdcs 3600 NS  corpsvr01.cpandl.com.
_gc._tcp.Default-First-Site-Name._sites [Aging:35265] 600 SRV 0 100 3268 corps
vr02.cpandl.com.
_kerberos._tcp.Default-First-Site-Name._sites [Aging:35235] 600 SRV0 100 88
 corpsvr02.cpandl.com.
_ldap._tcp.Default-First-Site-Name._sites [Aging:35335] 600 SRV    0 100 38
9 corpsvr02.cpandl.com.
_gc._tcp [Aging:3534265] 600 SRV         0 100 3268 corpsvr02.cpandl.com.
_kerberos._tcp [Aging:3534235] 600 SRV   0 100 88 corpsvr02.cpandl.com.
_kpasswd._tcp [Aging:3534235] 600 SRV    0 100 464 corpsvr02.cpandl.com.
corpsvr02 [Aging:3534281] 3600 A         192.168.1.50
corpsvr17 3600 A      192.168.15.22
DomainDnsZones [Aging:3534265] 600 A     192.168.1.50
_ldap._tcp.Default-First-Site-Name._sites.DomainDnsZones [Aging:35365] 600 SRV
       0 100 389 corpsvr02.cpandl.com.
_ldap._tcp.DomainDnsZones [Aging:3534265] 600 SRV     0 100 389 corpsvr02.cpan
dl.com.
ForestDnsZones [Aging:3534265] 600 A     192.168.1.50
_ldap._tcp.Default-First-Site-Name._sites.ForestDnsZones [Aging:35365] 600 SRV
       0 100 389 corpsvr02.cpandl.com.
_ldap._tcp.ForestDnsZones [Aging:35365] 600 SRV       0 100 389 corpsvr02.cpan
dl.com.
ny 3600 NS      ns1.ny.cpandl.com.
ns1.ny 3600 A   10.10.10.52
www 3600 CNAME  corpsvr17.cpandl.com.
```

As you can see from the listing, DNSCMD /ZONEPRINT shows all the records, even the ones created by Active Directory. This is particularly useful because it means you don't have to try to navigate the many subfolders in which these SRV records are stored.

Chapter 28

Implementing and Maintaining WINS

Windows Internet Naming Service (WINS) enables computers to register and resolve NetBIOS names. WINS is maintained primarily for backward support and compatibility with early versions of Microsoft Windows, including Windows 95, Windows 98, and Windows NT, that used WINS for computer name resolution; or for networks running Windows 2000 or later that don't have Active Directory directory service deployed and thus don't require DNS. On most large networks, WINS is needed to support Windows 95, Windows 98, and Windows NT computers.

If you are setting up a new network, you probably don't need WINS. On an existing network running all Microsoft Windows 2000, Windows XP, and Windows Server 2003 systems, only the Domain Name System (DNS) is needed because these computers rely exclusively on DNS for name resolution if Active Directory is deployed. Because WINS is not required, WINS support could be removed from the network. Doing so, however, would mean that applications and services that rely on NetBIOS, such as the computer Browser service, would no longer function.

WINS Essentials

Like DNS, WINS is a client/server protocol. All Windows servers have a WINS service that can be installed to provide WINS services on the network. All Windows computers have a WINS client that is installed automatically. The Workstation and Server services on computers are used to specify resources that are available, such as file shares. These resources have NetBIOS names as well.

NetBIOS Namespace and Scope

WINS architecture is very different from DNS. Unlike DNS, WINS has a flat namespace and doesn't use a hierarchy or tree. Each computer or resource on a Windows network has a NetBIOS name, which can be up to 15 characters long. This name must be unique on the network—no other computer or resource can have the same name. Although there are no extensions to this name per se that indicate a domain, a NetBIOS scope can be set in Dynamic Host Configuration Protocol (DHCP).

The NetBIOS scope is a hidden 16th character (suffix) for the NetBIOS name. It is used to limit the scope of communications for WINS clients. Only WINS clients with the same NetBIOS scope can communicate with each other. See the section entitled "Configuring TCP/IP Options" on page 831 for details on setting the NetBIOS scope for computers that use DHCP.

NetBIOS Node Types

The ways WINS works on a network is determined by the node type set for a client. The node type defines how name services work. WINS clients can be one of four node types:

- **B-Node (Broadcast Node)** Broadcast messages are used to register and resolve names. Computers that need to resolve a name broadcast a message to every host on the local network, requesting the IP address for a computer name. Best for small networks.
- **P-Node (Peer-to-Peer Node)** WINS servers are used to register and resolve computer names to Internet Protocol (IP) addresses. Computers that need to resolve a name send a query message to the server and the server responds. Best if you want to eliminate broadcasts. In some cases, however, resources might not be seen as available if the WINS server isn't updated by the computer providing the resources.
- **M-Node (Mixed Node)** A combination of B-Node and P-Node. WINS clients first try to use broadcasts for name resolution. If this fails, the clients then try using a WINS server. Still means a lot of broadcast traffic.
- **H-Node (Hybrid Node)** A combination of B-Node and P-Node. WINS clients first try to use a WINS server for name resolution. If this fails, the clients then try broadcasts for name resolution. Best for most networks that use WINS servers because it reduces broadcast traffic.

> **Tip** **Small networks might not need a WINS server**
> On a small network without subnets and a limited number of computers, WINS clients can rely on broadcasts for name resolution. In this case, it isn't necessary to set up a WINS server.

WINS Name Registration and Cache

WINS maintains a database of name-to-IP-address mappings automatically. Whenever a computer or resource becomes available, it registers itself with the WINS server to tell the server the name and IP address it is using. As long as no other computer or resource on the network is using that name, the WINS server accepts the request and registers the computer or resource in its database.

Name registration isn't permanent. Each name that is registered has a lease period associated with it, which is called its Time to Live (TTL). A WINS client must reregister its name before the lease expires and attempts to do so when 50 percent of the lease period has elapsed or when it is restarted. If a WINS client doesn't reregister its name, the lease expires and is marked for deletion from the WINS database. During normal shutdown, a WINS client will send a message to the WINS server requesting release of the registration. The WINS server then marks the record for deletion. Whenever records are marked for deletion, they are said to be *tombstoned*.

As with DNS clients, WINS clients maintain a cache of NetBIOS names that have been looked up. WINS cache, however, is designed to hold only names looked up recently. By default, names are cached for up to 10 minutes and the cache is limited to 16 names. You can view entries in the NetBIOS cache by typing **nbtstat-c** at the command prompt.

WINS Implementation Details and New Features

On most networks that use WINS, you'll want to configure at least two WINS servers for name resolution. When there are multiple WINS servers, you can configure replication of database entries between the servers. Replication allows for fault tolerance and load balancing by ensuring that entries in one server's database are replicated to its replication partners. These replication partners can then handle renewal and release requests from clients as if they held the primary registration in the first place.

For Windows Server 2003, WINS has several important updates, including the following:

- **Persistent connections** In a standard configuration, replication partners establish and release connections each time they replicate WINS database changes. With persistent connections, replication partners can be configured to maintain a persistent connection. This reduces the overhead associated with opening and closing connections and speeds up the replication process.
- **Automatic replication partners** Using automatic replication partners, WINS can automatically configure itself for replication with other WINS servers. To do this, WINS sends periodic multicast messages to announce its availability. These messages are addressed to the WINS multicast group address (224.0.1.24), and any other WINS

servers on the network that are listening for datagrams sent on this group address can receive and process the automatic replication request. Once replication is set up with multicast partners, the partners use standard replication with either persistent or non-persistent connections.

- **Manual tombstoning** Manual tombstoning allows administrators to mark records for deletion. A record marked for deletion is said to be tombstoned. This state is then replicated to a WINS server's replication partners, which prevents the record from being re-created on a replication partner and then being replicated back to the original server on which it was marked for deletion.
- **Record export** The record export feature allows administrators to export the entries in the WINS database to a file that can be used for tracking or reporting on which clients are using WINS.

Setting Up WINS Servers

To make a computer running Windows Server 2003 into a WINS server, you must install the WINS service. This service doesn't require a dedicated server and uses limited resources in most cases. This means you could install the WINS service on a DNS server, DHCP server, or domain controller. The only key requirement is that the WINS service can be installed only on a computer with a static IP address. Although you can install WINS on a server with multiple IP address or multiple network interfaces, this isn't recommended because the server might not be able to replicate properly with its replication partners. In most cases, you won't want to configure a domain controller as a WINS server.

Installing WINS

You can install the WINS service using the Add Or Remove Programs utility or using the Configure Your Server Wizard. Follow these steps for using the Add Or Remove Programs utility to do this:

1. In Control Panel, double-click Add Or Remove Programs. Then in the Add Or Remove Programs dialog box, click Add Windows Components to start the Windows Components Wizard.
2. On the Windows Components page, select Networking Services, and then click Details.
3. In the Networking Services dialog box, ensure the correct components are selected but don't clear selections if a service has already been installed. Click OK.
4. Click Next to begin the installation, and then click Finish.

Follow these steps for using the Configure Your Server Wizard to install the WINS service:

1. Select Configure Your Server Wizard on the Administrative Tools menu.
2. When the wizard starts, click Next twice. The server's current roles are shown.
3. Select WINS Server, and then click Next twice.
4. The wizard will then install WINS. When the installation ends, click Finish.

WINS Postinstallation Tasks

After you install the WINS service, the WINS console is available on the Administrative Tools menu. Start the console by clicking Start and selecting Programs (or All Programs as appropriate), Administrative Tools, and finally WINS. Then select the WINS server you are working with to see its entries, as shown in Figure 28-1.

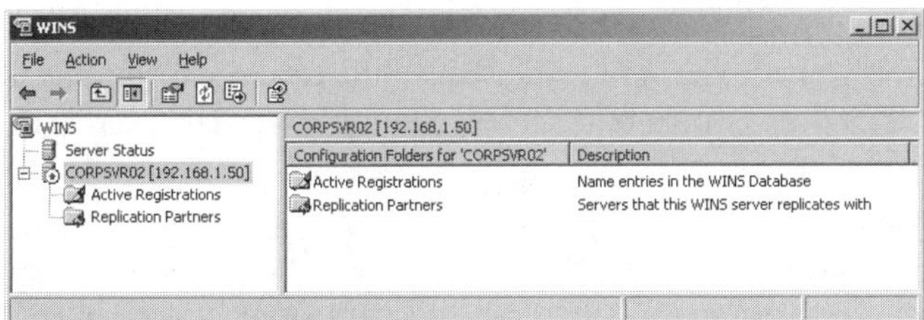

Figure 28-1. The WINS console.

The only key postinstallation task for the WINS service is to configure replication partners. However, you should check the Transmission Control Protocol/Internet Protocol (TCP/IP) configuration of the WINS server. It should have only itself listed as the WINS server to use and shouldn't have a secondary WINS server. This prevents the WINS client on the server from registering itself with a different WINS database, which can cause problems.

To set the server's primary WINS server address to its own IP address and clear out any secondaries from the list, access Network Connections in Control Panel, and then select or double-click the primary network connection. In the Status dialog box, click Properties. In the Properties dialog box, open the Internet Protocol (TCP/IP) Properties dialog box by double-clicking Internet Protocol (TCP/IP). Click Advanced to display the Advanced TCP/IP Settings dialog box, and then select the WINS tab. Set the WINS server's IP address as the WINS server to use and remove any additional WINS server addresses. When you're finished, click OK.

You can remotely manage and configure WINS. Simply start the WINS console on your workstation, right-click the WINS node in the left pane, and select Add Server. In the Add Server dialog box, select This Server, type the name or IP address of the WINS server, and then click OK.

The command-line counterpart to the WINS console is Netsh WINS. From the command prompt on a computer running Windows Server 2003, you can use Netsh WINS to perform all the tasks available in the WINS console as well as to perform some additional tasks that can't be performed in the WINS console. To start Netsh WINS and access a particular WINS server, follow these steps:

1. Start a command prompt, and then type **netsh** to start Netsh. The command prompt changes to netsh>.
2. Access the WINS context within Netsh by typing **wins**. The command prompt changes to netsh WINS>.
3. Type **server** followed by the Universal Naming Convention (UNC) name or IP address of the WINS server, such as **\\ns2** or **\\10.10.15.2**. If the WINS server is in a different domain from your logon domain, you should type the fully qualified domain name (FQDN) of the server, such as **\\ns2.cpandl.com**.
4. The command prompt changes to netsh WINS server>. You can now work with the selected server. If you later want to work with a different server, you can do this without having to start over. Simply type **server** followed by the UNC name or IP address of that server.

Note Technically, you don't need to type the double backslashes (\\) when you specify an IP address. You must, however, type **** when you specify a server's name or FQDN. Because of this discrepancy, you might want to use \\ all the time so that you won't leave it out by accident when you need it.

Troubleshooting

Resolving WINS replication errors

Most WINS replication errors involve incorrectly configured WINS servers. If you see replication errors in the event logs, check the TCP/IP configuration of your WINS servers. Every WINS server in the organization should be configured as its own primary, and any secondary WINS servers should be deleted. This ensures that WINS servers register their NetBIOS names only in their own WINS database. If you don't configure WINS in this way, WINS servers may register their names with other WINS servers. This can result in different WINS servers owning the NetBIOS names that a particular WINS server registers and, ultimately, to problems with WINS itself. For more information on this issue, see Microsoft Knowledge Base article 321208 (*http://support.microsoft.com/default.aspx?scid=kb;en-us;321208*).

Configuring Replication Partners

When you have two or more WINS servers on a network, you should configure replication between them. When servers replicate database entries with each other, they are said to be *replication partners.*

Replication Essentials

There are two replication roles for WINS servers:

- **Push partner** A push partner is a replication partner that notifies other WINS servers that updates are available.
- **Pull partner** A pull partner is a replication partner that requests updates.

By default, all WINS servers have replication enabled and replication partners are configured to use both push and pull replication. After a replication partner notifies a partner that there are changes using push replication, the partner can request the changes using pull replication. This pulls the changes down to its WINS database. In addition, all replication is done using persistent connections by default to increase efficiency.

Because replication is automatically enabled and configured, all you have to do to start replication is tell each WINS server about the other WINS servers that are available. On a small network, you can do this using the automatic replication partners feature. Because this can cause a lot of broadcast traffic on medium or large networks that contain many clients and servers, you'll probably want to designate specific replication partners to reduce broadcast traffic.

Configuring Automatic Replication Partners

To configure automatic replication partners, follow these steps:

1. Start the WINS console. Right-click the WINS node in the left pane, and select Add Server. In the Add Server dialog box, select This Server, type the name or IP address of the WINS server, and then click OK.
2. Expand the server entry, right-click the Replication Partners entry in the left pane, and then select Properties. In the Replication Partners Properties dialog box, select the Advanced tab, as shown in Figure 28-2.

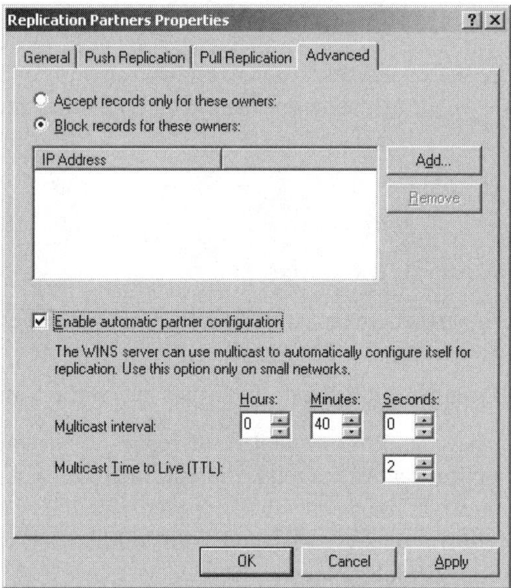

Figure 28-2. Enable automatic replication.

3 Select Enable Automatic Partner Configuration.

4 Use the Multicast Interval options to set the interval between multicast broadcasts to the WINS server group address. These broadcasts are used to tell other WINS servers about the availability of the server you are configuring. The default interval is 40 minutes.

Tip **Registrations remain until restart**

Once a server is discovered and added as a partner through multicasting, the server remains as a configured partner until you restart the WINS service or until you restart the server. When WINS is shut down properly, part of the shutdown process is to send messages to current replication partners and remove its registration.

5 Use the Multicast Time To Live (TTL) combo box to specify how many links multicast broadcasts can go through before being discarded. The default is 2, which would allow the broadcasts to be relayed through two routers.

6 Click OK.

Tip Multicast through routers is possible

The TTL is used to allow the discovery broadcasts to be routed between subnets. This means you could use automatic replication partners on networks with subnets. However, routing isn't automatic just because a datagram has a TTL. You must configure the routers on each subnet to forward multicast traffic received from the WINS multicast group address (224.0.1.24).

Using Designated Replication Partners

To designate specific replication partners, start the WINS console. Right-click the WINS node in the left pane, and select Add Server. In the Add Server dialog box, select This Server, type the name or IP address of the WINS server, and then click OK.

Right-click the Replication Partners entry in the left pane, and select New Replication Partners. In the New Replication Partners dialog box, type the name or IP address of the WINS server that should be used as a replication partner, and then click OK. The replication partner is added and listed as available in the WINS console. As shown in Figure 28-3, replication partners are listed by server name, IP address, and replication type.

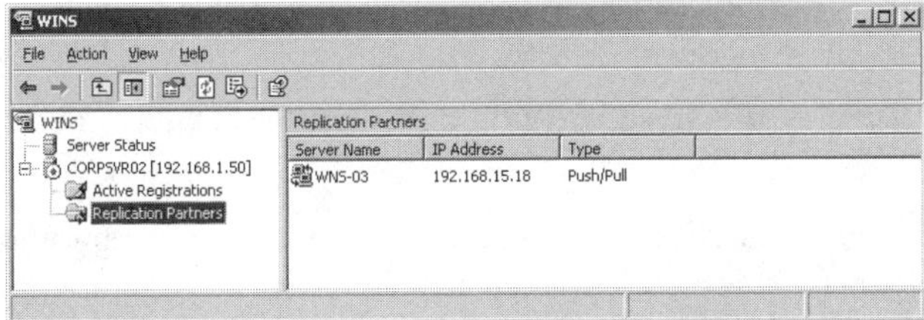

Figure 28-3. View replication partners in the WINS console.

By default, the replication partner is configured to use both push and pull replication as well as persistent connections. Once you configure a replication partner, the configuration is permanent. If you restart a server, you do not need to reconfigure replication partners.

To view or change the replication settings for a replication partner, start the WINS console. Expand the server entry for the server you want to work with, and then select the Replication Partners entry in the left pane. Double-click the replication partner in the details pane. This displays the replication partner's Properties dialog box. Click the Advanced tab, as shown in Figure 28-4.

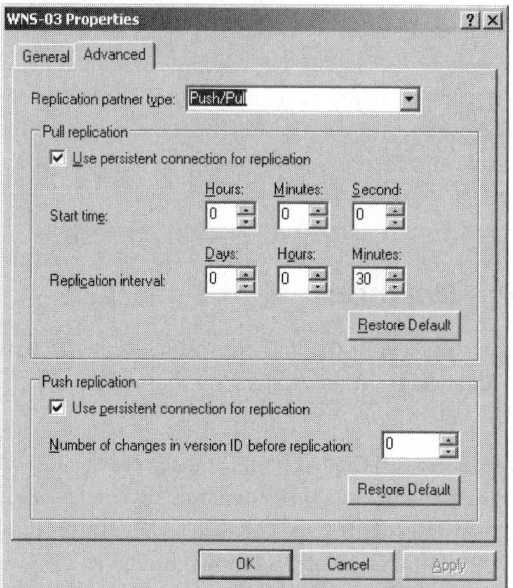

Figure 28-4. Configure replication partner settings.

The configuration options are used as follows:

- Replication Partner Type—Sets the replication type as push, pull, or push/pull.
- Pull Replication
  - *Use Persistent Connection For Replication*—Configures pull replication so a persistent connection is used. This reduces the time spent opening and closing connections and improves performance.
  - *Start Time*—Sets the hour of the day when replication should begin using a 24-hour clock.
  - *Replication Interval*—Sets the frequency of replication. The default is every 30 minutes.
- Push Replication
  - *Use Persistent Connection For Replication*—Configures push replication so a persistent connection is used. This reduces the time spent opening and closing connections and improves performance.
  - *Number Of Changes In Version ID Before Replication*—Can be used to limit replication by allowing replication to occur only when a set number of changes have occurred in the local WINS database.

> **Note** By default Number Of Changes In Version ID Before Replication is set to 0, which allows replication at the designated interval whenever there are changes. If you set a specific value, that many changes must occur before replication takes place.

Configuring and Maintaining WINS

WINS is fairly easy to configure and maintain once it is set up and replication partners are configured. The key configuration and maintenance tasks are related to the following issues:

- Configuring burst handling as the network grows
- Checking server status and configuration
- Checking active registrations and scavenging records if necessary
- Maintaining the WINS database

Configuring Burst Handling

If you configured the WINS server on a network with more than 100 clients, you should enable burst handling of registrations. As your network grows, you should change the burst-handling sessions as appropriate for the number of clients on the network. To configure burst handling of registration and name refresh requests, start the WINS console. Right-click the server entry in the WINS console, and then select Properties. In the Properties dialog box, click the Advanced tab, as shown in Figure 28-5.

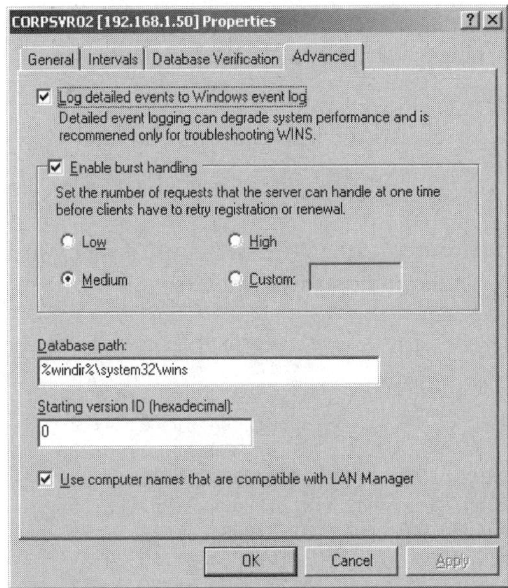

Figure 28-5. Set burst handling for medium and large networks.

Select Enable Burst Handling, and then select a burst-handling setting. The settings available are the following:

- Low for handling up to 300 registration and name refresh requests
- Medium for handling up to 500 registration and name refresh requests
- High for handling up to 1,000 registration and name refresh requests

Tip Set a custom threshold for burst handling
You can also set a custom threshold value for burst handling. To do this, click Custom and then enter a threshold value between 50 and 5,000. For example, if you set the threshold to 5,000, up to 5,000 requests could be queued at once. Keep in mind that you would do this only if your network environment needs this setting. If you set the value to 5,000 but only need a queue that allows up to 100 name registration requests, you would waste a lot of server resources maintaining a very large queue that you don't need.

Checking Server Status and Configuration

Using the WINS console, you can do the following:

- View the status of all WINS servers on the network by clicking the Server Status entry in the left pane. The status of the servers is then displayed in the right pane.
- View the current replication partners for a server by expanding the server entry and selecting Replication Partners in the left pane. The replication partners for that server are displayed in the right pane.
- View server statistics for startup, replication, queries, releases, registrations, and replication partners by right-clicking the server entry in the left pane and selecting Display Server Statistics.

Using Netsh WINS, you can view server statistics by typing the command

```
netsh wins server ServerName show statistics
```

where *ServerName* is the name or IP address of the WINS server you want to work with, such as \\WINS02 or 10.10.12.15. An example of the statistics follows:

```
***You have Read and Write access to the server corpsvr02.cpandl.com***

WINS Started                             : 3/10/2004 at 14:46:1
Last initialization                      : 3/12/2004 at 02:14:12
Last planned scavenging                  : 3/19/2004 at 12:30:25
Last admin triggered scavenging          : 3/10/2004 at 16:52:24
Last replicas tombstones scavenging      : 3/21/2004 at 09:12:26
Last replicas verification scavenging    : 3/23/2004 at 12:38:9
Last planned replication                 : 3/10/2004 at 16:20:39
Last admin triggered replication         : 3/27/2004 at 08:27:30
Last reset of counter                    : 4/01/2004 at 18:23:45
```

```
Counter Information :
                     No of U and G Registration requests = (250 222)
                     No of Successful/Failed Queries = (812/67)
                     No of U and G Refreshes = (213 144)
                     No of Successful/Failed Releases = (68/12)
                     No of U. and G. Conflicts = (12 10)
~~~~~~~~~~~~~~~~~~~~~~~~~~~~~~~~~~~~~~~~~~~~~~~~~~~~~~~~~~~~~~~~~~~~~~~~~~~~~~
WINS Partner IP Address    - No. of Replication      - No. of Comm Failure
~~~~~~~~~~~~~~~~~~~~~~~~~~~~~~~~~~~~~~~~~~~~~~~~~~~~~~~~~~~~~~~~~~~~~~~~~~~~~~
        192.168.15.18      -    153                       -   2
```

These statistics are useful for troubleshooting registration and replication problems. Scavenging and replication are automatic once configured. Problems to look for include the following:

- **Replication** If there are problems with replication, you should see a high number of communication failures relative to the number of replications. Check the links over which replication is occurring to see if there are intermittent failures or times when links aren't available.
- **Name resolution** If WINS clients are having problems with name resolution, you'll see a high number of failed queries. You might need to scavenge the database for old records more frequently. Check the server statistics for the renew interval, extinction interval, extinction timeout, and verification interval or the Intervals tab in the server's Properties dialog box.
- **Registration release** If WINS clients aren't releasing registrations properly, you'll see a high number of failed releases. Clients might not be getting shut down properly.

You can view the configuration details for a WINS server by typing the command

```
netsh wins server ServerName show info
```

where *ServerName* is the name or IP address of the WINS server. The output looks like this:

```
WINS Database backup parameter
~~~~~~~~~~~~~~~~~~~~~~~~~~~~~~~~~~~~~~~~~~~~~~~~~~~~~~~~
Backup Dir                                  :
Backup on Shutdown                          : Disabled

Name Record Settings(day:hour:minute)
~~~~~~~~~~~~~~~~~~~~~~~~~~~~~~~~~~~~~~~~~~~~~~~~~~~~~~~~
Refresh Interval                            : 006:00:00
Extinction(Tombstone) Interval              : 004:00:00
Extinction(Tombstone) TimeOut               : 006:00:00
Verification Interval                       : 024:00:00
```

```
Database consistency checking parameters :
~~~~~~~~~~~~~~~~~~~~~~~~~~~~~~~~~~~~~~~~~~~~~~~~~~~~~~~~
Periodic Checking                             : Disabled

WINS Logging Parameters:
~~~~~~~~~~~~~~~~~~~~~~~~~~~~~~~~~~~~~~~~~~~~~~~~~~~~~~~~

Log Database changes to JET log files         : Enabled
Log details events to System Event Log        : Enabled

Burst Handling Parameters :
~~~~~~~~~~~~~~~~~~~~~~~~~~~~~~~~~~~~~~~~~~~~~~~~~~~~~~~~

Burst Handling State                          : Enabled
Burst handling queue size                     : 500
Checking, Scavenging and Tombstoning Registrations
```

Checking Active Registrations and Scavenging Records

Using the WINS console, you can view the active registrations in the WINS database by expanding the server entry, right-clicking Active Registrations, and choosing Display Records. In the Display Records dialog box, click Find Now without making any selections to see all the available records or use the filter options to specify the types of records you want to view, and then click Find Now. To tombstone a record manually, right-click it, and then select Delete. This deletes it from the current server, and this deletion is then replicated to other WINS servers; that is, the record will be replicated marked as Tombstoned.

Netsh provides many ways to examine records in the WINS database. Because this is something you won't use that frequently, the easiest way to do it is to list all available records and write the information to a file that you can search. To do this, type the command

```
netsh wins server ServerName show database Servers={}
```

where *ServerName* is the name or IP address of the WINS server. The output shows you the registration entries in the database as follows:

```
~~~~~~~~~~~~~~~~~~~~~~~~~~~~~~~~~~~~~~~~~~~~~~~~~~~~~~~~~~~~~~~~~~~~~~~~~~~~~~
     NAME           -T-S- VERSION -G-   IPADDRESS      - EXPIRATION DATE
~~~~~~~~~~~~~~~~~~~~~~~~~~~~~~~~~~~~~~~~~~~~~~~~~~~~~~~~~~~~~~~~~~~~~~~~~~~~~~
 Retrieving database from the Wins server 192.168.1.50
 ??__MSBROWSE__?[01h]-D-A- 5     -N- 192.168.1.50    -3/16/2004 2:46:01 PM
 CPANDL          [1Bh]-D-A- 2     -U- 192.168.1.50    -3/16/2004 2:46:01 PM
 CORPSVR02       [00h]-D-A- 7     -U- 192.168.1.50    -3/16/2004 2:46:01 PM
 CORPSVR02       [20h]-D-A- 6     -U- 192.168.1.50    -3/16/2004 2:46:01 PM
 CPANDL          [00h]-D-A- 4     -N- 192.168.1.50    -3/16/2004 2:46:01 PM
 CPANDL          [1Ch]-D-A- 3     -I- 192.168.1.50    -3/16/2004 2:46:01 PM
 CPANDL          [1Eh]-D-A- 1     -N- 192.168.1.50    -3/16/2004 2:46:01 PM
```

WINS automatically scavenges the database to mark old records for deletion. To see when this is done, check the server statistics for the renew interval, extinction interval, extinction timeout, and verification interval or the Intervals tab in the server's Properties dialog box.

You can initiate scavenging (referred to as an admin-triggered scavenging in the server statistics) by right-clicking the server entry in the WINS console and selecting Scavenge Database. To initiate scavenging at the command prompt, type **netsh wins server *ServerName* init scavenge**, where *ServerName* is the name or IP address of the WINS server.

After scavenging, the renew interval, extinction interval, extinction timeout, and verification interval are used to mark each record as follows:

- If the renew interval has not expired, the record remains marked as Active.
- If the renew interval has expired, the record is marked as Released.
- If the extinction interval has expired, the record is marked as Tombstoned.

If the record was tombstoned, it is deleted from the database. If the record is active and was replicated from another server but the verification interval has expired, the record is revalidated.

Maintaining the WINS Database

The WINS database, like any database, should be maintained. You should routinely perform the following maintenance operations:

- Verify the database consistency
- Compact the database
- Back up the database

Verifying the WINS Database Consistency

WINS can be configured to verify the database consistency automatically. This operation checks and verifies the registered names. To configure automatic database consistency checks, follow these steps:

1. Start the WINS console. Right-click the WINS node in the left pane, and select Add Server. In the Add Server dialog box, select This Server, type the name or IP address of the WINS server, and then click OK.
2. Right-click the server entry in the WINS console, and select Properties. In the Properties dialog box, click the Database Verification tab, as shown in Figure 28-6.

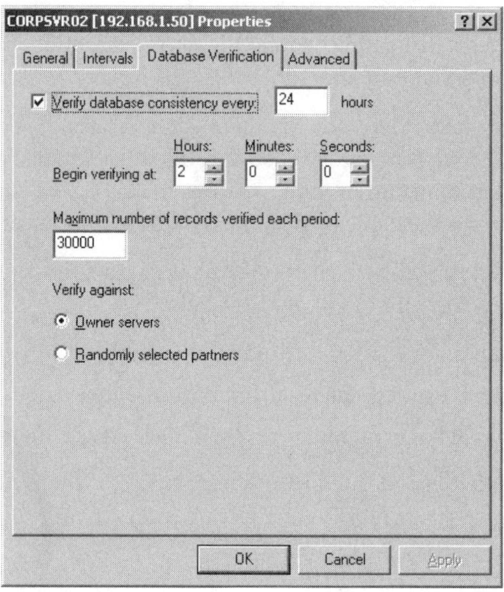

Figure 28-6. Set automatic verification of the WINS database.

3. Select the Verify Database Consistency Every option, and then set a check interval. Typically, you'll want to perform this operation no more frequently than once every 24 hours.
4. Use the Begin Verifying At section to set the time at which verification checks are started. This time is on a 24-hour clock and the default time is 2 hours, 0 minutes, and 0 seconds, meaning 2:00 A.M. If you wanted verification checks to begin at 2:00 P.M. instead, you would set the time to 14 hours, 0 minutes, and 0 seconds.
5. Set other options as necessary, and then click OK.

Compacting the WINS Database

The WINS database should be compacted periodically, at least once a month or once every other month, depending on how often computers are added to or removed from your network. In addition to reducing the size of the database by squeezing out unneeded space that has been allocated and is no longer needed, compacting the database can improve performance and make the database more reliable.

At the command prompt, you can compact the WINS database by following these steps:

1. Change to the WINS directory by typing **cd %SystemRoot%\System32\Wins.**
2. Stop the WINS service by typing **net stop wins.**

3. Compact the WINS database by typing **jetpack wins.mdb winstemp.mdb.**
4. Start the WINS service by typing **net start wins.**

> **Note** With Windows Server 2003 Service Pack 2 or later, you might be able to use the NETSH WINS SERVER INIT COMPACT command. This is a proposed extension for a Netsh revision. By entering the following line in a script and configuring the script as a scheduled task, you can perform this procedure automatically: **netsh wins server *ServerName* init compact**, where *ServerName* is the name or IP address of the WINS server.

Backing Up the WINS Database

By default, the WINS database is not backed up—but it should be. You can perform manual or automatic backups. To back up the WINS database manually, follow these steps:

1. Start the WINS console. Right-click the server entry, and then select Back Up Database.
2. In the Browse For Folder dialog box, select the folder where the WINS server should store the database backup files, and then click OK.
3. The WINS server will then write the backup files to a subfolder of the designated folder called Wins_bak. When it finishes, click OK.

To configure automatic backups of the WINS database, follow these steps:

1. Start the WINS console. Right-click the server entry, and then select Properties.
2. In the Properties dialog box, click Browse in the General tab.
3. Use the Browse For Folder dialog box to select the folder where the WINS server should store the database backup files, and then click OK. The WINS server will write backup files to a subfolder of the designated folder called Wins_bak.
4. Select Back Up Database During Shutdown.
5. Click OK. Now whenever you shut down the server or the WINS service on the server, the WINS service will back up the database to the designated folder.

Restoring the WINS Database

If something happens to the WINS database, you can use the backup files to recover it to the state it was in prior to the problem. To restore the WINS database from backup, follow these steps:

1. Start the WINS console. Right-click the server entry, point to All Tasks, and then select Stop. This stops the WINS service.
2. Right-click the server entry again, and select Restore Database.

3. In the Browse For Folder dialog box, select the parent folder of the Wins_bak folder created during backup (not the Wins_bak folder itself), and click OK.
4. The WINS server will then restore the database from backup. When it finishes, click OK.
5. The WINS service will be restarted automatically.

Enabling WINS Lookups Through DNS

You can enable WINS lookups through DNS. This integration of WINS and DNS provides for an additional opportunity to resolve an IP address to a host name when normal DNS lookups fail. Typically, this might be necessary for clients that can't register their IP addresses in DNS using dynamic updates.

You enable WINS name resolution on a zone-by-zone basis from within the DNS console. Follow these steps:

1. In the DNS console, right-click the zone you want to work with, and then select Properties.
2. In the Properties dialog box, select the WINS or WINS-R tab as appropriate for the type of zone. The WINS tab is used with forward lookup zones and the WINS-R tab is used with reverse lookup zones.
3. Select Use WINS Forward Lookup or Use WINS Reverse Lookup as appropriate.
4. If you're not using DNS servers running on Windows 2000 or later as secondary servers, select Do Not Replicate This Record. This ensures the WINS record that is created during this configuration won't be replicated to servers that don't support this feature.
5. Type the IP address of a WINS server you want to use for name resolution, and click Add. Repeat this step for other WINS servers that should be used.
6. Click OK.

Chapter 29

Installing and Maintaining Print Services

Print services have changed substantially over the years and the changes for Microsoft Windows Server 2003 offer many new features and improvements. The techniques for installing and maintaining print services are what this chapter is about. When you point to Print in an application and click, the document is supposed to print on a printer somewhere. Most users don't care to know how or why printing works; they only care that it works. In that respect, printing is like networking services—something most people take for granted until it doesn't work the way they expect it to or it stops working altogether. The problem with this way of thinking is that next to file and networking services, print services are the most used feature of the Windows operating system. It takes a lot of behind-the-scenes work to ensure printing is as easy as point and click.

Understanding Windows Server 2003 Print Services

In a perfect world, the printers used by an organization would be selected after careful planning. You'd select the best printer for the job based on the expected use of the printer and the features required. The reality is that in many organizations printers are purchased separately by departments and individuals without much thought given to how the printer will be used. Someone sees that a printer is needed and one is purchased. The result is that many organizations have a hodgepodge of printers. Some printers are high-volume and others are low-volume, low-cost. The high-volume printers are designed to handle heavy, daily loads from multiple users, and the low-volume, low-cost printers are designed to handle printing for small groups or individuals. If you are responsible for printers in your department or the organization as a whole, you might want to look at ways to consolidate or standardize so the hodgepodge of printers spread around the department or throughout the organization is easier to manage and maintain.

All printers regardless of type have one thing in common: A device is needed to manage the communication between the printer and the client computers that want to print to the printers. This device is called a *print server*. In most cases, a print server is a computer running the Windows operating system. When a Windows computer acts as a print server, it provides many services. It provides clients with the drivers they need for printing. It stores documents that are spooled for printing and maintains the associated print queue. It provides for security and auditing of printer access.

From a process perspective, it helps to understand how printing works so that you can better manage and better troubleshoot printing problems. The way printing works depends on the data type of the printer driver being used. There are two main data types for printer drivers:

- **Enhanced Meta File (EMF)** EMF uses the Printer Control Language (PCL) page description language. EMF documents are sent to the print server with minimal processing and are then further processed on the print server.
- **RAW** RAW is most commonly used with the PostScript page description language. RAW documents are fully processed on clients before being sent to a print server and aren't modified by the print server.

When you print a document, many processes are involved. Figure 29-1 shows the standard EMF printing process.

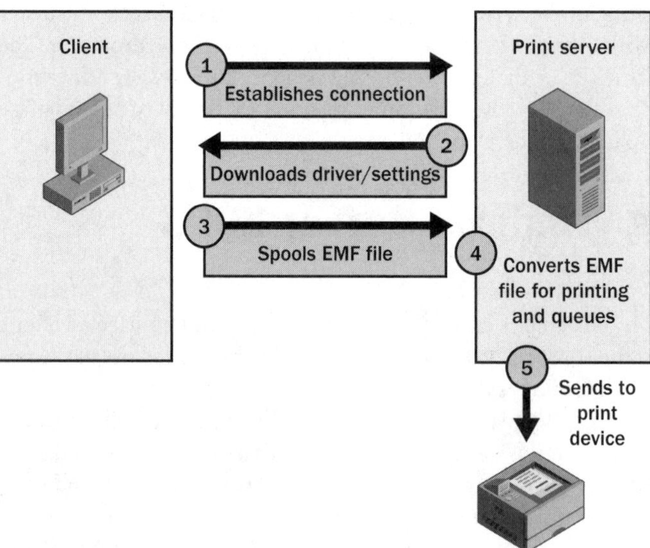

Figure 29-1. The standard EMF printing process.

Here, the client establishes a connection to the print server. If it needs a print driver or if there is a new driver available, it downloads the driver and the associated settings. The client first uses the print driver to partially render the document into EMF and then spools the EMF file to the print server. The print server converts the EMF file to final form and then queues the file to the printer queue (printer). When the document reaches the top of the print queue it is sent to the physical print device.

Figure 29-2 shows the standard RAW printing process. Here, the client establishes a connection to the print server. If it needs a print driver or if there is a new driver available, it downloads the driver and the associated settings. The client then fully processes the file for printing and spools the RAW file to the print server. The print server queues the file to the logical print device (printer). When the document reaches the top of the print queue it is sent to the physical print device.

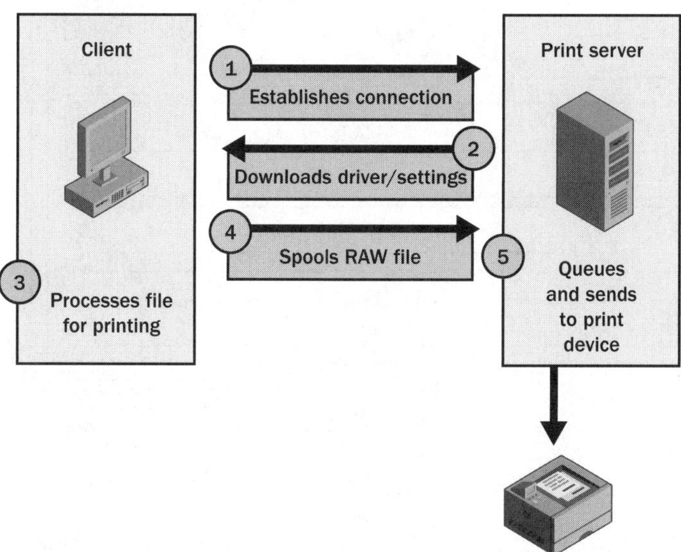

Figure 29-2. The standard RAW printing process.

Okay, so that's the version at 10,000 feet—the fine details are much more complicated, as Figure 29-3 shows. The model can be applied to the mechanics of the initial printing of a document on a client to the handling on the print server to the actual printing on the print device.

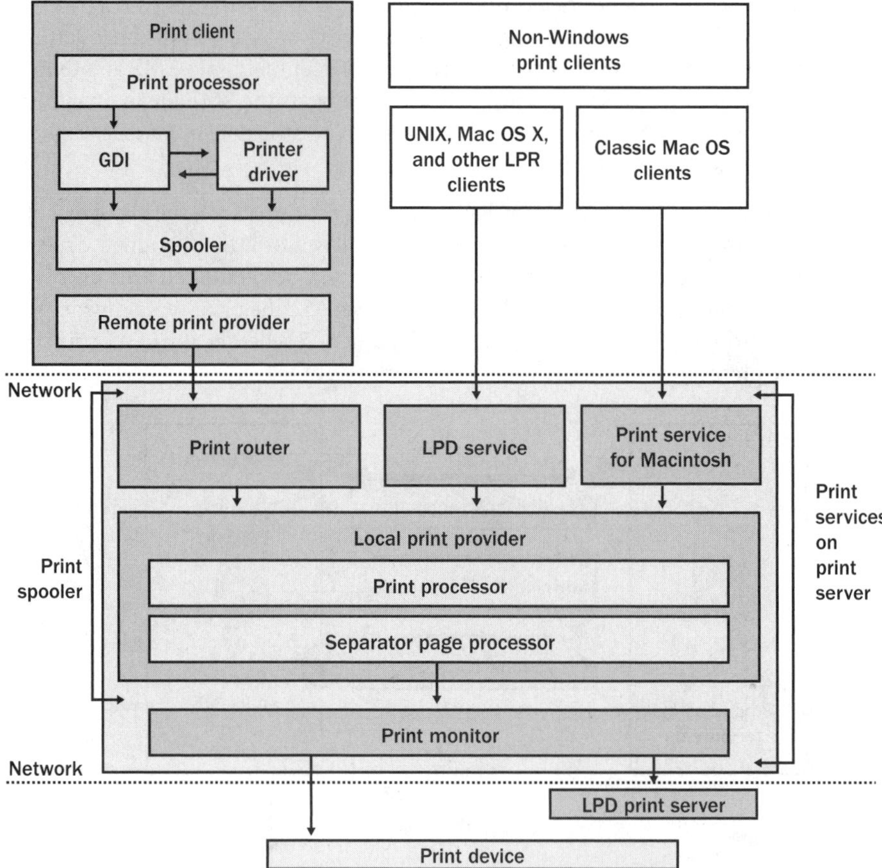

Figure 29-3. A representation of printing from the client to the server to the print device.

Print drivers are stored in the %SystemRoot%\System32\Spool\Drivers folder on the print server. Assuming that a client already has the current print drivers, the printing process works like this:

1. On a client running Microsoft Windows 2000 or later, the application you're printing from calls the Graphics Device Interface (GDI), which uses the printer driver to determine how to format the document for the selected print device. The GDI is responsible for any necessary preprocessing (converting into EMF or RAW format) of the document, which, depending on the printer driver type and configuration settings, might or might not be necessary. When it's finished with the document, the GDI passes the document to the local print spooler (Winspool.drv).
2. The local print spooler makes a remote procedure call (RPC) connection to the Print Spooler service (Spoolsv.exe) on the print server. The Print Spooler service calls the

print router (Spoolss.dll). The print router makes an RPC connection to the remote print provider (Win32spl.dll) on the client. The remote print provider then connects directly to the Print Spooler service on the print server and sends the document.

3 The local print provider on the print server saves the document in the print queue as a print job. By default, all print jobs for all printers on a print server are stored in the %SystemRoot%\System32\Spool\Printers folder. The primary spool file has a .spl extension and the control information needed to print the spool file is stored in a .shd file.

4 The local print provider is responsible for any necessary postprocessing of the document, which, depending on the printer driver type and configuration settings, might or might not be necessary. The local print provider uses the print processor to do any necessary processing or conversion and the separator page processor to insert any separator pages if necessary. The local print provider processes the document when it reaches the top of the print queue and before it sends the print job to the print monitor.

5 The print monitor sends the print job to the physical print device, where it is actually printed. The way spooling works depends on the print queue configuration and the printer buffer. If possible, the entire document is transferred to the print device. Otherwise, the print monitor sends the print job gradually as the print buffer allows.

Like the Registry, printing is one of those areas of the Windows operating system that is obfuscated by varying use of terminology. From a user perspective, a printer is the device that prints out their documents. From a technical perspective, a logical print device or printer is a software component used for printing. Because it is where documents are queued before printing, it is also referred to as a print queue. When you add or install a printer on a Windows system, you are installing the software—the logical print device—as opposed to the physical print device itself.

Print Services Changes for Windows Server 2003

Windows Server 2003 has built-in support for over 3,800 printer drivers, including both 32-bit and 64-bit printer drivers. Support for 64-bit printer drivers is important because systems running 64-bit editions of Windows need 64-bit drivers. As with previous versions of Windows, printer drivers are installed automatically on clients when they first try to print to a new printer device on a print server.

In Microsoft Windows NT 4, all printer drivers operate in kernel mode and are said to be version 2 drivers. With a kernel-mode driver, an error with a printer driver can cause the server to crash. This happens because the driver is running in the operating system kernel process. In Windows 2000 and later, printer drivers operate in user mode and support kernel-mode drivers only for backward compatibility. User-mode drivers are referred to as version 3 drivers.

User-mode drivers operate in a process separate from the operating system kernel process. An error in a user-mode driver affects only its related process. Typically, this means the Print Spooler process hangs up and has to be restarted. Because Windows Server 2003 is configured by default to restart the Print Spooler process automatically within 1 minute if it stops with an error or hangs up, no administrator action is required.

Inside Out

Automatic restart of services is for errors only

When a service is configured to restart automatically, the restart is performed only when an error occurs. Two general types of errors can occur: either the service will hang up and stop responding or the service will stop running and exit with an error code. In these cases, automatic restart can usually recover the service and get the service to resume normal operations. If you stop a service manually, automatic restart does not take place.

Windows 2000 and later also use the Microsoft Universal Printer Driver (Unidrv) rather than the Raster Device Driver (Rasdd) interface, which was used in Windows NT 4. The Universal Printer Driver provides core printing functions that printer driver manufacturers can use. These functions are implemented in two print engines:

- **Unidrv.dll** Provides the core printing functions for PCL print devices. Uses EMF-formatted files.
- **PScript5.dll** Provides core printing functions for PostScript print devices. Uses RAW-formatted files.

The availability of these print engines gives printer manufacturers several options for developing printer drivers. They can create a mini driver that implements only the unique functionality of a particular print device and rely on the appropriate print engine for print services, or they can make their own custom driver that uses its own print engine.

Inside Out

Automatic print driver distribution on clusters

On clusters, any print driver that you install on a virtual cluster is automatically distributed from the cluster spooler resource to all nodes of the cluster. This is an important new feature that simplifies installation and management of print clusters. Administrators must install drivers only once rather than once in each node in the cluster. Additionally, Terminal Services and print services can coexist. This important change allows Terminal Services and print services to be installed on the same nodes in a cluster.

Printing has been enhanced in several areas. Print spooling has been optimized to improve read/write performance from disk. This allows higher-volume printing and faster printing of documents. The Standard TCP/IP Port Monitor used for network-attached print devices has been updated. The updates improve the way print servers establish connections with network-attached print devices and monitor print jobs for error messages, progress, and completion. You can now monitor the status of network-attached printers using a Web browser. To do this, type in the Internet Protocol (IP) address of the network-attached printer.

Also new for Windows Server 2003 are a set of tools for managing print services from the command line. These tools include the following:

- **PrintDriverInfo** A Windows Server 2003 Resource Kit tool for obtaining information about the printers installed on a system
- **SplInfo** A Windows Server 2003 Resource Kit tool for tracking print spool information and usage statistics
- **PrnMngr** A built-in tool for installing printers and managing printers configured on a computer
- **PrnCnfg** A built-in tool for setting printer configuration, including printer name, printer properties, printer sharing, and printer publishing in the Active Directory directory service
- **PrnDrv** A built-in tool for listing and managing print drivers
- **PrnJobs** A built-in tool for viewing and managing print jobs in a print queue
- **PrnPort** A built-in tool for creating and managing Transmission Control Protocol/Internet Protocol (TCP/IP) ports for printers
- **PrntQctl** A built-in tool for managing print queues

Upgrading Windows NT 4 Print Servers to Windows Server 2003

Before upgrading a Windows NT 4 print server to Windows Server 2003, you should uninstall all printer drivers and reinstall the latest versions of those drivers for Windows Server 2003. The reason for doing this is to ensure that kernel-mode print drivers are replaced with user-mode drivers. Replacing these drivers ensures that print servers experience fewer Stop errors and improves print performance overall substantially.

A utility that helps you uninstall and replace kernel-mode printer drivers is available on the Windows Server 2003 distribution CD-ROM. This utility, called FixPrnSv, is located in the Printers\Fixprnsv folder. You must run this utility prior to upgrading from Windows NT 4. When you run FixPrnSv, it identifies bad printer drivers and replaces them with compatible drivers. If there isn't a replacement on the distribution CD for a bad driver, the utility lets you know that you must obtain an updated driver from the printer manufacturer.

To use FixPrnSv, follow these steps:

1. Insert the Windows Server 2003 distribution CD. When the Autorun dialog box is displayed, click Perform Additional Tasks, and then select Browse This CD. This starts Windows Explorer with the Windows Server 2003 distribution CD selected.
2. Double-click Printers, and then double-click FixPrnSv. In the FixPrnSv folder, double-click FixPrnSv.exe. This opens a command prompt and runs FixPrnSv, as shown in Figure 29-4.

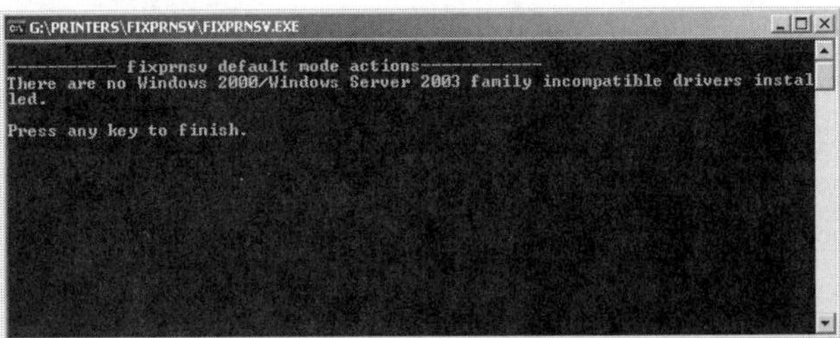

Figure 29-4. FixPrnSv finds and replaces kernel-mode printer drivers; use it prior to upgrading from Windows NT 4.

3. FixPrnSv examines all the printer drivers on the computer and replaces kernel-mode drivers with user-mode drivers automatically. You are prompted if printer drivers are found that aren't on the CD.
4. When FixPrnSv finishes, press any key to finish and exit the utility.

After you upgrade drivers, you can upgrade the system to Windows Server 2003. Be sure to perform any other necessary upgrade procedures as discussed in Chapter 8, "Upgrading to Windows Server 2003."

Migrating Print Servers from One System to Another

Often you'll find that you must replace an existing print server with a new machine. Sometimes this happens because the current hardware doesn't perform well enough to handle the current load. Other times this happens because you are moving from one operating system to another.

When you deploy a new print server to replace an existing server, you can use the migration techniques discussed in Part 3, "Windows Server 2003 Upgrades and Migrations," to do the following:

- Reduce the amount of time it takes to configure the new server
- Ensure the configuration of the new server is the same as the old server

- Consolidate print servers by moving printers from multiple print servers to a single print server

As with standard operating system migration, you can migrate print servers manually, automatically, or using a combination of the techniques.

Manually Migrating Print Servers

The manual migration process starts with documentation. Document the print server's configuration. Note the printers that are set up on the server and write down the details of their configuration, making sure to include the following information:

- Printer names and models
- Printer drivers and the additional types of drivers made available to clients
- Printer ports and the configuration used
- Advanced printer settings, such as priority and availability schedule
- Printer security settings and the users and groups with access

After you thoroughly document the existing print server configuration, you can install the new print server and configure its print services in the same way as the server you are replacing. By migrating a print server by hand, you can ensure that the latest drivers are used and can use the opportunity to standardize the printer information. The obvious disadvantage is that manual migration can take a lot of time and is prone to errors.

Automating Print Server Migration

Microsoft provides a utility for migrating print services called Printer Migrator. Using Printer Migrator version 3.1 or later, you can

- Migrate print services from a print server running Windows NT 4, Windows 2000, Windows XP, or Windows Server 2003 to a print server running Windows 2000, Windows XP, or Windows Server 2003
- Migrate print services from a stand-alone Windows NT 4 or Windows 2000 printer server to a clustered print server running Windows 2000 or Windows Server 2003

Printer Migrator is available as a download from the Microsoft Web site at *http://www.microsoft.com/printserver/*. After you obtain and install the Printer Migrator, don't run it until you consider how you want to handle printer drivers. Printer Migrator migrates the current print environment from an existing source server to a target server exactly as the environment exists on the source server, which includes printers, printer drivers, printer ports, print processors, and print monitors that are configured, as well as the associated

Registry settings and files. It won't, however, update driver versions. Because of this, if you are migrating from Windows NT 4, you might first want to upgrade printer drivers using FixPrnSv as discussed in the section entitled "Upgrading Windows NT 4 Print Servers to Windows Server 2003" earlier in this chapter.

When you work with Printer Migrator, you use it to back up the print services configuration of a target server and restore it on another target server. This allows you to migrate print services to and from multiple systems from a central location, which can be your desktop system. To allow you to consolidate the print services of multiple servers to a single server, Printer Migrator doesn't delete the existing printer configurations when you perform restore operations. Instead, it performs a merge operation, which replaces any existing settings with this defined in the configuration you backed up and adding any additional configuration settings.

When you are ready to migrate print services, follow these steps:

1. Log on to the print server that you want to migrate using an account that is a member of the Administrators or Print Operators group. Then start Printer Migrator by double-clicking the executable you obtained. This should be PrintMig.exe.
2. When Printer Migrator starts, it will examine the current print environment. As shown in Figure 29-5, this means Printer Migrator enumerates all printers, printer drivers, printer ports, print processors, and print monitors and stores their configuration information. You can examine this information by expanding the related entries.

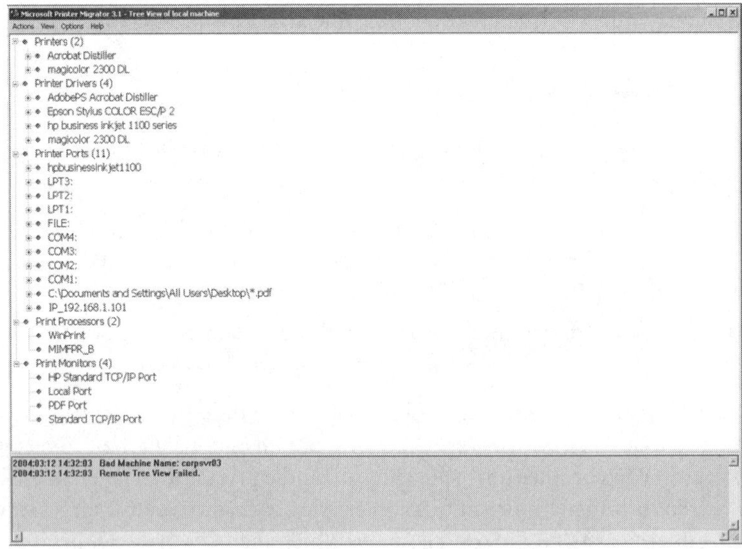

Figure 29-5. Printer Migrator examines the print server.

3. Create a backup of the print server's configuration. Select Backup from the Actions menu. In the Printer Configuration Backup dialog box, shown in Figure 29-6, you can

now select a save location for the printer configuration using the Look In selection list. Once you find a save location, type a name for the backup file.

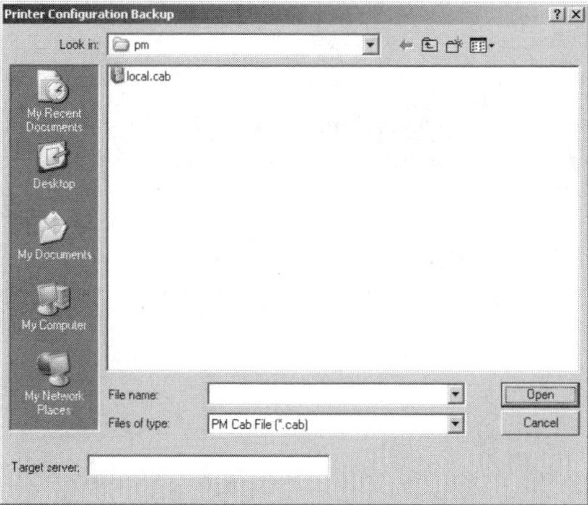

Figure 29-6. Backup the configuration.

4 When you click Open, Printer Migrator will save the printer configuration to the named file as a compressed .cab file. This process can take a few minutes, depending on the number of printers configured, and each step in the backup operation is displayed, as shown in Figure 29-7. Scroll back through the logged text and check for any critical error, such as the inability to save a configuration file in the cabinet. If there are no substantive errors, continue with the migration process.

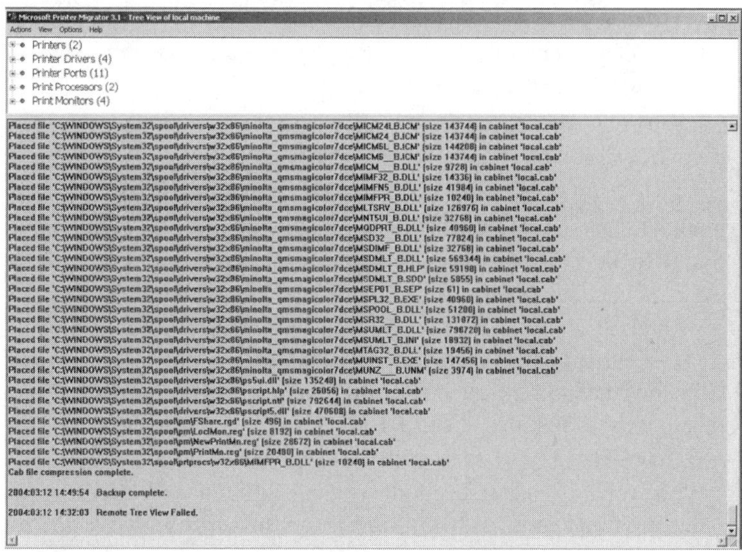

Figure 29-7. Each step in the backup operation is recorded.

Note Typically, errors occur if you don't have appropriate permissions to perform the backup operation. In this case, use Run As to run the Printer Migrator using an account with the appropriate permissions or log off and then log back on using an account with appropriate permissions.

5. When the .cab file creation process is completed, select Restore from the Actions menu. In the Printer Configuration Restore dialog box, shown in Figure 29-8, select the previously saved .cab file.

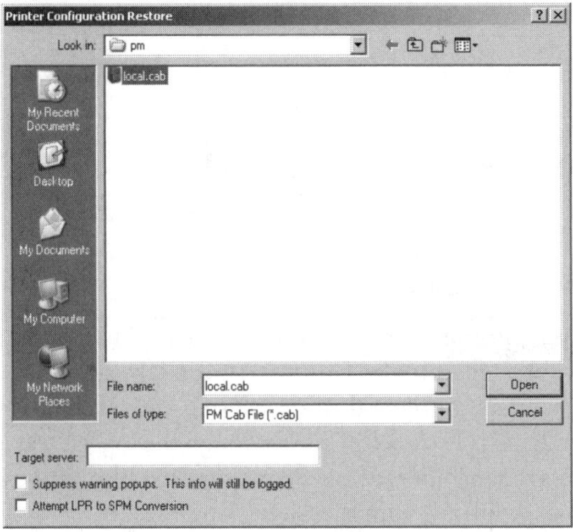

Figure 29-8. Restore the configuration on the destination server.

6. In the Target Server field, type the name or IP address of the print server to which you want to migrate the print services.
7. If you don't want to see popups showing errors, select Suppress Warning Popups. Errors will still be recorded in the logged text.
8. Printer Migrator can attempt to convert legacy Line Printer Remote (LPR) printer ports to Standard TCP/IP Port Monitor ports. If you want to do this, select Attempt LPR To SPM Conversion.

Note With LPR, a port is used in conjunction with a line printer daemon (LPD) print queue. Most current printers use Standard TCP/IP Port Monitor ports and the RAW protocol. With RAW, data is sent unmodified over the port to the printer using a designated port number. In most cases, this is port 9100.

9. When you are ready to begin the restore, click Open. Printer Migration will then use the .cab file to configure print services on the target server. Again this process can take

a few minutes, depending on the number of printers configured. Each step in the restore operation is displayed and you can scroll back through the logged text to check for any critical errors.

> **Note** As part of the restore process, Printer Migrator will stop the Print Spooler service on the target system so it can replace driver files. Once the driver files are copied from the .cab file to the target system, Printer Migrator will restart the Print Spooler service.

10. If you are consolidating print servers, repeat steps 1 through 9 to migrate other print services to the print server.

Planning for Printer Deployments and Consolidation

Print servers and printers are the key components needed for printing. You can size and optimize both print servers and printers in many ways.

> **Tip** **Optimize and monitor after installation as well**
> After sizing and optimization, you should consider optimizing the way printing is handled using print queues. To better support deployed print services, you can periodically monitor performance, check for and install print driver upgrades, and prepare for print server failure.

Sizing Print Server Hardware and Optimizing Configuration

The maximum load and performance level of a print server depends on its configuration. Print servers can be configured in many ways, and as a print server's workload changes over time, so should its configuration. As the workload of the print server scales, so does the amount of processing and memory required to handle print services. Any computer, including a desktop-class system, can act as a print server. The print server's central processing unit (CPU) speed, total random access memory (RAM), and network card speed should be considered.

When PCL printers and EMF print drivers are used, most of the document processing is performed on the server and the server will need a fairly fast processor and sufficient RAM to process documents. When PostScript printers and RAW print drivers are used, most of the document processing is performed on clients before documents are transferred to the server and the server's processor speed and memory are less important. In many cases, a printer server will provide services for multiple printers so there's a good chance that some of the printers will be PCL and some of the printers will be PostScript. In this case, the processing power and total RAM of the print server are again important.

Complex print jobs, such as those containing graphics, can use additional resources on the print server. They require more memory to process and more processing power. The number of clients connecting to a print server can also affect resource requirements:

- Most print clients running Windows 2000 or later establish RPC connections to print servers. With RPC, a connection between a client and server remains open as long as there is one or more open handles. Typically, applications open handles to a print server when a user prints but don't close those open handles until the user shuts down or exits the application. If a user accesses the printer folder or views the printer queue on the print server, this opens handles to the print server because the folders or queues are open as well. As a result, there can be many open handles to a print server using resources even when a printer server isn't busy.
- Most non-Windows clients establish Server Message Block (SMB) connections to print servers. If Print Services for Unix are configured, SMB clients running UNIX, Mac OS X, or other operating systems can use the LPR service to communicate with the LDP service on the print server. Because these clients maintain their own printer spools, the print server acts as the gateway between the client and the printer. These clients use very little resources on the server, but have very few options.

Note Microsoft Windows 95, Windows 98, and Windows Millennium Edition (Windows Me) clients use SMB connections as well. These clients do not, however, use LPR or the LPD service. They render files using the GDI and spool RAW-formatted files to the print server. This means they perform their own processing of printed documents.

Print servers must have sufficient disk space to handle print jobs. The amount of disk space required depends on the size of print jobs and the number of print jobs that are queued for printing at any one time. It also depends on the print server configuration because in some cases a print server can be configured to save documents after they have been spooled for faster reprinting. By default, print jobs are spooled to files on the print server's system drive (%SystemRoot%\System32\Spool\PRINTERS), but this is completely configurable, as discussed in the section entitled "Configuring Print Spool, Logging, and Notification Settings" later in this chapter.

Print servers perform a substantial amount of disk input/output (I/O) operations. To ensure optimal performance, you should consider moving the spool folder to a separate drive or array of drives that isn't used for other purposes. A separate drive should help to ensure disk space isn't a constraint on the number of jobs the print server can handle and that the disk I/O operations related to the spooler are separate from that of other disk I/O operations.

Tip Paging and spooling are both disk I/O-intensive operations. If possible, use a separate disk that uses a separate Small Computer System Interface (SCSI) controller rather than the disk and controller used for the server's paging file.

The network interfaces on a print server are also important, but often overlooked. The print server needs sufficient connectivity to communicate with both clients and printers. You should use 100-megabits-per-second (Mbps) network cards when possible.

Finally, when working with a dedicated print server, you should configure the Server service to Maximize Performance For File Sharing, as discussed in the section entitled "Tuning Data Throughput" on page 452. This setting optimizes Windows for file and printer sharing by increasing the amount of memory reserved for the system cache and maximizing data throughput for file sharing.

Sizing Printer Hardware and Optimizing Configuration

Many types of printers are available including ink-jet and laser. Both types have advantages and disadvantages.

Ink-jet printers typically have lower upfront costs but higher costs later because they often require more maintenance and use consumables (ink cartridges) quicker. A typical ink-jet printer will print several hundred pages before you have to replace its ink cartridges. Higher-capacity cartridges are available for some business-class models. As part of periodic maintenance, you must perform nozzle checks to check for clogged nozzles and then clean the print heads if they are clogged. You might also need to align the print heads periodically.

Laser printers typically have higher upfront costs and moderate incremental costs because these printers typically require less maintenance and use consumables (ink cartridges and OPC kits) less frequently. A typical laser printer will print several thousand pages before you have to replace ink cartridges and about 10,000 pages before you have to replace the OPC kit. Higher-capacity ink cartridges are also available for most business-class models. Replacing the ink cartridges and the OPC kit are the key maintenance tasks.

Tip **Use laser printers for high-volume printing**
In most cases, laser printers have a lower per-sheet print cost than ink-jet printers. This is true for black-and-white as well as color printing. Because of the lower cost, longer life cycle of consumables, and less frequent preventative maintenance schedule, laser printers are better suited to high-volume printing.

For either printer type, you should look at the included features and the expansion options available (if any). Most business-class printers can be expanded. The options available depend on the printer model and can include the following:

- **RAM expansion modules** The amount of RAM on a printer determines how much information it can buffer. At a minimum, a printer should be sized so that the average document being printed can be buffered in RAM in its entirety. As the workload of the printer increases, the RAM should allow for buffering of multiple documents simultaneously, which allows for faster and more efficient printing.

Tip **Consider the type of document being printed**

Most word-processing documents are relatively small—several hundred pages of text use only a few hundred kilobytes. When you add in graphics, such as with presentations or Portable Document Format (PDF) files, even files with few pages can use several megabytes of disk space. Digital art, computer-aided design (CAD), and other types of files with high-resolution graphics can use hundreds of megabytes.

- **Paper or envelope trays** Add-on paper or envelope trays can improve performance substantially—more than you'd think. If a group within the organization routinely prints with different paper sizes or prints transparencies or envelopes, you should consider getting an add-on tray to accommodate the additional paper size or type. Otherwise, every time someone prints to the alternate paper size or type, the printer can stop and wait for the user to insert the appropriate type of paper. On a busy printer, this can lead to big delays in printing, frustrated users, and major problems.
- **Duplexers** Duplexers allow for printing on both sides of a sheet of paper. If a printer has a duplexer, Windows Server 2003 will use that feature automatically to reduce the amount of paper used by the printer. This doesn't necessarily save time, but it does mean the printer's tray will have to be refilled less frequently. Users can of course change the default settings and elect not to duplex.
- **Internal hard disks** An internal hard disk shifts much of the printing burden from the print server to the printer itself. A printer with an internal hard disk is able to store many documents internally and queue them for printing directly. Because the documents are stored on the server, printing is more efficient and can be quicker than if the printer had to wait for documents to be transferred over the network.

Many groups of users have specific needs, so if you are purchasing a printer for a particular group be sure to ask their needs, which might include the need for the following:

- **Photo printing** Usually an option for ink-jet printers rather than laser jet printers
- **Large-format printing** The capability to print documents larger than 11 by 17 inches

Both ink-jet and laser jet printers are available in direct-attached and network-attached models. Direct-attached printers (more commonly known as *local printers*) connect directly to a print server by a parallel, universal serial bus (USB) or FireWire (IEEE 1394) interface. For faster transmission speeds and easier configuration, consider printers with USB 2 or FireWire interfaces and stay away from those with slower parallel interfaces. USB and FireWire interfaces are also fully Plug and Play–compliant.

Network-attached printers have a network card and connect to the network like other devices with network cards. A printer with a built-in network interface gives you flexibility in where you place the printer relative to the print server. Unlike a local printer, which must be placed in close proximity to the print server, a network-attached printer can be placed just anywhere with a network connection. If you have a choice, choose a network-attached printer over a local printer.

Inside Out

The ins and outs of color printing

The price of color printers and the per-sheet cost of printing in color have both dropped substantially over the years. This makes color printing more affordable than ever and that has led many organizations to increase their use of color printers. If your organization is considering the use of color printers, you should look closely at the type of ink or toner cartridges used by the printer.

Most business-class color printers have separate cartridges for each basic color—cyan, magenta, and yellow—and black. Some high-end printers have additional cartridges for producing true-to-life colors, and these printers are often referred to be the number of ink/toner cartridges, such as a six-color printer. Look closely at the capacity options for cartridges. Some printers can use both standard-capacity and high-capacity cartridges, but not always for both color and black ink.

If a group or individual needs a printer for photo printing, it is important to consider whether special photo ink/toner cartridges are available. For example, some Hewlett-Packard (HP) DeskJet models have the option to use a photo ink cartridge. This special cartridge prints digital photos with richer colors that are more true to life. Also, don't assume a color laser printer will be able to print on specialty photo paper because this might or might not be the case. See the section entitled "Configuring Color Profiles" later in this chapter for details on how Integrated Color Management (ICM) is used in Windows Server 2003.

Setting Up Printers

Windows Server 2003 allows you to set up local printers as well as network-attached printers. Either type of printer can be shared on the network so that it is available to other computers and users. The computer sharing the printer is called a *print server*, regardless of whether it is actually running a server version of the Windows operating system.

As discussed previously, you can configure more than one logical print device (printer) for a physical print device. The key reason to do this is when you want to use different options, such as when you want to create a priority or scheduled print queue. If you configure multiple printers, you must use a different local name and share name each time. Other than that, you can choose the exact same initial settings each time and modify them as desired.

Note Windows Server 2003 supports printing for clients running any version of Windows. To support Macintosh and UNIX clients, you must install additional print services. Install Print Services For Macintosh to support Mac users on classic Mac. Install Print Services For Unix to support UNIX and Macintosh OS X (which is built on UNIX).

Adding Local Printers

Typically, a local printer is a desktop version for use by an individual or a small group. Most desktop printers allow you to connect to them using either a parallel printer interface or a USB or FireWire interface. All of these techniques require a cable to connect from the computer to the printer. You might also have the option of using wireless infrared (IrDA or Bluetooth), which doesn't require a cable. Windows Server 2003 supports all of these options.

Inside Out

Choosing an interface type

With any available printer interface option, your key concern shouldn't be having to spend additional money on a cable—spend the money if you have to—it should be on getting the best performance. Consider the following:

- A standard parallel printer interface (IEEE 1284–compliant) has a maximum transmission speed of 250 kilobits per second (Kbps).
- A high-speed parallel printer interface (ECP/EPP-compliant) has a maximum transmission speed of 3–5 Mbps.
- A wireless interface that is IrDA-compliant has a maximum transmission speed of around 4 Mbps; a wireless interface that is Bluetooth-compliant has a speed of 2–3 Mbps.
- A USB interface has a maximum transmission speed of 12 Mbps for USB 1 and 480 Mbps for USB 2.
- A FireWire (IEEE 1394–compliant) interface has a transmission speed of 100 to 400 Mbps.

Given these transmission speeds and that USB and FireWire are Plug and Play–compliant, they should be the preferred interfaces to use when you have a choice. With USB 2, it is important to note that you get only the speed benefit if both the computer interface and the printer interface are USB 2–compliant.

To set up a local printer, you'll need to use an account that is a member of the Administrators or Print Operators group. To get started, connect the print device to the server. If Windows Server 2003 automatically detects the print device, it begins installing the printer and its drivers. If the drivers aren't found, you might need to insert the Windows Server 2003 distribution CD into the CD-ROM drive or use a driver disk. Windows Server 2003 will then automatically share the printer for network access. The share name is set to the first eight characters of the printer name with spaces removed. You can rename the printer share later if necessary.

If Windows Server 2003 doesn't detect the print device automatically, you must install the print device using the Add Printer Wizard. Follow these steps:

1. Access the Printers And Faxes folder either by clicking Start and then clicking Printers And Faxes or by clicking Start, pointing to Settings, and then selecting Printers And Faxes.
2. Select or double-click Add Printer to start the Add Printer Wizard. Click Next.
3. Select Local Printer Attached To This Computer, as shown in Figure 29-9, and then select Automatically Detect And Install My Plug And Play Printer. Click Next.

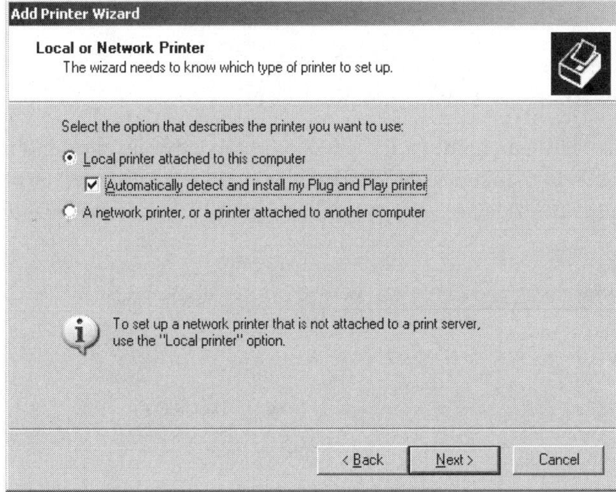

Figure 29-9. Select the local printer option for a directly connected printer.

4. If Windows is able to detect the printer and it is Plug and Play–compatible, the New Hardware Found dialog box is displayed and the operating system installs the printer using drivers if they are available or prompts you to insert the Windows Server 2003 distribution CD into the CD-ROM drive or use a driver disk. Windows Server 2003 will then complete the installation by automatically sharing the printer for network access.
5. If the printer wasn't detected, you must continue with manual installation. On the Select A Printer Port page, select Use The Following Port, and then choose the port to which the printer is attached, as shown in Figure 29-10. Click Next.

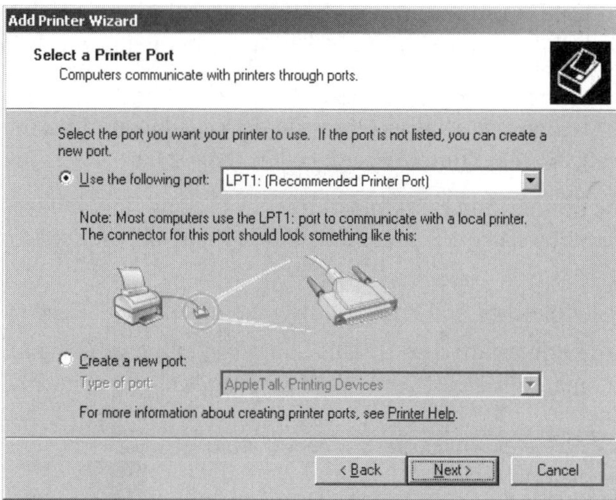

Figure 29-10. Select the printer port to use.

6 On the Install Printer Software page, choose the manufacturer and model of the printer, as shown in Figure 29-11. This allows Windows Server 2003 to assign a printer driver to the print device. After you choose a print device manufacturer, choose a printer model.

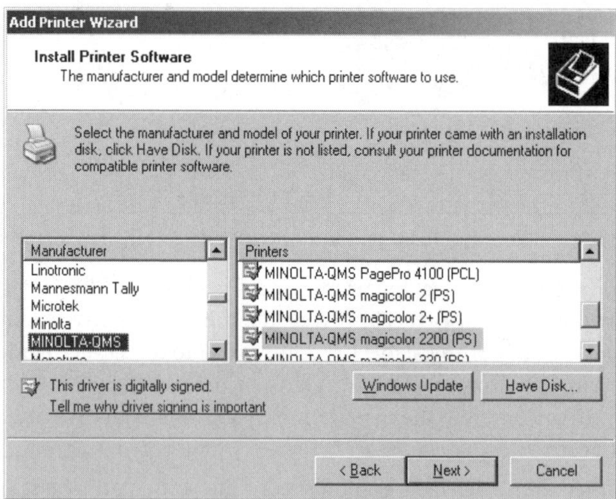

Figure 29-11. Specify the printer manufacturer and model.

> **Tip** **Use a driver disk or check Windows Update**
> If the print device manufacturer and model you're using aren't displayed in the list or you have a newer driver from the manufacturer, click Have Disk to install a new driver. If you want to check for and download new drivers from the Microsoft Web site automatically, click Windows Update. Make sure the driver you use is digitally signed. This is indicated after you select a manufacturer and model and means that Microsoft has certified the driver for use with Microsoft products. Any drivers downloaded from Windows Update are digitally signed and therefore certified.

7. Click Next. If a driver is already installed for the printer, as would be the case if you are creating an additional print queue or are installing a second identical print device, you see the Use Existing Driver Page. You can choose to keep the existing driver or replace it. It is recommended that you keep the existing driver. However, if you have a newer driver, you will probably want to use that driver if it is digitally signed and certified by Microsoft. Click Next.
8. On the Name Your Printer page, type a name for the printer, as shown in Figure 29-12. The name you use is the one you'll see in the Printers And Faxes folder of Control Panel. It shouldn't contain special characters such as commas, backward slashes, or exclamation points, but can contain spaces. You can also set the printer as the local default for the local computer. Click Next.

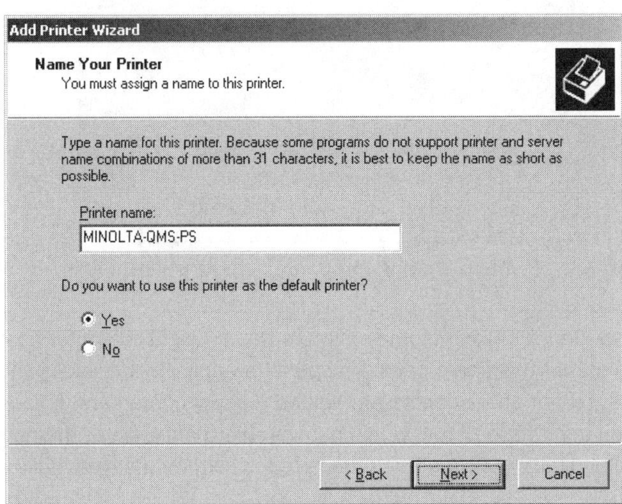

Figure 29-12. Specify a name for the printer.

Tip Choose names that have the widest compatibility

Although you can use just about any name for a printer, you should keep the printer name as short as possible. For maximum compatibility, it is recommended that the printer name be no more than 31 characters and not contain spaces. This will make the printer easier to work with from the command line and in applications that have printer name limitations.

9 Choose whether to share the printer by selecting either Do Not Share This Printer or Share Name, as shown in Figure 29-13. If you're sharing the printer, type a share name, and then click Next. Keep in mind the best printer share names are descriptive and help you determine what the printer is used for and where it is. With this in mind, you might name a printer EngPrinter to indicate it is the printer for the Engineering department.

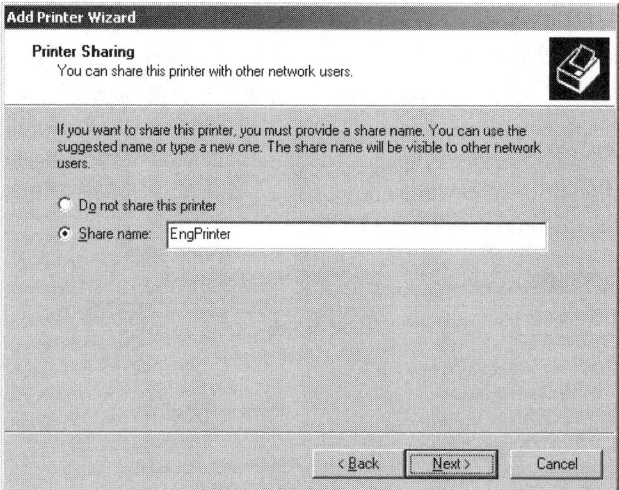

Figure 29-13. If you're sharing the printer, type a share name.

Note Windows Server 2003 automatically creates an eight-character name for the print share. You can accept this share name or type a new one. For backward compatibility with MS-DOS clients, printer share names are limited to eight characters. If you don't have MS-DOS clients, you don't have to follow this naming rule. Simply enter the name you want to use, click Next, and then click Yes when prompted to confirm that you really want to use the share name.

10 On the Location And Comment page, enter an optional location and comment. Use the comment to describe the printer and its capabilities. Use the location to detail where the printer is located. Computers running Windows 95, Windows 98, and

Windows NT 4 will display the comment in printer-related dialog boxes. Computers running Windows 2000 or later will display both the location and the comment in printer-related dialog boxes, which makes it easier for users to browse Active Directory to find printers by searching according to location. Click Next.

11 Next you have the opportunity to print a test page. This is a good idea to make sure the printer works and that files can be printed to the print device using this configuration. Choose Yes to print a test page or No to continue without printing a test page, and then click Next.

12 As shown in Figure 29-14, the final page displays a summary of the configuration settings you selected. Review the information and when you are ready, click Finish to complete the setup and save the configuration. The wizard will then copy the printer drivers as necessary and, if selected, print a test page.

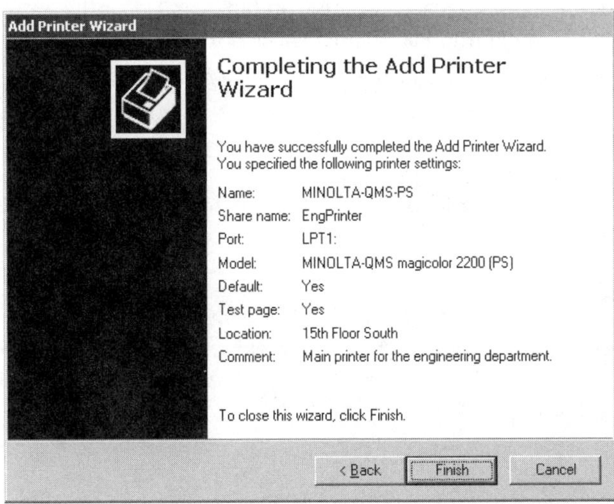

Figure 29-14. Review the printer settings and click Finish when you are done.

> **Note** All printers configured for sharing on Windows Server 2003 systems are automatically listed in Active Directory. Printers can be removed from the directory as necessary, however.

Adding Network-Attached Printers

Network-attached printers are printers that have their own network cards. Typically, a network-attached printer is a workgroup-class printer for use by groups of users. Most network-attached printers use the RAW protocol or the LPR protocol to communicate over a standard TCP/IP port. This includes network-attached printers that use TCP/IP as well as those that use network devices such as Hewlett-Packard JetDirect or Intel NetPort.

In some case, you might need to configure other types of network printer connections. To communicate with printers connected to a UNIX computer or using the LPD service, you can configure the printer to use LPR and connect to the LPD service. To communicate with an AppleTalk printer, you can configure the printer to use AppleTalk.

Adding Standard TCP/IP Printers

You can set up a network-attached printer using a standard TCP/IP port using an account that is a member of the Administrators or Print Operators group. Follow these steps:

1. Access the Printers And Faxes folder either by clicking Start and then clicking Printers And Faxes or by clicking Start, pointing to Settings, and then selecting Printers And Faxes.
2. Select or double-click Add Printer to start the Add Printer Wizard. Click Next.
3. Select Local Printer Attached To This Computer, and clear the Automatically Detect And Install My Plug And Play Printer check box. Click Next.
4. On the Select A Printer Port page, select Create A New Port, and then choose Standard TCP/IP Port, as shown in Figure 29-15. Click Next to start the Add Standard TCP/IP Printer Port Wizard.

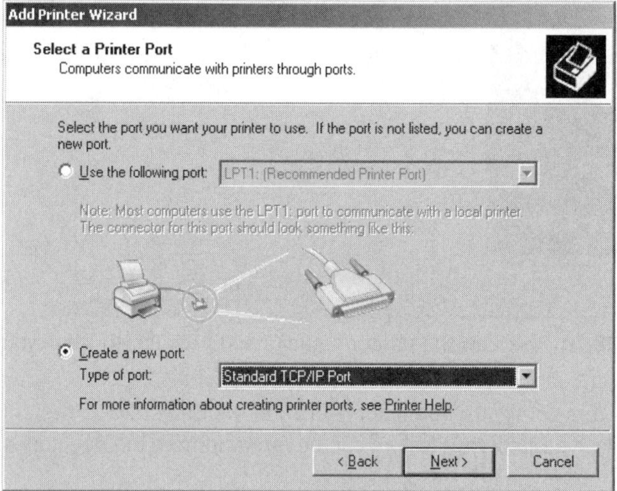

Figure 29-15. Select Standard TCP/IP Port.

5. Make sure the printer is connected to the network and turned on. One way to do this is to ping the printer's IP address. As a final check of the printer, you might want to print its configuration or check its network settings to ensure it has the appropriate IP address and subnet mask. When you are ready to continue, click Next.
6. On the Add Port page, shown in Figure 29-16, type the printer name or IP address. This must be the actual printer name or IP address as specified in the printer configuration. A port name is filled in for you automatically. Because this port name must be

unique on the print server, you can't have two printers with the same port name on a print server.

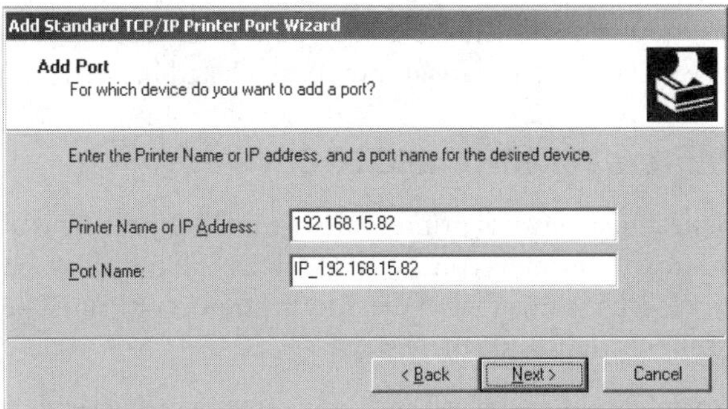

Figure 29-16. Type the printer name or IP address as it is set in the printer configuration.

7 When you click Next, the wizard will look for the printer on the network. If the wizard is unable to find the print device or needs additional information, select the printer device type using the Standard list, as shown in Figure 29-17.

Note If the wizard is unable to find the print device on the network, make sure that you entered the printer name or IP address correctly. If you have, make sure the device is on, that it is properly configured, and that the network is set up correctly. If the wizard still can't detect the printer, select the device type and continue with the installation. You will mostly likely need to change the standard TCP/IP port monitor settings before you can use the printer. You can do this by selecting Custom and clicking Settings now, or you can perform the necessary changes later. Both techniques are discussed in the section entitled "Changing Standard TCP/IP Port Monitor Settings" later in this chapter.

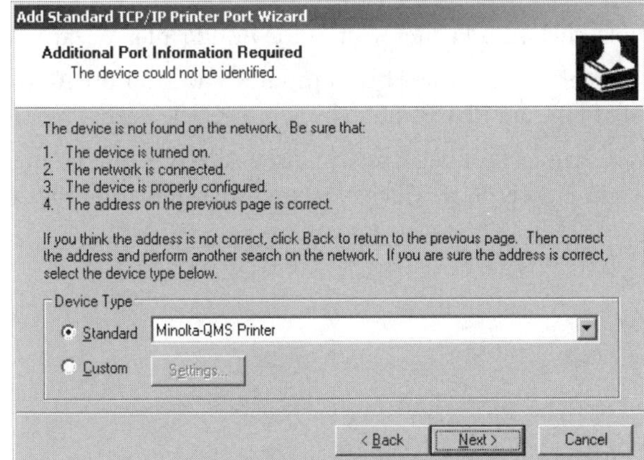

Figure 29-17. Select the printer device type.

8. Click Next, review the port configuration, and then click Finish. In the Add Printer Wizard, the configuration will continue as it did with local printers. With that in mind, continue with steps 7 through 12 in the section entitled "Adding Local Printers" earlier in this chapter. As noted previously, all printers configured for sharing on Windows Server 2003 systems are automatically listed in Active Directory.

Adding LPR Printers for UNIX and LPD

Another way to connect to a network printer is to use an LPR port. This allows the print server to communicate with printers connected to UNIX computers or that use the LPD service. Using an account that is a member of the Administrators or Print Operators group, you can add the LPR printer by following these steps:

1. Connect the printer to the network and configure the printer with the appropriate TCP/IP settings for the network. Print the configuration if possible so you have it handy.
2. Next start the installation process for Print Services For Unix. In Control Panel, double-click Add Or Remove Programs. Then in the Add Or Remove Programs dialog box, click Add Windows Components to start the Windows Components Wizard.
3. On the Windows Components page, select Other Network File And Print Services, and then click Details.
4. In the Other Network File And Print Services dialog box, select Print Services For Unix. Don't clear other selections if a service has already been installed. Click OK.
5. Click Next to begin the installation, and then click Finish. This completes the installation process for Print Services For UNIX.
6. Access the Printers And Faxes folder either by clicking Start and then clicking Printers And Faxes or by clicking Start, pointing to Settings, and then selecting Printers And Faxes.
7. Select or double-click Add Printer to start the Add Printer Wizard. Click Next.
8. Select Local Printer Attached To This Computer, and clear the Automatically Detect And Install My Plug And Play Printer check box. Click Next.
9. On the Select A Printer Port page, select Create A New Port, and then choose LPR Port, as shown in Figure 29-18. Click Next to display the Add LPR Compatible Printer dialog box.

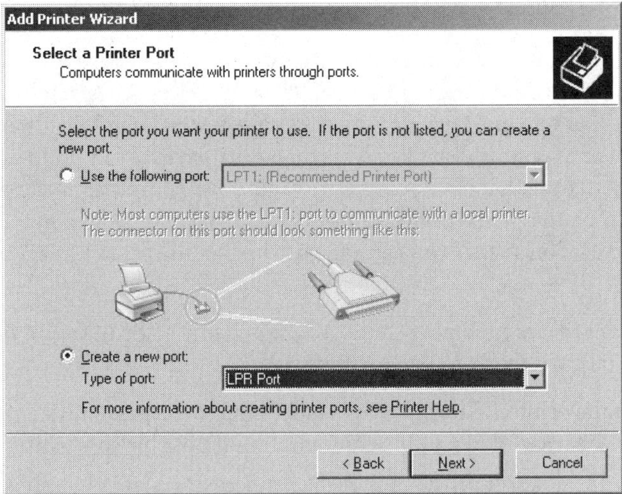

Figure 29-18. Select the printer device type.

10 Type the name or IP address of the server running LPD, as shown in Figure 29-19.

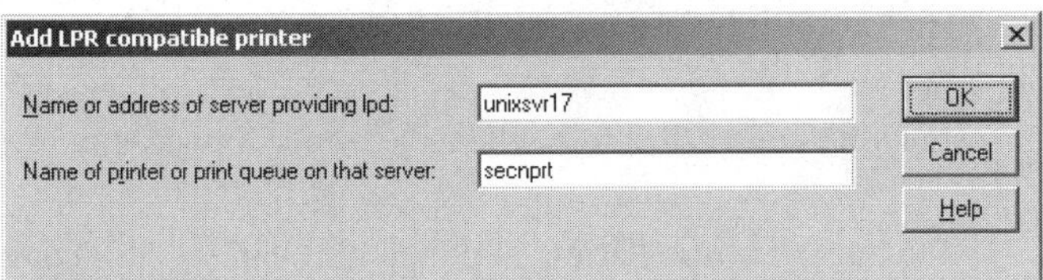

Figure 29-19. Configure the LPR port.

11 Type the name of the printer or the name of the print queue on the LPD server.

12 When you click OK, the computer will create the port and attempt to connect to the printer or the LPD server. If the wizard is unable to find the print device or needs additional information, click OK at the prompt.

13 In the Add Printer Wizard, the configuration will continue as it did with local printers. With that in mind, continue with steps 6 through 12 in the section entitled "Adding Local Printers" earlier in this chapter. As noted previously, all printers configured for sharing on Windows Server 2003 systems are automatically listed in Active Directory.

Adding AppleTalk Printers

When you have computers running classic Mac OS, you might need to use a Windows server as the print server. To do this, you must install Print Services For Macintosh and then configure the print server to communicate with the AppleTalk printer. It is important to note that Print Services For Macintosh isn't available for 64-bit versions of Windows Server 2003. It is also important to note that once you set up a Windows computer as the print server for an AppleTalk printer, the print service can only be managed by and connected to the Windows print server. This means you cannot also connect the printer to a Macintosh print server.

Using an account that is a member of the Administrators or Print Operators group, you can add the AppleTalk printer by following these steps:

1. Connect the printer to the network and configure the printer with the appropriate settings for the network. Print the configuration if possible so you have it.
2. Start the installation process for Print Services For Macintosh. In Control Panel, double-click Add Or Remove Programs.
3. In the Add Or Remove Programs dialog box, click Add Windows Components to start the Windows Components Wizard. On the Windows Components page, select Other Network File And Print Services, and then click Details.
4. In the Other Network File And Print Services dialog box, select Print Services For Macintosh. Don't clear other selections if a service has already been installed. Click OK.
5. Click Next to begin the installation, and then click Finish. This completes the installation of Print Services for Macintosh.
6. Access the Printers And Faxes folder either by clicking Start and then clicking Printers And Faxes or by clicking Start, pointing to Settings, and then selecting Printers And Faxes.
7. Select or double-click Add Printer to start the Add Printer Wizard. Click Next.
8. Select Local Printer Attached To This Computer, but do not select Automatically Detect And Install My Plug And Play Printer. Click Next.
9. On the Select A Printer Port page, select Create A New Port, and then choose AppleTalk Printing Devices, as shown in Figure 29-20.
10. When you click Next, Windows searches the network for AppleTalk printers. Choose the printer in the Available AppleTalk Printing Devices dialog box, and then click OK to install the printer. When prompted to capture the port, click Yes.
11. In the Add Printer Wizard, the configuration will continue as it did with local printers. With that in mind, continue with steps 6 through 12 from the section entitled "Adding Local Printers" earlier in this chapter. As noted previously, all printers configured for sharing on Windows Server 2003 systems are automatically listed in Active Directory.

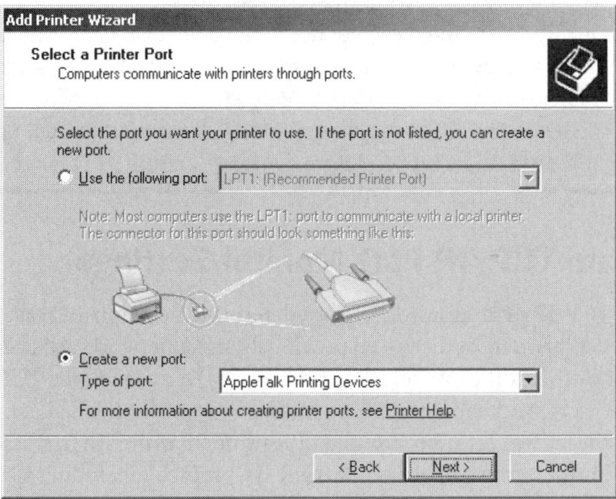

Figure 29-20. Select the print device type.

Inside Out

Setting permissions for Mac users

With an AppleTalk printer, you can't set permissions on a per-user basis. AppleTalk doesn't support client user names or passwords. You can set permissions for all Macintosh users as a group, however. This would give all Macintosh users the same printer permissions. To do this, you must create a new user account, set print permissions for this account, and then configure Print Services For Macintosh to use this account. Follow these steps:

1. Create a new user account as discussed in Chapter 37, "Managing Users, Groups, and Computers."
2. Configure the printer security as discussed in the section entitled "Managing Printer Permissions" later in this chapter. Be sure to add the account you created and then set the permissions you want to use for all classic Mac OS clients.
3. Start the Services utility from the Administrative Tools menu.
4. In the Services utility, double-click Print Server For Macintosh. You can now set properties for this service.
5. In the Log On tab, select This Account. Type the name of the user account you created, and then type and confirm the password for this account.
6. When you click OK, the service is updated to use this account. The account will be granted the right to Log On As A Service on the print server. Click OK twice.
7. The changes won't take effect until you stop and then start the Print Server For Macintosh service. In the Services utility, right-click Print Server For Macintosh, and then select Restart.

To ensure spooling works for the new user account, you should check the permissions on the spool folder. Users, of which the new user account is a member, are given access to the spool folder and to create files and folders by default. The necessary permissions include Traverse Folder/Execute File, Read Attributes, Read Extended Attributes, Create Files/Write Data, and Create Folders/Append Data.

Changing Standard TCP/IP Port Monitor Settings

The standard TCP/IP port monitor settings determine how a print server connects to a network-attached printer. As discussed previously, most network-attached printers use the RAW protocol or the LPR protocol to communicate over a standard TCP/IP port. If the Add TCP/IP Port Wizard had problems detecting a network-attached printer, the chances are good the printer was set up to use the LPR protocol rather than the RAW protocol. Unfortunately, most current printers use the RAW protocol, including laser printers from HP, Minolta, Epson, and other printer manufacturers.

To change a printer's standard TCP/IP port monitor settings, follow these steps:

1. If you are currently working with the Add Standard TCP/IP Printer Port Wizard, skip to step 3. Otherwise, access the Printers And Faxes folder either by clicking Start and then clicking Printers And Faxes or by clicking Start, pointing to Settings, and then selecting Printers And Faxes.
2. Right-click the printer, and select Properties. In the printer's Properties dialog box, select the Ports tab. The port used by the printer is selected and highlighted by default. Click Configure Port.
3. In the Configure Standard TCP/IP Port Monitor dialog box, shown in Figure 29-21, select the protocol that the printer uses, either RAW or LPR, as follows:
   - When you select RAW, the Raw Settings panel is available and you can set a port number. Because the default port number used by most RAW printers is 9100, this value is filled in for you. Only change the default setting if the printer documentation instructs you to do so.
   - When you select LPR, the LPR Settings panel is available. Set the queue name to be used by the port. Because the default queue name used by most LPR printers is crownnet, this value is filled in for you. Only change the default setting if the printer documentation instructs you to do so.

Note With LPR, you also have the option to enable LPR Byte Counting. When this option is enabled, the printer server counts the bytes in a document before sending it to the printer, and the byte count can be used by the printer to verify that a complete document has been received. However, this option slows down printing and uses processor resources on the print server.

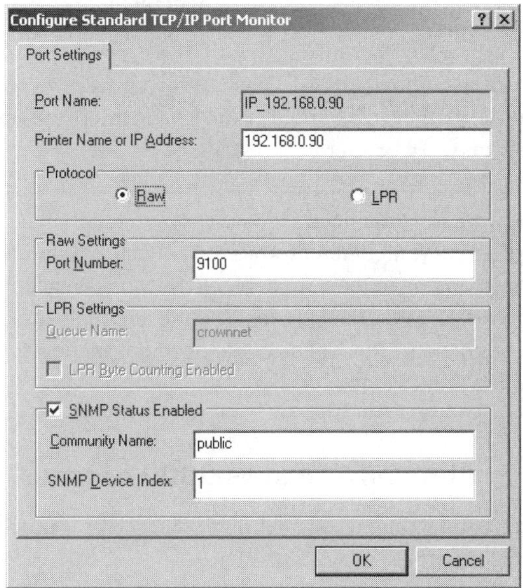

Figure 29-21. Configure the standard TCP/IP port monitor for the printer.

4 Click OK when you are finished configuring the TCP/IP port monitor settings.

Connecting Users to Shared Printers

Once a printer is configured and shared, users on client machines can connect to it. The technique is similar for all versions of Windows.

Accessing Shared Printers on Windows 95, Windows 98, or Windows NT 4

For Windows 95, Windows 98, or Windows NT 4 clients, you install a printer by completing the following steps:

1 With the user logged on, double-click the Printers icon in Control Panel or select Settings in the Start menu, and then choose the Printers option.

2 Double-click the Add Printer icon to open the Add Printer Wizard.

3 Select the Network Printer Server option, and then click Next.

4 Using the Connect To Printer dialog box, select the shared printer. Click the items in the Shared Printers list to work your way down to the shared printer to which you want to connect. When the printer is selected, click OK.

5. Determine whether the printer is the default used by Windows applications. Choose Yes or No, and then click Next.
6. Choose Finish to complete the operation. The user can now print to the network printer by selecting the printer in an application. The Printers tab on the user's computer shows the new network printer.

Tip **Connect through Network Neighborhood**
As you might expect, there are several different ways to connect to a network printer. You can also set up a printer by browsing to the print server in Network Neighborhood and then accessing the server's Printers folder by double-clicking it. Next, double-click the icon of the printer to which you want to connect. This opens a management window for the printer. Finally, select Install from the Printer menu.

Accessing Shared Printers on Windows 2000 or Later

For Windows 2000 or later, connecting to a printer on a print server is much easier. Users can use any of the following techniques to install a printer:

- **UNC Path** Click Start, and then click Run. In the Run dialog box, shown in the following screen, type the Universal Naming Convention (UNC) path to the printer share, and click OK. That's it. The syntax for UNC paths to printer shares is *ServerName**PrintShareName*, where *ServerName* is the name or IP address of the print server and *PrintShareName* is the name of the printer share, such as **\\CorpSvr02\EngMain**.

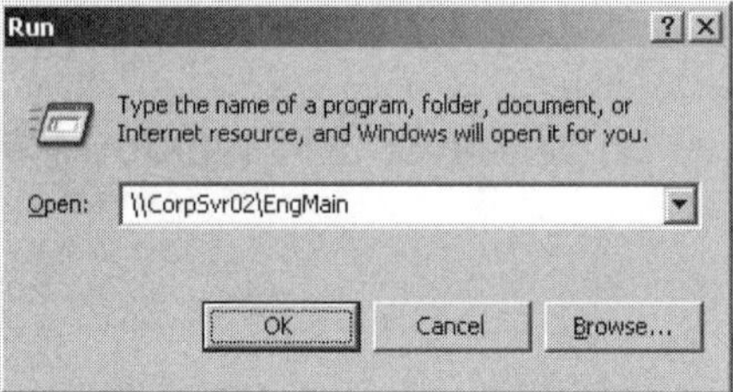

- **My Network Places** In Windows Explorer, expand Control Panel so that the Printers And Faxes entry is visible, and then navigate My Network Places to the print server, as shown in the following screen. With the print server selected in the left pane under My Network Places, select the printer and drag it to the Printers And Faxes folder.

Chapter 29

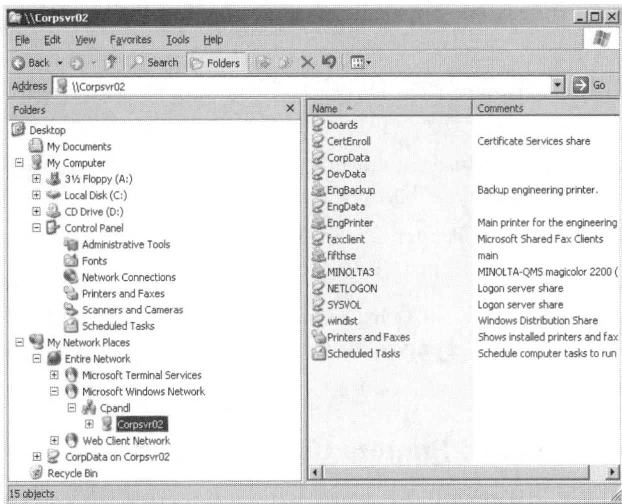

- **Add Printer Wizard** In the Printers And Faxes folder, select or double-click Add Printer to start the Add Printer Wizard. Afterward, as shown in the following screen, select A Network Printer, and then click Next.

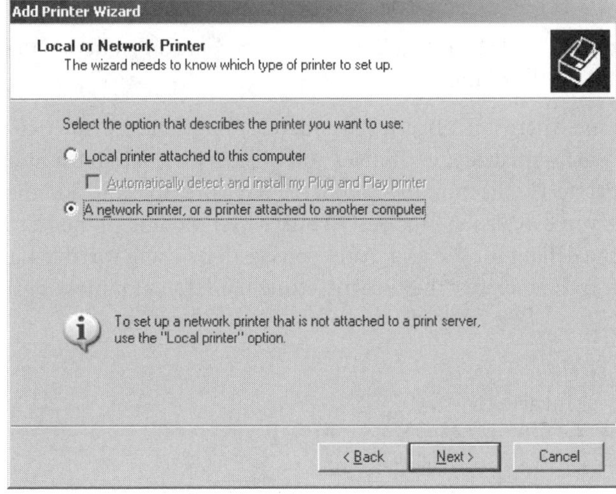

In the Specify A Printer dialog box, choose a method for finding the network printer as follows:

- Choose Find A Printer In The Directory if you want to search Active Directory for the printer.
- Choose Connect To This Printer, and type the printer name or browse the network for shared printers just as you'd browse in My Network Places.
- Choose Connect To A Printer On The Internet if you want to enter the Uniform Resource Locator (URL) of an Internet printer.

When the printer is selected, click OK. Select whether the printer is the default used by Windows applications by selecting Yes or No and then clicking Next. Choose Finish to complete the operation.

Connecting to Shared Printers Using the Command Line and Scripts

With any Windows operating system, you can connect users to shared printers using the command line and scripts. In a logon script that uses batch scripting or at the command line, you can use the NET USE command to connect to a network printer. Consider the following example:

```
net use \\corpsvr02\engmain /persistent:yes
```

Here, you use the NET USE command to add a persistent connection to the EngMain printer on CORPSVR02. That's all there is to it.

You could also use Microsoft VBScript in a logon script to set a printer connection. With VBScript, you must initialize the variables and objects you plan to use and then call the AddWindowsPrinterConnection method of the Network object to add the printer connection. If desired, you can also use the SetDefaultPrinter method of the Network object to set the printer as the default for the user. After you are done using variables and objects, it is good form to free the memory they use by setting them to vbEmpty. Consider the following example:

```
Option Explicit
Dim wNetwork, printerPath
Set wNetwork = WScript.CreateObject("WScript.Network")
printerPath = "\\corpsvr02\engmain"

wNetwork.AddWindowsPrinterConnection printerPath
wNetwork.SetDefaultPrinter printerPath

Set wNetwork = vbEmpty
Set printerPath = vbEmpty
```

Here, you use the AddWindowsPrinterConnection method to add a connection to the Eng-Main printer on CORPSVR02. You then use the SetDefaultPrinter method to set the printer as the default for the user.

Note In Windows 95 and Windows 98, the AddWindowsPrinterConnection method expects to be passed the name of the printer as a second parameter.

Managing Printer Permissions

By default, everyone with access to the network can print to a shared printer. This means any user with a domain account or any user logged on as a guest can print to any available printer. Because this isn't always what is wanted, you might want to consider whether you need to restrict access to a printer. Restricting access to printers ensures that only those users with appropriate permissions can use a printer.

With specialty printers, such as those used for color or large-format printing, you'll find that restricting access to specific groups or individuals makes the most sense. But you might also want to restrict access to other types of printers as well. For example, you might not want everyone with network access to be able to print. Instead, you might want only users with valid domain accounts to be able to print. While you are configuring printer security, you might also want to configure printer auditing to track who is using printers and what they are doing.

Understanding Printer Permissions

Printer permissions set the maximum allowed access level for a printer. These permissions are applied whenever someone tries to print, whether the person is connected locally or remotely, and include both special and standard permissions.

Special permissions are assigned individually and include the following:

- **Read Permissions** Allows users to view permissions
- **Change Permissions** Allows users to change permissions
- **Take Ownership** Allows users to take ownership of a printer, its print jobs, or both

The standard printer permissions available are the following:

- **Print** With this permission, users can connect to a printer and submit documents for printing. They can also manage their own print jobs. If a user or group has print permission, it also has the special permission called Read Permissions for any documents it prints.
- **Manage Printers** With this permission, users have complete control over a printer and can set printer permissions. This means they can share printers,

change permissions, assign ownership, pause and restart printing, and change printer properties. If a user or group has the Manage Printers permission, it also has the special permissions called Read Permissions, Change Permissions, and Take Ownership for any documents on the printer.

- **Manage Documents** With this permission, users can manage individual print jobs. This allows them to pause, restart, resume, or cancel documents. It also allows them to change the order of documents in the queue. It doesn't, however, allow them to print, because this permission is assigned separately. If a user or group has Manage Documents permission, it also has the special permissions called Read Permissions, Change Permissions, and Take Ownership for the printer.

By default, the permissions on printers are assigned as shown in Table 29-1.

Table 29-1. Default Printer Permissions

Group	Print	Manage Documents	Manage Printers
Creator Owner		Yes	
Everyone	Yes		
Administrators	Yes	Yes	Yes
Power Users	Yes	Yes	Yes
Print Operators	Yes	Yes	Yes
Server Operators	Yes	Yes	Yes

As you examine printer permissions, keep in mind that if a user is a member of a group that is granted printer permissions, the user also has those permissions and the permissions are cumulative. This means that if one group of which the user is a member has Print permission and another has Manage Printers permission, the user has both permissions. To override this behavior, you must specifically deny a permission.

Troubleshooting

Check permissions on the spool folder

By default, the spool folder is located on the system drive. The default permissions give Full Control to Administrators, Print Operators, Server Operators, and the System user. System is the account under which the Print Spooler service runs, and this account needs Full Control to be able to create and manage spool files. Administrators, Print Operators, and Server Operators are given full control so that they can spool documents and clear out the spool folder if necessary. Creator Owner has special permissions that grant Full Control so that anyone that prints a document can manage it. Authenticated Users are given Read & Execute permissions so that an authenticated user can access the spool folder and to create files and folders. If these permissions get changed, print spooling might fail.

Configuring Printer Permissions

To view or manage the permissions of a printer, right-click the printer in the Printers And Faxes folder, and then select Properties. In the Properties dialog box, select the Security tab, shown in Figure 29-22. You can now view the users and groups that have printer permissions and the type of permissions they have.

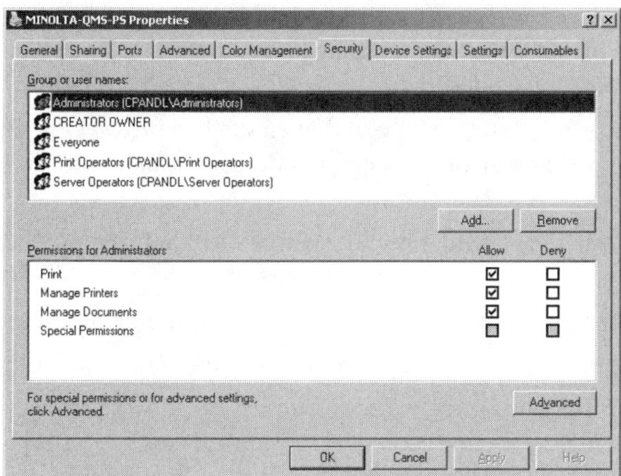

Figure 29-22. View or set printer permissions.

You can grant or deny printer permissions by following these steps:

1. In Printers And Faxes, right-click the printer, and then select Properties. In the printer Properties dialog box, select the Security tab.
2. In the Security tab, choose Add. This opens the Select Users, Computers, Or Groups dialog box, as shown in Figure 29-23.

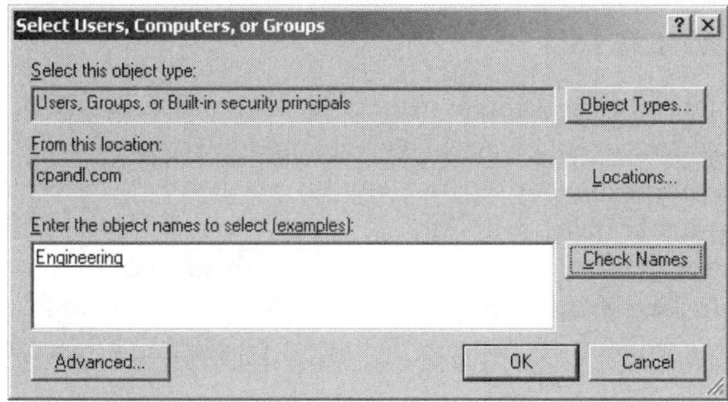

Figure 29-23. Specify the users or groups to add.

Chapter 29

3. The default location is the current domain. Click Locations to see a list of the available domains and other resources that you can access. Because of the transitive trusts in Windows Server 2003, you can usually access all the domains in the domain tree or forest.
4. Type the name of a user or group account in the selected or default domain, and then click Check Names. The options available depend on the number of matches found as follows:
   - When a single match is found, the dialog box is automatically updated as appropriate and the entry is underlined.
   - When no matches are found, you've either entered an incorrect name part or you're working with an incorrect location. Modify the name and try again, or click Locations to select a new location.
   - If multiple matches are found, select the name(s) you want to use, and then click OK.
5. To add additional users or groups, type a semicolon (;), and then repeat this process.
6. When you click OK, the users and groups are added to the Name list for the printer.
7. Configure access permissions for each user and group added by selecting an account name and then allowing or denying access permissions. If a user or group should be granted access permissions, select the permission in the Allow column. If a user or group should be denied access permissions, select the permission in the Deny column.

> **Note** If you give a group a permission, such as Print, the related special permission, Read Permissions, is also granted. For this reason, you usually need not configure special permissions for printers.

8. When you're finished, click OK.

Assigning Printer Ownership

The owner of a printer has permission to manage its documents. By default, the Administrators group is listed as the current owner of a printer and the printer's actual creator is listed as a person who can take ownership. Ownership can be taken or transferred in several ways. Any administrator can take ownership. Any user or group with the Take Ownership permission can take ownership. You can take ownership using the printer's Properties dialog box. Right-click the printer, and then select Properties. In the Security tab of the Properties dialog box, display the Advanced Security Settings dialog box by clicking Advanced. Next, select the Owner tab, as shown in Figure 29-24.

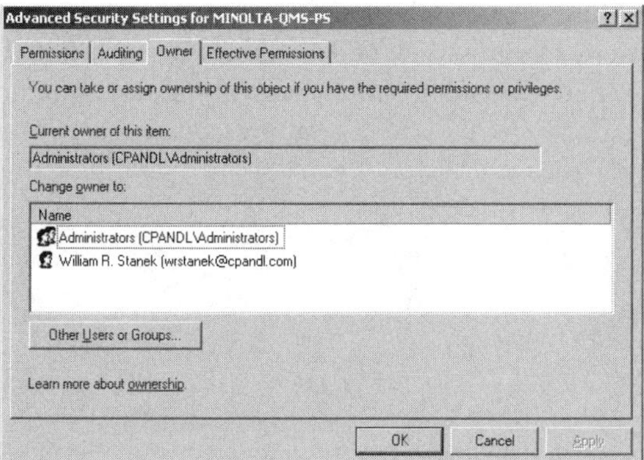

Figure 29-24. Assigning printer ownership.

If you are an administrator or a current owner of a file or folder, you can grant permission to take ownership of the printer. Click Other Users Or Groups to display the Select User, Computer, Or Group dialog box. Type the name of a user or group, and click Check Names. If multiple names match the value you entered, you'll see a list of names and will be able to choose the one you want to use. Otherwise, the name will be filled in for you, and you can click OK.

Auditing Printer Access

Auditing printer access can help you track who is accessing printers and what they are doing. You configure auditing policies on a per-printer basis. In Printers And Faxes, right-click the printer to be audited, and then select Properties. In the Properties dialog box, select the Security tab, and then click Advanced. In the Advanced Security Settings dialog box, select the Auditing tab, shown in Figure 29-25.

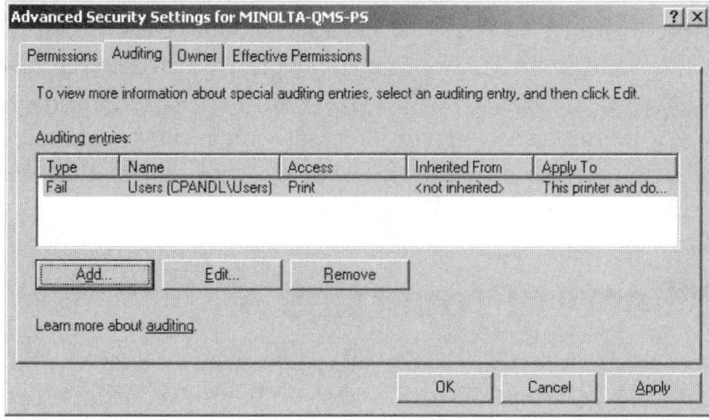

Figure 29-25. Specify to which users and groups auditing should apply.

Now use the Auditing Entries list box to select the users, groups, or computers whose actions you want to audit. To add specific accounts, click Add, and then use the Select User, Computer, Or Group dialog box to select an account name to add. If you want to audit actions for all users, use the special group Everyone. Otherwise, select the specific user groups or users, or both, that you want to audit. When you click OK, you'll see the Auditing Entry For dialog box, shown in Figure 29-26.

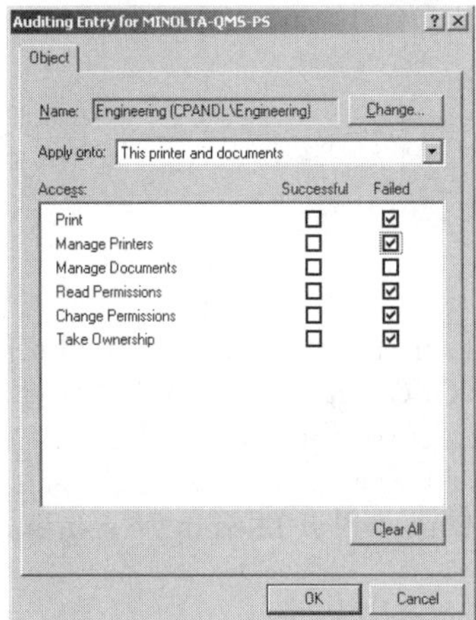

Figure 29-26. Specify the actions to audit for the designated user, group, or computer.

The Apply Onto drop-down list box allows you to specify whether the actions should be audited for

- This Printer Only
- Documents Only
- This Printer And Documents

After you make a selection, under Access, select the Successful or Failed options, or both, for each of the events you want to audit. The events you can audit are the same as the printer permissions discussed previously. Choose OK when you're finished. Repeat this process to audit other users, groups, or computers. Any time printers for which you've configured for auditing are accessed, the action is written to the system's security log, where it's stored for your review. The security log is accessible from Event Viewer.

Managing Print Server Properties

Print server properties control the global settings for all printers on a server. You can access print server properties from the Printers And Faxes folder. In the Printers And Faxes window, select Server Properties from the File menu. Or right-click an open area of the Printers And

Faxes window, and select Server Properties. If you want to configure a print server remotely, start Windows Explorer, expand My Network Places, and navigate to the Printers And Faxes folder of the remote print server.

Using the Print Server Properties dialog box, you can configure settings for all printers, including the following:

- Forms
- Ports
- Drivers
- Advanced settings

Viewing and Creating Printer Forms

Forms are used by print servers to define the standard sizes for paper, envelopes, and transparencies. Print servers have many predefined forms from which you can choose, but you can also define your own forms.

To view the current settings for a printer form, right-click an open area of the Printers And Faxes window, and select Server Properties. Then click the Forms tab, as shown in Figure 29-27. Use the Forms On list to select the form you want to view. The form settings are shown in the Form Description (Measurements) area. You can't change or delete the default system forms.

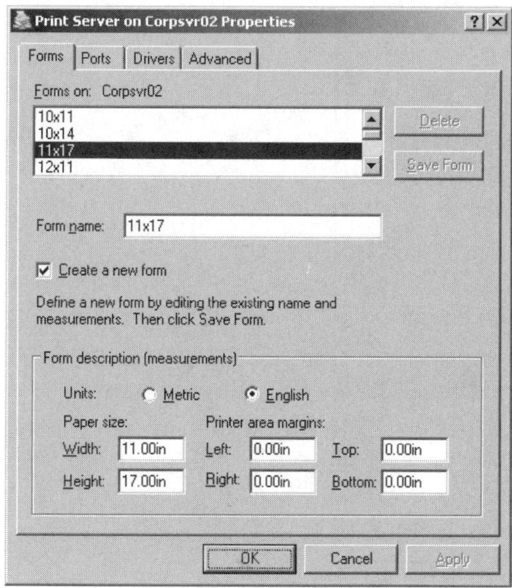

Figure 29-27. View and configure forms for paper, envelopes, and transparencies.

To create a new form, follow these steps:

1. Access the Forms tab of the Print Server Properties dialog box. Use the Forms On list box to select the existing form on which you want to base the new form.
2. Select the Create A New Form option, and then enter a new name for the Form in the Form Description For field.
3. Use the fields in the Form Description (Measurements) area to set the paper size and margins. When you are finished, click the Save Form button to save the form.

Viewing and Configuring Printer Ports

Ports are used to define the interfaces and TCP/IP addresses to which the print server can connect. Using the Print Server Properties dialog box, you can view and manage all the ports configured for use on the printer server. This gives you one location for viewing, adding, deleting, and configuring ports.

To work with ports, right-click in an open area of the Printers And Faxes window, and select Server Properties. Then click the Ports tab, as shown in Figure 29-28. If you want to view or change a port's settings, select it in the Ports On This Server list and then click Configure Port. For details on configuring TCP/IP ports, see the section entitled "Changing Standard TCP/IP Port Monitor Settings" earlier in this chapter.

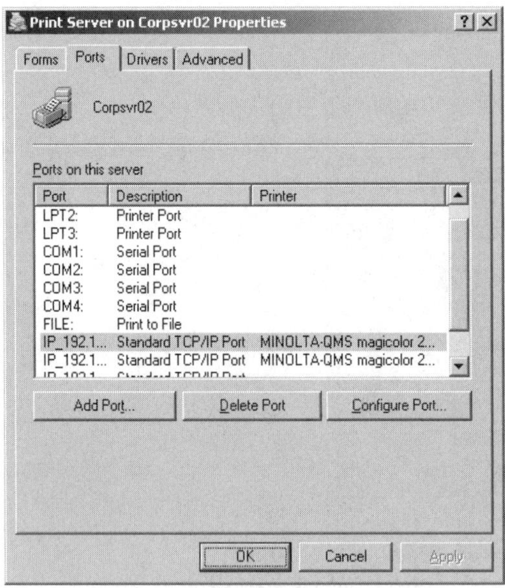

Figure 29-28. View and configure printer ports.

Viewing and Configuring Print Drivers

As discussed in the section entitled "Installing and Updating Print Drivers on Clients" later in this chapter, printer clients download print drivers the first time they access a printer and anytime the print drivers have been updated. Once you've configured each printer so that clients can download drivers, you can manage the installed printer drivers through the Print Server Properties dialog box. As with ports, the key here is convenience. Not only can you view all the print drivers that are available but you can add, remove, and reinstall drivers as well.

To work with drivers, right-click in an open area of the Printers And Faxes window and select Server Properties. Then click the Drivers tab. As shown in Figure 29-29, drivers are listed by

- **Name** Typically, this is the manufacturer and model number of the printer.
- **Processor** The chip architecture for the listed driver.
- **Version** The operating systems with which a particular driver is compatible.

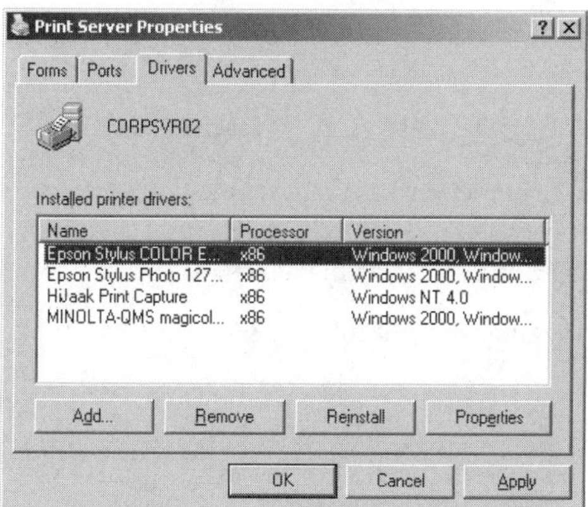

Figure 29-29. View and configure print drivers.

You can now do the following:

- **View driver properties and file associations** If you select a driver and click Properties, you'll see detailed information on the driver, which includes all the files associated with the driver. This includes all related help, configuration, data, driver settings, and dependent files.
- **Add or update an existing print driver** If you want to add or update an existing print driver, click Add to start the Add Printer Driver Wizard, and then follow these steps:
  1. In the Add Printer Driver Wizard, click Next. On the Printer Driver Selection page, choose the manufacturer and model of the printer for which you are adding support. If the print device manufacturer and model you're using aren't displayed in the list or you have a newer driver from the manufacturer, click Have

Disk to install a new driver. In either case, make sure the driver you use is digitally signed. This is indicated after you select a manufacturer and model and means that the driver is certified for use by Microsoft.

2. On the Processor And Operating System Selection page, choose all the Windows clients that will be connecting to this printer from the network. To install additional print drivers for clients, you need access to the installation files for the appropriate driver version either on the network or on CD.
3. When you click Next, Windows will install any available drivers and then prompt you to provide additional drivers as necessary. Click Finish when you are done.

- **Remove print drivers** If you want to remove a driver, select it, and then click Remove. When prompted to confirm the action, click Yes.
- **Reinstall print drivers** If you select a print driver and click Reinstall, Windows will reinstall the print driver. This is useful if you suspect a print driver or some of its files might have been corrupted.

Configuring Print Spool, Logging, and Notification Settings

Using the Advanced tab of the Print Server Properties dialog box, you can configure properties related to spooling. Not only can you change the location of the spool folder but you can also control event logging and notification actions related to the Print Spooler service.

To configure the print spool, logging, and notification settings, right-click in an open area of the Printers And Faxes window, and select Server Properties. Then click the Advanced tab. As shown in Figure 29-30, you can configure the following options:

- **Spool Folder** Shows the current location of the print spool folder. To change the spool folder location, type a new folder path, click Apply, and then when prompted, click Yes.

Tip **Spooling changes immediately**

The changes to the spool folder will occur immediately. This means the Print Spooler folder will look to this folder for documents to print and any previously spooled documents in the old spool folder will not print. Because of this, you should allow all current documents to print before changing the spool folder location.

Caution The security on the selected folder will not be changed and this could affect spooling of files to the selected folder. For best results, you should set security permissions on the new folder so they are the same as the original spool folder. See the Troubleshooting sidebar "Check Permissions on the Spool Folder" earlier in this chapter.

- **Log Spooler Error Events** Writes error events related to the Print Spool service to the event logs.
- **Log Spooler Warning Events** Writes warning events related to the Print Spool service to the event logs.
- **Log Spooler Information Events** Writes information events related to the Print Spool service to the event logs.
- **Beep On Errors Of Remote Documents** Windows 2000 and Windows XP clients display a warning balloon in the notification area when a document has failed to print. This warning is displayed for 10 seconds or until clicked. Don't use this if you have earlier client versions, because they will actually get alerts.
- **Show Informational Notification For Local Printers** Displays the status of all jobs sent to this print server on the computer of the user that submitted the print job.
- **Show Informational Notification For Network Printers** Displays the status of print jobs sent by users on this computer to print services on other print servers.
- **Notify When Remote Documents Are Printed** Notifies Windows 95, Windows 98, and Windows NT users when a remote document is printed. This is minimally useful because the prompt can become annoying.
- **Notify Computer, Not User, When Remote Documents Are Printed** For Windows 95, Windows 98, and Windows NT clients, sends notification to the computer from which a document was printed rather than the particular user. Again, this is minimally useful because the prompt can become annoying.

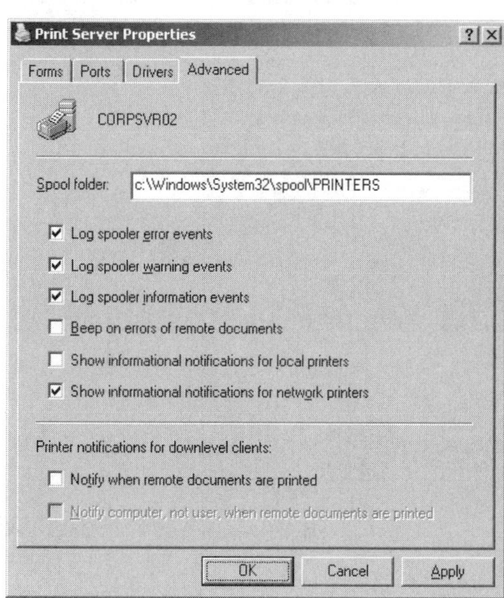

Figure 29-30. Configure the print spool, logging, and notification.

Chapter 29

Managing Printer Properties

Printer properties control the settings for an individual printer. You can access a printer's properties from the Printers And Faxes folder. In the Printers And Faxes window, right-click the printer and select Properties. If you want to configure a printer on a remote print server, start Windows Explorer, expand My Network Places, and navigate to the Printers And Faxes folder of the remote print server. You can then right-click the printer and select Properties.

Note The specific properties displayed depend to some extent on the make and model of printer you are working with. Because of this, some of the settings described below won't necessarily apply to all printers.

Setting General Properties, Printing Preferences, and Document Defaults

To help users find printers and ensure that they don't have to waste time trying to configure default settings such as paper size and paper tray to use, you should take a close look at the general properties, printing preferences, and document defaults assigned to a printer after you install it. Although this will take you a few minutes to go through, it will save users much more time, especially when you consider that this is something that every user in the organization would otherwise have to do.

As Figure 29-31 shows, the general settings are accessed from the General tab of the printer's Properties dialog box.

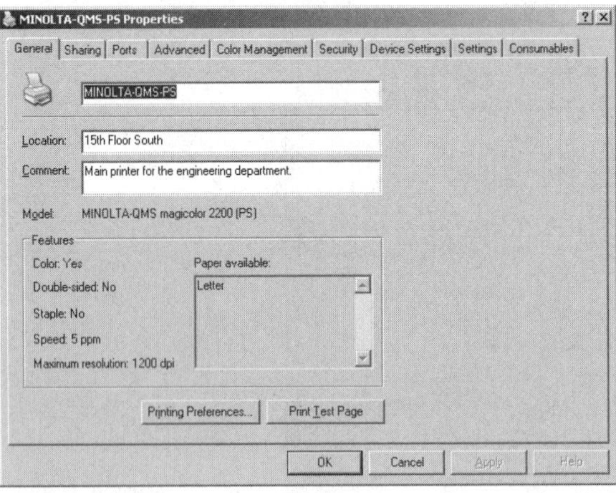

Figure 29-31. Configure general settings.

In the Printers And Faxes window, right-click the printer, and then select Properties. In the General tab, you can view or change the following options:

- **Local printer name** The name of the printer on the print server
- **Location** The location description of the printer
- **Comment** An additional comment about the printer

To make sure the printer is ready for use, you should next go through the printing preferences and device settings to configure the settings that will be used by default on the printer. Click Printing Preferences in the lower portion of the General tab. Check the settings in the following tabs:

- **Layout** Controls the paper orientation and page order for printing
- **Paper/Quality** Controls the paper source (tray), the media (paper type), and the printing preference for black and white or color

In the Printing Preferences dialog box, click OK. Then in the printer's Properties dialog box, click the Device Settings tab, as shown in Figure 29-32. Check the following device settings and change them as necessary and applicable to your printer:

- **Form To Tray Assignment** Form To Tray Assignment options ensure the printer trays are configured for the proper paper types. Selecting a tray entry highlights it and displays a selection list that you can use to set the paper type for the tray.
- **Job Timeout** Job Timeout optimizes the print job wait times. Job Timeout specifies the maximum amount of time the printer allows for a job to get from the computer to the printer. If this time is exceeded, the printer will stop trying to print the document. The default value is 0, which means the printer will continue trying to print a document indefinitely. To change this value, select Job Timeout, and then type a new timeout.
- **Wait Timeout** Wait Timeout optimizes in-process printing wait times. Wait Timeout specifies how long the printer waits for additional information from the printer. If this time elapses, the printer stops trying to print the document and prints an error message. Typically, the default wait timeout is 300 seconds. Although this is sufficient for most types of print jobs, a print server that is under a heavy load or processing very complex documents might exceed this. If you notice that the printer unexpectedly stops printing photos, CAD drawings, digital art, or other types of complex documents, try increasing the wait timeout to resolve this problem. To change this value, select Wait Timeout, then type a new timeout.
- **Installed Memory/Installable Options** Installed Memory (sometimes known as Installable Options) tells the computer about the amount of memory installed on the printer. Although you should never use a value less than the default setting for the printer, you can use this option to tell the print server about additional RAM that you installed on the printer. This ensures the computer knows the extra RAM is available.

To change this value, select Installed Memory, then choose the appropriate value on the selection list.

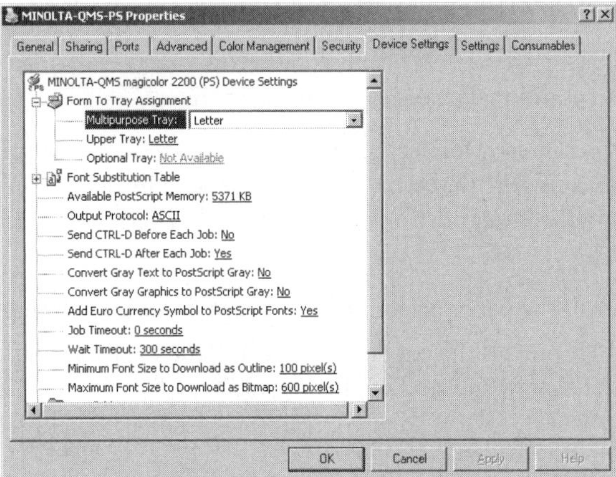

Figure 29-32. Configure Form To Tray Assignment and other device settings.

Setting Overlays and Watermarks for Documents

In secure environments, it might be necessary to set a watermark in the background of every page that is printed. A watermark is a word or phrase, such as DRAFT, CONFIDENTIAL, or TOP SECRET, that is printed lightly in the background of every page using a very large font size—typically 72-point Courier. If your printer supports this feature, you can print the watermark in the background of every page or only the first page of a document.

To clear or set a default watermark for all printed documents, follow these steps:

1. In the Printers And Faxes window, right-click the printer, and select Properties. In the General tab, click Printing Preferences. Then in the Printing Preferences dialog box, select the Overlays tab.
2. To clear a default watermark, select None as the watermark type. Afterward, click OK and skip the remaining steps.
3. To set a default watermark, select a watermark type. Available types include CONFIDENTIAL, COPY, DRAFT, FINAL, ORIGINAL, and PROOF.
4. To create a new watermark, click Add, then use the Watermarks dialog box to set the watermark name, text, and options. The watermark text sets the word or phrase that will be printed lightly in the background.
5. To set the watermark on the first page only, select First Page Only.
6. Click OK.

Installing and Updating Print Drivers on Clients

When a print server runs Windows Server 2003, print drivers can be installed and updated automatically on clients as discussed in the section entitled "Understanding Windows Server 2003 Print Services" earlier in this chapter. A client downloads print drivers the first time it accesses a printer and any time the print drivers have been updated.

> **Note** The drivers that are available for a printer depend on when the printer was installed and whether the system was upgraded from Windows NT 4. If the system was upgraded from Windows NT 4 and the printer was installed prior to the upgrade, level 2 kernel-mode drivers are installed and available to clients. Otherwise, a printer should have level 3 user-mode drivers installed and available to clients. Level 2 print drivers are needed to support Windows NT 4 clients. Level 3 print drivers are needed to support Windows 2000 or later clients.

By default, printers installed on a Windows Server 2003 network support only Windows NT 4 or later with kernel-mode drivers or Windows 2000 or later with user-mode drivers. Four types of drivers can be made available to clients for automatic download:

- **Itanium-based drivers** Used on 64-bit Windows XP and Windows Server 2003 systems that use the Intel Itanium processor architecture
- **x86 user-mode drivers** Used on Windows 2000, Windows XP, and Windows Server 2003
- **x86 kernel-mode drivers** Used on Windows NT 4
- **x86 desktop drivers** Used by Windows 95, Windows 98, and Windows Me clients

You confirm and configure print driver availability on a per-printer basis by following these steps:

1. In Control Panel, access Printers And Faxes, then right-click the printer you want to work with, and then select Properties.
2. In the Properties dialog box, select the Sharing tab, and then click Additional Drivers. This displays the Additional Drivers dialog box, as shown in Figure 29-33.
3. Select the option for any client drivers to be installed, and then click OK.
4. To install additional print drivers for clients, you need access to the installation files for the appropriate driver version either on the network or on CD.

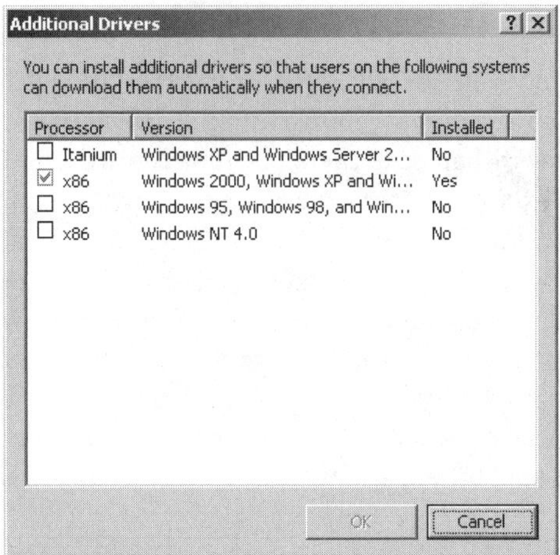

Figure 29-33. Select the additional operating systems that should be supported.

Once you've installed the print drivers for clients, clients will download them when they first connect to the print server. If you update the drivers, all clients except those running Windows 95, Windows 98, and Windows Me will get the updated drivers automatically. Windows 95, Windows 98, and Windows Me clients do not automatically check for updated drivers and must be updated manually.

Configuring Printer Sharing and Publishing

When you set up a printer, you are given the chance to share it. If you share a printer, it is published in Active Directory automatically. Published printers can be searched for by users in a variety of ways, including when a user is attempting to connect to a network printer using the Add Printer Wizard. You can check or change the printer sharing and publishing options using the Sharing tab of the printer's Properties dialog box. In the Printers And Faxes window, right-click the printer, and then select Properties.

In the Sharing tab, you have the following options, as shown in Figure 29-34:

- **Do Not Share This Printer** Selecting this option stops printer sharing and makes the printer available only as a local printer to users who log on to the computer.
- **Share This Printer** Selecting this option shares the printer so that it is accessible to users as discussed in the section entitled "Connecting Users to Shared Printers" earlier in this chapter.
- **List In The Directory** For a shared printer, selecting this option lists the printer in Active Directory, and clearing the option removes the listing from Active Directory.

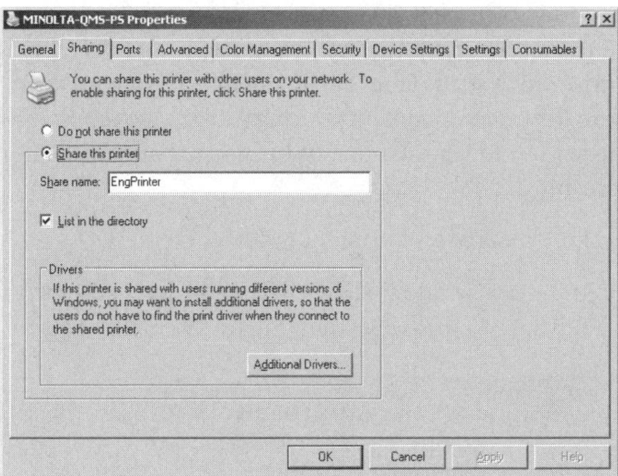

Figure 29-34. Configure sharing settings.

Optimizing Printing Through Queues and Pooling

A printer queue is a logical print device. You can have one logical print device associated with a printer, or you can have multiple logical print devices associated with a printer. It is the latter option that gives you more flexibility and can help improve printing in general, especially if you create different logical print devices for different purposes and educate users how they should be used. With multiple logical print devices, you can use print queue priority and scheduling settings to control how and when a logical print device is used.

Configuring Queue Priority and Scheduling

Queue priority lets you prioritize printing based on the type of document being printed. Queue scheduling lets you schedule when documents in a queue can be printed—it doesn't restrict spooling to the queue, only printing from the queue. Print queue priority and scheduling settings can be used separately or together. Consider the following scenarios:

- **A printer has a normal queue and a priority queue** You configure the normal queue so that it can be used for all routine print jobs. You configure the priority queue so that it is used for all urgent print jobs. Because the priority queue has a higher priority than the normal queue, any documents printed to the priority queue are printed before and preempt documents in the normal queue. To ensure the priority queue isn't abused, you might want to restrict access to those groups or individuals that actually have priority printing needs on a printer.
- **A printer has a normal queue and a scheduled bulk queue** You configure the normal queue so that it can be used any time for all routine print jobs. You configure the bulk print queue so that it is used for large documents and only after hours or during

nonpeak hours. Any document spooled to the normal queue can be printed immediately. Any document spooled to the bulk queue is printed only within the scheduled availability hours, which keeps large documents from tying up the printer and causing a lengthy backup for other documents during peak usage times. If you set the priority of the bulk queue to be lower than that of the normal queue, the normal queue will always have priority.

To set printer availability schedule and priority, follow these steps:

1. In the Printers And Faxes window, right-click the printer, and then select Properties. Then select the Advanced tab, as shown in Figure 29-35.

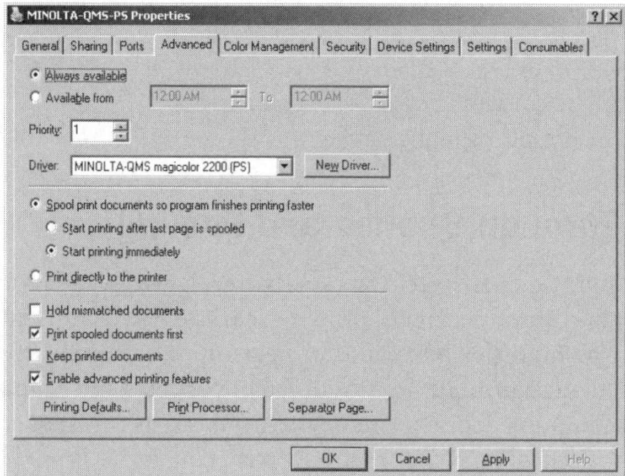

Figure 29-35. Use the Advanced tab to set the printer availability schedule and priority.

2. Printers are either always available or available only during the hours specified. Select Always Available to make the printer available at all times, or select Available From to set specific hours of operation.
3. Use the Priority box to set the default priority for the print queue. The priority range goes from 1, which is the lowest priority, to 99, which is the highest priority. Print jobs always print in order of priority, and jobs with higher priority print before jobs with lower priority. The priority you use is assigned to all print jobs spooled to this printer.
4. If you are configuring a priority queue, select the Security tab, and configure permissions to allow only those users and groups that you want to print at this priority. Remove or deny print permissions for users and groups that should have a different priority level. These users will use the normal priority queue that you've configured for the printer. If you haven't configured one yet, do so now.
5. When you are finished, click OK. Repeat this process for all other logical print devices you configured for this printer.

Configuring Printer Pooling

Using a technique called printer pooling, a single logical print device can also be associated with multiple physical print devices. In this configuration, you have one print queue but multiple printers and jobs are sent to the first available physical printer. To take advantage of printer spooling, the printers must use the same printer driver. Typically, this means they must be from the same manufacturer and have the same model. They must also have the same amount of memory installed.

Figure 29-36 shows an example of printer pooling. As the figure shows, the advantage of printer pooling is that users see a single print queue but multiple printers are available to handle their print jobs. Behind the scenes, administrators are free to add or remove physical printers without affecting the users' configuration.

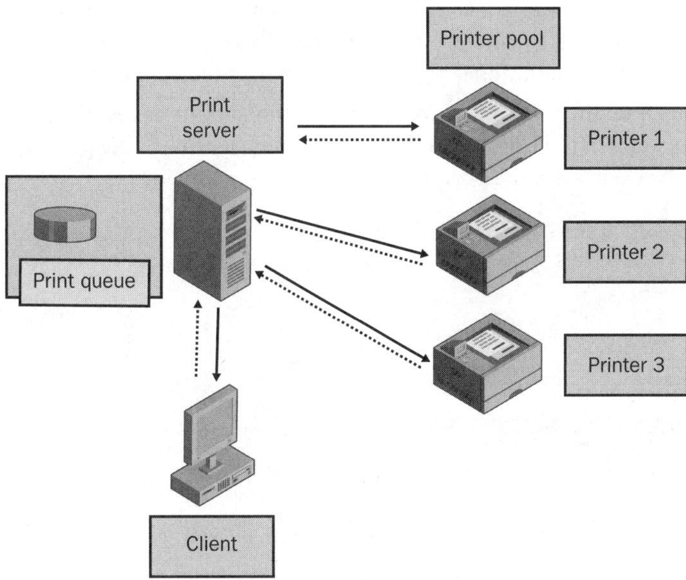

Figure 29-36. Printer pooling.

Printer pooling is useful in several scenarios:

- **Print-capacity scaling** To scale print capacity, you can place two, three, four, or more identical printers side by side and then use printer pooling to effectively double, triple, quadruple, or more your printing capacity. In this arrangement, users have one queue for printing to these printers, and the only changes you must make are on the print server. On the print server, you enable printer pooling so that the first available printer prints a document.
- **Printer maintenance and replacement** Printer pooling can facilitate printer maintenance and replacement as well. If you must maintain or repair a printer that is part of a printer pool, you can take it offline whenever necessary without impacting print

operations. Users will still be able to print to the print queue and the additional printers in the pool will handle printing for their documents.

Tip **Cluster the print server**
Printer pooling provides high availability and fault tolerance for the printers themselves. It doesn't provide high availability or fault tolerance for the print server. If a group of users requires high performance and high reliability, you can set up a print cluster as discussed in the section entitled "Managing Server Clusters and Their Resources" on page 577. Setting up a print cluster provides additional capacity and fault tolerance should one of the print servers stop responding.

You can configure printer pooling by following these steps:

1. Printer pooling is managed using a single logical print device and multiple ports. This means you must add a printer so that it uses a particular port and then add one additional port for each additional physical print device you want to pool.
2. After you set up the printer and configure additional ports, access the printer's Properties dialog box. In the Printers And Faxes window, right-click the printer, and select Properties. Then select the Ports tab, as shown in Figure 29-37.

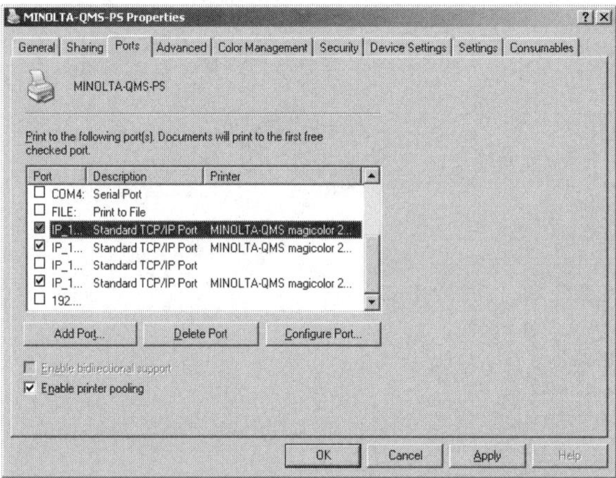

Figure 29-37. Select the ports to use for pooling.

3. Select Enable Printer Pooling, and then select all the ports to which printers in the pool are attached. These ports can be local ports as well as network ports. As long as the physical print devices to which they connect are all identical, meaning they are from the same manufacturer, have the same model, and have the same amount of memory installed.
4. When you are finished configuring printer pooling, click OK.

> **Tip** **Put pooled printers next to each other and consider using separator pages**
> Printer pooling works best when the pooled printers are all in the same location. You might want to put the printers back to back or side by side. It also helps if you use separator pages. Separator pages help to keep print jobs organized and make it easier for users to identify which printouts are theirs.

Configuring Print Spooling

The way print spooling is configured on a printer affects how clients perceive printing performance and the actual printing options. You can configure printers to start printing immediately after a print job is received or to wait until the last page is spooled. If a print server's drives are full or can't be written to, you can change printer spooling settings so clients can print directly. Although this can slow printing down on a busy printer, it allows clients to continue printing. Other spooling options allow you to keep printed documents for faster reprinting and to hold mismatched documents so that jobs using alternate types of paper or envelopes don't cause the printer to stop and wait.

To configure print spooling options, access the printer's Properties dialog box. In the Printers And Faxes window, right-click the printer, and select Properties. Then select the Advanced tab, as shown previously in Figure 29-35. You can now use the following options to configure print spooling:

- **Spool Print Documents So Program Finishes Printing Faster** Spools print jobs to the print server, allowing clients to finish faster so they can perform other tasks.
- **Start Printing After Last Page Is Spooled** Ensures that the entire document is spooled to the print server and available to the printer when printing begins. This option gives more control over the print job. If printing is canceled or not completed, the job won't be printed. If a higher-priority job becomes available, it will print first.
- **Start Printing Immediately** Reduces the time it takes to print by allowing the printing to begin immediately when the print device isn't already in use. This option is preferred if you want print jobs to be completed faster and if you want to ensure that the client finishes faster.
- **Print Directly To The Printer** Turns off spooling completely and documents are sent directly to the printer. This option can seriously degrade print performance. Only use this option if there is a problem writing to the spool folder and you want to ensure printing can continue.
- **Hold Mismatched Documents** Holds documents that don't match the setup for the print device without affecting other documents in the print queue. This speeds up the overall printing throughput by keeping the printer from waiting for alternate paper and envelope types. For example, if a user prints a transparency, rather than stopping printing and waiting for the user to insert transparency paper, the printer holds the document and continues printing.

- **Print Spooled Documents First** Allows jobs that have completed spooling to print before jobs in the process of spooling without regard to priority. The document with the highest priority that is already spooled will print even if a higher-priority document is in the process of spooling. This speeds up the overall printing throughput by keeping the printer from waiting for documents that are in the process of spooling.
- **Keep Printed Documents** Keeps a copy of documents in the print queue in case users need to print the same document again. When selected, if a user reprints a document that's already in the queue, the document can be taken directly from the queue rather than having to be transferred and spooled again. In most cases, you'll want to consider using this option only when users print specialty types of documents that can take a long time to transfer and spool. Enabling this option substantially increases the amount of disk space required for spooling.
- **Enable Advanced Printing Features** Enables advanced printing features for metafile (EMF) spooling, including Page Order, Booklet Printing, and Pages Per Sheet. Typically, this option is enabled because metafile spooling is desired.

Viewing the Print Processor and Default Data Type

Every printer has a print processor. The default print processor for Windows systems is Winprint. Other print processors can be installed when you set up a printer. The print processor and the default data type for the processor determine how much processing the printer performs. As discussed previously, the RAW data type is processed on the client and minimally processed on the print server. The EMF data type is sent to the print server for processing.

Generally speaking, you do not need to change either the print processor or the default data type. However, if you want to determine the print processor and default data type used by a printer, you can access the printer's Properties dialog box, select the Advanced tab, and then click Print Processor. This displays the Print Processor dialog box. As shown in Figure 29-38, the current print processor and default data type are selected and highlighted by default.

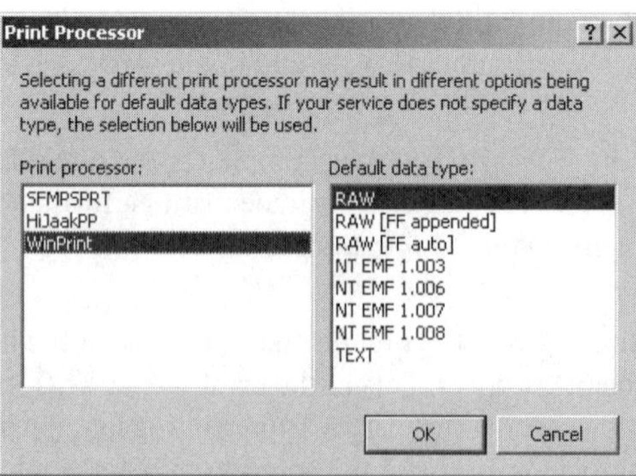

Figure 29-38. The current print processor and default data type are highlighted.

Chapter 29

Configuring Separator Pages

On a busy printer or when you use printer pooling, you might need some help keeping print jobs organized so that users can easily find their print jobs among other print jobs. This is where separator pages come in handy. Separator pages are used at the beginning of each print job to help identify the related document and who printed it.

Using Separator Pages

By default, printers don't use separator pages. If you want to use separator pages, you must configure them on a per-printer (logical print device) basis. Windows Server 2003 includes four default separator pages. These default separator pages are stored in the %SystemRoot%\System32 folder and are defined using standard American Standard Code for Information Interchange (ASCII) text. This means you can view and edit them using any standard text editor, including Notepad.

The default separator pages include the following types:

- **Pcl.sep** Sets the print device to PCL mode and prints a separator page before each document. The separator page shows the print job ID, date, and time. The Pcl.sep file uses the PCL page definition language and has the following contents:

```
\
\H1B\L%-12345X@PJL ENTER LANGUAGE=PCL
\H1B\L&l1T\0
\M\B\S\N\U
\U\LJob : \I
\U\LDate: \D
\U\LTime: \T
\E
```

- **Pscript.sep** Sets a dual-language printer to PostScript mode but doesn't print a separator page. The Pscript.sep file uses the PostScript page definition language and has the following contents:

```
\
\H1B\L%-12345X@PJL ENTER LANGUAGE=POSTSCRIPT\0
```

- **Sysprint.sep** Sets the print device to PostScript mode and prints a separator page before each document. The separator page has banner text to help easily identify who printed the document and when. The Sysprint.sep file uses the PostScript page definition language. The key definition assignments are the following:

```
@L/name (@N@L) def
@L/jobid(@I@L) def
@L/date (@D@L) def
@L/time (@T@L) def
```

- **Sysprtj.sep** Sets the print device to PostScript mode and prints a separator page before each document. The Sysprtj.sep file uses the PostScript page definition language and is essentially an alternate version of the Sysprint.sep that uses a different version of the banner text.

Other separator pages can be installed in the %SystemRoot%\System32 folder as well. Some printers install their own separator pages. Typically, they do this because they can't use any of the standard separator pages. For example, Minolta QMS MagiColor Laser printers install their own separator page. The default name of this separator page is Msep01_b.sep. The contents of this file are as follows:

```
\
\M\B\S\N\U
\U\LJob : \I
\U\LDate: \D
\U\LTime: \T
\E
```

Here, the user name is printing in banner text and then job ID, date, and time are printed in standard text. It is important to know what the definitions look like in a separator page because all separator pages can be customized. The way you do this is to modify existing definitions or add definitions.

Setting a Separator Page

To use one of the default separator pages, access the printer's Properties dialog box, select the Advanced tab, and then click Separator Page. In the Separator Page dialog box, shown in Figure 29-39, click Browse. This opens a Find dialog box in the %SystemRoot%\System32 folder so you can easily choose available separator pages. Click a separator page that uses the same page description language as the printer, and then click Open. Afterward, in the Separator Page dialog box, click OK.

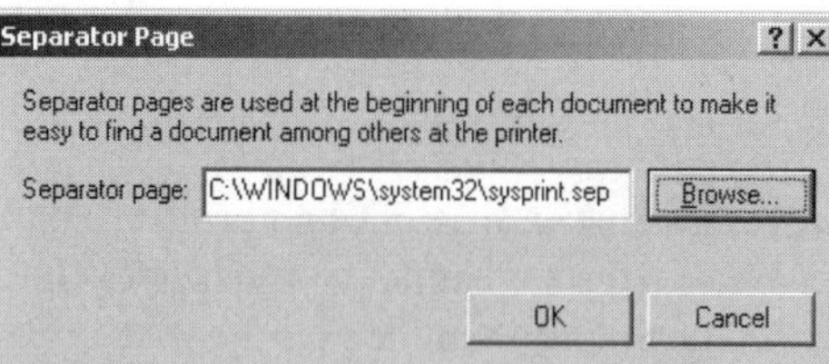

Figure 29-39. Select a separator page.

> **Tip** Test the separator page
>
> After you select a separator page, you should print a test document to ensure printing works as expected. To do this, click Print Test Page in the General tab of the printer's Properties dialog box. If there's any printing error, you've chosen an incompatible separator page and will need to try a different one.

Customizing Separator Pages

You can customize separator pages for your organization. Although PCL, PostScript, and other types of separator pages use a different syntax, they all use the same variables. These variables are summarized in Table 29-2.

Table 29-2. Separator Page Variables

Variable	Usage
B	Turns on banner printing of text for which each character is block printed using pound signs (#) until you exit banner printing with the U variable.
D	Prints the date the document was printed using the default date format.
E	Inserts a page break. Typically used at the end of the separator page so that the document starts printing on a new sheet of paper.
F*filepath*	Prints the contents of the specified text file to the separator page. The specified file must contain only text and the formatting of the text is not retained.
H*nn*	Sets a printer-specific code, which is used to control printer functions. Refer to the printer manual for control codes that might be available.
I	Prints the job ID. The job ID is set when a document is spooled to the printer.
L*text*	Prints the literal text following the variable until the next escape code or variable is reached.
L%	Marks the start of comment text that isn't printed. The next escape code or variable marks the end of the comment.
M	Turns on emphasis (bold) print. Switch off with S.
N	Prints the logon name of the user who submitted the print job.
N	Skips *n* lines, where *n* is a number from 0 to 9.
S	Switches off emphasis (bold).
T	Prints the time the document was printed using the default time format.
U	Turns off banner text printing.
W*nn*	Sets the line character width. Any lines with more characters than the specified width are truncated. The default width is 80 characters.

Knowing the available variables and their meaning, you can now examine the separator page listings shown previously to see exactly what they are doing.

Now that we know what the variables mean, let's take another look at Pcl.sep:

1. The first line sets the escape code for the separator page:

   ```
   \
   ```

2 On the second and third lines, the separator page uses control codes to set the page description language to PCL:

```
\H1B\L%-12345X@PJL ENTER LANGUAGE=PCL
\H1B\L&l1T\0
```

3 On the fourth line, the separator page switches to bold banner text mode and then prints the name of the logon user:

```
\M\B\S\N\U
```

Note The order of these elements must be as follows. Enable Emphasis (M), Enable Banner Text (B), Stop Emphasis (S), Print Name (N), Stop Banner Text (U). If you don't follow this order, the emphasis, banner text format, or both may be enabled for the entire separator page.

4 On lines 5 through 8, the separator page prints literal text followed by a value—either the job ID, date, or time:

```
\U\LJob : \I
\U\LDate: \D
\U\LTime: \T
```

5 On the last line, the separator page inserts a page break:

```
\E
```

The PostScript separator pages are a bit more difficult to follow but have similar definitions. With PostScript, @ typically is used as an escape character to mark the start of variables instead of \. However, the first line of the separator page specifies the escape code that will be used.

With both PCL and PostScript, you have two options for customizing separator pages: you can either try to edit the existing separator pages or create your own. Before you edit an existing separator page, you should make a backup copy and work with the copy instead of the original file. If you elect to make your own separator page, you can do so using Notepad.

When you start from scratch, you can use either \ and @ as escape codes or $. Set the escape code on the first line of the document and stick with the escape code you start with. With that in mind, if you want to print out the user name, date, and time in bold banner text, you would create a separator page with the following contents:

```
$
$M$B$S$N$U
$M$B$S$D$U
$M$B$S$T$U
$E
```

You would then save the file to the %SystemRoot%\System32 folder and name it with the .sep extension, such as Working.sep. To use the custom separator page, set it as the one to use as discussed previously.

Configuring Color Profiles

With more and more color printers being used, it has become increasingly important to ensure color printers accurately reproduce colors. Windows Server 2003 supports Integrated Color Management (ICM). ICM uses color profiles to ensure colors are printed consistently. By default, Windows chooses the best color profile based on what is being printed.

By default, Windows includes only a few color profiles. When you install a color printer or graphics software on a computer, additional color profiles typically are installed. All color profiles are stored in the %SystemRoot%\System32\Spool\Drivers\Color folder. In most cases, color profiles installed with a printer are set as the defaults to use.

To view or configure color profiles, follow these steps:

1. In the Printers And Faxes window, right-click the printer, and select Properties. Then select the Color Management tab, as shown in Figure 29-40.

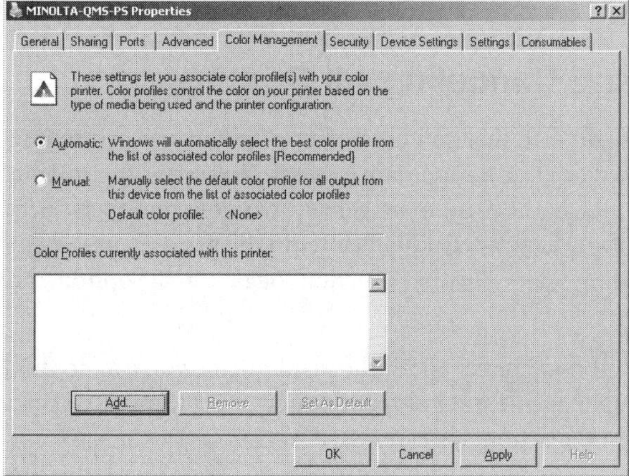

Figure 29-40. Check the color profile settings.

> **Tip** **Create a separate printer for experimenting**
> Before you change the default color profiles, you might want to create a separate printer (logical print device). This way you can experiment with the printer's color settings without affecting other users.

2. Select the Automatic option to have Windows choose the best color profile.
3. To set a color profile to use manually, select Manual, and then select a profile from the list of available profiles or click Add to add an additional profile association for the printer. Any profile selected in the profile list is used as the current profile. To make the current profile the default profile for the printer, click Set As Default.
4. Click OK.

> **Tip** **Copy needed color profiles to the print server**
> Color profiles available to users, such as graphic designers using Adobe PhotoShop, are installed with the software. These profiles will exist on the user's desktop but not on the print server. To make the profiles available for use, you can copy available profiles from a user's desktop to the print server.

Managing Print Jobs

To manage a printer and its print jobs, you use the print management window. You can access a printer's management window from the Printers And Faxes folder. Simply double-click the printer you want to work with. If you want to manage print jobs on a remote print server, start Windows Explorer, expand My Network Places, and navigate to the Printers And Faxes folder of the remote print server. You can then double-click the printer to access its management window.

Pausing, Starting, and Canceling All Printing

Occasionally, you might find that you must temporarily pause printing so that you can replace a toner cartridge, clear a paper jam, or perform some other maintenance procedure. To do this, click Printer in the print management window, and then select Pause Printing. You can resume printing later by clicking Printer in the print management window and then selecting Pause Printing again. The first selection toggles on the option, the second toggles off the option.

If you need to clear all documents out of the print queue, you can do this as well. Click Printer in the print management window, and then select Cancel All Documents. When prompted to confirm the action, click Yes.

Viewing Print Jobs

Every document in the process of printing is shown in a print management window. In the print management window, documents are listed by the following information:

- **Document Name** The full name of the document
- **Status** The print status of the document
- **Owner** The user that printed the document
- **Pages** The number of pages in the document
- **Size** The file size of the document
- **Submitted** The date and time the document was spooled to the printer
- **Port** The ports used for printing

Managing Print Jobs

When you select a document in the print management window, you can manage it using the Document menu or by right-clicking in much the same way as you manage the printer itself. To stop the document from printing or to pause printing if it is currently being printed, right-click the document, and then select Pause. You can enable or resume printing later by right-clicking the document and selecting Resume. If you need to clear a document out of the print queue, right-click the document, and then select Cancel. When prompted to confirm the action, click Yes.

You can change a document's properties by right-clicking the document and selecting Properties. This opens the document's Properties dialog box, as shown in Figure 29-41. To change a document's properties when it is in the process of printing, you should pause the print job first.

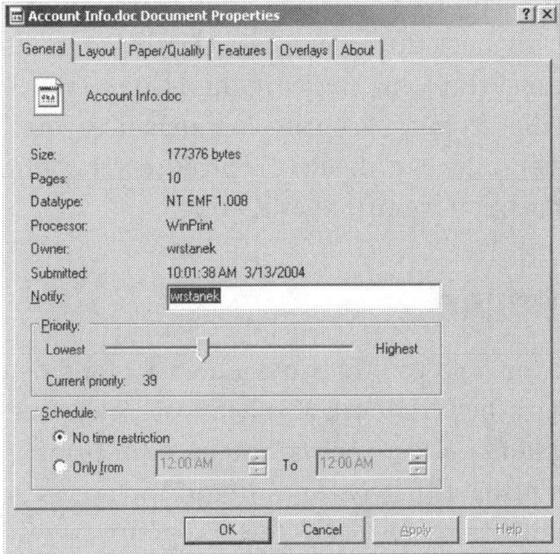

Figure 29-41. You can change the properties of documents in the print queue.

Typically, you might want to edit a document's properties to set its priority. For example, if someone printed a very long document and you want to ensure other documents print before it, you could lower the long document's priority. Similarly, if there's an important document that you want to be printed ahead of other documents, you can raise the document's priority.

Troubleshooting

Clear out stuck documents

The Print Spooler service is configured to restart automatically if there's a problem. Sometimes it won't completely freeze or it will hang up in such a way that it can't be restarted automatically. You can tell this because the print queue will have error documents that you can't clear manually. In this case, restart the Print Spooler service manually. In the Administrative Tools folder, select Services, and then select Print Spooler in the right pane. Right-click Print Spooler, and then select Start or Restart as appropriate.

Printer Maintenance and Troubleshooting

Regular printer maintenance is an important part of printer administration. In addition to checking the print queue periodically for stuck documents and clearing them out as discussed in the section entitled "Managing Print Jobs" earlier in this chapter, you should check to see how the print server is performing. As part of routine maintenance, you should also prepare for print server failure by periodically backing up the print server configuration. Finally, when things go wrong, you must perform troubleshooting.

Monitoring Print Server Performance

Monitoring print server performance can help you track usage statistics and determine whether a print server is performing as expected. It can also help you determine whether changes or upgrades are needed and plan for future needs. You monitor print server performance using the performance objects available in System Monitor. You access System Monitor from within the Performance Monitor console. Click Start, Programs or All Programs, Administrative Tools, Performance. Or type **perfmon** at the command line.

Get started by following the techniques discussed in Chapter 16, "Comprehensive Performance Analysis and Logging," for establishing performance baselines and detecting performance bottlenecks. These topics are discussed in the sections entitled "Establishing Performance Baselines" on page 486, and "Resolving Performance Bottlenecks" on page 495, respectively. Once you've done this, zero in on the server's print spooling and queuing performance using the SpoolSv instance of the Process object and the Print Queue object as detailed in the following steps:

1. On a server you want to use for remote monitoring, start Performance Monitor, and then select System Monitor in the left pane.
2. Press Ctrl+R to use the View Report display, and then press Ctrl+E to start a new counter set.

3 Press Ctrl+I to display the Add Counters dialog box. In the Add Counters dialog box, choose Select Counters From Computer, and then type the UNC name or IP address of the print server you want to monitor remotely. An UNC computer name or IP address begins with \\. So, for instance, you could enter **\\PrintServer02** or **\\192.168.12.15**.

4 After you type the UNC computer name or IP address, press Tab or click the Performance Object list. When you do this, Performance Monitor will attempt to connect to the remote computer and retrieve a list of available performance objects to monitor.

5 Choose Process, and then in Select Instances From List choose Spoolsv, as shown in Figure 29-42.

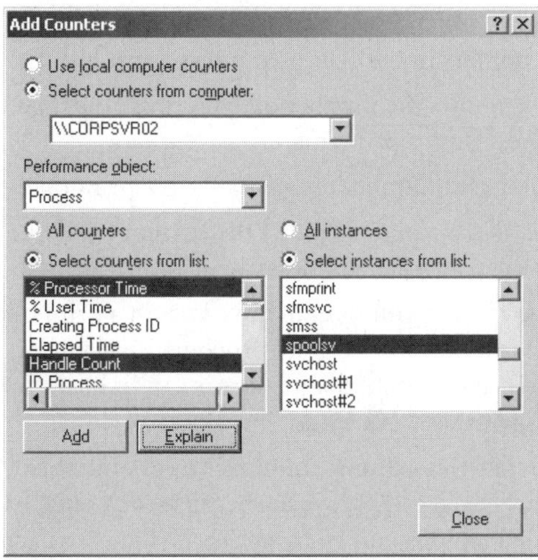

Figure 29-42. Monitor the Process object's Spoolsv instance.

6 Choose the following counters in the Select Counters From List box:

- *% Processor Time*—Shows the percentage of elapsed time of all process threads used by the Print Spooler service. A dedicated print server that is very busy will have a relatively high amount of processor time.
- *Handle Count*—Shows the total number of handles open by the Print Spooler process. This is important to track because each open handle uses resources, and open handles can be from clients that aren't actively printing.
- *Virtual Bytes/Virtual Bytes Peak*—Shows the current/peak size in bytes of the virtual address spaced used by the Print Spooler process.
- *Page File Bytes*—Shows the current amount in bytes of the virtual memory that the Print Spooler process has reserved in the paging file.

- *Pool Paged Bytes*—Shows the current size in bytes of the paged pool used by the Print Spooler process. Memory in the paged pool can be written to disk when it is not in use.
- *Pool Nonpaged Bytes*—Shows the current size in bytes of the nonpaged pool used by the Print Spooler process. Memory in the nonpaged pool cannot be written to disk and must remain in physical memory.
- *Working Set/Working Set Peak*—Shows the current/peak size in bytes of the set of memory pages (working set) used by the Print Spooler process.

7. Click Add to add the selected counters to the chart.
8. Under Performance Object, choose Print Queue, and then choose All Instances to track all print queues on the server.
9. Choose the following counters in the Select Counters From List list:
   - *Bytes Printed/Sec*—Shows the number of bytes printed per second and is a relative indicator of how busy a printer is.
   - *Jobs*—Shows the current number of print jobs in a print queue.
   - *Jobs Spooling/Max Jobs Spooling*—Shows the current/peak number of print jobs being spooled to the print queue. These are incoming print jobs.
   - *Job Errors*—Shows the total number of job errors in a print queue since the last restart. Job errors can occur if there are problems transferring print jobs to the printer. A relatively high number of job errors can indicate networking problems or problems with network cards.
   - *References/Max References*—Shows the current/peak number of handles open to a print queue. This is important to track because each open handle uses resources, and open handles can be from clients that aren't actively printing.
   - *Not Ready Errors*—Shows the total number of printer not ready errors in a print queue since the last restart. These errors occur if the printer is waiting or not ready for printing.
   - *Out Of Paper Errors*—Shows the total number of out of paper errors in a print queue since the last restart. If a printer is frequently running out of paper, paper might not be getting refilled properly or you might need an additional paper tray.
   - *Total Jobs Printed*—Shows the total number of jobs printed on a print queue since the last restart. This is a relative indicator of how busy a printer is.
   - *Total Pages Printed*—Shows the total number of pages printed on a print queue since the last restart. This is a relative indicator of how busy a printer is.

Note Total Pages Printed doesn't show pages printed by Windows 95, Windows 98, Windows Me, and non-Windows clients. These clients use SMB.

10 Click Add to add the selected counters to the chart, and then click Close.

You can now monitor the print server to determine activity levels and how many system resources are being used for printing.

Preparing for Print Server Failure

As part of your print services optimization and maintenance process, you should consider how you are going to handle printer and print server failure. Several techniques have been discussed previously for increasing availability and fault tolerance. These techniques include print queue pooling and print clusters as discussed in the section entitled "Optimizing Printing Through Queues and Pooling" earlier in this chapter. Because these options aren't practical for all environments, you should have other backup plans ready.

Start by considering how you would handle printer failure. If you have an identical printer available as a spare, you can configure this printer to take the place of the failed printer. As long as the printer uses the same print drivers, users can access it from the same print queue. If you have other printers available, you could instruct users how to access one of these printers or, ideally, already have a second printer added for use on their computer as a backup in case the primary printer fails. Trust me, you'll have happier users if you do this.

Next, consider how you would handle print server failure, which could mean that several printers are inaccessible. It's often a good idea to have a secondary print server available if a primary print server fails. You could then switch users from the primary print server to the secondary print server. Assuming the print server is already configured to provide print services for the printers originally serviced by the primary, you could simply tell users how to access the print queues on the secondary print server.

A more complete disaster recovery plan for a print server would be similar to the following:

1. As part of periodic backups, back up the printer configuration on the print server using Printer Migrator. This would create a .cab file that should be stored on a network share that is itself regularly backed up to tape.
2. In the event the primary print server failed, you would disconnect the primary server from the network. Then use Printer Migrator to restore the .cab file containing the printer configuration on the secondary server.
3. You would then change the secondary print server's IP address and computer name to match that of the original print server. Users would then be able to access printers and resume printing.

Solving Printing Problems

Windows Server 2003 has many improvements that reduce the amount of printing problems you'll encounter. The biggest change is the automatic restart of spooling if the Print Spooler service hangs up due to errors, which takes a lot of guesswork out of troubleshooting. However, if the Print Spooler has a critical problem, such as when the volume on which the spool folder is located runs out of space, the Print Spooler can stop running.

Printer Troubleshooting Essentials

When you are troubleshooting printing problems, as with troubleshooting any problems, first try to figure out where the problem is and then try to fix it. As with most problems, you'll usually want to start with the client experiencing the printing problem before you start troubleshooting on the print server. Of course, the printer might also have a problem and the network might be a culprit as well. So, this gives you four key areas to examine:

- **Client/Application software** The client or the application software on the client might be improperly configured. This could include problems with print drivers, permissions, and print settings.
- **Printer hardware** The printer might have a problem. This could include being out of paper, out of toner, or having a paper jam.
- **Printer server** The print server might have a problem. This could include the spool folder running out of space, permissions set for a printer or the spool folder, print drivers used by the server, and device status.
- **Network connectivity** The network might have a problem, or the network card on the client, server, or printer might be misconfigured or bad.

Troubleshooting

Running out of space may indicate a deeper problem

Occasionally, the .spl and .shd files won't get cleared out of the spool folder. This can happen if print spooling is not functioning as it should. To correct this problem, manually clear out the print spooler folder and then restart the Print Spooler service. And if Windows won't allow you to delete the files, stop the Print Spooler service first, delete the files, and restart the service.

Start by trying to figure out which area has a problem. If the user is asking you directly for help, make sure the user is connected to the right printer and knows which print device is associated with the printer he or she is using. Try printing to the printer from your machine. You can print a test page from the printer's Properties dialog box by clicking Print Test Page in the General tab. If you can print a test page, printing is working and the problem might have to do with permissions or the user's system or configuration. Try printing from someone else's computer. If this succeeds, the problem might be with this particular user's system or configuration. If this fails, try printing from the print server. If this fails, the problem might be with the printer configuration or with the network.

While you are printing test pages, be sure to keep track of the printer status. Most current printers have a mini Hypertext Transfer Protocol (HTTP) server and an online status page that you can check simply by typing the printer's IP address in your Web browser. If you can't check current status that way, start Windows Explorer, expand My Network Places, and navigate to the Printers And Faxes folder of the print server. You can then double-click the printer to access its management window. If there's a document with an error status at the top of the print queue, remove it, which should restore printing, and then see the section entitled "Configuring Print Spooling" earlier in the chapter to see how you can try to prevent that type of error from happening again. If all documents have a printing error or if each time you clear a bad document out of the queue, the status changes to Error-Printing, there might be a problem with the network or the printer itself. If the title bar shows the printer is paused, click Printer, and then select Pause Printing to resume printing.

When you can't check the status of the printer online, don't spend more than five minutes on a printer problem without walking over to the printer and checking its status. Most printers with an error status will have a blinking yellow light and the display will state the problem. Also, you might want to check the event logs on the print server for error or warning events.

Hopefully, after performing these procedures, you'll have isolated the problem to a particular area or have a better understanding of where the problem might exist. With that said, let's delve into specific scenarios and troubleshooting options.

Inside Out

Solve the printing problem with a clear plan

Few things frustrate users more than when printing goes awry. One of the most important things you can do is to communicate with the user or users having the problem, but don't do this too many times. Don't forget that your account might have permissions and privileges other user accounts don't, so you might want to have a default user account for troubleshooting. In this case, you would log on to your computer or a spare computer at your desk and try printing. Try to solve the problem without taking over a user's machine for troubleshooting. If you must access a user's machine, do this when you are fairly sure the problem is specific to a user or a group of users. If the problem cannot be resolved within a reasonable amount of time or you know it's going to be a long time, such as when the print server has stopped working, you should consider implementing your recovery plan as discussed in the section "Preparing for Print Server Failure" earlier in this chapter.

Comprehensive Printer Troubleshooting

When someone states there is a printing problem, you should try to determine who is affected by the problem. Try printing from your machine and other machines. Try printing from the print server. Hopefully, after doing this you'll know whether the problem affects

- Everyone, meaning no one can print. In these circumstances, the problem likely has to do with the printer itself or the network. Perform the following actions:
  - Check the printer status either by walking over to the printer or using a browser to check the printer's status page. (Try typing the printer's IP address in your Web browser.) Afterward, check the event logs on the print server. Look for error or warning events that might indicate a problem.
  - Check the print queue (logical print device). Look to see if the printer is paused or if there are documents with a status of Error-Printing. Clear out these documents by right-clicking them and selecting Cancel.
  - Print or check the configuration of the printer. Someone might have set it to use Dynamic Host Configuration Protocol (DHCP) and might not have made a reservation for it. In this case, if the printer was shut down and then restarted, it might have a different IP address. The printer port would then point to the wrong IP address. Check the printer's subnet mask as well.
  - Check the network. See if you can ping the printer's IP address from your system and from other systems. At the command line, type **ping *PrinterIP***, where *PrinterIP* is the IP address of the printer. If you can't ping the printer's IP address from any system, the printer might be turned off or its network cable might be disconnected. The printer might also have a bad network card. The problem could also be in the switch into which the printer is plugged or with routing to the printer.
  - Determine when the last time the printer worked and if the printer configuration has been changed. If the printer never worked, it might not have been configured correctly in the first place. If the printer configuration was changed, change the configuration back to the previous settings if possible. If you suspect a problem with the print driver, try reinstalling it or installing a new driver as discussed in the section entitled "Viewing and Configuring Print Drivers" earlier in this chapter.
  - Check the free space on the volume on which the spool folder is located. If the volume is low on space or out of space, the print server won't be able to create spool files and, therefore, documents won't print. Also check the permissions on the spool folder. If the permissions are set incorrectly, the spooling won't work. See the section entitled "Configuring Print Spool, Logging, and Notification Settings" and the Troubleshooting sidebar "Check Permissions on the Spool Folder" earlier in this chapter.

- Check the print monitor and separator page settings to ensure they are correct. If an incorrect print monitor is set, the printer might print garbled pages or might not print at all. Try using the RAW data type or the EMF data type to see if this clears up the problem. If the separator page is set incorrectly, the printer might print out the contents of the separator page or it might not print at all. See the sections entitled "Viewing the Print Processor and Default Data Type" and "Configuring Separator Pages" earlier in this chapter.
- Check the Print Spooler service. It is configured for automatic restart, but if restart fails twice within a minute, the Print Spooler service won't try to start again. Also, if the print queue has error documents and you can't clear them out, it is usually the fault of the Print Spooler. In this case, restart the service manually. In the Administrative Tools folder, select Services, and then select Print Spooler in the right pane. Right-click Print Spooler, and select Start or Restart as appropriate.

- Some people, meaning only some users can't print and some can. If some people can't print, the problem likely has to do with the permissions, application software, or the network. Perform the following actions:
  - Check the network using a computer in the same subnet as the people having the problem. See if you can ping the printer's IP address. At the command line, type **ping *PrinterIP***, where *PrinterIP* is the IP address of the printer. If you can't ping the printer's IP address from any system on the subnet, a switch or routing between the user's computer and the printer might be bad or disconnected. This happens a lot if local switches/hubs are under people's desks.
  - Check the printer permissions and the permissions on the spool folder to see if the groups of which the users are members have appropriate access. If the permissions are set incorrectly, the spooling won't work. See the section entitled "Configuring Print Spool, Logging, and Notification Settings" and the Troubleshooting sidebar "Check Permissions on the Spool Folder" earlier in this chapter.
  - Check the print monitor. Windows 95, Windows 98, and Windows Me clients can print only if the print monitor uses the RAW data type. See the section entitled "Viewing the Print Processor and Default Data Type" earlier in this chapter.
  - Check the application being used for printing. The application might be incorrectly configured or the default printer might not be what users think it is.
  - Check the error message generated when printing. If the client gets an error stating it must install a printer driver when connecting to a printer, this means the correct drivers are installed on the server but aren't available to the client. Additionally, Windows 95, Windows 98, and Windows Me clients do not automatically check for updated drivers and must be updated manually. See the section entitled "Installing and Updating Print Drivers on Clients" earlier in this chapter.

- One person, meaning only one user can't print. If only one person can't print, the problem likely has to do with application software, the user's computer, or permissions. Start with the user's computer and perform the following actions:
  - Check the application being used for printing. The application might be incorrectly configured, or the default printer might not be what the user thinks it is.
  - Check the user's computer. The Print Spooler service must be running for the user to print. The computer must have sufficient temporary space to generate the initial spool file. The computer must have other essential services configured. The list goes on. Essentially, it is better if you restart the computer if you suspect the problem has to do with that computer specifically.
  - Check to make sure the user's computer can connect over the network to other resources. Try pinging the router or the printer in question.
  - Check the error message generated when printing. If the client gets an error stating it must install a printer driver when connecting to a printer, this means the correct drivers are installed on the server but aren't available to the client. See the section "Installing and Updating Print Drivers on Clients" earlier in this chapter. If the client gets an "Access Denied" error, this is a permissions issue.
  - Check the printer permissions and the permissions on the spool folder to see if the user or groups of which the user is a member have appropriate access. If the permissions are set incorrectly, the spooling won't work. See the section entitled "Configuring Print Spool, Logging, and Notification Settings" and the Troubleshooting sidebar "Check Permissions on the Spool Folder" earlier in this chapter.

Resolving Garbled or Incorrect Printing

If the printer prints garbled or incorrect pages, this can be a sign that the printer is incorrectly configured. You should check the print driver and the port monitor settings. You might want to reinstall the print driver as discussed in the section entitled "Viewing and Configuring Print Drivers" earlier in this chapter. You might want to change the port monitor data type to RAW or EMF to see if this clears up the problem. See the section entitled "Viewing the Print Processor and Default Data Type" earlier in this chapter.

To resolve this problem, check the following:

- Ensure that the complete document is transferred to the printer before printing starts by selecting the Start Printing After Last Page Is Spooled option. See the section entitled "Configuring Print Spooling" earlier in this chapter.
- Try using the RAW data type or the EMF data type to see if this clears up the problem. See the section entitled "Viewing the Print Processor and Default Data Type" earlier in this chapter.

- Try removing any separator page that is used, because this might be setting the printer page description language incorrectly. See the section entitled "Configuring Separator Pages" earlier in this chapter.
- Try clearing the Enable Advanced Printing Features option on the Advanced tab. This disables metafile spooling. Windows 95, Windows 98, and Windows Me clients use SMB connections and spool RAW-formatted files to the print server. See the section entitled "Configuring Print Spooling" earlier in this chapter.

Chapter 30

Using Remote Desktop for Administration

Remote support is an important part of administration. Using Remote Desktop for Administration, you can manage remote servers and workstations. Remote Desktop for Administration is a feature of Microsoft Windows Server 2003 Terminal Services and is built on the Microsoft Windows 2000 Terminal Services in Remote Administration mode. You can use it to connect to and manage remote systems as if you were logged on locally. Because all the application processing is performed on the remote system, only the data from devices such as the display, keyboard, and mouse are transmitted over the network. You can use Remote Desktop for Administration to manage computers running Windows 2000 Server, Windows XP Professional, and Windows Server 2003.

Remote Desktop for Administration Essentials

Using Remote Desktop for Administration, you can use a local area network (LAN), wide area network (WAN), or Internet connection to manage computers remotely with the Windows graphical interface. Remote Desktop for Administration is part of Terminal Services. For Windows Server 2003, Microsoft has separated Terminal Services into two operating modes:

- **Remote Desktop for Administration mode** This feature was known as *Remote Administration* mode in Windows 2000. You enable Remote Desktop for Administration using the System utility in Control Panel.
- **Terminal Server mode** Known as *Application Server* mode in Windows 2000 Server. You enable Terminal Services by adding the Terminal Server component using the Add/Remove Programs utility in Control Panel.

To be operational, Remote Desktop for Administration and Terminal Server both depend on the Terminal Services service being installed and running on the server. By default, Terminal Services is installed and configured to run automatically. Both features use the same client, Remote Desktop Connection (RDC), for connecting to remote systems. Administrators can also use the Remote Desktops snap-in for the Microsoft Management Console (MMC).

Note Remote Desktop for Administration isn't designed for application serving. Most productivity applications such as Microsoft Office Word, Outlook, and Excel require specific environment settings that are not available through this feature. If you want to work with these types of applications (rather than server applications), you should install and use Terminal Server.

No Terminal Server Client Access License (TS CAL) is required to use Remote Desktop for Administration. One console session and two remote administration sessions are provided for with this service. Most remote sessions are created as console sessions. The reason for this is that the console session provides full functionality for administration. Unlike standard Terminal Services connections, which are created as virtual sessions, console sessions are always created as Session 0.

Why is this important? Using a console session, you can interact with the server just as if you were sitting at the keyboard. This means all notification area messages directed to the console are visible remotely. For security, only one console session—either local or remote—is allowed. If you log on locally to the console and someone is logged on remotely to the console, you will be prompted to end that person's user session so that you can log on. The same is true if you log on remotely to the console.

Although it is recommended that administrators use console sessions, you can use remote administration sessions—hey, that's what they're there for. Remote administration sessions are created as virtual sessions on the server. They can perform most administration tasks, and their key limitation is in their ability to interact with the console session itself. This means users logged on using a remote administration session do not see console messages or notifications, cannot install some programs, and cannot perform tasks that require console access.

You'll want to formalize a general policy on how Remote Desktop for Administration should be used in the organization. You don't want more than one administrator trying to perform administration tasks on a remote system because this could cause serious problems. For example, if two administrators are both working with Disk Management, this could cause serious problems with the volumes on the remote system. Because of this, you'll want to coordinate administration tasks with other administrators.

Configuring Remote Desktop for Administration

The two components of Remote Desktop for Administration you will need to support and configure are Terminal Services for the server portion and the Remote Desktop Connection (RDC) for the client portion. An alternative to using RDC is the Remote Desktops snap-in, which lets you connect to and manage multiple remote desktops.

Enabling Remote Desktop for Administration on Servers

Enabling the Remote Desktop for Administration mode on all servers on your network is recommended, especially for servers in remote sites that have no local administrators. To enable the Remote Desktop on the server, access Control Panel, and then double-click System to start the System utility. In the Remote tab, select Allow Users To Connect Remotely To This Computer, as shown in Figure 30-1.

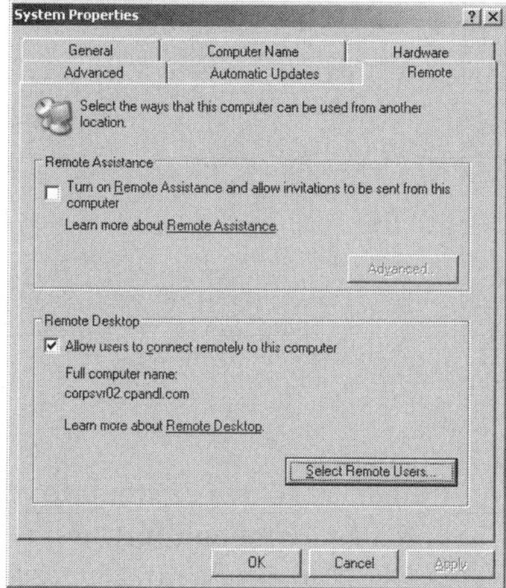

Figure 30-1. Enabling Remote Desktop.

When the warning prompt is displayed, click OK, but keep the following details about using Remote Desktop for Administration in mind:

- All remote connections must be established using accounts that have passwords. If a local account on the system doesn't have a password, you can't use the account to connect to the system remotely.
- If you are running a personal firewall on the system, you must open a port on the firewall to allow the Remote Desktop Protocol (RDP) connection to be established. The default port used is TCP port 3389. The Registry value HKEY_LOCAL_MACHINE\System\CurrentControlSet\Control\TerminalServer\WinStations\RDP-Tcp\PortNumber controls the actual setting.

Permitting and Restricting Remote Logon

By default, all members of the Administrators group can log on remotely. The Remote Desktop User group has been added to Windows Server 2003 Active Directory to ease managing Terminal Services users. Members of this group are allowed to log on remotely as well once you enable this in Group Policy.

If you want to add a member to this group, access Control Panel, and then double-click System to start the System utility. In the Remote tab, click Select Remote Users. As shown in Figure 30-2, any current members of the Remote Desktop Users group are listed in the Remote Desktop Users dialog box. To add users or groups to the list, click Add. This opens the Select Users Or Groups dialog box.

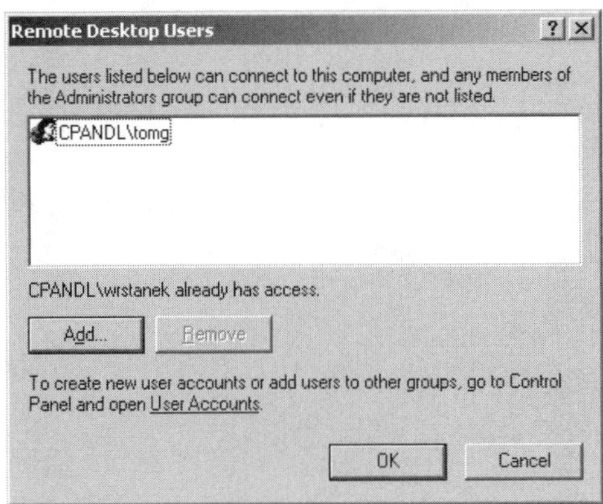

Figure 30-2. Configuring Remote Desktop users.

In the Select Users Or Groups dialog box, type the name of a user or group account in the selected or default domain, and then click Check Names. If multiple matches are found, select the name(s) you want to use, and then click OK. If no matches are found, you've either entered an incorrect name part or you're working with an incorrect location. Modify the name and try again, or click Locations to select a new location. To add additional users or groups, type a semicolon (;), and then repeat this process. When you click OK, the users and groups are added to the list in the Remote Desktop Users dialog box.

Once you add users to the Remote Desktop Users group, you will need to explicitly allow members of this group to log on. Typically, you will want to do this through local policy on a per-machine basis. You can also do this through site, domain, and organizational policy. Access the appropriate Group Policy object and select Computer Configuration, Windows Settings, Security Settings, Local Policies, and User Rights Assignments. Double-click Allow

Log On Through Terminal Services. In the policy Properties dialog box, select Define These Policy Settings, and then click Add User Or Group. In the Add User Or Group dialog box, click Browse. This displays the Select Users, Computers, or Groups dialog box, type Remote Desktop Users, and then click OK. You can add other groups as well if desired.

Inside Out

Restrict remote logon through Group Policy

If you want to restrict users or groups from remotely administering a server, access the appropriate Group Policy object and expand Computer Configuration\Windows Settings\Security Settings\Local Policies\User Rights Assignments. Double-click Deny Log On Through Terminal Services. In the policy Properties dialog box, select Define These Policy Settings, and then click Add User Or Group. In the Add User Or Group dialog box, click Browse. This displays the Select Users, Computers, or Groups dialog box, type the name of the user or group for which you want to deny logon through Terminal Services, and then click OK. You can also change the default permissions for groups in the Terminal Services Configuration tool. For instance, you could remove Administrators from having Full Control of the Terminal Services objects. For more information on the Terminal Services Configuration tool, see the section entitled "Terminal Services Servers" on page 1036.

Configuring Remote Desktop for Administration Through Group Policy

Remote Desktop for Administration is part of Terminal Services, and you can use Group Policy to configure Terminal Services. Microsoft recommends using Group Policy as the first choice when you are when configuring Terminal Services for use with Remote Desktop for Administration. The precedence hierarchy for Terminal Services configuration is as follows:

- Computer-level Group Policy
- User-level Group Policy
- Local computer policy using the Terminal Services Configuration tool
- User policy on the Local User and Group level
- Local client settings

You can configure local policy on individual computers or on an organizational unit (OU) in a domain. You can use Group Policy to configure Terminal Services settings per connection, per user, per computer, or for groups of computers in an OU of a domain. The Group Policy settings for Terminal Services are modified using the Group Policy Object Editor and are located in Computer Configuration\Administrative Templates\Windows Components\Terminal Services and in User Configuration\Administrative Templates\Windows Components\Terminal Services.

> **Tip** **Create a separate OU for Terminal Services**
> Typically, Remote Desktop for Administration is used throughout an organization and Terminal Servers are isolated to a particular group of servers operating in a separate OU. So, if you plan to use Terminal Services as well in the organization, you should consider creating a separate OU for the Terminal Servers. In this way, you can manage Terminal Servers separately from Remote Desktop for Administration.

Supporting Remote Desktop Connection Clients

The Remote Desktop Connection client is the new Terminal Services client. It uses the Microsoft Remote Desktop Protocol (RDP) version 5.2 or later. Clients can use the Remote Desktop Connection client to connect to a remote server or workstation that has been set up to be administered remotely.

New Features for the Remote Desktop Connection Client

The latest Remote Desktop Connection client has been substantially improved. The new features an administrator should be aware of when supporting RDC are the following:

- Connection Manager is now fully integrated into RDC. This allows the clients to save connection settings locally and provides the capability to deploy connection profiles.
- Improved interface allows high-color and full-screen viewing. A connection bar has been added to allow quick switching between a remote session and the local desktop.
- Support for high encryption of the data sent between the client and the server. By default, the encryption is at the maximum key strength supported by the client. New for RDP 5.2 is the ability to use 128-bit encryption, and this level of encryption can be required on the client. If you set RDP to require high encryption, a client can make a connection only if it supports this level of encryption.
- Support for automatic restoration of connections and automatic completion of processes even if the connection is lost. If a connection is interrupted or lost while an administrator is performing a task, the client will reconnect to the session and in the

interim, processing continues on the server so that any running processes can be finished without interruption.

- Support for client resource redirection. Resource redirection allows audio, mapped drives, ports, printers, and certain keyboard combinations to be handled by the client computer. If an application generates audio feedback, such as an error notification, this can be redirected to the client. Key combinations that perform application functions are passed to the remote server except for Ctrl+Alt+Delete, which is handled by the client computer. In addition, local devices such as drives, printers, and serial ports are also available. Because both local and network drives are available on the client, users can easily access local drives and transfer files between the client and the server.

Installing Remote Desktop Connection Clients

The Remote Desktop Connection client comes installed on Windows XP and Windows Server 2003 systems and can be installed on other platforms such as Windows 2000 Server and workstations. The Remote Desktop Connection client installation software is available for the following operating systems: Microsoft Windows 95, Windows 98, Windows Millennium Edition (Windows Me), Windows NT 4, and Windows 2000.

For these operating systems, you can use these deployment options to make the Remote Desktop Connection client available to remote users:

- Install from the Windows Server 2003 installation CD. On the Windows Server 2003, the client setup is in the Support\Tools folder. The client setup and the install shield are included in a single executable: Msrdpcli.exe. Simply copy to the client to the target computer and double-click to run it. On the Internet, the client can be downloaded from *http://www.microsoft.com/windowsxp/remotedesktop/*.
- Copy from a server system and install. On a Windows Server 2003 system, the client setup and the related installer programs are in the %SystemRoot%\System32\Clients\Tsclient\Win32 folder. The installer package is named Msrdpcli.msi. If you start the Setup.exe program in this folder, it will check for the necessary version of the Windows Installer Package and install this as part of the client tool installation. Two installer packages are provided: Instmsia.exe and Instmsiw.exe.

> **Note** Windows Server 2003 uses Remote Desktop Protocol (RDP) version 5.2. The Remote Desktop Connection client that was originally shipped with Windows XP uses RDP version 5.1. When you install Service Pack 1 or later, the Remote Desktop Connection client is updated so that it works with RDP version 5.2.

Other deployment options include storing the client installation software on a network share and publishing the location or using Microsoft Systems Management Server (SMS) to publish the Windows installer RDC. RDC also supports Microsoft Windows CE and can be installed on Windows CE–based handheld professional devices and Windows CE–based terminals. A Windows CE version of RDC is included in the Windows CE .NET Platform Builder and can also be installed by Windows CE hardware vendors.

Running the Remote Desktop Connection Client

As discussed previously, you now can open two remote virtual sessions and one console session on computers that run Windows Server 2003 without needing a TS CAL. Previously, Windows 2000 Terminal Services required a license for each client. The addition of the console session is a new feature that greatly enhances your capabilities as an administrator to execute successfully many programs, applications, and processes that would not run on previous versions.

There are several ways to start the Remote Desktop Connection client.

- **Run in console mode** Console mode is used by administrators to enable full interaction with the console of the remote system. To run the client in console mode, you can do either of the following:
  - Type **mstsc /console** at the command prompt or in the Run dialog box
- **Run in virtual session mode** Virtual session mode is used by administrators as well as users to start a virtual session on a remote system. To run the client in virtual session mode, you can do either of the following:
  - Type **mstsc** at the command prompt or in the Run dialog box
  - Click Start and select Programs or All Programs, Accessories, Communications, and finally Remote Desktop Connection

Once the client is started, enter the name or Internet Protocol (IP) address of the computer to which you want to connect, as shown in Figure 30-3. If you don't know the name of the computer, use the drop-down list provided to choose an available computer, or select Browse For More on the drop-down list to display a list of domains and computers in those domains.

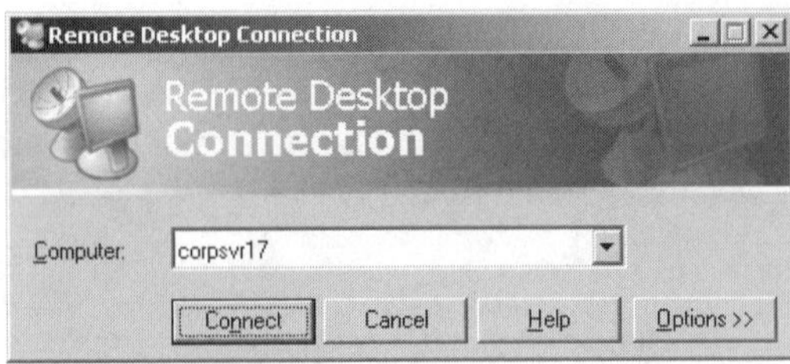

Figure 30-3. Specifying the remote computer with which to establish a connection.

By default, Windows uses your current user name and domain to log on to the remote computer. If you want to use different account information, click Options, and then enter values in the related User Name, Password, and Domain fields, and select the Save My Password check box to enable automatic logon if desired.

Note Even if you select the Save My Password check box, you might be prompted to enter your password during the logon process depending on your network's policies and the configuration of the terminal server.

As shown in Figure 30-4, you can change other client settings as well when you click Options.

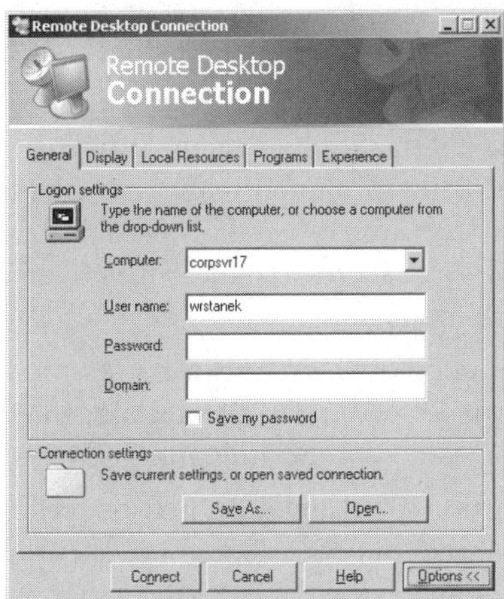

Figure 30-4. RDC options.

There are five tabs you can use to change the client settings:

- **General** You might want to use these options to save keystrokes by adding logon information. Rather than typing in your settings each time, you can save the connection settings and load them when you want to make a connection.

  To save the current connection settings, click Save As, then use the Save As dialog box to save the .rdp file for the connection.

  To load previously saved connection settings, click Open, and then use the Open dialog box to find and open the previously saved connection settings.
- **Display** The default settings for RDC are full-screen and high-color. You can modify these settings here.

  Use the Remote Desktop Size option to set the screen size. The size options available depend on the display size on the local computer.

Use the Colors option to choose the preferred color depth. The default is 16-bit high color, but settings on the remote computer might override this setting.

- **Local Resources** You can modify the way the new redirection features work, including audio redirection, keystroke combination redirection, and local device redirection.

  By default, remote computer sound is redirected to the local computer. Using the Remote Computer Sound option, you can change the default setting by selecting Do Not Play or Leave At Remote Computer.

  By default, when you are working in full-screen mode, key combinations such as Alt+Tab and Ctrl+Esc are redirected to the remote system, and Ctrl+Alt+Delete is handled locally. Using Apply Windows Key Combinations, you change this behavior so key combinations are sent to the local computer or the remote computer only. However, if you send key combinations to the remote computer only, you could get in a situation where you cannot log on locally.

  By default, local printers are connected automatically when users are logged on to the remote computer. This makes it easy to print to your currently configured printers when you are working with a remote system. You can also connect local disk drives and serial ports for the same reason. With local drives connected, you can easily transfer files between the local and remote computer.

- **Programs** You can configure the execution of programs when a session starts from this dialog box. Select Start The Following Program On Connection, and then set the program path or file name and the start folder for the program.
- **Experience** You can select the connection speed and other network performance settings. For optimal performance, choose the connection speed you are using, such as Modem (56 Kbps) or LAN (10 Mbps or higher), and allow only bitmap caching.

  Other options you can allow include Desktop Background, Show Contents Of Window While Dragging, Menu And Window Animation, and Themes. If you choose these additional options, you cause additional processing on the remote system and additional network traffic, which can slow down performance.

  By default, Reconnect If Connection Is Dropped is selected. If the session is interrupted, the RDC will try to reconnect it automatically. Getting disconnected from a connection doesn't stop processing. The session will go into a disconnected state and continue executing whatever processes the sessions was running.

When you click Connect, you are connected to the remote system. Enter your account password if prompted, and then click OK. If the connection is successful, you'll see the Remote Desktop window on the selected computer, as shown in Figure 30-5, and you'll be able to work with resources on the computer. In the case of a failed connection, check the information you provided and then try to connect again.

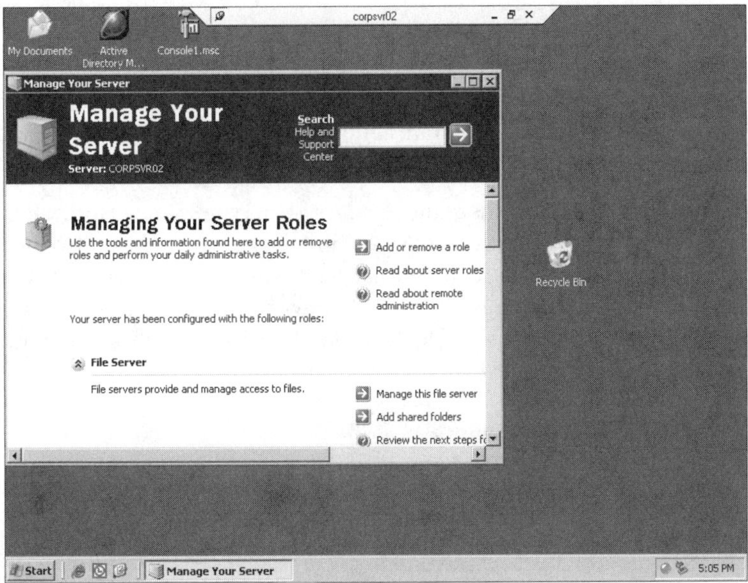

Figure 30-5. A connection to a remote system.

When you are working in full-screen mode, a connection bar is displayed at the top of the screen. On the left side of the connection bar is a push pin. If you click the push pin, it unpins the connection bar so that the bar disappears when you move the mouse away. To make the bar appear again, you would then need to point the mouse to the top part of the screen. On the right side of the connection bar are several other buttons. The first button switches you to the local desktop. The second button switches between full mode and tile display mode. The third button disconnects the remote session.

Disconnecting from a session does not end a session. The session continues to run on the server, which uses resources and may prevent other users from connecting because only one console session and two virtual sessions are allowed. The proper way to end a session is to log off the remote computer just as you would a local computer. In the Remote Desktop Connection window, click Start, and then click Shutdown. In the Shut Down Windows dialog box, select Log Off, and then click OK.

> **Caution** Don't try to log off the remote session by pressing Ctrl+Alt+Delete and clicking Logoff. Doing this will log you off the console session on your local client but still leave the remove session running on the terminal server.

Running Remote Desktops

Remote Desktops allows you to connect to a number of computers running Remote Desktop for Administration and to switch between them within one window. To start Remote Desktops, click Start, Programs or All Programs, Administrative Tools, Remote Desktops, or type **tsmmc.msc** at the command prompt.

You can then establish connections to the remote systems you want to work with. Right-click the Remote Desktops node in the console root, and then select Add New Connection. In the Add New Connection dialog box, enter the name or IP address of the computer to which you want to connect, as shown in Figure 30-6. Click Browse to display a list of domains and available computers in those domains. The Connection Name field is filled in automatically for you based on the server name or IP address you entered.

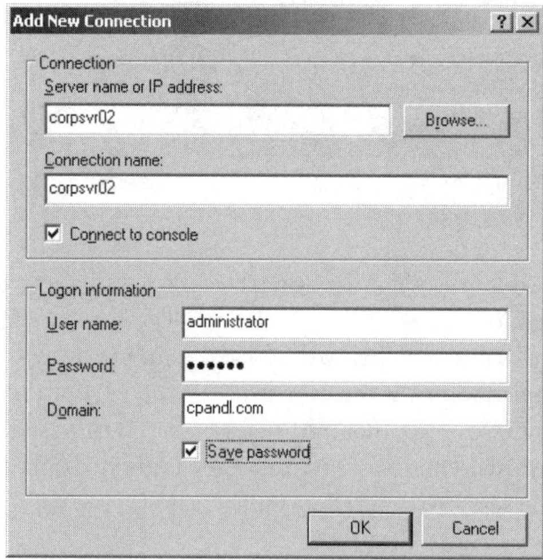

Figure 30-6. Connecting to a remote system in Remote Desktops.

The Connect To Console option controls whether you are connected to a console session or a virtual session. By default, this option is selected, meaning console mode is used. Clear this option to establish a virtual session with the remote computer. In the Logon Information area, type the user name, password, and domain that you want to use for logon. To save the password, click Save Password. When you are finished setting connection options, click OK.

As shown in Figure 30-7, an entry is added below Remote Desktops for the computer. Clicking this entry automatically connects to the remote system. Each configured connection can be selected and switched between without you having to log off each time. Following this, you could switch to a different remote system simply by clicking its entry in the left pane. To disconnect from a remote system, right-click the related entry in the left pane, and select Disconnect.

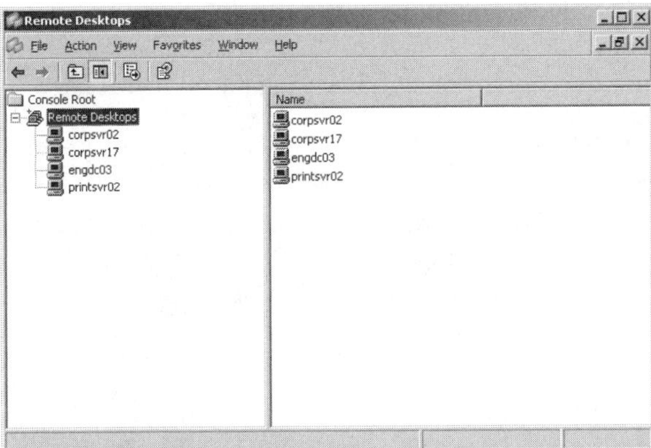

Figure 30-7. Each configured connection can be selected and switched between.

Disconnecting from a session does not end a session. The session will go into a disconnected state and continue executing whatever processes the session was running. The proper way to end a session is to log off the remote computer just as you would a local computer. In the right pane of the Remote Desktops window, click Start, and then click Shutdown. In the Shut Down Windows dialog box, select Log Off, and then click OK.

When you connect to a remote system, the screen on the remote system fills the right pane, as shown in Figure 30-8. Before you make a connection, you should maximize the Remote Desktops window. If you don't do this, you'll end up with a small screen that cannot be resized.

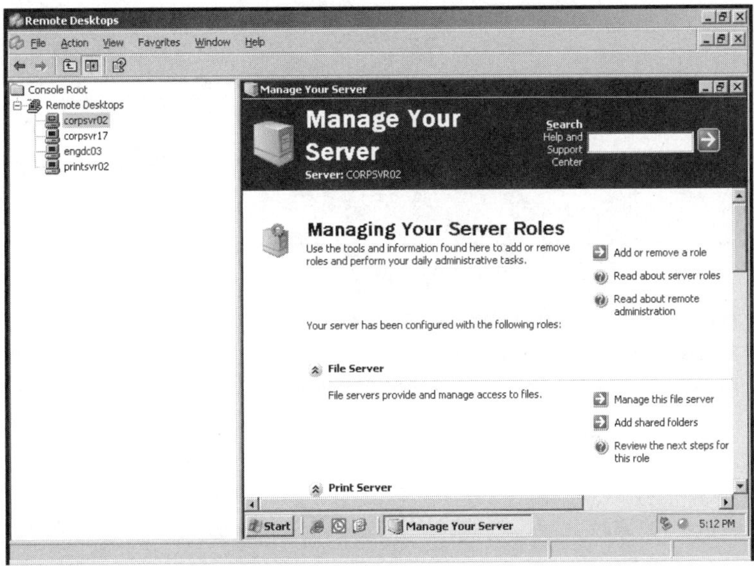

Figure 30-8. A remote connection.

To change this behavior or configure additional options, right-click the related entry in the left pane of Remote Desktops, and select Properties. In the Properties dialog box, shown in Figure 30-9, you can change the connection options using the following tabs:

- **General** You can set the connection options as discussed previously. You can also use this to change the connection mode and the password associated with the logon.
- **Screen Options** You can choose a desktop size or custom size to use for the connection. The screen size options available depend on the size of the display on your local computer. In most cases, you'll want to use the default option Expand To Fill MMC Result Pane.
- **Other** You can configure the execution of programs when a session starts and enable redirection of local drives when logged on to the remote computer. Drive redirection makes it easier to transfer files to and from the remote computer.

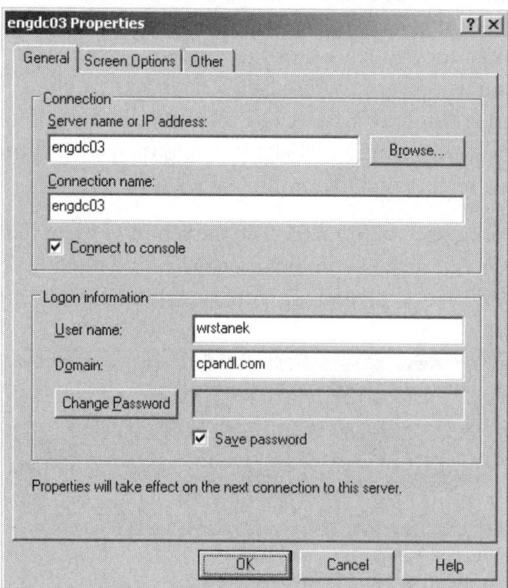

Figure 30-9. Modify connection options.

When you are finished configuring the connections you want to use for administration, you should save the Remote Desktops configuration. This ensures the connections remain available if you exit the console. To save the options, press Ctrl+S or click File, Save.

Tracking Who's Logged On

When you deploy Terminal Services, you can use the Terminal Services Manager to view and manage logon sessions. With Remote Desktop for Administration, you can use this as well, but you typically don't need all the additional options and details. A more basic way to keep track of who is logged on to a server is to use the QUSER command. Type **quser** to see who is logged on to the system on which you are running the command prompt, or type **quser /server:*ServerName*** to see who is logged on to a remote server. Consider the following example:

```
USERNAME  SESSIONNAME ID   STATEIDLE TIME  LOGON TIME
wrstanek  console     0    Active            9/16/2004 1:33 PM
administrator  rdp-tcp#4   1    Active       1    9/16/2004 5:05 PM
```

Here, there are two active sessions:

- Wrstanek is logged on to an active console session. The session ID is 0, meaning it is Session 0.
- Administrator is logged on to an active virtual session. The session ID is 1, meaning it is Session 1.

You can also use the Task Manager to view user sessions. Press Ctrl+Alt+Delete, and then click Task Manager. In the Task Manager dialog box, select the Users tab, as shown in Figure 30-10. Similar details are shown as with the command line. The one useful addition is the name of the client machine from which the connection was established.

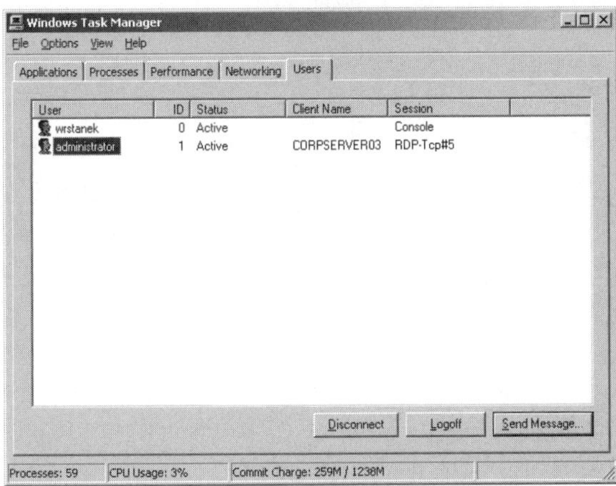

Figure 30-10. View and manage remote sessions from Task Manager.

You can also use Task Manager to manage remote user sessions:

- To disconnect a user session, select the user entry, click Disconnect, and then click Yes when prompted to confirm the action.
- To log off a user, select the user entry, click Logoff, and then click Yes when prompted to confirm the action.

The difference between disconnecting a session and logging off a session is important. When you disconnect a session, the session goes into a disconnected state and continues executing current processes. If you log off a user, you end that user's session, closing any applications the user was running and ending any foreground processes the person was running as well. A foreground process is a process being run by an active application as opposed to a background or batch process being run independently from the user session.

Chapter 31

Deploying Terminal Services

Terminal Services lets users run Microsoft Windows–based applications on a remote server. When users run an application on a terminal server, the execution and processing take place on the server, and only the data from devices such as the display, keyboard, and mouse are transmitted over the network. A client logged on to a terminal server and running applications remotely is said to be using a *virtual session*. Although there may be dozens or hundreds of users simultaneously logged on to a terminal server, users see only their own virtual session.

Using Terminal Services

You can use Terminal Services to rapidly deploy and centrally manage Windows-based applications. One advantage of this method is that you can be sure that all users are running the same version of an application and that they can do so from any computer. Another advantage is that organizations with older computers running earlier versions of Windows can get more mileage out of their computers by having users run applications on terminal servers instead of locally on their desktops. Terminal Services involves these key elements:

- Terminal Services clients
- Terminal Services servers
- Terminal Services licensing

Terminal Services Clients

The primary client used to establish connections to a terminal server is the Remote Desktop Connection client. This client comes installed on the Microsoft Windows XP and Windows Server 2003 operating systems and is available for installation on Microsoft Windows 95, Windows 98, Windows Millennium Edition (Windows Me), Windows NT 4, Windows 2000, and Windows CE. For details on the use and features of this client, see the section entitled "Supporting Remote Desktop Connection Clients" on page 1024.

By sending only the data required for I/O devices to and from the server, Terminal Services significantly reduces the amount of data transferred between a client and a server. This reduces the amount of network bandwidth used, allowing Terminal Services to operate in low bandwidth environments. In addition, users are able to optimize performance based on the speed of their connection. On a 28.8 Kbps modem, a user has only the essential features to ensure the best overall performance possible. As a user goes from a 28.8 Kbps modem connection to a LAN connection at 10 Mbps or higher, Windows features are automatically added to enhance the user experience. Administrators can also configure Terminal Services to restrict the additional features. For example, if hundreds of users are using a terminal server, you may need to restrict enhancements to ensure the overall performance of the server. If you don't do this and the terminal server is overworked, it may fail.

Terminal Services Servers

It's very easy to set up a terminal server. What isn't so easy is getting the infrastructure right before you do so and maintaining the installation once it's in place. Before you install Terminal Services, it is essential to plan the environment and to deploy Terminal Services before you install applications on the terminal server. Once you deploy Terminal Services, you will configure the environment, install applications, and make those applications available to remote users.

The new features for the Remote Desktop Connection client were discussed in the section entitled "New Features for the Remote Desktop Connection Client" on page 1024. For Windows Server 2003, there are many standard features and enhancements as well. The administration tools for Terminal Services include the following:

- **Terminal Services Manager** Terminal Services Manager is the primary tool for managing terminal servers and client connections. Unlike previous versions, the current version doesn't automatically enumerate all the terminal servers that are available. Instead, it gives direct access to a local server if it is running Terminal Services and allows you to selectively enumerate servers and add servers to a list of favorites for easier management. In a large installation with many terminal servers, this makes Terminal Services Manager more responsive.

Note It is important to note that certain features of Terminal Services Manager work only when you run the tool from a client. For example, if you run Terminal Services Manager on a terminal server, you won't be able to use the Remote Control and Connect features.

- **Terminal Services Licensing Manager** Terminal Services Licensing Manager is used to install licenses and activate a Terminal Services license server. The enhanced interface makes it easier to install licenses and to activate or deactivate license servers.
- **Terminal Services Configuration** Terminal Services Configuration is used to manage terminal server connections as well as global and default server settings. Terminal server connections and the Remote Desktop Protocol (RDP) make the enhancements to the Remote Desktop Connection possible. Server settings also enable you to easily set terminal server policy. A key policy addition is the single session policy, which, when activated, limits a user to a single session, whether the session is active or not.

Terminal Services has many changes for security as well. In previous editions of Terminal Services, you had to assign user access permissions using the Terminal Services Configuration tool. For Windows Server 2003, you have the additional option of adding users and groups to the Remote Desktop Users group. This is a standard group for which you can configure membership in Active Directory Users And Computers. By adding the Domain Users group to the Remote Desktop Users group, you allow all authenticated users to use Terminal Services. If instead you were to add the special group Everyone, anyone with access to the network could use Terminal Services.

Other important security changes involve additional encryption options. Terminal Services now supports 128-bit encryption as well as encryption compliant with the Federal Information Processing Standard (FIPS). Using 128-bit encryption ensures a high level of encryption, which provides powerful protection of the data sent between a Terminal Services client and a server. FIPS encryption is added to provide compliance with FIPS 140-1 and FIPS 140-2, which are standards for Security Requirements for Cryptographic Modules, a necessity for some organizations.

Terminal Services Licensing

A Terminal Services license server is required to set up Terminal Services (see Figure 31-1). The license server, responsible for issuing licenses and tracking their usage, maintains a pool of all available licenses. The assigned licenses are also tracked so that they can be validated. Unlike Windows NT 4, which allowed the license server to trust that you had acquired the number of licenses you specified, Terminal Services requires that you get official licenses from Microsoft and activate them through the Microsoft Clearinghouse.

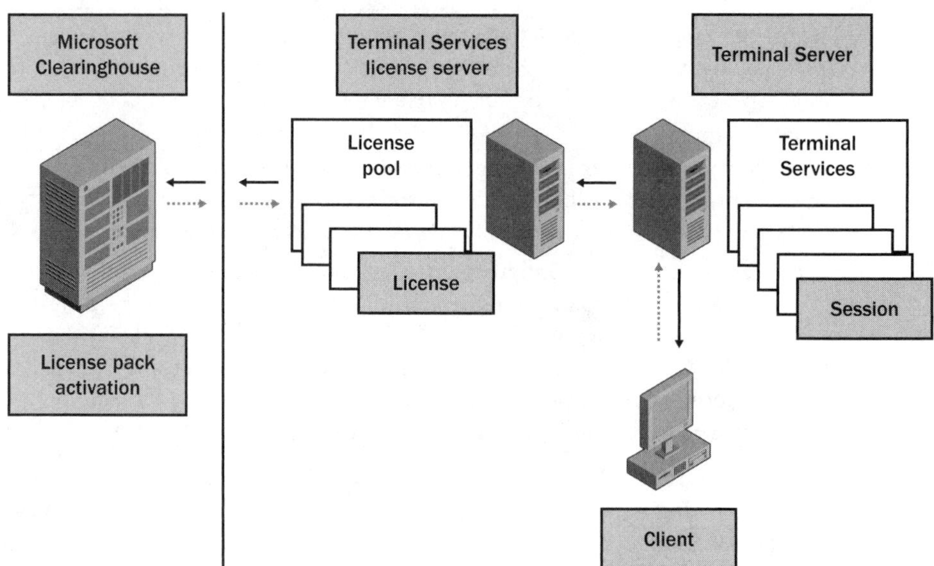

Figure 31-1. Terminal Services implementation with a license server.

The first time a client connects to a terminal server, the terminal server checks for a license. If the client has a license, the terminal server validates it and allows the client to connect. If the client doesn't have a license, the terminal server locates a license server (using a network broadcast in workgroups or through Active Directory in domains) and requests a new license. If that license server doesn't have a license to offer, the client is not allowed to connect.

> **Note** For the first 120 days after deployment, clients can be granted a temporary license if an activated license server is not available. After this grace period, Terminal Services will stop serving unlicensed clients.

Provided that the server has a license, it will give the license to the terminal server, which in turn issues it to the client. Client access licenses provided by Terminal Services are issued per device or per user, so the way licensing works depends on the licensing configuration—which can be mixed and matched as necessary. With per-device licensing, the license is valid only for a particular computer and will be validated in the future to the globally unique identifier (GUID) of the machine on which the client is running. With per-user licensing, the license is valid only for that user and will be validated in the future to the GUID of the user's account.

> **Note** Terminal Services client access licenses are issued per device or per user only. They are not available in per-server mode because Windows sessions are not allowed in per-server mode.

An issued license is valid for a period of 52 to 89 days; the interval is assigned randomly. When the client later disconnects or logs off the terminal server, the license is not returned to the pool. The expiration date serves to return unused licenses to the license pool. Each time a client connects to a terminal server, the expiration date of its license is checked. If the current date is within seven days of the expiration date, the license server renews the license for another 52 to 89 days. If a client doesn't log back in to the terminal server before its license expires, the license is returned to the license pool, which makes it available to other clients.

Unlike previous implementations of Terminal Services, the current version lets you reassign a client access license from one device to another device or from one user to another user. However, there are some limitations. The license must be either permanently reassigned away from its existing owner (device or user), or it must be temporarily reassigned to a loaner device while a permanent device is out of service, or to a temporary worker while a regular employee is absent.

Inside Out

Terminal Services Licensing Changes

Anyone who wants to use Terminal Services must have a client access license. This remains true whether a user connects to the terminal server using Microsoft Remote Desktop Protocol (RDP) or uses another vendor's protocol. You can purchase client access licenses using the licensing programs discussed in the section entitled "Product Licensing" on page 82. This means that small companies can purchase licenses in packs of 5, 20, or more, while bigger companies can purchase licenses under programs such as the Microsoft Open License.

When you purchase licenses in packs, you'll receive a product activation code that can be used one time to activate the number of licenses purchased. When you use Open Licensing or other programs, you purchase a set number of licenses. With Open Licensing, you are then issued an Open License Authorization and a set of license numbers that you can use to activate licenses. Under Select and Enterprise licensing agreements, you provide your Enrollment Agreement Number to activate licenses.

In the past, the requirement for a Terminal Services client access license was waived if the device accessing the terminal server was running the same or later version of an equivalent desktop operating system. For example, a client running Windows XP Professional could access a Windows 2000 terminal server without needing a Terminal Services client access license. With the release of Windows Server 2003, all clients are required to have a Terminal Services client access license.

Designing the Terminal Services Infrastructure

Terminal Services can be deployed in single-server and multi-server environments. The first thing to plan is Terminal Services capacity. Capacity planning can help you determine the actual number of users that a specific Terminal Services configuration can support.

Capacity Planning for Terminal Services

It is important to note that Windows Server 2003 has significant scalability advantages over its predecessors. Primarily this is because the Windows Server 2003 kernel provides better use of the 32-bit virtual address space. Because a terminal server must allocate virtual resources for all users who are logged on, whether they are active or in a disconnected state, the improved memory handling in Windows Server 2003 gives it significant advantages over Windows 2000 Server. In addition, Windows Server 2003 is more effective at using faster processors and system buses. This again gives Windows Server 2003 significant advantages over Windows 2000 Server.

Because remote serving of applications is both processor-intensive and memory-intensive, the most significant limits on the number of users a server can support are imposed by a server's processing power and available RAM. Network bandwidth and disk performance can also be factors, but typically, a server's capacity to handle requests will be exhausted well before the network bandwidth and disk drive subsystems have reached maximum utilization.

Planning should start by looking at not only the number of users you need to support but also the following factors:

- The type of users you need to support
- The applications users will be running
- The way users work

These latter characteristics play a significant role in the actual usage of a server. Users can be divided into three general types:

- **Data entry worker** Data entry workers provide data input. They typically perform data entry, transcription, order entry, or clerical work. Data entry workers typically have low impact on a server on a per-user basis. This means a server used primarily by data entry workers could scale to a larger number of users than a server used by other types of workers.
- **Knowledge worker** Knowledge workers perform day-to-day tasks using business applications. Rather than providing strictly data input, knowledge workers create documents, spreadsheets, presentations, and reports. Knowledge workers typically have moderate impact on a server on a per-user basis. This means a server being used primarily by knowledge workers would not scale as well as a server being used by data entry workers.

- **Productivity worker** Productivity workers are the high-performance workers in the business environment. Their daily tasks include specialized applications for graphic design, CAD, 3D animation, and applications that perform complex calculations or require a high amount of processing. Productivity workers typically have high impact on a server on a per-user basis. This means a server being used primarily by productivity workers would scale to a lower number of users than a server used by other types of workers.

The impact of these types of users can best be illustrated graphically. Consider the scenario in Figure 31-2. The chart shows the number of different types of users that can be supported on three different server configurations.

- Server A is a 4-processor system with high-end processors and 4 GB RAM.
- Server B is a 2-processor system with high-end processors and 4 GB RAM.
- Server C is a 1-processor system with a high-end processor and 4 GB RAM.

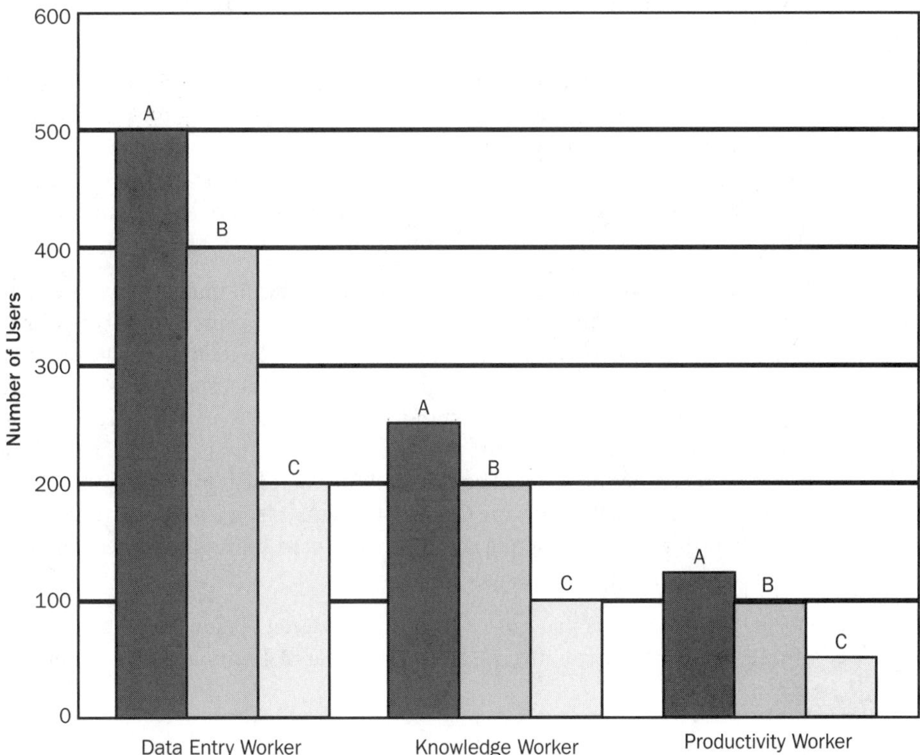

Figure 31-2. Terminal Services capacity example.

As you can see from the example, each server can handle a large number of data entry workers relative to other types of workers. Because CPU power and RAM are so important, the servers are given fast processors and a lot of RAM. These results are based on using Intel Xeon Processors operating at 3.2 gigahertz (GHz) and using a 2 megabyte (MB) L2 Cache with a 533 megahertz (MHz) front size bus.

While the example takes into account the types of users and the types of applications being used, it doesn't take into account the way users work. The way users work can also have a significant impact on Terminal Services. You should also consider these factors:

- Users' typing speed
- Users' work habits
- Experience settings on the client

Believe it or not, typing speed can affect performance. Many users who type very quickly will make more updates and require more processing than a group of users who type slowly. You don't want to tell users to type more slowly, but you do want to take their typing skills into account.

Users with poor work habits can have a significant impact on performance. Consider the case of a user who exits applications rather than switching among them: The user starts Microsoft Outlook to check his mail, exits Outlook, starts Microsoft Word to type a document, exits Word, starts Outlook again to check his e-mail, exits Outlook, and so on—and does this all day long. Starting and exiting applications requires more processing and resources than simply switching among applications as you use them.

The experience settings on the client can have a significant impact on performance as well. If users have optimized their experience settings for LAN connections of 10 Mbps or higher, they will have desktop backgrounds, themes, menu and window animation, and other extras that require a lot more processing on the server. The only experience setting that actually improves performance is bitmap caching, which ensures that caching is used as much as possible to reduce the amount of data that has to be passed to the client. Client display settings also affect server performance. The default display setting is for High Color (16 bit). An additional option is available for True Color (24 bit). As 24-bit color requires a lot more processing than 16-bit color, this setting should only be used by those who need high-end color resolution, such as graphic designers.

Having covered factors that can affect performance, let's take a closer look at how to plan for capacity. Start by determining the average number of Terminal Services users. Remember that both active users and those with inactive or disconnected sessions use system resources. Then consider the types and average numbers of applications users will be running. Run those applications and use the techniques discussed in Chapter 15, "Performance Monitoring and Tuning," and Chapter 16, "Comprehensive Performance Analysis and Logging," to determine how much physical and virtual memory each application uses on average. This should give you a good baseline for capacity planning.

If a server will have 100 users, who each run four applications on average, and those applications collectively use 10 MB of physical memory and 24 MB of virtual memory on average, you know the system will need a minimum of 1 gigabyte (GB) of RAM for good performance. That's the baseline. You typically want to have 50 percent capacity above the baseline to ensure that the server can handle peak usage loads and can support additional users if necessary. Therefore, in this scenario you'd want to have a minimum of 1.5 GB of RAM.

Processing power is as important as RAM. A server's processors need to be able to keep up with the processing workload. As you scale up, you need to be able to add processors to handle the additional processing load of additional users. If you are monitoring server performance, pay particular attention to the Copy Read Hits % performance counter of the Cache performance object. This counter tracks the percentage of cache copy read requests that did not require a disk read to provide access to the page in cache. For best performance, you want this counter to be at 95 percent or above (optimally at 99 percent). If the counter is below 95 percent, the server is reading from the page file on disk frequently and this can affect performance. You can resolve this problem by adding RAM to the system.

Also consider network bandwidth and disk configuration in capacity planning. A network running at 100 megabits per second (Mbps) can handle hundreds of Terminal Services users. A network running at 1,000 Mbps (Gigabit Ethernet) can handle thousands of Terminal Services users. Consider existing traffic on the network before Terminal Services is deployed a limiting factor. For capacity planning, you can test the average amount of bandwidth a client uses when working with a terminal server by monitoring the Bytes Total/sec counter of the Network Interface performance object. If a client uses 1,250 bytes per second on average, this is 10,000 bits per second. In theory, a network running at 100 Mbps could handle 10,000 of these clients. Reduce this by 50 percent to shift from the theoretical to what is probably possible, and then subtract current bandwidth usage to come up with a working number.

Disk subsystem performance can also have a substantial impact on overall performance, especially on a server that makes moderate to heavy use of the paging file. Because the number and frequency of standard read/write operations for files affects the design of the disk subsystem, these operations will also affect overall performance. Ideally, the disk subsystem on a terminal server will be configured with hardware RAID and multiple RAID controllers rather than software RAID. When multiple SCSI/RAID controllers are used, disks should be configured to distribute the load. When you install applications that will be used with Terminal Services, you can help spread the load by installing and configuring applications to use different disk sets on different SCSI/RAID controllers.

Planning Organizational Structure for Terminal Services

When you are deploying Terminal Services, your planning should include deciding where in the organizational structure your terminal servers should be located. As discussed in Chapter 30, "Using Remote Desktop for Administration," servers running in Terminal Server mode should be clearly separated from servers running in Remote Desktop for Administration mode. This ensures that administrators and support personnel can use Remote Desktop for Administration throughout the organization and that selected users can make use of terminal servers.

The best way to achieve separation of these services is to deploy terminal servers in a separate Organizational Unit, which I will call the Terminal Services OU. You can then implement policies and restrictions for Terminal Services separately from those for the rest of the organization. To start, you should place the computer accounts for your terminal servers in the Terminal Services OU. When you do this, you can apply systemwide restrictions to terminal servers and enforce these restrictions using a computer-based policy. These restrictions then replace or are added to the restrictions a Terminal Services user usually has when logging on to the domain.

If you need to provide additional restrictions for Terminal Services users, you can do so on a per-user basis by placing the user account in the Terminal Services OU and defining user-based policy restrictions. In this way, the restrictions are enforced wherever the user logs on to the domain.

Deploying Single-Server Environments

Deploying Terminal Services in a single-server environment is much easier than deploying Terminal Services in a multi-server environment. In a single-server deployment, a group of clients always connects to the same server, so that although your organization may have three terminal servers, Group A always uses Server 1, Group B always uses Server 2, and Group C always uses Server 3, as shown in Figure 31-3.

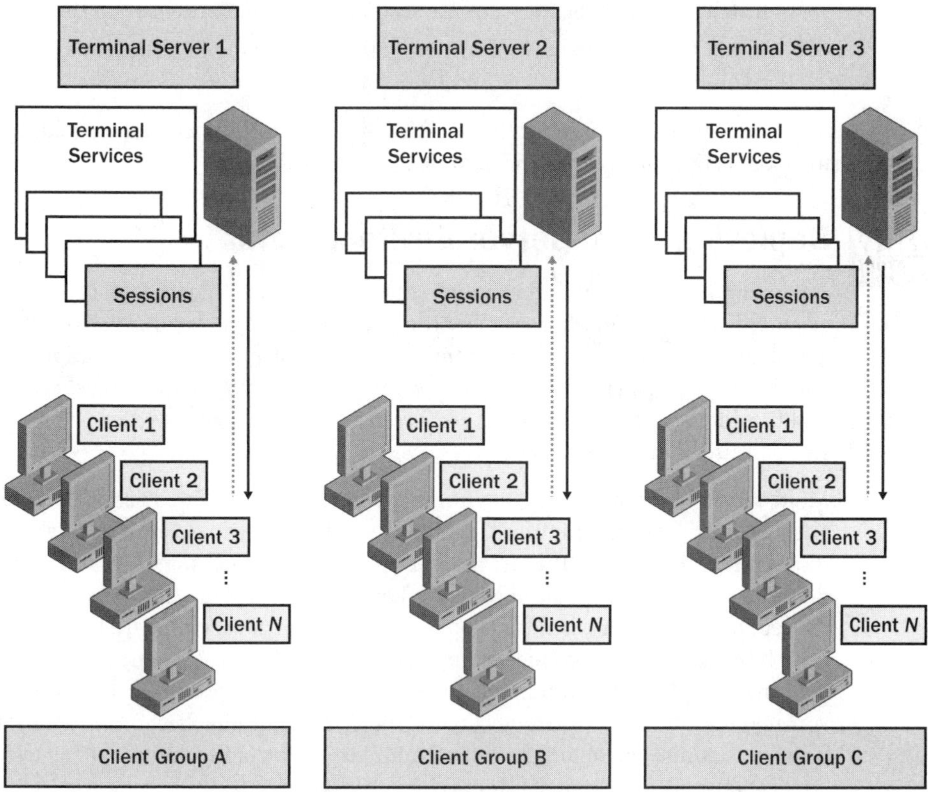

Figure 31-3. Terminal Services in a single-server environment.

A single-server configuration is the easiest to set up, as you need to perform only the following steps:

1. Install the operating system on your designated server and configure the server so it is optimized for file sharing.
2. Install Terminal Services using Add Or Remove Programs to make Terminal Services available to clients.
3. Install applications to be used by clients using Add Or Remove Programs, which ensures that the applications are set up using Install Mode for Terminal Services rather than Execute Mode.

4 Install a Terminal Services license server and configure licenses for use.

5 Install terminal clients and configure them to use the Remote Desktop Connection client.

Steps 2 through 4 are discussed in detail in this chapter. Chapter 30 discussed Remote Desktop Connection client setup and support.

Deploying Multi-Server Environments

Deploying Terminal Services in a multi-server environment requires a lot of planning and an advanced setup. In a multi-server environment, you use load balancing to create a farm of Terminal Servers whose incoming connections are distributed across multiple servers. Clients see the load-balanced Terminal Server farm as a single server. The farm has a single virtual IP address, and client requests are directed to this virtual IP address, allowing for seamless use of multiple servers.

Multi-server Terminal Services environments can be implemented using Network Load Balancing. A variety of techniques is possible, including Microsoft Network Load Balancing as discussed in Chapter 18, "Preparing and Deploying Server Clusters." Terminal Services introduces a wrinkle to the standard Network Load Balancing configuration by introducing the concept of a session. A client that connects to a Terminal Server is said to be in a virtual session. If that session is disconnected, processing continues in a disconnected state and the client can be configured to automatically try to reconnect the session. In a load-balanced farm, you always want a client to connect to the server it was originally working with. This enables users to continue where they left off without loss of data and without having to restart their applications, open documents, and so on.

For multi-server Terminal Services environments, session information can be managed using a Session Directory server (see Figure 31-4). A Session Directory server maintains a session directory database, which contains a record for each session. The record includes the user name under which the session was established, the session ID, and the server to which the session is connected in the load-balanced farm. Session Directory servers are a new feature for Windows Server 2003.

Whenever a client tries to establish a Terminal Services connection and the user is authenticated, the session database is queried to see if a session record for that user exists. In this way, a user who was disconnected from a session can reconnect to the original session on the correct server. Without session management, the user might be connected to a different server and have to start a new session.

The Session Directory server can be a separate server running the Session Directory service as shown in Figure 31-4, or it can be one of the servers in the load-balanced farm running the Session Directory service. There are several advantages to using a separate server. First of all, if you don't use a separate server, you need to use a multiple network interface configuration for Microsoft Network Load Balancing. This configuration ensures that Terminal Services can communicate with the Network Load Balancing cluster and the Session Directory server. In addition, as you scale Terminal Services, you have the option of clustering Session Directory services to provide for greater availability.

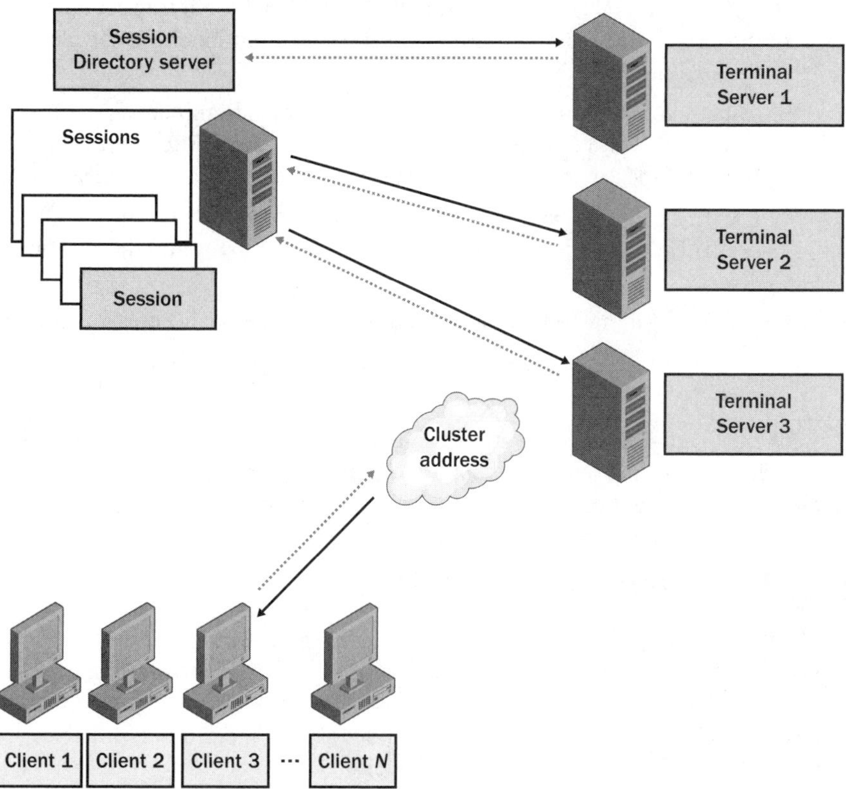

Figure 31-4. A multi-server Terminal Services deployment.

To use a session directory, all servers in the farm must be running Windows Server 2003 Enterprise Edition or Windows Server 2003 Datacenter Edition. A multi-server environment is more complex to set up than a single-server environment. To configure Terminal Services in a multi-server environment, you must follow these steps:

1. Install the operating system on your designated servers and configure the servers so they are optimized for file sharing.

2. Install Terminal Server service on each Terminal Server using Add Or Remove Programs to make Terminal Services available to clients.
3. Install applications to be used by clients using Add Or Remove Programs, which ensures that the applications are set up using Install Mode for Terminal Services rather than Execute Mode.
4. Enable Terminal Services Session Directory service for automatic startup, then start the service on a separate Session Directory server or on one of the member servers in the load-balanced farm.
5. Install Microsoft Network Load Balancing on each terminal server. Make a note of the cluster name and IP address used. A multiple network interface configuration should be used if the Session Directory server is a member of the load-balanced farm.
6. Use the Terminal Services Configuration tool to set the Join Session Directory properties. These properties tell clients about the cluster name and the Session Directory Server.
7. Install a Terminal Services license server and configure licenses for use.
8. Install terminal clients and configure them to use the Remote Desktop Connection client.

Steps 2 through 4, 6, and 7 are discussed in detail in this chapter. Chapter 18 discussed Network Load Balancing setup and support. Chapter 30 discussed Remote Desktop Connection client setup and support.

Setting Up Terminal Services

The tasks required to set up Terminal Services in single-server and multi-server environments are discussed in the sections that follow. As you read these sections, remember that if you want to use a multi-server environment with Session Directory service, all the servers involved must be running Windows Server 2003 Enterprise Edition or later.

Installing Terminal Services

Two components are required for Terminal Services to work:

- Terminal Services service, which is installed by default and configured to run automatically on Windows Server 2003
- Terminal Server service, which is installed using Add Or Remove Programs

To install Terminal Server service, open the Control Panel and double-click Add Or Remove Programs. In the Add Or Remove Programs dialog box, click Add/Remove Windows Components to start the Windows Components Wizard. On the Windows Components page, select Terminal Server. If Internet Explorer Enhanced Security is configured (which is the default on servers), you see the prompt shown in Figure 31-5.

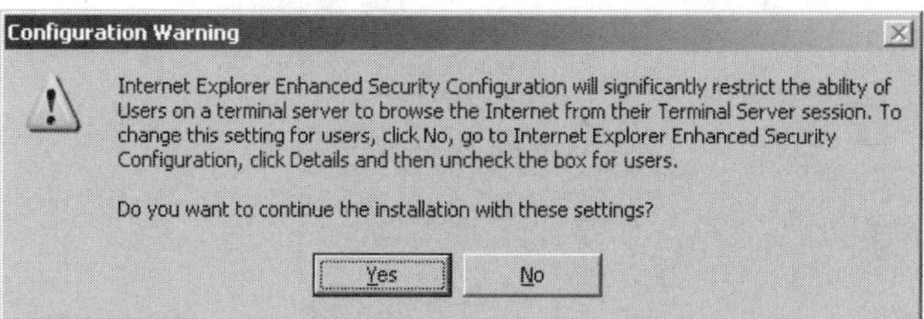

Figure 31-5. Consider whether to continue with Internet Explorer Enhanced Security.

> **Note** By default, Internet Explorer Enhanced Security disables support for ActiveX controls and scripting. A user who visits a site that has these features is prompted to add the site to the Trusted sites security zone so that the content on the World Wide Web can run. For local intranet servers, servers must be added to the Local Intranet security zone so that users can run Web-based applications.

If you are prompted, you have two options:

- If you want to continue and use Internet Explorer Enhanced Security, click Yes. Then click Next to begin the installation, and then click Finish.
- If you want to stop using Internet Explorer Enhanced Security, click No, clear the Internet Explorer Enhanced Security option on the Windows Components page, and then select Terminal Server. Then click Next to begin the installation, and next click Finish.

Otherwise, click Next to display the Terminal Server Setup page. This page tells you the basic rules for using Terminal Services After you read the information, click Next again.

On the next page of the wizard, as shown in Figure 31-6, you can select the default permissions for application compatibility as follows:

- **Full Security** Full Security restricts user access to certain areas of the Registry and to system files. This safeguards the terminal server so that remote users running a virtual session cannot modify system files or the Registry arbitrarily. Most applications designed for Windows XP can run under full security; most programs designed for earlier versions of Windows cannot.
- **Relaxed Security** Relaxed Security is the standard configuration for Windows 2000 Terminal Services. This mode doesn't restrict user access to the Registry or to system files. It is designed for maximum compatibility with applications, particularly those designed for Windows 2000 or earlier versions of Windows.

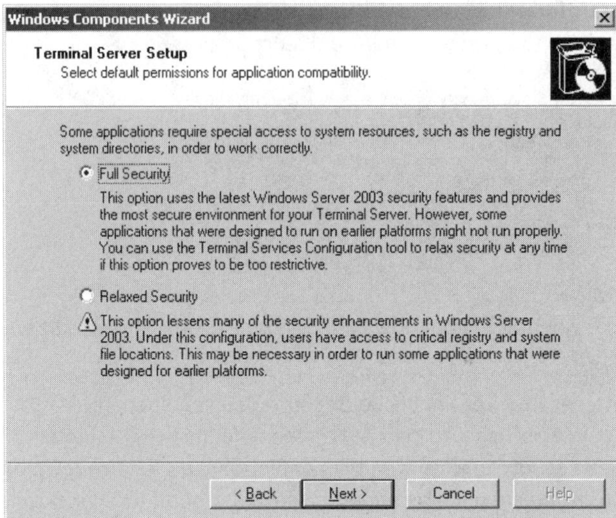

Figure 31-6. Review the details for using Terminal Services.

> **Note** If you are not sure which setting to use, you might try using Full Security, and then perform pre-deployment testing after configuring applications. Don't worry; the security mode can be changed using the Terminal Services Configuration tool. See the section entitled "Configuring Server Settings" later in this chapter.

After you make a selection, click Next to begin the installation. When the installation is complete, click Finish to exit the Windows Component Wizard. If you are prompted to restart the computer, click Yes to restart the computer so that the installation can take effect or click No to restart the computer later.

Installing Applications for Clients to Use

Once you install Terminal Services, there are decisions to make about the applications that you want to make available to users. Not all applications work well in multi-user environments. Some applications simply shouldn't be used; others can be used with some modifications or using a compatibility script. Regardless, all applications must be installed so that they are made available to users correctly.

Choosing Applications for Terminal Services Users

The best applications to run on a terminal server are those that can run multiple instances and perform well in a multi-user environment. The characteristics of applications that perform well in a multi-user environment include the following:

- Storing global data separately from local data
- Storing user data by user rather than by machine
- Identifying users by user name rather than by computer name

Although Terminal Services can be used to run Win16, MS-DOS, and Win32 applications, Terminal Services works best with Win32 applications. With Win16 and MS-DOS applications, Windows Server 2003 creates a virtual MS-DOS machine and runs the 16-bit or MS-DOS application within that context. Because 16-bit and MS-DOS applications are run in a different context, there is additional overhead and the applications won't perform as well as Win32 applications.

If possible, you should limit the use of MS-DOS applications altogether as they are designed for single-user and non-multi-tasking environments and can cause serious performance problems. In addition, you should avoid using applications with known memory bugs or leaks; running multiple instances of such programs only multiplies the problem.

Application Licensing for Terminal Services Users

Unlike client access licensing, application licensing for Terminal Services users is pretty straightforward. Essentially, the licensing that is set for the product in a single-user environment is used in the Terminal Services environment. With Office, for example, licensing is per seat, so every computer that runs Office needs a license whether one user or several use the computer. Thus, a client computer connecting to a terminal server and using Office needs a license per seat. If the client computer already has a license for Office, another license is not needed.

Installing Applications for Terminal Services Users

Terminal Server has two operating modes:

- **Execute mode** Execute mode is used for working with clients. When a client connects to a terminal server, the client and server use Execute mode.
- **Install mode** Install mode is used to install applications on a terminal server. When you install an application, you use this mode to ensure that the application is configured for use with multiple users.

You really don't have to do anything complicated to ensure that you install applications in Install mode: Merely install the application through Add Or Remove Programs rather than using the application's normal setup program, as follows:

1. In Control Panel, select or double-click Add Or Remove Programs.
2. In Add Or Remove Programs, click Add New Programs, and then click CD or Floppy.

3. Click Next. Add Or Remove Programs will then look for a Setup.exe program on the floppy disk first, and then on CD-ROM.
4. If Add Or Remove Programs finds the appropriate Setup.exe program, click Next to begin installation. Otherwise, click Browse to find the appropriate Setup.exe program, and then click Next to begin the installation.

When you install an application on a terminal server using Add Or Remove Programs, Add Or Remove Programs uses a compatible configuration. Any configuration information that an application writes under HKCU or HKLM is written to HKLM\Software\Microsoft\Windows NT\Current Version\Terminal Server\Install as well. Any later changes to an application's configuration that affect HKCU or HKLM are also written to HKLM\Software\Microsoft\Windows NT\Current Version\Terminal Server\Install.

Any time a client using Terminal Services runs an application and that application attempts to read HKCU or HKLM, Terminal Services uses HKLM\Software\Microsoft\Windows NT\Current Version\Terminal Server\Install instead and copies the necessary information to the appropriate location under HKCU. User-specific .ini files or DLLs are copied to the user's home directory. If a user doesn't have a designated home directory, the .ini files or DLLs are copied to the user's profile. All this works to ensure that the core settings for an application are machine specific and that users can customize applications to meet their needs.

Note Some applications come with multi-user installation packages. An example is Office. If you try to install one of these programs on a terminal server, you will see a prompt telling you how to install the application in a multi-user environment. Typically, this involves copying over an initialization or transform file before using Add Or Remove Programs to install the application.

In addition to using Add Or Remove Programs to install applications in Install mode, you can explicitly put a session in Install mode using the CHANGE USER command. CHANGE USER accepts three parameters:

- **/QUERY** Displays the current mode as either "Application EXECUTE mode is enabled" or "Application INSTALL mode is enabled"
- **/EXECUTE** Changes Terminal Services to Execute mode
- **/INSTALL** Changes Terminal Services to Install mode

If you want to install an application using its setup program, you can do this by typing **change user /install** at the command prompt and then running the setup program. Any changes you make to the application in Install mode will apply to all users who use the application for the first time.

When you use CHANGE USER, you may also want to use CHANGE LOGON. The CHANGE LOGON command is used to enable or disable user logon to the terminal server. It can also be used to query the logon state. CHANGE LOGON accepts three parameters:

- **/QUERY** Displays the current logon status as either "Session logins are currently ENABLED" or "Session logins are currently DISABLED"
- **/ENABLE** Enables user logon
- **/DISABLE** Disables user logon

Tip A related but less frequently used command is CHANGE PORT. This command is used to map COM ports for MS-DOS compatibility. Type **change port /?** to learn more about this command.

After you install an application, you will probably need to optimize its configuration for a multi-user environment. Two techniques can be used: application compatibility scripts, discussed in the following section, "Using Application Compatibility Scripts," and hand-tuning, discussed in the section of this chapter entitled "Modifying Applications After Installation."

Using Application Compatibility Scripts

Some applications need a compatibility script to work properly in a multi-user environment. For these applications, you can develop an application compatibility script or use the techniques discussed in the section of this chapter entitled "Modifying Applications After Installation." Three application compatibility scripts are provided with Windows Server 2003:

- **Eudora4.cmd** For Eudora 4
- **Msvs6.cmd** For Microsoft Visual Studio 6
- **Outlk98.cmd** For Outlook 98

These scripts are located in the %SystemRoot%\Application Compatibility Scripts\Install folder. After you install an application with an application compatibility script, you run the application compatibility script from the Install folder. For example, to run MSVS6, you would change the directory to the %SystemRoot%\Application Compatibility Scripts\Install folder, and then type **msv6** at the command prompt.

The application compatibility scripts customize the application's setup so that it works with Terminal Services. This involves setting up the command environment, making changes to the Registry, and configuring file and folder paths for multi-user use. The scripts are written as batch programs and can be edited if you do not want to accept the default values.

Modifying Applications After Installation

After installation, you'll often need to manipulate an application to get it to work well in a multi-user environment. Here are some techniques you can use:

- **Configure application settings in Install mode** You should make changes to application settings in Install mode. This ensures that the configuration settings are available to all users.

- **Set user file paths to drive letters** Many applications have settings for file paths that need to be set on a per-user basis. In this case, you can enter a drive letter, and then map the drive letter to a network share as appropriate for each user. For example, you could set the file path to X: and map X: to the user's home directory. Every user has a separate Terminal Services profile, which you can use for mapping home folders.
- **Configure Registry settings under HKLM\Software\Microsoft\Windows NT\Current Version\Terminal Server\Compatibility\Applications** Only a limited set of application settings can be changed through the Registry. If you need to tune an application's Registry settings, you must do this in Install mode and make changes only to keys and values under HKLM\Software\Microsoft\Windows NT\Current Version\Terminal Server\Compatibility\Applications. This means you would type **change user /install** and then start the Registry Editor.

Some applications don't work well in multi-user environments. If an application performs poorly or hogs system resources, you may need to fine-tune its configuration in the Registry. Each application configured on a terminal server should have a separate subkey under HKLM\Software\Microsoft\Windows NT\Current Version\Terminal Server\Compatibility\Applications. The name of the application subkey is the same as the name of the application's executable without the .exe extension.

Table 31-1 shows the values you can use under an application's subkey to modify the behavior of the application. All these values must be set as the REG_DWORD type. Create or edit the values as discussed in Chapter 14, "Managing the Registry." Any changes you make are applied the next time the application is started.

Table 31-1. Performance-Tuning Registry Values for 16-Bit and 32-Bit Windows Applications

Value Entry	Description	Default Value
FirstCountMsgQPeeks-SleepBadApp	Sets the number of times the application must query the message queue before Terminal Services decides that it is a bad application. The lower this value, the more often the application will be deemed to be bad and the more quickly the application will be suspended so that it uses less CPU time.	0xF (15 decimal)
MsgQBadAppSleep-TimeInMillisec	Sets the number of milliseconds the application is suspended when Terminal Services has decided that it is a bad application. The higher this value is set, the longer the application will be suspended. If this value is zero, polling detection is disabled.	0

Table 31-1. Performance-Tuning Registry Values for 16-Bit and 32-Bit Windows Applications

Value Entry	Description	Default Value
NthCountMsgQPeeks-SleepBadApp	Sets the number of times the application must query the message queue before it is suspended again. The lower this value, the more often the application will be deemed to be bad and the more quickly the application will be suspended so that it uses less CPU time.	0x5 (5 decimal)
Flags	Describes the type of Windows application. Valid values are: 0x4 for Win16 applications; 0x8 for Win32 applications; 0xC for either Win16 or Win32 applications	0x8 (Win32 only)

Note The hyphens inserted in the names in the Value Entry column are not part of the actual name.

Enabling and Joining the Session Directory Service

When you are using a load-balanced terminal server farm, you need to configure a Session Directory server and configure Terminal Services to join the Session Directory. As discussed previously, the Session Directory server can be a member of the load-balanced farm or it can be a separate server. If you use a separate Session Directory server, it probably doesn't need to be a high-end server. The session management workload on the Session Directory server typically is very light, but depends on the number of clients connecting to Terminal Services. Regardless of configuration, the Session Directory server and all terminal servers in the load-balanced farm must be running Windows Server 2003 Enterprise Edition or later.

To set up the Session Directory server, you need to enable the Terminal Services Session Directory service for automatic startup, and then start the service. This service is installed automatically but disabled on all Windows Server 2003 systems. Next, you need to tell the Session Directory server about the computers that can connect to the service. The Terminal Services Session Directory service will not accept any connections from servers that it doesn't know are authorized. To tell the service which servers are authorized, add the computer account for each server in the load-balanced farm to a local computer group called Session Directory Computers. This group is created automatically when you configure the Terminal Services Session Directory service.

To complete the process, you need to configure each server in the farm so that it knows the cluster name, cluster IP address, and Session Directory server IP address. These settings enable Terminal Services to use load balancing and the Session Directory server. To make these changes, you use the Terminal Services Configuration tool.

Enable and Start the Terminal Services Session Directory Service

Follow these steps to enable and start the Terminal Services Session Directory service:

1. Start Computer Management by clicking Start, Programs or All Programs, Administrative Tools, Computer Management. To work with a remote system, right-click the Computer Management entry in the left pane and select Connect To Another Computer on the shortcut menu. This displays the Connect To Another Computer dialog box. Type the domain name or IP address of the system whose drives you want to manage, and then click OK.
2. In Computer Management, expand Services And Applications, and then select Services. In the right pane, double-click Terminal Services Session Directory. This displays a Properties dialog box.
3. In the General tab, select Automatic as the Startup Type as shown in Figure 31-7, and then click OK. In Computer Management, right-click the Terminal Services Session Directory service entry and select Start.

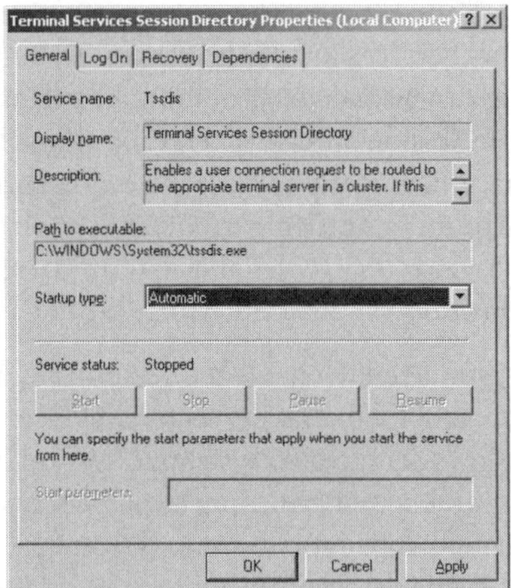

Figure 31-7. Configure the Terminal Services Session Directory service startup.

Authorize Terminal Servers to Use the Terminal Services Session Directory Service

When the Terminal Services Session Directory service is started, the service looks for a computer group named Session Directory Computers. If this group doesn't exist, the service creates it. You need to add the computer account for each server in the load-balanced farm to the Session Directory Computers group.

In an Active Directory domain, you add the computer account for each server by following these steps:

1. Start Active Directory Users And Computers by clicking Start, Programs or All Programs, Administrative Tools, Active Directory Users And Computers.
2. In Active Directory Users And Computers, expand the OU you created for Terminal Servers or the Users folder, and then double-click the Session Directory Computers group.
3. In the Session Directory Computers Properties dialog box, select the Members tab, and then click Add. This displays the Select Users, Contacts, Computers, Or Groups dialog box.
4. Click Object Types to display the Object Types dialog box as shown in Figure 31-8. In the Object Types dialog box, select Computers, and then click OK.

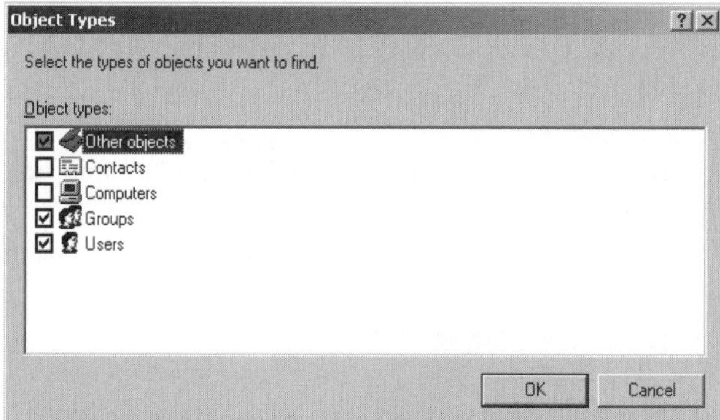

Figure 31-8. Add Computers as a permitted object type.

5. In the Select Users, Contacts, Computers, Or Groups dialog box, you can now type and validate the names of computer accounts, as shown in Figure 31-9. Type a computer account name, and then click Check Names. If multiple matches are found, select the name or names you want to use, and then click OK. If no matches are found, either you've entered an incorrect name part or you're working with an incorrect location. Modify the name and try again or click Locations to select a new location. To add additional computer accounts, type a semicolon (;), and then repeat this process.

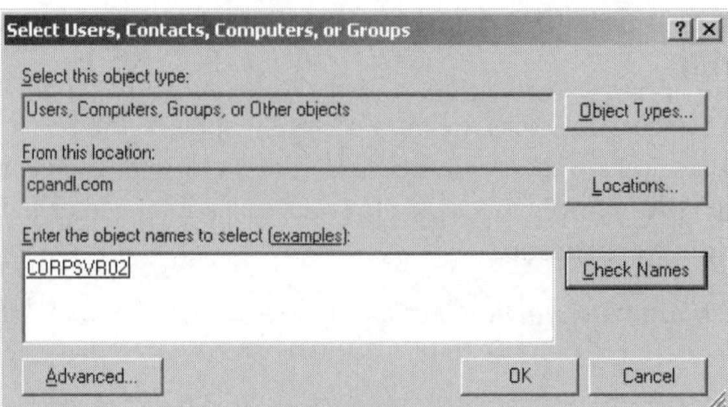

Figure 31-9. Select the computer accounts that should be members of the group.

6 When you click OK, the computer accounts are added to the list in the Session Directory Computers Properties dialog box. Click OK again to close the Properties dialog box.

In a workgroup, you add the computer account for each server by following these steps:

1 Start Computer Management by clicking Start, Programs or All Programs, Administrative Tools, Computer Management. To work with a remote system, right-click the Computer Management entry in the left pane, and then select Connect To Another Computer on the shortcut menu. This displays the Connect To Another Computer dialog box. Type the domain name or IP address of the system whose drives you want to manage, and then click OK.
2 In Computer Management, expand Services And Applications, and then select Services. In the right pane, double-click Terminal Services Session Directory. This displays a properties dialog box.
3 Click Add, and then use the Select Users dialog box to add each of the computer accounts in turn.
4 Click OK when you are finished.

Configure Each Server to Join the Session Directory

Now that you've set up the Session Directory server and authorized servers to use it, you need to tell the terminal servers in the farm about the load-balancing and session directory configuration. You do this using the Terminal Services Configuration tool to set the Join Session Directory properties. These properties tell clients about the cluster name and the Session Directory server.

On each server in the load-balanced farm, complete these steps:

1. Start the Terminal Services Configuration tool by clicking Start, Programs or All Programs, Administrative Tools, Terminal Services Configuration, or by typing **tscc.msc** at the command prompt.
2. In the Terminal Services Configuration tool, select Server Settings in the left pane, and then, in the details pane, right-click Session Directory and select Properties.
3. In the Properties dialog box, select Join Session Directory.
4. In the Cluster Name field, type the fully qualified domain name of the cluster. With Microsoft Network Load Balancing, this is the Full Internet Name of the cluster as set in the section entitled "Creating a New Network Load Balancing Cluster" on page 55.
5. In the Session Directory Server Name field, type the name or IP address of the Session Directory server.
6. Click OK.

Note Some third-party load-balancing solutions act as routers as well as load balancers. For these devices, you must clear the IP Address Redirection check box to allow the load balancer to use router token redirection. If you clear this check box, you will need to set the Network Adapter And IP Address Session Directory ... field to the IP address to which client computers should connect.

Setting Up a Terminal Services License Server

Licensing is required to use Terminal Services, which means you must do the following:

1. Install a Terminal Services license server.
2. Activate the license server.
3. Configure licenses for use.

Considerations for Installing a Terminal Services License Server

A Terminal Services license server is a server running the Terminal Server Licensing service. While you can use any server in the organization, the license server should be well connected in the domain. The Terminal Services license server will need network access to the organization's terminal servers and to the Internet for the following reasons:

- The internal network connection is required to issue and validate client licenses.
- The connection to the Internet is needed to connect to the Microsoft Clearinghouse server for activation of the license server and any licenses you've purchased.

Note The connection to the Microsoft Clearinghouse uses HTTP ports 80 and 443 for the connection. If you've set up a proxy or Network Address Translation (NAT) server and enabled Web browsing in the organization, the license server shouldn't have a problem connecting to the Internet over these ports. If, however, you do not allow Web browsing or you restrict Web browsing, you will need to activate the license server and its licenses over the telephone.

You can configure the Terminal Services license server for enterprise-wide use or for use in a specific domain or workgroup.

- If you choose enterprise-wide use, you only need one license server regardless of how many single-server or multi-server Terminal Services environments you've implemented in the organization.
- If you choose domain or workgroup use, you need one license server for each domain or workgroup that uses Terminal Services.

Think carefully about the approach, as it determines how licenses are issued and made available to Terminal Services clients. If you want all client access licenses to be available to all clients, you might want to use the enterprise-wide configuration. If you want to organize licensing by department or functional groups, you might want to use a domain or workgroup approach to restrict users' access to licenses per domain or per workgroup. When making infrastructure design decisions, keep the following in mind:

- In a single-server Terminal Services environment, the terminal server and the Terminal Services license server can be the same system.
- In a multi-server Terminal Services environment, you probably don't want one of the terminal servers to be a license server as well. If you have a separate Session Directory Server, however, you may want to make this server the Terminal Services license server as well.

Prior to activation of a license server, you have a 120-day grace period during which you can perform unlimited testing and client connections. Use this time to ensure that your Terminal Services environment is as you want it to be. Once you activate the license server, you will need to configure actual licenses for use, and those licenses will work only on the license server for which you've activated them. The activation code necessary for the license server is the product ID.

Installing a Terminal Services License Server

To install the Terminal Services Licensing service, access the Control Panel and double-click Add Or Remove Programs. In the Add Or Remove Programs dialog box, click Add/Remove Windows Components to start the Windows Components Wizard. On the Windows Components page, select Terminal Server Licensing, and then click Next.

As shown in Figure 31-10, you can specify the role of the license server as either Your Entire Enterprise or Your Domain or Workgroup. By default, the license server database is installed in the %SystemRoot%\System32\LServer folder. You can accept this setting or click Browse to specify a new location. When you are ready to continue, click Next to begin the installation, and then click Finish.

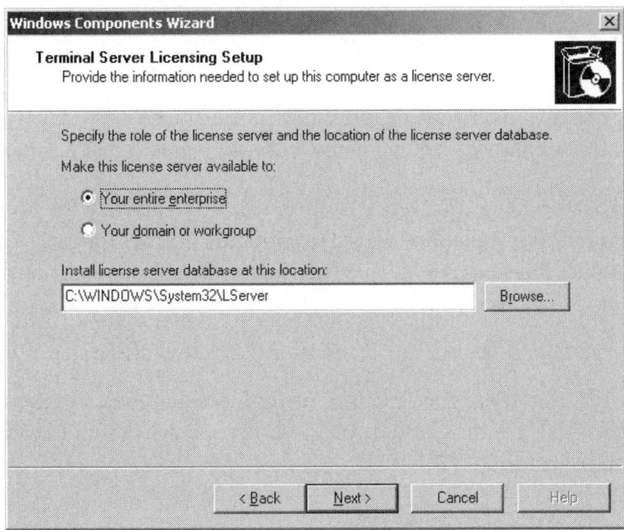

Figure 31-10. Select the role of the license server.

Tip **Consider the license database location**

Every time a client attempts to connect to a terminal server, a lookup is made to the license server database. If the client has an existing license, the terminal server to which the client is connected queries the license server about the client's license and the license server performs a lookup to validate it. If the client doesn't have an existing license, the terminal server to which the client is connected queries the availability of licenses and the license server performs a lookup to determine if licenses are available. If a license is available, it is issued to the client. For optimal performance in a large network with many hundreds or thousands of clients, you might want to consider putting the license database on a separate physical disk from that used by the operating system.

Activating the License Server and Configuring Licenses for Use

Once you install the Terminal Services Licensing service, you can activate the license server and configure licenses for use with the Terminal Server Licensing tool. To start the Terminal Server Licensing tool, click Start, Programs, or All Programs, Administrative Tools, Terminal Server Licensing, or type **licmgr.exe** at the command prompt.

When you first start the Terminal Server Licensing tool, it will search for license servers on the network, and then list the ones it has found, as shown in Figure 31-11. Here, a license server is present but not yet activated (as indicated by a red dot on its icon).

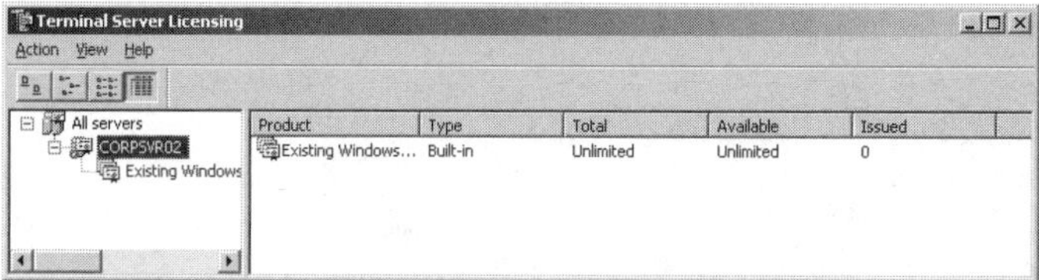

Figure 31-11. Available license servers are listed in the Terminal Server Licensing tool.

You use the Terminal Server License Server Activation Wizard to activate the license server, and the Terminal Server CAL Installation Wizard to configure licenses for use. (The acronym CAL stands for Client Access License.) When you activate a server, both wizards can be run in turn if desired.

To activate the license server and configure licenses for use, follow these steps:

1 Right-click the server entry in the Terminal Server Licensing tool, and then select Activate Server. Click Next. On the Connection Method page, select the activation method to use, as shown in Figure 31-12.

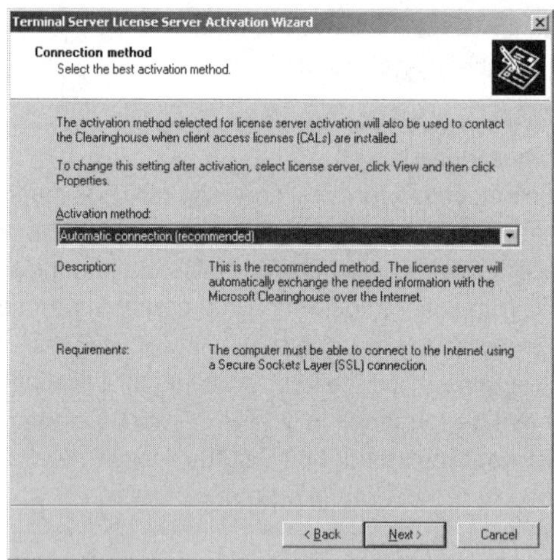

Figure 31-12. Select a connection method.

2 The default technique used for license server and license activation is an Automatic Connection to the Microsoft Clearinghouse. You can also use specify Web Browser or Telephone if you want to get an activation code manually.

- *With the Automatic Connection method*—When you click Next, the wizard attempts to connect over the Internet to the Microsoft Clearinghouse, as shown in the following screen. If you choose this method, you will need to identify yourself and your organization to obtain an authorization code, which is automatically sent to the server.

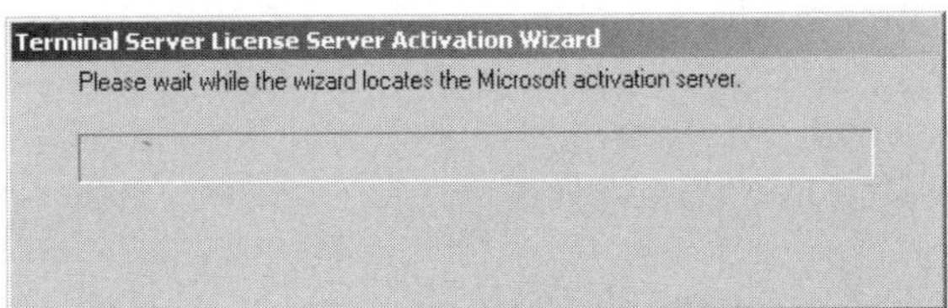

- *With the Web Browser method*—When you click Next, the wizard tells you that you need to go the Terminal Server Activation and Licensing Web site (*https://activate.microsoft.com*) and provide your product ID, as shown in the following screen. You will then get a license server ID to use.

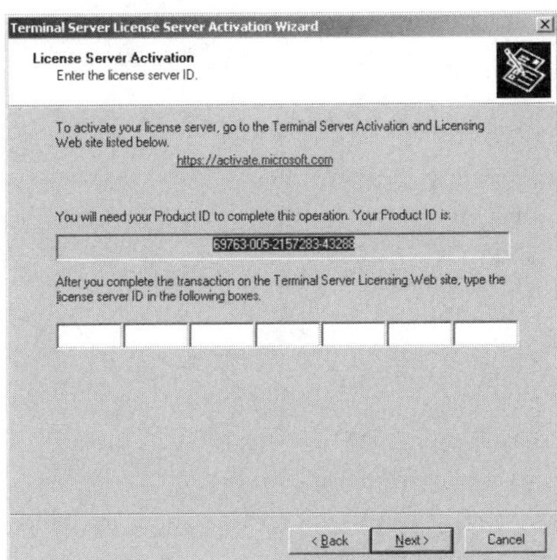

- *With the Telephone method*—When you click Next, the wizard prompts you to select your country or region. After you select your country or region and click Next, you will see a telephone number specific to your region or country to call, and you will be given your product ID to provide during the call, as shown in the following screen. You will then get a license server ID to use.

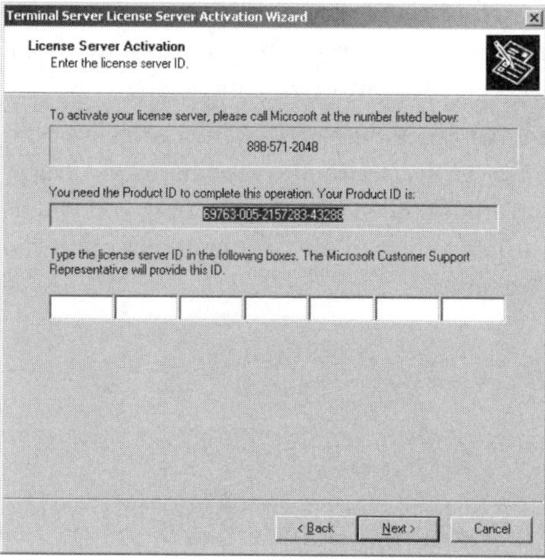

3 When you finish this process, you'll see the Completing The Terminal Server Activation Wizard page as shown in Figure 31-13. On this page, Start Terminal Server Client Licensing Wizard is automatically selected so that if you click Next from here, the wizard starts.

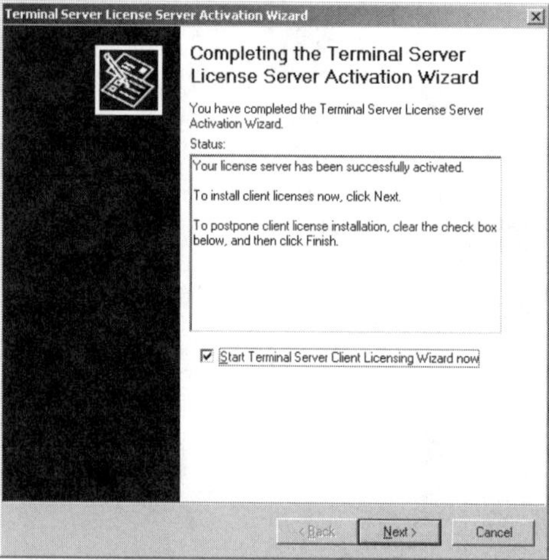

Figure 31-13. Finishing the activation and starting the client licensing wizard.

4 The Terminal Server Client Licensing Wizard uses the previously selected connection method to activate client licenses. You will need to click Next twice and then enter a license code from your retail product packaging, Select Enterprise Agreement or Open license contract. As before, the way this works depends on the connection method.

To install licenses separately or at a later date, right-click the server entry in the Terminal Server Licensing tool, and then select Install Licenses. This starts the Terminal Server Client Licensing Wizard, which you can use to configure licenses for use.

The Terminal Server License Server Activation Wizard and the Terminal Server CAL Installation Wizard store information about the connection method and your contact information. If you want to use a different connection method or change contact information, you need to edit the default properties for the license server. To do this, right-click the server entry in the Terminal Server Licensing tool and select Properties. You can then make changes as necessary using the Licensing Wizard Properties dialog box shown in Figure 31-14.

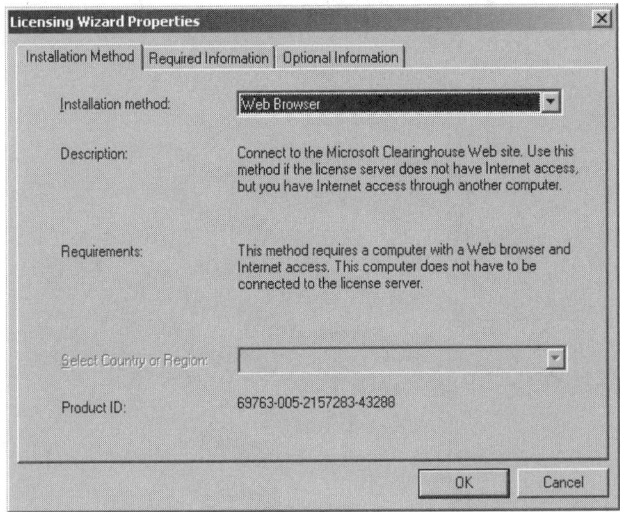

Figure 31-14. Change wizard defaults using the Licensing Wizard Properties dialog box.

Using the Terminal Services Configuration Tool

The Terminal Services Configuration tool is found in the Administrative Tools program group on the Start menu. Click Start, Programs or All Programs, Administrative Tools, and Terminal Service Configuration, or else type **tssc.msc** at a command prompt. As shown in Figure 31-15, you can configure connections and server settings using the Terminal Services Configuration tool. Each terminal server must be configured separately.

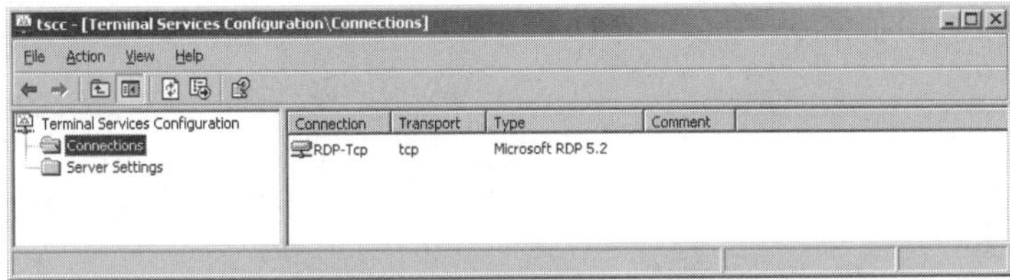

Figure 31-15. Editing settings with the Terminal Services Configuration tool.

Configuring Global Connection Settings

With Terminal Services and Remote Desktop for Administration, data transmission between the server and the client uses Remote Desktop Protocol (RDP), which is encapsulated and encrypted within TCP. RDP version 5.2 is the default version of the protocol used with Windows Server 2003. In the Terminal Services Configuration tool, you can configure the settings for RDP. RDP settings are used to set global defaults and to override the local and default settings used by clients.

To modify the RDP settings for the server you are currently working with, in the Details pane right-click on RDP-Tcp, and then select Properties. This displays the RDP-Tcp Properties dialog box as shown in Figure 31-16. If any of these settings are unavailable, they have probably been configured using Group Policy.

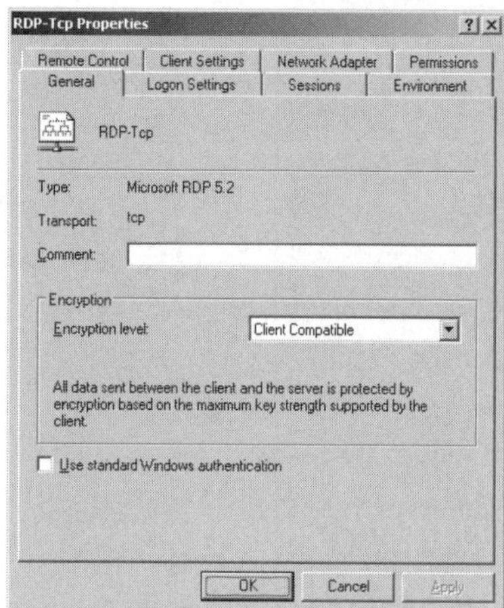

Figure 31-16. Configuring RDP-Tcp Properties and settings.

The RDP-Tcp Properties dialog box has the following tabs:

- **General** Sets the encryption level for the server. Use Client Compatible if you are using a mixed environment that may include computers running Windows 2000. You can also require High (128-bit) or FIPS-compliant encryption.
- **Logon Settings** Configures specific logons to use. In most cases, however, you'll want to use the default setting Use Client-Provided Logon Information. If you want clients always to be prompted for a password regardless of their client settings, choose Always Prompt For Password.

- **Sessions** Configures session reconnection and timeout. Any settings used here override the user settings. You can configure whether and when Terminal Services ends disconnected sessions, limits active sessions, or limits idle sessions.
- **Environment** Sets an initial program to run. This setting overrides client settings for Remote Desktop clients.
- **Remote Control** Determines whether remote control of user sessions is enabled, and sets remote control options. Remote control can allow an administrator to view a user's Terminal Services sessions, interact with a user's Terminal Services sessions, or both. These remote control options set the global defaults used by all users.
- **Client Settings** Determines how the client screen resolution and redirection features are managed. By default, the connection settings from the Remote Desktop clients are used, and clients are limited to a maximum color depth of 16-bits. Additionally, audio mapping is disabled by default.
- **Network Adapter** Determines the network adapters on the server to which Terminals Services connections can be made. The All Network Adapters option is selected by default.
- **Permissions** Lets you view or modify security permissions for the server. Rather than configuring permissions per server, it is much easier to add users to the Remote Desktop Users group in Active Directory Users And Computers if they should have access to Terminal Services. It should be noted that this group has limited permissions. By default, members of the Remote Desktop Users group have User Access and Guest Access permission. This means users can log on to a session on the server, query information about a session, connect to other user sessions, and connect to another session.

Configuring Server Settings

As shown in Figure 31-17, the Server Settings folder contains options for all connections on a terminal server.

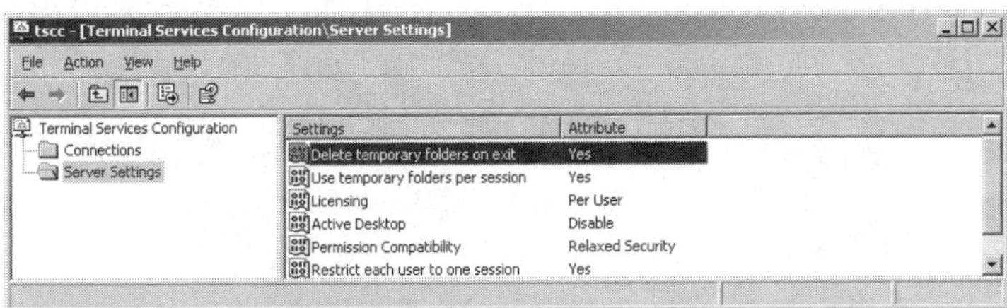

Figure 31-17. Configure general server settings for all connections.

The settings available depend on the Terminal Services configuration and include the following:

- **Delete Temporary Folders On Exit** Determines whether temporary folders created by clients are deleted automatically when a user logs off. By default, this setting is enabled, so temporary folders are deleted when a user logs off the terminal server. To change this setting, right-click it and select Yes or No as appropriate.
- **Use Temporary Folders Per Session** Determines whether temporary folders are used on a per-session basis. By default, this setting is enabled, so each session has its own set of temporary folders. To change this setting, right-click it and select Yes or No as appropriate.
- **Licensing** Determines whether the licensing mode for clients is set Per Device or Per User. To change this setting, right-click it, select Properties, and then select Per Device or Per User as appropriate. Click OK.
- **Active Desktop** Determines whether users are permitted to use Active Desktop. By default, this setting is enabled, so users are able to use Active Desktop. To reduce the amount of overhead for processing and network bandwidth, you might want to disable this option. To change this setting, right-click it and select Enable or Disable as appropriate.
- **Permission Compatibility** Determines the default permissions for compatibility with applications. Full Security restricts user access to areas of the Registry and to system files, and is designed to safeguard the terminal server so that remote users running a virtual session cannot arbitrarily modify system files or the Registry. Relaxed Security doesn't restrict user access to the Registry or system files, and is designed for maximum compatibility with applications, particularly those designed for Windows 2000 or earlier versions of Windows. To change this setting, right-click it, select Properties, and then select Full Security or Relaxed Security as appropriate. Click OK.
- **Restrict Each User To One Session** Determines whether users are limited to a single session on the terminal server. By default, this is enabled to conserve resources on the terminal server. To change this setting, right-click it and select Yes or No as appropriate.
- **Join Session Directory** Determines whether the server uses a Session Directory, and sets the Session Directory properties. To change this setting, right-click it, select Properties, and then configure it as discussed in the section entitled "Configure Each Server to Join the Session Directory" earlier in this chapter. Click OK.

> **Note** Note that the word "join" is part of this setting name only if the Terminal Services Session Directory service is running. If it's not running, then this option is simply named Session Directory and has the value Disabled.

Configuring Terminal Services Security

Terminal Services permissions set the maximum allowed permissions for a Terminal Services connection. These permissions are applied whenever a client connects to a terminal server. The basic permissions for Terminal Services are the following:

- **Full Control** Users have full control over their own sessions as well as the sessions of other users. In addition to setting user access permissions, they can set information, take control of or view other user sessions, disconnect sessions, or establish virtual channels.
- **User Access** Users have limited control over their own sessions. This means users can log on to a session on the server, query information about a session, or connect to another session.
- **Guest Access** Users can log on to a terminal server. They do not have other permissions.

If users have a basic permission, they also have special permissions built into the basic permission, as shown in Table 31-2. Note that the Logon permission implicitly gives users the right to log off their own session and the Connect permission implicitly gives users the right to disconnect their own session.

Table 31-2. Special Permissions for Terminal Services

Special Permission	Description	Included In
Query Information	Allows a user to gather information about users connected to the terminal server, processes running on the server, etc.	Full Control, User Access
Set Information	Allows a user to configure connection properties.	Full Control
Remote Control	Allows a user to view or remotely control another user's session.	Full Control
Logon	Allows a user to log on to a session on the server.	Full Control, User Access, Guest Access
Logoff	Allows a user to log off another user from a session. This is different from being able to log off your own session.	Full Control
Message	Allows a user to send a message to another user's session.	Full Control

Table 31-2. Special Permissions for Terminal Services

Special Permission	Description	Included In
Connect	Allows a user to connect to another session.	Full Control
Disconnect	Allows a user to disconnect another user from a session.	Full Control
Virtual Channels	Allows a user to use virtual channels.	Full Control

With Windows Server 2003, you must use the Remote Desktop Users group to control access to Terminal Services. In addition, to have default security permission, this group is given default user rights, which allow members of the group to log on to a terminal server.

To view or manage the permissions of a terminal server, start the Terminal Services Configuration tool on the server. In the left pane select Connections, and then, in the details pane, right-click the connection you want to work with and select Properties. In the Properties dialog box, select the Permissions tab, shown in Figure 31-18. You can now view the users and groups that have Terminal Services permissions and their permissions.

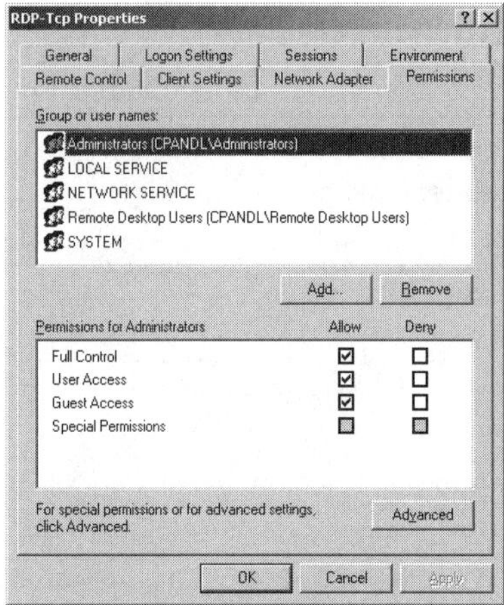

Figure 31-18. View or set Terminal Services permissions.

You can grant or deny Terminal Services permissions. In the Terminal Services Configuration tool, select Connections, and then, in the details pane, right-click the connection you want to work with and select Properties. In the Properties dialog box, select the Permissions tab.

In the Permissions tab, configure access permissions for each user and group added by selecting an account name, and then allowing or denying access permissions. To grant a user or group access permissions, select the permission in the Allow column. To deny a user or group access permissions, select the permission in the Deny column.

You can set special permissions for Terminal Services using the Terminal Services Configuration tool as well. Right-click the connection you want to work with and select Properties. In the Properties dialog box, select the Permissions tab, and then click Advanced. This displays the dialog box shown in Figure 31-19.

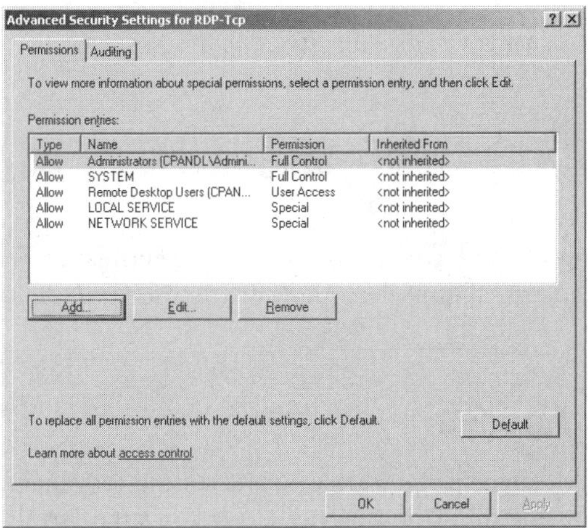

Figure 31-19. The Advanced Security Settings dialog box shows the special permissions assigned to each user or group.

You now have the following options:

- **Add** Adds a user or group. Click Add to display the Select User, Computer, Or Group dialog box. Type the name of a user or group and click Check Names. If multiple names match the value you entered, you'll see a list of names and will be able to choose the one you want to use. Otherwise, the name will be filled in for you. When you click OK, the Permission Entry For dialog box shown in Figure 31-20 appears.
- **Edit** Edits an existing user or group entry. Select the user or group whose permissions you want to modify, and then click Edit. The Permission Entry For dialog box appears.
- **Remove** Removes an existing user or group entry. Select the user or group whose permissions you want to remove, and then click Remove.

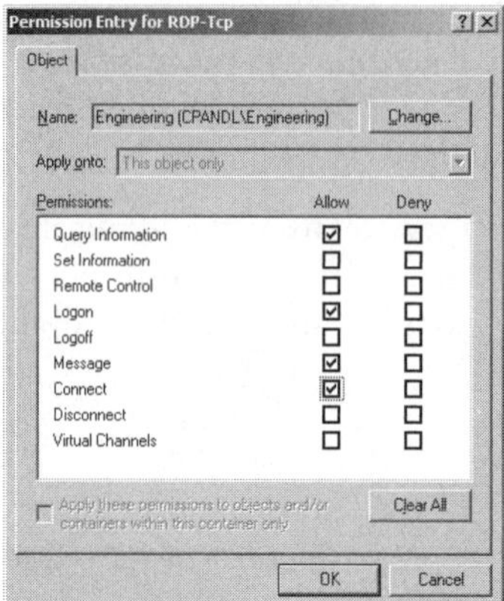

Figure 31-20. Use the Permission Entry For dialog box to set special permissions.

If you are adding or editing entries for users or groups, you use the Permission Entry For dialog box to grant or deny special permissions. Select Allow or Deny for each permission as appropriate.

Auditing Terminal Services Access

Auditing Terminal Services access can help you track who is accessing Terminal Services and what they are doing. You configure auditing policies per server. Click the Terminal Services Configuration tool, select Connections, and then, in the details pane, right-click the connection you want to work with and select Properties. In the Properties dialog box, select the Permissions tab, and then click Advanced. In the Advanced Security Settings dialog box, select the Auditing tab, shown in Figure 31-21.

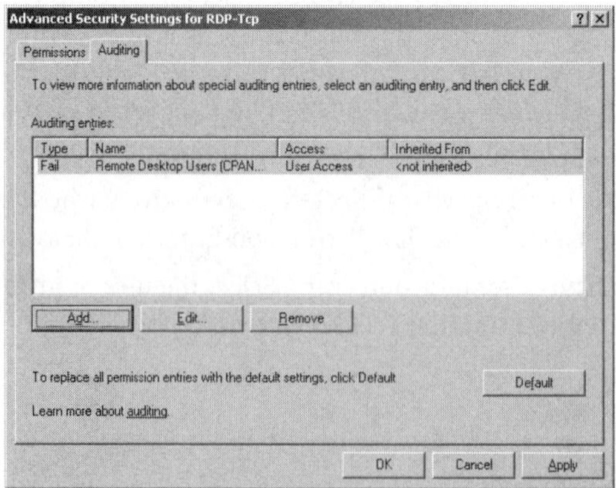

Figure 31-21. Specify to which users and groups auditing should apply.

Use the Auditing Entries list to select the users, groups, or computers whose actions you want to audit. To add specific accounts, click Add, and then use the Select User, Computer, Or Group dialog box to select an account name to add. If you want to audit actions for all Terminal Services users, use the Remote Desktop Users group. Otherwise, select the specific user groups or users, or both, that you want to audit. When you click OK, you'll see the Auditing Entry For ... dialog box, shown in Figure 31-22.

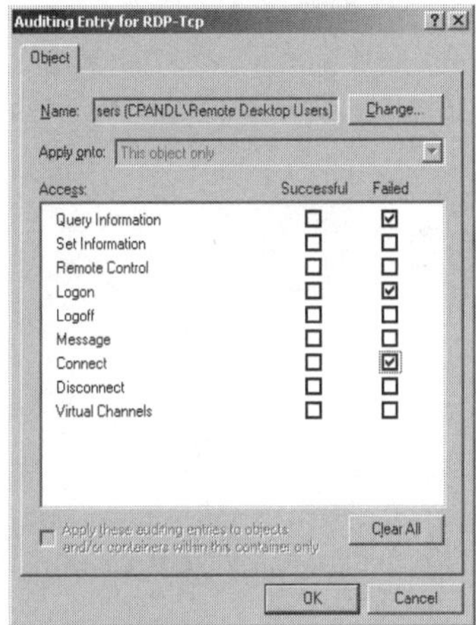

Figure 31-22. Specify the actions to audit for the designated user, group, or computer.

After you make a selection, under Access, select the Successful or Failed check boxes, or both, for each event you want to audit. The events you can audit are the same as those for which you control Terminal Services permissions, as discussed previously. Choose OK when you're finished. Repeat this process to audit other users, groups, or computers. Any time permissions that you've configured for auditing are used, the action is written to the system's security log, where it's stored for your review. The security log is accessible from Event Viewer.

Using the Terminal Services Manager

You can use the Terminal Services Manager, shown in Figure 31-23, to inspect data about terminal servers in trusted domains. You can examine users, connections, sessions, or processes as well as execute certain administrative commands against the remote terminal servers. Start Terminal Services Manager from the Administrative Tools menu or by typing **tsadmin.exe** at the command prompt.

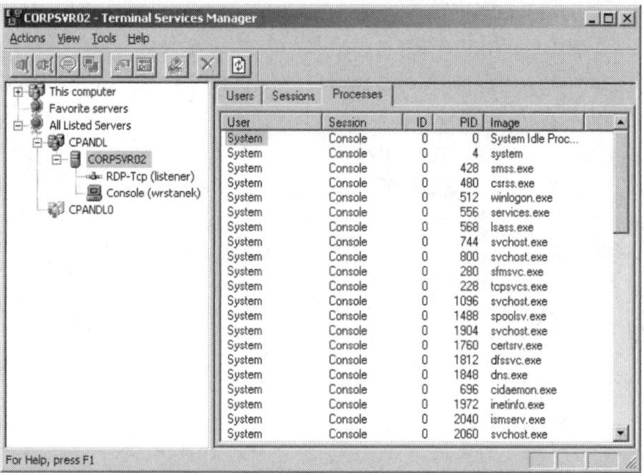

Figure 31-23. Terminal Services Manager.

Connecting to Terminal Servers

Unlike previous versions of Terminal Services Manager, the current version does not automatically enumerate all the terminal servers that are available. By right-clicking All Listed Servers, you can perform the following actions:

- **Connect To Computer** Connect to a terminal server by name or IP address.
- **Refresh Servers In All Domains** Refresh the list of current servers in all the domains you are working with.

> **Caution** Using Refresh Servers In All Domains starts a series of network broadcast messages to all domains in the Active Directory forest. Broadcasting in this way can cause significant network traffic and slow server response. If you want to limit the broadcasts to a particular domain, right-click the domain and select Refresh Servers In The Domain.

- **Disconnect From All Servers** Disconnect from all terminal servers in all domains.

Once a server is listed, you can right-click its entry to perform one of these actions:

- **Connect** Connects to the server so you can view the current users, sessions, and processes
- **Disconnect** Disconnects from the server
- **Add To Favorites** Adds the server to the Favorite Servers list so it's connected automatically when you start Terminal Services Manager
- **Remove From Favorites** Removes the server from the Favorite Servers list

Getting Terminal Services Information

In the Terminal Services Manager window, terminal servers are organized by domain. Once you expand a domain entry, you can click on a terminal server in the left pane, and the detail pane on the right will display information about the related users, sessions, and processes.

- When you select the Users tab in the right pane, you can view and manage user sessions. Each user with a current session is shown regardless of whether the session is active or inactive. See the following section entitled "Managing User Sessions in Terminal Services Manager" for more information.
- When you select the Sessions tab in the right pane, you can view and manage user and listener sessions. If users are permitted multiple sessions, this lets you see the individual sessions separately from the users who started them.
- When you select the Processes tab in the right pane, you can view and manage all running process on the server. If you right-click a process, you can select End Process to stop the process.

Below the server entry in the left pane, you'll have an entry for each active session as well as for the RDP-Tcp listener session. The listener session waits and accepts new Remote Desktop Protocol (RDP) connections. If you right-click the listener entry and select Reset, you can reset all the sessions using RDP-Tcp.

Managing User Sessions in Terminal Services Manager

Whenever you select a user entry or session in Terminal Services Manager, you can right-click the related entry to perform one of the following actions:

- **Connect** Allows you to connect to a user's session if you have the appropriate permissions. After you choose Connect, you are prompted to enter the user's password if the user running the session is different from your current user account. Note that the Connect option is available only if Terminal Services Manager is running on a remote machine and not locally on the terminal server.
- **Disconnect** Disconnects an active session. When a session is disconnected, all the processes in that session continue to run in a disconnected state. This means that no information is transmitted to the remote client. To disconnect multiple sessions, simply select all the sessions you want to disconnect, and then choose Disconnect from the Actions menu.
- **Log Off** Logs the user off and ends any processes the user is currently running. You can use this option to free resources being used by a session. However, this can result in the loss of data if the user hasn't saved work. This option is available only when you select the server entry in the left pane and the Users tab in the right pane.
- **Send Message** Sends the user a console message. The message is displayed in a pop-up dialog box.

- **Remote Control** Allows you to view or interact with a user's session. When you select Remote Control, you are prompted to set the hot key that can be used to log off the remote control session. The default hot key is Ctrl+asterisk (*). By default, when you take remote control of a session, the user is notified and prompted to give permission. You won't be able to continue until the user clicks Yes to accept the request. If you don't want users to be prompted, you can change this behavior using the Remote Control tab in the RDP-Tcp Properties dialog box. Note that the Remote Control option is available only if Terminal Services Manager is running on a remote machine and not locally on the terminal server.

  It is important to note that remote control can be enabled or disabled globally through the Terminal Services Configuration tool and per user in each user's Properties dialog box.
- **Reset** Resets a user session that is frozen or unresponsive. When you reset a session, you terminate the session and free up all resources being used by the session. Unlike logging a user off, this action does not use the normal logoff processes. This means that not only could users lose data, but any changes they've made to their profiles or settings could also be lost. Only use Reset when a session cannot be logged off.
- **Send Message** Sends a console message to the user. To send the same console message to several users, simply select all the users to whom you want to send a message, and then choose Send Message from the Actions menu.

Managing Terminal Services from the Command Line

In addition to the tools in Terminal Services Manager, there are quite a few command-line tools for working with Terminal Services. These commands can be divided into two categories:

- Gathering information
- Controlling user sessions

Gathering Terminal Services Information

Several commands are available for gathering Terminal Services information from the command line including the following:

- QUERY PROCESS [* | *ProcessId* | *UserName* | *SessionName* | /ID:*SessionId* | *ProgramName*] [/Server:*ServerName*]—Displays information about processes being run in Terminal Services sessions on the server
- QUERY SESSION [*SessionName* | *UserName* | *SessionId*] [/Server:*ServerName*]—Displays information about Terminal Services sessions
- QUERY TERMSERVER [*ServerName*] [/Domain:*domain*] [/Address]—Displays the available application terminal servers on the network. The /Address parameter adds network and node addresses to the output.
- QUERY USER [*UserName* | *SessionName* | *SessionId*] [/Server:*ServerName*]—Display information about users logged on to the system

These commands accept many common parameters, including the following:

- *ProcessId*—The ID of the process on the terminal server that you want to examine
- *ServerName*—The name of the remote terminal server you want to work with
- *SessionId*—The ID of the session on the terminal server that you want to examine
- *SessionName*—The name of the session on the terminal server that you want to examine
- *UserName*—The name of the user whose sessions or processes you want to examine

These commands are very helpful when you are looking for Terminal Services information and you do not have to use parameters to obtain information. If you type **query process** at the command line, you get a list of all processes being run in Terminal Services sessions on the local terminal server, for example:

```
USERNAME        SESSIONNAME      ID      PID      IMAGE
>wrstanek       console          0       3204     explorer.exe
>wrstanek       console          0       3372     mshta.exe
>wrstanek       console          0       3656     licmgr.exe
```

If you type **query session** at the command line, you get a list of all sessions on the local terminal server, for example:

```
SESSIONNAME       USERNAME         ID      STATE    TYPE     DEVICE
>console          wrstanek         0       Active   wdcon
 rdp-tcp                           65536   Listen   rdpwd
```

If you type **query user** at the command prompt, you get a list of all users who have sessions on the local server, for example:

```
USERNAME          SESSIONNAME      ID      STATE    IDLE TIME     LOGON TIME
>wrstanek         console          0       Active           .     9/16/2004 10:31 AM
tomc              rdp-tcp#4        1       Active           1     9/16/2004 5:05 PM
```

If you type **query termserver** at the command prompt, you get a list of all known terminal servers in the enterprise:

```
Known Terminal servers
----------------------
TSSVR02
TSSVR03
TSSVR04
```

> **Tip** **QUERY is a server command in Windows Server 2003**
> The QUERY command is available in Windows Server 2003 but not from a desktop computer. If you are using Windows XP Professional as your desktop system, however, you can resolve this dilemma by copying the Query.exe command from a server to your desktop. Type **where query.exe** at the command line on the server to locate the command, and then copy the command to your desktop.

Managing User Sessions from the Command Line

When you want to manage user sessions from the command line, you can use these commands:

- SHADOW [*SessionName* | *SessionId*] [/Server:*ServerName*] [/v]—Allows you to take remote control of a user's session
- TSCON [*SessionName* | *SessionId*] [/Password:*password*] [/v]—Allows you to connect to a user's session if you know that user's password
- TSDISCON [*SessionName* | *SessionId*] [/Server:*ServerName*] [/v]—Allows you to disconnect a user's session
- RESET SESSION [*SessionName* | *SessionId*] [/Server:*ServerName*] [/v]—Allows you to reset a user's session
- LOGOFF [*SessionName* | *SessionId*] [/Server:*ServerName*] [/v]—Allows you to log off a user's session

As you can see, all these commands accept similar parameters. These parameters include the following:

- *SessionName*—The name of the session on the terminal server that you want to work with
- *SessionId*—The ID of the session on the terminal server that you want to work with
- *ServerName*—The name of the remote terminal server you want to work with

These commands also allow you to set verbose output using the /V parameter.

Using these commands is fairly straightforward. For example, if you want to disconnect a user session with the session ID 2 on the remote server TS06, you'd type the command **tsdiscon 2 /server:ts06**.

If you are logged on locally to the Terminal Server, it's even easier, as all you have to type is **tsdiscon 2**.

Other Useful Terminal Services Commands

There are a few other useful commands for working with Terminal Services, including the following:

- MSG [*UserName* | *SessionName* | *SessionId* | *] [/Server:*ServerName*] [*Message*]—Use MSG to send a console message to users by user name, session name, and session ID. Use the asterisk wildcard (*) to send the same message to all sessions on a designated server.
- TSKILL *ProcessId* | *ProcessName* [/Server:*ServerName*] [/ID:*SessionId* | /a] [/v]—Use TSKILL to end a process using the process ID or process name. A process can be shut down for a particular session ID using /ID:*SessionID* or for all sessions running the process by using the option /a.
- TSSHUTDN [*SecondsToWait*] [/Server:*ServerName*] [/Reboot] [/Powerdown] [/Delay:*LogoffDelay*] [/v]—Use TSSHUTDN to remotely shut down a terminal server. By default, TSSHUTDN logs off all connected user sessions, waits 30 seconds, and then shuts down. You can set a different delay using the /Delay option. The /Powerdown option allows a server to prepare for powering off; only use this if you aren't rebooting. /Reboot sets the server to restart after shutting down.

Configuring Terminal Services Per-User Settings

When you install Terminal Services, the properties pages of users are updated to include two additional tabs: Remote Control and Terminal Services Profile. The settings on these tabs can be used to configure per user settings for Terminal Services.

Getting Remote Control of a User's Session

Being able to get remote control of a user's session is helpful for troubleshooting. Rather than guess what a user is trying to do when working with an application, you can view the user's session and see the mistakes yourself. If allowed, you can also take over a user's session and manipulate the session from your desktop while still allowing the user to view the session from the desktop. By watching the task being performed correctly, the user should be better able to perform the task independently next time.

By default, remote control is enabled and administrators are allowed to interact with user sessions. However, this occurs only if the user gives permission for an administrator to do so. Although global remote control settings for all users are set with the Terminal Services Configuration tool, you can change the settings for individual users as necessary. To do this, follow these steps:

1. Click Start, Programs or All Programs, Administrative Tools, and Active Directory Users And Computers. In Active Directory Users and Computers, expand the organizational unit or container in which the user's account was created, and then double-click the account to display its Properties dialog box.

2 As shown in Figure 31-24, select the Remote Control tab. If you want to configure the account so that it cannot be controlled remotely, clear Enable Remote Control. Otherwise, select Enable Remote Control and configure the way in which remote control works as follows:

- If you want to ensure that permission is required to view or interact with a user's account, select Require User's Permission.
- If you want to be able to remotely control a user's account without explicit permission, clear Require User's Permission.

3 Afterward, set the level of control allowed as follows:

- If you want only to be able to view the account, select View The User's Session.
- If you want to be able to view and take control of the account, select Interact With The Session.

4 Click OK.

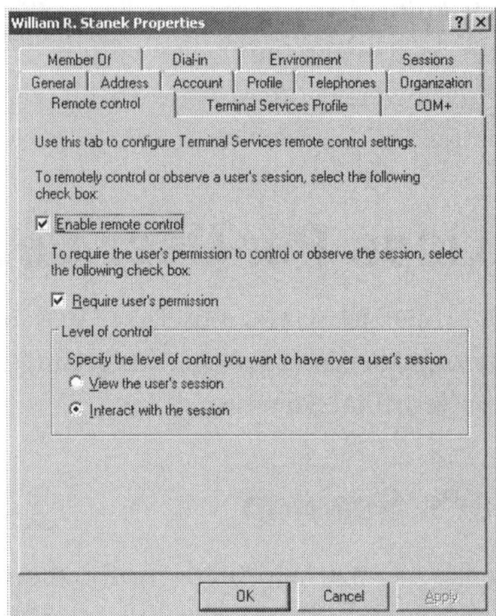

Figure 31-24. Enable and configure remote control of an individual user's account.

Setting Up the Terminal Services Profile for Users

All user accounts have a separate Terminal Services profile and home directory, which is used when the users log on to a terminal server. To configure these optional settings, follow these steps:

1 Click Start, Programs or All Programs, Administrative Tools, and Active Directory Users And Computers. In Active Directory Users and Computers, expand the organizational unit or container in which the user's account was created, and then double-click the account to display its Properties dialog box.

2 As shown in Figure 31-25, select the Terminal Services Profile tab. Using this tab, you can set the following fields:

- *Profile Path*—The path to the user's Terminal Services profile. Terminal Services profiles provide the environment settings for users when they connect to a terminal server. Each time a user logs on to a terminal server, that user's profile determines desktop and control panel settings, the availability of menu options and applications, and so on. Typically, you set the profile path to a network share and use the %UserName% environment variable to set a user-specific profile path.
- *Terminal Services Home Folder*—The directory in which the user should store files when connected to Terminal Services. Assign a specific directory for the user's files as a local path on the user's system or a connected network drive. If the directory is available to the network, the user can access the directory regardless of which computer is used to connect to Terminal Services.

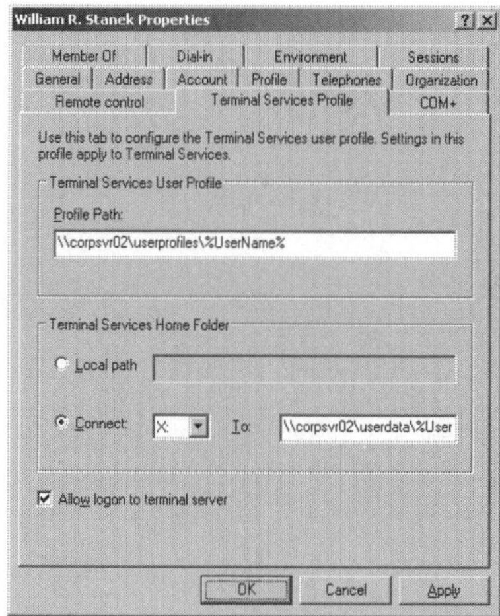

Figure 31-25. Configure the Terminal Services Profile for a user as necessary to help customize an individual environment.

3 The Allow Logon To Terminal Server option controls whether a user can log on to a terminal server. If this option is cleared, a user who tries to connect to Terminal Services will get an error message stating that the logon privilege has been disabled.

4 Click OK.

Part 7

Managing Active Directory and Security

Chapter 32

Active Directory Architecture

Active Directory is an extensible directory service that enables you to manage network resources efficiently. A directory service does this by storing detailed information about each network resource, which makes it easier to provide basic lookup and authentication. Being able to store large amounts of information is a key objective of a directory service, but the information must be also organized so that it is easily searched and retrieved.

Active Directory provides for authenticated search and retrieval of information by dividing the physical and logical structure of the directory into separate layers. Understanding the physical structure of Active Directory is important for understanding how a directory service works. Understanding the logical structure of Active Directory is important for implementing and managing a directory service.

Active Directory Physical Architecture

Active Directory's physical layer controls the following features:

- How directory information is accessed
- How directory information is stored on the hard disk of a server

Active Directory Physical Architecture: A Top-Level View

From a physical or machine perspective, Active Directory is part of the security subsystem (see Figure 32-1). The security subsystem runs in user mode. User-mode applications do not have direct access to the operating system or hardware. This means that requests from user-mode applications have to pass through the executive services layer and must be validated before being executed.

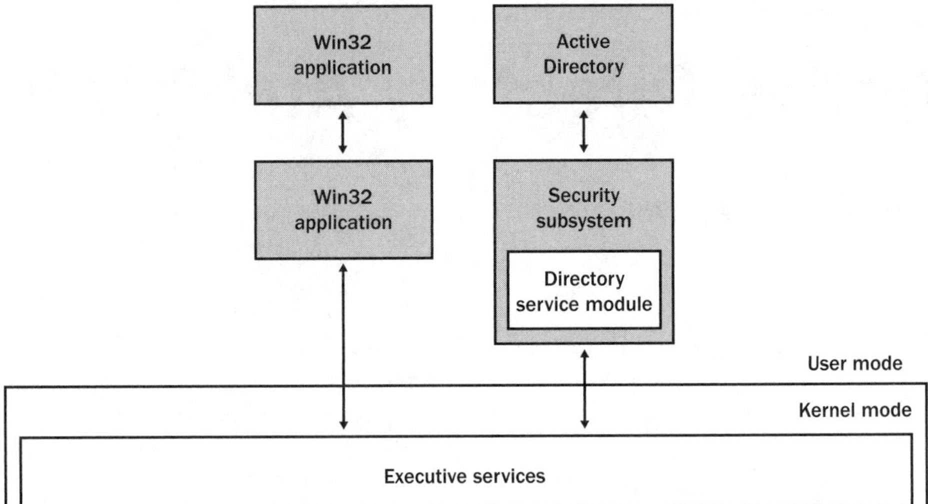

Figure 32-1. Top-level overview of Active Directory architecture.

> **Note** Being part of the security subsystem makes Active Directory an integrated part of the access control and authentication mechanism built into Microsoft Windows Server 2003. Access control and authentication protect the resources in the directory.

Each resource in Active Directory is represented as an object. Anyone who tries to gain access to an object must be granted permission. Lists of permissions that describe who or what can access an object are referred to as Access Control Lists (ACL). Each object in the directory has an associated ACL.

You can restrict permissions across a broader scope by using policy. The security infrastructure of Active Directory uses policy to enforce security models on several objects that are grouped logically. Trust relationships between groups of objects can also be set up to allow for an even broader scope for security controls between trusted groups of objects that need to interact. From a top-level perspective, that's how Active Directory works, but to really understand Active Directory, you need to delve into the security subsystem.

Active Directory Within the Local Security Authority

Within the security subsystem, Active Directory is a subcomponent of the Local Security Authority (LSA). As shown in Figure 32-2, the LSA consists of many components which provide the security features of Windows Server 2003 and ensure that access control and authentication function as they should. Not only does the LSA manage local security policy, it also performs the following functions:

- Generates security identifiers
- Provides the interactive process for logon
- Manages auditing

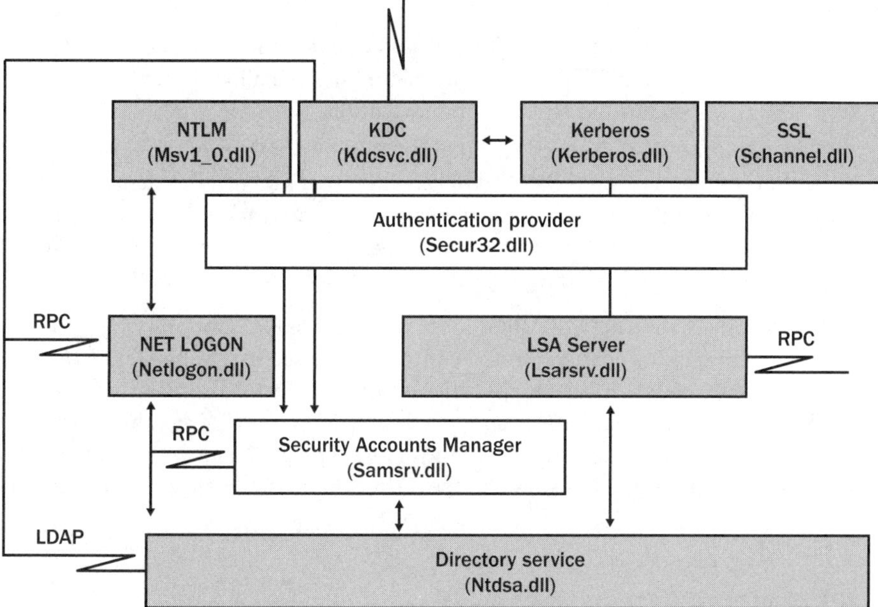

Figure 32-2. Windows Server 2003 security subsystem using Active Directory.

When you work through the security subsystem as it is used with Active Directory, you'll find the three following key areas:

- Authentication mechanisms
  - NTLM (Msv1_0.dll) used for Windows NT LAN Manager (NTLM) authentication
  - Kerberos (Kerberos.dll) and Key Distribution Center (Kdcsvc.dll) used for Kerberos V5 authentication
  - SSL (Schannel.dll) used for Secure Sockets Layer (SSL) authentication
  - Authentication provider (Secur32.dll) used to manage authentication
- Logon/access control mechanisms
  - NET LOGON (Netlogon.dll) used for interactive logon via NTLM. For NTLM authentication, NET LOGON passes logon credentials to the directory service module and returns the security identifiers for objects to clients making requests.

  - LSA Server (Lsasrv.dll) used to enforce security policies for Kerberos and SSL. For Kerberos and SSL authentication, LSA Server passes logon credentials to the directory service module and returns the security identifiers for objects to clients making requests.
  - Security Accounts Manager (Samsrv.dll) used to enforce security policies for NTLM.
- Directory service component
  - Directory service (Ntdsa.dll) used to provide directory services for Windows Server 2003. This is the actual module that allows you to perform authenticated searches and retrieval of information.

As you can see, users are authenticated before they can work with the directory service component. Authentication is handled by passing a user's security credentials to a domain controller. Once authenticated on the network, users can work with resources and perform actions according to the permissions and rights they have been granted in the directory. At least, this is how the Windows Server 2003 security subsystem works with Active Directory.

When you are on a network that doesn't use Active Directory or when you log on locally to a machine other than a domain controller, the security subsystem works as shown in Figure 32-3. Here, the directory service is not used. Instead, authentication and access control are handled through the Security Accounts Manager (SAM). This is, in fact, the model used for authentication and access control in Microsoft Windows NT 4. In this model, information about resources is stored in the SAM, which itself is stored in the Registry.

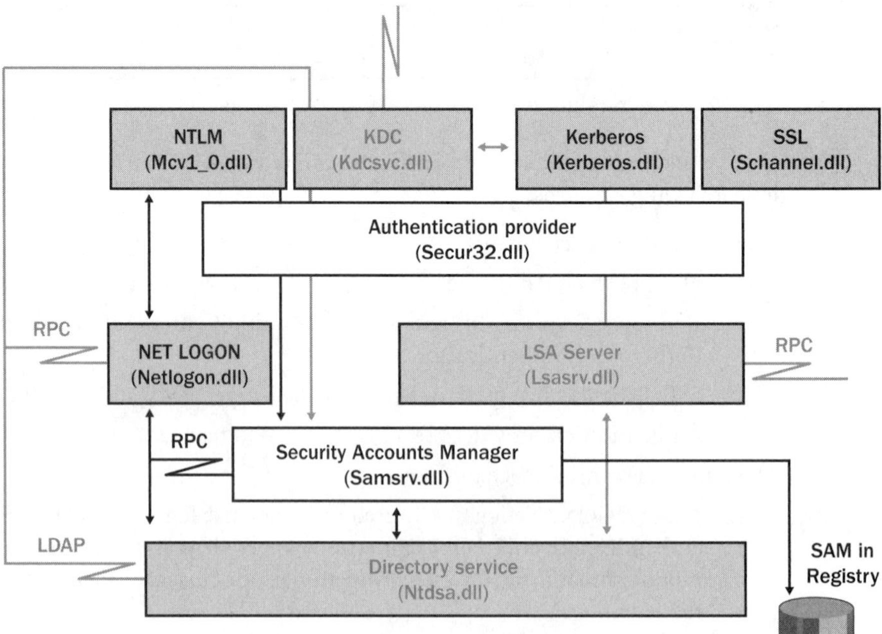

Figure 32-3. Windows Server 2003 security subsystem without Active Directory.

Directory Service Architecture

As you've seen, incoming requests are passed through the security subsystem to the directory service component. The directory service component is designed to accept requests from many different kinds of clients. As shown in Figure 32-4, these clients use specific protocols to interact with Active Directory.

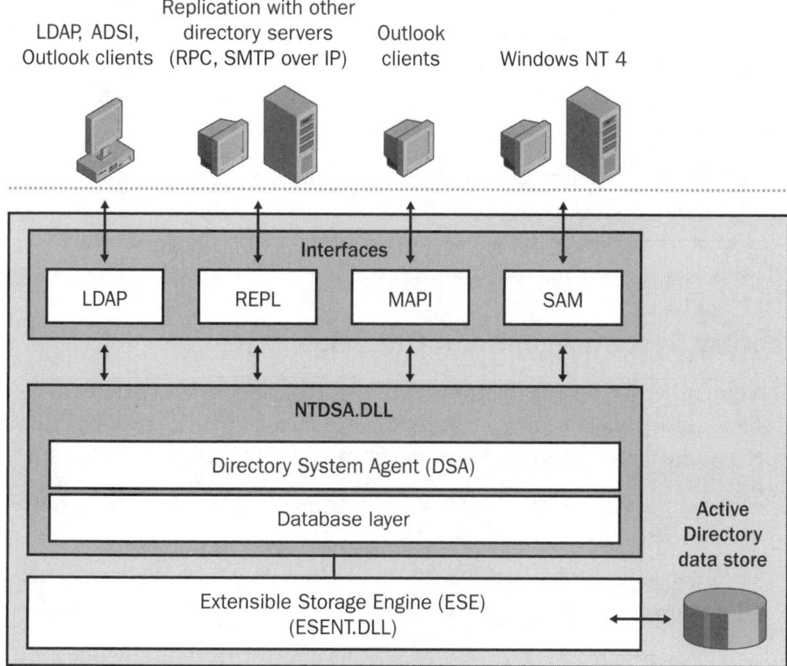

Figure 32-4. The directory service architecture.

Protocols and Client Interfaces

The primary protocol for Active Directory access is Lightweight Directory Access Protocol (LDAP). LDAP is an industry-standard protocol for directory access that runs over TCP/IP. Active Directory supports LDAP versions 2 and 3. Clients can use LDAP to query and manage directory information, depending on the level of permissions they have been granted, by establishing a TCP connection to a computer, called a *domain controller,* running the directory service. The default TCP port used by LDAP clients is 389 for standard communications and 636 for SSL.

Active Directory supports intersite and intrasite replication through the REPL interface, which uses either Remote Procedure Calls (RPCs) or Simple Mail Transport Protocol over Internet Protocol (SMTP over IP), depending on how replication is configured. Each domain controller is responsible for replicating changes to the directory to other domain controllers, using a multimaster approach. Unlike Windows NT 4, which used a single primary domain controller and one backup domain controller, the multimaster approach used in Active Directory allows updates to be made to the directory, via any domain controller and then replicated to other domain controllers.

For older messaging clients, Active Directory supports the Messaging Application Programming Interface (MAPI). MAPI allows messaging clients to access Active Directory (which is used by Microsoft Exchange for storing information), primarily for address book lookups. Messaging clients use Remote Procedure Calls (RPCs) to establish connection with the directory service. UDP port 135 and TCP port 135 are used by the RPC Endpoint Mapper. Current messaging clients use LDAP instead of RPC.

For clients running Windows NT 4, Active Directory supports the Security Accounts Manager (SAM) interface, which also uses RPCs. This allows Windows NT 4 clients to access the Active Directory data store the same way they would access the SAM database. The SAM interface is also used during replication with Windows NT 4 backup domain controllers.

Directory System Agent and Database Layer

Clients and other servers use the LDAP, REPL, MAPI, and SAM interfaces to communicate with the directory service component (Ntdsa.dll) on a domain controller. From an abstract perspective, the directory service component consists of the following:

- Directory System Agent (DSA), which provides the interfaces through which clients and other servers connect
- Database Layer, which provides an Application Programming Interface (API) for working with the Active Directory data store

From a physical perspective, the DSA is really the directory service component, and the database layer resides within it. The reason for separating the two is that the database layer performs a vital abstraction. Without this abstraction, the physical database on the disk would not be protected from the applications the DSA interacts with. Furthermore, the object-based hierarchy used by Active Directory would not be possible. Why? Because the data store is in a single data file using a flat (record-based) structure, while the database layer is used to represent the flat file records as objects within a hierarchy of containers. Like a folder that can contain files as well as other folders, a container is simply a type of object that can contain other objects as well as other containers.

Each object in the data store has a name relative to the container in which it is stored. This name is aptly called the object's relative distinguished name (RDN). An object's full name, also referred to as an object's distinguished name (DN), describes the series of containers, from the highest to the lowest, of which the object is a part.

To make sure every object stored in Active Directory is truly unique, each object also has a globally unique identifier (GUID), which is generated when the object is created. Unlike an object's RDN or DN, which can be changed by renaming an object or moving it to another container, the GUID can never be changed. It is assigned to an object by the DSA and it never changes.

The DSA is responsible for ensuring that the type of information associated with an object adheres to a specific set of rules. This set of rules is referred to as the *schema*. The schema is stored in the directory and contains the definitions of all object classes and describes their attributes. In Active Directory, the schema is the set of rules that determine the kind of data that can be stored in the database, the type of information that can be associated with a particular object, the naming conventions for objects, and so on.

Inside Out

The schema saves space and helps validate attributes

The schema serves to separate an object's definition from its actual values. Thanks to the schema, Active Directory doesn't have to write information about all of an object's possible attributes when it creates the object. When you create an object, only the defined attributes are stored in the object's record. This saves a lot of space in the database. Furthermore, as the schema not only specifies the valid attributes but also the valid values for those attributes, Active Directory uses the schema both to validate the attributes that have been set on an object and to keep track of what other possible attributes are available.

The DSA is also responsible for enforcing security limitations. It does this by reading the security identifiers (SIDs) on a client's access token and comparing it with that of the SID for an object. If a client has appropriate access permissions, it is granted access to an object. If a client doesn't have appropriate access permissions, it is denied access.

Finally, the DSA is used to initiate replication. Replication is the essential functionality that ensures that the information stored on domain controllers is accurate and consistent with changes that have been made. Without proper replication, the data on servers would become stale and outdated.

Extensible Storage Engine

The Extensible Storage Engine (ESE) is used by Active Directory to retrieve information from and write information to the data store. The ESE uses indexed and sequential storage with transactional processing, as follows:

- **Indexed storage** Indexing the data store allows the ESE to access data quickly without having to search the entire database. In this way, the ESE can rapidly retrieve, write, and update data.

- **Sequential storage** Sequentially storing data means that the ESE writes data as a stream of bits and bytes. This allows data to be read from and written to specific locations.
- **Transactional processing** Transactional processing ensures that changes to the database are applied as discrete operations that can be rolled back if necessary.

Any data that is modified in a transaction is copied to a temporary database file. This gives two views of the data that is being changed: one view for the process changing the data and one view of the original data that is available to other processes until the transaction is finalized. A transaction remains open as long as changes are being processed. If an error occurs during processing, the transaction can be rolled back to return the object being modified to its original state. If Active Directory finishes processing changes without errors occurring, the transaction can be committed.

As with most databases that use transactional processing, Active Directory maintains a transaction log. A record of the transaction is written first to an in-memory copy of an object, then to the transaction log, and finally to the database. The in-memory copy of an object is stored in the version store. The version store is an area of physical memory (RAM) used for processing changes. If a domain controller has 400 megabytes (MB) of RAM or more, the version store is 100 MB. If a domain controller has less than 400 MB of RAM, the version store is 25 percent of the physical RAM.

The transaction log serves as a record of all changes that have yet to be committed to the database file. The transaction is written first to the transaction log to ensure that even if the database shuts down immediately afterward, the change is not lost and can take effect. To ensure this, Active Directory uses a checkpoint file to track the point up to which transactions in the log file have been committed to the database file. Once a transaction is committed to the database file, it can be cleared out of the transaction log.

The actual update of the database is written from the in-memory copy of the object in the version store and not from the transaction log. This reduces the number of disk I/O operations and helps ensure that updates can keep pace with changes. When many updates are made, however, the version store can reach a point where it is overwhelmed. This happens when the version store reaches 90 percent of its maximum size. When this happens, the ESE temporarily stops processing cleanup operations that are used to return space after an object is modified or deleted from the database.

Because changes need to be replicated from one domain controller to another, an object that is deleted from the database isn't fully removed. Instead, most of the object's attributes are removed and the object's isDeleted attribute is set to TRUE to indicate that it has been deleted. The object is then moved to a hidden Deleted Objects container where its deletion can be replicated to other domain controllers. In this state, the object is said to be *tombstoned*. To allow the tombstoned state to be replicated to all domain controllers, and thus removed from all copies of the database, an attribute called tombstoneLifetime is also set on the object. The tombstoneLifetime attribute specifies how long the tombstoned object should remain in the Deleted Objects container. The default lifetime is 60 days.

The ESE uses a garbage-collection process to clear out tombstoned objects after the tombstone lifetime has expired and performs automatic online defragmentation of the database after garbage collection. The interval at which garbage collection occurs is a factor of the value set for the garbageCollPeriod attribute and the tombstone lifetime. By default, garbage collection occurs every 12 hours. When there are more than 5,000 tombstoned objects to be garbage-collected, the ESE removes the first 5,000 tombstoned objects, and then uses the CPU availability to determine if garbage collection can continue. If no other process is waiting for the CPU, garbage collection continues for up to the next 5,000 tombstoned objects whose tombstone lifetime has expired and the CPU availability is again checked to determine if garbage collection can continue. This process continues until all the tombstoned objects whose tombstone lifetime has expired are deleted or another process needs access to the CPU.

Data Store Architecture

Once you have examined the operating system components that support Active Directory, the next step is to see how directory data is stored on a domain controller's hard disks. As Figure 32-5 shows, the data store has a primary data file and several other types of related files, including working files and transaction logs.

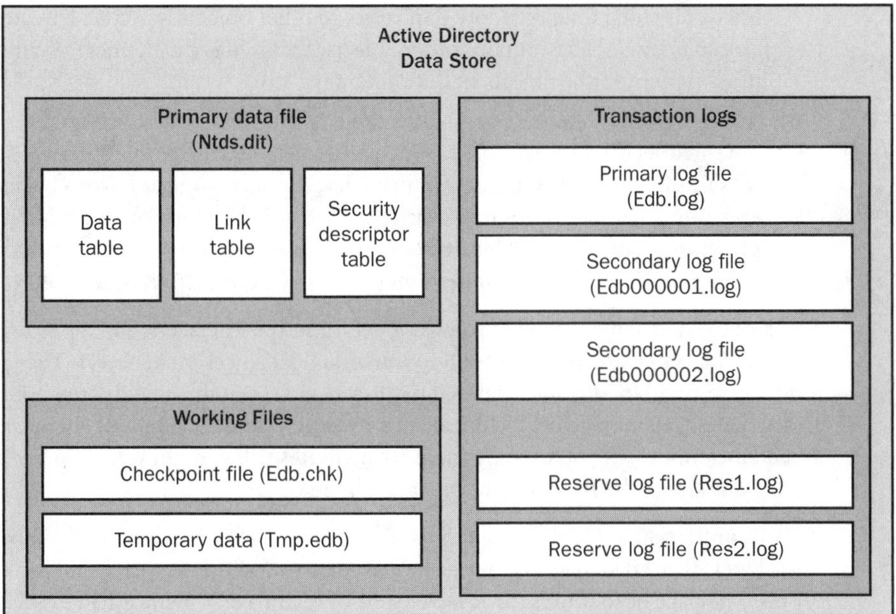

Figure 32-5. The Active Directory data store.

These files are used as follows:

- **Primary data file (Ntds.dit)** Physical database file that holds the contents of the Active Directory data store
- **Checkpoint file (Edb.chk)** Checkpoint file that tracks the point up to which the transactions in the log file have been committed to the database file
- **Temporary data (Tmp.edb)** Temporary workspace for processing transactions
- **Primary log file (Edb.log)** Primary log file that contains a record of all changes that have yet to be committed to the database file
- **Secondary log files (Edb00001.log, Edb00002.log, …)** Additional logs files that are used as needed
- **Reserve log files (Res1.log, Res2.log, …)** Files that are used to reserve space for additional log files if the primary log file becomes full

The primary data file contains three indexed tables:

- **Active Directory data table** The data table contains a record for each object in the data store, which can include object containers, the objects themselves, and any other type of data that is stored in Active Directory.
- **Active Directory link table** The link table is used to represent linked attributes. A linked attribute is an attribute that refers to other objects in Active Directory. For example, if an object contains other objects (that is, it is a container), attribute links are used to point to the objects in the container.

- **Active Directory security descriptor table** The security descriptor table contains the inherited security descriptors for each object in the data store. Windows Server 2003 uses this table so that inherited security descriptors no longer have to be duplicated on each object. Instead, inherited security descriptors are stored in this table and linked to the appropriate objects. This makes Active Directory authentication and control mechanisms much more efficient than they were in Microsoft Windows 2000.

Think of the data table as having rows and columns; the intersection of a row and a column is a field. The table's rows correspond to individual instances of an object. The table's columns correspond to attributes defined in the schema. The table's fields are populated only if an attribute contains a value. Fields can be a fixed or a variable length. If you create an object and define only 10 attributes, only these 10 attributes will contain values. While some of those values might be fixed length, other might be variable length.

Records in the data table are stored in data pages that have a fixed size of 8 kilobytes (KB, or 8,192 bytes). Each data page has a page header, data rows, and free space that can contain row offsets. The page header uses the first 96 bytes of each page, leaving 8,096 bytes for data and row offsets. Row offsets indicate the logical order of rows on a page, which means that offset 0 refers to the first row in the index, offset 1 refers to the second row, and so on. If a row contains long, variable-length data, the data may not be stored with the rest of the data for that row. Instead, Active Directory can store an 8-byte pointer to the actual data, which is stored in a collection of 8-KB pages that aren't necessarily written contiguously. In this way, an object and all its attribute values can be much larger than 8 KB.

The primary log file has a fixed size of 10 MB. When this log fills up, Active Directory creates additional (secondary) log files as necessary. The secondary log files are also limited to a fixed size of 10 MB. Active Directory uses the reserve log files to reserve space on disk for log files that may need to be created. As several reserve files are already created, this speeds up the transactional logging process when additional logs are needed.

By default, the primary data file, working files, and transaction logs are all stored in the same location. On a domain controller's system volume, you'll find these files in the %SystemRoot%\NTDS folder. While these are the only files used for the data store, there are other files used by Active Directory. For example, policy files and other files, such as startup and shutdown scripts used by the DSA, are stored in the %SystemRoot%\SYSVOL folder.

> **Note** A distribution copy of Ntds.dit is also placed in the %SystemRoot%\System32 folder. This is used to create a domain controller when you install Active Directory on a server running Windows Server 2003. If the file doesn't exist, the Active Directory Installation Wizard will need the installation CD to promote a member server to be a domain controller.

Active Directory Logical Architecture

Active Directory's logical layer determines how you see the information contained in the data store and also controls access to that information. The logical layer does this by defining the namespaces and naming schemes used to access resources stored in the directory. This provides a consistent way to access directory-stored information regardless of type. For example, you can obtain information about a printer resource stored in the directory in much the same way that you can obtain information about a user resource.

To better understand Active Directory's logical architecture, you need to understand the following topics:

- Active Directory objects
- Active Directory domains, trees, and forests
- Active Directory trusts
- Active Directory namespaces and partitions
- Active Directory data distribution

Active Directory Objects

Because so many different types of resources can be stored in the directory, a standard storage mechanism was needed and Microsoft developers decided to use the LDAP model for organizing data. In this model, each resource that you want to represent in the directory is created as an object with attributes that define information you want to store about the resource. For example, the user object in Active Directory has attributes for a user's first name, middle initial, last name, and logon name.

An object that holds other objects is referred to as a *container object* or simply a *container*. The data store itself is a container that contains other containers and objects. An object that doesn't contain other objects is a *leaf object*. Each object created within the directory is of a particular type or class. The object classes are defined in schema and include the following types:

- User
- Group
- Computer
- Printer

When you create an object in the directory, you must comply with the schema rules for that object class. Not only do the schema rules dictate the available attributes for an object class, they also dictate which attributes are mandatory and which attributes are optional. When you create an object, mandatory attributes must be defined. For example, you can't create a user object without specifying the user's full name and logon name. The reason is that these attributes are mandatory.

Some rules for attributes are defined in policy as well. For example, the default security policy for Windows Server 2003 specifies that a user account must have a password and the password must meet certain complexity requirements. If you try to create a user account without a password or with a password that doesn't meet these complexity requirements, the account creation will fail because of the security policy.

The schema can be extended or changed as well. This allows administrators to define new object classes, to add attributes to existing objects, and to change the way attributes are used. However, you need special access permissions and privileges to work directly with the schema.

Active Directory Domains, Trees, and Forests

Within the directory, objects are organized using a hierarchical tree structure called a *directory tree*. The structure of the hierarchy is derived from the schema and is used to define the parent-child relationships of objects stored in the directory.

Active Directory Architecture

A logical grouping of objects that allows central management of those objects is called a *domain*. In the directory tree, a domain is itself represented as an object. It is in fact the parent object of all the objects it contains. Unlike Windows NT 4, which limited the number of objects you could store in a domain, an Active Directory domain can contain millions of objects. Because of this, you probably do not need to create separate user and resource domains as was done commonly with Windows NT 4.0. instead, you can create a single domain that contains all the resources you want to manage centrally. In Figure 32-6, a domain object is represented by a large triangle and the objects it contains are as shown.

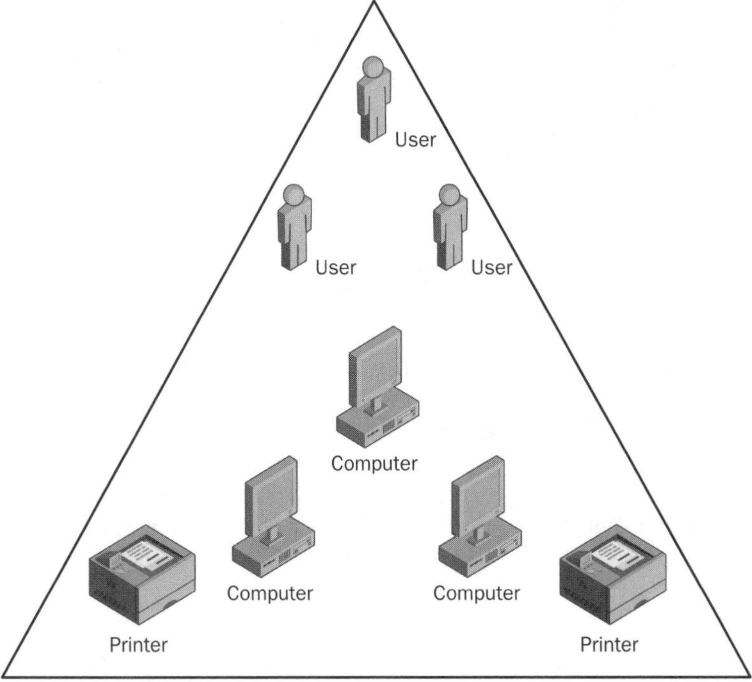

Figure 32-6. An Active Directory domain.

Domains are only one of several building blocks for implementing Active Directory structures. Other building blocks include the following:

- Active Directory trees, which are logical groupings of domains
- Active Directory forests, which are logical groupings of domain trees

As described above, a directory tree is used to represent a hierarchy of objects, showing the parent-child relationships between those objects. Thus, when we're talking about a domain tree, we're looking at the relationship between parent and child domains. The domain at the top of the domain tree is referred to as the *root domain (think of this as an upside-down tree)*. More specifically, the root domain is the first domain created in a new tree within Active Directory. When talking about forests and domains, there is an important distinction made between the first domain created in a new forest—a forest root domain—and the first domain created in each additional tree within a forest—a root domain.

In the example shown in Figure 32-7, cohovineyard.com is the root domain in an Active Directory forest with a single tree, that is, it is the forest root domain. As such, cohovineyard.com is the parent of the sales.cohovineyard.com domain and the mf.cohovineyard.com domain. The mf.cohovineyard.com domain itself has a related subdomain: bottling.mf.cohovineyard.com. This makes mf.cohovineyard.com the parent of the child domain bottling.mf.cohovineyard.com.

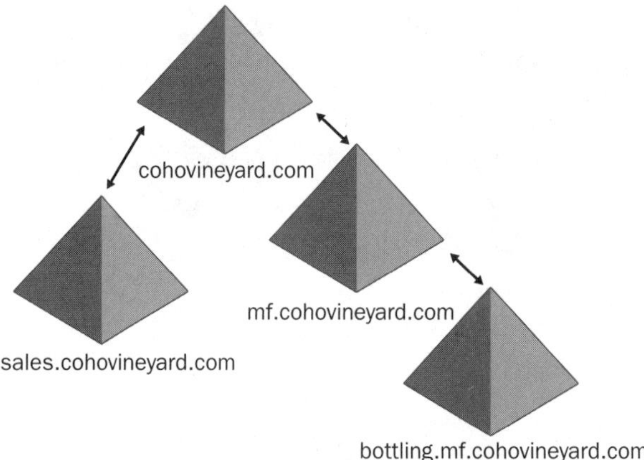

Figure 32-7. An Active Directory forest with a single tree.

The most important thing to note about this and all domain trees is that the namespace is contiguous. Here, all the domains are part of the cohovineyard.com namespace. If a domain is a part of a different namespace, it can be added as part of a new tree in the forest. In the example shown in Figure 32-8, a second tree is added to the forest. The root domain of the second tree is cohowinery.com, and this domain has cs.cohowinery.com as a child domain.

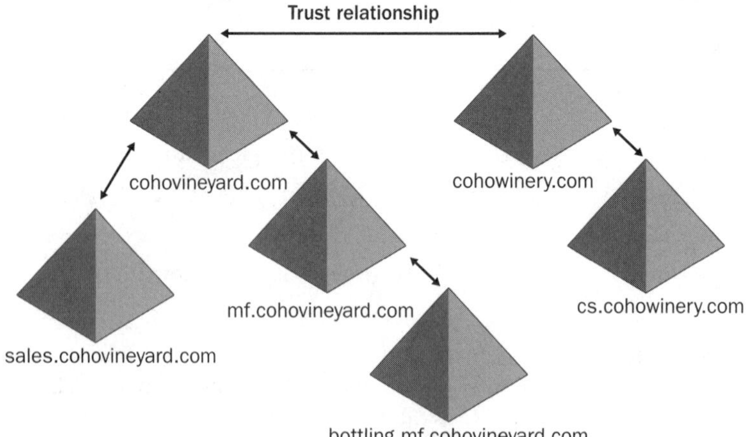

Figure 32-8. An Active Directory forest with multiple trees.

You create a forest root domain by installing Active Directory on a stand-alone server and establishing the server as the first domain controller in a new forest. To add an additional tree to an existing forest, you install Active Directory on a stand-alone server and configure the server as a member of the forest, but with a domain name that is not part of the current namespace being used. You make the new domain part of the same forest to allow associations called trusts to be made between domains that belong to different namespaces.

Active Directory Trusts

In Active Directory, two-way transitive trusts are established automatically between domains that are members of the same forest. Trusts join parent and child domains in the same domain tree and join the roots of domain trees. Because trusts are transitive, this means that if domain A trusts domain B and domain B trusts domain C, domain A trusts domain C as well. As all trusts in Active Directory are two-way and transitive, by default every domain in a forest implicitly trusts every other domain. It also means that resources in any domain are available to users in every domain in the forest. For example, with the trust relationships in place, a user in the sales.cohovineyard.com domain could access a printer or other resources in the cohovineyard.com domain or even the cs.cohowinery.com domain.

However, the creation of a trust doesn't imply any specific permission. Instead, it implies only the ability to grant permissions. No privileges are automatically implied or inherited by the establishment of a trust relationship. The trust doesn't grant or deny any permission. It only exists to allow administrators to be able to grant permissions.

There are several key terms used to describe trusts, including the following:

- **Trusting domain** A domain that establishes a trust is referred to as a trusting domain. Trusting domains allow access by users from another domain (the trusted domain).
- **Trusted domain** A domain that trusts another domain is referred to as a trusted domain. Users in trusted domains have access to another domain (the trusting domain).

To make it easier for administrators to grant access throughout a forest, Active Directory allows you to designate two types of administrators:

- **Enterprise administrators** Enterprise administrators, which are the designated administrators of the enterprise. Enterprise administrators can manage and grant access to resources in any domain in the Active Directory forest.
- **Domain administrators** Domain administrators, which are the designated administrators of a particular domain. Domain administrators in a trusting domain can access user accounts in a trusted domain and set permissions that grant access to resources in the trusting domain.

Going back to the example, an enterprise administrator in this forest could grant access to resources in any domain in the forest. If Jim, in the sales.cohovineyard.com domain, needed access to a printer in the cs.cohowinery.com domain, an enterprise administrator could grant this access. As cs.cohowinery.com is the trusting domain and sales.cohovineyard.com is the trusted domain in this example, a domain administrator in the cs.cohowinery.com could grant permission to use the printer as well. A domain administrator for sales.cohovineyard.com could not, however, as the printer resource exists in a domain other than the one the administrator controls.

To continue working with Figure 32-8, take a look at the arrows that designate the trust relationships. For a user in the sales.cohovineyard.com domain to access a printer in the cs.cohowinery.com domain, the request must pass through the following series of trust relationships:

1. The trust between sales.cohovineyard.com and cohovineyard.com
2. The trust between cohovineyard.com and cohowinery.com
3. The trust between cohowinery.com and cs.cohowinery.com

The *trust path* defines the path that an authentication request must take between the two domains. Here, a domain controller in the user's local domain (sales.cohovineyard.com) would pass the request to a domain controller in the cohovineyard.com domain. This domain controller would in turn pass the request to a domain controller in the cohowinery.com domain. Finally, the request would be passed to a domain controller in the cs.cohowinery.com domain, which would ultimately grant or deny access.

In all, the user's request has to pass through four domain controllers—one for each domain between the user and the resource. Because the domain structure is separate from your network's physical structure, the printer could actually be located right beside the user's desk and the user would still have to go through this process. If you expand this scenario to include all the users in the sales.cohovineyard.com domain, you could potentially have many hundreds of users whose requests have to go through a similar process to access resources in the cs.cohowinery.com domain.

Omitting the fact that the domain design in this scenario is very poor—because if many users are working with resources, those resources are ideally in their own domain or a domain closer in the tree—one solution for this problem would be to establish a shortcut trust between the user's domain and the resource's domain. With a shortcut trust, you could specify that cs.cohowinery.com explicitly trusts sales.cohovineyard.com. Now when a user in the sales.cohovineyard.com requests a resource in the cs.cohowinery.com domain, the local domain administrator knows about the cs.cohowinery.com and can directly submit the request for authentication. This means that the sales.cohovineyard.com domain controller sends the request directly to a cs.cohowinery.com domain controller.

Shortcut trusts are meant to help make more efficient use of resources on a busy network. On a network with a lot of activity, the explicit trust can reduce the overhead on servers and on the network as a whole. Shortcut trusts shouldn't be implemented without careful planning. They should only be used when resources in one domain will be accessed by users in another domain on a regular basis. They don't need to be used between two domains that have a parent-child relationship, because a default trust already exists explicitly between a parent and a child domain.

With Active Directory, you can also make use of external trusts that work the same they did in Windows NT 4. External trusts are manually configured and are always nontransitive. One of the primary reasons for establishing an external trust is to create a trust between an Active Directory domain and a legacy Windows NT domain. In this way, existing Windows NT domains continue to be available to users while you are implementing Active Directory. For example, you could upgrade your company's main domain from Windows NT 4 to Windows Server 2003, and then create external trusts between any other Windows NT domains. These external trusts should be created as two-way trusts to ensure that users can access resources as their permissions allow.

Active Directory Namespaces and Partitions

Any data stored in the Active Directory database is represented logically as an object. Every object in the directory has a relative distinguished name (RDN). That is, every object has a name relative to the parent container in which it is stored. The relative name is the name of the object itself and is also referred to as an object's *common name*. This relative name is stored as an attribute of the object and must be unique for the container in which it is located. Following this, no two objects in a container can have the same common name, but two objects in different containers could have the same name.

In addition to an RDN, objects also have a distinguished name (DN). An object's DN describes the object's place in the directory tree and is logically the series of containers from the highest to the lowest of which the object is a part. It is called a distinguished name because it serves to distinguish like-named objects and as such must be unique in the directory. No two objects in the directory will have the same distinguished name.

Every object in the directory has a parent, except the root of the directory tree, which is referred to as the rootDSE. The rootDSE represents the top of the logical namespace for a directory. It has no name *per se*. Although there is only one rootDSE, the information stored in the rootDSE specifically relates to the domain controller on which the directory is stored. In a domain with multiple domain controllers, the rootDSE will have a slightly different representation on each domain controller. The representation relates to the capability and configuration of the domain controller in question. In this way, Active Directory clients can determine the capabilities and configuration of a particular domain controller.

Below the rootDSE, every directory tree has a root domain. The root domain is the first domain created in an Active Directory forest and is also referred to as the forest root domain. Once it is established, the forest root domain never changes, even if you add new trees to the forest. The LDAP distinguished name of the forest root domain is: DC=*ForestRootDomainName* where DC is an LDAP identifier for a domain component and *ForestRootDomainName* is the actual name of the forest root domain. Each level within the domain tree is broken out as a separate domain component. For example, if the forest root domain is cohovineyard.com, the domain's distinguished name is DC=cohovineyard,DC=com.

When Active Directory is installed on the first domain controller in a new forest, three containers are created below the rootDSE:

- Forest Root Domain container, which is the container for the objects in the forest root domain
- Configuration container, which is the container for the default configuration and all policy information
- Schema container, which is the container for all objects, classes, attributes, and syntaxes

From a logical perspective, these containers are organized as shown in Figure 32-9. The LDAP identifier for an object's common name is CN. The DN for the Configuration container is CN=configuration, DC=*ForestRootDomainName* and the DN for the Schema container is CN=schema,CN=configuration,DC=*ForestRootDomainName*. In the cohovineyard.com domain, the DNs for the Configuration and Schema containers are CN=configuration,DC=cohovineyard,DC=com and CN=schema,CN=configuration,DC=cohovineyard,DC=com, respectively. As you can see, the distinguished name allows you to walk the directory tree from the relative name of the object you are working with to the forest root.

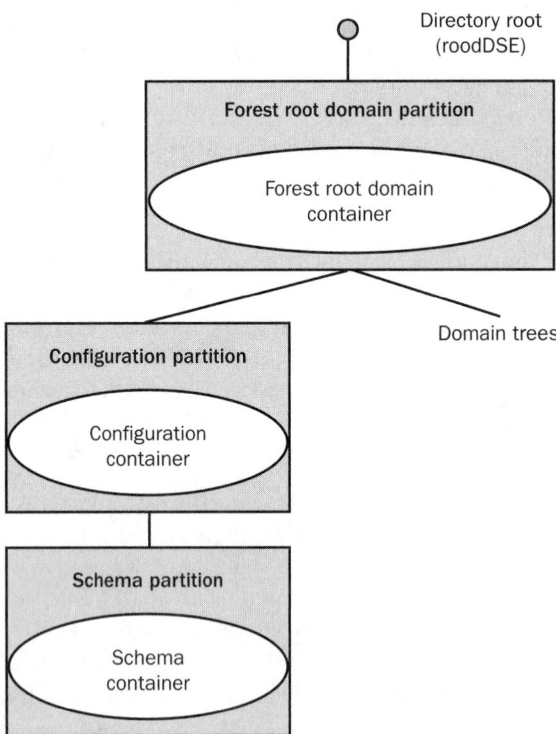

Figure 32-9. The directory tree in a new forest.

As shown in the figure, the forest root domain and the Configuration and Schema containers exist within their own individual partitions. Active Directory uses partitions to logically apportion the directory so that each domain controller does not have to store a complete copy of the entire directory. To do this, object names are used to group objects into logical categories so that the objects can be managed and replicated as appropriate. The largest logical category is a directory partition. All directory partitions are created as instances of the domainDNS object class.

As far as Active Directory is concerned, a domain is a container of objects that is logically partitioned from other container objects. When you create a new domain in Active Directory, you create a new container object in the directory tree, and that container is in turn contained by a domain directory partition for the purposes of management and replication.

Active Directory Data Distribution

Active Directory uses partitions to help distribute three general types of data:

- Domain-wide data, which is data replicated to every domain controller in a domain
- Forest-wide data, which is data replicated to every domain controller in a forest
- Application data, which is data replicated to an arbitrary set of domain controllers

Every domain controller stores at least one domain directory partition as well as two forest-wide data partitions: the schema partition and the configuration partition. Data in a domain directory partition is replicated to every domain controller in the domain as a writeable replica.

Forest-wide data partitions are replicated to every domain controller in the forest. The configuration partition is replicated as a writeable replica. The schema partition is replicated as a read-only replica and the only writeable replica is stored on a domain controller that is designated as having the schema operations master role. Other operations master roles are defined as well.

Active Directory can replicate application-specific data that is stored in an application partition such as the default application partitions used with zones in Domain Name System (DNS) that are integrated with Active Directory. Application partition data is replicated on a forest-wide, domain-wide, or other basis to domain controllers that have a particular application partition. If a domain controller doesn't have an application partition, it doesn't receive a replica of the application partition.

Note Application partitions can only be created on domain controllers running Windows Server 2003 and later. Domain controllers running Windows 2000 or earlier versions of Windows do not recognize application partitions.

In addition to full replicas that are distributed for domains, Active Directory distributes partial replicas of every domain in the forest to special domain controllers designated as global catalog servers. The partial replicas stored on global catalog servers contain information on every object in the forest and are used to facilitate searches and queries for objects in the forest. Because only a subset of an object's attributes is stored, the amount of data replicated to and maintained by a global catalog server is significantly smaller than the total size of all object data stored in all the domains in the forest.

Every domain must have at least one global catalog server. By default, the first domain controller installed in a domain is set as that domain's global catalog server. The global catalog server can be changed, and additional servers can be designated as global catalogs as necessary.

Chapter 33

Designing and Managing the Domain Environment

As you learned in the previous chapter, the physical structure of Active Directory is tightly integrated with the security architecture of the Microsoft Windows operating system. At a high level, Active Directory provides interfaces to which clients can connect, and the directory physically exists on disk in a database file called Ntds.dit. When you install Active Directory on a computer, the computer becomes a domain controller. When you implement Active Directory, you can have as many domain controllers as are needed to support the directory service needs of the organization.

Before you implement or modify the Active Directory domain environment, you need to consider the limitations and architecture requirements for the following processes:

- Replication
- Search and global catalogs
- Compatibility and functional levels
- Authentication and trusts
- Delegated authentication
- Operations masters

Remember that planning for Active Directory is an ongoing process that you should think about whether you are planning to deploy Active Directory for the first time or have already deployed Active Directory in your organization. Why? Because every time you consider making changes to your organizational structure or network infrastructure, you should consider how this affects Active Directory and plan accordingly.

In planning for Active Directory, few things are outside the scope of the design. When you initially deploy Active Directory, you need to develop an Active Directory design and implementation plan that involves every level of your organization and your network infrastructure. Once Active Directory is deployed, any time you plan to change your organizational structure or network infrastructure, you should determine the impact on Active Directory. You then need to plan for and implement any changes to Active Directory that are required.

Design Considerations for Active Directory Replication

Because Active Directory uses a multimaster replication model, there are no primary or backup domain controllers. Every domain controller deployed in the organization is autonomous, with its own copy of the directory. When you need to make changes to standard directory data, you can do so on any domain controller and you can rely on Active Directory's built-in replication engine to replicate the changes to other domain controllers in the organization as appropriate.

As shown in Figure 33-1, the actual mechanics of replication depend on the level and role of a domain controller in the organization. To help manage replication, Active Directory uses partitions in the following ways:

- Forest-wide data is replicated to every domain controller in the forest and includes the configuration and schema partitions for the forest. A domain controller designated as the schema master maintains the only writeable copy of the schema data. Every domain controller maintains a writeable copy of the configuration data.
- Domain-wide data is replicated to every domain controller in a domain and includes only the data for a particular domain. Every domain controller in a domain has a writeable copy of the data for that domain.

Note Domain controllers designated as DNS servers also replicate directory partitions for DNS. Every domain controller that is designated as a DNS server has a copy of the ForestDNSZones and DomainDNSZones partitions.

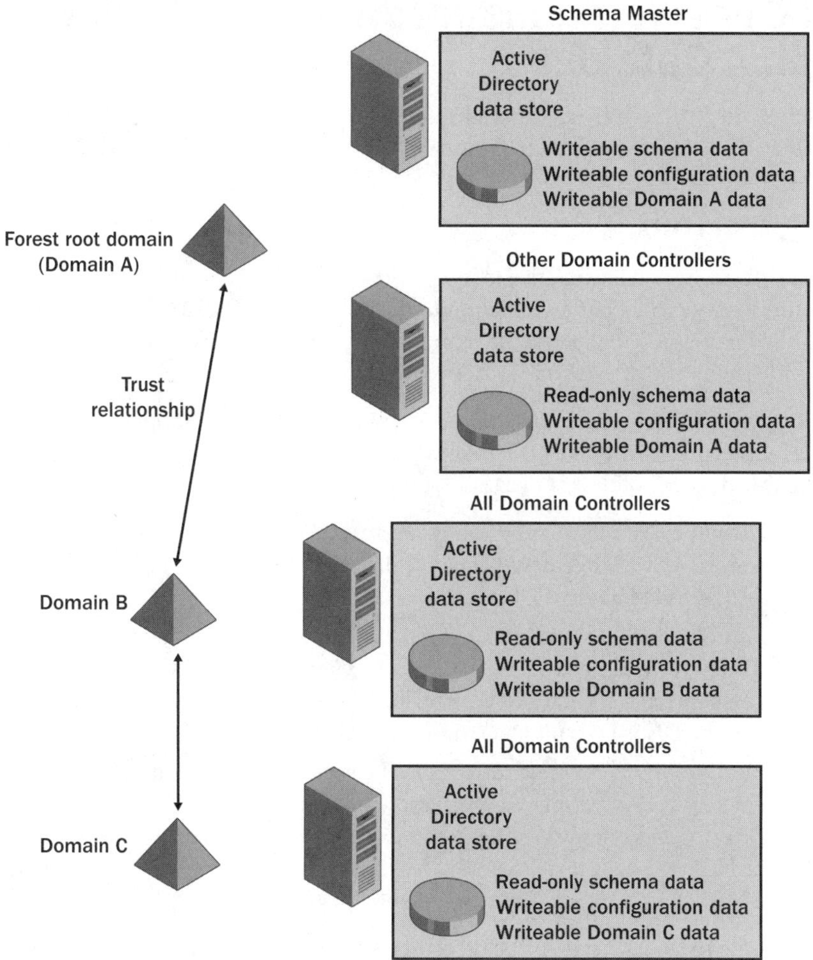

Figure 33-1. Replication of data in the Active Directory data store.

Design Considerations for Active Directory Search and Global Catalogs

Active Directory uses the Lightweight Directory Access Protocol (LDAP) model to query and manage directory information. Objects in the directory can be located using an LDAP query.

Searching the Tree

Every object has a name relative to its location in the directory and a distinguished name that points to its exact location in relation to the root of the directory tree. The relative distinguished name (RDN) is the actual name of the object. The distinguished name (DN) is the complete object name as seen by Active Directory.

When you work your way down the tree, you add a naming component for each successive level. In Figure 33-2, the relative names of several objects are shown on the left and the distinguished names of those objects are shown on the right.

- **cohovineyards.com** The cohovineyards.com domain object is near the top of the tree. In Active Directory, its relative distinguished name is DC=cohovineyards and its distinguished name is DC=cohovineyards,DC=com.
- **mf.Cohovineyards.com** The mf.cohovineyards.com domain object is at the next level of the tree. In Active Directory, its relative name is DC=mf and its distinguished name includes the path to the previous level as well as its relative name. This means that the DN is DC=mf,DC=cohovineyards,DC=com.
- **Bottling.Mf.Cohovineyards.com** The bottling.mf.cohovineyards.com domain object is below the mf.cohovineyards.com domain in the directory tree. In Active Directory, its relative distinguished name is DC=bottling and its distinguished name includes the path to all the previous levels as well as its relative name. This means the DN is DC=bottling,DC=mf,DC=cohovineyards,DC=com.

Being able to find objects in the directory efficiently regardless of their location in the directory tree is extremely important. If objects can't be easily located, users won't be able to find resources that are available and administrators won't be able to manage the available resources either. To make it easier to find resources, Active Directory uses special-purpose domain controllers that function as global catalog servers.

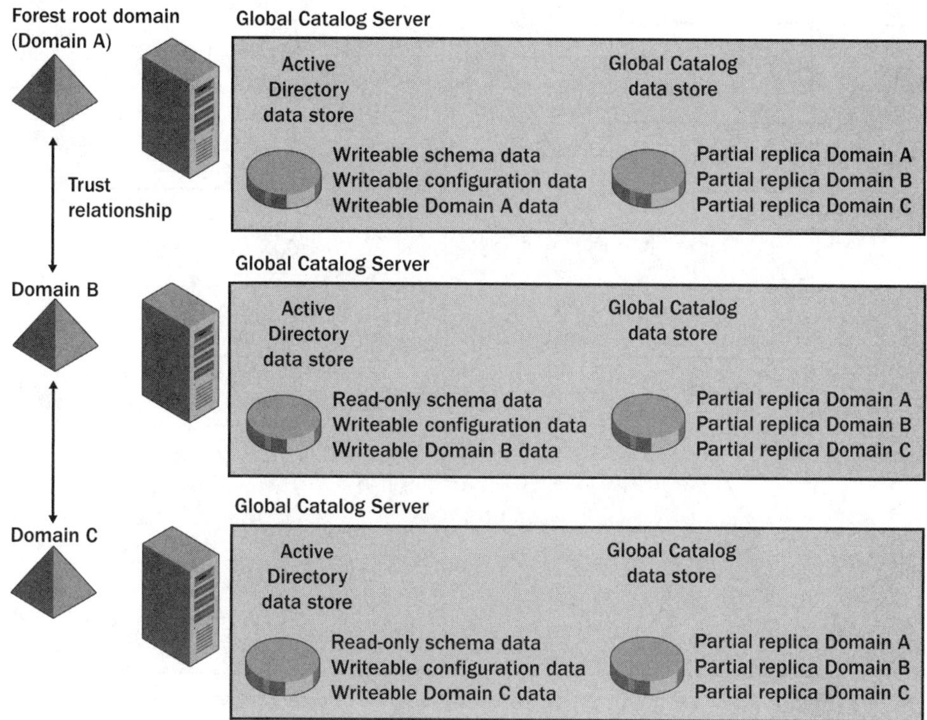

Figure 33-2. Active Directory uses the LDAP model to query and manage the directory.

Accessing the Global Catalog

A domain controller designated as a global catalog server contains an additional data store called the global catalog, as shown in Figure 33-3. The global catalog contains a partial, read-only replica of all the domains in the Active Directory forest. Although the catalog is a partial replica, it does contain a copy of every object in the directory, but only the base attributes of those objects. Queries to global catalog servers are made over TCP port 3268 for standard communications and TCP port 3269 for secure communications.

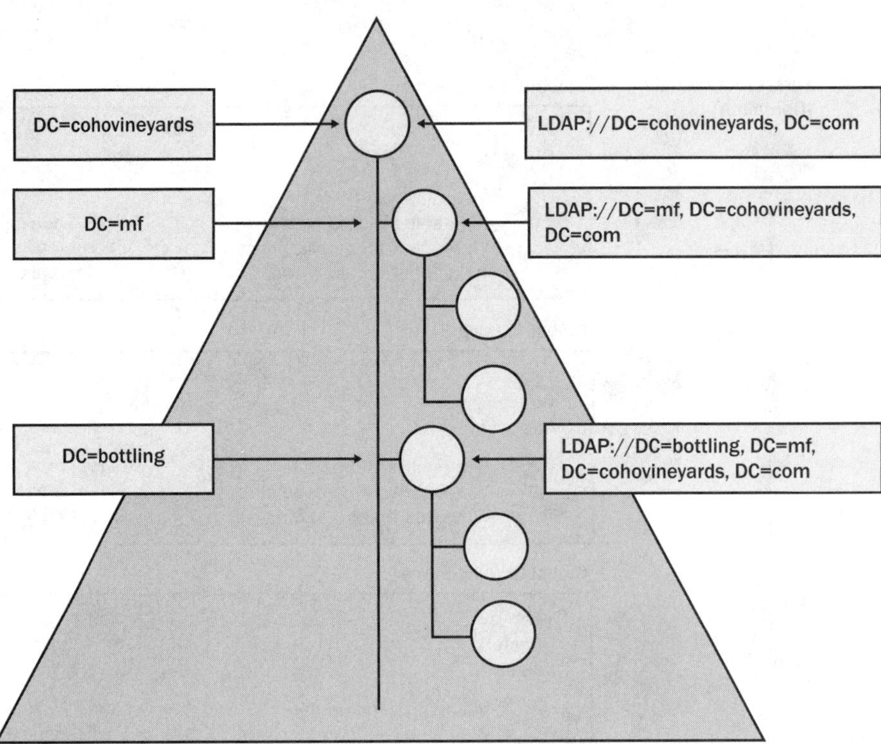

Figure 33-3. Global catalog servers in an Active Directory forest.

Global catalog data is replicated to global catalog servers using the normal Active Directory replication process. In an Active Directory forest with domains A, B, and C, this means that any domain controller designated as a global catalog server has a partial replica of all three domains. If a user in domain C searches for a resource located in domain A, the global catalog server in domain C can respond to the query using an attribute that has been replicated to the global catalog without needing to refer to another domain controller. Without a global catalog server, a domain controller in domain C would need to forward the query to a domain controller in another domain.

Designating Global Catalog Servers

The first domain controller installed in a domain is automatically designated as a global catalog server. You can designate additional domain controllers to be global catalog servers as well. To do this, you use the Active Directory Sites And Services tool to set the Global Catalog Server option for the domain controller you want to be a global catalog server.

Start Active Directory Sites And Services by clicking Start, Programs or All Programs, Administrative Tools, and Active Directory Sites And Services. Expand the site you want to work with, such as Default-First-Site-Name, expand the related servers node, and then select the server you want to designate as a global catalog, as shown in the following screen:

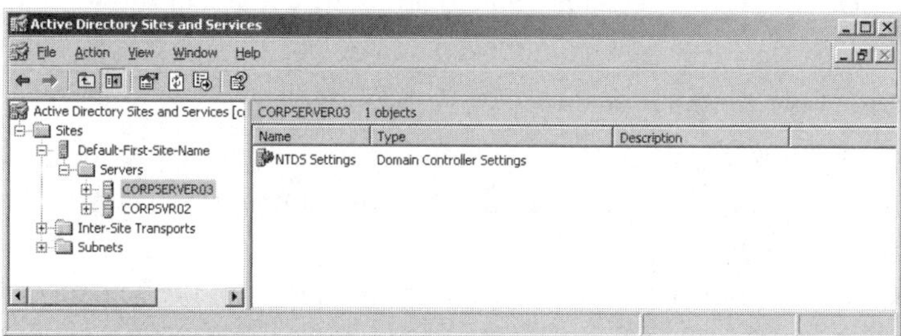

In the right pane, right-click NTDS Settings, and then select Properties. This displays the NTDS Settings Properties dialog box, as shown in the following screen:

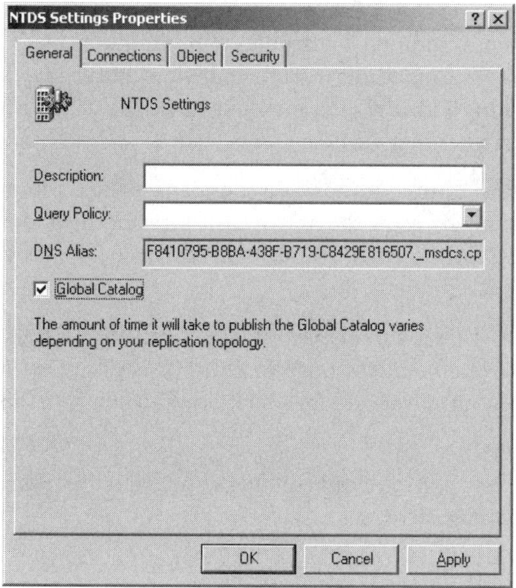

If you want the selected server to be a global catalog, select the Global Catalog option. If you want the selected server to stop being a global catalog, clear the Global Catalog option. When you designate a new global catalog server, the server will request a copy of the global catalog from an existing global catalog server in the domain. The amount of time it takes to replicate the global catalog depends on the size of the catalog and the network configuration.

Designating Replication Attributes

The contents of the global catalog are determined by the attributes that are replicated for each object class. Common object classes you'll work with include the following:

- **Computer** Represents a computer account in the domain or forest
- **Contact** Represents a contact in the domain or forest
- **Domain** Represents a domain
- **Group** Represents a group account in the domain or forest
- **InetOrgPerson** Represents a special type of user account, which typically has been migrated from another directory service
- **PrintQueue** Represents a logical printer (print queue) in the domain or forest
- **Server** Represents a server account in the domain or forest
- **Site** Represents an Active Directory site
- **Subnet** Represents an Active Directory subnet
- **User** Represents a user account in the domain or forest

Schema administrators can configure additional attributes to be replicated by global catalog servers. The primary reason for replicating additional attributes is to add attributes for which users routinely search. You shouldn't add attributes for which users search infrequently. You should rarely, if ever, remove attributes that are being replicated.

If you are a member of the Schema Admins groups, you can manage the attributes that are replicated through the global catalog by using the Active Directory Schema snap-in for the Microsoft Management Console (MMC). When you start this snap-in, it makes a direct connection to the schema master for the forest.

The Active Directory Schema snap-in is not available by default. You must install the Administration Tools (Adminpak.msi) from the Microsoft Windows Server 2003 CD-ROM, or, if you are working with a server, you can simply double-click Adminpak.msi in the %SystemRoot%\System32 folder.

Once you install the Administrative Tools, you can add the Active Directory Schema snap-in to a custom console by following these steps:

1. Open a blank MMC in Author mode. Click Start, select Run, type **mmc** in the Open field, and then click OK.
2. Choose Add/Remove Snap-In from the File menu in the main window. Choose Add, which displays the Add Standalone Snap-in dialog box shown in the screen on the following page.

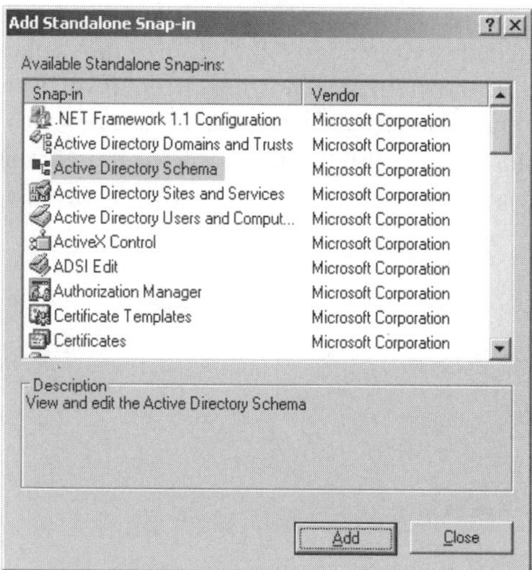

3 Click Active Directory Schema, and then choose Add. The Active Directory Schema snap-in is added to the list of snap-ins in the Add/Remove Snap-In dialog box. Click Close, and then click OK.

After you add the snap-in to a custom console, you can edit the schema for the object whose attribute you want to replicate in the global catalog. In Active Directory Schema, expand the Active Directory Schema node, and then select the Attributes node. A list of the attributes for all objects in the directory appears in the right pane as shown in the following screen:

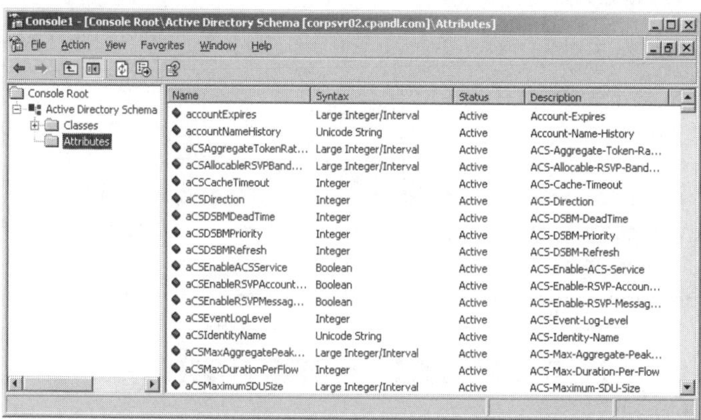

Double-click the attribute you want to replicate to the global catalog. In the attribute's Properties dialog box, mark the attribute to be replicated by selecting the Replicate This Attribute To The Global Catalog option as shown in the following screen. If you want the attribute to be indexed in the database for faster search and retrieval, select Index This Attribute In The Active Directory. Although indexing an attribute allows it to be found more quickly, each index you create slightly increases the size of the Active Directory database.

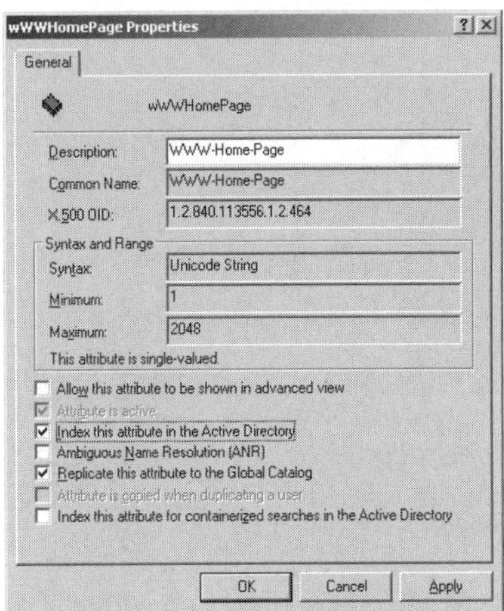

Troubleshooting

You cannot change an attribute even though you are a member of the Administrators group

As a member of the Administrators group, you can view Active Directory schema. To change schema, you must be a member of the Schema Admins group. The Active Directory Schema snap-in doesn't check to ensure that you are a member of the Schema Admins group until you try to change attribute settings. If you aren't a member of the group, it states that you have insufficient permissions.

Design Considerations for Compatibility

In Windows Server 2003, each forest and each domain within a forest can be assigned a functional level. The functional level for a forest is referred to as the *forest functional level*. The functional level for a domain within a forest is referred to as the *domain functional level*.

Inside Out

Functional levels affect compatibility

Functional levels affect the inner workings of Active Directory and are used to enable features that are compatible with the installed server versions of the Windows operating system. For backward compatibility with previous versions of Windows, Active Directory is configured by default to be compatible with Windows NT domains and clients. Windows NT domains have a primary domain controller and one or more backup domain controllers rather than multiple domain controllers that are all equally accountable. When a domain is operating in the default mode, a domain controller running Windows 2000 or later is designated as a primary domain controller (PDC) emulator. The PDC emulator role is a special operations master role that allows the domain controller to act as the primary domain controller for Windows NT clients in the domain.

Understanding Domain Functional Level

When a functional level is set for a domain, the level of functionality applies only to that domain. This means that other domains in the forest can have a different functional level.

As shown in Table 33-1, there are several domain functional levels. The default domain functional level is Windows 2000 mixed. Changing a functional level changes the operating systems that are supported for domain controllers. For example, in Windows 2000 mixed functional level, the domain can have domain controllers running Windows Server 2003 or Windows 2000, with backup domain controllers running Windows NT 4.

Note Although you can raise the domain functional level, you can never lower it. This means that if you raise the domain functional level to Windows Server 2003, only Windows Server 2003 domain controllers can be configured in the domain.

Table 33-1. Domain Functional Levels

Domain Functional Level	Supported Domain Controllers
Windows 2000 mixed (default)	Windows Server 2003 Windows 2000 Windows NT 4 backup domain controller (BDC)
Windows 2000 native	Windows Server 2003 Windows 2000
Windows Server 2003 interim	Windows Server 2003 Windows NT 4 BDC
Windows Server 2003	Windows Server 2003

Understanding Forest Functional Level

Forest functional level is a bit simpler, as shown in Table 33-2. The default forest functional level is Windows 2000. Before you can raise the forest functional level to Windows Server 2003, all domains in the forest must be set to the Windows 2000 native or Windows Server 2003 functional level. Then, when you raise the forest functional level to Windows Server 2003, all domains using the Windows 2000 native domain functional level will automatically be raised to the Windows Server 2003 domain functional level. As with the domain functional level, once you raise the forest functional level, you cannot lower it.

Table 33-2. Forest Functional Levels

Forest Functional Level	Supported Domain Controllers
Windows 2000 (default)	Windows Server 2003 Windows 2000 Windows NT 4 BDC
Windows Server 2003 interim	Windows Server 2003 Windows NT 4 BDC
Windows Server 2003	Windows Server 2003

Raising the Domain or Forest Functional Level

You can raise the domain or forest functional level using Active Directory Domains And Trusts. To raise the domain functional level, follow these steps:

1. Click Start, choose Programs or All Programs as appropriate, choose Administrative Tools, and then select Active Directory Domains And Trusts.
2. In the console tree, right-click the domain you want to work with, and then select Raise Domain Functional Level. The current domain name and functional level appear in the Raise Domain Functional Level dialog box.
3. To change the domain functionality, select the new domain functional level using the selection list provided, and then click Raise.

> **Warning** You can't reverse this action. Once you raise the functional level, there's no going back, so you should consider the implications carefully before you do this.

4. When you click OK, the new domain functional level will be replicated to each domain controller in the domain. This operation can take some several minutes or longer in a large organization.

You can raise the forest level functionality by completing the following steps:

1. Click Start, choose Programs or All Programs as appropriate, choose Administrative Tools, and then select Active Directory Domains And Trusts.

2. Right-click the Active Directory Domains And Trusts node in the console tree, and then select Raise Forest Functional Level. The current forest name and functional level appear in the Raise Forest Functional Level dialog box.
3. To change the forest functionality, select the new forest functional level using the selection list provided, and then click Raise.

> **Warning** You can't reverse this action. Once you raise the functional level, there's no going back, so you should consider the implications carefully before you do this.

4. When you click OK, the new forest functional level will be replicated to each domain controller in each domain in the forest. This operation can take several minutes or longer in a large organization.

As a planning option, you can determine the steps you need to take to raise the forest functional level by clicking Save As in the Raise Forest Functional Level dialog box. When you click Save As, a Save As dialog box appears, allowing you to select a save location for a log file. As shown in the following screen, the log file details show the following information:

- The forest root domain and the current forest functional level.
- The domains and the domain controllers in those domains that are running versions of Windows earlier than Windows Server 2003. These are the servers that need to be upgraded.
- The domain functional level of each domain whose functional level must be raised. As long as the domain functional level of all domains is set to at least Windows 2000 native, you can raise the forest functional level—doing so raises the domain functional level in all the domains to Windows Server 2003 and sets the forest functional level to Windows Server 2003 as well.

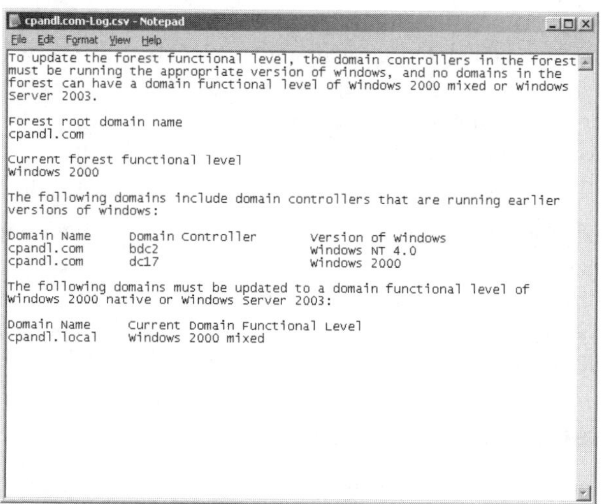

cpandl.com-Log.csv - Notepad

File Edit Format View Help

```
To update the forest functional level, the domain controllers in the forest
must be running the appropriate version of Windows, and no domains in the
forest can have a domain functional level of Windows 2000 mixed or Windows
Server 2003.

Forest root domain name
cpandl.com

Current forest functional level
Windows 2000

The following domains include domain controllers that are running earlier
versions of Windows:

Domain Name     Domain Controller        Version of Windows
cpandl.com      bdc2                     Windows NT 4.0
cpandl.com      dc17                     Windows 2000

The following domains must be updated to a domain functional level of
Windows 2000 native or Windows Server 2003:

Domain Name     Current Domain Functional Level
cpandl.local    Windows 2000 mixed
```

Design Considerations for Active Directory Authentication and Trusts

Authentication and trusts are integral parts of Active Directory. Before you implement any Active Directory design or try to modify your existing Active Directory infrastructure, you should have a firm understanding of how both authentication and trusts work in an Active Directory environment.

Universal Groups and Authentication

When a user logs on to a domain, Active Directory looks up information about the groups of which the user is a member to generate a security token for the user. The security token is needed as part of the normal authentication process and is used whenever a user accesses resources on the network.

Understanding Security Tokens and Universal Group Membership Caching

To generate the security token, Active Directory checks the domain local and global group memberships for the user. When a domain is operating in Windows 2000 native functional level or higher, an additional type of group is also available, called a *universal group*. As universal groups can contain user and group accounts from any domain in the forest, and global catalog servers are the only servers in a domain with forest-wide domain data, the global catalog is essential for logon in any domain operating at the Windows 2000 native functional level or higher.

Because of problems authenticating users when global catalog servers are not available, Windows Server 2003 introduces a technique for caching universal group membership. In a domain with domain controllers running Windows Server 2003, universal group membership caching can be enabled. Once caching is enabled, the cache is where domain controllers store universal group membership information that they have previously looked up. Domain controllers use the cache for the next time the user logs on to the domain. The cache is maintained indefinitely and updated periodically to ensure that it is current. By default, domain controllers check the consistency of the cache every eight hours.

Thanks to universal group membership caching, remote sites running Windows Server 2003 domain controllers don't necessarily have to have global catalog servers configured as well. This gives you additional options when configuring the Active Directory forest. The assignment of security tokens is only part of the logon process. The logon process also includes authentication and the assignment of a user principal name (UPN) to the user.

Enabling Universal Group Membership Caching

In a domain with domain controllers running Windows Server 2003, you use the Active Directory Sites And Services tool to configure universal group membership caching. You enable caching on a per-site basis. Start Active Directory Sites And Services by clicking Start, Programs or All Programs, Administrative Tools, and Active Directory Sites And Services. Expand the site in which you want to enable universal group membership caching, as shown in the following screen:

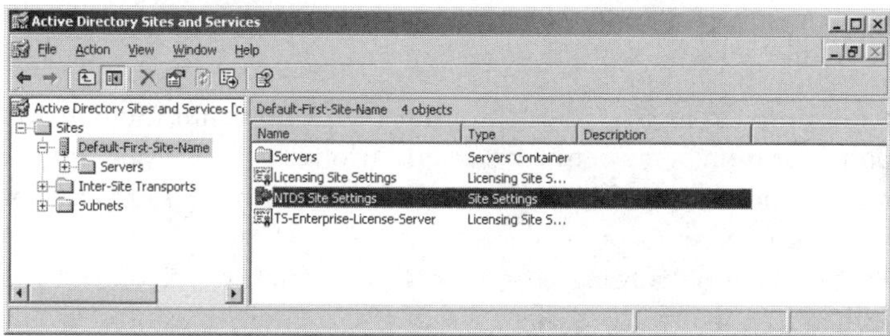

In the right pane, right-click NTDS Site Settings, and then select Properties. This displays the NTDS Site Settings Properties dialog box as shown in the following screen:

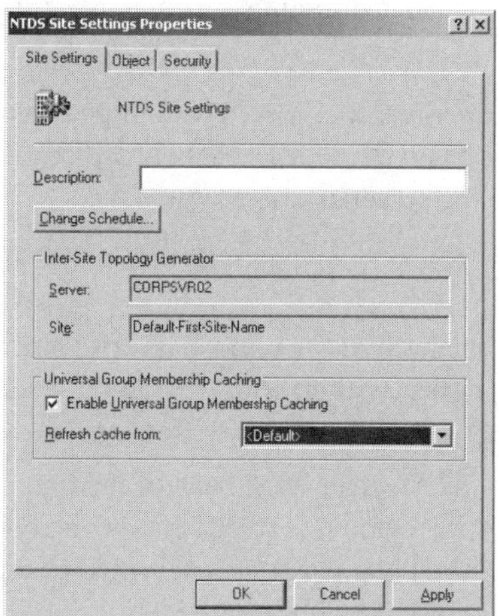

To enable universal group membership caching for the site, select Enable Universal Group Membership Caching and continue as follows:

- If the directory has multiple sites, you can replicate existing universal group membership information from a specific site's cache by selecting the site on the Refresh Cache From List. With this option, universal group membership information doesn't need to be generated and then replicated; it is simply replicated from the other site's cache.
- If the directory has only one site or you'd rather get the information from a global catalog server in the nearest site, accept the default setting <Default>. With this option, universal group membership information is generated and then replicated.

When you are finished configuring universal group membership caching, click OK.

NTLM and Kerberos Authentication

Windows NT 4 uses a form of authentication known as NT LAN Manager (NTLM). With NTLM, an encrypted challenge/response is used to authenticate a user without sending the user's password over the network. The system requesting authentication must perform a calculation that proves it has access to the secured NTLM credentials. It does this by sending a one-way hash of the user's password that can be verified.

NTLM authentication has interactive and non-interactive authentication processes. Interactive NTLM authentication over a network typically involves a client system from which a user is requesting authentication, and a domain controller on which the user's password is stored. As the user accesses other resources on the network, non-interactive authentication may take place as well to permit an already logged-on user to access network resources. Typically, non-interactive authentication involves a client, a server, and a domain controller that manages the authentication.

To see how NTLM authentication works, consider the situation that occurs when a user tries to access a resource on the network and she is prompted for her user name and password. Assuming the resource is on a server that is not also a domain controller, the authentication process would be similar to the following:

1. When prompted, the user provides a domain name, user name, and password. The client computer generates a cryptographic hash of the user's password, discards the actual password, then sends the user name to the server as unencrypted text.
2. The server generates a 16-byte random number, called a *challenge*, and sends it to the client.
3. The client encrypts the challenge with the hash of the user's password and returns the result, called a *response*, to the server. The server then sends the domain controller the user name, the challenge sent to the client, and the response from the client.
4. The domain controller uses the user name to retrieve the hash of the user's password from the Security Account Manager (SAM) database. The domain controller uses this password hash to encrypt the challenge then compares the encrypted challenge it computed to the response computed by the client. If they are identical, the authentication is successful.

Starting with Windows 2000, Active Directory uses Kerberos as the default authentication protocol, and NTLM authentication is only maintained for backward compatibility with older clients. Whenever a client running Windows 2000 or later tries to authenticate with Active Directory, the client tries to use Kerberos. Kerberos has a number of advantages over NTLM authentication, including the use of mutual authentication. Mutual authentication in Kerberos allows for two-way authentication, so that not only can a server authenticate a client, but a client can also authenticate a server. Thus, mutual authentication ensures that not only is an authorized client trying to access the network, but also that an authorized server is the one responding to the client request.

Kerberos uses the following three main components:

- A client that needs access to resources
- A server that manages access to resources and ensures that only authenticated users can gain access to resources
- A Key Distribution Center (KDC) that acts as a central clearinghouse

Establishing the Initial Authentication

All domain controllers run the Kerberos Key Distribution Center service to act as KDCs. With Kerberos authentication, a user password is never sent over the network. Instead, Kerberos authentication uses a shared secret authentication model. In most cases, the client and the server use the user's password as the shared secret. With this technique, authentication works as shown in Figure 33-4.

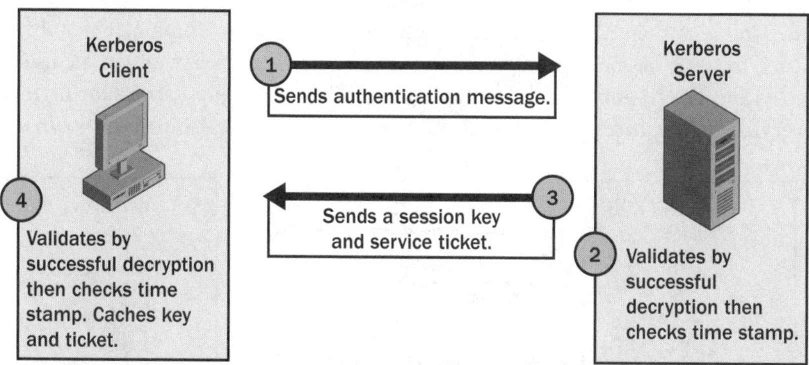

Figure 33-4. The Kerberos authentication process.

The details of the initial authentication of a user in the domain are as follows:

1. When a user logs on to the network, the client sends the KDC server a message containing the user name, domain name, and a request for access to the network. In the message is a packet of information that has been encrypted using the shared secret information (the user's password), which includes a time stamp.
2. When the KDC server receives the message, the server reads the user name, and then checks the directory database for its copy of the shared secret information (the user's password). The KDC server then decrypts the secret part of the message and checks the message time stamp. As long as the message time stamp is within five minutes of the current time on the server, the server can then authenticate the user. If the decryption fails or the message time stamp is more than five minutes off the current time, the authentication fails. Five minutes is the default value; the allowable time difference can be configured through domain security policy, using the Kerberos policy Maximum Tolerance For Computer Clock Synchronization.

3 Once the user is authenticated, the KDC server sends the client a message that is encrypted with the shared secret information (the user's password). The message includes a session key that the client will use when communicating with the KDC server from now on and a session ticket that grants the user access to the domain controller. The ticket is encrypted with the KDC server's key, which makes it valid only for that domain controller.

4 When the client receives the message, the client decrypts the message and checks the message time stamp. As long as the message time stamp is within five minutes of the current time on the server, the client can then authenticate the server and assume that the server is valid. The client then caches the session key so it can be used for all future connections with the KDC server. The session key is valid until it expires or the user logs off. The session ticket is cached as well, but it isn't decrypted.

Accessing Resources After Authentication

After initial authentication, the user is granted access to the domain. The only resource to which the user has been granted access is the domain controller. When the user wants to access another resource on the network, the client must request access through the KDC. An overview of the process for authenticating access to network resources is shown in Figure 33-5.

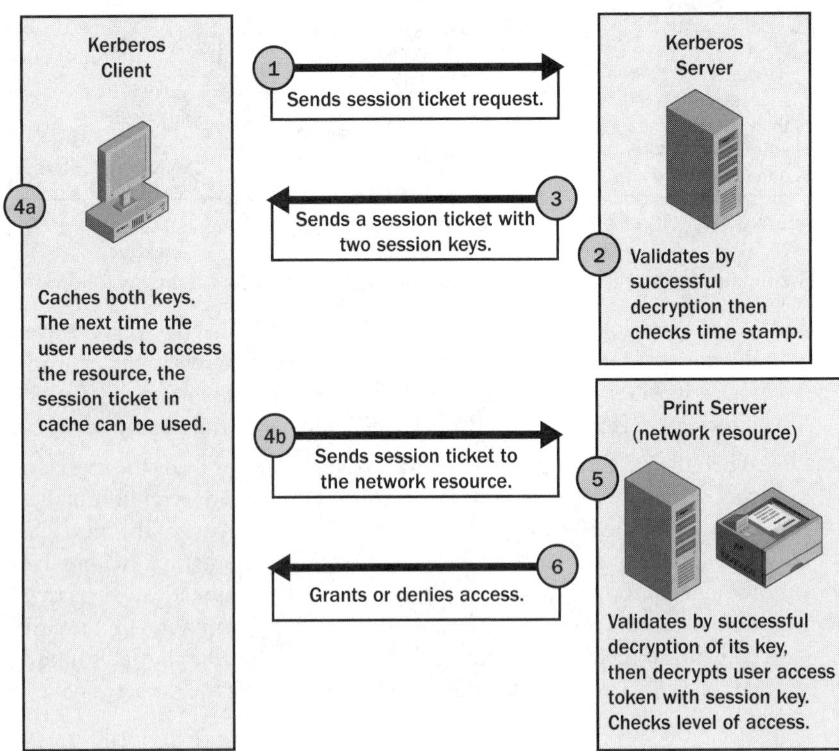

Figure 33-5. The Kerberos authentication process.

The details of an access request for a network resource are as follows:

1. When a user tries to access a resource on the network, the client sends the KDC server a session ticket request. The message contains the user's name, the session ticket the client was previously granted, the name of the network resource the client is trying to access, and a time stamp that is encrypted with the session key.
2. When the KDC server receives the message, the server decrypts the session ticket using its key. Afterward, it extracts the original session key from the session ticket and uses it to decrypt the time stamp, which is then validated. The validation process is designed to ensure that the client is using the correct session key and that the time stamp is valid.
3. If all is acceptable, the KDC server sends a session ticket to the client. The session ticket includes two copies of a session key that the client will use to access the requested resource. The first copy of the session key is encrypted using the client's session key. The second copy of the session key contains the user's access information and is encrypted with the resource's secret key known only by the KDC server and the network resource.
4. The client caches the session ticket, and then sends the session ticket to the network resource to gain access. This request also contains an encrypted time stamp.
5. The network resource decrypts the second session key in the session ticket, using the secret key it shares with the KDC server. If this is successful, the network resource has validated that the session ticket came from a trusted KDC. It then decrypts the user's access information, using the session key, and checks the user's access permissions. The time stamp sent from the client is also decrypted and validated by the network resource.
6. If the authentication and authorization are successful (meaning that the client has the appropriate access permissions), the user is granted the type of access to the network resource that the particular permissions allow. The next time the user needs to access the resource, the session ticket in cache is used, as long as it hasn't expired. Using a cached session ticket allows the client to send a request directly to the network resource. If the ticket has expired, however, the client must start over and get a new ticket.

Authentication and Trusts Across Domain Boundaries

Active Directory uses Kerberos security for server-to-server authentication and the establishment of trusts, while allowing older clients and servers on the network to use NTLM if necessary. Figure 33-6 shows a one-way trust in which one domain is the trusted domain and the other domain is the trusting domain. In Windows NT 4, you typically implemented one-way trusts when you had separate account and resource domains. The establishment of the trust allowed users in the account domain to access resources in the resource domain.

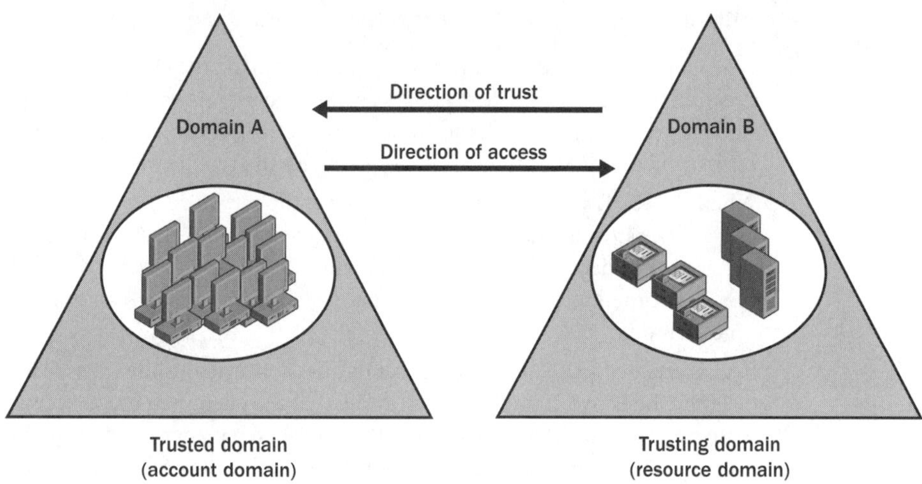

Figure 33-6. One-way trust with a trusted domain and a trusting domain.

Two-Way Transitive Trusts

With Active Directory, trusts are automatically configured between all the domains in a forest and are implemented as two-way, transitive trusts. As a result, users in domain A can automatically access resources in domain B and users in domain B can automatically access resources in domain A. Because the trusts are automatically established between all domains in the forest, no setup is involved and there are many more design options for implementing Active Directory domains.

> **Note** The physical limitation on the number of objects that necessitated having separate account and resource domains in Windows NT 4 no longer applies. Active Directory domains can have millions of objects, a fact that changes the fundamental reason for creating additional domains.

As trusts join parent and child domains in the same domain tree and join the roots of domain trees, the structure of trusts in a forest can be referred to as a *trust tree*. When a user tries to access a resource in another domain, the trust tree is used, and the user's request has to pass through one domain controller for each domain between the user and the resource. This type of authentication takes place across domain boundaries. Authentication across domain boundaries also applies when a user with an account in one domain visits another domain in the forest and tries to log on to the network from that domain.

Consider the example shown in Figure 33-7. If a user from domain G visits domain K and tries to log on to the network, the user's computer must be able to connect to a domain controller in domain K. Here, the user's computer sends the initial logon request to the domain K domain controller. When the domain controller receives the logon request, it determines that the user is located in domain G. The domain controller refers the request to a domain controller in the next domain in its trust tree, which in this case is domain J. A domain controller in domain J refers the request to domain I. A domain controller in domain I refers the request to domain H. This process continues through domains A, E, and F until the request finally gets to domain G.

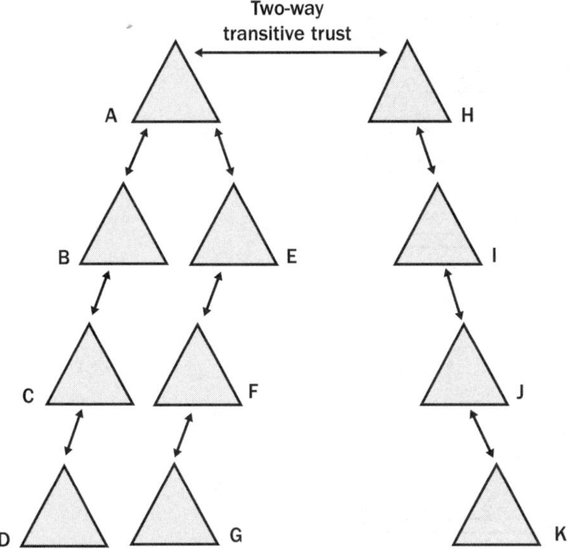

Figure 33-7. A forest with many domains.

Shortcut Trusts

This rather lengthy referral process could be avoided if you established an explicit trust between domain G and domain K as shown in Figure 33-8. Technically, explicit trusts are one-way transitive trusts, but you can establish a two-way explicit trust by creating two one-way trusts. Thus unlike standard trusts within the trust tree, which are inherently two-way and transitive, explicit trusts can be made to be two-way if desired. As they can be used to establish authentication shortcuts between domains, they are also referred to as *shortcut trusts*. In this example, it was decided to create two one-way trusts: one from domain G to domain K and one from domain K to domain G. With these shortcut trusts in place, users in domain G could visit domain K and be rapidly authenticated and users in domain K could visit domain G and be rapidly authenticated.

If you examine the figure closely, you'll see that several other shortcut trusts were add to the forest as well. Shortcut trusts have been established between B and E and between E and I. Establishing the shortcut trusts in both directions allows for easy access to resources and rapid authentication in several combinations, such as the following:

- Using the B to E shortcut trust, users in domain B can rapidly access resources in domain E.
- Using the B to E and E to I shortcut trusts, users in domain B can also rapidly access resources in domain I.

- Using the B to E shortcut trust, users in domain B can visit domain E and be rapidly authenticated.
- Using the B to E and E to I shortcut trusts, users in domain B can visit domain I and be rapidly authenticated.

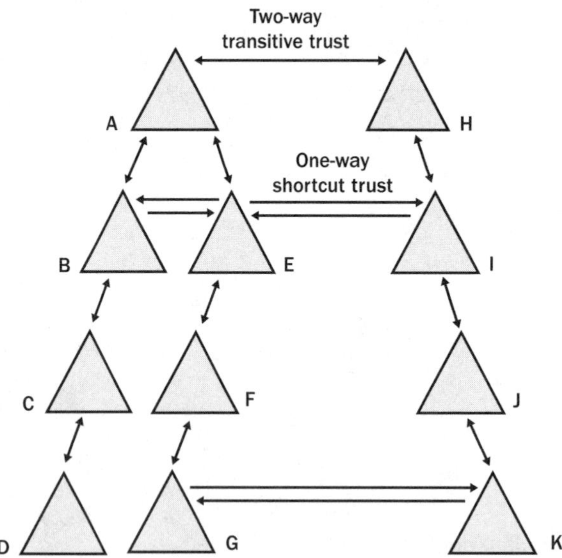

Figure 33-8. A forest with several shortcut trusts.

The trusts work similarly for users in domain E. Users in domain E have direct access to both domain B and domain I. Imagine that domain B is sales.cohovineyard.com, domain E is mf.cohovineyard.com, and domain I is cs.cohowinery.com, and you may be able to better picture how the shortcut trusts allow users to cut across trees in the Active Directory forest. Hopefully, you can also imagine how much planning should go into deciding your domain structure, especially when it comes to access to resources and authentication.

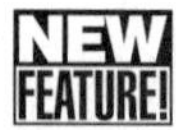

Authentication and Trusts Across Forest Boundaries

Authentication and trusts can be established across forest boundaries as well. As discussed in Chapter 32, while you are upgrading your network to implement Active Directory, you can establish external trusts to Windows NT domains to ensure that Windows NT domains continue to be available to users.

One-way external trusts, such as the one depicted in Figure 33-9, are nontransitive. This means that if, as in the example, a trust is established between domain H and domain L only, a user in any domain in forest 1 could access a resource in domain L but not in any other domain in forest 2. The reason for this limitation is that the trust doesn't continue past domain L and it does not matter that a two-way transitive trust does exist between domain L and domain M or that a two-way trust also exists between domain L and domain O.

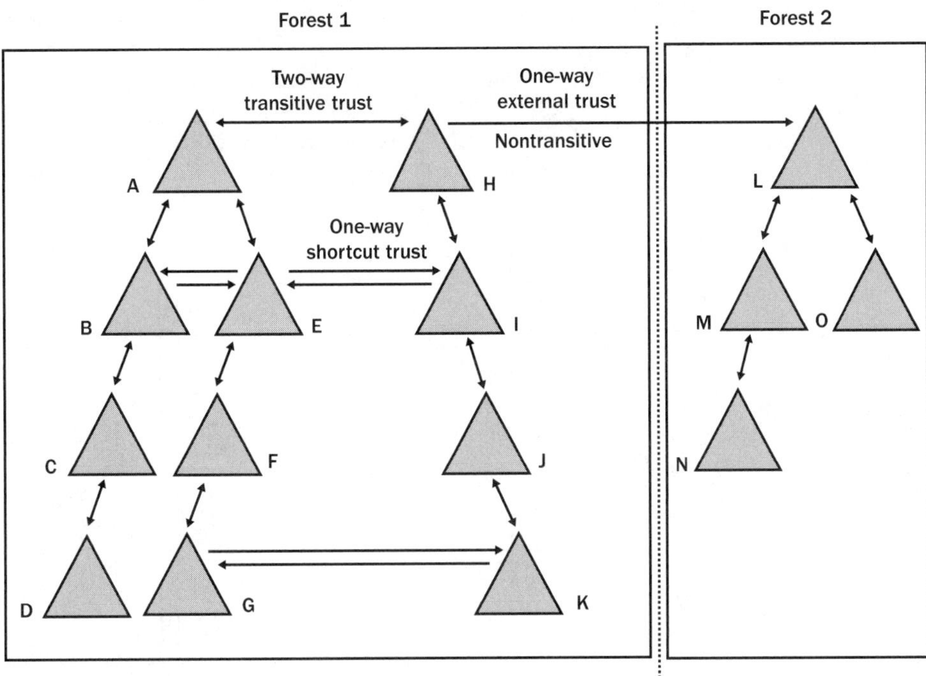

Figure 33-9. A one-way external trust that crosses forest boundaries but is nontransitive.

New in Windows Server 2003 is the addition of the cross-forest transitive trust also referred to simply as a *forest trust*. With this type of trust, you can establish a one-way or two-way transitive trust between forests to share resources and to authenticate users. With a two-way trust, as shown Figure 33-10, you enable cross-forest authentication and cross-forest authorization. Before you can use cross-forest trusts, all domain controllers in all domains of both forests must be upgraded to Windows Server 2003 and the forest must be running at the Windows Server 2003 functional level.

As discussed in the section "NTLM and Kerberos Authentication" earlier in this chapter, Kerberos is the default authentication protocol, but NTLM can also be used. This allows current clients and servers as well as older clients and servers to be authenticated. Once you establish a two-way cross-forest trust, users get all the benefits of Active Directory regardless of where they sign on to the network. With cross-forest authentication, you ensure secure access to resources when the user account is in one forest and the computer account is in another forest, and when the user in one forest needs access to network resources in another trusted forest. As part of cross-forest authorization, administrators can select users and global groups from trusted forests for inclusion in local groups. This ensures the integrity of the forest security boundary while allowing trust between forests.

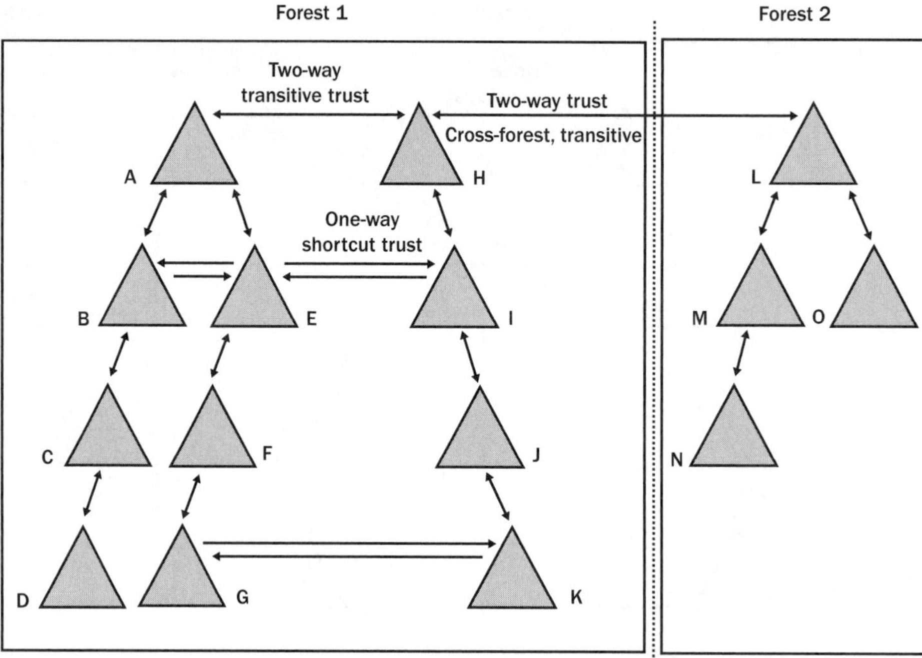

Figure 33-10. A two-way transitive trust between forests.

When you connect two or more forests using cross-forest trusts, the implementation is referred to as a *federated forest design*. The federated forest design is most useful when you need to join two separate Active Directory structures, for example, when two companies merge, when one company acquires another, or when an organization has a major restructuring. Consider the case in which two companies merge, and, rather than migrate their separate Active Directory structures into a single directory tree, the staff decides to link the two forests using cross-forest trusts. As long as the trusts are two-way, users in forest 1 can access resources in forest 2 and users in forest 2 can access resources in forest 1.

Having separate forests with cross-forest trusts between them is also useful when you want a division or group within the organization to have more autonomy but still have a link to the other divisions or groups. By placing the division or group in a separate forest, you ensure strict security and give that division or group ownership of the Active Directory structure. If users in the forest needed access to resources in another forest, you could establish a one-way cross-forest trust between the forests. This would allow users in the secured forest to gain access to resources in the second forest, but would not allow users in the second forest to gain access to the secure forest.

Organizations that contain groups or divisions with high security requirements could use this approach. For example, consider Figure 33-11.

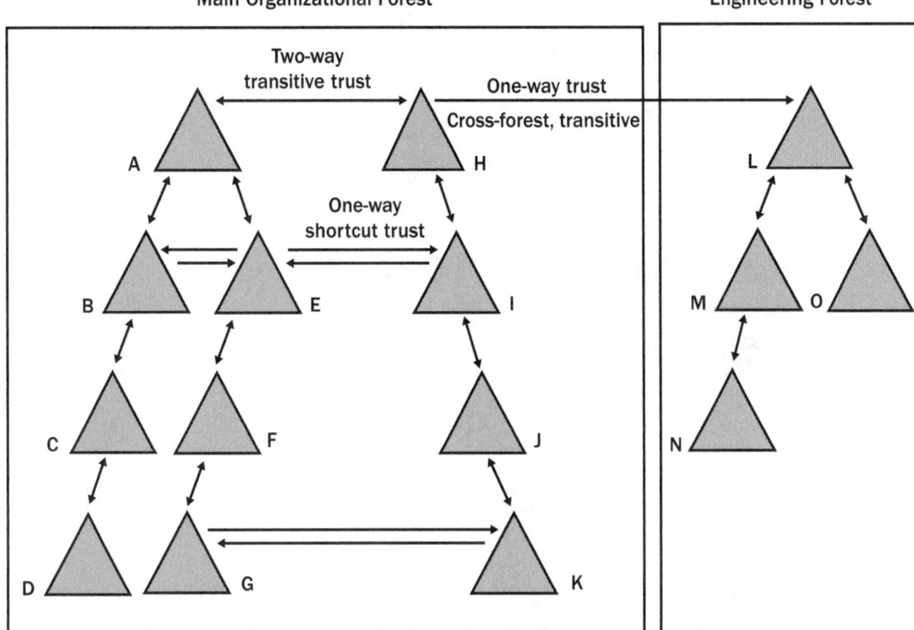

Figure 33-11. A one-way transitive trust between forests.

In this situation, the users in the organization's Engineering department need access to resources in other departments, but for security reasons they should be isolated from the rest of the organization. Here the organization has implemented two forests: a main organizational forest and a separate Engineering forest. Using a one-way cross-forest trust from the main forest to the Engineering department forest, the organization allows Engineering users to access other resources, but ensures that the Engineering department is secure and isolated.

Examining Domain and Forest Trusts

You can examine existing trusts using Active Directory Domains And Trusts. Click Start, choose Programs or All Programs as appropriate, choose Administrative Tools, and then select Active Directory Domains And Trusts. As shown in the following screen, you see a list of available domains:

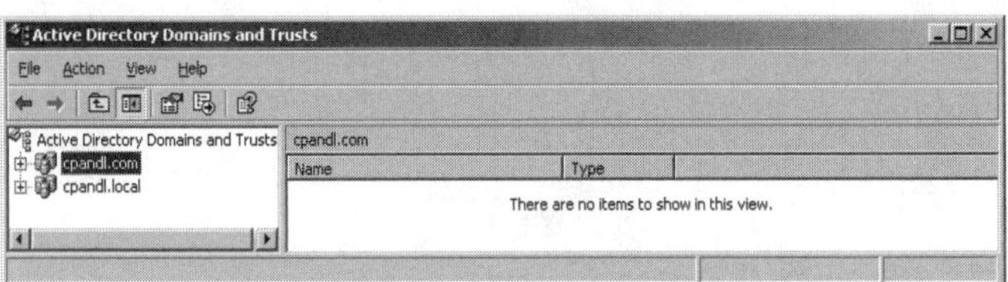

To examine the existing trusts for a domain, right-click the domain entry, and then select Properties. Then, in the domain's Properties dialog box, click the Trust tab as shown in the following screen. The Trust tab is organized into two panels:

- **Domains Trusted By This Domain (Outgoing Trusts)** Lists the domains that this domain trusts (the trusted domains).
- **Domains That Trust This Domain (Incoming Trusts)** Lists the domains that trust this domain (the trusting domains).

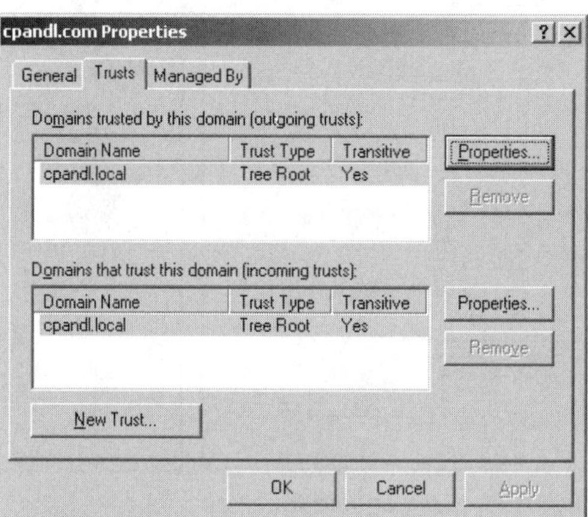

To view the details of a particular trust, select it, and then click Properties. The following screen shows the trust's Properties dialog box:

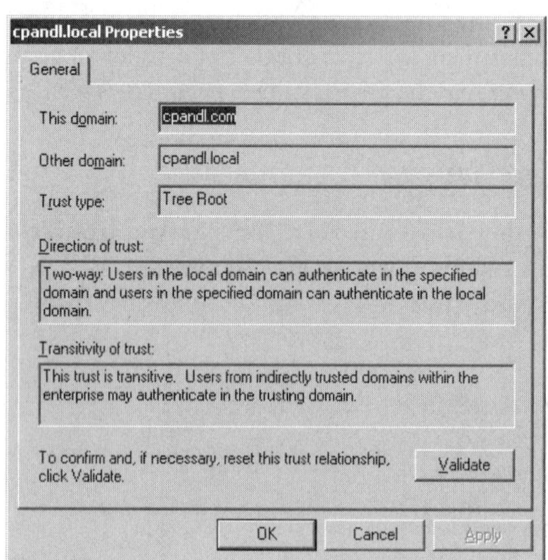

The Properties dialog box contains the following information:

- **This Domain** The domain you are working with.
- **Other Domain** The domain with which the trust is established.
- **Trust Type** The type of trust. By default, two-way transitive trusts are created automatically when a new domain is added to a new domain tree within the forest or a subdomain of a root domain. There are two default trust types: Tree Root and Parent And Child. When a new domain tree is added to the forest, the default trust that is established automatically is a tree-root trust. When a new domain is a subdomain of a root domain, the default trust that is established automatically is a parent and child trust. Other trust types that may appear include the following:
  - External, which is a one-way or two-way nontransitive trust used to provide access to resources in a Windows NT 4.0 domain or to a domain in a separate forest that is not joined by a forest trust
  - Forest, which is a one-way or two-way transitive trust used to share resources between forests
  - Realm, which is a transitive or nontransitive trust that can be established as one way or two way between a non-Windows Kerberos realm and a Windows Server 2003 domain
  - Shortcut, which is a one-way or two-way transitive trust used to speed up authentication and resource access between domain trees
- **Direction Of Trust** The direction of the trust. All default trusts are established as two-way trusts. This means that users in the domain you are working with can authenticate in the other domain and users from the other domain can authenticate in the domain you are working with.
- **Transitivity Of Trust** The transitivity of the trust. All default trusts are transitive, which means that users from indirectly trusted domains can authenticate in the other domain.

Establishing External, Shortcut, Realm, and Cross-Forest Trusts

All trusts, regardless of type, are established in the same way. For all trusts there are two sides: an incoming trust and an outgoing trust. To configure both sides of the trust, keep the following in mind:

- For domain trusts, you need to use two accounts: one that is a member of the Domain Admins group in the first domain and one that is a member of the Domain Admins group in the second domain. If you don't have appropriate accounts in both domains, you can establish one side of the trust and allow another administrator in the other domain to establish the other side of the trust.
- For forest trusts, you will need to use two accounts: one that is a member of the Enterprise Admins group in the first forest and one that is a member of the Enterprise

Admins group in the second forest. If you don't have appropriate accounts in both forests, you can establish one side of the two-way trust and allow another administrator in the other forest to establish the other side of the trust.

- For realm trusts, you will need to establish the trust separately for the Windows domain and for the Kerberos realm. If you don't have appropriate administrative access to both the Windows domain and the Kerberos realm, you can establish one side of the trust and allow another administrator to establish the other side of the trust.

To establish a trust, follow these steps:

1. Click Start, choose Programs or All Programs as appropriate, choose Administrative Tools, and then select Active Directory Domains And Trusts.
2. Right-click the domain for which you want to establish a one-way incoming, one-way outgoing, or two-way trust. For a cross-forest trust, this must be the forest root domain in one of the participating forests.
3. In the domain Properties dialog box, select the Trust tab, and then click the New Trust button. This starts the New Trust Wizard. Click Next to skip the welcome page.
4. On the Trust Name page, specify the domain name of the other domain, as shown in Figure 33-12. For a cross-forest trust, this must be the name of the forest root domain in the other forest.

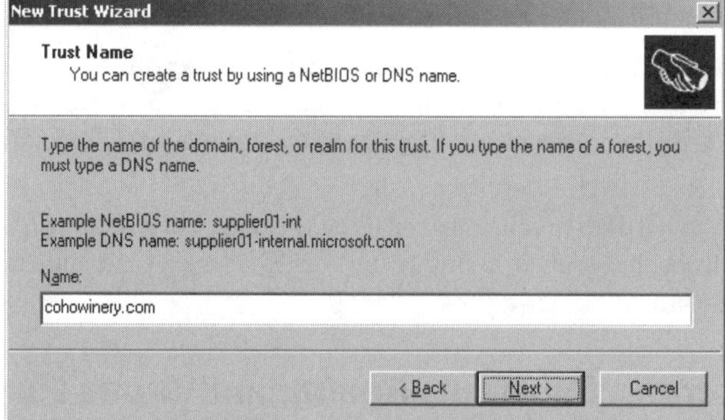

Figure 33-12. Specify the name of the other domain.

5. When you click Next, the wizard tries to establish a connection to the other domain. The options on the next page depend on whether you are connecting to a Windows domain, a Windows forest or a non-Windows forest.
   - If the domain is determined to be a Windows forest, you have the option of creating an external trust that is nontransitive or a forest trust that is transitive. Choose either External Trust or Forest Trust, and then click Next.
   - If the domain is determined to be a Windows domain, it is assumed that you are creating a shortcut trust, and the wizard goes directly to the Direction Of Trust page.

- If the domain is determined to be a non-Windows domain, you have the option of creating a realm trust with a Kerberos version 5 realm. Select Realm Trust, and then, on the Transitivity Of Trust page, select either Nontransitive or Transitive, and then click Next.

6 On the Direction Of Trust page, shown in Figure 33-13, choose the direction of Trust and then click Next. The following options are available:

- Two-way—Users in the domain initially selected and in the designated domain can access resources in either domain or realm.
- One-way: Incoming—Users in the domain initially selected will be able to access resources in the designated domain. Users in the designated domain will not be able to access resources in the domain initially selected.
- One-way: Outgoing—Users in the designated domain will be able to access resources in the domain initially selected. Users in the domain initially selected will not be able to access resources in the designated domain.

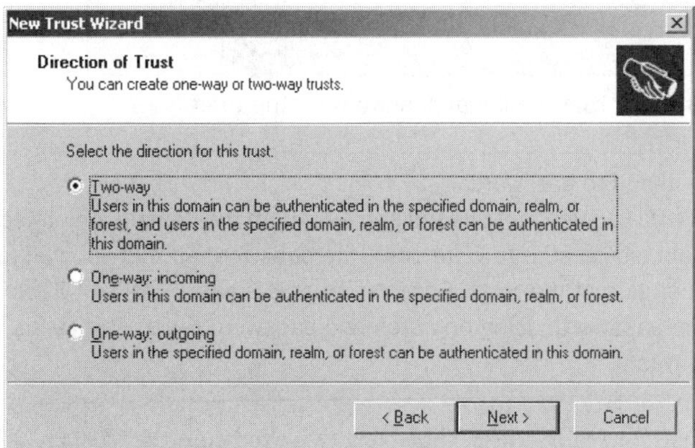

Figure 33-13. Choose the direction of trust.

7 For shortcut or forest trusts, the next page you see is the Sides Of Trust page. To begin using a trust, you must create both sides of the trust. You have the option of setting the sides of the trust for This Domain Only or for Both This Domain And The Specified Domain.

- If you are creating only one side of the trust, select This Domain Only, and then click Next.
- If you are setting both sides of the trust or the administrator from the other domain is at your desk, select Both This Domain And The Specified Domain, and then click Next. When prompted, type, or let the other administrator type, the name and password of an appropriate account in the other domain or forest, and then click OK.

8 On the Trust Password page, shown in Figure 33-14, type and then confirm the initial password you want to use for the trust. The password is arbitrary but must follow the strong security rules, meaning that it must have at least eight characters, contain a combination of upper case and lowercase characters, and contain either numerals or special characters.

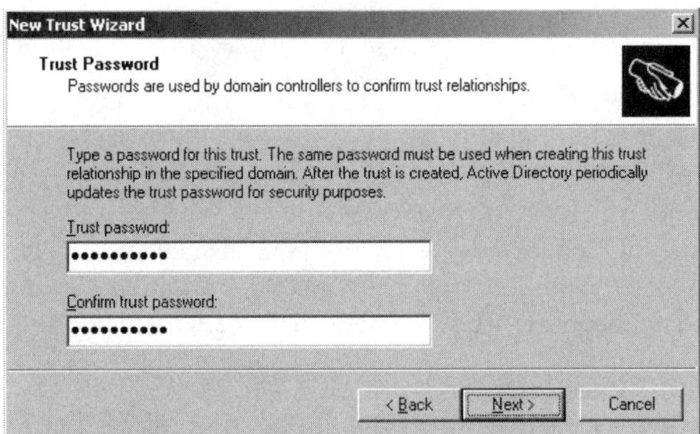

Figure 33-14. Set the initial password for the trust.

Tip **You may need the password**

The trust password you use must be the same for both the domain initially selected and the specified domain, so be sure to write down the password so that you can use it when configuring the other side of the trust. Once the trust is created, Active Directory will periodically update the password, using an automatic password reset. This helps safeguard the integrity of the trust.

9 For domain or realm trusts, click Next twice to begin the trust creation process.

10 For forest trusts, you can set the outgoing trust authentication level as either Domain-Wide Authentication or Selective Authentication. With domain-wide authentication, users in the trusted domain can be authenticated to use all the resources in the trusting domain (and any trusted domains). This means that authentication is automatic for all users. With Selective Authentication, only the users or groups to which you explicitly grant permission can access resources in the trusting domain. This means that authentication is not automatic and you will need to grant individual access to each server that you want to make available to users in the trusting domain. Click Next twice.

11 After the trust is created, you are given the opportunity to verify the trust.

Verifying and Troubleshooting Trusts

By default, Windows validates all incoming trusts automatically. If the credentials used to establish the trust are no longer valid, the trust will fail verification. If you want to revalidate a trust by providing new credentials or to specify that incoming trusts should not be validated, follow these steps:

1. Click Start, choose Programs or All Programs as appropriate, choose Administrative Tools, and then select Active Directory Domains And Trusts.
2. Right-click the trusted domain whose incoming trust you want to verify, and then select Properties.
3. In the domain's Properties dialog box, select the Trust tab, and then click Validate and select one of the following options:
   - If you want to stop validation of the incoming trust, select No, Do Not Validate The Incoming Trust.
   - If you want to revalidate the incoming trust, select Yes, Validate The Incoming Trust, and then type the user account and password for an administrator account in the other (trusting) domain.
4. Click OK. For a two-way trust, repeat this procedure for the other (trusting) domain.

You may want to revalidate trusts or specify that incoming trusts should not be validated for the following reasons:

- If clients are unable to access resources in a domain outside the forest, the external trust between the domains may have failed. In this case, you should verify the trust for the trusted domain. Note that a PDC emulator must be available to reset and verify the external trust.
- If clients cannot connect to a domain controller running Windows 2000, check the service pack level on the domain controller. The Windows 2000 domain controller should be running Service Pack 3 or later. If it isn't, upgrade it.
- If clients or servers get trust errors within an Active Directory forest, there could be several causes. The time on the clients or servers trying to authenticate may be more than five minutes off, which is the default maximum time difference allowed for Kerberos authentication. In this case, synchronize the time on the clients and servers. The problem could also be that the domain controller may be down or the trust relationship could be broken. For the latter case, you can run NETDOM to verify or reset the trust.
- If clients are experiencing trust errors connecting to a Windows NT 4 domain, the automatic password reset for the trust may not have reached the PDC emulator. You can run NETDOM to verify or reset the trust. If this doesn't resolve the problem, see Knowledge Base article 317178 for more information.
- After upgrading a Windows NT 4 domain that has existing trusts with one or more Active Directory domains, you need to delete and recreate all the previously existing

trusts. These trusts are not automatically upgraded from Windows NT 4 trusts. If this doesn't resolve the problem, see Knowledge Base article 275221 for more information.

Delegating Authentication

The delegation of authentication is often a requirement when a network service is distributed across several servers, such as when the organization uses Web-based application services with front-end and back-end servers. In this environment, a client connects to the front-end servers and the user's credentials may need to be passed to back-end servers to ensure that the user only gets access to information to which she has been granted access.

Delegated Authentication Essentials

In Windows 2000, this functionality is provided using Kerberos authentication, either using proxy tickets or using forwarded tickets:

- With proxy tickets, the client sends a session ticket request to a domain controller acting as a KDC, asking for access to the back-end server. The KDC grants the session ticket request and sends the client a session ticket with a PROXIABLE flag set. The client can then send this ticket to the front-end server, and the front-end server in turn uses this ticket to access information on the back-end server. In this configuration, the client needs to know the name of the backend server, which in some cases is problematic, particularly if you need to maintain strict security for the back-end databases and don't want their integrity to be compromised.
- With forwarding tickets, the clients sends an initial authorization request to the KDC, requesting a session ticket that the front-end server will be able to use to access the back-end servers. The KDC grants the session ticket request, and sends it to the client. The client can then send the ticket to the front-end server, which then uses the session ticket to make a network resource request on behalf of the client. The front-end server then gets a session ticket to access the back-end server using the client's credentials.

Note In the Windows 2000 model, the front-end server is not constrained in terms of the network resources it can request on the client's behalf. That means the front-end server could try to access any network resource using the client's credentials.

While both techniques are effective, the requirement to use Kerberos in Windows 2000 limits the types of clients that can be used. In this scenario, only clients running Windows 2000 or later can be used. With Windows Server 2003, you can use both NTLM and Kerberos for authentication, which allows clients running Microsoft Windows 95, Windows 98, and Windows NT to be used, as well as clients running Windows 2000 or later. In addition, with Windows Server 2003, you can use constrained delegation. Constrained delegation allows you to configure accounts so that they are delegated only for specific purposes. This kind of delegation is based on service principal names. Thus, unlike Windows 2000, in which the front-end server can access any network service on the client's behalf, in Windows Server 2003, a front-end server can only access network resources for which delegation has been granted.

Configuring Delegated Authentication

To use delegated authentication, the user account, as well as the service or computer account acting on the user's behalf, must be configured to support delegated authentication.

Configuring the Delegated User Account

For the user account, you must ensure that the account option Account Is Sensitive And Cannot Be Delegated is not selected, which by default it isn't. If you want to check this option, use Active Directory Users And Computers, as shown in the following screen. Double-click the user's account entry in Active Directory Users And Computers, and then select the Account tab. You'll find the Account Is Sensitive And Cannot Be Delegated option under Account Options. Scroll through the list until you find it.

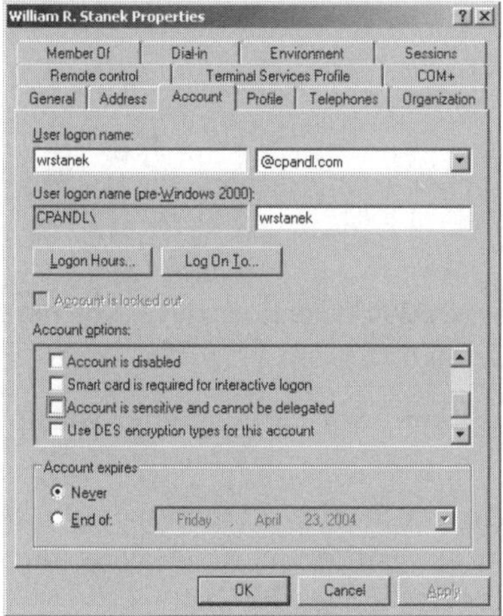

Configuring the Delegated Service or Computer Account

For the service acting on the user's behalf, you must first determine if the service is running under a normal user account or under a special identity, such as LocalSystem. If the service runs under a normal user account, check the account in Active Directory Users And Computers and ensure that the Account Is Sensitive And Cannot Be Delegated option is not selected. If the service runs under a special identity, you need to configure delegation for the computer account of the front-end server.

When the domain is operating in Windows 2000 Mixed or Windows 2000 Native functional level, you have limited options for configuring a computer for delegation. In Active Directory Users and Computers, double-click the computer account. On the General tab, select the Trust This Computer For Delegation option to allow delegation. This option sets the Windows 2000 level of authentication, which allows the service to make requests for any network resources on the client's behalf.

In Active Directory Users And Computers, double-click the computer account to display its Properties dialog box, and then select the Delegation tab, as shown in the following screen:

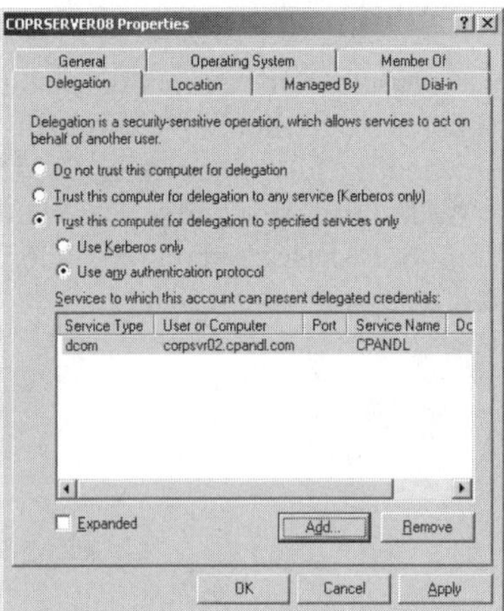

When the domain is operating in Windows Server 2003 functional level, you have the following options for configuring a computer for delegation:

- **Do Not Trust This Computer For Delegation** Select this option if you don't want the computer to be trusted for delegation.
- **Trust This Computer For Delegation To Any Service (Kerberos Only)** Select this option to use the Windows 2000 level of authentication, which allows the service to make requests for any network resources on the client's behalf.
- **Trust This Computer For Delegation To Specified Services Only** Select this option to use the Windows Server 2003 level of authentication, which allows the service to make requests only for specified services. You can then specify whether the client must authenticate using Kerberos only or can use any authentication protocol.

When you are using the Windows Server 2003 level of authentication, you must next specify the services to which the front-end server can present a client's delegated credentials. To do this, you need to know the name of the computers running the services and the types of services you are authorizing. Click Add to display the Add Services dialog box shown in the screen on the following page, and then click Users Or Computers to display the Select Users Or Computers dialog box.

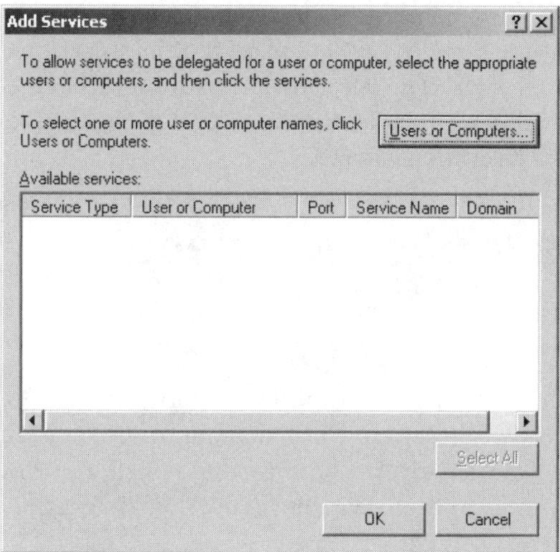

In the Select Users Or Computer dialog box, type the name of the computer proving the service, such as CORPSVR02, and then click Check Names. If multiple matches are found, select the name or names you want to use, and then click OK. If no matches are found, you've either entered an incorrect name or you're working with an incorrect location. Modify the name and try again or click Locations to select a new location. To add additional computers, type a semicolon (;), and then repeat this process. When you click OK, the Add Services dialog box is updated with a list of available services on the selected computer or computers, as shown in the following screen:

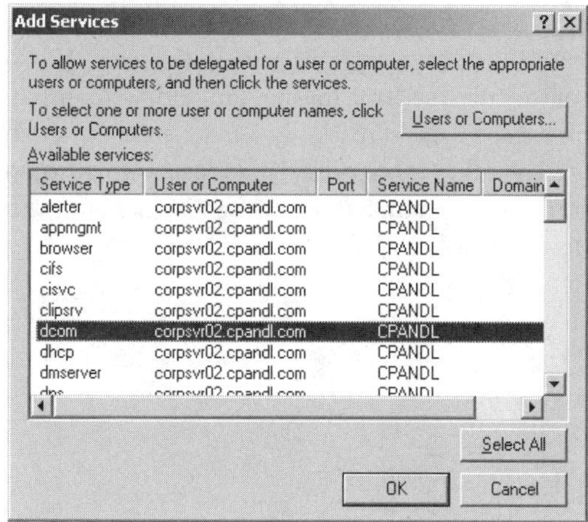

Use the Add Services dialog box to select the services for which you are authorizing delegated authentication. You can use Shift+click or Ctrl+click to select multiple services. Once you've selected the appropriate services, click OK. The selected services are added to the Services To Which This Account Can Present Delegated Credentials list. Click OK to close the computer's Properties dialog box and save the delegation changes.

Design Considerations for Active Directory Operations Masters

Active Directory's multimaster replication model creates a distributed environment that allows any domain controller to be used for authentication and allows changes to be made to standard directory information without regard to which domain controller is used. The approach works well for most Active Directory operations—but not all. Some Active Directory operations can only be performed by a single authoritative domain controller called an *operations master*.

Operations Master Roles

A designated operations master has a flexible single-master operations (FSMO) role. The five designated roles are

- Schema master
- Domain naming master
- Relative ID (RID) master
- PDC emulator
- Infrastructure master

As depicted in Figure 33-15, two of the roles, schema master and domain naming master, are assigned on a per-forest basis. This means that there is only one schema master and only one domain naming master in a forest. The other three roles, RID master, infrastructure master, and PDC emulator, are assigned on a per-domain basis. For each domain in the forest, there is only one of these operations master roles.

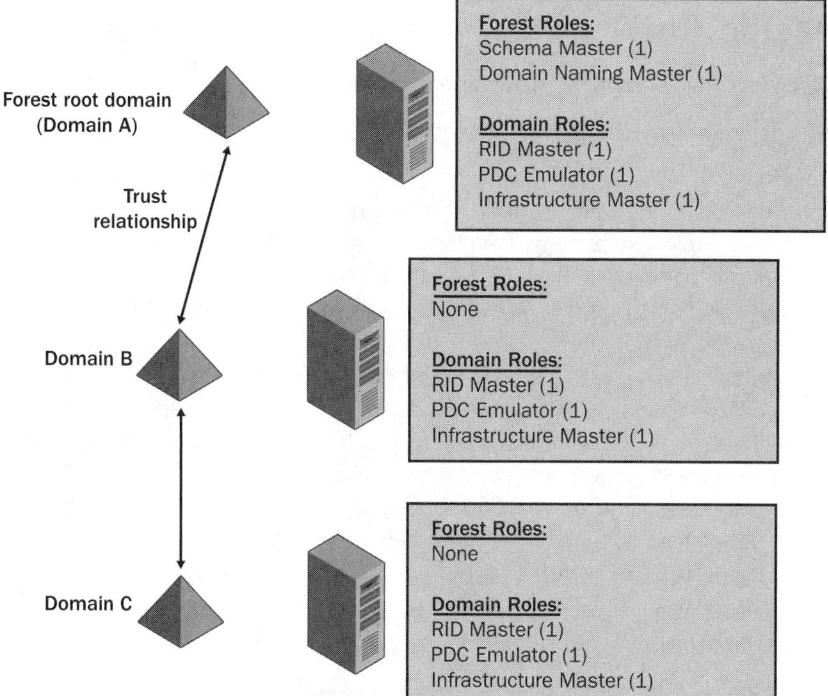

Figure 33-15. Operations masters in forests and domains.

When you install Active Directory and create the first domain controller in a new forest, all five roles are assigned to that domain controller. As you add domains, the first domain controller installed in a domain is automatically designated the RID master, infrastructure master, and PDC emulator for that domain.

As part of domain design, you should consider how many domain controllers you need per domain, and whether you need to transfer operations master roles after you install new domain controllers. In all cases, you'll want to have at least two domain controllers in each domain in the forest. The reasons for transferring the operations master roles depend on several factors. First, you might want to transfer an operations master role to improve performance, as you might do when a server has too heavy a workload and you need to distribute some of the load. Second, you might need to transfer an operations master role if you plan to take the server with that role offline for maintenance or if the server fails.

Inside Out

Recommended placement of operations master roles

Microsoft recommends the following configuration:

- Ideally, the forest-wide roles, schema master and domain naming master, should be placed on the same domain controller. There is very little overhead associated with these roles, so placement on the same server adds very little load overall. However, it is important to safeguard this server, because these are critical roles in the forest. In addition, the server acting as the domain naming master should also be a global catalog server.
- Ideally, the relative ID master and PDC emulator roles should be placed on the same domain controller. The reason for this is that the PDC emulator uses more relative IDs than most other domain controllers. If the relative ID master and PDC emulator roles aren't on the same domain controller, the domain controllers on which they are placed should be in the same Active Directory site, and the domain controllers should have a reliable connection between them.
- Ideally, the infrastructure master should not be placed on a domain controller that is also a global catalog server. The reason for this is a bit complicated, and there are some important exceptions to note.

  The infrastructure master is responsible for updating cross-domain group membership and determines whether its information is current or out of date by checking a global catalog and then replicating changes to other domain controllers as necessary. If the infrastructure master and the global catalog are on the same server, the infrastructure master doesn't see that changes have been made and thus doesn't replicate them.

  The exceptions are for a single-domain forest or a multi-domain forest where all domain controllers are global catalog servers. In the case of a single domain forest, there are no cross-group references to update, so it doesn't matter where the infrastructure master is located. In the case of a multi-domain forest where all domain controllers are global catalog servers, all the domain controllers know about all the objects in the forest already, so the infrastructure master doesn't really have to make updates.

Using, Locating, and Transferring the Schema Master Role

The schema master is the only domain controller in the forest with a writeable copy of the schema container. This means that it is the only domain controller in the forest on which you can make changes to the schema. You make changes to the schema using the Active Directory Schema snap-in. When you start the Active Directory Schema snap-in, it makes a direct connection to the schema master, allowing you to view the schema for the directory.

To make changes to the schema, however, you must use an account that is a member of the Schema Admins group.

By default, the schema master is the first domain controller installed in the forest root domain. This role can be transferred using the Active Directory Schema snap-in or the NTDSUTIL command-line utility.

To locate the schema master, open the Active Directory Schema snap-in in a custom console. Right-click the Active Directory Schema node, and then select Operations Master. The Change Schema Master dialog box, shown in the following screen, shows the current schema master:

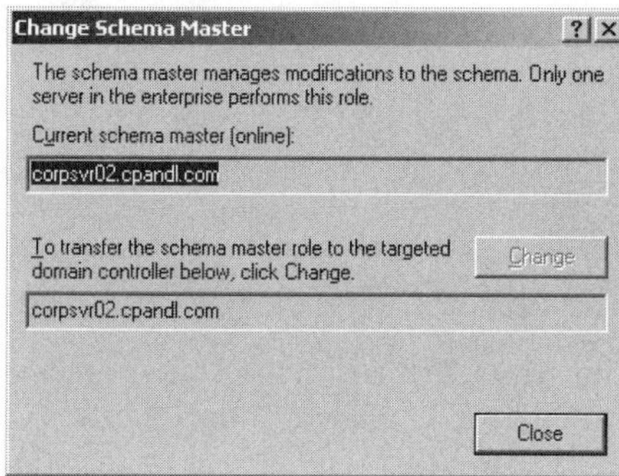

To transfer the schema master role to another server, follow these steps:

1. Open the Active Directory Schema snap-in in a custom console. Right-click the Active Directory Schema node, and then select Change Domain Controller.
2. In the Change Domain Controller dialog box, type the fully qualified domain name of the domain controller to which you want to transfer the schema master role, and then click OK.
3. Right-click the Active Directory Schema node, and then select Operations Master. In the Change Schema Master dialog box, click Change, and then click Close.

Using, Locating, and Transferring the Domain Naming Master Role

The domain naming master is responsible for adding or removing domains from the forest. Any time you create a domain, a Remote Procedure Call (RPC) connection is made to the domain naming master, which assigns the domain a globally unique identifier (GUID). Any time you remove a domain, an RPC connection is made to the domain naming master and the previously assigned GUID reference is removed. If you cannot connect to the domain naming master when you are trying to add or remove a domain, you will not be able to create or remove the domain.

To locate the domain naming master, start Active Directory Domains And Trusts. Right-click the Active Directory Domains And Trusts node, and then select Operations Master. The Change Operations Master dialog box, shown in the following screen, shows the current domain naming master:

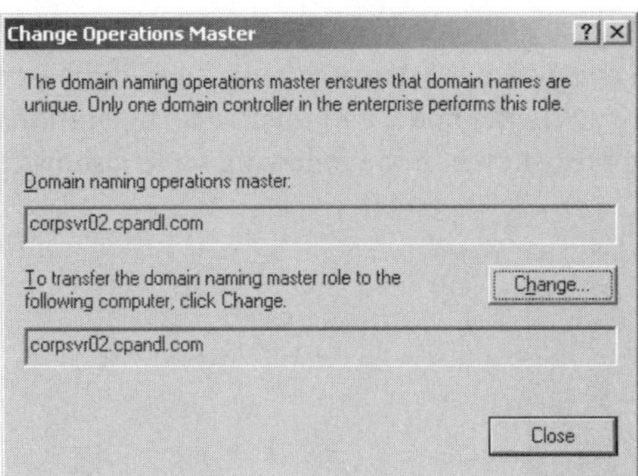

To transfer the domain naming master role to another server, follow these steps:

1. Start Active Directory Domains And Trusts. Right-click the Active Directory Domains And Trusts node, and then select Connect To Domain Controller.
2. In the Connect To Domain Controller dialog box, type the forest root domain name in the Domain Name field, and then press Tab. Select an available domain controller to which you want to transfer the role, and then click OK.
3. Right-click the Active Directory Domains And Trusts node, and then select Operations Master. In the Change Operations Master dialog box, click Change, and then click Close.

Using, Locating, and Transferring the Relative ID Master Role

The relative ID (RID) master controls the creation of new security principals such as users, groups, and computers throughout its related domain. Every domain controller in a domain is issued a block of relative IDs by the RID master. These relative IDs are used to build the security IDs that uniquely identify security principals in the domain. The actual security ID generated by a domain controller consists of a domain identifier, which is the same for every object in a domain, and a unique relative ID that differentiates the object from any other objects in the domain.

The block of relative IDs issued to a domain controller is called a RID pool. Typically, blocks of relative IDs are issued in lots of 10,000. When the RID pool on a domain controller is nearly exhausted, the domain controller requests a new block of 10,000 RIDs. It is the job of the RID master to issue blocks of RIDs and it does so as long as it is up and running. If a domain controller cannot connect to the RID master and for any reason runs outs of RIDs, no new objects can be created on the domain controller and object creation will fail. To resolve this problem, the RID master must be made available or the RID master role must be transferred to another server.

To locate the RID master, start Active Directory Users And Computers. Right-click the domain you want to work with, and then select Operations Masters. The Operations Masters dialog box, shown in the following screen, shows the current RID master on the RID tab:

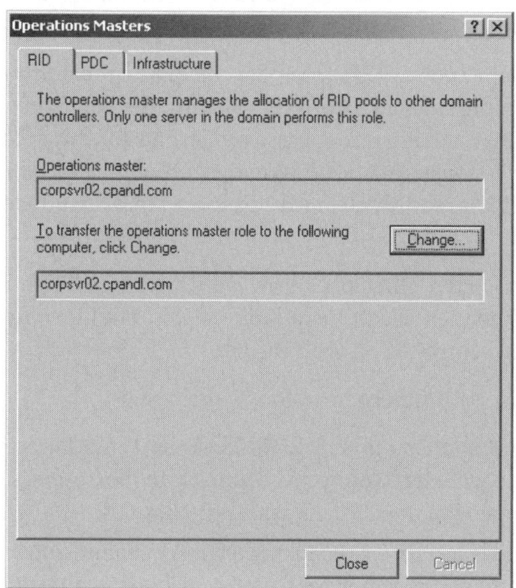

To transfer the RID master role to another server, follow these steps:

1. Start Active Directory Users And Computers. Right-click the Active Directory Users And Computers node, and then select Connect To Domain. In the Connect To Domain dialog box, type the DNS name of the domain, and then click OK.
2. Right-click the domain node, and then select Connect To Domain Controller. In the Connect To Domain Controller dialog box, select an available domain controller to which you want to transfer the role, and then click OK.
3. Right-click the domain node again, and then select Operations Masters. In the Operations Masters dialog box, the RID tab is selected by default. Click Change, and then click Close.

Using, Locating, and Transferring the PDC Emulator Role

The PDC emulator role is required for Windows Server 2003 to coexist with Windows NT 4 domain controllers. In a domain using the Windows 2000 mixed or Windows Server 2003 interim functional level, the Windows Server 2003 domain controller with this role acts as the primary domain controller (PDC) for all Windows NT 4 backup domain controllers

(BDCs). In these environments, the job of the PDC emulator is to authenticate Windows NT logons, process password changes, and replicate domain changes to BDCs. It also runs the domain master browser service.

In a domain using the Windows 2000 native or Windows Server 2003 functional level, the Windows Server 2003 domain controller with this role is still responsible for processing password changes. When a user changes a password, the change is first sent to the PDC emulator, which in turn replicates the change to all the other domain controllers in the domain.

All domain controllers in a domain know which server has the PDC emulator role. If a user tries to log on to the network but provides an incorrect password, the domain controller checks the PDC emulator to see that it has a recent password change for this account. If so, the domain controller retries the logon authentication on the PDC emulator. This approach is designed to ensure that if a user has recently changed a password they are not denied logon with the new password.

To locate the PDC emulator, start Active Directory Users And Computers. Right-click the domain you want to work with, and then select Operations Masters. The Operations Masters dialog box shows the current PDC emulator on the PDC tab.

To transfer the PDC emulator role to another server, follow these steps:

1. Start Active Directory Users And Computers. Right-click the Active Directory Users And Computers node, and then select Connect To Domain. In the Connect To Domain dialog box, type the DNS name of the domain, and then click OK.
2. Right-click the domain node, and then select Connect To Domain Controller. In the Connect To Domain Controller dialog box, select an available domain controller to which you want to transfer the role, and then click OK.
3. Right-click the domain node again, and then select Operations Master. In the Operations Masters dialog box, select the PDC tab. Click Change, and then click Close.

Using, Locating, and Transferring the Infrastructure Master Role

The infrastructure master is responsible for updating cross-domain group-to-user references. This means that the infrastructure master is responsible for ensuring that changes to the common name of a user account are correctly reflected in the group membership information for groups in other domains in the forest. The infrastructure master does this by comparing its directory data to that of a global catalog. If the data is outdated, it updates the data and replicates the changes to other domain controllers in the domain. If for some reason the infrastructure master is unavailable, group-to-user name references will not be updated, and cross-domain group membership may not accurately reflect the actual names of user objects.

To locate the infrastructure master, start Active Directory Users And Computers. Right-click the domain you want to work with, and then select Operations Masters. The Operations Masters dialog box shows the current infrastructure master on the Infrastructure tab.

To transfer the infrastructure master role to another server, follow these steps:

1. Start Active Directory Users And Computers. Right-click the Active Directory Users And Computers node, and then select Connect To Domain. In the Connect To Domain dialog box, type the DNS name of the domain, and then click OK.
2. Right-click the domain node, and then select Connect To Domain Controller. In the Connect To Domain Controller dialog box, select an available domain controller to which you want to transfer the role, and then click OK.
3. Right-click the domain node again, and then select Operations Masters. In the Operations Masters dialog box, select the Infrastructure tab. Click Change, and then click Close.

Chapter 34

Organizing Active Directory

Whether you are implementing a new Active Directory environment or updating your existing environment, there's a lot to think about when it comes to design. Every Active Directory design is built from the same basic building blocks. These basic building blocks include the following:

- **Domains** A domain is a logical grouping of objects that allows central management and control over replication of those objects. Every organization has at least one domain, which is implemented when Active Directory is installed on the first domain controller.
- **Domain Trees** A domain tree is a single domain in a unique namespace or a group of domains that share the same namespace. The domain at the top of a domain tree is referred to as the *root domain*. Two-way transitive trusts join parent and child domains in the same domain tree.
- **Forests** A forest is a single domain tree or a group of domain trees that are grouped together to share resources. The first domain created in a new forest is referred to as the forest root domain. Domain trees in a forest have two-way transitive trusts between their root domains.

Many organizations have only one domain and while I'll discuss reasons why you might want to have additional domains, domain trees, and forests in this chapter, you might also want to add structure to a domain. The building block you use to add structure to a domain is the organizational unit (OU), which I'll discuss in depth in this chapter.

Creating an Active Directory Implementation or Update Plan

Creating or modifying an existing domain and forest plan is the single most important design decision you will make when implementing Active Directory. As such, this isn't a decision you should make alone. When you design Active Directory for an organization of any size, you should get the organization's management involved in the high-level design process.

Involvement doesn't mean letting other groups decide on all aspects of the design. There are many complex components that all have to fit together, and the actual implementation of Active Directory should be the responsibility of the IT group. Involvement means getting feedback from and working with the business managers of other groups to ensure that the high-level design meets their business requirements.

In addition, you will almost certainly need to get approval of the high-level design goals with regard to security, access, usability, and manageability. Plan for this as you are developing the initial implementation plan. Your plan should start with the highest-level objects and work toward the lowest-level objects. This means that you must do the following:

1. Develop a forest plan
2. Develop a domain plan that supports the forest plan
3. Develop an organizational unit plan that supports the domain and forest plan

The sections that follow discuss how to develop the necessary plans. Once you have completed the planning and the plans are approved, you can implement the plan.

Developing a Forest Plan

Forest planning involves developing a plan for the namespace and administration needs of the organization as a whole. As part of this planning, you should decide who are the owners of the forest or forests implemented. From an administration standpoint, the owners of a forest are the users who are the members of the Schema Admins and Enterprise Admins groups of the forest as well as users who are members of the Domains Admins group in the root domain of the forest. Although these users have direct control over the forest structure, they typically don't make the final decisions when it comes to implementing forest-wide changes. Typically, the final authority for making forest-wide changes is an IT or business manager who is requesting changes based on a specific business need or requirement and acting after coordinating with business managers from other groups as necessary.

Forest Namespace

The top structure in any Active Directory implementation is the forest root domain. The forest root domain is established when you install Active Directory on the first domain controller in a new forest. Any time you add a new domain that is part of a different namespace to an existing forest, you establish a root domain for a new tree. The name given to a root domain—either the forest root domain itself or the root domain of a new tree in a forest—acts as the base name for all domains later created in that tree. As you add subsequent domains, the domains are added below an established root domain. This makes the domains child domains of a root domain (see Figure 34-1).

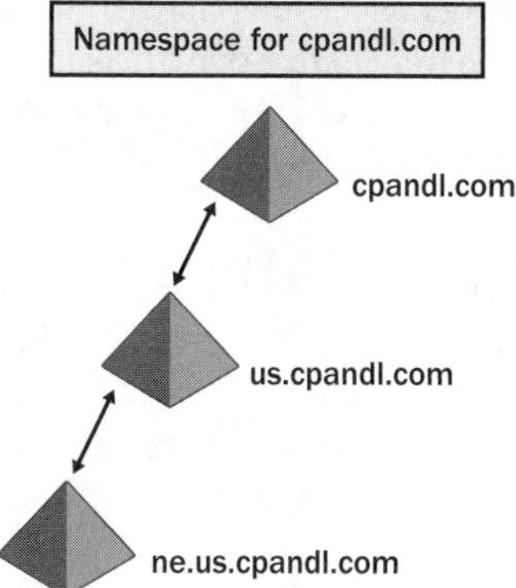

Figure 34-1. A hierarchy of domains.

Regardless of whether your forest uses a single namespace or multiple namespaces, additional domains in the same forest have the following characteristics:

- **Share a common schema** All domain controllers in the forest have the same schema and a single schema master is designated for the forest.
- **Share a common configuration directory partition** All domain controllers share the same configuration container, and it stores the default configuration and policy information.
- **Share a common trust configuration** All domains in the forest are configured to trust all the other domains in the forest, and the trust is two-way and transitive.
- **Share a common global catalog** All domains in the forest have the same global catalog, and it stores a partial replica of all objects in the forest.
- **Share common forest-wide administrators** All domains in the forest have the same top-level administrators: Enterprise Admins and Schema Admins, who have the following roles.
  - Enterprise Admins are the only administrators with forest-level privileges, which let them add or remove domains. The Enterprise Admins group is also a member of the local Administrators group of each domain, so, by default, these users can manage any domain in the forest.
  - Schema Admins are the only administrators who have the right to modify the schema.

Single vs. Multiple Forests

Part of creating a forest plan is deciding how many forests you will need or whether you need additional forests. This isn't an easy decision or a decision that should be made lightly. With a single forest, you have a single top-level unit for sharing and managing resources. You can share information across all domains in the forest. However, this requires a great deal of trust and cooperation among all the groups in the organization.

With multiple forests you change the dynamic considerably. You no longer have a single top-level unit for sharing and managing resources. You have separate structures that are fully autonomous and isolated from one another. The forests do not share schema, configuration information, trusts, global catalogs, or forest-wide administrators. If desired, you can join the forests with a cross-forest trust.

Should you decide to implement a cross-forest trust between the forests, you can control whether a trust is one-way or two-way and the trust authentication level. Unlike inter-forest trusts, which are two-way and transitive by default, cross-forest trusts are either two-way or one-way. With a two-way trust, users in either forest have access to resources in the other forest. With a one-way trust, users in one forest have access to resources in the other forest but not vice versa.

The trust authentication level is set on outgoing trusts and is either domain-wide or selective. Domain-wide authentication is open and implies a certain level of trust as users in the trusted forest can be authenticated to use all of the resources in the trusting forest. Selective authentication is closed and more secure, because only the users or groups to which you explicitly grant permission can access resources in the trusting domain.

Tip **Consider the size of the organization**

You should consider the size of the organization when deciding forest structure. However, the size of an organization alone is not a reason for deploying multiple forests. A forest can contain multiple domains. The domains can be deployed in multiple namespaces. Each domain is a separate unit of administration and each domain can have millions of objects.

Inside Out

Geographically separated sites

Geographically separated business units may want completely separate forests or domains. Although there may be business reasons for this, the decision should not be made based on perceived limitations in Active Directory. As long as a connection can be made between locations, there is no need for separate forests or domains. Active Directory sites provide the solution for connecting across limited bandwidth links. With the automatic compression feature for site bridgehead servers, replication traffic is compressed 85 to 90 percent, meaning that it is 10 to 15 percent of its non-compressed size. This means that even low bandwidth links can often be used effectively for replication. For more information on sites, see Chapter 35, "Configuring Active Directory Sites and Replication."

Forest Administration

Most companies opt to deploy a single forest, and it is only through merger or acquisition that additional forests enter the picture. In part, this is because there is no easy way to merge forests if you decide to do so later: You must migrate objects from one forest to the other, which can be a very long process. For this and other reasons, you should decide from the start how many forests are going to be implemented and you should justify the need for each additional forest. Sometimes additional forests are deployed because of organizational politics or the inability of business units to decide how to manage the top-level forest functions. At other times, additional forests are deployed to isolate business units or give complete control of the directory to a business unit.

The organization should consider the following factors before creating additional forests:

- Additional forests make it more difficult for users to collaborate and share information. For example, users have direct access to the global catalog and can search for resources easily only for their own forest. Access to resources in other forests must be configured, and the users will not be able to directly search for available resources in other forests.
- Additional forests mean additional administrative overheard and duplication of infrastructure. Each forest will have its own forest-level configuration and one or more additional domain-level configurations that need to be managed. The ability to share resources and synchronize information across forests must be specifically configured rather than implemented by using built-in trusts and synchronization.

Sometimes, however, the additional controls put in place with additional forests are needed to give reasonable assurance that administrators from other domains in a forest do not make harmful changes to the directory, which are then replicated throughout the organization. All the domain controllers in a forest are tightly integrated. A change made on one domain controller will be replicated to all other domain controllers. Replication is automatic, and there are no security checks other than the fact that the person making the change must have the appropriate permissions in the first place, that is, the person must be a member of the appropriate administrator group for the type of change being made. If such an administrator is acting maliciously in making changes, those changes will be replicated regardless of the effect on the organization.

That said, reasonable assurance can be addressed by putting strict administration rules and procedures in place. With strict rules and procedures, the organization will have the following multiple levels of administrators:

- Top-level administrators with enterprise-wide privileges who are trusted with forest-wide administration. These administrators are members of the Enterprise Admins group.
- High-level administrators with domain-wide privileges who are trusted with domain-wide administration. These administrators are members of the Domain Admins, Administrators, Server Operators, or Backup Operators groups.

- Administrators who are delegated responsibilities for specific tasks, which might include being a member of the Server Operators, Backup Operators, or similar groups.

To give reasonable assurance, the organization will also need to physically secure domain controllers, set policies about how administrators use their accounts, such as running tasks as an administrator only when needed for administration, and configure auditing of all actions performed by both users and administrators.

Developing a Domain Plan

Once you determine how many forests are needed based on the current namespace and administration needs of the organization as a whole, you next need to determine the domain structure that needs to be implemented. Whether your organization has an existing Active Directory structure or is implementing Active Directory for the first time, this means assessing the current environment and determining what changes are needed.

You will need to thoroughly document the existing infrastructure and determine what—if anything—needs to be restructured, replaced, or upgraded. You will also need to determine if it is even possible or practical to update the existing infrastructure as proposed. In some cases, you may find that current design is not ideal for updating as proposed and you may need to revise your plans.

That's all acceptable, because design is usually an iterative process in which you go from the theoretical to the practical during successive revisions. Just remember that it is difficult to change the domain namespace as well as the number of forests and domains once you've started implementing the design. Other parts of a design, such as the OU and site structure, are easier to change after implementation.

Note For tips and techniques on naming domains and establishing a naming hierarchy, see Chapter 26, "Architecting DNS Infrastructure." You'll also find detailed information on using DNS (Domain Name System) with Active Directory in Chapter 27, "Implementing and Managing DNS."

Domain Design Considerations

Domains allow you to logically group objects for central management and control over replication of those objects. You use domains to partition a forest into smaller components. As part of domain design, you should consider the following:

- **Replication** Domains set the replication boundary for the domain directory partition and for domain policy information stored in the Sysvol folder on every domain controller in the domain. Any changes made to the domain directory partition or domain policy information on one of the domain controllers is replicated automatically to the other domain controllers in the domain. Although other directory partitions, such as the schema and configuration, are replicated throughout a forest, the domain information is only replicated within a particular domain, and the more objects in the domain container, the more data that potentially needs to be replicated.

- **Resource access** The trusts between and among domains in a forest do not by themselves grant permission to access resources. A user must be specifically given permission to access a resource in another domain. By default, an administrator of a domain can only manage resources in that domain and cannot manage resources in another domain. This means that domain boundaries are also boundaries for resource access and administration.
- **Policy** The policies that apply to one domain are independent from those applied to other domains. This means that policies for user and computer configuration and security can be applied differently in different domains. Certain policies can be applied only at the domain level. These policies, referred to as *domain security policies*, include password policies, account lockout policies, and Kerberos policies, and are applied to all domain accounts.
- **Language** For organizations in which multiple languages are used, servers within a domain should all be configured with the same language. Although English is supported by all installations, any additional language should be the same on all servers within a domain. This is a consideration for administration purposes but not a requirement.

Single vs. Multiple Domains

With domain design, part of the decision involves the number of domains that are needed. You may need to implement additional domains or continue using a single domain. A single domain is the easiest to manage. It is also the ideal environment for users, because it is easier for users to locate resources in a single domain environment than in a multi-domain or multi-tree forest.

Inside Out

Moving from Windows NT

For most companies moving from Microsoft Windows NT domains, you can implement Active Directory domains with fewer domains, a process known as domain consolidation. Windows NT imposes less than ideal limits on the number of objects you can have in a domain, which forces many organizations to have multiple domains. As a result, organizations using Windows NT domains often have separate user account domains and resource domains. This is not the case with Active Directory. With Active Directory, you can have millions of objects in a single domain, so the reason for using multiple domains is not based solely on the number of objects—although the number of objects is certainly still a factor to consider from a manageability standpoint. It is important to note that when you are upgrading from Windows NT with a multiple-domain environment, you typically keep the existing domain infrastructure until after the upgrade. When you finish upgrading, you can then merge the additional domains so that there are fewer domains.

Beyond simplicity, there are several other reasons for implementing or keeping to a single domain design, such as the following:

- You do not need to create additional domains to limit administrative access, delegate control, or create a hierarchical structure. In Active Directory, you can use OUs for these purposes.
- You may want to make authentication and resource access easier to configure and less prone to problems. A single domain doesn't have to rely on trusts or the assignment of resource access in other domains.
- You may want to make domain structure easier to manage. A single domain only has one set of domain administrators and one set of domain policy. A single domain doesn't need duplicate domain-wide infrastructure for domain controllers.
- Your organization may frequently restructure its business units. It is easy to rename OUs, but very difficult to rename domains. It is easy to move accounts and resources between OUs, but much more difficult to move accounts and resources between domains.

That said, using multiple domains sometimes make sense, particularly if your organization has multiple business locations. With multiple locations, domain changes need to be replicated to all domain controllers and geographic separation is often—but not always—a key factor in deciding to use multiple domains. Primarily, this is because there is less replication traffic between domains than within domains (relatively speaking), and if business locations are geographically separated, it makes sense to limit the replication traffic between locations if possible.

The need to limit replication traffic is a key reason for using multiple domains even within a single business location. For example, a large organization with groups of users spread out over several floors of a building or in multiple buildings in a campus setting may find that the connection speed between locations isn't adequate. In this case, using multiple domains may make sense, because it will limit the scope of updates that initiate replication of changes.

Restricting access to resources and the need to enforce different sets of security policies are also reasons for using multiple domains. Using multiple domains creates boundaries for resource access and administration. It also creates boundaries for security policy. So, if you need to limit resource access or tighten security controls for both users and administrators, you will probably want to use multiple domains.

Like additional forests, multiple domains require additional administrative and infrastructure overhead. Each domain will have its own domain-level configuration, which will require server hardware and administrators to manage that hardware. Because users may be accessing, authenticating, and accessing resources across trusts, there is more complexity and there are more points of failure.

Forest Root Domain Design Configurations

The forest root domain can be either a dedicated root or a non-dedicated root. A dedicated root, also referred to as an *empty root*, is used as a placeholder to start the directory. No user or group accounts are associated with it other than accounts created when the forest root is installed and accounts that are needed to manage the forest. Because no additional user or group accounts are associated with it, a dedicated root domain is not used to assign access to resources. A non-dedicated root is used as a normal part of the directory. It has user and group accounts associated with it and is used to assign access to resources.

For an organization that is going to use multiple domains anyway, using a dedicated root domain makes a lot of sense. The forest root domain contains the forest-wide administrator accounts (Enterprise Admins and Schema Admins) and the forest-wide operations masters (domain naming master and schema master). It must be available when users log on to domains other than their home domain and when users access resources in other domains.

A dedicated root domain is easier to manage than a root domain that contains accounts. It allows you to separate the root domain from the rest of the forest. The separation also helps safeguard the entire directory, which is important, as the forest root domain cannot be replaced. If the root domain is destroyed and cannot be recovered, you must recreate the entire forest.

Changing Domain Design

Ideally, after you implement a domain structure, the domain names will never need to change. In the real world, however, things change. Organizations change their names, merge with other companies, are acquired, or restructure more often than we'd like. With Active Directory, you have several options for changing structure. If you find that you need to move a large number of objects from one domain to another, you can use the migration techniques discussed in Chapter 9, "Migrating to Windows Server 2003." You can rename domains as long as the forest is running at the Windows Server 2003 functional level. Changing the domain design after implementation is difficult, however, and involves using the Domain Rename utility (Rendom.exe), which is provided on the CD-ROM that accompanies this book.

You can rename domains in the following key ways:

- Rename domains to move them within a domain tree. For example, you could rename a child domain from eng.it.cohowinery.com to eng.cohowinery.com.
- Rename domains so that a new tree is created. For example, you could change the name of a child domain from vineyard.cohowinery.com to cohovineyard.com.
- Rename domains to move them to a new tree. For example, you could change the name of a child domain from it.cohowinery.com to it.cohovineyard.com.

- Rename domains to set new domain names without changing the parent-child structure. For example, if the company name changes from Coho Vineyard to Coho Winery, you could change the existing domain names to use cohowinery.com instead of cohovineyard.com.

You *cannot* use the Domain Rename utility to change which domain is the forest root domain. Although you *can* change the name of the forest root domain so that it is no longer the forest root logically, the domain will remain the forest root domain physically in Active Directory. It will still contain the forest-wide administrator accounts (Enterprise Admins and Schema Admins) and the forest-wide operations masters (domain naming master and schema master). This occurs because there is no way to change the forest root domain assignment within Active Directory once the forest root has been established.

You cannot use Domain Rename to make changes to a domain in which Microsoft Exchange 2000 is deployed. Exchange 2000 does not have its own directory service functionality. It uses Active Directory for this purpose.

On the CD-ROM that accompanies this book, you'll find a step-by-step guide for implementing Domain Rename. As you might imagine, renaming a domain in a single-domain forest is the easiest renaming operation. As you increase the number of domains within a forest, you increase the complexity of the Domain Rename operation. Regardless of how many domains you are working with, you should always plan the project completely from start to finish and back up the entire domain infrastructure before trying to implement Domain Rename.

The reason for this planning and backup is that when you rename domains, even if you rename only one domain in a forest of many domains, you will need to make a change to every domain controller in the forest so that it recognizes the renamed domain. When you are finished, you will need to reboot each domain controller. If you don't perform the rename change on every domain controller, you will need to remove from service the domain controllers that did not get the updates. Furthermore, from the time you start the rename operation to the time you reboot domain controllers, the forest will be out of service.

To complete the process after renaming a domain and updating domain controllers, each workstation or member server in the renamed domain will need to be rebooted twice. Any computers running Windows NT 4 in the renamed domain will need to be unjoined from the domain and then rejoined to the domain. While you are working with domain controllers and other computers that don't use Dynamic Host Configuration Protocol (DHCP) in the renamed domain, you should rename the computer so the DNS name is correct and make other DNS name changes as appropriate.

Developing an Organizational Unit Plan

So far in this book, I've discussed domains, domain trees, and forests. These are the components of Active Directory that can help you scale the directory to meet the needs of any organization regardless of its size. Sometimes, however, what you want to do is not scale the directory but create hierarchical structures that represent parts of the organization or to limit or delegate administrative access for a part of the organization. This is where OUs come in handy.

Using Organizational Units (OUs)

An *organizational unit* (OU) is a logical administrative unit that is used to group objects within a domain. Within a domain, OUs can be used to delegate administrator privileges while limiting administrative access and to create a hierarchy that mirrors the business's structure or functions. So rather than having multiple domains to represent the structure of the organization or its business functions, you can create OUs within a domain to do this.

At its most basic level, an OU is a container for objects that can contain other OUs as well as the following objects:

- Computers
- Contacts
- Groups
- inetOrgPerson
- Printers
- Shared Folders
- Users

Note OUs are used to contain objects within a domain. They cannot, however, contain objects from other domains.

Tip An inetOrgPerson object is used to represent user accounts that have been migrated from other directory services. Except for having a different object name, inetOrgPerson objects are managed the same way as user objects.

For administrative purposes, OUs can be used in two key ways. First, you can use OUs to delegate administrative rights. This allows you to give someone limited or full administrative control over only a part of a domain. For example, if you have a branch office, you could create an OU for all the accounts and resources at that office, and then delegate administration of that OU to the local administrator.

Second, you can use OUs to manage a group of objects as a single unit. Unlike domains, OUs are not a part of DNS structure. Within Active Directory, OUs are seen as container objects that are part of a domain. In the directory tree, they are referenced with the OU= identifier, such as OU=Sales for an OU named Sales. The distinguished name (DN) of an OU includes the path to its parent as well as its relative name. As you may recall, the DC= identifier is used to reference domain components. This means that the Sales OU in the cpandl.com domain has a DN of OU=Sales,DC=cpandl,DC=com.

Because OUs can contain other OUs, you can have multiple levels of OUs. For example, if you had a USA OU and a Europe OU within the Sales OU, the DNs of these OUs would be OU=USA,OU=Sales,DC=cpandl,DC=com and OU=Europe,OU=Sales,DC=cpandl, DC=com, respectively. When you nest OUs in this way, the nested OUs inherit the Group Policy settings of the top-level OUs by default, but you can override inheritance if you want to use unique Group Policy settings for a particular OU.

From a user perspective, OUs are fairly transparent. As OUs aren't a part of DNS structure, users don't have to reference OUs when they log on, during authentication, or for searches of Active Directory. This makes multiple OUs much easier to work with than multiple domains. Also, it is fairly easy to change the names and structures of OUs, which isn't the case with domains.

Using OUs for Delegation

Although you will want to centrally manage Active Directory structure, many other administrative tasks related to Active Directory can be delegated to specific groups or individuals. Delegating administrative rights allows a user to perform a set of assigned administrative tasks for a specific OU. The tasks allowed depend on the way you configure delegation and include allowing an individual to perform the following actions:

- Create, delete, and manage accounts
- Reset user passwords and force password changes at next logon
- Read all user information
- Create, delete, and manage groups
- Modify the membership of a group
- Manage Group Policy links
- Generate Resultant Set of Policy

One of the common reasons for delegating administrative rights is to allow an individual in a department or business unit to reset user passwords. When you delegate this right, you allow a trusted person to change someone's password should the need arise. As the right is delegated to a user within a particular OU, this right is limited to that specific OU. In many organizations, this type of right is granted to Help Desk staff to allow them to reset passwords while preventing the Help Desk staff from changing other account properties.

Using OUs for Group Policy

Group Policy allows you to specify a set of rules for computer and user configuration settings. These rules control the working environment for computers and users. Although I'll discuss Group Policy in depth in Chapter 37, "Managing Users, Groups, and Computers," the important thing to know about Group Policy is that you can use it to set default options, to limit options, and to prevent changing options in virtually every aspect of computer and user configuration.

Every domain you create has a default Group Policy rule set, referred to as the *Default Domain Policy.* Group Policy can also be applied to OUs, which makes OUs important in helping administrators manage groups of accounts and resources in a particular way. By default, OUs inherit the Group Policy settings of their parent object. For top-level OUs within a domain, this means that the Default Domain Policy is inherited by default. For lower-level OUs, this means that the OUs inherit the Group Policy of the OUs above them (and if the higher-level OUs inherit Group Policy from the domain, so do the lower-level OUs).

To manage Group Policy, you can use the Group Policy Object Editor or the Group Policy Management Console. Group Policy is a very important part of Active Directory. Not only can you use it to manage the functionality available to users, you can also use it to enforce security, standardize desktop configuration, install software, specify scripts that should be run when a computer starts or shuts down and when a user logs on or logs off, and so on.

Because Group Policy is so important in Active Directory, you should plan your OU structure with Group Policy in mind. You do this by grouping objects that require the same Group Policy settings. For example, if a group of users requires a specific environment configuration to use an application or if a group of users requires a standard set of mapped drives, you can configure this through Group Policy.

Creating an OU Design

OUs simplify administration by organizing accounts and resources in ways that best fit the organizational structure. When designing OU structure, you should plan the structure before you try to implement it. Often you'll find that you need multiple levels of OUs. This is fine. The levels of OUs will form a hierarchy, much like the hierarchy formed when you use multiple levels of domains. The key thing to understand about any OU design is that it is really for administrators. As such, the design needs to be meaningful for your organization's administrators—and ideally, it should help make administration easier.

Creating a good OU design isn't always as easy as it seems. It is a good idea to go through several possible scenarios on paper before trying to implement a design. Through successive revisions on paper, you should be able to improve the design substantially. Common design models for OUs are discussed in the sections that follow.

OU Design: Division or Business Unit Model

With a division or business unit model, you use OUs to reflect the department structure within the organization. The advantage to this model is that users will know and understand it. The disadvantage to this model is that when the company restructures, you may need to redesign the OU structure.

In the example shown in Figure 34-2, OUs are organized by department within the company, and, to allow for separate controls for accounts and resources, the related objects are put in second-level OUs. If you want to only have one level of OUs, you could do this by putting all the objects in the top-level OU.

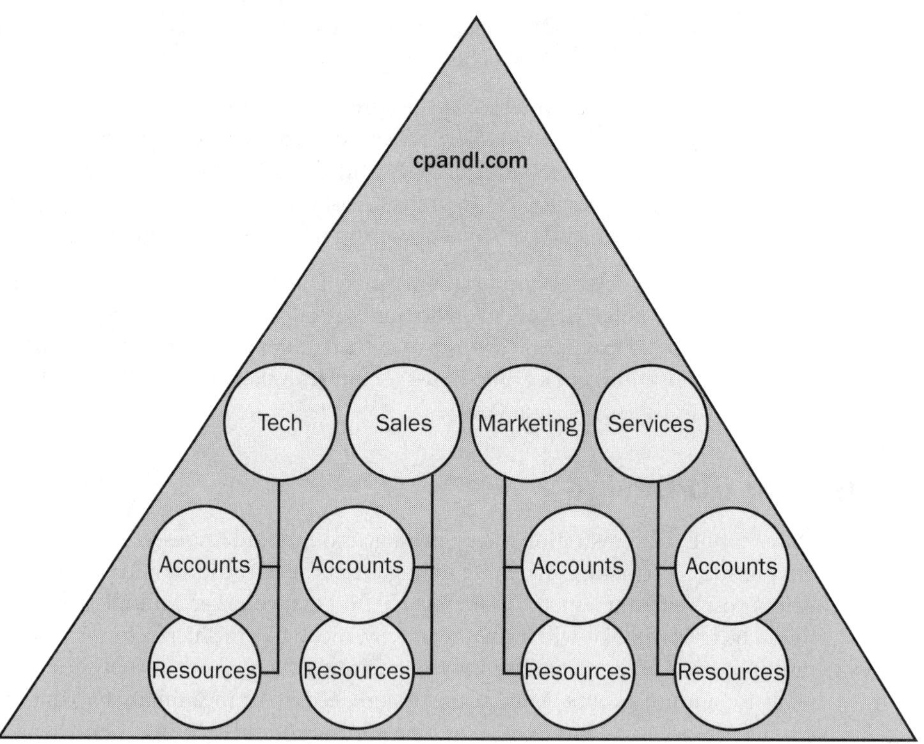

Figure 34-2. The division or business unit model.

OU Design: Geographic Model

With a geographic model, you use OUs to reflect geographic location. In this model, top-level OUs represent the largest geographic units, such as continents, and the lower-level OUs represent successively smaller geographic units, such as countries (see Figure 34-3).

There are several advantages to this model. A geographic structure is fairly stable. Many companies reorganize internally frequently, but only rarely change geographic structure. Additionally, when you use a geographic model, it is easy to determine where accounts and resources are physically located.

The disadvantages to this model have to do with its scope. For a global company, this design would put all accounts and resources in a single domain. As a result, changes made to Active Directory at any location would be replicated to every office location. Additionally, the OU structure doesn't relate to the business structure of the organization.

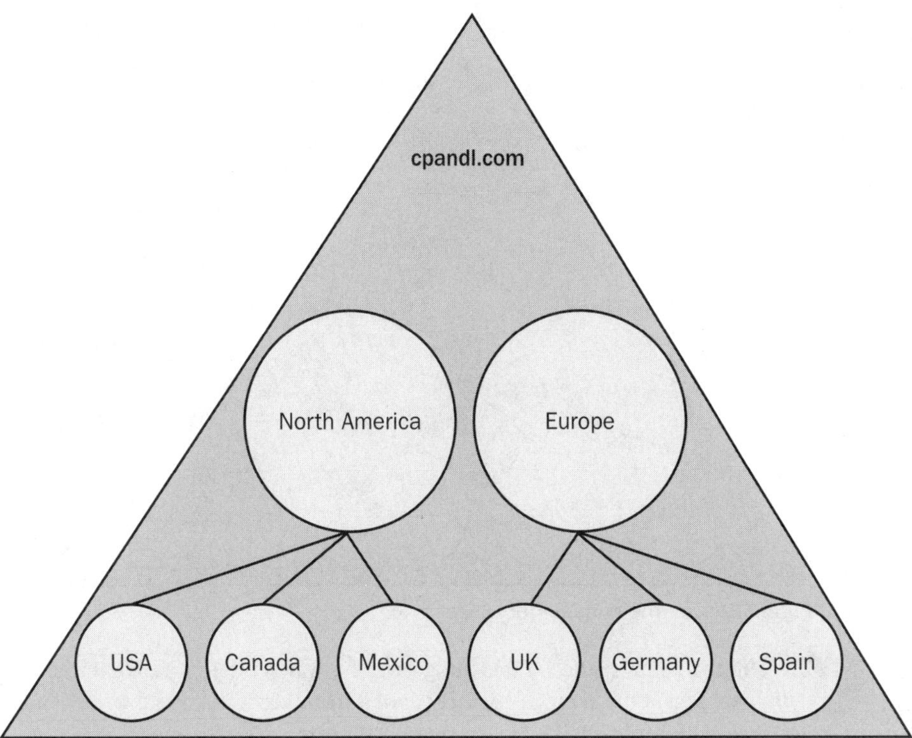

Figure 34-3. The geographic model.

OU Design: The Cost Center Model

With a cost center model, you use OUs to reflect cost centers. In this model, top-level OUs represent the major cost centers within the organization and the lower-level OUs represent geographic locations, projects, or business structures, as shown in Figure 34-4. In a company where budget is the top priority, the cost center model may be an effective way to reflect this priority. Cost centers could also be independent divisions or business units within the company that have their own management and cost controls.

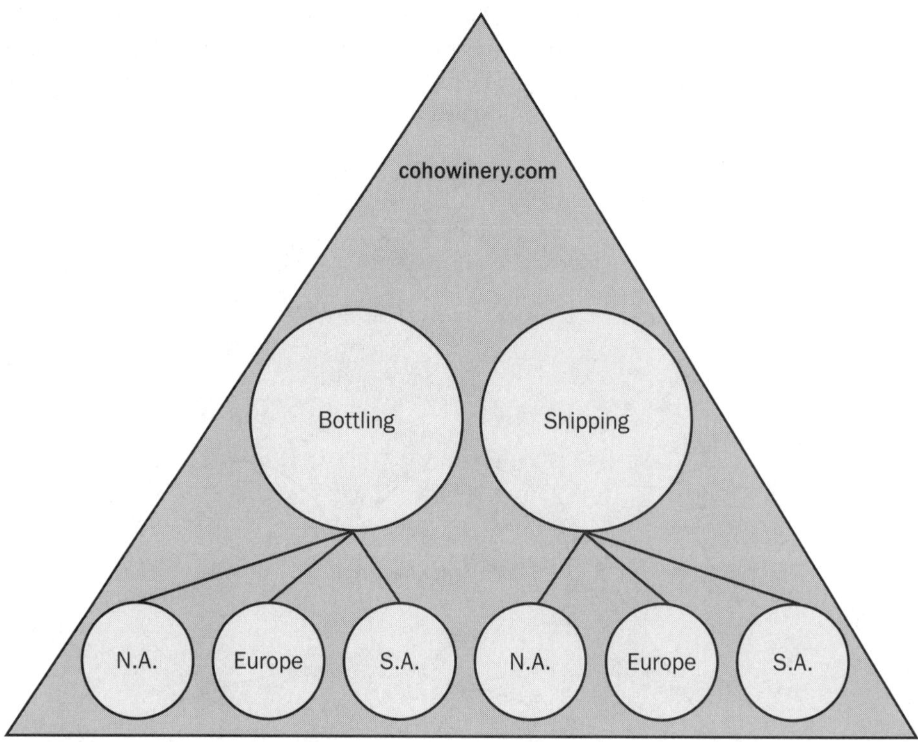

Figure 34-4. The cost center model.

The ability to represent costs and budgets in this way is a definite advantage but could also be a disadvantage. Cost center structure is not a structure well known to most administrators, and it may be confusing.

OU Design: The Administration Model

With an administration model, you use OUs to reflect the way resources and accounts are managed. As this model reflects the business structure of a company, it is very similar to the division or business unit model. The key difference is that the top-level OU is for administrators and second-level OUs are for business structure (see Figure 34-5). If successive levels are needed, they can be organized by resource type, geographic location, project type, or some combination of the three.

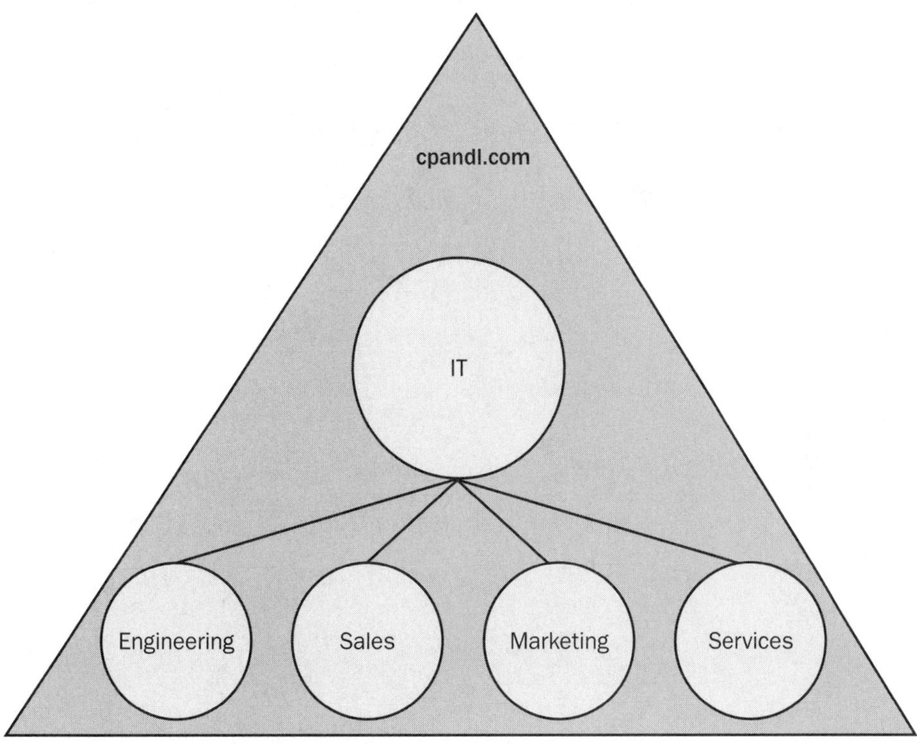

Figure 34-5. The administration model.

In a large company, you may use multiple implementations of this model for each division or business unit. In this case, the top-level administrative group would be for the division or business unit and the second-level OUs would be for groups within the division.

The advantage to this model is that it is designed around the way administrators work and represents the business structure of the company. The disadvantage to this model is that when the company or divisions within the company restructure, you may need to redesign the OU structure.

Chapter 35

Configuring Active Directory Sites and Replication

As part of the design of Active Directory directory service, you should examine the network topology and determine if you need to manage network traffic between subnets or business locations. To manage network traffic related to Active Directory, you use sites, which can be used to reflect the physical topology of your network. Every Active Directory implementation has at least one site. An important part of understanding sites involves understanding Active Directory replication. Active Directory uses two replication models: one model for replication within sites and one model for replication between sites. You need a solid understanding of these replication models to plan your site structure.

Working with Active Directory Sites

A *site* is a group of Transmission Control Protocol/Internet Protocol (TCP/IP) subnets that are implemented to control directory replication traffic and isolate logon authentication traffic between physical network locations. Each subnet that is part of a site should be connected by reliable, high-speed links. Any business location connected over slow or unreliable links should be part of a separate site. Because of this, individual sites typically represent the individual local area networks (LANs) within an organization, and the wide area network (WAN) links between business locations typically mark the boundaries of these sites. However, sites can be used in other ways as well.

Sites do not reflect the Active Directory namespace. Domain and site boundaries are separate. From a network topology perspective, a single site can contain multiple TCP/IP subnets as well. However, a single subnet can be in only one site. This means that the following conditions apply:

- A single site can contain resources from multiple domains.
- A single domain can have resources spread out among multiple sites.
- A single site can have multiple subnets.

As you design site structure, you have many options. Sites can contain a domain or a portion of a domain. A single site can have one subnet or multiple subnets. It is important to note that replication is handled differently between sites than it is within sites. Replication that occurs within a site is referred to as *intrasite replication*. Replication between sites is referred to as *intersite replication*. Each side of a site connection has one or more designated bridgehead servers.

Figure 35-1 shows an example of an organization that has one domain and two sites at the same physical location. Here, the organization has an East Campus site and a West Campus site. As you can see, the organization has multiple domain controllers at each site. The domain controllers in the East Campus site perform intrasite replication with each other, as do the domain controllers in the West Campus site. Designated servers in each site, referred to as site *bridgehead* servers, perform intersite replication with each other.

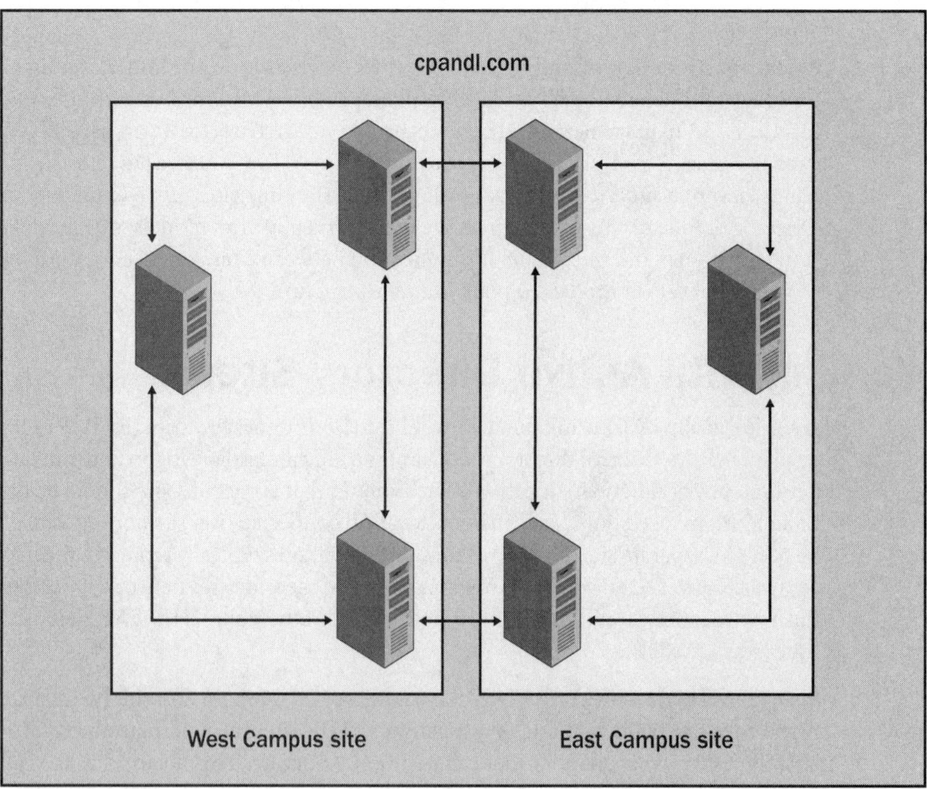

Figure 35-1. Multiple sites at the same location.

Figure 35-2 shows an example of an organization that has two different physical locations. Here, the organization has decided to use two domains and two sites. The Main site is for the cohowinery.com domain and the Seattle site is for the sea.cohowinery.com domain. Again, replication occurs both within and between the sites.

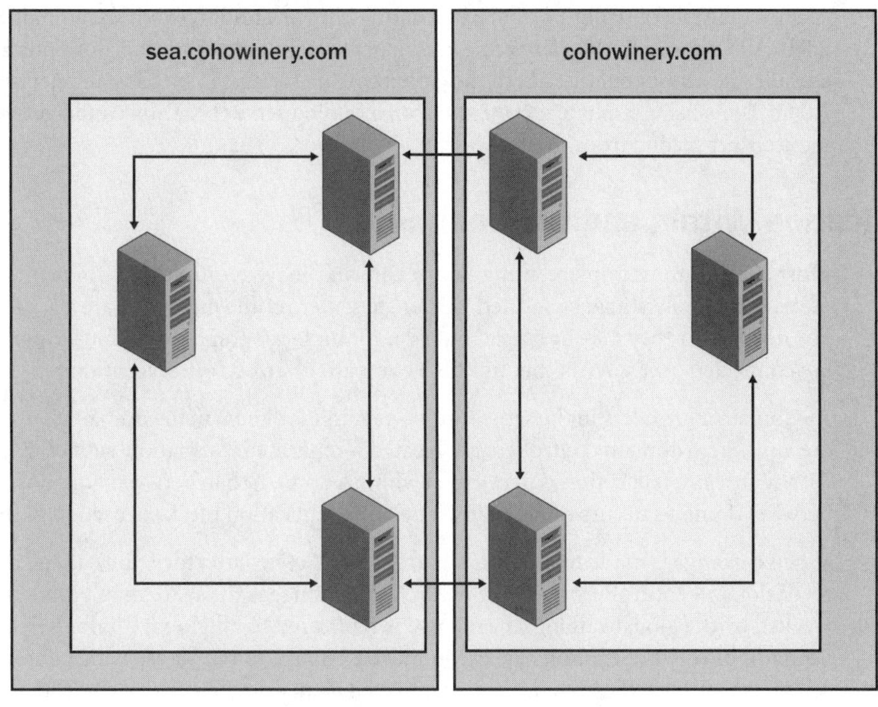

Figure 35-2. Multiple sites at different locations.

Single Site vs. Multiple Sites

One reason to create additional sites at the same physical location is to control replication traffic. Replication traffic between sites is automatically compressed, reducing the amount of traffic passed between sites by 85 to 90 percent of its original size. Because network clients try to log on to network resources within their local site first, this means that you can use sites to isolate logon traffic as well.

It is recommended that each site have at least one domain controller and one global catalog for client authentication. For name resolution and IP address assignment, it is also recommended that each site have at least one Domain Name System (DNS) server and one Dynamic Host Configuration Protocol (DHCP) server. Then, by creating multiple sites in the same physical location and establishing a domain controller, global catalog, and DNS and DHCP server within each site, you can closely control the logon process.

Sites should also be designed with other network resources in mind, including distributed file system (DFS) file shares, certificate authorities, and Microsoft Exchange 2000 servers. You want to configure sites so that clients' network queries can be answered within the site. If every client query for a network resource has to be sent to a remote site, there could be substantial network traffic between sites which could be a problem over slow WAN links.

A good example of the importance of locating network resources within a site is Exchange 2000. All Exchange 2000 clients contact a global catalog server for the global address list. As a result, the number of queries to the global catalog server can be substantial. On a site with 1,000 clients using Exchange 2000, the global catalog server typically would get two to three requests per second from these clients.

Replication Within and Between Sites

Most organizations implementing Active Directory have multiple domain controllers. The domain controllers may be located in a single server room where they are all connected to a fast network or they may be spread out over multiple geographic locations, from which they are connected over a WAN that links the company's various office locations.

All domain controllers in the same forest—regardless of how many domain controllers there are and where domain controllers are located—replicate information with each other. Although more replication is performed within a domain than between domains, replication between domains occurs nonetheless. The same replication model is used in both cases.

When a change is made to a domain partition in Active Directory, the change is replicated to all domain controllers in the domain. If the change is made to an attribute of an object tracked by the global catalog, the change is replicated to all global catalog servers in all domains of the forest. Similarly, if you make a change to the forest-wide configuration or schema partitions, these changes are replicated to all domain controllers in all the domains of the forest.

Authentication within and between domains is also handled by domain controllers. If a user logs in to his or her home domain, the local domain control authenticates the logon. If a user logs in to a domain other than the home domain, the logon request is forwarded through the trust tree to a domain controller in the user's home domain.

Active Directory's replication model is designed for consistency, but the consistency is loosely defined. By loosely defined, I mean that at any given moment the information on one domain controller can be different from the information on a different domain controller. This can happen when changes on the first domain controller have not been replicated to the other domain controller. Over time, the changes made to one domain controller will be replicated to all domain controllers as necessary.

When multiple sites are involved, the replication model is used to store and then forward changes as necessary between sites. In this case, a domain controller in the site where the changes were originally made forwards the changes to a domain controller in another site. This domain controller in turn stores the changes, and then forwards the changes to all the domain controllers in the second site. In this way, the domain controller on which a change is made doesn't have to replicate directly with all the other domain controllers. It can instead rely on the store-and-forward technique to ensure that the changes are replicated as necessary.

Determining Site Boundaries

When trying to determine site boundaries, you should configure sites so that they reflect the physical structure of your network. Use connectivity between network segments to determine where site boundaries should be located. Areas of the network that are connected with fast connections should all be part of the same site, unless you have specific requirements for controlling replication or the logon process. Areas of the network that are connected with limited bandwidth or unreliable links should be part of different sites.

As you examine each of the organization's business locations, determine whether placing domain controllers and other network resources at that location is necessary. If you elect not to place a domain controller at a remote location, you cannot make the location a part of a separate site. This has the following advantages:

- No Active Directory replication between the business locations
- No remote domain controllers to manage
- No additional site infrastructure to manage

There are also several disadvantages to this approach:

- All logon traffic will have to cross the link between the business locations.
- Users may experience slow logon and authentication to network resources.

In the end, the decision to establish a separate site may come down to the user experience and the available bandwidth. If you have fast connections between sites—which should be dedicated and redundant—you may not want to establish a separate site for the remote business location. If you have limited bandwidth between business locations and want to maintain the user experience, you may want to establish a separate site and place domain controllers and possibly other network resources at the site. This will speed up the logon and authentication process and allow you to better control the network traffic between sites.

Understanding Active Directory Replication

When you are planning site structure, it is important that you understand how replication works. As discussed previously, Active Directory uses two replication models; each of which is handled differently. The intrasite replication model is used for replication within sites and is optimized for high bandwidth connections. The intersite replication model is used for replication between sites and is optimized for limited bandwidth connections. Before I get into the specifics of replication and the replication models, let's look at the way replication has changed between Microsoft Windows 2000 and Windows Server 2003.

Replication Enhancements for Windows Server 2003

The replication model used for Windows Server 2003 has changed in several important ways from the model in Windows 2000. In Windows 2000, the smallest unit of replication is an individual attribute. At first examination, this seems to be what is wanted; after all, you don't want to have to replicate an entire object if only an attribute of that object has changed. The problem with this approach is that some attributes are multivalued. That is, they have multiple values. An example is the membership attribute of a universal group. This attribute represents all the members of the universal group.

In Windows 2000, by adding or removing a single user from the group, you caused the entire group membership to be replicated. In large organizations, a significant amount of replication traffic was often generated because universal groups might have several thousand members. Windows Server 2003 resolves this problem by replicating only the attribute's updated value. With universal group membership, this means that only the users you've added or removed are updated, rather than the entire group membership.

As discussed in the section entitled "Extensible Storage Engine" on page 1091, Active Directory uses transactional processing. When there are many changes, Active Directory processes the changes in batches of 5,000 at a time. This means that Active Directory processes a single transaction or multiple transactions in sequence until it reaches 5,000 changes, then it stops and checks to see if other processes are waiting for the CPU. Because a transaction must be completed before processing stops in this way, this places a practical limit on the number of changes that can be made in a single transaction—that number is 5,000.

In Windows 2000, because all the members of a group were processed any time a group's membership was changed, the limit on transactions also placed a practical limit on the number of members in a group. Again, this value is 5,000. The change in the way Windows Server 2003 replicates multivalued attributes also removes the limitation of 5,000 members for groups.

Note When a forest is running at Windows Server 2003 functional level or Windows Server 2003 interim functional level, the members of the forest can take advantage of the previously discussed replication enhancements. For Windows Server 2003 functional level, this means that all domain controllers in all domains within the forest must be running Windows Server 2003. For Windows Server 2003 interim functional level, this means that all domain controllers in all domains within the forest must be running either Windows Server 2003 or Microsoft Windows NT.

Other replication enhancements for Windows Server 2003 involve intersite replication. Windows Server 2003 introduces the ability to turn off compression for intersite replication and to enable notification for intersite replication. Windows Server 2003 also has an improved knowledge consistency checker (KCC), which allows Active Directory to support a greater number of sites. These changes affect intersite replication in the following key ways:

- In Windows 2000 and Windows Server 2003, all intersite replication traffic is compressed by default. Although this significantly reduces the amount of traffic between sites, it increases the processing overhead required on the bridgehead servers to replicate traffic between sites. Therefore, if processor utilization on bridgehead servers is a concern, and you have adequate bandwidth connections between sites, you may want to disable compression, which Windows Server 2003 allows you to do.

- In Windows 2000 and Windows Server 2003, replication between sites occurs at scheduled intervals according to the site link configuration. In Windows Server 2003, you can enable notification for intersite replication, which allows the bridgehead server in a site to notify the bridgehead server on the other side of a site link that changes have occurred. This allows the other bridgehead server to pull the changes across the site link and thereby get more frequent updates.
- In Windows 2000, the maximum number of sites you can have in a forest is greatly influenced by the knowledge consistency checker (KCC). As a result, there's a practical limit of about 100 sites per forest. Because the KCC in Windows Server 2003 has been revised, the KCC itself is no longer the limiting factor. This means that you can have many hundreds of sites per forest.

> **Note** To turn off compression or enable notification, you need to edit the related site link or connection object. See the section entitled "Configuring Site Link Replication Options" on page 1342.

Replication Architecture: An Overview

Active Directory replication is a multipart process that involves a source domain controller and a destination domain controller. From a high level, replication works much as shown in Figure 35-3.

The step-by-step procedure goes like this:

1. When a user or a system process makes a change to the directory, this change is implemented as an LDAP write to the appropriate directory partition.
2. The source domain controller begins by looking up the IP address of a replication partner. For the initial lookup or when the destination DNS record has expired, the source domain controller does this by querying the primary DNS server. Subsequent lookups can be done using the local resolver cache.
3. The source and destination domain controllers use Kerberos to mutually authenticate each other.
4. The source domain controller then sends a change notification to the destination domain controller using RPC over IP.
5. The destination domain controller sends a request for the changes using RPC over IP, including information that allows the source domain controller to determine if those changes are needed.
6. Using the information sent by the destination domain controller, the source domain controller determines what changes (if any) need to be sent to the destination domain controller, and then sends the required changes using RCP over IP.
7. The destination domain controller then uses the replication subsystem to write the changes to the directory database.

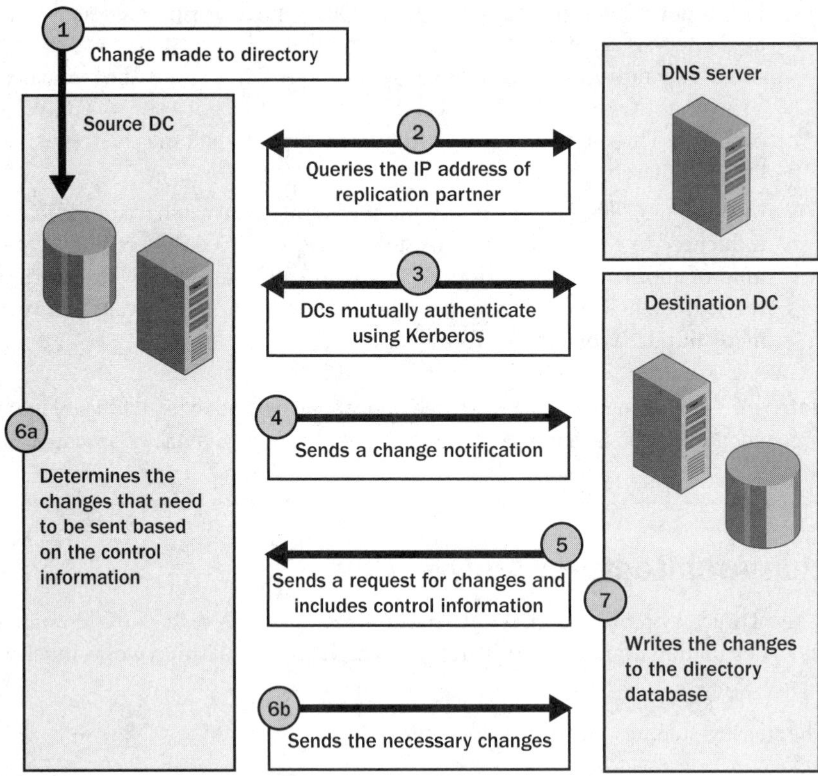

Figure 35-3. An overview of replication.

> **Note** For intersite replication, two transports are available: RPC over IP and SMTP. With this in mind, SMTP could also be used as an alternate transport. SMTP uses TCP port 25.

As you can see from this overview, Active Directory replication depends on the following key services:

- LDAP
- Domain Name System (DNS)
- Kerberos version 5 Authentication
- Remote Procedure Call (RPC)

These Windows services must be functioning properly to allow directory updates to be replicated. Active Directory also uses File Replication Service (FRS) to replicate files in the System Volume (SYSVOL) shared folders on domain controllers. The User Datagram Protocol (UDP) and TCP ports used during replication are summarized in Table 35-1.

Table 35-1. Ports Used During Active Directory Replication

Service/Component	Port	
	UDP	**TCP**
LDAP	389	389
LDAP Secure Sockets Layer (SSL)		686
Global Catalog (LDAP)		3268
Kerberos version 5	88	88
DNS	53	53
Server Message Block (SMB) over IP	445	445

Inside Out

How is FRS used with Active Directory?

A lot of people have asked me what exactly FRS is—and it can be confusing to see how it fits in with Active Directory. File Replication Service (FRS) is a replication service that uses the Active Directory replication topology to replicate data files. On behalf of Active Directory, FRS replicates files and folders in the System Volume (SYSVOL) shared folders on domain controllers. The SYSVOL folder contains domain policy, as well as scripts used for log on, log off, shutdown, and startup, and other related files used by Active Directory.

FRS is used to transfer the physical data files themselves. The replication topology used is the one implemented by Active Directory. The way this works is that FRS checks with the KCC to determine the replication topology that has been generated for Active Directory replication, and then uses this replication topology to replication SYSVOL files to all the domain controllers in a domain.

Intrasite Replication Essentials

Active Directory's multimaster replication model is designed to ensure that there is no single point of failure. In this model, every domain controller can access changes to the database, and those changes can be replicated to all other domain controllers. When replication occurs within a domain, the replication follows a specific model that is very different from the replication model used for intersite replication.

With intrasite replication, the focus is on ensuring that changes are rapidly distributed. Intrasite replication traffic is not compressed, and replication is designed so that changes are replicated almost immediately after a change has been made. The main component in Active Directory responsible for the replication structure is the KCC. One of the main responsibilities of the KCC is to generate the replication topology—that is, the way replication is implemented.

As domain controllers are added to a site, the KCC configures a ring topology for intrasite replication with pull replication partners. Why use this model? For the following reasons:

- In a ring topology model, there are always at least two paths between connected network resources to provide redundancy. Creating a ring topology for Active Directory replication ensures that there are at least two paths that changes can follow from one domain controller to another.
- In a pull replication model, two servers are used. One is designated the push partner, the other the pull partner. It is the responsibility of the push partner to notify the pull partner that changes are available. The pull partner can then request the changes. Creating push and pull replication partners allows for rapid notification of changes and for updating once a request for changes has been made.

The KCC uses these models to create a replication ring. As domain controllers are added to a site, the size and configuration of this ring change. When there are at least three domain controllers in a site, each domain controller is configured with at least two incoming replication connections. As the number of domain controllers changes, the KCC updates the replication topology.

When a domain controller is updated, it waits approximately 15 seconds before initiating replication. This short wait is implemented in case additional changes are made. The domain controller on which the change is made notifies one of its partners, using an RPC, and specifies that changes are available. The partner can then pull the changes. Once replication with this partner is completed, the domain controller waits approximately 3 seconds, and then notifies its second partner of changes. The second partner can then pull the changes. Meanwhile, the first partner is notifying its partners of changes as appropriate. This process continues until all the domain controllers have been updated.

Inside Out

Replicating urgent changes

The 15-second delay for replication applies to Windows Server 2003. For Windows 2000, the default delay is 300 seconds. In either case, however, the delay is overridden to allow immediate replication of priority changes. Priority (urgent) replication is triggered if you perform one of the following actions:

- Lock out an account, change the account lockout policy, or if an account is locked out automatically due to failed logon attempts
- Change the domain password policy
- Change the password on a domain controller computer account
- Change the relative ID master role owner
- Change a shared secret password used by the Local Security Authority (LSA) for Kerberos authentication

Urgent replication means that there is no delay to initiate replication. Note that all other changes to user and computer passwords are handled by the designated primary domain controller (PDC) emulator in a domain. When a user changes a normal user or computer password, the domain controller to which that user is connected immediately sends the change to the PDC emulator. This way, the PDC emulator always has the latest password for a user. This is why the PDC emulator is checked for a new password if a logon fails initially. Once the new password is updated on the PDC emulator, the PDC emulator replicates the change using normal replication. The only exception is when a domain controller contacts the PDC emulator requesting a password for a user. In this case, the PDC emulator immediately replicates the current password to the requesting domain controller so that no additional requests are made for that password.

Figure 35-4 shows a ring topology that a KCC would construct if there were three domain controllers in a site.

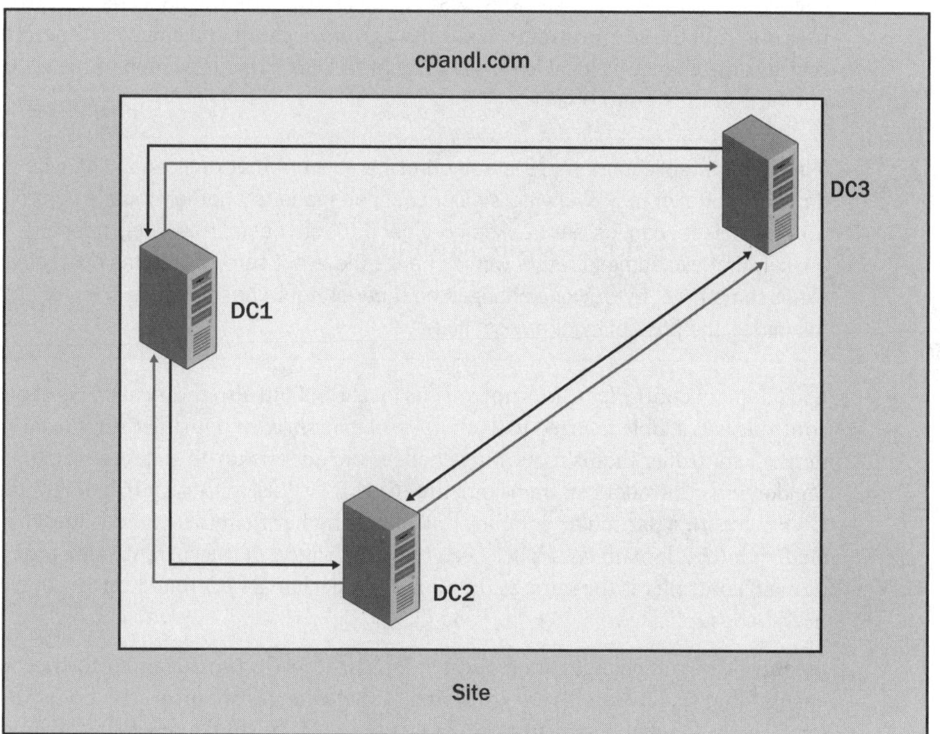

Figure 35-4. Intrasite replication using a ring topology.

As you can see from the figure, replication is set up as follows:

- DC1 has incoming replication connections from DC2 and DC3.
- DC2 has incoming replication connections from DC1 and DC3.
- DC3 has incoming replication connections from DC1 and DC2.

If changes were made to DC1, DC1 would notify DC2 of the changes. DC2 would then pull the changes. Once replication was completed, DC1 would notify DC3 of the changes. DC3 would then pull the changes. Because all domain controllers in the site have now been notified, no additional replication would occur. However, DC2 would still notify DC3 that changes were available. DC3 would not pull the changes, however, because it would already have them.

Domain controllers track directory changes using Update Sequence Numbers (USNs). Any time a change is made to the directory, the domain controller assigns the change a USN. Each domain controller maintains its own local USNs and increments their values each time a change occurs. The domain controller also assigns the local USN to the object attribute that changed. Each object has a related attribute called uSNChanged. The uSNChanged attribute is stored with the object and identifies the highest USN that has been assigned to any of the object's attributes.

To see how this works, consider the following example. The local USN for DC1 is 125. An administrator connected to DC1 changes the password on a user's account. DC1 registers the change as local USN 126. The local USN value is written to the uSNChanged attribute of the user object. If the administrator next edits a group account and changes its description, DC1 registers the change as local USN 127. The local USN value is written to the uSNChanged attribute of the Group object.

Note With replication, there is sometimes a concern that replication changes from one domain controller may overwrite similar changes made to another domain controller. However, as object changes are tracked on a per-attribute basis, this rarely happens. It is very unlikely that two administrators would change the exact same attributes of an object at the exact same time. By tracking changes on a per-attribute basis, Active Directory effectively minimizes the possibility of any conflict.

Each domain controller tracks not only its local USN but also the local USNs of other domain controllers in a table referred to as an *up-to-dateness vector*. During the replication process, a domain controller that is requesting changes includes its up-to-dateness vector. The receiving domain controller can then compare the USN values to those it has stored. If the current USN value for a particular domain controller is higher than the stored value, changes associated with that domain controller need to be replicated. If the current value for a particular domain controller is the same as the stored value, changes for that domain controller do not need to be replicated.

As only necessary changes are replicated, this process of comparing up-to-dateness vectors ensures that replication is very efficient and that changes are propagated only when necessary. The up-to-dateness vectors are in fact the mechanism that enables domain controllers with redundant connections to know that they've already received the necessary updates.

Inside Out

Schema changes have priority

Several types of replication changes have priority. If you make changes to object attributes in the schema, these changes take precedence over most other changes. In this case, Active Directory blocks replication of normal changes and replicates the schema changes. Active Directory will continue to replicate schema changes until the schema configuration is synchronized on all domain controllers in the forest. This ensures that schema changes are applied rapidly. Still, it's a good idea to make changes to the schema during off-hours, since schema changes need to be propagated throughout the forest before other changes such as resetting passwords can be made to Active Directory.

The Windows Server 2003 schema adds 25 indexed attributes to the schema directory partition. When you upgrade or install the first Windows Server 2003 domain controller, these changes are replicated throughout the forest. Because of this, it is recommended that Windows 2000 domain controllers have Service Pack 3 or later installed before you upgrade or install the first Windows Server 2003 domain controller.

Intersite Replication Essentials

While intrasite replication is focused on speed, intersite replication is focused on efficiency. The primary goal of intersite replication is to transfer replication information between sites while making the most efficient use of the available resources. With efficiency as a goal, intersite replication traffic uses designated bridgehead servers and a default configuration that is scheduled rather than automatic, and compressed rather than uncompressed.

- With designated bridgehead servers, the ISTG limits the points of replication between sites. Instead of allowing all the domain controllers in one site to replicate with all the domain controllers in another site, the ISTG designates a limited number of domain controllers as bridgehead servers. These domain controllers are then the only ones used to replicate information between sites.
- With scheduled replication, you can set the valid times during which replication can occur and the replication frequency within this scheduled interval. By default, when you configure intersite replication, replication is scheduled to occur every 180 minutes 24 hours a day. When there's limited bandwidth between sites, you might want to change the default schedule to better accommodate the users who also use the link. For example, you might want to allow replication to occur every 180 minutes 24 hours a day on Saturday and Sunday, but during the week set the schedule to allow more bandwidth during the day. For example, you might set replication to occur every 60 minutes from 6 A.M. to 8 A.M. and from 7 P.M. to 3 A.M. Monday through Friday.
- With compression, replication traffic is compressed 85 to 90 percent, meaning that it is 10 to 15 percent of its uncompressed size. This means that even low bandwidth links can often be used effectively for replication. Compression is triggered when the replication traffic is more than 32 kilobytes (KB) in size.

As discussed previously, there are two key ways to change intersite replication, as follows:

- Turn off automatic compression if you have sufficient bandwidth on a link and are more concerned about the processing power used for compression.
- Enable automatic notification of changes to allow domain controllers on either side of the link to indicate that changes are available. Automatic notification allows those changes to be requested rather than making domain controllers wait for the next replication interval.

Regardless of the site link configuration, replication traffic is sent through dedicated bridgehead servers rather than through multiple replication partners. When changes are made to the directory in one site, those changes are replicated to the other site via the designated bridgehead servers. The bridgehead servers then initiate replication of the changes exactly as was discussed in the section entitled "Intrasite Replication Essentials" earlier in this chapter, except that SMTP can be used instead of RPC over IP if SMTP is being used as a transport. Thus, intersite replication is really concerned with getting changes from one site to another across a site link.

Figure 35-5 shows an example of intersite replication using a single dedicated bridgehead server on each side of a site link. In this example, DC3 is the designated bridgehead server for Site 1 and DC4 is the designated bridgehead server for Site 2.

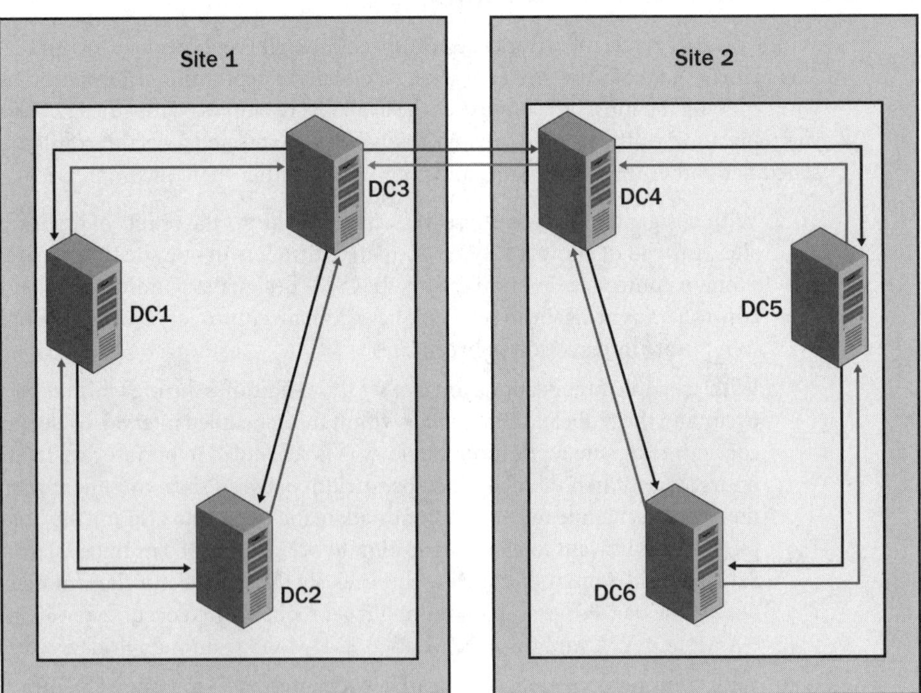

Figure 35-5. Replication between two sites.

As you can see from the figure, replication is set up as follows:

- DC1 has incoming replication connections from DC2 and DC3.
- DC2 has incoming replication connections from DC1 and DC3.
- DC3 has incoming replication connections from DC1 and DC2.
- DC4 has incoming replication connections from DC5 and DC6.
- DC5 has incoming replication connections from DC4 and DC6.
- DC6 has incoming replication connections from DC4 and DC5.

If changes were made to DC1 in Site 1, DC1 would notify DC2 of the changes. DC2 would then pull the changes. Once replication was completed, DC1 would notify DC3 of the changes. DC3 would then pull the changes. Because all domain controllers in the Site 1 have now been notified, no additional replication would occur within the site. However, DC2 would still notify DC3 that changes were available. DC3 would not pull the changes, however, because it would already have them.

According to the site link configuration between Site 1 and Site 2, DC3 would notify DC4 that changes were available. DC4 would then pull the changes. Next DC4 would notify DC5 of the changes. DC5 would then pull the changes. Once replication was completed, DC4 would notify DC6 of the changes. DC6 would then pull the changes. Because all domain controllers in Site 2 have now been notified, no additional replication would occur. However, DC5 would still notify DC6 that changes were available. DC6 would not pull the changes, however, because it would already have the changes.

So far, I've talked about designated bridgehead servers but haven't said how bridgehead servers are designated. That's because it is a rather involved process. When you set up a site, the knowledge consistency checker (KCC) on a domain controller that Active Directory has designated the Inter-Site Topology Generator (ISTG) is responsible for generating the intersite topology. Each site has only one ISTG and its job is to determine the best way to configure replication between sites.

The ISTG does this by identifying the bridgehead servers that are to be used. Replication between sites is always sent from a bridgehead server in one site to a bridgehead server in another site. This ensures that information is replicated only once between sites. As domain controllers are added and removed from sites, the ISTG regenerates the topology automatically.

The ISTG also creates the connection objects that are needed to connect bridgehead servers on either side of a site link. This is how Active Directory logically represents a site link. The ISTG continuously monitors connections and will create new connections when a domain controller acting as a designated bridgehead server is no longer available. In most cases, there will be more than one designated bridgehead server, and I'll discuss why in the following section, "Replicating Rings and Directory Partitions."

> **Note** You can manually configure intersite replication in several ways. In addition to the techniques discussed previously for scheduling, notification, and compression, you can also configure site link costs, configure connection objects manually, and designate preferred bridgehead servers.

Replication Rings and Directory Partitions

The knowledge consistency checker (KCC) is responsible for generating the intrasite replication topology, and the ISTG uses the KCC to generate the intersite replication topology. The KCC always configures the replication topology so that each domain controller in a site has at least two incoming connections if possible, as already discussed. The KCC also always configures intrasite replication so that each domain controller is no more than three hops from any other domain controller. This also means that *maximum replication latency*, the delay in replicating a change across an entire site, is approximately 45 seconds for normal replication.

When there are two domain controllers in a site, each domain controller is the replication partner of the other. When there are between three and seven domain controllers in the domain, each domain controller will have two incoming connections and two replication partners. Figure 35-6 shows the replication topology for City Power & Light's Sacramento campus. Here the network is spread over two buildings that are connected with high-speed interconnects. Because the buildings are connected over redundant high-speed links, the organization uses a single site with three domain controllers in each building. The replication topology for the six domain controllers as shown ensures that no domain controller is more than three hops from any other domain controller.

When the number of domain controllers increases beyond seven, additional connection objects are added to ensure that no domain controller is more than three hops from any other domain controller in the replication topology. To see an example of this, consider Figure 35-7. Here, City Power & Light has built a third building that connects its original buildings to form a U-shaped office complex. The administrators have placed two new domain controllers in building 3. As a result of adding the additional domain controllers, some domain controllers now have three replication partners.

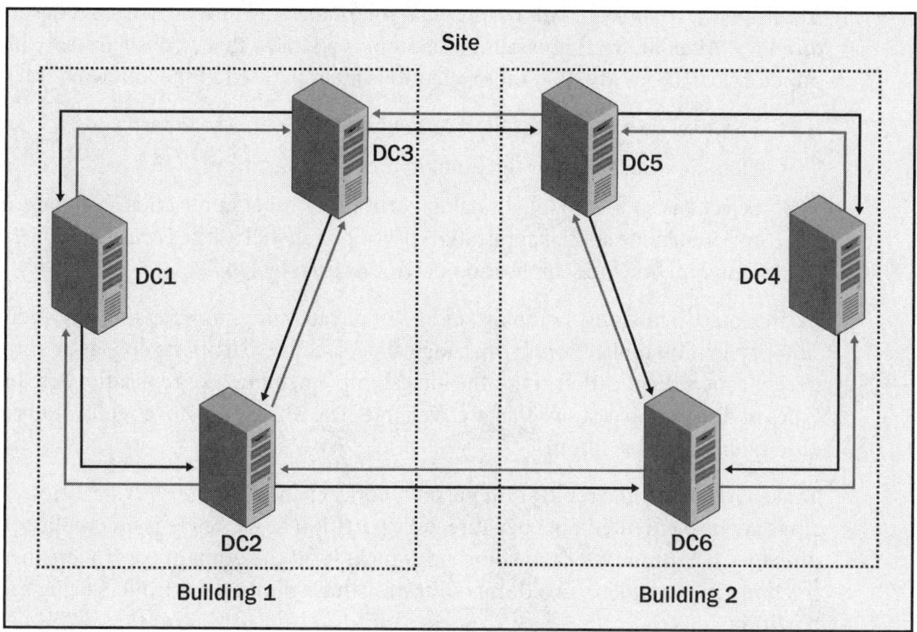

Figure 35-6. Campus replication with two buildings and three domain controllers in each building.

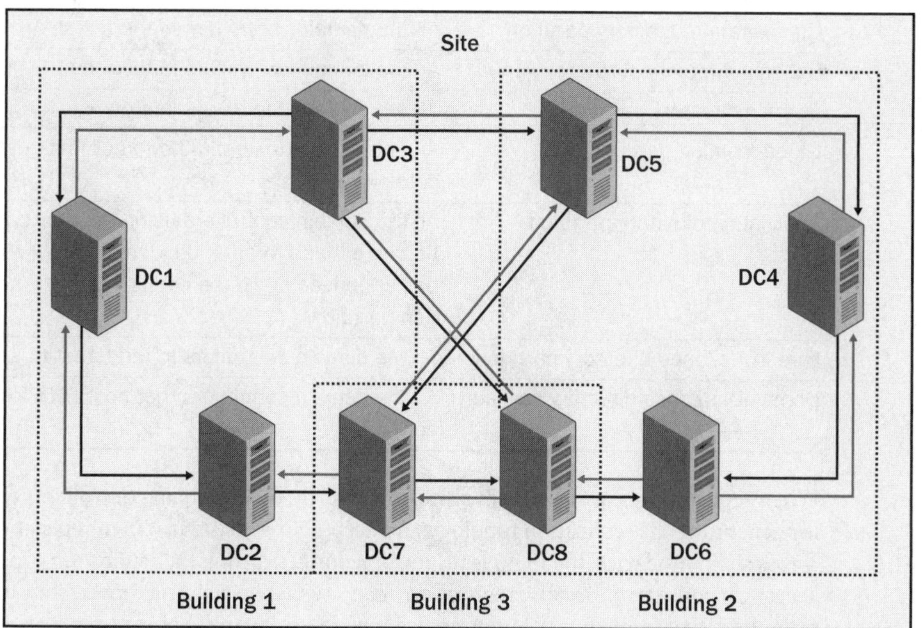

Figure 35-7. Campus replication with three buildings and eight domain controllers.

At this point, you may be wondering what role, if any; directory partitions play in replication topology. After all, from previous discussions, you know that Active Directory has multiple directory partitions and that those partitions are replicated in the following ways:

- Forest-wide basis for configuration and schema directory partitions
- Domain-wide basis for the domain directory partition
- Select basis for the global catalog partition or other application-specific partitions, which include special application partitions as well as the ForestDnsZones and DomainDnsZones application partitions used by DNS

In previous discussions, I didn't want to complicate things unnecessarily by adding a discussion of partition replication. From a logical perspective, partitions do play an important role in replication. Replication rings, the logical implementation of replication, are based on the types of directory partitions that are available. The KCC generates a replication ring for each kind of directory partition.

Table 35-2 details the replication partners for each kind of directory partition. Replication rings are implemented on a per-directory partition basis. There is one replication ring per directory partition type, and some rings include all the domain controllers in a forest, all the domain controllers in a domain, or only those domain controllers using application partitions.

Table 35-2. Per-Directory Partition Replication Rings

Directory Partition	Replication Partners
Configuration directory partition	All the domain controllers in the forest
Schema directory partition	All the domain controllers in the forest
Domain directory partition	All the domain controllers in a domain
Global catalog partition	All domain controllers in the forest that host global catalogs
Application directory partition	All the domain controllers using the application partition on either a forest-wide, domain-wide, or selective basis, depending on the configuration of the application partition
ForestDnsZones directory partition	All the domain controllers in the forest that host DNS
DomainDnsZones directory partition	All the domain controllers that host DNS for that domain.

When replication rings are within a site, the KCC on each domain controller is responsible for generating the replication topology and keeping it consistent. When replication rings go across site boundaries, the ISTG is responsible for generating the replication topology and keeping it consistent. Because replication rings are merely a logical representation of replication, the actual implementation of replication rings is expressed in the replication topology by using connection objects. Regardless of whether you are talking about intrasite or intersite replication, there is one connection object for each incoming connection. The KCC and ISTG do not create additional connection objects for each replication ring. Instead, they reuse connection objects for as many replication rings as possible.

When you extend the reuse of connection objects to the way intersite replication is performed, this is how multiple bridgehead servers might be designated. Typically, each site will also have a designated bridgehead server for replicating the domain, schema, and configuration directory partitions. Other types of directory partitions may be replicated between sites by domain controllers that host these partitions. For example, if two sites have multiple domain controllers and only a few have application partitions, a connection object may be created for the intersite replication of the application partition.

Figure 35-8 shows an example of how multiple bridgehead servers might be used. Here, the domain, schema, and configuration partitions are replicated from Site 1 to Site 2 and vice versa using the connection objects between DC3 and DC5. A special application partition is replicated from Site 1 to Site 2 and vice versa using the connection objects between DC2 and DC6.

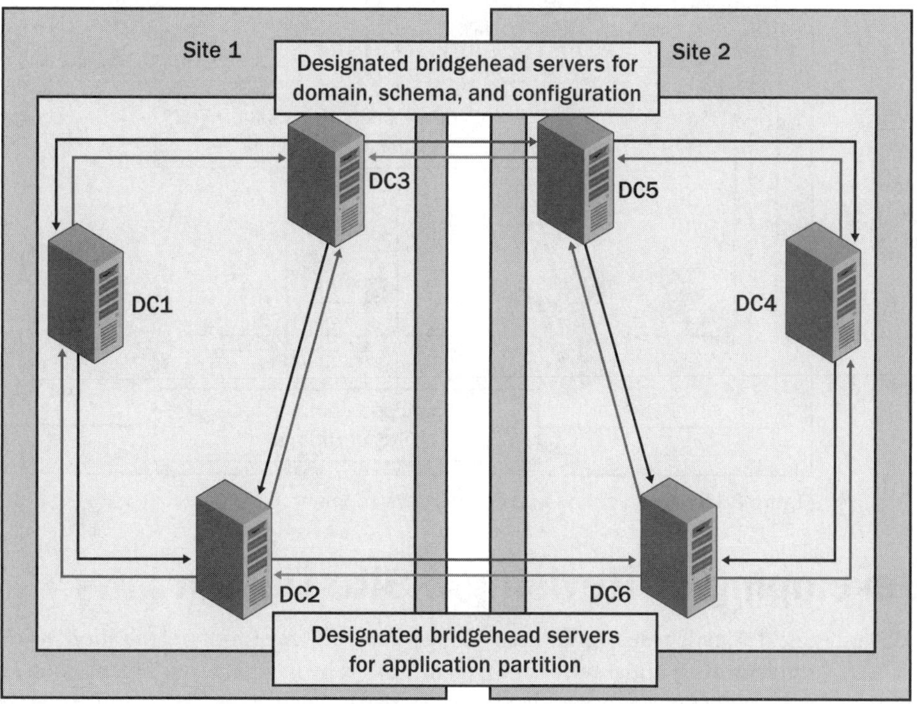

Figure 35-8. Replication between sites using multiple bridgehead servers.

The global catalog partition is a special exception. The global catalog is built from all the domain databases in a forest. Each designated global catalog server in a forest must get global catalog information from the domain controllers in all the domains of the forest. This means that a global catalog server must connect to a domain controller in every domain and there must be an associated connection object to do this. Because of this, global catalog servers are another reason for having more than one designated bridgehead server per site.

Figure 35-9 provides an example of how replication might work for a more complex environment that includes domain, configuration, and schema partitions as well as DNS and global catalog partitions. Here, the domain, schema, and configuration partitions are replicated from Site 1 to Site 2 and vice versa using the connection objects between DC3 and DC5. The connection objects between DC1 and DC4 are used to replicate the global catalog partition from Site 1 to Site 2 and vice versa. In addition, the connection objects between DC2 and DC6 are used to replicate the DNS partitions from Site 1 to Site 2 and vice versa.

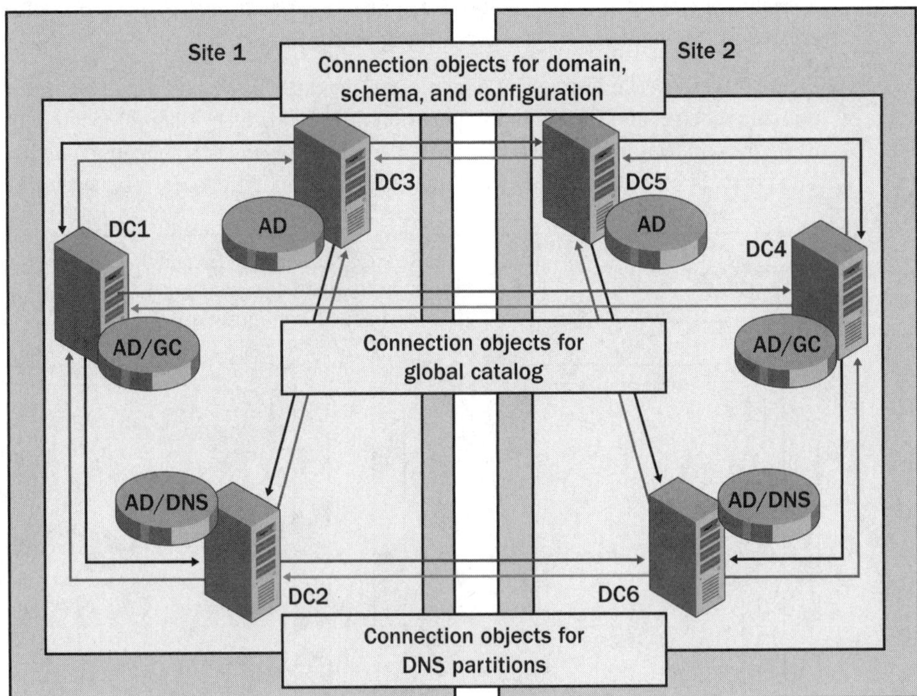

Figure 35-9. Replication in a complex environment.

Developing or Revising a Site Design

Site design depends on the networking infrastructure of your organization. As you set out to implement an initial site design, you must start by mapping your organization's existing network topology. Any time you plan to revise your network infrastructure, you must also plan the necessary revisions to your existing site design.

Mapping Network Infrastructure

Although site design is relatively independent from domain structure, the replication topology depends on how available domain controllers are and how they are configured. The KCC running on each domain controller monitors domain controller availability and configuration, and updates replication topology as changes occur. The ISTG performs similar monitoring to determine the best way to configure intersite replication. This means that as you implement or change the domain controller configuration, you may change the replication topology.

To develop a site design, you should start by mapping your existing network architecture. Be sure to include all the business locations in the organization that are part of the forest or forests for which you are developing a site plan. Document the subnets on each network segment and the connection speed on the links connecting each network segment.

- You need to document the subnets because each site in the organization will have separate subnets. Although a single subnet can only exist in one site, a single site can have multiple subnets associated with it. After you create sites, you will create subnet-to-site associations by adding subnets to these sites.
- You need to document the connection speeds for links because the available bandwidth on a connection affects the way you configure site links. Each site link is assigned a link cost, which determines its priority order for replication. If there are several possible routes to a site, the route with the lowest link cost is used first. In the event that a primary link fails, a secondary link can be used.

Because site design and network infrastructure are so closely linked, you'll want to work closely with your organization's network administrators. If you wear both hats, start mapping the network architecture by listing each network location, the subnets at that location, and the links that connect the location. For an organization with its headquarters in Chicago and four regional offices, in Seattle, New York, Los Angeles (LA), and Miami, this information might come together as shown in Table 35-3. Notice that I started with the hubs and worked my way to the central office. This way, the multiple connections to the central office are all accounted for when I finally make this entry.

Table 35-3. Mapping Network Structure

Location	Subnets	Connections
Seattle	10.1.11.0/24, 10.1.12.0/24	256 kilobits per second (Kbps) Seattle–Chicago, 128 Kbps Seattle–LA
LA	10.1.21.0/24, 10.1.22.0/24	512 Kbps LA–Chicago, 128 Kbps LA–Seattle
New York	10.1.31.0/24, 10.1.32.0/24	512 Kbps New York–Chicago, 128 Kbps New York–Miami
Miami	10.1.41.0/24, 10.1.42.0/24	256 Kbps Miami–Chicago, 128 Kbps Miami–New York
Chicago	10.1.1.0/24, 10.1.2.0/24	256 Kbps Seattle–Chicago, 512 Kbps LA–Chicago, 512 Kbps New York–Chicago, 256 Kbps Miami–Chicago

I then used the table to create a diagram similar to the one shown in Figure 35-10, in which I've depicted each network and the connections between them. I've also noted the subnets at each location. Although it is also helpful to know the number of users and computers at each location, this information alone isn't enough to help you determine how links connecting sites are used. The only certain way to know that is to monitor the network traffic going over the various links.

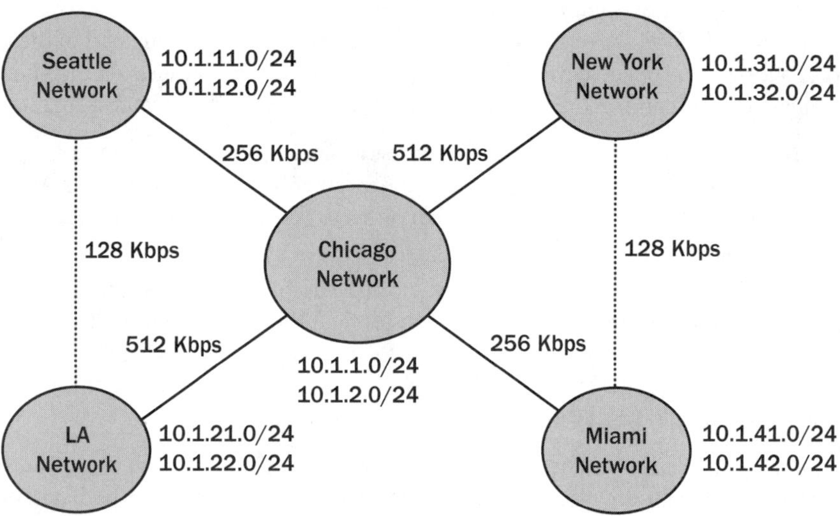

Figure 35-10. Network diagram for a wide area network (WAN).

Creating a Site Design

Once you've mapped the network structure, you are ready to create a site design. Creating a site design involves the following steps:

1. Mapping the network structure to site structure
2. Designing each individual site
3. Designing the intersite replication topology
4. Considering the impact of site link bridging
5. Planning the placement of servers in sites

Each of these steps is examined in the sections that follow.

Mapping the Network Structure to Site Structure

To map the network structure to site structure, start by examining each network location and the speed of the connections between those locations. In general, if you want to make separate network locations part of the same site, the sites should have at least 512 Kbps of available bandwidth. If the sites are in separate geographic locations, I also recommend that the network locations have redundant links for fault tolerance.

These recommended speeds are for replication traffic only, not for other user traffic. Smaller organizations with fewer than 100 users at branch locations may be able to scale down to dedicated 128-Kbps or 256-Kbps links. Larger organizations with 250 or more users at branch locations may need to scale up.

Following the previous example, the Chicago-based company would probably be best served by having separate sites at each network location. With this in mind, the site-to-network mapping would be as shown in Figure 35-11. By creating the additional sites at the other network locations, you help control replication over the slow links, which can significantly improve the performance of Active Directory. More good news is that sites are relatively low maintenance once you configure them, so you get a significant benefit without a lot of additional administration overhead.

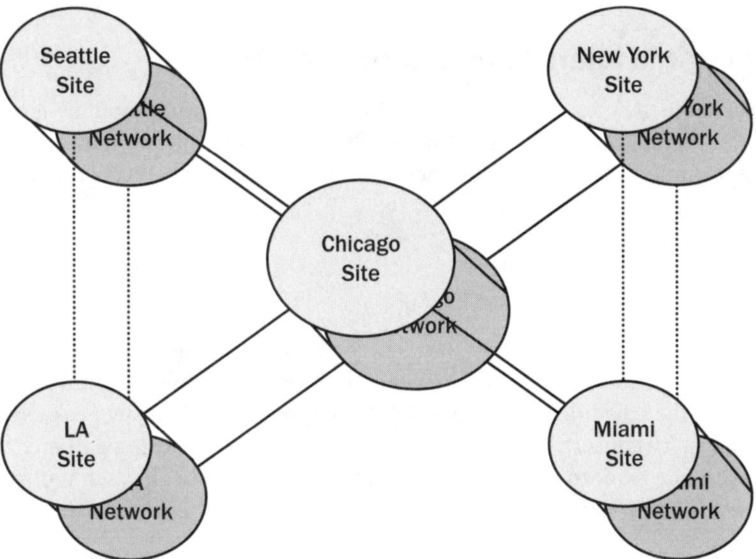

Figure 35-11. Initial site-to-network mapping.

Designing Each Individual Site

After you have determined how many sites you will have, you next need to consider the design of each site. A key part of the site design has to do with naming the sites and identifying the subnets that are associated with each site. Site names should reflect the physical location of the site. The default site created by Active Directory is Default-First-Site-Name, and most site names should follow a similar naming scheme. Continuing the example, you might use the following site names:

- Seattle-First-Site
- LA-First-Site
- NewYork-First-Site
- Miami-First-Site
- Chicago-First-Site

I've used dashes instead of spaces, following the style Active Directory uses for the default site. I've named the sites *City*-First-Site rather than *City*-Site to allow for easy revision of the site architecture to include additional sites at each location. Now, if a location receives additional sites, the naming convention is very clear, and it is also very clear that if you have a Seattle-First-Site, Seattle-Second-Site, and Seattle-Third-Site, these are all different sites at the Seattle location.

To determine the subnets that should be associated with each site, use the network diagram developed in the previous section. It already has a list of the subnets. In your site documentation, simply note the IP subnet associations that are needed and update your site diagram to include the subnets.

Designing the Intersite Replication Topology

After you name the sites and determine subnet associations, you should design the intersite replication topology. You do this by planning the details of replication over each link designated in the initial site diagram. For each site link, plan the following components:

- Replication schedule
- Replication interval
- Link cost

Typically, you'll want replication to occur at least every 180 minutes, 24 hours a day, 7 days a week. This is the default replication schedule. If you have limited bandwidth, you may need to alter the schedule to allow user traffic to have priority during peak usage times. If bandwidth isn't a concern or if you have strong concerns about keeping branch locations up to date, you may want to increase the replication frequency. In all cases, if possible you should monitor any existing links to get a sense of the bandwidth utilization and the peak usage periods.

Calculating the link cost can be a bit complicated. When there are multiple links between locations, you need to think carefully about the appropriate cost of each link. Even if there is only one link between all your sites now, you should set an appropriate link cost now to ensure that if links are added between locations, all the links are used in the most efficient way possible.

Valid link costs range from 1, which assigns the highest possible preference to a link, to 99999, which assigns the lowest possible preference to a link. When you create a new link, the default link cost is set to 100. If you were to set all the links to this cost, all the links would have equal preference for replication. But would you really want replication to go over a 128-Kbps link when you have a 512-Kbps link to the same location? Probably not.

In most cases, the best way to set link cost is to assign a cost based on the available network bandwidth over a link. Table 35-4 provides an example of how this could be done.

Table 35-4. Setting Link Cost Based on Available Bandwidth

Available Bandwidth	Link Cost	Preference
100 megabits per second (Mbps) or greater	20	Very high
100 Mbps to 10 Mbps	40	Moderately high
10 Mbps to 1.544 Mbps	100	High
1.544 Mbps to 512 Kbps	200	Above normal
512 Kbps to 256 Kbps	400	Normal
256 Kbps to 128 Kbps	800	Below normal
128 Kbps to 56 Kbps	1600	Moderately low
56 Kbps or less	3200	Low

You can use the costs in the table to assign costs to each link you identified in your site diagram. Once you do this, update your site diagram so that you can determine the route that will be used for replication if all the links are working. As Figure 35-12 shows, your site diagram should now show the names of the sites, the associated subnets, and the cost of each link.

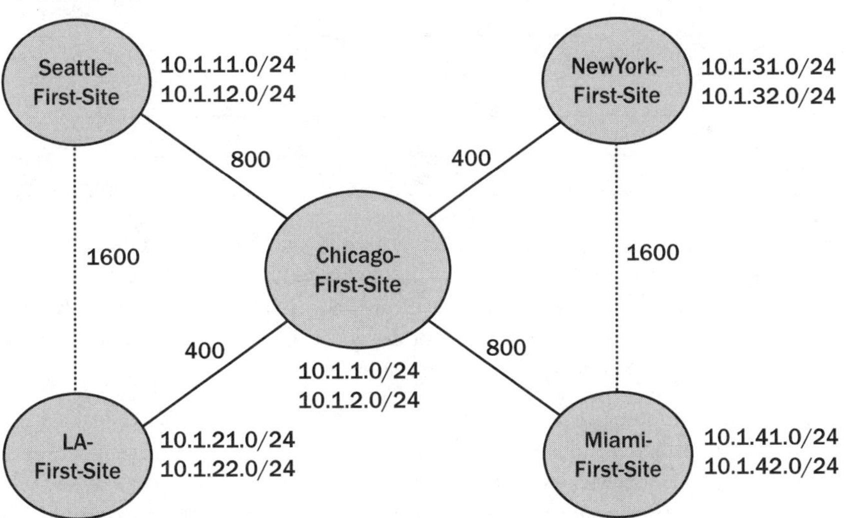

Figure 35-12. Updated site design to show site names, subnet associations, and link costs.

Considering the Impact of Site Link Bridging

By default, Active Directory automatically configures site link bridges, which makes links transitive between sites in much the same way that trusts are transitive between domains.

When a site is bridged, any two domain controllers can make a connection across any consecutive series of links. The site link bridge cost is the sum of all the costs of the links included in the bridge. Let's calculate the site link bridge costs using the links shown in Figure 35-12. Because of site link bridges, the domain controllers at the Chicago headquarters have two possible routes for replication to each of the branch office locations. The costs of these routes are summarized in Table 35-5.

Table 35-5. Link and Bridge Costs

Site/Link	Link/Bridge Cost
Seattle Site	
Chicago–Seattle	800
Chicago–LA–Seattle	2000
LA Site	
Chicago–LA	400
Chicago–Seattle–LA	2400
New York Site	
Chicago–New York	400
Chicago–Miami–New York	2400
Miami Site	
Chicago–Miami	800
Chicago–New York–Miami	2000

Knowing the costs of links and link bridges, you can calculate the effects of a network link failure. In this example, if the primary link between Chicago and Seattle went down, replication would occur over the Chicago-LA-Seattle site link bridge. It's relatively straightforward in this example, but if you were to introduce additional links between network locations, the scenarios become very complicated very quickly.

The network topology used in the previous example is referred to as a *hub-and-spoke* design. The headquarters in Chicago is the hub, and the rest of the offices are spokes. Automatic site link bridging works well with a hub-and-spoke design. It doesn't work so well when you have multiple hubs. Consider the example shown in Figure 35-13. In this example, Chicago is the main hub, but because Seattle and LA have a spoke, they are also considered hubs.

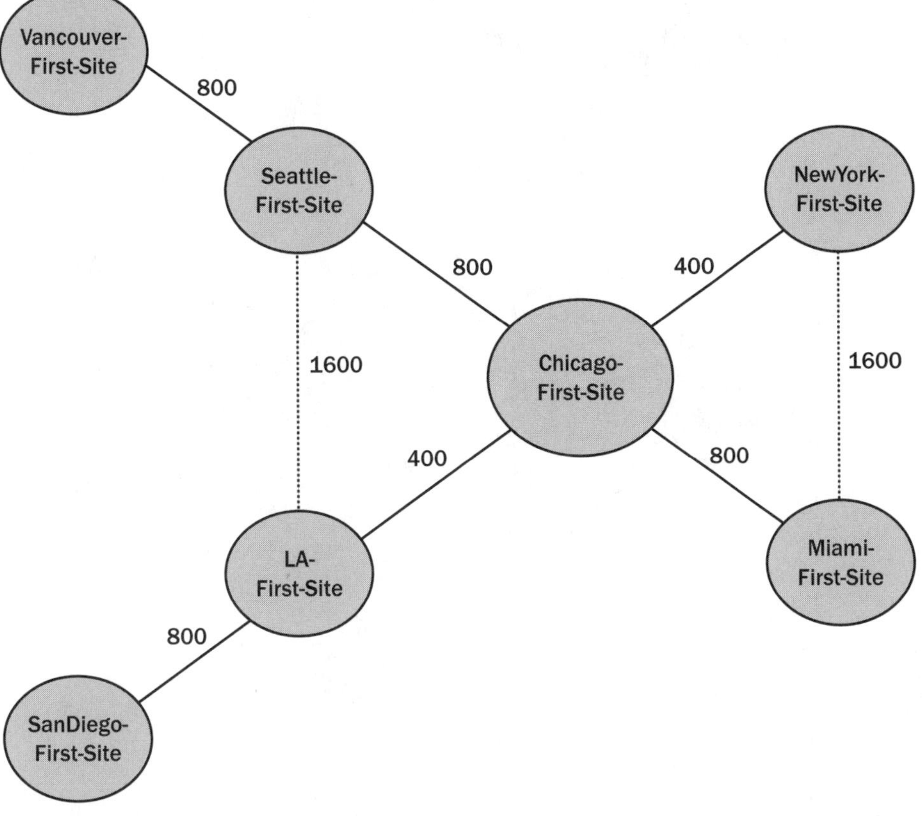

Figure 35-13. Additional sites added to original site design, making Seattle and LA hubs.

Site link bridging can have unintended consequences when you have multiple hubs and spokes on each hub. Here, when the bridgehead servers in the Chicago site replicate with other sites, they will replicate with Seattle, New York, LA, and Miami bridgehead servers as before, but they will also replicate with the Vancouver and San Diego bridgehead servers across the site bridge from Chicago-Seattle-Vancouver and from Chicago-LA-San Diego. This means that the same replication traffic could go over the Chicago-Seattle and Chicago-LA links twice. This can happen because of the rule of three hops for optimizing replication topology.

The repeat replication over the hub links is made worse as additional spokes are added. Consider Figure 35-14. Here, the LA hub has connections to sites in Sacramento, San Diego, and San Francisco. As a result of site link bridging, the same replication traffic could go over the Chicago-LA links four times. This happens because of the rule of three hops for optimizing replication topology.

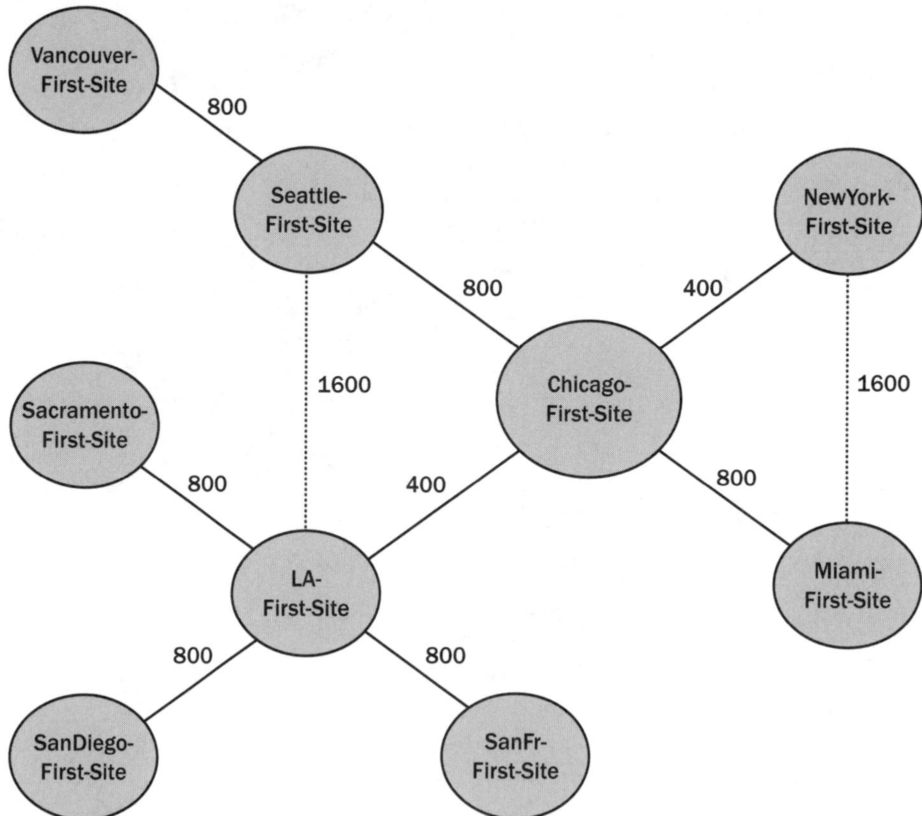

Figure 35-14. A site design with multiple spokes at hubs.

The solution to the problem of repeat replication traffic is to disable automatic site bridging. Unfortunately, the automatic bridging configuration is all or nothing. This means that if you disable automatic site link bridging and still want some site links to be bridged, you will need to configure those bridges manually. You can enable, disable, and manually configure site link bridges as discussed in the section entitled "Configuring Site Link Bridges" on page 1336.

Planning the Placement of Servers in Sites

When you are finished configuring site links, you should plan the placement of servers in the sites. Think about which types of domain controllers and how many of each will be located in a site. Answer the following questions:

- Will there be domain controllers? If so, how many?
- Will any of the domain controllers host a global catalog? If so, how many?
- Will any of the domain controllers host DNS? If so, how many?

- Will any of the domain controllers have an operations master role? If so, what roles and on which domain controllers?

Think about which Active Directory partitions will be replicated between the sites as a result of the domain controller placement, and about any additional partitions that may need to be replicated to a site. Answer the following questions:

- Will domain, configuration, and schema partitions be replicated to the site?
- Will a global catalog be replicated to the site?
- Will ForestDnsZones and DomainDnsZones partitions be replicated to the site?
- Will any special application partitions be replicated to the site? If so, what partitions, how are they used, and which domain controllers will host them?

By answering all these questions, you will know what servers will be placed in each site as well as what information will be replicated between sites. Don't forget about dependent services for Active Directory. At a minimum, each site should have at least one domain controller, a global catalog, and DNS. This configuration allows intrasite replication to occur without having to go across site links for dependent services. To improve the user experience, keep in mind the following facts:

- Global catalogs are needed for logon (unless universal group membership caching is enabled). If there is a local global catalog, logon can complete without a request having to go across a site link.
- DHCP servers are needed for dynamic IP addressing. If there is a local DHCP server, clients with dynamic IP addressing will be able to start up and get an IP address assignment without having to go across a site link.
- DNS servers are needed for forward and reverse lookups. If there is a local DNS server, clients will be able to perform DNS queries without having to go across a site link.

Chapter 36

Implementing Active Directory

Once you've completed planning, the process of implementing Active Directory is similar whether you are installing Active Directory for the first time or extending your existing Active Directory infrastructure. In either case, you need to take the following steps:

1. Install the necessary domain controllers and assign any other needed roles to these servers
2. Create the necessary organizational units (OUs) and delegate administrative control over these OUs as necessary
3. Create any necessary user, group, and computer accounts as well as the resources that are required for use in a domain
4. Use group policy and local security policy to set default settings for user and computer environments in any domains and OUs you've created
5. Create the necessary sites and configure those sites for use and replication

In this chapter, I examine the steps for installing domain controllers, creating OUs, and delegating administrative control. Chapter 37, "Managing Users, Groups, and Computers," discusses creating user, group, and computer accounts as well as related group policy. Chapter 38, "Managing Group Policy," discusses managing group policy and local security policy. Chapter 39, "Active Directory Site Administration," discusses creating sites and managing replication.

Preinstallation Considerations for Active Directory

Whenever you work with a Microsoft Windows component as complex as Active Directory, you should take time to carefully consider the physical implementation. As with the installation of Microsoft SQL Server, Microsoft Exchange Server, or Microsoft Internet Information Systems (IIS), you should evaluate hardware requirements, plan for the system's backup needs, and consider how the system will be used.

Hardware and Configuration Considerations for Domain Controllers

Every domain controller is essentially a database server with a complex replication system, and as such, when you select hardware for and configure domain controllers, you should use all the care and attention that you'd give to one of your mainstay database servers. The hardware you choose for the domain controllers should be as robust as the hardware for your database servers.

The following guidelines should be taken into consideration:

- **Processor** The CPU for a domain controller needs to be relatively fast. As soon as you install the second domain controller in a forest, a process called the *knowledge consistency checker (KCC)* begins running on every domain controller. The KCC is responsible for generating the replication topology and dynamically handling changes and failures within the replication topology. By default, the KCC on every domain controller recalculates the replication topology every 15 minutes. The more complex the replication topology, the more processing power it takes to perform, and, in many cases, even in small domain environments, the calculations performed by the KCC will cause the CPU to go to 100 percent utilization. This is acceptable for short durations. However, if the domain controller doesn't have a fast enough CPU, generating the replication topology in a complex environment could take several minutes rather than several seconds, which would severely affect the performance of all other processes running on the server.
- **Multiprocessing** Some installations may benefit from having domain controllers with multiple CPUs. With multiple processors, you may see significant performance improvements. However, rather than having a single beefy domain controller, it is better to have multiple domain controllers placed appropriately.
- **Memory** Domain controllers may use more memory than other servers. In addition to running standard processes, domain controllers must run special processes, such as storage engine processes, knowledge consistency checking, replication, and garbage collection. Therefore, most domain controllers should have at least 512 megabytes (MB) of RAM as a starting point. Be sure to monitor memory usage and upgrade as necessary.
- **Disks** The data storage capacity you need depends entirely on the number of objects related to users, computers, groups, and resources that are stored in the Active Directory database. The initial installation of Active Directory requires only about 25 MB of available space. By default, the database is stored in the Ntdis.dit database file on the system volume, as are related log files. When the database and log files are stored together, the storage volume should have free disk space of at least 20 percent of the combined size of the database and log files. When the database and log files are stored separately, each storage volume should have free disk space of at least 20 percent of either the database or the log files, as appropriate.

- **Data protection** Domain controllers should use fault-tolerant drives to protect against hardware failure of the system volume and any other volumes used by Active Directory. I recommend using a redundant array of independent disks (RAID), either RAID 1 or RAID 5. Hardware RAID is preferable to software RAID.

As part of the hardware configuration, you should consider where you will install the files used by Active Directory. Active Directory database and log files are stored by default in the %SystemRoot%\NTDS folder, while the Active Directory system volume (Sysvol), which is created as a shared folder, and contains policy, scripts, and other related files, is stored by default in the %SystemRoot%\SYSVOL folder. These locations are completely configurable during installation; some consideration should be given to whether you want to accept the defaults or store the files elsewhere. You'll get much better scalability and performance if you put the database and log files on different volumes, each on a separate drive. The Active Directory Sysvol can remain in the default location in most cases.

Note If you decide to move the Sysvol, it must be moved to an NTFS-5 volume. Because of this requirement, a volume formatted under Microsoft Windows NT is not acceptable. For security reasons, the database and log folders should be on NTFS-5 volumes as well, but this isn't a requirement.

Active Directory is dependent on network connectivity and the Domain Name System (DNS). Domain controllers should be configured to use static Internet Protocol (IP) addresses and have the appropriate primary and secondary DNS servers set in their Transmission Control Protocol/Internet Protocol (TCP/IP) configuration, as discussed in Chapter 24, "Managing TCP/IP Networking." If DNS isn't available on the network, you have the opportunity to make DNS available during the installation of Active Directory. Implement DNS as discussed in Chapter 26, "Architecting DNS Infrastructure," and Chapter 27, "Implementing and Managing DNS," and be sure to configure the DNS server to use itself for DNS resolution. If you previously deployed Microsoft DNS, as discussed in Chapters 26 and 27, the DNS environment should already be set to work with Active Directory.

If you are using a Domain Name System (DNS) server that does not use the Windows DNS, you can verify that the DNS server will work properly with Active Directory by using the Domain Controller Diagnostic Utility (Dcdiag.exe). This utility is included as part of the Windows Support Tools. Once you've installed the Support Tools, you can run Dcdiag and test the DNS configuration by typing the following command at the command prompt:

```
dcdiag /test:dcpromo /dnsdomain:DomainName /newforest
```

where *DomainName* is the name of the DNS domain in which the domain controller is located. Consider the following example:

```
dcdiag /test:dcpromo /dnsdomain:cpandl.com /newforest
```

Here, you run a test of the Active Directory Installation Wizard (Dcpromo.exe) to see if the DNS domain cpandl.com is compatible for creating a new forest. Any errors in the output of the test would need to be examined closely and resolved.

Configuring Active Directory for Fast Recovery with Storage Area Networks

Domain controllers are backed up differently than other servers are. To back up Active Directory, you must back up the System State. A backup of the System State includes the Active Directory database and log files, the Sysvol, the Registry, system boot files, and the COM+ registration database. These items must be backed up as a set and cannot be divided. To keep the System State intact when you place the volumes related to Active Directory on a Storage Area Network (SAN), you must also place the operating system (system and boot volume) on the SAN. This means that you must then boot from the SAN.

Booting from a SAN and configuring Active Directory so that the related volumes are on a SAN enables several fast recovery scenarios—most of which make use of the Volume Shadow Copy service (VSS). For instance, a domain controller is using the C, D, and E volumes: C for the operating system and Sysvol, D for the Active Directory database, and E for the Active Directory logs. Using a third-party backup utility that makes use of the Volume Shadow Copy service, you may be able to use that backup software to create shadow copies of the System State on separate Logical Unit Numbers (LUNs) on the SAN.

On the SAN, let's say that volumes C, D, and E correspond to LUNs 1, 2, and 3 and that the current shadow copy of those volumes is on LUNs 7, 8, and 9. If Active Directory were to fail at this point, you could recover by performing the following steps:

1. Use the DiskRAID utility to mask the failed LUNs (1, 2, and 3) so that they are no longer accessible.

> **Note** The DiskRaid utility is a command-line tool for configuring and managing RAID storage subsystems, such as those associated with network-attached storage (NAS) and storage area networks (SANs). When you install the Windows Server 2003 Resource Kit, this tool is available for use.

2. Use the DiskRAID utility to unmask the shadow-copied LUNs (7, 8, and 9) so they are usable.
3. You would then boot the domain controller to BIOS, set the boot device to LUN 6, and then reboot.
4. You've now recovered Active Directory. When the domain controller starts, it will recover the Active Directory database and synchronize with the rest of the domain controllers in the organization through regular replication.

Connecting Clients to Active Directory

Network clients connect to Active Directory for logon and authentication and to perform Lightweight Directory Access Protocol (LDAP) lookups. In a standard configuration of Active Directory running on Microsoft Windows Server 2003, communications between clients and servers are secure and use either Server Message Block (SMB) signing or secure channel encryption and signing. Secure communications are used by default because the default security policy for Windows Server 2003 has higher security settings than the security policies for previous versions of Windows.

Windows clients running versions earlier than Microsoft Windows 2000 do not natively support either of these secure communications methods. Therefore, these Windows clients cannot log on or authenticate in a Windows Server 2003 domain until you update them.

- To allow Microsoft Windows 95 and Microsoft Windows 98 clients to securely communicate with Active Directory, you need to install the Directory Services Client on these systems.
- To allow Windows NT clients with Service Pack 3 and earlier to securely communicate with Active Directory, you need to install the Directory Services Client or Service Pack 4 or later on these systems.

Windows clients running Windows 2000 or later do not need to have a separate client installed. These clients all natively support SMB signing, secure channel encryption and signing, or both.

Note Note that Microsoft Windows for Workgroups does not support secure communications in this way and cannot be updated. This means that you'll need to upgrade any clients running Windows for Workgroups.

Inside Out

Secure communications for domain controllers

One reason for configuring secure communications by default is to prevent certain types of security attacks. Secure communications specifically thwarts man-in-the-middle attacks, among others. In this attack, a third machine gets between the client and the server and pretends to be the other machine to each. This allows the man-in-the-middle machine to intercept and modify data that is transmitted between the client and the server. That said, if you must disable secure communications, you can do so. Remember that disabling the secure communications requirement won't allay the need to install an Active Directory client on Windows clients running versions earlier than Windows 2000—they'll still need a client, but there is an unsecured client for Windows for Workgroups as well as Windows NT 4 clients with Service Pack 3 and earlier.

To disable the secure communications requirement, follow these steps:

1. Start Active Directory Users And Computers. Right-click Domain Controllers in the console tree, and then select Properties.
2. In the Properties dialog box, select the Group Policy tab, and then click Edit.
3. In the Group Policy Object Editor, expand Computer Configuration, Windows Settings, Security Settings, Local Policies, and Security Options.
4. Under Security Options, right-click Domain Member: Digitally Encrypt Or Sign Secure Channel Data (Always), and then select Properties.
5. In the Properties dialog box, select Disabled, and then click OK.

Installing Active Directory

Installing Active Directory on a computer running Windows Server 2003 makes that computer a domain controller. During installation, you are given the option of setting the domain controller type as a domain controller either for a new domain or as an additional domain controller in an existing domain. If you make the domain controller part of a new domain, you can create a new domain in a new forest, a child domain in an existing domain tree, or a new domain tree in an existing forest. In fact, this is how you extend Active Directory structure from the first domain in a new forest to include additional domains and domain trees.

Active Directory Installation Options and Issues

You have several options for installing Active Directory. You can use one of the following:

- Configure Your Server Wizard
- Manage Your Server
- Active Directory Installation Wizard
- Active Directory Installation Wizard with backup media

All these installation techniques have one thing in common: at some point they all use the Active Directory Installation Wizard (Dcpromo.exe) to install Active Directory. They all also require that you use an account with administrator privileges. The administrator privileges you need depend on whether you are as follows:

- **Creating a domain controller in a new forest** If you are creating a domain controller in a new forest, you should log on to the local machine using either the local Administrator account or an account that has administrator privileges on the local machine, and then start the installation.

- **Creating a domain controller in a new domain or a domain tree** If you are creating a domain controller in a new domain or a new domain tree in an existing forest, you should log on to the local machine using either the local Administrator account or an account that has administrator privileges on the local machine, and then start the installation.

  You will also be required to provide the credentials for an account that is a member of the Enterprise Admins group in the forest of which the domain will be a part.
- **Creating an additional domain controller in an existing domain** If you are creating an additional domain controller in an existing domain, you should consider whether you want to restore a backup of Active Directory from media rather than creating the domain controller from scratch. With either technique, you will need to log on to the local machine using either the local Administrator account or an account that has administrator privileges on the local machine, and then start the installation.

  You will also be required to provide the credentials for an account that is a member of the Domain Admins group in the domain of which the domain controller will be a part. It is not necessary for the server to be a member of the domain, as you will be given the opportunity to join the domain controller to the domain if necessary.

Before starting the Active Directory installation, you should examine local accounts and check for encrypted files and folders. As domain controllers do not have local accounts or separate cryptographic keys, making a server a domain controller deletes all local accounts and all certificates and cryptographic keys from the server. Any encrypted data on the server, including data stored using the Encrypting File System (EFS), must be decrypted before installing Active Directory or it will be permanently inaccessible.

Inside Out

Finding encrypted files

To search an entire volume for encrypted files, change directories to the root directory using the CD command, and then examine the entire contents of the directory by using the EFS-Info utility as follows:

```
efsinfo /s:DriveDesignator /i | find ": Encrypted"
```

where *DriveDesignator* is the drive designator of the volume to search, such as C:, as shown in the following example:

```
efsinfo /s:c: /i | find ": Encrypted"
```

Here, EFSInfo is used to search the root directory of C: and all its subdirectories and display the encryption status of all files and folders. As you care about only the encrypted file and folders, you pipe the output to the Find utility and search it for the string ": Encrypted", which is a text string that appears only in the output for encrypted files and folders.

Using the Configure Your Server Wizard

You can start an Active Directory installation using the Configure Your Server Wizard. Select Configure Your Server Wizard from the Administrative Tools menu. When the wizard starts, as shown in Figure 36-1, click Next twice. The wizard will then gather information about the server configuration. On the Server Role page, select Domain Controller (Active Directory), and then click Next twice. Configure Your Server then starts the Active Directory Installation Wizard, which is discussed next.

Figure 36-1. The Configure Your Server Wizard.

Using the Active Directory Installation Wizard

You can start the Active Directory Installation Wizard via the Configure Your Server Wizard or by typing **dcpromo** at the command prompt. Once you start the wizard, the Welcome page appears, as shown in Figure 36-2. The way you continue depends on whether you are adding an additional domain controller for an existing domain or creating a domain controller in a new domain.

Active Directory Installation Wizard

Welcome to the Active Directory Installation Wizard

This wizard helps you install Active Directory services on this server, making the server a domain controller.

If this is the first time you have installed Active Directory, it is recommended that you first read the overview in Active Directory Help.

To continue, click Next.

< Back | Next > | Cancel

Figure 36-2. The Active Directory Installation Wizard.

Creating Additional Domain Controllers for an Existing Domain

To create an additional domain controller for an existing domain, follow these steps:

1. Start the Active Directory Installation Wizard as discussed previously. Click Next twice to skip the Operating System Compatibility page; I've discussed the compatibility needs in the section entitled "Connecting Clients to Active Directory" earlier in this chapter. Continue with the installation.
2. On the Domain Controller Type page, shown in Figure 36-3, select Additional Domain Controller For An Existing Domain. Click Next.

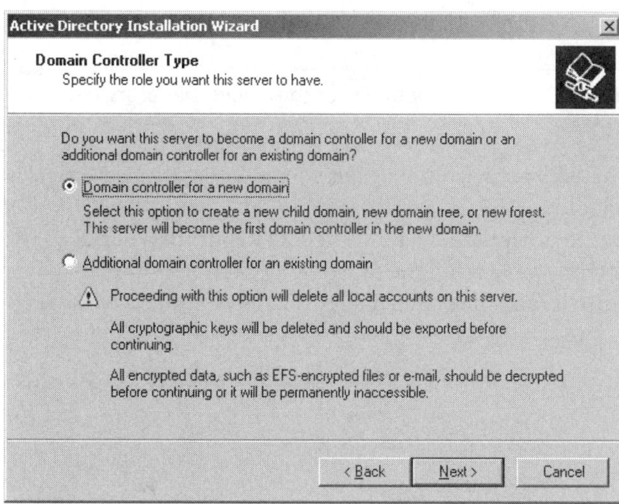

Figure 36-3. Specify the role for the domain controller.

> **Caution** Before continuing, make sure you check for encrypted files and folders as discussed in the section entitled "Active Directory Installation Options and Issues" earlier in this chapter. If you don't do this and there are encrypted files and folders present, you will no longer be able to decrypt them.

3. On the Network Credentials page, type the user name, password, and user domain of an account with Domain Admins privileges. Click Next.
4. On the Database And Log Folders page, shown in Figure 36-4, select a location to store the Active Directory database folder and log folder. The default location for both is %SystemRoot%\NTDS. As discussed in the section entitled "Hardware and Configuration Considerations for Domain Controllers" earlier in this chapter, you'll get better performance if these folders are on two separate volumes, each on a separate disk. Click Next when you are ready to continue.

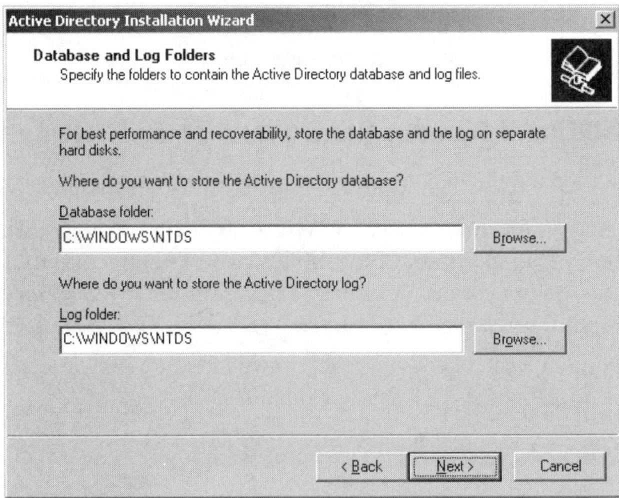

Figure 36-4. Specify the location for the Active Directory database and log folders.

5. On the Shared System Volume page, shown in Figure 36-5, select a location to store the Sysvol folder. The default location is %SystemRoot%\Sysvol. In most cases, you'll want to accept the default. The File Replication Service (FRS), which is responsible for replicating the Sysvol folder to other domain controllers as well as to other distributed file system (DFS) shares on the server, stores its database in the

%SystemRoot%\NTFRS folder anyway, so by keeping the folders on the same volume, you reduce the need to move files between drives.

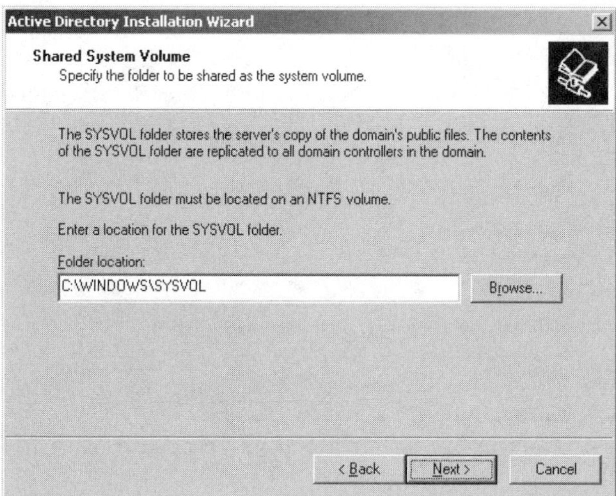

Figure 36-5. Specify the location for the Sysvol folder.

6 When you click Next, the wizard examines the network environment and attempts to register the domain and the domain controller in DNS. If it has any problems with registration, the wizard displays a diagnostics page like the one shown in Figure 36-6. Here, you have the opportunity to correct the problem with DNS and check again, to install and configure Microsoft DNS on the server, or to configure DNS later. In most cases, you'll want to use one of the first two options—either by making necessary changes to the server's DNS configuration or by allowing the wizard to install DNS. If you choose the third option, you'll need to create several advanced modifications to DNS and create a number of records manually—don't do this when the wizard can do it for you.

Note If you choose to let the wizard install DNS, the DNS Server service will be installed and the domain controller will also act as a DNS server. A primary DNS zone will be created as an Active Directory–integrated zone with the same name as the new domain you are setting up. The wizard will also update the server's TCP/IP configuration so that its primary DNS server is set to itself—unless you forgot to change the server's dynamic IP address to a static one, in which case you'll be prompted to configure the TCP/IP settings yourself.

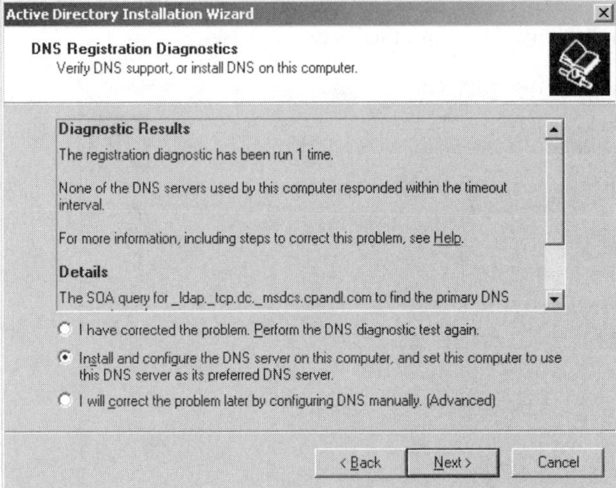

Figure 36-6. Verify DNS support and optionally choose to install the DNS Server service.

7 Click Next to display the Permissions page, and then select the default permissions for users and groups, as shown in Figure 36-7.

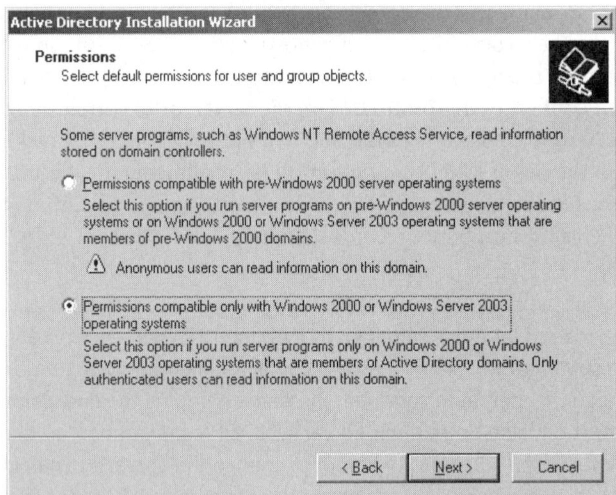

Figure 36-7. Specify the default permissions for users and groups.

The available options on this page are as follows:

- *Permissions Compatible With Pre–Windows 2000 Server Operating Systems*—Select this option to reduce the default security and allow anonymous user logons. Select this option only if the domain will have Windows NT servers running Windows NT applications or services that require anonymous user logons, such as Remote Access Service (RAS) or SQL Server running on Windows NT 4. By selecting this option, you are telling the wizard to add the special groups Everyone and Anonymous Logon to the Pre-Windows 2000-Compatible Access domain local group on the server and to fully allow anonymous logon and anonymous access to Active Directory data.

- *Permissions Compatible Only With Windows 2000 Or Windows Server 2003 Operating Systems*—Select this option to enforce the default security and prevent anonymous user logons. If the domain will have Windows 2000 or later computers running Windows 2000 or later services and applications, choose this option. When this option is selected, only authorized users can log on to the domain and access Active Directory data.

Tip In a domain where permissions have been configured to be compatible with Windows NT 4 services and applications, you can later change the domain environment so that anonymous logon and anonymous access are no longer allowed. Once you've upgraded all Windows NT 4 servers, services, and applications in the domain, you should do this to enhance security. Simply remove the members from the Pre-Windows 2000-Compatible Access group in Active Directory Users And Computers.

8. Click Next, and then type and confirm the password that should be used when you want to start the computer in Directory Services Restore Mode, as shown in Figure 36-8. Be sure to track this password carefully. This special password is used only in Restore mode and is different from the Administrator account password.

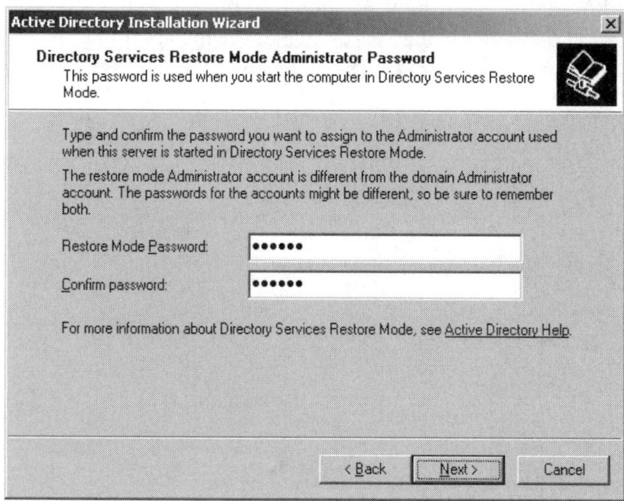

Figure 36-8. Specify the password for Directory Services Restore Mode.

9. Click Next. Review the installation options. When you click Next again, the wizard will use the options you've selected to install and configure Active Directory. This process can take several minutes. Your options are as follows:
   - If you specified that the DNS Server service should be installed, the server will also be configured as a DNS Server at this time. In this case, the wizard will also check to make sure that the server isn't using a dynamic IP address. If it is, you'll see the Choose Connection dialog box. You'll need to choose a network connection, and then click Properties. This displays the Internet Protocol (TCP/IP) Properties dialog box, which you can use to set a static IP address and the necessary TCP/IP settings for the computer. Click OK twice to close these dialog boxes and continue with the DNS server installation.
   - If you are installing an additional domain controller in an existing domain, the domain controller will need to obtain updates of all the directory partitions from other domain controllers and will do this by initiating a full synchronization. The only way to avoid this is to make a media backup of Active Directory on an existing domain controller, start the Active Directory Installation Wizard in Advanced mode, and then specify the backup media to use during installation of Active Directory.
10. When the wizard finishes configuring Active Directory, click Finish. You are then prompted to restart the domain controller. Click Restart Now to reboot.

After installing Active Directory, you should verify the installation by doing the following (in no particular order):

- Examine the log of the installation, which is stored in the Dcpromo.log file in the %SystemRoot%\Debug folder. As shown in the following screen, the log is very detailed and takes you through every step of the installation process, including the creation of directory partitions and the securing of the Registry for Active Directory.

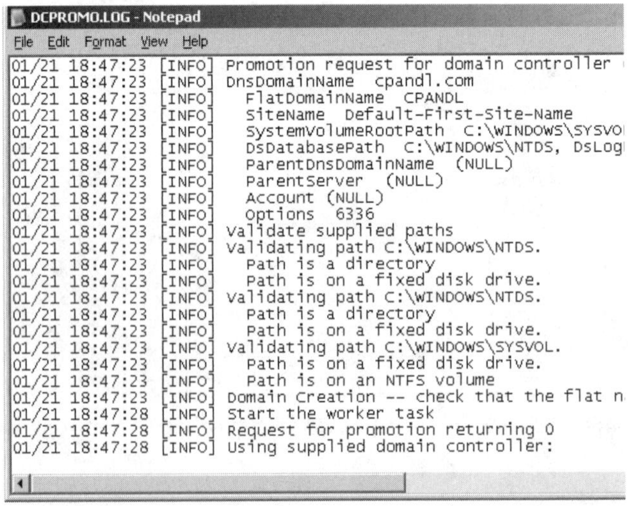

DCPROMO.LOG - Notepad

File Edit Format View Help

```
01/21 18:47:23 [INFO] Promotion request for domain controller
01/21 18:47:23 [INFO] DnsDomainName  cpandl.com
01/21 18:47:23 [INFO]   FlatDomainName  CPANDL
01/21 18:47:23 [INFO]   SiteName  Default-First-Site-Name
01/21 18:47:23 [INFO]   SystemVolumeRootPath  C:\WINDOWS\SYSVO
01/21 18:47:23 [INFO]   DsDatabasePath  C:\WINDOWS\NTDS, DsLog
01/21 18:47:23 [INFO]   ParentDnsDomainName  (NULL)
01/21 18:47:23 [INFO]   ParentServer  (NULL)
01/21 18:47:23 [INFO]   Account (NULL)
01/21 18:47:23 [INFO]   Options  6336
01/21 18:47:23 [INFO] Validate supplied paths
01/21 18:47:23 [INFO] Validating path C:\WINDOWS\NTDS.
01/21 18:47:23 [INFO]   Path is a directory
01/21 18:47:23 [INFO]   Path is on a fixed disk drive.
01/21 18:47:23 [INFO] Validating path C:\WINDOWS\NTDS.
01/21 18:47:23 [INFO]   Path is a directory
01/21 18:47:23 [INFO]   Path is on a fixed disk drive.
01/21 18:47:23 [INFO] Validating path C:\WINDOWS\SYSVOL.
01/21 18:47:23 [INFO]   Path is on a fixed disk drive.
01/21 18:47:23 [INFO]   Path is on an NTFS volume
01/21 18:47:23 [INFO] Domain Creation -- check that the flat n
01/21 18:47:28 [INFO] Start the worker task
01/21 18:47:28 [INFO] Request for promotion returning 0
01/21 18:47:28 [INFO] Using supplied domain controller:
```

- Check for DNS updates in the DNS console shown in the following screen. If you added a domain controller to an existing domain, DNS is updated to add SRV records for the server. If you created a new domain, DNS is updated to include a Forward Lookup Zone for the domain.

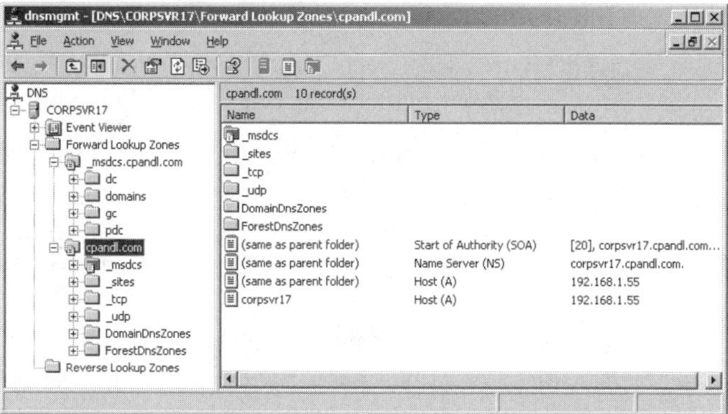

- Check for updates in Active Directory Users And Computers. For example, check to make sure the new domain controller is listed in the Domain Controllers OU, as shown in the following screen:

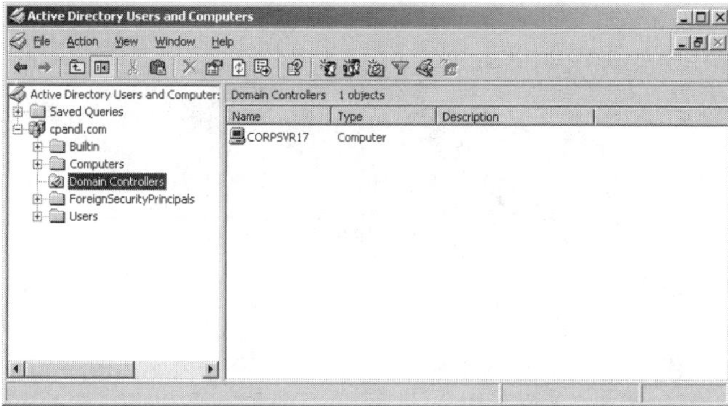

If you created a new domain, the following containers are created and populated as appropriate:

- Builtin contains the built-in accounts for administration, including Administrators and Account Operators.
- Computers contains computer accounts for the domain.
- Domain Controllers contains the domain controller accounts and should have an account for the domain controller you installed.
- ForeignSecurityPrinicipals is a container for security principals from other domain trees.
- Users is the default container for user accounts in the domain.

Creating Domain Controllers in a New Domain

To create a domain controller in a new domain, start the Active Directory Installation Wizard as discussed previously. Click Next twice to skip the Operating System Compatibility page; I've discussed the compatibility needs in the section entitled "Connecting Clients to Active Directory" earlier in this chapter. Continue with the installation.

On the Domain Controller Type page, select Domain Controller For A New Domain. Click Next. You will next need to choose whether to do one of the following:

- **Create a root domain in a new forest** Choose this option to establish the first domain controller in the organization or to install a new forest that is completely separate from any existing forests. By choosing this option, you are establishing the forest root domain. This means that the domain controller will have operations master roles across both the forest and the domain.

  1. When you click Next, you will go directly to the New Domain Name page, skipping the Network Credentials page. You don't need specific credentials because you are establishing a new forest with its own set of security groups.
  2. Click Next again to display the New Domain Name page shown in the following screen. Type the full DNS name for the new domain. Domain names are not case-sensitive and use the letters A to Z, the numerals 0 to 9, and the hyphen (-) character. Each component of the domain name must be separated by a dot (.) and cannot be longer than 63 characters.

- **Create a child domain in an existing domain tree** Choose this option to establish the first domain controller in a domain that is a child domain of an existing domain. By choosing this option, you are specifying that the necessary parent domain already exists. For example, you would choose this option if the parent domain cpandl.com had already been created and you wanted to create the tech.cpandl.com domain as a child of this domain.

  1. When you click Next, you will see the Network Credentials page. On this page, type the user name, password, and user domain of an account with Enterprise Admins privileges.
  2. Click Next again to display the Child Domain Installation page shown in the following screen. In the Parent Domain field, type the full DNS name for the parent domain, such as cpandl.com, or click Browse to search for an existing domain to use. In the Child Domain field, type the name component of the child domain, such as tech.

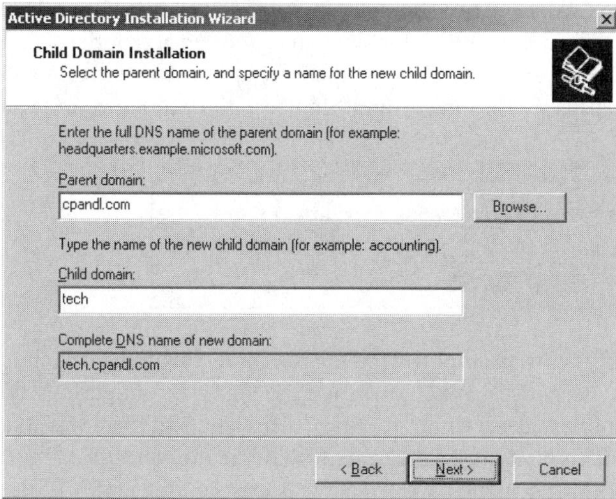

- **Create a domain tree in an existing forest** Choose this option to establish a new domain tree that is separate from any existing trees in the existing Active Directory forest. By choosing this option, you are specifying that there isn't an existing parent domain with which the new domain should be associated. For example, you would choose this option if the cohowinery.com domain already existed and you wanted to establish the cohovineyard.com domain in a new tree in the existing forest.

    1. When you click Next, you will see the Network Credentials page. On this page, type the user name, password, and user domain of an account with Enterprise Admins privileges.
    2. Click Next again to display the New Domain Tree page shown in the following screen. Type the full DNS name for the new domain. The domain name you use should not be a subdomain of an existing parent domain in any tree of the forest.

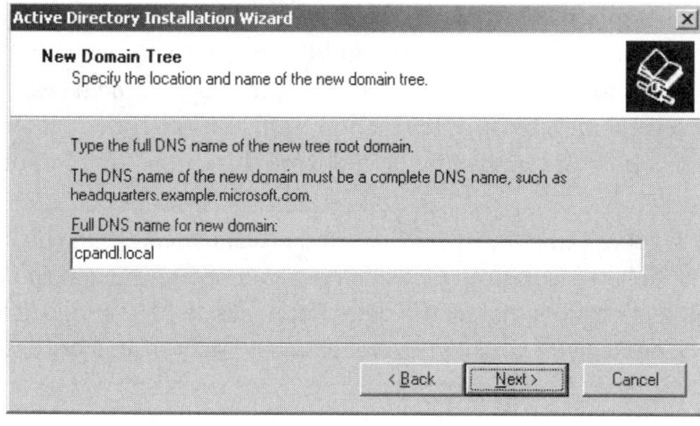

When you click Next, the Active Directory Installation Wizard will use the domain name you specified to set a default NetBIOS domain name. You can accept the default or type a new NetBIOS name of up to 15 characters. If there are any problems creating the default name, the wizard will display a warning prompt similar to the one shown in the following screen.

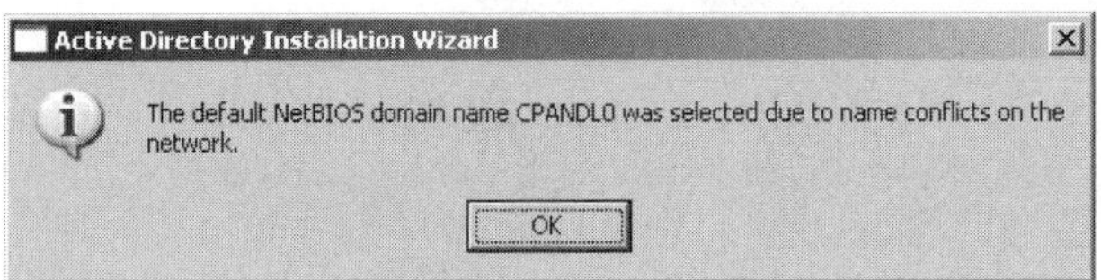

The wizard displays this prompt when there is a conflict with the default name originally selected and an alternative name has to be used. Here, I was configuring a domain tree named cpandl.local for internal use within City Power & Light, and there was an existing tree for cpandl.com. The conflict caused the wizard to choose the NetBIOS name CPANDL0 since a domain with NETBIOS name CPANDL already exists on the network.

The rest of the installation will proceed as previously discussed. Continue with steps 4-10 and the post-installation checks discussed in the previous section.

NEW FEATURE! Using the Active Directory Installation Wizard with Backup Media

Whenever you install an additional domain controller in an existing domain, you should consider whether you want to restore a backup of Active Directory from media rather than creating the domain controller from scratch. Doing so allows the Active Directory Installation Wizard to get the initial data for the Configuration, Schema, and Domain directory partitions from backup media rather than performing a full synchronization over the network.

Not only does this reduce the amount of network traffic, which is especially important when installing domain controllers in remote sites that are connected by low bandwidth WAN links, it can also greatly speed up the process of installing an additional domain controller and getting the directory partition data synchronized. This means that rather than having to get the full data in Configuration, Schema, and Domain directory partitions, the domain controller only needs to get the changes made since the backup media was made. This can mean that only several megabytes of replication traffic are generated rather than several gigabytes, and on a busy or low-bandwidth network this can be very important.

Note Restoring Active Directory from backup media is not designed to be used to restore failed domain controllers. To restore failed domain controllers, you should use System State restore as this ensures that all the data that needs to be restored is recovered as necessary, including Registry settings, Sysvol data, and Active Directory data.

There are a few guidelines that you should follow when installing Active Directory from backup media:

- Always try to use the most recent backup of Active Directory as possible. This will reduce the number of updates that must be replicated to the domain controller, which in turn will minimize the post-installation replication traffic.
- Always use a backup of a domain controller in the same domain in which the new domain controller is being created, and always use a backup from another Windows Server 2003 domain controller and not from a Windows 2000 domain controller.
- Always restore the backup to a local drive on the server for which you are installing Active Directory. You cannot use backup media from Universal Naming Convention (UNC) paths or mapped drives.
- Never use backup media that is older than the tombstone lifetime of the domain. The default value is 60 days. If you try to use backup media older than 60 days, the Active Directory installation will fail. For more information on tombstone lifetime and why it is important, see the section entitled "Extensible Storage Engine," on page 1091.

With these guidelines in mind, you can create an additional domain controller from backup media by completing the following steps:

1. Create a System State backup on a domain controller in the domain using the Backup utility. You can start Backup by typing **ntbackup** at the command line or in the Run dialog box, or by clicking Start, Programs or All Programs, Accessories, System Tools, Backup. By default, Backup starts in wizard mode. To change this behavior, clear Always Start In Wizard Mode, and then click Advanced Mode. This takes you to the main Backup interface.
2. Select the Backup tab, and then select the System State check box as shown in the following screen. You can then configure the rest of the backup as you would any other backup. This includes selecting the other data you want to back up, specifying the backup media to use, and clicking Start Backup to begin the backup process.

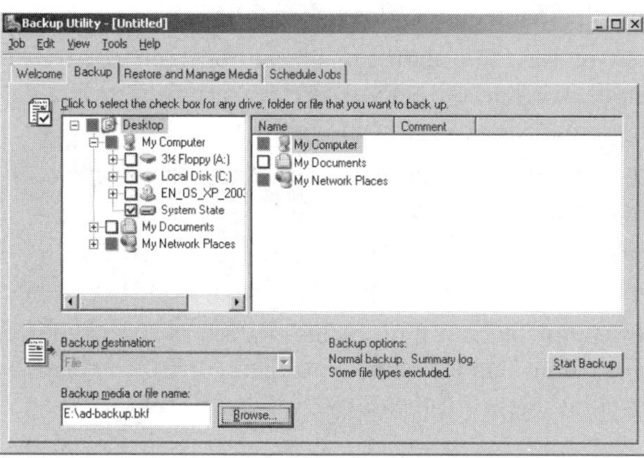

Chapter 36

3 Restore the System State backup to the server you want to be a domain controller. For example, write the backup to a DVD, and then access the DVD using the NTBACKUP command on the server that you want to be a domain controller. Start NTBACKUP, and then click Restore And Manage Media as shown in the following screen.

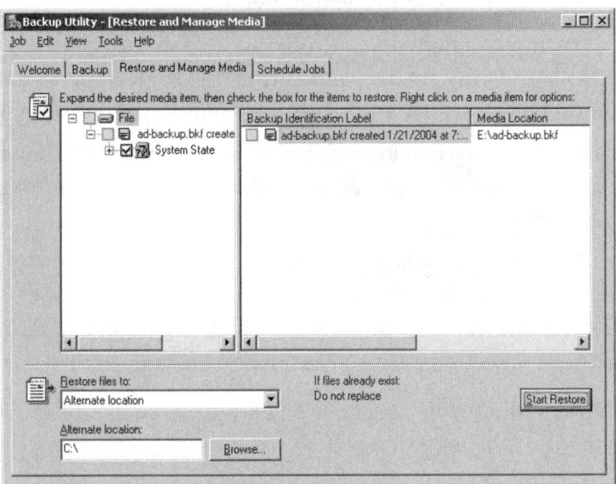

4 Catalog the backup file so that its details are available on the current computer. From the Tools menu, select Catalog A Backup File. In the Open Backup File dialog box, type the full file path to the backup file on the DVD or click Browse to file the backup file, and then click OK.

5 Expand the backup media entry, and then select System State, which is what you want to restore.

6 Under Restore Files To, select Alternate Location, and then, under Alternate Location, select the folder in which to restore the backup. Click Start Restore. When notified that you aren't restoring the System State, click OK. This is as it should be. Click OK again to begin the restore. Click Close when the restore finishes.

7 On the server you want to make a domain controller, install Active Directory in Advanced mode. You start the Active Directory Installation Wizard in Advanced mode by typing **dcpromo /adv** at a command prompt.

8 On the Domain Controller Type page, select Additional Domain Controller For An Existing Domain, and then click Next.

9 On the Copying Domain Information page, select From These Restored Backup Files, and then type the location of the restore backup files or click Browse to find them.

10 You can now complete the rest of the installation as discussed in the section entitled "Creating Additional Domain Controllers for an Existing Domain" earlier in this chapter. Continue with steps 3 to 10 and perform the post-installation checks as well.

Uninstalling Active Directory

You uninstall Active Directory using the same techniques as you used to install it. You can run Configure Your Server and remove the Domain Controller (Active Directory) role, which in turn will start the Active Directory Installation Wizard, or you can simply type **dcpromo** at a command prompt to start the Active Directory Installation Wizard directly. When you uninstall Active Directory, you demote the domain controller and make it a member server in the domain. If you remove Active Directory from the last domain controller in the domain, the computer becomes a stand-alone server in a workgroup. You must be a member of the Domain Admins group to remove an additional domain controller in a domain, and a member of the Enterprise Admins group to remove the last domain controller from a domain.

Considerations for Removing Global Catalogs

If you run the Active Directory Installation Wizard on a domain controller that is also a global catalog server, you will see the warning prompt shown in the following screen:

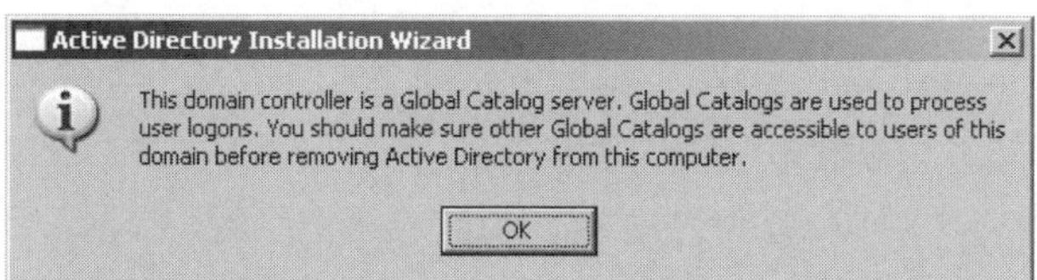

This prompt appears because you don't want to remove the last global catalog from the domain accidentally. If you remove the last global catalog from the domain, users won't be able to log on to the domain. A quick way to check to determine the global catalog servers in a domain is to type the following command at a command prompt:

```
dsquery server -domain DomainName | dsget server -isgc -dnsname
```

where *DomainName* is the name of the domain you want to examine. Consider the following example:

```
dsquery server -domain cpandl.com | dsget server -isgc -dnsname
```

Here, you are examining the cpandl.com domain to obtain a list of the global catalog servers according to their DNS names. The output is shown in two columns, for example:

```
dnsname                        isgc
corpsvr15.cpandl.com           no
corpsvr17.cpandl.com           yes
```

The first column is the DNS name of each domain controller in the domain. The second column is a flag that indicates whether the domain controller is also a global catalog. Thus, if the *isgc* value is set to *yes* for a domain controller, it is also a global catalog server.

When the wizard starts, click Next to display the Remove Active Directory page shown in Figure 36-9. If this is the last domain controller in the domain and you want to demote it, select This Server Is The Last Domain Controller In The Domain before you continue. After you remove the last domain controller in the domain, you will no longer be able to access any application partition data, domain accounts, or encrypted data. Therefore, before you uninstall the last domain controller in a domain, you should examine domain accounts and look for encrypted files and folders.

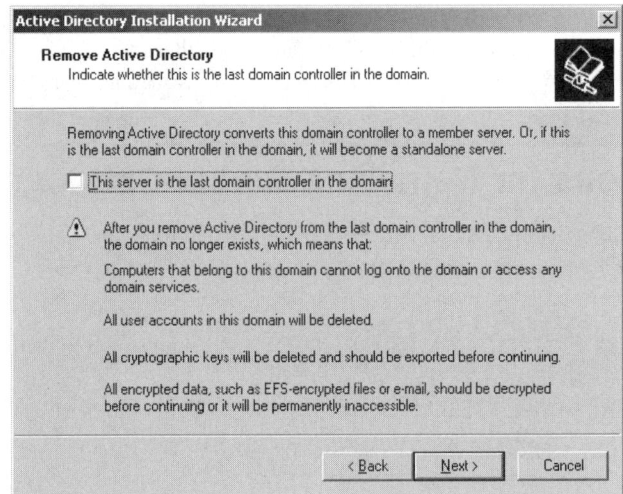

Figure 36-9. Removing Active Directory from a server.

Note Because the domain will no longer exist, its accounts and cryptographic keys are no longer applicable, and this results in the deletion of all domain accounts and all certificates and cryptographic keys from the server. Any encrypted data on the server, including data stored using the Encrypting File System (EFS), must be decrypted before removing Active Directory or it will be permanently inaccessible.

When you are ready to continue, click Next. The Active Directory Installation Wizard shows you any default application data partitions that will be lost if you proceed, as shown in Figure 36-10. If the domain controller is also a DNS server, the DNS data in the ForestDnsZones and DomainDnsZones partitions will be removed. If the domain controller is the last DNS server in the domain, this will result in the last replica of the DNS information being removed from the domain. All associated DNS records will be lost and may need to be recreated.

Click Next. Confirm that you really want to permanently delete the previously listed application partitions by selecting Delete All Application Directory Partitions On This Domain Controller, and then click Next again.

Active Directory Installation Wizard

Application Directory Partitions
Applications create these partitions for storing and replicating data.

This domain controller holds the last replica of the following application directory partitions:

Partition Distinguished Name	Description
DC=DomainDnsZones,DC=cpandl,D...	Microsoft DNS Directory
DC=ForestDnsZones,DC=cpandl,DC...	Microsoft DNS Directory

Update List

You should usually remove an application partition with the utility provided by the application that installed it. For more information, see Help.

If you want the wizard to remove all partitions from this domain controller, click Next.

< Back Next > Cancel

Figure 36-10. Carefully check the application partitions that will be lost.

Next, you are prompted to type and confirm the password for the local Administrator account on the server, as shown in Figure 36-11. This is necessary because domain controllers don't have local accounts but member or stand-alone servers do, so this account will be recreated as part of the Active Directory removal process. To complete the Active Directory removal process, click Next, and then click Finish.

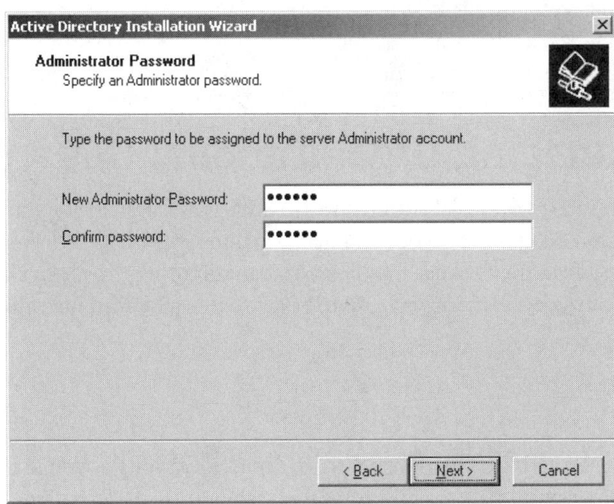

Figure 36-11. Set the local administrator password.

At this point, the actions the Active Directory Installation Wizard performs depend on whether you are removing an additional domain controller or removing the last domain controller from a domain. If you are removing an additional domain controller from a domain, the wizard does the following:

- Removes Active Directory and all related services from the server and makes it a member server in the domain
- Changes the computer account type and moves the computer account from the Domain Controllers container in Active Directory to the Computers container
- Transfers any operations master roles from the server to another domain controller in the domain
- Updates DNS to remove the domain controller SRV records
- Creates a local Security Accounts Manager (SAM) account database and a local Administrator account

If you are removing the last domain controller from a domain, the wizard verifies that there are no child domains of the current domain before continuing. If child domains are found, removal of Active Directory fails with an error telling you that you cannot remove Active Directory. When the domain being removed is a child domain, the wizard notifies a domain controller in the parent domain that the child domain is being removed. For a parent domain in its own tree, a domain controller in the forest root domain is notified. Either way, the domain object is tombstoned, and this change is then replicated to other domain controllers. The domain object and any related trust objects are also removed from the forest. As part of removing Active Directory from the last domain controller in a domain, all domain accounts, all certificates, and all cryptographic keys are removed from the server. The wizard creates a local SAM account database and a local Administrator account. It then changes the computer account type to a stand-alone server and puts the server in a new workgroup.

Creating and Managing Organizational Units (OUs)

Organizational units (OUs) are logical administrative units that can help you limit the scope of a domain. They can contain many types of objects, including those for computers, contacts, groups, printers, or users. Because they can also contain other OUs, you can build a hierarchy of OUs within a domain. You can also use OUs to delegate administrator privileges on a limited basis.

Creating an OU

You can create OUs in Active Directory Users And Computers. As long as you use an account that is a member of the Administrators group, you'll be able to create OUs anywhere in the domain. The only exception is that you cannot create OUs within the default containers created by Active Directory.

> **Note** Note that you can create OUs within the Domain Controllers container. This is possible because this container is created as an OU. Creating OUs within Domain Controllers is useful if you want to organize domain controllers.

To create an OU, follow these steps:

1. Click Start, Programs or All Programs, Administrative Tools, and Active Directory Users And Computers. This starts Active Directory Users And Computers.
2. By default, you are connected to your logon domain. If you want to create OUs in a different domain, right-click the Active Directory Users And Computers node in the console tree, and then select Connect To Domain. In the Connect To Domain dialog box, type the name of the domain to which you want to connect, and then click OK. Alternatively, in the Browse For Domain dialog box, you can click Browse to find the domain to which you want to connect.
3. You can now create the OU. If you want to create a top-level OU (that is, an OU that has the domain container as its parent), right-click the domain node in the console tree, point to New, and then select Organizational Unit. If you want to create a lower-level OU, right-click the OU in which you want to create the new OU, point to New, and then select Organizational Unit.
4. In the New Object–Organizational Unit dialog box, type a new name for the OU, as shown in Figure 36-12, and then click OK. Although the OU name can be any string of up to 256 characters, the best OU names are short and descriptive.

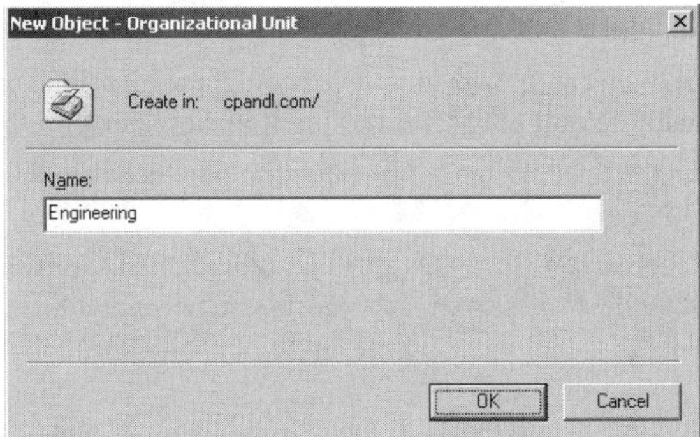

Figure 36-12. Specify the name of the OU to create.

Setting OU Properties

OUs have properties that you can set to add descriptive information. This will help other administrators know how the OU is used.

To set the properties of an OU, double-click the OU in Active Directory Users And Computers. This displays the OU's Properties dialog box, as shown in Figure 36-13.

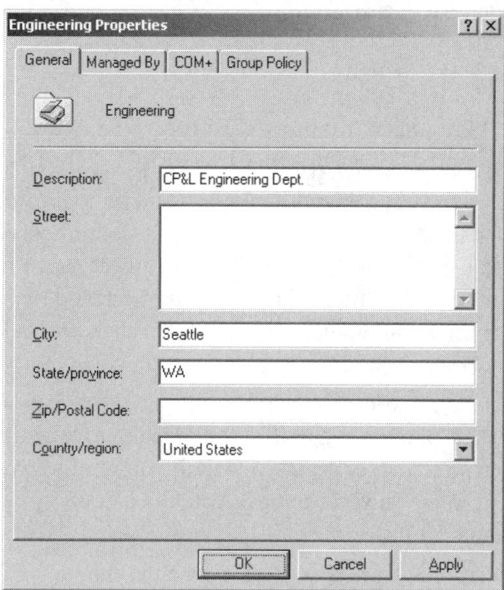

Figure 36-13. The OU properties dialog box.

- On the General tab, you can enter descriptive information about the OU, including a text description and address information.
- On the Managed By tab, you can specify the user or contact responsible for managing the OU. This gives a helpful point of contact for questions regarding the OU.
- On the COM+ tab, you can specify the COM+ partition of which the OU should be a member (if any).
- On the Group Policy tab, you can create Group Policy Objects that specify a set of rules for resources in the OU. These rules control the working environment for computers and users.

Creating or Moving Accounts and Resources for Use with an OU

After you create an OU, you might want to place accounts and resources in it. In Active Directory Users And Computers you follow one of these procedures:

- You create accounts in the OU, right-click the OU, point to New, and then select the type of object to create, such as Computer, Group, or User.

- You move existing accounts or resources to an OU, and then select the account or resources in its existing container by clicking and holding the left mouse button. You can then drag the account or resource to the OU. When you release the mouse button, the account or resource is moved to the OU. Using Ctrl+Click or Shift+Click, you can select and move multiple accounts as well.

Delegating Administration of Domains and OUs

When you create domains and OUs, you'll often want to be able to delegate control over them to specific individuals. This is useful if you want to give someone limited administrative privileges for a domain or OU. Before you delegate administration, you should carefully plan the permissions to grant. Ideally, you want to delegate the permissions that will allow a user to perform necessary tasks, while preventing your delegate from performing tasks he or she should not. Often, figuring out the tasks that a user with limited administrative permissions should be able to perform requires talking to the department or office manager or the individual.

Understanding Delegation of Administration

You delegate control of Active Directory objects to grant users permission to manage users, groups, computers, OUs, or other objects stored in Active Directory. You can grant permissions in the following ways:

- **Grant full control over an OU** Useful when you have local administrators within departments or at branch offices and you want those individuals to be able to manage all objects in the OU. Among other things, this allows local administrators to create and manage accounts in the OU.
- **Grant full control over specific types of objects in an OU** Useful when you have local administrators who should only be able to manage specific types of objects in an OU. For example, you might want local administrators to be able to manage users and groups but not to be able to manage computer accounts.
- **Grant full control over specific types of object in a domain** Useful when you want to allow an individual to be able only to manage specific types of objects in a domain. Rather than adding the user as a member of the Administrators group, you grant the user full control over specific objects. For example, you might allow the user to manage user and group accounts in the domain but not to perform other administrative tasks.
- **Grant rights to perform specific tasks** Useful when you want to allow an individual to perform a specific task. For example, you might want to allow a department manager to read information related to user accounts in Active Directory Users And Computers or you might want to allow help desk staff to be able to reset user passwords.

When you delegate permissions, it is important to remember how inheritance works in Active Directory. As you may recall from previous discussions of permissions, lower-level objects inherit permissions from top-level objects. In a domain, the top-level object is the domain object itself. This has the following results:

- Any user designated as an administrator for a domain automatically has full control over the domain.
- If you grant permissions at the domain level, the user will have those permissions for all OUs in the domain as well.
- If you grant permissions in a top-level OU, the user will have those permissions for all OUs that are created within the top-level OU.

Delegating Administration

To delegate administration of a domain or OU, follow these steps:

1. Start Active Directory Users And Computers. Click Start, Programs or All Programs, Administrative Tools, and Active Directory Users And Computers.
2. Right-click the domain or OU for which you want to delegate administration, and then select Delegate Control. When the Delegation Of Control Wizard starts, click Next.
3. On the Users Or Groups page shown in Figure 36-14, click Add to display the Select Users, Computers, Or Groups dialog box.

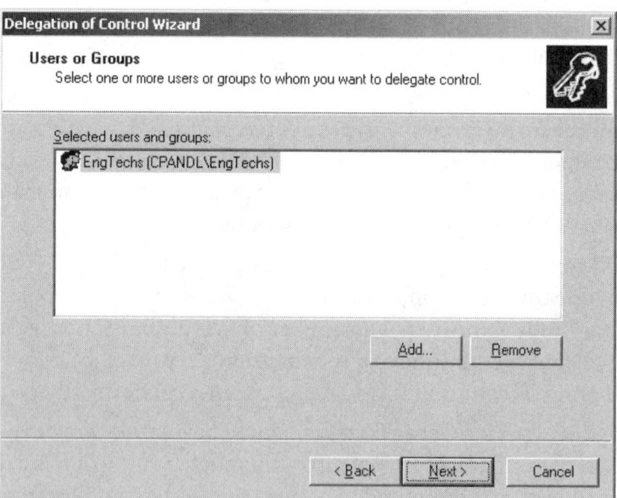

Figure 36-14. Select the users and groups for which you want to delegate control.

4. The default location is the current domain. Click Locations to see a list of the available domains and other resources that you can access. Because of the transitive trusts in

Windows Server 2003, you can usually access all the domains in the domain tree or forest.

5 Type the name of a user or group account in the selected or default domain, and then click Check Names. The options available depend on the number of matches found as follows:

- When a single match is found, the dialog box is automatically updated as appropriate and the entry is underlined.
- When no matches are found, you've either entered an incorrect name part or you're working with an incorrect location. Modify the name and try again or click Locations to select a new location.
- If multiple matches are found, select the name(s) you want to use, and then click OK.

6 To add additional users or groups, type a semicolon (;), and then repeat this process.

7 When you click OK, the users and groups are added to the Selected Users And Groups list in the Delegation Of Control Wizard. Click Next to continue.

8 On the Tasks To Delegate page, select the tasks you want to delegate. As shown in Figure 36-15, a list of common tasks is provided.

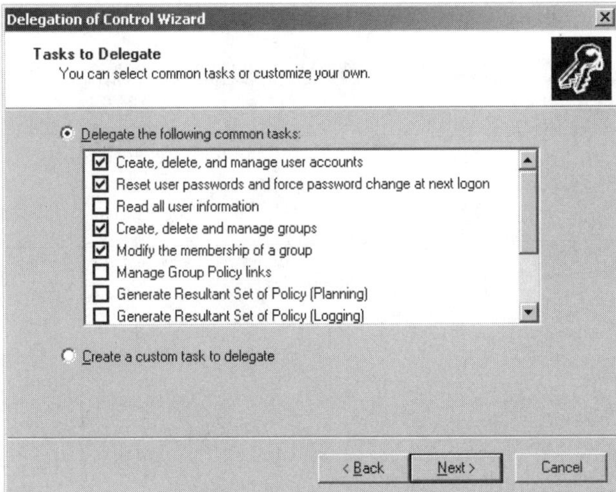

Figure 36-15. Select the tasks to delegate or choose to create a custom task.

9 If you want to delegate any of these common tasks, select the tasks. Afterward, click Next, and then click Finish. Skip the remaining steps.

10 If you want to create a custom task to delegate, choose Create A Custom Task To Delegate, and then click Next. On the Active Directory Object Type page, shown in Figure 36-16, you can now choose to delegate management of all objects in the container or limit the delegation to specific types of objects.

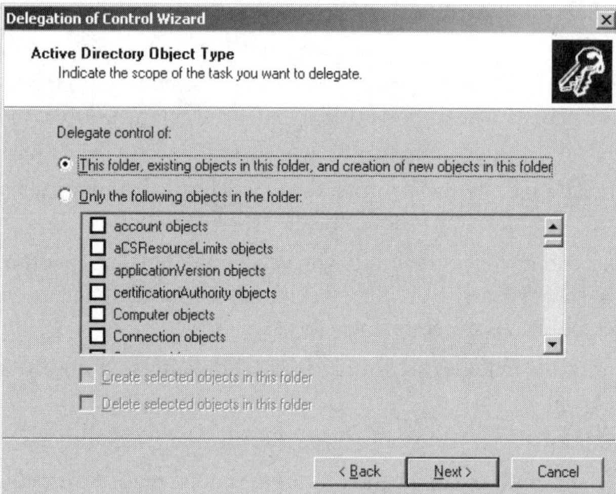

Figure 36-16. Select the tasks to delegate or choose to create a custom task.

11 On the Permissions page, shown in Figure 36-17, you can select the levels of permissions to delegate for the previously selected objects. You can choose to allow Full Control over the object or objects, or you can delegate very specific permissions.

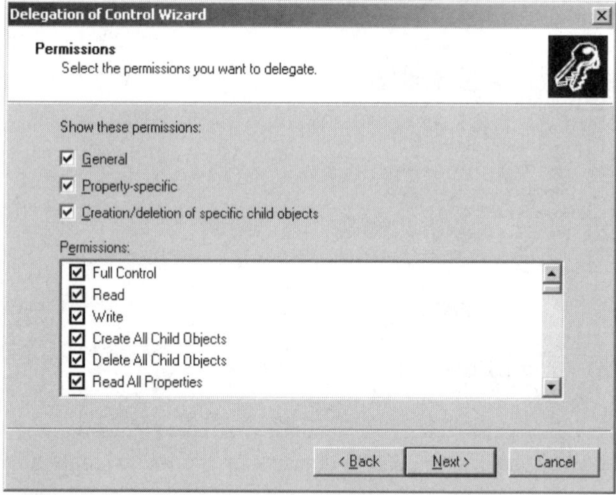

Figure 36-17. Specify the permissions to delegate for the previously selected objects.

12 Click Next, and then click Finish.

Chapter 37

Managing Users, Groups, and Computers

As an administrator, managing users, groups, and computers will probably be a significant part of your duties and responsibilities. Managing users, groups, and computers encapsulates the important duties of a system administrator because of the way convenience, performance, fault tolerance, and security must be balanced.

Managing Domain User Accounts

Microsoft Windows operating systems have come a long way from Microsoft Windows NT 4 when all you had was User Manager for Domains, two default users on installation, and only global and local groups. Managing users in Windows Server 2003 can be a daunting task for Windows NT administrators. Yet, when moving from Microsoft Windows 2000, there is little difference in the handling of users. The next part of this chapter is dedicated to helping you plan, manage, and administer user accounts in a secure and efficient manner.

Types of Users

It is a good idea to have a solid grasp of fundamental concepts that underpin the managing of users. In the first part of the chapter, I will describe the types of users Microsoft Windows Server 2003 defines.

- **User** In Windows Server 2003, you can have local user accounts or domain user accounts. On a domain controller, local users and groups are disabled. In Active Directory, the domain user account contains username, password, the groups of which the user is a member, and other descriptive information, such as address and phone numbers, as well as many other user descriptions and attributes, such as security and remote control configurations.
- **InetOrgPerson** InetOrgPerson is a new type of user in Windows Server 2003. InetOrgPerson has attributes based on Request for Comments (RFC) 2798 such as vehicle license number, department number, display name, employee number, JPEG

photograph, and preferred language. Used by X.500 and Lightweight Directory Access Protocol (LDAP) directory services, the InetOrgPerson account is used when you migrate non-Microsoft LDAP directories to Active Directory. Derivative of the user class, the InetOrgPerson can be used as a security principal. The InetOrgPerson is compatible with X.500 and LDAP directory services.

- **Contact** Sometime you may want to create an account that will only be used as an e-mail account. This is when you would create a contact. It is not a Security Principal and does not have a Security ID (SID). There are neither passwords nor logon functionality available with a contact account. However, it can be a member of a distribution group.
- **Default user accounts** These are the built-in user accounts created when a Windows Server 2003 installation or stand-alone server is configured to be a domain controller and Active Directory is installed. It is a good idea to rename the Administrator account for security reasons. The default user accounts are found by opening Active Directory Users And Computers, then examining the contents of the Builtin and Users containers. They include the following accounts:
  - *Administrator*—This is the account that has full control over the computer or domain. You should have a very strong password for this account. The Administrator is a member of these groups: Administrators, Domain Admins, Domain Users, and Group Policy Creator Owners. In a forest root domain, the Administrator is also a member of the Enterprise Admins and Schema Admins groups. The Administrator account can never be deleted. However, you can disable it (which is a new feature for Windows Server 2003) or rename it. Either of these actions is a good practice to ensure a secure domain and network.
  - *Guest*—The Guest account does not require a password and can be used by users who don't have an account in the domain. It is a member of the Guests domain local group and the Domain Guests global group. The Guest account is disabled by default when you make a stand-alone Windows Server 2003 server a domain controller.
  - *HelpAssistant*—This account is a dynamic object created when a Remote Assistance session is started, and is deleted by the Remote Desktop Help Session Manager service when there is no session pending or active.

Naming User Accounts

Think about the naming scheme you plan to use for user accounts. As the organization changes and grows, the original naming scheme may need to change but not the need for a naming scheme of some kind. While account names for operating systems earlier than Windows 2000 are limited to 20 characters for a user name, Windows Server 2003 has a 256-character limitation for a user name.

Small organizations commonly use a person's first name and last name initial for their user account. In a larger organization, it may be a better idea to use their full name for their user account name. For example, in a small organization, John Smith could have a user name of JohnS. However, in a larger organization, John Smith should have a username of JohnSmith.

This becomes a problem when an organization has more than one John Smith who needs a user account. Full names are likely to be an issue; using middle name initials can solve it. However, administrators may implement a numbering system. For example: JSmith1, Jsmith2. Another naming system uses a dot-delimited scheme, such as John.W.Smith@cpandl.com. Regardless of the naming scheme you choose, the key is to be as consistent as possible and to allow for exceptions as needed.

Configuring User Account Policies

Because domain controllers share the domain accounts database, user account policies must be consistent across all domain controllers. The way consistency is ensured is by having domain controllers obtain user account policies only from the domain container and only allowing one account policy for domain accounts. The one account policy allowed by domain accounts must be defined in the Default Domain Policy. The account policy is then enforced by the domain controllers in the domain. Domain controllers always obtain the account policy from the Default Domain Policy Group Policy Object (GPO), even if there is a different account policy applied to the organizational unit (OU) that contains the domain controller.

By default, computers joined to a domain will also receive the same account policy for their local accounts. However, local account policies can be different from the domain account policy, such as when you specifically define an account policy for local accounts. For example, if you configure an account policy for a GPO linked to the Boston OU, when users in Boston log on to Active Directory they'll obtain their account policy from the Default Domain Policy instead of the GPO linked to their OU. The only exception is when users in Boston log on locally to their machine instead of logging on to Active Directory, in that case any account policy in their OU GPO is applied to their machine's local GPO and enforced.

Tip Some security options are also obtained from the Default Domain Policy GPO
Two policies in Computer Configuration\Windows Settings\Security Settings\Local Policies\Security Options also behave like account policies. These policies are Network Access: Allow Anonymous SID/NAME Translation and Network Security: Force Logoff When Logon Hours Expire. For domain accounts, the settings for these policies are only obtained from the Default Domain Policy GPO. For local accounts, the settings for these policies can come from a local OU GPO if one is defined and applicable.

Account policies in a domain are configured through the Group Policy Editor (GPE) in Active Directory Users and Computers. Right-click the domain name, select Properties, and then click the Group Policy tab, as shown in the following screen. Afterward, double-click the Default Domain Policy GPO. The account policies are located in Computer Configuration\Windows Settings\Security Settings\Account Policies.

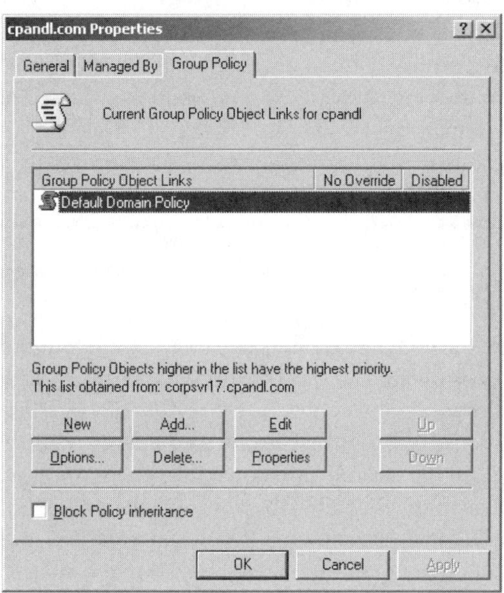

For local accounts, you can configure alternate account polices for an OU. Right-click the OU name, select Properties, and then click the Group Policy tab. By default, user policies for an OU are inherited from domain policy. You can define a specific OU policy by clicking New. The Account Policies are located in Computer Configuration\Windows Settings\Security Settings\Account Policies.

To change group policies, you must be a member of the Domain Admins group or Enterprise Admins group in Active Directory. Group policy is configured with the Group Policy Editor. You edit group policies for the account policies by double-clicking a policy, and then defining the policy setting. The account policies for a domain contain three subsets—Password Policy, Account Lockout Policy, and Kerberos Policy. While account policies for OUs include Password Policy and Account Lockout Policy, they do not include Kerberos Policy. Kerberos Policy can only be set at the domain level.

Enforcing Password Policy

Password policies for domain user accounts and local user accounts are very important in preventing unauthorized access. There are six settings for password policies that enable you to control how passwords are managed. As shown in Figure 37-1, these policies are located in Computer Configuration\Windows Settings\Security Settings\Account Policies\Password Policy.

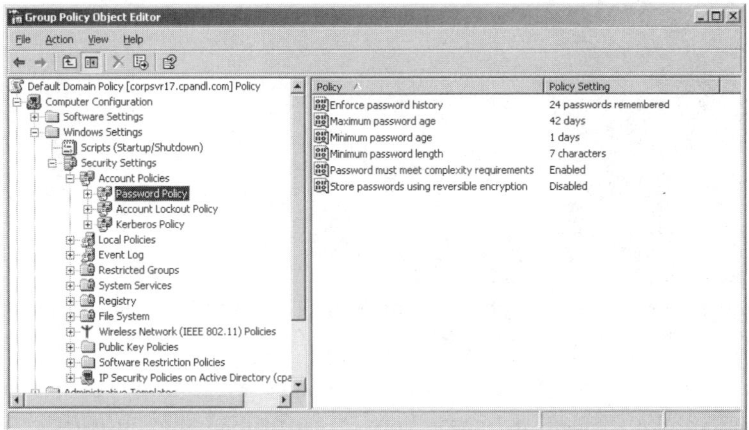

Figure 37-1. Managing Password Policy in the Default Domain Policy.

The settings are as follows:

- **Enforce Password History** When users change their passwords, this setting determines how many old passwords will be maintained and associated with each user. On a domain controller, the default is 24 passwords, on a stand-alone server, it is zero passwords.
- **Maximum Password Age** This determines when users are required to change their passwords. For example, if this is set to 90 days, on the 91st day the user will be required to change his or her password. The default on domain controllers is 42 days. The minimum number of days is 0, which effectively means that the password never changes. The maximum number of days is 999. In an environment where security is critical, you probably want to set the value low—in contrast, for environments where security is less stringent, you could set the password age high (rarely requiring users to change passwords).
- **Minimum Password Age** How long users must use passwords before they are allowed to change the password is determined by this setting. It must be more than zero days for the Enforce Password History Policy to be effective. In an environment where security is critical, you would probably set this to a shorter time, and to a longer time where security not as tight. This setting must be configured to be less than the Maximum Password Age policy. The default is 1 day on a domain controller and 0 days on stand-alone servers.
- **Minimum Password Length** This is the number of characters that sets the minimum requirement for the length of the password. Again, a more critically secure environment may require longer password lengths than one with reduced security requirements. As shown in Figure 37-2, the default length is seven characters on domain controllers. The default is zero characters on stand-alone servers.

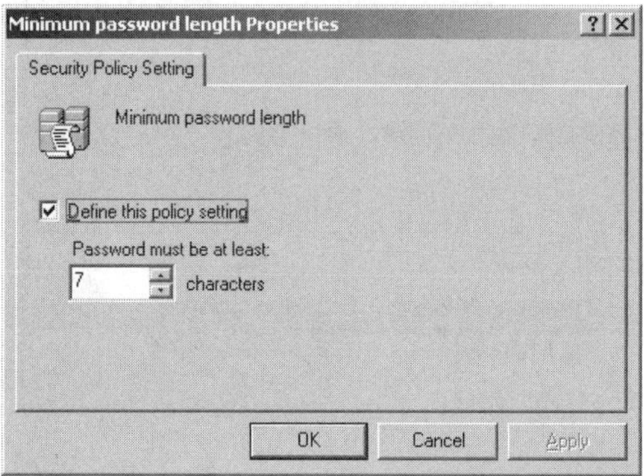

Figure 37-2. Configuring domain user Minimum Password Length in the Default Domain Policy.

- **Password Must Meet Complexity Requirements** Complexity requirements for passwords for the domain user accounts are set at a higher requirement than previously, in Windows 2000. If this policy is defined, passwords can't contain the user account name, must contain at least six characters, and must consist of uppercase letters, lowercase letters, numerals, and special non-alphabetical characters, such as the percentage sign (%) and the asterisk (*). (Complexity requirements are enabled by default on domain controllers and disabled by default on stand-alone servers for Windows Server 2003.)
- **Store Passwords Using Reversible Encryption** This is basically an additional policy that allows for plain text encryption of passwords for applications that may need it. By default, it is disabled on Windows Server 2003. Enabling this policy is basically the same as storing passwords as plain text and is used when applications use protocols that need information about the user's password. Because this policy degrades the overall security of the domain, it should be used only when necessary.

Configuring Account Lockout Policy

The Account Lockout Policy is invoked after a local user or a domain user has been locked out of his or her account. There are three settings for account lockout policies, located in Computer Configuration\Windows Settings\Security Settings\Account Policies\Account Lockout Policy. They are the following:

- **Account Lockout Duration** If a user does become locked out, this setting determines how long the user will be locked out before the user account is unlocked. There is no default setting, because this setting is dependent on the account lockout threshold setting. The range is from 0 through 99,999 minutes. The account will be locked out indefinitely when this is set to 0 and therefore will require an administrator to unlock it.

- **Account Lockout Threshold** This setting determines how many failed attempts at logon before a user will be locked out of the account. The range is from 0 to 999. If this setting is 0, the account will never be locked out and the Account Lockout Duration security setting is disabled. The default setting is 0.
- **Reset Account Lockout Counter After** This setting is the number of minutes after a failure to log on before the logon counter is reset to zero. This must be less than or equal to the Account Lockout Duration setting if the Account Lockout Threshold policy is enabled.

Setting Kerberos Policy

Kerberos is an authentication system designed for secure exchange of information as discussed in the section entitled "NTLM and Kerberos Authentication" on page 1120. Windows Server 2003 has five settings for Kerberos Policy, which are applied only to domain user accounts. The policies are located in Computer Configuration\Windows Settings\Security Settings\Account Policies\Kerberos Policy. They are as follows:

- **Enforce User Logon Restrictions** If you want to validate every ticket session request against the user rights, keep the default setting enabled.
- **Maximum Lifetime For Service Ticket** The default is 600 minutes, but this setting must be greater than 10 minutes, and also must be less than or equal to what is configured for the Maximum Lifetime For User Ticket setting. The setting does not apply to sessions that have already been validated.
- **Maximum Lifetime For User Ticket** This is different from the Maximum Lifetime For Service Ticket setting. Maximum Lifetime For User Ticket sets the maximum amount of time that a ticket may be used before either a new one must be requested or the existing one is renewed, whereas the Maximum Lifetime For Service Ticket setting is used to access a particular service. The default is 10 hours.
- **Maximum Lifetime For User Ticket Renewal** This user account security policy object configures the maximum amount of time the ticket may be used. The default is seven days.
- **Maximum Tolerance For Computer Clock Synchronization** Sometimes workstations and servers have different local clock times. This setting allows you to configure a tolerance level (defaults to 5 minutes) for this possible difference so that Kerberos authentication does not fail.

> **Note** In Windows Server 2003 Standard and Enterprise editions using Active Directory with all Password Policies disabled, if you change the Minimum Password Length setting to less than seven characters (the default), you will not be able to create a new user or change a user's password. To work around this limitation, set the password length to seven or higher.

Understanding User Account Capabilities, Privileges, and Rights

All user accounts have specific capabilities, privileges, and rights. When you create a user account, you can grant the user specific capabilities by making the user a member of one or more groups. This gives the user the capabilities of these groups. You then assign additional capabilities by making a user a member of the appropriate groups or withdraw capabilities by removing a user from a group.

In Windows Server 2003, some capabilities of accounts are built in. The built-in capabilities of accounts are assigned to groups and include the group's automatic capabilities. Although built-in capabilities are predefined and unchangeable, they can be granted to users by making them members of the appropriate group or delegated by granting the capability specifically, for example, the ability to create, delete, and manage user accounts. This capability is assigned to administrators and account operators. Thus, if a user is a member of the Administrators group, the user can create, delete, and manage user accounts.

Other capabilities of accounts, such as permissions, privileges and logon rights, can be assigned. The access permissions for accounts define the operations that can be performed on network resources. For example, permissions control whether a user can access a particular shared folder. You can assign access permissions to users, computers, and groups as discussed in Chapter 21, "File Sharing and Security." The privileges of an account grant permissions to perform specific tasks, such as the ability to change the system time. The logon rights of an account grant logon permissions, such as the ability to log on locally to a server.

An important part of an administrator's job is being able to determine and set permissions, privileges, and logon rights as necessary. Although you can't change a group's built-in capabilities, you can change a group's default privileges and logon rights. For example, you could revoke network access to a computer by removing a group's right to access the computer from the network. Table 37-1 provides an overview of the default privileges assigned to groups. Table 37-2 provides an overview of the default logon rights assigned to groups.

Table 37-1. Default Privileges Assigned to Groups

Privilege	Description	Groups Assigned by Default in Domains
Act As Part Of The Operating System	Allows a process to authenticate as any user. Processes that require this privilege must use the LocalSystem account, which already has this privilege.	None
Add Workstations To Domain	Allows users to add new computers to an existing domain.	Authenticated Users on domain controllers
Adjust Memory Quotas For A Process	Allows users to set the maximum amount of memory a process can use.	Administrators, Local Service, and Network Service

Table 37-1. Default Privileges Assigned to Groups

Privilege	Description	Groups Assigned by Default in Domains
Back Up Files And Directories	Allows users to back up the system regardless of the permissions set on files and directories.	Administrators, Backup Operators, and Server Operators
Bypass Traverse Checking	Allows users to go through directory trees even if a user doesn't have permissions to access the directories being passed through. The privilege doesn't allow the user to list directory contents.	Authenticated Users and Administrators on domain controllers; on member servers and workstations, Administrators, Backup Operators, Power Users, Users, and Everyone
Change The System Time	Allows users to set the time for the computer's clock.	Administrators and Server Operators on domain controllers; on member servers and workstations, Administrators and Power Users
Create A Pagefile	Allows users to create and modify the paging file size for virtual memory.	Administrators
Create A Token Object	Allows processes to create token objects that can be used to gain access to local resources. Processes that require this privilege must use the LocalSystem account, which already has this privilege.	None
Create Global Objects	Allows a process to create global directory objects. Most components already have this privilege and it's not necessary to specifically assign it.	None
Create Permanent Shared Objects	Allows processes to create directory objects in the Windows object manager. Most components already have this privilege and it's not necessary to specifically assign it.	None
Debug Programs	Allows users to perform debugging.	Administrators
Enable User And Computer Accounts To Be Trusted For Delegation	Permits users and computers to change or apply the trusted account for delegation setting, provided they have write access to the object.	Administrators on domain controllers

Table 37-1. Default Privileges Assigned to Groups

Privilege	Description	Groups Assigned by Default in Domains
Force Shutdown Of A Remote System	Allows users to shut down a computer from a remote location on the network.	Administrators and Server Operators on domain controllers; on member servers and workstations, Administrators
Generate Security Audits	Allows processes to make security log entries for auditing object access.	Local Service and Network Service
Increase Quotas	Allows processes with write access to a process to increase the processor quota assigned to those processes.	Administrators
Increase Scheduling Priority	Allows processes with write access to a process to increase the scheduling priority assigned to those processes.	Administrators
Load And Unload Device Drivers	Allows users to install and uninstall Plug and Play device drivers. This doesn't affect device drivers that aren't Plug and Play, which can only be installed by administrators.	Administrators and Printer Operators
Lock Pages In Memory	In Windows NT, allowed processes to keep data in physical memory, preventing the system from paging data to virtual memory on disk.	Not used in Windows 2000 or Windows Server 2003
Manage Auditing And Security Log	Allows users to specify auditing options and access the security log. You must turn on auditing in the group policy first.	Administrators
Modify Firmware Environment Values	Allows users and processes to modify system environment variables (not user environment variables).	Administrators
Perform Volume Maintenance Tasks	Allows administration of removable storage, disk defragmenter, and disk management.	Administrators
Profile A Single Process	Allows users to monitor the performance of non-system processes.	Administrators on domain controllers; on member servers and workstations, Administrators and Power Users
Profile System Performance	Allows users to monitor the performance of system processes.	Administrators

Table 37-1. Default Privileges Assigned to Groups

Privilege	Description	Groups Assigned by Default in Domains
Remove Computer From Docking Station	Allows undocking a laptop and removing from network.	Administrators, Power Users, and Users
Replace A Process Level Token	Allows processes to modify the default token for subprocesses.	Local Service and Network Service
Restore Files And Directories	Allows restoring backed-up files and directories, regardless of the permissions set on files and directories.	Administrators, Backup Operators, Server Operators on domain controllers; on member servers and workstations, Administrators and Backup Operators
Shut Down The System	Allows shutting down the local computer.	Administrators, Backup Operators, and Server Operators on domain controllers; on member servers, Administrators, Backup Operators, and Power Users; on workstations includes Users
Synchronize Directory Service Data	Allows users to synchronize directory service data on domain controllers.	None
Take Ownership Of Files Or Other Objects	Allows users to take ownership of any Active Directory objects.	Administrators

Table 37-2. Default Logon Rights Assigned to Groups

Logon Right	Description	Groups Assigned by Default in Domains
Access This Computer From The Network	Permits remote access to the computer.	Administrators, Authenticated Users, Everyone on domain controllers; on member servers and workstations, Administrators, Backup Operators, Power Users, Users, and Everyone
Allow Logon Locally	Grants permission to log on to the computer interactively at the console.	On domain controllers, Administrators, Account Operators, Backup Operators, Print Operators, and Server Operators; on member servers and workstations, Administrators, Backup Operators, Power Users, Users, and Guest

Table 37-2. Default Logon Rights Assigned to Groups

Logon Right	Description	Groups Assigned by Default in Domains
Allow Logon Through Terminal Services	Allows access through Terminal Services; necessary for remote assistance and remote desktop.	Administrators on domain controllers; on member servers and workstations, Administrators, Remote Desktop Users
Deny Access To This Computer From The Network	Denies remote access to the computer through network services.	None
Deny Logon As Batch Job	Denies the right to log on through a batch job or script.	None
Deny Logon As Service	Denies the right to log on as a service.	None
Deny Logon Locally	Denies the right to log on to the computer's keyboard.	None
Deny Logon Through Terminal Services	Denies right to log on through Terminal Services.	None
Log On As A Batch Job	Grants permission to log on as a batch job or script.	Local Service
Log On As A Service	Grants permission to log on as a server. LocalSystem account has this right. Services that run under separate accounts should be assigned this right.	Network Service

Assigning User Rights

The most efficient way to assign user rights is to make the user a member of a group that already has the right. In some cases, however, you might want a user to have a particular right but not have all the other rights of the group. One way to resolve this problem is to give the user the rights directly. Another way to resolve this is to create a special group for users that need the right. This is the approach used with the Remote Desktop Users group, which was created by Microsoft to grant Allow Logon Through Terminal Services to groups of users.

You assign user rights through the Local Policies node of Group Policy. Local policies can be set on a per-computer basis using a computer's local security policy or on a domain or OU basis through an existing group policy for the related domain or OU. When you do this, the local policies apply to all accounts in the domain or OU.

Assigning User Rights for a Domain or OU

You can assign user rights for a domain or OU by completing the following steps:

1. User policies in a domain are configured through the Group Policy Editor in Active Directory Users And Computers. Right-click the domain or OU name, select Properties, and then click the Group Policy tab.
2. Select the policy you want to work with, and then click Edit. Access the Local Policies node by working your way down the console tree. Expand Computer Configuration, Windows Settings, Security Settings, Local Policies, and User Rights Assignment, as shown in Figure 37-3.

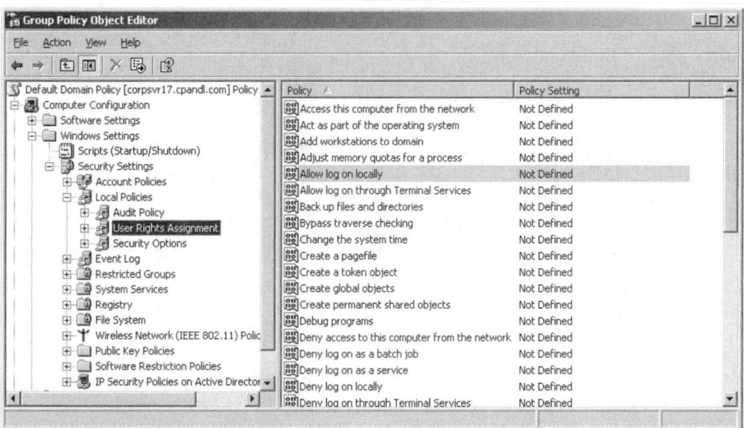

Figure 37-3. Configuring user rights in Group Policy.

3. To configure a user right, double-click a user right or right-click it and select Security. This opens a Properties dialog box, as shown in Figure 37-4. If the policy isn't defined, select Define These Policy Settings. To apply the right to a user or group, click Add User Or Group. Then, in the Add User Or Group dialog box, click Browse. This opens the Select Users, Computers, Or Groups dialog box.
4. Type the name of the user or group you want to use in the field provided, and then click Check Names. By default, the search is configured to find built-in security principals, groups, and user accounts. After you select the account names or groups to add,

click OK. The Add User Or Group dialog box should now show the selected accounts. Click OK again.

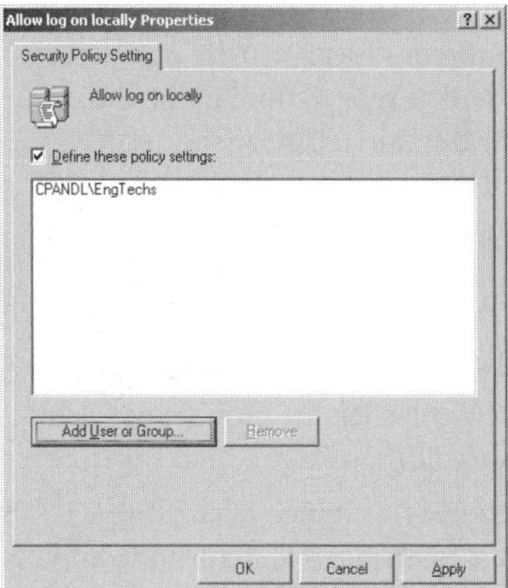

Figure 37-4. Define the user right, and then assign the right to users and groups.

5. The Properties dialog box is updated to reflect your selections. If you made a mistake, select a name and remove it by clicking Remove. When you're finished granting the right to users and groups, click OK.

Assigning User Rights on a Specific Computer

User rights can also be applied to a specific computer. However, remember that domain and OU policy take precedence over local policy. This means that any settings in these policies will override settings you make on a local computer.

You can apply user rights locally by completing the following steps:

1. Start Local Security Policy by clicking Start, Programs or All Programs, Administrative Tools, Local Security Policy.
2. Under Security Settings, expand Local Policies and then User Rights Assignment.
3. Double-click the user right you want to modify. The Properties dialog box shows current users and groups that have been given the user right.
4. You can apply the user right to additional users and groups by clicking Add User Or Group. This opens the Select Users Or Groups dialog box, which you can use to add users and groups.
5. Click OK twice to close the open dialog boxes.

> **Note** If the options in the Properties dialog box are dimmed, it means the policy has been set at a higher level and can't be overridden locally.

Creating and Configuring Domain User Accounts

As a member of the Account Operators, Enterprise Admins, or Domain Admins group, you can use Active Directory Users And Computers to create user accounts. Follow these steps:

1. Click Start, Programs or All Programs, Administrative Tools, and Active Directory Users And Computers. This starts Active Directory Users And Computers.
2. By default, you are connected to your logon domain. If you want to create OUs in a different domain, right-click the Active Directory Users And Computers node in the console tree, and then select Connect To Domain. In the Connect To Domain dialog box, type the name of the domain to which you want to connect, and then click OK. Alternatively, you can click Browse to find the domain to which you want to connect in the Browse For Domain dialog box.
3. You can now create the user account. Right-click the container in which you want to create the user, point to New, and then select User. This will start the New Object–User Wizard.
4. When you create a new user, you're prompted for the first name, initials, last name, full name, and logon name, as shown in Figure 37-5. The pre–Windows 2000 logon name then appears automatically. This logon name is used when a user logs on to Windows NT, Microsoft Windows 95, or Microsoft Windows 98.

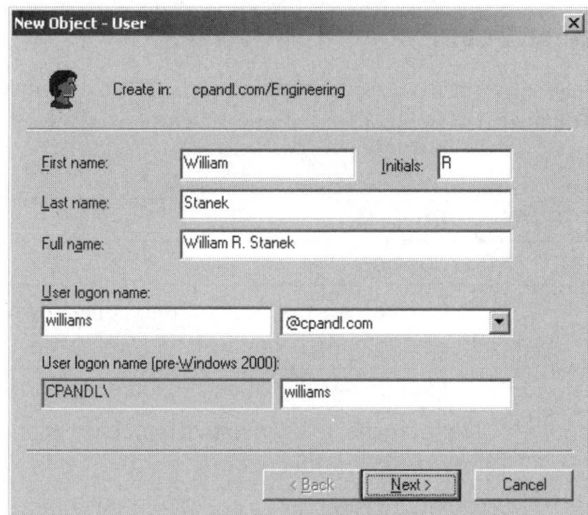

Figure 37-5. Creating a user account.

5. When you click Next, you can set the user's password and account options. The password must meet the complexity requirements set in the group policy. As shown in Figure 37-6, these options are as follows:
   - User Must Change Password At Next Logon
   - User Cannot Change Password
   - Password Never Expires
   - Account Is Disabled

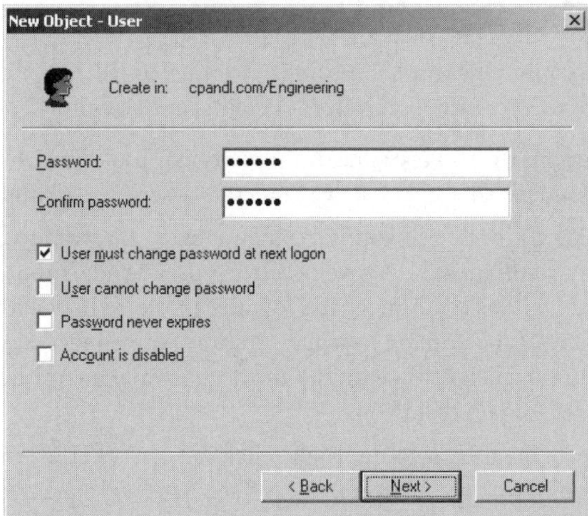

Figure 37-6. Set the user's password and account options.

6 Click Next, and then click Finish. If you use a password that doesn't meet the complexity requirements of group policy, you'll see an error and you'll have to click Back to change the user's password before you can continue.

Viewing and Setting User Account Properties

If you double-click a user account in Active Directory Users And Computers, a Properties dialog box appears, with tabs allowing you to configure the user's settings. Table 37-3 lists the user account properties.

Table 37-3. User Account Properties

Account Tab	Description
General	Used to manage the account name, display name, e-mail address, telephone number, and Web page
Address	Used to manage geographical address information
Account	Used to manage logon name, account options, logon times, and account lockout
Profile	Used to manage the user profile configuration (profile path, logon script) and Home Folder
Telephones	Used to manage home phone, pager, fax, IP phone, and cell-phone numbers
Organization	Used to manage the user's title and corporate information (department, manager, direct reports)
Environment	Used to manage the Terminal Services startup environment

Table 37-3. **User Account Properties**

Account Tab	Description
Sessions	Used to manage Terminal Services timeout and reconnection settings
Remote Control	Used to manage remote control settings for Terminal Services
Terminal Services Profile	Used to manage the user profile for Terminal Services
COM+	Used to select the user's COM+ partition set
Published Certificates	Used to install or remove user's X.509 certificates
Member Of	Used to add the user to or remove the user from selected groups
Dial-in	Used to set the user's dial-in or virtual private network (VPN) access controls as well as callback, IP address, and routing options for dial-in or VPN
Object	Displays the canonical name of the user object with dates and Update Sequence Numbers
Security	Used to configure advanced permissions for users and groups that can access this user object in Active Directory

Note The number of tabs in a user's Properties dialog box will vary depending upon the software installed. For example, adding Exchange mail services will add multiple property sheets (tabs) to each user's Active Directory account. Also, to view the Published Certificates, Objects, or Security property sheets, you must be in Advanced view. To access Advanced view, select Advanced Features from the View menu in Active Directory Users And Computers.

Most of the time, as the administrator, you will use a number of the account settings regularly. The General tab has the name and e-mail for the user. The Account tab has the user name and lets you configure logon hours or logon settings. There is also an area on the Account tab that allows the account to be unlocked. This latter setting is a quick way to unlock an account when a user has forgotten a password or is locked out of the account for some other reason. The Profile tab lets you set a user profile, logon script, and home folder. The Member Of tab lets you add the user to various groups. The Security tab lets you set the way permissions for groups or users are configured and provides access to the Effective Permissions tool via the Advanced Button.

Obtaining Effective Permissions

In Active Directory, user accounts are defined as objects—as are group and computer accounts. This means that user accounts have security descriptors that list the users and groups that are granted access. Security descriptors also define ownership of the object and specify the permissions that those users and groups have been assigned with respect to the object.

Individual entries in the security descriptor are referred to as access control entries (ACEs). Active Directory objects can inherit ACEs from their parent objects. This means that permissions for a parent object can be applied to a child object. For example, all members of the Account Operators group inherit permissions granted to this group.

Because of inheritance, sometimes it isn't clear whether a particular user, group, or computer has permission to work with another object in Active Directory. This is where the Effective Permissions tool comes in handy. The Effective Permissions tool allows you to examine the permissions that a user, group, or computer has with respect to another object. For example, if you wanted to determine what permissions, if any, a user who has received delegated control has over another user or group, you could use Effective Permissions to do this.

The Effective Permissions tool is available in Active Directory Users And Computers—but only if you are in the Advanced view. Select Advanced Features from the View menu if necessary, and then double-click a user, group, or computer name to display the related Properties dialog box. In the Properties dialog box, click the Advanced button on the Security tab, and then select the Effective Permissions tab. Next click Select, type the name of the user or group for which you want to see the effective permissions, and then click OK.

The Effective Permissions for the selected user or group with relation to the previously selected object appear, as shown in Figure 37-7. The Effective Permissions window will have check marks showing which permissions are in effect. If there are no effective permissions, none of the permissions will be selected.

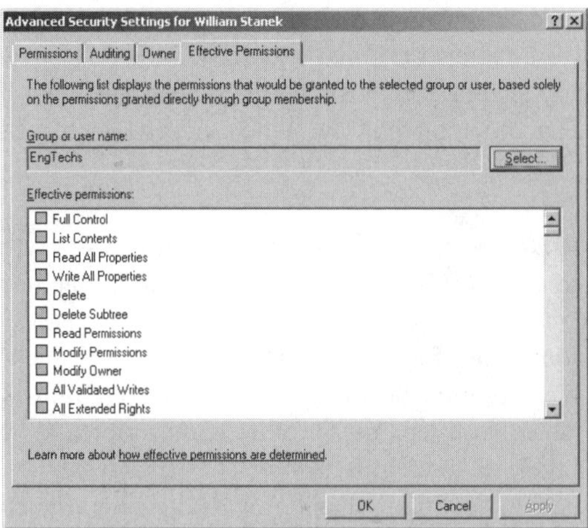

Figure 37-7. Obtaining Effective Permissions for a user, group, or computer.

Configuring Account Options

Every user account created in Active Directory has account options that control logon hours, the computers to which a user can log on, account expiration, and so on. To manage these settings for a user, double-click the user account in Active Directory Users And Computers, and then select the Account tab, as shown in Figure 37-8.

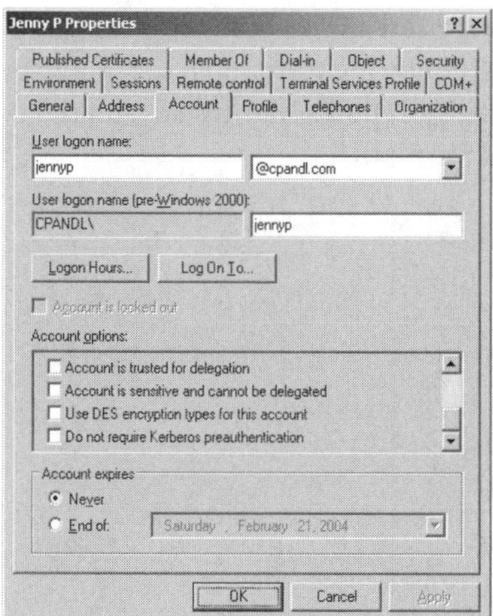

Figure 37-8. Display of logon settings in the User Account Properties dialog box.

Below the general account name fields, the account options areas are divided into three main areas. The first area that you can configure controls the Logon Hours and Log On To computer options.

- **Setting Logon Hours** Click Logon Hours to configure when a user can log on to the domain. By default, users can log on 24 hours a day, seven days a week. To deny a user a specific day or time, select the area that you want to restrict them from logging on, and then select the Logon Denied option, as shown in the following screen. For example, this option can be used to restrict shift workers to certain hours or to restrict working days to weekdays.

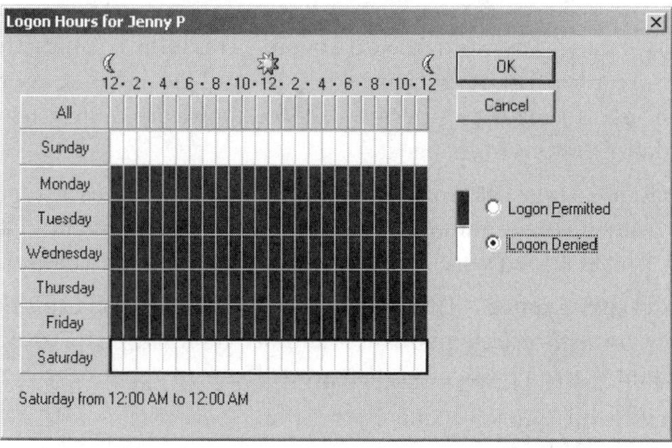

- **Configuring Logon Computer** When you click Log On To, you can restrict which computers a user can log on from. The NetBIOS protocol is required for this functionality, as well as a computer name from an operating system earlier than Windows 2000. The default setting allows users to log on from all computers. To restrict which computers a user can log on from, click The Following Computers, as shown in the following screen. Type a computer name in the Computer Name field, and then click Add. Repeat this procedure to set other logon computers.

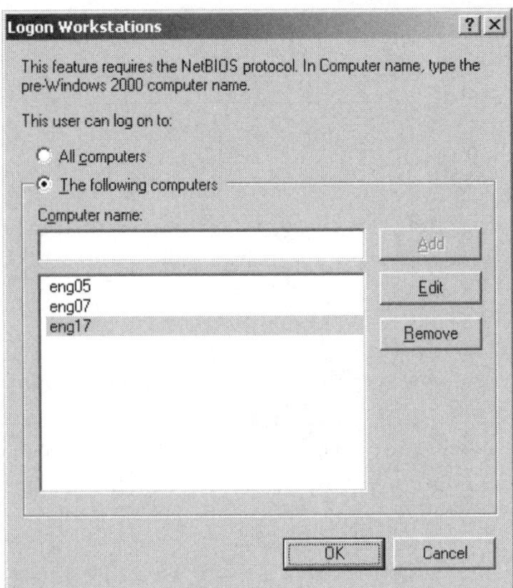

Below the Logon Hours and Log On To buttons is a check box called Account Is Locked Out. It will be dimmed if the account is not locked out. If the user has locked herself or himself out by trying to log on with the wrong password too many times, you can unlock the account here. Next is the Account Options list, which includes a number of account options you can configure. These options include the following:

- **User Must Change Password At Next Logon** This is the default setting when a user is created. It requires the user to change the password the first time he or she logs on. This allows the user to be the only person with the knowledge of the password, though you as the administrator can change it.
- **User Cannot Change Password** This setting prevents the user from changing the password and gives the administrator more control over accounts like the Guest account. This is a good setting for service and application accounts.
- **Password Never Expires** This prevents passwords from ever expiring. It is a good idea to use this on service accounts. This is another good setting for an application or service account where a password is hard-coded into an application or service.
- **Store Password Using Reversible Encryption** Saves the user password as encrypted clear text. Check this box if you have computers from Apple Computer, Inc., in your domain, because they store passwords as plaintext.

- **Account Is Disabled** This prevents a user from logging on to his or her account. It enables network administrators to immediately disable an account for security reasons.
- **Smart Card Is Required For Interactive Logon** To ensure higher security on a network, smart card technology can be implemented. Enabling the setting requires all users to use a smart card and reader to log on and to be authenticated. This domain setting also requires a personal identification number (PIN) configured on the smart card. This option also sets the Password Never Expires option to be enabled.
- **Account Is Trusted For Delegation** If a service is running under a user account rather than as a local system, you can set a user account to execute procedures on behalf of a different account on the network. By enabling this option, you can mimic a client to gain access to network resources on the local computer. This is only available on Windows Server 2003 domain controllers where domain functionality has been set to Windows 2000 mixed or Windows 2003 native mode.
- **Account Is Sensitive And Cannot Be Delegated** Select this option if this account cannot be assigned for delegation by another account. This is the opposite of the above setting, and could be used in a high-security network environment.
- **Use DES Encryption Types For This Account** Data Encryption Standard (DES) is used for many encryption protocols, including Microsoft Point-to-Point Encryption (MPPE) and Internet Protocol Security (IPSec) and supports up to 128-bit strong encryption. Enable this option if you want to use DES encryption.
- **Do Not Require Kerberos Preauthentication** You should enable this if the account uses a different implementation of the Kerberos protocol.

Finally, the Account Expires panel lets you set expiration options for the account. The default is Never, but some users may need to have this setting configured. For example, temporary, contract, summer help, or consultants may be working on your network for only a specified amount of time. If you know how long they need access to resources in your domain, you can use the Account Expires settings to automate the disabling of their account.

Tip **Disabling accounts**

In most network environments, administrators to whom managing users has been delegated will not be able to remove users immediately upon their leaving the company, creating a window of vulnerability. Yet, when accounts have scheduled end points, you can schedule them to be disabled on a specific date. So, it is good idea to schedule accounts to be disabled if you are sure that the user will no longer be working. If the account is automatically disabled, but the user needs access, he or she will let you know. But, if the account is not disabled automatically, it can represent a big security problem. To handle this on an enterprise level, many businesses are reviewing (or implementing) provisioning applications to automate the process of taking away access to company resources when employees leave the company.

Configuring Profile Options

User accounts can also have profiles, logon scripts, and home directories associated with them. To configure these options, double-click a user account in Active Directory Users And Computers, and then select the Profile tab, as shown in the following screen:

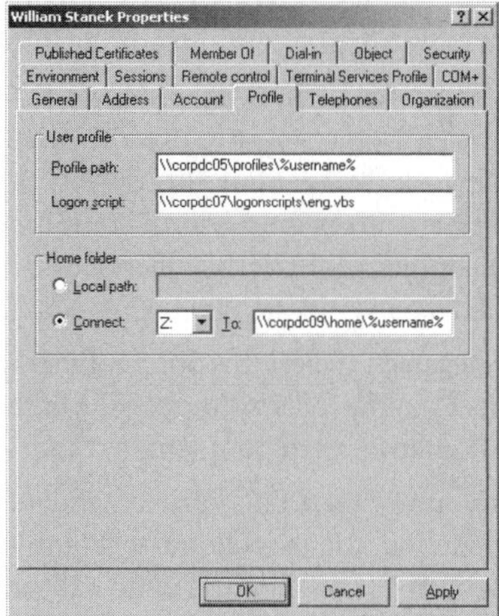

As the screen shows, you can set the following options in the Profile tab:

- **Profile Path** Profiles provide the environment settings for users. Each time a user logs on to a computer, that user's profile is used to determine desktop and Control Panel settings, the availability of menu options and applications, and so on. Setting the profile path and working with profiles is covered in the section entitled "Managing User Profiles" later in this chapter.
- **Logon Script** As the name implies, logon scripts are accessed when users log on to their accounts. Logon scripts set commands that should be executed each time a user logs on. One user or many users can use a single logon script, and, as the administrator, you control which users run which scripts. You can specify a logon script to use by typing the path to the logon script in the Logon Script field. Be sure to set the full path to the logon script, such as \\Corpdc05\LogonScripts\eng.vbs.

> **Note** You shouldn't use scripts to set environment variables. Environment settings used by scripts aren't maintained for subsequent user processes. Also, you shouldn't use logon scripts to specify applications that should run at startup. You should set startup applications by placing the appropriate shortcuts in the user's Startup folder.

- **Home Folder** A home folder can be assigned to each user account. Users can store and retrieve their personal files in this directory. Many applications use the home folder as the default for File Open and Save As operations, helping users find their resources easily. Home directories can be located on a user's local hard drive or on a shared network drive. If you don't assign a home folder, Windows Server 2003 uses a default local home folder.

To specify a home folder, do either of the following:

- You specify a local home folder by clicking the Local Path option button, and then typing the path to the home folder on the user's computer. Here's an example: C:\Home\%*UserName*%.
- You specify a network home folder by clicking the Connect option button in the Home Folder section, and then selecting a drive letter for the home folder. For consistency, you should use the same drive letter for all users. Also, be sure to select a drive letter that won't conflict with any currently configured physical or mapped drives. To avoid problems, you might want to use Z as the drive letter. After you select the drive letter, type the complete path to the home folder, using the Universal Naming Convention (UNC) notation, such as: \\Corpdc09\Home\%*UserName*%.

Managing User Profiles

User profiles contain global user settings and configuration information and are stored for each user account created on a server or in a domain. A user profile allows a user to maintain his or her desktop environment so it is the same whenever they log on. The profile is created the first time a user logs on. Different profiles are created for local user accounts and domain user accounts.

Profile Essentials

The following three types of user profiles can be used:

- **Local** Local user profiles are the means for saving user settings and restoring them when the user logs on to the local machine.
- **Roaming** Roaming profiles allow user settings to move with a user from computer to computer by storing the information on domain controllers and then downloading it when the user logs on to the domain. For an administrator, roaming profiles allow you to roam from server to server and not have to reconfigure the desktop each time you log on. For instance, in your roaming profile, Microsoft Windows Explorer can be configured through the Default Domain Policy to show file details regardless of where you log on or whether it was the first time you logged on to a particular computer.
- **Mandatory** Mandatory profiles are roaming profiles, originated by you and kept on a server, that are applied to users or groups, and that can only be changed by system administrators. For instance, a company may want all its sales clerks to have the same desktop settings at every workstation. This requires the creation of a preconfigured profile.

When a user has a local profile, all the user data is stored locally on that user's machine. When a user has a roaming profile, all the user data is stored in the profile itself and can be located on a network share. Inside a profile are the following folders:

- *Application Data* Includes program-specific settings as well as user security settings
- *Cookies* Includes cookies that have been downloaded while using a World Wide Web browser
- *Desktop* Includes the complete settings for the user's desktop, including any files, folders, and shortcuts that have been placed on the desktop
- *Favorites* Includes shortcuts to favorite locations on the local computer, network, or the Internet that the user has set
- *Local Settings* Includes application data as well as history and temporary files for the user's browser
- *My Recent Documents* Includes shortcuts to the documents the user has recently opened
- *NetHood* Includes shortcuts to My Network Places
- *PrintHood* Includes shortcuts to the Printers folder
- *SendTo* Includes items on the SendTo menu
- *StartMenu* Includes menu items on the user's Start Menu
- *Templates* Includes application templates

You can examine the contents of these folders using Windows Explorer. However, many of the folders are hidden from view by default. To configure Windows Explorer so that you can view the additional folders, choose Folder Options from the Tools menu, and then click the View tab. Under Advanced Settings, select Show Hidden Files And Folders.

Profile Changes and New Features

There are new features in Windows Server 2003 for handling user profiles, and changes to existing user profile features. These include the following:

- Windows Server 2003 will now save roaming profiles to a server when a user logs off, even if an application has the Registry open.
- The user profile error messages now have more detail, and unique IDs are associated with the error events that are logged in the Windows event logs.
- The System Properties dialog box (available via the System tool in Control Panel) has changed—the user profile store is now found on the Advanced tab of the System dialog box.
- When a user logs on to a domain or that user's profile is in use on the network, the Delete and Copy To buttons in the Advanced tab of the System Properties dialog box are not available.

Tip You may need to delete a user profile that is in use. To delete a user profile while someone is using it, take ownership of it using Windows Explorer. Right-click the profile file, and then select Properties. Click the Advanced button on the Security tab. Then select the Owner tab in the Advanced Security dialog box to set ownership to your account. You can then delete the profile in Windows Explorer.

Group Policy Changes for User Profiles

There are changes in applying group policy settings to user profiles in Windows Server 2003. Policies for user profiles have their own node in Group Policy. They are located in Computer Configuration\Administrative Templates\System\User Profiles.

These policies affect caching, slow network connections, timeouts, ownership, retries to load profiles, and wait times. The following group policy changes are included:

- To add roaming user profiles to the Administrators security group, use the Add The Administrator Security Group To Roaming User Profiles policy. This allows an administrator full control over the folder containing the user's profile. Only computers running Microsoft Windows XP Professional or later are affected by this policy.
- To deny access to a user's roaming profile on a per-computer basis, use the Only Allow Local Users Profiles policy. This prevents a user from getting his or her roaming profile on a particular computer or in the domain. Only computers running Windows XP Professional or later are affected by this policy.
- You can also prevent changes to a user's roaming profile on a local machine from being sent back to the server when the user logs off. To do this, enable the Prevent Roaming Profile Changes From Propagating To The Server policy. Users will receive their roaming profile when they log on, but if they change anything on their desktop, those changes will not be retained when they log off. Only computers running Windows XP Professional or later are affected by this policy.

Note The Group Policy snap-in now has an Extended tab in the right window. By selecting any of the user group policies, when the Extended tab is chosen the description explains what the policy will do in each configuration and indicates which operating system supports the policy.

By default, local user profiles are stored in the %SystemDrive%\Documents and Settings folder. However, if you are upgrading from Windows NT 4 to Windows Server 2003, the original profile path is not changed. It will remain as %SystemRoot%\Profiles.

Implementing and Creating Preconfigured Profiles

Preconfigured user profiles are used to define default user configuration and environment settings. They make it easier for new users to get started in a new environment and can be used for local, roaming, or mandatory profiles. For instance, you could have one preconfigured user profile for each department in the organization. Any of these preconfigured profiles could be saved and then used as a local, roaming, or mandatory profile for new users.

Before creating a preconfigured user profile, you should be aware of these guidelines:

- Use NTFS file system volumes for user profiles that are on shares. This allows you to configure profiles with different file and share permissions. By doing this you can have multiple roaming user profiles for users or groups. It also allows for higher security than a file allocation table (FAT) or FAT32 volume does.
- Do not use Encrypted File System for shared profiles. Encryption is configured on a per-user basis and the user logging on won't have access to the profile.
- It is a good idea to use a test computer that has video and hardware components similar to the production computers.

For mandatory user profiles, the shares where the mandatory user profiles are stored should have permissions set to read-only. A mandatory profile must also be created before a user logs on to a computer for the first time. This is required because the contents of the Default User folder are copied to the new user's profile folder with the Common Program Group settings from the All Users folder. The user account itself contains username, passwords, and the groups of which the user is a member.

To create a preconfigured user profile, follow these steps:

1. Log on to the test computer. (If you are creating multiple profiles, it is a good idea to create a separate account for each preconfigured profile to ensure that the configurations are correct.)
2. Install or configure all programs that meet the requirements of the department or group of users for which you are creating the profile. Arrange the Desktop and the Start menu as desired. Configuring the applications and the user desktop will create a model desktop profile template.
3. Log off, and then log on again as a member of the Administrators group.
4. Right-click My Computer, and then select Properties to display the System Properties dialog box (or simply select or double-click System in Control Panel). Select the Advanced tab, and then, under User Profiles, click Settings. The User Profiles dialog box appears, as shown in Figure 37-9.
5. Select the user profile you just created, and then click Copy To. In the Copy To dialog box, shown in Figure 37-10, type the path where you want to save a copy of the selected profile. Save a local profile to the %SystemDrive%\Documents and Settings\Default User folder. If you want a default profile for the domain, copy the preconfigured profile to a location on a network share. Then, when you set up a user's account, you can copy the saved profile to the path for the user's profile. For example, if the path for the user's profile is \\CorpSvr17\Profiles\JennyP, you would enter this as the Copy Profile To path.

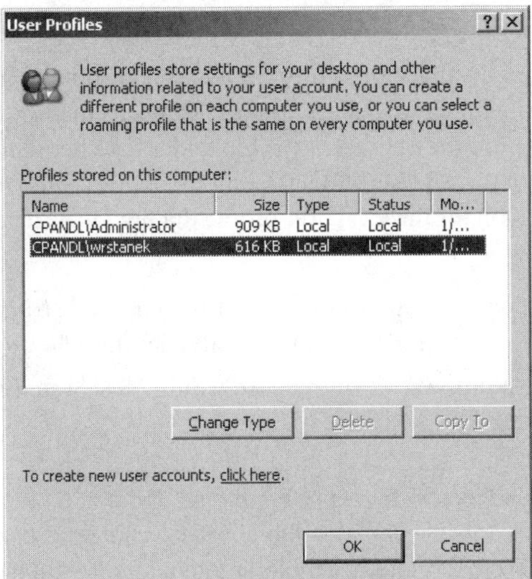

Figure 37-9. The User Profiles dialog box.

> **Note** In Windows Explorer, you must enable the Show Hidden Files And Folders option to access profile folders. To do this, select Folder Options from the Tools menu. This displays the Folder Options dialog box. On the View tab, select Show Hidden Files And Folders, and then click OK.

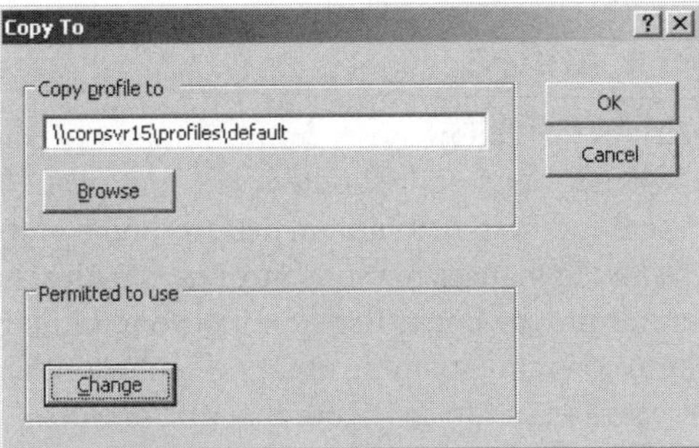

Figure 37-10. Set the profile path.

6. Set the profile permissions so that the profile can be used by other users. To do this, click Change under Permitted To Use, and then, in the Select User Or Group dialog box, type Everyone or the name of the specific user or group which should have access to the profile, and then click OK.
7. Click OK twice to close the open dialog boxes.

Configuring Local User Profiles

Local user profiles are created the first time a user logs on to a computer, unless there is a roaming or mandatory profile previously configured. This means that the contents of the Default User folder are copied to the new user's profile folder together with the Common Program Group settings from the All Users folder. Combined, this creates the user's desktop. Each new user has a unique path for the local user profile that includes the user's logon name as a subdirectory of the path.

- In a new Windows Server 2003 environment, or for an upgrade from Windows 2000, the path would be %SystemDrive%\Documents and Settings\%*UserName*%.
- For an upgrade from Windows NT 4, the path would be %SystemRoot%\Profiles\%*UserName*%.

Note In the user's main subdirectory for his or her profile, there is a file with a default name of Ntuser.ini. By default, this file contains the items that will be excluded from the copy process. For example, Microsoft Internet Explorer temporary files and history files, and individual application data are not copied as part of the user profile.

Configuring local user profiles is similar to configuring domain profiles. On the local machine, start Computer Management and access the Local Users And Groups node. Double-click a user's local account, and then select the Profiles tab. Type the local path for the profile. Domain controllers do not have local accounts, so you cannot access Local Users And Groups on a domain controller.

Configuring Roaming User Profiles

Roaming user profiles are settings that follow a user from computer to computer. They are especially valuable for administrators or troubleshooters who may need to log on to many different workstations or servers and need to maintain desktop and common settings for security and convenience reasons. To manage roaming profiles, you must be a member of the Account Operators, Domain Admins, or Enterprise Admins group in Active Directory, or have been delegated the right to configure roaming user profiles. Use either Active Directory Users And Computers or Server Manager to configure roaming profiles.

If you are using Active Directory Users And Computers to configure roaming profiles, double-click the user's account to display the related Properties dialog box. Select the Profile tab. Type the unique path of the roaming user profile chosen for that user in the Profile Path field. The path can be a local path on the user's computer such as C:\Profiles\%*UserName*% or a path to a network share on a remote server.

If you choose to put the user profiles on a remote server, the path should be in the Uniform Naming Convention (UNC) form such as *ServerName**ShareName*\%*UserName*% where *ServerName* is the name of the server, *ShareName* is the name of the share created for storing roaming profiles, and %*UserName*% is an environment variable that allows the profile path to be unique for each user. For example, if you set the profile path to \\CorpSvr15\Profiles\%User-

Name%, as shown in Figure 37-11, and were configuring the account for JennyP, the profile path would be set as \\CorpSvr15\Profiles\JennyP. The subfolder, JennyP, is created automatically, and the roaming profile is then stored in the folder as Ntuser.dat.

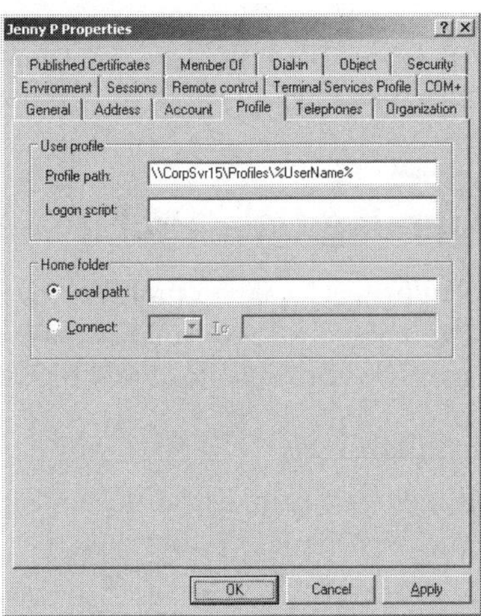

Figure 37-11. Set the profile path in the user's Properties dialog box.

> **Caution** When logged on to multiple computers using roaming profiles, changes to the profile settings and configuration may be lost if the order of logging off is incorrect. Imagine you are using a roaming profile and are logged on to two computers. You then change or install an application or program on the first computer. If you then log off that computer, any changes you made will be lost if you go to a second computer and log off without making the same changes, because your roaming profile on the second computer will be the one that is saved to the server and will not contain the changes made on the first computer. When using roaming profiles, the profile stored on the server is the one from the computer you logged off last.

Implementing Mandatory User Profiles

Mandatory user profiles are a type of roaming user profile. They can be used to maintain a higher security level and consistent environment for users. Although users can log on to different computers and get the same desktop settings, changes made to the desktop on the local computer will not be saved to the server where the mandatory user profiles are stored. Mandatory user profiles have the .man extension, for example, Ntuser.man.

To configure a mandatory user profile for a user, you set the user's profile path as previously discussed for roaming profiles. Then copy the profile that you want the user to have to the profile folder and change the name from Ntuser.dat to Ntuser.man. That's it—you rename the Ntuser.dat file to Ntuser.man using Windows Explorer, and it becomes a mandatory user profile.

Note Because profiles are hidden system files, they aren't automatically displayed in Windows Explorer. Choose Folder Options from the Tools menu, and then click the View tab. Under Advanced Settings, select Show Hidden Files And Folders. Note also that a mandatory profile must be available for a user to log on. If for some reason the user profile becomes unavailable, the user will not be able to log on. Because of this, you should check the security on the profile to ensure that the user can access it.

Switching Between a Local and a Roaming User Profile

Sometimes you may want to switch from a roaming to a local user profile or vice versa. This could be for personal preference, you may be troubleshooting, or you may have a slow network connection and the roaming profile takes too long to download to the local computer.

To switch between local and roaming profiles, complete these steps:

1. Right-click My Computer, and then select Properties to display the System Properties dialog box (or simply select or double-click System in Control Panel).
2. Select the Advanced tab, then, under User Profiles, click Settings. The User Profiles dialog box appears.
3. After selecting the profile that is to be changed, click Change Type, and then select Roaming Profile or Local Profile as appropriate.
4. Click OK twice.

Note Note that you can only change to the profile type if the profile was originally a roaming profile. If the change options aren't available, the user's profile was originally created as a local profile.

Managing User Data

It is important that users have access to the business data, software code, or accounting data on the network. They need access to the data to get their work done, and the organization needs to be operational 24 hours a day, seven days a week. Managing user data using folder redirection, group policy, offline files, and synchronization can help increase the network reliability and the availability of data. It can also reduce the time it takes to restore data in the event of hardware or software failures.

You want to make access to the data that each user and group requires invisible and seamless, and at the same time provide the most efficient process for restoring the data in case of a failure. Managing user data for fault tolerance and to reduce the amount of administrative load is accomplished using the Intellimirror technology. This technology allows users to have their data available to them regardless of which operating system (Windows 2000, Windows XP, or Windows Server 2003) and computer they log on. Using a combination of folder redirection, offline files, group policy, and synchronization, user data can be made available efficiently and reliably.

Using Folder Redirection

One useful approach to managing user data is folder redirection. In this process, the administrator uses group policy to configure where on the network the user's data, for example, the My Documents folder, is saved. This data is synchronized between the network storage site and the local copies in the background. This allows the user to change machines or to work offline and always have the same data available.

Using Group Policy, you can redirect four different folders: Application Data, Desktop, My Documents, and Start Menu. Before configuring the policy, however, you must first create a share to hold the user data. Create the share on a file server and configure the share so that the special group Everyone can List Contents, Read, and Write to it. Once you do this, you can configure group policy settings in order to implement folder redirection.

> **Note** Are you wondering what happens if the user's computer fails and folder redirection is in effect? Because the data is stored on the network server, if the user's local computer has a disk failure the network-stored data will not be lost and can be accessed from a different machine or from the original machine once it is rebuilt.

Folder redirection for domain users can be set in the domain policy or at an OU level. In Active Directory Users And Computers, right-click the domain or OU for which you want to implement folder redirection, and then select Properties. On the Group Policy tab, select the group policy you want to work with, and then click Edit. This displays the Group Policy Object Editor. In the Group Policy Object Editor, expand User Configuration\Windows Settings\Folder Redirection. As Figure 37-12 shows, the four folders that can be redirected are listed separately. This allows you to configure redirection of each folder separately.

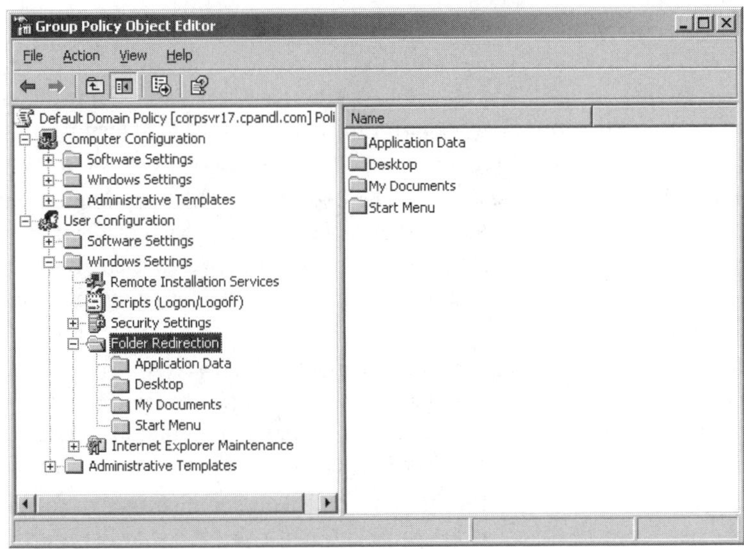

Figure 37-12. Select the folder you want to redirect.

In the Group Policy Object Editor, right-click the folder you want to redirect, and then select Properties. The default tab for the Properties dialog box is the Target tab. The Setting option of this tab provides three choices for configuring how folder redirection behaves. You can select from the following choices:

- **Not Configured** Use this setting to disable redirection of the selected folder.
- **Basic—Redirect Everyone's Folder To The Same Location** Use this setting to designate one location where all the related folders for users will be redirected. This would normally be a share on a server that is part of the daily backup schedule. The redirected folder data would then be available in the event of a disk crash. In most cases, the individual user folders will then be a subfolder of the designated folder. For example, if you wanted the My Documents folders for all users to be redirected to \\CorpSvr15\UserData, this folder would contain subfolders for each domain user, and the user's My Documents data would be stored in the appropriate subfolder.
- **Advanced—Specify Locations For Various User Groups** Use this setting if you want to set different user data locations for various groups. If you select this option, you can set an alternative target folder location for each group. Depending on the size of your network and domain, and its business model, this may be beneficial. You could, for example, set different folders for the Sales, Engineering, and Customer Service groups.

> **Note** Remember, the group policy you are working with only applies to user accounts that are in the container for which you are configuring Group Policy. So if you set a redirection policy for a user account that isn't defined in the domain or OU you are working with, the user's data will not be redirected.

If you choose basic redirection, the Target tab is updated, as shown in Figure 37-13, and you have the following options:

- **Redirect To The User's Home Folder** This setting applies only to redirection of a user's My Documents Folder. If you have configured the user's home folder in their account properties, you can use this setting to redirect the My Documents folder to the home folder. Use this setting only if the home folder has already been created.
- **Create Folder For Each User Under The Root Path** This is a common setting. It appends the user's name to the file share created on a file server, allowing a folder to be created automatically under the file share root path for each user. The folder name is based on the %*UserName*% variable. This option is not available with redirection of the Start Menu.
- **Redirect To The Following Location** This setting allows you to specify a root path to a file share and folder location for each user. If you add %*UserName*% to the path, you can create individual folders for each user as in the previous option. If you do not include a user-specific environment variable, all the users are redirected to the same folder.
- **Redirect To The Local User Profile Location** This setting causes the default location of the user's profile to be used as the location for the user data. This is the default

configuration if no redirection policies are enabled. If you use this option, the folders are not redirected to a network share and you essentially undo folder redirection. This option is not available with redirection of the Start menu.

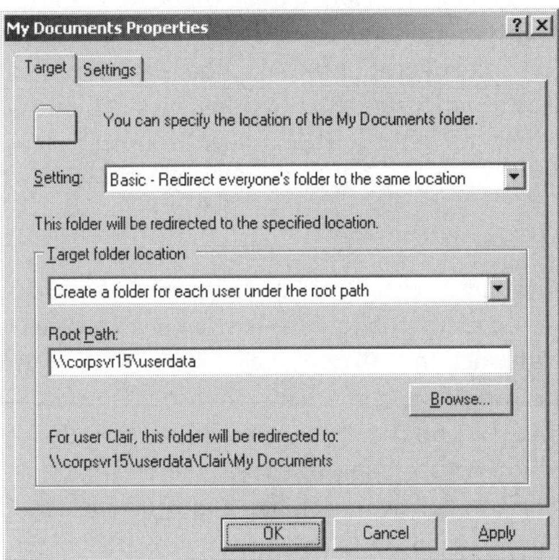

Figure 37-13. Configure basic folder redirection to redirect all the folders to the same location.

If you choose advanced redirection, the Target tab is updated so that you can define different redirection settings for different groups of users. Click Add to display the Specify Group And Location dialog box shown in Figure 37-14.

Figure 37-14. Configure advanced folder redirection to define different redirection settings for different groups.

In the Specify Group And Location dialog box, click Browse to display the Select Group dialog box. Type the name of a group account in the selected container, and then click Check Names. When a single match is found, the dialog box is automatically updated as appropriate and the entry is underlined. When you click OK, the group is added to the Security Group Membership list in the Specify Group And Location dialog box. You now have the same options for setting the Target Folder Location and the Root Path as you have with basic redirection. When you are finished configuring these options, click OK. You can then repeat this process to configure the redirection of the selected folder for other groups.

Using Offline Files

Offline files offer another way to manage user data. Think about how many of your users travel with their computers and may not be able to have a network connection to needed data. Using offline files in conjunction with folder redirection and synchronization, you ensure that user data will be available and consistent. To use offline files with folder redirection, you simply enable offline files on the shares created for redirection. By default, when you create shares, only the files and programs that users specify will be available for offline use. You can change this configuration so that all files and programs that users open from a share are automatically available offline. Or you can configure the share so that files and programs will not be available offline.

Note Offline files work by storing client data and documents in the file system cache on the client computer, making the data and documents available if there is no network connection.

Configuring Offline Files on File Servers

The quickest way to configure offline files is to use Computer Management. After you start Computer Management and connect to the computer you want to work with, expand System Tools and Shared Folders, and then select Shares to display the current shares on the system you are working with.

You can then configure offline settings for a shared folder by right-clicking the share in the details pane, and then selecting Properties. In the share's Properties dialog box, click Offline Settings on the General tab to display the Offline Settings dialog box. As shown in Figure 37-15, there are three settings:

- **Only The Files And Programs That Users Specify Will Be Available Offline.** This allows the user to decide which files will be available offline and is the default setting.
- **All Files And Programs That Users Open From The Share Will Be Automatically Available Offline.** If a user opens a file from a share, this setting makes it automatically available offline. The subsetting, Optimized For Performance, allows programs and application data to be available offline as well. Checking this box will help network

performance when applications are run over the network. Clear this box if you are not going to use folder redirection or offline files for application data.

- **Files Or Programs From The Share Will Not Be Available Offline.** This setting blocks users from storing files on the client computer for offline use.

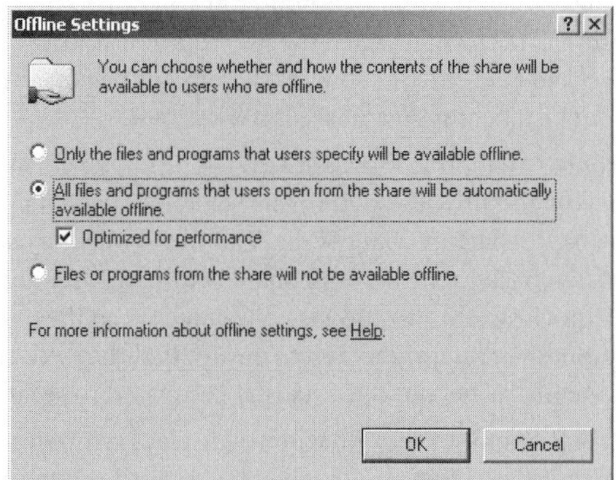

Figure 37-15. Configuring Offline Files settings on the server.

Configuring Offline Files on Clients

You can configure offline files for users on a client by completing the following steps:

1. Start Windows Explorer by right-clicking My Computer and selecting Explore.
2. Select Folder Options from the Tools menu. In the Folder Options dialog box, select the Offline Files tab, as shown in Figure 37-16.

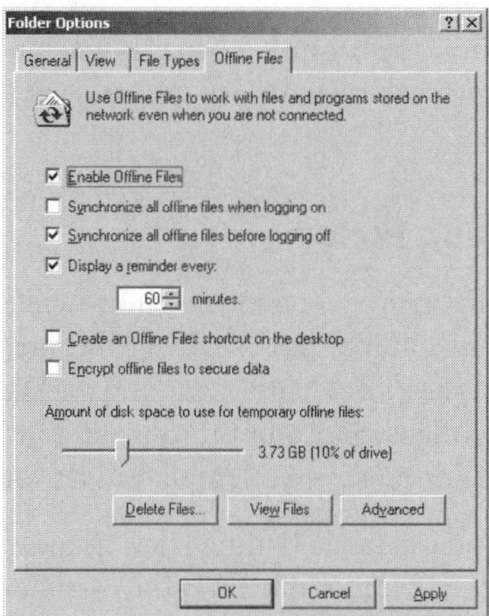

Figure 37-16. Enabling Offline Files on a client computer.

3. Select the Enable Offline Files check box. Offline files are now enabled on the client.

The Folder Options dialog box has a number of settings you can configure:

- The setting Synchronize All Offline Files When Logging On does a full synchronization when the user logs on. This synchronization is designed to ensure that any changes made to files while the user is offline are saved to the network share and that the most recent versions of files are on the user's computer. If you don't select this option, a quick synchronization is performed when the user logs on. With a quick synchronization, the files are checked to ensure that they exist both on the network share and in the file cache, but the data isn't compared to see if it is current.
- The setting Synchronize All Offline Files Before Logging Off performs a full synchronization when logging off and provides a complete version of the data. This synchronization is designed to ensure that any changes made to files while the user is logged on to the network are written back to the network share before the user logs off. If you don't select this option, a quick synchronization is performed when the user logs off. With a quick synchronization, the files are checked to ensure that they exist both on the network share and in the file cache, but the data isn't compared to see if it is current.
- The setting Display A Reminder Every … Minutes displays reminder balloons over the notification area at an interval that you specify whenever the computer is offline. As this can be distracting, you may want to set a long interval or disable this option.
- The setting Create An Offline Files Shortcut On The Desktop places a shortcut to the Offline Files folder on the desktop.
- The setting Encrypt Offline Files To Secure Data enables encryption for offline files. Only files on the local machine are encrypted, and files are not encrypted during movement across the network. Keep in mind that encryption requires the system partition to be formatted using NTFS and that only Administrators can enable encryption. Because some applications create temporary files in other folders, you might want to encrypt the working folders as well.
- The Advanced button configures how the computer behaves when network connectivity is lost, either allowing the user to continue to work offline or not allowing offline work to continue.

Configuring Offline Files in Group Policy

Group policy can manage access and configuration of offline files more efficiently than the methods mentioned previously. You can use Offline Files to manage the most common user data, including Application Data, My Documents, the Start Menu, and the Desktop. Offline Files policy objects are located in Computer Configuration\Administrative Templates\Network\Offline Files, and in User Configuration\Administrative Templates\Network\Offline Files.

When you use Group Policy to manage user data via Offline Files, be aware that precedence and dependencies are varied. For example: If you enable Prohibit User Configuration Of Offline Files in User Configuration, but enable it in Computer Configuration, offline files will be enabled, because the Computer Configuration setting has precedence over the User Configuration setting.

Managing File Synchronization

When you are managing files in a network using folder redirection or offline files, you need to make sure that the files on the network share remain synchronized with the files on the user's system. This allows you to ensure availability and that the latest version of the user's data is stored and available. Full synchronization provides the latest version, whereas Quick synchronization provides a complete version of the user data but not necessarily the most current version. By configuring the synchronization in Group Policy, you can ensure a full synchronization for either a logging on or logging off scenario.

There are three times for configuring Offline Files caching on a workstation:

- Logging on or off by the user
- Scheduled times
- During specific intervals of idleness on the computer

You will need to configure synchronization of redirected or offline files by using the Synchronization Manager. You run the Synchronization Manager using the Run dialog box. Click Start, and then select Run. In the Run dialog box, type **mobsync** and then click OK. This will display the Items To Synchronize dialog box, which you can use to manually synchronize folders and files and configure the Synchronization settings for each folder or file that is configured for offline use. If you click the Setup button, you see the three tabs representing the settings for automatic synchronization:

- To have synchronization performed during logging on or off (or both), select the Logon/Logoff tab, and set the When I Log On To My Computer and When I Log Off My Computer options.
- On the On Idle tab, click the Advanced button to configure how long your computer is idle before synchronization is executed and how often after your computer remains idle synchronization is repeated. For laptop support, a check box can be selected to prevent synchronization when running on a battery.
- The Scheduled tab allows you to schedule synchronization. Click Add to start the Scheduled Synchronization Wizard and schedule synchronization much like any other scheduled task.

Maintaining User Accounts

User accounts are fairly easy to maintain once they've been configured. Most of the maintenance tasks you need to perform involve user profiles and group membership, which are covered in separate sections of this chapter. Other than these areas, you may also need to perform the following tasks:

- Delete user accounts
- Disable, enable, or unlock user accounts
- Move user accounts

- Rename user accounts
- Reset a user's domain password
- Set logon scripts and home folders
- Creating a local user account password backup

Each of these tasks is examined in the sections that follow.

Deleting User Accounts

Each user account created in the domain has a unique security identifier (SID) and that SID is never reused. If you delete an account, you cannot create an account with the same name and regain all the same permissions and settings. The SID for the new account will be different than the old one, and you will have to redefine all the necessary permissions and settings. Because of this, you should delete accounts only when you know they are not going to be used again. If you are unsure, disable the account rather than deleting it.

To delete an account, select the account in Active Directory Users And Computers and press Delete. When prompted to confirm the deletion, click Yes and the account is permanently deleted. Deleting a user account doesn't delete a user's on-disk data. It only deletes the user account from Active Directory. This means the user's profile and other personal data will still be available on disk until you manually delete them.

Caution The permissions on users are internally characterized within Active Directory by unique SIDs that are allocated when the user is created. If you delete a user account and then recreate it, it will have a new SID and thus new permissions.

Disabling and Enabling User Accounts

If you need to deactivate a user account temporarily so that it cannot be used for logon or authentication, you can do this by disabling the account. While disabling an account makes it unusable, you can later enable the account so that it can be used again. To disable an account, right-click the account in Active Directory Users And Computers, and then select Disable Account.

When prompted that the account has been disabled, click OK. A red circle with an X is added to the account's icon to show that it is disabled. If you later need to enable the account, you can do so by right-clicking the account in Active Directory Users And Computers and then selecting Enable Account.

Moving User Accounts

When there is a reorganization or a user otherwise changes departments, you may need to move the user account to a new container in Active Directory Users and Computers. To move a user account, right-click the account, and then select Move. The Move dialog box appears allowing you to select the container to which you want to move the user account. Alternatively, you can drag the user account into a new container. You can also select multiple users to move by using windows keyboard shortcuts such as CTRL then selecting multiple users, or using Shift and selecting the first and last user.

Renaming User Accounts

Active Directory tracks objects by their SID. This allows you to safely rename user, computer, and group accounts without worrying about having to change access permissions as well. That said, however, the process of renaming a user account is not as easy as renaming other types of accounts. The reason is that users have several name components that are all related to a user's last name, including a full name, display name and user logon name. So when a person's last name changes as the result of a marriage, adoption or divorce, you not only need to update the user's account name in Active Directory but the rest of the related name components as well. To simplify the process of renaming user accounts, Active Directory Users And Computers provides a new dialog box (shown in the following screen) that you can use to rename a user's account and all the related name components.

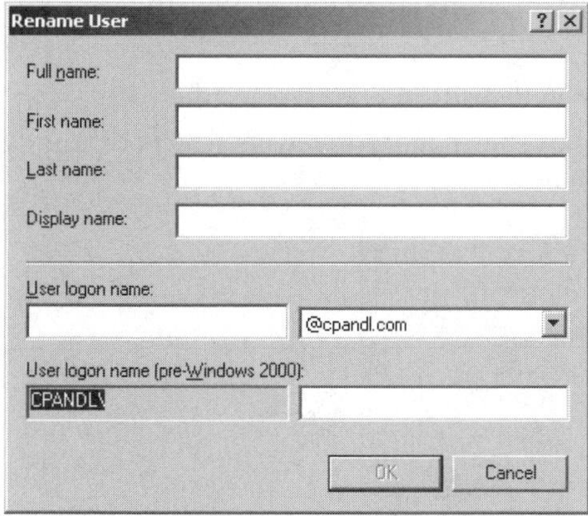

With the addition of the Rename User dialog box, the process for renaming user accounts is as follows:

1. Find the user account that you want to rename in Active Directory Users And Computers.
2. Right-click the user account and then select Rename. Active Directory Users And Computers then highlights the account name for editing. Press Backspace or Delete to erase the existing name and then press Enter to open the Rename User dialog box.
3. Make the necessary changes to the user's name information and then click OK. If the user is logged on, you'll see a warning prompt telling you that the user should log off and then log back on using the new account logon name.

4. The account is renamed and the SID for access permissions remains the same. You may still need to modify other data for the user in the account properties dialog box, including the following:
   - *User Profile Path*—As necessary change the Profile Path on the Profile tab, and then rename the corresponding directory on disk.
   - *Logon Script Name*—If you use individual logon scripts for each user, change the Logon Script Name on the Profile tab, and then rename the logon script on disk.
   - *Home Folder*—As necessary change the home folder path on the Profile tab, and then rename the corresponding directory on disk.

Resetting a User's Domain Password

One of the good things about using domain policy to require users to change their password is that the overall security of the network is improved by doing so. One of the downsides of frequent password changes is that users occasionally forget their password. If this happens, it is easy to fix by doing the following:

1. Find the user account whose password you want to reset in Active Directory Users And Computers.
2. Right-click the user account and then select Reset Password.
3. In the Reset Password dialog box shown in the following screen, type and then confirm the new password for the user.

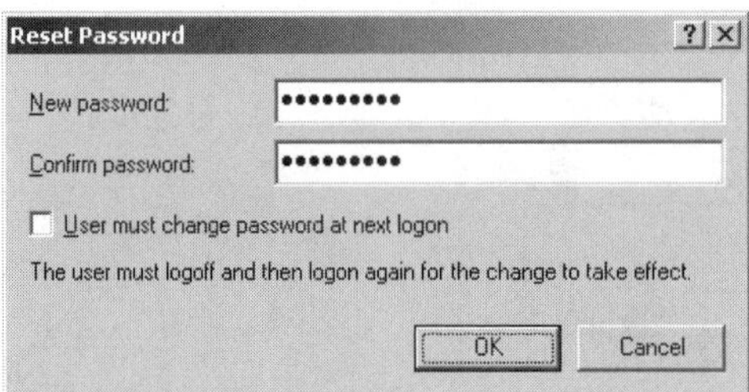

4. If you want, select the User Must Change Password At Next Logon option, and then click OK.

> **Note** The password change is immediately replicated to the PDC emulator as discussed in the section entitled "Using, Locating, and Transferring the PDC Emulator Role" on page 1145. This makes the password available for the user to log on anywhere in the domain.

Unlocking User Accounts

Whenever a user violates group policy such as when they fail to change their password before it expires or exceed the limit for bad logon attempts, Active Directory locks the account. Once the account is locked, the user can no longer log on. As accounts can also be locked because someone is trying to break into an account, you shouldn't automatically unlock accounts. Instead, either wait until the user asks you to unlock their account or go speak to the user when you notice their account has been locked.

You can unlock accounts by completing the following steps:

1. In Active Directory Users And Computers, right-click the locked account and then select Properties.
2. In the Properties dialog box, select the Account tab.
3. Clear the Account Is Locked Out check box and then click OK.

Creating a Local User Account Password Backup

Sometimes a user (or even an admin) will forget the local Administrator's or another local user account password on their server. If you manually reset a local user's account password, and the user has encrypted e-mail, files that have been encrypted, or passwords they use for Internet accounts, that data will be lost or not available with the new or reset password. With Windows Server 2003 you can reset a user's password without losing that encrypted data. You can consider this as backing up a local user password and you do this by creating a Reset Disk.

Be careful of the following when creating a Reset Disk:

- You are not allowed to create a Reset Disk and change your password from the Logon screen simultaneously.
- Reset Disks can only be used for local accounts, not for domain accounts.
- You do not have to create a new Reset Disk each time you change a local user's password; you only need to create the Reset Disk once for an account.
- Users should create their own Reset Disk for each local account they use.

You can make a reset disk for a Windows Server 2003 server that is a member of a domain or is a stand-alone server in a workgroup. You can also make a reset disk for a Windows XP Professional system that is a member of a domain or is a stand-alone workstation in a workgroup. You cannot, however, make a reset disk for a domain controller. Domain controllers do not have local accounts.

Follow these steps to make a password reset disk for a local account:

1. Log on to the computer using the local user account whose password you want to backup.
2. Press Ctrl+Alt+Delete, and then click Change Password.
3. In the User Name dialog box, type the name of the local user account login. In Log On To, type or select the name of the local host.

4. Click the Backup button. This starts the Forgotten Password Wizard.
5. Put a blank formatted 1.4 MB floppy disk into the A: drive.
6. The wizard asks for your current password, then a progress meter will display. When the process is complete, click Finish, and then click Cancel to get back to the desktop.

Troubleshooting

The Backup button doesn't appear

Sometimes the Backup button doesn't appear when you go through the Reset Disk creation process. The workaround is to use the Backspace key to delete the user name in the first field of the Security dialog box.

Store the floppy disk in a secure place, because now anyone can use it to gain access to the server. If you lose your local user password and need to gain access as a local administrator on your server, you can use the Reset Disk. Here's how to use the Reset Disk to get into a local user account:

1. Try to log on and fail. Select Reset when the Logon Failed Dialog box appears, to run the Forgotten Password Wizard.
2. Put the Reset Disk created earlier into the A: drive.
3. Type a new password and confirm. Then type a password hint and click OK.
4. The password should be changed and you should be able to log on using that password.

Inside Out

How the Password Reset Disk works

The Reset Disk process generates a public/private key pair. There are no passwords stored on the Reset Disk. The Reset Disk contains the private key and the public key encrypts the local account password. When a user forgets the local account password, the restore process uses the private key on the Reset Disk to decrypt the current password and create a new one that is encrypted with the same key. Data is not lost because the same encryption is used for any other encrypted data.

Managing Groups

Active Directory groups are objects that may hold users, contacts, computers, or other groups. When you want to manage users, computers, and other resources, such as files, directories, printers, network shares, and e-mail distribution lists, using groups can decrease administration time and improve network performance.

Understanding Groups

Types of groups and group scope are essential topics in planning and managing an efficient network. Planning an environment that uses Active Directory and groups is critical—failing to plan or taking shortcuts could negatively affect network traffic and create more administrative work in the long run. There are two types of groups and three group scopes.

Group management has been enhanced with two new features for universal groups. Before Windows Server 2003, all changes to universal groups would be replicated to all global catalog servers across the enterprise. Thus, if you used universal groups on your network, and you had slow network connectivity between global catalog servers, careful implementation of universal groups was crucial to preventing slow network throughput. To alleviate this possible bottleneck in network traffic, Microsoft has enhanced universal groups with caching of universal group membership and global catalog replication.

Caching universal groups may be useful in a Windows Server 2003 domain when the functional level is set to Windows 2000 Native functional level. You configure caching of a universal group when Active Directory sites are widely scattered geographically or connected by slow network and you want to minimize network traffic and increase logon efficiency and authentication. For instance, suppose you have a small remote office that has a slow wide area network (WAN) connection to the main office. Instead of the users having to connect to a domain controller in the main office, a domain controller can be configured in the remote office to cache the universal groups. This way you do not have to have the global catalog on the remote domain controller. When someone logs on in the remote office, the process uses cached logon credentials on the remote domain controller. By default, this cached data is refreshed every eight hours.

To improve dependability and performance, Microsoft has made some primary changes in replication and synchronization of Active Directory data. Within groups, all group membership data is no longer replicated between global catalog sites when group members are added, deleted, or changed. Rather, only the changed group member data is replicated. This helps reduce network traffic and also lowers the amount of required processing.

Types of Groups

There are two types of groups used in Windows Server 2003: security groups and distribution groups.

- Security groups are used to control access to resources. This is the kind of group you will probably use most often, and it may already be familiar. Security groups are listed in Discretionary Access Control Lists (DACLs). DACLs are part of an object's descriptor and are used to define permissions on objects and resources.
- Distribution groups are used for unsecured e-mail lists. Distribution lists do not use the functionality of the DACL permissions that security groups do. Distribution groups are not security-enabled but can be used by e-mail servers such as Microsoft Exchange Server.

Understanding the Scopes of Groups

Windows Server 2003 uses three types of groups: domain local, global, and universal. Each of these groups has a different scope that determines the types of objects that can be included as members of a group and the permissions and rights those objects can be granted. In practice, you will almost always use security groups, because they include distribution group functionality and are the only types of groups that have DACLs.

Domain Local Groups Consider using domain local groups first when you are giving groups or users access to local domain resources. For instance, if you have a domain named northwind.com and you want users or groups in that local domain to access a shared folder in the northwind.com local domain, you could create a domain local group called SalesPersons, insert in the SalesPersons group the users and global groups you want to give access to the shared folder, and then assign the SalesPersons group permissions on the resource.

Access policies for domain local groups are not stored in Active Directory. This means that they do not get replicated to the global catalog and thus queries performed on the global catalog will not return results from domain local groups. This is because domain local groups cannot be determined across domains. Domain local groups are analogous to local groups in Windows NT when used in Windows 2000 Mixed functional level.

Global Groups Use global groups to give users or groups access to resources according to how they have been organized. For instance, users from the Marketing or Development departments could be put in separate global groups in order to simplify administration of their need to access resources like printers and network shares.

Global groups behave differently depending on the functional level of your domain. In Windows 2000 Mixed functional level, global groups can only be put into the security descriptors of objects that are in the same domain. In Windows 2000 Native functional level, global groups can be nested in order to grant access to any domain in the forest.

Universal Groups Universal groups have very few fundamental restrictions. Universal groups are available only in Windows 2000 Native functional level or higher. Universal groups can be a tempting shortcut for administrators to use, because they can be used across domains in the forest. Memberships in universal groups can be drawn from any domain, and permissions can be set within any domain. However, using universal groups as your main method of grouping users, groups, and computers has a significant caveat.

Universal groups are stored in the global catalog, and whenever changes are made to a universal group, it must be replicated to other domain controllers configured as global catalog servers. For networks with slow network links, judicious use of universal groups to prevent network bottlenecks or slowed performance during authentication and global catalog changes is essential to reduce administrative and ownership costs.

Which Group Scope Should You Use? There is a strategy in choosing when to use a group scope and which group scope to use. A common strategy is to organize user accounts into logical groups based on the permissions they need to access specific resources. In a business model, this often can be determined according to the department the user belongs to. For instance, the Development department of a software business may put all their developers in a Dev group, and then assign permissions to a network share to the Dev group. On the other hand, in a Windows Server 2003 environment it becomes more complex than this, because there are different scopes for groups. Furthermore, groups may contain not only users, but also computers and even other groups, and can be nested to any scale.

Some important constraints on group scope in Windows Server 2003 include the following:

- Universal groups are available only in Windows 2000 Native functional level or higher.
- Universal groups are stored in the global catalog and replicated across the network. However, Windows Server 2003 has new features that allow caching of the global catalog and replication of only the changes in it.
- When the domain functional level is in Windows 2000 Mixed functional level, global groups can be included in an object's security data structure only if that object is in the same domain as the global group. In Windows 2000 Native functional level or higher, global groups can be nested in order to grant access to any domain in the forest.
- Domain local groups cannot be processed in other domains.

Group scope functionality and limitations include member inclusion and permissions. Table 37-4 lists how the three scopes function.

Table 37-4. How Group Scope Functions Using Windows Server 2003 Domain Functional Levels

Group	Member Inclusion	Permissions
Universal	You can include users, computer accounts, global groups, and universal groups from any domain.	Within any domain, universal groups can be added to other groups and granted permissions.
Global	You can put in a global group, any user or computer account or other global groups from the same domain.	Global groups can be added to other global groups in any domain in the forest and assigned permissions.
Domain local	Same as universal groups, but you can also include domain local groups from the same domain.	Domain local groups can be added only to other domain local groups in the same domain and assigned permissions.

In Native mode, Windows Server 2003 groups have nesting limitations that are dependent on the group scope. Limitations for nesting are listed in Table 37-5.

Table 37-5. Group Scope Nesting in Windows 2000 Native Functional Levels

Group Type	Can Nest in Universal?	Can Nest in Global?	Can Nest in Domain Local?
Universal	No	Yes	Yes
Global	Yes	Yes (only in the same domain)	Yes
Domain local	No	No	No

Why Use Domain Local Groups? Domain local groups are used when you want to give users, computers, or specific groups access to resources in a single local domain. In a domain local group, you can include other domain local groups with domain local scope, global groups, or universal groups. You can also include single accounts in the domain local group. However, including single user accounts can increase the amount of administration for you instead of reducing it, so unless management has specifically requested a special permission, this may not be the best route.

A common scenario for using domain local groups is to provide access to printers for members of a department (such as the Developers department).

In this scenario, you would use Active Directory Users And Computers:

1. Create a domain local group by right-clicking an OU, and then selecting New, Group.
2. Assign permissions to use the printer by adding the new domain local group to the printer by opening Control Panel, Printers and Faxes, then right-clicking Properties, selecting the Security tab, and finally adding the domain local group to the printer.
3. Create a global group.
4. Add the user accounts from the Development department to the global group
5. Add the global group to the domain Local group you created at the beginning.

This way, if you ever add a new printer, all you have to do is add access to it in the domain local group, and the Developers automatically get access because their global group is part of the domain local group.

If a new domain is added, all you have to do to give the people in the new domain access to the printer is add the new global groups from the new domain to the domain local group.

Why Use Global Groups? An important aspect of global groups is they are not replicated outside their own domain. They are not part of the global catalog replication. Thus, you should use global group membership for objects that need high regular maintenance or modifications. These changes will not be replicated across your network and thus will not slow network traffic over slow links. Therefore, a main reason to use Global groups is to organize users with similar needs within a domain to give them access to resources. For instance, you have two domains, one in the United States, the other in India. In each domain you have developers. Because your business model requires that neither group of developers needs access to the other's source code, you could create two global groups, USA\Dev and India\Dev, and give the global groups permissions to different source code shares.

Why Use Universal Groups? Using universal groups extends this idea so that users in groups of different domains may be able to access resources without affecting network traffic because of global catalog replication. By creating a universal group and adding global groups to it, you can give users from different domains in the forest access to the same resource. For instance, in the above scenario, a third group could be created for the developers, called UniDev. This would be a universal group to which you would add both global groups, USA\Dev and India\Dev, and assign permissions to perhaps even a second network share of source code that both groups of users must access. This is a good strategy, because if you add new user accounts to the global groups, the changes are not replicated to the global catalog and little if no impact to network traffic is incurred. However, be careful about changing memberships to universal groups, because those changes are replicated across all links to other domain controllers configured with global catalogs.

Creating a Group

You may create groups in the Users container or in a new OU that you have created in the domain. To create a group, start Active Directory Users And Computers. Right-click the Users container or the OU in which you want to place the group, point to New, and then select Group. This displays the New Object–Group dialog box shown in Figure 37-17. Type a group name, and then select Group Scope and Group Type. Afterward, click OK to create the group.

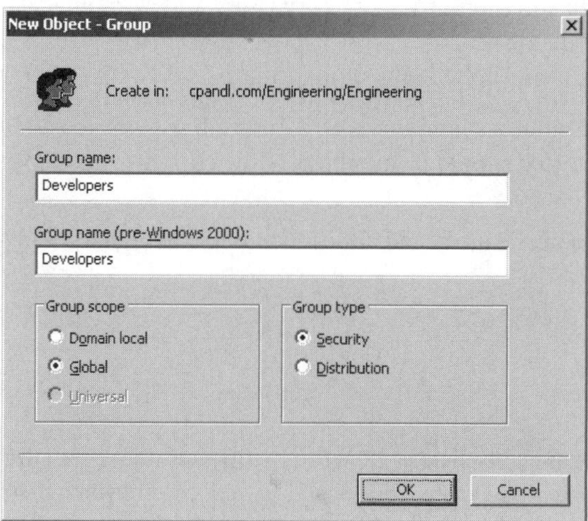

Figure 37-17. Creating a group.

In Windows 2000 Native and Windows Server 2003 domain functional levels, you have three group scopes and two group types you can select from (Universal scope is not available in Mixed mode). This allows you to create six different combinations of groups. You must be a member of the Account Operators, Domain Admins, or Enterprise Admins group to create new groups.

> **Note** The built-in accounts for Active Directory in Windows Server 2003 are located in two places. The built-in domain local groups such as Administrators, Account Operators, and Backup Operators, are located in the Builtin container. Built-in global groups such as Domain Admins and Enterprise Admins are located in the Users container.

Adding Members to Groups

The easiest way to add users to a group is to right-click the user in the details pane of Active Directory Users And Computers, and then select Add To A Group. The Select Group dialog box appears and you can select the group of which the user is to become a member. You can also get to the same dialog box by right-clicking on the user name, selecting Properties, and then choosing the Member Of tab and clicking Add.

> **Tip** To add multiple users to a group, select more than one user, using Shift+click or Ctrl+click, and follow the same steps.

If you want to add both users and groups as members of a group, you can do this by performing the following steps:

1. Double-click the group entry in Active Directory Users And Computers. This opens the group's Properties dialog box.
2. On the Members tab, click Add to add accounts to the group.
3. Use the Select Users, Contacts, Computers, Or Groups dialog box to choose users, computers, and groups that should be members of the currently selected group. Click OK.
4. Repeat steps 2 and 3 as necessary to add additional users, computers, and groups as members.
5. Click OK.

Deleting a Group

Deleting a group is as simple as right-clicking the group name within Active Directory Users And Computers, and then selecting Delete. You should be very careful when deleting groups because, though it does not delete the user accounts contained by the group, the permissions you may have assigned to the group are lost and cannot be recovered by merely recreating the group with the same name.

> **Caution** The permissions on groups are internally characterized within Active Directory by unique SIDs that are allocated when the group is created. If you delete a group and then recreate it, it will have a new SID and thus new permissions.

Modifying Groups

There are a number of modifications, property changes, and management procedures you may want to apply to groups. You can change the scope, the members and other groups contained in the group, move a group, delegate management of a group, and send mail to a group.

Find a Group

When you have a substantial number of groups, you can use the Find function to locate the one you need to manage. Just right-click the domain or OU, and then select Find. In the Find Users, Contacts, And Groups dialog box, you can specify what type of object to find, change the starting point, or structure a search query from the available tabs. Once the query has run, many administrative or management functions can be performed on the objects returned in the results window.

Inside Out

Saved queries in Active Directory

Part of the new enhanced user interface in Active Directory, a new feature for Windows Server 2003 is the ability to reuse and save queries. This allows you to find groups quickly and repeatedly when you want to manage and modify them. You can locate the new Saved Queries folder in the default position at the top of the Active Directory Users And Computers console tree (left pane). You cannot save queries from the Find menu when you right-click a group. You can only save them using the Saved Query procedure that is found in the uppermost part of the tree in Active Directory Users And Computers and creating a new query.

Managing the Properties of Groups

When you double-click a group name in Active Directory Users And Computers, the Group Properties dialog box appears. You can configure the following six areas or functions:

- **General** You change the description or group e-mail address here. In addition, you may be able to change the type of group or the scope of the group. When in Windows Server 2003 domain functional level, there are limitations on changing Group Scope, as shown in Table 37-6.
- **Members** You can list, add, and remove group members.
- **Member Of** Lists the groups the current group is a member of. These can be domain local groups or universal groups from the local domain or universal groups from other domains in the current domain tree or forest.
- **Managed By** Add, clear, or modify the user account you want to make responsible for managing this group.
- **Object** View the canonical name of the group object. This tab is visible only in Advanced view. To access Advanced view, select Advanced Features from the View menu in Active Directory Users And Computers.
- **Security** Used to configure advanced permissions for users and groups that can access the group object in Active Directory. This tab is visible only in Advanced view.

Table 37-6. Group Scope Conversions in Windows Server 2003 Domain Functional Level

Scope of Group	Can be Converted to Universal	Can be Converted to Global	Can be Converted to Domain Local
Universal	NA	Yes	Yes
Global	Yes	NA	No
Domain local	Yes	No	NA

Modifying Other Group Settings

You can modify other group settings using Active Directory Users And Computers. You can perform the following tasks:

- **Move a Group** To move a group, right-click it, and then select Move. The Move dialog box appears, allowing you to select the container to which you want to move the group. Alternatively, you can drag the group icon into a new container. You can also select multiple groups to move by using Windows keyboard shortcuts such as Ctrl, then selecting multiple groups, or using Shift and selecting the first and last group.
- **Rename a Group** Right-click the group name, and then select Rename. Type the new group name, and then press Enter. Multiple group selection is disabled for this function.
- **Send Mail to a Group** Right-click the group name, and then select Send Mail. An error will occur if no e-mail address has been configured on the General tab of Group Properties. Otherwise, the default mail client will be used to open a new mail message addressed to the group, which you can complete and send.

> **Note** Moving or renaming groups can alter the Effective Permissions of users and groups in unpredictable ways. With this in mind, you may want to check the Effective Permissions for member users and groups to ensure that the permissions are as expected.

Managing Computer Accounts

Computer accounts are managed and configured using Active Directory Users And Computers. By default, computer accounts are stored in the Computers container and domain controller accounts are stored in the Domain Controllers container. Computer accounts can also be stored in other containers, such as the OUs you've created. Computers may be joined and removed from a domain using Computer Management or the System tool in Control Panel.

Creating a Computer Account in Active Directory

When you create a new computer account in your domain, you must be a member of the Account Operators, Domain Admins, or Enterprise Admins groups in Active Directory. To create a new computer account, start Active Directory Users And Computers. Right-click the container in which you want to create the new computer account, point to New, and then select Computer. This starts the New Object–Computer Wizard shown in Figure 37-18.

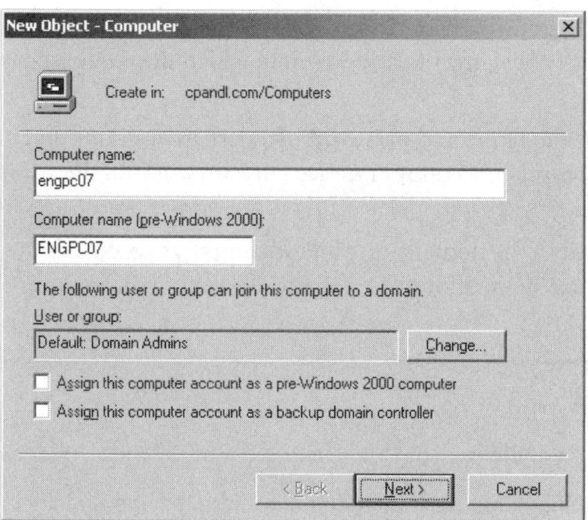

Figure 37-18. Creating a computer account.

Type a computer name. By default, only members of Domain Admins can join computers to the domain. To allow a different user or group to join the computer to the domain, click Change, and then use the Select User Or Group dialog box to select a user or group account that is authorized to join the computer to the domain. If Windows NT systems can use this account, select Assign This Computer Account As A Pre–Windows 2000 Computer. Afterward, click Next twice, and then click Finish.

Note Creating a computer account does not join the computer to the domain. It merely creates the account to simplify the process of joining a domain. You can, however, create a computer account when you join a computer to a domain.

Joining Computers to a Domain

When you join a computer to a domain, you must supply the credentials for creating a new computer account in Active Directory. The new computer will be placed in the default Computer container in Active Directory. Most of the time, there is a dialog box for joining a computer to the domain when you install or set up Windows 2000 or Windows Server 2003 the first time. You must be a member of the Administrators group on the local computer to join it to the domain. Windows Server 2003 allows any authenticated user to join workstations to the domain—up to a total of 10. To join a server to a domain, you must be a member of the Account Operators, Domain Admins, or Enterprise Admins group.

To join a server or workstation to a domain, follow these steps:

1. Start the System utility. On the desktop, right-click My Computer, and then select Properties. Alternatively, in Control Panel, select or double-click System.
2. On the Computer Name tab, click Change.
3. Select Domain and type the name of the domain to which the computer should join. Click OK.
4. When prompted, type the name and password of a domain account that has the permissions to create a computer account in Active Directory or join the computer to the domain, or both. Click OK.
5. The computer is joined to the domain, and a new computer account is created as necessary. If the changes are successful, you'll see a confirmation dialog box.

Troubleshooting

The computer won't join the domain

If there are problems joining the computer to the domain, there may be an existing computer in the domain with the same name. In this case, you would repeat this procedure and change the computer name. The computer must also have Transmission Control Protocol/Internet Protocol (TCP/IP) properly configured. If you suspect a problem with the TCP/IP configuration, check the configuration settings by typing **ipconfig /all** at the command prompt.

Moving a Computer Account

A corporation may have organizational changes requiring you to move a computer account. The computer account may be moved from one container to another. Plan and test moving the computer account to ensure that possible conflicts in permissions or rights don't occur. You can use the Effective Permissions tool in planning mode to simulate moving computer accounts and to determine if there could be conflicts.

To move a computer account, you can drag and drop the computer entry from one container to another within the Details pane of Active Directory Users And Computers. Alternatively, you can right-click the computer account name, select Move, and then select the container to which you want to move the account using the Move dialog box. You cannot move computer accounts across domains.

Disabling a Computer Account

Security issues, such as malicious viral attacks or rogue user actions may require you to temporarily disable a computer account. Perhaps a critical software bug has caused an individual computer to repeatedly try to receive authentication from a domain controller. You disable a computer account to prevent it from authenticating until you fix the problem.

You disable a computer account by right-clicking it in Active Directory Users And Computers and selecting Disable Account. This prevents the computer from logging on to the domain but does not remove the related account from Active Directory.

Deleting a Computer Account

When you delete a computer account using Active Directory Users And Computers, you cannot just re-create a new computer account with the same name and access. The SID of the original computer account will be different from that of the new account.

To remove a computer account, right-click the computer account name in Active Directory Users And Computers, and then select Delete.

Managing a Computer Account

Managing a remote computer is a common task when troubleshooting server or workstation problems. You see and configure computer management settings such as shares, system settings, services and applications, and the event log of the remote computer. Care should be taken when changing settings or re-starting services on remote machines.

Right-click the computer account name in Active Directory Users And Computers, and then select Manage to bring up the Microsoft Management Console (MMC) for that computer.

Resetting a Computer Account

Computer accounts, like user accounts, have passwords. Unlike user account passwords, computer account passwords are managed automatically. Sometimes, however, the password can get out of sync or there can be another issue that doesn't allow the computer account to be authenticated in the domain. If this happens, the computer account can no longer access resources in the domain and you should reset the computer account.

To reset a computer account, right-click the computer account name in Active Directory Users And Computers, and then select Reset Account.

Configuring Properties of Computer Accounts

As with users and groups, there are many configuration tabs you can select when you are modifying a computer account. Right-click the computer name in Active Directory Users And Computers, and then select Properties. The following tabs are available:

- **Delegation** Allows you to configure delegation for the computer account as discussed in the section entitled "Configuring the Delegated Service or Computer Account" on page 1137. This tab is available only when the domain is operating in Windows Server 2003 functional level.
- **General** Shows the computer's name and role and allows you to set a description. When the domain is operating in Windows 2000 Mixed or Windows 2000 Native functional level, you configure the computer for delegation by selecting the Trust This Computer For Delegation option.
- **Location** Allows you to set a location for the computer.
- **Managed By** Allows you to specify the person or group responsible for the computer.
- **Member Of** Allows you to configure the group membership for the computer.
- **Object** Displays the canonical name of the user object with dates and Update Sequence Numbers. This tab is visible only in Advanced view.
- **Operating System** Displays the operating system version and service pack used by the computer.
- **Remote Install** Allows you to set the unique identifier (globally unique identifier [GUID]/universal unique identifier [UUID]) and the remote installation server to use for a managed computer. This tab is available only for a managed computer.
- **Security** Used to configure advanced permissions for users and groups that can access this computer object in Active Directory. This tab is visible only in Advanced view.
- **Dial-In** Used to set the computer's dial-in or VPN access controls as well as callback, IP address, and routing options for dial-in or VPN or both.

As you can see, much of the data for computer account properties is informational. The data you may need to change is probably in the Security tab area, where you can add users or groups to the account and change permissions for users and groups that already exist or that you have added. You may also have to change the dial-in configuration as well as allow or deny dial-in access using the computer.

Chapter 38

Managing Group Policy

Group Policy is designed to simplify administration by allowing administrators to configure user and computer settings in the Active Directory directory service and then have those policies automatically applied to computers throughout an organization. Not only does this provide central management of computers, it also helps to automate key administrative tasks. Using Group Policy, you can accomplish the following tasks:

- Configure security policies for account lockout, passwords, Kerberos, and auditing
- Redirect special folders such as My Documents to centrally managed network shares
- Lock down computer desktop configurations
- Define logon, logoff, shutdown, and startup scripts
- Automate the installation of application software
- Maintain Microsoft Internet Explorer and configure standard settings

Some of these features such as security policies and folder redirection have been discussed in previous chapters. Other features are discussed in this chapter. The focus of this chapter, however, is on the management of Group Policy, which is the most challenging aspect of implementing Group Policy in an organization.

Understanding Group Policy

You can think of Group Policy as a set of rules that help you manage users and computers. Like any set of rules, Group Policy is effective only under certain conditions. You can use Group Policy to manage servers running Microsoft Windows 2000 and Windows Server 2003 and client workstations running Windows 2000 and Windows XP Professional. You cannot use Group Policy to manage Windows NT, Windows 95, or Windows 98.

Note Like Active Directory, Group Policy has gone through several revisions. As a result of these revisions, some policies work only with a version of the Windows operating system that is compatible with a particular revision. For example, some group policies are compatible with Windows 2000, Windows XP Professional, and Windows Server 2003, while others are compatible only with Windows XP Professional and Windows Server 2003.

Local and Active Directory Group Policy

Two types of group policies are available. The first type is local group policy, which is stored locally on individual computers in the %SystemRoot%\System32\GroupPolicy folder and applies only to a particular computer. Every computer running Windows 2000 or later has one local group policy. For a computer in a workgroup, the local group policy is the only group policy available. A computer in a domain also has a local group policy, but it is not the only group policy available, and this is where the second type of group policy called Active Directory group policy (or more commonly just "group policy") comes into the picture.

Active Directory group policy is stored in the Sysvol folder used by Active Directory for replicating policies and is represented logically as an object called a Group Policy Object (GPO). A GPO is simply a container for the policies you configure and their settings that can be linked to sites, domains, and organizational units (OUs) in your Active Directory structure. You can create multiple GPOs, and by linking those objects to different locations in your Active Directory structure, you can apply the related policy settings to the users and computers in those Active Directory containers.

When you create a domain, two Active Directory group policies are created:

- **Default Domain Policy** Used to configure domain-wide settings
- **Default Domain Controller Policy** Used to configure baseline security for domain controllers

Inside Out

Create additional GPOs rather than editing the default GPOs

The Default Domain Policy and Default Domain Controller Policy GPOs provide the baseline policy for a domain. These policies are vital to the health of Active Directory in that domain. You should edit the Default Domain Policy only to set account policy. For other types of policy, you should create a new GPO and link it to the domain. You should edit the Default Domain Controller Policy only to set users rights and audit policies. Otherwise, it is recommended that you do not make other changes to the Default Domain Controller Policy. If for some reason these policies become corrupted, Group Policy will not function properly. To resolve this, see the section entitled "Fixing Default Group Policy" later in this chapter.

You can create additional GPOs as necessary and link them to the sites, domains, and OUs you've created. Linking a GPO to Active Directory structure is how you apply Group Policy. For example, you could create a GPO called Technology Policy and then link it to the Technology OU. The policy then applies to that OU.

Group Policy Settings

Group Policy applies only to users and computers. Although groups can be used to specify to which users a particular policy applies, the actual policies are applied only to member users. Group Policy settings are divided into two categories: Computer Configuration and User Configuration. Computer Configuration contains settings that apply to computers. User Configuration contains settings that apply to user accounts.

Figure 38-1 shows the Default Domain Policy for a computer. As you can see in the figure, both Computer Configuration– and User Configuration–related settings are divided into three major classes, each of which contains several subclasses of settings:

- **Software Settings** Allow you to install software on computers and then maintain it by installing patches or upgrades. You can also uninstall software.
- **Windows Settings** Allow you to manage key Windows settings for both computers and users including scripts and security. For users, you can also manage Remote Installation Services, folder redirection, and Internet Explorer maintenance.
- **Administrative Templates** Allow you to control Registry settings that configure the operating system, Windows components, and applications. Administrative Templates are implemented for specific operating system versions.

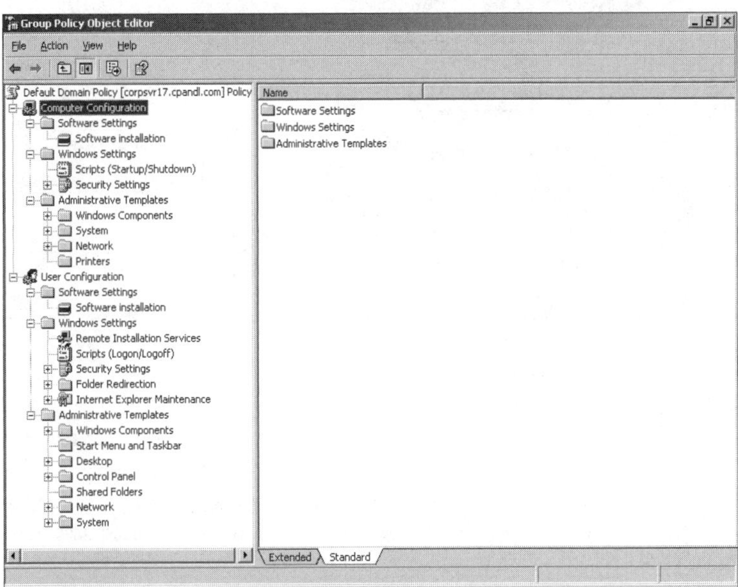

Figure 38-1. The Default Domain Policy.

Group Policy Architecture

Within the Windows operating system, the components of Group Policy have separate server and client implementations (see Figure 38-2). Each Group Policy client has client-side extensions that are used to interpret and apply Group Policy settings. The client-side extensions are implemented as dynamic-link libraries (DLLs) that are installed with the operating system. The main DLL for processing Administrative Templates is Userenv.dll.

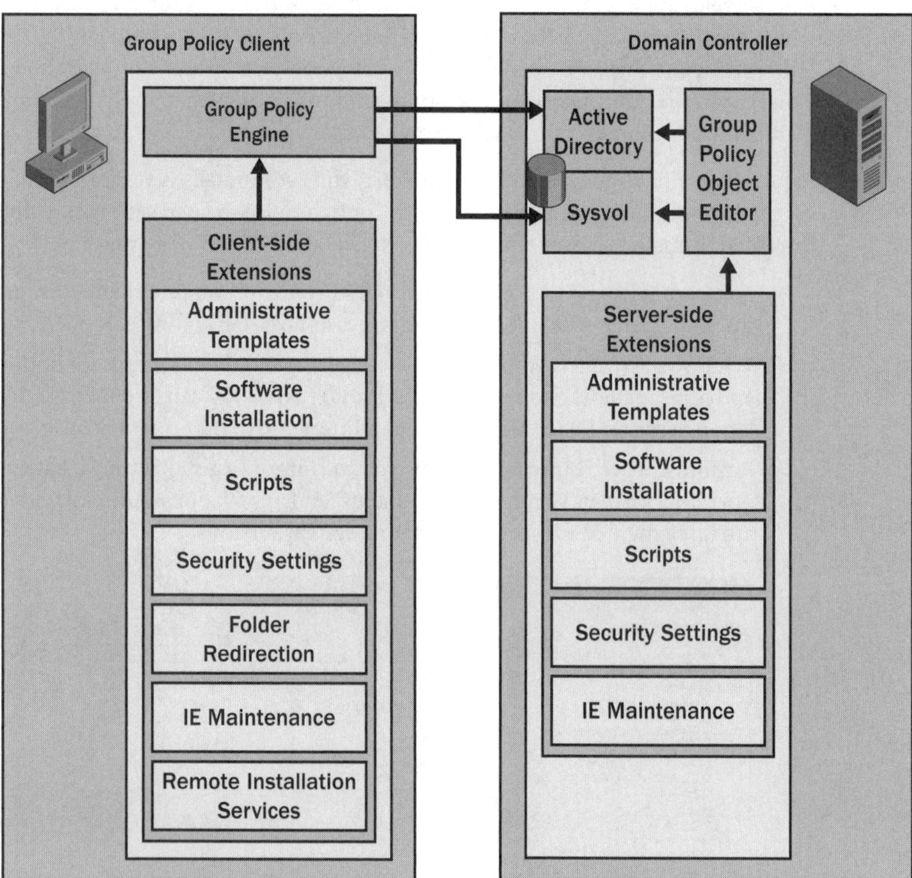

Figure 38-2. Group Policy architecture.

The Group Policy engine running on a client triggers the processing of policy when one of two events occurs: either the system is started or a user logs on to a computer. When a system is started and the network connection is initialized, computer policy settings are applied and then a history of the Registry-based settings that were applied is written to %AllUsersProfile%\Ntuser.pol. When a user logs on, user policy settings are applied and then a history of the Registry-based settings that were applied is written to %UserProfile%\Ntuser.pol.

> **Note** Any errors that occurred during processing of the Registry-based settings in the Administrative Templates are written to a log file called Gptext.log in the %SystemRoot%\Debug\Usermode folder. Warnings and informational events can also be written to Userenv.log if verbose logging is enabled. This log is also stored in the %SystemRoot%\Debug\Usermode folder.

Administrators use the Group Policy Object Editor to manage Group Policy. This snap-in for the Microsoft Management Console (MMC) provides the three top-level classes (Software Settings, Windows Settings, and Administrative Templates) that can be managed and makes use of a number of extensions. These extensions provide the functionality that allows you to configure various Group Policy settings. Some client-side extensions don't have specific implementations on the server because they are Registry-based and can be configured through Administrative Templates.

Although GPOs are represented logically in Active Directory and replicated through normal replication, most server-side Group Policy components are represented on the Sysvol as physical files. The default location for the Sysvol folder is %SystemRoot%\Sysvol with the subfolder %SystemRoot%\Sysvol\sysvol shared as SYSVOL. Within the shared Sysvol folder, you'll find subfolders organized by domain and the globally unique identifier (GUID) of each GPO created in a particular domain.

In these subfolders are files that are used to store the actual settings as implemented for a particular client-side extension on a per-GPO basis. The files available depend on the extensions that you use and include those summarized in Table 38-1.

Table 38-1. Essential Files Stored on the Sysvol

Client-Side Extension/ Sysvol File	Description
Administrative Templates	
Admfiles.ini	Initialization file for Administrative Templates that tracks the available template files.
System.adm	Provides policy settings for the operating system. Available for Windows 2000, Windows XP Professional, and Windows Server 2003.
Inetres.adm	Provides policy settings for Internet Explorer. Available for Windows 2000, Windows XP Professional, and Windows Server 2003.

Table 38-1. Essential Files Stored on the Sysvol

Client-Side Extension/ Sysvol File	Description
Conf.adm	Provides policy settings for Net Meeting. Available for Windows 2000, Windows XP Professional, and Windows Server 2003. Not available for 64-bit Windows editions.
Wmplayer.adm	Provides policy settings for Microsoft Windows Media Player. Available for Windows 2000, Windows XP Professional, and Windows Server 2003. Not available for 64-bit Windows editions.
Wuau.adm	Provides policy settings for Windows Update. Available for Windows 2000 Service Pack 3 or later, Windows XP Professional Service Pack 1 or later, and Windows Server 2003.
Software Installation	
AppGUID.aas	Stores the actual settings for a specific application installation according to the GUID of the application and includes the location of the application installation package. Although the .aas file is stored in the Sysvol, the actual application installer is not.
AppName.msi	A software installation package that is stored on disk separately from the related .aas file.
Security Settings	
Gptmpl.inf	Stores the actual security settings that apply to event auditing, Registry values, and privilege rights assignment.
Folder Redirection	
Fdeploy.ini	Stores the folder redirection settings for the GPO.
Other Settings	
Registry.pol	Stores miscellaneous Registry-based settings for Administrative Templates, Disk Quotas, EFS Recovery, QoS Packet Scheduler, and so forth.

Note Copies of Administrative Templates are also stored on the local computer. You'll find them in the %SystemRoot%\Inf folder.

Sysvol Replication Using the File Replication Service

Sysvol files are replicated using the File Replication Service (FRS). Although FRS uses Active Directory replication to distribute the Sysvol files, there is a separate database for replication (see Figure 38-3). This database uses the Microsoft JET database technology. The base location of this database is %SystemRoot%\Ntfrs\Jet and the primary data file for replication, Ntfrs.jdb, is stored in this folder.

The FRS storage engine uses transactional processing to manage the database. Any data that is modified in a transaction is copied to a temporary database file. If FRS finishes processing changes without errors occurring, the transaction can be committed. A record of the transaction is written to the transaction log and then to the database. The primary log file, Edb.log, has a fixed size of 5 megabytes (MB). FRS uses the reserve log files to reserve space on disk for additional log files that might need to be created. Because several 5 MB reserve files are already created, this speeds up the transactional logging process when additional logs are needed.

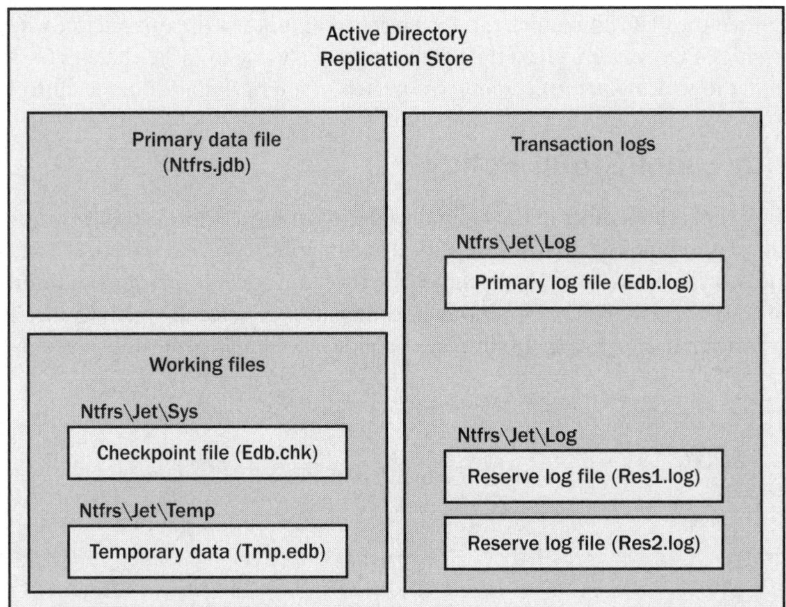

Figure 38-3. Active Directory replication store.

Implementing Group Policy

As discussed previously, there are two types of Group Policy: local group policy and Active Directory group policy. Local group policy applies to a local machine only, and there is only one local GPO per local machine. Active Directory group policy, on the other hand, can be implemented separately for sites, domains, and OUs. Two GUI tools are available to work with Active Directory group policy. You can use the Group Policy Object Editor, which is included with a standard installation of Windows Server 2003, or the Group Policy Management Console (GPMC), which is available as a free download from the Microsoft Downloads center (*http://www.microsoft.com/downloads*).

When you use either of these tools to create a new GPO or modify an existing GPO, the related changes are made on the domain controller acting as the PDC Emulator if it is available. The reason the PDC Emulator is used is so that there is a central point of contact for GPO creation and editing, and this in turn helps to ensure that only one administrator is granted access to a particular GPO at a time. This also simplifies replication of the changes because changes are always replicated from the same point of origin—the PDC Emulator. However, if the PDC Emulator cannot be reached or is otherwise unavailable when you try to work with GPOs, you are given the opportunity to choose to make changes on the domain controller to which you are currently connected or any available domain controller.

Working with Local Group Policy

Any user that is a member of the Domain Admins or local Administrators group can work with local group policy. To work with local group policy, you use the Local Security Policy tool, which can be accessed by clicking Start, Programs or All Programs, Administrative Tools, Local Security Policy. On a domain controller, you select Domain Controller Security Policy instead. In either case, this displays a dialog box similar to the one shown in Figure 38-4.

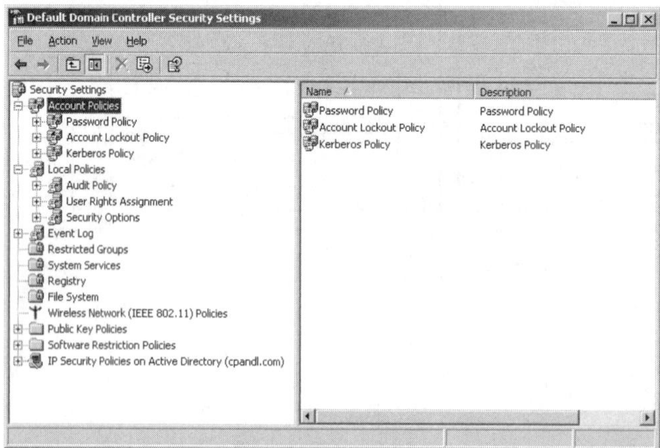

Figure 38-4. Using local group policy.

Inside Out

Accessing local group policy remotely

You can access the local group policy on another computer using the Group Policy Object Editor snap-in. Follow these steps:

1. Click Start, select Run, type **mmc** in the Open field, and then click OK.
2. Choose Add/Remove Snap-In from the File menu in the main window. In the Add/Remove Snap-In dialog box, click Add.
3. In the Add Standalone Snap-In dialog box, click Group Policy Object Editor, and then choose Add. This starts the Group Policy Wizard.
4. The Select Group Policy Object page is displayed. Click Browse.
5. In the Browse For A Group Policy Object dialog box, click the Computers tab, select Another Computer, and then click Browse again.
6. This displays the Select Computer dialog box. Enter the name of the computer whose local group policy you want to access, and click Check Names. When you have the right computer, click OK.
7. Click OK again and then click Finish in the Group Policy Wizard.
8. In the Add Standalone Snap-In dialog box, click Close. Then in the Add/Remove Snap-In dialog box, click OK.

In local group policy, you can configure security settings that apply to users and the local computer itself. Any changes you make to policy are applied to that computer the next time Group Policy is refreshed. In a domain environment these settings include the following:

- Account policies for passwords, account lockout, and Kerberos
- Local policies for auditing, user rights assignment, and security options
- Event logging options for configuring log size, access, and retention options for the application, system, and security logs
- Security restriction settings for groups, system services, Registry keys, and the file system
- Security settings for wireless networking, public keys, and Internet Protocol Security (IPSec)
- Software restrictions that specify software applications that aren't allowed to run on the computer

Local group policy is configured in the same way as Active Directory group policy. If you want to apply a policy, you must define it and set its values as appropriate. For example, let's say you are concerned about someone possibly cracking into the local system using the local Administrator account and you want to use Group Policy to rename this account so that it is more difficult to locate. To do this, you would define the Accounts: Rename Administrator

Account policy and set a new name for the local Administrator account by following these steps:

1. Start the Local Security Policy tool by clicking Start, Programs or All Programs, Administrative Tools, Local Security Policy.
2. Expand Security Options, and then double-click Accounts: Rename Administrator Account.
3. In the Accounts: Rename Administrator Account dialog box, shown in Figure 38-5, you would select the Define This Policy Setting option, type a new name for the local Administrator account, and then click OK.

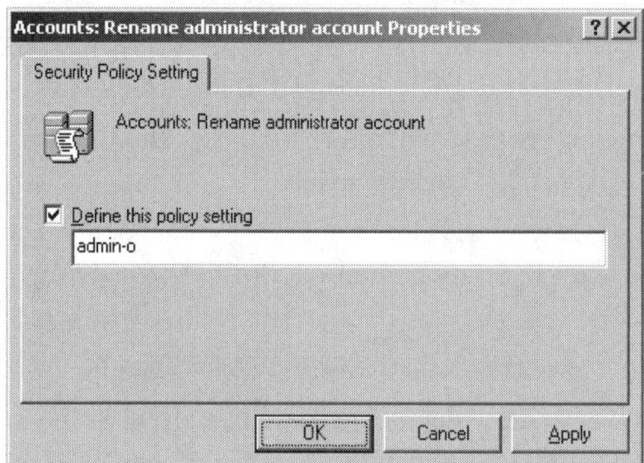

Figure 38-5. Defining a local policy.

Working with the Group Policy Object Editor

Any user that is a member of the Domain Admins or Enterprise Admins group can work with Active Directory group policy. Working with Active Directory group policy is a bit different than working with local group policy. With Active Directory group policy, object creation and linking are separate. You can create GPOs and then later link them to a container in Active Directory. You can also create objects and simultaneously link them to the appropriate container. Linking GPOs to a container is what tells Active Directory to apply the related settings.

The Group Policy Object Editor is used to open specific GPOs. Although you could open a new MMC and add the Group Policy Object Editor snap-in set to the GPO you want to work with (as discussed previously in the sidebar entitled "Accessing Local Group Policy Remotely"), there are easier ways to access linked GPOs. The technique you use depends on the type of object to which the GPO is linked, as follows:

- **For a domain** Start Active Directory Users and Computers. In the console tree, right-click the domain you want to work with, and then select Properties. In the Properties dialog box, click the Group Policy tab, as shown in Figure 38-6.

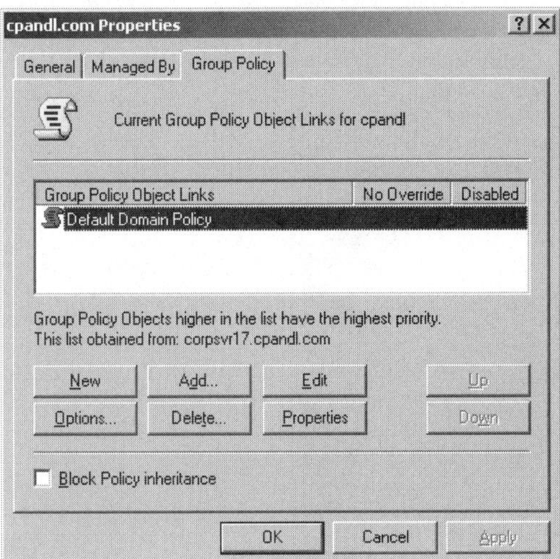

Figure 38-6. Accessing GPOs.

- **For an OU** Start Active Directory Users and Computers. In the console tree, right-click the OU you want to work with, and then select Properties. In the Properties dialog box, click the Group Policy tab.
- **For a site** Start Active Directory Sites and Services. In the console tree, right-click the site you want to work with, and then select Properties. In the Properties dialog box, click the Group Policy tab.

The New, Add, Edit, and Delete options in the Group Policy tab are discussed in the sections that follow.

> **Note** Once you install the Group Policy Management Console, the Group Policy tab options shown in Figure 38-6 are no longer available. You can click only Open to start the Group Policy Management Console—the use of which, I'll discuss in detail later in the chapter.

Creating and Linking a New GPO Using the Group Policy Object Editor

In the Group Policy tab, you can click New to create a new GPO that will be linked to the selected container. This link means any policy settings you define will be applied to the selected container according to the inheritance and preference options used by Active Directory. After you create the GPO by clicking New, an entry is added to the Group Policy Object Links list with the name highlighted, as shown in Figure 38-7. Type in a name, and then press Enter. Use the Up and Down buttons to change the preference order of the policy as necessary.

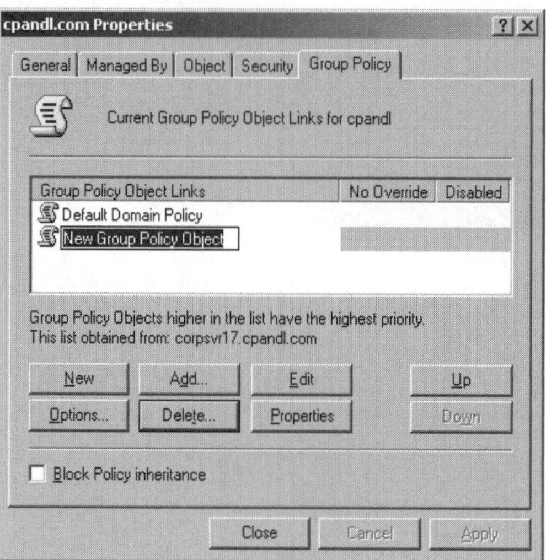

Figure 38-7. Creating a new GPO.

Editing an Existing GPO Using the Group Policy Object Editor

In the Group Policy tab, you can edit an existing GPO linked to the selected container by selecting it and then clicking Edit. This displays the Group Policy Object Editor dialog box, as shown in Figure 38-8. You can then make changes to Group Policy as necessary. The changes will be applied the next time Active Directory is refreshed, according to the inheritance and preference options used by Active Directory.

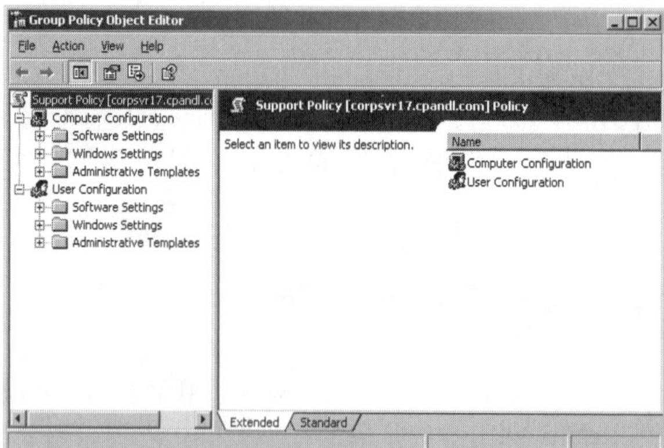

Figure 38-8. Creating a new GPO.

Linking to an Existing GPO Using the Group Policy Object Editor

Linking a GPO to a container applies the object to the container. In the Group Policy tab, you can link to an existing GPO by clicking Add. This displays the Add A Group Object Link dialog box, as shown in Figure 38-9.

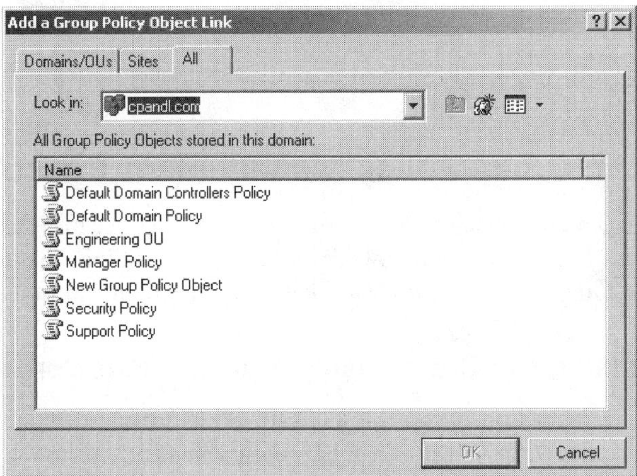

Figure 38-9. Linking to an existing GPO.

The container you are currently working with is selected in the Look In list, and any applicable policies are listed in the tab selected by default, which is either Domains/OUs or Sites depending on the type of container you are working with. If you select the All tab, you'll see all the GPOs that are available in the domain. Select the one you want to use, and then click OK. The linked policy will be applied the next time Active Directory is refreshed, according to the inheritance and preference options used by Active Directory.

Deleting an Existing GPO by Using the Group Policy Object Editor

In the Group Policy tab, you can remove an existing GPO by selecting it and then clicking Delete. This displays the Delete dialog box, as shown in Figure 38-10. You can now select the following options:

- **Remove The Link From The List** Selecting this option removes the link to the GPO in this container and means the GPO no longer applies to the objects in the container.
- **Remove The Link And Delete** Selecting this option removes the link to the GPO as well as the object itself. This permanently deletes the GPO. If the object is linked to other containers, those links will be removed as well.

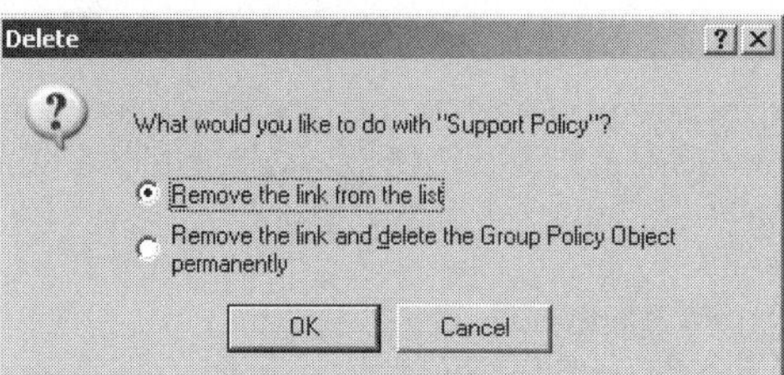

Figure 38-10. Removing a GPO.

Working with the Group Policy Management Console

The Group Policy Management console provides an integrated interface for working with GPOs. This console was introduced in Windows Server 2003. The sections that follow provide an overview of installing and using the Group Policy Management Console.

Installing and Running the Group Policy Management Console

The Group Policy Management Console (GPMC) is available as a free download from the Microsoft Downloads Center (*http://www.microsoft.com/downloads*). This tool can be installed on computers running Windows Server 2003 or Windows XP Professional Service Pack 1 with QFE 326469 or later, providing Microsoft .NET Framework is also installed. Once you've downloaded the Group Policy Management Console you can install it by completing the following steps:

1. Double-click the installer file Gpmc.msi. When the Microsoft Group Policy Management Console Setup Wizard starts, click Next.
2. Accept the license agreement by selecting I Agree, and then click Next again to begin the installation process.
3. When the wizard completes the installation, click Finish.

You can run the Group Policy Management console from the Administrative Tools menu. Click Start, Programs or All Programs, Administrative Tools, and Group Policy Management Console.

> **Caution** You cannot install Group Policy Management Console on computers running Windows 2000 or any previous versions of Windows. These operating systems are not compatible with the extensions used by the Group Policy Management console. Once you install the Group Policy Management console on a computer, you can no longer access the Group Policy tab options discussed in the section entitled "Working with the Group Policy Object Editor" earlier in this chapter.

Using the Group Policy Management Console

When you start Group Policy Management Console, the tool connects to Active Directory running on the domain controller acting as the PDC Emulator for your logon domain and obtains a list of all GPOs and OUs in that domain. It does this using Lightweight Directory Access Protocol (LDAP) to access the directory store and Server Message Block (SMB) protocol to access the Sysvol. The result, as shown in Figure 38-11, is that for each domain to which you are connected, you have all the related GPOs and OUs available to work with in one location.

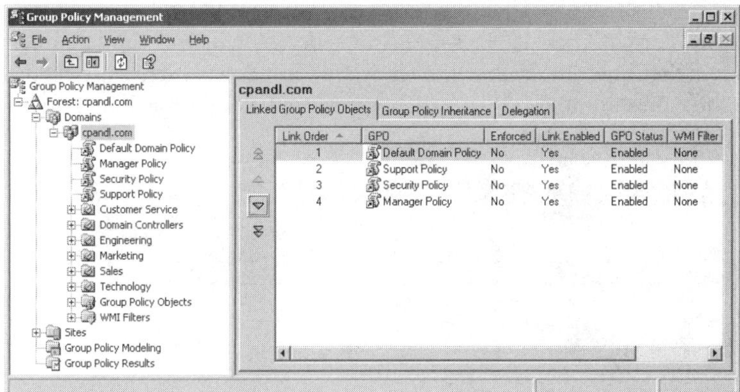

Figure 38-11. The Group Policy Management Console.

Accessing Forests, Domains, and Sites in Group Policy Management Console

Working with forests, domains, and sites in Group Policy Management Console is fairly straightforward, as follows:

- **Accessing forests** The forest root is listed for each forest to which you are connected. You can connect to additional forests by right-clicking the Group Policy Management node in the console tree and selecting Add Forest. In the Add Forest dialog box, shown in the following screen, type the name of a domain in the forest to which you want to connect, and then click OK. As long as there is an external trust to the domain, you can establish the connection and obtain forest information—even if you don't have a forest trust with the entire forest.

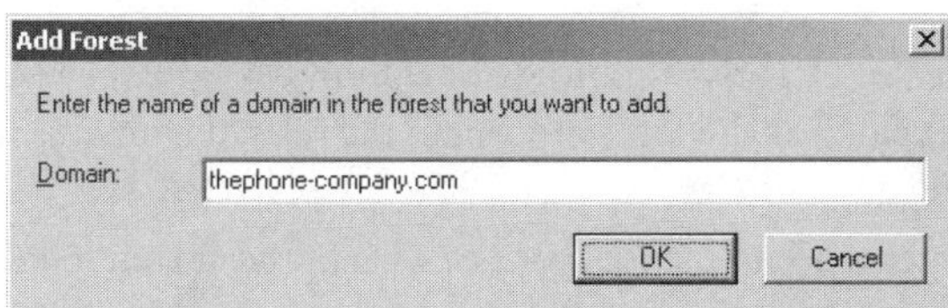

- **Accessing domains** You can view the domain to which you are connected in a forest by expanding the forest node and then expanding the related Domains node. By default, you are connected to your logon domain in the current forest. If you want to work with other domains in a particular forest, right-click the Domains node in the designated forest, and then select Show Domains. In the Show Domains dialog box, which has the same options as the Show Sites dialog box, select the options for the domains you want to work with and clear the options for the domains you don't want to work with. Then click OK.
- **Accessing sites** Because Group Policy is primarily configured for domains and OUs, sites are not shown by default in GPMC. If you want to work with the sites in a particular forest, right-click the Sites node in the designated forest, and then select Show Sites. In the Show Sites dialog box, shown in the following screen, select the options for the sites you want to work with and clear the options for the domains you don't want to work with. Then click OK.

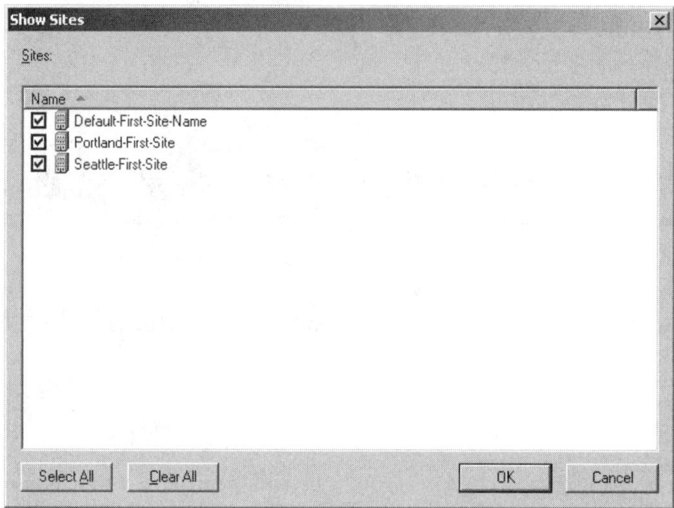

Creating and Linking a New GPO in Group Policy Management Console

In the Group Policy Management Console you can create and link a new GPO by completing the following steps:

1. Access the domain or OU you want to work with in Group Policy Management Console. Do this by expanding the forest node and the related Domains node as necessary, with the following guidelines:
   - If you selected a domain node, you see a list of the current GPOs and OUs in the domain.

- If you selected an OU node, you see a list of the current GPOs for the OU (if any).

2 Right-click the domain or OU node, and select Create And Link A GPO Here.

3 In the New GPO dialog box, type a name for the GPO, and then click OK.

Note Group Policy Management console doesn't let you create and link a new GPO for sites. You can, however, use the Group Policy Management console to link a site to an existing GPO. For more information, see the section "Linking to an Existing GPO in the Group Policy Management Console" later in this chapter.

The new GPO is added to the current list of linked GPOs. If you select the domain or OU node, you can change the preference order of the GPO by selecting it in the Linked Group Policy Objects tab and then using the Move Link Up or Move Link Down buttons to change the preference order (see Figure 38-12).

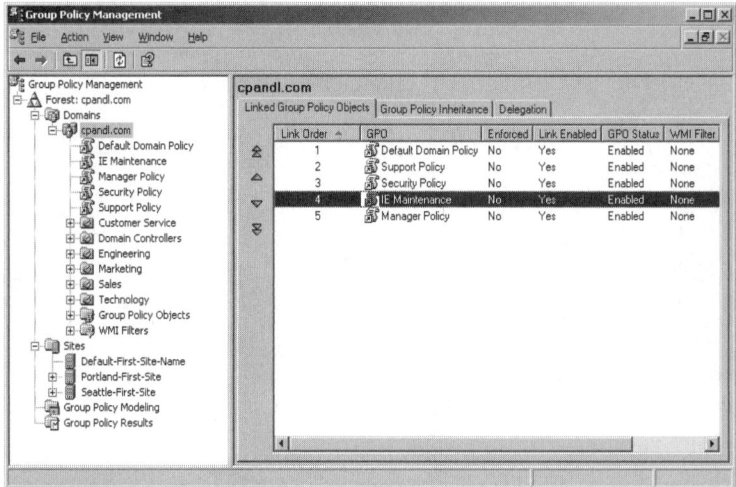

Figure 38-12. Changing the preference order of a GPO.

Editing an Existing GPO in the Group Policy Management Console

In the Group Policy Management console, you can edit an existing GPO linked to the selected container by right-clicking it and then selecting Edit. This displays the Group Policy Object Editor dialog box. You can then make changes to Group Policy as necessary. The changes will be applied the next time Active Directory is refreshed, according to the inheritance and preference options used by Active Directory.

Linking to an Existing GPO in the Group Policy Management Console

Linking a GPO to a container applies the object to the container. In the Group Policy Management console, you can link an existing GPO to a domain, OU, or site by completing the following steps:

1. Access the domain or OU you want to work with in Group Policy Management Console. Do this by expanding the forest node and the related Domains node as necessary.
2. Right-click the domain, OU, or site node, and select Link An Existing GPO.
3. In the Select GPO dialog box, shown in Figure 38-13, select the GPO to use, and then click OK.

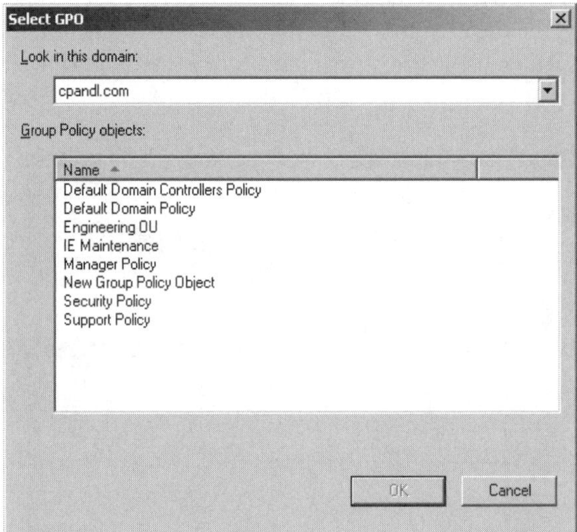

Figure 38-13. Choose the GPO that you want to link to the currently selected container.

4. The linked policy will be applied the next time Active Directory is refreshed, according to the inheritance and preference options used by Active Directory.

Deleting an Existing GPO in the Group Policy Management Console

In the Group Policy Management console, you use different techniques to remove GPO links and the GPOs themselves, as follows:

- If you want to remove a link to a GPO, you right-click the GPO in the container to which it is linked and then select Delete. When prompted to confirm that you want to remove the link, click OK.
- If you want to remove a GPO and all links to the object, expand the forest, the Domains node, and the Group Policy Objects node. Right-click the GPO, and then select Delete. When prompted to confirm that you want to remove the GPO and all links to it, click OK.

Managing Group Policy Inheritance and Processing

GPOs can be linked to sites, domains, and OUs in Active Directory. When you create and link a GPO to one of these containers in Active Directory, the GPO is applied to the user and computer objects in that container according to the inheritance and preference options used by Active Directory. Computer-related policies are processed during startup of the operating system. User-related policies are processed when a user logs on to a computer. Once applied, Group Policy settings are automatically refreshed at a specific interval to ensure they are current. Group Policy settings can also be refreshed manually.

Group Policy Inheritance

Active Directory uses inheritance to determine how Group Policy is applied. By default, Group Policy settings are inherited from top-level containers by lower-level containers. The order of inheritance goes from the site level to the domain level to the OU level. This means the Group Policy settings for a site are passed down to the domains within the site, and the settings for a domain are passed down to the OUs within that domain.

When multiple group policies are in place, the policies are applied in the following order:

1. **Local group policies** Each computer running Windows 2000 or later has one local group policy. The local policy is the first one applied.
2. **Site group policies** Policies linked to sites are processed second. If there are multiple site policies, they are processed synchronously in the listed preference order.
3. **Domain group policies** Policies linked to domains are processed third. If there are multiple domain policies, they are processed synchronously in the listed preference order.
4. **OU group policies** Policies linked to top-level OUs are processed fourth. If there are multiple top-level OU policies, they are processed synchronously in the listed preference order.
5. **Child OU group policies** Policies linked to child OUs are processed fifth. If there are multiple child OU policies, they are processed synchronously in the listed preference order. When there are multiple levels of child OUs, policies for higher-level OUs are applied first and policies for the lower-level OUs are applied next.

The order in which policies are applied determines which policy settings take effect if multiple policies modify the same settings. Most policies have three configuration options: Not Configured, Enabled, and Disabled. The default state of most policies is Not Configured, meaning the policy setting is not configured and does not apply. If a policy is set to Enabled, the policy is enforced and does apply to users and computers that are subject to the GPO. If a policy is set to Disabled, the policy is not enforced and does not apply to users and computers that are subject to the GPO.

To override a policy that is enabled in a higher-level container, you can specifically disable it in a lower-level policy. For example, if the user policy Prohibit Access To The Control Panel is enabled for a site, users in the site should not be able to access Control Panel. However, if domain policy specifically disables the user policy Prohibit Access To The Control Panel, users in the domain would be able to access Control Panel. On the other hand, if the domain policy was set to Not Configured, the policy setting would not be modified and would be inherited as normal from the higher-level container.

To override a policy that is disabled in a higher-level container, you can specifically enable it in a lower-level policy. For example, if the user policy Force Classic Control Panel Style is disabled for a domain, users in the domain would be able to choose whether they wanted to use Classic or Simple Control Panel. However, if the Engineering OU policy specifically enables the user policy Force Classic Control Panel Style, users in the Engineering OU would be able to use only the Classic Control Panel style. Again, if the OU policy was set to Not Configured instead, the policy setting would not be modified and would be inherited as normal from the higher-level container.

Modifying Inheritance

Because of inheritance, every computer and user object in a domain, no matter which container it is stored in, is affected by Group Policy. Often you'll find that you must modify inheritance to either block inheritance or enforce inheritance.

You block inheritance so that no policy settings from higher-level containers are applied. For example, if you didn't want a domain to inherit the site policy, you could configure the domain to block inheritance from higher-level containers. The way you block inheritance depends on the tool you are using:

- In Active Directory Users and Computers, you block inheritance by right-clicking the domain or OU that should not inherit settings from higher-level containers and selecting Properties. In the Group Policy tab of the Properties dialog box, select Block Policy Inheritance, and then click OK.
- Using Group Policy Management Console, you block inheritance by right-clicking the domain or OU that should not inherit settings from higher-level containers and selecting Block Inheritance. If Block Inheritance is already selected, selecting it again removes the setting.

> **Note** When you block inheritance in the Group Policy Management console, a blue circle with an exclamation point is added to the container's node in the console tree. This way you can quickly tell whether any domain or OU has the Block Inheritance setting enabled.

You enforce inheritance to prevent administrators who have been delegated authority over a container from overriding the inherited Group Policy settings. For example, if you want to ensure the domain group policy settings are applied to all OUs, you can do this by enforcing inheritance. Because enforced inheritance cannot be blocked, top-level administrators in an organization can always ensure policy settings are applied as necessary.

The way you enforce inheritance depends on the tool you are using as follows:

- In the Group Policy tab, accessed from either Active Directory Users and Computers or Active Directory Sites and Services, you enforce policy inheritance by selecting the policy and then clicking Options. In the Options dialog box, select No Override, and then click OK.
- In the Group Policy Management console, you enforce policy inheritance by expanding the container to which the policy is linked, right-clicking the policy, and then selecting Enforced. If Enforced is already selected, selecting it again removes the enforcement.

In the Group Policy Management console, it is easy to tell which policies are inherited and which policies are enforced. This information is displayed automatically in a GPO's Scope tab for all locations to which the GPO is linked (see Figure 38-14). To display similar scope information for any GPO, expand any container to which the policy is linked or the Group Policy Objects node, and then select the policy.

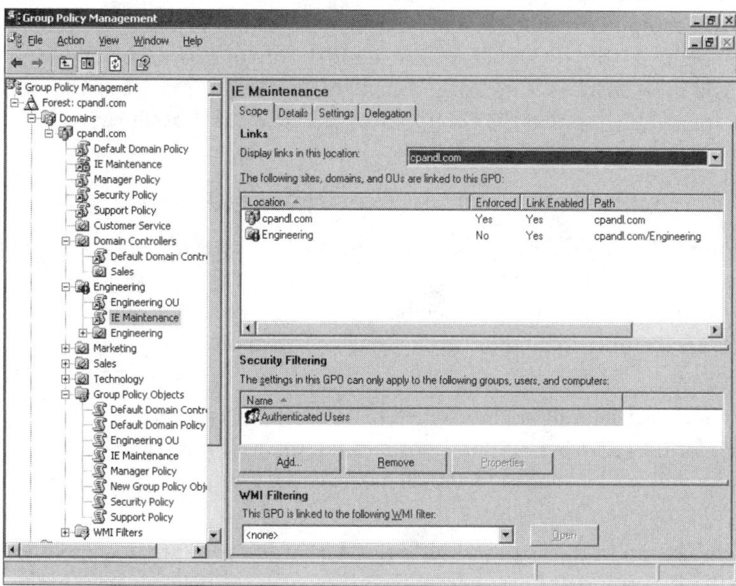

Figure 38-14. Use the Group Policy Management console to determine whether a GPO is applied.

Filtering Group Policy Application

By default, GPOs apply to all users and computers in the container to which the GPO is linked. The GPO applies to all users and computers in this way because of the security settings on the GPO, which specify that Authenticated Users have Read permission as well as Apply Group Policy permission. Thus, all users and computers with accounts in the domain are affected by the policy. Permissions are also assigned to administrators and the operating system. All members of the Enterprise Admins and Domain Admins groups as well as the LocalSystem account have permission to edit GPOs and manage their security.

You can modify which users and computers are affected by a particular group policy by changing the accounts for which the Apply Group Policy permission is set. In this way, you can selectively apply a GPO, which is known is filtering Group Policy. For example, say that you create an Engineering OU with a separate Group Policy for users and managers. You want the user GPO to apply to all users who are members of the EngUsers group and the manager GPO to apply to all users who are members of the EngMgr group. To do this, you must configure the user policy so that the Read and Apply Group Policy permissions apply to the EngUsers group only and configure the manager policy so that the Read and Apply Group Policy permissions apply to the EngMgr group only.

Before you selectively apply a GPO, you must carefully consider the types of policies it sets. If the GPO sets computer policies, you must ensure the computer accounts are included so that the computer reads the GPO and applies it at the startup of networking. If the GPO sets user policies, you must ensure the groups in which the users are members or the individual user accounts are included so that the Group Policy engine reads the GPO and applies it when users log on.

Use the following guidelines to help you determine how permissions should be configured:

- **Group Policy should be applied to all members of a group** Add the group to the access control list (ACL) for the GPO. Set Read to Allow and set Apply Group Policy to Allow. The group policy will then be applied to all members of the group except those who are members of another group to which Read or Apply Group Policy is set to Deny.
- **Group Policy should not be applied to members of a group** Add the group to the ACL for the GPO. Set Read to Deny and set Apply Group Policy to Deny. The group policy will not be applied to any members of the group regardless of which other groups members belong.
- **Membership in this group should not determine whether Group Policy is applied** Remove the group from the ACL for the GPO. Or clear both Allow and Deny for the Read permission as well as the Apply Group Policy permission. Once you do this, membership in the group will determine whether the GPO is applied.

In the Group Policy Management console, you can selectively apply a GPO by completing the following steps:

1. Select the policy in a container to which it is linked or in the Group Policy Objects node.
2. In the Details pane, select the Delegation tab, and then click the Advanced button in the lower-right corner of the dialog box. This displays the policy's Security Settings dialog box, as shown in Figure 38-15.

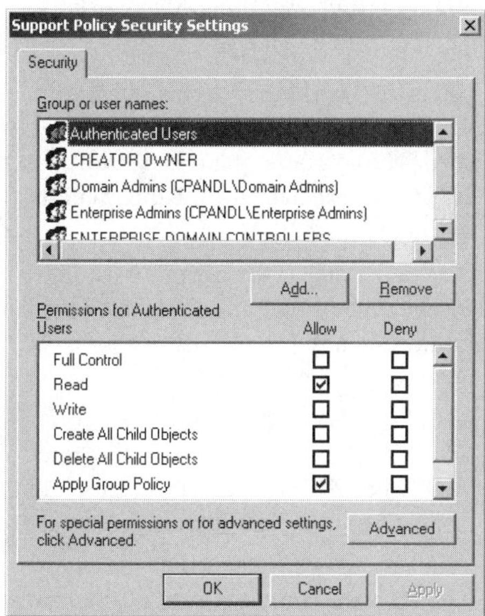

Figure 38-15. Accessing the security settings for a GPO.

3. You can then add or remove groups as necessary. Once a group is added, you can select Allow or Deny for the Read and Apply Group Policy permissions as necessary.
4. When you are finished configuring the ACL for the GPO, click OK until all open dialog boxes are closed.

In Active Directory Users and Computers, you can selectively apply a GPO by completing the following steps:

1. Right-click the domain or OU, and then select Properties. In the Group Policy tab of the Properties dialog box, click Properties.
2. In the Security tab, you have options identical to those shown previously in Figure 38-15. You can then add or remove groups as necessary. Once a group is added, you can select Allow or Deny for the Read and Apply Group Policy permissions as necessary.
3. When you are finished configuring the ACL for the GPO, click OK until all open dialog boxes are closed.

Group Policy Processing

Group Policy settings are divided into two categories:

- **Computer Configuration settings** Policies that apply to computer accounts only
- **User Configuration settings** Policies that apply to user accounts only

Normally, Computer Configuration settings are applied during startup of the operating system and User Configuration settings are applied when a user logs on to a computer. The sequence of events is often important in troubleshooting system behavior. The events that take place during startup and logon are as follows:

1. When the client computer starts, networking is started as part of the normal system startup. The computer reads the Registry to determine the Active Directory site in which the computer is located. The computer then sends a query to its primary Domain Name System (DNS) server to determine the Internet Protocol (IP) addresses of domain controllers in the site.
2. When the DNS server replies to the query, the computer connects to a domain controller in the local site. The client computer and domain controller authenticate each other. The client computer then requests a list of all the GPOs that apply to the computer.
3. The domain controller sends a list of GPOs that apply to the computer. The computer processes and applies the GPOs, starting with the local policy and continuing as discussed in the section entitled "Group Policy Inheritance" earlier in this chapter. It is important to note that only the Computer Configuration settings are sent at this point.
4. After processing computer policies, the computer runs any startup scripts. Startup scripts are hidden from view by default, and if there are multiple startup scripts, the scripts run in sequential order by default. Each script must finish running before the next one can be started. The default timeout for scripts is 600 seconds. Both the synchronous processing of scripts and their timeout value can be modified using Group Policy.
5. When a user logs on to the computer and is validated, the computer loads the user profile, and then requests a list of all the GPOs that apply to the user.
6. The domain controller sends a list of GPOs that apply to the user. The computer processes and applies the GPOs, starting with the local policy and continuing as discussed in the section entitled "Group Policy Inheritance" earlier in this chapter. Although only the User Configuration settings are sent and applied at this point, it is important to note that any computer policy settings that overlap with user policy settings are overwritten by default. User policy settings have precedence by default.

7 After processing user policies, the computer runs any logon scripts. Logon scripts are hidden from view by default, and if there are multiple startup scripts, the scripts run asynchronously by default. Thus, unlike startup scripts for which each script must finish running before the next one can be started, logon scripts are all started and run simultaneously. The default timeout for scripts is 600 seconds.

8 The user interface as defined in the user's profile and governed by the policy settings that are in effect is displayed. If the user logs off the computer, any logoff scripts defined for the user are run. If the user shuts down the computer, logoff is part of the shutdown process, so the user is first logged off and any logoff scripts defined for the user are run. Then the computer runs any shutdown scripts defined for the computer.

Inside Out

All Group Policy processing is handled as a refresh

Technically, all Group Policy processing is handled as a Group Policy refresh. Thus, processing during startup and logon is technically a refresh, which is handled as discussed in the section entitled "Group Policy Refresh" later in this chapter. The most important note about refresh is that if the client computer detects that it is using a slow network connection, only the Security Settings and Administrative Templates are processed. Although there is no way to turn off processing of these extensions, you can configure other extensions so that they are processed even across a slow network connection. For more information, see the section entitled "Modifying Group Policy Refresh" later in this chapter.

Modifying Group Policy Processing

You can modify Group Policy processing by disabling a policy in whole or in part. Disabling a policy is useful if you no longer need a policy but might need to use that policy again in the future. Disabling part of a policy is useful so that the policy applies only to either users or computers but not both.

In the Group Policy Management console, you can enable and disable policies partially or entirely by completing the following steps:

1. Select the policy in a container to which it is linked or in the Group Policy Objects node.
2. In the right pane, select the Details tab, and then use the GPO Status selection menu to choose a status as one of the following:
   - Enabled
   - All Settings Disabled

- Computer Configuration Settings Disabled
- User Configuration Settings Disabled

In Active Directory Users and Computers, you can enable and disable policies partially or entirely by completing the following steps:

1. Right-click the domain or OU, and select Properties. In the Group Policy tab of the Properties dialog box, click Properties.
2. To disable the policy entirely, select the policy, and then click Options. In the Options dialog box, select Disabled, and then click OK. If you later want to enable the policy, you would repeat this process and clear the Disabled option.
3. To disable the policy partially, select the policy, and then click Properties. In the Properties dialog box, select or clear Disable Computer Configuration Settings and Disable User Configuration Settings as necessary.

Modifying User Policy Preference Using Loopback Processing

When a user logs on, the client computer applies User Configuration settings. Because user policy settings have precedence by default, any computer policy settings that overlap with user policy settings are overwritten. However, for some computers, particularly special-use computers in classrooms, labs, or public places, you might want to restrict the computer to a specific configuration. In this case, you might not want less-restrictive user policy settings to be applied.

To change the default behavior that gives preference to user policy, you can enable the loopback processing policy. By enabling the loopback processing policy, you ensure that the Computer Configuration settings always apply. Loopback processing can be set in one of two ways, either with Replace or Merge. When you use the Replace option, only Computer Configuration settings are processed and User Configuration settings are not processed. When you use the Merge option, Computer Configuration settings are processed first, then User Configuration settings are processed, and then Computer Configuration settings are processed again. This serves to combine the settings and if there are any conflicts in the settings, the Computer Configuration settings have preference and overwrite the User Configuration settings.

To configure loopback processing, follow these steps:

1. Start the Group Policy Object Editor. In Group Policy Management Console, right-click the Group Policy you want to modify, and then select Edit.
2. Double-click the User Group Policy Loopback Processing Mode in the Computer Configuration\Administrative Templates\System\Group Policy folder.

3 Define the policy by selecting Enabled, as shown in Figure 38-16, then use the Mode selection menu to set the processing mode as either Replace or Merge.

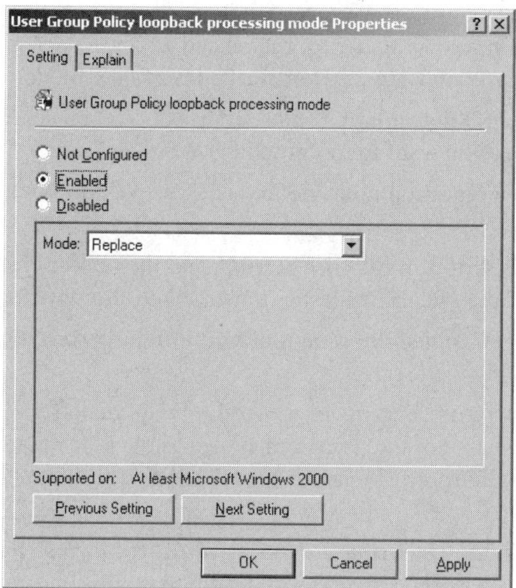

Figure 38-16. Configure loopback processing to give Computer Configuration settings preference.

4 Click OK. This policy is supported by all computers running Windows 2000 or later.

Using Scripts in Group Policy

In Windows Server 2003 you can configure computer startup and shutdown scripts as well as user logon and logoff scripts. You can write these scripts as command-shell batch scripts ending with the .bat or .cmd extension or as scripts that use the Windows Script Host (WSH). WSH is a feature of Windows Server 2003 that lets you use scripts written in a scripting language, such as Microsoft JScript and Microsoft VBScript.

Configuring Computer Startup and Shutdown Scripts

You can assign computer startup and shutdown scripts as part of a group policy. In this way, all computers in a site, domain, or OU run scripts automatically when they're started or shut down.

To configure a script that should be using during computer startup or shutdown, follow these steps:

1. For easy management, copy the scripts you want to use to the Machine\Scripts\Startup or Machine\Scripts\Shutdown folder for the related policy. By default, policies are stored in the %SystemRoot%\Sysvol\Domain\Policies folder on domain controllers.
2. Start the Group Policy Object Editor. In the Group Policy Management console, right-click the Group Policy you want to modify, and then select Edit.
3. In the Computer Configuration node, double-click the Windows Settings folder, and then click Scripts.
4. To work with startup scripts, right-click Startup, and then select Properties. Or right-click Shutdown, and then select Properties to work with shutdown scripts.
5. Click Show Files. If you copied the computer script to the correct location in the Policies folder, you should see the script.
6. Click Add to assign a script. This opens the Add A Script dialog box. In the Script Name field, type the name of the script you copied to the Machine\Scripts\Startup or the Machine\Scripts\Shutdown folder for the related policy. Repeat this step to add other scripts.
7. During startup or shutdown, scripts are run in the order in which they're listed in the Properties dialog box. Use the Up or Down button to reposition scripts as necessary.
8. To delete a script, select the script in the Script For list, and then click Remove.

Configuring User Logon and Logoff Scripts

You can assign logon and logoff scripts as part of a group policy. In this way, all users in a site, domain, or OU run scripts automatically when they log on or log off.

To configure a script that should be executed when a user logs on or logs off, complete the following steps:

1. For easy management, copy the scripts you want to use to the User\Scripts\Logon or the User\Scripts\Logoff folder for the related policy. By default, policies are stored in the %SystemRoot%\Sysvol\Domain\Policies folder on domain controllers.
2. Start the Group Policy Object Editor. In the Group Policy Management console, right-click the Group Policy you want to modify, and then select Edit.
3. Double-click the Windows Settings folder in the User Configuration node, and then click Scripts.
4. To work with logon scripts, right-click Logon, and then select Properties. Or right-click Logoff, and then select Properties to work with logoff scripts.
5. Click Show Files. If you copied the user script to the correct location in the Policies folder, you should see the script.

6. Click Add to assign a script. This opens the Add A Script dialog box. In the Script Name field, type the name of the script you copied to the User\Scripts\Logon or the User\Scripts\Logoff folder for the related policy. Repeat this step to add other scripts.
7. During logon or logoff, scripts are executed in the order in which they're listed in the Properties dialog box. Use the Up or Down button to reposition scripts as necessary.
8. To delete a script, select the script in the Script For list, and then click Remove.

Applying Group Policy Through Security Templates

Security templates take the guesswork out of configuring a computer's initial security. You use security templates to apply customized sets of Group Policy definitions that are security-related. These policy definitions generally affect the following components:

- Account policy settings that control security for passwords, account lockout, and Kerberos
- Local policy settings that control security for auditing, user rights assignment, and other security options
- Event log policy settings that control security for event logging
- Restricted groups policies that control security for local group membership and administration
- System services policy settings that control the startup mode for local services
- File system policy settings that control security for the local file system
- Registry policy settings that control the values of security-related Registry keys

Working with Security Templates

Security templates are available in all Windows Server 2003 installations and can be imported into any GPO. The templates are stored in the %SystemRoot%\Security\Templates folder by default, and you can access them using the Security Templates snap-in. You can also use the snap-in to create new templates. The standard templates distributed with Windows Server 2003 include the following:

- **Compatws** Relaxes the default file and Registry permissions to meet the security requirements of most non-certified applications.
- **Dc security** Default security settings for domain controllers
- **Rootsec** Default permissions for the %SystemRoot% folder and all the files and subfolders it contains.
- **Setup security** Default security settings for member servers
- **Securedc** Moderate security settings for domain controllers
- **Securews** Moderate security settings for workstations

- **Hisecdc** Stringent security settings for domain controllers
- **Hisecws** Stringent security settings for workstations

After you select the template that you want to use, you should go through each setting that the template will apply and evaluate how the setting will affect your environment. If a setting doesn't make sense, you should modify or delete it as appropriate.

You use the Security Templates snap-in only for viewing templates. You apply templates using the Security Configuration and Analysis snap-in. You can also use Security Configuration and Analysis to compare the settings in a template to the existing settings on a computer. The results of the analysis will highlight areas in which the current settings don't match those in the template. This is useful to determine whether security settings have changed over time.

You can access the security snap-ins by completing the following steps:

1. Open the Run dialog box by clicking Start and then clicking Run. Type **mmc** in the Open field, and then click OK. This opens the MMC.
2. In the MMC, click File, and then click Add/Remove Snap-In. This opens the Add/Remove Snap-In dialog box.
3. In the Standalone tab, click Add. In the Add Standalone Snap-In dialog box, click Security Templates, and then click Add. Click Security Configuration And Analysis, and then click Add.
4. Close the Add Standalone Snap-In dialog box by clicking Close, and then click OK.

Applying Security Templates

You use the Security Templates snap-in to view existing templates or to create new templates. Once you've created a template or determined that you want to use an existing template, you can then configure and analyze the template by completing the following steps:

1. Access the Security Configuration And Analysis snap-in. Right-click the Security Configuration And Analysis node, and then select Open Database. This displays the Open Database dialog box.
2. Type a new database name in the File Name field, and then click Open. The Import Template dialog box is displayed next. Select the security template that you want to use, and then click Open.
3. Right-click the Security Configuration And Analysis node, and then choose Analyze Computer Now. When prompted to set the error log path, type a new path or click OK to use the default path.
4. Wait for the snap-in to complete the analysis of the template. Afterward, review the findings and update the template as necessary. You can view the error log by right-clicking the Security Configuration And Analysis node and choosing View Log File.

5. When you're ready to apply the template, right-click the Security Configuration And Analysis node, and choose Configure Computer Now. When prompted to set the error log path, click OK. The default path should be fine.
6. View the configuration error log by right-clicking the Security Configuration And Analysis node and choosing View Log File. Note any problems and take action as necessary.

Maintaining and Troubleshooting Group Policy

Most Group Policy maintenance and troubleshooting tasks have to do with determining when policy is refreshed and applied and then changing the refresh options as appropriate to ensure policy is applied as expected. Thus, maintaining and troubleshooting Group Policy require a keen understanding of how Group Policy refresh works and how it can be changed to meet your needs. You also need tools for modeling and viewing the GPOs that would be or have been applied to users and computers. Group Policy Management Console provides these tools through the Group Policy Modeling and Group Policy Results Wizards,which can be used instead of the running the Resultant Set Of Policy (RSoP) Wizard in logging mode or planning mode.

Group Policy Refresh

Computer policies are applied when a computer starts, and user policies are applied when a user logs on. Once applied, Group Policy settings are automatically refreshed to ensure they are current. The default refresh interval for domain controllers is every 5 minutes. For all other computers, the default refresh interval is every 90 minutes with up to a 30-minute variation to avoid overloading the domain controller with numerous client requests at the same time.

> **Tip** **Change the refresh interval through Group Policy**
> You can change the Group Policy refresh interval if desired. The related policies are stored in the Computer Configuration\Administrative Templates\System\Group Policy folder. To set the refresh interval for domain controllers define the Group Policy Refresh Interval For Domain Controllers policy. Select Enabled, set the refresh interval, and then click OK. To set the refresh interval for all other computers define the Group Policy Refresh Interval For Computers policy. Select Enabled, set the refresh interval and random offset, and then click OK.

During Group Policy refresh, the client contacts an available domain controller in its local site. If one or more of the GPOs defined in the domain have changed, the domain controller provides a list of all the GPOs that apply to the computer and to the user that is currently logged on, as appropriate. The domain controller does so regardless of whether the version numbers on all the listed GPOs have changed.

By default, the computer processes the GPOs only if the version number of at least one of the GPOs has changed. If any one of the related policies has changed, all of the policies have to be processed again. This is required because of inheritance and the interdependencies within policies. Security Settings are a noted exception to the processing rule. By default, Security Settings are refreshed every 16 hours (960 minutes) regardless of whether GPOs contain changes. Additionally, if the client computer detects that it is connecting over a slow network connection, it tells the domain controller this and only the Security Settings and Administrative Templates are transferred over the network, which means only the Security Settings and Administrative Templates are applied.

Modifying Group Policy Refresh

Group Policy refresh can be changed in several ways. First, client computers determine that they are using a slow network connection by pinging the domain controller to which they are connected with a zero-byte packet. If the response time from the domain controller is more than 10 milliseconds, the computer then pings the domain controller three times with a 2-kilobyte (KB) message packet to determine if it is on a slow network. The computer uses the average response time to determine the network speed. By default, if the connection speed is determined to be less than 500 kilobits per second (Kbps), the computer interprets that as having a slow network connection, and in which case, it notifies the domain controller of this. As a result, only the Security Settings and Administrative Templates in the applicable GPOs are sent by the domain controller.

You can configure slow link detection using the Group Policy Slow Link Detection policy, which is stored in the Computer Configuration\Administrative Templates\System\Group Policy folder. To configure this policy, follow these steps:

1. Start the Group Policy Object Editor. In the Group Policy Management console, right-click the group policy you want to modify, and then select Edit.
2. Double-click the Group Policy Slow Link Detection policy in the Computer Configuration\Administrative Templates\System\Group Policy folder.
3. Define the policy by selecting Enabled, as shown in Figure 38-17, and then use the Connection Speed combo box to specify the speed that should be used to determine whether a computer is on a slow link. For example, if you want connections less than 128 Kbps to be deemed as "slow connections," you'd type **128**. If you want to disable slow link detection, you'd type **0** in the Connection Speed box.

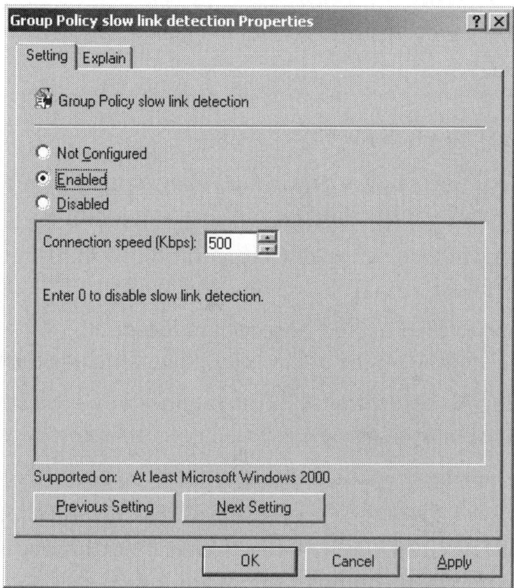

Figure 38-17. Configure slow link detection as necessary.

4 Click OK. This policy is supported by all computers running Windows 2000 or later.

If there is any area of Group Policy for which you want to configure refresh, you can do this in the Group Policy Object Editor. The related policies are stored in the Computer Configuration\Administrative Templates\System\Group Policy folder and include the following:

- Internet Explorer Maintenance Policy Processing
- Software Installation Policy Processing
- Folder Redirection Policy Processing
- Scripts Policy Processing
- Security Policy Processing
- IP Security Policy Processing
- Wireless Policy Processing
- EFS Recovery Policy Processing
- Disk Quota Policy Processing

Note You use Registry Policy Processing to control the processing of all other Registry-based extensions.

To configure refresh of an extension, follow these steps:

1. Start the Group Policy Object Editor. In Group Policy Management Console, right-click the group policy you want to modify, and then select Edit.
2. Double-click the policy in the Computer Configuration\Administrative Templates\System\Group Policy folder.
3. Define the policy by selecting Enabled, as shown in Figure 38-18. The options you have differ slightly depending on the policy selected and include the following:
   - Allow Processing Across A Slow Network Connection—Select this option to ensure the extension settings are processed even on a slow network.
   - Do Not Apply During Periodic Background Processing—Select this option to override refresh when extension settings change after startup or logon.
   - Process Even If The Group Policy Objects Have Not Changed—Select this option to force the client computer to process the extension settings during refresh even if the settings haven't changed.

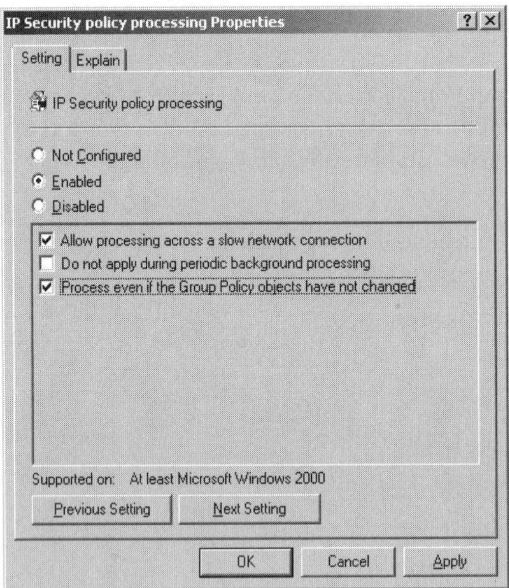

Figure 38-18. Change the way refresh works as necessary.

4. Click OK.

Viewing Applicable GPOs and Last Refresh

In the Group Policy Management console, you can view all of the GPOs that apply to a computer as well as the user logged on to that computer. You can also view the last time the applicable GPOs were processed (refreshed). To do this, you run the Group Policy Results Wizard.

To start the Group Policy Results Wizard and view applicable GPOs and the last refresh, follow these steps:

1. Start the Group Policy Management console. Right-click Group Policy Results, and then select Group Policy Results Wizard.
2. When the Group Policy Results Wizard starts, click Next. On the Computer Selection page shown in Figure 38-19, select Local Computer to view information for the local computer. If you want to view information for a remote computer, select Another Computer and then click Browse. In the Select Computer dialog box, type the name of the computer, and then click Check Names. Once the correct computer account is selected, click OK.

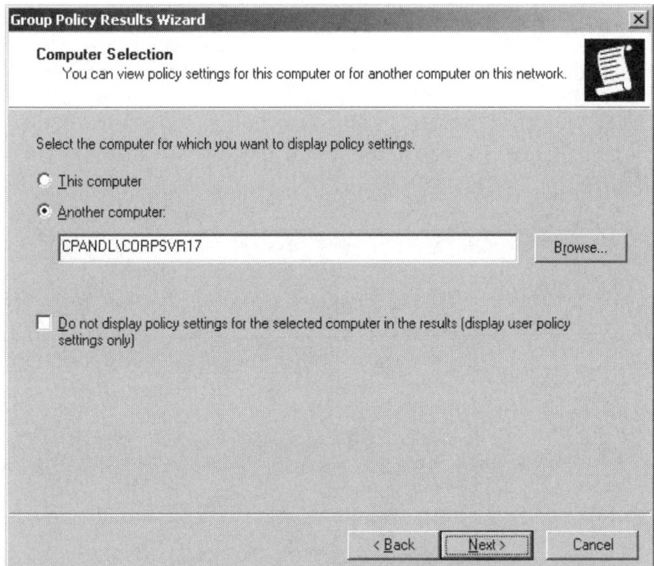

Figure 38-19. Select the computer to work with.

3. In the Group Policy Results Wizard, click Next. On the User Selection page, shown in Figure 38-20, select the user whose policy information you want to view. You can view policy information for any user that has logged on to the computer.

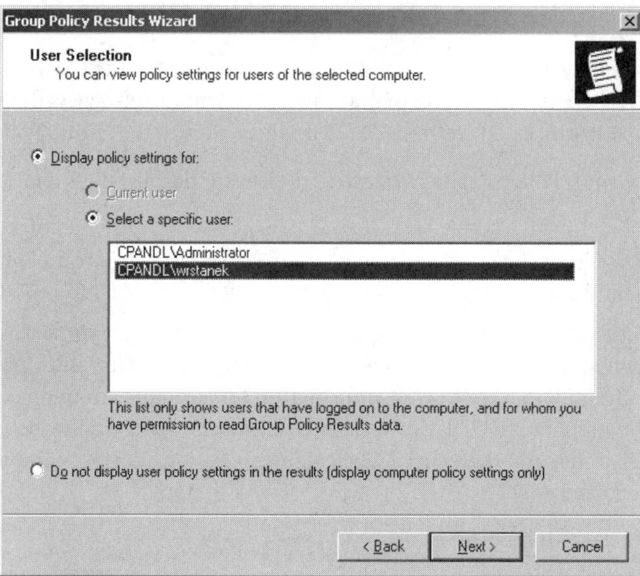

Figure 38-20. Select the user whose policy information you want to view.

4 Click Next, and then after the wizard gathers the policy information, click Finish. The wizard then generates a report, the results of which are displayed in the Details pane as shown in Figure 38-21.

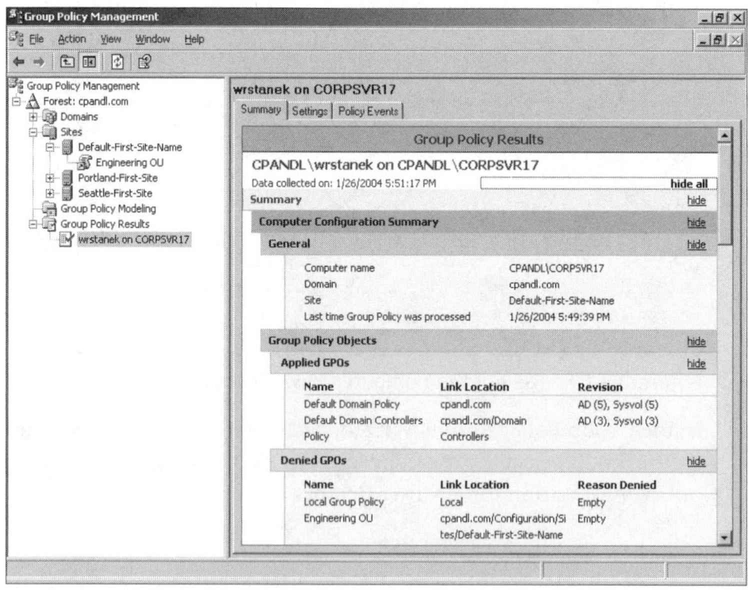

Figure 38-21. Use the report to view policy information.

5 On the report, click Show All to display all of the policy information that was gathered.

Computer and user policy information is listed separately. Computer policy information is listed under the Computer Configuration Summary. User policy information is listed under the User Configuration Summary as follows:

- To view the last time the computer or user policy was refreshed, look under Computer Configuration Summary, General for the Last Time Group Policy Was Processed entry.
- To view all applicable GPOs, look under Computer Configuration Summary, Group Policy Objects.

User policy information is listed under the User Configuration Summary as follows:

- To view the last time the computer or user policy was refreshed, look under User Configuration Summary, General for the Last Time Group Policy Was Processed entry.
- To view all applicable GPOs, look under User Configuration Summary, Group Policy Objects.

The Applied GPOs entry shows all GPOs that have been applied. The Denied GPOs entry shows all GPOs that should have been applied but weren't processed for some reason such as because they were empty or did not contain any computer policy settings. The GPO also might not have been processed because inheritance was blocked. If so, the Reason Denied is Blocked SOM.

Modeling GPOs for Planning

In the Group Policy Management console, you can test different scenarios for modifying Computer Configuration and User Configuration settings. For example, you can model the effect of a slow link or the use of loopback processing. You can also model the effect of moving a user or computer to another container in Active Directory or adding the user or computer to an additional security group. To do this, you run the Group Policy Modeling Wizard.

To start the Group Policy Modeling Wizard and test various scenarios, follow these steps:

1 Start the Group Policy Management console. Right-click Group Policy Modeling, and then select Group Policy Modeling Wizard.

2 When the Group Policy Modeling Wizard starts, click Next. On the Domain Controller Selection page, as shown in Figure 38-22, under Show Domain Controllers In This Domain, select the domain for which you want to model results. Next either select Any Available Domain Controller or This Domain Controller, and then choose a specific domain controller. Click Next.

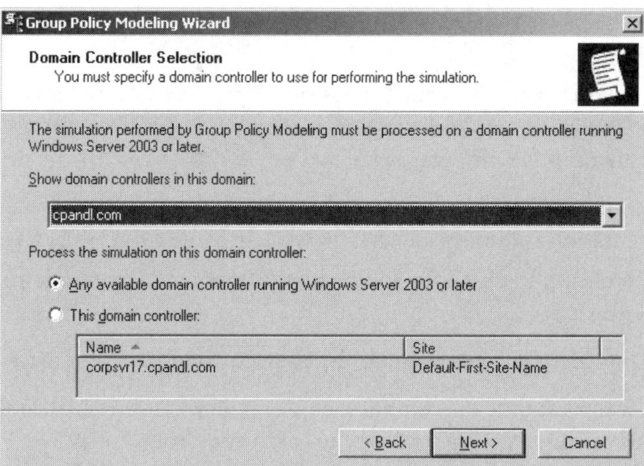

Figure 38-22. Select the domain controller to work with.

3 On the User And Computer Selection page, shown in Figure 38-23, select the modeling options for users and computers.

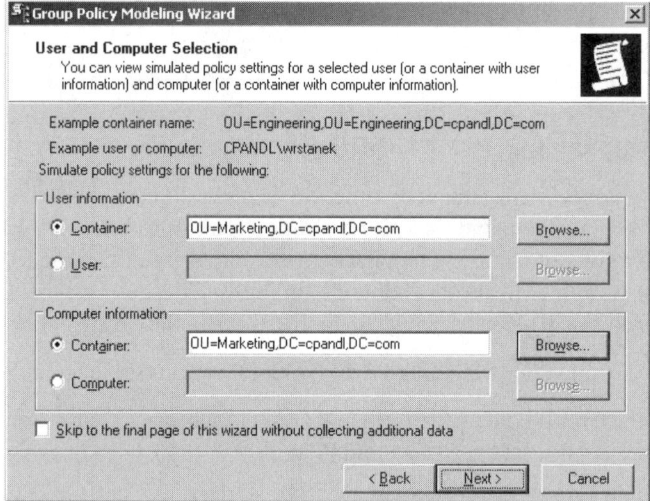

Figure 38-23. Select the modeling options for users and computers.

Typically, you'll want to model policy for a specific container using user and computer information. In this case, the following would apply:

- Under User Information, select Container, and then click Browse to display the Choose User Container dialog box, which you can use to choose any of the available user containers in the selected domain.

- Under Computer Information, select Container, and then click Browse to display the Choose Computer Container dialog box, which you can use to choose any of the available computer containers in the selected domain.

4 Click Next. On the Advanced User And Computer Selection page, as shown in Figure 38-24, select any advanced options for slow network connections, loopback processing, and sites as necessary, and then click Next.

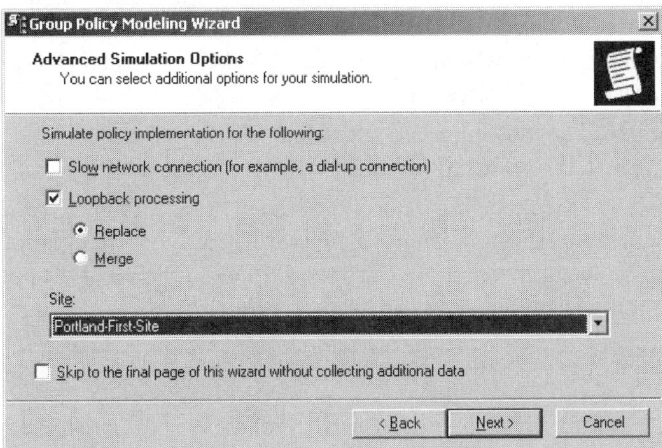

Figure 38-24. Select advanced options as necessary.

5 On the User Security Groups page, shown in Figure 38-25, you can simulate changes to security group membership to model the results on Group Policy. Any changes you make to group membership affect the previously selected user container. For example, if you want to see what would happen if a user in the designated user container is a member of the Domain Admins group, you could add this group to the Security Groups list. Click Next to continue.

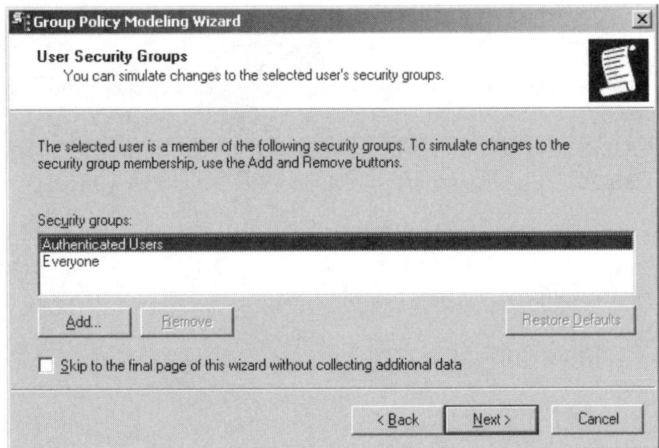

Figure 38-25. Simulate changes to security groups for users.

6. On the Computer Security Groups page, you can simulate changes to security group membership to model the results on Group Policy. Any changes you make to group membership affect the previously selected computer container. For example, if you want to see what would happen if a computer in the designated computer container is a member of the Domain Controllers group, you could add this group to the Security Groups list. Click Next to continue.
7. WMI filters can be linked to GPOs. By default, it is assumed that the selected users and computers meet all the WMI filter requirements, which is what you want in most cases for modeling, so click Next twice to skip past the WMI Filters For Users and WMI Filters For Computers pages.
8. To complete the modeling, click Next, and then click Finish. The wizard then generates a report, the results of which are displayed in the Details pane.
9. The name of the modeling report is generated based on the containers you chose and highlighted for editing, as shown in Figure 38-26. Type a new name as required, and then press Tab. On the report, click Show All to display all of the policy information that was modeled.

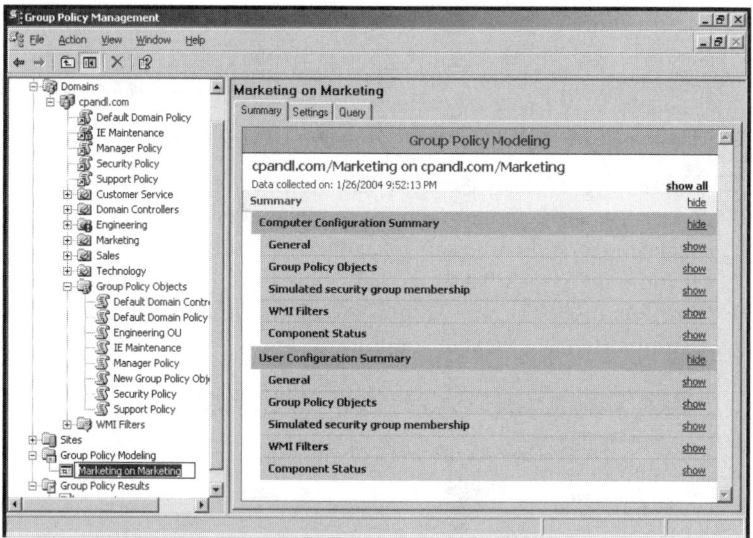

Figure 38-26. Use the report to examine the Group Policy model.

Refreshing Group Policy Manually

You can refresh Group Policy manually using the Gpupdate command-line utility. Gpupdate replaces the SECEDIT /refreshpolicy tool provided in Windows 2000. If you type **gpupdate** at a command prompt, both the Computer Configuration settings and the User Configuration settings in Group Policy are refreshed on the local computer.

You can also selectively refresh Group Policy. If you want to refresh only Computer Configuration settings, you type **gpupdate /target:computer** at the command prompt. If you want to refresh only User Configuration settings, you type **gpupdate /target:user** at the command prompt. By default, only policy settings that have changed are processed and applied. You can change this behavior using the /Force parameter. This parameter forces a refresh of all policy settings.

Gpupdate can also be used to log off a user or restart a computer after Group Policy is refreshed. This is useful because some group policies are applied only when a user logs on or when a computer starts up. To log off a user after a refresh, add the /Logoff parameter. To restart a computer after a refresh, add the /Boot parameter.

Backing Up GPOs

In the Group Policy Management console, you can back up GPOs so that you can restore them at a later time to recover Group Policy to the state it was in when the backup was performed. The ability to backup and restore GPOs is one of the reasons why the Group Policy Management console is more useful than the older Group Policy tools that come with Windows Server 2003. It is also important to add that you can backup and restore GPOs only when you have installed the Group Policy Management console.

You can either back up an individual GPO in a domain or all GPOs in a domain by completing the following steps:

1. Start the Group Policy Management console. Expand the forest, the Domains node, and the Group Policy Objects node.
2. If you want to back up all GPOs in the domain, right-click the Group Policy Objects node, and then select Back Up All.
3. If you want to back up a specific GPO in the domain, right-click the GPO, and then select Back Up.
4. In the Back Up Group Policy Object dialog box, shown in Figure 38-27, click Browse, and then use the Browse For Folder dialog box to set the location in which the GPO backup should be stored.

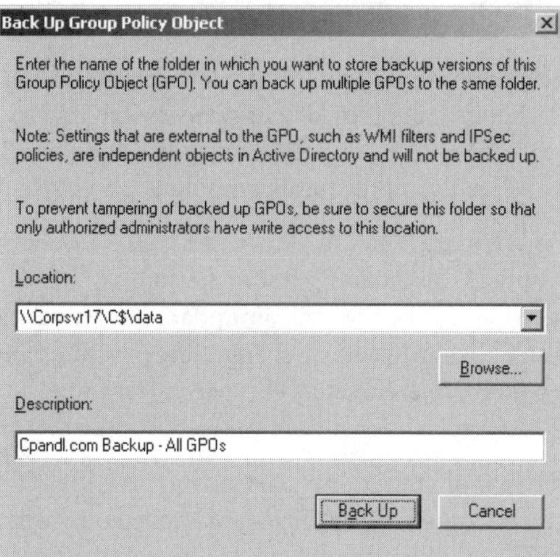

Figure 38-27. Set the backup location and description.

5. In the Description field, type a clear description of the contents of the backup.
6. Click Backup to start the backup process. The Backup dialog box, shown in Figure 38-28, shows the progress and status of the backup. If a backup fails, check the permissions on the GPO and the folder to which you are writing the backup. You need Read permission on a GPO and Write permission on the backup folder to create a backup. By Default, members of the Domain Admins and Enterprise Admins groups should have these permissions.

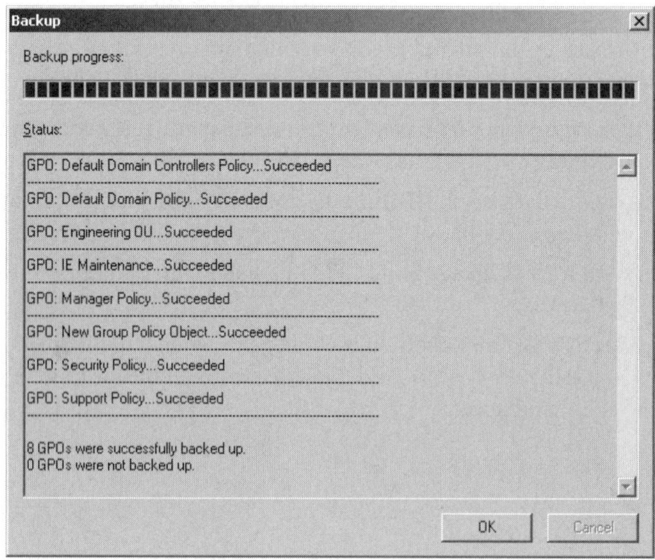

Figure 38-28. The Backup dialog box shows the backup progress and status.

Restoring GPOs

Using the Group Policy Management console, you can restore a GPO to the state it was in when it was backed up. The Group Policy Management console tracks the backup of each GPO separately, even if you back up all GPOs at once. Because version information is also tracked according to the backup time stamp and description, you can restore the last version of each GPO or a particular version of any GPO.

You can restore a GPO by completing the following steps:

1. Start the Group Policy Management console. Expand the forest, the Domains node, and the Group Policy Objects node.
2. If you want to back up all GPOs in the domain, right-click the Group Policy Objects node, and then select Manage Backups. This displays the Manage Backups dialog box (see Figure 38-29).
3. In the Backup Location field, type the folder path to the backup or click Browse to use the Browse For Folder dialog box to find the folder.
4. All GPO backups in the designated folder are listed under Backup GPOs. To show only the latest version of the GPOs according to the time stamp, select Show Only The Latest Version Of Each GPO.
5. Select the GPO you want to restore. If you want to confirm its settings, click View Settings, and then verify the settings are as expected using Internet Explorer. When you are ready to continue, click Restore. Confirm that you want to restore the selected GPO by clicking OK.

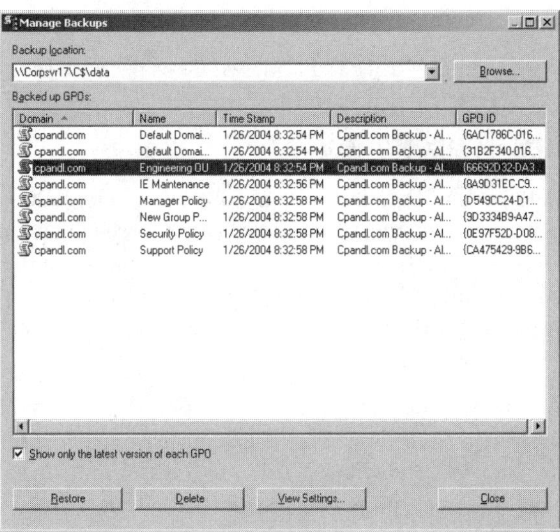

Figure 38-29. Use the Manage Backups dialog box to restore a GPO.

Chapter 38

6 The Restore dialog box, shown in Figure 38-30, shows the progress and status of the restore. If a restore fails, check the permissions on the GPO and the folder from which you are reading the backup. To restore a GPO, you need Edit, Delete, and Modify permissions on the GPO and Read permission on the folder containing the GPO backup. By default, members of the Domain Admins and Enterprise Admins groups should have these permissions.

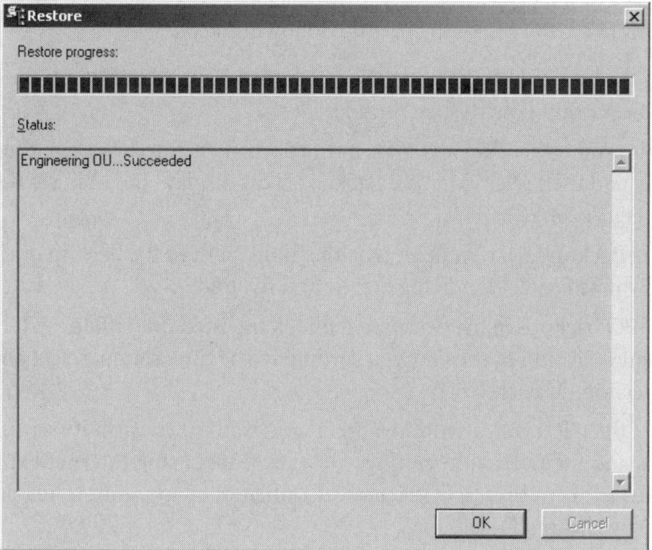

Figure 38-30. The Restore dialog box shows the restore progress and status.

7 Click OK, and then either restore additional GPOs as necessary or click Close.

Fixing Default Group Policy

The Default Domain Policy and Default Domain Controller Policy GPOs are vital to the health of Active Directory in a domain. If for some reason these policies become corrupted, Group Policy will not function properly. To resolve this, you must run the Dcgpofix utility. This utility restores the default GPOs to their original, default state, meaning the state they are in when you first install Active Directory in a new domain. You must be a member of Domain Admins or Enterprise Admins to run Dcgpofix.

By default, when you run Dcgpofix, both the Default Domain Policy and Default Domain Controller Policy GPOs are restored and you will lose any base changes made to these GPOs. The only exceptions are for the following extension settings: Remote Installation Services (RIS), Security Settings, and Encrypting File System (EFS). These extension settings are maintained separately and will not be lost. Nondefault Security Settings are not maintained, however, which means Security Settings configured by Microsoft Exchange Server 2000, migrated during an upgrade from Windows NT to Windows 2000, as well as policy object changes made through Systems Management Server (SMS) are lost as well. All other extensions settings are restored to their default postinstallation state, and any changes you've made are lost.

To run Dcgpofix, log on to a domain controller in the domain in which you want to fix default Group Policy, and then type **dcgpofix** at the command prompt. Dcgpofix checks the Active Directory schema version number to ensure compatibility between the version of Dcgpofix you are using and the Active Directory schema configuration. If the versions are not compatible, Dcgpofix exits without fixing the default Group Policy. By specifying the /Ignoreschema parameter, you can enable Dcgpofix to work with different versions of Active Directory. However, default policy objects might not be restored to their original state. Because of this, you should always be sure to use the version of Dcgpofix that is installed with the current operating system.

You also have the option of fixing only the Default Domain Policy or the Default Domain Controller Policy GPO. If you want to fix only the Default Domain Policy, type **dcgpofix /target: domain**. If you want to fix only the Default Domain Controller Policy, type **dcgpofix /target: dc**.

Chapter 39

Active Directory Site Administration

In this chapter, I discuss administration of sites, subnets, site links, and related components. Active Directory sites are used to control directory replication traffic and isolate logon authentication traffic between physical network locations. Every site has one or more subnets associated with it. Ideally, each subnet that is part of a site should be connected by reliable, high-speed links. Any physical location connected over slow or unreliable links should be part of a separate site, and these individual sites are linked to other sites using site links.

Managing Sites and Subnets

When you install the Active Directory directory service in a new forest, a new site called the Default-First-Site-Name is created. As you add additional domains and domain controllers to the forest, these domains and domain controllers are added to this site as they are installed unless you have configured other sites and associated subnets with those sites as necessary.

Administration of sites and subnets involves determining the sites and subnets you need and creating those sites and subnets. All sites have one or more subnets associated with them. It is in fact the subnet assignment that tells Active Directory where the site boundaries are established. As you create additional sites, you might also need to specify which domain controllers are a part of the sites. You do this by moving domain controllers to the site containers with which they should be associated. Thus, the most common administrative tasks for sites involve the following:

- Creating sites
- Creating subnets and associating them with sites
- Moving domain controllers between sites

Creating an Active Directory Site

As part of Active Directory design, discussed in Chapter 35, "Configuring Active Directory Sites and Replication," you must consider whether separate sites are needed. If your organization has multiple locations with limited bandwidth or unreliable connections between locations, you will typically want to create additional sites. In some cases you might also want to create additional sites to separate network segments even if they are connected with high-speed links; the reason for doing this is to isolate logon authentication traffic between the network segments.

To create an additional site, follow these steps:

1. Start Active Directory Sites and Services by clicking Start, Programs or All Programs, Administrative Tools, and Active Directory Sites And Services.

> **Tip** **Connect to the forest you want to work with**
> Active Directory Sites and Services is used to view a single forest. If your organization has multiple forests, you might need to connect to another forest. To do this, right-click the Active Directory Sites And Services node in the console tree, and then select Connect To Forest. In the Connect To Forest dialog box, type the name of the root domain in the forest to which you want to connect, and then click OK.

2. Right-click the Sites container in the console tree, and select New Site. This displays the New Object–Site dialog box, as shown in Figure 39-1.

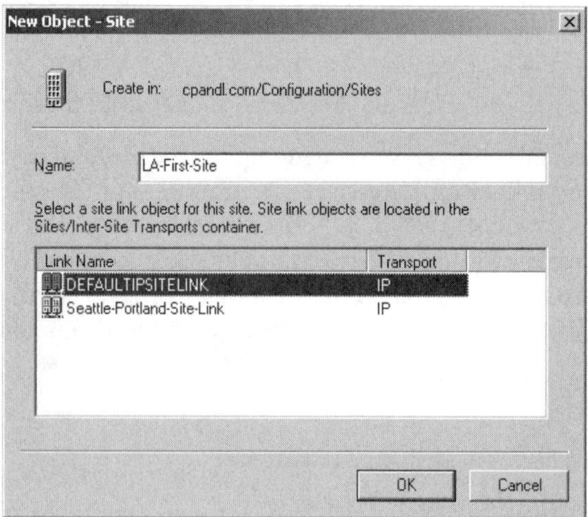

Figure 39-1. Use the New Object–Site dialog box to create a new site.

3. In the New Object—Site dialog box, type a descriptive name for the site. The site name serves as a point of reference for administrators and should clearly depict the purpose or physical location of the site.
4. Choose which site link will be used to connect this site to other sites. If the site link you want to use doesn't exist, that's okay—the site must exist before you can create links to it. Select the default site link DEFAULTIPSITELINK for now, and change the site link settings once you've created the necessary site link or links.
5. When you are ready to continue, click OK. A prompt is displayed detailing the steps you must complete to finish the site configuration. Click OK again. As the prompt details, you should do the following:
   - Ensure the links to this site are appropriate by creating the necessary site links. The catch in this is that both endpoints in a site link—the sites you want to link—must exist before you can create a site link.
   - Create subnets and associate them with the site. This tells Active Directory the network addresses that belong to a site.

Each site should have one or more domain controllers. Ideally, this domain controller should also be a global catalog server. Because of this, you should install one or more domain controllers in the site or move existing domain controllers into the site.

Creating a Subnet and Associating It with a Site

You create subnets and associate them with sites to allow Active Directory to determine the network segments that belong to the site. Any computer with an Internet Protocol (IP) address on a network segment associated with a site is considered to be located in the site. A site can have one or more subnets associated with it. Each subnet, however, can be associated with only one site.

You can create a subnet and associate it with a site by completing the following steps:

1. Start Active Directory Sites and Services by clicking Start, Programs or All Programs, Administrative Tools, and Active Directory Sites And Services.
2. Right-click the Subnets container in the console tree, and select New Subnet. This displays the New Object—Subnet dialog box, as shown in Figure 39-2.
3. In the Address field, type the network address for the subnet. Typically, the subnet address ends with a 0, such as 192.168.1.0. If subnetting is used as discussed in Chapter 24, "Managing TCP/IP Networking," the network address could end in a different value, however.

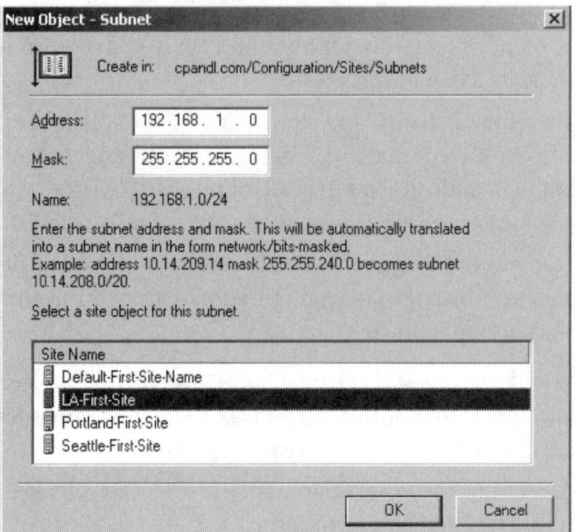

Figure 39-2. Use the New Object—Subnet dialog box to create a new subnet.

4 In the Mask field, type the subnet mask for the network segment. The network address and the subnet mask are used to set the subnet name. The name uses the network prefix notation, which is also referred to as the classless interdomain routing (CIDR) notation. For example, if the network address is 192.168.1.0 and the subnet mask is 255.255.255.0, the subnet name is set to 192.168.1.0/24.

5 Select the site with which the subnet should be associated, and then click OK. If you ever need to change the site association for the subnet, double-click the subnet in the Subnets folder and then, in the General tab, use the Site selection menu to change the site association.

Associating Domain Controllers with a Site

Once you associate subnets with a site, any domain controllers you install will automatically be located in the site when the IP address subnet matches the domain controller's IP address. Any domain controllers installed before you established the site and associated subnets with it will not, however, be moved to the site automatically. You must do this manually. In addition, if you associate a subnet with a different site, you might need to move domain controllers in that subnet to the new site.

You can move a domain controller to a site by completing the following steps:

1 Start Active Directory Sites and Services by clicking Start, Programs or All Programs, Administrative Tools, and Active Directory Sites And Services.

2 Domain controllers associated with a site are listed in the site's Servers node. To locate the domain controller that you want to move, expand the site node, and then expand the related Servers node.

3. Right-click the domain controller, and then select Move. This displays the Move Server dialog box.
4. In the Move Server dialog box, select the site that should contain the server, and then click OK.

> **Note** Another way to move a domain controller from one site to another in Windows Server 2003 is to drag the domain controller from its current site to the new site. But don't move a domain controller to a site arbitrarily. Move a domain controller to a site only if it is on a subnet associated with the site.

Managing Site Links and Intersite Replication

Site links are used to connect two or more sites together for the purpose of replication. When you install Active Directory in a new forest, a new site link called the DEFAULTIPSITELINK is created. As you add additional sites to the forest, these sites are included in the default site link unless you have configured other site links. If all of the network connections between sites are the same speed and priority, the default configuration can work. In this case, the intersite replication configuration for all sites will have the same properties. If you were to change these properties, the changes would affect the replication topology for all sites. By creating additional site links, you can configure different replication properties when the network connections between sites have different speeds and priorities.

Creating additional site links helps the designated Inter-Site Topology Generator (ISTG) for a site to prioritize the site links and determine when a site link should be used. It doesn't, however, change the way intersite replication works. Replication traffic between sites is always sent from a bridgehead server in one site to a bridgehead server in another site. Although it is the job of the ISTG to generate the intersite replication topology and designate bridgehead servers, you can manually designate bridgehead servers as well. Once you've established site links and designated bridgehead servers as necessary, you might want to change the way replication between sites is handled. For example, you might want to disable compression or enable notification so changes can be replicated more quickly between sites.

Following this, the most common administrative tasks related to site links involve the following:

- Creating site links
- Configuring site link bridges
- Determining the ISTG
- Configuring site bridgehead servers
- Setting site link replication options

Before looking at these administrative tasks, however, let's first look at the available replication transports.

Understanding IP and SMTP Replication Transports

When you create a site link, you will have to select a replication transport protocol. Two replication transports are available: IP and Simple Mail Transfer Protocol (SMTP). All replication connections within sites are synchronous and use RPC over IP. In this configuration, domain controllers establish an RPC over IP connection with a single replication partner at a time and replicate Active Directory changes. By default, the remote procedure call (RPC) connection uses dynamic port mapping. During replication, a replication client establishes a connection to a server on the RPC endpoint mapper port 135 and determines which port is to be used for replication on the server. Any additional replication traffic is sent over the ports defined in Table 35-1 on page 1175. When RPC over IP is used for intersite replication, these same ports are used. If there are firewalls between the sites, the appropriate ports on the firewalls must be opened to allow replication to occur.

Because RPC over IP is synchronous, both replication partners must be available at the time the connection is established. This is important because of the transitive nature of site links. For example, if Site 1 has a link to Site 2, and Site 2 has a link to Site 3, there is an automatic bridge between Site 1 and Site 3 that allows Site 1 to replicate traffic directly to Site 3. Because of this, you must carefully configure site link schedules so that all potential RPC over IP replication partners are available as necessary—more on this in a moment.

Replication between sites can also be configured to use SMTP. By using SMTP as the transport, all replication traffic is converted to e-mail messages that are sent between the sites. Because SMTP replication is asynchronous, it can be a good choice when you do not have a permanent connection between sites or when you have unreliable connections between sites. It is also a good choice when you have to replicate between locations over the public Internet.

Before you use SMTP as the replication protocol, there are several important considerations. First, SMTP can be used only to replicate information between domain controllers in different domains because the domain directory partition cannot be replicated using SMTP—only the configuration, schema, and global catalog directory partitions can be replicated. Second, SMTP messages are digitally signed and encrypted to ensure that replication traffic is secure even if replication traffic is routed over the public Internet. All domain controllers that will use SMTP for replication require additional components to create, digitally sign, and then encrypt e-mail messages. Specifically, you must install the SMTP Service subcomponent of Microsoft Internet Information Services (IIS) on each domain controller and you must install a Microsoft certificate authority (CA) in your organization. The certificates from the CA are used to digitally sign and encrypt the SMTP messages sent between the sites.

Tip **Configure replication through firewalls**

If you plan to use SMTP for replication, you must open port 25 on the firewall between sites. Port 25 is the default port used for SMTP. Although SMTP has definite security advantages over standard IP, you can encrypt RPC communications between domain controllers using IP Security (IPSec) and then open the appropriate ports on your firewalls for RPC over IP. Encrypting the RPC traffic between domain controllers would then be a viable alternative for replication over the public Internet when you have a dedicated connection between sites.

Creating a Site Link

After you create the sites that your organization needs, you can create site links between those sites to better manage intersite replication. Each site link must have at least two sites associated with it. These sites establish the endpoints or transit points for the link. For example, if you create a site link and add Portland-First-Site and LA-First-Site to the link, the Portland and LA sites are the endpoints for the link and the ISTG will use the link to create the connection objects that are required to replicate traffic between these sites.

Before you create a site link, you should determine the transport that you want to use as discussed previously in the section entitled "Understanding IP and SMTP Replication Transports" earlier in this chapter. You should also consider the following:

- **Link cost** The cost for a site link determines the relative priority of the link in relationship to other site links that might be available. If there are multiple possible routes to a site, the route with the lowest link cost is used first. In the event a primary link fails, a secondary link can be used. Typically, the link cost reflects the bandwidth available for a specific connection. It can also reflect the actual cost of sending traffic over a particular link if the organization has to pay a fee based on bandwidth usage.
- **Replication schedule** The replication schedule determines the times during the day that the site link is available for replication. By default, replication is allowed 24 hours a day. If you have a limited-bandwidth connection or you want user traffic to have priority at certain times of the day, you might want to configure a different availability schedule.
- **Replication interval** The replication interval determines the intervals at which the bridgehead servers in each site check to see if there are directory updates available. By default, the interval is set to 180 minutes. Following this, if the replication schedule is configured to allow replication from 7 P.M. to 7 A.M. each day, the bridgehead servers will check for updates at 7 P.M., 10 P.M., 1 A.M., 4 A.M., and 7 A.M. daily.

You can create a site link between two or more sites by completing the following steps:

1. Start Active Directory Sites and Services by clicking Start, Programs or All Programs, Administrative Tools, and Active Directory Sites And Services. If your organization has multiple forests, you might need to connect to another forest. To do this, right-click the Active Directory Sites And Services node in the console tree, and then select Connect To Forest. In the Connect To Forest dialog box, type the name of the root domain in the forest to which you want to connect, and then click OK.
2. Expand the Sites container, and then expand the Inter-Site Transports container. Right-click the container for the transport protocol you want to use, either IP or SMTP, and select New Site Link. This displays the New Object—Site Link dialog box, as shown in Figure 39-3.
3. In the New Object—Site Link dialog box, type a descriptive name for the site link. The site name serves as a point of reference for administrators and should clearly depict the sites the link connects.

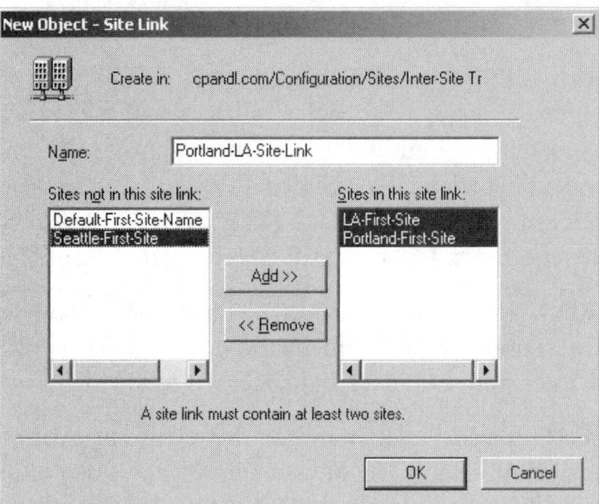

Figure 39-3. Create the site link.

4 In the Sites Not In This Site Link list, select a site that should be included in the link, and then click Add to add the site to the Sites In This Link list. Repeat this process for each site you want to add to the link. The link must include at least two sites.

5 Click OK to close the New Object—Site Link dialog box.

6 In Active Directory Sites And Services, the site link is added to the appropriate transport folder (IP or SMTP). Select the transport in the console tree, and then double-click the site link in the right pane. This displays the Link Properties dialog box, as shown in Figure 39-4.

7 Use the Cost combo box to set the relative cost of the link. The default cost is 100. For pointers on determining what cost to use, see the sections entitled "Mapping Network Infrastructure" on page 1186, and "Designing the Intersite Replication Topology" on page 1190.

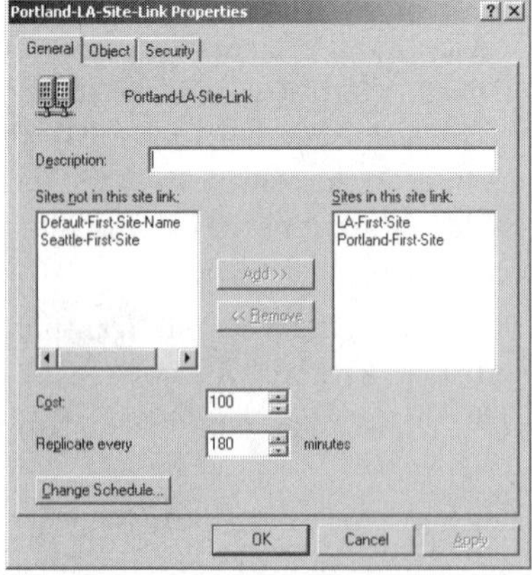

Figure 39-4. Set the site link properties.

8 Use the Replicate Every combo box to set the replication interval. The default interval is 180 minutes.

9 By default, the site link is available for replication 24 hours a day. To set a different schedule, click Change Schedule, and then use the Schedule For dialog box to set the desired replication schedule. When you are finished, click OK.

10 Click OK to close the site link's Properties dialog box.

Inside Out

The transitive nature of site links

Site links are transitive and follow the three hops rules as discussed in Chapter 35. This means that if Site 1 is linked to Site 2, Site 2 is linked to Site 3, and Site 3 is linked to Site 4, the domain controllers in Site 1 can replicate with Site 2, Site 3, and Site 4. Because of the transitive nature of site links, site link replication schedules and intervals for each site link are combined to determine the effective replication window and interval. To see the impact of combining replication schedules and intervals, consider the following examples:

- Site 1 to Site 2 link has a replication schedule of 7 P.M. to 7 A.M. and an interval of 60 minutes.
- Site 2 to Site 3 link has a replication schedule of 9 P.M. to 5 A.M. and an interval of 60 minutes.
- Site 3 to Site 4 link has a replication schedule of 1 P.M. to 3 A.M. and an interval of 180 minutes.

Because of the overlapping windows and intervals, replication between Site 1 and Site 2 could occur every 60 minutes from 7 P.M. to 7 A.M. Replication between Site 1 and Site 3 could occur every 60 minutes from 9 P.M. to 5 A.M. Replication between Site 1 and Site 4 could occur every 180 minutes from 9 P.M. to 3 A.M. This occurs because the replication availability window must overlap for replication to occur using transitive links.

If the site replication schedules do not overlap, replication is still possible between multiple sites. To see how replication would work if schedules do not overlap, consider the following example:

- Site 1 to Site 2 link has a replication schedule of 11 P.M. to 3 A.M. and an interval of 60 minutes.
- Site 2 to Site 3 link has a replication schedule of 6 P.M. to 9 P.M. and an interval of 60 minutes.
- Site 3 to Site 4 link has a replication schedule of 1 A.M. to 5 A.M. and an interval of 180 minutes.

Assuming there are no alternate links between the sites, replication between Site 1 and Site 2 could occur every 60 minutes from 11 P.M. to 3 A.M. Site 1 would not be able to replicate with Site 3 and Site 4, however. Instead, Site 2 would replicate changes to Site 3 every 60 minutes from 6 P.M. to 9 P.M. daily. Site 3 would in turn replicate changes to Site 4 every 180 minutes from 1 A.M. to 5 A.M. daily. In this configuration, there is significant replication latency (delay). Changes made at 5 P.M. in Site 1 would not be replicated to Site 2 until 11 P.M. The following day the changes would be replicated to Site 3 at 6 P.M., and then at 1 A.M. on the third day the changes would be replicated to Site 4.

Configuring Site Link Bridges

Be default, all site links are transitive, which allows Active Directory to automatically configure site link bridges between sites. When a site is bridged, any two domain controllers can make a connection across any consecutive series of links as long as the site links are all using the same transport. The site link bridge cost is the sum of all the links included in the bridge.

A significant advantage of automatically created site link bridges is that fault tolerance is built in whenever there are multiple possible routes between sites. Another significant advantage is that Active Directory automatically manages the site link bridges and the ISTG monitors for changes and reconfigures the replication topology accordingly—and all without any administrator involvement required. Site link bridges are discussed in more detail in the section entitled "Considering the Impact of Site Link Bridging" on page 1191.

You can enable or disable site link bridges on a per-transport basis. By default, both the IP and SMTP transports have site link bridging enabled. If you disable site link bridging, Active Directory will no longer manage site link bridges for the transport. You must then create and manage *all* site link bridges for that transport. Any sites you add to a site link bridge are considered to be transitive with each other. Site links that are not included in the site link bridge are not transitive.

To see how this would work, consider the previous example in which Site 1 is linked to Site 2, Site 2 is linked to Site 3, and Site 3 is linked to Site 4. If you disable site link bridging and then create a site link bridge that includes Site 1, Site 2, and Site 3, only those sites would have a transitive site link. Site 4 would be excluded. This would mean Site 1 could replicate changes to Site 2 and Site 1 could replicate changes to Site 3. Site 1 could not, however, replicate changes to Site 4. Only Site 3 would replicate changes to Site 4. This would occur because adjacent sites can always replicate changes with each other.

Note One reason to create site link bridges manually is to reduce the processing overhead on the designated ISTGs in each site. When you disable transitive links, the ISTGs no longer have to create and manage the site link bridges, and this reduces the number of computations required to create the intersite replication topology.

To turn off transitive site links and manually configure site link bridges, follow these steps:

1. Start Active Directory Sites and Services by clicking Start, Programs or All Programs, Administrative Tools, and Active Directory Sites And Services.
2. Expand the Sites container, and then expand the Inter-Site Transports container. Right-click the container for the transport protocol you want to work with, either IP or SMTP, and then select Properties. This displays a Properties dialog box (see Figure 39-5).

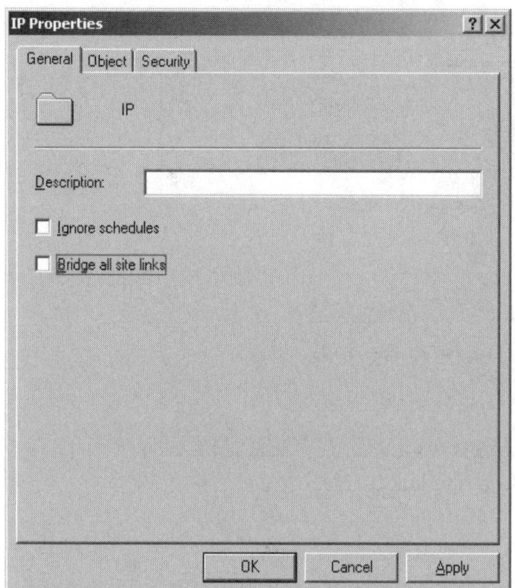

Figure 39-5. Disabling automatic transitive site links.

3. Clear Bridge All Site Links, and then click OK. If you later want to enable transitive links and have Active Directory ignore the site link bridges you've created, you can select Bridge All Site Links.

Once you've disabled transitive links, you can manually create a site link bridge between two or more sites by completing the following steps:

1. In Active Directory Sites and Services, expand the Sites container, and then expand the Inter-Site Transports container. Right-click the container for the transport protocol you want to use, either IP or SMTP, and then select New Site Link Bridge. This displays the New Object—Site Link Bridge dialog box, as shown in Figure 39-6.
2. In the New Object—Site Link Bridge dialog box, type a descriptive name for the site link bridge. This name serves as a point of reference for administrators and should clearly depict all the site links that are a part of the bridge.

3. In the Site Links Not In This Site Link Bridge list, select a site link that should be included in the bridge and then click Add to add the site link to the Site Links In This Site Link Bridge list. Repeat this process for each site link you want to add to the bridge. The bridge must include at least two site links.
4. Click OK to close the New Object—Site Link Bridge dialog box.

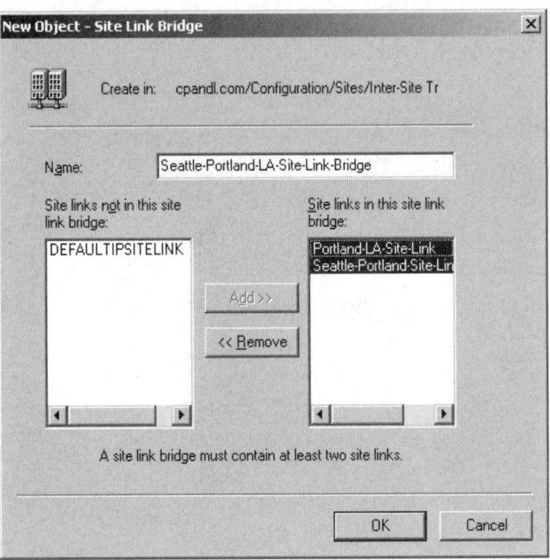

Figure 39-6. Create a site link bridge.

Determining the ISTG

Each site has an ISTG that is responsible for generating the intersite replication topology. As your organization grows and you add domain controllers and sites, the load on the ISTG can grow substantially because each addition means the ISTG must perform additional calculations to determine and maintain the optimal topology. When it is calculating the replication topology, its processor typically will reach 100 percent utilization. As the topology becomes more and more complex, the process will stay at maximum utilization longer and longer.

Because there is the potential for the ISTG to get overloaded, you should monitor the designated ISTG in a site more closely than other domain controllers. You can determine the ISTG by completing the following steps:

1. In Active Directory Sites and Services, expand the Sites container, and then select the site whose ISTG you want to locate in the console tree.
2. In the Details pane, double-click NTDS Site Settings.
3. In the NTDS Site Settings dialog box, the current ISTG is listed in the Inter-Site Topology Generator panel, as shown in Figure 39-7.

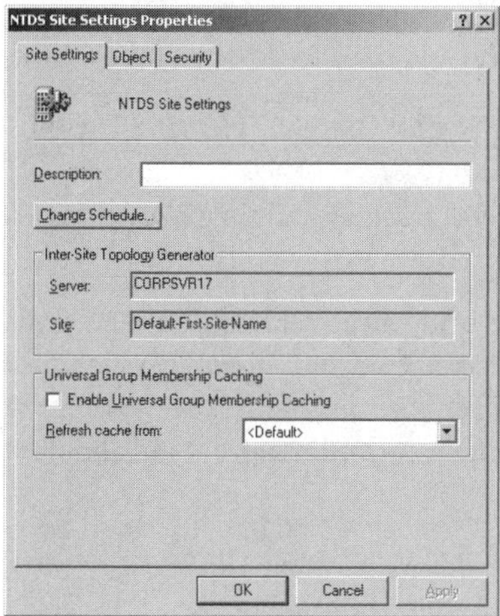

Figure 39-7. Locating the ISTG.

Configuring Site Bridgehead Servers

Replication between sites is performed by bridgehead servers in each site. A bridgehead server is a domain controller designated by the ISTG to perform intersite replication. Bridgehead servers are discussed in detail in the sections entitled "Intersite Replication Essentials" on page 1175, and "Replication Rings and Directory Partitions" on page 1182.

As with the ISTG role, operating as a bridgehead server can add a significant load to a domain controller. This load increases with the number and frequency of replication changes. Because of this, the designated bridgehead servers should also be closely monitored to make sure they don't become overloaded.

> **Tip** **Determine bridgehead servers**
> You can determine the current bridgehead servers throughout the enterprise using Replication Monitor, which I discuss in the section entitled "Monitoring and Troubleshooting Replication" later in this chapter. If you want to examine the bridgehead servers in the current site, type **repadmin /bridgeheads** at the command prompt.

In situations in which you have domain controllers that are already overloaded or not equipped to possibly handle the additional load of being a bridgehead server, you might want to control which domain controllers operate as bridgehead servers. You do this by designating preferred bridgehead servers in a site.

There are several important considerations for designating bridgehead servers. First, once you designate a preferred bridgehead server, the ISTG will use only the preferred bridgehead server for intersite replication. This means if the domain controller acting as the bridgehead server goes offline or is unable to replicate for any reason, intersite replication will stop until the server is again available for replication or you change the preferred bridgehead server configuration options. In the latter case, you would need to do one of the following:

- Remove the server as a preferred bridgehead server and then specify a different preferred bridgehead server
- Remove the server as a preferred bridgehead server and then allow the ISTG to select the bridgehead servers that should be used

Because you can designate multiple preferred bridgehead servers, you can prevent this situation simply by specifying more than one preferred bridgehead server. When there are multiple preferred bridgehead servers, the ISTG will choose one of the servers you've designated as the preferred bridgehead server. If this server fails, it would then choose another server from the list of preferred bridgehead servers.

An additional consideration to make when designating preferred bridgehead servers is that you must configure a bridgehead server for each partition that needs to be replicated. This means you must configure at least one domain controller with a replica of each directory partition as a bridgehead server. If you don't do this, replication of the partition will fail and the ISTG will log an event in the Directory Services event log detailing the failure. Consider the example shown in Figure 39-8.

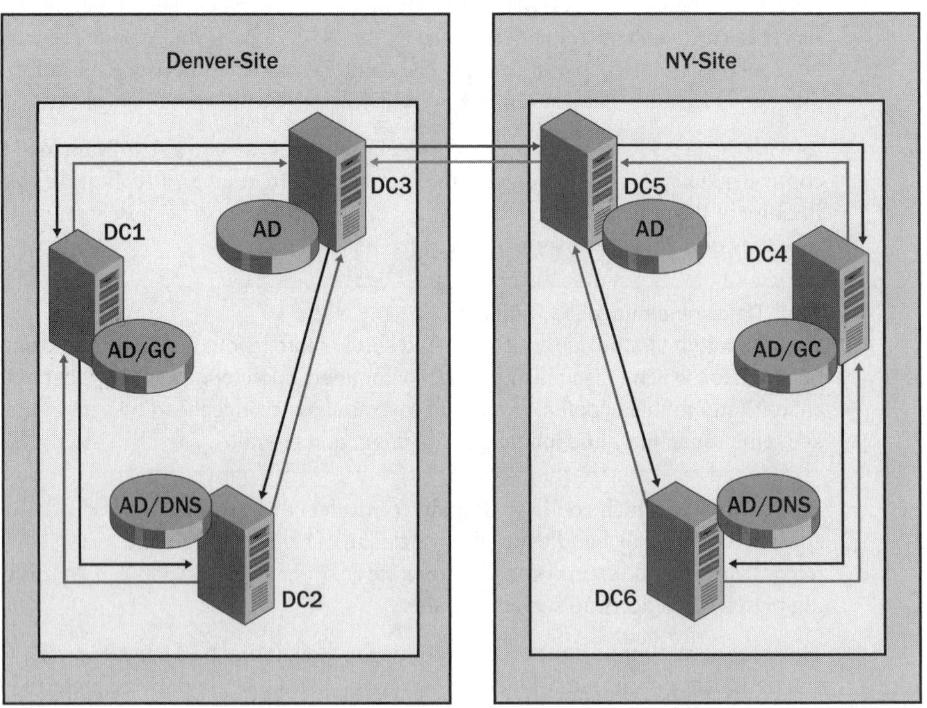

Figure 39-8. Directory partitions in separate sites must have a designated bridgehead server.

Here, the Denver-Site and the NY-Site are part of the same domain, ThePhone-Company.com. Each site has a global catalog and a DNS server that is integrated with Active Directory. In this configuration, the bridgehead servers must replicate the following directory partitions: domain, configuration, schema, global catalog, and DNS (for the Domain Name System). If you designated DC3 and DC5 as the preferred bridgehead servers, only the domain, configuration, schema directory partitions would be replicated. This means replication for the global catalog and the DNS partition would fail and the ISTG would log an event in the Directory Services event log specifying the reason for the failure. On the other hand, if you designated DC1 and DC2 as the preferred bridgehead servers for the Denver site and DC4 and DC6 as the preferred bridgehead servers for the NY site, all the directory partitions would be replicated.

To configure a domain controller as a preferred bridgehead server, complete the following steps:

1. Start Active Directory Sites and Services by clicking Start, Programs or All Programs, Administrative Tools, and Active Directory Sites And Services.
2. Domains controllers associated with a site are listed in the site's Servers node. To locate the domain controller that you want to work with, expand the site node, and then expand the related Servers node.
3. Right-click the server you want to designate as a preferred bridgehead, and then select Properties.
4. In the Properties dialog box, shown in Figure 39-9, you have the option of configuring the server as a preferred bridgehead server for either IP or SMTP. Select the appropriate transport in the Transports Available For list, and then click Add. If you later want the server to stop being a preferred bridgehead, select the transport in the This Server Is A Preferred Bridgehead Server list, and then click Remove.

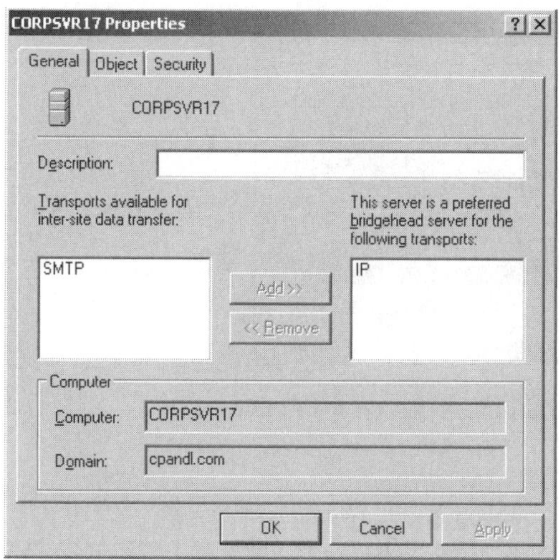

Figure 39-9. Designating a preferred bridgehead server.

5. Click OK.

Configuring Site Link Replication Options

Once you've configured a site link, you might want to change the site's configuration options, including whether replication compression and notification are enabled or disabled. You do this by editing the Options attribute on either the site link object or the connection object related to the site link you want to modify. Only members of the Enterprise Admins group can change these options.

If you are a member of the Enterprise Admins groups, you can manage the site option attributes for compression and notification using the ADSI Edit snap-in for the Microsoft Management Console (MMC). When you start this snap-in, you must make a connection to a replica of the Configuration container. Because every domain controller has a writeable copy of the configuration data, any domain controller to which you are connected when you start ADSI Edit will suffice.

You can access and use ADSI Edit to configure the site link object's Options attribute by following these steps:

1. Open a blank MMC in Author mode. Click Start, select Run, type **mmc** in the Open field, and then click OK.
2. Choose Add/Remove Snap-in from the File menu in the main window. Choose Add, which displays the Add Standalone Snap-In dialog box.
3. Click ADSI Edit, and then choose Add. The ADSI Edit snap-in is added to the list of snap-ins in the Add/Remove Snap-In dialog. Click Close, and then click OK.
4. When you first start ADSI Edit, it won't have any connections to containers within Active Directory. Because of this, you must add the connections to the Configuration container. Right-click the ADSI Edit node in the left pane, and then click Connect to. This displays the Connections Settings dialog box, as shown in Figure 39-10.

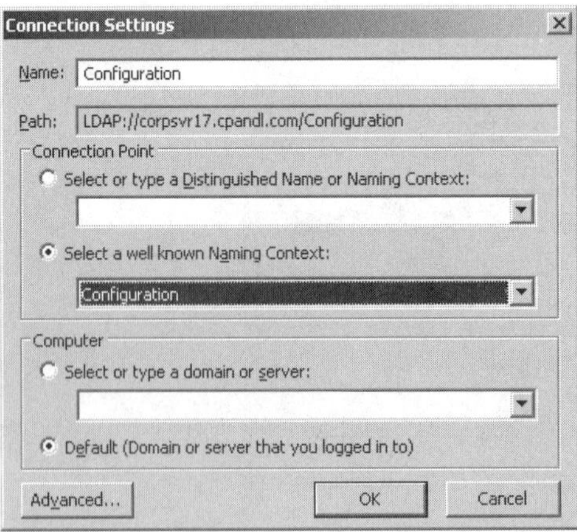

Figure 39-10. The Connection Settings dialog box.

5. In the Connection Point panel, choose Select A Well Known Naming Context, and then select Configuration. This specifies that you want to make a connection to the Configuration Container in Active Directory. Click OK.

6 After you add the snap-in to a custom console and connect to the Configuration container in Active Directory, you can edit site link objects. In ADSI Edit, expand the ADSI Edit node, expand Configuration, and then expand the configuration container for the forest; it is named with its distinguished name, as shown in Figure 39-11.

7 Next expand CN=Sites, CN=Inter-Site Transports, and then select the container for the appropriate transport type, either CN=IP for the link's IP transport or CN=SMTP for the link's SMTP transport.

8 In the details pane, right-click the site link you want to work with, and select Properties. This displays the link Properties dialog box.

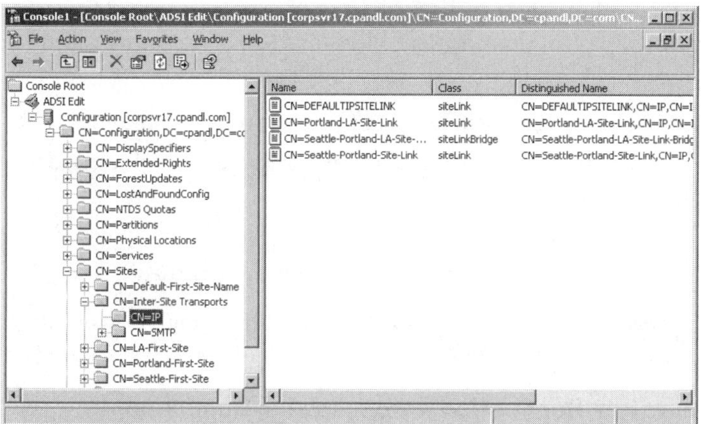

Figure 39-11. Access the site link object.

9 Scroll through the list of attributes until you find the Options attribute. When you find this attribute, click it to select it, and then click Edit.

10 In the Integer Attribute Editor dialog box, you can now do the following:

- Type 1 to enable notification for intersite replication. This means the bridgehead servers on either side of the link will no longer use compression. Use this option only when you have sufficient bandwidth for a site connection and are concerned about high processor utilization on the affected bridgehead servers.
- Type 4 to turn off compression for intersite replication. This means the bridgehead servers on either side of the link can notify each other that changes have occurred. This allows the bridgehead server receiving the notification to pull the changes across the site link and thereby get more frequent updates.
- Type 5 to set both options. This means compression will be turned off and notification for intersite replication will be enabled.
- Click Clear to reset the Options attribute to its default value <not set>. When Options is not set, notification for intersite replication is disabled and compression is turned on.

11 Click OK twice.

Monitoring and Troubleshooting Replication

Two helpful tools for monitoring and troubleshooting replication issues are provided in the Support Tools. The first tool is the Replication Administrator (RepAdmin), which is a command-line utility. The second tool is the Replication Monitor (ReplMon), which is a graphical user interface (GUI) utility. Both tools provide similar functionality, albeit one from the command line and one from the GUI.

Using the Replication Administrator

You run the Replication Administrator from the command line. Most command-line parameters accept a list of the domain controllers you want to work with called *DCList* and specified as follows:

- * is a wildcard that includes all domain controllers in the enterprise.
- *PartialName** is a partial server name that includes a wildcard to match the remainder of the server name.
- Site:*SiteName* includes only domain controllers in the named site.
- Gc: includes all global catalog servers in the enterprise.

Knowing this, there are many tasks you can perform using the Replication Administrator. These tasks are summarized in Table 39-1.

Table 39-1. Key Replication Administrator Commands

Command to Type	Description
repadmin /bridgeheads *DCList*] [/verbose]	Lists bridgehead servers.
repadmin /failcache *DCList*	Lists failed replication events that were detected by the Knowledge Consistency Checker (KCC).
repadmin istg *DCList* [/verbose]	Lists the name of the ISTG for a specified site.
repadmin /kcc *DCList* [/async]	Forces the KCC to recalculate the intrasite replication topology for a specified domain controller. By default, this recalculation occurs every 15 minutes. Use the /Async options to start the KCC and not wait for it to finish the calculation.
repadmin /latency *DCList* [/verbose]	Lists the amount of time between intersite replications using the ISTG Keep Alive timestamp.
repadmin /queue *DCList*	Lists tasks waiting in the replication queue.
repadmin /replsummary *DCList*	Displays a summary of the replication state.
repadmin /showcert *DCList*	Displays the server certificates loaded on the specified domain controllers.

Table 39-1. Key Replication Administrator Commands

Command to Type	Description
repadmin /showconn *DCList*	Displays the connection objects for the specified domain controllers. Defaults to the local site.
repadmin /showctx *DCList*	Lists computers that have opened sessions with a specified domain controller.
repadmin/showoutcalls *DCList*	Lists calls that were made by the specified server to other servers but that have not yet been answered.
repadmin /showrepl *DCList*	Lists the replication partners for each directory partition on the specified domain controller.
repadmin /showtrust *DCList*	Lists all domains trusted by a specified domain.

Using the Replication Monitor

The Replication Monitor (ReplMon) is a graphical utility that can perform many of the same tasks as the Replication Administrator. Once you've installed the Support Tools, the easiest way to start the Replication Monitor is to type **replmon** at a command prompt.

After you start the Replication Monitor, you must add the domain controllers that you want to monitor. You do this by right-clicking the Monitored Servers node in the console tree and selecting Add Monitored Server. In the Add Monitored Server Wizard, access the default option to Add The Server Explicitly By Name, and then click Next. On the Add Server To Monitor page, type the name of the domain controller you want to monitor, and then click Finish. The domain controller will then be added to the Replication Monitor.

As shown in Figure 39-12, each directory partition maintained by the server is listed. If you right-click a partition, you have the option of synchronizing the partition with all other domain controllers or showing change notifications to replication partners.

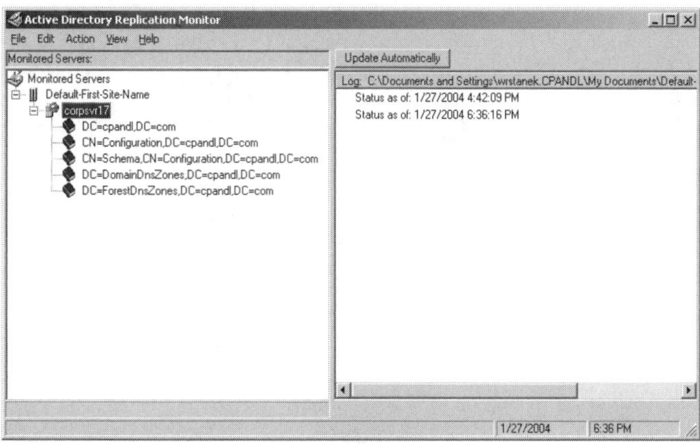

Figure 39-12. The Replication Monitor.

If you right-click the domain controller node in the console tree, you can perform many standard replication monitoring tasks. These tasks include the following:

- Checking the replication topology
- Synchronizing all directory partitions with all other domain controllers
- Generating a status report
- Showing the domain controllers in the current domain
- Showing the replication topology
- Showing the GPO status
- Showing current performance data for the server
- Showing a list of all the global catalog servers in the forest
- Showing the bridgehead servers in the site or in the forest
- Showing trust relationships
- Showing attribute metadata for Active Directory objects

Viewing replication errors for all domain controllers is another important task that you can perform in Replication Monitor. To do this, click the Action menu, point to Domain, and then select Search Domain Controllers For Replication Errors.

Part 8

Windows Server 2003 Disaster Planning and Recovery

Chapter 40

Disaster Planning

Ask three different people what their idea of a disaster is and you'll probably get three different answers. For most administrators, the term *disaster* probably means any scenario in which one or more essential system services cannot operate and the prospects for quick recovery are less than hopeful—that is, a disaster is something a service reset or system reboot won't fix.

To ensure that operations can be restored as quickly as possible in a given situation, every network needs a clear disaster recovery plan. In this chapter, I'm not going to mince words and try to explain why you need to plan for disasters. Instead, I'm going to focus on what you need to do to get ready for the inevitable, because worst-case scenarios can and do happen. I'm also going to discuss predisaster preparation procedures.

Preparing for a Disaster

Chapter 17, "Planning for High Availability," went into detail about planning for highly available, scalable, and manageable systems. Many of the same concepts go into disaster planning. Why? Because, at the end of the day, disaster planning involves implementing plans that ensure the availability of systems and services. Remember that part of disaster planning is applying some level of contingency planning to every essential network service and system. You need to implement problem escalation and response procedures. You also need a standing problem-resolution document that describes in great detail what to do when disaster strikes.

Developing Contingency Procedures

You should identify the services and systems that are essential to network operations. Typically, this list will include the following components:

- Network infrastructure servers running Active Directory, Domain Name System (DNS), Dynamic Host Configuration Protocol (DHCP), Terminal Services, and Routing and Remote Access Service (RRAS).

- File, database, and application servers, such as servers with essential file shares or those that provide database or e-mail services
- Networking hardware, including switches, routers, and firewalls

Use Chapter 17 to help you develop plans for contingency procedures in the following areas:

- **Physical security** Place network hardware and servers in a locked, secure access facility. This could be an office that is kept locked or a server room that requires a passkey to enter. When physical access to network hardware and servers requires special access privileges, you prevent a lot of problems and ensure that only authorized personnel can get access to systems from the console.
- **Data backup** Implement a regular backup plan that ensures that multiple datasets are available for all essential systems, and that these backups are stored in more than one location. For example, if you keep the most current backup sets on-site in the server room, you should rotate another backup set to off-site storage. In this way, if disaster strikes, you will be more likely to be able to recover operations.
- **Fault tolerance** Build redundancy into the network and system architecture. At the server level, you can protect data using a redundant array of independent disks (RAID) and guard against component failure by having spare parts at hand. These precautions protect servers at a very basic level. For essential services such as Active Directory, DNS, and DHCP, you can build in fault tolerance by deploying redundant systems using techniques discussed throughout this book. These same concepts can be applied to network hardware components such as routers and switches.
- **Recovery** Every essential server and network device should have a written recovery plan that details step by step what to do to rebuild and recover it. Be as detailed and explicit as possible and don't assume that the readers know anything about the system or device they are recovering. Do this even if you are sure that you'll be the one performing the recovery—you'll be thankful for it, trust me. Things can and do go wrong at the worst times, and sometimes, under pressure, you might forget some important detail in the recovery process—not to mention that you might be unavailable to recover the system for some reason.
- **Power protection** Power-protect servers and network hardware using an uninterruptible power supply (UPS) system. Power protection will help safeguard servers and network hardware from power surges and dirty power. Power protection will also help prevent data loss and allow you to power down servers in an appropriate fashion through manual or automatic shutdown.

Inside Out

Using and configuring UPS

Putting in a UPS requires a bit of planning, because you need to look not only at servers but also at everything in the server room that requires power. If the power goes out, you want to have ample time for systems to shut down in an orderly fashion. You may also have some systems that you do not want to be shut down, such as routers or servers required for security key cards. In most cases, rather than using individual UPS devices, you should install enterprise UPS solutions that can be connected to several servers or components.

Once you install a UPS, you can configure servers to take advantage of UPS using the Power Options utility in Control Panel. Select or double-click Power Options to open the Power Options dialog box, and then choose the UPS tab. You can then configure the way a server reacts when it switches to battery power. Typically, you'll want servers to start an orderly shutdown within a few minutes of switching to battery power.

In your planning, remember that 90 percent of power outages last less than 5 minutes and 99 percent of power outages last less than 60 minutes. With this in mind, you may want to plan your UPS implementation so that you can maintain 5 to 7 minutes of power for all server and network components and 60 to 70 minutes for critical systems. You would then configure all non-critical systems to shut down automatically after 5 minutes, and critical systems to shut down after 60 minutes.

Implementing Problem Escalation and Response Procedures

As part of planning, you need to develop well-defined problem escalation procedures that document how to handle problems and emergency changes that might be needed. You need to designate an incident response team and an emergency response team. Although the two teams could consist of the same team members, the teams differ in fundamental ways.

- **Incident response team** The incident response team's role is to respond to security incidents, such as the suspected cracking of a database server. This team is concerned with responding to intrusion, taking immediate action to safeguard the organization's information, documenting the security issue thoroughly in an after-action report, and then fixing the security problem so that the same type of incident cannot recur. Your organization's security administrator or network security expert should have a key role in this team.
- **Emergency response team** The emergency response team's role is to respond to service and system outages, such as the failure of a database server. This team is concerned with recovering the service or system as quickly as possible and allowing normal operations to resume. Like the incident response team, the emergency response team needs to document the outage thoroughly in an after-action report, and then, if applicable, propose changes to improve the recovery process. Your organization's system administrators should have key roles in this team.

Creating a Problem Resolution Policy Document

Over the years, I've worked with and consulted for many organizations, and I've often been asked to help implement information technology (IT) policy and procedure. In the area of disaster and recovery planning, there's one policy document that I always use, regardless of the size of the company I am working with. I call it the problem resolution policy document.

The problem resolution policy document has the following six sections:

- **Responsibilities** The overall responsibilities of IT and engineering staff during and after normal business hours should be detailed in this section. For an organization with 24/7 operations, such as a company with a public World Wide Web site maintained by internal staff, the after-hours responsibilities section should be very detailed and let individuals know exactly what their responsibilities are. Most organizations with 24/7 operations will designate individuals as being "on call" 7 days a week, 365 days a year, and in that case, this section should detail what being "on call" means, and what the general responsibilities are for an individual on call.
- **Phone roster** Every system and service that you've identified in your planning as essential should have a point of contact. For some systems, you'll have several points of contact. Consider, for example, a database server. You might have a system administrator who is responsible for the server itself, a database administrator who is responsible for the database running on the server, and an integration specialist responsible for any integration components running on the server.

Note The phone roster should include both on-site and off-site contact numbers. Ideally, this means that you'll have the work phone number, cell phone number, and pager number of each contact. It should be the responsibility of every individual on the phone roster to ensure that contact information is up to date.

- **Key contact information** In addition to a phone roster, you should have contact numbers for facilities and vendors. The key contacts list should include the main office phone numbers at branch offices and data centers, and contact numbers for the various vendors that installed infrastructure at each office, such as the building manager, Internet service provider (ISP), electrician, and network wiring specialist. It should also include the support phone numbers for hardware and software vendors and the information you'll be required to give in order to get service, such as customer identification number and service contract information.
- **Notification procedures** The way problems get resolved is through notification. This section should outline the notification procedures and the primary point of contact in case of outage. If many systems and services are involved, notification and primary

contacts can be divided into categories. For example, you may have an external systems notification process for your public Internet servers and an internal systems notification process for your intranet services.

- **Escalation** When problems aren't resolved within a specific timeframe, there should be clear escalation procedures that detail whom to contact and when. For example, you might have level 1, level 2, and level 3 points of contact, with level 1 contacts being called immediately, level 2 contacts being called when issues aren't resolved in 30 minutes, and level 3 contacts being called when issues aren't resolved in 60 minutes.

> **Note** You should also have a priority system in place that dictates what types of incidents or outages take precedence over others. For example, you could specify that service-level outages, such as those that involve the complete system have priority over an isolated outage involving a single server or application, but that suspected security incidents have priority over all other issues.

- **Post-action reporting** Every individual involved in a major outage or incident should be expected to write a post-action report. This section details what should be in that report. For example, you would want to track the notification time, actions after notification, escalation attempts, and other items that are important to improving the process or preventing the problem from recurring.

Every IT group should have a general policy with regard to problem resolution procedures, and this policy should be detailed in a problem resolution policy document or one like it. The document should be distributed to all relevant personnel throughout the organization, so that every person who has some level of responsibility for ensuring system and service availability knows what to do in case of an emergency. After you implement the policy, you should test it to help refine it so that the policy will work as expected in an actual disaster.

Predisaster Preparation Procedures

Just as you need to perform planning before disaster strikes, you also need to perform certain predisaster preparation procedures. These procedures ensure that you are able to recover systems as quickly as possible when a disaster strikes and include the following:

- Backups
- Automated System Recovery (ASR) disks
- Boot disks
- Startup and recovery options
- Recovery Console

Performing Backups

You should perform regular backups of every Microsoft Windows Server 2003 system. Backups can be performed using several techniques. Most organizations choose a combination of dedicated backup servers and per-server backups. If you use professional backup software, you can use one or more dedicated backup servers to create backups of other servers on the network, and then write the backups to media on centralized backup devices. If you use per-server backups, you run backup software on each server that you want to back up and store the backup media on a local backup device. By combining the techniques, you get the best of both worlds.

With dedicated backup servers, you purchase professional backup software, a backup server, and a scalable backup device. The initial costs for purchasing the required equipment and the time required to set up the backup environment can be substantial. However, once the backup environment is configured, it is rather easy to maintain. Centralized backups also offer substantial time savings for administrators, because the backup process itself can be fully automated.

With per-server backups, you use a backup utility to perform manual backups of individual systems. The primary tool for performing per-server backups is the NT Backup utility, which is discussed in Chapter 41, "Backup and Recovery." Because this tool is included with Windows Server 2003, there is no initial cost for implementation. However, because you perform per-server backup manually, in the end the process requires more time than using centralized backup servers.

Creating and Using ASR Disks

Unlike Microsoft Windows NT and Windows 2000, Windows Server 2003 doesn't use Emergency Repair Disks. Instead, Windows Server 2003 uses ASR disks. Every Windows Server 2003 system should have an ASR disk. ASR disks contain essential information that can be used in conjunction with a tape backup of your local system partition to recover a failed system. This information includes essential system files, partition boot sector information, the startup environment, and Registry data. This means that you can use the ASR disk to fix system files, the boot sector, the startup environment, and the Registry.

Whenever you install new services, components, or applications on a server, it's a good idea to make an ASR backup before and after you make the change. The pre-installation backup of the ASR can be used to help you recover the system if something goes wrong during or immediately after the installation. The post-installation backup of the ASR should be created when you are sure that the installation has worked and the system is stable. The ASR then records the current configuration of the server, so that the server can be recovered to its current state.

You create and use the ASR disk as discussed in the section entitled "Backing Up and Restoring the Registry," on page 434. When you create an ASR backup of a system, only part of the information is written to the ASR disk. The rest of the information is written to backup media. This means that to create an ASR backup you need a blank floppy disk and a backup tape. When you later want to recover a system using Automated System Recovery, you need the ASR floppy disk and the ASR backup media. The recovery process restores the full configuration of the server, including environment settings, shares, and other options you've set.

If you're wondering what exactly is on the ASR floppy disk, you can look after creating an ASR backup. You'll find the following three files:

- **Asr.sif** A setup information file that details the disks, partitions, and volumes on the system as well as the computer name and the location of the backup media used
- **Arpnp.sif** A setup information file that contains information on the plug-and-play devices installed on the system
- **Setup.log** A log file that contains a list of all the system files that were backed up

> **Tip** **Keep multiple copies of the ASR disk**
> Just as you keep multiple backups of data, you should keep multiple ASR disks. Floppy disks are cheap, so you might as well use a new one each time and keep several versions of the ASR disk handy. The ASR disk and the ASR backup media should be clearly labeled so that you know which ASR disk goes with which set of ASR backup media.

Creating and Using Boot Disks

With Windows Server 2003, you can use boot disks to help you recover from common boot problems. When it comes to specific information needed to boot a system, you'll find that using a boot disk to recover a system is often faster than trying to use ASR. Unlike boot disks for some previous versions of Windows, which allowed you to get to a command prompt, this type of boot disk allows you to fully boot the system so that you can log on the way you normally would, and then make the necessary repairs.

Boot disks can be helpful if a system has the following problems:

- A virus infection in the master boot record
- A missing or corrupt boot (Ntldr or Ntdetect.com) file
- A Boot.ini file with bad entries

Because a boot disk contains a system's Boot.ini file, each system should have its own boot disk. However, you can create one boot disk for systems with identically configured boot partitions. That is, if every system has the boot partition on the same controller, SCSI bus adapter, disk, and partition, all the systems can use the same boot disk.

A boot disk is not an MS-DOS startup disk, and you don't need to format the boot disk as an MS-DOS startup disk. To create a boot disk, follow these steps:

1. Insert a blank floppy disk into the system's floppy drive.
2. At the command prompt, type **format a:**.
3. Copy the Ntldr and Ntdetect.com files from the i386 folder of the Windows Server 2003 CD-ROM to the floppy disk.
4. Copy the Boot.ini file from the system drive to the floppy disk.

In a typical scenario for using a boot disk, you try to boot a system and startup fails, telling you that Ntldr or Ntdetect.com is missing or corrupted. The system may also tell you that you have a bad boot device. Although this could happen because the boot sector or the master boot record is corrupted, it can also happen because the Boot.ini file is pointing to the wrong device. In any of these situations, you could boot the system using the boot disk, and then use the files on the boot disk to repair the system, in the following ways:

- If Ntldr or Ntdetect.com were corrupted, you would copy the Ntldr file from the boot floppy disk to the system drive.
- If Boot.ini had bad entries, you could edit the Boot.ini file so that it pointed to the correct boot device.
- If you suspected that the master boot record has been corrupted by a virus, you could run a virus checker on the disk immediately. You should also make sure that the antivirus program has an up-to-date virus definitions file.

Note After you remove a virus, you may need to use the Recovery Console to repair the master boot record. See the section "Installing and Using the Recovery Console," later in this chapter, for details.

Editing Boot.ini

Editing the Boot.ini file is the trickiest part of a boot disk recovery, so let's take a look at a typical Boot.ini file:

```
[boot loader ]
timeout=30
default=multi(0)disk(0)rdisk(0)partition(2)\WINDOWS

[operating systems ]
multi(0)disk(0)rdisk(0)partition(2)\WINDOWS="Microsoft Windows Server 2003" /
fastdetect
```

Boot.ini entries tell Windows Server 2003 where to find the operating system files. When you add partitions to a physical drive that contains the Windows Server 2003 operating system, the number of the boot partition might change. If this happens, Windows will normally update the boot partition information for you. Sometimes, however, this doesn't happen or you may want to start with an alternate boot partition. The part of the Boot.ini entry that tells Windows Server 2003 which boot partition to use is the following entry:

```
multi(0)disk(0)rdisk(0)partition(2)\WINDOWS
```

This entry contains the following information:

- *multi(0)*—Indicates the hard disk controller to use, which in this case is controller 0. In some systems, you may have multiple controllers, and if you want to use a different controller, you need to enter its number. For example, to use controller 1 you would use multi(1).
- *disk(0)*—Indicates the SCSI bus adapter, which in this case is adapter 0. Typically, this is 0 unless the system has multiple SCSI bus adapters.
- *rdisk(0)*—Indicates the ordinal number of the disk on the adapter, which in this case is drive 0. With SCSI drives that use SCSI BIOS, you'll see numbers from 0 to 6. With other SCSI drives, this number is always 0. With Integrated Drive Electronics (IDE), you'll see either 0 or 1.
- *partition(2)*—Indicates the partition that contains the operating system, which in this case is 2.

Boot.ini entries are in the Advanced RISC Computer (ARC) name format. On SCSI systems that don't use SCSI BIOS, the first field in the entry `is scsi(`*n*`)`, where *n* is the controller number, and the second entry is `scsi(`*n*`)`, where *n* is the SCSI bus adapter. If the boot partition for Window Server 2003 changed from 2 to 3, you'd update the Boot.ini file shown earlier as follows (the changes appear in bold):

```
[boot loader ]
timeout=30
default=multi(0)disk(0)rdisk(0)partition(3)\WINDOWS

[operating systems ]
multi(0)disk(0)rdisk(0)partition(3)\WINDOWS="Microsoft Windows Server 2003" /
fastdetect
```

Chapter 40

Setting Startup and Recovery Options

As part of planning for the worst-case scenarios, you need to consider how you want systems to start up and recover in case a stop error is encountered. The options you choose can add to the boot time or they can mean that if a system encounters a stop error it does not reboot.

You can configure startup and recovery options by completing the following steps:

1. Access Control Panel, and then start the System utility. On the Advanced tab, click Settings in the Startup And Recovery panel. This displays the dialog box shown in Figure 40-1.

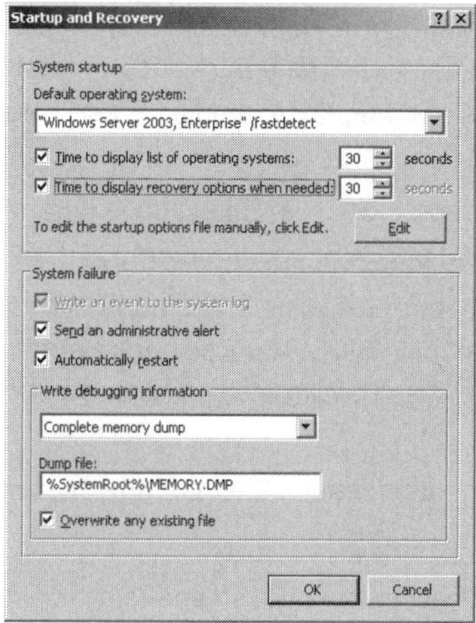

Figure 40-1. Configuring startup and recovery options.

2. In the Startup And Recovery dialog box, you configure the settings as follows:
   - If a server has multiple operating systems, you can set the default operating system by selecting one of the operating systems in the Default Operating System list. These options are obtained from the operating system section of the system's Boot.ini file.
   - When multiple operating systems are installed, the Time To Display List Of Operating Systems option controls how long the system waits before booting to the default operating system. In most cases, you won't need more than a few seconds to make a choice, so reduce this wait time to perhaps 5 or 10 seconds. Alternatively, you can have the system automatically choose the default operating system by clearing this option.
   - When you install the Recovery Console, the operating system uses the Time To Display Recovery Options When Needed setting to determine how long to wait for you to choose a recovery option. The default wait time is 30 seconds. If you

don't choose a recovery option in that time, the system boots normally without recovery. As with operating systems, you won't need more than a few seconds to make a choice, so reduce this wait time to perhaps 5 or 10 seconds.

- Under System Failure, you have several important options for determining what happens when a system experiences a stop error. By default, the Write An Event To The System Log option is selected so that the system logs an error in the system log. The option is dimmed, so it cannot normally be changed. The Send An Administrative Alert option sends an alert over the network to administrators. The Automatically Restart option is selected to ensure that the system attempts to reboot when a stop error occurs.

> **Note** In some cases, you may want the system to halt rather than reboot. For example, if you are having problems with a server, you may want it to halt so that an administrator will be more likely to notice that it is experiencing problems. Don't, however, prevent automatic reboot without a specific reason.

- The Write Debugging Information options allow you to choose the type of debugging information that should be created when a stop error occurs. In most cases, you will want debug information to be dumped, so that you can use it to determine the cause of a crash.

> **Note** If you choose a complete memory dump, you dump all physical memory being used at the time of the failure. You can create the dump file only if the system is properly configured. The system drive must have a paging file at least as large as RAM and adequate disk space to write the dump file.

- By default, dump files are written to the %SystemRoot% folder. If you want to write the dump file to a different location, type the file path in the Dump File box. Select the Overwrite Any Existing File option to ensure that only one dump file is maintained.

3. Click OK twice to close all open dialog boxes.

Installing and Using the Recovery Console

The Recovery Console was introduced with Windows 2000. Using the Recovery Console, you can boot a system to display a recovery command prompt and resolve many common startup problems by using commands that are built into the console. You can perform the following recovery tasks:

- Fixing the boot sector and the master boot record
- Enabling and disabling device drivers

- Enabling and disabling system services
- Changing the attributes of files on file allocation table (FAT)
- Copying files from floppy or CD-ROM to hard drives
- Running Check Disk to correct disk errors

The recovery command prompt is a *secure command prompt* from which you have access to any drives that are formatted with FAT, FAT32, or the NTFS file system (NTFS). However, unlike a standard command prompt, the recovery command prompt only gives you access to the root folder of drives, the %SystemRoot% folder and its subfolders, and removable media drives. In addition, although you can copy files from a floppy disk to a hard disk or from one hard disk to another, you cannot copy files from a hard disk to a floppy disk. The security restrictions are enforced through Group Policy.

Speaking of security, the Recovery Console is referred to as a secure command prompt because you must log in to access it. On systems that are not domain controllers, you use the local system administrator password. For domain controllers, the required password is the directory services restore password.

Inside Out

Use Group Policy to configure Recovery Console security

Several policies in Group Policy control the way security in the Recovery Console works. The first policy is Recovery Console: Allow Automatic Administrative Logon, which, if enabled, allows automatic logon to the Recovery Console, meaning that you do not need to know the system administrator password. The second is Recovery Console: Allow Floppy Copy And Access To All Drives And All Folders, which, if enabled, removes the copy and folder access restrictions, meaning that you will be able to copy files to floppy disks and access any folder on any drive. You'll find these policies in the Computer Configuration\Windows Settings\Security Settings\Local Policies\Security Options folder. Typically, you will want to set these options for specific machines, using either Local Security Policy or Domain Controller Security Policy rather than site, domain, or organizational unit policy.

You have two options for using the Recovery Console. You can preinstall it on systems or you can run it from the Windows Server 2003 CD-ROM. When you preinstall the Recovery Console, it becomes a startup option that you can use. You must use an account that is a member of the Administrators group to install the Recovery Console.

To install the Recovery Console as a startup option, complete the following steps:

1. With the Windows Server 2003 CD in the CD-ROM drive, click the Start menu, and then click Run. This displays the Run dialog box.

2. Type **d:\i386\winnt32.exe /cmdcons** in the Open box, where *d* is the CD-ROM drive.
3. Click OK. You are prompted as shown in Figure 40-2. Click Yes to continue.

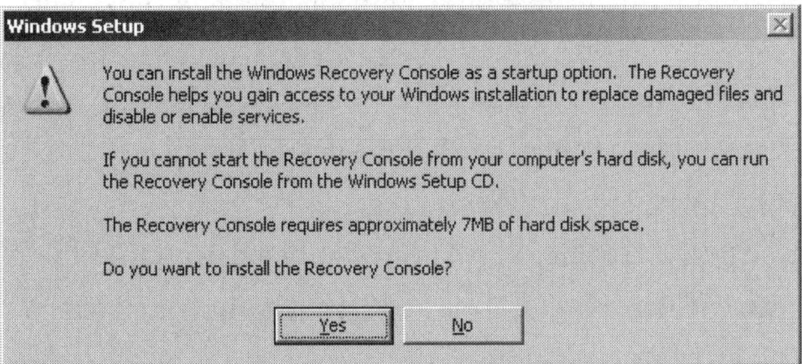

Figure 40-2. Installing the Recovery console.

4. Setup will then copy some files from the installation CD. The Recovery Console is then installed as a startup option.

If a computer won't start and you haven't installed the Recovery Console as a startup option, you can start the computer and access the Recovery Console by completing the following steps:

1. Boot from the Windows Server 2003 CD or Setup disk. Press F10 while Windows Setup is loading (before it displays menu options) or press R after Setup gives you the startup options.
2. Press C to access the Recovery Console. When prompted, type the required password. If the system is not a domain controller, this is the local system administrator password. For domain controllers, this is the directory services restore password.
3. When the system starts, you'll see a command prompt at which you can type Recovery Console commands. To exit the console and restart the computer when you are finished, type **exit**.

The Recovery Console is run in a special command prompt. At this prompt, you can use any of the following commands:

- ATTRIB Changes the attributes of a file or folder.
- BATCH Executes a series of commands set in a text file and sends the output to the command prompt or another text file.
- BOOTCFG Allows you to restore the default Boot.ini file, rebuild the boot list, and perform other operations to modify the Boot.ini file.
- CD Changes the current directory. Note that in the Recovery Console this command behaves a bit differently from what you may be used to, so if a directory path contains a space, enclose the path in quotation marks.
- CHKDSK Runs the Check Disk utility, which allows you to check for and repair disk errors. You can also mark bad sectors on disks.

- **CLS** Clears the screen.
- **COPY** Copies a single file to another location.
- **DEL** Deletes a file. Note that this command doesn't accept wildcard characters, so you can't use the asterisk (*).
- **DIR** Displays a directory listing.
- **DISABLE** Disables a system service or a device driver.
- **DISKPART** Manages partitions on hard disk drives.
- **ENABLE** Starts or enables a system service or a device driver.
- **EXIT** Exits the Recovery Console and restarts your computer.
- **EXPAND** Expands a compressed file.
- **FIXBOOT** Writes a new partition boot sector to the boot partition. This can be used to fix a corrupt boot sector.
- **FIXMBR** Repairs the Master Boot Record (MBR) on the boot partition. This can be used to fix a damaged MBR that is preventing Windows Server 2003 from starting.

> **Caution** Don't use the FIXMBR command if you suspect that the MBR is infected with a virus. Instead, you should boot the system and check for viruses. Make sure the antivirus program has an up-to-date virus definitions file. If the MBR is corrupted as a result of the virus infection, you should be able to start the system using a boot disk, as discussed in the section entitled "Creating and Using Boot Disks" earlier in this chapter.

- **FORMAT** Formats a disk.
- **HELP** Displays a list of Recovery Console commands.
- **LISTSVC** Lists the services and drivers available on the computer as well as their startup types. The information listed comes from the %SystemRoot%\System32\Config\System hive file. If this file has been corrupted, the service information will not be available.
- **LOGON** Lists all detected installations of Windows and allows you to log on with the local service administrator password. If you log on incorrectly three times, the Recovery Console will exit and the computer will restart.
- **MAP** Lists the drive letters and their mappings to physical devices as well as the associated file system types and partition sizes.
- **MD** Creates a directory.
- **MORE** Displays the contents of a text file one page at a time.

- **RD** Removes an empty directory. Note that the command doesn't accept wildcard characters, so you can't use the asterisk (*), and the command will fail if the directory has contents.
- **REN** Renames a single file in the current folder. You cannot specify a new file path or drive path.
- **SET** Allows you to display and set the following Recovery Console environment variables:
  - AllowWildCards—Makes it possible to use wildcard characters in the Recovery Console—in which case the caveats described above with some of these commands (such as RD) don't apply any longer.
  - AllowAllPaths—Makes it possible to access all folders
  - AllowRemovableMedia—Makes it possible to copy files to removable media devices
  - NoCopyPrompt—Makes it possible to overwrite files while copying without prompting for confirmation

> **Note** Group Policy also controls whether you can use the SET command. To allow the use of the SET command, you need to configure and enable the Enable The Set Command For The Recovery Console policy in the Configuration\Windows Settings\Security Settings\Security Options folder. Typically, you want to set these options for specific machines, using either Local Security Policy or Domain Controller Security Policy rather than site, domain, or organizational unit policy.

- **SYSTEMROOT** Changes to the %SystemRoot% directory.
- **TYPE** Displays the entire contents of a text file.

Once you've made any necessary changes or repairs, you use the EXIT command to quit the console and restart the computer.

Chapter 41

Backup and Recovery

In this chapter, I look at backup and recovery. Every Microsoft Windows Server 2003 system on your network represents a major investment in time, resources, and money. It requires a great deal of planning and effort to deploy a new server successfully. It requires just as much planning and effort—if not more—to ensure that you can restore a server when disaster strikes. Why? Because you not only need to plan and implement backup for each and every server on your network, you also need to perform backups regularly and test the backup process and procedures to ensure that when disaster strikes you are prepared.

Developing Backup Strategies

Backups are insurance plans plain and simple—and every administrator should see them that way. When disaster strikes, your backup implementation will either leave you out of harm's way or drowning without a life preserver. Trust me: you don't want to be drowning when it should be your moment to shine. After all, if you've implemented a well-thought-out backup plan and practiced the necessary recovery procedures until they are second nature, a server that has stopped working is nothing more than a bump in the road that you can smooth out even if you have to rebuild a server from scratch to do it.

Creating Your Backup Strategy

So where to start? Start by outlining a backup and recovery plan that describes the servers and the data that need to be backed up. Ask yourself the following questions:

- How important is the role that the server is performing?
- How important is the data stored on the server?
- How often does the data change?
- How much data in total is there to back up?

- How long does each backup take?
- How quickly do you need to recover the data?
- How much historical data do you need to store?
- Do you have the equipment needed to perform backups?
- Do you need to store backups off site?
- Who will be responsible for performing backups?

The answers to these questions will help you develop your backup and recovery plan. Often you'll find that your current resources aren't enough and that you'll need to obtain additional backup equipment. It may be one of the ultimate ironies in administration, but you'll often need more justification for backup equipment than for any other type of equipment. Fight to get the backup resources you need and do so without reservation. If you have to make incremental purchases over a period of several months to get the backup equipment and supplies, do so without hesitation.

Backup Strategy Considerations

In most cases, your backup strategy should involve performing some type of backup of every server daily and full backups of these servers at least once a week. You should also regularly inspect the backup log files and periodically perform test restores of the data to ensure that data is being properly written to the backup media.

Tip **It's all about the data**
Much of your backup strategy depends on the importance of the data, the frequency of change, and the total amount of data to back up. Data that is of higher importance or frequently changed needs to be backed up more often than other types of data. As the amount of data you are backing up increases, you will need to be able to scale your backup implementation. If you are starting out with a large amount of data, you will need to consider how much time a complete backup of the data set will take. To ensure that backups can be performed in a timely manner, you might have to purchase faster equipment or purchase backup devices with multiple tape drives.

Plan separate backup strategies for system files and data files.

- *System files* are used by the operating system and applications. These files only change when you install new components, service packs, or patches. They include system state data.

Note For systems that aren't domain controllers, the system state data includes essential boot files, key system files, and the COM+ class registration database as well as the Registry data. For domain controllers, the Active Directory database and System Volume (Sysvol) files are included as well.

- *Data files* are created by applications and users. Application files contain configuration settings and data. User files contain the daily work of users and can include documents, spreadsheets, media files, and so on. These files change every day.

Administrators often back up an entire machine and dump all the data into a single backup. There are several problems with this strategy. First, system files don't change that often but data files change frequently. Second, you'll typically need to recover data files more frequently than system files. You recover data files when documents are corrupted, lost, or accidentally deleted. You recover system files when you have serious problems with a system and typically are trying to restore the whole machine.

Look at the timing of backups as well. With Microsoft Windows 2000 and earlier versions of the Microsoft Windows operating systems, you are often concerned about the time that backups are performed. You want backups to be performed when the systems usage is low, so that more resources are available and few files are locked and in use. With the advances in backup technology made possible by the Shadow Copy API built into Windows Server 2003, the backup time is less of a concern than it was previously. Any backup programs that implement the Shadow Copy API allow you to back up files that are open or locked. This means that you can perform backups when applications are using files and no longer have to worry about backups failing because files are being used.

Selecting the Optimal Backup Techniques

When it comes to backup, there is no such thing as a one-size-fits-all solution. Often you'll implement one backup strategy for one system and a different backup strategy for a different system. It will all come down to the importance of the data, the frequency of change, and how much data there is to back up on each server. But don't overlook the importance of recovery speed. Different backup strategies take longer to recover than others and there may be differing urgencies involved in getting a system or service back online. Because of this, I recommend a multipronged backup strategy that is optimized on a per-server basis.

Key services running on a system have backup functions that are unique. Implement and use those backup mechanisms as your first line of defense against failure. Remember that a backup of the System State includes a full backup of a server's Registry, and that system configuration includes the configuration of all services running on a system. However, if a specific service fails, it is much easier and faster to recover that specific service than to try to recover the whole server. You'll have fewer problems, and it is less likely that something will go wrong.

Specific backup and recovery techniques for key services are as follows:

- With Dynamic Host Configuration Protocol (DHCP), you should periodically back up the DHCP configuration and the DHCP database as discussed in the sections entitled "Saving and Restoring the DHCP Configuration," on page 845, and "Managing and Maintaining the DHCP Database," on page 845, respectively.

- With the Windows Internet Name Service (WINS), you should periodically back up the WINS database as discussed in the section entitled "Maintaining the WINS Database,"on page 941.
- With Domain Name System (DNS), your backup strategy will depend on whether you are using Active Directory-integrated zones, standard zones, or both. When you are using Active Directory-integrated zones, DNS configuration data is stored in Active Directory. By default, when you are using standard zones, DNS configuration data is stored in the %SystemRoot%\System32\DNS folder and backups of zone data are stored in the %SystemRoot%\System32\DNS\backup folder.
- With Group Policy, you should periodically back up the Group Policy Object (GPO) configuration as discussed in the section entitled "Maintaining and Troubleshooting Group Policy," on page 1131.
- With printer servers, you should periodically back up the printer configuration as discussed in the section entitled "Preparing for Print Server Failure," on page 1011.
- With file servers, you should implement Volume Shadow Copy (VSS), as discussed in Chapter 22, "Using Volume Shadow Copy," for all network file shares. This makes it easier to restore previous versions of files. In addition, you should back up all user data files on the file server regularly.

The disaster preparation techniques discussed in the section entitled "Predisaster Preparation Procedures," on page 1353, are your next line of defense. Every system should have periodic Automated System Recovery (ASR) backups as well as a boot disk. This way you can recover a system to a bootable state and fix startup issues without having to rebuild a system from scratch.

Finally, you will also need to perform regular backups of both system and user data. Most backup programs, including Windows Backup, which is included in Windows Server 2003, support several types of backup jobs. The type of backup job determines how much data is backed up and what the backup program does when it performs a backup.

Inside Out

How backup programs use the archive bit

Most backup operations make use of the archive attribute that can be set on files. The archive attribute, a bit included in the directory entry of each file, can be turned on or off. In most cases, a backup program will turn off (clear) the archive attribute when it backs up a file. The archive bit is turned on (set) again when a user or the operating system later modifies a file. When the backup program runs again, it knows that only files with archive attributes that are set need to be backed up—because these are the only files that have changed.

Understanding Backup Types

The basic types of backups include the following:

- **Normal** A normal backup is a full backup of all the files and folders you select, regardless of the archive attribute's setting. When a file is backed up, the archive attribute is turned off.
- **Copy** A copy backup is a full backup of all files and folders you select, regardless of the archive attribute's setting. Unlike a normal backup, the archive attribute on files isn't turned off by the backup. This means that you can use a copy backup to create an additional or supplemental backup of a system without interfering with the existing backup strategy.
- **Incremental** An incremental backup is used to create a backup of all files that have changed since the last normal or incremental backup. As such, an incremental backup is a partial backup. The backup program uses the archive attribute to determine which files should be backed up and turns off the archive attribute after backing up a file. This means that each incremental backup contains only the most recent changes.
- **Differential** A differential backup is used to create a backup of all files that have changed since the last normal backup. Like an incremental backup, in a differential backup the backup program uses the archive attribute to determine which files should be backed up. However, the backup program does not change the archive attribute. This means that each differential backup contains all changes.
- **Daily** A daily backup uses the modification date on a file rather than the archive attribute. If a file has been changed on the day the backup is performed, the file will be backed up. This technique doesn't change the archive attributes of files and is useful when you want to perform an extra backup without interfering with the existing backup strategy.

As part of your backup strategy, you'll probably want to perform normal backups on a weekly basis and supplement this with daily, differential, or incremental backups. The advantage of normal backups is that they are a complete record of the files you select. The disadvantage of normal backups is that they take longer to make and use more storage space than other types of backups. Incremental and differential backups, on the other hand, use less space and are faster because they are partial backups. The disadvantage is that recovery of systems and files using incremental and differential backups is slower than when you only have to perform a normal backup. To see why, consider the following backup and recovery examples:

- **Normal backup with daily incremental backups** You perform a normal backup every Sunday and incremental backups Monday through Saturday. Monday's incremental backup contains changes since Sunday. Tuesday's incremental backup contains changes since Monday, and so on. If a server malfunctions on Thursday and you need to restore the server from backup, you would do this by restoring the normal backup from Sunday, the incremental backup from Monday, the incremental backup from Tuesday, and the incremental backup from Wednesday—in that order.

- **Normal backup with daily differential backups** You perform a normal backup every Sunday and differential backups Monday through Saturday. Monday's differential backup contains changes since Sunday as does Tuesday's differential backup, Wednesday's differential backup, and so on. If a server malfunctions on Thursday and you need to restore the server from backup, you would do this by restoring the normal backup from Sunday and then the differential backup from Wednesday.

Using Media Rotation and Maintaining Additional Media Sets

As part of your backup strategy, you might also want to use copy backups to create extended backup sets for monthly and quarterly use. You may also want to use a media rotation scheme to ensure that you always have a current copy of your data as well as several previous data sets. The point of a media rotation scheme is to reuse tapes in a consistent and organized manner. If you use a media rotation scheme, monthly and quarterly media sets can simply be media sets that you are rotating to offsite storage. Consider the following media rotation scenarios:

- **Media rotation with three weekly media sets and one monthly media set** In a 24/7 environment, you use a total of 14 tapes as a media set. Seven of those tapes contain your normal weekly backups for a set of servers. The other seven tapes contain your daily incremental backups for that set of servers—one tape for each day of the week. Three weekly media sets are maintained on site. Once a month, you rotate the previous week's media set to offsite storage.
- **Media rotation with three weekly media sets, one monthly media set, and one quarterly media set** In a 9 to 5 environment, you use a total of 14 tapes as a media set. Nine of those tapes contain your normal weekly backups for a set of servers. The other five tapes contain your daily incremental backups for that set of servers—one tape for each workday. Three weekly media sets are maintained on site. Once a month, you rotate the previous week's media set to offsite storage. Once a quarter, you rotate the previous week's media set to offsite storage.

Backing Up and Recovering Your Data

Windows Server 2003 includes a backup utility called Backup that was developed by Veritas Software Corporation. Backup is a versatile utility designed to perform backups of individual systems. You use Backup to perform the following tasks:

- Create backup archives of files and folders
- Create backups of the System State
- Create Automated System Recovery backups

- Access media pools reserved for Backup
- Restore archived files and folders
- Restore the System State

You can also use Backup to schedule recurring backups. Scheduling backups gives you the ability to create a backup job once and then run it repeatedly. For example, you could configure a backup job to run daily, weekly, monthly, or on an ad hoc basis. The only disadvantage of scheduled backups compared to manual backups is that you'll need to remember to change the media as necessary, so that backups are written to the proper media as per your rotation scheme.

Using the Backup Utility

To perform backup and recovery operations, you must use an account that is a member of the Administrators or Backup Operators group. Only members of these groups have authority to back up and restore files regardless of ownership and permissions. File owners and those who have been given control over files can also back up files, but only the files that they own or the files that they have permission to access.

You can start Backup by clicking Start, Programs, or All Programs, Accessories, System Tools, and then clicking Backup, or by typing **ntbackup** at the command prompt. The first time you use the Backup utility, it starts in basic, or wizard, mode, as shown in Figure 41-1.

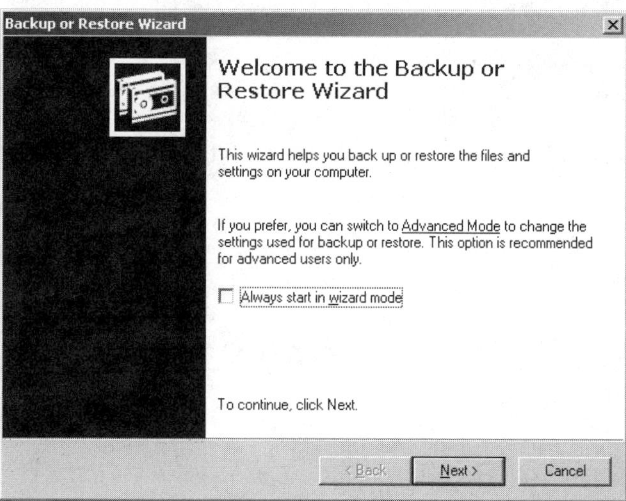

Figure 41-1. The Backup utility in basic mode.

Chapter 41

As an administrator, you'll want to use the Backup utility in advanced mode. The advanced mode gives you many additional options. With this in mind, clear Always Start In Wizard Mode, and then click the Advanced Mode link. You should now see the main Backup Utility interface.

As shown in Figure 41-2, the advanced mode interface provides the following four tabs:

- **Welcome** Provides a quick link to return to basic mode and options for starting the Backup Wizard in advanced mode, the Restore Wizard in advanced mode, and the Automated System Recovery Wizard.
- **Backup** Provides the main interface for configuring backups manually. With manually configured backups, you can create a selection script to save the files and folders you've selected for backup. You can then use the selection script to create an identical backup job during subsequent backup sessions.
- **Restore and Manage Media** Provides the main interface for manually configured restoration of archived files and folders. You can restore data to the original location, to an alternative location anywhere on the network, or to a single folder.
- **Schedule Jobs** Provides the main interface for scheduling backup jobs. You can view previously executed jobs as well as jobs scheduled for upcoming dates.

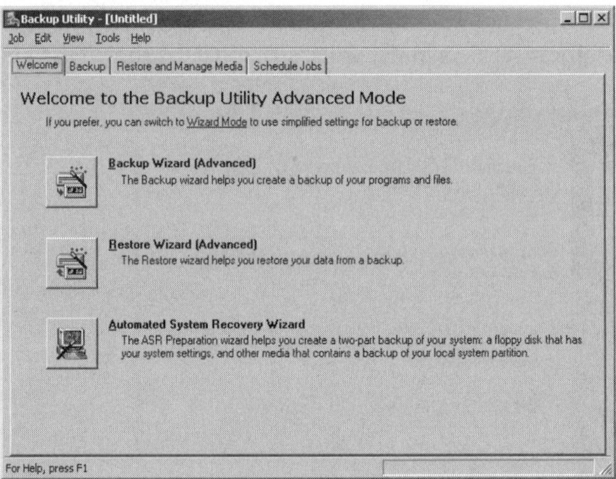

Figure 41-2. The Backup utility in advanced mode.

Setting Default Options for Backup

You create backups using the Backup utility's tabs or wizards. Both techniques use default options set for the Backup utility. You can view or change the default options only in advanced mode. Click Tools, and then select Options. The five categories of default options are as follows: General, Restore, Backup Type, Backup Log, and Exclude Files. Each of these categories is examined in the sections that follow.

General Backup and Restore Options

The configuration settings on the General tab in the Options dialog box help you control the way backup and restore operations are performed in general. Table 41-1 summarizes the available options.

Table 41-1. General Options for the Backup Utility

Option	Description	Default Setting
Compute Selection Information Before Backup And Restore Operations	Sets Backup so that before the backup or restore procedure, it calculates the number of files and bytes involved and displays this information. Otherwise, this data does not appear and the progress bar will not function.	Enabled
Use The Catalogs On The Media To Speed Up Building Restore Catalogs On Disk	Sets Backup to use archive logs on the media instead of scanning the entire archive to determine what files are included. Clear this option *only* when the catalog is missing, damaged, or otherwise unavailable.	Enabled
Verify Data After The Backup Completes	Sets Backup so that it checks the archive data against the original data to ensure that the data is the same. If the data isn't the same, there might be a problem with the backup media, and you should run the backup again using different media.	Disabled
Back Up The Contents Of Mounted Drives	Sets Backup so that you can back up data on mounted network drives. Otherwise, only the path information for mounted drives will be backed up.	Enabled
Show Alert Message When I Start The Backup Utility And Removable Storage Is Not Running	Displays an alert if you start Backup and the Removable Storage service isn't running. It's a good option to use if you work with removable media.	Enabled
Show Alert Message When I Start The Backup Utility And There Is Recognizable Media Available	Displays an alert if you start Backup and there is new media available in the import media pool. It's useful if you work with removable media.	Enabled

Table 41-1. General Options for the Backup Utility

Option	Description	Default Setting
Show Alert Message When New Media Is Inserted	Displays an alert when Removable Storage detects new media. It's useful if you work with removable media.	Enabled
Always Allow Use Of Recognizable Media Without Prompting	Allows Removable Storage to move new media to the backup pool automatically. Select this option if you use Removable Storage and you want new media to be available to Backup.	Disabled

Setting Restore, Backup Type, and Backup Log Options

In addition to setting general options, you can also set specific defaults that control restore, backup type, and backup logging. The related options and tabs are summarized in Table 41-2. The first column shows the tab where the option is available. The second column shows the name of the option.

Table 41-2. Restore, Backup Type, and Backup Log Options

Tab	Option	Description	Default Setting
Restore			
	Do Not Replace The Files On My Computer (Recommended)	Select this option to restore files that have been deleted from the hard disk. This means if the files don't exist on disk, they will be restored.	Selected
	Replace The File On Disk Only If The File On Disk Is Older	Select this option to replace older files on the hard disk with newer files from the backup. If files don't exist on disk, they will be restored as well.	Not selected
	Always Replace The File On My Computer	Select this option to replace all files on the hard disk with files from the backup. This option could cause users to lose changes they've made to files, because whatever is on the archive is fully restored.	Not selected
Backup Type			
	Default Backup Type	Select this option to set the default backup type. Available types are Normal, Copy, Differential, Incremental, and Daily.	Normal

Table 41-2. Restore, Backup Type, and Backup Log Options

Tab	Option	Description	Default Setting
Backup Log			
	Detailed	Select this option to save a detailed recovery log of the backup and restore operations, including the names of all files and folders.	Not selected
	Summary	Select this option to save an abbreviated summary of backup and restore operations.	Selected
	None	Select this option to disable logging for backup and restore operations.	Not selected

Excluding Files from Backup

Even when you are performing a normal backup, there are certain types of files you probably do not want to back up, such as the paging file and other temporary files. For this reason, Backup automatically excludes certain types of files from backup. You can view current exclusions on the Exclude Files tab in the Options dialog box. In Backup, select Options from the Tools menu, and then click the Exclude Files tab as shown in Figure 41-3.

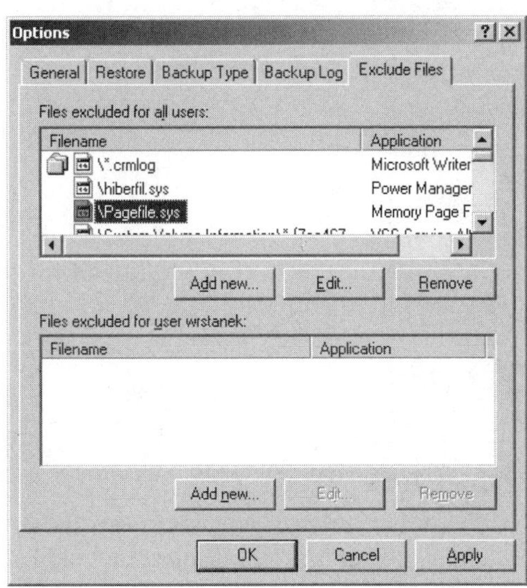

Figure 41-3. Displaying current file exclusions.

The actual exclusions listed will depend on the type of system you are working with and the roles for which the system is configured. The following exclusions are among those that may appear:

- On a laptop or any other computer configured for Power Management, the hibernation system file (Hiberfil.sys) is excluded.
- On a domain controller, many Active Directory files are excluded, in particular those files used by Volume Shadow Copy (VSS), the NT File Replication Service (NTFRS), and the NT Directory Service (NTDS).
- On a DNS server, the DNS logs are excluded.

In most cases, you won't want to remove exclusions unless you have a specific reason for doing so. You can and should, however, add exclusions as necessary. To do so, complete the following steps:

1 In Backup, select Options from the Tools menu, and then click the Exclude Files tab. You can exclude files for all users or files that you specifically own as follows:

  - To exclude files that are owned by any user, click Add New under the Files Excluded For All Users list. This displays the Add Excluded Files dialog box shown in Figure 41-4.

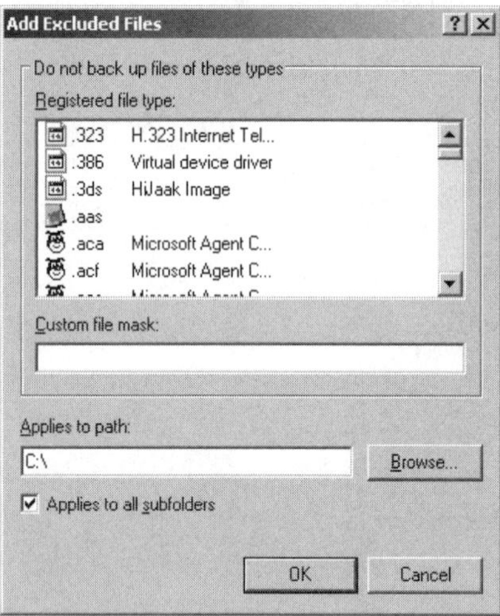

Figure 41-4. Set file exclusions using registered or custom file types.

  - To exclude only files that you or the currently logged-on user owns, click Add New under the Files Excluded For User list. This displays the Add Excluded Files dialog box.

2 You can exclude files by registered file type by clicking a file type in the Registered File Type list. Alternatively, you can exclude files by custom file type by typing a period followed by the file extension in the Custom File Mask box. For example, you could choose .BMP or enter the custom type .BMP-BAK.

Tip **Select multiple registered file types at once**
Use Ctrl+click or Shift+click to select more than one option at a time. When you highlight multiple registered file types this way, you set several exclusions at once.

Note You can't enter multiple custom types in one entry. If you enter more than one custom type—even if you use semicolons or other punctuation—Backup sees this as a single file type. For example, if you were to enter **.bak;.tmp**, Backup would look for files with the extension .bak;.tmp rather than files with the .bak extension and files with the .tmp extension.

3 In the Applies To Path box, enter the backslash (\) as the path to specify matching files on any file system or on a specific drive or file path. Files from all subfolders of that path will then be excluded unless you clear the Applies To All Subfolders check box.

4 Click OK. Repeat this process as necessary to add other exclusions.

Backing Up Your Data

Regardless of whether you want to back up data using the Backup Wizard or the Backup tab, the techniques are similar. In this section, I am going to discuss using the Backup tab options so that you know how to configure backup manually. I will also discuss creating and using the following:

- **Backup selection scripts** Backup selection scripts allow you to save the file and folder selections you've made so that they can be reused.
- **Scheduled jobs** Scheduled jobs allow you to configure recurring backups that run according to a daily, weekly, monthly, or ad hoc schedule.

To configure backups, follow these steps:

1 Start Backup by clicking Start, Programs or All Programs, Accessories, and System Tools, and then clicking Backup, or by typing **ntbackup** at the command prompt. If wizard mode is enabled, click Advanced Mode, and then select the Backup tab as shown in Figure 41-5. Otherwise, just click the Backup tab.

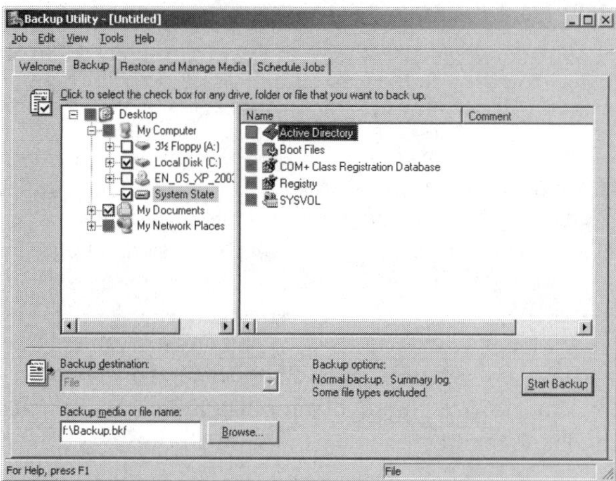

Figure 41-5. Use the Backup tab to configure backups manually without using a wizard.

2 Choose the data you want to back up in one of the following ways:

- Make selections by selecting or clearing the check boxes associated with a particular drive or folder. When you select a drive's check box, all files and folders on the drive are selected. When you clear a drive's check box, all files and folders on the drive are cleared.
- To work with individual files and folders on a drive, click the plus sign (+) to the left of the drive icon. You can now select and clear individual directories and files by clicking their associated check boxes. When you do this, the drive's check box shows a shaded checkmark. This indicates that you haven't selected all the files on the drive.
- To back up system state data, select System State under the My Computer node. For servers that aren't domain controllers, system state data includes essential boot and system files, the Windows Registry, and the COM+ class registration database. For domain controllers, system state data additionally includes Active Directory data and Sysvol files.
- To be able to recover a server running Microsoft Exchange Server, you must back up Exchange Server data. So, if you're backing up a server running Exchange Server, select the Microsoft Exchange icon under the My Computer node. When you do this, you'll be prompted to type the Universal Naming Convention (UNC) name of the Exchange server you want to back up, such as **\\ExchSvr06**. Only systems running Exchange Server have this type of data.

> **Tip** **Archiving Removable Storage and Remote Storage data**
> Removable Storage data is stored in %SystemRoot%\System32\Ntmsdata. If you back up this data, you can use the advanced restore option Restore Removable Storage Database to recover the Removable Storage configuration. Remote Storage data is stored in %SystemRoot%\System32\Remotestorage. If you back up this data, you can restore Remote Storage by copying the data back to this directory.

3 Next use the Backup Destination selection list to choose the media type for the backup. Choose File if you want to back up to a file. Choose a storage device if you want to back up files and folders to a tape or removable disk.

> **Note** When you write a backup to a file, the archive file normally has the .BKF file extension. However, you can use another file extension if you want.
>
> Remember that Removable Storage is used to manage tapes and removable disks. If no media are available, you'll be prompted to allocate media to the backup media pool. Follow the instructions given in the section entitled "Managing Media Pools," on page 761.

4 In Backup Media Or File Name, select the backup file or medium you want to use. If you're backing up to a file, type a path and file name for the backup file, or click Browse to find a file. If you're backing up to a tape or other removable media, choose the tape or medium you want to use.

5 To start the backup process, click Start Backup. This displays the Backup Job Information dialog box shown in Figure 41-6.

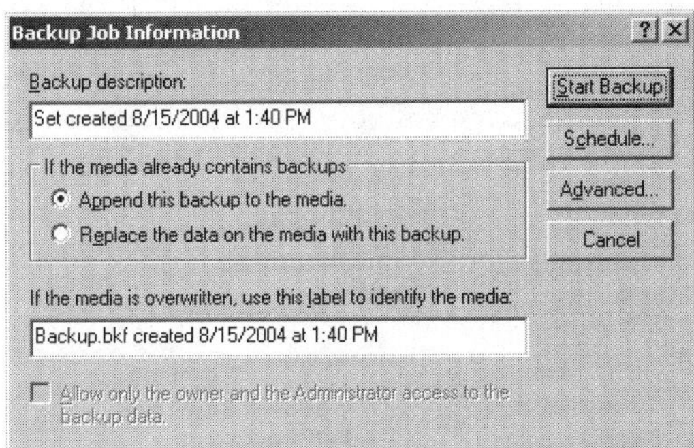

Figure 41-6. Use the Backup Job Information dialog box to configure backup options.

The options in this dialog box are as follows:

- *Backup Description*—Sets the backup label, which applies to the current backup only.
- *Append This Backup To The Media*—Adds the backup after existing data.
- *Replace The Data On The Media With This Backup*—Overwrites existing data.
- *If The Media Is Overwritten, Use This Label To Identify The Media*—Sets the media label, which is changed only when you're writing to a blank tape or overwriting existing data.
- *Allow Only The Owner And The Administrator Access To The Backup Data*—If you're overwriting data, you can specify that only the owner and an administrator can access the archive file by selecting this option.

6 Click Advanced if you want to override the default backup options. The following advanced options are available:

- *Back Up Data That Is In Remote Storage*—Archives placeholder files for Remote Storage with the backup. This ensures that you can recover an entire file system with necessary Remote Storage references intact.
- *Verify Data After Backup*—Instructs Backup to verify data after the backup procedure is completed. If selected, every file on the backup tape is compared to the original file. Verifying data can protect against write errors or failures.
- *If Possible, Compress Backup Data To Save Space*—Allows Backup to compress data as it's written to the storage device. This option is available only if the device supports hardware compression, and only compatible drives can read the compressed information, which might mean that only a drive from the same manufacturer can recover the data.
- *Automatically Back Up System Protected Files With The System State*—Backs up all the system files in the %SystemRoot% folder, in addition to the boot files that are included with the system state data.
- *Disable Volume Shadow Copy*—Tells the Backup Utility not to perform volume shadow copies. Volume shadow copies are used to back up files that are being written to. Thus, by disabling this feature, the Backup Utility will skip files that are locked for writing.
- *Backup Type*—Indicates the type of backup to perform. The available types are Normal, Copy, Differential, Incremental, and Daily.

7 If you want to create a backup selection script, set a backup schedule, or both, click Schedule and complete steps 8 to 14. Otherwise, skip to step 15.

8 When prompted to save the backup settings, as shown in the following screen, click Yes. In the Save As dialog box, type a name for the backup selection script, and then click Save.

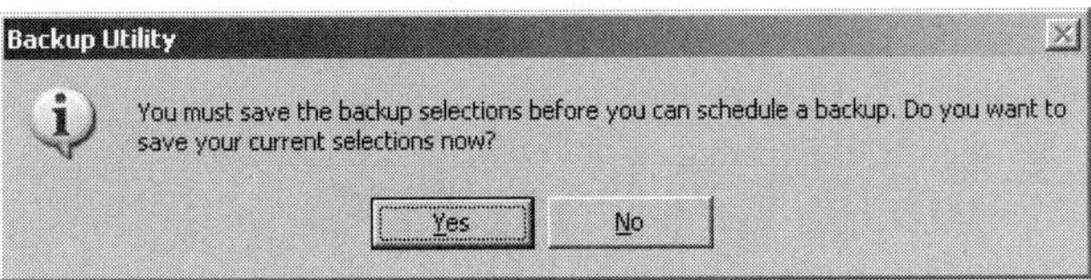

Note By default, Backup selection scripts are stored in %UserProfile%\Local Settings\Application Data\Microsoft\WindowsNT\NTBackup\Data with the .BKS extension. The account under which a scheduled backup runs must have access to this folder. If you are concerned about access permissions, change the save location as appropriate before clicking Save.

9 Next, as shown in the following screen, you are prompted to set the user name and password under which the backup selection script should run. Type the account name in *DOMAIN\UserName* format, for example, CPANDL\Wrstanek. Afterward, type and confirm the password for this account, and then click OK. When the Account Information Warning prompt appears, click OK again. It is hoped that you have already ensured that the backup selection script is in a location accessible to the account designated in this step.

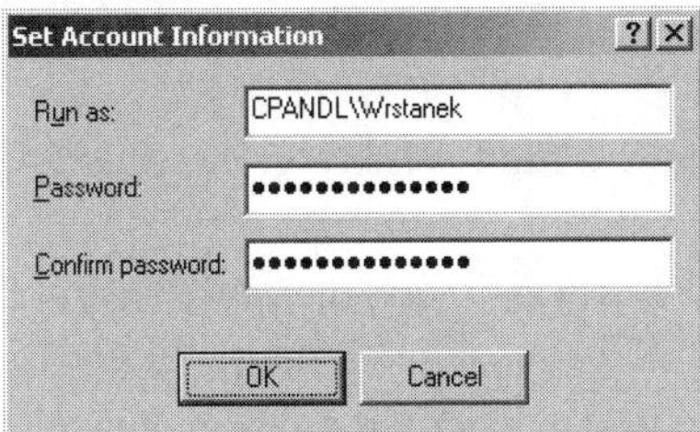

10 In the Scheduled Job Options dialog box, type a job name, and then click Properties.

11 In the Schedule Jobs dialog box, shown in the following screen, use the Schedule tab options to set a run schedule.

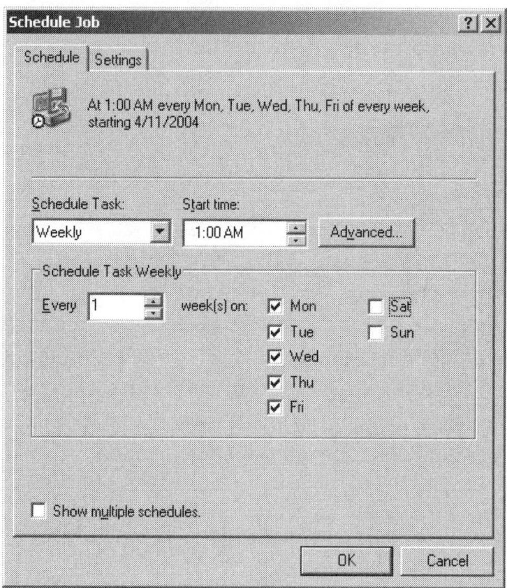

Daily scheduled backups can be configured to run

- *Every Day*—Seven days a week.
- *Weekdays*—Monday through Friday only.
- *Every … Days*—Every 2, 3, or *n* days.

Weekly scheduled backups can be configured to run using the following options:

- *Start Time*—Sets the start time of the task.
- *Every … Weeks*—Allows you to run the task every week, every two weeks, or every *n* weeks.
- *Select The Day(s) Of The Week Below*—Sets the day or days of the week when the task runs, for example, on Monday or on Monday and Friday.

Monthly scheduled backups can be configured to run using the following options:

- *Start Time*—Sets the start time of the task.
- *Day*—Sets the day of the month the task runs. For example, if you select 5, the task runs on the fifth day of the month.
- *The … Day*—Sets task to run on the *n*th occurrence of a day in a month, such as the second Monday or the third Tuesday of every month.
- *Of The Month(s)*—These check boxes let you select which months the task runs.

12 In the Schedule Jobs dialog box, use the Settings tab options, shown in the following screen, to set additional options.

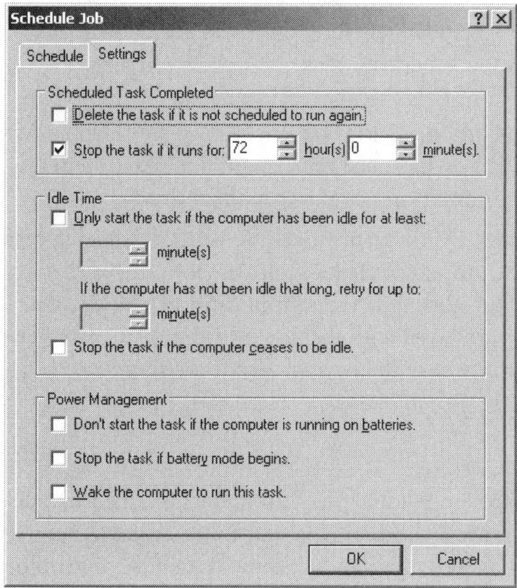

The additional options are as follows:

- *Scheduled Task Completed*—Use these options to delete the backup task automatically if it is not scheduled to run again and to stop the backup task if it runs for more than a set amount of time. In most cases, you won't want a backup to run for more than 24 hours. If a backup runs more than 24 hours, you may have a problem with your configuration that should be investigated. For example, you may need to obtain additional backup hardware or an additional drive for current backup hardware.
- *Idle Time*—With backups, you'll rarely use the Idle Time options, because you typically don't want to stop and start backups. With this in mind, you probably don't want to set Idle Time options.
- *Power Management*—Use these options to determine how power management affects backups. If you are using an uninterruptible power supply (UPS) and you've configured the computer to detect when it is running on battery, you can use the Don't Start… and Stop The Task… options to control the backup in the event of a power outage. If you've configured backups on a laptop, the computer can detect when it is running on battery power.

13 When you are finished scheduling the backup, click OK to close the Schedule Job dialog box. Next you are prompted to set the user name and password under which the scheduled backup task should run. Type the account name in *DOMAIN\UserName* format, such as **CPANDL\Wrstanek**. Afterward, type and confirm the password for this account, and then click OK.

Note In step 9, you entered credentials for the backup selection script. In this step, you are entering credentials for the scheduled task.

14 In the Scheduled Job Options dialog box, click OK again. The backup is now set to run as a scheduled task. You do not need to perform the final step in this scenario because the backup will run automatically at the scheduled time(s).

15 To start a backup manually, click Start Backup. When the backup has completed, click Close to complete the process or click Report to view the backup log. Backup logs are stored in %UserProfile%\Local Settings\Application Data\Microsoft\WindowsNT\NTBackup\Data and are saved with the .log extension. You can view log files from within the Backup utility or with any standard text editor.

Recovering Your Data

Using Backup, you can restore individual files and folders or an entire backup archive to its original location, an alternative location, or a single folder. For example, if Mary loses a spreadsheet and there isn't an available shadow copy of the file, you could recover the individual file from the backup archive. If John accidentally deletes an important folder, you can recover the folder and all its contents from a backup archive. If a system crashes and you are restoring it, you could recover all system and data files for the system as well.

You restore files using the Restore Wizard or the options of the Restore And Manage Media tab. With either option, you'll see a list of the backup files you created, unless you are recovering a system or restoring data to a different system. If the list is available, Backup can access details about the backup files and should have access to the catalog of the backup set that was created with the backup file.

Tip **Create a new catalog**
If Backup cannot find a catalog, you can force the program to create a new one by selecting Catalog A Backup File from the Tools menu. Backup then catalogs the file by reading the contents of the archive and creating the catalog. As this process can take nearly as long as it took to create the archive in the first place, only select this option if the original catalog is missing or damaged.

Backup accesses the catalog whenever you select backup media from the list for restoration. If a backup archive spans two or more tapes, the catalog is stored on the last tape of the set. In this case, when you insert the proper tape into the tape drive, Backup reads the catalog and shows the contents of the tape, using the same file and folder structure that Windows uses for normal storage of file and folders on disk drives. You can select drives, folders, and files to restore just as you selected them for backup.

To recover data using the Backup utility, follow these steps:

1. Start Backup by clicking Start, Programs, or All Programs, Accessories, System Tools, and then clicking Backup, or by typing **ntbackup** at the command prompt. If wizard mode is enabled, click the Advanced Mode button, and then select the Restore And Manage Media tab as shown in Figure 41-7. Otherwise, just click the Restore And Manage Media tab.

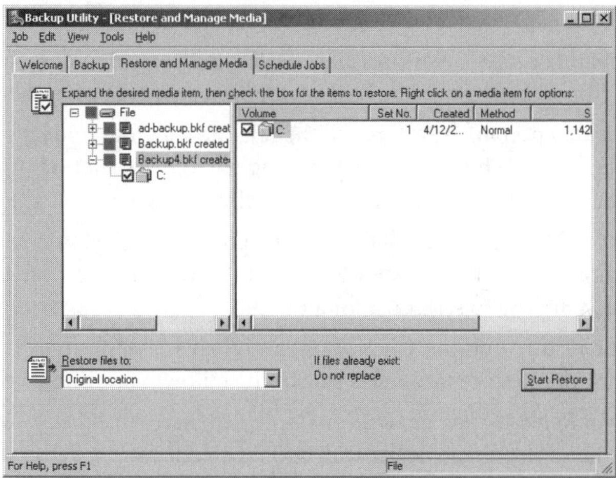

Figure 41-7. Use the Restore And Manage Media tab to recover data manually.

2. Select the check box next to any drive, folder, or file that you want to restore. If the media set you want to work with isn't shown, right-click File in the left view, select Catalog, and then type the name and path of the catalog you want to use. Keep the following in mind:

   - For system state data, select the check box for System State as well as for the other data you want to restore. If you're restoring to the original location, the current System State will be replaced by the system state data you're restoring. You can only restore system state data on a local system. If you restore to an alternate location, only the Registry, Sysvol, and system boot files are restored. You can't restore the Active Directory database, Certificate Services database, or the COM+ database to an alternative location.
   - For domain controllers, Active Directory and other replicated data, such as Sysvol, aren't restored. Instead, this information is replicated to the domain controller you are restoring after you restart it. This prevents accidental overwriting of essential domain information. To learn how to restore Active Directory, see the section entitled "Backing Up and Restoring Active Directory," later in this chapter.

- For Exchange Server, select the Exchange Server data to restore. Before the restore starts, you'll see the Restoring Microsoft Exchange dialog box. If you're restoring the Information Store, type the UNC name of the Exchange server you want to restore, such as **ExchSvr06**. If you're restoring to a different server, select Erase All Existing Data. This destroys all existing data and creates a new Information Store.

3 Use the Restore Files To list to choose the restore location. The following options are available:

- *Original Location*—Restores all the selected files and folders to the original location from which they were backed up, preserving the original folder structure.
- *Alternate Location*—Restores all the selected files and folders to a location that you designate while preserving the original folder structure. After you select this option, enter the folder path to use or click Browse to select the folder path.
- *Single Folder*—Restores all the selected files to a single folder without preserving the directory structure. After you select this option, enter the folder path to use or click Browse to select the folder path.

4 Next, set the restore options. Click Tools, and then select Options. In the Options dialog box, click the Restore tab. Select one of the following options, and then click OK:

- *Do Not Replace The Files On My Computer (Recommended)*—Restores only the files that don't already exist at the designated location. Select this option if you are restoring files that have been deleted and don't want to accidentally copy over other existing files.
- *Replace The File On Disk Only If The File On Disk Is Older*—Performs a comparison of the last modification date of identically named files, and overwrites files at the designated location only if the archived file is newer. Select this option to replace older files on the hard disk with newer files from the backup.
- *Always Replace The File On My Computer*—Restores all the selected files to the designated location, overwriting any existing files with identical names. Select this option to replace all files on the hard disk with files from the backup.

5 When you click Start Restore, the Confirm Restore dialog box appears. If you want to set advanced restore options, click Advanced, and then set any of the following options:

- *Restore Security*—Specifies whether Backup should restore all the security settings for each file and folder, including permissions, ownership, and auditing entries. Select this option to restore security settings for files and folders on NTFS volumes. Note that the files and folders must have been backed up from an NTFS volume as well.

- *Restore Junction Points, And Restore File And Folder Data Under Junction Points To The Original Location*—Specifies whether Backup should restore junction points created with mounted drives as well as the data that the junction points reference. Select this option to restore network drive mappings and the actual data to mapped network drives. Choose this option only if you're trying to recover a drive on a remote system. Otherwise, clear this option to restore folder references to network drives only. When this option is disabled or not selected, Backup restores the junction point but won't typically restore the referenced data.
- *When Restoring Replicated Data Sets, Mark The Restored Data As The Primary Data For All Replicas*—Specifies whether Backup should restore File Replication Service (FRS) data so that it is replicated to other servers. Select this option if you're restoring replicated data and want the restored data to be replicated to other servers. When this feature is disabled or not selected, Backup restores the FRS data, but this data might not be replicated because it will appear older than existing data on the subscribing computers.
- *Restore The Cluster Registry To The Quorum Disk And All Other Nodes*—Specifies whether Backup should restore the cluster registry to the quorum disk and replicate the cluster registry to all other nodes in the cluster. The cluster registry contains cluster configuration and state information. Select this option if you're restoring a cluster and want the restored data to be replicated to all nodes in the cluster. When this feature is disabled or not selected, Backup restores the cluster registry but it might not be replicated because it will appear older than existing data on other nodes.
- *Preserve Existing Volume Mount Points*—Specifies whether Backup should preserve existing volume mount points when restoring data. Select this option if you're restoring an entire file system (which includes the volume mount points) and want to retain the current mount points rather than those in the archive. This option is useful if you've remapped a drive and created additional volumes, and now you want to keep the current volume mappings. When this feature is not selected, Backup will overwrite existing volume mount points if mount points were saved in the archive.

6. In the Confirm Restore dialog box, click OK to start the restore operation. If prompted, enter the path and name of the backup set to use. You can cancel the backup by clicking Cancel in the Operation Status and Restore Progress dialog boxes.
7. When the restore is completed, you can click Close to complete the process or click Report to view a backup log containing information about the restore operation. Backup logs are stored in %UserProfile%\Local Settings\Application Data\Microsoft\WindowsNT\NTBackup\Data and are saved with the .log extension. You can view log files from within the Backup utility or with any standard text editor.

Recovering Configuration Data

Configuration data is stored in the System State. When you make a backup of the computer's System State, you can restore the computer's configuration in much the same way that you restore the computer's data. With System State, the recovery options take on a somewhat different meaning.

When you restore the System State to the original location, you tell Backup to replace the computer's current System State with the system state data from the backup archive. This means that the computer's boot files, key system files, COM+ class registration database, and the Registry will be restored to the state they were in when the backup archive was made. However, you can't restore the System State fully on a domain controller. On a domain controller, Active Directory is not restored as part of the System State restore. To restore a domain controller and restore Active Directory, you must first start the computer in Directory Services restore mode. For more information, see the following section.

When you restore the System State to an alternative location, only the Registry, Sysvol, and system boot files are restored to the alternative location. You can't restore the Active Directory database, Certificate Services database, or the COM+ database to an alternative location.

Backing Up and Restoring Active Directory

Backing up Active Directory is easy. To back up Active Directory, all you need to do is back up the System State on a domain controller. However, recovery of Active Directory is different from recovery for other types of network services. A key reason for this involves the way Active Directory data is replicated and restored. Because of this, let's look at backup and recovery strategies for Active Directory, and then look at various restore techniques.

Backup and Recovery Strategies for Active Directory

Domain controllers have replication partners with whom they share information. When you have multiple domain controllers in a domain and one fails, the other domain controllers automatically detect the failure and change their replication topology accordingly. You can repair or replace the failed domain controller from backup. However, the restore doesn't recover Active Directory information stored on the domain controller.

To restore Active Directory on the failed domain controller, you use either a nonauthoritative or authoritative approach. A *nonauthoritative restore* allows the domain controller to come back on line, and then get replication updates from other domain controllers. An *authoritative restore* makes the restored domain controller the authority in the domain, and its data is replicated to other domain controllers.

In most cases, you'll have multiple domain controllers in a domain, giving you flexibility in your disaster recovery plan. If one of the domain controllers fails, you can install a new domain controller or promote an existing member server so that it can be a domain controller. In either case, the directory on the new domain controller is updated automatically through replication. You could also recover the failed domain controller, and then perform a nonauthoritative restore. In this case, you would restore Active Directory on the domain controller and obtain directory updates from other domain controllers in the domain.

In some cases, you may need to perform an authoritative restore of Active Directory. For example, if a large number of objects were deleted from Active Directory, the only way to recover those objects would be to use an authoritative restore. In this case, you would restore Active Directory on a domain controller and use the recovered data as the master copy of the directory database. This data is then replicated to all other domain controllers.

The disaster recovery strategy you choose for Active Directory may depend on whether you have dedicated or nondedicated domain controllers, for the following reasons:

- When you have dedicated domain controllers that perform no other domain services, you can implement a very simple disaster recovery procedure for domain controllers. As long as you have multiple domain controllers in each domain, you can restore a failed domain controller by installing a new domain controller and then populating the directory on the new domain controller through replication or by recovering the domain controller using a nonauthoritative restore. You should always back up one or more of the domain controllers and their System State as well, so that you always have a current snapshot of Active Directory in the backup archives. If you need to recover from a disaster that has caused all your domain controllers to fail or Active Directory has been corrupted, you can recover using an authoritative restore in the Directory Services restore mode.
- When you have nondedicated domain controllers, you should back up the System State whenever you perform a full backup of a domain controller. This stores a snapshot of Active Directory along with the other pertinent system information that can be used to fully recover the domain controller. If a domain controller fails, you can recover the server the way you recover any server. You then have the option of restoring the system state data and Active Directory to allow the server to resume operating as a domain controller, by using a nonauthoritative restore in the Directory Services restore mode. If you need to recover from a disaster that has caused all your domain controllers to fail or Active Directory has been corrupted, you also have the option of using an authoritative restore in the Directory Services restore mode.

When planning backups of Active Directory, you should also remember the tombstone lifetime. As you may recall from Chapter 33, "Designing and Managing the Domain Environment," Active Directory doesn't actually delete objects when you remove them from the directory. Instead, objects are tombstoned (marked for deletion) and the tombstone is replicated to all the other domain controllers. By default, the tombstone lifetime is 60 days, meaning that a tombstone will remain in the directory for 60 days and then be deleted. To ensure that you don't accidentally restore objects that have actually been removed from Active Directory, you are prevented from restoring Active Directory if the backup archive is older than the tombstone lifetime. This means that, by default, you cannot restore a backup of Active Directory that is older than 60 days.

Other system information is contained in the System State besides Active Directory. So, any restore of Active Directory includes all that information, and that information will be restored to its previous state as well. If a server's configuration changed since the backup, the configuration changes will be lost.

Performing a Nonauthoritative Restore of Active Directory

When a domain controller fails, you can restore it the way you restore any other server except when it comes to Active Directory. With this in mind, first fix the problem that caused the server to fail. You can use a boot disk, Automated System Recovery, or the Recovery Console as discussed in Chapter 40, "Disaster Planning." Once you've restored the server, you can then work to restore Active Directory.

You recover Active Directory by restoring the System State on the domain controller, using a special recovery mode called Directory Services Restore Mode. If you have made changes to Active Directory since the backup, the System State backup will not contain those changes. However, other domain controllers in the domain will have the most recent changes, and the domain controller will be able to obtain those changes through the normal replication process.

When you want to restore Active Directory on a domain controller and have the domain controller get directory updates from other domain controllers, you perform a nonauthoritative restore. A nonauthoritative restore allows the domain controller to come back on line and then get replication updates from other domain controllers.

You can perform a nonauthoritative restore by completing the following steps:

1. Repair the failed domain controller or rebuild the domain controller by reinstalling Windows Server 2003. Once you've repaired or rebuilt the server, restart the server and press F8 during startup to access the Windows Advanced Options menu. You must press F8 before the Windows splash screen appears.
2. On the Windows Advanced Options menu, select Directory Services Restore Mode (Windows Domain Controllers Only). Windows will then restart in Safe Mode without loading Active Directory components.

3. You will next need to choose the operating system you want to start.
4. Log on to the server using the Administrator account with the Directory Services Restore password that was configured on the domain controller when Active Directory was installed.
5. The Desktop prompt warns you that you are running in Safe Mode, which allows you to fix problems with the server but makes some of your devices unavailable. Click OK.
6. Start the Backup utility and use it to restore the system state information on the server to its original location (see Figure 41-8).

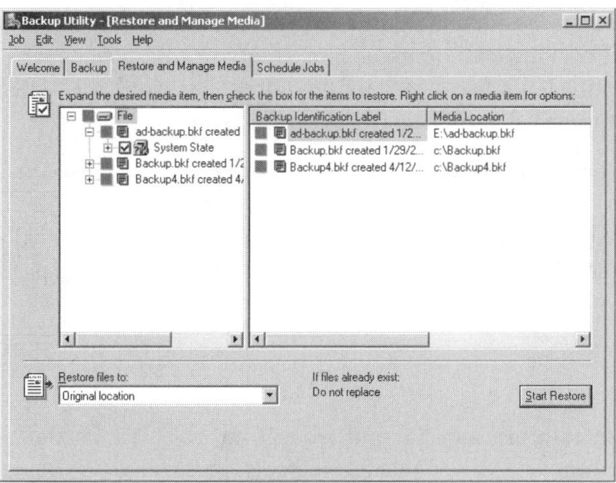

Figure 41-8. Restore the System State.

7. After the data is restored, restart the computer as instructed. Once the server restarts, it can act as a domain controller and it has a directory database that is current as of the date of the backup. The domain controller then connects to its replication partners and begins updating the database so that any changes since the backup are reflected.

Performing an Authoritative Restore of Active Directory

An authoritative restore is used when you need to recover Active Directory to a specific point in time and then replicate the restored data to all other domain controllers. Consider the following example: John accidentally deleted the Marketing organizational unit (OU) and all the objects it contained. Because the changes have already been replicated to all domain controllers in the domain, the only way to restore the OU and the related objects would be to use an authoritative restore. Similarly, if Active Directory were somehow corrupted, the only way to recover Active Directory fully would be to use an authoritative restore.

When performing authoritative restores, there are several significant issues that you should consider. The first and most important issue has to do with passwords used for computers and Windows NT LAN Manager (NTLM) trusts. These passwords are changed automatically every seven days. If you perform an authoritative restore of Active Directory, the restored data will contain the passwords that were in use when the backup archive was made. If you monitor the event logs after the restore, you may see related events or you may hear from users who are experiencing problems accessing resources in the domain.

Computer account passwords allow computers to authenticate themselves in a domain using a computer trust. If a computer password has changed, the computer may not be able to reauthenticate itself in the domain. In this case, you may need to reset the computer account password by right-clicking on the computer account in Active Directory Users And Computers, and then selecting Reset Account. If the reset of the password doesn't work, you may need to remove the computer account from the domain, and then add it back.

NTLM trusts are trusts between Active Directory domains and Microsoft Windows NT domains. If a trust password has changed, the trust between the domains may fail. In this case, you may need to delete the trust, and then recreate it as discussed in the section entitled "Establishing External, Shortcut, Realm, and Cross-Forest Trusts," on page 1131.

Another significant issue when performing an authoritative restore has to do with group membership. Problems with group membership can occur after an authoritative restore for several reasons.

In the first case, an administrator has updated a group object's membership on a domain controller that has not yet received the restored data. In this case, the domain controller may replicate the changes to other domain controllers, causing a temporary inconsistency. The changes shouldn't be permanent, however, because when you perform an authoritative restore, the update sequence number (USN) of all restored objects is incremented by 100,000. This ensures that the restored data is authoritative and overwrites any existing data.

Another problem with group membership can occur if group objects contain user accounts that do not currently exist in the domain. In this case, if group objects are replicated before these user objects are, the user accounts that do not currently exist in the domain will be seen as invalid user accounts. As a result, the user accounts will be deleted as group members. When the user accounts are later replicated, the user accounts will not be added back to the groups.

Although there is no way to control which objects are replicated first, there is a way to correct this problem. You must force the domain controller to replicate the group membership list with the group object. You can do this by creating a temporary user account and adding it to each group that contains user accounts that are currently not valid in the domain. Here's how this would work: You authoritatively restore and then restart the domain controller. The domain controller begins replicating its data to other domain controllers. When this initial replication process finishes, you create a temporary user account and add it to the requisite groups. The group membership list will then be replicated. If any domain controller has removed previously invalid user accounts as members of these groups, the domain controller will then return the user accounts to the group.

You can perform an authoritative restore by completing the following steps:

1. Follow steps 1 through 6 in the section entitled "Performing a Nonauthoritative Restore of Active Directory," but do *not* restart the computer when the restore is complete.
2. Click Start, click Run, type **cmd** in the Open field, and then click OK.
3. At the command prompt, type **ntdsutil**. This starts the Directory Services Management Tool.
4. At the Ntdsutil prompt, type **authoritative restore**. You should now be at the Authoritative Restore prompt, where you have the following options:
   - You can authoritatively restore the entire Active Directory database by typing **restore database**. If you restore the entire Active Directory database, there will be a significant amount of replication traffic generated throughout the domain and the forest. You should restore the entire database only if Active Directory has been corrupted or there is some other significant reason for doing so.
   - You can authoritatively restore a container and all its related objects (referred to as a subtree) by typing **restore subtree *ObjectDN*** where *ObjectDN* is the distinguished name of the container to restore. For example, if someone accidentally deleted the Marketing OU in the cpandl.com domain, you could restore the OU and all the objects it contained by typing the command **restore subtree ou=marketing,dc=cpandl,dc=com**.
   - You can authoritatively restore an individual object by typing **restore object *ObjectDN*** where *ObjectDN* is the distinguished name of the object to restore. For example, if someone accidentally deleted the Sales group from the default container for users and groups (**cn=users**) in the cpandl.com domain, you could restore the group by typing the command **restore object cn=sales,cn=users,dc=cpandl,dc=com**.
5. When you type a restore command and press Enter, the Authoritative Restore Confirmation dialog box appears, which prompts you to click Yes if you're sure you want to perform the restore action. Click Yes to perform the restore operation.
6. Type **quit** twice to exit Ntdsutil, and then restart the server.

> **Note** Every object that is restored will have its USN incremented by 100,000. When you are restoring the entire database, you cannot override this behavior, which is necessary to ensure that the data is properly replicated. For subtree and object restores, you can override this behavior by setting a different version increment value using the Verinc option. For example, if you wanted to restore the Sales group in the cpandl.com domain and increment the USN by 500 rather than 100,000, you could do this by typing the command **restore object cn=sales,cn=users,dc=cpandl,dc=com verinc 500**.

Performing a Primary Restore of Sysvol Data

The Sysvol folder is backed up as part of the system state information and contains critical domain information including GPOs, group policy templates, and scripts used for startup, shutdown, logging on and logging off. If you restore a domain controller, the Sysvol data will be replicated from other domain controllers. Unlike Active Directory data, Sysvol data is replicated using the File Replication Service (FRS).

You restore Sysvol data using a primary restore. A primary restore reestablishes the Sysvol folder and the File Replication Service, and sets the restored data as authoritative. This means that the restored Sysvol would be replicated to all other domain controllers. For example, if someone were to delete several scripts used for startup or logon and there were no backups of these scripts, you could restore them using a primary restore.

To perform a primary restore, you use Backup to restore the System State using either an authoritative or a nonauthoritative restore. During the restore, you do not accept the default restore settings. Instead, you access the advanced restore options shown in Figure 41-9, and then select the When Restoring Replicated Data Sets, Mark The Restored Data As The Primary Data For All Replicas option. This marks the Sysvol data as the primary data so that it is replicated to other servers. The Restore Security, Restore Juncture Points And Restore File And Folder Data Under Junction Points To The Original Location, and Preserve Existing Volume Mount Points options should all be selected by default. These options should remain selected to ensure proper recovery of the Sysvol data.

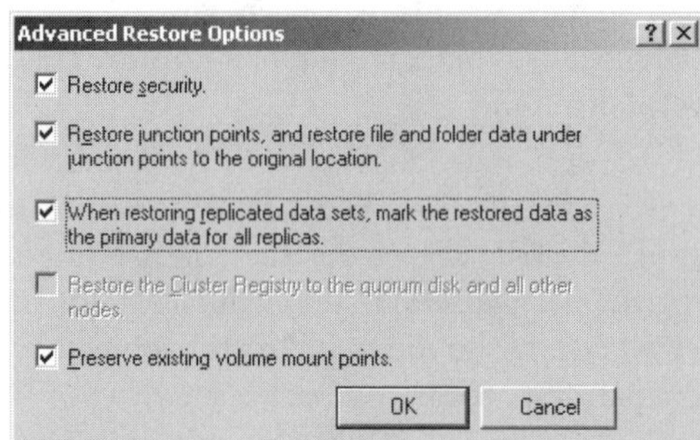

Figure 41-9. Configuring a primary restore.

Restoring a Failed Domain Controller by Installing a New Domain Controller

Sometimes you won't be able to or won't want to repair a failed domain controller and may instead elect to install a new domain controller. You can install a new domain controller by promoting an existing member server so that it is a domain controller or by installing a new computer, and then promoting it. Either way, the domain controller will get its directory information from another domain controller.

Installing a new domain controller is the easy part. When you've finished that, you need to clean up references to the old domain controller so that other computers in the domain don't try to connect to it anymore. You need to remove references to the server in DNS, and you need to examine any roles that the failed server played. If the failed server was a global catalog server, you should designate another domain controller as a global catalog server. If the failed server held an operations master role, you will need to seize the role and give it to another domain controller. Let's start with DNS and roles.

- To clean up DNS, you need to remove all records for the server in DNS. This includes SRV records that designate the computer as domain controller and any additional records that designate the computer as a global catalog server or PDC emulator if applicable.
- To designate another server as a global catalog server, see the section entitled "Designating Global Catalog Servers," on page 1110.
- To transfer operations master roles, see the section entitled "Changing Operations Masters," on page 243.

To clean up references to the failed domain controller in Active Directory, you are going to need to use Ntdsutil. You must use an account with Administrator privileges in the domain. You can, however, run Ntdsutil from any computer running Microsoft Windows 2000 or later. The cleanup process is as follows:

1. Click Start, click Run, type **cmd** in the Open field, and then click OK.
2. At the command prompt, type **ntdsutil**. This starts the Directory Services Management Tool.
3. At the Ntdsutil prompt, type **metadata cleanup**. You should now be at the Metadata Cleanup prompt.
4. Access the Server Connections prompt so that you can connect to a domain controller. To do this, type **connections** and then type **connect to server *DCName*** where *DCName* is the name of a working domain controller in the same domain as the failed domain controller.
5. Exit the Server Connections prompt by typing **quit**. You should now be back at the Metadata Cleanup prompt.
6. Access the Select Operation Target prompt so that you can work your way through Active Directory from a target domain to a target site to the actual domain controller you want to remove. Type **select operation target**.
7. List all the sites in the forest by typing **list sites** and then type **select site *Number***, where *Number* is the number of the site containing the failed domain controller.

8. List all the domains in the site by typing **list domains in site** and then type **select domain *Number***, where *Number* is the number of the domain containing the failed domain controller.
9. List all the domain controllers in the selected domain and site by typing **list servers in site** and then type **select server *Number***, where *Number* is the number of the server that failed.
10. Exit the Select Operation Target prompt by typing **quit**. You should now be back at the Metadata Cleanup prompt.
11. Remove the selected server from the directory by typing **remove selected server**. When prompted, confirm that you want to remove the selected server.
12. Type **quit** twice to exit Ntdsutil. Next, remove the related computer object from the Domain Controllers OU in Active Directory Users And Computers. Finally, remove the computer object from the Servers container for the site in which the domain controller was located, using Active Directory Sites And Services.

Troubleshooting Startup and Shutdown

Troubleshooting startup and shutdown are also part of system recovery. When problems occur, you need to be able to resolve them, and the key techniques are discussed in this part of the chapter. Don't forget about boot disks, ASR, and the Recovery Console—all of which were discussed in the section entitled "Predisaster Preparation Procedures," on page 1353.

Resolving Startup Issues

When you have problems starting a system, think about what has changed recently. If you and other administrators keep a change log, access the log to see what has changed on the system recently. A new device driver might have been installed or an application might have been installed that incorrectly modified the system configuration.

Often you can resolve startup issues using Safe Mode to recover or troubleshoot system problems. In Safe Mode, Windows Server 2003 loads only basic files, services, and drivers. Because Safe Mode loads a limited set of configuration information, it can help you troubleshoot problems. You start a system in Safe Mode by completing the following steps:

1. If the system is currently running and you want to troubleshoot startup, shut down the server, and then start it again. If the system is already powered down or has previously failed to start, start the server again.
2. Press F8 during startup to access the Windows Advanced Options menu. You must press F8 before the Windows splash screen appears.

3 In the Windows Advanced Options menu, select a startup mode. The key options are as follows:

- *Safe Mode*—Starts the computer and loads only basic files, services, and drivers during the initialization sequence. The drivers loaded include the mouse, monitor, keyboard, mass storage, and base video. No networking services or drivers are started.
- *Safe Mode With Command Prompt*—Starts the computer and loads only basic files, services, and drivers, and then starts a command prompt instead of the Windows Server 2003 graphical interface. No networking services or drivers are started.
- *Safe Mode With Networking*—Starts the computer and loads only basic files, services, and drivers, and the services and drivers needed to start networking.
- *Enable Boot Logging*—Starts the computer with boot logging enabled, which allows you to create a record of all startup events in a boot log.
- *Enable VGA Mode*—Starts the computer in Video Graphics Adapter (VGA) mode, which is useful if the system display is set to a mode that can't be used with the current monitor.
- *Last Known Good Configuration*—Starts the computer in Safe Mode using Registry information that Windows Server 2003 saved at the last shutdown.

4 If a problem doesn't reappear when you start in Safe Mode, you can eliminate the default settings and basic device drivers as possible causes. If a newly added device or updated driver is causing problems, you can use Safe Mode to remove the device or roll back the update.

5 Make other changes as necessary to resolve startup problems. If you are still having a problem starting the system, you may need to uninstall recently installed applications or devices to try to correct the problem.

Repairing Missing or Corrupted System Files

Automated System Recovery data can often help you recover a system that won't boot. If you can't start or recover a system in Safe Mode, from the Recovery Console, or with a boot disk, the next step is to try to recover the system using the last Automated System Recovery (ASR) backup. You can repair a system using the recovery data by completing the following steps:

1 Insert the Windows Server 2003 CD-ROM into the appropriate drive, and then restart the computer. Make sure that you boot from the CD-ROM, so when prompted to press a key to boot from the CD, do so.

2 As soon as the text-mode Setup begins to run, press F2 to start the Automated System Recovery (ASR) process.

3. Insert the ASR disk when prompted and press any key. Files will then be copied from the disk to the computer and the system configuration will be initialized.
4. The computer will then reboot. When the system restarts, it will reboot and start Windows Server 2003. The graphical Setup will begin, and then the ASR Wizard will start.
5. The ASR Wizard allows you to specify the location of the full system backup to be restored.
6. The computer will reboot again. When it restarts, it should start normally. At this point, the recovery of the system is complete. The system is restored with the configuration and settings it had when the ASR backup was made. Remember that, for a domain controller, ASR performs a nonauthoritative restore of both Active Directory and the Sysvol.

Resolving Restart or Shutdown Issues

Normally, you can shut down or restart Windows Server 2003 by clicking Start, selecting Shutdown, selecting Restart or Shutdown in the Shutdown Windows dialog box, and finally clicking OK. Sometimes, however, Windows Server 2003 won't shut down or restart normally and you are forced to take additional actions. In those cases, follow these steps:

1. Press Ctrl+Alt+Delete. The Windows Security dialog box should appear. If the Windows Security dialog box doesn't appear, skip to step 4.
2. Click Task Manager, and then look for an application that is not responding. If all programs appear to be running normally, skip to step 4.
3. Select the application that is not responding, and then click End Task. If the application fails to respond to the request, you'll see a prompt that allows you to end the application immediately or cancel the end task request. Click End Now.
4. Try shutting down or restarting the computer. Press Ctrl+Alt+Delete, and then click Shutdown. As a last resort, you might be forced to perform a hard shutdown by powering down or unplugging the computer. If you do this, run Check Disk the next time you start the computer to check for errors and problems that may have been caused by the hard shutdown.

Index to Troubleshooting Topics

Index

Numbers and Symbols

A

D

H

J

K

N

About the Author

William R. Stanek (williamstanek@aol.com) has more than 20 years of hands-on experience with advanced programming and development. He is a leading technology expert and an award-winning author. Over the years, his practical advice has helped millions of programmers, developers, and network engineers all over the world. He has written more than 25 computer books. Current or forthcoming books include *Microsoft Windows Command-Line Administrator's Pocket Consultant, Microsoft Windows 2000 Administrator's Pocket Consultant 2nd Edition, Microsoft Windows Server 2003 Administrator's Pocket Consultant*, and *Microsoft IIS 6.0 Administrator's Pocket Consultant.*

Mr. Stanek has been involved in the commercial Internet community since 1991. His core business and technology experience comes from more than 11 years of military service. He has substantial experience in developing server technology, encryption, and Internet solutions. He has written many technical white papers and training courses on a wide variety of topics. He is widely sought after as a subject matter expert.

Mr. Stanek has an MS in Information Systems degree with distinction and a BS Computer Science degree *magna cum laude*. He is proud to have served in the Persian Gulf War as a combat crew member on an electronic warfare aircraft. He flew on numerous combat missions into Iraq and was awarded nine medals for his wartime service, including one of the U.S. government's highest flying honors, the Air Force Distinguished Flying Cross. Currently, he resides in the Pacific Northwest with his wife and children.